D1537475

MANAGEMENT SCIENCE

MANAGEMENT SCIENCE

David F. Groebner
Boise State University

Patrick W. Shannon
Boise State University

Dellen Publishing Company
an imprint of

Macmillan Publishing Company
New York

Maxwell Macmillan Canada
Toronto

On the cover: "Pride" is an eighteen color lithograph and three color serigraph by Los Angeles artist Lawrence Gipe. Gipe's work is about memory—about facing the dreams of the past and acknowledging where they have failed us—and we them. The locomotive is a dynamic symbol that could be seen as the failed promise of modernity. The romantic image is made to function within the realm of the contemporary by the addition of the word "pride." The two elements create a synthesis of remembrance—and hope. Gipe's work is in the collection of the Laguna Art Museum, Laguna Beach, California. Gipe is represented by the Karl Bornstein Gallery in Santa Monica, California.

© Copyright 1992 by Dellen Publishing Company, an imprint of Macmillan Publishing Co.

Printed in the United States of America.

Macmillan Publishing Company
866 Third Avenue, New York, New York 10022

Macmillan Publishing Company is
part of the Maxwell Communication
Group of Companies.

Maxwell Macmillan Canada, Inc.
1200 Eglinton Avenue East
Suite 200
Don Mills, Ontario M3C 3N1

All rights reserved. No part of this book may be reproduced or transmitted in any form or by any means, electronic or mechanical, including photocopying, recording, or any information storage and retrieval system, without permission in writing from the Publisher.

Permissions: Dellen Publishing Company
400 Pacific Avenue
San Francisco, California 94133

Orders: Dellen Publishing Company
c/o Macmillan Publishing Company
Front and Brown Streets
Riverside, New Jersey 08075

Maxwell Macmillan Canada, Inc.
1200 Eglinton Avenue East
Suite 200
Don Mills, Ontario M3C 3N1

Library of Congress Cataloging-in-Publication Data

Groebner, David F.
Introduction to management science / David F. Groebner, Patrick W. Shannon.
p. cm.
Includes index.
ISBN 0-02-347850-0
1. Management science. I. Shannon, Patrick W. II. Title.
T56.G76 1991
658—dc20 90-21826
CIP

Printing: 1 2 3 4 5 6 7 8 9 Year: 2 3 4 5 6 7

ISBN 0-02-347850-0

CONTENTS

PREFACE

Recently a commercial was playing on the radio. The setting involved a group of new college graduates meeting with a recruiter from a major company. The recruiter asked the group why his company should hire them. They responded in unison, "I have a 3.50 GPA and I like people." The recruiter replied by saying "Don't call us; we'll call you."

While a good grade point average and the ability to get along with people are important factors in getting a job in business, the point of the commercial was that students need to do something to distinguish themselves from their peers. In today's competitive business climate, companies — more than ever before — are taking advantage of management science tools such as those covered in this text. Students who graduate with a fundamental knowledge of these management science techniques will have separated themselves from others and will be in demand by industry.

This introductory textbook on management science presents a number of the quantitative tools most frequently used by managers and is targeted for use by business students in the first undergraduate or MBA-level management science course. While some texts on management science are impressive from the standpoint of their mathematical eloquence and detailing of subareas of the discipline, such emphasis is often of limited practical value to most business students. This textbook is different because it has been written specifically with the student in mind: the writing style is clear and enjoyable to read; the focus is on the *application* of management science and not on the mathematical development of the techniques; the only prerequisite for understanding is a basic college algebra course.

The text contains a number of useful features that help the beginning student. Every chapter starts with a section ("Why You Need To Know") that provides a commonsense reason for learning the chapter material. A list of chapter objectives provides a focus for the important concepts of each chapter. The text is packed with tables and illustrations that clarify key concepts. The management science techniques are introduced through the use of business applications that clearly demonstrate how each technique is utilized in a decison making situation. Important concepts are highlighted in boxes, and the chapters are divided into subsections to ease both reading and comprehension.

Computers, of course, have greatly benefited the practice of solving real-world problems with management science tools. Thus, in all chapters where appropriate, a section on computer applications has been included. These sections illustrate how a computer can be used to perform the required mathematical computations, and the text explains how to interpret the computer output.

The text is loaded with applications problems, concept questions, and library assignments. Each chapter contains a section ("Solved Problems") that shows the steps required to set up and solve an applications problem. Each chapter also contains at least one Mini Case, which presents a real managerial setting and a decision problem that is a bit less defined than those found in the applications problems. These cases provide invaluable practice for students who will enter the organizational world where decision making situations are not formatted quite like textbook homework problems.

Complementing the many features in the text itself is a full array of accompanying supplemental materials:

Student Study Guide

The *Student Study Guide* contains two very useful sections. First, there is an outline of each chapter, which is comparable to a set of notes and which serves as an excellent review of the chapter material. Secondly, solutions to all the odd-numbered problems are given. These solutions allow students not only to check their answers, but also to determine how the problem was formulated and to see the steps required to reach the correct solution.

Instructor's Manual

The *Instructor's Manual* contains worked-out solutions to all even-numbered problems and solutions to all the Mini Cases in the text.

Computerized Test Bank

A computerized test bank with well over 1000 objective test questions has been developed by Professor Charles Lienart of the University of Denver. From this test bank instructors can pull quiz and exam problems that directly apply to any section in the text.

Transparency Masters

The instructor will be provided a complete set of transparency masters, which consist of useful instructional aids.

MASTER Computer Software and User's Manual

Available at no cost to schools adopting the text is a PC compatible software package called MASTER, which is an easy-to-use menu driven package containing modules for nearly all the management science topics covered in the text. Students can use the software as a computational tool and can then focus on interpreting the computer output. The *User's Manual* provides complete documentation for the use of the MASTER software. Ask your instructor about this software.

Problem Data Diskette

The instructor will be provided with a data diskette containing data files for selected problems in the text. These diskettes can be duplicated and given to the students at the instructor's discretion. Even though MASTER's data entry process is easy to use, this data diskette would relieve the data entry burden for the student and allow even greater emphasis on interpretation of results.

A great many people contributed to the development of this text. We are indebted to them for their comments, suggestions, and other contributions. Paul Hruska and Rick Mortensen were largely responsible for the software development. Susan Fry spent many hours proofing the manuscript and providing suggestions for improvements. Our colleague, Phil Fry, served as a sounding board and contributed several special applications problems and Mini Cases. Matthew Groebner provided valuable assistance in developing the *Student Study Guide*. We are especially grateful to the following people who carefully reviewed our manuscript in its early form and provided valuable suggestions for improvement:

Joseph R. Biggs, California State Polytechnic University, San Luis Obispo
Joseph D. Blackburn, Vanderbilt University
Robert S. Boothe, Memphis State University
Daniel G. Brooks, Arizona State University
Belva J. Cooley, Indiana State University
Peter Ellis, Utah State University
Charles E. Lienert, Metropolitan State College
Richard L. Schwaller, Montana State University
Susan L. Solomon, California State University, Sacramento
Charles J. Teplitz, University of San Diego
Richard A. Toelle, University of Idaho
William H. Turnquist, Eastern Washington University

We are also indebted to our publisher, Don Dellen, and his staff at Dellen Publishing for their support and commitment throughout this project. The work of Janet Bollow in design and Tralelia Twitty in technical editing was most appreciated. Ann Lee from our own office did so many things to help us, and we appreciate it all very much.

Finally, we are grateful for the support of our families who stuck with us through the writing of this text.

David F. Groebner

Patrick W. Shannon

Chapter 1

INTRODUCTION TO MANAGEMENT SCIENCE TECHNIQUES AND DECISION MODELING

Chapter Outline

Chapter 1

Why You Need to Know

The essence of business is decision making. What you are learning in college will help prepare you to make sound business decisions. Courses in the arts, humanities, and social sciences provide insights into the complexities of living in our rapidly changing environment. Business courses build upon these insights and provide a framework for decision making with a wide variety of decision tools and analytic methods.

This management science course will probably introduce you to more tools and analytic techniques that have direct application for business decision making than any other course you will take. If you learn how to use these tools and how to recognize the types of situations for which they should be used, you will have taken an important step in preparing for your professional future.

The management science techniques introduced in this text are applicable in virtually every type of public or private organization. These techniques, also referred to as operations research techniques and quantitative methods, can be used in a wide variety of decision-making situations. No matter what functional business area you have chosen as a major, you will encounter opportunities to apply these techniques. This will be true in the classes you take, and certainly in the work you do following graduation. Decision makers who are familiar with management science techniques and know how to apply them have a distinct advantage over their colleagues who do not have such expertise.

We urge you to read the chapters in this text carefully and to actively participate in this course. The efforts you make now will prove to be a valuable investment.

Chapter Objectives

While this text covers a wide range of management science techniques, the emphasis is on determining how and when the various techniques should be used. We will first describe decision-making situations which lend themselves to quantitative analysis and then will clearly explain what the appropriate technique is and how it is to be applied.

Chapter 1 lays the important groundwork you will need to fully understand the material in the remainder of the text.

The objectives of Chapter 1 are:

1. To provide a short description of each management science technique covered in this text.
2. To present examples of decision-making situations in which each of the techniques is applied.
3. To discuss the steps in decision making and to illustrate the role of management science models in this process.
4. To introduce the concept of decision modeling and to discuss some important terminology associated with it.
5. To discuss the role of computers in the application of management science techniques.

1-1 INTRODUCING MANAGEMENT SCIENCE TECHNIQUES

The extensive array of decision-making tools collectively referred to as management science or operations research techniques grows larger every year. This text focuses mainly on a group of widely applicable techniques. For most students, this course will provide your first exposure to these techniques. To give you an idea of what is in store, this section presents a brief overview of the techniques covered in later chapters and examples of applications for which they are best suited.

An important point to remember throughout this course is that people in business are continually making decisions. They must decide when to hire employees, how much inventory to carry in stock, whether to build a new plant, whether to introduce a new product in a particular market — the list is endless. But in order to make good decisions, people need good information. The management science techniques covered in this text are designed to provide such information.

Figure 1-1 lists the topics presented in this text, by chapter. The following paragraphs provide a brief introduction to these topics.

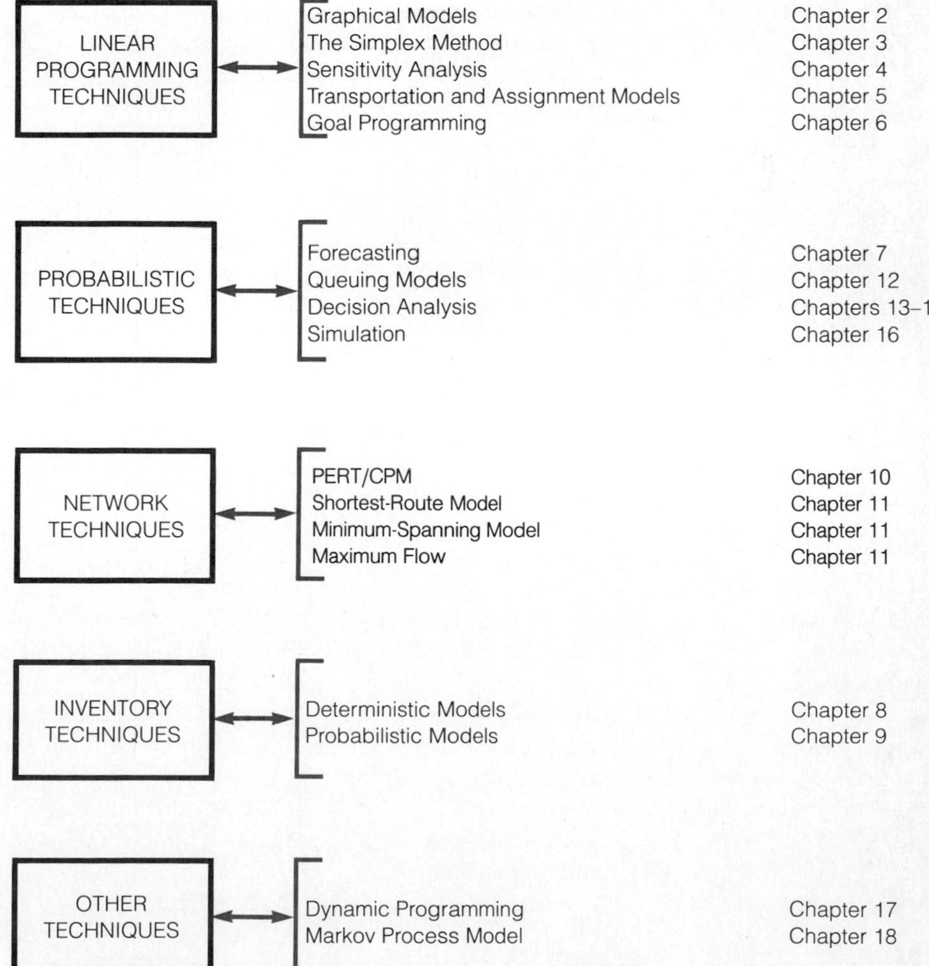

Figure 1-1
Management science topics by chapter

LINEAR PROGRAMMING

Linear programming is probably the best-known management science technique. It is part of a broad range of techniques referred to as mathematical programming. Linear programming is particularly useful in situations which require the allocation of scarce resources. In the following example, you will see how this technique might be used by the manager of a plywood mill to schedule weekly production.

The Hoopa Mill makes plywood in three thicknesses (3/8-, 1/2-, and 3/4-inch) and in two grades (common and construction). The sales department has firm orders for specific amounts of each thickness and grade combination, but might be able to sell more if it were available. The profit margins on the various products differ due to market conditions and manufacturing costs.

The plywood is made from logs kept on hand in the mill yard. The quantity of each type of plywood that can be made from the inventory of logs depends on the quantity of each size and grade of peeler core available. In addition, the mill has a maximum production capacity, which cannot be exceeded. The manager must determine how many units of each type of plywood to make each week in order to optimize profits. The decision is constrained by a variety of factors, including product demand, raw material inventory, and mill capacity.

Before the mill can begin operations for the week, the manager must decide what is going to be produced. Because he will be using linear programming, the manager will establish an *objective function* to maximize the total weekly profit. He will also specify the **constraints**, or restrictions, which must be satisfied in the final solution to the linear programming problem. For example, one constraint might be that total production of 3/8-inch plywood must be at least 4000 sheets but not more than 7000 sheets. Another constraint might require that the production of common-grade plywood be at least two times that of construction-grade. The linear programming solution procedure will determine the quantities of each type of plywood to produce to generate the maximum total profit while satisfying all defined constraints.

Linear programming is used in many different types of industries concerned with the allocation of scarce resources. In addition to wood products, these industries include oil, chemical, and food processing; transportation, and brewing. Linear programming has also been adapted to help companies define optimal shipping schedules and transportation routes for their products. And financial managers can use linear programming to help determine the best mix of investments for a pension portfolio. Chapters 2 through 6 cover a range of linear programming topics. After studying the material in these chapters, you should better understand the potential of this important management science tool.

FORECASTING

In any business, much of a manager's time is spent planning future activities. For instance, a production manager in a garment factory needs to plan production levels for the next few days, weeks, and even months to most effectively utilize the plant's personnel, equipment, and materials. The manager must decide whether the present number of workers is adequate, whether new equipment is needed, whether storage space is sufficient, whether enough raw material is on hand or on order, and on and on. Since each of these decisions depends on how many units will be sold during the planning time period, a significant input into this planning process is a *forecast* of future garment sales.

A **forecast** is a prediction of some future activity. No business, large or small, can get along without some form of forecasting. Among the wide variety of forecasting techniques, some are based on professional judgment, intuition, and general experience with the operations of an organization. We will explore some of these *qualitative* forecasting approaches, such as the delphi method, in Chapter 7.

In addition to the qualitative forecasting techniques, there is a wide range of *quantitative* techniques which provide a formal means of analyzing historical data as a basis for making predictions. Chapter 7 introduces a variety of quantitative techniques for analyzing past data and making forecasts. Figure 1-2 is an example of graphical output produced in a quantitative forecasting analysis.

INVENTORY CONTROL MODELS

The purchasing manager for an office products firm in Kansas is responsible for maintaining an inventory of more than 2000 different products. Let us focus on one of these products: the three-drawer metal file cabinet. The company needs to have enough of these file cabinets on hand to meet customer demand and ensure that no sales are lost. To accomplish this, the purchasing manager might keep a large supply of file cabinets in inventory to make sure that one is available when requested. However,

Figure 1-2
Forecasting output

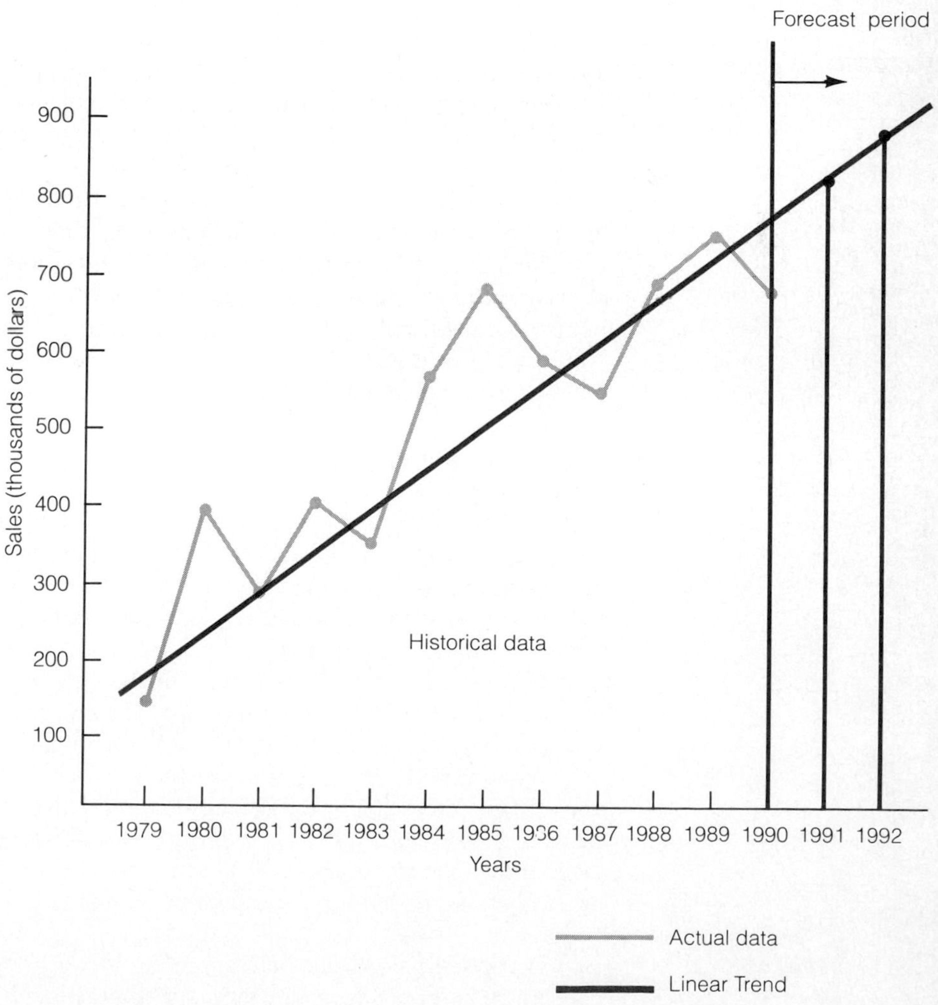

the large inventory will require a large storage area, which is costly. In addition, large inventories tie up capital that could be used for other purposes. Thus, because having cabinets sitting around is costly, a small inventory of file cabinets is desirable.

Having too few cabinets on hand will result in lost sales, while having too many increases operating costs. The purchasing manager has to determine how many file cabinets to carry in inventory to minimize overall costs to the company. Closely connected with this is the need to determine how many units to order and at what point to place the order. Chapters 8 and 9 introduce several *inventory control models* for dealing with issues like these. Inventory models have been developed for virtually every type of business.

NETWORK MODELS

For some organizations, the daily functions involve repetitious activities. For example, many operations in a bank are quite repetitious, the operation of a grocery store is basically the same every day, and the methods used to assemble computers are quite stable. In these types of organizations, once the operation is developed, the process continues with only fine-tuning from time to time.

However, for other organizations, the operations may consist of a variety of one-time activities. For instance, large engineering and construction firms, such as Morrison-Knudsen and Bechtel, take on a number of very specialized, one-of-a-kind projects during a year. Each project becomes a major undertaking and must be managed separately. Consider a construction project to build a large office building. There might be 10,000 or more different activities involved in completing the project, and the activities must be completed in some predetermined sequence. The project must be managed so that the building matches the design specifications. It also must be completed on schedule and within budget. To do all this, someone must decide when to order materials, when to hire workers, and when to move crews from one part of the building to the next.

The construction manager needs to know which tasks or activities have flexible starting dates and which ones have no flexibility. The manager also needs to know how the project's completion date will be affected if a particular task is started later than planned or takes longer than planned. The manager would be interested in knowing what improvement would result if more workers were available to speed the time to complete a particular task.

Decision makers involved with this type of management activity make extensive use of *network models*. The term *network* refers to the use of a network or flow diagram to show the sequence of activities. Figure 1-3 shows a relatively small network that defines the activities required for completing a market survey.

The two most widely used network models are the Program Evaluation and Review Technique (PERT) and the Critical Path Method (CPM). Because these models are very similar, they are discussed as one technique (PERT/CPM) in Chapter 10.

While PERT/CPM is commonly applied to one-time decision situations, other network models are useful for making more repetitive decisions. For instance, a parcel delivery service might use the *shortest-route model* to determine the path each truck will take through the city to minimize total travel distance. The shortest-route model and other network models are discussed in Chapter 11.

WAITING-LINE MODEL

How many stalls should be built at a new car wash? How many teller windows are needed at a new branch bank? How many emergency-room beds does a hospital need? How many phone operators does a magazine need to handle responses to its ads for

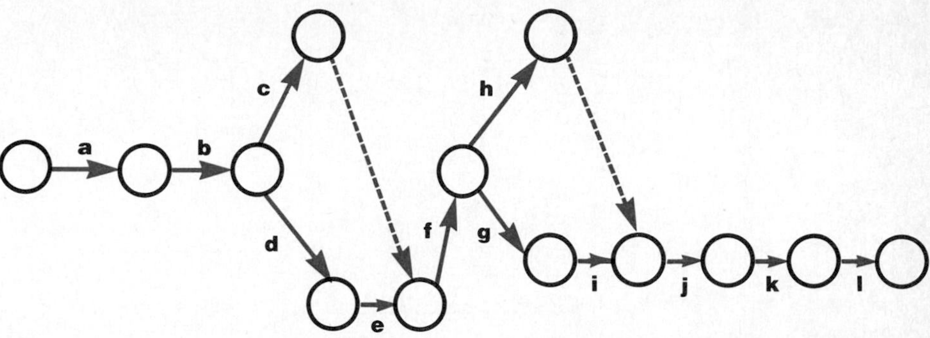

	ACTIVITY	TIME
a	Define objectives	3 days
b	Determine population	2 days
c	Calculate sample size	1 day
d	Construct survey instrument	3 days
e	Test survey instrument	3 days
f	Administer survey	6 days
g	Follow up on survey	5 days
h	Prepare computer programs	3 days
i	Key data	4 days
j	Run programs	2 days
k	Analyze data	4 days
l	Write report	5 days

Figure 1-3
PERT/CPM network model for market survey

special subscription rates? How many taxis does a taxi company need to have posted at the airport between 4:00 and 6:00 P.M.?

All these questions are about situations in which customers demand a service and an organization wants to provide the service. Let's look at the taxi example more closely. Figure 1-4 presents a graphical view of the situation. A customer wants a taxi available when he or she gets off the airplane. A short wait in line for the next available taxi might be tolerable, but long waits will cause complaints and/or a change to another form of transportation. From the customer's perspective, the ideal situation would be for the taxi company to post a very large number of taxis at the airport. The taxi company, on the other hand, must concern itself not only with meeting the demand for service but also with incurring excessive costs by having too many taxis available.

Since so many business organizations must decide how many service facilities to provide, a series of management science techniques called *waiting-line models,* or *queuing models,* have been developed. Chapter 12 discusses several frequently used waiting-line models. These models take into account such factors as customer arrival rates and services rates, and provide the decision maker with information about average length of the line, expected waiting time, average facility idle time, and service facility utilization. By modeling changes in the service levels (e.g., the number of taxis at the airport), the decision-maker can observe the potential impact on both the customers and the service facilities. As is true in most business situations, the ultimate choice of service level will represent a trade-off between customer service and effective use of resources.

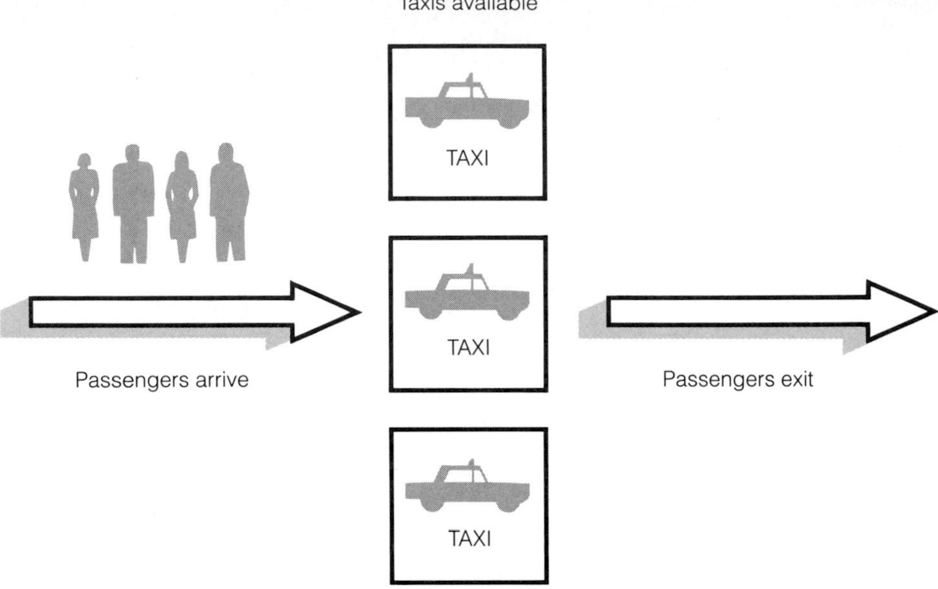

Figure 1-4
Waiting-line example

DECISION ANALYSIS

The decision maker, operating in an environment filled with uncertainty, is often faced with making a decision involving several choices. In addition, each choice may have several possible outcomes, none of which can be known with certainty.

Consider, for example, decisions to be made by the manager in charge of short-term investments for a large computer manufacturer. The manager's job is to place the company's excess cash in short-term investments to earn the largest possible return. But there are a number of possible investment options, ranging from certificates of deposit to market securities. For some of these options, the return is known; but for others, such as market securities, the return is not certain. Sometimes, selecting the "best" alternative will depend on knowing what decisions will be made in the future. Since making decisions on the basis of possible future outcomes is difficult to do intuitively, the manager may rely on *decision analysis* to determine how to invest the company's money. Decision analysis is useful in situations involving choices among many alternatives.

Chapters 13 through 15 introduce a number of decision analysis techniques, including *decision tree analysis, posterior analysis,* and *risk preference analysis.* These and other decision analysis techniques can be combined to model a situation and enable a person to make the most informed choice among alternatives. Figure 1-5 is a simplified version of a decision tree. In this case, a college athlete is deciding whether to finish his last year of college basketball eligibility or go into the National Basketball Association draft after his junior year. By considering the possible outcomes of each decision, the athlete is better informed and thus better prepared to make his choice.

COMPUTER SIMULATION

The topics introduced so far are analytical techniques which provide a solution that is "optimal," given the inputs and assumptions of the models. Generally, these models involve mathematical procedures which can be applied to numerous decision-making situations. However, there are many other cases where the decision problem to be modeled either contains so much uncertainty or is so complex that a traditional

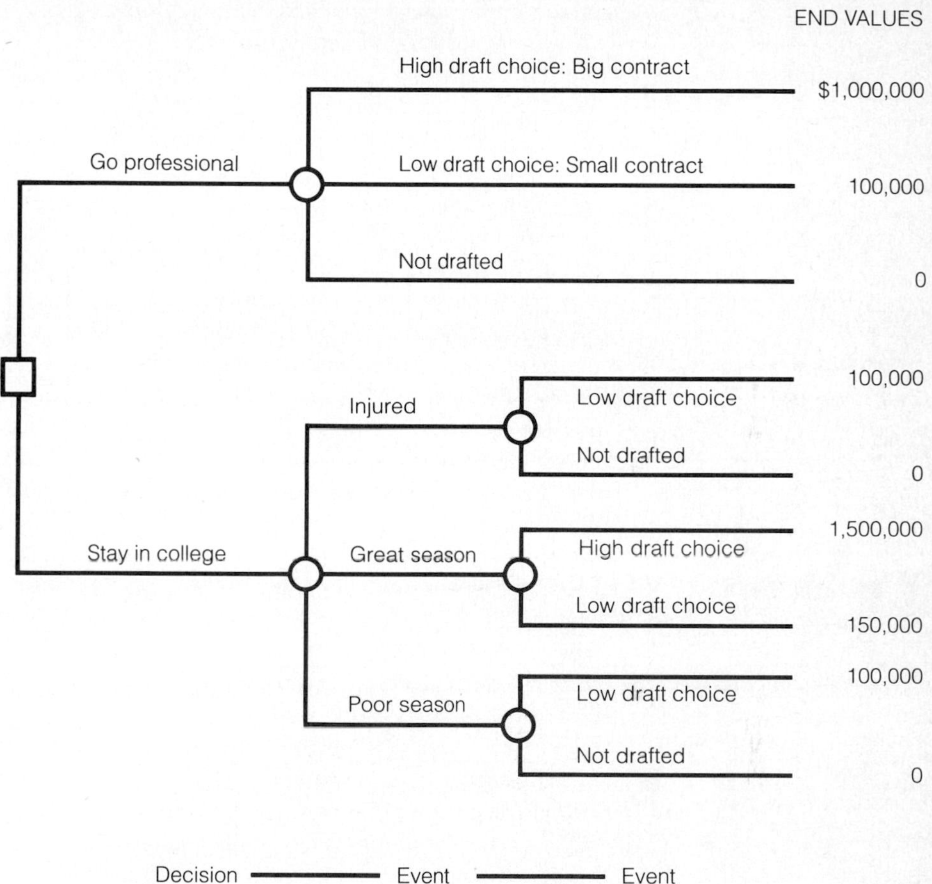

Figure 1-5
Decision tree for basketball player

management science model cannot be formed. In these instances, decision makers turn to *simulation*. More specifically, they turn to computer simulation, since virtually any practical simulation is performed on a computer.

A computer simulation model is a computer program which mimics a real-world situation or system. The behavior of the real system can be studied by examining the behavior of the computer simulation model. Simulation models are used to answer "What if?" questions about the modeled system. For instance, a simulation model of an airport might be used to explore the impact that different landing and take-off schedules would have on air traffic congestion or on customer service in the baggage pickup and flight check-in areas. The model could account for such uncertainties as weather problems, mechanical problems, and other factors affecting airport operations.

Chapter 16 discusses the steps in developing and using computer simulation models.

OTHER MODELS

The management science techniques discussed so far account for many of the applications encountered in business situations. However, there are other important techniques which are applicable in more limited circumstances. One of these is *dynamic programming*. As you will see in Chapter 17, a dynamic programming solution involves breaking a large, complex problem into a series of smaller problems. With dynamic programming, the solutions to the smaller problems (or stages) will lead to the general solution to the original larger problem.

For example, a company that builds airplanes might use a dynamic programming model to help in scheduling production for a 6-month time period. Whereas linear programming might be used to determine the optimal allocation of production resources at a particular time, dynamic programming can be used to show how these resources should be allocated over the planning period on a month-by-month basis.

The *Markov process model* is another quantitative model which has applications in situations where a decision maker wants to track the performance of a system over time. For example, in a manufacturing environment, the Markov model can be used to analyze whether a piece of equipment which has been functioning properly in one period will continue to function properly in the next period. Such analysis is helpful in establishing maintenance schedules. A Markov process model might also be used to analyze the effectiveness of inventory policies over time by projecting the costs incurred under various ordering plans.

Chapter 18 introduces the Markov technique and illustrates how it can be applied in different business situations.

WHAT MANAGEMENT SCIENCE MODELS MEAN TO YOU

From our experience with students, we are aware that at least some of you are now saying, "Hey, I'm going to be an accountant (or a marketing manager, or a financial analyst . . .). I'll never have to use these models." Chances are you are wrong. Many surveys of managers have shown that large percentages of organizations use these tools: 90% use forecasting, 80% use linear programming, 87% use simulation, 59% use queuing theory, and so forth. (For examples, see Shannon et al. and Forgionne, listed in the Chapter References.)

If you go to work for an organization that uses management science models as an aid to decision making, you will obviously be a more valuable employee if you already know something about the models. And if you go to work for an organization that could benefit from management science models but is not using them, your knowledge can provide valuable assistance to your employer. The first step in any decision situation is to determine which, if any, management science technique is appropriate. Because this is a crucial step, throughout the text we will stress the importance of identifying the correct model for the problem being considered.

1-2 THE MANAGEMENT SCIENCE MODELING CONCEPT

In the preceding sections, we introduced the management science topics covered in this text and discussed their potential importance to you as future decision makers. However, before we move to Chapter 2 and begin to discuss the tools of management science in detail, we will provide an overview of the steps involved in developing a management science model. In addition, we will introduce some terms which need to be defined to aid your understanding and ability to apply these techniques.

We have used the term *model* a number of times before when discussing management science techniques: A **model** is a representation of a real situation or system. Most people have had some experience with models in one form or another, such as a model train, a model car, or a doll when you were a child. In high school, you may have had access to a driving simulator which allowed you to practice driving without running the risk of wrecking a real car. Or you may have participated in a computer business simulation game in another course. You may have developed accounting spreadsheets in which you could ask questions such as, "If we changed sales by $25,000, what would be the impact on cash flow?"

In each of these instances, a model is used to represent reality. There are several types of models. An **iconic model** is a physical representation of a real object. A doll and a model car are examples of iconic models. An **analog model** is a physical system used to represent a different physical system. For instance, systems as complex as our national economic system have been modeled using electrical analog models. A thermometer might be thought of as a model of the molecular activity which we perceive as warmth.

While iconic and analog models have value in some decision-making situations, in most cases when models and decision-making are connected, the types of models referred to are mathematical models. A **mathematical model** is one which uses mathematical equations and logical operations to represent a real system. For instance, a very simple mathematical model used to represent a real system involves the cost of renting a car. An equation can be developed to represent the rental company's pricing structure, such as:

$$\text{Price} = (\$19.95 \times \text{days used}) + (\$.13 \times \text{miles driven})$$

The price depends on how many days the vehicle is used plus the number of miles driven. We could complicate the model by including the possibility of being charged for damage to the vehicle or for returning the car late, or any number of other factors.

Organizations use models as decision-making aids because they are cheaper and less time-consuming than experimenting with the real system. For instance, if you were debating the effect of changing an assembly line, one alternative would be to physically make the change and look at the results. But this would be an expensive and time-consuming process. If the change was not effective, you have wasted both time and money. If you have a model that accurately represents the assembly line, you can first try out changes on the model and then implement only those that seem most promising.

You should always remember that models rarely duplicate the real system perfectly. Instead, they represent an approximation of the real system. If a model can approximate the real system within acceptable limits, it can be used to provide information for the decision process; if not, then it shouldn't be used. We will expand on this concept later in the text.

MODEL CLASSIFICATIONS

All of the management science models discussed in this text are mathematical representations of actual systems. Mathematical models can be divided into two distinct classes: *deterministic* and *stochastic*.

Deterministic Models

Keep in mind that a model is a representation of a real system or situation. If the system or situation can be adequately modeled by assuming that all the factors which influence the outputs are known with certainty, a **deterministic model** will be used. For many situations, decision makers find deterministic models very appropriate. For instance, accountants and financial analysts set up deterministic models to measure the impact of various investment alternatives on taxes. Such factors as tax rates and investment return are assumed to be known with certainty. The users then obtain answers to various "What if?" questions by changing the values of one or more factors in the model.

Many of the management science techniques presented in this text fall within the deterministic classification. For instance, most inventory control models are considered deterministic, since the costs and demands used in the models are assumed to be known with certainty. The recommended inventory decisions are optimal, given the levels of costs and demands used in the model. A variety of "What if?" questions can be posed by changing the values of costs or demands. A network model of an accounting audit is deterministic if the activities and their completion costs and times are known with certainty.

Some management science authors and practitioners claim that deterministic models are limited in scope and represent only gross approximations of the real system being modeled. Although we don't totally disagree with this position, we believe that deterministic models have a place in business decision making and should be considered for situations in which the deterministic assumptions are reasonable or the impact of uncertainty is minimal. Also, developing a deterministic model is sometimes the first step in formulating a more realistic model. We will have more to say about these issues as we discuss various management science techniques in the text.

Stochastic Models

If in modeling a system we encounter parts of the system that are not known with certainty, the model must provide some means for incorporating uncertainty. In management science models, uncertainty is introduced by using probability. Models which have at least one uncontrolled component whose value is unknown but assumed to vary according to a probability distribution are called **stochastic models.**

For example, one uncontrollable factor in an inventory system is demand for the product. A deterministic model would assume demand to be fixed at some specific level or rate. But this may not be realistic, since actual demand might vary from the assumed fixed level. A stochastic model would attempt to incorporate this variation by using a probability distribution to represent demand. For instance, the demand during a given week might be assumed to be normally distributed with a certain mean and standard deviation. The model's output would reflect the uncertain demand through that probability distribution.

Computer simulation models which directly use probability distributions are called **Monte Carlo models.** The use of Monte Carlo models is analogous to sampling in a statistical study. Each run of the computer model is thought of as one trial of the experiment. Consider, for example, development of a computer simulation model for a small manufacturer of office desks. Probability distributions might be used to represent the potential uncertainty in several areas, including demand, machine downtime, and quality. Each run of the model will produce a potentially different shipping quantity because different values occur for demand, machine downtime, and quality. However, a long-run average shipping quantity can be determined and the results associated with a specified production plan can be analyzed by observing many runs of the model and by using inferential statistical methods.

Stochastic models probably reflect reality in most situations better than do deterministic models, but they are also generally more costly to develop and more complex to operate. As with any form of information gathering, one must be careful that the cost of collecting information does not exceed the value of the information. The choice between employing a deterministic model versus a stochastic model should be based on the ratio of cost to perceived benefit.

1-3 THE MANAGEMENT SCIENCE PROBLEM-SOLVING APPROACH

If making good business decisions were always simple, there would be no need for management science models. In reality, however, the complex operational environments of many organizations make decision making far from simple—and also make quantitative tools a necessity for the people who make decisions.

Before we discuss more specifically the role of management science models, let's review the decision-making process and its relationship to management science. Figure 1-6 summarizes the steps involved in the management science approach to decision making. Note that these steps closely parallel the process known as the scientific method.

IDENTIFY AND DEFINE THE PROBLEM

The first step in the decision-making process is to determine that a problem exists and to define that problem. Although seemingly obvious, this step is often overlooked, or at least not formalized. But without a clear definition of the problem, making effective decisions that will lead to a solution will be difficult, if not impossible.

In order to define the problem, the *problem environment* must be carefully observed. This may involve nothing more than visits with the people involved in the system or process under consideration, or it may require lengthy study and extensive data collection. In either case, the problem definition will evolve; and in most instances, it can be classified into one of a number of forms which the decision maker or the organization has had experience with in the past. This will serve to narrow the focus of the decision process.

An important point in the problem definition step is to try to get everyone to agree on precisely what the problem is. A sure prescription for disaster is to have everyone working very hard, and very diligently, but on different definitions of the problem. One additional point: When we say that the first step in the decision process is to define the problem, we are thinking of problem in the widest sense. The problem may involve a difficulty, but it may also involve the choice between two or more very positive alternatives. Thus a problem is not necessarily a bad situation.

FORMULATE THE MODEL

As we have indicated, the subject of management science deals with the development and application of mathematical models. The mathematical model is made of one or more equations which describe the system. For example, suppose the county highway district is responsible for paving all the roads in the county. The paving projects require a gravel base and an asphalt top. The gravel base costs the county $1.55 per cubic foot, and the asphalt costs $5.44 per cubic foot. A model (or linear equation) which indicates total paving cost for the county is:

$$Z = \$1.55g + \$5.44a$$

In this model, g represents the number of cubic feet of gravel to be used per paving unit, a represents the cubic feet of asphalt, and Z represents the total cost. g, a, and Z are the *variables* in the model. A **variable** is a factor in the model that can change. In this

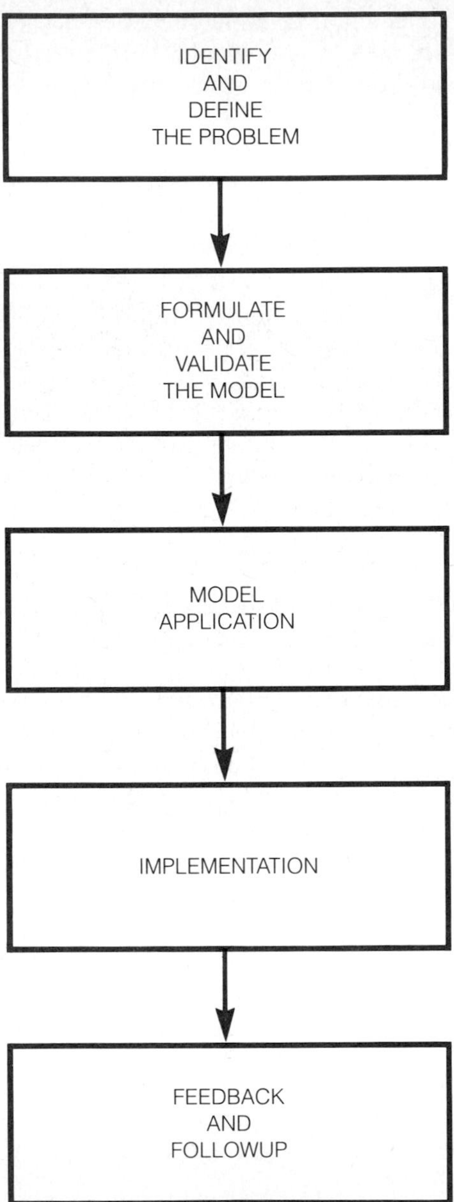

Figure 1-6
Summary of steps in the decision-making process

example, the values for *g* and *a* are determined by the decision maker, based on engineering requirements. Variables that are inputs to the model are called **independent variables** or **endogenous variables.** Once the choice is made for *g* and *a*, their values are substituted into the model and a value of *Z* is output. Output variables are called **dependent variables** because their value depends on the values of the input variables. Dependent variables are also referred to as **exogenous variables.**

A model also contains **parameters**, or constants. In the paving example, $1.55 and $5.44 are the model's parameters because they are fixed. The value of a parameter is often established by studying data. In this case, the county's cost accountants would probably have examined a variety of data before coming up with the $1.55 and $5.44

values. Keep in mind that the quality of the model depends on the accuracy of the parameters and the correctness of the model formulation. Thus, if we are quite certain that these cost values are correct and that there are no other costs involved in paving the road, the total cost model should be of high quality and produce reliable results.

Suppose that in the problem identification phase the county defined a need to determine the appropriate mix of gravel (g) and asphalt (a) so that paving could be done at a minimum cost. Thus, the county's *objective* is to minimize the cost of paving a road of any length. This can be expressed as the following objective function:

$$\text{Minimize } Z = \$1.55g + \$5.44a$$

We see that Z can be minimized by setting g and a to zero, but then no paving would be done. Another option would be to use all gravel ($g > 0$) and no asphalt ($a = 0$), since gravel has a coefficient of \$1.55 versus \$5.44 for asphalt. But if this were done, the road would be gravel, not paved. As in most decision situations, there are *constraints* which place limits on the values of the independent variables. These constraints may also be represented in mathematical form.

Suppose design criteria specify that a combination of 2 parts gravel and 1 part asphalt must make up at least 1.1 cubic feet per paving unit. This constraint can be expressed as follows:

$$2.0g + 1.0a \geq 1.1$$

Another restriction is that the mix must contain at least .15 cubic foot of gravel per paving unit. This can be written as:

$$1.0g \geq .15$$

Also, the maximum amount of gravel in the mix is .80 cubic foot per unit, which can be written as:

$$1.0g \leq .80$$

Likewise, the asphalt must be between .20 and 3.00 cubic feet per unit. This requirement can be expressed using two inequalities, as follows:

$$1.0a \geq .20 \qquad \text{and} \qquad 1.0a \leq 3.00$$

We can now state the model as:

Objective:

$$\text{Minimize } Z = \$1.55g + \$5.44a$$

Subject to:

$$\begin{aligned} 2.0g + 1.0a &\geq 1.10 \\ 1.0g &\geq .15 \\ 1.0g &\leq .80 \\ 1.0a &\geq .20 \\ 1.0a &\leq 3.00 \end{aligned}$$

This model now represents the situation facing the county highway district. Or does it? Once a model is formulated, it must be validated. The **validation** is a check to see that in fact the model does represent the decision system as we know it and that the model performs in a manner consistent with the underlying system. In this case, we need to be sure that the objective function accurately represents the cost function and that the constraints are correctly formulated and complete.

MODEL APPLICATION

Once the model has been formulated and validated, it can be used to provide information about the decision at hand. The county highway department officials are interested in determining the mix of gravel and asphalt which will result in an acceptable paving job (meets the constraints) at a minimum cost. Suppose the department is currently using .80 cubic foot of gravel ($g = .80$) and .30 cubic foot of asphalt ($a = .30$) per paving unit. These quantities satisfy all the constraints and result in the following cost:

$$Z = \$1.55(.80) + \$5.44(.30)$$
$$Z = \$2.872 \text{ per paving unit}$$

The question is whether this is the mix which will yield the minimum cost. To determine the answer, we need to solve for g and a such that Z is minimized and the constraints are satisfied.

Linear programming is the management science technique used to solve a model of this type. Chapters 2 through 6 cover linear programming and its solution procedure. We won't attempt to explain the solution method here, but we will tell you that the "optimal" values for the paving model were found to be:

$$g = .45 \qquad \text{and} \qquad a = .20$$

At these levels, all the constraints are satisfied and the total cost (Z) is minimized:

$$Z = \$1.55(.45) + \$5.44(.20)$$
$$Z = \$1.786$$

This solution represents a saving of $1.086 per paving unit over the cost of the current mix.

IMPLEMENTATION

The results from solving the model are one source of information for the highway district decision makers. In this case, the model shows that a sizable reduction in cost can be achieved by changing to the suggested mix of gravel and asphalt. After this and any other bits of information have been received, the decision maker must process the information and make a decision on the initial problem.

The information provided by management science techniques is often just a primary input to the selection of the "best" course of action. As we will emphasize throughout this text, the value of the information provided by a model depends on how well the model represents reality. It is the decision maker's responsibility to combine the information from all sources in arriving at a decision. However, when management science models are carefully constructed and employed, and when the decision maker understands their potential, the information from the models will play a larger role in the decision process.

FEEDBACK AND FOLLOWUP

While implementing the steps to solve the problem, the decision maker develops an action plan, indicating what improvements should be made and when they should occur. Followup should be done to confirm that the decision actually has the desired result. Often this followup consists of comparing the actual results with those that were forecast by the model.

THE ROLE OF MANAGEMENT SCIENCE MODELS

While management science models are not always needed as part of the decision-making process, there are many situations in which the process can be aided significantly by applying the appropriate technique. For instance, a major U.S. brewery uses linear programming to help determine the best distribution system for its products. Organizations that need more effective management of parts and materials may turn to inventory models for assistance. Recently, a national food processor turned to linear programming for help in evaluating the consequences associated with closing a plant in the Midwest. A major manufacturer of construction components used a PERT/CPM model to help manage the construction of a production line for a new product. A U.S. automobile manufacturer has designed and implemented a large-scale computer simulation model to help analyze its production scheduling worldwide.

These are but a few of the many areas where management science models have a role in the decision-making process. *Management science applications succeed when the problem is defined before the technique is selected.* In those instances where a management science tool has failed, all too often the cause has been an attempt to use a technique inappropriate to the problem. Just because linear programming was successful in one situation does not mean that it can help solve all problems. *The technique employed must fit the problem.* Professor Gene Woolsey, in the November–December 1986 issue of *Interfaces,* reminds us all of the proper role of management science techniques when he says, "MS/OR is the application of mathematics and logic to a real-world problem in such a way that the answer doesn't get in the way of common sense."

1-4 THE ROLE OF COMPUTERS IN MODELING

Since most management science techniques were developed before the widespread use of computers, it may be an overstatement to say that without computers, management science would not exist. However, we are sure that without computers the application of management science models would be far less entrenched in business than it is today. Computers are ideally suited to working with large-scale mathematical models. The largest computers can perform millions of computations per second with virtually no chance for a mathematical error. Thus, decision makers can explore many alternatives in a short amount of time.

Software programs are needed to make computers function. Sometimes these programs are available as software packages and can be used for a variety of applications. Packages such as SAS-OR (Statistical Analysis System–Operations Research) and LINDO are commercially available and are used by many companies. Accompanying this text is a microcomputer software package called MASTER which is designed for smaller-scale problems, like those you will be working with in this course. Sometimes, custom programs must be developed for specific applications, such as those involving simulation. In these instances, special programming languages have been developed to make the task easier for the decision maker.

Computers play a very special role in the application of management science. However, you should never forget that people are required to identify the problems and ultimately make the decisions for their organizations. The proper role of management science models is not this:

Data → Model → Decision

but this:

Data → Model → Information → Decision

1-5 SUMMARY AND CONCLUSIONS

This chapter has introduced you to the subject of management science. Although the collection of quantitative techniques included under this subject heading is quite extensive, this text focuses on those that are used most often. While management science models are based on mathematical procedures, we will not stress these manipulations. Instead, our emphasis will be on recognizing the types of situations for which each technique is appropriate and on how to use the technique to provide information for the decision process.

This chapter has also introduced models and discussed their role in the decision-making process. Recall that *a model is a representation of a real system or situation.* As you continue with this course, and as you read about new topics in the text, we hope you will recognize that each management science technique is a model for a particular type of situation. Since management science models have proven so valuable to business decision makers—largely because of the wide variety of situations to which they can be applied—familiarizing yourself with the techniques in this text should be of lasting benefit.

General Questions and Assignments

1. The term *model* is used throughout Chapter 1. In your own words, define the term and describe an example of a model based upon your own experience.
2. Using the information in this chapter, discuss in your own terms what a management science model is.
3. The chapter briefly discusses waiting-line models. Describe two business situations in which you think a waiting-line model might be used. Discuss the specific decision for which the model might be used to supply information.
4. Using the brief description of forecasting in this chapter, describe two business situations in which forecasting models could be applied. Discuss in your own terms what forecasting models are used for in business decision making.
5. Discuss the difference between a deterministic model and a stochastic model.
6. Go to the library and locate one of the articles listed in the References Section for this chapter. Read it and write a short review discussing the main points and the single most informative feature of the article. While you are at the library, look around to become familiar with where the management science materials are located.
7. Describe the steps in the management science decision-making process. Identify a decision you have to make in the near future. Explain how you could use these steps in making your decision.

8. Valliview Manufacturing makes and sells a residential alarm system. The company's cost accountants have determined that the per unit production cost is $140. Valliview sells the alarm systems for $300 each. The company also has a monthly fixed cost (salaries, insurance, property lease, etc.) of $11,000. In their planning process, the sales managers are interested in the number of units which need to be sold to break even.
   a. In your own words, define the problem facing Valliview Manufacturing.
   b. Develop a mathematical model to represent the problem the Valliview managers face, but do not solve it.
   c. Identify the input variable(s) in the model you developed for part **b**. Define *input variable*.
   d. What is the output variable in the part **b** model? Define *output variable*.
   e. What are the parameters in the part **b** model? Define *parameter*.
   f. Solve the model you developed for part **b**.
   g. Discuss how the results of the model should be used in this application.
9. Suppose the following model has been formulated by the production manager at the Decatur Lumber Company:

$$\text{Maximize } Z = \$3.40x_1 + \$5.76x_2$$

Subject to:

$$8x_1 + 5x_2 \leq 30{,}000$$
$$1.5x_1 + 3.0x_2 \leq 17{,}500$$

where:

Z = total profit
x_1 = sheets of ⅜-inch plywood
x_2 = sheets of ½-inch plywood

   a. What are the input variables in this model?
   b. What is the output variable(s) in this model?
   c. What are the parameters of this model? Why are these items referred to as parameters?
   d. The value $3.40 is the profit coefficient for ⅜-inch plywood. Discuss how this value might have been determined by the lumber company.
   e. Identify the objective function in this model. Define *objective function*.
   f. Identify the constraint(s) in the model. Discuss what the constraint(s) represent.
10. At a recent staff meeting, an assistant department manager remarked, "We used a computer model to determine how many units to produce this week, and it said to produce 30,000 units. But how can we produce this many units? We don't have enough materials or machines. It's just not possible. But if that's what the model says, I must be wrong."

    Write a short management letter discussing this situation. Be sure to specifically address the issue of depending on model output. Also indicate what, if anything, might be wrong with the model.

Chapter Glossary

Analog model A model in which one physical system is used to represent a different physical system.

Constraint Limitation placed on a model. A constraint is usually expressed as a mathematical relationship which represents a limited resource or range of acceptable activity.

Dependent variable A variable which is an output from a model and whose value is based on the values of the independent variables.

Deterministic model A model in which all functional relationships, and coefficients in those relationships, are assumed to be known with certainty.

Endogenous variable A variable which is an input to a model and whose value is often controlled by the decision maker. An endogenous variable is also called an *independent variable.*

Exogenous variable A variable which is an output from a model and whose value is based on the values of the independent variables. An exogenous variable is also referred to as a *dependent variable.*

Forecast A prediction of some future activity.

Iconic model A scaled physical representation of a real object.

Independent variable A variable which is an input to a model and whose value is often controlled by the decision maker. An independent variable is also called an *endogenous variable.*

Mathematical model A model in which a physical system is represented by a set of mathematical relationships and logical operations.

Model A representation of a real system or situation.

Monte Carlo models Models that incorporate uncertainty by sampling values from probability distributions.

Parameter A fixed value or constant in a model.

Stochastic model A model in which uncertainty is incorporated in the functional relationships through the use of probability distributions. It is also known as a *probabilistic model.*

Validation The process of checking to determine whether a model accurately represents the system being modeled.

Variable A factor in a model that can change.

Chapter References

BOOKS

Ackoff, Russell L., and Maurice W. Sasieni. *Fundamentals of Operations Research.* New York: Wiley, 1968.

Beer, Stafford. *Management Sciences: The Business Use of Operations Research.* New York: Doubleday, 1967.

Churchman, C. W., R. L. Ackoff, and E. L. Arnoff. *Introduction to Operations Research.* New York: Wiley, 1957.

Hillier, F. S., and G. J. Lieberman. *Operations Research,* 3d ed. Oakland: Holden-Day, 1980.

Wagner, Harvey M. *Principles of Management Science.* Englewood Cliffs, N.J.: Prentice-Hall, 1975.

ARTICLES

Forgionne, G. A. "Corporate Management Science Activities: An Update." *Interfaces,* Vol. 13, No. 3, 1983.

Gaither, N. "The Adoption of Operations Research Techniques by Manufacturing Organizations." *Decision Sciences,* Vol. 6, No. 4, 1975.

Grayson, C. J., Jr. "Management Science and Business Practice." *Harvard Business Review,* Vol. 51, 1973.

Ledbetter, W., and J. Cox. "Are OR Techniques Being Used?" *Industrial Engineering,* Vol. 9, 1977.

Radnor, M., and R. D. Neal. "The Progress of Management Science Activities in Large U.S. Industrial Corporations." *Operations Research,* Vol. 21, 1973.

Shannon, R. E., S. S. Long, and B. P. Buckles. "Operations Research Methodologies in Industrial Engineering: A Survey." *AIIE Transactions,* Vol. 12, No. 4, 1980.

Sharda, R. "The State of the Art of Linear Programming on Personnel Computers." *Interfaces,* Vol. 18, July–August 1988.

Thomas, G., and J. DaCosta. "A Sample Survey of Corporate Operations Research." *Interfaces,* August 1979.

Thomas, G., and M. Mitchell. "OR in the U.S. Marine Corps: A Characterization." *Interfaces,* June 1983.

Ward, S. C. "Arguments for Constructively Simple Models." *Journal of the Operations Research Society,* Vol. 40, February 1989.

Woolsey, Gene. "The Fifth Column: The Case of the Unused Forecast, or, When Trying to Forecast What's to Be, First Try $Y - MX + B$." *Interfaces,* Vol. 16, No. 6, 1986.

Mini Case

CASE 1
ORE-IDA FOODS

Ore-Ida Foods, a subsidiary of H. J. Heinz Corporation, is a widely recognized retail brand in the United States. Ore-Ida dominates the retail market for frozen potato products, is in the top 10 among all food brands in retail sales, and is one of the top 3 in frozen food sales. It is a major player in the food services market for frozen potato products (sales to such fast-food companies as McDonald's and Burger King). In addition, Ore-Ida owns Foodways National, the packer of Weight Watchers brand frozen foods. The company is a major, and in some cases dominant, player in a very large retail market.

However, while Ore-Ida has achieved a leading position in its industry, the company is a rather recent entry in the retail food market. Ore-Ida was started by Nephi and Golden Grigg in 1951, when they acquired a small freezing plant in Ontario, Oregon, near the Idaho border. Initially, the plant processed only corn, but soon the Griggs switched to frozen French-fried potatoes. Ore-Ida was a pioneer in that market.

In making French fries, part of the potato is unused and may go to waste. In 1958, the Grigg brothers introduced a product they called Tater Tots, which uses potato scraps left over from the French-fry operation. This product not only greatly increased the yield from the raw potato, it also increased overall profitability for the company.

The company grew, and in 1961 it went public under its current name of Ore-Ida Foods, Inc. Ore-Ida opened a second processing plant that same year. Under the direction of D. B. Berelson and Co., a food broker which had purchased the rights to Ore-Ida brand's retail sales, an expanded line of frozen products (including additional potato products, corn on the cob, and onion rings) was introduced.

By 1965, the company had about 23% of the U.S. market for frozen potatoes and annual sales of $38 million. That year, Ore-Ida was acquired by H. J. Heinz for stock valued at $29.7 million.

The new owners brought in a consulting firm, McKinsey & Company, to study ways of making the operations more efficient. In their studies, McKinsey found indications of conflict of interest among the managers from the period before the Heinz takeover. The McKinsey consultants also pointed out problems associated with rundown and poorly operated plants. The first finding led to a dismissal of the previous managers. The second finding prompted McKinsey to construct a management science model to use in improving the operational efficiency of the two processing plants.

In 1967, Scott Robertson, who had recently earned a master's degree from Northwestern University, was hired to operate and maintain the model. His first step was to study the model and try to relate it to the operations at the Ontario, Oregon, plant. After extensive analysis, Scott was convinced that the model did not accurately represent the current plant operation. He met with J. Wray Connolly, the director of procurement, who had hired him, and recommended that the outdated McKinsey model be scrapped. Connolly agreed. Scott Robertson stayed on, and today he continues to promote the use of management science tools in Ore-Ida's decision-making process. Partly as a result of Robertson's leadership, Ore-Ida now makes extensive use of management science tools—and it uses them successfully.

ASSIGNMENTS

1. Do research to find out more about Ore-Ida Foods and the frozen food industry. Specifically, locate information which describes the processing involved in the frozen food industry. Write a report which summarizes your findings.
2. Search out in your own community one or more companies which use management science techniques in decision making. Arrange an interview with a key person who uses management science techniques in that company. If possible, obtain permission to meet with him or her throughout the school term to discuss management science applications at that company.

Chapter 2

INTRODUCTION TO LINEAR PROGRAMMING

Chapter Outline

Chapter 2

Why You Need to Know

Possibly the most important function of a business decision maker is to allocate resources efficiently. Good decision making is often an effort to use resources — such as time, production capacity, money, personnel, and materials — in a manner that will result in a maximum payoff or a minimum cost. Linear programming is a management science technique that is helpful in formulating decision strategies to maximize such outputs as profits, total production yield, and total investment return. It is also used in situations where the objective is to minimize such factors as production costs, investment risks, or marketing expenses. Since it was developed in 1947 by George Dantzig, linear programming has become perhaps the most widely used management science decision tool. It has applications in every functional business area, including accounting, finance, marketing, human resources, and operations. All the applications have one feature in common: the allocation of scarce resources in an optimal manner.

Because linear programming applications cover all the functional areas of business, you will very likely have a need to work with this technique. Therefore you need to understand how to formulate linear programming problems and how to interpret their solutions.

Chapter Objectives

This is the first of several chapters on the topic of linear programming. After a brief historical review of the subject, we will introduce the basics of linear programming. We will spend considerable time on formulating linear programming problems. We will also demonstrate how to graphically solve small linear programming problems and will introduce a number of important concepts associated with linear programming.

Specifically, the objectives of this chapter are:

1. To help you understand the meaning of the important terms associated with linear programming.
2. To convey the objectives of linear programming by demonstrating both maximization and minimization applications.
3. To assist you in identifying linear programming applications and to aid you in learning how linear programming problems are formulated.
4. To illustrate how linear programming problems involving two variables can be solved graphically and, through the graphical solution process, demonstrate some important concepts associated with linear programming.

2-1 MANAGEMENT SCIENCE AND THE SEARCH FOR OPTIMAL SOLUTIONS

One way to look at management science is as a long campaign, conducted on many fronts, to apply the logic and discipline of the physical sciences to managerial decision making. The first step in this effort is to construct a model, usually a mathematical model, to describe the physical decision-making situation. If such a model can be successfully constructed, some of the uncertainty associated with managerial decisions can be removed and the best, or "optimal," alternative can be selected.

However, the idea of generating an "optimal solution" to a decision problem must be taken with a degree of caution. First, not all management science techniques are designed to produce optimal solutions. Second, even for those techniques where optimality is guaranteed, the guarantee is valid only within the assumptions and limitations of the model. If the wrong model is used, or if the right model is incorrectly specified, the outcome can be very misleading. The solution can be truly optimal only if the model accurately represents the real system being studied. To the extent that the model departs from reality, the solution will be less than optimal. But if the decision maker can specify an appropriate model and live with the assumptions and limitations underlying that model, the *information* produced can be very valuable in the decision-making process.

As a decision-making tool, linear programming has two advantages. First, it can be used to represent a wide variety of physical situations. Second, the structure of the model is such that the linear programming solution technique will provide a mathematically optimal result for the formulated problem.

2-2 THE BEGINNINGS OF LINEAR PROGRAMMING

The history of linear programming is extremely rich and full of major contributors, including Nobel prize winners. Any effort to give a condensed version is certain to omit some of the people who have made important contributions. (We apologize in advance for any such omissions.) Thus, we will concentrate our description on theory and time frames and will minimize our discussion of individuals. A more complete exploration of the beginnings of this technique can be found in *Linear Programming and Extensions,* by George Dantzig (Princeton, 1963).

The present form of linear programming, and its application in the world today, is the product of three approaches to problem solving—mathematics, economic modeling, and military planning—and the accelerated development necessitated by World War II. We will examine these factors in the following paragraphs.

A major factor in the development of linear programming involves the set of mathematical tools associated with solving a system of inequalities. (Many of the techniques developed to deal with systems of inequalities are discussed in linear algebra courses.) Baron Jean Baptiste Joseph Fourier, a French mathematician, seems to have been the first to recognize the importance of systems of inequalities, in the early 1800s. The first person to structure a decision problem in what is now related to a linear programming format was Russian mathematician L. V. Kantorovich, in 1939. Unfortunately, his work was universally ignored for about 20 years.

John Von Neumann, an American born in Hungary, was generally regarded as the greatest mathematician of his lifetime (1903–57). He made at least two major contributions in this area during the time before linear programming. First, his development of game theory with Oskar Morgenstern was important since it, like linear programming, is based on linear inequalities. Second, he was instrumental in developing the logic of present computer programming, without which realistic linear programming models could not be solved.

The second factor was economic modeling, particularly the modeling of the U.S. economy. This modeling, beginning as early as the 1700s, was vastly increased after the crash of the stock market in 1929. During the Great Depression, economists in the federal government and elsewhere tried to find an explanation for what was happening to the economy and how to stimulate a rebound. While many people contributed to this effort, of particular importance was mathematician John Von Neumann. His 1932 paper titled "A Model of General Economic Equilibrium" proposed what was later to be formulated as a dynamic linear programming model for producing commodities and contributed to applications of modeling techniques. In addition, Wassily Leontief's quantitative model of the American economy was important because it was an empirical rather than a theoretical model of an economic system. Leontief's model was structured in matrix form, the form linear programming was to eventually assume.

The third factor was the increasing complexity of planning for future military operations. In times of peace, military staffs spend a great deal of time on such planning. While at one time an experienced commander could personally plan most of a military action, as the numbers of people and areas involved became larger, planning staffs were added solely for this purpose. These staffs were concerned with developing methods to deliver the personnel and equipment necessary to meet any potential military threat. As the military range of operations increased, these plans became increasingly complex and were subdivided into areas of specialization. The function of a commander then became selecting from a group of alternatives based on some set of objectives, and the commander's staff was actively involved in looking for tools to aid the selection process.

When World War II began, the United States found itself involved in a truly global war of previously unexperienced proportions. The requirements for both people and equipment became gigantic, as did the planning efforts necessary to ensure that enough of everything was on hand for the planned actions. The process was so complex the plans were often divided into subcomponents and worked on individually. In addition, the planners soon realized they could not be bound by tradition in their efforts and were willing to look for new ways to attack their problems.

In 1943, this willingness led the U.S. Air Corps to form a program monitoring group. The purpose of this group was to develop a system to plan and coordinate the efforts of the Air Corps to achieve a set of objectives. During the latter part of the war, the program monitoring group decided the effort was so complex that some scientific programming techniques were required. The developmental programs, which continued after the end of the war, led to the introduction, in 1947, of the *simplex method* to solve linear programming problems. While this procedure is most commonly associated with George Dantzig, who was at the time working as part of Project SCOOP (Scientific Computation of Optimal Programs) for the U.S. Air Force, certainly his work was founded on the efforts of many people.

Rapid advances were made after the introduction of the simplex method. In a meeting with Dantzig in 1947, John Von Neumann was able to translate the theorems of game theory into equivalent inequality constraints. In addition, he developed the concept of duality (discussed in Chapter 4) during these discussions. (One rumor has it that he scratched out his ideas on the back of napkins at a cocktail party!) Beginning in 1947, T. C. Koopmans brought to the attention of the nation's economists the potential of linear programming for addressing a large number of economic concerns. Perhaps more importantly, in 1949 Koopmans organized a conference of the Cowles Commission for Research in Economics that was devoted to linear programming. This conference was attended by most of the people who were to set the trend for applying linear programming to economic decision making, including Paul Samuelson, Robert Dorfman, and Robert Solow.

The first industrial application of linear programming came in 1951, when it was used in oil refinery scheduling. After that it was applied in 1953 to the food distribution and the metal working industries, in 1954 to papermill scheduling, and in 1955 to electrical power generation and distribution. Since 1955, the applications and extensions of linear programming have expanded until it is now perhaps the most widely used management science tool.

Note, however, the original applications were in industries that produced large volumes of a standard product. Such a situation is the easiest place to apply this tool, and probably the most successful applications are still in these industries. We will illustrate some areas of application through the examples and problems in this and subsequent chapters. The Chapter References contain many examples of works describing how linear programming has been applied.

Much work has also been done to develop new and better solution techniques for linear programming. The simplex method, which is introduced in Chapter 3, is still the most frequently used technique. However, for large industrial problems, it has been found to be fairly inefficient. In 1984, a management scientist at the Bell Laboratories, Narendra Karmarkar, pioneered a new solution procedure which, for large linear programming problems, is reputed to be as much as 50 times faster than the simplex method. This finding was so newsworthy it was featured in *Time* magazine and the *Wall Street Journal* and in a number of scholarly journals. Even as you read this, much work is being done to further improve linear programming as a decision-making tool.

2-3 LINEAR PROGRAMMING APPLICATIONS AND FORMULATION

Probably the chief reason that linear programming has achieved its position of importance as a management science tool is its very broad range of applications in business decision making. While not every possible application area can be addressed in this text, this section does describe a variety of situations in which linear programming can be applied. We will also discuss how linear programming problems are formulated or modeled. The formulations are critical, since the solution techniques presented later in this chapter and in Chapter 3 depend on a correctly formulated model. We will begin with a very basic application and then extend into more complex examples.

A PRODUCT MIX APPLICATION

A major application area for linear programming is determining product mix. In these situations, the decision maker is commonly faced with trying to determine how many units of two or more different products to produce and/or market. The per unit profits are known for each product, and the objective may be to maximize total profit from the business activity during some specified time period. There are usually one or more constraints that restrict the decision maker's choice of how many of each product to produce. Linear programming has proven very useful in a wide variety of industries for problems fitting this description.

Our purpose here is to provide an elementary example of a product mix application. In addition, we will carefully take you through the steps in formulating the appropriate linear programming problem.

Richards Paint Company

The Richards Paint Company, headquartered in Jackson, Mississippi, makes paint base for sale and distribution in the southeastern United States. The company produces two types of paint base, oil and latex. A problem facing the company each month is how many gallons of oil base and how many gallons of latex base paint to make.

Richards Paint sells its base to large retailers, who add coloring pigments and then market the paint as their own house brand. Potential customers for Richards Paint are large retailers such as Sears and K-Mart. In this example, Richards has a sales contract for next month that will net $.40 profit per gallon from the latex base and $.50 per gallon from the oil base.

Initially, you might conclude that since oil base is more profitable than latex, Richards Paint should produce only oil base. While this might be the correct decision in some cases, it is akin to saying General Motors should produce only Cadillacs, since this is its most profitable car. Obviously, for General Motors, as for Richards Paint, the product mix decision depends on more than per unit profitability. Linear programming provides a format that allows consideration of the numerous factors affecting realistic decision-making situations. In this example, we will show how Richards Paint can use linear programming to determine the "optimal" product mix. We will also introduce some of the key terminology associated with linear programming.

Although a certain amount of creativity and experience may be required, the basic process of converting a decision-making situation to a linear programming problem can be very structured. The steps in formulating a linear programming problem are:

1. Define the decision variables.
2. Specify the objective function.
3. Determine the constraints.

In the following paragraphs, we will explain these steps as we discuss the Richards Paint production mix problem.

Step 1 **Define the decision variables.** The first step in formulating a linear programming model is to define the decision variables in the physical situation. **Decision variables** are those factors under the decision maker's control during the time frame of the decision. Since Richards makes only two types of paint base, and since the company is trying to decide how much of each type to make, the decision variables are (1) the number of gallons of latex and (2) the number of gallons of oil base. In typical linear programming notation, we define these variables as follows:

x_1 = number of gallons of latex produced

x_2 = number of gallons of oil base produced

Step 2 **Specify the objective function.** The net profit for each paint base is known: $.40 for each gallon of x_1 (latex) and $.50 per gallon of x_2 (oil base). The company's net profit function (assuming it sells all that is produced) can be written in the following form:

$$\text{Net profit} = Z = .40x_1 + .50x_2 \qquad (2\text{-}1)$$

The coefficients on the variables in the objective function are called the **contribution rates.** For instance, each gallon of latex (x_1) contributes \$.40 to profit and each gallon of oil base (x_2) contributes \$.50 to profit.

Since the company is in business to make a profit, let's assume its objective for the month should be to *maximize* net profit. Thus, we can reformulate equation 2-1 as the **objective function**, which tells us what the net profit is for any combination of x_1 (latex) and x_2 (oil base) production:

$$\text{Maximize } Z = .40x_1 + .50x_2 \qquad (2\text{-}2)$$

where Z = net profit.

Since the objective function states that Richards Paint wants to maximize the total net profit, the company needs to decide how many gallons of latex base paint (x_1) and oil base paint (x_2) to produce in order to maximize Z (net profit).

Step 3 **Determine the constraints.** In looking at Richards' objective function, the managers should want to produce huge volumes of both types of paint base, since the equation indicates that the more of each type produced, the higher the company's profit. Unfortunately, since Richards does not have unlimited resources, there will be constraints on its production capability. A **constraint** is any condition which limits a decision maker's flexibility in assigning values to the decision variables. The constraints for the Richards Paint production mix example are described below.

Richards has contracts which require the company to produce *at least* 200,000 gallons of latex and *at least* 300,000 gallons of oil base. Further, the capacity of the paint plant allows for *at most* 500,000 gallons of latex base and *at most* 800,000 gallons of oil base to be produced.

These conditions are practical constraints on Richards' production. *In a linear programming application, the constraints are formulated as equalities and/or inequalities involving the decision variables.* For instance, we can formulate the minimum-production constraints as follows:

$$x_1 \geq 200{,}000 \text{ gallons of latex}$$
$$x_2 \geq 300{,}000 \text{ gallons of oil base}$$

These constraints are linear inequalities of the "greater than or equal to ($\geq$)" variety. The inequality concept is important in linear programming. While strict equalities (=) are used in mathematics to represent equations, there are many business situations (such as the minimum-production constraints above) which cannot be described by an equation. In these cases, inequalities are used. Inequalities provide the flexibility to solve a wider range of business problems than do equations. The mathematical solution technique which will be introduced in the next chapter requires that the constraints contain all the decision variables. Therefore, we will write the constraint inequalities as:

(a) $1x_1 + 0x_2 \geq 200{,}000$
(b) $0x_1 + 1x_2 \geq 300{,}000$

In constraints (a) and (b), coefficients have been placed in front of each decision variable. Called *constraint coefficients,* they determine the rate at which the decision variables impact the right-hand-side limiting value. When the constraint is "greater than or equal to (≥)," the coefficient indicates the rate at which each unit of a decision variable will add to the right-hand-side requirement.

For instance, in constraint (a), for latex base, the 1 coefficient on the x_1 variable means that each gallon of latex base produced will contribute 1 gallon toward the demand requirement of 200,000 gallons of latex shown on the right-hand side. The 0 coefficient on variable x_2, oil base, means the demand for latex paint, shown on the right-hand side, is not affected by the variable x_2.

Most companies have limits on their total sales and production volumes. In this example, Richards has plant capacity limitations which make it impossible to produce more than 500,000 gallons of latex paint and more than 800,000 gallons of oil base paint. These capacity limitations can be arranged in the constraint format as follows:

(c) $1x_1 + 0x_2 \leq 500{,}000$
(d) $0x_1 + 1x_2 \leq 800{,}000$

The capacity constraint coefficients can be interpreted in a manner similar to those for the minimum production constraints. When the constraint is "less than or equal to (≤)," the coefficient indicates the rate at which the decision variable consumes (or subtracts from) the limiting quantity on the right-hand side. In constraint (c), each gallon of latex (x_1) produced uses 1 unit of the production limit for latex. The coefficients in constraint (d) indicate that each unit of oil base (x_2) uses 1 unit of the oil base production limit.

The linear programming model to this point, including the objective function and four constraints, is:

Maximize $Z = .40x_1 + .50x_2$

Subject to:
Delivery requirement constraints

(a) $1x_1 + 0x_2 \geq 200{,}000$
(b) $0x_1 + 1x_2 \geq 300{,}000$

Plant capacity constraints

(c) $1x_1 + 0x_2 \leq 500{,}000$
(d) $0x_1 + 1x_2 \leq 800{,}000$

The company's available supply of color pigment material is 1,000,000 units. This provides a further capacity constraint. The combined production of latex and oil base cannot use more than 1,000,000 units of color pigments. Each gallon of latex requires 1 unit of pigment and each gallon of the oil base paint requires 1.5 units of color pigment. This constraint can be written as:

(e) $1.0x_1 + 1.5x_2 \leq 1{,}000{,}000$

Note that the constraint coefficient for variable x_2 is 1.5. This indicates that each gallon of oil base uses 1.5 units of color pigment, a rate half again that of latex paint.

Finally, Richards can acquire enough of all the other raw materials for any reasonable level of production but one, a patented silicate which makes the paint bases exceptionally durable. Presently, the company's supplier has the capability of producing a maximum of 30,000 gallons of silicate a month. None is available from any other sources. Richards' chemist says that the proper mix is 1 gallon of silicate for 40 gallons of latex and 1 gallon of silicate for 45 gallons of oil base.

We can formulate this information into constraint form as follows:

(f) $.025x_1 + .022x_2 \leq 30{,}000$

Note that the .025 coefficient for variable x_1 is equal to 1/40, which means that each gallon of latex requires 1/40 gallon of silicate. Also, .022 equals 1/45, meaning that 1 gallon of oil base requires 1/45 gallon of silicate.

Because Richards cannot produce negative gallons of paint, we must establish *nonnegativity constraints*. These constraints force the values of the decision variables to be greater than or equal to zero. The nonnegativity constraints can be stated as follows:

(g) $x_1 \geq 0$
(h) $x_2 \geq 0$

These constraints ensure that the decision variables have values greater than or equal to zero. However, in this example the minimum supply constraints have already accomplished this purpose, so the nonnegativity constraints are redundant.

The final formulation, including the objective function and all the constraints, is:

Maximize $Z = .40x_1 + .50x_2$

Subject to:

(a) $1.0x_1 + 0.0x_2 \geq 200{,}000$
(b) $0.0x_1 + 1.0x_2 \geq 300{,}000$
(c) $1.0x_1 + 0.0x_2 \leq 500{,}000$
(d) $0.0x_1 + 1.0x_2 \leq 800{,}000$
(e) $1.0x_1 + 1.5x_2 \leq 1{,}000{,}000$
(f) $.025x_1 + .022x_2 \leq 30{,}000$
(g) $1.0x_1 + 0.0x \geq 0$
(h) $0.0x_1 + 1.0x_2 \geq 0$

This is a formal representation. A less formal but equally valid formulation is:

Maximize $Z = .40x_1 + .50x_2$

Subject to:

$$
\begin{aligned}
x_1 \qquad\qquad &\geq 200{,}000 \\
x_2 &\geq 300{,}000 \\
x_1 \qquad\qquad &\leq 500{,}000 \\
x_2 &\leq 800{,}000 \\
x_1 + 1.5x_2 &\leq 1{,}000{,}000 \\
.025x_1 + .022x_2 &\leq 30{,}000 \\
x_1, x_2 &\geq 0
\end{aligned}
$$

While both presentations are correct, most computer software—including MASTER, which accompanies this text—requires that the full set of constraint coefficients be used.

SUMMARY OF MODEL FORMULATION STEPS

Throughout this and the following chapters, we will introduce many linear programming applications. In each case, the method used to formulate the linear programming model is the same. First, you should consider just what factors in the decision situation are within the decision maker's control. These factors will yield the decision variables. Second, you should consider the model's purpose. If it is to maximize or minimize some decision criterion, you can use the decision variables to establish an objective function. Finally, you should consider the limitations facing the decision maker; these become the constraints in the model.

Once the formulation is completed, you have "modeled" the decision system. This model must be evaluated carefully to determine that it represents the decision situation accurately. Once that has been established to your satisfaction, the linear programming problem can be solved to provide the "optimal values" for the decision variables. Later in this chapter, we will illustrate the graphical solution technique for solving linear programming problems. Chapter 3 will introduce a mathematical solution procedure called the *simplex method*.

INGREDIENT MIX AND BLENDING APPLICATIONS

Linear programming has been widely used to model decision-making situations in which the objective is to determine the appropriate mix of ingredients making up an end product. Among the many industries that use linear programming for this type of situation are oil and gasoline, cattle feeding, chemicals, and pharmaceuticals. Food processors use linear programming to determine ingredient mixes for such products as breakfast cereal, bread, pet food, and many others. Ingredient mix problems are also common in the construction industry, as the Justice Construction Company example shows.

Justice Construction Company

Consider the situation facing the Justice Construction Company. A team of managers and engineers is preparing a bid for the construction of an airport runway in Trenton, New Jersey. One factor that must be considered in the bid is the amount and type of fill to use to ensure that the runway meets the minimum design "bearing ratio." The design on which the bid is being based has been converted to show the minimum number of cubic yards of material needed to meet the bearing ratio requirements. Four types of materials are used as runway fill: BR-60, BR-50, BR-40, and BR-8.

Engineers have determined that the runway will require a minimum of 226,000 cubic yards of fill. Available supplies of the four fill materials are:

BR-60	65,000 cubic yards
BR-50	25,000 cubic yards
BR-40	70,000 cubic yards
BR-8	130,000 cubic yards

In addition, the project specifications call for at least 50,000 cubic yards of BR-60 and at least 112,000 cubic yards of BR-8 material in the fill. There is no specific requirement that either BR-50 or BR-40 be used in this project.

The different materials require different amounts of compaction time per 1000 cubic yards. BR-60 requires 200 hours per 1000 cubic yards, BR-50 requires 100 hours, BR-40 requires 133 hours, and BR-8 requires 33 hours of compaction time per 1000 cubic yards. Justice Construction has 22,000 hours of compaction time available.

The material source for BR-60 is 3 miles from the airport runway, BR-50 is 2 miles away, BR-40 is only 1 mile from the airport, and BR-8 is 3 miles away. The equipment that the company has available is sufficient to haul an equivalent of 600,000 cubic yard–miles. (A cubic yard–mile is equivalent to hauling 1 cubic yard of material 1 mile.)

The materials also have different prices per cubic yard. BR-60 costs $2.80 per cubic yard; BR-50, $3.00; BR-40, $3.20; and BR-8 costs only $2.00 per cubic yard.

The issue facing Justice is to determine what mix of fill materials to use to build the runway at a minimum cost. This is a blending problem and can be modeled as a linear programming problem. We first need to formulate the LP model. Recall that the steps in formulating a linear programming problem are:

1. Define the decision variables.
2. Specify the objective function.
3. Determine the constraints.

Decision variables. As explained earlier, the decision variables are those that can be controlled by the decision maker. In this case, there are four decision variables:

x_1 = cubic yards of BR-60 used to fill material

x_2 = cubic yards of BR-50 used to fill material

x_3 = cubic yards of BR-40 used to fill material

x_4 = cubic yards of BR-8 used to fill material

Objective function. The objective is to determine how many cubic yards of each material would be needed to complete the project at a minimum cost. We can translate this into the following linear programming objective function:

$$\text{Minimize } Z = \$2.80x_1 + \$3.00x_2 + \$3.20x_3 + \$2.00x_4$$

where: Z = total materials cost

The values $2.80, $3.00, $3.20, and $2.00 are the per cubic yard costs for the four materials. In the objective function, these are referred to as the *objective-function coefficients.*

Constraints. In a linear programming model, the constraints are the limitations placed on the decision maker in choosing values for the decision variables. A linear programming model incorporates these constraints through equations and inequalities. Often the most difficult task in correctly formulating a linear programming problem is determining how these constraints should be expressed. In the Justice Construction Company example, several constraints affect the number of cubic yards of each type of fill material that can be used. One of these is the available supply of each fill material. We can express these constraints as:

$$x_1 \leq 65{,}000$$
$$x_2 \leq 25{,}000$$
$$x_3 \leq 70{,}000$$
$$x_4 \leq 130{,}000$$

Two additional constraints are the contract specifications which call for minimum amounts of R-60 and R-8 materials. We can express these constraints as:

$$x_1 \ge 50{,}000 \qquad \text{and} \qquad x_4 \ge 112{,}000$$

The company is also limited by the amount of compacting time it has available: 22,000 hours. Based on the time required to compact 1000 cubic yards of each fill material (the times were given earlier in this example) the compacting-time constraint (restated in terms of a single yard) is as follows:

$$.200x_1 + .100x_2 + .133x_3 + .033x_4 \le 22{,}000$$

Note that the fractional constraint coefficients represent the *per yard* compacting time. For instance, each cubic yard of material x_1 (BR-60) will require .200 hour (based on the rate of 200 hours per 1000 cubic yards given earlier).

The total hauling capacity is limited to 600,000 cubic yard miles. This means that when the travel distance is multiplied by the number of cubic yards hauled, the product can't exceed 600,000. Based upon the distances the materials are from the runway, the following constraint can be formulated:

$$3x_1 + 2x_2 + 1x_3 + 3x_4 \le 600{,}000$$

Another constraint which impacts the model is the requirement that the runway fill must total at least 226,000 cubic yards. This constraint is expressed as:

$$x_1 + x_2 + x_3 + x_4 \ge 226{,}000$$

Finally, a constraint included in all linear programming problems discussed in this text is the one which indicates that the decision variables must be nonnegative, which we show as follows:

$$x_1, x_2, x_3, x_4 \ge 0$$

When we combine the objective function and all the constraints, the model for the Justice Company example becomes:

$$\text{Minimize } Z = \$2.80x_1 + \$3.00x_2 + \$3.20x_3 + \$2.00x_4$$

Subject to:

$$\begin{array}{rrrrl}
x_1 & & & & \le 65{,}000 \\
 & x_2 & & & \le 25{,}000 \\
 & & x_3 & & \le 70{,}000 \\
 & & & x_4 & \le 130{,}000 \\
x_1 & & & & \ge 50{,}000 \\
 & x_2 & & & \ge 112{,}000 \\
.200x_1 + & .100x_2 + & .133x_3 + & .033x_4 & \le 22{,}000 \\
3x_1 + & 2x_2 + & 1x_3 + & 3x_4 & \le 600{,}000 \\
x_1 + & x_2 + & x_3 + & x_4 & \ge 226{,}000 \\
 & & & x_1, x_2, x_3, x_4 & \ge 0
\end{array}$$

PERSONNEL MANAGEMENT APPLICATIONS

Organizations can sometimes make effective use of linear programming in their staffing decisions. These types of applications are similar to blending problems, since the linear programming model is used to "blend together" people with different expertise and abilities to perform a job function or make up a work shift. To illustrate, the following paragraphs describe a hospital staffing problem.

Blaire County Hospital

The Blaire County Hospital has three main shifts: 7:00 A.M.–3:00 P.M., 3:00–11:00 P.M., and 11:00 P.M.–7:00 A.M. Three types of nursing staff are needed: registered nurses (RNs), licensed practical nurses (LPNs), and nurse's aides (NAs). Full-time RNs earn \$23.00 per hour, full-time LPNs earn \$19.00 per hour, and full-time NAs earn \$7.50 per hour. Also, RNs and LPNs earn an additional \$2.00 per hour for working the late night shift. NAs are paid \$8.50 per hour for working the late shift.

Hospital requirements call for 1 hour of RN time for every 3 hours of LPN time on each shift, and there can be no more than 200 hours of NA time on each shift. To meet hospital accreditation standards, the early morning shift must have at least 400 hours of total LPN and RN time. The swing shift is required to have at least 376 hours of RN and LPN time. The late night shift must have at least 270 hours of RN and LPN time. The total staffing for each of the three shifts must be at least 600 hours.

The question facing the hospital administrators is how to minimize costs while meeting all the staffing requirements. This type of situation can be modeled as a linear programming problem. To do so, we need to formulate the problem, showing the objective function and constraints. Recall the steps in formulating a linear programming problem:

1. Define the decision variables.
2. Specify the objective function.
3. Determine the constraints.

Decision variables. The decision variables are those that can be controlled by the decision maker. In this case, there are nine decision variables, one for each of the three types of nursing staff for each of the three shifts:

x_1 = RN hours, early morning shift

x_2 = LPN hours, early morning shift

x_3 = NA hours, early morning shift

x_4 = RN hours, afternoon shift

.

.

.

x_9 = NA hours, late night shift

Objective function. The personnel administrator wants to adequately staff the hospital at the minimum possible cost. Based on the information available, the following objective function describes the hospital's situation:

$$\text{Minimize } Z = \$23x_1 + \$19x_2 + \$7.5x_3 + \$23x_4 + \$19x_5 + \$7.5x_6 + \$25x_7 + \$21x_8 + \$8.5x_9$$

Constraints. Constraints are limitations regarding the values that can be used for the decision variables. If there were no constraints, the administrator could minimize costs by not hiring any nursing staff. But in this example there are several constraints that can be formulated as inequalities.

First, there is the requirement that no shift can have more than 200 hours of NA time. Since there are three shifts, we write this as:

$$x_3 \leq 200$$
$$x_6 \leq 200$$
$$x_9 \leq 200$$

There is also the requirement that the morning shift have at least 400 hours of RN and LPN time. This constraint can be written as:

$$x_1 + x_2 \geq 400$$

Likewise, there is a minimum RN-LPN requirement for the other two shifts. We write these constraints as:

$$x_4 + x_5 \geq 376 \qquad \text{and} \qquad x_7 + x_8 \geq 270$$

Each shift must have a total of 600 nursing-staff hours. We write the constraints for the three shifts as follows:

$$x_1 + x_2 + x_3 \geq 600$$
$$x_4 + x_5 + x_6 \geq 600$$
$$x_7 + x_8 + x_9 \geq 600$$

The hospital also requires that for every 3 hours of LPN time there must be 1 hour of RN time. This will hold for each shift. For the morning shift we could set this constraint as follows:

$$3x_1 = x_2$$

This formulation may not seem immediately obvious, but consider the fact that we want to ensure that for every 3 hours of LPN (x_2) time we have 1 hour of RN (x_1) time. In our formulation, if x_2 is 300 hours, in order for the equality to hold, x_1 must be 100 hours, thus preserving the 3-to-1 ratio.

The simplex technique for solving linear programming models, which we will discuss in Chapter 3, requires that the constraints be formulated so that *all* decision variables are on the left-hand side. Thus, we need to rewrite the constraint. By subtracting x_2 from both sides we get:

$$3x_1 - x_2 = 0$$

We can follow this format for establishing the 3-to-1 ratio constraints for the other two shifts as follows:

$$3x_4 - x_5 = 0 \qquad \text{and} \qquad 3x_7 - x_8 = 0$$

As will always be the case, we add the nonnegativity constraints:

$$x_1, x_2, x_3, x_4, x_5, x_6, x_7, x_8, x_9 \geq 0$$

We can now consolidate the objective function and constraints to form the linear programming model for the Blaire County Hospital problem as follows:

$$\text{Minimize } Z = \$23x_1 + \$19x_2 + \$7.5x_3 + \$23x_4 + \$19x_5$$
$$+ \$7.5x_6 + \$25x_7 + \$21x_8 + \$8.5x_9$$

Subject to:

$$
\begin{aligned}
x_3 &\le 200\\
x_6 &\le 200\\
x_9 &\le 200\\
x_1 + x_2 &\ge 400\\
x_4 + x_5 &\ge 376\\
x_7 + x_8 &\ge 270\\
x_1 + x_2 + x_3 &\ge 600\\
x_4 + x_5 + x_6 &\ge 600\\
x_7 + x_8 + x_9 &\ge 600\\
3x_1 - x_2 &= 0\\
3x_4 - x_5 &= 0\\
3x_7 - x_8 &= 0
\end{aligned}
$$

and the nonnegativity constraints:

$$x_1, x_2, x_3, x_4, x_5, x_6, x_7, x_8, x_9 \ge 0$$

FINANCIAL ANALYSIS APPLICATIONS

There are many areas within the financial arena in which linear programming is applied. Among these is investment portfolio management. Companies which have employee pension funds frequently hire an investment analyst whose job is to select stocks, bonds, and other investments to form the pension portfolio. The analyst's objective is to maximize the total rate of return on the money invested. However, the analyst will be required to make the investments subject to certain requirements. For instance, there will probably be restrictions placed on the ratio of common stock to bonds in the portfolio. Additionally, there may be requirements limiting the percentage of the portfolio tied up in any one security. Other likely considerations relate to the portfolio mix relative to the degree of risk associated with the investments. Linear programming can be used to help determine the "best" mix of investments subject to the various restrictions placed on the portfolio.

The financial applications of linear programming do not end with portfolio analysis. Companies involved in large-scale growth and development often need financing for their expansion efforts. They need to know what is the best mix of financial instruments to use for this purpose. Linear programming can help supply the answer by minimizing the cost of borrowing subject to certain provisions about timing on payback, quantities borrowed from any one source, and so forth.

The Farthington Group

The Farthington Group is a holding company composed of a number of smaller companies in Vermont. Like all companies, the Farthington Group has the problem of managing its cash assets. Cash can be put into short-term investments when the company has cash on hand. And when the company needs cash, it must seek the least-expensive short-term loans. The financial manager wishes to establish a cash management plan which will allow the company to achieve the maximum possible return on cash assets.

The company's forecast of its cash receipts and cash payments over the next 3 months is as follows:

Month	Cash Receipts	Cash Payments
1	\$20,000	\$30,000
2	\$40,000	\$80,000
3	\$60,000	\$70,000
Totals	\$120,000	\$180,000

Farthington can delay a cash payment for a maximum of 1 month but will have to pay an interest penalty of 1.5% of the amount delayed. There is a short-term security (security A) in the asset portfolio. This security matures the first day of month 3 and will yield \$70,000. However, the security can be redeemed early in any amount up to the \$70,000 face value. If the security is redeemed early, a penalty must be paid. Redeeming 1 month early results in a 1% penalty on the amount redeemed; 2 months early causes a 1.9% penalty on the amount redeemed.

Farthington can use its line of credit for short-term loans with an interest rate of 1.6% per month. Assuming any short-term loan will be repaid on the first day of month 4, a loan taken on the first day of month 1 will incur a total interest charge of 4.8%; a loan taken on the first day of month 2 will incur an interest charge of 3.2%; and a loan taken on the first day of month 3 will incur an interest charge of 1.6%.

Any excess cash available during a month can be invested in 1- or 2-month securities. The interest earned for 1 month will be .875%. Interest earned for 2 months will be 1.75%.

The question facing the financial manager is how to best manage the company's cash over the next 3 months. A linear programming model can be used to provide this information. Thus, we need to formulate the model. (The formulation to this problem is somewhat complex. We have included it at this point in the text to give you a feeling for the type of linear programming problems which are actually used in business decision making. As you work through the remainder of this chapter and through Chapters 3 and 4, you should become much more comfortable with formulating linear programming problems like this one.)

We hope that by now the steps in formulating a linear programming problem are familiar:

1. Define the decision variables.
2. Specify the objective function.
3. Determine the constraints.

Decision variables. The decision variables are those that can be controlled by the decision maker. In this case, there are 14 decision variables:

x_1 = \$ from line of credit at beginning of month 1

x_2 = \$ from line of credit at beginning of month 2

x_3 = \$ from line of credit at beginning of month 3

x_4 = \$ from selling security A at beginning of month 1

x_5 = \$ from selling security A at beginning of month 2

x_6 = \$ from selling security A at beginning of month 3

x_7 = \$ paid out in month 1 due in month 1

x_8 = \$ paid out in month 2 due in month 1

x_9 = \$ paid out in month 2 due in month 2
x_{10} = \$ paid out in month 3 due in month 2
x_{11} = \$ paid out in month 3 due in month 3
x_{12} = \$ invested in short-term securities in month 1 held to month 2
x_{13} = \$ invested in short-term securities in month 1 held to month 3
x_{14} = \$ invested in short-term securities in month 2 held to month 3

Objective function. The objective for the financial manager is to develop a cash management plan for the 3-month period which maximizes the net return. This objective can be translated into an objective function in a linear programming model. First, we can consider the revenue side of the picture. If the Farthington Group has the cash available to invest in short-term securities, interest can be earned. This is shown as:

$$.00875x_{12} + .0175x_{13} + .00875x_{14}$$

Next, we consider the various costs. For instance, if the company uses its line of credit, it must pay interest. These costs are shown as:

$$.048x_1 + .032x_2 + .016x_3$$

The company has a security that can be redeemed early but must pay a penalty according to whether the redemption occurs 1 or 2 months early. We express these costs as:

$$.019x_4 + .01x_5$$

The company also incurs a cost anytime it delays its cash payments to the following month. We express these costs as:

$$.015x_8 + .015x_{10}$$

Now we can combine the revenues and costs into one equation, as follows:

$$.00875x_{12} + .0175x_{13} + .00875x_{14} - (.048x_1 + .032x_2 + .016x_3) - (.019x_4 + .01x_5) - (.015x_8 + .015x_{10})$$

This can be rewritten in the usual format for a linear programming objective function as:

$$\text{Maximize } Z = .00875x_{12} + .0175x_{13} + .00875x_{14} - .048x_1 - .032x_2 - .016x_3 - .019x_4 - .01x_5 - .015x_8 - .015x_{10}$$

This objective function does not contain all 14 decision variables because the omitted variables have no positive or negative impact on the objective function. For example, variable x_{11} is the cash paid out by the company in month 3 that was due in month 3. No interest is earned on such a payment; nor is there any late penalty, since the payment was made when due. Thus, the objective-function coefficient for this variable is zero. The same is true for variables x_6, x_7, and x_9. However, these decision variables should be included in the objective function. After rearranging, it becomes:

$$\text{Maximize } Z = -.048x_1 - .032x_2 - .016x_3 - .019x_4 - .01x_5 + 0x_6 + 0x_7 - .015x_8 + 0x_9 - .015x_{10} + 0x_{11} + .00875x_{12} + .0175x_{13} + .00875x_{14}$$

Constraints. Constraints are the limitations placed on the decision maker with respect to what values he or she can select for the decision variables. In this situation, several constraints need to be included in the model.

To begin with, the amount of cash available in each month must equal the total payments plus any investments made. For instance, in month 1 the company will have \$20,000 in cash receipts. In addition, it can borrow on its line of credit (x_1). Because the interest rate on the line of credit for a loan taken out in period 1 is 4.8%, only $100 - 4.8 = 95.2\%$ of the loan amount will actually be available. The company can also sell its short-term security (x_4) in month 1 at a 1.9% penalty. Thus, only $100 - 1.9 = 98.1\%$ of the dollar volume of short-term securities redeemed in period 1 will be available. The company could not receive any interest income from securities it might invest in during month 1. That interest becomes a source of cash in month 2.

Since cash cannot disappear, for month 1 the cash outflow for payments and any investments must equal the inflow from receipts, loans, or sales of securities. Thus, we can formulate the following constraint for month 1:

$$.952x_1 + .981x_4 + 20{,}000 = x_7 + x_{12} + x_{13}$$

which we can rewrite as:

$$.952x_1 + .981x_4 - x_7 - x_{12} - x_{13} = -20{,}000$$

Constraints for months 2 and 3 are developed in a similar manner. Note that in the following constraints, we have also accounted for potential investment interest from the purchase of short-term securities. The constraint for month 2 is:

$$.968x_2 + .990x_5 + 1.00875x_{12} - 1.015x_8 - x_9 - x_{14} = -40{,}000$$

and for month 3:

$$.984x_3 + 1.0x_6 + 1.0175x_{13} + 1.00875x_{14} - 1.015x_{10} - x_{11} = -60{,}000$$

We agree that formulating these constraints is fairly difficult. You should spend some time to make sure you understand how each constraint was developed and how the constraint coefficients are determined.

In addition to the above constraints, a few others must be included to complete the model. First, the cash payments for month 1 must equal \$30,000. This constraint is:

$$x_7 + x_8 = 30{,}000$$

For months 2 and 3 we get:

$$x_9 + x_{10} = 80{,}000$$
$$x_{11} = 70{,}000$$

Also, the Farthington Group has a security with a value of \$70,000 which matures in month 3. The amounts of this security redeemed through month 3 must sum to \$70,000. This constraint is shown as follows:

$$x_4 + x_5 + x_6 = 70{,}000$$

Other than nonnegativity requirements for the decision variables, this should conclude the constraints facing the financial manager for the Farthington Group. Thus, we can state the linear programming model which represents the cash management system as:

$$\begin{aligned}\text{Maximize } Z = & -.048x_1 - .032x_2 - .016x_3 - .019x_4 - .01x_5 + 0x_6 + 0x_7 \\ & - .015x_8 + 0x_9 - .015x_{10} + 0x_{11} + .00875x_{12} + .0175x_{13} \\ & + .00875x_{14}\end{aligned}$$

Subject to:

$$\begin{aligned}
.952x_1 + .981x_4 - x_7 - x_{12} - x_{13} &= -20{,}000 \\
.968x_2 + .990x_5 + 1.00875x_{12} - 1.015x_8 - x_9 - x_{14} &= -40{,}000 \\
.984x_3 + 1.0x_6 + 1.0175x_{13} + 1.00875x_{14} - 1.015x_{10} - x_{11} &= -60{,}000 \\
x_7 + x_8 &= 30{,}000 \\
x_9 + x_{10} &= 80{,}000 \\
x_{11} &= 70{,}000 \\
x_4 + x_5 + x_6 &= 70{,}000
\end{aligned}$$

OTHER LINEAR PROGRAMMING APPLICATIONS

Resource Assignment

An area where linear programming has proven to be very useful is resource assignment. For example, a manufacturing plant might have several machines capable of performing the same task but these machines might have different unit costs. Therefore, the total cost of performing the task is at least partly determined by the machine that is used to complete the task. Constraints generally exist which preclude the plant manager from assigning all work to the low-cost machine. Linear programming can be used to determine which tasks are assigned to which machines to minimize total operating costs.

Of course, instead of machines the resource could be people. Then linear programming would be used to help schedule the workload of employees.

Transportation Problems

Many companies produce products at several locations and ship these products to warehouses throughout the country. The production facilities are often located close to the sources of supplies and raw materials. The warehouses are located near the product's major markets. Breweries are an example of this type of business. A large company may have 10 or more breweries where its beer is made. These are probably located close to an area where barley and hops are grown or close to a supply of high-quality water. The brewery company will also have storage warehouses located in every major city in its market area. Linear programming models can be used to determine how many units of a given product to ship from each plant to each warehouse to minimize transportation costs while meeting demand for the product.

Summary

This section has introduced a sampling of business areas in which linear programming has proven to be very useful. But they are only a few of the many areas where linear programming is currently being applied in industry. We have demonstrated the steps involved in formulating a linear programming model. Proper formulation is extremely important. The problems and cases at the end of this chapter (and in Chapters 3–6) provide more opportunities to improve your model formulation skills.

2-4 LINEAR PROGRAMMING ASSUMPTIONS

The examples in the previous section illustrated how to formulate linear programming models. A great many applications exist where linear programming can be used to help a decision maker. However, these situations have to satisfy certain assumptions before linear programming can be applied. There are four basic assumptions associated with linear programming: *linearity, additivity, divisibility*, and *certainty*. These assumptions are discussed below.

LINEARITY

A basic assumption of linear programming is that the objective function and constraints are all linear. This means that when the objective function or a constraint is graphed it will appear as a straight line. To ensure this, the decision variables (x_1, x_2, etc.) cannot appear to any power higher than 1 and there can be no cross-product terms involving two or more variables.

For example, an objective function of this form:

$$\text{Maximize } Z = 100x + 200y$$

is linear. Each additional unit of variable x adds 100 to the objective function no matter what value x takes on. Likewise, the variable y adds 200 per unit over the entire range of y.

An objective function of this form:

$$\text{Maximize } Z = 100x^2 + 200y^3$$

is not linear. The decision variables are raised to powers higher than 1. If variable x is increased from 0 to 1, the objective function would increase by 100. However, if x is increased from 1 to 2, x^2 would go from 1 to 4 and the objective function would increase from 100 to 400. Thus, the contribution of the variable x to the objective function depends on the level of x. The same is true for the y variable which is raised to the third power.

The following objective function would also violate the linearity assumption:

$$\text{Maximize } Z = 400x_1x_2 + 300x_2$$

because the decision variables appear in cross-product form.

Problems which require nonlinear objective functions and/or constraints are called *nonlinear programming* problems and are not discussed in this text.

ADDITIVITY

Another assumption of a linear programming model is *additivity*. When considering the use of scarce resources, additivity means that the total amount of the resource used by several activities must equal the sum of the resources used by the individual activities.

To describe a situation for which the additivity assumption would not be satisfied, suppose the Richards Paint Company produced a third product which is made from the residue left over from producing latex and oil base paints. This residue by-product is used to coat the back of flooring materials such as linoleum. The primary raw materials, silicates, and color pigments needed to produce latex and oil base paints need to be available regardless of whether any residue is produced. However, if only the residue by-product were produced, we would still need silicates and color pigments. Thus, the total resource requirements when all three products are produced is less than the sum of the requirements when each is produced individually.

Another way of thinking of additivity is with respect to the objective function. The total value of the objective function must equal the sum of the individual variables times their own contribution rates. For instance, in the Richards Paint example, the contribution rate for latex is \$.40 per gallon and the contribution rate for oil base paint is \$.50 per gallon. If no oil base paint was produced, then total profit would be $\$.40x_1$. If no latex paint was produced, total profit would be $\$.50x_2$. We have additivity only if, when both products are produced at levels x_1 and x_2, respectively, the total profit is $\$.40x_1 + \$.50x_2$. If the contribution rate for one or both products must be changed when both are produced, then we would not have additivity.

DIVISIBILITY

Suppose the optimal solution to the Richards Paint problem showed the company should produce 500,000 gallons of latex and 333,333.33 gallons of oil base. The solutions to a linear programming problem need not always be an integer value. The linear programming model assumes that the decision variables are continuous and infinitely divisible. This means that all decision variables are allowed to assume fractional as well as integer values.

A technique known as integer programming can be used to generate integer solutions if the need exists. Chapter 6 presents a general discussion of integer programming.

CERTAINTY

The solution to a linear programming problem is based on the assumption that *parameters* of the model are known with certainty. The parameters are such things as capacities, resource supplies, contribution rates, and constraint coefficients. In the Richards Paint example, the \$.40 and \$.50 contribution rates for latex and oil base paints were assumed to be known with certainty. The available quantity of color pigment and plant capacity were also assumed to be known. In many business situations, however, the parameters will not be known and the linear programming solution will be conditional on the values used for the parameters. When uncertainty exists in the model, *sensitivity analysis* on the solution can be used to determine how much the parameters could change without altering the solution. Chapter 4 introduces the topic of sensitivity analysis.

2-5 THE GRAPHICAL LINEAR PROGRAMMING SOLUTION

In section 2-3, we introduced just a few decision situations where linear programming could be used. We began by introducing the Richards Paint Company problem, a simple application involving only two decision variables. The other examples were a bit more complex, involving several decision variables. Of course, the next step after formulating the linear programming model is to solve it for the "optimal" values of the decision variables. Chapter 3 presents a numerical solution technique, the simplex method, which can be used to determine the optimal solution for all linear programming problems, simple and complex.

However, before moving to the simplex solution method, this section takes you through a graphical approach for solving small linear programming problems with two decision variables. When the objective function contains only two decision variables, a graph can be used to provide a good approximation of the values of x_1 and x_2 that will maximize (or minimize) the objective function while satisfying the applicable constraints. More importantly, the graphical solution can provide insight into the solution procedure for all linear programming problems.

Now let us return to the Richards Paint example. To demonstrate the graphical solution procedure, we develop a graph that displays all possible x_1 (latex) and x_2 (oil base) values. The technique begins with the assumption that all values of x_1 and x_2 are possible, even though some of them may violate one or more of the constraints. Graphically, the set of all possible solution values is called the feasible region. The **feasible region** consists of all combinations of values of the decision variables which simultaneously satisfy all the constraints imposed on the problem. We are presently assuming all values of x_1 and x_2 are possible (or that the problem has no constraints). This graph is shown in Figure 2-1.

We will reduce the feasible region by adding constraints to the model. We will first consider the nonnegativity constraints. Recall that paint production cannot be negative. Figure 2-2 illustrates the reduced feasible region when nonnegativity is considered. As you can see, the feasible values are limited to the upper right-hand quadrant (quadrant I). Thus, we need only consider values for the decision variables which fall in this region.

Figure 2-1
Richards Paint Co. problem: graph of all possible values (x_1, x_2)

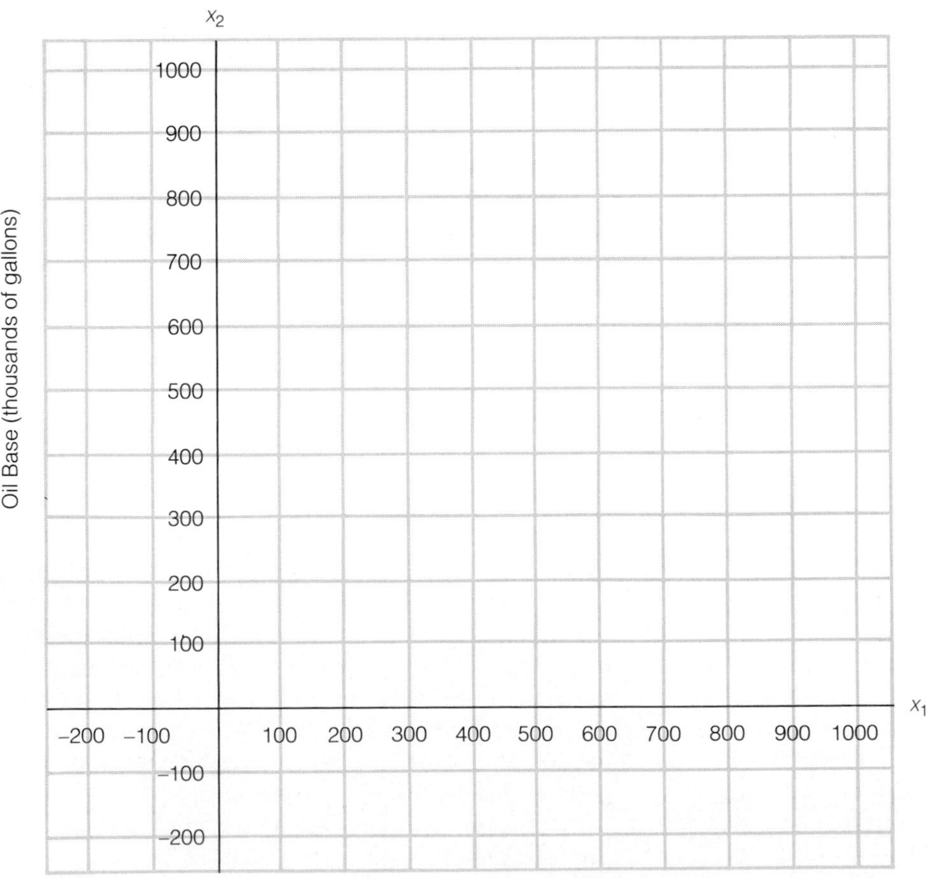

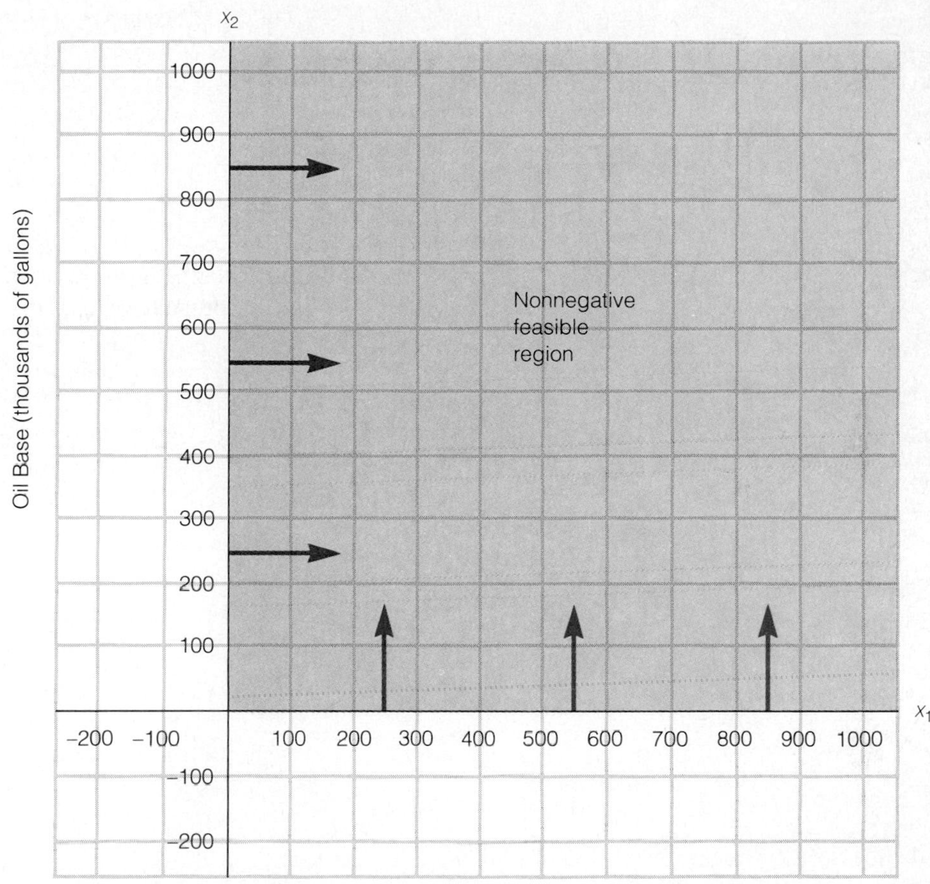

Figure 2-2
Richards Paint Co. problem: nonnegativity considered

The next step in developing the graphical solution is to further limit the feasible solution region by graphically representing the other constraints. Consider the minimum production constraint on latex base:

(a) $1x_1 + 0x_2 \geq 200{,}000$

Figure 2-3 illustrates this constraint and shows the new feasible region. All values of x_1 and x_2 within the shaded area are currently feasible.

The feasible region is reduced further when we consider the minimum production constraint on oil base:

(b) $0x_1 + 1x_2 \geq 300{,}000$

Figure 2-4 shows this constraint added to the graph and the resulting feasible region. Note that these two constraints require values of $x_1 \geq 200{,}000$ and $x_2 \geq 300{,}000$ but place no upper limit on them. Thus, if these were the only constraints, Richards could generate huge profits by producing unlimited quantities of latex and oil base paints. However, plant capacity limits how many gallons of each type that Richards Paint can

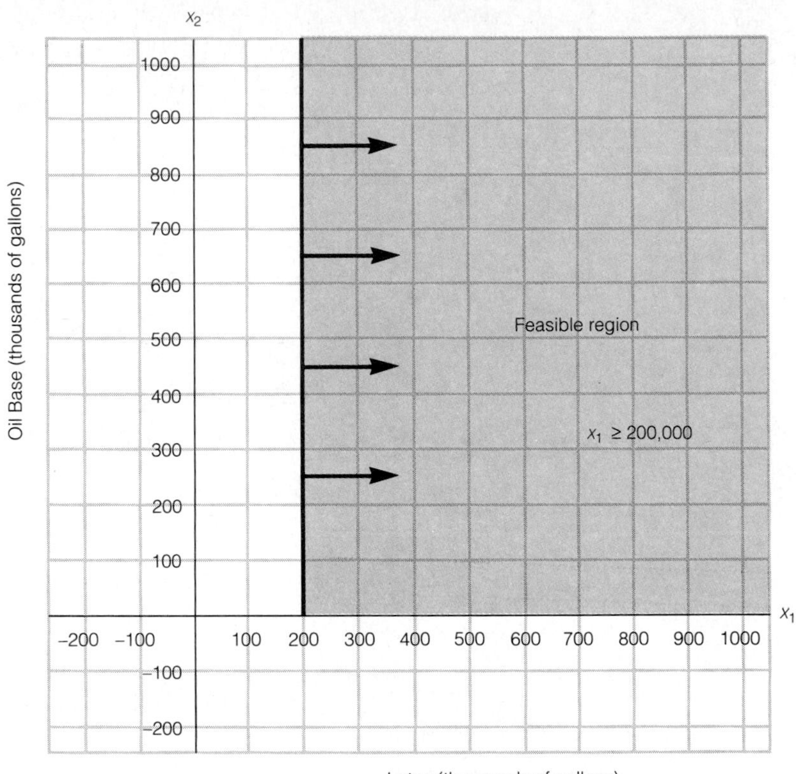

Figure 2-3
Richards Paint Co. problem: minimum latex constraint (*a*) included

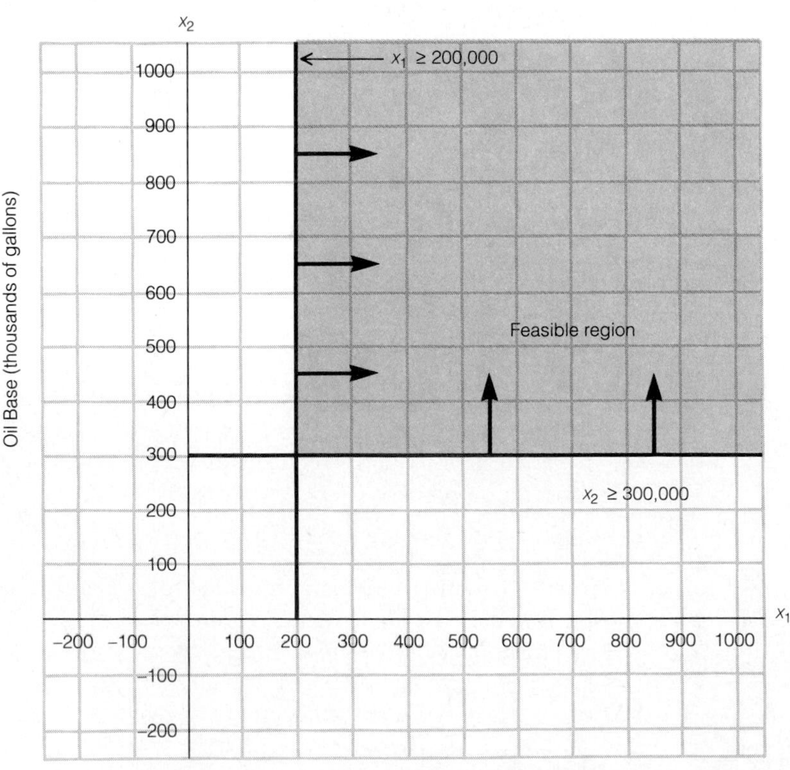

Figure 2-4
Richards Paint Co. problem: minimum oil base constraint (*b*) included

produce. Figure 2-5 adds the constraint on latex base:

(c) $1x_1 + 0x_2 \leq 500{,}000$

Figure 2-6 shows the feasible region after the maximum production constraint for oil base has been included:

(d) $0x_1 + 1x_2 \leq 800{,}000$

Note that the feasible region has been reduced to a small rectangle. Any values of x_1 and x_2 falling within the shaded area will satisfy the constraints considered thus far.

Two further constraints were imposed on Richards' decision. The first deals with available pigments:

(e) $1x_1 + 1.5x_2 \leq 1{,}000{,}000$

To graph this constraint, we perform the following steps:

Step 1 Treat the constraint as an equality and graph the equation as a straight line. Since we need only two points to determine the straight line, we can set each

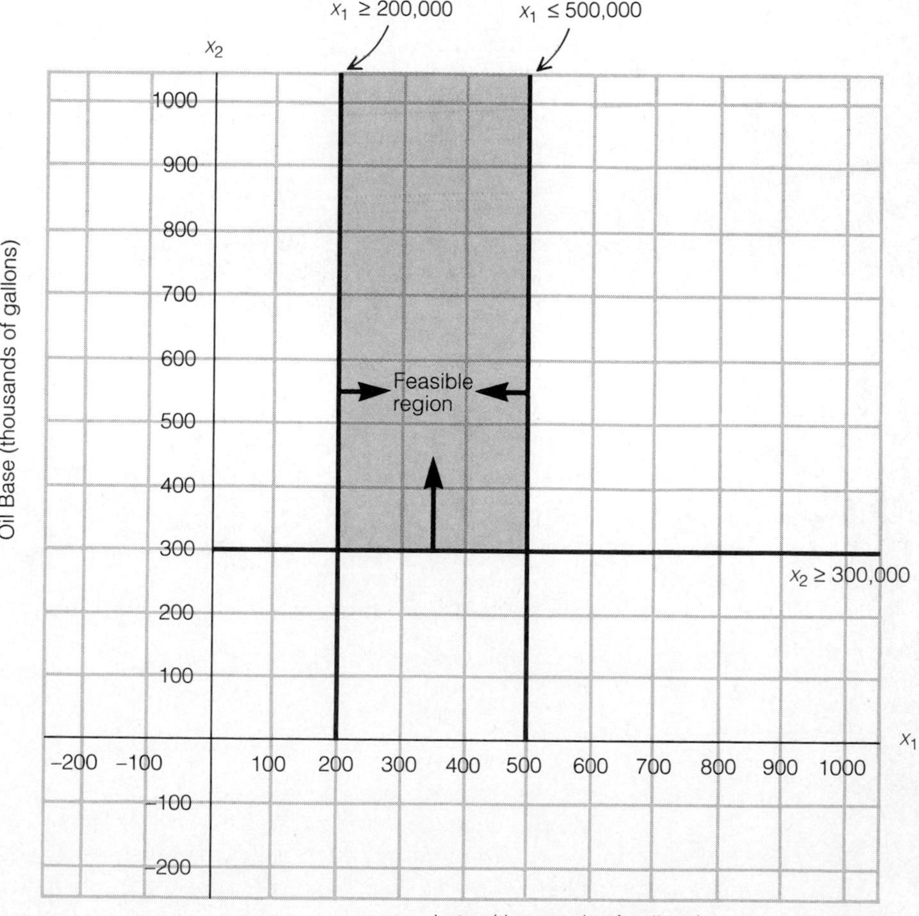

Figure 2-5
Richards Paint Co. problem: maximum latex constraint (c) included

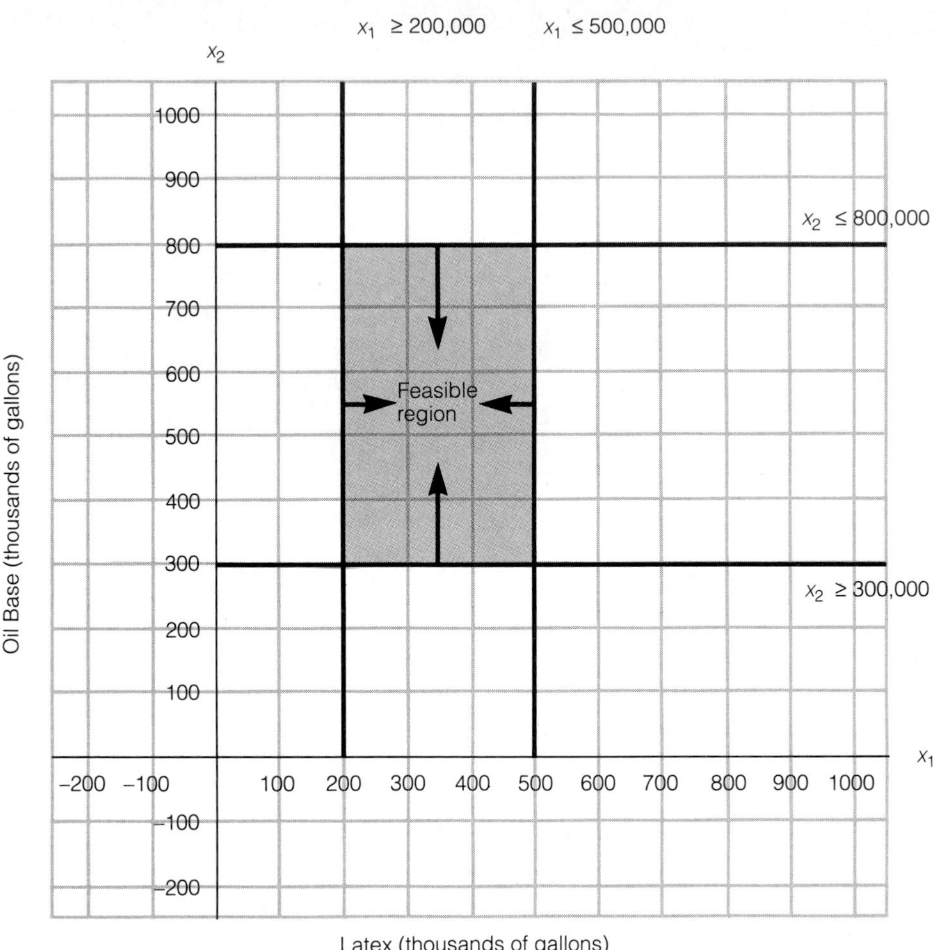

Figure 2-6
Richards Paint Co. problem: maximum oil base constraint (*d*) included

variable equal to zero and solve for the other. If $x_2 = 0$:

$$\begin{aligned} 1x_1 + 1.5(0) &= 1{,}000{,}000 \\ x_1 \qquad &= 1{,}000{,}000 \end{aligned}$$

Thus, we locate one point at $x_1 = 1{,}000{,}000$ and $x_2 = 0$.

Step 2 Next we solve for x_2 by setting $x_1 = 0$:

$$\begin{aligned} 1(0) + 1.5x_2 &= 1{,}000{,}000 \\ x_2 &= \quad 666{,}666.67 \end{aligned}$$

We locate a second point at $x_1 = 0$ and $x_2 = 666{,}666.67$. The line is determined by connecting these two points as shown in Figure 2-7.

To determine on which side of the constraint the feasible region falls, we can pick a point, often the origin, and see whether the constraint is satisfied by substituting the coordinates of this point into the constraint inequality. If we use the origin ($x_1 = 0$,

$x_2 = 0$) and the constraint is satisfied, the feasible region lies below the constraint line. Otherwise, the feasible region lies above the constraint line. In this case, as shown in Figure 2-7, the feasible region lies below the constraint line. The final constraint reflects silicate availability:

(f) $.025x_1 + .022x_2 \leq 30{,}000$

Again, we plot this inequality constraint by first assuming equality. Now, solving for x_1 when $x_2 = 0$:

$$
\begin{aligned}
.025x_1 + .022(0) &= 30{,}000 \\
x_1 &= 30{,}000/.025 \\
x_1 &= 1{,}200{,}000
\end{aligned}
$$

We then solve for x_2 when $x_1 = 0$:

$$
\begin{aligned}
.025(0) + .022x_2 &= 30{,}000 \\
x_2 &= 30{,}000/.022 \\
x_2 &= 1{,}363{,}636.40
\end{aligned}
$$

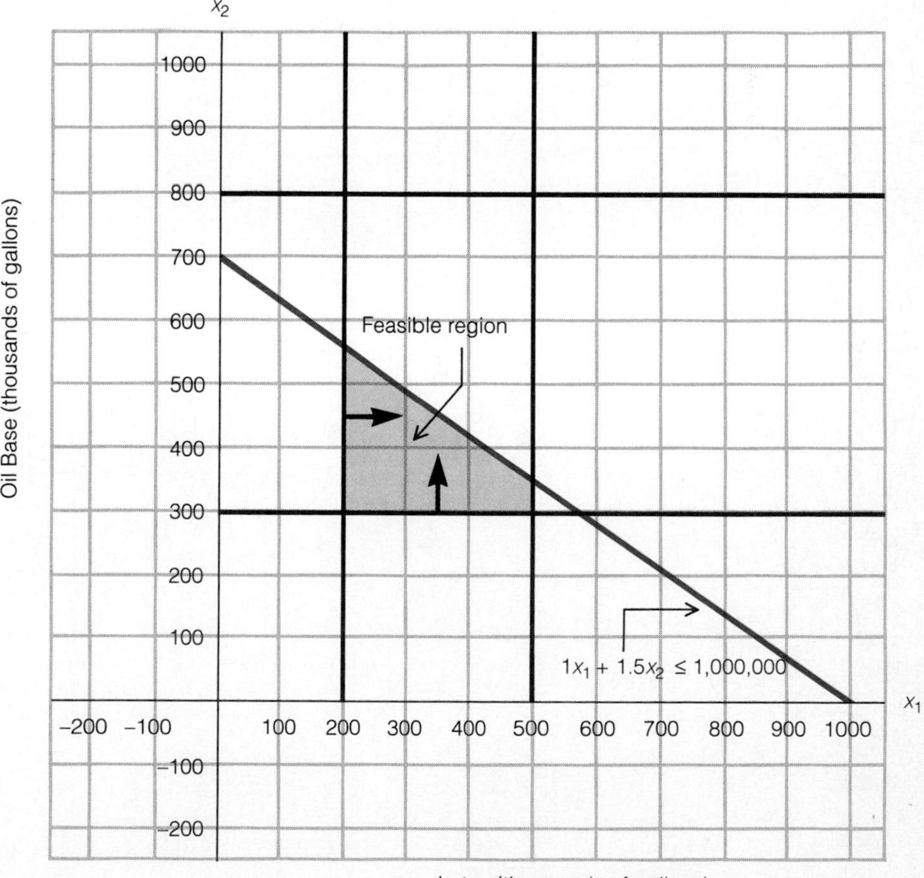

Figure 2-7
Richards Paint Co. problem: total pigment capacity constraint (e) included

These points are connected by a straight line as shown in Figure 2-8. You can see the silicate constraint does not reduce the feasible region. A constraint which does not reduce the feasible region is called a *redundant constraint*. This means the company is not constrained by the quantity of silicate available because before the silicate is exhausted, paint production will already be halted due to one of the other constraints. You should also note that the maximum production constraint for oil base is redundant now that the other constraints have been added.

DETERMINING THE OPTIMAL SOLUTION

Remember, the managers at the Richards Paint needed to determine how many gallons of latex (x_1) and oil base (x_2) to produce in order to maximize net profits. However, constraints limited their production alternatives. The feasibility region in Figure 2-8 represents the combinations of x_1 and x_2 which satisfy all the constraints. Any value of x_1 and x_2 within this area will produce a net profit, but what values of x_1 and x_2 will give the greatest net profit?

To answer this question, we begin with the objective function:

Maximize $Z = .40x_1 + .50x_2$

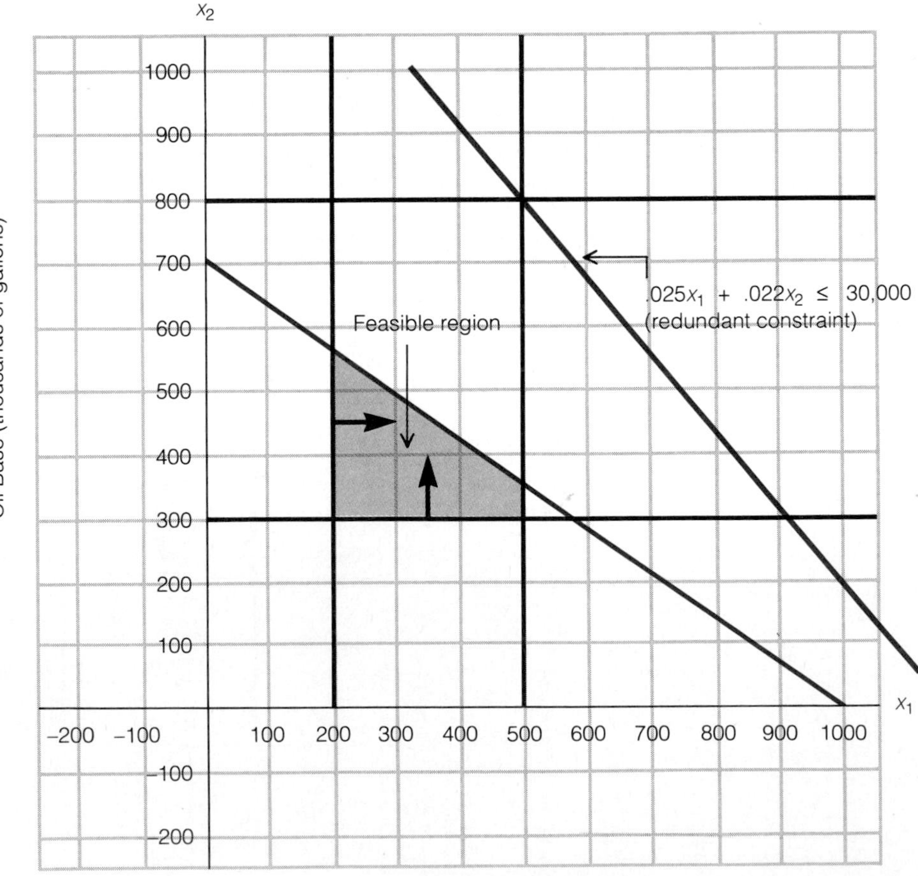

Figure 2-8
Richards Paint Co. problem: redundant constraint (*f*) included

Where

Z = profit
x_1 = gallons of latex produced
x_2 = gallons of oil base produced

Profit is determined by multiplying the number of gallons of latex (x_1) and oil base (x_2) by their respective profit coefficients. The objective function can be shown on our graph by selecting an arbitrary profit level, say \$300,000. (The value we start with could have been \$200,000 or \$800,000, or any other value.) Since the objective function is linear, we can graphically show this profit level by determining values of x_1 and x_2 which would yield \$300,000, as follows:

First let:

$$x_2 = 0$$
$$300{,}000 = .40(x_1) + .50(0)$$
$$x_1 = 750{,}000$$

Then let:

$$x_1 = 0$$
$$300{,}000 = .40(0) + .50x_2$$
$$x_2 = 600{,}000$$

Now we locate the points (750,000; 0) and (0; 600,000) on the graph in Figure 2-9 and connect these points with a straight line, giving Isoprofit line 1. Any production combinations of x_1 and x_2 on this line will give a profit of \$300,000. The points on the **isoprofit line** passing through the feasible region represent feasible solutions to the linear programming problem.

In order to graphically locate the production levels which will maximize profit, we can continue to form isoprofit lines for higher profit levels (see lines 2 and 3 in Figure 2-10) until the isoprofit line touches the outermost boundary of the feasible region. Figure 2-10 illustrates this, and also shows that for a given linear programming problem, *all isoprofit lines are linear and parallel*. Isoprofit line 3 touches the boundary of the feasible region at a corner. This **corner point** is formed by the intersection of constraints (c) and (e). This means the linear programming solution is constrained by the capacity to produce latex base (500,000 gallons) and by the company's total pigment capacity (1,000,000 units). The constraints that form this corner are called **binding constraints**. Therefore, of the five constraints, only two are binding.

We can use Figure 2-10 to find the approximate solution to the linear programming problem. Because of the constraints we know that x_1 must equal 500,000, and from the graph we see that x_2 is in the range of 300,000 to 350,000. However, since we know which two constraints are binding, we can determine the exact values of x_1 and x_2 at the optimal corner. We use the linear equations for the two constraints and solve for the point where these two lines intersect:

$$\text{(c)}\quad 1x_1 + 0x_2 = 500{,}000$$
$$\text{(e)}\quad 1x_1 + 1.5x_2 = 1{,}000{,}000$$

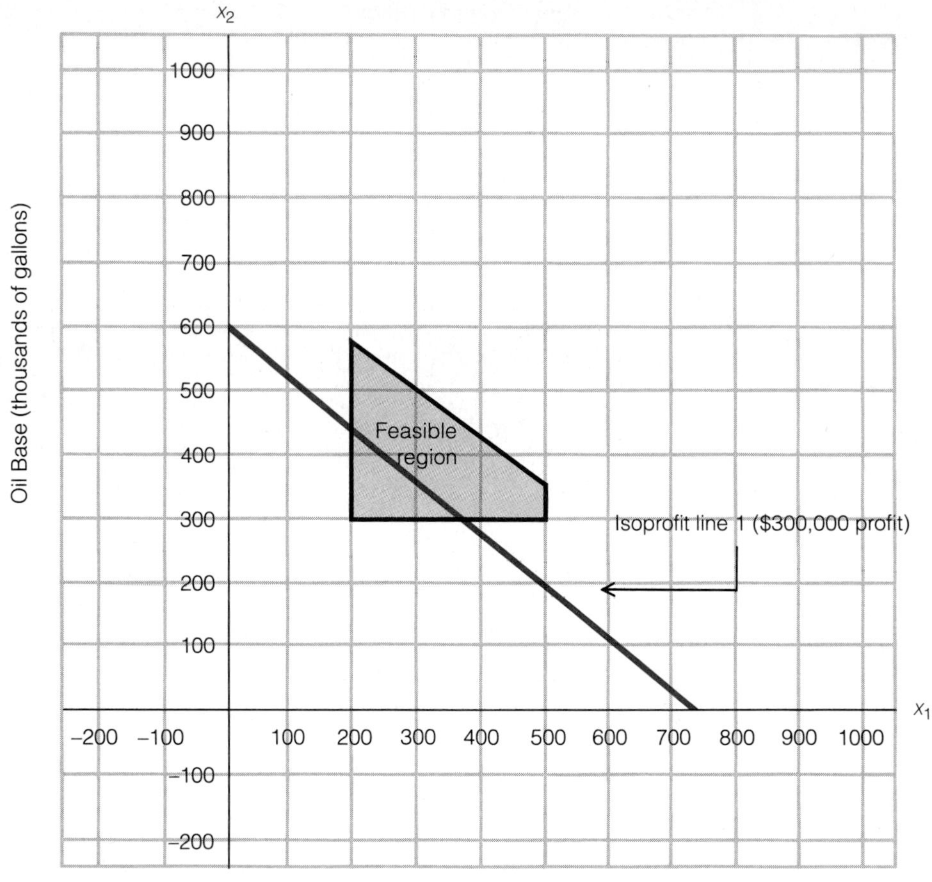

Figure 2-9
Richards Paint Co. problem: isoprofit line 1

We can solve equation (c) directly for x_1:

$$\text{(c)}\quad 1x_1 + 0x_2 = 500{,}000$$
$$x_1 = 500{,}000$$

Now we substitute this value for x_1 into equation (e) and solve for x_2 as follows:

$$\text{(e)}\quad 1(500{,}000) + 1.5x_2 = 1{,}000{,}000$$
$$1.5x_2 = 1{,}000{,}000 - 500{,}000$$
$$x_2 = 500{,}000/1.5$$
$$x_2 = 333{,}333.33$$

The corner point is $x_1 = 500{,}000$ and $x_2 = 333{,}333.33$. Thus, Richards Paint should produce 500,000 gallons of latex base and 333,333.33 gallons of oil base. The total net profit from this decision is determined by substituting these values into the objective function:

$$\text{Profit} = Z = (\$.40)500{,}000 + (\$.50)333{,}333.33$$
$$Z = \$366{,}666.67$$

By inspecting Figure 2-10 you can see that the optimal solution point will be at a corner of the feasible region, given that we have linear constraints and a linear objective function. Put a ruler on the graph parallel to the isoprofit lines. Now change the slope of the ruler. No matter what the slope of the profit line, its optimal value will be at a corner of the feasible region. (If the isoprofit line is parallel to one side of the feasible region, alternative optimal solutions will exist. We will discuss this in more detail in section 2-7.) The conclusion that the optimal solution to a linear programming problem will be at a corner point is formally expressed as:

The Fundamental Theorem of Linear Programming

If an optimal value of the objective function exists, it will occur at a corner of the feasible region.

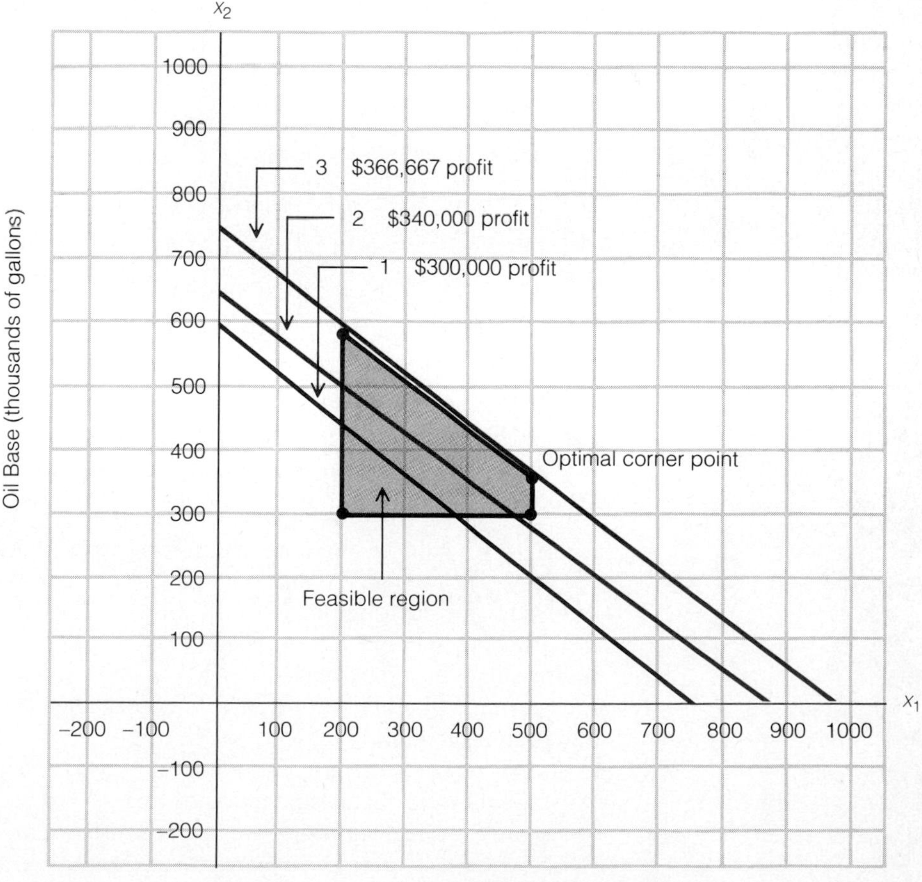

Figure 2-10
Richards Paint Co. problem: optimal solution

Determining the Optimal Solution by Inspecting Corners

Since the optimal solution must be at a corner, we can determine the optimal solution to any linear programming problem by inspecting all corners of the feasible region. For instance, the values:

$$x_1 = 200{,}000$$

and

$$x_2 = 300{,}000$$

determine the lower left-hand corner of the feasible region in the Richards Paint Company example. The profit associated with this point is:

$$\begin{aligned} \text{Profit} &= Z \\ &= \$.40(200{,}000) + \$.50(300{,}000) \\ &= \$80{,}000 + \$150{,}000 \\ &= \$230{,}000 \end{aligned}$$

Figure 2-11 shows all corners of the feasible region. These corner points have the following values of x_1, x_2, and profit:

	Corner	x_1	x_2	**Profit**
	C_1	200,000	300,000	\$230,000
	C_2	200,000	533,333.33	\$346,666.67
Optimal	C_3	500,000	333,333.33	\$366,666.67
	C_4	500,000	300,000	\$350,000

As indicated, corner point C_3 will maximize profits; thus, the company should produce 500,000 gallons of latex base and 333,333.33 gallons of oil base next month. These quantities will satisfy all constraints and result in a maximum net profit of \$366,666.67.

Here is a summary of the steps in the graphical solution process:

1. Identify the decision variables.
2. Formulate the objective function.
3. Formulate the constraints.
4. Determine whether the objective function and constraints appropriately model the decision situation.
5. Graph the constraints to determine the feasible region.
6. Graph the isoprofit line and move the line toward the outer boundary of the feasible region, or evaluate the objective function at each corner point of the feasible region.
7. The optimal solution in a maximization application is the corner point which yields the highest value for the objective function.

Figure 2-11
Richards Paint Co. problem: corner points

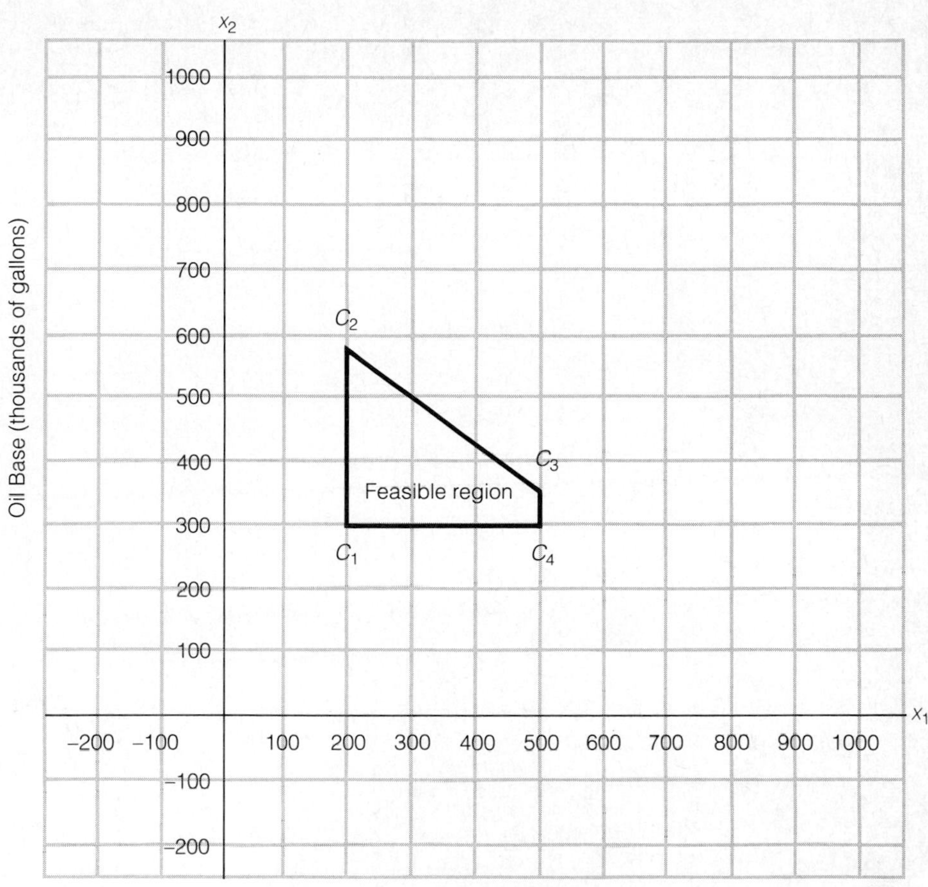

2-6 A MINIMIZATION EXAMPLE

Many business decision-making situations that can be represented by linear programming models have objectives that involve minimization rather than maximization. For example, consider the S. E. Fields Corporation, a Minneapolis-based advertising agency. The company represents a variety of large and small clients. Its services range from creating full-fledged advertising campaigns to simply preparing spot commercials and placing those commercials in the appropriate media.

S. E. FIELDS CORPORATION

The situation considered here is one in which the S. E. Fields Corporation has been retained by a bank to determine the "best" advertising mix for its radio and television commercials.

When the bank approached S. E. Fields, it imposed several restrictions on the advertising plan:

1. At least 20, but not more than 70, minutes of television spots must be played during the advertising period.

2. The radio spots must total at least 50 minutes during the period. No maximum is placed on radio minutes.
3. At least 80 minutes of radio and television spots must be aired during the period.
4. The total customer index rating for the period must be at least 500,000.
5. Achieve conditions 1–4 at the least possible cost.

Assuming that radio and television commercials can be of any time length, the situation described here can be formulated and solved as a linear programming problem.

Formulating the Linear Programming Problem

We have previously suggested a three-step approach for developing a linear programming model:

1. Define the decision variables.
2. Formulate the objective function.
3. Formulate the constraints.

Decision variables. In this example, the decision variables are:

$R =$ the number of radio minutes

$T =$ the number of television minutes

Objective function. From a study of the radio and television advertising rates in the bank's market area, executives at S. E. Fields have determined that the average cost per radio minute will be \$200 and the average cost per television minute will be \$2500. The charge given S. E. Fields was to *minimize* the bank's total advertising costs. Therefore, we establish the following objective function:

$$\text{Minimize } Z = 200R + \$2500T$$

Where:

$Z =$ total advertising cost

$R =$ radio minutes

$T =$ television minutes

Constraints. Obviously, the bank's advertising expense could be minimized by not playing any radio or television spots. However, the bank has imposed several constraints which make this approach unreasonable. For instance, the television spots must total at least 20, but not more than 70, minutes during the period. From this, two formal constraints can be stated:

(a) $0R + 1T \geq 20$
(b) $0R + 1T \leq 70$

The constraint coefficient for variable T in constraint (a) indicates that each television minute aired adds 1 to the required 20 minutes. The coefficient for R in constraint (a) indicates that radio spots add nothing to the television requirement.

The bank also imposed constraints on the minutes of radio spots by requesting that at least 50 radio minutes be aired during the period. This constraint can be written as follows:

(c) $1R + 0T \geq 50$

The combined radio and television spots must total at least 80 minutes during the period. This constraint is written as:

(d) $1R + 1T \geq 80$

Finally, the bank requires that the customer index rating be at least 500,000 during the period. The customer index rating is a scale used by S. E. Fields and other advertising agencies to measure the effectiveness of different media. The exact numbers used for this index rating depend on the market area. For the bank's market area, each radio minute is worth 5000 rating points. Each television minute is worth 25,000 rating points. (This shows why television time costs so much more than radio time in this market.) This constraint can be stated in linear programming terms as follows:

(e) $5000R + 25{,}000T \geq 500{,}000$

Since these are the only constraints to be considered, we can restate the entire linear programming problem as follows:

Minimize $Z = 200R + \$2500T$

Subject to:

(a) $0R + 1T \geq 20$
(b) $0R + 1T \leq 70$
(c) $1R + 0T \geq 50$
(d) $1R + 1T \geq 80$
(e) $5000R + 25{,}000T \geq 500{,}000$

and $R, T \geq 0$

Of course, having a negative amount of radio or television time is impossible, so the nonnegativity constraints have been added.

This formulation is a model of the situation facing the S. E. Fields Corporation. Remember, a model is a representation of a real situation. The quality of the information supplied by the model is largely dependent upon how accurately the model represents reality. (This is a point we will stress throughout this text!)

The Graphical Solution

To determine the solution graphically, we begin with the feasible region determined by the nonnegativity constraints, as shown in Figure 2-12. Next we graph the constraints, using the methods previously discussed in the Richards Paint Company example. The constraint lines are shown in Figure 2-13. These constraints form a revised (and reduced) feasible region. Note that we have labeled the corners of the feasible region as C_1, C_2, and C_3. Remember that if an optimal solution exists, it will lie at a corner of the feasible region.

The next step in determining the graphical solution is to graph the objective function or isocost line. Recall that the cost function to be minimized is:

$Z = 200R + 2500T$

We use the same procedure to graph the isocost line that we used for graphing the isoprofit line in the Richards Paint example. Start by selecting any value for the total cost, say, \$5,000. We can represent the cost line by determining values for R and T that

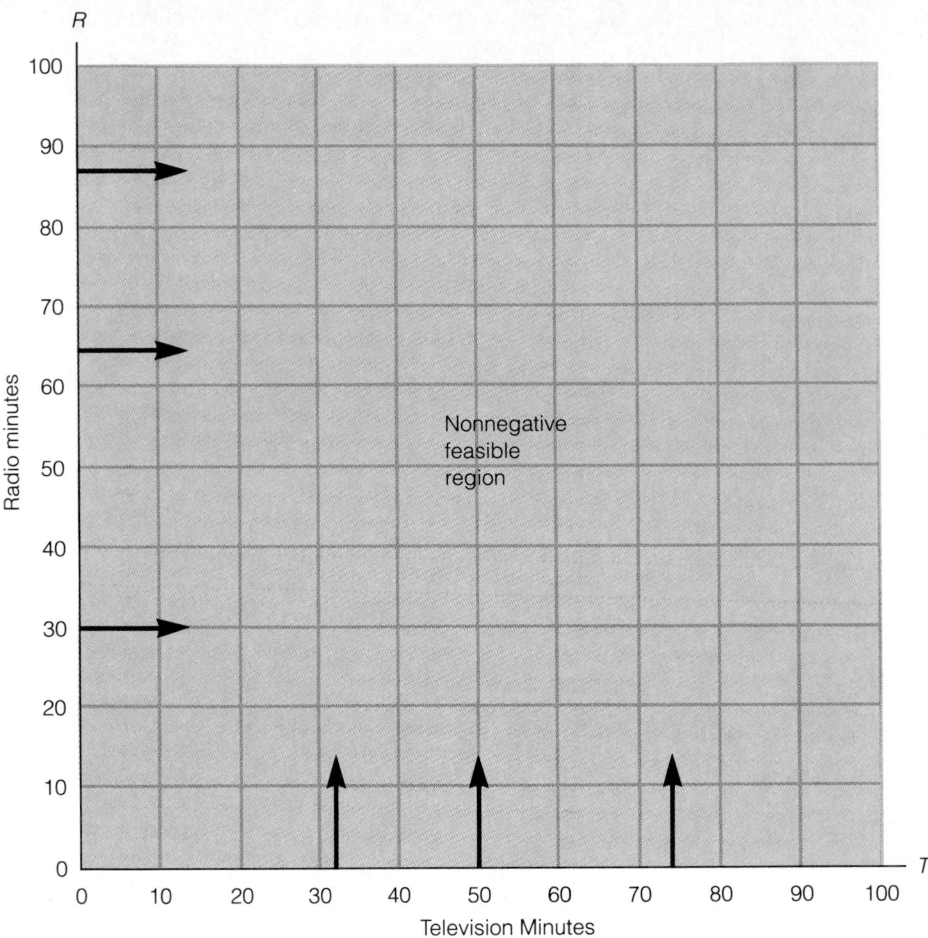

Figure 2-12
S. E. Fields Corp. problem: nonnegativity considered

will yield a total cost of \$5000. First, let $R = 0$:

$$200(0) + 2500T = 5000$$

Solving for T gives:

$$T = 2$$

Then, let $T = 0$:

$$200R + 2500(0) = 5000$$

Solving for R gives:

$$R = 25$$

Now we locate the points ($R = 0$, $T = 2$) and ($R = 25$, $T = 0$) on the graph and connect these points with a straight line, as shown in Figure 2-14. Note that this isocost line falls below the feasible region, so values of R and T on this cost line do not represent feasible solutions. The total cost line must be moved upward until it comes into contact with the feasible region. Recall that all isoprofit lines for a given profit function are linear and parallel. The same is true for isocost lines. Recall, too, the optimal solution to a linear programming problem (if one exists) will lie at one of the corner points. Therefore, in this example, if we move the cost line out, parallel to the original cost line, until it hits a corner of the feasible region, we will have located a corner-point solution for the S. E. Fields problem. This is shown in Figure 2-14 as corner point C_1. Because the objective is to minimize cost, we stop at the first corner point touched by the isocost line. (If the first isocost line had been above the feasible region, we would have moved the isocost line toward the origin until we reached the optimal corner.)

Now we can determine the values of R and T corresponding to the solution to the linear programming problem. Since constraints (a) and (d) intersect to form the corner representing the solution point, we can set up the constraints as linear equations and solve for the two unknowns.

(a) $0R + 1T = 20$
(d) $1R + 1T = 80$

Figure 2-13
S. E. Fields Corp. problem: constraints and feasible region

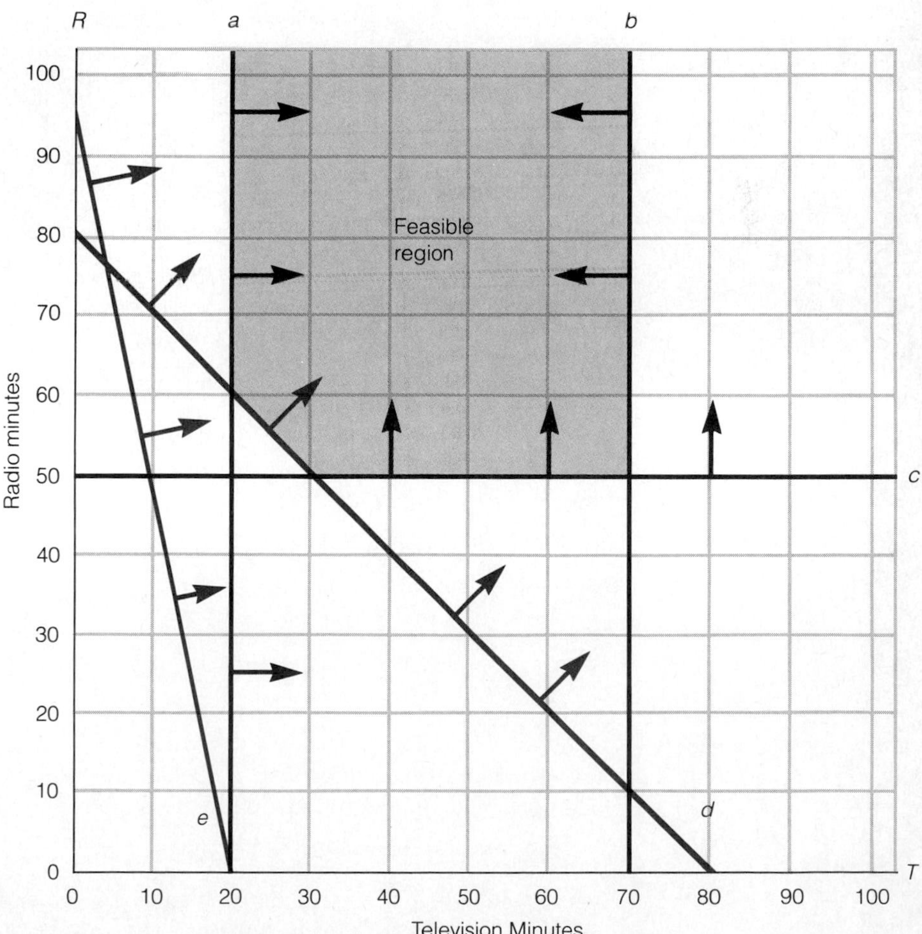

Note: Constraint *e* is a redundant constraint since it does not reduce the feasible region.

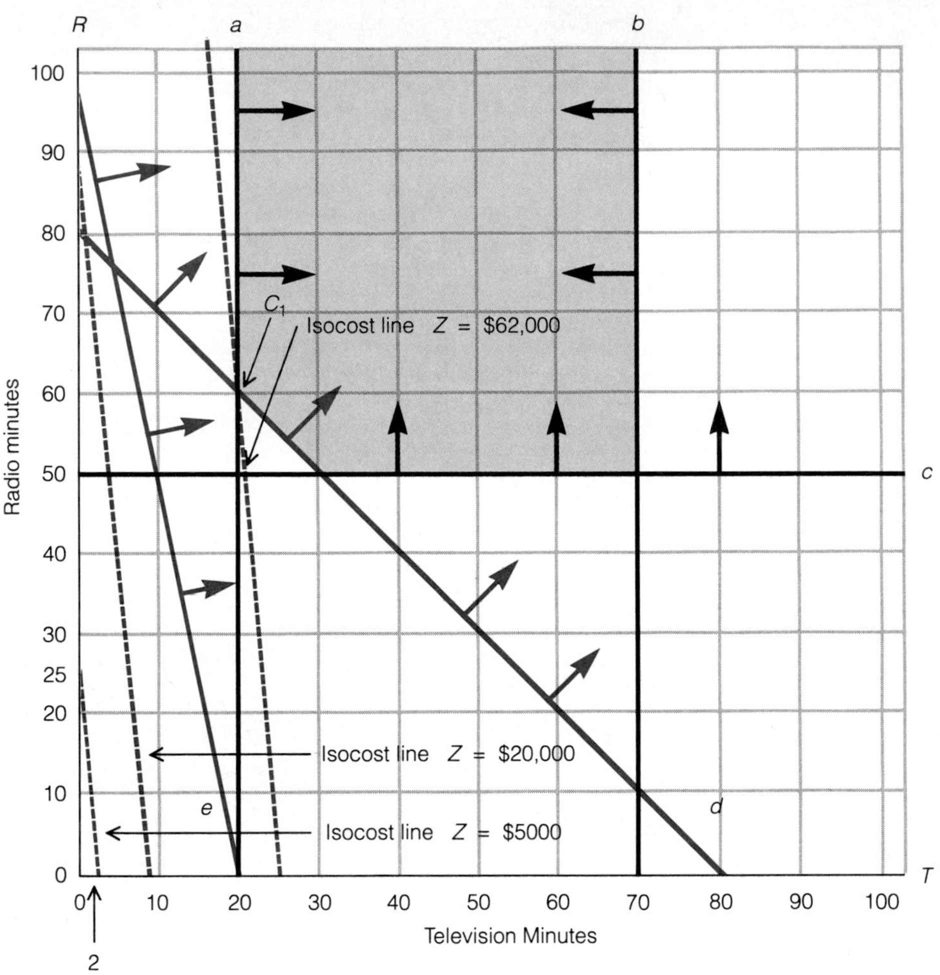

Figure 2-14
S. E. Fields Corp. problem: constraints, feasible region, and isocost lines

Note: The Isocost lines are parallel. The optimal solution is at the least-cost corner point (C_1).

Solving for R and T, we get

$$T = 20$$

and:

$$R = 80 - T$$

$$R = 60$$

Therefore, the solution for S. E. Fields is to purchase 20 minutes of television time and 60 minutes of radio time during the period. The total cost for this solution is:

$$\$200(60) + \$2500(20) = \$62,000$$

Given the constraints of this problem, S. E. Fields can establish no advertising mix to give a lower cost than the solution arrived at through linear programming. You should inspect other feasible values for R and T to verify that \$62,000 is the minimum cost solution.

2-7 OTHER LINEAR PROGRAMMING CONSIDERATIONS

As decision makers expand their use of linear programming, they may encounter some of the following special situations: *infeasibility, alternate optimal solutions,* and *unbounded solutions.* A brief discussion of these conditions follows.

INFEASIBILITY

Infeasibility occurs when the constraints of a linear programming problem cannot be satisfied simultaneously. This happens because the constraints are in conflict and there is no feasible region. For instance, consider the following objective function and constraints:

$$\text{Maximize } Z = 30x_1 + 50x_2$$

Subject to:

(a) $10x_1 \leq 100$
(b) $5x_1 \geq 60$
(c) $20x_2 \leq 300$
(d) $x_1, x_2 \geq 0$

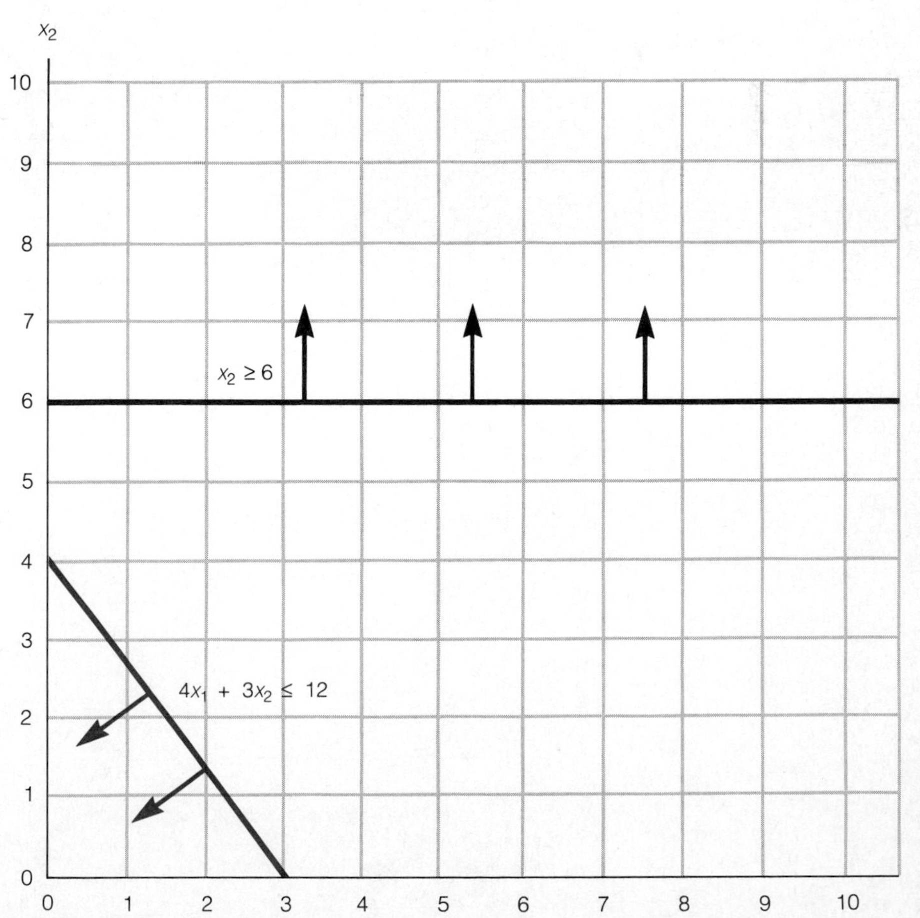

Figure 2-15
An infeasible linear programming problem

Constraint (a) restricts x_1 to a maximum value of 10 to satisfy the right-handside limit of 100. However, constraint (b) indicates that x_1 must be at least 12 to ensure that $5x_1 \geq 60$. Because these two constraints cannot both be satisfied, the linear programming problem is infeasible. Situations like this may mean that additional resources are required or that certain requirements must be reduced before the linear programming problem can be solved. Infeasibility may also mean the constraints have been formulated incorrectly and that revising the constraints is required. Figure 2-15 graphically demonstrates another situation when two constraints combine to produce an infeasible linear programming problem.

ALTERNATE OPTIMAL SOLUTIONS

A linear programming problem with more than one optimal solution is said to have **alternate optimal solutions.** In a graphical representation, alternate optimal solutions occur when the profit or cost line runs parallel to a binding constraint. When this happens, there are an infinite number of possible optimal solutions. Figure 2-16 illustrates this concept. A linear programming problem will have 0, 1, or an infinite number of solutions. From a management viewpoint, alternate optimal solutions are desirable, since the decision maker has a choice among the alternatives and can base the decision on qualitative factors not considered in the linear programming formulation.

UNBOUNDED SOLUTIONS

A linear programming problem is **unbounded** if the objective function can become infinitely large (or small) without violating any of the constraints. In practical applications of linear programming, if an unbounded solution results, it is safe to conclude that the constraints have not been formulated correctly and further specification is required. Figure 2-17 shows the profit line and constraints in graphical form for an unbounded solution example.

Figure 2-16
Alternate optimal solutions

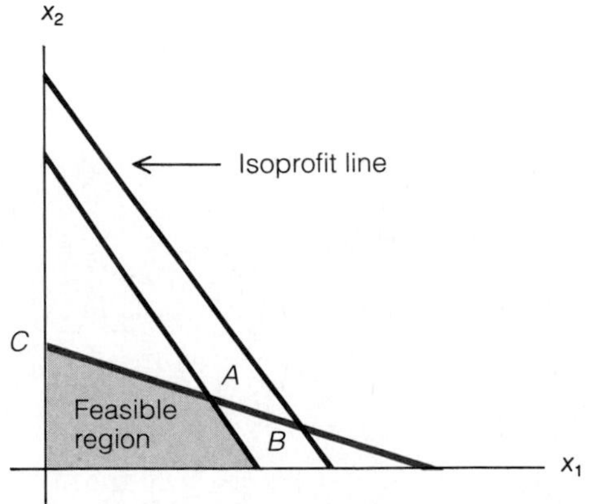

Note: The isoprofit line is parallel to side *AB* of the feasible region. All solutions on line *AB* will be optimal.

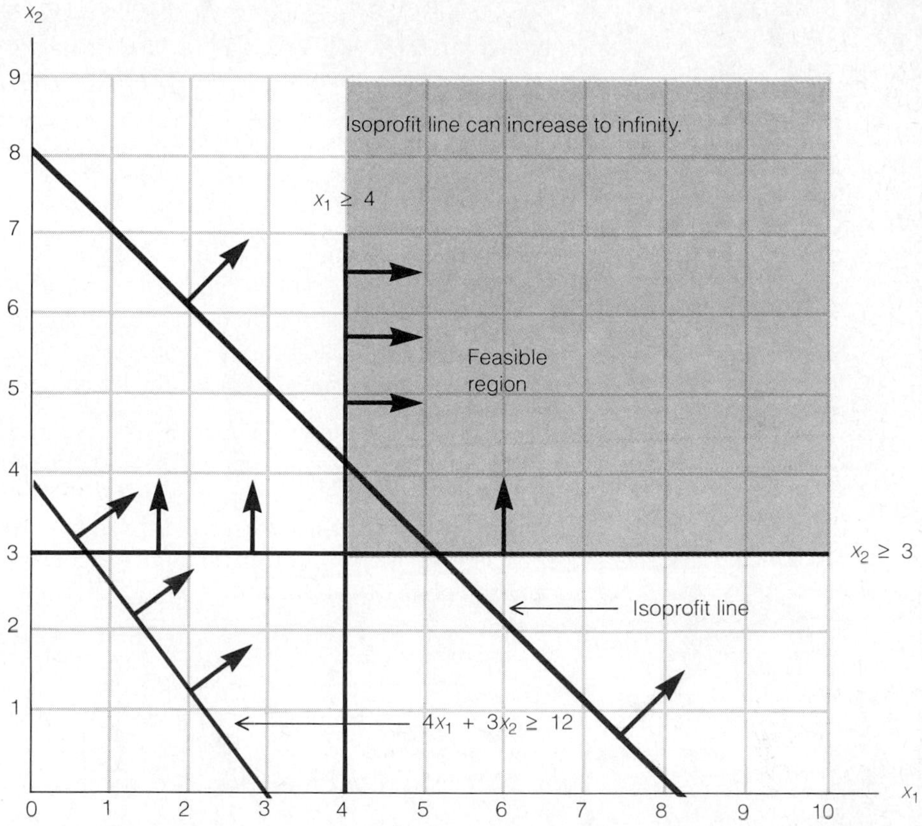

Figure 2-17
Unbounded solution

2-8 SUMMARY AND CONCLUSIONS

The idea of determining an optimal solution to a problem is very appealing to a decision maker. Linear programming is a management science technique developed to provide an optimal solution to particular types of decision problems. The trick for the decision maker is to use linear programming to model a given situation. Fortunately, even in situations where using linear programming requires considerable simplifying assumptions, the solutions obtained may provide useful starting points for further analysis.

There have been, and continue to be, many applications of linear programming in business situations. Most applications center on a common theme involving the effective allocation of resources. The Chapter References contain articles describing a variety of linear programming applications.

The purpose of this chapter has been to introduce the concepts of linear programming and to show how a basic situation can be modeled in a linear programming format. We have introduced the graphical solution procedure. While no real problem would be solved graphically, our purpose in going through this method was to demonstrate some important concepts which apply to all linear programming applications. We demonstrated how the feasible region is constructed based upon constraints on the decision variables. We also showed that the optimal solution (if one exists) lies at a corner point of the feasible region. You will see the importance of this in the next chapter, where we introduce a general solution procedure for solving larger-scale linear programming problems.

The graphical solution procedure consists of the following steps:

1. Determine the decision variables.
2. Define the objective function.
3. Formulate the constraints.
4. Identify the feasible region by plotting the constraints.
5. Determine the optimal solution either by evaluating the objective function at all corner points or by plotting the profit (or cost) line on the graph and moving parallel lines toward the extreme of the feasible region.

While linear programming applications cross all business disciplines, a situation must meet four primary assumptions before the procedure can be used. As discussed in this chapter, those assumptions are *linearity, additivity, divisibility,* and *certainty.*

Solving problems using the graphical technique, or by examining all corner solutions, is adequate for linear programming problems involving only two variables but is not acceptable for problems with more than two variables. To handle these larger situations, we must develop a more formal mathematical procedure. In the next chapter, we relate linear programming to systems of linear equations. Specifically, we will show how to reformulate a linear programming problem with linear inequality constraints into a system of linear equalities. We will also introduce a mathematical technique (the simplex procedure) for solving linear programming problems with two or more decision variables.

Solved Problems

PROBLEM 1 The Conrad-Krinkle Corporation manufactures two styles of designer jeans, standard and deluxe. Each pair of standard jeans nets the company $6 in profit, and the deluxe jeans net $7 each. An employee has suggested a procedure which makes available an additional 12 hours of time on machine A and 8 hours of time on machine B in the production process. These machines, used for cutting and sewing, are the only resources required to produce the designer jeans.

The production manager wants to determine the mix of standard (s) and deluxe (d) jeans which will generate the maximum profit for the company from the additional machine time subject to resource limitations. She knows that each pair of standard jeans requires 2 hours of machine A time and 2 hours of machine B time. Each pair of deluxe jeans requires 3 hours of machine A time and 1 hour of machine B time.

Formulate the decision situation facing the Conrad-Krinkle Corporation as a linear programming problem.

Solution The three steps in formulation are:

1. Define the decision variables.
2. Develop the objective function.
3. Specify the constraints.

In this example, there are two decision variables:

s = number of standard jeans

d = number of deluxe jeans

The objective facing Conrad-Krinkle is to determine the mix of jeans (standard and deluxe) which will maximize profits. Since standard jeans net \$6 each and deluxe jeans net \$7 each, the objective function is:

Maximize $Z = 6s + 7d$

The constraints, which must be part of the model, deal with machine capacity. Machine A has a maximum of 12 hours available. Each pair of standard jeans requires 2 hours of machine A time and deluxe jeans require 3 hours each. With this information, we can formulate the following constraint for machine A:

$$2s + 3d \leq 12$$

Likewise, machine B has a maximum of 8 hours available. The standard jeans require 2 hours per unit on machine B, and the deluxe jeans require 1 hour per unit. The constraint is written as:

$$2s + 1d \leq 8$$

Finally, we can add the nonnegativity constraints:

$$s, d \geq 0$$

Thus, the following formulation describes the decision situation facing Conrad-Krinkle:

Maximize $Z = 6s + 7d$

Subject to:

$$2s + 3d \leq 12$$
$$2s + 1d \leq 8$$

and

$$s, d \geq 0$$

PROBLEM 2 Use the graphical solution technique to solve the linear programming problem formulated in Problem 1. Determine how many standard and deluxe jeans to produce with the extra machine time.

Solution The linear programming formulation shown in Problem 1 is:

Maximize $Z = 6s + 7d$

Subject to:

$$2s + 3d \leq 12$$
$$2s + 1d \leq 8$$

and

$$s, d \geq 0$$

First we graph the two constraints as shown in Figure 2-18. (The feasible region is indicated by the shaded area on the graph.) Next we graph the profit function using any value for profit, say, \$42.

As seen in Figure 2-18, this is not the optimal profit, since the line is entirely outside the feasible region of the graph. We move the profit line toward the feasible region, keeping it parallel to the original profit line, until it touches the feasible region at the corner close to the values of $s = 3$ and $d = 2$. To be sure of the correct values for s and d, we will solve the system of equations formed by the two constraints that intersect to give that specific corner point.

$$2s + 3d = 12$$
$$2s + 1d = 8$$

We can solve these equations by multiplying the second equation by -1 and then adding the two equations, as follows:

$$\begin{array}{r} 2s + 3d = 12 \\ \underline{-2s + (-1d) = -8} \\ 2d = 4 \end{array}$$

Then:

$$d = 4/2$$
$$d = 2$$

If $d = 2$, we can solve for s using either of the two original equations, as follows:

$$\begin{aligned} 2s + 3(2) &= 12 \\ 2s &= 12 - 6 \\ 2s &= 6 \\ s &= 6/2 \\ s &= 3 \end{aligned}$$

Thus, the solution for the Conrad-Krinkle Company is use the additional machine time to make 3 pairs of standard (s) jeans and 2 pairs of deluxe jeans (d), for a total profit of $\$6(3) + \$7(2) = \$32$.

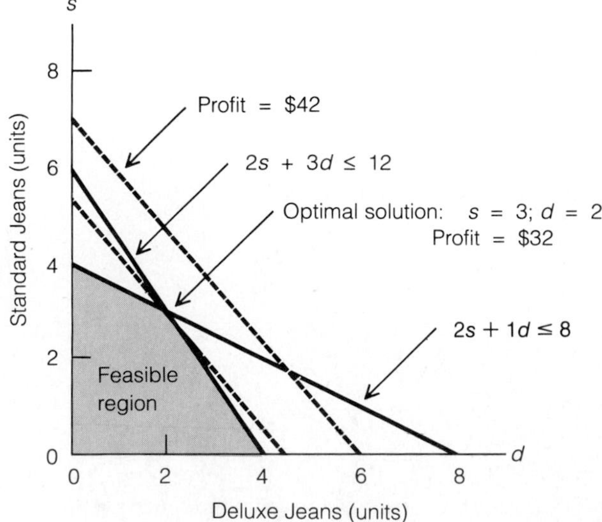

Figure 2-18
Graphical solution for Problem 2

General Questions and Assignments

1. What are some of the problems associated with generating an *optimal solution* to a decision problem?
2. What are the advantages of using linear programming as a decision-making tool?
3. What are the three-approaches to problem solving that led to the present form of linear programming?
4. What was the global event that contributed to the development of linear programming? Discuss its significance.
5. What are the three steps in formulating a linear programming problem?
6. What is the purpose of *constraints* in a linear programming problem?
7. Contact a local business and determine whether it uses linear programming as an aid to decision making. If so, write a short report describing the applications. If not, write a short report outlining an area where the company might be able to use linear programming.
8. Locate three articles in the library which describe applications of linear programming. Write a report summarizing the articles. Comment on how successful these applications were.

Exercises and Application Problems

1. The production manager for the Littleton Company is preparing the weekly production schedule. There will be 160 hours of drilling time and 80 hours of sanding time available next week. The available inventory of raw material is 500 units, and each product requires 2 units of raw material. Product A requires .8 hour of drilling time and .1 hour of sanding time per unit. Product B requires .4 hour of drilling time and .16 hour of sanding time per unit. Product C requires .30 hour of drilling time and .18 hour of sanding time per unit. The profit margin on product A is $30, the profit margin on B is $11, and the profit margin on C is $15. Formulate this production scheduling problem as a linear programming problem assuming that the objective is to maximize profits. Do not solve.
2. Referring to problem 1, suppose an agreement has already been made with a customer that requires the company to make at least 250 units of product C. Further assume that because of a poor demand forecast for product A, no more than 100 units of that product are to be made this period. Considering this new information, reformulate the problem as a linear programming problem but do not solve.
3. A dairy products company is considering blending artificial cream with whole milk to form a new product to be used on breakfast cereals. The artificial cream costs the company $.50 per unit and whole milk costs $.80 per unit. The total fat content of the blended product cannot exceed 40 grams per gallon. Each unit of artificial cream contains 6 grams of fat, and each unit of whole milk contains 10 grams of fat. It takes 5 units of whole milk by itself to make a gallon, and it takes 8 units of the artificial cream to make a gallon. Tests have shown that there needs to be at least twice as much artificial cream as whole milk in the finished product. Formulate a linear programming problem which will indicate how much of each ingredient should go into a gallon of the finished product, if the company wishes to meet the requirements and minimize costs. Do not solve.
4. An individual has $100,000 to invest and has several alternatives to choose from. Municipal bonds will return 7.5%, certificates of deposit will return 6%, treasury bills will return 9.7%, and a mutual fund will return 13% on average. Because each investment alternative has a different risk level, the

investor wishes to diversify her investments. When she talked with her investment adviser, they agreed on the following:

a. No more than 25% of the investment should be in mutual funds.
b. The amount invested in CDs should be no more than the total of the other three investments.
c. At least 30% of the investment should be in treasury bills and municipal bonds.
d. The amount invested in municipal bonds should be no more than one-third the amount invested in any other alternative.
e. The investor wishes to invest the entire $100,000.

Formulate this investment decision as a linear programming problem in which the objective is to maximize the return on investment. Do not solve.

5. A cereal company makes a product which it claims will meet the minimum daily requirements for vitamins A and D. Three main ingredients go into this product: wheat, oats, and barley. These ingredients contain various quantities of vitamins A and D. The question is, How much of each ingredient should be in each box if the objective is to minimize costs and still meet the minimum daily requirements? The following table lists the vitamin contribution per box for each ingredient and the total requirement:

	Vitamin A	Vitamin D	Cost per Ounce
Wheat	15	10	$.05
Oats	25	20	$.07
Barley	12	16	$.04
Requirement	150	100	

Formulate as a linear programming problem but do not solve.

6. Referring to problem 5, suppose the company wishes to have twice as much barley in each box as the other two products combined. Reformulate the problem with this new constraint included.

7. As the investment manager for Lanier Consultants, it is your responsibility to invest any excess funds for the firm. The company currently has $1.5 million in excess funds. You can invest in either stock A, bond B, or U.S. Treasury bills (a risk-free asset). You are required to invest all of the funds. The firm has a policy that at most 75% of the funds can be invested in risky assets. The firm also requires that no more than 30% of the funds be invested in stocks. The expected returns on stock A, bond B, and U.S. T-bills are 15%, 13%, and 10%, respectively. Formulate this problem to maximize the return on dollars invested in each of the assets. (No solution is required.)

8. The advertising manager of Badeaux Boutique has asked you to determine the advertising strategy for print advertising for the following month. You have three choices: magazines, billboards, and newspapers. The following table gives some relevant information about each type of advertising:

	Magazines	Billboards	Newspapers
Cost per advertisement	$1,000	$5,000	$1,200
Consumer exposure per ad	10,000	20,000	15,000
Revenue per advertisement	$5,000	$8,000	$5,950

This month's advertising budget is $20,000. The company president wants no more than 3 billboards and wants at least as many newspaper ads as magazine ads. The policy is to always have no more than 20 units of print advertising per month. The president has told you that she wants to reach at least 85,000 people with the advertisements. Formulate a linear programming model for this problem, assuming the goal is to maximize profits. (No solution is required.)

9. Wake-up Coffee has two types of gourmet coffee: premium blend, which sells for $6.00 per pound, and deluxe blend, which sells for $4.50 per pound. Both coffees are made from three types of beans: Haitian, Colombian, and Peruvian. The following information is known about each type of bean:

Bean	Maximum Amount Available	Cost per Pound
Haitian	300 pounds	$1.00
Colombian	500 pounds	2.50
Peruvian	350 pounds	3.00

Each type of coffee requires a different blend of beans, as follows:

Coffee	Blend of Beans
Premium	Maximum 30% Haitian Minimum 30% Colombian Minimum 50% Peruvian
Deluxe	Minimum 40% Haitian Minimum 40% Colombian Maximum 20% Peruvian

Wake-up Coffee can sell at least 400 pounds of premium blend and 500 pounds of deluxe blend. Formulate this as a linear programming problem, assuming the objective is to maximize profit. (No solution is required.)

10. The Zarruk Calculator Company has 5 assembly stations (A–E) that it needs to keep in operation. Currently there are 4 employees who can operate any of the stations. Their degree of expertise is such that the employees can produce a different number of calculators per hour, depending on which station they operate. The following table provides this information:

	Units Produced per Hour, by Station				
Employee	**A**	**B**	**C**	**D**	**E**
Sharon	5	8	4	6	5
Eddie	4	1	3	9	8
Charlene	3	3	9	7	8
Darlene	3	8	1	5	4

Sharon could be assigned to 2 stations if necessary, but the other employees can only be assigned to 1. However, each station must have an assigned worker. Formulate this as a linear programming problem, assuming the goal is to maximize the number of calculators produced per hour. (No solution is required.)

11. Come-Back Yo-Yo Company must determine how many Sleeper and Spinner yo-yos to manufacture this month. The Sleeper requires 1 minute to assemble and 2 square inches of wood. The Spinner requires 2 minutes of assembly time and 8 square inches of wood. The company, however, is limited to 240 hours of assembly time and 48,000 square inches of wood. Both types of yo-yo generate $2 each in profits.

    Formulate this as a linear programming problem, assuming that profit maximization is the company's objective. (No solution is required.)

12. Bearcat Sports, Inc., makes footballs and basketballs in its small plant in Keystone, Colorado. The footballs take 1 hour each to make and require .5 yard of leather (allowing for waste). Basketballs also take 1 hour to make, but they require 1 yard of leather. The company's labor force can provide 300 hours of labor this week. Leather supplies are limited to the current inventory of 450 yards. If the footballs and basketballs net $5 and $10 in profits, respectively, how many of each should Bearcat Sports produce this week to maximize profits? (Assume the company can sell all it produces.)

    Formulate this problem as a linear programming problem. (No solution is required.)

13. Luebke Recreation Company produces two models of golf shoes: the Driver and the Master. During the upcoming month, Luebke has more orders than it is capable of filling. Both models involve the same production processes of cutting, assembly, and finishing. The production requirements and availabilities are shown below:

Process	Driver	Master	Time Available
Cutting (minutes)	2	2	166⅔ hours
Assembly (minutes)	1	3	150 hours
Finishing (minutes)	2	3	200 hours

Assuming that Driver nets the company $11 per pair and Master nets $13 per pair, establish the appropriate objective function and constraints if Luebke Recreation wishes to maximize net profit. (No solution is required.)

14. A small winery near Sonoma, California, bottles two types of wine: rosé and burgundy. The rosé sells for $20 a quart and the burgundy sells for $28.50 a quart, at the wholesale level. It takes an estimated 5 minutes of employee time to make a quart of rosé and 12 minutes to make a quart of burgundy. The small winery has only 2 employees, who together work a total of 15 hours per day, 5 days a week.

It takes 10 pounds of grapes to make each quart of burgundy and 14 pounds of grapes to make each quart of rosé. Because the grapes must be picked at just the right time, only 4000 pounds of grapes are available each week. Because of customer demand, the winery has agreed to supply at least 50 quarts of each type of wine each week. Formulate this problem as a linear programming problem, assuming that the winery wishes to produce the mix of wines that will maximize revenues given the constraints imposed on production. (No solution is required.)

15. Problem 14 states that the winery has 2 employees but does not mention the work that each employee does in making the wine. Suppose employee 1, whose specialty is making rosé, works 8 hours per day. Making rosé requires at least 5 hours per day. However, because of management's desire to have both employees involved in making both wines, employee 1 must work at least 1 hour per day making burgundy. Using these new constraints, along with the others stated in problem 14, formulate the linear programming problem. (Do not solve.)

16. The Cedar Falls Manufacturing Company recently discontinued production of one of its product lines because of the line's poor profitability. This has resulted in excess production capacity, which management would like to allocate to one or more of the other three product lines: X, Y, and Z. The milling department now has an extra 600 hours available per week, the grinder has an extra 480 hours available per week, and the polishing department has an extra 400 hours of time available per week. The following table shows the number of hours for each process required to produce each unit of X, Y, and Z.

Product	Milling	Grinding	Polishing
X	11	8	6
Y	9	10	7
Z	8	8	13

Because of the great effort of the sales department, demand for X, Y, and Z will exceed any potential production level. The profit per unit for X is $24; for Y, $15; and for Z, $19. Formulate this as a linear programming problem, assuming profit maximization is the objective. (No solution is required.)

17. The Delta Manufacturing Company makes two sizes of file cabinets, letter size and legal size. The letter-size cabinet sells to the distributor for $138, and the legal size cabinet sells for $176.50. The cabinets are constructed from sheet metal that is ordered with a special coloring and finish. It takes 36 square feet of sheet metal to make a letter-size file cabinet and 54 square feet of sheet metal to make a legal-size cabinet. Because of a problem at the supplier's plant, Delta will not be able to get

any more of the special sheet metal until next year and has only 120,000 square feet to use for the rest of this year. Making cabinets requires two major operations: cutting the metal and bending it into parts, and then assembling the different parts. The cutting and bending operations take 2 hours for a letter-size cabinet and 3 hours for a legal-size cabinet. The company has 10,000 hours of time available for this operation. Assembly takes 4 hours for a letter-size cabinet and 2 hours for a legal-size cabinet. The company has 8000 hours available for this operation.

Both indirect and direct labor costs are assigned to the products that Delta makes. Each letter-size cabinet requires $41 in direct labor charges. The legal-size cabinets require $52 in direct labor. The board of directors has allocated $375,000 for direct labor.

The company's cost accountants have determined that the total direct and indirect costs assigned to the letter-size cabinet are $87. The total costs allocated to the legal-size cabinet are $121.

Formulate the objective function and the constraints for this problem, assuming that Delta wishes to determine the optimal number of each type of file cabinet to make in order to maximize profits within the given constraints. (No solution is required.)

18. The Dilmart Department Store carries three lines of men's suits: Budget, Career, and Insignia. The more expensive the suit is, the more profit Dilmart makes on each suit. However, the expensive suits also require more time by the sales personnel and more display space. When Dilmart orders suits for the coming season, it always orders at least 1000 suits of each line in order to maintain the inventory variety that the customers have come to expect. The Dilmart buyers order suits with the objective of maximizing profits. However, the buyers must consider certain limitations. For instance, for the coming season, sales personnel will have a maximum of 6400 hours available and the sales area (including displays) will be limited to 6000 square feet. The following table provides some useful information on each suit line.

Suit Line	Profit per Suit	Sales Hours per 1000 Suits	Display Space per 1000 Suits
Budget	$ 6	300	200
Career	$13.20	500	400
Insignia	$28.50	2000	800

Formulate this as a linear programming problem, assuming that Dilmart wishes to maximize profits and that all suits ordered will be sold. (Do not solve.)

19. Discuss in your own terms what is meant by the *divisibility assumption* in linear programming. Describe two examples, one in which the divisibility assumption holds and the other where it would not be reasonable.

20. Discuss in your own terms what the *linearity assumption* in linear programming is. Show an example of an objective function which would violate the linearity assumption.

21. Describe in your own terms what the *additivity assumption* in linear programming means. Present an example which demonstrates this assumption.

22. One of the linear programming assumptions is *certainty*. Explain what this assumption means. Also discuss some of the problems this assumption might cause in actual linear programming applications.

23. Use the graphical approach to determine the feasible region for the following set of constraints:

$$2x_1 + 4x_2 \leq 12$$
$$3x_1 + 2x_2 \geq 6$$
$$x_1, x_2 \geq 0$$

24. Use the graphical approach to determine the feasible region for the following set of constraints:

$$\begin{aligned} 8x_1 + 12x_2 &\le 48 \\ x_1 \qquad &\le 4 \\ x_2 &\ge 1 \\ 14x_1 + 10x_2 &\ge 28 \\ x_1, x_2 &\ge 0 \end{aligned}$$

25. Use the graphical approach to determine the feasible region for the following set of constraints:

$$\begin{aligned} 10x_1 + 12x_2 &\le 100 \\ x_1 \qquad &\ge 5 \\ 20x_1 - 10x_2 &\le 120 \\ x_1, x_2 &\ge 0 \end{aligned}$$

26. Use the graphical solution procedure to determine the solution to the following linear programming problem:

Maximize $Z = 100x_1 + 50x_2$

Subject to:

$$\begin{aligned} 50x_1 + 80x_2 &\le 500 \\ 25x_1 + 10x_2 &\ge 50 \\ x_1 \qquad &\le 5 \\ x_2 &\ge 3 \\ x_1, x_2 &\ge 0 \end{aligned}$$

27. Use the graphical solution method to solve the following linear programming problem:

Maximize $Z = 7x_1 + 3x_2$

Subject to:

$$\begin{aligned} 4x_1 + 5x_2 &\le 23 \\ 2x_1 + 5x_2 &\le 17 \\ x_1, x_2 &\ge 0 \end{aligned}$$

28. Use the graphical solution method to solve the following linear programming problem:

Maximize $Z = 10x_1 + 12x_2$

Subject to:

$$\begin{aligned} 5x_1 + 9x_2 &\le 140 \\ 9x_1 + 5x_2 &\le 55 \\ x_1, x_2 &\ge 0 \end{aligned}$$

29. Use the graphical solution method to solve the following linear programming problem:

Maximize $Z = .07x_1 + .03x_2$

Subject to:

$$4x_1 + 5x_2 \leq 15$$
$$2x_1 + 5x_2 \leq 26$$
$$x_2 \geq 1.5$$
$$x_1, x_2 \geq 0$$

30. Use the graphical solution method to solve the following linear programming problem:

$$\text{Maximize } Z = 245x_1 + 103x_2$$

Subject to:

$$.25x_1 + .4x_2 \leq 300$$
$$2x_1 + 5x_2 \geq 170$$
$$x_1, x_2 \geq 0$$

31. Use the graphical solution method to solve the following linear programming problem:

$$\text{Maximize } Z = .5x_1 + 1.5x_2$$

Subject to:

$$4x_1 + 5x_2 = 500$$
$$2x_1 + 4x_2 \leq 2400$$
$$8x_1 \geq 600$$
$$x_1, x_2 \geq 0$$

32. The Rawlene Manufacturing Company makes two sizes of picnic tables, small and large. The small table sells to distributors for \$200, and the large table sells for \$300. The tables are constructed from sheet metal that has been ordered with a special coloring and finish. It takes 60 square feet of sheet metal to make a small table and 95 square feet of sheet metal to make a large table. Because of shipping problems, Rawlene has on hand only 250,000 square feet of sheet metal to use during the production period.

Labor costs are \$45 for the small tables and \$61 for the large tables. The management has budgeted \$400,000 for labor.

Total direct and indirect costs assigned to the small table are \$88.00 each, and for the large table, \$103 each.

a. Formulate the objective function and the constraints for this problem, assuming that Rawlene wishes to determine the optimal number of each type of table to make in order to maximize profits within the given constraints.

b. Use the objective function and constraints you formulated in part **a** to solve the linear programming problem, using the graphical solution procedure.

33. Nix Brothers Fencing, Inc., manufactures fence posts and fence panels in its small plant in Keystone, Colorado. The posts require 4 minutes each to manufacture and require 4.0 units of wood (allowing for waste). Fence panels take 12 minutes to manufacture and require 10.5 units of wood. The company's workers can provide 300 hours of labor this week. Wood supplies are limited to the current inventory of 2450 units. Posts and fence rails net the company \$1.50 and \$2.00, respectively.

a. Formulate the problem as a linear programming problem. (Assume that maximizing revenues is the objective and that they can sell all that they produce.)

b. Solve graphically the linear programming problem. How many fence posts and how many fence panels should Nix Brothers produce?

c. Which constraints are binding? Indicate which, if any, resource has not been completely used.

34. Homeco Construction develops property for residential subdivisions. It generally buys a tract of land and then puts in sewer, water, utilities, and streets. It currently owns land in Medford, Oregon, and Tacoma, Washington. Records indicate that the sales price per lot in Medford is $18,000, and the sales price for a lot in Tacoma is $16,500. The company is prepared to develop more lots in either or both of these locations but wishes to carry out the development in a manner that will optimize sales revenues. Homeco is assured that any lot that is ready for sale — with utilities, water, sewer, and streets — can be sold at the prices indicated.

There are 88 lots available in Medford and 54 lots available in Tacoma. Further, the company has a total of 900 available hours for planning and supervision between the two sites. Each lot in Medford requires 25 hours of planning and supervision, while lots in Tacoma require 20 hours each. The cost of street improvement is $4500 per lot in Medford and $3450 in Tacoma. Homeco has allocated $275,000 this year for street improvements. The electric utilities cost $500 per lot at each location, and the budget for installing electric utilities is $42,700. The sewer costs are $2300 per lot in Medford and $3100 per lot in Tacoma. The company has available $230,400 to spend on sewers during the period. Finally, installing water service costs $1475 per lot in Medford and $300 in Tacoma. Homeco has budgeted $115,000 for water installation.

a. Develop the linear programming formulation, including objective function and constraints, for optimizing the sales revenue for the Homeco Company.

b. Solve using the graphical solution approach.

35. Cruiser Bicycle Company makes two models of bicycles: the Traveler and the Tourister. Both models use the same frame and tires, but the Traveler requires 1 hour of assembly and painting while the Tourister requires 3 hours for the same work. Overall styling is the reason the Tourister can command a premium $400 price, as opposed to the Traveler's selling price of $200. The company has available 300 bicycle frames and 360 hours of labor. Each Tourister bike costs $175 to make, and the Traveler costs $140 to make.

How many of each model should the company produce in order to maximize profits? Solve by the graphical method.

36. Volume Manufacturers is in the process of determining the monthly production schedule. The company makes two products at its Atlanta plant, sunroofs and porthole windows. Both of these products are used in van customizing by independent shops around the country. A sunroof requires 30 minutes of labor to cut and finish. It also requires 6 square feet of glass. The porthole requires 45 minutes of labor and 4 square feet of glass. The company is limited to 240 hours of labor time and 4800 square feet of glass. Each sunroof nets the company $22, and each porthole nets $15.

a. Formulate this as a linear programming problem, assuming that profit maximization is the company's objective.

b. Solve using the graphical method. How many units of each type of product should be made to maximize profit?

37. The winery near Sonoma, California (see problem 14), bottles two types of wine, rosé and burgundy. The rosé sells for $20 a quart and the burgundy sells for $28.50 a quart, at the wholesale level. It takes an estimated 5 minutes to make a quart of rosé and 12 minutes to make a quart of burgundy. The small winery has only 2 employees, who together work a total of 15 hours per day, 5 days a week. It takes 10 pounds of grapes to make each quart of burgundy and 14 pounds of grapes to make each quart of rosé. Because the grapes must be picked at just the right time, only 4000 pounds of grapes are available each week. Because of customer demand, the winery has agreed to supply at least 50 quarts of each type of wine each week.

Formulate this as a linear programming problem, assuming that the winery wishes to produce the mix of wines that will maximize revenues given the constraints imposed on production. What is the optimal mix of wine to maximize revenues for the winery? Use the graphical solution technique. Check your solution by evaluating all the corners of the feasible region.

38. It has been stated as a rule of linear programming that if a solution exists, it will correspond to a corner of the feasible region. Discuss why this is true. If you need to, draw a graph to facilitate your discussion.

39. A local supermarket has asked you to perform a survey of the community to determine information on grocery purchases. The manager of the store feels that information from at least 200 homes is necessary. You determine that you can contact people either by telephone or by mail. The cost to contact customers by telephone is $1.50 each; the cost to contact them by mail is $1.00 each. The response rate for telephone contacts is expected to be 50 percent, and the response rate for a mail survey should be 35 percent. Because the manager feels that you may get a more accurate response if the survey is done by telephone, he wants at least 3 times as many telephone responses as mail responses. Formulate a linear programming model that will minimize cost.

40. The A & B Supermarket has decided to have its larger stores remain open 7 days a week for 8 hours per day. The regional manager has determined the minimum number of employees needed each day of the week, as given below:

Day	Minimum Employees
Sunday	900
Monday	500
Tuesday	300
Wednesday	700
Thursday	600
Friday	700
Saturday	1000

Each clerk will work 5 consecutive days, starting any day of the week. Determine the linear programming formulation if the goal is to minimize the number of employees needed.

41. The Fry Appliance Company has stores in three cities: Baton Rouge, Fayetteville, and Salina. It also has three warehouses, in Boise, Minneapolis, and Kansas City. Fry is preparing to send food processors to all three stores for the holiday shipping rush. The warehouses in Boise, Minneapolis, and Kansas City have in stock 300, 800, and 600 food processers, respectively. The stores have submitted the following orders: 200 for Baton Rouge, 400 for Fayetteville, and 500 for Salina. The shipping costs per food processor are given below.

	Boise	Minneapolis	Kansas City
Baton Rouge	$7	$6	$2
Fayetteville	4	8	2
Salina	1	3	4

Formulate a linear programming problem to minimize shipping costs.

42. Use the graphical solution procedure to solve the following linear programming problem:

Minimize $Z = 4x_1 + 6x_2$

Subject to:

$$
\begin{aligned}
10x_1 + 12x_2 &\leq 100 \\
x_1 \qquad &\geq 5 \\
x_2 &\geq 2 \\
20x_1 - 10x_2 &\leq 120 \\
x_1, x_2 &\geq 0
\end{aligned}
$$

43. Use the graphical solution procedure to solve the following linear programming problem:

$$\text{Minimize } Z = 12x_1 + 10x_2$$

Subject to:

$$\begin{aligned} 8x_1 + 10x_2 &\le 64 \\ x_1 \quad\quad &\ge 3 \\ 4x_1 + 5x_2 &\ge 25 \\ x_2 &\ge 2 \\ x_1, x_2 &\ge 0 \end{aligned}$$

44. Use the graphical solution procedure to solve the following linear programming problem:

$$\text{Minimize } Z = .05x_1 + .04x_2$$

Subject to:

$$\begin{aligned} 7x_1 + 5x_2 &\ge 58 \\ x_1 + 2x_2 &\ge 22 \\ x_1, x_2 &\ge 0 \end{aligned}$$

45. Use the graphical solution procedure to solve the following linear programming problem:

$$\text{Minimize } Z = 85x_1 + 50x_2$$

Subject to:

$$\begin{aligned} 4x_1 + 3x_2 &\ge 28 \\ x_1 + x_2 &\ge 6 \\ 3x_1 + 5x_2 &\ge 14 \\ x_1, x_2 &\ge 0 \end{aligned}$$

46. Use the graphical solution procedure to solve the following linear programming problem:

$$\text{Minimize } Z = 5x_1 + 3x_2$$

Subject to:

$$\begin{aligned} 2x_1 + 10x_2 &\ge 20 \\ 6x_1 + 6x_2 &\ge 36 \\ x_1 \quad\quad &\ge 2 \\ x_1, x_2 &\ge 0 \end{aligned}$$

47. Use the graphical solution procedure to solve the following linear programming problem:

$$\text{Minimize } Z = 55x_1 + 80x_2$$

Subject to:

$$\begin{aligned} x_1 + 3x_2 &\ge 6 \\ x_1 + x_2 &\ge 4 \\ 6x_1 + 2x_2 &\ge 12 \\ x_1, x_2 &\ge 0 \end{aligned}$$

48. Use the graphical solution procedure to solve the following linear programming problem:

Minimize $Z = 15x_1 + 25x_2$

Subject to:

$$2x_1 + 5x_2 \geq 45$$
$$x_1 + x_2 \geq 14$$
$$x_2 \leq 8$$
$$x_1, x_2 \geq 0$$

49. The North Tablet Company produces vitamin supplements. It is considering marketing an inexpensive pill called More-Power, which will supply the minimum daily adult requirement of vitamins D and E. A bottle of 200 More-Power tablets requires a minimum of 20 units of vitamin D and 80 units of vitamin E. After considerable research, the company found that a unit of lamb heart extract contains .25 unit of vitamin D and a unit of soybean oil contains 1 unit of vitamin D. Conversely, a unit of lamb heart extract contains 2 units of vitamin E and a unit of soybean oil contains .5 unit of vitamin E. The company also notes that a unit of lamb heart extract costs \$.04 and a unit of soybean oil costs \$.06. Given this information, the firm wishes to know what amounts of lamb heart extract and soybean oil to use per bottle of More-Power in order to minimize the cost of supplying the minimum requirements of vitamins D and E. Solve, using the graphical linear programming solution procedure.

50. The Great Start Cereal Company makes breakfast cereal products. The base product in all of the company's cereals is wheat. However, each cereal has different "additives" that make it distinct from the others. For example, the Nut N Raisin cereal has two additives, peanuts and raisins. Raisins are used to add potassium at the rate of 5 mg per raisin. The peanuts supply protein, at the rate of .05 gram per peanut. Raisins also supply protein, at the rate of .005 gram each.

Raisins cost the company \$.25 per pound (1 pound = 1000 raisins), and peanuts cost \$.40 per pound (1 pound = 250 peanuts). The question facing the nutritionists at Great Start is how many raisins and peanuts to add to a box of Nut N Raisin cereal if they want the added protein to be at least 10 grams and the added potassium to be at least 600 mg. The company wishes to meet these requirements while minimizing the total costs of the added products. Solve, using the graphical technique.

51. Walsh Oil Company has accepted an offer to produce at least 3200 gallons of a high-powered racing fuel. The company has two raw products, liquid A and liquid B, which may be processed to satisfy the requirements. These are the only ingredients in the fuel. The two liquids, each of which can be obtained for \$1 per gallon, have different potencies: while 2 gallons of liquid A can be processed to yield a gallon of the racing fuel, it takes 4 gallons of liquid B to yield a gallon of racing fuel. Management has 550 gallons of liquid A. It wishes to free the tank for other storage purposes and wants to use all of that liquid. In addition, the company has an incoming shipment of 400 gallons of liquid B, which it wishes to process immediately to avoid the danger of storing such a high quantity of highly explosive liquid. More liquid A and B can be acquired if need be.

How should the company allocate liquids A and B in order to minimize the cost of filling its racing fuel order? Set this problem up in linear programming form and solve using the graphical technique.

52. Benjaminson Electrical Company has begun planning its personnel needs for a week-long project. In deciding how many master electricians and apprentices to hire for the job, Mr. Benjaminson recognizes that the former receives a \$450 per week salary, while apprentices need only be paid \$120 per week. Since this is the company's first project, a job service was contracted to provide all the labor. As part of that contract, Mr. Benjaminson agreed to hire at least 30 workers. Additionally,

the local Building Safety Council recommends that each master electrician provide 3 hours of inspection time during the project. A project of this nature should require 25 hours of inspection. In order to accomplish the project at the least cost, yet still meet the contract and safety requirements, how many of each type of worker should be hired? Solve, using the graphical technique. Do you see any problems in implementing this solution?

Chapter Glossary

Alternate optimal solutions The situation in which a linear programming problem has more than one optimal solution. It occurs when the profit (or cost) line lies parallel to one of the binding constraints.

Binding constraint A constraint which limits the final solution to a linear programming problem.

Corner point A corner, or point where constraint lines intersect in the linear programming feasible region. The optimal solution will occur at one of the corner points.

Constraint An equality or inequality involving the decision variables which determine limitations on, or requirements of, the use of resources.

Contribution rates The objective-function coefficients of the decision variables indicating the rate at which each unit of each variable affects the objective function.

Decision variables The variables in a linear programming problem that can be controlled by the decision maker.

Feasible region The graph of all values of the decision variables that satisfy all constraints. The feasible region is always located in quadrant I.

Infeasibility A situation that sometimes occurs in a linear programming problem in which all constraints cannot be satisfied simultaneously.

Isoprofit line On a two-dimensional graph, a line connecting both axes such that the profit is the same for all ordered pairs (x_1, x_2) on the line. All linear programming profit and cost lines are linear and parallel.

Objective function A function containing the decision variables and their contribution rates or coefficients. The goal is to maximize or minimize the objective function subject to the constraints.

Unbounded solution A solution in which the feasible region contains no upper limit in a maximization problem.

Chapter References

BOOKS

Charnes, A., and W. W. Cooper. *Management Models and Industrial Applications of Linear Programming.* New York: Wiley, 1961.

Driebeek, Normal J. *Applied Linear Programming.* Reading, Mass.: Addison-Wesley, 1969.

Dantzig, G. B. *Linear Programming and Extensions.* Princeton, N.J.: Princeton, 1963.

Hillier, F., and G. J. Lieberman. *Introduction to Operations Research,* 4th ed., Oakland, Calif.: Holden-Day, 1986.

Loomba, N. P., and E. Turban. *Applied Programming for Management.* New York: Holt, 1974.

Wagner, H. *Principles of Operations Research with Applications to Managerial Decisions.* Englewood Cliffs, N.J.: Prentice-Hall, 1975.

ARTICLES

Charnes, A., and W. W. Cooper. "Blending Aviation Gasolines: A Study in Programming Interdependent Activities in an Integrated Oil Company." *Econometrica,* Vol. 20, No. 2, 1952.

———. "Management Models and Industrial Applications of Linear Programming." *Management Science,* Vol. 4, No. 1, 1957.

Dantzig, G. B. "Recent Advances in Linear Programming." *Management Science,* Vol. 2, No. 2, 1956.

Fabozzi, E. J., and J. Valente. "Mathematical Programming in American Companies: A Sample Survey." *Interfaces,* Vol. 7, No. 1 (November), 1976.

Hooker, J. N. "Karmarkar's Linear Programming Algorithm." *Interfaces,* Vol. 16, No. 4, 1986.

Karmarkar, N. "A New Polynomial–Time Algorithm for Linear Programming." Technical Report, AT&T/Bell Laboratories, 1984.

Mini Cases

CASE 2A

SOUTH-HAMPTON INVESTMENT COMPANY

Alexander Joiner hung up the telephone and turned slowly in his plush swivel chair. The conversation he had just finished with Dr. Susan Avery was going through his mind as he gazed out his window. Dr. Avery, who heads the most prestigious health clinic in the South-Hampton area, had just inquired about investing a large sum of money in the two mutual funds managed by the South-Hampton Investment Company. Alexander knew how important Dr. Avery's business would be to the company and, in turn, how important it would be to his career if he could convince Dr. Avery to invest with South-Hampton. But it wouldn't be easy. An experienced investor, Dr. Avery had set forth very specific conditions for her investment and asked Alexander to respond with a proposal within two days.

Each of the two mutual funds consists of a portfolio of stocks traded publicly on the New York Stock Exchange. However, the two funds are quite different in the types of stocks held. The Freedom Fund is the company's largest fund, with just over \$21 million invested. The Freedom Fund portfolio consists primarily of blue chip stocks such as IBM and General Motors. The expected return (based on past history) for the Freedom Fund is 9.3%.

The Freedom Fund is considered a low-risk fund because the historical return has been fairly stable from year to year. The South-Hampton Investment Company has devised a measure of risk for its portfolios called the risk rate. This is a number between 1 and 10 assigned to any portfolio (1 indicates the lowest possible risk). An investor can then determine the "risk points" of his or her investment by multiplying the risk rate for a particular fund times the dollar amount invested in the fund. The Freedom Fund portfolio currently has a risk rate of 3.5.

The second fund managed by the South-Hampton Investment Company is called the Equity-Growth Fund. The stocks in this fund include ones which traditionally have paid high dividends and others which are more speculative in nature. The expected return of the Equity-Growth Fund is 16.5%, based on historical data. However, due to the type of fund it is, the Equity-Growth Fund is much more risky than the Freedom Fund. The Risk Rate for the Equity-Growth Fund is currently 6.4. The South-Hampton Investment Company charges an annual fee to investors in each fund. The Freedom Fund annual fee is 1.5% of the dollars invested, and the Equity-Growth Fund has an annual fee of 1%.

All of these factors were spinning through Alexander Joiner's mind as he considered the requirements outlined by Dr. Avery over the phone. First, she is willing to invest up to \$1.4 million with South-Hampton, but no more than 70% can be in any one mutual fund. Further, she wants the total risk points to be no more than 6 million points. Of course, she wishes to maximize the expected return from her investment within these constraints. As Alexander rocked back and forth in his chair, he thought there must be a way of determining the "best" mix of investment in the two funds for Dr. Avery.

CASE 2B

MAMA IRENE'S COOKIE COMPANY

The special meeting of the production department had just adjourned, and Jaclyn Granger walked briskly back to her office on the second floor of the corporate office building. She had worked for Mama Irene's Cookie Company for two years, coming to the company immediately following graduation from a leading college of business. Meetings like this morning's were by now familiar to her.

While Jaclyn was used to the production manager calling special meetings to announce the need for changes in the company's production mix, it always bothered her that the need for changes usually occurred because the marketing department could not accurately forecast cookie sales.

Today, Jaclyn was informed that sales for the cream-filled cookies over the past few weeks had been far below the sales forecast. Because of the need to sell fresh cookies, Jaclyn's boss decided that next week's production of cream-filled cookies would be cancelled and all sales orders would be filled from existing inventories. This would help clear out the inventory of cream-filled cookies before they lost their freshness and were no longer salable.

Jaclyn recognized that eliminating the production of cream-filled cookies would free up resources which could potentially be used next week to produce the other two types of cookies made by the company.

As Jaclyn reached her office, she immediately began her production planning for the next week. Her production schedule and accompanying working papers contained a variety of information regarding the production quantities, resource requirements, inventory levels, and production costs.

At first glance, Jaclyn thought that she would just increase production of honey-nut cookies and chocolate wafers proportional to the schedule already set until all the freed-up production resources had been utilized. But after giving this matter some thought, she realized that the planned production of these two cookies had been originally determined under the assumption that cream-filled cookies were also going to be produced. This caused a nagging feeling that maybe the most cost-effective mix of honey-nut and chocolate wafers would be different if the production plan were recalculated from scratch assuming no cream-filled cookie production.

With this in mind, she pulled information from her working papers together and developed a table (see Table C-1). In addition to these data, Jaclyn noted that honey-nut cookies have a standard production cost of $.35 per dozen, while the chocolate wafers are produced at a cost of $.45 per dozen. Further, marketing sales forecasts for honey-nut cookies and chocolate wafers next week are 4200 dozen and 3300 dozen, respectively. Jaclyn noted that, with current inventories, in order to meet these forecasts, production the next week must total at least 1500 dozen honey-nut and 2000 dozen chocolate wafers. Finally, Jaclyn recalled the union contract that requires at least 60 hours of baking time each week.

Table C-1 COOKIE TYPE

	Honey-Nut	Chocolate Wafer	
Department	Resource Usage Rates		Resource Capacity
Baking	.01 hour/dozen	.02 hour/dozen	80 hours
Inspection	.03 hour/dozen	.02 hour/dozen	120 hours
Packaging	.005 hour/dozen	.005 hour/dozen	50 hours
Storage	1 unit/dozen	1.5 units/dozen	600 units

CASE 2C

LINEAR PROGRAMMING AT ORE-IDA FOODS

As you should recall from our brief review of the history of linear programming, the food processing and distribution industry was one of the earliest users. Therefore, you should not be surprised that Ore-Ida Foods makes extensive use of linear programming, and has done so since 1968.

In Chapter 1, we mentioned that the consulting firm of McKinsey and Company had been retained by Ore-Ida to help develop a linear programming model for allocating raw production. After careful analysis, Scott Robertson and his staff decided the McKinsey and Company model did not realistically represent the production situation in the Ore-Ida plant and the model was discarded. Scott understood that for a model to be of value in decision making at Ore-Ida, it must accurately reflect the system being modeled. If not, the results from the model would not be valid and could lead the company to incorrect decisions. The experience at Ore-Ida hammers home a point we will be making throughout this text: *Don't blindly accept a model as being useful without checking its validity.*

One unusable linear programming model did not shake the Ore-Ida managers' faith in linear programming as a tool. Instead, Scott Robertson initiated efforts to apply linear programming at Ore-Ida where he and the other managers thought it could best be used. The first actual in-house application of linear programming occurred in connection with a large farm operation owned by Ore-Ida. The decision variables were the different crops that could be grown on the farm and the constraints were factors such as land and water availability. Work was also started on developing a production allocation model, similar in concept to the McKinsey model but covering all production facilities. This model was completed and operational in 1972. The model contained many variables and constraints and required a large computer. At the time, Ore-Ida did not have a large-scale linear programming software package on its own computer system and was running the linear programming on a contracted time-share system. Because of the expense involved with this process, the model was not frequently used.

In 1976, the production allocation model was expanded to include distribution costs in addition to production costs. This was done in connection with deciding where to locate a new production facility. Ore-Ida also acquired in-house software for running the linear programming model to make it more accessible. This same model has been continually improved and refined since that time and is now an important tool in Ore-Ida's planning process.

While the models we have considered in this chapter contain two decision variables and a few constraints, the production allocation model at Ore-Ida now contains about 3200 constraints and 1400 decision variables. The model is used as often as every week, as managers seek to determine the results associated with various changes under consideration.

One major finding which has resulted from use of the linear programming model is that the profitability of many of Ore-Ida's institutional food contracts depends on the negotiated price and mix of products being turned out by the manufacturing plants. A contract that is profitable one month may not be profitable the next. Presently, efforts are being made to make the constraints represent seasonal production changes rather than annual data.

A smaller linear programming model was developed in 1981 to help in packaging-materials negotiations. Ore-Ida purchases large quantities of boxes and other packaging materials from major paper companies, such as Weyerhauser and Boise-

Cascade. However, the price that any of these companies charges for each type of packaging material depends on the quantities of *all* materials a purchaser buys from that company.

The model developed to help in these negotiations is much smaller than the production model and has 55 constraints and 124 decision variables. The savings associated with using the packaging model were determined to be several millions of dollars each year. Ore-Ida used the model to make much more efficient purchasing decisions.

THE SIMPLEX SOLUTION PROCEDURE FOR LINEAR PROGRAMMING

Chapter Outline

Chapter 3

Why You Need to Know

Chapter 2 introduced the important management science tool of linear programming. One of the most widely used management science techniques, it is regularly applied in all areas of business. The common theme running through all linear programming applications is the need to maximize or minimize a linear objective function subject to a set of linear constraints.

After studying Chapter 2, you should understand how to formulate a linear programming problem. You should also know how to solve simple linear programming problems using the graphical solution process. While the graphical solution process is useful for learning the underlying logic of linear programming, it won't get you far in real-life situations because it is limited to problems with only two decision variables. Probably no realistic linear programming problems can be defined using two variables. In fact, most realistic applications involve hundreds or even thousands of variables.

Since the graphical solution technique has no practical uses, you need to know a linear programming solution method which can be used for problems involving any number of variables. The simplex method is the mathematical technique most frequently used to solve linear programming problems. While in actual business applications a computer is used to solve linear programming problems, you need to understand the manual solution process. By working several small linear programming problems using the simplex method, you will gain a better understanding of linear programming and be better able to interpret the results when you do use a computer.

Chapter Objectives

An objective of this chapter is to further your understanding of linear programming by introducing the simplex mathematical solution procedure. This chapter will show you how the simplex method is used in maximization and minimization problems. By using a number of examples and problems in this chapter, we will expose you to a variety of business applications for linear programming. We will also introduce several important terms associated with linear programming and the simplex method. Finally, the chapter will illustrate some situations where the focus is on formulating the linear programming problem and interpreting the computer output.

The specific objectives of this chapter are:

1. To introduce the simplex method for solving linear programming problems.
2. To illustrate how to interpret the results of the simplex solution.
3. To introduce several important linear programming concepts, such as slack and surplus variables.
4. To present computer applications and to show how to interpret the computer solutions.

3-1 THE FAIRVIEW MANUFACTURING COMPANY: A MAXIMIZATION EXAMPLE

The Fairview Manufacturing Company, located near Orlando, Florida, makes and distributes two models of pool tables. The Golden Eagle is considered the Cadillac of pool tables and is a high-profit item, netting Fairview \$1000 per table. The other model, called the Excell, is a more standard table, used in homes and pool halls. Because of competition with other manufacturers, Fairview has priced the Excell at a level which yields the company \$600 per table in net profit.

The two models require the same type of resources: hardwood, slate, plastic, felt, and human labor. However, the quantities of each of these are different. Table 3-1 shows the requirements of each resource for the two models. Table 3-1 also shows the available supplies of each resource during the upcoming production period.

Fairview can sell all of either model pool table it produces. The question is, How many of each model should it make during the production period to maximize net profits?

FORMULATING THE LINEAR PROGRAMMING PROBLEM

The decision situation facing the Fairview Manufacturing Company can be modeled as a linear programming problem. To do so, we begin by specifying the decision variables. Recall from Chapter 2 that the **decision variables** are those factors that are, for the short run, controlled by the decision maker. In this problem, there are two decision variables: the number of Golden Eagle pool tables to make and the number of Excell pool tables to make.

We define the decision variables as:

x_1 = number of Golden Eagle tables

x_2 = number of Excell tables

Once the decision variables have been identified, the next step is to determine the **objective function**. Since we are interested in profit maximization, we set up the following objective function:

$$\text{Maximize } Z = \$1000x_1 + \$600x_2$$

The data in Table 3-1 describe the production constraints facing Fairview. The first constraint deals with hardwood availability and can be written as follows:

(a) $20x_1 + 15x_2 \leq 600$

Thus, the combined production of Golden Eagle and Excell tables cannot use more than 600 board feet of hardwood.

Next, the production is constrained by the available supply of slate. Based upon the data in Table 3-1, the slate constraint is written as follows:

(b) $2x_1 + 1x_2 \leq 70$

The Golden Eagle uses 2 sheets of slate and the Excell uses only 1 sheet. The total slate available is 70 sheets.

Production is also constrained by the 1000 squares of available plastic. Based upon the usage rates in Table 3-1, we can formulate the following constraint for plastic:

(c) $20x_1 + 30x_2 \leq 1000$

In addition, the supply of felt constrains pool table production. There are 2000

Table 3-1 FAIRVIEW MANUFACTURING CO. PROBLEM: RESOURCE REQUIREMENTS

Resource	Required for Golden Eagle	Required for Excell	Amount Available
Hardwood (board feet)	20	15	600
Slate (sheets)	2	1	70
Plastic (squares)	20	30	1000
Felt (square feet)	80	40	2000
Labor (hours)	40	30	2000

square feet of felt available. The Golden Eagle model requires 80 square feet of felt, and the Excell model uses 40 square feet. We can write this constraint as:

(d) $80x_1 + 40x_2 \leq 2000$

Finally, the pool tables are crafted by skilled workers. The company has 2000 available labor hours during the upcoming production period. According to Table 3-1, each Golden Eagle table requires 40 hours of labor and the Excell model requires 30 hours each. We can formulate this as the following linear programming constraint:

(e) $40x_1 + 30x_2 \leq 2000$

The linear programming model for the Fairview Manufacturing Company is:

Maximize $Z = \$1000x_1 + \$600x_2$

Subject to:

(a) $20x_1 + 15x_2 \leq 600$
(b) $2x_1 + 1x_2 \leq 70$
(c) $20x_1 + 30x_2 \leq 1000$
(d) $80x_1 + 40x_2 \leq 2000$
(e) $40x_1 + 30x_2 \leq 2000$

and the nonnegativity constraints: $x_1, x_2 \geq 0$

THE GRAPHICAL SOLUTION

Since this problem has only two decision variables, x_1 and x_2, we can use a graph to help model the system. Figure 3-1 shows the constraints and the resulting shaded feasible region. Note that since constraints (b), (slate) and (e), (labor) do not help form the feasible region, they are redundant constraints. This means that resources other than slate and labor will limit production of pool tables. Note, too, the four corner points labeled (1), (2), (3), and (4). Recall the Fundamental Theorem of Linear Programming (Chapter 2) says that if a solution to a linear programming problem exists, it will exist at a corner point of the feasible region. The importance of this theorem is that we do not need to consider all points in the feasible region, we simply have to consider the four corner points and pick the optimal one.

Figure 3-2 shows the feasible region and all corner-point solutions. To solve for the values of x_1 and x_2 at each corner point, we first note the constraints which form the corner. In some cases, such as corner (1) determined by the intersection of the x_1 axis and the felt constraint, the values of x_1 and x_2 are easy to determine, since x_2 is zero. The same reasoning applies to finding the values of x_1 and x_2 for corner (4), except that here x_1 is zero.

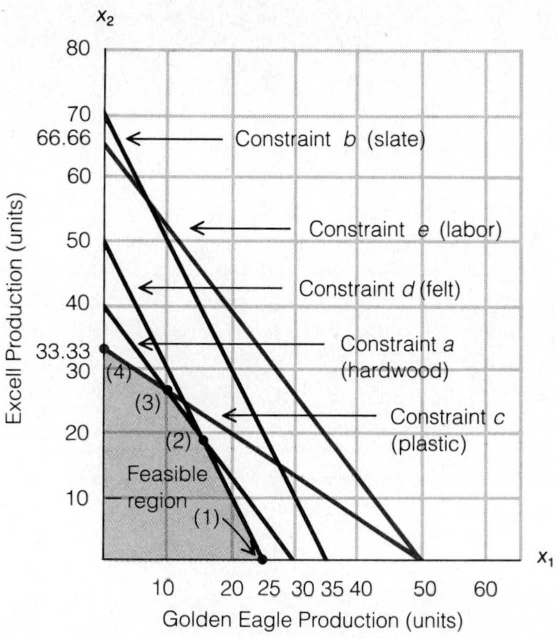

Figure 3-1
Fairview Manufacturing Co. problem: constraints and feasible region

The values of x_1 and x_2 at corner (2) are a little more difficult to find. This corner is determined by constraints (a), (hardwood) and (d), (felt). As shown in Chapter 2, we write these constraints as linear equations and solve for x_1 and x_2 as follows:

(a) $20x_1 + 15x_2 = 600$
(d) $80x_1 + 40x_2 = 2000$

Step 1 Multiply the equation for constraint (a) by -4 and add to equation (d):

$$\begin{array}{lrcr} \textbf{(a)} & -80x_1 - 60x_2 & = & -2400 \\ \textbf{(d)} & 80x_1 + 40x_2 & = & 2000 \\ \hline & -20x_2 & = & -400 \end{array}$$

Then: $x_2 = 20$

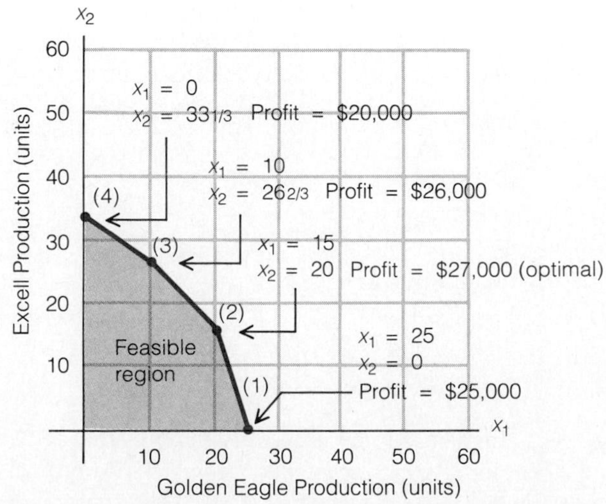

Figure 3-2
Fairview Manufacturing Co. problem: all corner-point solutions

Step 2 Substitute $x_2 = 20$ into either equation (a) or equation (d) and solve for x_1:

(d) $80x_1 + 40x_2 = 2000$

Then:

$$\begin{aligned} \textbf{(d)}\quad 80x_1 + 40(20) &= 2000 \\ 80x_1 &= 1200 \\ x_1 &= 15 \end{aligned}$$

The same process is used to find the x_1 and x_2 values at corner (3). The profit values at each corner point are found by substituting the appropriate values of x_1 and x_2 in the objective function. We see from Figure 3-2 that the optimal solution occurs at corner (2). The optimal solution for the Fairview Manufacturing Company is to make 15 Golden Eagle pool tables and 20 Excell pool tables during the upcoming production period. The total net profit from this production mix decision would be:

$$Z = \$1000x_1 + \$600x_2$$
$$Z = \$1000(15) + \$600(20) = \$27{,}000$$

THE SIMPLEX SOLUTION METHOD

Finding the solution by evaluating all possible corners is a viable option for Fairview. The enumeration approach worked fine in this case, since only two decision variables were involved. However, identifying and solving for all corner points formed in a problem with thousands of decision variables and thousands of constraints is not feasible. Thus, for linear programming to be useful as a decision-making tool, an efficient general solution procedure is required. The simplex method, introduced by George Dantzig in 1947, was the breakthrough needed for solving large-scale linear programming problems. The **simplex method** is a mathematical technique which tests a limited number of potential corner solutions to a linear programming problem until it reaches and stops at the optimal corner. Since it was introduced, the simplex method has become the most frequently used linear programming solution procedure.

To introduce you to the simplex method, we will apply it to the Fairview Manufacturing Company example just solved, wherein the managers want to determine how many Golden Eagle and Excell pool tables to make during the upcoming production period. The simplex method is a mathematical process which uses basic algebra to solve a system of simultaneous equations such that the value of the objective function is maximized (or minimized.) To put this in context, let's return to the linear program problem formulation for the Fairview example:

Maximize $Z = \$1000x_1 + \$600x_2$

Subject to:

(a) $20x_1 + 15x_2 \le 600$
(b) $2x_1 + 1x_2 \le 70$
(c) $20x_1 + 30x_2 \le 1000$
(d) $80x_1 + 40x_2 \le 2000$
(e) $40x_1 + 30x_2 \le 2000$

and the nonnegativity constraints: $x_1, x_2 \ge 0$

The simplex solution procedure requires that all decision variables be nonnegative. Therefore the nonnegativity constraints do not need to be explicitly listed.

As you can see, the constraints are represented by a set of inequalities. The first step in the simplex process is to convert the inequalities to a corresponding set of equalities. We do this by adding a new variable to (or subtracting from) each constraint such that an equality is formed. For example, consider constraint (a), which represents hardwood availability:

(a) $20x_1 + 15x_2 \leq 600$

Since this is a less-than-or-equal-to ($\leq$) constraint, to make an equality, a slack variable is added to the left-hand side, as follows:

(a) $20x_1 + 15x_2 + s_1 = 600$

The variable, s_1, is called a **slack variable** because it represents the potential unused (or idle) amount of this constraint. Slack variables have no impact on the value of the objective function and are used only to achieve the necessary equalities. Thus, a slack variable takes on any value which is needed to convert the inequality to an equality. For instance, at corner point (1) in Figure 3-2, $x_1 = 25, x_2 = 0$, and $s_1 = 100$, which means Fairview still has 100 board feet of hardwood available at this point. We arrive at $s_1 = 100$ as follows:

$$20x_1 + 15x_2 + s_1 = 600$$

If $x_1 = 25$ and $x_2 = 0$, then:

$$\begin{aligned} 20(25) + 15(0) + s_1 &= 600 \\ 500 + 0 + s_1 &= 600 \end{aligned}$$

Solving for s_1, we find: $s_1 = 100$

At corner point (2), $x_1 = 15$ and $x_2 = 20$. When we solve for s_1 we find $s_1 = 0$, indicating that for this solution the entire available supply of hardwood would be used.

Once a slack variable has been added to each inequality, the linear programming problem has been converted to its **standard form**, the formulation in which all the constraints are written as equalities. For the Fairview example, the standard form is:

$$\text{Maximize} \quad Z = 1000x_1 + 600x_2 + 0s_1 + 0s_2 + 0s_3 + 0s_4 + 0s_5$$

Subject to:

$$\begin{aligned}
&\text{(a)}\ 20x_1 + 15x_2 + s_1 &&= 600 \\
&\text{(b)}\ \ 2x_1 + \ 1x_2 \quad + s_2 &&= 70 \\
&\text{(c)}\ 20x_1 + 30x_2 \quad\quad + s_3 &&= 1000 \\
&\text{(d)}\ 80x_1 + 40x_2 \quad\quad\quad + s_4 &&= 2000 \\
&\text{(e)}\ 40x_1 + 30x_2 \quad\quad\quad\quad + s_5 &&= 2000 \\
&\quad x_1, x_2, s_1, s_2, s_3, s_4, s_5 \geq 0
\end{aligned}$$

Note that since we have five $\leq$ constraints in the example, we need five slack variables. Note also that not only does the simplex method require that the decision variables, x_1 and x_2, be nonnegative, but that the slack variables, s_1, s_2, s_3, s_4, and s_5, are also nonnegative. Finally, in standard form, the slack variables are added to the objective function. But since they have no effect on the objective-function value, their coefficients are set to zero.

Figure 3-3 shows the values of the decision variables and the slack variables at each corner point of the feasible region. At each corner point the value of each slack variable represents the remaining amount of each constraining factor.

Once in standard form, the constraints *a* through *e* form a system of five simulta-

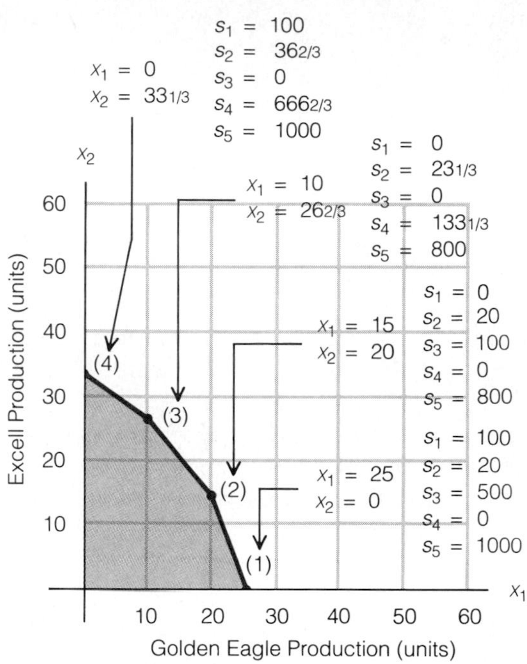

Figure 3-3
Fairview Manufacturing Co. problem: corner-point solutions with slack variables

neous equations with seven variables. You might recall from your math courses that when a system of equations has more variables than equations, an infinite number of solutions are possible. Remember, the simplex method is an algebraic technique for solving systems of simultaneous equations with more variables than equations. Not only will the simplex method solve the system of equations, it will identify the solution which optimizes the objective function.

Finding a Basic Feasible Solution

The simplex method solves a system of linear equations having more variables than constraints by setting some variables equal to zero and then solving for the rest using conventional algebraic techniques. While the fundamental theorem assures us we need only consider corner points, the solution procedure must be able to determine answers to a set of three questions:

1. At what corner do we start our search for the optimal solution?
2. Once we are at a corner, where do we go next?
3. When do we stop searching for better solutions?

In simplex terminology, any corner point is called a basic solution. In general terms, given a system of linear equations with k variables and m equations, and where $k > m$, a **basic solution** is determined when k-m variables are set to zero and the m linear equations are solved for the remaining m variables. The simplex method refers to the k-m variables set equal to zero as the nonbasic variables. The remaining m variables are called the basic variables or the **variables in basis.**

The Initial Solution

The simplex solution technique requires that the decision variables be nonnegative. To ensure this, the simplex method begins by setting the k-m decision variables equal to zero and solving for the other variables. In the Fairview example, we let $x_1 = 0$ and $x_2 = 0$ and solve:

$$
\begin{array}{llcl}
\text{(a)} & s_1 & = & 600 \\
\text{(b)} & \quad + s_2 & = & 70 \\
\text{(c)} & \qquad + s_3 & = & 1000 \\
\text{(d)} & \qquad\quad + s_4 & = & 2000 \\
\text{(e)} & \qquad\qquad + s_5 & = & 2000
\end{array}
$$

Now the five slack variables are basic variables (in basis) and the two decision variables are nonbasic. All variables are nonnegative. The simplex method always uses this basic solution as the starting point in solving the linear programming problem. Figure 3-4 shows this initial basic solution in graphical form. The constraints are also graphed and the feasible region defined.

In Figure 3-4, we see the initial solution is at a corner of the feasible region. When a solution is at a corner point of the feasible region, it is called a basic feasible solution. The logic of the simplex is to move, in an orderly manner, from one basic feasible solution to the next (i.e., from one corner point of the feasible region to an adjacent corner point) until no further improvement in the objective-function value is possible. This is easy to visualize in a two-dimensional graph like Figure 3-4. The simplex method might move from the initial solution at the origin to corner 1, then to corner 2, which we established earlier as the optimal solution. It might also move from the initial solution to corner 4, then to corner 3, and finally to corner 2. However, in this example, no matter which route is taken, the procedure will make it to corner 2 and then stop.

Through an iterative process, the simplex method reaches the **optimal feasible solution** to the linear programming problem. However, in problems with more than two decision variables, we are unable to chart, graphically, the progress of the simplex method around the corners of the feasible region. Instead, we rely on the algebraic process to get us to the optimal solution. A **simplex tableau** is typically used to help keep the algebraic steps in order and to provide us with information about the solution status as we move toward the optimal solution.

Figure 3-4
Fairview Manufacturing Co. problem: initial basic solution

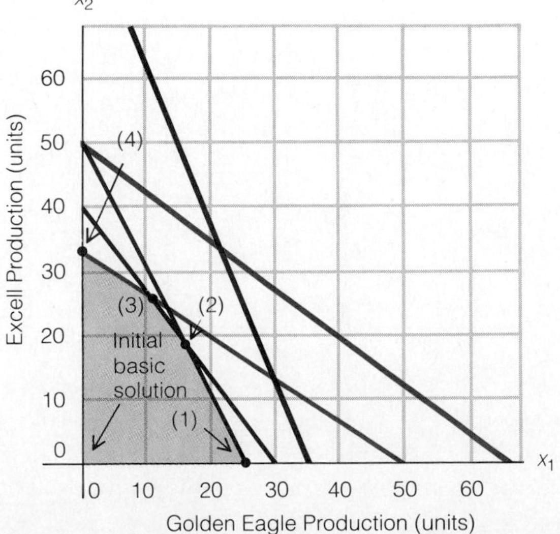

The Simplex Tableau

Recall that the standard form for the Fairview Manufacturing Company example is as follows:

$$\text{Maximize} \quad Z = 1000x_1 + 600x_2 + 0s_1 + 0s_2 + 0s_3 + 0s_4 + 0s_5$$

Subject to:

$$\begin{aligned}
&\text{(a)}\ 20x_1 + 15x_2 + s_1 &&= 600\\
&\text{(b)}\ \ 2x_1 + \ 1x_2 \qquad + s_2 &&= 70\\
&\text{(c)}\ 20x_1 + 30x_2 \qquad\qquad + s_3 &&= 1000\\
&\text{(d)}\ 80x_1 + 40x_2 \qquad\qquad\qquad + s_4 &&= 2000\\
&\text{(e)}\ 40x_1 + 30x_2 \qquad\qquad\qquad\qquad + s_5 &&= 2000\\
&\quad x_1, x_2, s_1, s_2, s_3, s_4, s_5 \geq 0
\end{aligned}$$

For ease of manipulation, we can ensure each equation contains all variables by remembering that we can add zero to *any* equation without changing the sense of the equality. In its fullest form, this problem becomes:

$$\text{Maximize} \quad Z = 1000x_1 + 600x_2 + 0s_1 + 0s_2 + 0s_3 + 0s_4 + 0s_5$$

Subject to:

$$\begin{aligned}
&\text{(a)}\ 20x_1 + 15x_2 + 1s_1 + 0s_2 + 0s_3 + 0s_4 + 0s_5 = 600\\
&\text{(b)}\ \ 2x_1 + \ 1x_2 + 0s_1 + 1s_2 + 0s_3 + 0s_4 + 0s_5 = 70\\
&\text{(c)}\ 20x_1 + 30x_2 + 0s_1 + 0s_2 + 1s_3 + 0s_4 + 0s_5 = 1000\\
&\text{(d)}\ 80x_1 + 40x_2 + 0s_1 + 0s_2 + 0s_3 + 1s_4 + 0s_5 = 2000\\
&\text{(e)}\ 40x_1 + 30x_2 + 0s_1 + 0s_2 + 0s_3 + 0s_4 + 1s_5 = 2000\\
&\quad x_1, x_2, s_1, s_2, s_3, s_4, s_5 \geq 0
\end{aligned}$$

At this point we develop a standard notation to represent all linear programming problems, the simplex tableau. The following notation is used in conjunction with the simplex method in defining a generalized initial simplex tableau:

c_j = objective-function coefficient for the jth variable

b_i = right-hand side of constraint i

a_{ij} = coefficient on variable j in constraint i

Then we can set up part of the simplex tableau as follows:

c row	c_1	c_2	c_3	. . .	c_k	*b* column
	a_{11}	a_{12}	a_{13}	. . .	a_{1k}	b_1
	a_{21}	a_{22}	a_{23}	. . .	a_{2k}	b_2
A matrix	⋮	⋮	⋮		⋮	⋮
	a_{m1}	a_{m2}	a_{m3}	. . .	a_{mk}	b_m

Table 3-2 shows the simplex tableau for the Fairview Manufacturing Company. Table 3-3 shows the same tableau with additional rows and columns, which are useful to keep track of different corner solutions. On the far left side of the tableau is a column labeled *Basis*, listing the variables in the current solution. These are the variables in

Table 3-2 FAIRVIEW MANUFACTURING CO. PROBLEM: INITIAL SIMPLEX TABLEAU

x_1	x_2	s_1	s_2	s_3	s_4	s_5	
1000	600	0	0	0	0	0	
20	15	1	0	0	0	0	600
2	1	0	1	0	0	0	70
20	30	0	0	1	0	0	1000
80	40	0	0	0	1	0	2000
40	30	0	0	0	0	1	2000

basis. The variables in basis are always those whose column has a 1 as the only nonzero entry in the A matrix. In the initial tableau, the variables in the basis are the five slack variables. As the simplex procedure moves from corner to corner, the variables in basis will change.

Next to the Basis column in Table 3-3 is a column labeled c_i. The values in this column correspond to the objective-function coefficients for the variables in basis. Note that the c_i values are all zero because the variables in basis are all slack variables which have zero values for coefficients in the original objective function. At the far right is a column labeled b_i/a_{ij}. Ratios in this column are used to determine which variable will enter basis at each iteration. For now, we have left this column blank. We will fill these values in shortly.

In a maximization problem, the row labeled Z_j represents the decrease in the objective function for each unit of the jth variable brought into basis. In the initial solution shown in Table 3-3, the values in the Z_j row are all zero, meaning there would be no reduction in the objective function if any variable not currently in the basis (x_1 or x_2) were brought into the basis. The Z_j values are computed by:

$$Z_j = \Sigma\, c_i(a_{ij}) \tag{3-1}$$

where:

c_i = objective-function coefficient for the ith basic variable

a_{ij} = tableau value in ith row, jth column

To understand why the Z_j values represent the per unit decrease in the objective function if one unit of a nonbasic variable is brought into basis, return to the original

Table 3-3 FAIRVIEW MANUFACTURING CO. PROBLEM:
COMPLETE FORMAT FOR INITIAL SIMPLEX TABLEAU

		x_1	x_2	s_1	s_2	s_3	s_4	s_5		
Basis	c_i	1000	600	0	0	0	0	0	b_i	b_i/a_{ij}
s_1	0	20	15	1	0	0	0	0	600	
s_2	0	2	1	0	1	0	0	0	70	
s_3	0	20	30	0	0	1	0	0	1000	
s_4	0	80	40	0	0	0	1	0	2000	
s_5	0	40	30	0	0	0	0	1	2000	
Z_j		0	0	0	0	0	0	0	0	
$c_j - Z_j$		1000	600	0	0	0	0	0		

basic solution. Remember that with the original solution we are producing no pool tables of either type. If we were to let the nonbasic variable x_1 (Golden Eagle pool table) enter the solution—meaning we would produce some number of these tables—different amounts of each resource would be required. Thus, given that we must satisfy the constraints, values of some slack variables are going to have to change to accommodate building Golden Eagle tables. The a_{ij} values, called the **exchange coefficients** or rates of substitution, indicate the per unit changes that will occur in the availability of each constraint if one Golden Eagle table is built.

To relate this to the simplex tableau, turn to Table 3-3, where the five slack variables are in basis. The values of these variables, found in the b_i column, represent the unused amount of each constraint when $x_1 = 0$ and $x_2 = 0$. Building 1 unit of x_1 will use some of this capacity. For instance, s_1, the slack variable for the hardwood resource, has a value of 600 board feet in the initial tableau. However, the exchange coefficient for variable x_1 indicates that each unit of x_1 uses 20 board feet of hardwood. Thus, the hardwood slack would be reduced by 20 board feet for every Golden Eagle table built. Since hardwood slack has no effect on the objective-function value, (i.e., its $c_i = 0$), the 20 units of lost slack will not reduce the objective-function value. The same is true for the other slack variables. Thus, the Z_j for variable x_1 is:

$$Z_j = 20(0) + 2(0) + 20(0) + 80(0) + 40(0) = 0$$

The same reasoning applies for decision variable x_2, since currently only slack variables are in basis.

The row labeled $c_j - Z_j$ in Table 3-3 is called the **net evaluation row**. The value c_j is the increase in the objective function due to adding 1 unit of variable j to the solution. We have seen that Z_j is the decrease in the objective function due to adding a unit of the jth variable. Therefore the $c_j - Z_j$ row represents the net change in the value of the objective function for each unit of a variable brought into basis.

In a maximization problem, a negative value in the $c_j - Z_j$ row would mean that bringing the corresponding variable into basis would reduce the value of the objective function. Therefore, in a maximization problem the objective function can be improved only when the $c_j - Z_j$ row contains a positive value. In Table 3-3, we see that x_1 and x_2 will add 1000 and 600 dollars per unit to the objective function, respectively.

The final value in the simplex tableau to consider is the 0 at the intersection of the Z_j row and the b_i column. This represents the value of the objective function for the current solution. With $x_1 = 0$ and $x_2 = 0$, the value of the objective function is 0.

Searching for an Improved Solution

Figure 3-4 shows the initial solution where $x_1 = 0$ and $x_2 = 0$ with a net profit of \$0. However, we know from Figure 3-2 that other corner points will yield higher profits. To move to an adjacent corner, one of the variables which is currently not in basis will become "basic" (in basis), while one of the variables currently in basis will be removed and become "nonbasic." The question is, Which nonbasic variable will move into basis and which basic variable will be replaced?

According to the simplex procedure, the next variable introduced into basis will be the variable with the largest net evaluation (or largest $c_j - Z_j$ value.) Since the net evaluation for variable $x_1 = 1000$ and the net evaluation for variable $x_2 = 600$, the next variable to be brought into basis is x_1. The column labeled x_1 is referred to as the **pivot column**. The pivot column is shaded in Table 3-4.

Table 3-4 FAIRVIEW MANUFACTURING CO. PROBLEM: ENTERING AND EXITING VARIABLES

		x_1	x_2	s_1	s_2	s_3	s_4	s_5		
Basis	c_i	1000	600	0	0	0	0	0	b_i	b_i/a_{ij}
s_1	0	20	15	1	0	0	0	0	600	30
s_2	0	2	1	0	1	0	0	0	70	35
s_3	0	20	30	0	0	1	0	0	1000	50
s_4	0	(80)	40	0	0	0	1	0	2000	25
s_5	0	40	30	0	0	0	0	1	2000	40
Z_j		0	0	0	0	0	0	0		
$c_j - Z_j$		1000	600	0	0	0	0	0		

Note: The pivot column and pivot row are shaded. This shading shows the entering and departing variables at the first iteration of the simplex method. The pivot element, 80, is circled.

The rightmost column in Table 3-4 shows the b_i/a_{ij} ratios, which are used to determine which variable will leave the basis. These ratios determine the maximum quantity of x_1 which can be produced if each constraint is considered individually. For instance, in the first row the ratio is 30, meaning that when $x_1 = 30$ the supply of hardwood would be depleted. This value is found by dividing the amount of hardwood available, 600, by the amount of hardwood used in each Golden Eagle table (x_1), 20.

Some constraints are less restrictive. For example, the available supply of plastic is 1000 squares ($s_3 = 1000$). Each unit of x_1 requires 20 squares of plastic. Dividing 1000 by 20 gives 50 as the maximum number of x_1 before the plastic supply is depleted. The other values in this column are computed in the same manner. Note that the divisor is always the exchange coefficient in the pivot column.

If profit maximization is the objective, we should make as many units of x_1 as possible, and the b_i/a_{ij} column in the simplex tableau (see Table 3-4) is used to determine how many this will be. The limit on x_1 is determined by the smallest ratio. Thus, when $x_1 = 25$, we will have used all 2000 square feet of felt. No additional x_1 units can be produced if we are to meet the constraints of the linear programming problem. Therefore, if we set $x_1 = 25$, the slack variable s_4 will leave the basis, showing there will be no unused felt. Table 3-4 shows that s_4 is the departing variable.

In Summary

The entering variable is the one whose net evaluation ($c_j - Z_j$) will do the most to improve the objective function. In a maximization problem, the entering variable will be the one with the largest positive ($c_j - Z_j$) value.

The departing variable will be the variable which is most restrictive. For a maximization problem, the departing variable will be the one with the smallest positive b_i/a_{ij} value.

If an a_{ij} exchange coefficient is zero, introducing the indicated variable will have no effect on the variable already in basis. Also, if the exchange coefficient is negative, introducing the variable into the basis implies an increase in the variable already in the basis. Thus, a simplex rule is: Don't compute the b_i/a_{ij} ratios in those instances where

$a_{ij} \leq 0$. Note, this also preserves the nonnegativity requirement of the simplex solution procedure.

The Next Tableau

The simplex method is an algebraic procedure for solving a system of simultaneous linear equations with more variables than equations. The simplex procedure uses the following algebraic *row operation rules.*

1. The elements in any equation (row) can be multiplied by a nonzero number without altering the system of equations.
2. Any equation (row) can be replaced by the result of adding or subtracting the multiple of another equation (row) to it without affecting the solution to the system of equations.

In applying the simplex method, we use these row operation rules to identify the next basic feasible solution to the linear programming problem and to determine the next entering and departing variables. The steps involved in this process are mechanical and are outlined in the next few paragraphs, continuing with the Fairview Manufacturing Company example. As we will show, the steps of the simplex procedure are equivalent to moving from one corner point of the solution space to an adjacent corner.

In examining Table 3-4, we see the set of basic variables can be identified from the body of the tableau, since their corresponding columns have one exchange coefficient equal to 1 and all other coefficients are equal to 0. This column structure is what identifies variables in the basis in a simplex tableau. Our task is to use the row operation rules to ensure this structure remains once the entering variable, x_1, is added to the solution and the departing variable, s_4, is replaced.

The process begins by identifying the pivot element. The **pivot element** occurs at the intersection of the **pivot row** (determined by the smallest b_i/a_{ij} value) and pivot column (determined by the largest $c_j - Z_j$ value). In Table 3-4, the exchange coefficient, 80, is circled. This is the pivot element, which is important in helping us arrive at the next simplex tableau. In following our progress graphically, we have started at the origin and decided to improve our objective function by adding variable x_1 to the solution. This means we will move to corner point (1), as shown in Figure 3-5. We now

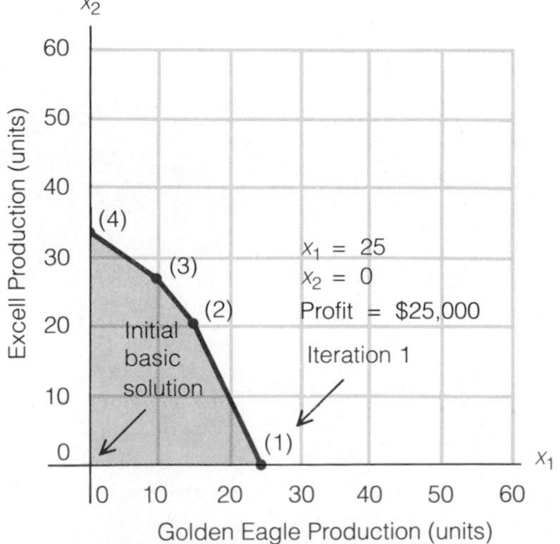

Figure 3-5
Fairview Manufacturing Co. problem: iteration 1 solution

Table 3-5 FAIRVIEW MANUFACTURING CO. PROBLEM: GENERATING THE NEXT TABLEAU, STEP 1

		x_1	x_2	s_1	s_2	s_3	s_4	s_5		
Basis	c_i	1000	600	0	0	0	0	0	b_i	b_i/a_{ij}
s_1	0	20	15	1	0	0	0	0	600	30
s_2	0	2	1	0	1	0	0	0	70	35
s_3	0	20	30	0	0	1	0	0	1000	50
s_4	0	1	40/80	0	0	0	1/80	0	2000	2000/80
s_5	0	40	30	0	0	0	0	1	2000	40
Z_j										
$c_j - Z_j$										

need to revise the simplex tableau to reflect this change. This means we need to convert the coefficients in column x_1, as follows:

From	To
20	0
2	0
20	0
80	1
40	0

Note that the pivot element will be converted to 1 and all other elements in the column to 0.

To make this conversion, we begin by dividing each element in the pivot row by 80 (the value of the pivot element). The results of this step are shown in Table 3-5. Now we must convert the other coefficients in column x_1 to 0. We begin with row 1, where the coefficient is 20. To convert the 20 to 0, we multiply every element in the newly created pivot row by 20 and then subtract this row, element for element, from row 1. The results are shown in Table 3-6. Make sure you can arrive at the values in row 1. For instance, the 5 in column x_2 is determined by first multiplying 40/80 by 20, giving 10. We

Table 3-6 FAIRVIEW MANUFACTURING CO. PROBLEM: GENERATING THE NEXT TABLEAU, STEP 2

		x_1	x_2	s_1	s_2	s_3	s_4	s_5		
Basis	c_i	1000	600	0	0	0	0	0	b_i	b_i/a_{ij}
s_1	0	0	5	1	0	0	−20/80	0	100	
s_2	0	2	1	0	1	0	0	0	70	
s_3	0	20	30	0	0	1	0	0	1000	
s_4	0	1	40/80	0	0	0	1/80	0	25	
s_5	0	40	30	0	0	0	0	1	2000	
Z_j										
$c_j - Z_j$										

then subtract 10 from the 15 in Table 3-5, giving 5. This process is repeated across the row.

We then change the remaining coefficients in the x_1 column to 0, using the same process for each row. Table 3-7 shows the results for row 2. The results for rows 3 and 5 are shown in Table 3-8. You should make sure that you can complete these row changes and arrive at the results in Table 3-8.

When all row operations have been completed, we compute the Z_j row using equation 3-1. Finally, we compute the $c_j - Z_j$ row as shown earlier.

Interpreting the Tableau

Table 3-9 shows the completed tableau. Note that the variable x_1 now appears in the Basis column. A lot of information is contained in this tableau. First, in the b_i column, the value 25 in the x_1 row means that 25 units of x_1 will be produced. The value of s_1, hardware slack, is now 100 board feet. The remaining slate, s_2, is 20 sheets. There are 500 squares of plastic (s_3) remaining. Just 1000 hours of labor (s_5) remain to be used. Finally, there are no felt (s_4) resources remaining, since producing 25 Golden Eagle pool tables used all the felt. Note that these are exactly the same values found at this corner point in Figure 3-3.

Table 3-7 FAIRVIEW MANUFACTURING CO. PROBLEM: GENERATING THE NEXT TABLEAU, STEP 3

		x_1	x_2	s_1	s_2	s_3	s_4	s_5		
Basis	c_i	1000	600	0	0	0	0	0	b_i	b_i/a_{ij}
s_1	0	0	5	1	0	0	$-20/80$	0	100	
s_2	0	0	0	0	1	0	$-2/80$	0	20	
s_3	0	20	30	0	0	1	0	0	1000	
s_4	0	1	$40/80$	0	0	0	$1/80$	0	25	
s_5	0	40	30	0	0	0	0	1	2000	
Z_j										
$c_j - Z_j$										

Table 3-8 FAIRVIEW MANUFACTURING CO. PROBLEM: GENERATING THE NEXT TABLEAU, FINAL STEP

		x_1	x_2	s_1	s_2	s_3	s_4	s_5		
Basis	c_i	1000	600	0	0	0	0	0	b_i	b_i/a_{ij}
s_1	0	0	5	1	0	0	$-20/80$	0	100	
s_2	0	0	0	0	1	0	$-2/80$	0	20	
s_3	0	0	20	0	0	1	$-20/80$	0	500	
x_1	1000	1	$40/80$	0	0	0	$1/80$	0	25	
s_5	0	0	10	0	0	0	$-40/80$	1	1000	
Z_j										
$c_j - Z_j$										

Table 3-9 FAIRVIEW MANUFACTURING CO. PROBLEM: COMPLETED TABLEAU

		x_1	x_2	s_1	s_2	s_3	s_4	s_5		
Basis	c_i	1000	600	0	0	0	0	0	b_i	b_i/a_{ij}
s_1	0	0	5	1	0	0	$-20/80$	0	100	
s_2	0	0	0	0	1	0	$-2/80$	0	20	
s_3	0	0	20	0	0	1	$-20/80$	0	500	
x_1	1000	1	$40/80$	0	0	0	$1/80$	0	25	
s_5	0	0	10	0	0	0	$-40/80$	1	1000	
Z_j		1000	500	0	0	0	$1000/80$	0	25,000	
$c_j - Z_j$		0	100	0	0	0	$-1000/80$	0		

The value 25,000, located at the bottom of the b_i column, indicates the current solution gives an objective-function value of \$25,000 (i.e., 25 units of $x_1 \times$ \$1000 per unit = \$25,000). Thus the solution has improved from \$0 to \$25,000.

The Z_j row also provides useful information. Recall that these values are computed using:

$$Z_j = \Sigma\, c_i(a_{ij}) \tag{3-1}$$

where:

c_i = objective-function coefficient for the ith basic variable

a_{ij} = tableau value in ith row, jth column

The Z_j values represent the decrease in the objective function for each additional unit of the jth variable brought into basis. The Z_j values reflect costs only. For instance, if we were to build one more unit of x_1 we would have to trade it for one of the x_1 units already planned. That reduction costs \$1000, the value of c_j. However, as shown in the $c_j - Z_j$ row, the net change is zero, since the loss in profit from giving up one unit of x_1 is offset by the additional \$1000 gained from building the new one. Thus, this type of exchange would serve no useful purpose.

However, the $Z_j = 500$ in the x_2 column means that building one unit of x_2, the Excell pool table, will immediately decrease the objective function by \$500. The reason for this is that in order to build a unit of x_2 we must give up $40/80 = .5$ unit of x_1. Although the supply of felt was exhausted by producing 25 units of x_1, each x_2 table requires 40 square feet of felt. This much would have to be taken from the x_1 supply. Since each x_1 table uses 80 square feet of felt, the amount taken represents exactly half of an x_1 table. Since an x_1 table nets the company \$1000, the .5 unit x_1 reduction represents a decline in the objective function of \$500, as indicated in the Z_j row. But at the same time we are giving up \$500, we are gaining \$600 in net profit by building the x_2 pool table. Thus, the net benefit as shown in the $c_j - Z_j$ row of Table 3-9 is +\$100.

The +\$100 value in the $c_j - Z_j$ row of Table 3-9 means the objective function can be improved by \$100 for each unit of x_2 produced. Therefore, *in a maximization example, if the net evaluation row contains a positive value, we know that we have not yet reached the optimal solution.* We must go through another iteration of the simplex method to determine how many units of x_2 to make.

At this point you might be curious about the $-1000/80$ at the bottom of the s_4 column. This number is called a **shadow price**. It represents the *marginal value* of a one unit change in of the s_4 resource. For example, an additional square foot of felt, if available, would add $1000/80 = \$12.50$ in profit, since it would allow an extra $1/80$ of an x_1 pool table to be constructed. At a profit of \$1000 per unit, $1/80$ of a table is worth \$12.50. Since we still have excesses of the other resources, their shadow prices are 0, meaning that additional units will not allow any more x_1 tables to be built and therefore will not increase the objective function. We will have more to say about shadow prices later in this chapter and in Chapter 4.

A Second Iteration

To begin the second iteration, we identify the variable which will enter the basis. In a maximization problem, the *entering variable* will be the one which has the largest positive net evaluation. In Table 3-10, we see that x_2, with $c_j - Z_j = 100$, is the variable to enter basis. Thus the column headed x_2 is the new pivot column. In the right-hand column of the tableau, under the b_i/a_{ij} heading, we see the ratios which will determine the departing variable. Recall that these values are computed by dividing each b_i value by the exchange coefficient in the pivot column (as long as the exchange coefficient is > 0). The *departing variable* is the one with the smallest ratio in the b_i/a_{ij} column in Table 3-10. This is the slack variable s_1, hardwood. We can produce 20 units of x_2 with the available supply of 100 board feet. Thus, the *pivot row* is the s_1 row.

At this point, a common question from many students is how, if in the original problem formulation 15 board feet of hardwood are required to make each unit of x_2, we can now make 20 units with only 100 board feet of hardwood. Please note that the exchange coefficient of the pivot row under column x_2 in Table 3-10 is 5. This value was derived during the first iteration of the simplex method, but we suggest you think of it using the following reasoning.

It actually takes 20 square feet of hardwood to make one unit of x_1 and 15 square feet of hardwood to make one unit of x_2. Once we get through the first iteration of the simplex, we will be building 25 units of x_1 and no units of x_2. The supply of felt is used up. However, in Table 3-10 the exchange coefficient in the pivot column for the x_1 row is $40/80 = .5$. We explained this earlier to mean that each unit of x_2 will require that we give up .5 unit of x_1 to make the necessary felt available. Therefore, if we give up .5 unit of x_1, we are reducing our need for hardwood by $.5 \times 20 = 10$ board feet. But an added unit of x_2 will use 15 board feet of hardwood. The net difference is $15 - 10 =$

Table 3-10 FAIRVIEW MANUFACTURING CO. PROBLEM: PIVOT COLUMN AND PIVOT ROW

		x_1	x_2	s_1	s_2	s_3	s_4	s_5		
Basis	c_i	1000	600	0	0	0	0	0	b_i	b_i/a_{ij}
s_1	0	0	(5)	1	0	0	$-20/80$	0	100	20
s_2	0	0	0	0	1	0	$-2/80$	0	20	*
s_3	0	0	20	0	0	1	$-20/80$	0	500	25
x_1	1000	1	$40/80$	0	0	0	$1/80$	0	25	50
s_5	0	0	10	0	0	0	$-40/80$	1	1000	100
Z_j		1000	500	0	0	0	$1000/80$	0	25,000	
$c_j - Z_j$		0	100	0	0	0	$-1000/80$	0		

Note: The pivot column and pivot row are shaded. The pivot element is circled.
* Ratio not computed, since $a_{ij} = 0$.

5 board feet. Thus, if the variable x_2 is brought into basis, $100/5 = 20$ units can be made with the remaining 100 square feet of hardwood. The a_{ij} values (the exchange coefficients) at any point apply to the current solution.

Now that we know which variable will enter basis and which will depart, we can proceed with the simplex method to arrive at the next tableau. The process, using row operation rules, is the same as before. We want to convert the x_2 column of exchange coefficients as follows:

From	To
5	1
0	0
20	0
40/80	0
10	0

The pivot element is 5, as shown in Table 3-10. The simplex method divides each element in the pivot row by 5, as shown in Table 3-11. Next we change the 20 in the x_2 column to 0 by multiplying the pivot row by 20 and subtracting the multiplied values from the s_3 row. The result is shown in Table 3-12. We continue to change coefficients in the pivot column to 0 using the same process. The result of these operations is shown in Table 3-13.

The completed tableau is shown in Table 3-14. We see the two decision variables

Table 3-11 FAIRVIEW MANUFACTURING CO. PROBLEM: ITERATION 2, FIRST STEP

		x_1	x_2	s_1	s_2	s_3	s_4	s_5		
Basis	c_i	1000	600	0	0	0	0	0	b_i	b_i/a_{ij}
x_2	600	0	1	1/5	0	0	−20/400	0	20	
s_2	0	0	0	0	1	0	−2/80	0	20	
s_3	0	0	20	0	0	1	−20/80	0	500	
x_1	1000	1	40/80	0	0	0	1/80	0	25	
s_5	0	0	10	0	0	0	−40/80	1	1000	
Z_j										
$c_j - Z_j$										

Table 3-12 FAIRVIEW MANUFACTURING CO. PROBLEM: ITERATION 2, SECOND STEP

		x_1	x_2	s_1	s_2	s_3	s_4	s_5		
Basis	c_i	1000	600	0	0	0	0	0	b_i	b_i/a_{ij}
x_2	600	0	1	1/5	0	0	−20/400	0	20	
s_2	0	0	0	0	1	0	−2/80	0	20	
s_3	0	0	0	−4	0	1	60/80	0	100	
x_1	1000	1	40/80	0	0	0	1/80	0	25	
s_5	0	0	10	0	0	0	−40/80	1	1000	
Z_j										
$c_j - Z_j$										

Table 3-13 FAIRVIEW MANUFACTURING CO. PROBLEM: ITERATION 2, FINAL STEP

		x_1	x_2	s_1	s_2	s_3	s_4	s_5		
Basis	c_i	1000	600	0	0	0	0	0	b_i	b_i/a_{ij}
x_2	600	0	1	1/5	0	0	−20/400	0	20	
s_2	0	0	0	0	1	0	−2/80	0	20	
s_3	0	0	0	−4	0	1	60/80	0	100	
x_1	1000	1	0	−1/10	0	0	30/800	0	15	
s_5	0	0	0	−2	0	0	0	1	800	
Z_j										
$c_j - Z_j$										

Table 3-14 FAIRVIEW MANUFACTURING CO. PROBLEM: ITERATION 2, COMPLETE TABLEAU

		x_1	x_2	s_1	s_2	s_3	s_4	s_5		
Basis	c_i	1000	600	0	0	0	0	0	b_i	b_i/a_{ij}
x_2	600	0	1	1/5	0	0	−20/400	0	20	
s_2	0	0	0	0	1	0	−2/80	0	20	
s_3	0	0	0	−4	0	1	60/80	0	100	
x_1	1000	1	0	−1/10	0	0	30/800	0	15	
s_5	0	0	0	−2	0	0	0	1	800	
Z_j		1000	600	20	0	0	7.5	0	27,000	
$c_j - Z_j$		0	0	−20	0	0	−7.5	0		

in the solution are x_1 and x_2 with $x_1 = 15$ and $x_2 = 20$ for a total net profit of \$27,000. The value of the objective function has increased \$2000 over the previous step. Figure 3-6 shows the steps taken by the simplex method. You should recognize the current solution as the optimal corner point determined earlier in Figure 3-2. We can see by examining the simplex tableau in Table 3-14 that we have reached the optimal solution since no variable has a positive value in the $c_j - Z_j$ row. *In a maximization problem, the simplex method stops, and the optimal solution is reached, when the net evaluation row contains no positive values.*

Interpreting the Final Tableau

The final tableau shown in Table 3-14 provides information about the optimal solution to the Fairview linear programming example. First both x_1 and x_2 are part of the basic solution. This means that the company will produce a mix of Golden Eagle and Excell pool tables—15 and 20, respectively. But beyond this, the slack variables s_1 and s_4, which relate to hardwood and felt, are not in basis in the final tableau. This means the production of x_1 and x_2 fully utilizes all available hardwood and felt. If more of these resources were available, more units of x_1 and/or x_2 could be made for higher profits. In fact, the shadow price for s_1 shown in the net evaluation row is −20. This indicates that an additional board foot of hardwood would be worth \$20 in additional profit for the company. This is the marginal value of hardwood. Likewise, an additional square foot

Figure 3-6
Fairview Manufacturing Co. problem: iteration 2 solution

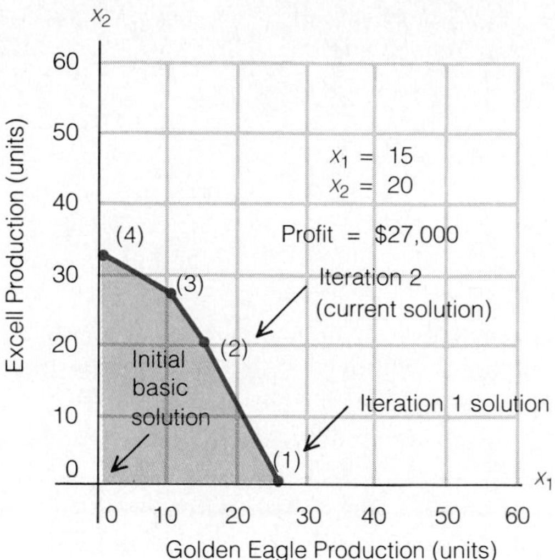

of felt is worth $7.50, and the company should be willing to pay up to $7.50 for each additional square foot of felt.

The other resources—slate, plastic, and labor—have not been fully utilized, since the slack variables s_2 (slate), s_3 (plastic), and s_5 (labor) are still in basis. The b_i column of the tableau shows that 20 units of slate are still available, as are 100 units of plastic and 800 hours of labor. Thus, adding more units of any of these three resources will not improve the value of the objective function. At this point, their marginal value (shadow price) is zero, as seen in the net evaluation row of the final simplex tableau. Also notice that the values for all seven variables in the final tableau are the same as those shown on Figure 3-3.

Linear programming has provided the Fairview Manufacturing Company with a solution to its production problem. But remember, this solution is optimal only so long as the model we have formulated accurately represents the situation facing the company.

3-2 THE WILLIAMS INVESTMENT COMPANY: A MAXIMIZATION EXAMPLE

The previous section has taken you through an example in which the simplex method for solving linear programming was used. As we demonstrated, that problem was solvable using the corner enumeration technique, shown on a graph, since only two decision variables were involved. We used this example to show that the simplex solution procedure just moves from corner to corner of the feasible region until no further improvement in the objective function is possible.

In this section, we present an example with three decision variables where a graphical representation is not feasible. In addition, this new example will show you how to handle situations with greater-than-or-equal-to (≥) constraints.

The Williams Investment Company is located in Bremerton, Washington. Although its employees will advise individual clients with over $1 million to invest, its principal business is managing private company pension funds. Naturally, the Williams advisers seek to achieve the highest possible return for their clients, but different clients have different requirements and so each client will have a different portfolio mix.

Suppose we consider a simplified example involving a medium-size trucking firm in Utah which has retained Williams to manage its \$24 million pension fund. The trucking firm will consider three categories of investment: growth-stock mutual funds, bond mutual funds, and U.S. Treasury notes. The company's directors want to invest some or all of the \$24 million. Anything not invested by Williams will be put into certificates of deposit yielding 5.5%.

The directors have told the Williams Company to invest at least \$10 million in U.S. Treasury notes, but they are concerned about the risk of the investment strategy. Williams has developed a risk scale for its clients. This scale ranges from 1, indicating a very high risk investment strategy, to 0, indicating a very low risk strategy. As an example of how this scale works, if \$100 is invested in a growth-stock issue which has been assigned a .9 risk rating, 90 risk points would be assigned to the investment. If the same \$100 is invested in a risk-free investment such as certificates of deposit (CDs), 0 risk points would be assigned. The growth-stock fund which Williams manages has been assigned a risk rating of .7. The bond fund has a risk rating of .5, and U.S. Treasury notes have a risk rating of .3. Based on the potential \$24 million original investment, the trucking firm wants the total risk points not to exceed 12 million. At the end of the year, the trucking firm will reevaluate its agreement with Williams.

For purposes of this example, suppose the Williams Company estimates the net return for its growth-stock fund to be 13% annually. The bond fund will net 9%, and the U.S. Treasury notes will yield 7%. The issue facing the Williams advisers is how to invest in each alternative so that the total return on investment is maximized subject to the constraints imposed by the trucking firm.

FORMULATING THE LINEAR PROGRAMMING PROBLEM

To formulate this situation as a linear programming problem, we first have to define the decision variables. Let:

G = dollars invested in the growth-stock mutual fund

B = dollars invested in the bond mutual fund

T = dollars invested in U.S. Treasury notes

Since we are interested in maximizing the value of the portfolio at the end of the year, the objective function becomes:

$$\text{Maximize} \quad Z = 1.13G + 1.09B + 1.07T$$

The three constraints can be represented as:

$$
\begin{aligned}
&\text{(a)} \quad 1G + 1B + 1T \leq 24 \\
&\text{(b)} \quad 1T \geq 10 \\
&\text{(c)} \quad .7G + .5B + .3T \leq 12 \\
&\quad \text{with:} \quad G, B, \text{ and } T \geq 0
\end{aligned}
$$

Constraint (a) deals with the requirement that no more than \$24 million be invested among the three alternatives. Constraint (b) relates to the requirement that at least \$10 million be invested in U.S. Treasury notes. Constraint (c) indicates that the total risk points must not exceed 12 million.

THE SIMPLEX METHOD

Since this linear programming problem has three decision variables, a graphical representation is impractical and we will move directly to the simplex method. Recall that the first step in using the simplex method is to convert the linear programming problem to its standard form. This means converting all inequality constraints to equalities to form a system of linear equations.

You can see that this linear programming problem has a greater-than-or-equal-to ($\geq$) constraint and two less-than-or-equal-to ($\leq$) constraints. In the previous section, we showed that a slack variable is needed for each $\leq$ constraint. Thus, constraints (a) and (c), are restructured as:

(a) $1G + 1B + 1T + 1s_1 = 24$
(c) $.7G + .5B + 3T + 1s_2 = 12$

Since the initial solution in the simplex procedure corresponds to the origin of the graphical solution, the initial basis will have $G = 0$, $B = 0$, and $T = 0$. Consequently, the initial feasible solution will have $s_1 = 24$ and $s_2 = 12$.

Dealing with Greater-than-or-Equal-to Constraints

Our logic in developing slack variables was that their value would become the amount needed to increase the left side of a $\leq$ constraint to equal the right-hand-side value. Since the left side was always less than or equal to the right side, the slack variable would always be the amount added to the left side.

Applying the same logic to a $\geq$ constraint, we need to subtract some amount from the left side to make it equal the right-side value. Thus, to transform constraint (b) into an equality we need a **surplus variable**. Subtracting the surplus variable from constraint (b) gives $1T - 1w_1 = 10$, where w_1 is a surplus variable.

Unfortunately, for the initial basic solution, where we know $T = 0$, the solution to the above equation gives $w_1 = -10$. But the simplex procedure does not allow any variable in the basic solution to be negative. Therefore, an **artificial variable** is introduced into the model for the express purpose of preventing the surplus variables from being negative. This artificial variable will be in basis in the initial solution but will not remain in the final solution. In a moment, we will show how this works. For now, the revised constraint (b) is $1T - 1w_1 + 1y_1 = 10$, where y_1 is an artificial variable.

To repeat: *Whenever a $\geq$ constraint occurs in a linear programming problem, we will include both a surplus variable and an artificial variable.* The surplus variable indicates how far any constraint is above the minimum required level. The artificial variable has no meaning and is added only to make the origin a feasible solution. Artificial variables must not remain in the final optimal solution set. If they do, the problem has no feasible solution.

The Model in Standard Form

In the Fairview Manufacturing Company example in the previous section, we saw that slack variables have a coefficient of zero in the objective function since slack adds nothing to the objective function. Surplus variables also have a coefficient of zero in the objective function, since they add nothing to the objective function.

The artificial variables are a different story. Recall that artificial variables are used for each greater-than-or-equal-to constraint. These variables will begin in basis but must be forced out of the solution before the optimal corner is found. While alternative methods exist for forcing artificial variables out of the basis, perhaps the easiest to understand is the "big M method." The idea is that since we are interested in maximizing the objective function, if we give the objective-function coefficient of the artificial variable some large negative value, the simplex method will force it from the solution set as the iterations are performed. Thus, in a maximization application, $-M$ is used as the objective-function coefficient for all artificial variables. The M is assumed to be some very large number.

The standard form model for the Williams Investment Company, including all slack, surplus, and artificial variables, is:

$$\text{Maximize} \quad Z = 1.13G + 1.09B + 1.07T + 0s_1 + 0s_2 + 0w_1 - My_1$$

subject to:

$$\begin{aligned}
&\text{(a)}\quad 1G + 1B + 1T + 1s_1 &&= 24\\
&\text{(b)}\quad 1T - 1w_1 + 1y_1 &&= 10\\
&\text{(c)}\quad .7G + .5B + .3T + 1s_2 &&= 12
\end{aligned}$$

Determining the Pivot Column and Pivot Row

Table 3-15 shows the initial simplex tableau for the Williams Investment example. The first step in the simplex process is to determine which variable will enter the solution. As in the last example, we look to the $c_j - Z_j$ row in the tableau in Table 13-15. In a maximization problem, the variable with the largest positive $c_j - Z_j$ will be the variable brought into basis. Since M is some huge number, $107/100 + M$ is greater than any other value in the net evaluation row; thus variable T will be the first variable brought into basis and identifies the pivot column.

The next step is to determine which variable will leave basis. Again, we examine the b_i/a_{ij} ratios on the right side of the tableau. Recall that these values determine how much each constraint restricts the amount of the pivot column variable that can be added to the present solution. The variable corresponding to the smallest ratio will leave basis first. As shown in Table 3-16, the departing variable will be the artificial variable, y_1.

To complete the first iteration of the simplex method, we must make the coefficient in the T column equal to 1 in the pivot row and 0 elsewhere. We do this using the row operations discussed previously. Table 3-17 shows the simplex tableau after the first iteration. Make sure that you understand the steps in moving from Table 3-16 to Table 3-17. At this point, \$10 million will be invested in treasury notes, \$14 million (s_1) remains to be invested, and 9 (s_2) million unused risk points remain. If this solution

Table 3-15 WILLIAMS INVESTMENT CO. PROBLEM: INITIAL TABLEAU

		G	B	T	s_1	s_2	w_1	y_1		
Basis	c_i	113/100	109/100	107/100	0	0	0	$-M$	b_i	b_i/a_{ij}
s_1	0	1	1	1	1	0	0	0	24	
y_1	$-M$	0	0	1	0	0	-1	1	10	
s_2	0	7/10	5/10	3/10	0	1	0	0	12	
Z_j		0	0	$-M$	0	0	M	$-M$	$-10M$	
$c_j - Z_j$		113/100	109/100	107/100 + M	0	0	$-M$	0		

Table 3-16 WILLIAMS INVESTMENT CO. PROBLEM: INITIAL TABLEAU, PIVOT ROW AND PIVOT COLUMN

		G	B	T	s_1	s_2	w_1	y_1		
Basis	c_i	113/100	109/100	107/100	0	0	0	$-M$	b_i	b_i/a_{ij}
s_1	0	1	1	1	1	0	0	0	24	24
y_1	$-M$	0	0	(1)	0	0	-1	1	10	10
s_2	0	7/10	5/10	3/10	0	1	0	0	12	40
Z_j		0	0	$-M$	0	0	M	$-M$	$-10M$	
$c_j - Z_j$		113/100	109/100	107/100 + M	0	0	$-M$	0		

Note: The pivot row and pivot column are shaded. The pivot element is circled.

Table 3-17 WILLIAMS INVESTMENT CO. PROBLEM: SIMPLEX TABLEAU, FIRST ITERATION

		G	B	T	s_1	s_2	w_1	y_1		
Basis	c_i	113/100	109/100	107/100	0	0	0	$-M$	b_i	b_i/a_{ij}
s_1	0	1	1	0	1	0	1	-1	14	
T	107/100	0	0	1	0	0	-1	1	10	
s_2	0	7/10	5/10	0	0	1	3/10	$-3/10$	9	
Z_j		0	0	107/100	0	0	$-107/100$	107/100	107/10 = 10.7	
$c_j - Z_j$		113/100	109/100	0	0	0	107/100	$-M - 107/100$		

stood for a year, the portfolio would be worth \$10.7 million, plus the interest earned from putting the \$14 million in CDs.

Improving the Solution

We recognize the solution is not complete, since one or more positive values exist in the net evaluation row. Based upon having the largest $c_j - Z_j$ value shown in Table 3-18, the next entering variable will be G, growth stocks. The departing variable will be s_2 because its b_i/a_{ij} ratio is the smallest. The next simplex tableau is formed by converting the coefficient at the intersection of the pivot row and pivot column to 1 and the remaining coefficients in the pivot column to zero, using row operations rules. This tableau is shown in Table 3-19.

At this point, the solution is to invest \$10 million in treasury notes, \$12.86 million in the growth-stock mutual fund, leaving \$1.14 million to go into CDs. Not counting the CD interest, the portfolio will be worth \$25.22 million at the end of a year.

The Next Tableau

The net evaluation row in Table 3-19 tells us that we have not yet reached the optimal solution, since positive values are present. The highest positive value is associated with the surplus variable, w_1. This variable will be the entering variable and forms the pivot column. The fact that this surplus variable is entering the solution means the next solution will show additional treasury note investment beyond the required \$10 million. Table 3-20 shows the pivot column. It also shows the pivot row is associated with the slack variable, s_1.

Table 3-18 WILLIAMS INVESTMENT CO. PROBLEM: SIMPLEX TABLEAU, PIVOT ROW AND PIVOT COLUMN, STEP 2

		G	B	T	s_1	s_2	w_1	y_1		
Basis	c_i	113/100	109/100	107/100	0	0	0	$-M$	b_i	b_i/a_{ij}
s_1	0	1	1	0	1	0	1	−1	14	14
T	107/100	0	0	1	0	0	−1	1	10	
s_2	0	(7/10)	5/10	0	0	1	3/10	−3/10	9	12.86
Z_j		0	0	107/100	0	0	−107/100	107/100	107/10	
$c_j - Z_j$		113/100	109/100	0	0	0	107/100	$-M -$ 107/100		

Note: The pivot row and pivot column are shaded.

Table 3-19 WILLIAMS INVESTMENT CO. PROBLEM: SIMPLEX TABLEAU, SECOND ITERATION

		G	B	T	s_1	s_2	w_1	y_1		
Basis	c_i	113/100	109/100	107/100	0	0	0	$-M$	b_i	b_i/a_{ij}
s_1	0	0	2/7	0	1	−10/7	4/7	−4/7	8/7 = 1.14	
T	107/100	0	0	1	0	0	−1	1	10	
G	113/100	1	5/7	0	0	10/7	3/7	−3/7	90/7 = 12.86	
Z_j		113/100	565/700	107/100	0	113/70	−41/70	41/70	1766/70 = 25.22	
$c_j - Z_j$		0	198/700	0	0	−113/70	41/70	$-M -$ 41/70		

Table 3-20 WILLIAMS INVESTMENT CO. PROBLEM: SIMPLEX TABLEAU, NEW PIVOT ROW AND PIVOT COLUMN

		G	B	T	s_1	s_2	w_1	y_1		
Basis	c_i	113/100	109/100	107/100	0	0	0	$-M$	b_i	b_i/a_{ij}
s_1	0	0	2/7	0	1	−10/7	(4/7)	−4/7	8/7	2
T	107/100	0	0	1	0	0	−1	1	10	
G	113/100	1	5/7	0	0	10/7	3/7	−3/7	90/7	30
Z_j		113/100	565/700	107/100	0	113/70	−41/70	41/70	1766/70	
$c_j - Z_j$		0	198/700	0	0	−113/70	41/70	$-M -$ 41/70		

Note: The pivot row and pivot column are shaded.

Table 3-21 WILLIAMS INVESTMENT CO. PROBLEM: SIMPLEX TABLEAU, THIRD ITERATION, FINAL TABLEAU

		G	B	T	s_1	s_2	w_1	y_1		
Basis	c_i	113/100	109/100	107/100	0	0	0	$-M$	b_i	b_i/a_{ij}
w_1	0	0	1/2	0	7/4	−5/2	1	−1	2	
T	107/100	0	1/2	1	7/4	−5/2	0	0	12	
G	113/100	1	1/2	0	−3/4	5/2	0	0	12	
Z_j		113/100	11/10	107/100	41/40	3/20	0	0	264/10 = 26.4	
$c_j - Z_j$		0	−1/100	0	−41/40	−3/20	0	$-M$		

The simplex tableau for the third (and final) iteration is shown in Table 3-21. This tableau is computed in the usual manner by making sure that the coefficient at the intersection of the pivot column and pivot row is 1 and all other coefficients in the pivot column are zero. In this solution, \$12 million is invested in treasury notes and \$12 million is invested in the growth-stock fund. This solution provides a surplus of \$2 million in treasury-note investment over the minimum \$10 million required by the trucking firm. All \$24 million has been invested. At year's end, the portfolio is expected to be worth \$26.4 million.

Dealing with Equal-to Constraints

The previous example involved greater-than-or-equal-to constraints. As seen in that example, the constraint can be converted to standard form by adding both a surplus and an artificial variable to the constraint. The purpose of the artificial variable was to satisfy the requirement that all variables in the solution be nonnegative and that the initial solution be at the origin of the solution space, with all decision variables equaling zero.

Sometimes a decision-making situation will have a restriction which is represented as an equal-to-constraint. For instance, in the making of a product, some exact amount of a component may be required, or a labor contract may require a project to employ some specific number of electricians or inspectors. For whatever reason, we may be faced with a constraint of this form:

$$x_1 = 10$$

With some thought, you should realize that this constraint will violate the requirement that the initial solution be at the origin of the solution space. We cannot have a decision variable equal to 0 when the constraint sets it equal to 10. To solve this problem, equal-to constraints are converted to standard form by adding an artificial variable. Therefore, the above constraint would be written as:

$$x_1 + y_1 = 10$$

At the end of this chapter, solved Problem 2 is an example of a situation with an equal-to constraint.

Reflections

This is a good time to reinforce the idea that what the Williams Investment Company has done is to model a decision problem. In doing so, the decision makers have made some assumptions on which the solution is based. A key assumption concerns the rates of return during the coming year for the three investment categories. Recall that certainty is an assumption in linear programming. If the rates of return reflected in the objective-function coefficients differ from those which actually do occur, the solution may not be optimal—and certainly the value of the objective function would be different. The results provided by a management science model are contingent on the validity of the assumptions on which the model is based.

However, the results of the model are more sensitive to some assumptions than to others. For instance, we might ask how much the objective-function coefficients in the Williams Investment example could change before the investment decision would change. We might also be interested in how much of a change in the investment restrictions could be made before an investment could be made in the bond-based mutual fund. This question of sensitivity in linear programming is the subject of

Chapter 4. However, the issue of sensitivity is important to all management science techniques and we will discuss the concept throughout this text.

If you have carefully followed the Fairview Manufacturing and Williams Investment Company examples, you should have a fairly good understanding of how the simplex solution method works for maximization problems. You should also have a feel for the time-consuming nature of the simplex process when worked manually. Our examples have been very small relative to actual applications, which might involve 1500 or more variables and as many or more constraints. It would be virtually impossible to attempt such a problem manually.

Computers and linear programming software have made actual applications of linear programming possible. Hopefully, you will have access to a computer and appropriate software. A software package called MASTER accompanies this text and is designed to work problems given here. Section 3-3 presents some linear programming computer examples using this software.

3-3 COMPUTER APPLICATIONS: MAXIMIZATION EXAMPLES

The purpose of presenting the simplex solution steps was to make you aware of how linear programming problems are solved mathematically. The math part of the solution process is not particularly difficult. However, even for relatively simple problems like those in this chapter, the calculations are tedious and even the most careful person can easily make an error that will totally invalidate the solution.

The simplex method is well suited to computers, and many linear programming software packages are available. Programs such as LINDO, developed by Linus E. Schrage at the University of Chicago, are available now for both mainframe and personal computers. Many companies have large-scale linear programming software for solving very large industrial problems.

A software package called MASTER has been prepared to accompany this text. In this section, we will use output from MASTER to illustrate using computers to solve linear programming problems. When using a computer, the decision maker can focus on formulating the problem and on interpreting the solution without getting bogged down in the computations required to reach the solution.

STONINGTON CYCLE COMPANY

The Stonington Cycle Company makes all-terrain four-wheel cycles for sale and distribution in the United States and Canada. It employs 100 skilled people at $12 per hour, based on a standard 40-hour week. The company's only product is the Blazer 444 cycle which, after all costs are considered, nets the company $300 per vehicle. While the company buys some of the parts that it uses in producing the cycle, it also makes three parts: seat bracket, front suspension unit, and automatic clutch. When sold to dealers for spare parts, these items net the company $60, $90, and $110, respectively, per unit.

Making the three parts requires three operations: machining, testing, and assembly. Only assembly time is necessary to make a finished Blazer 444 cycle, once the parts are available. Table 3-22 shows the resource limitations and requirements for parts and finished goods. Note that machine time, testing time, and assembly time relate to the equipment necessary to perform these processes. For instance, the company has 80 hours of machine time available each week.

Table 3-22 STONINGTON CYCLE CO. PROBLEM: RESOURCE REQUIREMENTS AND LIMITATIONS (HOURS)

	Resource			
Product	Machine Time	Testing Time	Assembly Time	Skilled Labor
Cycle	9	7	6	80
Seat bracket	2	2	1	14
Front suspension	4	2	3	16
Clutch	3	3	2	22
Availability	80	60	200	4000

The issue facing Stonington's production manager is how many complete cycles to make and how many of each part to produce. The actual decision variables can be defined as follows:

x_1 = number of seat brackets per week for spare parts

x_2 = number of front suspension units per week for spare parts

x_3 = number of clutch units per week for spare parts

x_4 = number of complete cycles (including seat bracket, front-end suspension, and clutch unit)

Since the company wants to maximize its net profit, the following linear programming formulation is appropriate:

Maximize $Z = 60x_1 + 90x_2 + 110x_3 + 300x_4$

Subject to:

$$
\begin{aligned}
2x_1 + 4x_2 + 3x_3 + 9x_4 &\le 80 \\
2x_1 + 2x_2 + 3x_3 + 7x_4 &\le 60 \\
1x_1 + 3x_2 + 2x_3 + 6x_4 &\le 200 \\
14x_1 + 16x_2 + 22x_3 + 80x_4 &\le 4000 \\
x_1, x_2, x_3, x_4 &\ge 0
\end{aligned}
$$

A User's Manual is available which shows in detail how to use MASTER. We will only summarize the steps required to take advantage of this software. The user selects the linear programming option from the main menu, as shown in Figure 3-7. Figure 3-8 shows the data entry screen for this problem. You can enter the constraints in any order. MASTER reorders them so that all $\le$ constraints come first followed by all $=$ constraints, and then all $\ge$ constraints. This problem has only $\le$ constraints. Figure 3-9 shows the linear programming output.

Interpreting the Solution

The solution to the original linear programming problem is given under the heading "Optimal Solution" (Figure 3-9). The decision variables have the following values:

Variable $x_2 = 2.000$ (front suspension spare parts)

Variable $x_4 = 8.000$ (completed cycles)

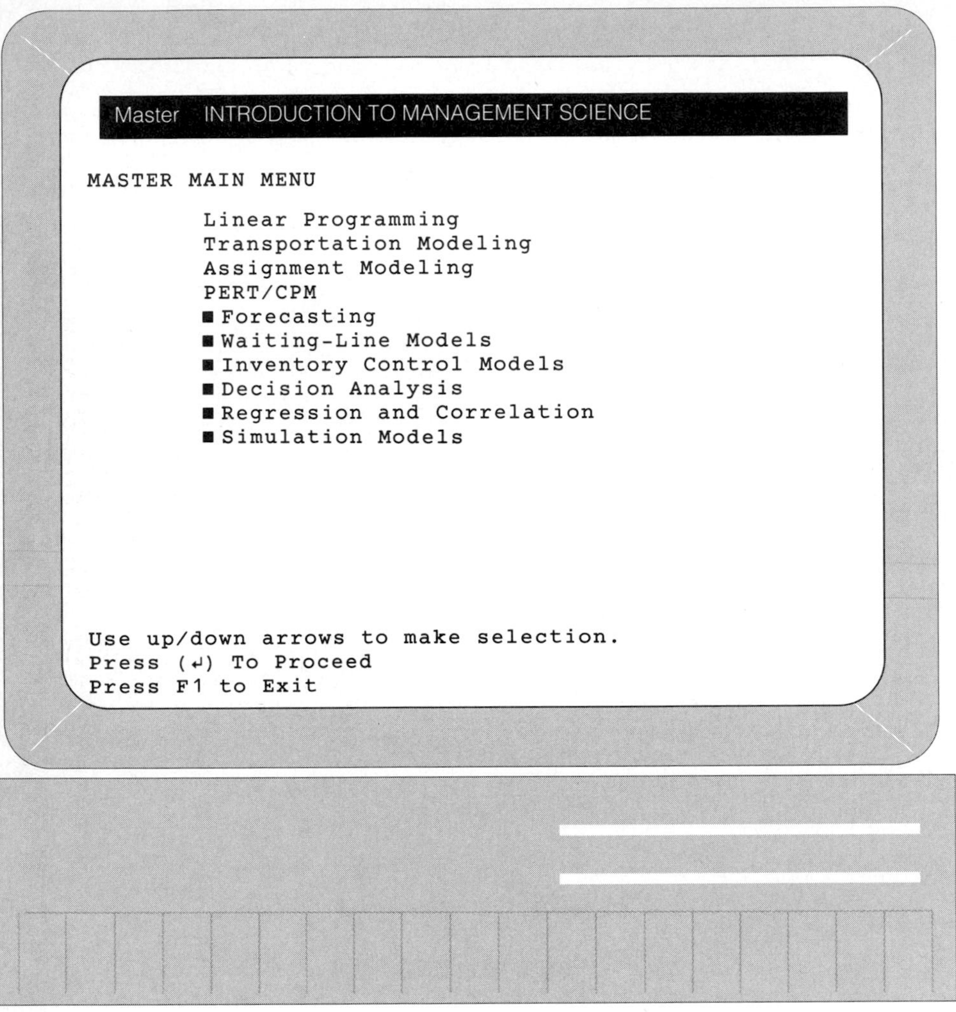

Figure 3-7
Main menu for MASTER computer software

Thus the optimal solution is to build 2 front suspension units as spare parts and 8 complete cycles. Decision variables x_1 and x_3 are not part of the optimal solution. This means their value is zero. In addition to the decision variables in the optimal solution, two slack variables are present, variables 7 and 8. These slack variables correspond to constraints 3 and 4. Variable 8 has a value of 146, which means that 146 hours of assembly time remains unused. Likewise, 3328 hours of skilled labor remain unused. Since machine time slack (variable 5) and testing time slack (variable 6) do not appear in the basic solution, we know that these resources have been completely used. The objective function has been maximized in 2 iterations at \$2580.

The values under the "Dual Results" heading provide additional information. Dual values will be discussed more completely in Chapter 4. For now, simply accept

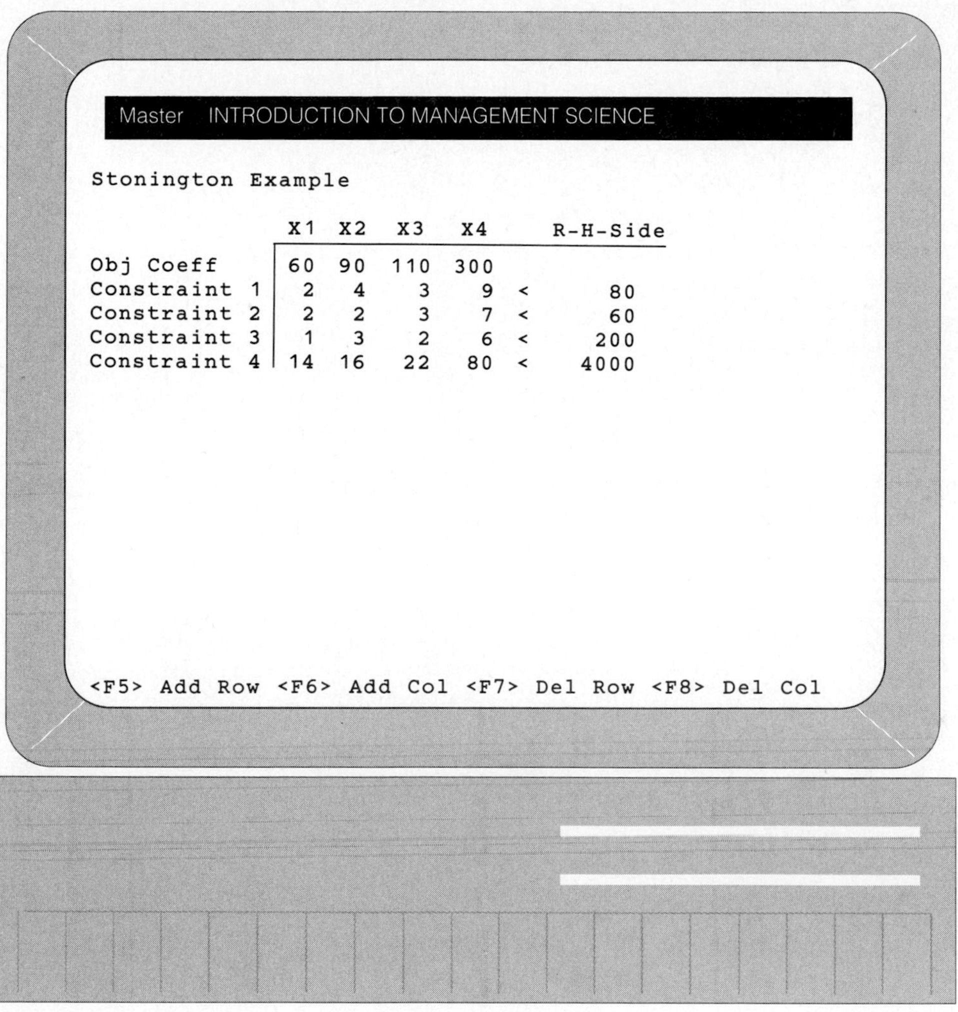

Figure 3-8
Stonington Cycle Co. problem: MASTER data entry screen

that the **dual values** are what we have referred to as shadow prices. They are the marginal values of each additional unit of the resource. For instance, each additional unit of machine time (constraint 1) will add \$3.00 to the objective function and each additional hour of testing time (constraint 2) will add \$39. The other two constraints already have slack, so additional amounts of these variables will add nothing to the objective function. Consequently, their dual values are zero.

The natural next step would be to analyze the sensitivity of the linear programming model. For instance, we might want to know how much the objective-function coefficients or the right-hand-side values of the constraints could change before the solution changed. The MASTER software package performs sensitivity analysis at the user's request, but we will postpone this request until sensitivity analysis is explained in Chapter 4.

```
                 LINEAR PROGRAMMING FORMULATION

OBJECTIVE FUNCTION:
  MAXIMIZE Z =
      60.00 X1 +    90.00  X2 +    110.00  X3 +    300.00  X4

SUBJECT TO:
      2.00X1 +   4.00X2 +    3.00X3 +    9.00X4  <=     80.00
      2.00X1 +   2.00X2 +    3.00X3 +    7.00X4  <=     60.00
      1.00X1 +   3.00X2 +    2.00X3 +    6.00X4  <=    200.00
     14.00X1 +  16.00X2 +   22.00X3 +   80.00X4  <=   4000.00

              THE DECISION VARIABLES ARE  1  THROUGH  4
              THE SLACK VARIABLES ARE      5  THROUGH  8


         OPTIMAL SOLUTION

ITERATIONS =   2

OBJECTIVE FUNCTION =        2580.000


DECISION VARIABLES:

VARIABLE  NAME    VALUE
   2      X2      2.000
   4      X4      8.000


SLACK OR SURPLUS VARIABLES:

VARIABLE  NAME            VALUE
 7        SLACK         146.000
 8        SLACK        3328.000


DUAL RESULTS

VARIABLE  NAME           VALUE
          X1            24.000
          X2             0.000
          X3            16.000
          X4             0.000
          CONSTRAINT  1   3.000
          CONSTRAINT  2  39.000
          CONSTRAINT  3   0.000
          CONSTRAINT  4   0.000
```

Figure 3-9
Stonington Cycle Co. problem: MASTER output

TEXAS-ANNA OIL AND GAS

The Texas-Anna Oil and Gas Company makes regular and unleaded gasoline. This business is very competitive, and the company has been able to net only $.04 per gallon of regular gasoline and $.05 per gallon of unleaded. Because of contracts with distributors, the company must produce at least 200,000 gallons of regular and at least 300,000 gallons of unleaded gas per week. The company figures it can sell no more than 500,000 gallons of regular and no more than 800,000 gallons of unleaded each week. The total refining capacity, defined in units, is 1,000,000. A gallon of regular gasoline uses 1 unit of production capacity, while each gallon of unleaded gasoline uses 1.5 units of capacity. Another limitation on the Texas-Anna Company is the available crude from which the gasoline is refined. The weekly supply is 30,000 barrels of crude. One barrel of crude yields 40 gallons of regular gasoline and 45 gallons of unleaded gasoline. Another way of stating this is that each gallon of regular gasoline requires 1/40 (.025) barrel of crude while each gallon of unleaded gasoline requires 1/45 (.022) barrel of crude.

The issue facing the Texas-Anna Oil and Gasoline Company is how many gallons of regular and unleaded to produce each week to maximize total net profits. To help answer this question, we can model the problem using linear programming as follows:

$$\text{Maximize} \quad Z = .04x_1 + .05x_2$$

Subject to:

$$\begin{aligned} 1x_1 + 0x_2 &\le 500{,}000 \\ 0x_1 + 1x_2 &\le 800{,}000 \\ 1x_1 + 1.5x_2 &\le 1{,}000{,}000 \\ .025x_1 + .022x_2 &\le 30{,}000 \\ 1x_1 + 0x_2 &\ge 200{,}000 \\ 0x_1 + 1x_2 &\ge 300{,}000 \\ x_1, x_2 &\ge 0 \end{aligned}$$

Figure 3-10 shows the input to the MASTER software. MASTER will automatically reorganize the constraints, putting all $\le$ first, followed by $=$, followed by the $\ge$ constraints. On the printout, variables 1 and 2 are the decision variables x_1 and x_2, respectively. Variables 3–6 are the slack variables corresponding to the $\le$ constraints. Variables 7 and 8 are the surplus variables for the two $\ge$ constraints, and variables 9 and 10 are the artificial variables for the $\ge$ constraints. These are identified on the computer printout in Figure 3-11, which shows the results of the linear program.

The linear programming output shows that the Texas-Anna Oil and Gas Company will maximize profits at $36,666.66 if it produces 500,000 gallons of regular gasoline (x_1) and 333,333.30 gallons of unleaded (x_2).

The value of variable 4 (slack) indicates that the optimal solution is 466,666.7 gallons short of the maximum sales volume for unleaded gasoline. The value for variable 6 (slack) indicates that 10,166.67 units of available crude remain, given the optimal solution. The decision to produce 500,000 gallons of regular gas exceeds the minimum requirement of 200,000 by 300,000 gallons (see the surplus variable 7). The unleaded production of 333,333.33 exceeds the requirements of 300,000 gallons by 33,333.30 gallons (see the surplus variable 8).

The dual result for constraint 1 indicates that each additional unit of regular gasoline beyond the current limit of 500,000 gallons which could be sold during the

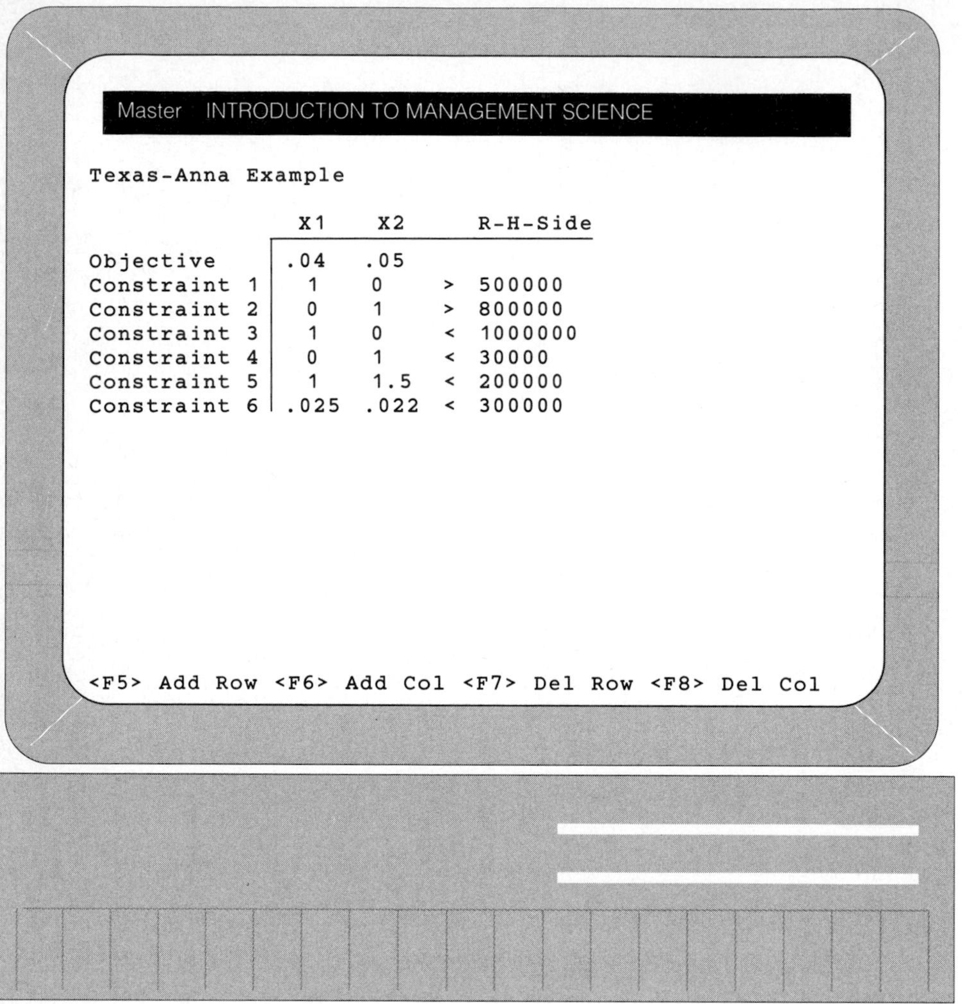

Figure 3-10
Texas-Anna Oil and Gas Co. problem: MASTER data entry screen

week would add \$.007 to the company's total profit. The dual result for constraint 3 indicates that each additional unit of refining capacity has a marginal value of \$.033.

3-4 THE MOTORPART CORPORATION: A MINIMIZATION EXAMPLE

The previous section has demonstrated that once a decision situation has been formulated as a linear programming problem, a computer can quickly solve the problem. Therefore the emphasis should be on interpreting the solution rather than working through the computations of the simplex method. However, we also feel that you should understand the basic solution procedure before jumping into computer applications. That is why sections 3-1 and 3-2 presented two complete examples using the simplex method manually. In those examples, the objective was to *maximize* the objective function.

```
                LINEAR PROGRAMMING FORMULATION

OBJECTIVE FUNCTION:
  MAXIMIZE Z =
       0.04  X1 +     0.05  X2

SUBJECT TO:
      1.00X1 +     0.00X2 <= 500000.00
      0.00X1 +     1.00X2 <= 800000.00
      1.00X1 +     1.50X2 <=1000000.00
      0.03X1 +     0.02X2 <=   30000.00
      1.00X1 +     0.00X2 >= 200000.00
      0.00X1 +     1.00X2 >= 300000.00

              THE DECISION VARIABLES ARE  1  THROUGH  2
              THE SLACK VARIABLES ARE       3  THROUGH  6
              THE SURPLUS VARIABLES ARE      7  THROUGH   8
              THE ARTIFICIAL VARIABLES ARE 9  THROUGH  10


       OPTIMAL SOLUTION

ITERATIONS = 4

OBJECTIVE FUNCTION =       36666.66


DECISION VARIABLES:

VARIABLE    NAME     VALUE
   1        X1       500000.000
   2        X2       333333.300


SLACK OR SURPLUS VARIABLES:

VARIABLE    NAME           VALUE
 4          SLACK      466666.700
 6          SLACK       10166.670
 7          SURPLUS    300000.000
 8          SURPLUS     33333.30


DUAL RESULTS

VARIABLE    NAME             VALUE
            X1               0.000
            X2               0.000
            CONSTRAINT  1    0.007
            CONSTRAINT  2    0.000
            CONSTRAINT  3    0.033
            CONSTRAINT  4    0.000
            CONSTRAINT  5    0.000
            CONSTRAINT  6    0.000
```

Figure 3-11
Texas-Anna Oil Co. example: MASTER output

Table 3-23 MOTORPART CORP. PROBLEM: ADVERTISING OPTIONS AND INFORMATION

Advertising Option	Potential Audience	Impact Rating*	Cost per Ad
Radio ads	3,000	10	$500
Television ads	20,000	40	$4000
Newspaper ads	14,000	20	$1000

* The impact rating is a numerical score which attempts to measure the effectiveness of advertising in the various media, taking into account factors such as demographic characteristics of the potential audience and the quality of the ad.

In this section, we consider a *minimization* example and show how the simplex method works in such applications. With a couple of important exceptions, the simplex method for minimization is the same as for maximization. Consider the following example.

The MotorPart Corporation makes and markets replacement automobile parts. The company has allotted $30,000 for its quarterly advertising budget in the Dover, Delaware, area. The vice-president for marketing has been instructed to devise an effective advertising campaign within the budgeted amount. Table 3-23 presents some information about advertising alternatives in the Dover area.

In their planning meetings, the members of the marketing department have established certain goals that the final advertising decision must satisfy. For instance, the total quarterly audience for the company's ads must be at least 300,000. Also, the total impact rating must be at least 300 points. The vice-president has indicated that these goals must be satisfied at a cost not to exceed $30,000.

FORMULATING THE LINEAR PROGRAMMING PROBLEM

The steps in formulating a linear programming model are:

1. Define the decision variables.
2. Formulate the objective function.
3. Formulate the constraints.

The decision variables in this application are:

x_1 = number of radio ads

x_2 = number of television ads

x_3 = number of newspaper ads

The objective function is:

$$\text{Minimize} \quad Z = 500x_1 + 4000x_2 + 1000x_3$$

The constraints are:

$$\begin{aligned}
&\text{(a)} \quad 3000x_1 + 20{,}000x_2 + 14{,}000x_3 \geq 300{,}000 \\
&\text{(b)} \quad 10x_1 + 40x_2 + 20x_3 \geq 300 \\
&\text{(c)} \quad 500x_1 + 4000x_2 + 1000x_3 \leq 30{,}000
\end{aligned}$$

and: $x_1, x_2, x_3 \geq 0$

Constraint (a) represents the total audience requirement, constraint (b) represents the impact requirement, and constraint (c) addresses the total budget issue. Since this problem involves three decision variables, we cannot determine its solution graphically. Instead, we will use the simplex method.

CONVERSION TO STANDARD FORM

The first step in employing the simplex method is to convert the problem to standard form. Recall, from our maximization examples in sections 3-1 and 3-2, that each ≤ constraint requires a slack variable. In addition, each ≥ constraint requires a surplus and an artificial variable. Recall also that the slack and surplus variables have coefficients of 0 in the objective function, since they do not affect its value.

In the previous maximization example, artificial variables were driven from the solution by assigning them a large negative coefficient, $-M$, in the objective function. These large negative coefficients ensure that the artificial variables will be forced out of basis and not be part of the final solution.

In a minimization problem, the "big M" is also used; but in this case, a $+M$ coefficient is assigned to the artificial variables in the objective function. This very large coefficient works against the minimization objective and ensures that the artificial variables will not be part of the final solution.

Given all this, the standard form for the MotorPart Corporation example is:

$$\text{Minimize} \quad Z = 500x_1 + 4000x_2 + 1000x_3 + 0s_1 + 0w_1 + 0w_2 + My_1 + My_2$$

Subject to:

$$\begin{aligned}
3000x_1 + 20{,}000x_2 + 14{,}000x_3 + 0s_1 - 1w_1 - 0w_2 + 1y_1 + 0y_2 &= 300{,}000 \\
10x_1 + 40x_2 + 20x_3 + 0s_1 - 0w_1 - 1w_2 + 0y_1 + 1y_2 &= 300 \\
500x_1 + 4000x_2 + 1000x_3 + 1s_1 - 0w_1 - 0w_2 + 0y_1 + 0y_2 &= 30{,}000
\end{aligned}$$

We have three decision variables, one slack variable, two surplus variables, and two artificial variables.

THE SIMPLEX TABLEAUS

Table 3-24 shows the initial simplex tableau with the entering and exiting variables identified. The principal difference between a maximization problem and a minimiza-

Table 3-24 MOTORPART CORP. PROBLEM: INITIAL SIMPLEX TABLEAU

		x_1	x_2	x_3	s_1	w_1	w_2	y_1	y_2		
Basis	c_i	500	4000	1000	0	0	0	M	M	b_i	b_i/a_{ij}
y_1	M	3000	20,000	14,000	0	-1	0	1	0	300,000	$300{,}000/20{,}000 = 15$
y_2	M	10	(40)	20	0	0	-1	0	1	300	$300/40 = 7.5$*
s_1	0	500	4000	1000	1	0	0	0	0	30,000	$30{,}000/4000 = 7.5$
Z_j		$3010M$	$20{,}040M$	$14{,}020M$	0	$-M$	$-M$	M	M	$300{,}300M$	
$c_j - Z_j$		$500 - 3010M$	$4000 - 20{,}040M$†	$1000 - 14{,}020M$	0	M	M	0	0		

Note: The pivot row and pivot column are shaded.
* Exiting variable.
† Entering variable (most-negative $c_j - Z_j$ value).

tion problem is how the entering variable at each step is selected. In a maximization problem, we select the variable with the largest positive $c_j - Z_j$ in the net evaluation row. Variables continue to be brought in as long as any $c_j - Z_j$ is greater than zero. In a minimization problem, the entering variable is the one with the most negative $c_j - Z_j$ value. We continue to bring variables into basis as long as there is a negative value in the net evaluation row.

From Table 3-24, we see the entering variable is x_2, the number of television ads. The artificial variable y_2 will leave the basis. (Actually, y_2 and s_1 both tie, with values of 7.5 in the tableau in Table 3-24. When this occurs and one of the variables is an artificial variable, it should be the variable removed. Thus we have chosen y_2 as the exiting variable.) The completed tableau after the first iteration is shown in Table 3-25. Notice that the coefficient for the pivot element in Table 3-24 is now 1, while the other coefficients in the pivot column are 0. This was accomplished using the row operation rules illustrated earlier. You should test your understanding by performing the calculations required to move from Table 3-24 to Table 3-25.

In Table 3-25, we see that the $c_j - Z_j$ row still has a negative value in the x_3 (newspaper ads) column. This will be the next entering variable. The departing variable will be x_2, the number of television ads. Table 3-26 shows the simplex tableau after the second iteration. Since there is still at least one variable with a negative $c_j - Z_j$ value, we have not reached the optimal solution. (Note also that y_1 still remains in the basis after the second iteration. This variable must be forced out before an optimal feasible solution is identified.) The next variable to enter basis is w_2, the surplus variable for rating impact points. The departing variable is y_2, the artificial variable.

Table 3-27 presents the results after the third iteration. This is the final iteration, since all variables in the $c_j - Z_j$ row are nonnegative. The final solution is to place $150/7 = 21.429$ newspaper ads and no radio or television ads. This strategy will exceed the minimum impact rating requirement by $900/7 = 128.571$ points. There will be $60{,}000/7 = \$8571.43$ of the original \$30,000 advertising budget unused, for a minimum total cost of $150{,}000/7 = \$21{,}428.57$. Given the objective function and constraints set forth in this situation, MotorPart cannot achieve a lower-cost advertising mix and still meet these requirements.

You might have noticed that the required number of ads is not an integer value. It may be hard to place .429 ad in the newspaper! Because linear programming is a mathematical tool, it produces solutions which are optimal without regard to whether they are meaningful. In some applications, fractional values cause no problems because the decision variable is divisible or because the solution is so large that rounding does not substantially change the optimal point. But in other situations, only integer values are meaningful. Where the divisibility assumption is not appropriate, a technique known as integer programming is used. Integer programming is discussed in Chapter 6.

Whether it be for minimization or maximization, the simplex method can be used to reach the optimal solution to a linear programming problem. However, as you have noticed from our examples and from any problems you may have worked already, the simplex process requires substantial computational effort. As we showed in section 3-3, linear programming problems are ideally suited to solving by computer. In the next section, we consider a computer solution to a linear programming minimization problem.

Table 3-25 MOTORPART CORP. PROBLEM: TABLEAU AFTER FIRST ITERATION

		x_1	x_2	x_3	s_1	w_1	w_2	y_1	y_2		
Basis	c_i	500	4000	1000	0	0	0	M	M	b_i	b_i/a_{ij}
y_1	M	-2000	0	4000	0	-1	500	1	-500	150,000	$150{,}000/4000 = 37.5$
x_2	4000	$1/4$	1	$1/2$	0	0	$-1/40$	0	$1/40$	$15/2$	$7.50/.5 = 15$*
s_1	0	-500	0	-1000	1.0	0	100	0	-100	0	
Z_j		$1000 - 2000M$	4000	$2000 + 4000M$	0	$-M$	$-100 + 500M$	M	$100 - 500M$	$30{,}000 + 150{,}000M$	
$c_j - Z_j$		$-500 + 2000M$	0	$-1000 - 4000M$†	0	M	$100 - 500M$	0	$501M - 100$		

Note: The pivot row and pivot column are shaded.
* Exiting variable.
† Entering variable (most-negative $c_j - Z_j$ value).

Table 3-26 MOTORPART CORP. PROBLEM: TABLEAU AFTER SECOND ITERATION

		x_1	x_2	x_3	s_1	w_1	w_2	y_1	y_2		
Basis	c_i	500	4000	1000	0	0	0	M	M	b_i	b_i/a_{ij}
y_1	M	−4000	−8000	0	0	−1	(700)	1	−700	90,000	90,000/700 = 128.57*
x_3	1000	½	2	1	0	0	−1/20	0	1/20	15	
s_1	0	0	2000	0	1	0	50	0	−50	15,000	15,000/50 = 300
Z_j		$500 - 4000M$	$2000 - 8000M$	1000	0	$-M$	$-50 + 700M$	M	$50 - 700M$	$15,000 + 90,000M$	
$c_j - Z_j$		$4000M$	$2000 + 8000M$	0	0	M	$50 - 700M$†	0	$-50 + 701M$		

Note: The pivot row and pivot column are shaded.
* Exiting variable.
† Entering variable (most-negative $c_j - Z_j$ value).

Table 3-27 MOTORPART CORP. PROBLEM: TABLEAU AFTER THIRD ITERATION, FINAL TABLEAU

		x_1	x_2	x_3	s_1	w_1	w_2	y_1	y_2		
Basis	c_i	500	4000	1000	0	0	0	M	M	b_i	b_i/a_{ij}
w_2	0	$-40/7$	$-80/7$	0	0	$-1/700$	1	$1/700$	-1	$900/7$	
x_3	1000	$3/14$	$10/7$	1	0	0	0	0	0	$150/7$	
s_1	0	$2000/7$	$10{,}000/7$	0	1	$50/700$	0	$-50/700$	0	$60{,}000/7$	
Z_j		$1500/7$	$10{,}000/7$	1000	0	0	0	0	0	$150{,}000/7 = 21{,}428.57$	
$c_j - Z_j$		$2000/7$	$18{,}000/7$	0	0	0	0	M	M		

3-5 COMPUTER APPLICATIONS: A MINIMIZATION EXAMPLE

Western Mills of South Dakota makes a feed supplement for cattle, with three main ingredients: alfalfa pellets, potato skins, and molasses. Each sack of the feed supplement must contain minimum quantities of four different nutrients. Table 3-28 shows the contribution to each nutrient type for 1 unit of each ingredient as well as the minimum required amounts of each ingredient.

The ingredients vary in cost from $.27 per unit for potato skins to $.62 for each unit of molasses. In order to advertise the product as containing all three ingredients, at least 5 units of each must be included in a sack of feed supplement. Due to food digestion requirements, no more than 25 units of potato skins can be included in a sack of feed supplement.

The question facing the Western Mills Company is what the proper mix of ingredients should be per bag to meet the nutrient requirements at a minimum cost per sack. To answer this, we can employ linear programming. We first define the decision variables as follows:

x_1 = units of alfalfa

x_2 = units of potato skins

x_3 = units of molasses

Next, we define the objective function as:

$$\text{Minimize} \quad Z = .35x_1 + .27x_2 + .62x_3$$

Table 3-28 WESTERN MILLS PROBLEM: NUTRIENT CONTRIBUTIONS, BY INGREDIENT

Nutrient	Alfalfa	Potato Skins	Molasses	Minimum Required
A	3	5	1	50
B	6	2	4	80
C	1	0	2	40
D	.5	2	0	25
Unit cost	$.35	$.27	$.62	

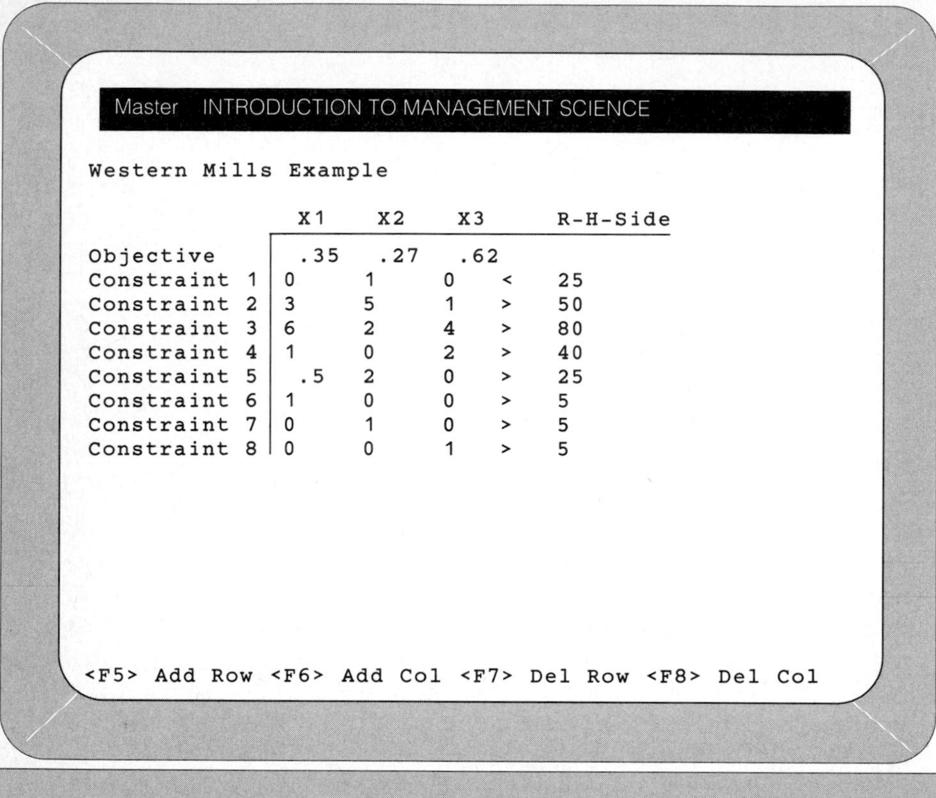

Figure 3-12
Western Mills example: MASTER data entry screen

The constraints are:

$$
\begin{aligned}
1x_2 \quad\quad\quad &\leq 25\\
3x_1 + 5x_2 + 1x_3 &\geq 50\\
6x_1 + 2x_2 + 4x_3 &\geq 80\\
1x_1 \quad\quad + 2x_3 &\geq 40\\
.5x_1 + 2x_2 \quad\quad &\geq 25\\
1x_1 \quad\quad\quad\quad &\geq 5\\
1x_2 \quad\quad &\geq 5\\
1x_3 &\geq 5
\end{aligned}
$$

Figure 3-12 shows the data input required by the MASTER software. The results are displayed in Figure 3-13.

```
                LINEAR PROGRAMMING FORMULATION

   OBJECTIVE FUNCTION:
     MINIMIZE Z =
          0.35  X1 +      0.27  X2 +      0.62  X3

   SUBJECT TO:
         0.00X1 +     1.00X2 +     0.00X3  <=   25.00
         3.00X1 +     5.00X2 +     1.00X3  >=   50.00
         6.00X1 +     2.00X2 +     4.00X3  >=   80.00
         1.00X1 +     0.00X2 +     2.00X3  >=   40.00
         0.50X1 +     2.00X2 +     0.00X3  >=   25.00
         1.00X1 +     0.00X2 +     0.00X3  >=    5.00
         0.00X1 +     1.00X2 +     0.00X3  >=    5.00
         0.00X1 +     0.00X2 +     1.00X3  >=    5.00

                THE DECISION VARIABLES ARE  1  THROUGH  3
                THE SLACK VARIABLES ARE      4  THROUGH  4
                THE SURPLUS VARIABLES ARE     5  THROUGH   11
                THE ARTIFICIAL VARIABLES ARE 12  THROUGH  18


           OPTIMAL SOLUTION

   ITERATIONS =   9

   OBJECTIVE FUNCTION =           14.950


   DECISION VARIABLES:

   VARIABLE  NAME    VALUE
       1      X1    30.000
       2      X2     5.000
       3      X3     5.000


   SLACK OR SURPLUS VARIABLES:

   VARIABLE    NAME          VALUE
    4          SLACK        20.000
    5          SURPLUS      70.000
    6          SURPLUS     130.000
    9          SURPLUS      25.000
   10          SURPLUS      -0.000
```

Figure 3-13
Western Mills example: MASTER output (figure continued on next page)

```
DUAL RESULTS

VARIABLE   NAME                 VALUE
           X1                   0.000
           X2                   0.000
           X3                   0.000
           CONSTRAINT     1     0.000
           CONSTRAINT     2     0.000
           CONSTRAINT     3     0.000
           CONSTRAINT     4    -0.283
           CONSTRAINT     5    -0.135
           CONSTRAINT     6     0.000
           CONSTRAINT     7     0.000
           CONSTRAINT     8    -0.055
```

Figure 3-13 Continued

The objective function is minimized at $14.95 with 30 units of alfalfa, 5 units of potato skins, and 5 units of molasses. The slack variable associated with the one ≤ constraint has a value of 20, meaning the optimal mix contains 20 fewer potato skin units than the limit of 25. The optimal solution has four surplus variables in basis. Variable 5, associated with the minimum requirement for nutrient A has a value of 70, indicating that the optimal solution exceeds the minimum requirement by 70 units. Note that variable 10 has a value of −0.000, indicating there really is no surplus. However, the simplex solution procedure requires that the number of variables in basis be the same as the number of constraints. Thus, variable 10 is included in basis in the final solution with a value of zero.

3-6 SPECIAL LINEAR PROGRAMMING SITUATIONS

In Chapter 2, we indicated that in some situations special results can occur from linear programming. Among these are (1) alternate optimal solutions, (2) unbounded solutions, and (3) no feasible solutions.

ALTERNATE OPTIMAL SOLUTIONS

In the graphical case, alternate optimal solutions occur when the isoprofit line is parallel to one of the binding constraints. The same situation can occur when the simplex method is used. For example, consider the following linear programming formulation:

$$\text{Maximize} \quad Z = 2x_1 + 4x_2$$

Subject to:

(a) $4x_1 + 8x_2 \leq 18$
(b) $6x_1 + 2x_2 \leq 24$
$x_1, x_2 \geq 0$

By comparing the coefficients of constraint (a) with those in the objective function, we can see the objective function (isoprofit line) is parallel to constraint (a). Table 3-29 shows the initial simplex tableau for this problem. Table 3-30 shows the simplex

Table 3-29 EXAMPLE OF ALTERNATE OPTIMAL SOLUTIONS: INITIAL TABLEAU

		x_1	x_2	s_1	s_2		
Basis	c_i	2	4	0	0	b_i	b_i/a_{ij}
s_1	0	4	8	1	0	18	2.25
s_2	0	6	2	0	1	24	12
Z_j		0	0	0	0		
$c_j - Z_j$		2	4	0	0		

Note: The entering and departing variables are shaded.

Table 3-30 EXAMPLE OF ALTERNATE OPTIMAL SOLUTIONS: FIRST ITERATION

		x_1	x_2	s_1	s_2		
Basis	c_i	2	4	0	0	b_i	b_i/a_{ij}
x_2	4	1/2	1	1/8	0	9/4	
s_2	0	5	0	−1/4	1	39/2	
Z_j		2	4	4/8	0	9	
$c_j - Z_j$		0	0	−4/8	0		

Note: The $c_j - Z_j$ for the nonbasis variable, x_1, is zero.

Table 3-31 EXAMPLE OF ALTERNATE OPTIMAL SOLUTIONS: SECOND ITERATION

		x_1	x_2	s_1	s_2		
Basis	c_i	2	4	0	0	b_i	b_i/a_{ij}
x_2	4	0	1	3/20	−1/10	3/10	
x_1	2	1	0	−1/20	1/5	39/10	
Z_j		2	4	1/2	0	9	
$c_j - Z_j$		0	0	−1/2	0		

tableau after the first iteration. This tableau is also the optimal solution, since no value in the $c_j - Z_j$ row is positive. The value of the objective function is 9.0 with $x_2 = 2.25$ and $s_2 = 19.5$.

Note, however, that the $c_j - Z_j$ value for variable x_1 is zero. This implies that adding variable x_1 to the basis will have no effect on the objective-function value. Thus, a new solution with $x_1 > 0$ will still yield 9 for the objective function. We can demonstrate this by forcing x_1 into the solution, as shown in Table 3-31. We see the solution is now $x_1 = 3.90$ and $x_2 = .30$, giving an objective-function value of 9, the same as before. Note that the nonbasic variable, s_2, now has a $c_j - Z_j = 0$, indicating this variable could come into the solution without changing the objective function.

Anytime a nonbasic variable has a net evaluation ($c_j - Z_j$) of zero in the final tableau, alternate optimal solutions exist.

Table 3-32 EXAMPLE OF NO FEASIBLE SOLUTIONS: INITIAL TABLEAU

		x_1	x_2	s_1	w_1	y_1		
Basis	c_i	20	50	0	0	$-M$	b_i	b_i/a_{ij}
s_1	0	1	2	1	0	0	20	10
W_1	$-M$	3/2	3	0	-1	1	50	50/3
Z_j		$-2M$	$-3M$	0	M	$-M$		
$c_j - Z_j$		$20 + 2M$	$50 + 3M$	0	$-M$	M		

Note: The entering and departing variables are shaded.

NO FEASIBLE SOLUTION

A linear programming problem has no feasible solution if the constraints are incompatible. For instance, consider the following linear programming formulation:

$$\text{Maximize} \quad Z = 20x_1 + 50x_2$$

Subject to:

(a) $x_1 + 2x_2 \leq 20$
(b) $3/2x_1 + 3x_2 \geq 50$
$x_1, x_2 \geq 0$

By graphing these two constraints, you will see the problem has no feasible solution space. How does this problem show up in the simplex procedure? Table 3-32 shows the initial tableau for this problem. Observe that we have included $-M$ in the objective-function row for the artificial variable associated with constraint (b). As noted, the entering variable is x_2 and the departing variable is s_1. After the first iteration, we get in trouble, as seen in Table 3-33. The net evaluation row indicates an optimal solution, since all values are ≤ 0; however, an artificial variable remains in the basis with a value > 0. This indicates no feasible solution is possible.

When using the simplex method, if an artificial variable is still in basis in the final solution with a positive value, there is no feasible solution to the problem. However, if an artificial variable is in basis with a value of zero, the solution may be both feasible and optimal, but the linear programming problem may have a *redundant constraint* or the solution may be degenerate. Computer packages will generally give a warning when a solution is not feasible.

Table 3-33 EXAMPLE OF NO FEASIBLE SOLUTIONS: FIRST ITERATION

		x_1	x_2	s_1	w_1	y_1		
Basis	c_i	20	50	0	0	$-M$	b_i	b_i/a_{ij}
x_2	50	1/2	1	1/2	0	0	10	
W_1	$-M$	0	0	$-3/2$	-1	1	20	
Z_j		25	50	$3M/2$	M	$-M$		
$c_j - Z_j$		-5	0	$-3M/2$	$-M$	0		

Note: The entering and departing variables are shaded.

DEGENERATE BASIC SOLUTION

If the final tableau contains a variable in basis with a value of zero, the solution is degenerate. Degeneracy can occur in the simplex procedure when two or more variables have equal b_i/a_{ij} ratios and are tied in terms of which variable should leave the solution when a new variable is added. Only one variable can depart; however, the tied variable, which remains in the solution, is also forced to zero. This condition may be temporary, with the variable having a zero value leaving basis in a subsequent iteration, or it may be permanent. (This condition existed in the MotorPart Corporation example, as shown in Table 3-25. In this case, the condition was temporary and didn't result in any problem.) Another possibility is that the optimal solution is never reached and the simplex method *cycles* back and forth between alternate solutions (or between corner points).

The major problem with degeneracy lies in the potential for cycling. Probably the easiest way to deal with cycling is to go back to the tableau where the tie occurred and select a different departing variable. This generally resolves the cycling problem and points you toward the optimal solution. If you are performing the simplex manually, you will observe cycling and can correct the situation. However, unless a computer is programmed to recognize cycling, it will be caught in a loop and will not stop until you intervene.

UNBOUNDED SOLUTIONS

We discussed the issue of an unbounded solution in Chapter 2. In a maximization problem, the solution is unbounded if the feasible region is open upward. Given the simplex requirement that all variables be ≥ 0, minimization problems don't typically have the problem of unboundedness.

The following linear programming problem illustrates a situation where the solution is unbounded.

$$\text{Maximize} \quad Z = 1x_1 + 5x_2$$

Subject to:

$$3x_1 - 2x_2 \leq 100$$
$$x_1 \leq 20$$

Decision variable x_2 is found only in the first constraint, and its negative coefficient implies we could add as many units of x_2 to the solution as we want without violating either constraint. Thus, the solution is unbounded, since the objective function could grow infinitely large.

Table 3-34 shows the initial tableau for this example. We see that the entering

Table 3-34 EXAMPLE OF UNBOUNDED SOLUTION: INITIAL TABLEAU

		x_1	x_2	s_1	s_2		
Basis	c_i	1	5	0	0	b_i	b_i/a_{ij}
s_1	0	3	−2	1	0	100	
s_2	0	1	0	0	1	20	
Z_j		0	0	0	0		
$c_j - Z_j$		1	5	0	0		

variable will be x_2, since it has the largest $c_j - Z_j$ value. However, the b_i/a_{ij} ratios for both basic variables will be infinite or negative. This means that an infinite amount of x_2 can be brought into basis without forcing any of the current variables to zero. Thus: *At any iteration where the entering variable has all zero or negative exchange coefficients, the solution will be unbounded.*

The problems just discussed can occur in linear programming applications, but they are not frequently encountered. In general, they occur because the linear programming problem has been incorrectly formulated. If you do uncover one of these problems, our first suggestion is to reexamine your initial problem formulation for possible errors.

3-7 SUMMARY AND CONCLUSIONS

Most linear programming applications involve many decision variables and constraints. These problems require something other than a graphical solution technique. The simplex solution procedure has been introduced in this chapter. The simplex method is a mathematical technique which systematically inspects corners of the feasible region until it reaches the optimal solution. For smaller problems, such as those presented in this chapter, the simplex method can be performed manually. We have taken you through several examples of maximization and minimization problems because we feel that a good understanding of the simplex solution process will better aid you in future application of linear programming. However, for larger problems, computers need to be used. This chapter demonstrated several computer applications using the software package MASTER. In these cases, the emphasis is on problem formulation and interpretation of the output.

A number of the important terms introduced in this chapter are listed in the Chapter Glossary. Chapters 4 through 6 will further our discussion of linear programming and give you more opportunities to use this very powerful management science technique.

Solved Problems

PROBLEM 1 Given the following linear programming problem:

$$\text{Minimize} \quad Z = 12x_1 + 4x_2 + 8x_3$$

Subject to:

$$\begin{aligned}
5x_1 + 2x_2 + 6x_3 &\geq 120 \\
12x_1 + 8x_2 + 4x_3 &\leq 350 \\
5x_1 \qquad\quad + 6x_3 &\leq 50 \\
x_1 \qquad\qquad\qquad &\geq 2 \\
x_1, x_2, x_3 &\geq 0
\end{aligned}$$

a. Put the problem in standard form.
b. Set up the initial simplex tableau.
c. Solve for the optimal solution using the simplex method.

Solutions

a. Minimize $Z = 12x_1 + 4x_2 + 8x_3 + 0w_1 + My_1 + 0s_1 + 0s_2 + 0w_2 + My_2$

Subject to:

$$5x_1 + 2x_2 + 6x_3 - w_1 + y_1 = 120$$
$$12x_1 + 8x_2 + 4x_3 + s_1 = 350$$
$$5x_1 + 6x_3 + s_2 = 50$$
$$x_1 - w_2 + y_2 = 2$$
$$x_1, x_2, x_3, w_1, y_1, s_1, s_2, w_2, y_2 \geq 0$$

b.

Initial Tableau

Basis	c_i	x_1 12	x_2 4	x_3 8	w_1 0	y_1 M	s_1 0	s_2 0	w_2 0	y_2 M	b_i
y_1	M	5	2	6	-1	1	0	0	0	0	120
s_1	0	12	8	4	0	0	1	0	0	0	350
s_2	0	5	0	6	0	0	0	1	0	0	50
y_2	M	1	0	0	0	0	0	0	-1	0	2
Z_j		$6M$	$2M$	$6M$	$-M$	M	0	0	$-M$	M	$122M$
$c_j - Z_j$		$12 - 6M$	$4 - 2M$	$8 - 6M$	M	0	0	0	M	0	

c.

Tableau after First Iteration

Basis	c_i	x_1 12	x_2 4	x_3 8	w_1 0	y_1 M	s_1 0	s_2 0	w_2 0	y_2 M	b_i
y_1	M	0	2	0	-1	1	0	-1	0	0	70
s_1	0	$26/3$	8	0	0	0	1	$-2/3$	0	0	$950/3$
x_3	8	$5/6$	0	1	0	0	0	$1/6$	0	0	$25/3$
y_2	M	1	0	0	0	0	0	0	-1	1	2
Z_j		$20/3 + M$	$2M$	8	$-M$	M	0	$4/3 - M$	$-M$	M	$200/3 + 72M$
$c_j - Z_j$		$16/3 - M$	$4 - 2M$	0	M	0	0	$-4/3 + M$	M	0	

Tableau after Second Iteration

Basis	c_i	x_1 12	x_2 4	x_3 8	w_1 0	y_1 M	s_1 0	s_2 0	w_2 0	y_2 M	b_i
x_2	4	0	1	0	$-1/2$	$1/2$	0	$-1/2$	0	0	35
s_1	0	$26/3$	0	0	4	-4	1	$10/3$	0	0	$110/3$
x_3	8	$5/6$	0	1	0	0	0	$1/6$	0	0	$25/3$
y_2	M	1	0	0	0	0	0	0	-1	1	2
Z_j		$20/3 + M$	4	8	-2	2	0	$-2/3$	$-M$	M	$206\frac{2}{3} + 2M$
$c_j - Z_j$		$16/3 - M$	0	0	2	$M - 2$	0	$2/3$	M	0	

Tableau after Third Iteration (Final Tableau)

		x_1	x_2	x_3	w_1	y_1	s_1	s_2	w_2	y_2	
Basis	c_i	12	4	8	0	M	0	0	0	M	b_i
x_2	4	0	1	0	$-1/2$	$1/2$	0	$-1/2$	0	0	35
s_1	0	0	0	0	4	-4	1	$10/3$	$26/3$	$-26/3$	$58/3$
x_3	8	0	0	1	0	0	0	$1/6$	$5/6$	$-5/6$	$20/3$
x_1	12	1	0	0	0	0	0	0	-1	1	2
Z_j		12	4	8	-2	2	0	$-2/3$	$-16/3$	$16/3$	$652/3$
$c_j - Z_j$		0	0	0	2	$M-2$	0	$2/3$	$16/3$	$M - 16/3$	

By looking at the final tableau, we see the solution is:

$x_1 = 2$, $x_2 = 35$, $x_3 = 20/3$, and $s_1 = 58/3$

PROBLEM 2 The Get-Wet Swimsuit Company makes three types of swimsusits: bikinis, racing suits, and swim trunks. The following information is available about profits, costs, material (nylon) needs, and labor needs for each type of swimsuit.

	Profit ($)	Cost ($)	Nylon (yards)	Labor (hours)
Bikini (women's)	10	6	1	4
Racing suit (women's)	15	12	3	2
Swim trunks (men's)	8	5	2	3

The maximum manufacturing budget this month for the swimsuit company is $2000. A total of 1000 yards of nylon is available. The company employs 5 people to make the swimsuits, and each employee works only 8 hours per day. (The company does not have any money in the budget for overtime.) Assume that this month has 20 working days. The marketing manager has determined that 100 women's swimsuits must be manufactured this month.

a. Assuming the company's goal is to maximize profits, formulate as a linear programming problem.

b. Set up the initial simplex tableau.

c. Determine the optimal solution using the simplex method.

Solutions

a. Maximize $Z = 10x_1 + 15x_2 + 8x_3$

Subject to:

$$
\begin{aligned}
6x_1 + 12x_2 + 5x_3 &\leq 2000 \\
x_1 + 3x_2 + 2x_3 &\leq 1000 \\
4x_1 + 2x_2 + 3x_3 &\leq 800 \\
x_1 + x_2 &= 100 \\
x_1, x_2, x_3 &\geq 0
\end{aligned}
$$

b.

Initial Simplex Tableau

Basis	c_j	x_1 10	x_2 15	x_3 8	s_1 0	s_2 0	s_3 0	y_1 $-M$	b_i
s_1	0	6	12	5	1	0	0	0	2000
s_2	0	1	3	2	0	1	0	0	1000
s_3	0	4	2	3	0	0	1	0	800
y_1	$-M$	1	1	0	0	0	0	1	100
Z_j		$-M$	$-M$	0	0	0	0	$-M$	$-100M$
$c_j - Z_j$		$10 + M$	$15 + M$	8	0	0	0	0	

Tableau after First Iteration

Basis	c_j	x_1 10	x_2 15	x_3 8	s_1 0	s_2 0	s_3 0	y_1 $-M$	b_i
s_1	0	-6	0	5	1	0	0	-12	800
s_2	0	-2	0	2	0	1	0	-3	700
s_3	0	2	0	3	0	0	1	-2	600
x_2	15	1	1	0	0	0	0	1	100
Z_j		15	15	0	0	0	0	15	1500
$c_j - Z_j$		-5	0	8	0	0	0	$-M - 15$	

Tableau after Second Iteration

Basis	c_j	x_1 10	x_2 15	x_3 8	s_1 0	s_2 0	s_3 0	y_1 $-M$	b_i
x_3	8	$-6/5$	0	1	$1/5$	0	0	$-12/5$	160
s_2	0	$2/5$	0	0	$-2/5$	1	0	$9/5$	380
s_3	0	$28/5$	0	0	$-3/5$	0	1	$26/5$	120
x_2	15	1	1	0	0	0	0	1	100
Z_j		$27/5$	15	8	$8/5$	0	0	$-21/5$	2780
$c_j - Z_j$		$23/5$	0	0	$-8/5$	0	0	$-M + 21/3$	

Tableau after Third Iteration

Basis	c_j	x_1 10	x_2 15	x_3 8	s_1 0	s_2 0	s_3 0	y_1 $-M$	b_i
x_3	8	0	0	1	$1/14$	0	$3/14$	$-9/7$	$1300/7$
s_2	0	0	0	0	$-5/14$	1	$-1/14$	$10/7$	$2600/7$
x_1	10	1	0	0	$-3/28$	0	$5/28$	$13/14$	$150/7$
x_2	15	0	1	0	$3/28$	0	$-5/28$	$1/14$	$550/7$
Z_j		10	15	8	$31/28$	0	$23/28$	$1/14$	$20{,}150/7$
$c_j - Z_j$		0	0	0	$-31/28$	0	$-23/28$	$-M - 1/4$	

The solution to this problem is:

Make $150/7 = 21.43$ bikinis

$550/7 = 78.57$ racing suits

$1300/7 = 185.71$ swim trunks

At the optimal point, $2600/7 = 471.43$ yards of nylon will remain.

Note that this solution requires making fractional numbers of all three products. The decision maker may want to consider using an integer programming model to solve this problem. This technique will be discussed in Chapter 6.

General Questions and Assignments

1. Discuss in your own terms how the simplex solution procedure relates to the idea of moving from one corner to another in the feasible region.
2. For a maximization problem, discuss the rule used to indicate when you have reached the final solution with the simplex method.
3. In employing the simplex solution method, how do you determine which variable will enter basis and which variable will leave basis? (Answer this question for both maximization and minimization problems.)
4. Discuss the conditions under which a linear programming model can result in alternate optimal decisions.
5. Discuss the purpose of artificial variables in the simplex linear programming solution procedure.
6. Locate three or more articles in the library which discuss applications of linear programming. For each application, determine the number of decision variables in the model and the number of constraints in the model.
7. Discuss in your own terms how you can determine the number of variables that will be in the initial basic solution to the linear programming model.
8. Discuss whether it is possible for the simplex solution procedure to provide a solution that violates one or more of the constraints.

Exercises and Application Problems

1. What is the *Fundamental Theorem of Linear Programming?*
2. Given the following linear programming problem:

   Maximize $Z = 3000x_1 + 5000x_2$

   Subject to:

$$
\begin{aligned}
500x_1 + 300x_2 &\geq 1500 \\
80x_1 + 100x_2 &\leq 800 \\
40x_1 - 20x_2 &\geq 100 \\
10x_1 + 30x_2 &\leq 150 \\
x_1, x_2 &\geq 0
\end{aligned}
$$

   a. Which constraints are binding? Which are nonbinding?
   b. Determine the solution at each corner point.
   c. What is the optimal solution?

3. Explain how the graphical solution method and the simplex method are similar.
4. What are slack variables?
5. Given the following linear programming problem:

$$\text{Maximize} \quad Z = 8x_1 + 6x_2$$

Subject to:

$$x_1 + x_2 \le 10$$
$$2x_1 + 3x_2 \le 24$$
$$3x_1 - x_2 \le 12$$
$$x_1, x_2 \ge 0$$

a. Determine the solution for each corner point.
b. Put the problem in standard form.
c. Set up the initial simplex tableau.

6. Given the following linear programming problem:

$$\text{Maximize} \quad Z = 7x_1 + 3x_2$$

Subject to:

$$4x_1 + 5x_2 \le 23$$
$$2x_1 + 5x_2 \le 17$$
$$x_1, x_2 \ge 0$$

a. Put the problem in standard form.
b. Set up the initial simplex tableau.
c. Which variable should enter the basis and which variable should leave the basis at the initial tableau?

7. Solve problem 5 using the simplex method. At each iteration compare the answer found using simplex with the corner-point solutions found using the graphical method.
8. The Delta Manufacturing Company makes two sizes of file cabinets, letter size and legal size. The letter-size cabinet sells to distributors for $138, and the legal-size cabinet sells for $176.50. The cabinets are constructed from sheet metal that has been ordered with a special coloring and finish. It takes 36 square feet of sheet metal to make a letter-size file cabinet and 54 square feet of sheet metal to make a legal-size cabinet. Because of a problem at the supplier's plant, Delta has on hand only 120,000 square feet of sheet metal to last the year. Making cabinets requires two major operations, cutting the metal and bending it into parts and then assembling the different parts. The cutting and bending operations take 2 hours for a letter-size cabinet and 3 hours for a legal-size cabinet. The company has 10,000 hours of time available for this operation. Assembly takes 4 hours for a letter-size cabinet and 2 hours for a legal-size cabinet. The company has 8000 hours available for this operation.

   Both indirect and direct labor costs are assigned to the products that Delta makes. Each letter-size cabinet requires $41 in direct labor charges. The legal-size cabinets require $52 in direct labor. The board of directors has allocated $375,000 for direct labor.

   The company's cost accountants have determined that the total direct and indirect costs assigned to the letter-size cabinet are $87. The total costs allocated to the legal-size cabinet are $121.

   Formulate the objective function and the constraints for this problem, assuming that Delta wishes to determine the optimal number of each type of file cabinet to make in order to maximize profits within the given constraints.

a. Solve this problem using the graphical procedure.
b. Solve using simplex and compare the solutions at each iteration with the corner points found in part a.

9. The Cedar Falls Manufacturing Company recently discontinued production of one of its product lines because of the line's poor profitability. This has resulted in excess production capacity that management would like to allocate to one or more of the other three product lines: X, Y, and Z. The milling department now has an extra 600 hours available per week, the grinder has an extra 480 hours available per week, and the polishing department has an extra 400 hours of time available per week. The following table indicates the number of hours of each process that are required for each unit of X, Y, and Z.

Product	Milling	Grinding	Polishing
X	11	8	6
Y	9	10	7
Z	8	8	13

Because of the great effort of the sales department, demand for X, Y, and Z will exceed any potential production level. The profit per unit for X is \$24; for Y, \$15; and for Z, \$19.

Formulate as a linear programming problem and solve.

10. The Dilmart Department Store carries three lines of men's suits: Budget, Career, and Insignia. The more expensive the suit is, the more profit Dilmart makes on the suit. However, the expensive suits also require more time by the sales personnel and more sales space for the kind of displays necessary to sell expensive suits. When Dilmart orders suits for the coming season, it orders at most 5000 suits of each line. The Dilmart buyers order suits with the objective of maximizing profits. However, the buyers must consider certain limitations. For instance, during the sales period for the coming season, there will be a maximum of 6400 sales personnel hours available and at most 6000 square feet of sales area, including displays. The following table provides some useful information regarding each suit line.

Suit Line	Profit per Suit (\$)	Sales Hours per 1000 Suits	Display Space per 1000 Suits (square feet)
Budget	6.00	300	200
Career	13.20	500	400
Insignia	28.50	2000	800

Formulate as a linear programming problem, assuming that Dilmart wishes to maximize profits, and solve.

11. What is a surplus variable in the simplex solution procedure and under what circumstances are surplus variables included? If a surplus variable is in the final basic solution to a linear programming problem, how would you interpret its value?

12. What is a slack variable in and why are slack variables used in the simplex solution procedure? If a slack variable is in the final basic solution, what does it mean?

13. Mr. Ran Dunn operates a Tough Wear carpet store that carries three lines of carpets: Easywear, Foreverwear, and Superwear. Ran needs to determine how many rolls of each line of carpet to order so that his goal of maximizing profit will be attained. The following information is available:

	Square Yards per Roll	Cost per Square Yard ($)	Selling Price per Square Yard ($)
Easywear	1000	40	75
Foreverwear	1500	70	100
Superwear	1300	80	105

Because of limited space, Ran can order no more than 25,000 square yards of carpet. He knows from past experience that he will need at least twice as many rolls of Foreverwear as Superwear. In order to take advantage of quantity discount costs, Ran must order at least 6 rolls of Easywear, 3 rolls of Foreverwear, and 2 rolls of Superwear. Formulate as a linear programming problem and solve using the simplex method.

14. The manager of Badeaux Boutique has asked you to determine the advertising strategy for the following month. You have three choices of media in which to advertise: magazines, billboards, and newspapers. The following table gives some relevant information about each type of advertising:

	Magazine	Billboard	Newspaper
Cost per advertisement	$1,000	$5,000	$1,200
Exposure per advertisement	10,000	20,000	15,000
Revenue per advertisement	$5,000	$8,000	$5,950

The advertising budget allocated this month is $20,000. The company policy dictates that no more than 3 billboards can be displayed in any one month and at least as many newspaper advertisements must appear as magazine advertisements. A maximum of 20 advertisements are allowed each month. The manager has indicated that total exposure must be at least 85,000. Formulate a linear programming model for this problem, assuming the goal of the Boutique is to maximize profits, and solve. (Disregard the fact that in practice the decision variables would be required to have integer values.)

15. Use the simplex method to determine the solution to the following linear programming problem:

Maximize $Z = 100x_1 + 50x_2$

Subject to:

$$
\begin{aligned}
50x_1 + 80x_2 &\leq 500 \\
25x_1 + 10x_2 &\geq 50 \\
x_1 \qquad &\leq 5 \\
x_2 &\geq 3 \\
x_1, x_2 &\geq 0
\end{aligned}
$$

16. Use the simplex method to determine the solution to the following linear programming problem:

Maximize $Z = 2x_1 + 7x_2$

Subject to:

$$
\begin{aligned}
8x_1 + 12x_2 &\leq 48 \\
x_1 \qquad &\leq 4 \\
x_2 &\geq 1 \\
14x_1 + 10x_2 &\geq 28 \\
x_1, x_2 &\geq 0
\end{aligned}
$$

17. A small winery near Sonoma, California, bottles two types of wine: rosé and burgundy. The rosé sells for \$20 a quart and the burgundy sells for \$28.50 a quart at the wholesale level. It takes an estimated 5 minutes of employee time to make a quart of rosé and 12 minutes to make a quart of burgundy. The winery has only 2 employees, who together work a total of 15 hours per day, 5 days a week. It takes 10 pounds of grapes to make each quart of burgundy and 14 pounds of grapes to make each quart of rosé. Because the grapes must be picked at just the right time, only 4000 pounds of grapes are available each week. Because of customer demand, the winery has agreed to supply at least 50 quarts of each type of wine each week. Formulate this as a linear programming problem, assuming that the winery wishes to produce the mix of wines that will maximize revenues given the constraints imposed on production. Solve using the simplex method.

18. Solve the following linear programming problem using the simplex method.

$$\text{Maximize} \quad Z = 8x_1 + 4x_2 + 6x_3$$

Subject to:

$$\begin{aligned} 2x_1 + x_2 + 4x_3 &\leq 100 \\ x_1 + 3x_2 + 2x_3 &\leq 700 \\ 2x_1 + 3x_2 &\geq 50 \\ x_1, x_2 &\geq 0 \end{aligned}$$

19. Use the simplex method to solve the following linear programming problem.

$$\text{Maximize} \quad Z = .07x_1 + .03x_2$$

Subject to:

$$\begin{aligned} 4x_1 + 5x_2 &\leq 15 \\ 2x_1 + 5x_2 &\leq 26 \\ x_2 &\geq 1.5 \\ x_1, x_2 &\geq 0 \end{aligned}$$

20. The Mark-up Store carries three brands of microwaves: Pamana, Sonyo, and Coldpoint. The profits from Pamana, Sonyo, and Coldpoint are \$200, \$125, and \$155, respectively. From past experience, the Mark-up Store knows that it wll need to carry at least as many Coldpoint as Pamana, and at least twice as many Sonyo as Pamana and Coldpoint combined. Because of limited space, the store cannot stock more than 50 total units. Formulate this as a linear programming problem, assuming the goal is to maximize profits. Solve using the simplex method. (Disregard the fact that in practice the decision variables would be required to have integer values.)

21. What are the major differences in the simplex technique when solving maximization and minimization problems?

22. What is the purpose of the "big *M*" technique when using the simplex method?

23. The Frame Shop carries three standard sizes of frames, ordered from an outside supplier: large (8″ × 10″), medium (5″ × 7″), and small (3″ × 5″). The costs for these frames are \$10.00, \$8.50, and \$5.00 for the large, medium, and small, respectively. This month's budget is \$1500. From past experience, the manager realizes that at least 100 frames should be ordered. She wants to order no more than twice as many small frames as other frames, and will need at least 10 large frames. Formulate as a linear programming problem, assuming that the goal is to minimize cost. Solve using the simplex method.

24. Sciacca Charter Bus Company owns three buses. The manager has just received calls from three organizations in nearby cities that each need to charter one bus. These groups are located in

Delphos, Barnard, and Ada. All three buses are in different locations. The distances they must travel to reach the areas where they are needed vary, depending on which bus is sent to which city. The distances are given below.

	Distance to Each City (miles)		
Bus	Delphos	Barnard	Ada
A	5	16	11
B	10	3	15
C	3	6	9

Determine which bus the manager should send to each city so that the distance traveled to get there will be minimized. Solve using the simplex method.

25. A local grocery store has asked you to conduct a survey in the community to collect information on grocery purchases. The manager of the store feels that information from at least 200 homes is necessary. You determine that you can contact people either by telephone or by mail. The cost to contact customers by telephone is $1.50, and the cost to contact them by mail is $1.00. The response rate for contacts by telephone is expected to be 50%; the response rate for a mail survey should be 35%. The manager feels that the results may be more accurate if the survey is done by telephone, so he wants at least 3 times as many telephone responses as mail responses. Formulate a linear programming model that will minimize cost. Solve using the simplex method.

26. Use the simplex method to solve the following linear programming problem:

Minimize $Z = 12x_1 + 10x_2$

Subject to:

$$8x_1 + 10x_2 \leq 64$$
$$x_1 \geq 3$$
$$4x_1 + 5x_2 \geq 25$$
$$x_2 \geq 2$$
$$x_1, x_2 \geq 0$$

27. Use the simplex method to solve the following linear programming problem:

Minimize $Z = 4x_1 + 6x_2$

Subject to:

$$10x_1 + 12x_2 \leq 100$$
$$x_1 \geq 5$$
$$x_2 \geq 2$$
$$20x_1 - 10x_2 \leq 120$$
$$x_1, x_2 \geq 0$$

28. The North Tablet Company produces sleeping pills and tranquilizers. The company is considering marketing an inexpensive pill called More-Power which will supply the user with the minimum daily adult requirement of vitamins D and E. A bottle of 200 More-Power tablets requires a minimum of 20 units of vitamin D and 80 units of vitamin E. After considerable research, the company found that a unit of lamb heart extract contains .25 unit of vitamin D and a unit of soybean oil contains 1 unit of vitamin D. Conversely, a unit of lamb heart extract contains 2 units of vitamin E and a unit of soybean oil contains .5 unit of vitamin E. The company also notes that a unit of lamb heart extract costs $.04 and a unit of soybean oil costs $.06. Given this information, the firm wishes to know what amounts of lamb heart extract and soybean oil to use per bottle of More-Power in order to minimize the cost of supplying the minimum requirements of vitamins D and E. Solve using the simplex method.

29. Walsh Oil Company has accepted an offer to produce at least 3200 gallons of a high-powered racing fuel. The company has two raw products, liquid A and liquid B, which may be processed to satisfy the requirements. These are the only ingredients in the fuel. The two liquids, each of which can be obtained for $1 per gallon, have different potencies: 2 gallons of liquid A can be processed to yield a gallon of the racing fuel, but it takes 4 gallons of liquid B to yield a gallon of racing fuel. The company has a 550-gallon tank of liquid A, which management wishes to free for other storage purposes by using all of that liquid as rapidly as possible. In addition, the company has an incoming shipment of 400 gallons of liquid B which it wishes to process immediately, to avoid the danger of storing such a large quantity of highly explosive liquid. More of liquids A and B can be acquired if need be. How should the company allocate the current amounts of liquids A and B in order to minimize the cost of filling its racing fuel order? Set this problem up in a linear programming form and solve using the simplex method.

30. Use the simplex method to determine the solution to the following linear programming problem:

Minimize $Z = 55x_1 + 80x_2$

Subject to:

$$
\begin{aligned}
x_1 + 3x_2 &\geq 6 \\
x_1 + x_2 &\geq 4 \\
6x_1 + 2x_2 &\geq 12 \\
x_1, x_2 &\geq 0
\end{aligned}
$$

31. After careful review, the securities analyst for an investment firm has identified eight potential investment opportunities for the firm's clients. The following information is available about these investments:

	Price per Unit ($)	Minimum Purchase (units)	Percentage Return
Banana Computer stock	160	100	15
NBM Computer stock	150		13
NBM Computer bonds (Aa)	940	10	8
Star Oil Co. stock	40		16
Star Oil Co. bonds (Aaa)	850	20	10
Benny's Dept. Store stock	80		9
Bear's Dept. Store stock	30	200	11
Bear's Dept. Store bonds (B)	1010	10	12

The firm has at most $24,000,000 to invest. Because of the risk involved, company policy is that no more than 40% be invested in one industry. Since bonds are generally less risky than stocks, the firm also requires that at least 60% of the funds be invested in bonds. Since some bonds are more risky than others, however, no more than 5% of the invested funds can be in bonds rated lower than A. Because of brokerage fees, some of the assets have a minimum number of shares of stock or number of bonds that can be purchased. The firm has also decided that no more than 40% of the funds invested can be in computer stocks.

Determine the dollar amount to be invested in each asset, assuming the goal is to maximize return. Solve on the computer using the simplex method.

32. The K & E Athletic Company makes several products that use a variety of materials and require labor time in five different departments. The president of the company has asked you to determine the optimal mix of products in order to maximize the profits of the firm.

The following table indicates the amount of each type of material needed to provide a finished product and the total amount of each material available.

	Materials (ounces)				
Product	Rubber	Wood	Fiberglass	Nylon	Leather
Fiberglass tennis racket			6	2	3
Wooden tennis racket		10		2	3
Baseball bat		24			
Baseballs	1			5	1
Fishing pole			10	3	
Golf balls	½			3	½
Tennis balls	2			4	2
Total material available (pounds)	10	40	30	70	20

The following table indicates the amount of time (in hours) spent on each product in each department.

Product	**Cutting**	**Shaping**	**Stringing/ Wrapping**	**Finishing**	**Packing**
Fiberglass tennis racket	½	1	2	1	¼
Wooden tennis racket	1	2	2	½	¼
Baseball bat	2	2	—	2	½
Baseballs	½	—	3	1	¼
Fishing pole	1	3/2	1	½	3/2
Golf balls	½	—	2	3/2	½
Tennis balls	1	—	—	3	3/2

The cost accounting department has determined the profit from each product and also the minimum demand for the products (in units). This information is given below.

Product	**Profit ($)**	**Minimum Demand**
Fiberglass tennis racket	10	20
Wooden tennis racket	8	15
Baseball bat	5	10
Baseballs	3.50	25
Fishing pole	12	30
Golf balls	2.50	25
Tennis balls	4	25

From past experience, management also knows that it is best to stock at least twice as many fiberglass tennis rackets as wooden tennis rackets, regardless of the minimum demand. The company currently has 1000 hours of labor available that can be divided between departments as needed. Use a computer to solve this problem.

33. The Nakamura Golf Resort is scheduled to open for business next month. The resort has decided to do an extensive advertising campaign during this month in an effort to obtain a significant number of memberships before the club opens. Mr. Nakamura has determined that six advertising media could be used to reach the largest number of potential members. He has asked you to determine the best advertising strategy, given the following information and restrictions on each type of advertising.

Type of Advertising	Cost per Ad or Campaign ($)	Customer Contacts per Ad or Campaign	Maximum Number of Ads or Campaigns
Golf magazine	5,000	15,000	4
Newspaper	3,000	9,000	10
Radio	7,500	25,000	20
Television	10,000	30,000	25
Flyers	1,500	6,000	5
Direct mail	2,500	10,000	5

The total amount of this month's advertising budget is $100,000. Mr. Nakamura has determined that he wants at least twice as many television advertisements as newspaper advertisements. Determine the optimal advertising strategy if the goal is to maximize customer contact. Solve using a computer.

34. Wake-up Coffee makes three gourmet blends: regular, premium, and deluxe. Each blend is made from three types of beans: Haitian, Colombian, and Peruvian. The following information is available about each type of bean:

Beans	Maximum Available (pounds)	Cost per Pound ($)
Haitian	700	1.00
Colombian	900	2.50
Peruvian	500	3.00

Each type of coffee requires a different blend of the beans, as follows:

Coffee	Blend of Beans	Selling Price per Pound ($)
Regular	Maximum 10% Peruvian	3.50
	Minimum 5% Peruvian	
	Minimum 60% Haitian	
	Minimum 20% Colombian	
Premium	Maximum 30% Haitian	6.00
	Minimum 30% Colombian	
	Minimum 50% Peruvian	
Deluxe	Minimum 40% Haitian	4.50
	Minimum 40% Colombian	
	Maximum 20% Peruvian	

Wake-up Coffee can sell at least 700 pounds of regular blend, 400 pounds of premium blend, and 500 pounds of deluxe blend. Formulate as a linear programming problem, assuming the goal is to maximize profit. Solve using a computer.

35. The Zarruk Calculator Company has five assembly stations that need to be in operation. Currently there are four employees who can operate any of the stations. Their degree of expertise is such that the employees can produce a different number of calculators per hour, depending on which station they operate. The following table provides this information:

	Station				
Employee	A	B	C	D	E
Sharon	7	4	8	5	5
Eddie	2	1	9	5	3
Clarita	7	6	7	2	1
Darlene	8	7	9	1	4

Darlene can be assigned to two stations, but the others can be assigned to only one. Each station must be assigned one worker. Formulate as a linear programming problem to maximize the number of calculators produced per hour. Solve using a computer.

36. The Northvale Supermarket has decided to have its larger stores remain open 7 days a week for 8 hours per day. The regional manager has determined the minimum number of employees needed each day of the week, as given below:

Day	**Minimum Number of Employees**
Sunday	900
Monday	500
Tuesday	300
Wednesday	700
Thursday	600
Friday	700
Saturday	1000

Each clerk will work 5 consecutive days, but can start on any day of the week. Determine the linear programming problem that will minimize the number of employees. Solve using a computer.

37. The Hottest Mexican Restaurant has restaurants in 5 Midwestern cities. They order their tortillas from the Laredo Tortilla Factory, which has warehouses in 6 cities. The shipping costs (in dollars per dozen tortillas) are given below:

	Restaurants				
Warehouse	Minneapolis	Salina	Kansas City	Lincoln	Wichita
Tulsa	3	9	6	5	7
Oklahoma City	6	4	5	4	5
Denver	7	3	7	1	2
St. Louis	3	7	9	2	2
Lawrence	4	3	3	8	4
Omaha	5	1	2	5	9

The demand for each restaurant and the tortillas available at each warehouse are shown below:

	Demand (dozens)		Available (dozens)
Minneapolis	52	Tulsa	77
Salina	99	Oklahoma City	45
Kansas City	83	Denver	85
Lincoln	71	St. Louis	50
Wichita	65	Lawrence	94
		Omaha	72

Formulate as a linear programming problem so that shipping costs will be minimized. Solve using a computer.

38. Solve the following linear programming problem using a computer.

Maximize $Z = 7x_1 + 4x_2 + 5x_3 + 8x_4 + 18x_5 + 20x_6 + 15x_7$

Subject to:

$$
\begin{aligned}
3x_1 + 5x_2 + 8x_3 &\geq 120 \\
3x_1 + 5x_2 + 8x_3 &\leq 240 \\
5x_1 - 6x_2 + 3x_3 + x_4 + 5x_5 + 6x_6 + 7x_7 &\geq 100 \\
6x_1 + 3x_2 + 4x_5 + 6x_6 &\leq 300 \\
x_1 + x_2 + x_3 + x_4 + x_5 + x_6 + x_7 &\leq 150 \\
3x_1 - 2x_2 - 4x_3 + x_4 + 7x_6 + 8x_7 &\geq 150 \\
x_7 &\leq 50 \\
x_1, x_2, x_3, x_4, x_5, x_6, x_7 &\geq 0
\end{aligned}
$$

39. Solve the following linear programming problem using a computer.

Minimize $Z = 5x_1 + 4x_2 + 6x_3 + 5x_4 + 3x_5$

Subject to:

$$
\begin{aligned}
x_1 + x_2 + x_3 + x_4 + x_5 &\geq 300 \\
x_1 + 2x_2 + 4x_3 + 5x_4 + 6x_5 &\leq 1000 \\
x_1 + 4x_2 + 5x_3 &\geq 55 \\
x_2 + 3x_4 + 2x_5 &\leq 300 \\
x_1 - 3x_2 + 3x_3 + 3x_4 - x_5 &\leq 850 \\
x_1 - 3x_2 + 3x_3 + 3x_4 - x_5 &\geq 300 \\
x_1 + 3x_2 + 4x_3 + 5x_4 &\leq 700 \\
x_1, x_2, x_3, x_4, x_5 &\geq 0
\end{aligned}
$$

40. Use a computer to solve the following linear programming problem.

Maximize $Z = 5x_1 + 6x_2 + 3x_3 + 4x_4$

Subject to:

$$
\begin{aligned}
3x_1 + 4x_2 + 2x_3 + x_4 &\geq 100 \\
5x_1 + 3x_2 + 6x_3 + 5x_4 &\leq 1000 \\
2x_1 + 4x_2 + 6x_3 + 8x_4 &\geq 300
\end{aligned}
$$

$$\begin{aligned} 3x_1 \qquad\qquad\quad + 5x_4 &\geq 100 \\ 4x_1 + 3x_2 + 4x_3 + 5x_4 &\leq 600 \\ 3x_3 \qquad &\geq 5 \\ x_2 \qquad\qquad &\leq 100 \\ 2x_2 \qquad + x_4 &\geq 210 \\ x_1, x_2, x_3, x_4 &\geq 0 \end{aligned}$$

41. The Boise City Council is concerned with the number of complaints they have been receiving about dogs running loose in the neighborhoods. They decided to perform a survey to determine how widespread the problem is. In order to have as accurate a survey as possible, some contacts will be made during the week and some on weekends, so working households will be contacted too. The cost for the weekday surveys is $12 per contact; for weekend surveys, the cost is $18 per contact. The council members also want to make sure they contact some citizens who own dogs and some citizens who do not. In order to do this, they will divide the citizens into 3 classes:
   a. People with no dogs
   b. People with one or two dogs
   c. People with more than two dogs

   The following requirements must be met to ensure a reasonably unbiased survey:
   a. There will be no more than twice as many weekday contacts as weekend contacts.
   b. At least as many citizens with no dogs will be contacted as citizens with dogs.
   c. At least 10%, but no more than 20%, of those contacted will own more than two dogs.
   d. A minimum of 2000 contacts will be made.

   Determine the optimal number of contacts in each category in order to minimize costs. Solve using a computer.

42. Use the simplex method to determine the solution to the following linear programming problem. If you encounter any problems, describe them and point out one or more potential causes.

   Maximize $Z = 15x_1 + 9x_2$

   Subject to:

$$\begin{aligned} x_1 + 2x_2 &\geq 5 \\ 2x_1 + 6x_2 &\geq 12 \\ x_1, x_2 &\geq 0 \end{aligned}$$

43. Use the simplex method to determine the solution to the following linear programming problem. If you encounter any problems, describe them and point out one or more potential causes.

   Maximize $Z = 5x_1 + 10x_2$

   Subject to:

$$\begin{aligned} 7x_1 + 14x_2 &\leq 42 \\ 2x_1 + x_2 &\geq 4 \\ x_2 &\geq 2 \\ x_1, x_2 &\geq 0 \end{aligned}$$

44. Use the simplex method to determine the solution to the following linear programming problem. If you encounter any problems, describe them and point out one or more potential causes.

Maximize $Z = 3x_1 + 5x_2$

Subject to:

$$\begin{aligned} x_1 + x_2 &\geq 12 \\ 2x_1 + x_2 &\leq 20 \\ 4x_1 + 6x_2 &\leq 72 \\ x_1, x_2 &\geq 0 \end{aligned}$$

45. Use the simplex method to determine the solution to the following linear programming problem. If you encounter any problems, describe them and point out one or more potential causes.

Maximize $Z = 10x_1 + 8x_2$

Subject to:

$$\begin{aligned} 10x_1 - 5x_2 &\geq 20 \\ x_2 &\leq 2 \\ 5x_1 + 3x_2 &\geq 15 \\ x_1, x_2 &\geq 0 \end{aligned}$$

46. Use the simplex method to determine the solution to the following linear programming problem. If you encounter any problems, describe them and point out one or more potential causes.

Minimize $Z = 17x_1 + 20x_2$

Subject to:

$$\begin{aligned} 5x_1 + 3x_2 &\leq 18 \\ 3x_1 &\geq 6 \\ 10x_1 - 5x_2 &\geq 20 \\ x_2 &\geq 2 \end{aligned}$$

47. Use the simplex method to determine the solution to the following linear programming problem. If you encounter any problems, describe them and point out one or more potential causes.

Minimize $Z = 6x_1 + 4x_2 + 8x_3 + 3x_4$

Subject to:

$$\begin{aligned} x_1 + x_2 &\leq 1 \\ x_3 + x_4 &\leq 1 \\ x_1 + x_3 &\leq 1 \\ x_2 + x_4 &\leq 1 \\ x_1, x_2, x_3, x_4 &\geq 0 \end{aligned}$$

48. Use the simplex method to determine the solution to the following linear programming problem. If you encounter any problems, describe them and point out one or more potential causes.

Minimize $Z = 5x_1 + 3x_3$

Subject to:

$$\begin{aligned} 2x_1 + 3x_2 &\geq 12 \\ x_1 + x_2 &\leq 1 \end{aligned}$$

$$3x_1 \geq 15$$
$$x_1, x_2 \geq 0$$

49. Use the simplex method to determine the solution to the following linear programming problem. If you encounter any problems, describe them and point out one or more potential causes.

Maximize $Z = 6x_1 + 4x_2 + 3x_3$

Subject to:

$$12x_1 + 9x_2 + 6x_3 \leq 100$$
$$x_1 + x_2 + x_3 \geq 15$$
$$x_1 + x_2 + x_3 \leq 20$$
$$x_1, x_2, x_3 \geq 0$$

Chapter Glossary

Artificial variable A variable with no physical meaning, which is included in a linear programming standard formulation to make sure that an initial basic feasible solution exists. An artificial variable is needed when there are greater-than-or-equal-to constraints to make sure no variables in basis have negative values. Artificial variables are also used when the constraints are of the equal-to variety.

Basic solution Any corner point on the feasible region. In general terms, given a system of linear equations with k variables and m equations, and where $k > m$, a basic solution is determined when $k - m$ variables are set to zero and the m linear equations are solved for the remaining m variables.

Decision variables The variables in a linear programming formulation which the decision maker can control. The linear programming solution determines values for the decision variables which will optimize the objective function.

Dual value The shadow price, or marginal value, of a constraining resource.

Exchange coefficients The a_{ij} values in the simplex tableau, often called *substitution rates.*

Net evaluation row The $c_j - Z_j$ row in a simplex tableau. This row represents the net change in the value of the objective function for each unit of a variable brought into basis.

Nonbinding constraint A constraint in a linear programming model that does not restrict the solution.

Objective function A linear function that is either maximized or minimized.

Optimal feasible solution The solution to the linear programming model which either maximizes or minimizes the objective function.

Pivot column The column in a simplex tableau associated with the variable that will be introduced into basis.

Pivot element The element in a simplex tableau which is at the intersection of the pivot row and pivot column.

Pivot row The row in a simplex tableau associated with the variable which will be removed from basis.

Shadow price The marginal value of an additional unit of a resource.

Simplex method An algebraic method for solving linear programming problems. This solution method, which employs elementary row operations, uses iterations to move from one extreme point to another until the optimal solution is reached.

Simplex tableau A table that is used to keep track of the computations required to solve a linear programming problem when the simplex method is used.

Slack variable A variable added to the left-hand side of a less-than-or-equal-to constraint to convert the constraint into an equality. In many applications, the value of a slack variable is interpreted as the amount of a resource that is unused in the final solution.

Standard form A linear programming formulation in which all the constraints are written as equalities. The standard form includes all necessary slack, surplus, and artificial variables.

Surplus variable A variable added to the left-hand side of a greater-than-or-equal-to constraint to change it to an equality. In many applications, the value of the surplus variable is the excess amount of a factor above some minimum requirement.

Variables in basis Those variables whose column in a simplex tableau has a 1 as the only nonzero entry. There will be the same number of variables in basis as there are constraints in the linear programming formulation.

Chapter References

BOOKS

Charnes, A., and W. W. Cooper. *Management Models and Industrial Applications of Linear Programming.* New York: Wiley, 1961.

Dantzig, G. B. *Linear Programming and Extensions.* Princeton, N.J.: Princeton, 1963.

Driebeek, Norman J. *Applied Linear Programming.* Reading, Mass.: Addison-Wesley, 1969.

Hillier, F., and G. J. Lieberman. *Introduction to Operations Research,* 4th ed. Oakland, Calif.: Holden-Day, 1986.

Loomba, N. P., and E. Turban. *Applied Programming for Management.* New York: Holt, 1974.

Wagner, H. *Principles of Operations Research with Applications to Managerial Decisions.* Englewood Cliffs, N.J.: Prentice-Hall, 1975.

ARTICLES

Charnes, A., and W. W. Cooper. "Blending Aviation Gasolines: A Study in Programming Interdependent Activities in an Integrated Oil Company." *Econometrica,* Vol. 20, No. 2, 1952.

———. "Management Models and Industrial Applications of Linear Programming." *Management Science,* Vol. 4, No. 1, 1957.

Dantzig, G. B. "Recent Advances in Linear Programming." *Management Science,* Vol. 2, No. 2, 1956.

Fabozzi, E. J., and J. Valente. "Mathematical Programming in American Companies: A Sample Survey." *Interfaces,* Vol. 7, No. 1 (November), 1976.

Hooker, J. N. "Karmarkar's Linear Programming Algorithm." *Interfaces,* Vol. 16, No. 4, 1986.

Karmarkar, N. "A New Polynomial–Time Algorithm for Linear Programming." Technical Report, AT & T/Bell Laboratories, 1984.

Mini Cases

CASE 3A
BAY HILL MANUFACTURING

Henry Artis, production manager for Bay Hill Manufacturing, is responsible for all aspects of production for the company's two key products: the X-53-C disc brake and the A-14-Y speedometer cable. Bay Hill sells its entire production output to a major automobile manufacturer. The monthly orders for these parts vary, depending on the car maker's production schedule and new car sales levels. Henry feels that his plant is more efficient when he uses a level production strategy instead of trying to match production levels with orders. For instance, on the basis of expected orders for the next two months, Henry has developed a production schedule calling for 4000 X-53-C brake parts and 2000 A-14-Y cables each month.

James Baker, the company's senior accountant, countered that even though the production department might like a level production schedule to "make their life easier," it might not be advisable from a total cost viewpoint. He reminded Henry about such factors as the costs of tied-up capital and inventory storage. He argued that when these costs are factored in, a fixed-rate production schedule might not be the least costly approach. He suggested that two categories of costs—production costs and inventory holding costs—be considered in setting the production schedule. While Henry was a little upset at Baker's intrusion into his domain, he agreed to collect data on these costs for the coming two months and present them to the management group. The results of Henry's investigation are given below.

	X-53-C		A-14-Y	
	Month 1	Month 2	Month 1	Month 2
Unit Production cost ($)	18.00	19.00	11.00	11.00
Unit Storage cost ($)	.18	.19	.11	.11

Henry also presented the management group with the following data on projected orders for the next two months:

	X-53-C	A-14-Y
Month 1	3800	1500
Month 2	3000	1200

As the management group met in company's main conference room, Henry was asked to review his original production proposal and bring the other managers up to date on the important considerations of production scheduling. Seizing the opportunity to redeem himself, Henry first explained that no matter what else happened, the company must meet the demand each month for each product. The following relationship must hold:

Beginning inventory + production ≥ current month's demand

Stated another way:

Current production + beginning inventory − current demand = current inventory

He indicated that current inventory for the X-53-C was 400 units, and for the A-14-Y the current inventory was 300 units. Henry also explained to the group that he had limitations to deal with in three areas: machine time, labor, and storage capacity. He showed the managers the following information regarding the production limitations:

	Available Capacity		**Requirements per Unit**	
Use Rates	Month 1	Month 2	X-53-C	A-14-Y
Machine time (hours)	3800	3900	.30	.40
Labor (hours)	2900	3000	.35	.24
Storage (square feet)	5000	4200	1.50	1.00

As the managers mulled over the information that Henry had presented, Jake Parsons, manager of customer relations, said that he would like to see at least 100 units of each product in inventory at the end of month 2 to take care of any special orders that the company might receive from auto parts stores. The managers were pondering all the data when the morning's coffee and sweet rolls were delivered.

When the group settled back to business, James Baker was the first to speak. "I am very impressed with the way Henry has presented this information. I am certain there is a systematic way in which we can incorporate the information to help us determine the best possible production schedule." A substantial amount of discussion took place following Baker's comments.

It was well past noon when Henry suggested that outside help was needed if they were going to devise a production schedule that was better than the one he had previously proposed. Henry was asked to contact the local university to see whether a student group might be available to help.

Chapter 4

DUALITY AND SENSITIVITY ANALYSIS

Chapter Outline

Chapter 4

Why You Need to Know

Only a few years passed between the introduction of the simplex solution procedure and its first organizational applications. This is unusually fast for what is essentially a mathematical matrix manipulation procedure. There seem to be two reasons for this quick response: first, linear programming models can be used to represent many practical decision-making situations; and second, the simplex procedure for solving linear programming problems quickly developed a full set of economic interpretations.

To expand on the first point, all successful management science tools were developed in response to important organizational problems. Linear programming models were developed rapidly because they allowed decision makers to address important issues, and the simplex procedure allowed easily understood economic principles to be incorporated in its interpretation. If the simplex procedure did not provide for economic interpretations, it would be much less widely used.

The rapid adoption of the simplex procedure for economic decision making is largely due to the fact that every linear programming model (referred to as a primal problem) has a dual, a kind of inverted mirror image of the original model. The economic interpretation of the simplex solution procedure is based on the relationship between the primal and dual models.

When we first discussed linear programming models, we stated that, to be successfully modeled, the physical situation had to satisfy three assumptions:

1. The relationships must be linear.
2. The decision variables must be infinitely divisible.
3. The model's objective function and constraints must be known with certainty.

Much of what is discussed in the next few chapters, and in more advanced texts, is an effort to show how to modify the simplex solution procedure to deal with practical applications which do not meet the last two of these restrictive assumptions.

In many cases, the most restrictive of these assumptions is the one requiring that the objective function and constraints be known with certainty. Organizations need models to help managers make decisions about the future, not to optimize the past. Yet whenever you look into the future, you add an element of uncertainty. For example, Rigley's Nursery presently makes a profit of $5 for each apple tree sold and $12 for each pine tree, but will these profit levels continue next year? By using the current profit figures as objective function coefficients in a linear programming planning model, the company would be assuming that the profit levels will stay the same.

Most practical decision-making situations have an element of uncertainty; and for linear programming to be useful, it must have some method of dealing with this uncertainty. The technique used to deal with uncertainty in the linear programming model is sensitivity analysis. While sensitivity analysis does not directly incorporate uncertainty in the model, it will indicate how much variation can be allowed in certain parts of the model, particularly in the objective function coefficients and the amounts of constraining resources available (the right-hand sides), before the current solution becomes nonoptimal.

This chapter introduces the concepts of duality and sensitivity analysis. You should become familiar with both to more fully appreciate the role of linear programming in business decision making.

Chapter Objectives

The purpose of this chapter is to extend the applications of the simplex technique introduced in Chapter 3. We will first consider economic interpretations of the simplex tableau and solution procedure. These economic interpretations contributed greatly to the acceptance of linear programming by business decision makers and economists. We will also introduce the concept and interpretation of the dual in linear programming.

Second, we will examine how uncertainty can be considered within the simplex model by showing how sensitivity analysis is performed. In particular, the objectives of this chapter are:

1. To show that every linear programming model has an accompanying dual model and that any problem can be solved by working with either the original model (the primal) or the dual.
2. To discuss the economic insights that can be gained by understanding the relationship between the solutions to the primal and dual problems.
3. To discuss the need to incorporate uncertainty in the linear programming model.
4. To relate the concept of sensitivity analysis to the graphical solution of a linear programming model.
5. To demonstrate how to perform sensitivity analysis on the objective function coefficients in a linear programming model.
6. To demonstrate how to perform sensitivity analysis on the constraint values (right-hand sides) in a linear programming model.

4-1 THE DUAL TO A LINEAR PROGRAMMING MODEL

In Chapters 2 and 3, we considered how to formulate and solve linear programming problems. But this is often the start, not the end, of a manager's task. Once the optimal solution has been found, the manager is interested in attaching economic interpretations to the optimal operating point. These economic interpretations extend beyond the optimal values of the decision variables. For instance, at the optimal operating point, some constraints will be binding. If the manager is able to acquire additional units of these binding constraints, how much should he or she be willing to spend? Or perhaps the manager will be approached by someone wanting to purchase some of the company's existing resources. Should they be sold, and if so, for what price?

The original linear programming problem is called the **primal problem**. Its solution can provide the answers to many questions. However, much terminology associated with the economic analysis of linear programming models is based on the relationship between the primal problem and a well-defined **dual problem**.

THE CONCEPT OF DUALITY

Soon after the simplex solution procedure was introduced in 1947, management scientists realized that the same procedure could be used to solve two related models: (1) the model formed by the original objective function and constraints, called the primal model, and (2) a related linear programming model called the dual.

Consider the following example involving The Dalles Windsurf Company, which was started 3 years ago in The Dalles, Oregon. The company presently makes two types of windsurfing boards, the Pro and the Master. It earns a profit of $50 on each Pro and $70 on each Master. Each polyurethane board is poured in a mold, put in a curing oven, and then hand-sanded and painted. The major limiting resources are the capacity of the curing ovens and the space needed to hand-sand and paint the boards. The company presently has 5 curing ovens, each operating 40 hours a week (200 total units of capacity), and 10 sanding and painting stations, each used for 40 hours a week (400 units of capacity). Each Pro board takes 3 hours in the curing oven, and each Master takes 2 hours. In addition, each Pro takes 4 hours to sand and paint and each Master takes 6 hours.

Assuming The Dalles Windsurf Company is interested in maximizing profit, the situation just described can be modeled as the following linear programming problem:

The objective function becomes:

$$\text{Maximize} \quad Z = 50x_1 + 70x_2$$

Subject to the following constraints:

$$3x_1 + 2x_2 \le 200 \text{ (5 ovens} \times \text{40 hours)}$$
$$4x_1 + 6x_2 \le 400 \text{ (10 stations} \times \text{40 hours)}$$

where:

x_1 = number of Pro boards produced

x_2 = number of Master boards produced

To solve this problem using the simplex procedure, we would first convert to the standard form by adding a slack variable for each constraint:

$$\text{Maximize} \quad Z = 50x_1 + 70x_2 + 0s_1 + 0s_2$$

Subject to:

$$3x_1 + 2x_2 + 1s_1 + 0s_2 = 200$$
$$4x_1 + 6x_2 + 0s_1 + 1s_2 = 400$$

This problem is graphed in Figure 4-1, where the optimal point is shown to be:

$x_1 = 40$

$x_2 = 40$

$s_1 = 0$ (all oven capacity is used)

$s_2 = 0$ (all painting/sanding capacity is used)

$Z = 40(\$50) + 40(\$70) = \$4800$

This linear programming problem can also be solved using the simplex technique. The final tableau for this procedure is shown in Table 4-1. Thus, if The Dalles

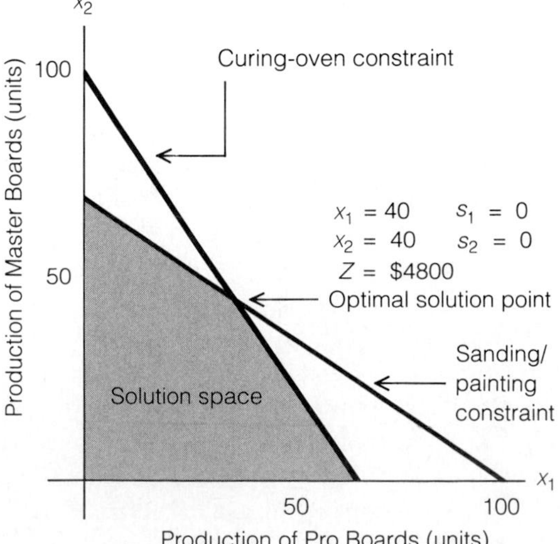

Figure 4-1
The Dalles Windsurf Co. primal problem

Table 4-1 THE DALLES WINDSURF COMPANY: FINAL TABLEAU FOR PRIMAL PROBLEM

		Variables				
		x_1	x_2	s_1	s_2	
Basis	c_j	50	70	0	0	b_i
x_1	50	1	0	3/5	−1/5	40
x_2	70	0	1	−2/5	3/10	40
	Z_j	50	70	2	11	4800
	$c_j - Z_j$	0	0	−2	−11	

Windsurf Company makes 40 Pro boards and 40 Master boards, under the current resource limitations it will maximize its profits at $4800.

Upon reviewing the linear programming results, the managers recognize that oven capacity and painting/sanding capacity would be completely used if production is set at the optimal point. The slack variables for these two resources equal zero in the optimal solution. Thus, the limited availability of these resources will limit the amount of profit which the company can generate from its operations. This finding leads the managers to view their situation from two perspectives. First, if additional resource capacity could be made available, how much would the company be willing to pay for each unit of added capacity? Second, if the company could rent out some of its oven or painting/sanding capacity (thereby lowering the amount it could use for its own production), what price should it charge for each of the resources?

In Chapter 3, we introduced this concept of **shadow prices**. There, we showed that the $c_j - Z_j$ row of the final simplex tableau contains the shadow prices, which represent the value of adding a unit of a constraining resource in the primal problem. Table 4-1 shows the final simplex tableau for the present problem. The values -2 and -11 in the $c_j - Z_j$ row for variables s_1 and s_2 indicate that an additional unit of oven capacity would be worth $2 and an additional unit of painting/sanding capacity would be worth $11. The values also represent the price The Dalles Windsurf Company should charge per unit if it were to rent out some of these resources.

FORMULATING THE DUAL TO A PRIMAL MAXIMIZATION MODEL

An alternative line of reasoning which involves formulating and solving the dual linear programming problem can be used to arrive at these same results. Consider the possibility that another company might wish to rent The Dalles Windsurf Company's oven and painting/sanding capacity. Potentially, 200 units of oven capacity and 400 units of painting/sanding capacity exist. The question is, What price should be charged per unit for each resource?

Suppose we let d_1 be the per unit price of oven capacity and d_2 be the per unit price for painting/sanding capacity. If the other company were to rent all available units of both resources, the cost would be:

$$\text{Total cost} = 200d_1 + 400d_2$$

The company renting the resources would naturally want to pay the lowest rental possible. Therefore, the problem facing The Dalles Windsurf Company is what price to charge to make sure that it is as well off as if it had used the resources to produce its own products.

The objective function for the other company can be stated as follows:

$$\text{Minimize} \quad Z = 200d_1 + 400d_2$$

Since The Dalles Windsurf Company will not rent out its resources unless it can realize as much profit as if it had used the resources itself, there are some constraints. First, to make a Pro board, 3 units of oven capacity and 4 units of painting/sanding capacity are needed. Since each Pro board earns a \$50 profit, the resources that go into making a Pro board would be rented out at:

$$3d_1 + 4d_2$$

The rental rates must be set so that the resources which are rented earn at least as much as could have been earned from making Pro boards. Thus, we can formulate the following constraint:

$$3d_1 + 4d_2 \geq 50$$

We can use similar thinking to formulate a constraint associated with not producing Master boards, as follows:

$$2d_1 + 6d_2 \geq 70$$

This change from thinking about the problem as one of maximizing profits from board production to one of minimizing resource rental cost has brought us to a new model formulation, which is called the dual to the original primal problem. We state the dual model as follows:

$$\text{Minimize} \quad Z = 200d_1 + 400d_2$$

Subject to:

$$3d_1 + 4d_2 \geq 50$$
$$2d_1 + 6d_2 \geq 70$$

To solve the dual problem, we first have to convert the problem into standard form. Because the constraints are "greater than or equal to (≥)," we do this by adding surplus and artificial variables. The standard form becomes:

$$\text{Minimize} \quad Z = 200d_1 + 400d_2 + 0w_1 + 0w_2 + My_1 + My_2$$

Subject to:

$$3d_1 + 4d_2 - 1w_1 + 0w_2 + 1y_1 + 0y_2 = 50$$
$$2d_1 + 6d_2 + 0w_1 - 1w_2 + 0y_1 + 1y_2 = 70$$

This problem is graphed in Figure 4-2. The optimal point is shown to be:

$$d_1 = 2$$
$$d_2 = 11$$
$$w_1 = 0$$
$$w_2 = 0$$
$$Z = 4800$$

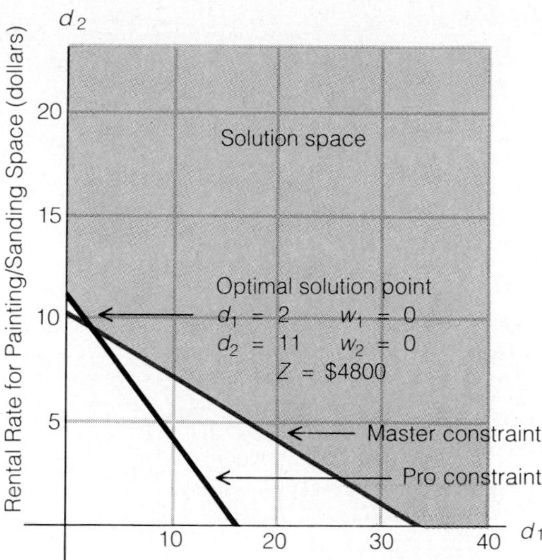

Figure 4-2
The Dalles Windsurf Co. dual problem

Table 4-2 shows the final tableau for the simplex solution procedure. To minimize rental costs, The Dalles Windsurf Company would have to charge \$2 per unit for the oven resource and \$11 per unit for the painting/sanding resource, for a total cost to the renter of \$4800.

This example demonstrates the steps required to formulate the dual to a linear programming problem. It also illustrates several important points about the relationship between the primal linear programming problem and the corresponding dual problem:

1. If the primal problem has a maximization objective function, the dual problem has a minimization objective function. Likewise, if the primal has a minimization objective, the dual will have a maximization objective.
2. For each constraint in the primal problem there is a corresponding decision variable in the dual problem. For this problem the dual decision variables are:

   d_1 = economic value per unit for the curing oven
   d_2 = economic value per unit of painting/sanding space
3. The right-hand-side values of the original problem become the objective-function coefficient values in the dual problem.
4. The constraining values (right-hand-side values) for the dual problem are determined by the objective-function coefficients of the original problem (50 and 70 in this case).
5. The constraint coefficients associated with a single decision variable (column) in the original problem become the coefficients of a constraint (row) in the corresponding dual problem. In addition, all "less than or equal to (≤)" constraints in the original problem become "greater than or equal to (≥)" constraints in the dual problem.

Table 4-2 THE DALLES WINDSURF COMPANY: FINAL TABLEAU FOR DUAL PROBLEM

		Variables						
		d_1	d_2	w_1	y_1	w_2	y_2	
Basis	c_j	200	400	0	M	0	M	b_i
y_1	200	1	0	$-3/5$	$3/5$	$2/5$	$-2/5$	2
y_2	400	0	1	$1/5$	$-1/5$	$-3/10$	$3/10$	11
	Z_j	200	400	-40	40	-40	40	4800
	$c_j - Z_j$	0	0	40	$M - 40$	40	$M - 40$	

4-2 COMPARING THE PRIMAL AND DUAL SOLUTIONS

Despite the fact that the objective of The Dalles Windsurf Company's primal problem is maximization and the dual problem's objective is minimization, both have an optimal objective-function value of \$4800. This is no coincidence. An important property of the primal-dual relationship is that *if both the primal and dual problems have solutions, the objective-function values of both problems will be equal at the optimal corner point.*

We can look at the two objective functions in greater depth:

1. *The primal objective function:* In the primal problem, the decision variables represent the two outputs. The primal objective function is formed by knowing the unit profitability of two products. The optimal point determines how much of each product must be produced to maximize profitability.
2. *The dual objective function:* In the dual problem, the decision variables represent the economic value of the two resources required in the production process: curing-oven time and painting/sanding space. The optimal point determines the value of each of these two resources such that the total cost of the input to the process is minimized.

In looking at the final tableaus for the two problems (Table 4-3), we can make some interesting comparisons. First, the solution values to the dual problem, $d_1 = 2$ and $d_2 = 11$, are the same (except for the negative signs) as the net contribution values, $c_j - Z_j$, for the slack variables in the primal problem. Recall from Chapter 3, and from our earlier discussion in this chapter, that the net contribution values are called shadow prices. The shadow prices reflect the marginal value of an additional unit of a resource. At the optimal solution point, the entire availability of curing-oven time, 200 hours, is used. None remains. The -2 in the net contribution row of the final primal tableau means that if 1 less hour of curing time (s_1) had been available (199 instead of 200), the objective-function value would be decreased by \$2. If decreasing the amount of curing-oven time by 1 hour will decrease the objective function by \$2, the implication is that increasing the amount of curing time by 1 hour (from 200 to 201) should increase the objective function by \$2. Since an additional unit of curing capacity will increase the objective function by \$2, this is the economic value to the company of acquiring an additional unit of curing capacity.

Table 4-3 THE DALLES WINDSURF COMPANY: COMPARISON OF FINAL TABLEAUS

Primal Problem

		x_1	x_2	s_1	s_2	
Basis	c_j	50	70	0	0	b_i
x_1	50	1	0	3/5	−1/5	40
x_2	70	0	1	−2/5	3/10	40
	Z_j	50	70	2	11	4800
	$c_j - Z_j$	0	0	−2	−11	

Dual Problem

		d_1	d_2	w_1	y_1	w_2	y_2	
Basis	c_j	200	400	0	M	0	M	b_i
d_1	200	1	0	−3/5	3/5	2/5	−2/5	2
d_2	400	0	1	1/5	−1/5	−3/10	3/10	11
	Z_j	200	400	−40	40	−40	40	4800
	$c_j - Z_j$	0	0	40	$M - 40$	40	$M - 40$	

Likewise, the $c_j - Z_j$ row of the primal tableau in Table 4-3 shows that a reduction in the sanding/painting capacity (s_2) of 1 unit will reduce the value of the objective function in the final solution by \$11. Conversely, if we add another unit of this resource, the objective function will increase by \$11. Thus, \$11 is the shadow price of this constraining resource.

The fact that the optimal solution to the dual provides values which are equivalent to the shadow prices in the final tableau of the primal problem illustrates the importance of the dual from an economic analysis viewpoint. *The solution to the dual problem provides the economic values of the resource constraints for the primal problem at its optimal solution.*

Many computerized linear programming packages—including MASTER, which accompanies this text—print out the solutions to both the primal and dual problems. Figure 4-3 shows the output produced by the MASTER software package for The Dalles Windsurf Company problem. The dual values provide the economic values of the constraints in the linear programming problem without having the final tableau printed out.

A second comparison between the primal and dual solutions is that all the information for both the primal and the dual can be found in the final tableau solution to either problem. For example, if we look at the $c_j - Z_j$ row for the dual in Table 4-3, we see the values 40 for w_1 and 40 for w_2. These values are the optimal production levels determined by the primal problem. Therefore, we see that any linear programming problem can be solved as either a primal or dual problem.

```
        LINEAR PROGRAMMING FORMULATION

OBJECTIVE FUNCTION:
   MAXIMIZE Z =
      50.00  Variab 1     70.00 Variab 2

SUBJECT TO:
      3.00Variab 1 +    2.00Variab 2 <=     200.00
      4.00Variab 1 +    6.00Variab 2 <=     400.00

     THE DECISION VARIABLES ARE    1. THROUGH   2.
     THE SLACK VARIABLES ARE       3. THROUGH   4.

        OPTIMAL SOLUTION

ITERATIONS =   2.

OBJECTIVE FUNCTION =       4800.000

DECISION VARIABLES:

VARIABLE   NAME    VALUE

    1.     Variab 1       40.000
    2.     Variab 2       40.000

SLACK OR SURPLUS VARIABLES:

VARIABLE   NAME            VALUE

DUAL RESULTS

VARIABLE   NAME             VALUE
           Variab 1         0.000
           Variab 2         0.000
           CONSTRAINT 1.    2.000
           CONSTRAINT 2.   11.000
```

Figure 4-3
The Dalles Windsurf Co. problem: MASTER output

A NOTE ON THE ECONOMIC INTERPRETATION OF SHADOW PRICES

We have indicated several times that the shadow prices for a primal problem can be used to determine the economic value of the right-hand-side resources. Likewise, the optimal values for the decision variables in the dual provide the same information. When a constraint's right-hand side represents the available amount of a particular resource, the shadow price (or dual value) is often interpreted as the amount one would be willing to pay for an additional unit of the resource. However, this interpretation needs a little explanation.

The key to correctly interpreting the shadow prices rests with understanding the difference between sunk costs and relevant costs. A **sunk cost** is one that will be incurred regardless of the level of the decision variables. For instance, in The Dalles Windsurf example, if the company owns the ovens and their cost will be incurred regardless of the number of units of Pro and Master boards that are made, then the oven cost is a sunk cost. However, if the company leases the ovens and is charged only for their use, then the oven cost would be considered a **relevant cost.**

When determining the objective-function coefficients, the relevant costs should be subtracted out so that the coefficients reflect the per unit profit. On the other hand, the objective-function coefficients do not take into account any sunk costs. When a resource cost is a sunk cost, the shadow price can be interpreted as the marginal value of an additional unit of the resource (in this case, increasing the oven capacity to 201). If the resource cost is a relevant cost, the shadow price must be interpreted as the amount by which the value of the resource exceeds its current cost on a per unit basis. Thus, for relevant cost resources, the shadow price is the amount over and above the normal cost that one would be willing to pay for an additional unit of the resource. In this example, if oven space was leased at \$20 per hour, the objective-function profit coefficient should reflect this cost. A shadow price of -2 means the company would be willing to pay \$22 for an additional hour of oven time.

When sunk costs are present in an application, they have to be deducted from the final objective-function value to arrive at the correct economic outcome. We will discuss this concept later in the chapter. We will also consider the economic interpretation of resources that have a zero shadow price.

FINAL COMMENTS ON THE PRIMAL-DUAL RELATIONSHIP

The primal-dual relationship assumes that, if the original problem is a maximization problem, all constraints are "less than or equal to ($\leq$)" and, if the original problem is a minimization problem, all constraints are "greater than or equal to ($\geq$)." This may seem to be a restricting assumption, until we remember that the direction of an inequality in a constraint can be reversed by multiplying the constraint by -1. For example, if the constraint is:

$$4x_1 + 6x_2 \leq 12$$

it can be converted to:

$$-4x_1 - 6x_2 \geq -12$$

In addition, an "equal to (=)" constraint can be changed to two constraints, one "greater than or equal to ($\geq$)" and the other "less than or equal to ($\leq$)." For instance, if the constraint is:

$$4x_1 + 6x_2 = 12$$

it can be converted into these two constraints:

$$4x_1 + 6x_2 \leq 12$$

and

$$4x_1 + 6x_2 \geq 12$$

4-3 THE NEED FOR SENSITIVITY ANALYSIS

The solution to a linear programming problem is "optimal" for the problem specified. That is, for a given objective function and set of constraints, the solution reached through linear programming will be a maximum or minimum, depending on the objective. When you, as a decision maker, encounter an application for linear programming, your role will be to correctly formulate the model. Once you know the precise values of the objective-function coefficients, and once you have correctly defined the constraints, including the right-hand sides, the solution will be optimal.

Unfortunately, in many applications, specifying the model won't be that easy. For instance, you may have difficulty determining the exact value of one or more of the objective-function coefficients. You might have a pretty good idea about what a constraint's right-hand-side value should be, but its exact value may be uncertain.

For example, suppose you are setting up a linear programming problem to maximize net income for a plywood manufacturing plant. Linear programming is to be used to determine the optimal product mix for the four types of plywood the plant makes. To specify the linear programming model, you must know the net profit per unit for each type of plywood. These profits become the objective-function coefficients. But the net profit per unit depends on the sales price and the direct costs of producing each type of plywood. Although you can look at past data for these values, you cannot know for certain whether the price and costs will be the same in the future planning period. Thus, there is some uncertainty about the objective-function coefficients.

You might also be able to identify the categories of capacity constraints on production, such as demand, maximum inventory, raw materials, labor, equipment, and so forth. However, are you really sure exactly how much of each you will actually have? For instance, you might plan for 1000 hours of production time on the peeler machine. But what if mechanical problems reduce that amount? Or what if the actual amounts of the various raw materials are not exactly what you had planned?

These questions about both the objective-function coefficients and the constraint right-hand sides introduce *uncertainty* into the situation. Linear programming assumes that all these values are known with certainty, but in reality this is usually not the case. One of the most important extensions of linear programming is **sensitivity analysis**, which allows decision makers to consider the uncertainties they face in setting up a linear programming model.

Sensitivity analysis gives the decision maker a means for determining how much change can be allowed in an objective-function coefficient or the right-hand side of a constraint before a new optimal corner point solution is reached.

Consider the following example. John Powers owns a winery and a 100-acre vineyard near Sonoma, California. He has signed a contract to produce both white (Reisling) and rosé wines for Taylor Brothers Winery this summer and is trying to decide how much of each type to produce. The contract calls for Taylor Brothers to pay \$4.00 per gallon for rosé and \$3.50 per gallon for the white wine. After estimating manufacturing expenses, John estimates his profit will be \$.60 for each gallon of rosé and \$.45 for each gallon of white wine.

John has 60 acres of green grapes, which he thinks will yield 1100 bushels per acre, and 40 acres of red grapes, which should yield 1200 bushels per acre. Each gallon of white wine takes 2 bushels of green grapes; each gallon of rosé takes 1 bushel of green and 2 bushels of red grapes. Because he knows that each gallon of either wine takes 1 pound of sugar, John has contracted for 40,000 pounds. From past records, he knows that producing 100 gallons of white wine takes 2 worker-hours and 100 gallons of rosé takes 3 hours. John will have 1000 worker-hours available this summer.

Linear programming can be used to help decide the optimal production mix.

The decision variables are:

x_1 = gallons of white wine

x_2 = gallons of rosé wine

Since John is interested in maximizing profits, the objective function is:

Maximize $Z = .45x_1 + .60x_2$

The constraints are determined by the four limiting resources: green grapes, red grapes, sugar, and worker-hours. The constraints become:

Green grapes	$2x_1 + 1x_2 \leq 66{,}000$	(60 acres × 1100)
Red grapes	$0x_1 + 2x_2 \leq 48{,}000$	(40 acres × 1200)
Sugar	$1x_1 + 1x_2 \leq 40{,}000$	
Worker-hours	$.02x_1 + .03x_2 \leq 1{,}000$	

The solution to this linear programming problem is:

Gallons of white wine produced = x_1 = 20,000

Gallons of rosé wine produced = x_2 = 20,000

Bushels of green grapes available = slack 1 = s_1 = 6000

Bushels of red grapes available = slack 2 = s_2 = 8000

Pounds of sugar available = slack 3 = s_3 = 0

Worker-hours available = slack 4 = s_4 = 0

Objective-function value = \$21,000

In analyzing this solution, John recognizes that:

1. He probably will not have exactly 66,000 bushels of green grapes available, since some acres will yield above or below his estimate of 1100 bushels per acre.
2. He also will not have exactly 48,000 bushels of red grapes available, since some acres will yield above or below his estimate of 1200 bushels per acre.
3. Because of spoilage and distributor errors, he may have more or less than 40,000 pounds of sugar available when it is needed.
4. For a variety of reasons, he will probably not have exactly 1000 worker-hours of labor available.

In addition:

5. John's estimate of profitability for each gallon of both wines is based on his estimate of expenses. Therefore, his estimates of \$.60 for each gallon of rosé and \$.45 for each gallon of white are likely not to be the exact profit figures.
6. Depending on the quality of this year's harvest, he may need more or less than the estimated amount of grapes to make each gallon of wine.
7. Since the natural sugar content of grapes varies from year to year, he may need more or less than 1 pound of sugar for each gallon of wine.
8. Depending on the skill of the workers he can hire, his estimate of worker-hours needed to make 100 gallons of wine may change.

Although all of these uncertainties complicate the situation for John, he can attempt to deal with them by using sensitivity analysis. He can count on sensitivity analysis to provide the answer to a basic question: By how much can the various parameters of the linear programming problem change before the optimal solution will change?

The sections that follow discuss how to use sensitivity analysis on the objective-function coefficients and on the right-hand-side values. The explanation of how to use sensitivity analysis on the constraint coefficients is left to a more advanced course in linear programming.

4-4 SENSITIVITY ANALYSIS ON THE OBJECTIVE-FUNCTION COEFFICIENTS

In the John Powers example, the objective-function coefficients indicate the per gallon profit from each type of wine. Recall that the per gallon profit for white wine is \$.45 and the profit for rosé is \$.60 per gallon. Even though rosé is more profitable, the linear programming model has determined that profit is maximized by producing an equal amount (20,000 gallons), of both wines. But how much could each objective-function coefficient change before the optimal number of gallons of each wine would change? To answer this question, we can perform sensitivity analysis on the objective-function coefficients.

In linear programming, sensitivity analysis works by using an *incremental change* approach. Thus, through sensitivity analysis, we can examine the effects that changes in the objective-function coefficients have on the linear programming solution. When the changes to an objective-function coefficient are small, the optimal solution may not change. But at a certain point, a change in the size of the objective coefficient will produce new optimal values for the decision variables. For example, small changes in the profitability of either wine would probably not cause the optimal product mix to change, but large changes in profitability would. Thus, increasing the profitability of rosé from \$.60 to \$.61 might not cause John to produce more rosé, but increasing its profitability to \$10.00 per gallon would most likely prompt him to make as much rosé as possible. Now the question is, At what point do the changes become large enough to cause the linear programming solution to move to a new corner point? We can answer this question by performing sensitivity analysis on the objective-function coefficients.

THE GRAPHICAL APPROACH

We will first use a graphical approach to sensitivity analysis to demonstrate the logic of the process and then extend it to the simplex solution procedure.

We begin by looking at the corner-point solution for the John Powers linear programming problem shown in Figure 4-4. Recall that in a maximization problem the

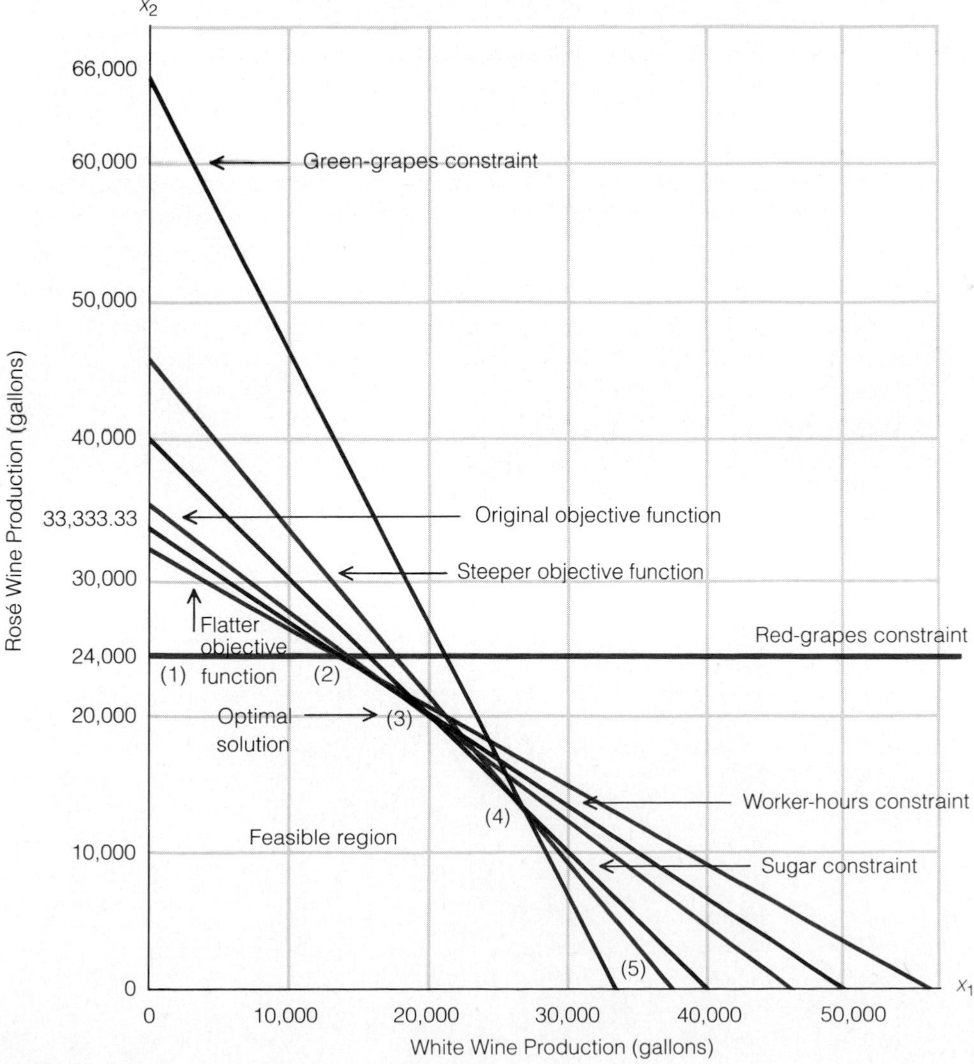

Figure 4-4
John Powers problem: small changes in the objective function

optimal point is at the corner of the solution space that allows the objective function to move as far away from the origin as possible. If we change the slope of the objective function by a small amount, the optimal solution will remain at the same corner point as in Figure 4-4. However, if the slope of the objective function is changed enough, a new corner in the solution space will become the optimal point. To determine how much change in the slope will be required to move the solution to a new corner, consider the following reasoning:

1. The corner-point solution to a linear programming problem is determined by the intersection of two or more (only two in this problem) constraints. For John Powers, the two constraints are sugar and worker-hour availability.
2. The slope of the objective function is determined by the objective-function coefficients, .45 and .60 in this example. Changing either of these coefficients will change the slope of the objective function. However, for small changes in the slope, corner 1 in Figure 4-4 will remain optimal.
3. If the objective-function slope becomes flatter, at some point the optimal solution will move to corner 2 in Figure 4-4. When this occurs, the slope of the objective function will become equal to the slope of the line determined by the labor constraint. As discussed in Chapter 3, this will result in **multiple optimal solutions.**
4. If the objective-function slope becomes steeper, at some point the optimal solution will move to corner 4 in Figure 4-4. When this occurs, the slope of the objective function will be equal to the slope of the line determined by the sugar constraint.

Thus, the sensitivity question is, How much can the objective-function slope change before the optimal point moves to an adjacent corner? The slope can be changed by changing the coefficient on variable x_1 or x_2. Consequently, we must examine each coefficient separately to determine the range of values that will retain the original solution for variables x_1 and x_2.

Sensitivity of the x_1 Coefficient

The constraints involving worker-hours and sugar availability form the optimal-solution corner point of the feasible region. To determine how much the objective-function coefficient on variable x_1 can change without changing the optimal solution, we must determine the slope of these two constraints.

The line forming the boundary of the worker-hour constraint is determined by this equation:

$$.02x_1 + .03x_2 = 1000$$

If we isolate x_2 on one side of the equation, we get:

$$x_2 = 33{,}333.33 - .02x_1/.03$$

Note that this equation has the form $Y = A + BX$, which is the equation for a straight line where $A =$ intercept and $B =$ slope. Therefore the slope of this line is $-.02/.03$, or $-2/3$, and the intercept on the x_2 axis is 33,333.33.

The line forming the boundary of the sugar constraint is determined by this equation:

$$x_1 + x_2 = 40{,}000$$

Converting this to the slope-intercept form for the equation of a straight line, we find:

$$x_2 = 40{,}000 - x_1$$

The slope of this line is -1, and the intercept on the x_2 axis is 40,000.

These two lines intersect to form the optimal corner point, given the present objective function. To move to corner 2 in Figure 4-4, the slope of the objective function must become at least as flat as the worker-hour constraint line having a slope of $-2/3$. To move to corner 4, the slope of the objective function must become at least as steep as the sugar constraint line with a slope of -1. Therefore, the current corner point will remain optimal if:

$$-1 \leq \text{slope of the objective function} \leq -2/3$$

We can determine the slope of the objective function for the John Powers problem by converting it to slope-intercept form using the following procedure:

$$Z = .45x_1 + .60x_2$$

Then we isolate x_2 on the left side:

$$x_2 = Z/.60 - .45x_1/.60$$

The slope of the objective function is $-.45/.60$, or $-3/4$, which is within the above range (-1 to $-2/3$). The coefficient of the x_1 decision variable (c_1) is currently .45. If it is increased to .60, the slope would change to -1, one of the limiting values. Likewise, if the coefficient is decreased to .40, the slope would become $-2/3$, the other limiting value. Therefore, as long as the objective coefficient, c_1, remains this range:

$$.40 \leq c_1 \leq .60$$

the corner-point solution 1 in Figure 4-4 will remain optimal.

Note that as the coefficient, c_1, changes value within the range \$.40 to \$.60, the value of the objective function will either increase or decrease but the values of x_1 and x_2 will not change. As long as the profit on the white wine stays within the range \$.40 to \$.60 (and the profit on rosé stays at \$.60), the production levels $x_1 = 20{,}000$ gallons and $x_2 = 20{,}000$ gallons will remain optimal. Of course, this assumes that the constraints remain as originally stated.

Sensitivity of the x_2 Coefficient

We determine the sensitivity range for the objective-function coefficient of the x_2 decision variable in the same manner as for the coefficient on variable x_1. In the previous section, we saw that the range of values over which the slope of the objective function can vary while maintaining the present solution point is:

$$-1 \leq \text{slope of the objective function} \leq -2/3$$

The slope of the objective function is currently $-.45/.60$, which falls within the range -1 to $-2/3$. The coefficient of the x_2 decision variable is presently .60. This coefficient on x_2 could decrease to .45 before the slope would reach -1. If the coefficient is decreased below .45, the slope would increase above -1 and the optimal corner-point solution would change.

Likewise, if the coefficient on x_2 increased to .675, the slope would become $-2/3$, the other limiting value. Therefore, as long as the coefficient, c_2, remains in this range:

$$.45 \leq c_2 \leq .675$$

the corner point 3 in Figure 4-4 will remain the optimal solution. This range assumes that we are holding the coefficient on x_1 constant at .45. Thus, if the per gallon profit on white wine is \$.45, the plan to produce 20,000 gallons of rosé and 20,000 gallons of white wine will be optimal as long as the profit on the rosé is in the range \$.45 to \$.675. Remember that as the coefficient, c_2, changes value, the objective function value (total profit) will either increase or decrease, but the optimal values of x_1 and x_2 will not change as long as c_2 is in the range .45 to .675.

THE SIMPLEX SOLUTION PROCEDURE

Sensitivity analysis using the graphical representation of a linear programming problem is limited to problems which have two decision variables. However, since actual applications have many more decision variables, we need to be able to extend the logic of sensitivity analysis to problems involving any number of decision variables. This means that we need a method for performing sensitivity analysis using the simplex tableau.

As we indicated earlier, you will use a computer software package to solve actual linear programming problems. These software packages typically use the simplex solution method and are capable of performing sensitivity analysis. But before moving to the computer examples, you need to understand how sensitivity analysis is performed using the simplex solution method.

The Simplex Tableau

To illustrate how sensitivity analysis is performed on the objective-function coefficients, we will continue with the John Powers example. The objective function and constraints, shown below, are represented in the initial tableau shown in Table 4-4.

$$\text{Maximize} \quad Z = .45x_1 + .60x_2$$

Subject to:

Green grapes	$2x_1 + 1x_2 \leq 66{,}000$
Red grapes	$0x_1 + 2x_2 \leq 48{,}000$
Sugar	$1x_1 + 1x_2 \leq 40{,}000$
Worker-hours	$.02x_1 + .03x_2 \leq 1{,}000$

Table 4-4 JOHN POWERS PROBLEM: INITIAL TABLEAU

		Variables						
		x_1	x_2	s_1	s_2	s_3	s_4	
Basis	c_j	.45	.60	0	0	0	0	b_i
s_1	0	2	1	1	0	0	0	66,000
s_2	0	0	2	0	1	0	0	48,000
s_3	0	1	1	0	0	1	0	40,000
s_4	0	$2/100$	$3/100$	0	0	0	1	1,000
	Z_j	0	0	0	0	0	0	0
	$c_j - Z_j$	.45	.60	0	0	0	0	

Table 4-5 JOHN POWERS PROBLEM: FINAL TABLEAU

		Variables						
		x_1	x_2	s_1	s_2	s_3	s_4	
Basis	c_j	.45	.60	0	0	0	0	b_i
s_1	0	0	0	1	0	−4	100	6,000
s_2	0	0	0	0	1	4	−200	8,000
x_2	.60	0	1	0	0	−2	100	20,000
x_1	.45	1	0	0	0	3	−100	20,000
	Z_j	.45	.60	0	0	.15	15	21,000
	$c_j - Z_j$	0	0	0	0	−.15	−15	

By following the simplex rules, the tableau shown in Table 4-4 is converted into the final tableau shown in Table 4-5.

To incorporate a small change in the objective-function coefficient of x_1, we allow coefficient c_1 to change by a small amount, Δc_1. The idea is to determine how this small change will affect the final tableau which contains the final values of all variables in the model. Incorporating the small change in c_1 changes the initial tableau, as shown in Table 4-6.

According to the mechanics of the simplex tableau, the c_j values are used only to determine the entering variables and thus show up only in the c_j and $c_j - Z_j$ rows. Therefore, the change in the initial tableau will be carried into the final tableau in the manner shown in Table 4-7.

The tableau shown in Table 4-7 will remain optimal as long as the values in the $c_j - Z_j$ row do not become positive. Therefore, to remain optimal, we must have:

$$-.15 - 3\Delta c_1 \le 0 \qquad \text{and} \qquad -15 + 100\Delta c_1 \le 0$$

Working with the first inequality, we can isolate c_1 as follows:

$$-.15 - 3\Delta c_1 \le 0$$

or

$$-3\Delta c_1 \le .15$$

$$\Delta c_1 \ge -.05$$

Table 4-6 JOHN POWERS PROBLEM WITH A SMALL CHANGE IN c_1: INITIAL TABLEAU

		Variables						
		x_1	x_2	s_1	s_2	s_3	s_4	
Basis	c_j	$.45 + \Delta c_1$	.60	0	0	0	0	b_i
s_1	0	2	1	1	0	0	0	66,000
s_2	0	0	2	0	1	0	0	48,000
s_3	0	1	1	0	0	1	0	40,000
s_4	0	2/100	3/100	0	0	0	1	1,000
	Z_j	0	0	0	0	0	0	0
	$c_j - Z_j$	$.45 + \Delta c_1$	.60	0	0	0	0	

Table 4-7 JOHN POWERS PROBLEM WITH A SMALL CHANGE IN c_1: FINAL TABLEAU

		Variables						
		x_1	x_2	s_1	s_2	s_3	s_4	
Basis	c_j	$.45 + \Delta c_j$	.60	0	0	0	0	b_i
s_1	0	0	0	1	0	-4	-100	6,000
s_2	0	0	0	0	1	4	200	8,000
x_2	.60	0	1	0	0	-2	100	20,000
x_1	$.45 + \Delta c_1$	1	0	0	0	3	-100	20,000
	Z_j	$.45 + \Delta c_1$	.60	0	0	$.15 + 3\Delta c_1$	$15 - 100\Delta c_1$	$21{,}000 + 20{,}000\Delta c_1$
	$c_j - Z_j$	0	0	0	0	$-.15 - 3\Delta c_1$	$-15 + 100\Delta c_1$	

From the second inequality, we find:

$$-15 + 100\Delta c_1 \le 0$$

or

$$100\Delta c_1 \le 15$$

$$\Delta c_1 \le .15$$

Combining these two inequalities, we find the range of values which Δc_1 can assume without changing the final tableau:

$$-.05 \le \Delta c_1 \le .15$$

This means that c_1 can be reduced by an amount up to .05, or increased by an amount up to .15, before the solution shown in Table 4-7 is no longer optimal.

Since c_1 has an initial value of .45, we can determine the range of values which it can take without changing the final set of variables in the solution by adding .45 to the above limits, giving:

$$.40 \le c_1 \le .60$$

If the value of c_1 were to go outside this range, either s_3 or s_4 would enter the basis. Thus, if c_2 is held constant at .60, the solution to produce 20,000 gallons of each type of wine will remain optimal as long as c_1 stays within the range \$.40 to \$.60.

The same steps can be used to find the range within which the coefficient c_2 can change without changing the variables in the final basic solution. The initial tableau is shown in Table 4-8, and the final tableau is shown in Table 4-9.

Again, using the logic of determining entering variables, this tableau will remain optimal as long as the values in the $c_j - Z_j$ row do not become positive. Therefore, to remain optimal, we must have:

$$-.15 + 2\Delta c_2 \le 0 \qquad \text{and} \qquad -15 - 100\Delta c_2 \le 0$$

Working with the first inequality, we isolate Δc_2 as follows:

$$.15 + 2\Delta c_2 \le 0$$

or

$$2\Delta c_2 \le .15$$

$$\Delta c_2 \le .075$$

From the second inequality, we find

$$-15 - 100\Delta c_2 \le 0$$

Table 4-8 JOHN POWERS PROBLEM WITH A SMALL CHANGE IN c_2: INITIAL TABLEAU

		Variables						
		x_1	x_2	s_1	s_2	s_3	s_4	
Basis	c_j	.45	$.60 + \Delta c_2$	0	0	0	0	b_i
s_1	0	2	1	1	0	0	0	66,000
s_2	0	0	2	0	1	0	0	48,000
s_3	0	1	1	0	0	1	0	40,000
s_4	0	2/100	3/100	0	0	0	1	1,000
	Z_j	0	0	0	0	0	0	0
	$c_j - Z_j$	.45	$.60 + \Delta c_2$	0	0	0	0	

or
$$-100\Delta c_2 \leq 15$$
$$\Delta c_2 \geq -.15$$

Combining these two inequalities gives the range of values which Δc_2 can assume without changing the final tableau:

$$-.15 \leq \Delta c_2 \leq .075$$

But since c_2 starts at .60, by adding .60 to these limits we get the range of values which c_2 can take without changing the final set of variables in the solution:

$$.45 \leq c_2 \leq .675$$

If the value of c_2 goes outside this range, either s_3 or s_4 would enter the basis. Therefore, as long as the white wine profit, c_1, is \$.45, the profit on rosé, c_2, can be anywhere in the range \$.45 to \$.675 without affecting the optimal solution to produce 20,000 gallons of each type of wine.

The results of the sensitivity analysis using the simplex tableau approach are the same as those obtained with the graphical method. The advantage of the simplex tableau approach is that it can be used to perform sensitivity analysis for linear programming problems with any number of decision variables.

Table 4-9 JOHN POWERS PROBLEM WITH A SMALL CHANGE IN c_2: FINAL TABLEAU

		Variables						
		x_1	x_2	s_1	s_2	s_3	s_4	
Basis	c_j	.45	$.60 + \Delta c_2$	0	0	0	0	b_i
s_1	0	0	0	1	0	−4	100	6,000
s_2	0	0	0	0	1	4	−200	8,000
x_2	$.60 + \Delta c_2$	0	1	0	0	−2	100	20,000
x_1	.45	1	0	0	0	3	−100	20,000
	Z_j	.45	$.60 + \Delta c_2$	0	0	$.15 - 2\Delta c_2$	$15 + 100\Delta c_2$	$21{,}000 + 20{,}000\Delta c_2$
	$c_j - Z_j$	0	0	0	0	$-.15 + 2\Delta c_2$	$-15 - 100\Delta c_2$	

```
OBJECTIVE FUNCTION SENSITIVITY ANALYSIS

                                          LOWER    CURRENT    UPPER
VARIABLE       NAME       STATUS          BOUND     VALUE     BOUND

   1           X1         BASIC           0.400     0.450     0.600
   2           X2         BASIC           0.450     0.600     0.675
```

Figure 4-5

John Powers problem: MASTER output for objective-function sensitivity analysis

Computer Applications

Because sensitivity analysis is such a powerful addition to linear programming, it is incorporated in many software packages. To illustrate the use of computerized sensitivity analysis, we have provided examples that can be solved with the MASTER software package that accompanies this text. Most other linear programming software performs in essentially the same manner.

After MASTER solves the linear programming problem you have specified, it will ask if you wish to perform sensitivity analysis. Suppose you have run the John Powers production mix example. If you request sensitivity analysis on the objective-function coefficients, the output screen will look like Figure 4-5. As you can see, these results are the same as those we found earlier using the manual approach. Computer software frees the decision maker from the computational burden of the simplex solution procedure and allows more time for problem formulation and interpretation of the results, including sensitivity analysis.

DECISION-MAKING ADVANTAGES

The final question to be answered in this section is, How does sensitivity analysis help John Powers? Remember that managerial decisions made about future events have an element of uncertainty. Sensitivity analysis will not eliminate this uncertainty, but it will limit it. If John Powers believes his estimates of profitability for each gallon of white and rosé wines will be accurate within $\pm$\$.02, he will probably feel comfortable with the product mix determined by the linear programming model. If, however, he thinks the actual profitability for a gallon of white wine may be between \$.30 and \$.80, then the product mix of 20,000 gallons of each type of wine may prove nonoptimal.

John has several options if he remains uncertain whether the profit coefficient on either of the two wines falls within its sensitivity range. The first would be to spend more time gathering information to use in making the profitability estimates. This information would be used to reduce the range of possible outcomes, but it would be needed only if the present estimates fall outside the range of values determined by sensitivity analysis. Another option John would have is to use a version of linear programming known as *chance-constrained programming,* which allows objective-function coefficients to be represented by a probability distribution. Chance-constrained programming is beyond the scope of this book, but it is covered in advanced linear programming texts.

4-5 SENSITIVITY ANALYSIS ON THE RIGHT-HAND-SIDE VALUES

Section 4-4 has shown the methodology for performing sensitivity analysis on the objective-function coefficients. This analysis allows the decision maker to determine the ranges within which the objective-function coefficients can fall without affecting the optimal solution to the linear programming problem. While this type of analysis is important in a linear programming application, decision makers are also concerned with the uncertainties associated with the right-hand-side values of the problem constraints. In this section, we introduce the methods for performing sensitivity analysis on the right-hand-side values.

We will continue with the John Powers wine-making example. John's production decision was constrained by limitations on four resources: green grapes, red grapes, sugar, and worker-hours. The central question is, How much change in the available capacity of any of the four resources can occur before the optimal solution will change? To answer this question, John will have to perform sensitivity analysis on the right-hand-side values.

Our discussion will begin with the graphical approach to sensitivity analysis of the objective-function coefficients. Then we will illustrate how sensitivity analysis is performed using the simplex tableau. Finally, we will demonstrate computerized sensitivity analysis.

THE GRAPHICAL APPROACH

Refer to the corner-point solution for the John Powers linear programming problem shown in Figure 4-4. The corner-point solution, corner 3, is formed by the intersection of the sugar constraint line and the worker-hour constraint line. These are the *binding constraints* in this solution. Since the red-grapes and green-grapes constraints are not

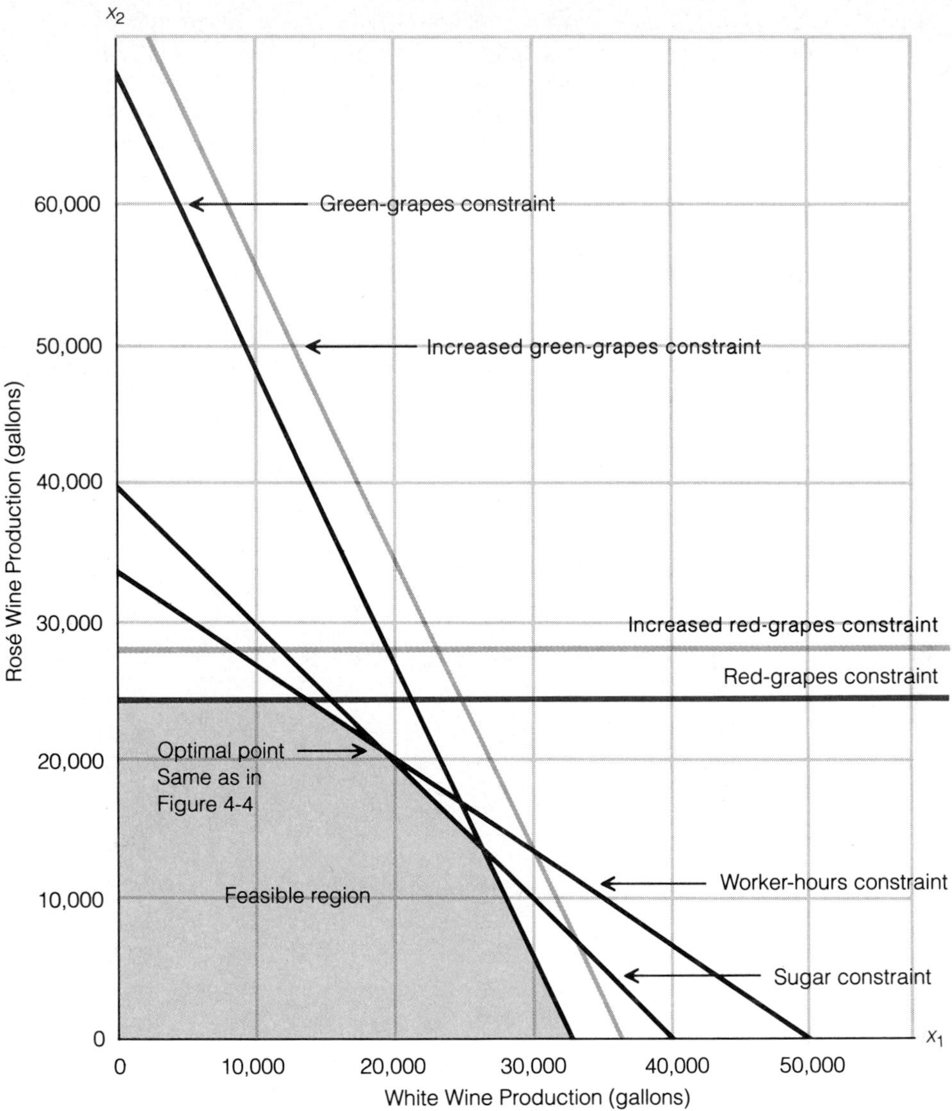

Figure 4-6
John Powers problem: increased availability of grapes

used in determining the optimal solution, they are *nonbinding constraints.* We are interested in performing sensitivity analysis on the right-hand sides for both the binding and nonbinding constraints.

To determine how much change in each of the resource capacities (right-hand sides) will be required to affect the present corner-point solution, we use the following reasoning:

1. Presently, neither of the two grapes constraints is involved in determining the optimal corner point. If the weather was exceptionally favorable and the harvest of red and/or green grapes was greater than expected, it would be reflected in Figure 4-6 by moving the constraints farther from the origin. Increasing the availability of a nonbinding constraint will not affect the corner point.

2. If the weather was unfavorable and the harvest was less than estimated, the two grapes constraint lines would move closer to the origin; and at some point, they would restrict the solution space enough to cause the corner-point solution to be determined by a different set of resources. For example, Figure 4-7 shows this situation for the red-grapes constraint line. Any further reduction in the availability of red grapes will cause the corner point to be determined by the intersection of the red-grapes and sugar availability lines.

Figure 4-7
John Powers problem: reduced availability of red grapes

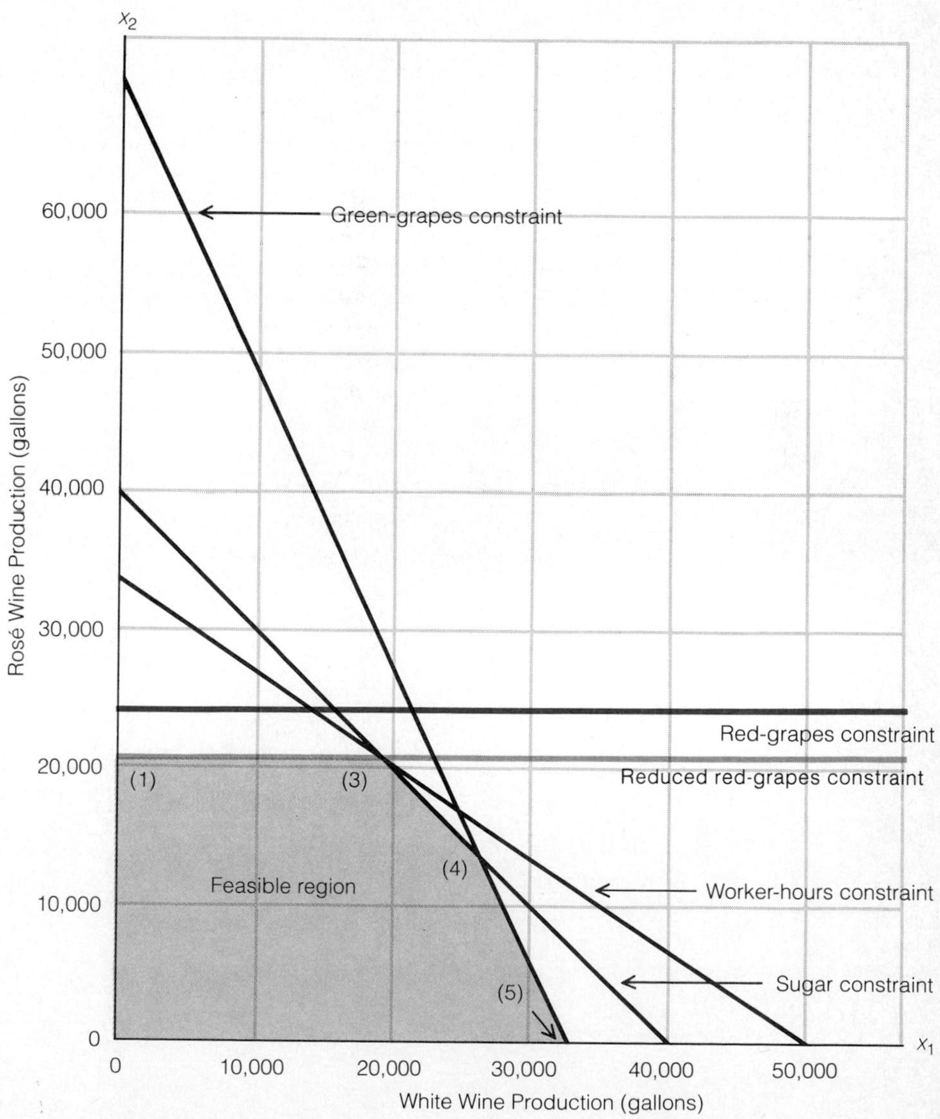

Note: Corner 2 will be eliminated when the red-grape constraint is reduced to pass through corner 3. Any further reduction will result in the corner point being formed by the red-grape constraint and the sugar constraint.

3. Changing the availability of either of the binding constraints will cause the corner-point solution to move, but small changes in either resource will still leave the corner point determined by the intersection of the sugar and worker-hour constraint lines.
4. Large changes in either of the binding constraints will cause the corner point to be determined by a different set of resources. For instance, in Figure 4-8 the worker-hour resource has been expanded so that the corner point is determined by the availability of sugar and red grapes. In Figure 4-9, the worker-hour constraint has

Figure 4-8
John Powers problem: expanded worker-hours constraint, worker-hours not binding

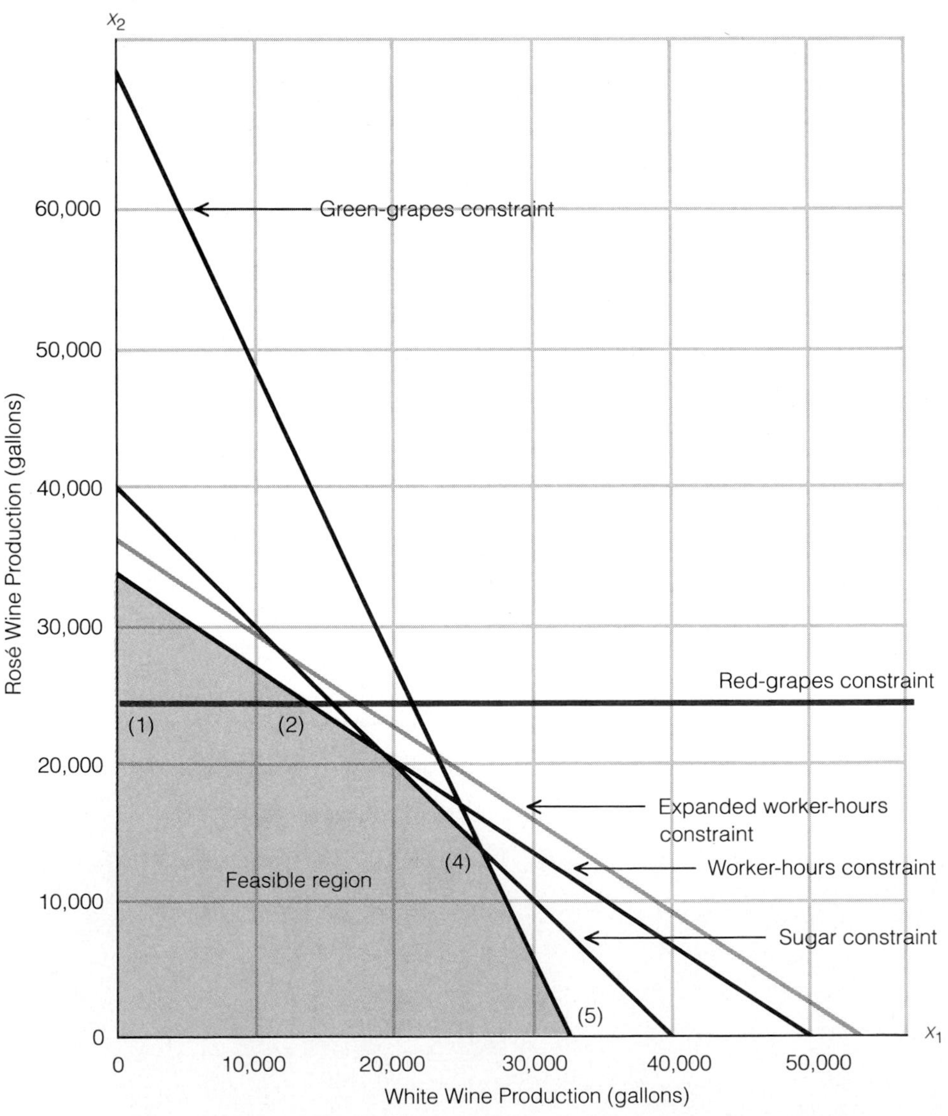

Note: Corner 3 is eliminated when worker-hours constraint is expanded. Corner 2 is formed by the red-grape constraint and sugar constraint. The worker-hours constraint is now nonbinding.

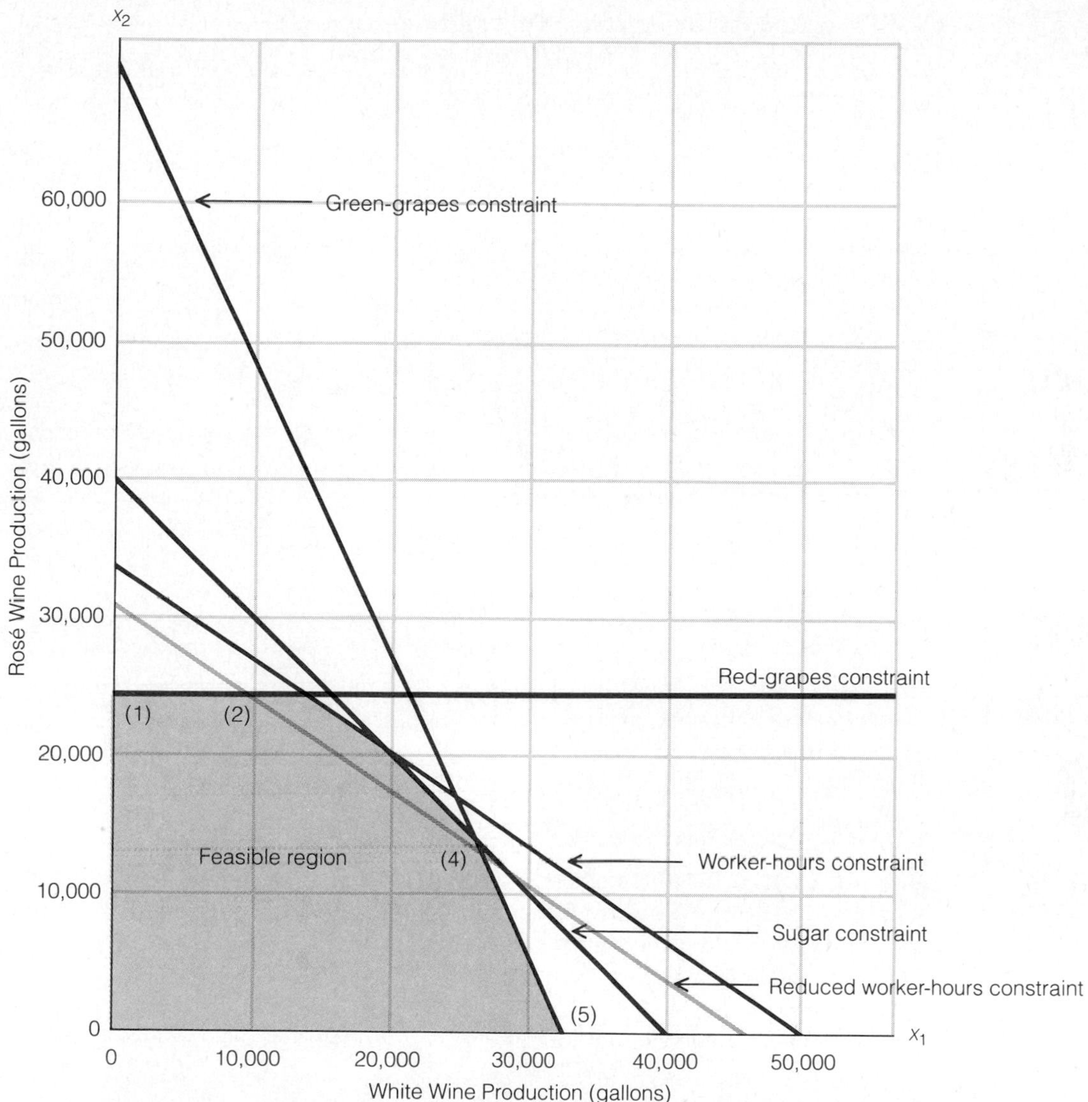

Note: A reduction in the worker-hours constraint will result in corner 3 being eliminated and corner 4 being formed by the green-grapes constraint and the worker-hours constraint. The sugar constraint becomes non-binding.

Figure 4-9
John Powers problem: reduced worker-hours constraint, sugar constraint not binding

been reduced to the point where the binding constraints are now worker-hours and green grapes.

> Performing sensitivity analysis on the right-hand-side values involves finding out how much each right-hand side can change before the optimal corner point is determined by a new set of constraints.

Sensitivity Analysis on a Nonbinding Constraint

The present optimal point indicates that John should produce 20,000 gallons of both white and rosé wines. The nonbinding constraints for red and green grapes are:

Green grapes $2x_1 + 1x_2 \leq 66{,}000$

Red grapes $0x_1 + 2x_2 \leq 48{,}000$

We have already observed that increasing the availability of either of these two resources will not affect the current solution. However, decreasing the availability of a nonbinding resource may reduce the solution space and cause a new corner point to become optimal. At the present solution point, we are using the following values:

$$2(20{,}000) + 1(20{,}000) = 60{,}000 \text{ bushels of green grapes}$$

Therefore, if we reduced the amount of green grapes from the current limit of 66,000 bushels to 60,000 bushels, it would be equivalent to moving the green-grapes constraint line toward the origin to the point where it just touches the present solution point. Any further reduction in green grapes will reduce the present solution space and affect the current corner-point solution. Therefore, the range over which green grapes can change without changing the present set of binding constraints is:

$$60{,}000 \leq b_1 \leq \infty$$

This shows that if the amount of green grapes is 60,000 pounds or more, the current solution will remain optimal. The infinity sign indicates that there is no upper bound on this constraint.

At the present solution point, we are using the following values:

$$0(20{,}000) + 2(20{,}000) = 40{,}000 \text{ bushels of red grapes}$$

Therefore, if we reduced the amount of red grapes from the current limit of 48,000 bushels to 40,000 bushels, it would be equivalent to moving the red-grapes constraint line toward the origin to the point where it just touches the present solution point. Any further reduction in red grapes will reduce the present solution space and affect the current corner-point solution. Therefore, the range over which red grapes can change without changing the present set of binding constraints is:

$$40{,}000 \leq b_2 \leq \infty$$

Again, this means that as long as the amount of red grapes is at least 40,000 bushels, the current solution will remain optimal. The infinity sign indicates that there is no upper bound on this constraint.

We should also point out that the sensitivity analysis on a given constraint is performed assuming that the right-hand-side values for each of the other constraints are held constant at their original levels. Sensitivity analysis performed simultaneously on two or more right-hand-side values is beyond the scope of this text, but it is covered in the text by Hillier and Lieberman cited in the References section for this chapter.

Sensitivity Analysis on a Binding Constraint

Performing sensitivity analysis on a binding constraint is more complicated than for a nonbinding constraint, since any change in constraint availability will change the location of the corner point. The question is, How much change can occur before a new binding constraint enters the solution? Looking at Figure 4-10, we see that if sugar

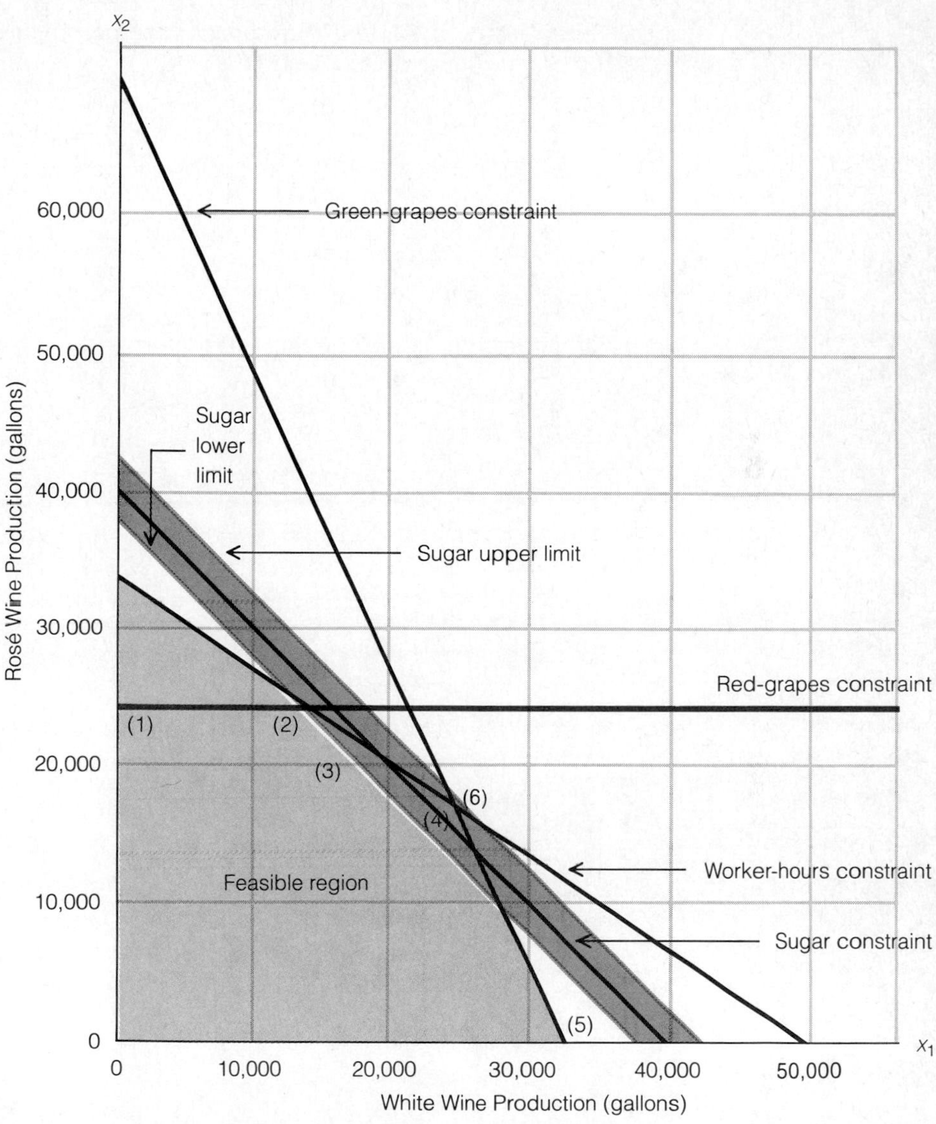

Figure 4-10
John Powers problem: range of values for sugar constraint

Note: The shaded area represents the range for the sugar constraint.

availability is increased enough, corner 6 will become the new optimal point, and if it is decreased enough, corner 2 will become the new optimal point.

Corner 6 is presently formed by the intersection of the green-grapes and worker-hour constraints. Our first step is to solve the equations for these two constraint lines to determine the corresponding values for x_1 and x_2. We set up a system of two equations with two unknowns, as follows:

$$2x_1 + 1x_2 = 66{,}000$$
$$.02x_1 + .03x_2 = 1{,}000$$

Solving this system gives:

$$x_2 = 17{,}000$$
$$x_1 = 24{,}500$$

The sugar availability that corresponds to corner point 6 is:

$$1(24{,}500) + 1(17{,}000) = 41{,}500 \text{ pounds}$$

Corner 2 is formed by the intersection of the red-grapes and worker-hour constraints. We set up another system of two equations with two unknowns and again solve for x_1 and x_2, as follows:

$$0x_1 + 2x_2 = 48{,}000$$
$$.02x_1 + .03x_2 = 1{,}000$$

Then we get:

$$x_2 = 24{,}000$$
$$x_1 = 14{,}000$$

The sugar availability that corresponds to this point is:

$$1(14{,}000) + 1(24{,}000) = 38{,}000 \text{ pounds}$$

As long as the changes in sugar availability are small enough so that its constraint line does not extend beyond corner point 2 or 6, sugar will remain a constraining resource. Therefore, sugar availability (b_3) can range from 38,000 to 41,500 pounds before a different set of constraints will determine the corner-point solution. Thus, we have determined that the *lower bound* on sugar is 38,000 pounds and the *upper bound* is 41,500 pounds:

$$38{,}000 \le b_3 \le 41{,}500$$

In Figure 4-11, we see that if worker-hour availability is increased enough, corner 6 will become the new optimal point; and if it is decreased enough, corner 4 will become the new optimal point.

Corner 6 is formed by the intersection of the red-grapes and sugar constraints. Using these two constraints, we set up a system of two equations with two unknowns and solve for x_1 and x_2:

$$1x_1 + 1x_2 = 40{,}000$$
$$0x_1 + 2x_2 = 48{,}000$$

Then we get:

$$x_2 = 24{,}000$$
$$x_1 = 16{,}000$$

The worker-hour availability that corresponds to this point is:

$$.02(16{,}000) + .03(24{,}000) = 1040 \text{ hours}$$

Likewise, corner 4 is formed by the intersection of the green-grapes and sugar constraints. As before, we solve the equations for these two constraint lines, to determine the values of x_1 and x_2:

$$1x_1 + 1x_2 = 40{,}000$$
$$2x_1 + 1x_2 = 66{,}000$$

Figure 4-11
John Powers problem: range for worker-hour constraint

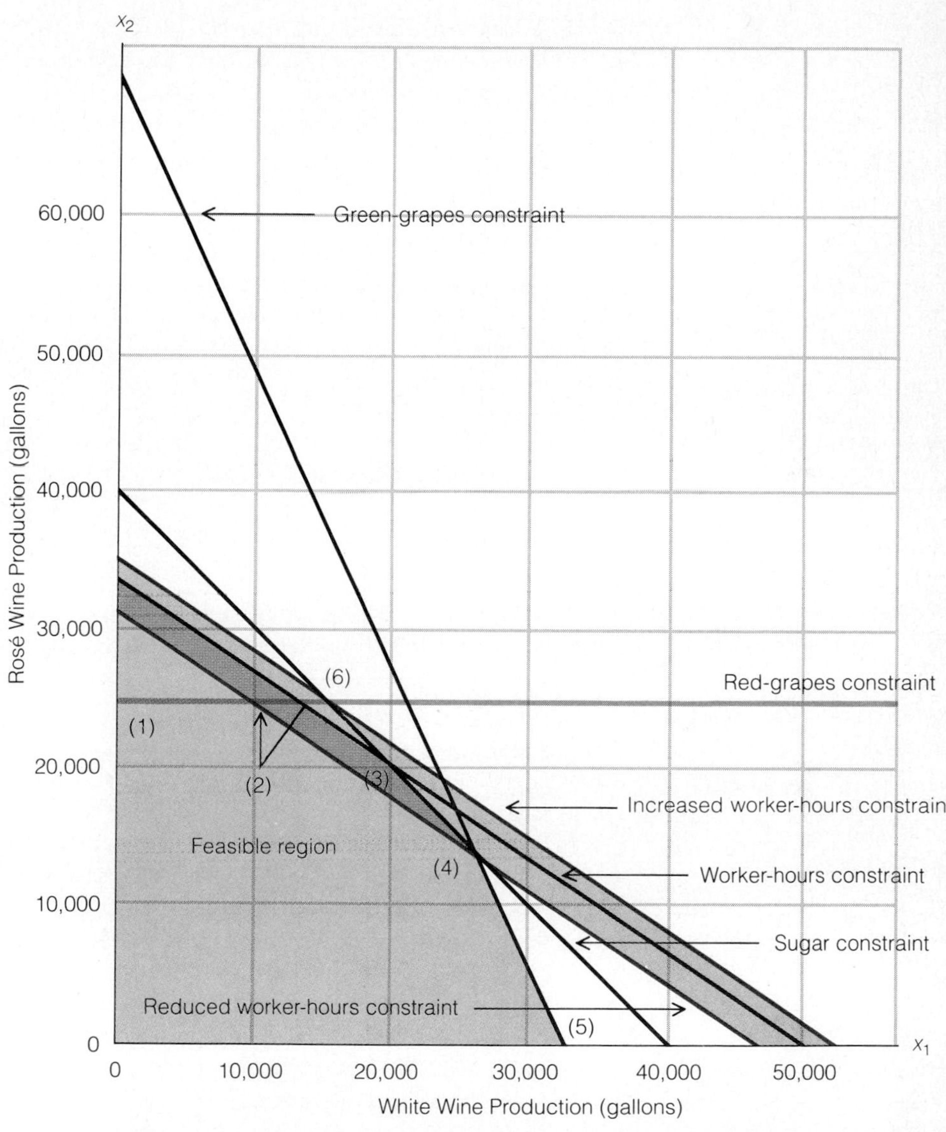

Note: The shaded area represent the range for the worker-hours constraint. Corner 3 is eliminated when the worker-hours constraint is expanded. Corner 2 becomes the optimal corner point. When the worker-hours constraint is reduced, a new corner 2 is developed and the optimal solution is at corner 4.

Then we get:

$$x_2 = 14{,}000$$
$$x_1 = 26{,}000$$

The worker-hour availability that corresponds to this point is:

$$.02(26{,}000) + .03(14{,}000) = 940 \text{ hours}$$

Thus, as long as the changes in worker-hour availability are small enough so that its constraint line does not extend beyond corner point 2 or 4, it will remain a constraining resource. Our computations show that worker-hour availability (b_4) can range from 940 to 1,040 hours before a different set of constraints will determine the corner-point solution. Thus, we have determined that the lower bound on the worker-hour constraint is 940 hours and the upper bound is 1040 hours:

$$940 \leq b_4 \leq 1040$$

Remember: *Any change in the right-hand-side value of a binding constraint will change the optimal solution, since the corner points of the feasible region will be changed.* Not only will the value of the objective function change, so will the values of the decision variables.

THE SIMPLEX SOLUTION PROCEDURE

Since the graphical approach for performing sensitivity analysis on the right-hand-side values is limited to problems having two decision variables, it has few practical applications. Our main reason for demonstrating it is to expand your understanding of the logic behind the process. As discussed earlier, sensitivity analysis can be extended to larger problems by using the simplex solution procedure. Problems can be solved either manually, using the simplex tableau, or by computer, using appropriate software. Both methods are examined below.

The Simplex Tableau

To illustrate how sensitivity analysis is performed on the right-hand-side coefficients, we will continue with the John Powers problem. The initial and final tableaus for the problem are given in Tables 4-4 and 4-5 (see section 4-4).

To use the simplex tableau to perform sensitivity analysis on the nonbinding constraint value b_1, we allow it to change by a small amount, Δb_1. This modification to the initial tableau is shown in Table 4-10. Notice that we have added an amount $1\Delta b_1$ to the first constraint, representing green grapes. We have added nothing to the other three constraints (shown by writing $0\Delta b_1$ in the remaining three rows). However, because of the row manipulation procedures in the simplex method, the $1\Delta b_1$ term in the first constraint will be carried to additional rows of the tableau any time a multiple of the first row is added to or subtracted from any other row. Therefore, the addition to the first constraint may be carried to all terms in the b_i column of the final tableau.

Table 4-10 JOHN POWERS PROBLEM WITH CHANGE IN b_1: INITIAL TABLEAU

		Variables						
		x_1	x_2	s_1	s_2	s_3	s_4	
Basis	c_j	.45	.60	0	0	0	0	b_i
s_1	0	2	1	1	0	0	0	$66{,}000 + 1\Delta b_1$
s_2	0	0	2	0	1	0	0	$48{,}000 + 0\Delta b_1$
s_3	0	1	1	0	0	1	0	$40{,}000 + 0\Delta b_1$
s_4	0	2/100	3/100	0	0	0	1	$1{,}000 + 0\Delta b_1$
	Z_j	0	0	0	0	0	0	0
	$c_j - Z_j$	.45	.60	0	0	0	0	

The logic behind performing sensitivity analysis on the constraining right-hand-side values is as follows:

> The simplex tableau is a matrix representation of the linear programming model's objective-function and constraint equations. By adding the term $1\Delta b_1$ to the first constraint and the term $0\Delta b_1$ to all the other constraints, we have added another column to the simplex tableau.
>
> Because the simplex procedure involves adding or subtracting some multiple of one row in the matrix to other rows, the new column just added will be affected by the same operations as an equivalent column in the matrix—in this case, the one under s_1.

The final simplex tableau reflecting a small change in the amount of green grapes would then be as shown in Table 4-11. In order for this tableau to remain optimal, all the right-hand side values must be greater than or equal to (≥) zero. In this case, since only the first row has a value affected by Δb_1:

$$6000 + \Delta b_1 \geq 0$$

or

$$\Delta b_1 \geq -6000$$

But since b_1 starts at 66,000, this means the amount of green grapes can go as low as 60,000 bushels (66,000 − 6000) before the variables in the basis will change. Similar reasoning, based on the initial and final tableaus, shows that red grapes (a nonbinding constraint) can drop as low as 40,000 pounds before a different set of constraints will be binding and different variables will be in the basis of the final tableau.

The two binding constraints, representing sugar and worker-hour availability, will lead to somewhat more complicated situations. Let's consider a small change in the sugar constraint, shown in the modified initial tableau, Table 4-12.

Using the same reasoning as for a small change in b_1, we look for a column with the sequence 0, 0, 1, 0. Since this is the column under s_3, everything that happens to the s_3 column will also happen to the column added to the right-hand side. Therefore, the final tableau will be as shown in Table 4-13.

Table 4-11 JOHN POWERS PROBLEM WITH CHANGE IN b_1: FINAL TABLEAU

		Variables						
		x_1	x_2	s_1	s_2	s_3	s_4	
Basis	c_j	.45	.60	0	0	0	0	b_i
s_1	0	0	0	1	0	−4	100	$6,000 + 1\Delta b_1$
s_2	0	0	0	0	1	4	−200	$8,000 + 0\Delta b_1$
x_2	.60	0	1	0	0	−2	100	$20,000 + 0\Delta b_1$
x_1	.45	1	0	0	0	3	−100	$20,000 + 0\Delta b_1$
	Z_j	.45	.60	0	0	.15	15	21,000
	$c_j - Z_j$	0	0	0	0	−.15	−15	

Table 4-12 JOHN POWERS PROBLEM WITH CHANGE IN b_3: INITIAL TABLEAU

		Variables						
		x_1	x_2	s_1	s_2	s_3	s_4	
Basis	c_j	.45	.60	0	0	0	0	b_i
s_1	0	2	1	1	0	0	0	$66{,}000 + 0\Delta b_3$
s_2	0	0	2	0	1	0	0	$48{,}000 + 0\Delta b_3$
s_3	0	1	1	0	0	1	0	$40{,}000 + 1\Delta b_3$
s_4	0	2/100	3/100	0	0	0	1	$1{,}000 + 0\Delta b_3$
	Z_j	0	0	0	0	0	0	0
	$c_j - Z_j$	.45	.60	0	0	0	0	

For this tableau to remain optimal, all right-hand sides must be greater than or equal to zero. Therefore:

From line 1: $6000 - 4\Delta b_3 \geq 0$ or: $\Delta b_3 \leq 1500$

From line 2: $8000 + 4\Delta b_3 \geq 0$ or: $\Delta b_3 \geq -2000$

From line 3: $20{,}000 - 2\Delta b_3 \geq 0$ or $\Delta b_3 \leq 10{,}000$

From line 4: $20{,}000 + 3\Delta b_3 \geq 0$ or: $\Delta b_3 \geq -6667$

We select the two most restrictive constraints (from lines 1 and 2) to determine the range of values which Δb_3 may assume. We get:

$$-2000 \leq \Delta b_3 \leq 1500$$

Since the limiting value of the sugar constraint starts at 40,000, we add 40,000 to each limit and get:

$$38{,}000 \leq \text{sugar availability} \leq 41{,}500$$

which is the same range we found using the graphical procedure.

Using a similar procedure on the worker-hour constraint, we find it can range from 940 to 1040 hours before a different set of constraints will determine the corner-point solution:

$$940 \leq \text{worker-hour availability} \leq 1040$$

Table 4-13 JOHN POWERS PROBLEM WITH CHANGE IN b_3: FINAL TABLEAU

		Variables						
		x_1	x_2	s_1	s_2	s_3	s_4	
Basis	c_j	.45	.60	0	0	0	0	b_i
s_1	0	0	0	1	0	−4	100	$6{,}000 - 4\Delta b_3$
s_2	0	0	0	0	1	4	−200	$8{,}000 + 4\Delta b_3$
x_2	.60	0	1	0	0	−2	100	$20{,}000 - 2\Delta b_3$
x_1	.45	1	0	0	0	3	−100	$20{,}000 + 3\Delta b_3$
	Z_j	.45	.60	0	0	.15	15	21,000
	$c_j - Z_j$	0	0	0	0	−.15	−15	

This process for performing sensitivity analysis using the simplex tableau approach is actually an extension of the logic presented for the graphical approach. The sensitivity analysis determines the amount by which each right-hand side can change before a different set of constraints become binding in the linear programming solution.

Computer Applications

As we said earlier, most actual linear programming and sensitivity analyses are done with computers. The purpose of our discussion of right-hand-side sensitivity analysis using the graphical approach and the simplex tableau is to explain the logic of sensitivity analysis. Although we believe that you will better understand linear programming and sensitivity analysis after having worked several problems manually with the simplex procedure, you also need to know how to interpret computer output for similar problems.

To illustrate, we will use the MASTER software package that accompanies this text. It allows you to perform sensitivity analysis on the right-hand-side values as well as on the objective-function coefficients. MASTER begins by solving the original linear programming problem and then asks you whether you want to perform sensitivity analysis. For the John Powers problem, MASTER provides the sensitivity analysis output shown in Figure 4-12. As you can see, the results are the same as those we computed using the graphical approach and the simplex tableau approach. Section 4-7 presents additional linear programming computer applications with sensitivity analysis.

DECISION-MAKING ADVANTAGES

Sensitivity analysis on the right-hand sides is a means for dealing with the uncertainty that usually exists in formulating a linear programming problem. It also tells the decision maker the range of capacity within which the associated dual price is valid.

For example, consider the binding worker-hour constraint in the John Powers problem. As shown in Figure 4-12, if the right-hand-side values of the other constraints are held constant, as long as the number of available worker-hours is between 940 and 1040 the current constraints remain binding. This means that the dual price of $15.00 is valid over this range. Thus, if John currently has 1000 worker-hours scheduled, he knows that he can spend an additional $15.00 per hour over his normal costs to acquire up to 40 additional worker-hours. Beyond the 1040 total hours, the dual price is not valid. Likewise, the sensitivity analysis range indicates that for each worker-hour reduced between 1000 hours and 940 hours, the amount of lost profit will be $15.00.

A similar analysis can be performed for each constraint. In each case, the sensitivity analysis determines the range within which the associated dual price is valid.

4-6 COMPUTER APPLICATIONS

In this section, we will use the MASTER software package that accompanies this text to further demonstrate linear programming, dual values, and sensitivity analysis. The following discussion explains how to use MASTER to solve the example problems. If

SENSITIVITY ANALYSIS FOR RIGHT-HAND-SIDE VALUES

VARIABLE	ORIGINAL CONSTRAINT	LOWER BOUND	CURRENT VALUE	UPPER BOUND
3	1	60000.000	66000.000	INFINITY
4	2	40000.000	48000.000	INFINITY
5	3	38000.000	40000.000	41500.000
6	4	940.000	1000.000	1040.000

Figure 4-12
John Powers problem: MASTER output for right-hand-side sensitivity analysis

you have access to a different software package, we suggest that you repeat the examples and compare output.

AMERICAN CEREAL COMPANY: A MAXIMIZATION EXAMPLE

The American Cereal Company makes four breakfast cereals for distribution in the United States and Canada. The company's current estimates of profit per 16-ounce box for each type of cereal are as follows: Krispy Flakes, \$.40; Oat Ohs, \$.55; Raisin Wheats, \$.39; and Mixed Grains, \$.45. Several limited resources are required to produce the cereals: labor, cooking time, drying time, raw materials (wheat, oats, and raisins), and packaging time. Each product requires certain quantities of these resources, as shown in Table 4-14. The limitations on these resources are also shown in the table.

The most profitable production mix for the American Cereal Company can be determined with linear programming using the MASTER software package. Figure 4-13 shows the data input requirements. As you can see, the problem has been

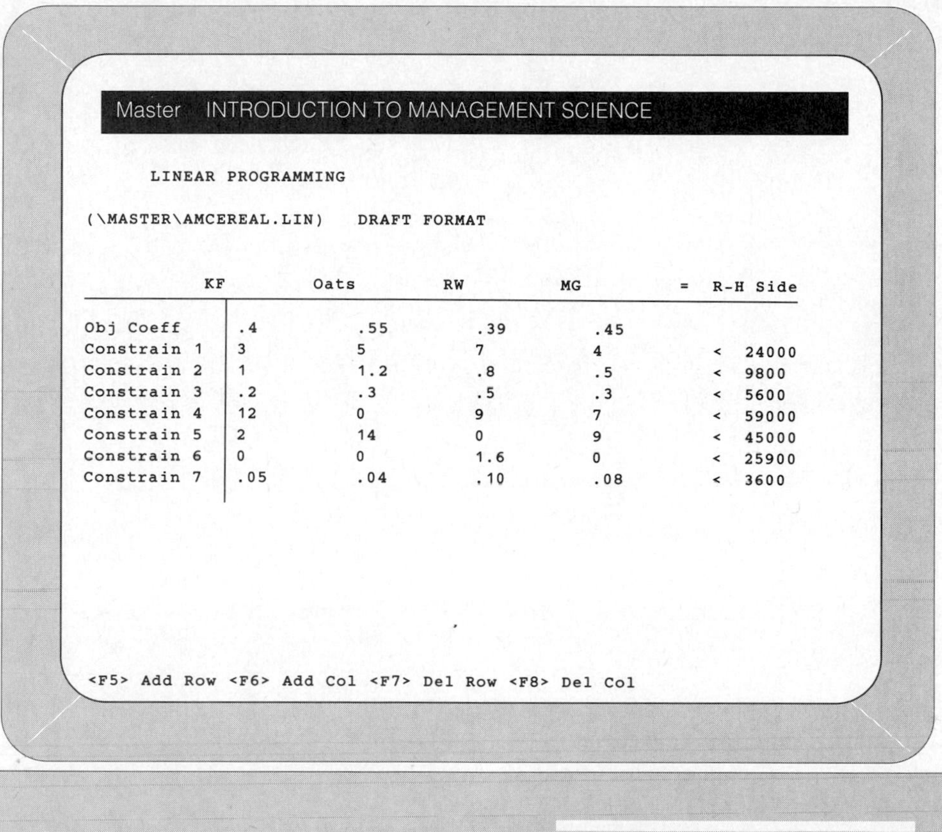

Figure 4-13
American Cereal Co. problem: MASTER software linear programming data requirements

Table 4-14 AMERICAN CEREAL COMPANY EXAMPLE: RESOURCE UTILIZATION TABLE

	Product				
Resource	Krispy Flakes	Oat Ohs	Raisin Wheats	Mixed Grains	Limit
Labor (minutes)	3	5	7	4	24,000
Cooking (minutes)	1	1.2	.8	.5	9,800
Drying (minutes)	.2	.3	.5	.3	5,600
Wheat (ounces)	12	0	9	7	59,000
Oats (ounces)	2	14	0	9	45,000
Raisins (ounces)	0	0	1.6	0	25,900
Packaging (minutes)	.05	.04	.10	.08	3,600

```
                LINEAR PROGRAMMING FORMULATION

OBJECTIVE FUNCTION:
  MAXIMIZE Z =
       0.40  KF +     0.55 OAT +     0.39  RW +    0.45  MG +

SUBJECT TO:
      3.00KF +    5.00OAT +    7.00RW +    4.00MG <=  24000.00
      1.00KF +    1.20OAT +    0.80RW +    0.50MG <=   9800.00
      0.20KF +    0.30OAT +    0.50RW +    0.30MG <=   5600.00
     12.00KF +    0.00OAT +    9.00RW +    7.00MG <=  59000.00
      2.00KF +   14.00OAT +    0.00RW +    9.00MG <=  45000.00
      0.00KF +    0.00OAT +    1.60RW +    0.00MG <=  25900.00
      0.05KF +    0.04OAT +    0.10RW +    0.08MG <=   3600.00

              THE DECISION VARIABLES ARE  1  THROUGH  4
              THE SLACK VARIABLES ARE      5  THROUGH  11


         OPTIONAL SOLUTION

ITERATIONS =   4

OBJECTIVE FUNCTION =       2984.167


DECISION VARIABLES:

VARIABLE   NAME    VALUE

   1         KF   4916.667
   2        OAT   1850.000


SLACK OR SURPLUS VARIABLES:

VARIABLE   NAME    VALUE
 6         SLACK  2663.334
 7         SLACK  4061.667
 9         SLACK  9266.667
10         SLACK 25900.000
11         SLACK  3280.167
```

Figure 4-14
American Cereal Co. problem: MASTER software linear programming output

```
DUAL RESULTS

VARIABLE    NAME                VALUE
           KF                   0.000
           OAT                  0.000
           RW                   0.433
           MG                   0.031
           CONSTRAINT  1        0.110
           CONSTRAINT  2        0.000
           CONSTRAINT  3        0.000
           CONSTRAINT  4        0.006
           CONSTRAINT  5        0.000
           CONSTRAINT  6        0.000
           CONSTRAINT  7        0.000
```

Figure 4-14 Continued

formulated with four decision variables and seven constraints. The MASTER software package first solves the linear programming problem as formulated. The results, shown in Figure 4-14, indicate that the American Cereal Company should produce 4916.667 boxes of Krispy Flakes, 1850 boxes of Oat Ohs, 0 boxes of Raisin Wheats, and 0 boxes of Mixed Grains for a total profit of $2984.167. Some of the resources were not totally used and have slack values, as shown in the output. For example, cooking time has 2663.334 minutes left from the original 9800 units; and since the optimal decision calls for no production of Raisin Wheats, the entire 25,900 ounces of raisins will still be available.

The Dual

Figure 4-14 also displays the dual values. These dual values are the shadow prices for each resource. As discussed earlier, the duals (shadow prices) reflect the economic value of the various resources. For resources that have *sunk costs* (costs that will be the same regardless of the level of production and are not reflected in the objective-function coefficients), the dual values represent the per unit amount that American Cereal would be willing to pay for additional units. For those resources with *relevant costs* (costs that will depend on the values of the decision variables and will therefore be reflected in the values of the objective-function coefficients), the dual value is interpreted to be the premium that American Cereal would be willing to pay per unit over and above the regular per unit price.

For example, the labor cost is fixed, regardless of production levels; it is therefore considered a sunk cost and is not factored into the value of the objective-function profit coefficients. The dual value for the labor constraint is .110, indicating that each additional minute of labor time that could be obtained would be worth $.11. The dual value for constraint 4, the wheat resource, has a dual value of .006. Because the cost of wheat is a relevant cost, the .006 is interpreted to mean that if additional wheat could be obtained, American Cereal would be willing to pay a maximum premium of $.006 per ounce over the standard price.

Note that the dual values for the resources with positive slack values are zero, indicating that adding more of these resources would not add anything to profit. For instance, constraint 6, cooking capacity, has 2663.334 units of slack in the optimal

OBJECTIVE-FUNCTION SENSITIVITY ANALYSIS

VARIABLE	NAME	STATUS	LOWER BOUND	CURRENT VALUE	UPPER BOUND
1	KF	BASIC	0.347	0.400	INFINITY
2	OAT	BASIC	0.481	0.550	0.667
3	RW	NON-BASIC	-INFINITY	0.390	0.823
4	MG	NON-BASIC	-INFINITY	0.450	0.481

SENSITIVITY ANALYSIS FOR RIGHT-HAND-SIDE VALUES

VARIABLE	ORIGINAL CONSTRAINT	LOWER BOUND	CURRENT VALUE	UPPER BOUND
5	1	14750.000	24000.000	27309.520
6	2	7136.667	9800.000	INFINITY
7	3	1538.334	5600.000	INFINITY
8	4	41625.000	59000.000	96000.000
9	5	35733.330	45000.000	INFINITY
10	6	0.000	25900.000	INFINITY
11	7	319.834	3600.000	INFINITY

Figure 4-15
American Cereal Co. problem: MASTER sensitivity analysis output

solution. The dual for constraint 2, cooking time, is zero, indicating that there is no economic value to acquiring additional units of the resource.

Sensitivity Analysis

The MASTER software will also perform sensitivity analysis on the objective-function coefficients and the right-hand side constraint. Figure 4-15 shows the output for the sensitivity analysis. For example, the Krispy Flake profit coefficient is $.40. The sensitivity analysis shows that the current optimal solution will not change until the profit on this product drops below $.347 per box. The upper bound is infinity, which means that the current optimal solution will not change no matter how high the per box profit on Krispy Flakes goes. Likewise, the profit per box for Oat Ohs can range between $.481 and $.667 without changing the current optimal solution.

The Raisin Wheats and Mixed Grains products do not enter the optimal solution as formulated. The sensitivity analysis on the objective coefficients shows that any reduction in profit will have no effect on this situation. However, if the profit on Raisin Wheats was increased to exceed $.823, the current solution would change and Raisin Wheats would be produced. For Mixed Grains, sensitivity analysis shows the profit only has to increase from $.45 per box to $.481 in order for this product to enter basis and be part of the optimal solution.

The sensitivity analysis on the right-hand sides shown in Figure 4-15 indicates the range within which the capacities could change without changing which constraints form the optimal corner of the feasible region. Note that those constraints which are not now binding constraints all have upper limits of infinity, since adding to their capacities will only add to the slack available and will not change the optimal corner point. However, reductions in capacity for any of these resources might change the corner-point solution. For example, if the capacity of cooking time was reduced from 9800 to 7136 minutes, this constraint would become binding.

WEST CITY BANK: A MINIMIZATION EXAMPLE

West City Bank is planning to expand its service day to 12 hours (8:00 A.M. to 8:00 P.M.). The personnel manager is responsible for rearranging the tellers' work schedule to fit the new hours and is developing a model for the task. For scheduling purposes, she has divided the workday into six 2-hour time periods. She knows that the minimum number of tellers needed during each of these 2-hour period is:

Time Period	Minimum Tellers
8:00–10:00 A.M.	6
10:00 A.M.–12:00 noon	10
12:00–2:00 P.M.	12
2:00–4:00 P.M.	11
4:00–6:00 P.M.	5
6:00–8:00 P.M.	4
Total	48

As we can see, the new schedule requires 48 teller work periods of 2 hours each. Each teller works a shift of 6 consecutive hours. At first glance it appears that this translates into $48 \div 6 = 8$ tellers required. However, can the bank get by with only 8 tellers, given the uneven distribution of need during the day? The personnel manager wishes to staff the bank with the minimum number of tellers required to meet all the bank's needs.

To help in setting up the new schedule, she developed a linear programming model. It assumes that tellers will start work at the beginning of one of the 2-hour time blocks. The decision variables are:

x_1 = number of tellers starting at 8:00 A.M.

x_2 = number of tellers starting at 10:00 A.M.

x_3 = number of tellers starting at 12:00 noon

x_4 = number of tellers starting at 2:00 P.M.

Note that no tellers will be scheduled to arrive later than 2:00 P.M., since the bank closes at 8:00 P.M. The objective function is:

$$\text{Minimize} \quad Z = 1.0x_1 + 1.0x_2 + 1.0x_3 + 1.0x_4$$

where Z is the total number of tellers starting work sometime during the day.

The constraints which have been imposed deal with the number of tellers needed to fill the six 2-hour time periods each day. For instance, between the hours of 8:00 and 10:00 A.M., at least 6 tellers must be working; between 10:00 A.M. and noon, at least 10 tellers must be working, and so forth. We can translate these requirements into the following constraints:

$$\begin{aligned}
x_1 \qquad\qquad\qquad &\geq 6 \\
x_1 + x_2 \qquad\qquad &\geq 10 \\
x_1 + x_2 + x_3 \qquad &\geq 12 \\
x_2 + x_3 + x_4 &\geq 11 \\
x_3 + x_4 &\geq 5 \\
x_4 &\geq 4
\end{aligned}$$

Thus, the linear programming model is:

Minimize $Z = 1.0x_1 + 1.0x_2 + 1.0x_3 + 1.0x_4$

Subject to:

$$\begin{aligned}
x_1 \qquad\qquad\qquad &\geq 6 \\
x_1 + x_2 \qquad\qquad &\geq 10 \\
x_1 + x_2 + x_3 \qquad &\geq 12 \\
x_2 + x_3 + x_4 &\geq 11 \\
x_3 + x_4 &\geq 5 \\
x_4 &\geq 4
\end{aligned}$$

The Primal Solution

We used MASTER to solve this linear programming problem. Figure 4-16 shows the resulting output. As indicated in this output, six iterations were required to reach the optimal solution. At the optimal solution, a total of 17 tellers will be scheduled to work during the 12-hour day. When the bank opens at 8:00 A.M., 6 tellers will be required ($x_1 = 6$). Then, at 10:00 A.M., 6 more tellers are scheduled to arrive ($x_2 = 6$). At 12:00 noon, 1 additional teller will arrive ($x_3 = 1$), and at 2:00 P.M., 4 tellers will begin their shifts ($x_4 = 4$).

This linear programming solution indicates that 17 is the minimum number of tellers needed to meet the bank's daily staffing needs. Thus, our earlier question about whether the personnel manager could get by with only 8 tellers has been answered.

The Dual Results

Interpreting the dual in this example is slightly different than in the other examples in this chapter. The reason is that in this case the Z value is not measured in dollars but instead is the total number of tellers that will have to be available for work each day. Thus, the dual value of -1 for constraint 1 (see Figure 4-16) is interpreted to mean that if the requirement for tellers during the period 8:00–10:00 A.M. could be reduced by 1, the total number of tellers required during the day could also be changed by -1, to 16 tellers.

Constraint 4 which also has a dual value of -1, deals with the number of tellers needed for the 2:00–4:00 P.M. time slot. The dual value indicates that if the teller requirement could be reduced by 1 person during this time period, the total number of tellers for the day could be changed by -1, to 16 tellers. For economic reasons, the personnel manager should therefore attempt to reduce the teller requirement for either the 8:00–10:00 A.M. or the 2:00–4:00 P.M. time slot, but only if the cost of the

```
MASTER                    Introduction to Management Science                    V1.09
______Linear Programming______________________________________________________________

OBJECTIVE FUNCTION:
   MINIMIZE Z =
       1.00  Variab 1 +     1.00  Variab 2 +     1.00  Variab 3 +    1.00 Variab 4
SUBJECT TO:
      1.00Variab 1 +  + 0.00Variab 2 +    0.00Variab 3 +    0.00Variab 4  >= 6
      1.00Variab 1 +    1.00Variab 2 +    0.00Variab 3 +    0.00Variab 4  >=10
      1.00Variab 1 +    1.00Variab 2 +    1.00Variab 3 +    0.00Variab 4  >=12
      0.00Variab 1 +    1.00Variab 2 +    1.00Variab 3 +    1.00Variab 4  >=11
      0.00Variab 1 +    0.00Variab 2 +    1.00Variab 3 +    1.00Variab 4  >=5
      0.00Variab 1 +    0.00Variab 2 +    0.00Variab 3 +    1.00Variab 4  >=4

     THE DECISION VARIABLES ARE     1. THROUGH   4.
     THE SURPLUS VARIABLES ARE      5. THROUGH  10.
     THE ARTIFICIAL VARIABLES ARE  11. THROUGH  16.


         OPTIMAL SOLUTION

ITERATIONS =  6.

OBJECTIVE FUNCTION =         17.000


DECISION VARIABLES:

VARIABLE    NAME             VALUE
    1.      Variab 1         6.000
    2.      Variab 2         6.000
    3.      Variab 3         1.000
    4.      Variab 4         4.000


SLACK OR SURPLUS VARIABLES:

VARIABLE    NAME             VALUE
 6.         SURPLUS          2.000
 7.         SURPLUS          1.000
```

Figure 4-16
West City Bank problem: MASTER output (figure continued on next page)

```
DUAL RESULTS

VARIABLE    NAME                VALUE
            Variab 1            0.000
            Variab 2            0.000
            Variab 3            0.000
            Variab 4            0.000
            CONSTRAINT 1.      -1.000
            CONSTRAINT 2.       0.000
            CONSTRAINT 3.       0.000
            CONSTRAINT 4.      -1.000
            CONSTRAINT 5.       0.000
            CONSTRAINT 6.       0.000
```

Figure 4-16 Continued

reduction (lost business, customer dissatisfaction, etc.) did not exceed the cost of hiring a teller.

Since the other constraints have dual values of zero, reducing the teller requirements for the time periods represented would not change the total number of tellers required for the day. Thus, there is no economic justification for trying to reduce the teller requirements for those time periods.

Sensitivity Analysis

The MASTER software provides sensitivity analysis on both the objective-function coefficients and the right-hand-side values. Suppose we first look at the section of the output in Figure 4-17 labeled "objective-function sensitivity analysis." Recall that the lower bound indicates the amount to which an objective-function coefficient can be *reduced* before the value of the corresponding decision variable will be changed in the optimal solution. Likewise, the upper bound is the amount to which an objective-function coefficient can be *increased* before the value of the decision variable will be changed in the optimal solution. Currently, the coefficients are 1.000 for all decision variables.

For variable x_1, the upper boundary is infinity, which indicates that no matter how much the coefficient is increased, there will be no change in the number of tellers scheduled to start work at 8:00 A.M.. The lower bound is zero. This means that the coefficient on variable x_1 could go as low as zero before the number of tellers required to start at 8:00 A.M. would be changed from the current level of 6. Note that if the coefficient was changed to zero, the implication would be that no tellers were actually needed during the 8:00 to 10:00 A.M. slot.

The sensitivity analysis output for the objective-function coefficients for variables x_3 and x_4 present an interesting result. Note that for variable x_3 both the upper and lower bounds are 1.00, the same as the current value of the objective-function coefficient. Likewise, the lower bound for variable x_4 is 1.00, the same as the current objective-function coefficient.

These results imply that there are multiple optimal solutions, since the "slope" of the objective function is parallel to a constraint "line." This concept was discussed earlier when we presented sensitivity analysis from a graphical perspective. In general, *anytime the maximum allowable increase or decrease in an objective-function coefficient is*

```
     OBJECTIVE FUNCTION SENSITIVITY ANALYSIS

                                          LOWER     CURRENT      UPPER
VARIABLE   NAME      STATUS               BOUND      VALUE       BOUND

     1.   Variab 1   BASIC                0.000      1.000     INFINITY
     2.   Variab 2   BASIC                0.000      1.000        1.000
     3.   Variab 3   BASIC                1.000      1.000        1.000
     4.   Variab 4   BASIC                1.000      1.000     INFINITY

**************************
**   CHECK FOR MULTIPLE  **
**   OPTIMAL SOLUTIONS   **
**************************
**************************
**   CHECK FOR MULTIPLE  **
**   OPTIMAL SOLUTIONS   **
**************************

      SENSITIVITY ANALYSIS FOR RIGHT-HAND-SIDE VALUES

                      ORIGINAL            LOWER     CURRENT     UPPER
VARIABLE             CONSTRAINT           BOUND      VALUE      BOUND

     5.                  1.                5.000      6.000   INFINITY
     6.                  2.            -INFINITY     10.000     12.000
     7.                  3.            -INFINITY     12.000     13.000
     8.                  4.               10.000     11.000   INFINITY
     9.                  5.                4.000      5.000      7.000
    10.                  6.                0.000      4.000      5.000
```

Figure 4-17
West City Bank problem: MASTER sensitivity output

zero, there will be multiple optimal solutions. As you can see in Figure 4-17, the MASTER software flags this with a warning about multiple optimal solutions.

Figure 4-17 also shows the sensitivity analysis on the right-hand-side values for each constraint. Recall that the constraints in this application refer to the minimum requirements for tellers during the 6 time slots. In each case in Figure 4-17, the distance between the lower bound and the upper bound is the range within which the teller requirements could change without changing the variables that are in basis in the optimal solution. For instance, constraint 5 corresponds to the time slot 4:00–6:00 P.M. The current teller requirement for that time period is 5 tellers. As long as the requirement is between 4 and 7 tellers during this time slot, the same variables that are in basis in the optimal solution will stay in basis.

Integer Solution

In this example we see that the decision variables in the optimal solution turn out to be integer values. An employee scheduling model obviously needs an integer solution, since there can be no "fractional" employees. However, linear programming does not guarantee that the solution will be integer. If faced with a noninteger solution, one might be tempted to simply round up or down to the nearest integer, but doing so will not guarantee an optimal integer solution. In general, though, when the noninteger values of the decision variables are large, rounding provides a close approximation to the actual optimal solution.

An extension of linear programming called *integer programming* is discussed in Chapter 6. This technique is designed to provide truly optimal results for problems where the solution must be integer. This is the approach we recommend when an integer solution is required and linear programming yields fractional values for an optimal solution.

4-7 SUMMARY AND CONCLUSIONS

Linear programming is one of the most widely used tools in management science, largely because it has such a broad variety of applications. Its results are easy to interpret in economic terms, and the incorporation of sensitivity analysis enhances its usefulness by allowing users to see the results of changing variable constraints in a problem.

Much initial work on the simplex tableau involved analyzing its operations in such widely developed economic terms as marginal rates of substitution. Much of the early work on the economic interpretation of linear programming problems was done in terms of the relationship between an original, or primal, problem and a related problem called the dual. While some of the importance of the primal-dual relationship has been lessened with the development of large, high-speed computers, many of the economic concepts associated with this procedure are best understood by knowing the primal-dual interaction. In this chapter, we have explained the relationship between any primal linear programming model and its dual. We have also shown that the solution to the dual problem is contained in the final tableau associated with the primal, and likewise the final dual tableau contains the solution to the primal problem. In particular, we have shown how the solution to the dual problem provides the economic value of adding a unit of any constraining resource in the decision-making situation.

We have also emphasized many times in this chapter — and will continue to do so throughout the text — the inherent uncertainty involved in managerial decision-making situations. Because of this uncertainty, managers are continually asking "What if?" questions. The ability to associate a well-defined method of performing sensitivity analysis with linear programming problems has enabled managers to begin to answer these questions.

Our introductory treatment of sensitivity analysis covered only the objective-function coefficients and right-hand-side values of the constraints. We restricted our treatment of these two types of sensitivity analysis to changes in only one value at a time. The calculations necessary to allow for simultaneously changing more than one objective-function coefficient or right-hand-side value (called parametric sensitivity analysis) are beyond the scope of this text.

We also did not discuss performing sensitivity analysis on the constraint coefficients. While we believe that students should recognize the importance of allowing these values to change in the linear programming model, a discussion of the techniques necessary to place limits on these changes is beyond the scope of an introductory text. Certain computer software packages allow for both sensitivity analysis on the constraint coefficients and parametric sensitivity analysis.

Several new terms have been introduced in this chapter. They are summarized in the Chapter Glossary. We suggest that you review them to be sure you understand them before you move on to Chapter 5.

Solved Problems

PROBLEM 1 Farley Manufacturing currently produces four different styles of hardwood speaker cabinets for expensive home entertainment centers. The marketing department identifies the four cabinets by their model numbers: X19, Y44, S17, and Z9. Profits for the cabinets are as follows: X19, \$55; Y44, \$70; S17, \$45; Z9, \$80.

Making each cabinet requires three operations: cutting, assembly and sanding, and finishing. Model X19 requires 2.5 hours of cutting time, 5 hours of assembly and sanding time, and 3 hours for finishing. The times required for the same operations for the Y44 are 3, 2, and 4 hours; for the S17: 5, 3, and 2 hours; and for the Z9: 4, 2, and 3 hours. For the current month, Farley Manufacturing has available 700 hours of cutting time, 800 hours of assembly and sanding time, and 550 hours of finishing time.

Use MASTER or another suitable computer software package to answer the following questions:

a. Susan Farley is trying to decide how many of each type of cabinet to produce next month. Given the present profits, what product mix would you recommend and how much monthly income should Susan project from the four speaker cabinets?

b. Farley Manufacturing could contract for additional cutting time at the rate of \$7 per hour. Would you recommend this option? Why or why not?

c. Susan is trying to decide whether she should arrange for additional capacity in any of the other operations. If she should, how much should she be willing to spend?

d. Farley Manufacturing has been experiencing quality control problems for the past 6 months. The company has responded by offering a price rebate to customers, amounting to \$10 on each cabinet. If quality problems occur again this month, would your product mix recommendation change?

e. The joiner used in the cutting operation breaks down periodically. Its downtime may effectively reduce the available cutting time by 100 hours this month. Could this cause a change in your product mix recommendation?

Solutions a. We can formulate this as a linear programming problem with the following decision variables:

x_1 = number of X19 cabinets

x_2 = number of Y44 cabinets

x_3 = number of S17 cabinets

x_4 = number of Z9 cabinets

Objective function:

$$\text{Maximize} \quad Z = 55x_1 + 70x_2 + 45x_3 + 80x_4$$

Subject to:

Cutting time	$2.5x_1 + 3x_2 + 5x_3 + 4x_4 \leq 700$
Assembly/sanding time	$5x_1 + 2x_2 + 3x_3 + 2x_4 \leq 800$
Finishing time	$3x_1 + 4x_2 + 2x_3 + 3x_4 \leq 550$

We used MASTER, the software package that accompanies this text, to solve the problem. Figure 4-18 shows the computer output, with the following results:

X19 cabinets $= x_1 = 0$

Y44 cabinets $= x_2 = 14.286$

S17 cabinets $= x_3 = 0$

Z9 cabinets $= x_4 = 164.286$

Remaining cutting time $= s_1 = 0$

Remaining assembly/sanding time $= s_2 = 442.857$

Remaining finish time $= s_3 = 0$

Objective function $= Z = 14{,}142.86$

b. This question can be approached in two ways. First, the problem can be reformulated in its dual form, since the solution to the dual problem gives the economic value of the constraining resources. The dual problem is:

Minimize $Z = 700d_1 + 800d_2 + 550d_3$

Subject to:

$$2.5d_1 + 5d_2 + 3d_3 \geq 55$$
$$3d_1 + 2d_2 + 4d_3 \geq 70$$
$$5d_1 + 3d_2 + 2d_3 \geq 45$$
$$4d_1 + 2d_2 + 3d_3 \geq 80$$

The simplex solution procedure could be used to solve the dual problem. The values of the decision variables will represent the economic values of the constraining resources in the original primal problem.

The second approach would be to look at the shadow prices in the final tableau of the simplex solution to the primal problem. These shadow prices will be equivalent to the dual values. We might use this method if we were working the problem manually and had the simplex tableaus available.

However, since linear programming software packages like MASTER usually output the dual values along with the primals, reformulation is not required. The output shown in Figure 4-18 provides the following dual values:

Constraint 1 (cutting) $= 15.714$

Constraint 2 (sanding) $= 0$

Constraint 3 (finishing) $= 5.714$

Since Farley Manufacturing can contract for additional cutting time at $7.00 per hour—a rate which is less than its economic value to the firm of $15.714—the company should arrange for the contract. (Since we are assuming that the cutting costs are sunk costs, we can consider the dual as the economic value of an additional unit of the resource.)

c. In looking at the solution to the dual problem and at the slack values in the optimal solution, we see

```
          LINEAR PROGRAMMING FORMULATION

OBJECTIVE FUNCTION:
   MAXIMIZE Z =
      55.00  X1 +    70.00  X2 +    45.00  X3 +   80.00 X4

SUBJECT TO:
      2.50X1 +    3.00X2 +    5.00X3 +    4.00X4  <=    700.00
      5.00X1 +    2.00X2 +    3.00X3 +    2.00X4  <=    800.00
      3.00X1 +    4.00X2 +    2.00X3 +    3.00X4  <=    550.00

     THE DECISION VARIABLES ARE      1. THROUGH   4.
     THE SLACK VARIABLES ARE         5. THROUGH   7.


         OPTIMAL SOLUTION

     ITERATIONS =   2.

     OBJECTIVE FUNCTION =        14142.860


     DECISION VARIABLES:

     VARIABLE   NAME    VALUE
         2.     X2       14.286
         4.     X4      164.286

     SLACK OR SURPLUS VARIABLES:

     VARIABLE   NAME           VALUE
         6.     SLACK          442.857


     DUAL RESULTS

     VARIABLE   NAME                VALUE
                X1                    1.429
                X2                    0.000
                X3                   45.000
                X4                    0.000
                CONSTRAINT 1.        15.714
                CONSTRAINT 2.         0.000
                CONSTRAINT 3.         5.714
```

Figure 4-18

Solved problem 1: MASTER linear programming output (figure continued on next page)

```
OBJECTIVE FUNCTION SENSITIVITY ANALYSIS

                                   LOWER      CURRENT      UPPER
VARIABLE    NAME    STATUS         BOUND      VALUE        BOUND

   1.       X1      NON-BASIC   -INFINITY     55.000       56.429
   2.       X2          BASIC      67.778     70.000      106.667
   3.       X3      NON-BASIC   -INFINITY     45.000       90.000
   4.       X4          BASIC      70.000     80.000       93.333


SENSITIVITY ANALYSIS FOR RIGHT-HAND-SIDE VALUES

              ORIGINAL             LOWER      CURRENT      UPPER
VARIABLE     CONSTRAINT            BOUND      VALUE        BOUND

   5.           1.               412.500     700.000     733.333
   6.           2.               357.143     800.000     INFINITY
   7.           3.               525.000     550.000     933.333
```

Figure 4-18 Continued

that the company already has an excess of assembly/sanding capacity; so Susan should not consider adding any more. However, since the finishing constraint is binding (slack = 0), she should try to add more of this capacity, if she can do so for less than the dual price of $5.714.

d. In looking at the linear programming output, we see that variables x_1 and x_3 are not in the final solution. Some thought should convince you that if the present profitability of the X19 and S17 cabinets is not enough to make them enter the solution, then decreasing their profitability by $10 will not cause some other cabinet to be built. Now the question is, What happens if the profitability of x_2 or x_4 is reduced? To answer this question, we perform sensitivity analysis on the coefficients of these two variables in the objective function.

The MASTER software package performs sensitivity analysis on both the objective function coefficients and the right-hand sides. The following sensitivity results for the objective function coefficients are shown in Figure 4-18.

Variable	Status	Lower	Current	Upper
x_1	Nonbasic	−Infinity	55.000	56.429
x_2	Basic	67.778	70.000	106.667
x_3	Nonbasic	−Infinity	45.000	90.000
x_4	Basic	70.000	80.000	93.333

This shows that the profit on variable x_2 (the Y44 cabinet) can drop only from $70 to $67.778 without affecting the product mix. Therefore, a quality problem in the Y44 cabinet could cause us to change the production mix.

Likewise, if the profit on variable x_4 (the Z9 cabinet) drops from $80 to anything below $70, the optimal production mix will be changed. Therefore, a quality problem in the Z9 cabinet could also cause us to change the production mix.

e. In looking at the final solution to the problem, we see that cutting time is a binding constraint; so a reduction in the time available would move the corner point. The question now is whether a reduction of 100 hours would be enough to cause the solution to move to a corner formed by a new set of constraints. To answer this question, we must perform sensitivity analysis on the right-hand-side value that corresponds to the cutting-time constraint.

MASTER performs sensitivity analysis on the right-hand sides. For this problem, the sensitivity outputs are as follows:

Constraint	Lower	Current	Upper
1	412.500	700.00	733.333
2	357.143	800.00	Infinity
3	525.000	550.00	933.333

Constraint 1 is cutting time. The sensitivity analysis indicates that the available hours could be reduced from 700 to 412.50 without changing corner points. Thus, a reduction of 100 hours would not change the variables which are in basis in the final solution.

General Questions and Assignments

1. Describe in your own terms what the dual of a linear programming problem is.
2. Develop an example to illustrate the economic interpretation of shadow prices. Discuss why the shadow prices for the primal model represent the solution to the dual model.
3. In performing a sensitivity analysis on the right-hand-side values, suppose one right-hand side has the following:

Lower Bound	Current Value	Upper Bound
−Infinity	2000	2400

Discuss what this means with respect to the linear programming model.

4. In performing a sensitivity analysis on the right-hand sides, we get the following results:

Lower Bound	Current Value	Upper Bound
600	2000	2400

Discuss what this means with respect to the linear programming solution.

5. Discuss why it is not necessary to solve the primal and dual models separately when using the simplex method, even if both solutions are required.
6. Suppose a sensitivity analysis on the objective-function coefficients produces the following results for one of the coefficients:

Lower Bound	Current Value	Upper Limit
1.59	3.60	Infinity

Discuss the proper interpretation for these results with respect to the linear programming solution.

7. Read at least three articles which describe applications for linear programming and sensitivity analysis. Write a paper summarizing the articles. Comment on the value of linear programming to these applications.
8. Visit a local firm that uses linear programming. Ask the analyst to discuss his or her use of sensitivity analysis. Write a short paper describing your interview.

Exercises and Application Problems

1. Consider the following primal linear programming problem:

   Maximize $Z = 6x_1 + 3x_2$

   Subject to:

$$3x_1 + 5x_2 \leq 30$$
$$5x_1 + 2x_2 \leq 20$$
$$x_1, x_2 \geq 0$$

   a. Formulate the dual to this problem.
   b. Solve both problems, either manually or using a software package.
   c. Compare the solutions to the primal problem with the solutions to the dual problem. Identify the shadow prices for both problems.

2. Consider the following primal linear programming problem:

   Maximize $Z = 8x_1 + 10x_2$

   Subject to:

$$6x_1 + 8x_2 \leq 130$$
$$9x_1 + 4x_2 \leq 65$$
$$x_1, x_2 \geq 0$$

   a. Formulate the dual to this problem.
   b. Solve both problems, either manually or using a software package.
   c. Compare the solutions to the primal problem with the solutions to the dual problem. Identify the shadow prices for both problems.

3. Consider the following primal linear programming problem:

   Minimize $Z = .08x_1 + .04x_2$

   Subject to:

$$2x_1 + 4x_2 \geq 18$$
$$4x_1 + 10x_2 \geq 40$$
$$x_2 \geq 3.5$$
$$x_1, x_2 \geq 0$$

   a. Formulate the dual to this problem.
   b. Solve both problems, either manually or using a software package.
   c. Compare the solutions to the primal problem with the solutions to the dual problem. Identify the shadow prices for both problems.

4. Consider the following primal linear programming problem:

   Minimize $Z = .5x_1 + 1.5x_2$

Subject to:

$$
\begin{aligned}
5x_1 + 4x_2 &\geq 600 \\
2x_1 + 4x_2 &\geq 2400 \\
8x_1 \qquad &\geq 600 \\
x_1, x_2 &\geq 0
\end{aligned}
$$

a. Formulate the dual to this problem.
b. Solve both problems, either manually or using a software package.
c. Compare the solutions to the primal problem with the solutions to the dual problem. Identify the shadow prices for both problems.

5. Suppose the financial investments class at your university has been asked by the dean of your school to invest part of the university's endowment fund as a class project. The amount you have been asked to invest is $10 million. You have identified four investment options: a growth stock mutual fund, a blue chip mutual fund, a recent junk bond offering, and U.S. Treasury bills (risk-free asset). The expected returns on these four options are: growth stock fund, 20%; blue chip fund, 15%; junk bonds, 17%; and U.S. Treasury bills, 10%.
The dean's requirements are:

No more than 50% of the funds can be invested in risky assets (growth stocks and junk bonds).

No more than 35% of the funds can be invested in any single area.

At least 25% of the funds must be invested in treasury bills.

The return on this investment should be as large as possible.

a. Formulate the appropriate linear programming problem to describe this situation.
b. Formulate the dual to this problem. Discuss the meaning of the dual formulation.
c. Solve both problems, either manually or using a software package.
d. Compare the solutions to the primal problem with the solutions to the dual problem. Discuss the meaning of the shadow prices for both problems.

6. The advertising manager of Bob and Ray's Shirt Shop has asked for your advice on the store's advertising strategy for next month. You have three choices for advertising; magazines, billboards, and newspapers. The following table gives some relevant information about each type of advertising.

	Magazines	**Billboards**	**Newspapers**
Cost per ad unit	$2,000	$6,000	$2,200
Consumer exposure per ad unit	10,000	20,000	15,000
Estimated increase in profit per ad unit	$15,000	$20,000	$12,000

Bob and Ray have two requirements; they want (1) no more than 3 billboard ad units and (2) at least twice as many newspaper ad units as magazine ad units. (Note: Fractional ad units are possible.) The advertising manager has a policy of limiting the total number of ad units to 15 per month, and she has told you that she wants to reach at least 100,000 people with the ads. The monthly advertising budget is $30,000. Assume the goal is to maximize profits.

a. Formulate the appropriate linear programming problem to describe this situation.
b. Formulate the dual to this problem. Discuss the economic reasoning behind the dual to this problem.
c. Solve both problems, either manually or using a software package.

d. Compare the solutions to the primal problem with the solutions to the dual problem. Write a report which fully discusses the results of the linear programming analysis.

7. The Treetop Software Company produces inventory control software for the IBM PC and compatible computers. The company provides a telephone support service for buyers of the five inventory packages. At present, the company has four employees assigned to telephone support. While all four employees can provide support on any of the packages, each is generally assigned to a specific hotline. The number of calls they can answer per hour depends on their expertise and on which package they support. The following table lists the average hourly number of calls that each employee can answer for each of the five packages.

	Software Package				
Employee	A	B	C	D	E
Vivian	5	8	4	6	5
Waylon	4	1	3	9	8
Jennifer	3	3	9	7	8
Howard	3	8	1	5	4

Vivian and Howard can work two support lines in the same shift if necessary, but the other employees can be assigned to only one line per shift. However, each hotline must have an assigned worker.

a. Assuming the goal is to maximize the number of calls that can be handled per hour, formulate the appropriate linear programming problem to describe this situation.

b. Formulate the dual to this problem. Discuss the meaning of the dual formulation.

c. Solve both problems, either manually or using a software package.

d. Compare the solutions to the primal problem with the solutions to the dual problem.

8. The Ambrose Plastic Molding Company makes three sizes of pet travel cages: small, medium, and large. The small cage sells to distributors for \$78; the medium and large sizes sell for \$110 and \$145 each. The cages are made of a special plastic that has been ordered with a specific coloring and density. Each small cage requires enough plastic to make 20 square feet of cage surface. Each medium cage requires enough plastic for 40 square feet of surface, and each large cage needs enough plastic for 75 feet of surface. Because of a fire at the supplier's refinery, Ambrose has on hand only enough plastic to make 160,000 square feet of cage area until the end of the year.

The company's accounting department assigns both direct and indirect costs to all the products Ambrose makes. Each small travel cage is assigned \$30 in direct costs; the medium and large cages have \$35 and \$38 in direct costs. The total costs allocated to the small, medium, and large cages are \$65, \$95, and \$125, respectively. Enough cages must be produced to cover the \$250,000 in indirect costs allocated to this product between now and the end of the year. The company has firm orders for 3000 small cages and 1200 medium cages.

a. Assuming the goal is to maximize profits, formulate the appropriate linear programming problem describing this situation.

b. Formulate the dual to this problem.

c. Solve both problems, either manually or using a software package.

d. Compare the solutions to the primal problem with the solutions to the dual problem. Discuss the meaning of the shadow prices for both problems.

9. Consider the following linear programming problem:

$$\text{Minimize} \quad Z = 3x_1 + 5x_2$$

Subject to:

$$\begin{aligned} 15x_1 + 18x_2 &\geq 140 \\ x_1 \qquad &\geq 6 \\ x_2 &\geq 3 \\ 10x_1 - 5x_2 &\leq 60 \\ x_1, x_2 &\geq 0 \end{aligned}$$

Find the optimal solution to this problem and determine the range within which the coefficients of the objective function can change before the solution point will change.

10. Consider the following linear programming problem:

Maximize $Z = 12x_1 + 10x_2$

Subject to:

$$\begin{aligned} 8x_1 + 10x_2 &\leq 64 \\ x_1 \qquad &\leq 5 \\ 6x_1 + 2x_2 &\leq 25 \\ x_2 &\leq 10 \\ x_1, x_2 &\geq 0 \end{aligned}$$

Find the optimal solution to this problem and determine the range within which the coefficients of the objective function can change before the solution point will change.

11. Consider the following linear programming problem:

Minimize $Z = 500x_1 + 800x_2 + 1200x_3$

Subject to:

$$\begin{aligned} 2x_1 + 3x_2 + 4x_3 &\geq 12 \\ x_1 + 2x_2 + x_3 &\geq 6 \\ 2x_1 + x_2 + x_3 &\geq 8 \\ x_1, x_2 &\geq 0 \end{aligned}$$

Find the optimal solution to this problem and determine the range within which the coefficients of the objective function can change before the solution point will change.

12. Consider the following linear programming problem:

Maximize $Z = 12x_1 + 4x_2 + 16x_3$

Subject to:

$$\begin{aligned} 2x_1 + 4x_2 + 2x_3 &\leq 1000 \\ 9x_1 \qquad + 6x_3 &\leq 1300 \\ 2x_1 + 8x_2 + 2x_3 &\geq 900 \\ x_1, x_2 &\geq 0 \end{aligned}$$

Find the optimal solution to this problem and determine the range within which the coefficients of the objective function can change before the solution point will change.

13. The Harrington Career Shop stocks three lines of fall coats: sport, career, and formal. The profit margin on sport coats is the lowest, and formal coats have the largest profit margins. However, the

formal coats also require more sales time and more display space. Because the store needs a base inventory to start the sales season, it orders a minimum of 1000 of each type of coat. When placing orders, the buyers must consider certain limitations. During the coming sales period, the store will have a maximum of 10,000 sales hours available and at most 10,000 square feet for sales area, including displays. The following table provides information for each coat line.

Coat Line	Profit per Coat	Sales Hours Required per 1000 Coats	Sales Area Required per 1000 Coats (square feet)
Sport	$20.00	600	300
Career	$28.00	700	400
Formal	$40.00	900	500

Find the optimal number of each type of coat for the Harrington Career Shop to order. Determine how much the profit margin on each type of coat can change before the optimal solution point will change.

14. LR Manufacturing makes picture frames, mirror frames, and coat racks at its small plant in Los Angeles. All three products are made of 1-inch walnut, which is in short supply this year. Presently the company has 3000 square feet of the wood on hand, but may not be able to get any more for the rest of this year. Counting waste, each picture frame takes 3 square feet of wood, each mirror frame takes 4 square feet, and each coat rack takes 2.5 square feet. LR's owner, Larry Reynoso, operates the company on a part-time basis and employs two family members as production workers. Each picture frame requires .5 hour of labor; each mirror frame takes .7 hour; and each coat rack, .9 hour. Larry can plan on having 800 hours of labor available for the rest of the year. He has already accepted orders for 100 picture frames and 300 coat racks. LR Manufacturing makes a $7.00 profit on each picture frame, $8.00 on a mirror frame, and $6.00 on a coat rack.
   a. How many of each product should be made between now and the end of the year?
   b. How much can each profit level change before your answer to question **a** will change?

15. Following are the initial and final tableaus for a linear programming problem.

Initial Tableau

Basis	c_j	x_1	x_2	x_3	s_1	s_2	s_3	
		7.5	15	10	0	0	0	b_i
s_1	0	2	0	3	1	0	0	8
s_2	0	.5	2	1	0	1	0	3
s_3	0	1	1	2	0	0	1	6
	Z_j	0	0	0	0	0	0	0
	$c_j - Z_j$	7.5	15	10	0	0	0	

Final Tableau

Basis	c_j	x_1	x_2	x_3	s_1	s_2	s_3	
		7.5	15	10	0	0	0	b_i
x_1	7.5	1	0	1	.5	0	0	4
x_2	15	0	1	.25	−.125	.5	0	.5
x_3	0	0	0	.75	−.375	−.5	1	1.5
	Z_j	7.5	15	11.25	1.375	7.5	0	37.5
	$c_j - Z_j$	0	0	−1.25	−1.375	−7.5	0	

a. Assume all relative revenue and cost information is measured in dollars. You are able to purchase an additional unit of any of the resources represented by the constraints for $5. Discuss which resource you would be willing to purchase and why.
b. If the profitability of decision variable 3 could be increased to 12, would this variable enter the basis? If so, which variable would leave the basis?
c. How much can the profitability of decision variable 1 change without changing the variables in the final tableau?

16. A local politician is considering running for governor and has asked you to recommend survey techniques to gather information on issues that concern state voters. You have decided on a possible mix of three data-gathering techniques: personal interviews, telephone surveys, and mail questionnaires. The potential candidate wants information from at least 700 voters. You know that telephone interviews will cost $4.00 each, with a usable-response rate of 40%, and that personal interviews will cost $7.00 each, with a usable-response rate of 60%. You also know that while mail questionnaires will cost only $1.00 each, their usable-response rate is only 10%. You estimate that you need information from at least 100 personal interviews, and from at least as many phone interviews as responses to mail questionnaires.
a. Formulate a linear programming model that will determine the number of personal interviews, telephone surveys, and mail questionnaires to use and the total cost to the candidate.
b. If the cost of a telephone interview increased to $5.00, would your answer to question **a** change?
c. If the cost of a mail questionnaire dropped to $.75, would your answer to question **a** change?
d. For each data-gathering technique, determine the range of costs within which your answer to question **a** will remain the same.

17. Consider the following linear programming problem:

$$\text{Minimize} \quad Z = 4x_1 + 7x_2$$

Subject to:

$$\begin{aligned} 5x_1 + 8x_2 &\leq 95 \\ x_1 \qquad &\geq 10 \\ x_2 &\geq 5 \\ 15x_1 - 8x_2 &\leq 125 \\ x_1, x_2 &\geq 0 \end{aligned}$$

Find the optimal solution to this problem and determine the range within which the right-hand-side constraint values can change before different variables will be brought into the final solution.

18. Consider the following linear programming problem:

$$\text{Maximize} \quad Z = 20x_1 + 15x_2$$

Subject to:

$$\begin{aligned} 2x_1 + 4x_2 &\leq 30 \\ x_1 \qquad &\leq 12 \\ 8x_1 + 5x_2 &\leq 90 \\ x_1, x_2 &\geq 0 \end{aligned}$$

Find the optimal solution to this problem and determine the range within which the right-hand-side constraint values can change before different variables will be brought into the final solution.

19. Consider the following linear programming problem:

$$\text{Minimize} \quad Z = 40x_1 + 60x_2 + 100x_3$$

Subject to:

$$4x_1 + 7x_2 + 5x_3 \geq 20$$
$$2x_1 + 2x_2 + x_3 \geq 12$$
$$x_1 + x_2 + 2x_3 \geq 7$$
$$x_1 \geq 2$$
$$x_2 \geq 1$$
$$x_1, x_2 \geq 0$$

Find the optimal solution to this problem and determine the range within which the right-hand-side constraint values can change before different variables will be brought into the final solution.

20. Consider the following linear programming problem:

$$\text{Maximize} \quad Z = 10x_1 + 8x_2 + 14x_3$$

Subject to:

$$3x_1 + 5x_2 + 4x_3 \leq 1100$$
$$8x_1 + 9x_3 \leq 900$$
$$3x_1 + 5x_2 + 7x_3 \geq 600$$
$$6x_2 + 4x_3 \leq 800$$
$$x_1, x_2 \geq 0$$

Find the optimal solution to this problem and determine the range within which the right-hand-side constraint values can change before different variables will be brought into the final solution.

21. J. M. Department Stores wants to expand its retail network. Current plans call for adding a store in Fort Rollins that will have 75,000 square feet of usable floor space. The total investment for the store cannot exceed \$1.5 million. Planners are attempting to allocate the new space among four departments. Past experience and the best forecasts available indicate the following levels of profitability for the four departments:

Men's clothing	\$3.00 per square foot
Women's clothing	\$5.00 per square foot
Housewares	\$2.50 per square foot
Auto supplies	\$2.75 per square foot

It is also known that different departments require different rates of investment:

Men's clothing	\$12.00 per square foot
Women's clothing	\$15.00 per square foot
Housewares	\$10.00 per square foot
Auto supplies	\$20.00 per square foot

Additionally, the planners know that the women's clothing department should not take more than 30% of the total space available and the space for auto supplies should be less than 25% of the space allocated for the other three departments. Finally, each department has a minimum space requirement:

Men's clothing	10,000 square feet
Women's clothing	15,000 square feet
Housewares	8,000 square feet
Auto supplies	5,000 square feet

a. Formulate this situation as a linear programming problem and solve.
b. Determine which constraints you would be willing to purchase additional amounts of. How much would you be willing to spend for each unit of these additional resources?
c. How much can each of the constraining relationships change before the variables in the basic solution will change?

22. The Hartman Company produces custom-made men's, women's, and children's hiking backpacks. Measurements are sent in to the factory from stores that sell Hartman products. Making the backpacks involves four operations: cutting the material, sewing the pack, making the frame, and testing the completed product for fit and balance on an instrumentized robot that Kathy Hartman developed. The men's pack has a unit profitability of $30, and the women's and children's packs have profit levels of $27 and $23. The company is trying to set distribution schedules for the next month. The only serious constraints involve labor availability in the four departments. The cutting department is scheduled for 800 hours, framing for 1200 hours, sewing for 1600 hours, and testing for 600 hours. Each man's pack requires .75 hour for cutting, .75 hour for sewing, 1 hour for making the frame, and .3 hour for testing. Each woman's pack requires .5 hour for cutting, .6 hour for sewing, .8 hour for making the frame, and .25 hour for testing. The children's pack requires .4 hour for cutting, .5 hour for sewing, .75 hour for making the frame, and .25 hour for testing.
    a. How many backpacks of each type should Hartman produce next month? How much profit will be made at this point?
    b. For which of the operations would you be willing to authorize overtime? Discuss your reasoning.
    c. How much can each of the time availabilities change before the variables in the basic solution will change?

23. The Okimbu Engineering Support Stores sell and install computer work stations purchased from manufacturers in Los Angeles and San Francisco. In a typical month, the company orders 500 work stations. Since on-time delivery of the product is critical, Mark Okimbu has established a policy of not relying on any one carrier or form of transportation in getting shipments from the West Coast. Okimbu presently uses three carriers; an air freight company, a trucking company, and a container company that piggybacks truck trailers on rail cars. Transporting a work station from California to the central Okimbu warehouse costs $200 by air freight, $150 by truck, and $125 by piggyback. Each month, the company ships at least 5 work stations by each form of transportation. In addition, if last month's pattern is continued, at least as many units will be shipped by air freight as by piggyback, and truck shipments will exceed both air freight and piggyback shipments combined.
    a. For the current month, how many work stations will be shipped by each method? What will be the cost of shipping?
    b. Using your knowledge of sensitivity analysis, would you recommend any changes in the present shipping schedule? Discuss your reasoning.

Chapter Glossary

Dual problem A linear programming problem associated with the primal problem by a specific set of relationships. Solving the dual problem also provides a solution to the primal problem.

Dual variable A decision variable in the dual problem associated with a constraint in the primal problem. The value of a dual variable is the economic value of adding a unit of the appropriate constraining resource in the primal problem.

Multiple optimal solutions A case in linear programming in which the objective function has the same slope as one of the constraint equations. Thus, there is no unique corner-point solution. This situation is detected when sensitivity analysis indicates that the maximum change allowed, up or down, in the objective-function coefficient is zero.

Primal problem The original formulation of a linear programming model.

Relevant cost A cost which varies according to the levels set for the decision variables in a linear programming model. These costs are factored into the objective-function constraints.

Sensitivity analysis A technique used to examine the effect that changes in specific values for the original linear programming model have on the optimal corner-point solution.

Shadow price The value of adding a unit of a constraining resource in the primal problem. The corresponding value of the variable in the dual problem.

Sunk cost A cost that must be incurred regardless of the levels set for the decision variables. This cost is not factored into the objective-function coefficients.

Chapter References

BOOKS

Anderson, D. R., D. J. Sweeney, and T. A. Williams. *Linear Programming for Decision Making.* St. Paul, Minn.: West, 1974.

Charnes, A., and W. W. Cooper. *Management Models and Industrial Applications of Linear Programming.* New York: Wiley, 1961.

Dantzig, G. B. *Linear Programming and Extensions.* Princeton, N.J.: Princeton, 1963.

Gass, S. *Linear Programming,* 4th ed. New York: McGraw-Hill, 1975.

Hillier, F., and G. J. Lieberman. *Introduction to Operations Research,* 4th ed. Oakland: Holden-Day, 1986.

Wagner, H. *Principles of Operations Research with Applications to Managerial Decisions,* 2d ed. Englewood Cliffs, N.J.: Prentice-Hall, 1975.

ARTICLES

Allman, W. P. "An Optimization Approach to Freight Car Collision under Fiscal-Mileage per Diem Rental Rates." *Management Science,* Vol. 18, No. 10 (June), 1972.

Anderson, D. "Models for Determining Least-Cost Investments in Electricity Supply." *The Bell Journal of Economics and Management Science,* Spring 1972.

Barken, J. D., and J. E. Bruno. "Operations Research in Planning Political Campaign Strategies." *Operations Research,* September–October 1972.

Bass, F. M., and R. T. Lonsdale. "An Exploration of Linear Programming in Media Selection." *Journal of Marketing Research,* Vol. 3, 1966.

Carino, H. F., and C. H. LeNoir, Jr. "Optimizing Wood Procurement in Cabinet Manufacturing." *Interfaces,* March–April 1988.

Charnes, A., W. W. Cooper, and R. Ferguson. "Blending Aviation Gasolines: A Study in Programming Interdependent Activities." *Econometrica,* Vol. 20, No. 2 (April), 1952.

———. "Optimal Estimation of Executive Compensation by Linear Programming." *Management Science,* Vol. 1, No. 2 (January), 1955.

Cohen, K. J., and F. S. Hammer. "Linear Programming and Optimal Bank-Asset Management Decisions." *Journal of Finance,* Vol. 21, 1967.

Drayer, W., and S. Seabury. "Facilities Expansion Model." *Interfaces: Practice of Management Science,* Vol. 5, No. 2 (February), 1975.

Engle, J. F., and M. W. Warshaw. "Allocating Advertising Research." *Journal of Advertising Research,* Vol. 4, No. 3, 1964.

Glassey, C. R., and V. K. Gupta. "A Linear Programming Analysis of Paper Recycling." *Management Science,* Vol. 21, No. 4 (December), 1974.

Hanssmann, F., and S. W. Hess. "A Linear Programming Approach to Production and Employment Scheduling." *Management Technology,* No. 1 (January), 1960.

Hess, W. H., J. Weaverm, H. Siegfeldt, J. Whelan, and P. Zitau. "Nonpartisan Political Redistricting by Computer." *Operations Research,* Vol. 13, No. 6 (November–December), 1965.

Kotak, D. B. "Application of Linear Programming to Plywood Manufacturing." *Interfaces,* Vol. 7, No. 1, Part 2 (November), 1976.

Reddy, J. "A Model to Schedule Sales Optimally Blended from Scarce Resources." *Interfaces,* Vol. 6, No. 2, Part 2 (November), 1975.

Sharda, R. "The State of the Art of Linear Programming on Personal Computers." *Interfaces,* July–August 1988.

Mini Case

CASE 4A

THE GROSSMAN DISTRIBUTION COMPANY, Part I

The commute between Jim Wilson's home in Tacoma and his downtown Seattle office is usually a pleasant trip, especially since he switched from driving his own car to riding the Puget Sound Express bus. The area's natural beauty had been a major factor in Jim's decision to leave Dallas several years ago to join the Grossman Distribution Company. But this morning, Jim found the ride was less relaxing than usual. Yesterday, he had received word that Ancil Fong, one of the three sales representatives in Jim's region, had resigned. Because the company has been having financial problems recently, H. P. Grossman, the president, has asked Jim not to hire a replacement for at least six months.

Before Fong's resignation, the three sales representatives had been calling on customers in five territories. The number of customers varied from territory to territory, as follows:

Territory 1	40
Territory 2	80
Territory 3	100
Territory 4	30
Territory 5	60

Figure C4-1, a map of the five territories, shows where the sales representatives live: Sandra Dunn (SD) lives in territory 2, and Nick Ferris (NF) lives in territory 1. The map also shows the relative sizes of the rectangular territories.

Throughout the 45-minute bus ride, Jim thought about how to handle the situation. He was absolutely sure that he didn't want to lose contact with the departed Fong's customer base. But to keep them, he would have to reassign the customers to Sandra and Nick. Now the puzzling question was how to allocate the customers. Jim's

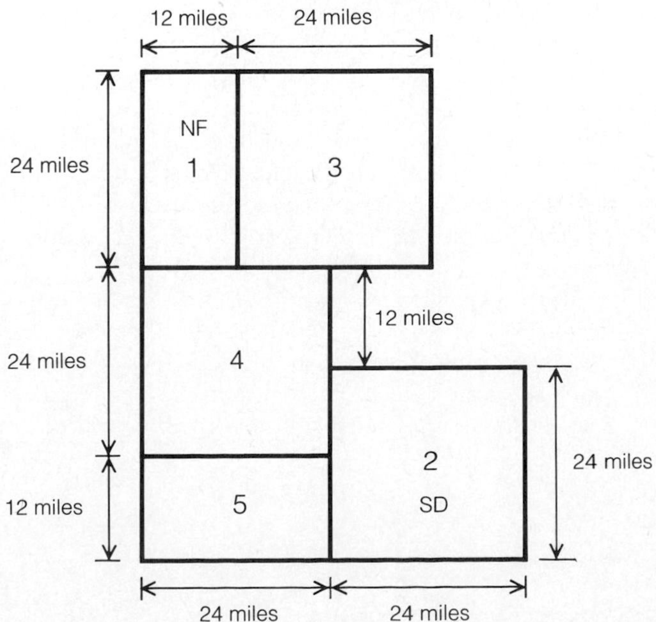

Figure C4-1
Sales territory map for Grossman Distribution Company

first instinct was to merely divide Fong's customers between the two remaining sales representatives.

While this seemed like a reasonable approach, Jim also recognized that now might be an opportune time to reduce the travel burden for Sandra and Nick. Since all the sales representatives had acquired customers in a random fashion over the years, each had customers scattered throughout all five sales territories. They also had somewhat frantic travel schedules. If Sandra and Nick had to take on Fong's customers, they would be doing even more traveling.

After a quick stop at the office coffee bar and some cordial bantering with a few of the office staff, Jim went to his office to try to work out a totally new customer allocation scheme. As he thought about it, he made the following notes:

Objective is to minimize travel time for Sandra and Nick

Must cover all customers

Distance traveled closely equates to travel time

Assign Sandra and Nick the same percentage of customers

Assume that travel occurs east-west, west-east, south-north, or north-south

Assume all customers are located at the center of each territory

Then he drew up several assignment plans, but each time the total travel distance was different. Short of listing all the possibilities, how was Jim to know if he had the most feasible customer allocation plan? Frustrated by not being able to find a quick solution to his problem, he finally called Professor Harrington at State University. Over the years, Jim had turned to the professor several times for help with similarly tricky problems. After listening to the entire story and going through Jim's notes over the phone, Professor Harrington said that he would have his management science class take on Jim's problem as a class project. He promised to report back very soon with a recommendation.

CASE 4B

THE GROSSMAN DISTRIBUTION COMPANY, Part II

Three days after his call to Professor Harrington (see Case 4A), the phone rang in Jim Wilson's office. It was Candice Weatherbe, a student in Professor Harrington's management science class. She explained that she was the project leader assigned to Jim's problem. She said that the class had developed a model which would allocate the customers in each territory in a pattern that minimized travel. However, before finalizing their conclusions, the students had a question for Jim. They were concerned about his assumption regarding travel distances between territories. Candice pointed out to Jim that her group's solution was based on the assumption that travel distances are known with certainty.

Jim acknowledged that the sales representatives would not actually travel just north-south and east-west, but he said he thought it was too complicated to deal with the problem any other way. He then asked Candice if her group could determine how much the travel distances could change before the optimal customer allocations change. She assured him that the information would be included in the group's report.

TRANSPORTATION, TRANSSHIPMENT, AND ASSIGNMENT MODELS

Chapter Outline

Chapter 5

Why You Need to Know

Decision makers in seemingly unrelated organizations often find themselves facing similar situations. For instance, many organizations need to transport a product from one or more sources of supply to one or more demand destinations and would like to determine a transportation schedule that minimizes shipping costs. This problem is found in numerous retail, wholesale, distribution, manufacturing, service, and government organizations. These situations are modeled by what management scientists call transportation or transshipment problems. Also, many organizations encounter situations where they need to assign workers, or teams, to alternative work sites or projects. The decision makers would like to have a systematic method for making these assignments. In management science terminology, these situations are called assignment problems.

Transportation, transshipment, and assignment problems were among the first to be tackled using quantitative decision-making tools. In addition, they were among the first to be formulated as linear programming models. However, as we shall show, transportation and assignment problems can become cumbersome to formulate and solve using linear programming. Fortunately, the special structure of these problems allows more efficient solution techniques to be developed. In this chapter we will look at both the linear programming and special solution procedures used to formulate and solve transportation, transshipment, and assignment problems.

Because transportation, transshipment, and assignment problems are so frequently encountered in many organizations, you need to become familiar with this class of decision problems and the techniques for solving them.

Chapter Objectives

The purpose of this chapter is to introduce three special types of linear programming problems. Because these three problem situations — transportation, transshipment, and assignment — are so commonly encountered in managerial decision making, special techniques have been developed to solve them. This chapter will discuss each of these three decision problems and will explore solution techniques used to deal with them.

The specific objectives of this chapter are:

1. To identify the type of decision-making situations which can be represented as transportation problems.
2. To demonstrate techniques necessary to formulate and solve transportation problems.
3. To identify the types of decision-making situations which can be represented as transshipment problems.
4. To demonstrate techniques necessary to formulate and solve transshipment problems.
5. To identify the types of decision-making situations which can be represented as assignment problems.
6. To demonstrate techniques necessary to formulate and solve assignment problems.
7. To show how computer software can be used to greatly reduce the time needed to solve these three types of decision problems.

5-1 A BRIEF HISTORY OF TRANSPORTATION, TRANSSHIPMENT, AND ASSIGNMENT PROBLEMS

While the problems solved by the techniques covered in this chapter have been present in organizations for a long time, the solution techniques are more recent, and are generally associated with the linear programming procedures discussed in earlier chapters. As we shall see, all three types of problems considered in this chapter—transportation, transshipment, and assignment—can be formulated as linear programming problems; therefore, the simplex solution procedure can be used to solve all three.

The fact that transportation, transshipment, and assignment problems are special forms of the general category of linear programming problems was recognized early on by management scientists such as Dantzig and Koopmans. However, the special structure of these problems, and the initial difficulty in solving large linear programming problems, led to the development of special solution procedures. In particular, the work of two Hungarian mathematicians, E. Egervary and D. Konig, during the 1930s and the extension of their work by H. W. Kuhn during the 1950s, led directly to the solution procedures discussed in this chapter.

5-2 GORMAN OUTERWARE: A TRANSPORTATION PROBLEM

Gorman Outerware has introduced a new medium-weight all-purpose jacket that seems to have a good chance of being a major product in the outerware market. The jacket contains a layer of water-repellant material that, unlike the waterproofing from competing materials, adds an insulation factor. This means the Gorman jacket with a given insulation rating is lighter in weight than any competing jacket with the same insulation rating.

Gorman Outerware has three manufacturing plants, located in Brainard, Minnesota; Macon, Georgia; and Waco, Texas. Gorman's capacity to produce new jackets at each of these locations for next season has been determined as follows:

Brainard	12,000 jackets
Macon	10,000 jackets
Waco	13,000 jackets

Total capacity at the three plants is 35,000 jackets.

Since its founding in 1973, Gorman has limited itself strictly to manufacturing clothing and has always entered into contracts with other companies to market and distribute its products. Gorman has a distribution agreement for the new jackets with a company which has four distribution centers. The four centers are in Reno, Nevada; Peoria, Illinois; Springfield, Massachusetts; and Oklahoma City, Oklahoma. After a series of meetings with Gorman officials, the distribution company has placed an order for 35,000 jackets to be delivered to its four distribution centers in the following amounts:

Reno	8,000 jackets
Peoria	9,000 jackets
Springfield	11,000 jackets
Oklahoma City	7,000 jackets

Notice that 35,000 jackets are required by the distribution outlet, an amount which equals Gorman's production capacity. Later in this chapter we will present an example which does not have equal demand and capacity.

The problem facing Gorman Outerware is to determine how many jackets to ship from each plant to each distribution center so that the total shipping cost is as small as possible. This is a classic **transportation problem**, involving the distribution of goods (jackets) from a set of sources (manufacturing plants) to a set of demands (distribution centers).

Gorman's accounting department has come up with the following set of shipping costs:

From	to	Cost per Jacket ($)
Brainard	Reno	1.40
	Peoria	.90
	Springfield	1.20
	Oklahoma City	1.00
Macon	Reno	1.50
	Peoria	1.30
	Springfield	1.05
	Oklahoma City	.80
Waco	Reno	.75
	Peoria	1.25
	Springfield	1.50
	Oklahoma City	.70

Since Gorman Outerware is interested in a shipping schedule that will minimize total transportation costs, it needs a solution procedure that will provide this minimization.

A LINEAR PROGRAMMING SOLUTION

Any transportation problem can be formulated and solved as a linear programming problem. We begin by defining the decision variables. In this case there are 12 decision variables, one for each possible plant to distribution center shipping route:

x_{11} = quantity shipped from Brainard to Reno

x_{12} = quantity shipped from Brainard to Peoria

x_{13} = quantity shipped from Brainard to Springfield

x_{14} = quantity shipped from Brainard to Oklahoma City

x_{21} = quantity shipped from Macon to Reno

x_{22} = quantity shipped from Macon to Peoria

x_{23} = quantity shipped from Macon to Springfield

x_{24} = quantity shipped from Macon to Oklahoma City

x_{31} = quantity shipped from Waco to Reno

x_{32} = quantity shipped from Waco to Peoria

x_{33} = quantity shipped from Waco to Springfield

x_{34} = quantity shipped from Waco to Oklahoma City

Since Gorman is trying to determine the shipping schedule which will minimize shipping costs, the objective function becomes:

$$\text{Minimize} \quad Z = 1.40x_{11} + .90x_{12} + 1.20x_{13} + 1.00x_{14} + 1.50x_{21} + 1.30x_{22} + 1.05x_{23} + .80x_{24} + .75x_{31} + 1.25x_{32} + 1.50x_{33} + .70x_{34}$$

The constraints are based on the fact that a limited number of jackets are available at each production plant and that the distribution centers must receive the number of jackets they require. We can group the constraints into two categories: supply and demand.

Supply Constraints
Ship no more than 12,000 from Brainard:

$$x_{11} + x_{12} + x_{13} + x_{14} \leq 12{,}000$$

Ship no more than 10,000 from Macon:

$$x_{21} + x_{22} + x_{23} + x_{24} \leq 10{,}000$$

Ship no more than 13,000 from Waco:

$$x_{31} + x_{32} + x_{33} + x_{34} \leq 13{,}000$$

Demand Constraints
Ship 8000 to Reno:

$$x_{11} + x_{21} + x_{31} = 8000$$

Ship 9000 to Peoria:

$$x_{12} + x_{22} + x_{32} = 9000$$

Ship 11,000 to Springfield:

$$x_{13} + x_{23} + x_{33} = 11{,}000$$

Ship 7000 to Oklahoma City:

$$x_{14} + x_{24} + x_{34} = 7000$$

Notice that the size of the linear programming formulation depends on the number of supply locations and the number of demand points. If n = supplies and m = demands, then the number of decision variables is determined by the product of $n \times m$, and the number of constraints is the sum of $n + m$. As you might guess, some transportation problems can become very large. A national brewery which has 22 production facilities and 200 distribution centers would have a linear programming formulation with 4400 decision variables and 222 constraints.

Once a transportation problem has been formulated as a linear programming problem, the solution can be achieved manually using the simplex method or more efficiently by using a computer linear programming software package. To demonstrate, we will use the linear programming module contained in the MASTER software which accompanies this text. Figure 5-1 shows the data entry screen. Figure 5-2 shows the resulting output when the program is executed. The values for the decision variables in the computer output in Figure 5-2 indicate the amounts to be shipped from each factory to each distribution center.

9000 from Brainard to Peoria

3000 from Brainard to Springfield

8000 from Macon to Springfield

2000 from Macon to Oklahoma City

8000 from Waco to Reno

5000 from Waco to Oklahoma City

Master INTRODUCTION TO MANAGEMENT SCIENCE

Gorman Outerware

	X11	X12	X13	X14	X21	X22	X23	X24	X31	X32	X33	X34	R-H-Side
Obj. Coef	1.40	.90	1.20	1.00	1.50	1.30	1.05	.80	.75	1.25	1.50	.70	
Const 1	1.0	1.0	1.0	1.0									≤12000.0
Const 2					1.0	1.0	1.0	1.0					≤10000.0
Const 3									1.0	1.0	1.0	1.0	≤13000.0
Const 4	1.0				1.0				1.0				= 8000.0
Const 5		1.0				1.0				1.0			= 9000.0
Const 6			1.0				1.0				1.0		=11000.0
Const 7				1.0				1.0				1.0	= 7000.0

Use arrows to select and change data. Press F1 to Exit.

<F5> Add Row <F6> Add Col <F7> Del Row <F8> Del Col

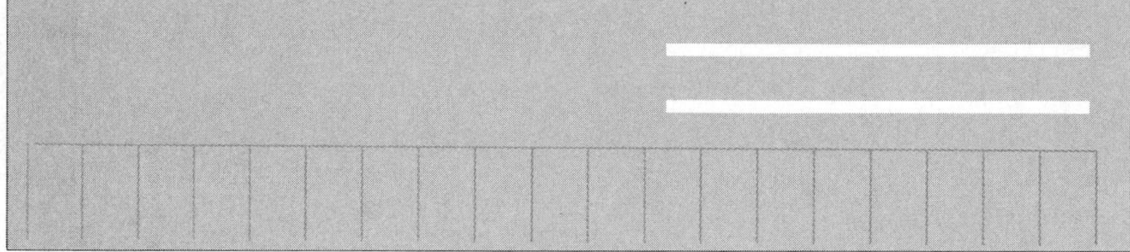

Figure 5-1
Gorman Outerware problem: MASTER data entry screen

The total cost of this shipping schedule is $31,200. The problem took 6 iterations of the simplex tableau to reach the optimal point. There is no other shipping schedule which will result in a lower total shipping cost.

AN ALTERNATIVE SOLUTION PROCEDURE

While the difficulty of solving large linear programming problems has decreased now that computer time has become relatively cheap, simpler models always have an advantage over more complicated models. Fortunately, the linear programming constraints have a structure that allows the model to be reformulated and solved by a different procedure, which we demonstrate next.

To appreciate this special procedure, and its equivalence to the linear programming formulation, notice in Figure 5-1 that in each constraint the coefficients on the decision variables are either 0 or 1. Notice also that each decision variable has a coefficient of 1 only once in the set of supply constraints and only once in the set of demand constraints. This special form of linear programming model allows a specialized solution technique.

```
                 LINEAR PROGRAMMING FORMULATION

   OBJECTIVE FUNCTION:
     MINIMIZE Z =
          1.40   X11 +      0.90   X12 +      1.20   X13 +      1.00   X14 +      1.50   X21
   +      1.30   X22 +      1.05   X23 +      0.80   X24 +      0.75   X31 +      1.25   X32
   +      1.50   X33 +      0.70   X34

   SUBJECT TO:
         1.00X11 +       1.00X12 +       1.00X13 +       1.00X14 +       0.00X21 +       0.00X22 +
       0.00X23 +       0.00X24 +       0.00X31 +       0.00X32 +       0.00X33 +       0.00X34   <=
     12000.00
         0.00X11 +       0.00X12 +       0.00X13 +       0.00X14 +       1.00X21 +       1.00X22 +
       1.00X23 +       1.00X24 +       0.00X31 +       0.00X32 +       0.00X33 +       0.00X34   <=
     10000.00
         0.00X11 +       0.00X12 +       0.00X13 +       0.00X14 +       0.00X21 +       0.00X22 +
       0.00X23 +       0.00X24 +       1.00X31 +       1.00X32 +       1.00X33 +       1.00X34   <=
     13000.00
         1.00X11 +       0.00X12 +       0.00X13 +       0.00X14 +       1.00X21 +       0.00X22 +
       0.00X23 +       0.00X24 +       1.00X31 +       0.00X32 +       0.00X33 +       0.00X34    =
      8000.00
         0.00X11 +       1.00X12 +       0.00X13 +       0.00X14 +       0.00X21 +       1.00X22 +
       0.00X23 +       0.00X24 +       0.00X31 +       1.00X32 +       0.00X33 +       0.00X34    =
      9000.00
         0.00X11 +       0.00X12 +       1.00X13 +       0.00X14 +       0.00X21 +       0.00X22 +
       1.00X23 +       0.00X24 +       0.00X31 +       0.00X32 +       1.00X33 +       0.00X34    =
     11000.00
         0.00X11 +       0.00X12 +       0.00X13 +       1.00X14 +       0.00X21 +       0.00X22 +
      0.00X23 +       1.00X24 +       0.00X31 +       0.00X32 +       0.00X33 +       1.00X34    =
      7000.00

                 THE DECISION VARIABLES ARE     1  THROUGH  12
                 THE SLACK VARIABLES ARE        13  THROUGH  15
                 THE ARTIFICIAL VARIABLES ARE   16  THROUGH  19
            OPTIMAL SOLUTION

   ITERATIONS =  6

   OBJECTIVE FUNCTION =        31200.000


   DECISION VARIABLES:

   VARIABLE  NAME             VALUE
       2       X12           9000.000
       3       X13           3000.000
       7       X23           8000.000
       8       X24           2000.000
       9       X31           8000.000
      12       X34           5000.000
```

Figure 5-2
Gorman Outerware problem: MASTER output (figure continued on next page)

```
SLACK OR SURPLUS VARIABLES:

VARIABLE    NAME               VALUE
13          SLACK              0.000


DUAL RESULTS

VARIABLE    NAME                      VALUE
            X11                       0.400
            X12                       0.000
            X13                       0.000
            X14                       0.050
            X21                       0.650
            X22                       0.550
            X23                       0.000
            X24                       0.000
            X31                       0.000
            X32                       0.600
            X33                       0.550
            X34                       0.000
            CONSTRAINT    1           0.000
            CONSTRAINT    2           0.150
            CONSTRAINT    3           0.250
            CONSTRAINT    4          -1.000
            CONSTRAINT    5          -0.900
            CONSTRAINT    6          -1.200
            CONSTRAINT    7          -0.950
```

Figure 5-2 Continued

Because each decision variable represents a possible distribution route, the objective-function coefficients can be represented by the matrix shown in Table 5-1. Also, since each decision variable has a coefficient of 1 only twice in the constraints—once in a supply constraint and once in a demand constraint—the matrix in Table 5-1 can be expanded to incorporate the constraints shown in Table 5-2. To parallel the linear programming formulation, x_{11} represents the quantity to be shipped from Brainard to Reno, x_{12} represents the quantity to be shipped from Brainard to Peoria, x_{13} is the quantity to be shipped from Brainard to Springfield, and x_{14} is the number shipped from Brainard to Oklahoma City. The first row of Table 5-2 would represent the constraint:

$$x_{11} + x_{12} + x_{13} + x_{14} = 12{,}000$$

Table 5-2 is just a different way of representing the linear programming model. As with all linear programming models, we will need to develop a solution procedure to answer the same three questions:

1. Where do we start looking for an optimal solution?
2. Where do we go next?
3. When can we stop looking?

Table 5-1 OBJECTIVE-FUNCTION COEFFICIENTS REPRESENTED IN MATRIX FORM

	Distribution Centers			
Plants	Reno	Peoria	Springfield	Oklahoma City
Brainard	1.40	.90	1.20	1.00
Macon	1.50	1.30	1.05	.80
Waco	.75	1.25	1.50	.70

Table 5-2 TRANSPORTATION TABLEAU FOR GORMAN OUTERWARE

	Distribution Centers				
Plants	Reno	Peoria	Springfield	Oklahoma City	**Supplies**
Brainard	1.40	.90	1.20	1.00	12,000
Macon	1.50	1.30	1.05	.80	10,000
Waco	.75	1.25	1.50	.70	13,000
Demands	8000	9000	11,000	7000	

Finding an Initial Starting Solution

The method used to solve transportation problems has many similarities with the simplex procedure: We find an initial starting solution and move in a systematic fashion to the final solution, looking at each step for the single largest incremental improvement. However, while we always started the simplex procedure at the origin, we can find several initial starting solutions for a transportation problem. The following paragraphs discuss two alternative starting methods: the northwest corner rule and the minimum-cost method.

The Northwest Corner Rule This is probably the easiest rule to use to find a starting solution. You simply start allocating supplies to demands beginning with the upper left-hand corner of the matrix and move to the lower right-hand corner. In each case we allocate the maximum amount to each cell in the matrix. Therefore, in the Gorman Outerware problem we start with the Brainard–Reno cell and allocate 8000, which will completely satisfy the demand from Reno. We will then move to the Brainard–Peoria cell to allocate the remaining output from the Brainard plant. We will continue to allocate the maximum amount to each cell until we have the initial transportation tableau shown in Table 5-3.

The advantage of the northwest corner rule is that the initial allocation is very easy to make. The disadvantage is that the method does not take into consideration costs (or profits, if we are maximizing rather than minimizing) in making the initial allocation.

Notice that this method gives six initial transportation routes. The number of allocated cells in any transportation tableau should always be $n + m - 1$. This will occasionally be an issue, as we will discuss shortly. The cost of this starting solution is

$$(1.40 \times 8000 + .90 \times 4000 + 1.30 \times 5000 + 1.05 \times 5000 + 1.50 \times 6000 + .70 \times 7000) = \$40{,}450.$$

Table 5-3 INITIAL TRANSPORTATION TABLEAU FOR GORMAN OUTERWARE—NORTHWEST CORNER RULE

	Distribution Centers				
Plants	Reno	Peoria	Springfield	Oklahoma City	**Supplies**
Brainard	1.40 8000	.90 4000	1.20	1.00	12,000
Macon	1.50	1.30 5000	1.05 5,000	.80	10,000
Waco	.75	1.25	1.50 6,000	.70 7000	13,000
Demands	8000	9000	11,000	7000	

Using Minimum Costs for the Initial Allocation The **minimum-cost method** of making the initial allocation, unlike the northwest corner rule, does take costs into consideration. To make the initial allocation, we search the transportation tableau (Table 5-4) for the lowest-cost shipping cell.

The lowest cost is the \$.70 per jacket shipping charge between Waco and Oklahoma City. We allocate as many as possible to this cell. This will be the 7000 also shown in Table 5-4. This allocation means that Oklahoma City's demand has been completely satisfied. This is indicated by lining out the appropriate column in Table 5-5. We no longer need to worry about Oklahoma City.

The second allocation is made by searching the remaining cells in Table 5-5 for the next lowest distribution cost. This is the \$.75 from Waco to Reno, and the maximum amount 6000, is put into this cell (Table 5-6). This eliminates Waco as a source of supply.

The next least expensive cell is the \$.80 per jacket shipping cost between Macon and Oklahoma City, but this route is not available since all of Oklahoma City's demand is satisfied from the Waco plant. However, the \$.90 cost from Brainard to Peoria is

Table 5-4 INITIAL TRANSPORTATION TABLEAU FOR GORMAN OUTERWARE—MINIMUM-COST METHOD

	Distribution Centers				
Plants	Reno	Peoria	Springfield	Oklahoma City	**Supplies**
Brainard	1.40	.90	1.20	1.00	12,000
Macon	1.50	1.30	1.05	.80	10,000
Waco	.75	1.25	1.50	.70 7000	13,000
Demands	8000	9000	11,000	7000	

Table 5-5 INITIAL ALLOCATION FOR GORMAN OUTERWARE

	Distribution Centers				
Plants	Reno	Peoria	Springfield	Oklahoma City	**Supplies**
Brainard	1.40	.90	1.20	1.00	12,000
Macon	1.50	1.30	1.05	.80	10,000
Waco	.75	1.25	1.50	.70 7000	13,000
Demands	8000	9000	11,000	7000	

Table 5-6 SECOND ALLOCATION FOR GORMAN OUTERWARE

	Distribution Centers				
Plants	Reno	Peoria	Springfield	Oklahoma City	**Supplies**
Brainard	1.40	.90	1.20	1.00	12,000
Macon	1.50	1.30	1.05	.80	10,000
Waco	.75 6000	1.25	1.50	.70 7000	13,000
Demands	8000	9000	11,000	7000	

available, and we can allocate 9000 to this route, as shown in Table 5-7. This also means that Peoria's entire demand has been satisfied.

Continuing our search for the next cheapest allocation in the cells that have not been lined out, we select the Macon–Springfield route and put 10,000 in this cell (Table 5-8). We have now eliminated everything except the Brainard–Reno and Brainard–Springfield routes. Putting the amounts needed to satisfy the Reno and Springfield demands in these two cells, we arrive at the minimum-cost starting allocation shown in Table 5-9.

Notice that we once again have designated six shipping routes, but the cost of this starting solution is $(1.40 \times 2000 + .90 \times 9000 + 1.20 \times 1000 + 1.05 \times 10{,}000 + .75 \times 6000 + .70 \times 7000) = \$32{,}000$. This is considerably less than the northwest corner rule starting-point cost. Thus, as you can see, the starting point for solving the transportation problem depends on which method you employ.

Too Few Initial Cells

Earlier we stated that the initial allocation of an m-source, n-destination transportation problem must contain $m + n - 1$ cells. This is required for the solution procedure we are going to discuss. For the Gorman Outerware problem, the initial allocations found

Table 5-7 THIRD ALLOCATION FOR GORMAN OUTERWARE

Plants	Distribution Centers: Reno	Peoria	Springfield	Oklahoma City	Supplies
Brainard	1.40	.90 9000	1.20	1.00	12,000
Macon	1.50	1.30	1.05	.80	10,000
Waco	.75 6000	1.25	1.50	.70 7000	13,000
Demands	8000	9000	11,000	7000	

Table 5-8 FOURTH ALLOCATION FOR GORMAN OUTERWARE

Plants	Distribution Centers: Reno	Peoria	Springfield	Oklahoma City	Supplies
Brainard	1.40	.90 9000	1.20	1.00	12,000
Macon	1.50	1.30	1.05 10,000	.80	10,000
Waco	.75 6000	1.25	1.50	.70 7000	13,000
Demands	8000	9000	11,000	7000	

Table 5-9 STARTING ALLOCATION FOR GORMAN OUTERWARE—MINIMUM-COST METHOD

Plants	Distribution Centers: Reno	Peoria	Springfield	Oklahoma City	Supplies
Brainard	1.40 2000	.90 9000	1.20 1000	1.00	12,000
Macon	1.50	1.30	1.05 10,000	.80	10,000
Waco	.75 6000	1.25	1.50	.70 7000	13,000
Demands	8000	9000	11,000	7000	

Table 5-10 MODIFIED INITIAL ALLOCATION FOR GORMAN OUTERWARE

	Distribution Centers				
Plants	Reno	Peoria	Springfield	Oklahoma City	**Supplies**
Brainard	1.40	.90	1.20	1.00	12,000
Macon	1.50	1.30	1.05	.80	10,000
Waco	.75	1.25	1.50	.70 7000	7,000
Demands	8000	9000	5000	7000	

using both the northwest corner rule and minimum-cost allocation procedures contained $3 + 4 - 1 = 6$ cells. Reviewing the two procedures, you will find that every time an allocation was made, either one supply was exhausted or one demand was completely satisfied. When the final allocation was made, both the last supply and last demand were satisfied. Eliminating either one supply or one demand from the matrix until the final allocation is made will ensure the initial set of routes will contain $m + n - 1$ cells. However, sometimes a single allocation will eliminate both a supply and a demand. When this happens, we are left with fewer than the required $m + n - 1$ cells. Consider the initial allocation made using the minimum-cost method, as shown previously in Table 5-5. We allocated 7000 to the Waco–Oklahoma City route, which totally satisified the demand from Oklahoma City and eliminated this column from the matrix. However, if the supply from Waco had been 7000 instead of 13,000, as shown in Table 5-10, this assignment would eliminate both the Waco supply and the Oklahoma City demand.

The result of this initial allocation is that the starting point would contain fewer than 6 cells and the solution procedure we will introduce will not work. To eliminate the problem, when any allocation, prior to the final one, eliminates both a row and column from the matrix we simply pick any cell in either the eliminated row or column and assign a zero to this cell. We then treat it the same as any other allocation. This technique allows us to retain the required number of cells needed to complete the solution technique which will be presented.

Summary of the Minimum-Cost Starting-Point Method

While the minimum-cost starting-point method requires slightly more work than the northwest corner rule, the fact that it provides a lower-cost starting point means it will generally move to the optimal solution faster. To summarize, the steps in arriving at the lowest-cost starting point are:

Step 1 Choose the cell in the transportation tableau with the minimum cost (or maximum profit, if solving a maximization problem) and allocate as many units as possible to this cell. In case of a tie, pick the cell which allows the greatest number of units to be allocated. If this still results in a tie, arbitrarily pick the starting cell.

Step 2 Eliminate the supply, or demand, that is exhausted by the allocation in step 1 by drawing a line through the appropriate row or column. Reduce the supply or demand that is not eliminated by the amount allocated.

Step 3 If step 2 eliminates both a row and a column, and additional rows or cells remain in the matrix, pick any cell in either the eliminated row or column and assign a zero to this cell.

Step 4 If step 2 has eliminated all rows and columns in the transportation tableau, you have a starting allocation. If not, return to step 1 and repeat steps 1–3.

Solving the Transportation Problem

Now that we have determined a starting point for the transportation problem, the next step is to determine whether we are at the optimal point, and if not, how to move to an improved solution. We will introduce two solution techniques: the stepping-stone method and the modified distribution method. Each technique begins by using either the northwest corner method or the minimum-cost method to find starting points.

The Stepping-Stone Solution Method The **stepping-stone method** is similar to the simplex procedure in that it starts with the present solution, looks to see if an improved solution can be found, and moves from the present solution to an improved solution. When considering the process necessary to determine the optimal shipping schedule using the stepping-stone method, remember the logic of the simplex procedure, which requires a set number of variables to be in basis. The simplex solution procedure performs a series of steps resulting in one new variable at a time being added to the basis and a current variable being removed.

We begin the stepping-stone method by considering the initial minimum-cost allocation for Gorman Outerware, reproduced in Table 5-11. (We also could have used the starting point indicated by the northwest corner method.) Since we have 12 possible shipping routes, we have 12 decision variables; and of these, 6 are in the initial solution. (There will always be $m + n - 1$ variables in the initial solution.) Using linear programming terminology, the decision variables and their values are:

Decision Variable	Value	Unit Cost ($)	Total Cost ($)
Brainard–Reno	2,000	1.40	2,800
Brainard–Peoria	9,000	.90	8,100
Brainard–Springfield	1,000	1.20	1,200
Macon–Springfield	10,000	1.05	10,500
Waco–Reno	6,000	.75	4,500
Waco–Oklahoma City	7,000	.70	4,900
			32,000

The cost of this distribution schedule (the value of the objective function) is $32,000. The question is whether this is the optimal transportation schedule or whether a lower-cost alternative exists.

The stepping-stone method starts with the present schedule, as shown in Table 5-11, and looks for an improved solution by testing each of the shipping routes not presently in the solution. The logic is to test each open cell to see if an improved solution can be found by including only that cell in the solution set. If an improved solution can be found, as many units as possible will be transferred to that cell. Of course, the new solution must ensure that all supply and demand constraints are

Table 5-11 STARTING ALLOCATION FOR GORMAN OUTERWARE—STEPPING-STONE METHOD

	Distribution Centers				
Plants	Reno	Peoria	Springfield	Oklahoma City	**Supplies**
Brainard	1.40 2000	.90 9000	1.20 1000	1.00	12,000
Macon	1.50	1.30	1.05 10,000	.80	10,000
Waco	.75 6000	1.25	1.50	.70 7000	13,000
Demands	8000	9000	11,000	7000	

satisfied and that the total number of decision variables in the solution remains at $m + n - 1$, or 6 in this example.

To start, let's pick the Macon–Reno route. We test to see if including this cell will give an improved solution by temporarily transferring one unit to this route, as shown in Table 5-12. If we ship one jacket from Macon to Reno, maintaining the supply constraint requires shipping one jacket less from Macon to Springfield. However, we now need to ship one more to Springfield to satisfy its demand constraint, and since the solution procedure requires considering only one additional decision variable, we will make this additional shipment from Brainard. However, to maintain Brainard's supply constraint, we must now ship one less to another distribution center. If we pick the Brainard–Reno route, we develop a closed loop that maintains all supply and demand constraints. This closed-loop system is shown in Table 5-12.

To determine whether this route will reduce the overall shipping cost, we have to analyze the marginal change in cost due to this one-unit shift. Moving one unit from Macon to Reno will increase costs by $1.50, but shipping one less from Macon to Springfield will reduce costs by $1.05. Shipping one more from Brainard to Springfield

Table 5-12 EVALUATION OF MACON–RENO ROUTE

	Distribution Centers				
Plants	Reno	Peoria	Springfield	Oklahoma City	**Supplies**
Brainard	1.40 (−1) 2000	.90 9000	1.20 (+1) 1000	1.00	12,000
Macon	1.50 (+1)	1.30	1.05 (−1) 10,000	.80	10,000
Waco	.75 6000	1.25	1.50	.70 7000	13,000
Demands	8000	9000	11,000	7000	

will increase costs by $1.20, but shipping one less from Brainard to Reno will decrease costs by $1.40. These changes, and the net effect of making this one-unit shift, are summarized below:

Change	Effect
1 unit to Macon – Reno	+$1.50
1 unit less, Macon – Springfield	−$1.05
1 unit more, Brainard – Springfield	+$1.20
1 unit less, Brainard – Reno	−$1.40
Net effect	+$ .25

Since this change will increase costs, it should not be made. Notice that we are doing the same thing here as we did when evaluating the $c_j - Z_j$ row in the simplex tableau to determine the entering variable. If the evaluation shows a variable will improve the solution, it becomes a candidate for inclusion in the solution set. Also, as long as one variable not presently in the solution could improve the objective function, the optimum solution has not been reached.

While we will not improve the solution by adding the Macon – Reno route, we have five other open routes to check. The marginal changes in costs for these cells are shown in Table 5-13, and the closed-route calculations are summarized in Table 5-14. When checking these values, note that all routes are designed so that:

1. The closed-loop route involves the cell being checked and *only* those cells that are already in the solution.
2. The closed loop is designed so each row that contains a +1 also contains a −1 and each column that contains a +1 also contains a −1.

The net-effect row in each evaluation is treated just like the $c_j - Z_j$ row in the simplex tableau. We search for the net effect with the largest negative value, and this route becomes the entering decision variable. In this example, the largest per unit

Table 5-13 EVALUATION OF ALL OPEN ROUTES

	Distribution Centers				
Plants	Reno	Peoria	Springfield	Oklahoma City	**Supplies**
Brainard	1.40 2000	.90 9000	1.20 1,000	1.00 (−.35)	12,000
Macon	1.50 (+.25)	1.30 (+.55)	1.05 10,000	.80 (−.40)	10,000
Waco	.75 6000	1.25 (+1.00)	1.50 (+.95)	.70 7000	13,000
Demands	8000	9000	11,000	7000	

Note: Value in ( ) reflects net effects.

Table 5-14 CLOSED-LOOP EVALUATION OF FIVE REMAINING OPEN ROUTES

Route	Change	Effect
Macon–Peoria	1 unit to Macon–Peoria	+1.30
	1 unit less, Macon–Springfield	−1.05
	1 unit more, Brainard–Springfield	+1.20
	1 unit less, Brainard–Peoria	− .90
	Net effect	+ .55
Brainard–Oklahoma City	1 unit to Brainard–Oklahoma City	+1.00
	1 unit less, Waco–Oklahoma City	− .70
	1 unit more, Waco–Reno	+ .75
	1 unit less, Brainard–Reno	−1.40
	Net effect	− .35
Macon–Oklahoma City	1 unit to Macon–Oklahoma City	+ .80
	1 unit less, Macon–Springfield	−1.05
	1 unit more, Brainard–Springfield	+1.20
	1 unit less, Brainard–Reno	−1.40
	1 unit more, Waco–Reno	+ .75
	1 unit less, Waco–Oklahoma City	− .70
	Net effect	− .40
Waco–Peoria	1 unit to Waco–Peoria	+1.25
	1 unit less, Waco–Reno	− .75
	1 unit more, Brainard–Reno	+1.40
	1 unit less, Brainard–Peoria	− .90
	Net effect	+1.00
Waco–Springfield	1 unit to Waco–Springfield	+1.50
	1 unit less, Waco–Reno	− .75
	1 unit more, Brainard–Reno	+1.40
	1 unit less, Brainard–Springfield	−1.20
	Net effect	+ .95

improvement is associated with the Macon–Oklahoma City route:

Change	Effect
1 unit to Macon–Oklahoma City	+$ .80
1 unit less, Macon–Springfield	−$1.05
1 unit more, Brainard–Springfield	+$1.20
1 unit less, Brainard–Reno	−$1.40
1 unit more, Waco–Reno	+$ .75
1 unit less, Waco–Oklahoma City	−$ .70
Net effect	−$ .40

We will want to add as many units as possible to this route because we save $.40 per unit in shipping costs by doing so. However, for every unit added to Macon–Oklahoma City, we must also remove one unit from three routes: Macon–Springfield, Brainard–Reno, and Waco–Oklahoma City.

The cells that lose units are all candidates to be the departing variable and are referred to as donor cells. The actual amount we can transfer to the Macon – Oklahoma City route is determined by the donor cell with the smallest present allocation. In this case, the 2000 units presently scheduled to be shipped from Brainard to Reno is the smallest.

The transportation problem after iteration 1 is shown in Table 5-15. To determine whether this is the optimal routing, we must again evaluate the free cells in the tableau. The results of this evaluation are shown in Tables 5-16 and 5-17.

We have checked all empty cells in the transportation tableau. Each of these checks yielded a positive evaluation value. Since we are trying to minimize costs, we can make no further improvements and are at the optimal shipping schedule:

Route	No. Jackets	Unit Cost	Total Cost
Brainard – Peoria	9,000	$ .90	$ 8,100
Brainard – Springfield	3,000	$1.20	$ 3,600
Macon – Springfield	8,000	$1.05	$ 8,400
Macon – Oklahoma City	2,000	$ .80	$ 1,600
Waco – Reno	8,000	$ .75	$ 6,000
Waco – Oklahoma City	5,000	$ .70	$ 3,500
	35,000		$31,200

Earlier we used linear programming to solve this transportation problem and reached the same solution. But in this problem, we reached the optimal solution at one iteration after the starting position was determined. If the first iteration had not yielded the optimal solution, we would have proceeded in the same manner through iteration 2 and so on until no cost reductions were possible. Large-scale transportation problems may require many iterations.

Maintaining the Required Number of Cells in the Solution

Earlier we stated the transportation tableau must have $m + n - 1$ filled cells. In the discussion of the minimum-cost initial allocation procedure, we showed how fewer than $m + n - 1$ cells might be allocated and how to correct the situation if it should

Table 5-15 TRANSPORTATION TABLEAU AFTER FIRST INTERATION

	Distribution Centers				
Plants	Reno	Peoria	Springfield	Oklahoma City	**Supplies**
Brainard	1.40	.90 9000	1.20 3000	1.00	12,000
Macon	1.50	1.30	1.05 8000	.80 2000	10,000
Waco	.75 8000	1.25	1.50	.70 5000	13,000
Demands	8000	9000	11,000	7000	

Table 5-16 EVALUATION OF OPEN ROUTES

Plants	Distribution Centers: Reno	Peoria	Springfield	Oklahoma City	Supplies
Brainard	1.40 (+1.50)	.90 9000	1.20 3000	1.00 (+.05)	12,000
Macon	1.50 (+1.30)	1.30 (+.55)	1.05 8000	.80 2000	10,000
Waco	.75 8000	1.25 (+.60)	1.50 (+.55)	.70 5000	13,000
Demands	8000	9000	11,000	7000	

occur. While the stepping-stone example just demonstrated maintained the number of assigned routes at 6, in some cases this solution procedure may lead to a reduced number of allocations. To demonstrate, we will alter the Gorman Outerware example slightly.

Table 5-18 shows the revised initial tableau. We have changed the supply and demand levels for Waco and Oklahoma City. Since the distribution costs have not changed, the initial assignment uses the same cells as in the previous example (see Table 5-11). To determine whether an improved shipping schedule exists, we use the stepping-stone method of evaluating all open routes. As before, the Macon–Oklahoma City route provides the greatest reduction in unit shipping costs:

Change	Effect
1 unit to Macon–Oklahoma City	+$ .80
1 unit less, Macon–Springfield	−$1.05
1 unit more, Brainard–Springfield	+$1.20
1 unit less, Brainard–Reno	−$1.40
1 unit more, Waco–Reno	+$ .75
1 unit less, Waco–Oklahoma City	−$ .70
Net effect	−$ .40

In order to add shipments between Macon and Oklahoma City, we need to reduce the Brainard–Reno and the Waco–Oklahoma City shipments. These will be the donor cells. However, when looking at the donor cells, we see that both Waco–Oklahoma City and Brainard–Reno have the same smallest value of 2000. This means that if we allocate 2000 to the Macon–Oklahoma City route, we will remove 2000 from both donor cells and the allocated routes will be reduced to 5 instead of the 6 required in this example.

Eliminating two cells while adding one means we will not be able to develop a closed-loop evaluation for all nonassigned cells. To solve this problem, we arbitrarily select either of the donor cells, Waco–Oklahoma City or Brainard–Reno, and make

Table 5-17 EVALUATION OF SIX OPEN ROUTES

Route	Change	Effect
Brainard–Reno	1 unit to Brainard–Reno	+1.40
	1 unit less, Brainard–Springfield	−1.20
	1 unit more, Macon–Springfield	+1.05
	1 unit less, Macon–Oklahoma City	− .80
	1 unit more, Waco–Oklahoma City	+ .70
	1 unit less, Waco–Reno	− .75
	Net effect	+ .40
Macon–Reno	1 unit to Macon–Reno	+1.50
	1 unit less, Macon–Oklahoma City	− .80
	1 unit more, Waco–Oklahoma City	+ .70
	1 unit less, Waco–Reno	− .75
	Net effect	+ .65
Macon–Peoria	1 unit to Macon–Peoria	+1.30
	1 unit less, Macon–Springfield	−1.05
	1 unit more, Brainard–Springfield	+1.20
	1 unit less, Brainard–Peoria	− .90
	Net effect	+ .55
Brainard–Oklahoma City	1 unit to Brainard–Oklahoma City	+1.00
	1 unit less, Macon–Oklahoma City	− .80
	1 unit more, Macon–Springfield	+1.05
	1 unit less, Brainard–Springfield	−1.20
	Net effect	+ .05
Waco–Peoria	1 unit to Waco–Peoria	+1.25
	1 unit less, Waco–Oklahoma City	− .70
	1 unit more, Macon–Oklahoma City	+ .80
	1 unit less, Macon–Springfield	−1.05
	1 unit more, Brainard–Springfield	+1.20
	1 unit less, Brainard–Peoria	− .90
	Net effect	+ .60
Waco–Springfield	1 unit to Waco–Springfield	+1.50
	1 unit less, Waco–Oklahoma City	− .70
	1 unit more, Macon–Oklahoma City	+ .80
	1 unit less, Macon–Springfield	−1.05
	Net effect	+ .55

an assignment of zero units to that route. This gives us the tableau shown in Table 5-19. Note that we treat a cell with the zero assignment like any other assigned cell. The problem is now continued in the same manner as before. The zero allocation will disappear if this cell ever becomes an acceptor cell in a future iteration.

The Modified Distribution Solution Procedure While the stepping-stone solution procedure will lead to an optimal solution in a transportation problem, the process of determining the closed-loop net change can be tedious. We are forced to evaluate loops for all empty cells. This is referred to as complete enumeration. The **modified**

Table 5-18 REVISED INITIAL TABLEAU FOR GORMAN OUTERWARE EXAMPLE

	Distribution Centers				
Plants	Reno	Peoria	Springfield	Oklahoma City	**Supplies**
Brainard	1.40	.90	1.20	1.00	
	2000	9000	1000		12,000
Macon	1.50	1.30	1.05	.80	
			10,000		10,000
Waco	.75	1.25	1.50	.70	
	6000			2000	8,000
Demands	8000	9000	11,000	2000	

Table 5-19 MODIFIED INITIAL TABLEAU FOR GORMAN OUTERWARE EXAMPLE

	Distribution Centers				
Plants	Reno	Peoria	Springfield	Oklahoma City	**Supplies**
Brainard	1.40	.90	1.20	1.00	
Brainard		9000	3000		12,000
Macon	1.50	1.30	1.05	.80	
			8000	2000	10,000
Waco	.75	1.25	1.50	.70	
	8000			0	8,000
Demands	8000	9000	11,000	2000	

distribution (MODI) solution procedure, an algorithm for determining the per unit improvement associated with shipping one unit over an unused route, can be used to solve transportation problems with a generally reduced number of computations.

The modified distribution method is based on the primal-dual relationship of the simplex linear programming solution procedure. Although a complete treatment of MODI is beyond the scope of this text, we will demonstrate how it works by using the Gorman Outerware example.

The MODI procedure requires that we determine an index, u_i, for each row of the transportation tableau and an index, v_j, for each column. As the MODI procedure progresses, the values of these indices, when summed, will equal the per unit cost of shipping from each source to each destination for the allocated cells in the transportation tableau. In more formal terms:

$$u_i + v_j = c_{ij} \text{ for all assigned cells}$$

where: $i = 1$ . . . the number of rows
$j = 1$ . . . the number of columns

We will be able to use this relationship to determine an equation for each assigned cell. Using the minimum-cost starting allocation in Table 5-20, we find the following six equations.

$$u_1 + v_1 = 1.40 \qquad u_2 + v_3 = 1.05$$
$$u_1 + v_2 = .90 \qquad u_3 + v_1 = .75$$
$$u_1 + v_3 = 1.20 \qquad u_3 + v_4 = .70$$

Since we have six equations and seven unknowns, we can pick any value we want for one of the index values. Selectively choosing $u_1 = 0$ (since it is in three of the six equations), we get the following set of equations:

$$0 + v_1 = 1.40 \qquad u_2 + v_3 = 1.05$$
$$0 + v_2 = .90 \qquad u_3 + v_1 = .75$$
$$0 + v_3 = 1.20 \qquad u_3 + v_4 = .70$$

Solving this set of equations, we find:

$$u_1 = 0 \qquad v_1 = 1.40$$
$$u_2 = -.15 \qquad v_2 = .90$$
$$u_3 = -.65 \qquad v_3 = 1.20$$
$$v_4 = 1.35$$

These index values play a very important role in arriving at the solution to the transportation problem. To illustrate, let e_{ij} be the net improvement associated with moving one unit from the present allocation system to a vacant cell identified by i and j. Then, for a given row i and column j, we get:

$$e_{ij} = c_{ij} - u_i - v_j$$

In Table 5-20, the Brainard–Oklahoma City route is vacant. Evaluating this cell, we find:

$$e_{14} = 1.00 - 0 - 1.35 = -.35$$

Likewise, the Macon–Reno route is empty in Table 5-20. Using the MODI method, we get:

$$e_{21} = 1.50 - (-.15) - 1.40 = .25$$

Table 5-20 STARTING ALLOCATION FOR GORMAN OUTERWARE—MODI

	Distribution Centers				
Plants	Reno	Peoria	Springfield	Oklahoma City	**Supplies**
Brainard	1.40 / 2000	.90 / 9000	1.20 / 1000	1.00	12,000
Macon	1.50	1.30	1.05 / 10,000	.80	10,000
Waco	.75 / 6000	1.25	1.50	.70 / 7000	13,000
Demands	8000	9000	11,000	7000	

Table 5-21 EVALUATION OF ALL OPEN ROUTES—MODI

	Distribution Centers				
Plants	Reno	Peoria	Springfield	Oklahoma City	**Supplies**
Brainard	1.40 2000	.90 9000	1.20 1,000	1.00 (−.35)	12,000
Macon	1.50 (+.25)	1.30 (+.55)	1.05 10,000	.80 (−.40)	10,000
Waco	.75 6000	1.25 (+1.00)	1.50 (+.95)	.70 7000	13,000
Demands	8000	9000	11,000	7000	

Note these are the same net improvement values found previously using the stepping-stone method. Table 5-21 shows the net improvement values, e_{ij}, for all empty cells. These are the same values shown earlier in Table 5-13. The MODI procedure requires substantially less effort.

Once the unallocated cell with the greatest per unit improvement is identified, the same sequence of acceptor and donor cells is identified and we make the maximum allowable changes through the closed loop. The MODI method is then used to evaluate the next tableau for an improved solution. When we reach a point where all net improvements found using the MODI calculation are positive, we know the least-cost transportation schedule has been identified.

5-3 UNBALANCED TRANSPORTATION PROBLEMS AND OTHER ISSUES

The Gorman Outerware example in section 5-2 is considered a **balanced transportation problem** because the demand for jackets was equal to the supply. In addition, there were no restrictions on the use of any distribution route and the solution techniques arrived at the optimal point with no procedural problems. Obviously, not all applications work out this well. However, in situations which are not as clear-cut as the Gorman example, the solution procedures we have presented can still be applied. In this section, we look at several transportation situations that can occur and show how they are handled.

SUPPLY EXCEEDS DEMAND

Very commonly, the supply from a company's manufacturing facilities does not exactly match the demand at the various receiving locations. We begin by examining a situation in which the capacity exceeds the demand. The example is an extension of the Gorman Outerware example from section 5-2. Assume that demand for Gorman jackets is the same as before at each distribution center. However, suppose that production capacity at the Brainard and Waco plants has been increased to 15,000 and 18,000 respectively. Now the system is not balanced, since total supply (43,000 jackets) exceeds total demand (35,000 jackets). The transportation tableau is shown in Table 5-22.

The problem of excess supply is taken care of by establishing a dummy distribution center. We then set the demand at this dummy center equal to the difference between supply and demand at the real distribution centers:

$$\text{dummy demand} = 43{,}000 - 35{,}000 = 8000 \text{ jackets}$$

No jackets will actually be shipped to this dummy distribution center. Thus, the distribution cost between each source and the dummy distribution center is zero. A new column is added to the transportation tableau, as shown in Table 5-23.

Adding the **dummy demand** results in a balanced system which we can solve using the procedures outlined in section 5-2. To make sure you understand the manual solution technique, use the stepping-stone method to solve this problem. You should

Table 5-22 TRANSPORTATION TABLEAU FOR GORMAN OUTERWARE WITH INCREASED PLANT CAPACITY

	Distribution Centers				
Plants	Reno	Peoria	Springfield	Oklahoma City	**Supplies**
Brainard	1.40	.90	1.20	1.00	15,000
Macon	1.50	1.30	1.05	.80	10,000
Waco	.75	1.25	1.50	.70	18,000
Demands	8000	9000	11,000	7000	

Table 5-23 TRANSPORTATION TABLEAU FOR GORMAN OUTERWARE WITH INCREASED CAPACITY AT DISTRIBUTION CENTERS

	Distribution Centers					
Plants	Reno	Peoria	Springfield	Oklahoma City	Dummy	**Supplies**
Brainard	1.40	.90	1.20	1.00	0	15,000
Macon	1.50	1.30	1.05	.80	0	10,000
Waco	.75	1.25	1.50	.70	0	18,000
Demands	8000	9000	11,000	7000	8000	

find the following shipping routes and amounts:

From	To	No. Jackets	Cost per Unit ($)	Total ($)
Brainard	Peoria	9,000	0.90	8,100
Brainard	Springfield	1,000	1.20	1,200
Brainard	Dummy	5,000	0.00	0
Macon	Springfield	10,000	1.05	10,500
Waco	Reno	8,000	0.75	6,000
Waco	Oklahoma City	7,000	0.70	4,900
Waco	Dummy	3,000	0.00	0

This schedule has a total shipping cost of $30,000. This schedule shows that the Brainard plant will ship 5000 jackets to the dummy distribution center and Waco will ship 3000 jackets to the dummy location. Because the dummy center does not actually exist, Brainard will actually produce 5000 fewer jackets than its capacity and Waco will underproduce by 3000 jackets. Hopefully, managers at these facilities can rechannel this capacity into some other product for which the company has excess demand.

DEMAND EXCEEDS SUPPLY

While the most common situation facing an organization is for capacity to exceed demand, in some cases demand will be greater than supply. When this occurs in a transportation problem, a **dummy supply** is added as a row in the transportation tableau. The total capacity of this dummy supply is set at a level just high enough to ensure that supply equals demand. The transportation cost between the dummy supply location and all demand points is set to zero. Then the transportation problem is solved as before. Any shipments scheduled in the final solution from the dummy supply will not be made and the affected distribution centers will actually receive fewer than the demanded units.

USING A MAXIMIZATION CRITERION

In some cases a decision maker is interested in making transportation decisions based upon a maximization objective. For instance, instead of minimizing transportation costs, the organization may wish to maximize profits or revenues. When maximization is the objective, an optimal distribution schedule can be determined using the procedures previously developed, with one change. To illustrate the solution procedure for a maximization problem, we introduce a new example.

Rumeal Mining has three potash mines in the western United States. The potash coming from each of these three mines is of different quality and can be shipped to four potential processing plants. The company managers are interested in establishing a plan which indicates how much potash should be shipped from each mine to each processing plant. The transportation plan should be based on all combinations of costs (mining and transportation) and revenue. Not only do transportation costs vary between different mines and processing plants, but contract revenues are determined by the quality of potash coming from the mine and the processing capability of the plant.

The cost accounting department at Rumeal Mining's central headquarters has arrived at the per ton operating profit figures for all combinations of mines and processing plants, shown in Table 5-24. For example, the profit per ton for potash shipped from mine M2 to processing plant P3 is $16.

The method used to solve this problem is the same as for a minimization problem, except we look for increases instead of decreases and positive values instead of negative values. The initial allocation is based on profit maximization, not cost mini-

Table 5-24 PER TON OPERATING PROFITS FOR RUMEAL MINING

	Processing Plants				
Mines	P1	P2	P3	P4	**Supplies**
M1	$12	$18	$20	$15	50
M2	$16	$21	$16	$14	20
M3	$22	$17	$19	$20	30
Demands	35	20	15	30	

Note: Supply and demand data are in thousands of tons per day.

mization. The highest profit ($22) occurs when Rumeal ships between M3 and P1. Mine M3 has a capacity of 25 tons and plant P1 has a demand of 35 tons. This means Rumeal would ship the full 25 tons from M3 to P1, leaving 10 tons to be shipped to P1 from one of the other mines. The next highest profit ($21) occurs between M2 and P2. The most profitable arrangement would be to ship all 20 tons of P2's demand from M2. This would leave 5 tons of capacity remaining at M2 which could be shipped to another processing plant. The next highest profit ($20) is for shipments between M1 and P3. Since P3's demand is 15 tons, that is the amount that will be shipped from M1, leaving it with 35 tons of capacity. We continue in this manner using up capacity and filling demands. The maximum profit criterion initial allocation becomes that shown in Table 5-25.

This initial allocation gives a daily profitability of $1,860,000. To determine

Table 5-25 INITIAL ALLOCATION FOR RUMEAL MINING

	Processing Plants				
Mines	P1	P2	P3	P4	**Supplies**
M1	$12 5	$18	$20 15	$15 30	50
M2	$16 5	$21 20	$16	$14	25
M3	$22 25	$17	$19	$20	25
Demands	35	20	15	30	

Tons	**Profit per Ton**	**Total Profit**
5,000	$12	$ 60,000
15,000	$20	$ 300,000
30,000	$15	$ 450,000
5,000	$16	$ 80,000
20,000	$21	$ 420,000
25,000	$22	$ 550,000
		$1,860,000

Note: Supply and demand data are in thousands of tons per day.

whether an improved transportation schedule exists, we can use the MODI method. The only change is that an improved solution will be determined by a positive e_{ij} value.

We establish the row and column indexes for the cells which have been assigned shipments as follows:

$u_i + v_j = c_{ij}$ for all assigned cells

where: $i = 1 \ldots$ the number of rows
$j = 1 \ldots$ the number of columns

Table 5-26 shows the computations for the net improvement indexes. Next, we determine the e_{ij} values for each empty cell. For example, e_{12} is computed as follows:

$$e_{12} = c_{12} - u_1 - v_2 = 18 - 0 - 17 = 1.0$$

This means that each additional ton shipped from M1 to P2 will add $1.00 to profit. Table 5-27 shows the e_{ij} values for each previously unassigned cell.

Looking at this tableau, we see that only one cell offers a profit improvement. This is the M1 – P2 route and is referred to as the acceptor cell. We want to transfer as many tons of potash into this cell as possible to improve the total profit. The number of tons tranferred to this cell is limited by the corner cell with the smallest quantity. This is cell

Table 5-26 DETERMINING NET IMPROVEMENTS FOR RUMEAL MINING

$$u_1 + v_1 = 12 \qquad u_2 + v_1 = 16$$
$$u_1 + v_3 = 20 \qquad u_2 + v_2 = 21$$
$$u_1 + v_4 = 15 \qquad u_3 + v_1 = 22$$

Again picking $u_1 = 0$ (since it is in three of the six equations), we get the following values:

$$u_1 = 0 \qquad v_1 = 12$$
$$u_2 = 4 \qquad v_2 = 17$$
$$u_3 = 10 \qquad v_3 = 20$$
$$v_4 = 15$$

Table 5-27 NET IMPROVEMENT TABLEAU FOR RUMEAL MINING

	Processing Plants				
Mines	P1	P2	P3	P4	**Supplies**
M1	$12 5	$18 (+1)	$20 15	$15 30	50
M2	$16 5	$21 20	$16 (−8)	$14 (−5)	25
M3	$22 25	$17 (−10)	$19 (−11)	$20 (−5)	25
Demands	35	20	15	30	

Note: Supply and demand data are in thousands of tons per day. Values in parentheses are e_{ij}.

Table 5-28 REVISED TABLEAU FOR RUMEAL MINING

Mines	Processing Plants P1	P2	P3	P4	Supplies
M1	\$12 (−1)	\$18 5	\$20 15	\$15 30	50
M2	\$16 10	\$21 15	\$16 (−7)	\$14 (−4)	25
M3	\$22 25	\$17 (−10)	\$19 (−10)	\$20 (−4)	25
Demands	35	20	15	30	

Note: Supply and demand data are in thousands of tons per day. Values in parentheses are e_{ij}.

M1 – P1 with 5 (5000 tons). Thus, we will transfer the 5 from cell M1 – P1 to cell M1 – P2. This keeps the sum of the allocations from row M1 equal to M1's capacity of 50. But when we place 5 in cell M1 – P2, we must reduce the value in cell M2 – P2 from 20 to 15 so that the total shipments to processing plant P2 stay at 20. This decrease of 5 units in cell M2 – P2 must be offset by adding 5 to cell M2 – P1, making it increase from 5 to 10. At this point, the transportation tableau is in balance. Table 5-28 shows the results of this reallocation. It also shows the e_{ij} values for the new tableau. Since there are no positive e_{ij} values, the transportation problem has reached the optimal solution:

Route	Amount	Profit per Ton	Total Profit
M1 – P2	5,000 tons	\$18	\$ 90,000
M1 – P3	15,000 tons	\$20	\$ 300,000
M1 – P4	30,000 tons	\$15	\$ 450,000
M2 – P1	10,000 tons	\$16	\$ 160,000
M2 – P2	15,000 tons	\$21	\$ 315,000
M3 – P1	25,000 tons	\$22	\$ 550,000
			\$1,865,000

This allocation has a maximum daily operating profitability of \$1,865,000.

As this example illustrates, the procedure for solving a maximization problem differs from that for a minimization problem only in that choosing the acceptor cell is based on picking the value with the largest positive net improvement instead of the one that is the most negative. The optimal solution is reached when no positive net improvements remain in the transportation tableau.

UNAVAILABLE TRANSPORTATION ROUTES

In some situations, certain potential transportation routes may not actually be available to an organization. This may be due to a physical limitation, such as not all locations being served by trains. Or a firm may have a shipping contract with a trucking firm which does not ship between two locations. Whatever the reason, if a decision maker is faced with a transportation problem where certain cells are not available for allocation, the final solution must not have any values in the unavailable cells.

This situation can be readily incorporated in our solution procedure. A relatively easy way to handle the problem when the objective is to minimize cost is to put a very high cost in the unavailable cell. We represent this high cost as M. If the objective is to maximize a variable such as profit, we place a large negative profit, $-M$, into all unavailable cells.

The large cost (or negative profit) ensures that an improved solution can never be found using this cell. The Solved Problem section at the end of this chapter contains an example with unavailable cells.

5-4 TRANSSHIPMENT PROBLEMS

In many situations a product is not transported directly from the source to its destination but instead makes one or more intermediate stops. If you send a package by Federal Express from Chicago to Denver, the actual route is Chicago–Memphis–Denver, since all packages are routed through Memphis. Wheat grown in North Dakota may make an intermediate stop at a storage facility in Fargo before being sent to a mill in Minneapolis. A person flying from Buffalo to Los Angeles may have to make an intermediate stop in Chicago.

Many actual problems do in fact involve intermediate stops. If this is the case, we now have to consider not only origin points and destination points, but also intermediate, or transshipment, points in our routing decisions. To demonstrate how to solve a **transshipment problem**, we will consider the case of Rice Farms Inc.

Rice Farms is a large agribusiness with extensive holdings in Kansas and North Dakota. Wheat produced in either location is first shipped to Rice Farms' temporary storage facilities in either Kansas City, Kansas, or Sioux Falls, South Dakota, where it is processed to separate any wheat stalks from the wheat heads. From these interim storage facilities, the wheat is shipped to numerous final destinations both in the United States and overseas. Rice Farms is presently developing shipping plans for 300,000 bushels of wheat grown in Kansas and 400,000 bushels of North Dakota wheat.

Rice Farms executives have signed contracts for delivery of 200,000 bushels of wheat in Cincinnati, 150,000 bushels in St. Louis, 170,000 bushels in Chicago, and 180,000 bushels in New Orleans. This situation can be represented in a node-arc configuration, or **network**, as shown in Figure 5-3.

The nodes in Figure 5-3 represent the origins and destinations of the wheat as well as the two intermediate storage facilities. The arcs represent the possible routes that Rice Farms could select. The supplies at the two origins are also shown, along with the demands at the four destinations. The per bushel shipping costs between each source and storage facility, and between each storage facility and final destination, are shown in Table 5-29.

A LINEAR PROGRAMMING SOLUTION

While the special-purpose transportation algorithm discussed previously can be expanded to solve transshipment problems, the tableau is much larger and the solution procedure more complicated. Alternatively, the problem can be formulated and solved as a linear programming problem. Most management scientists agree that the linear programming solution procedure is more straightforward and easier to use than the stepping-stone method for transshipment problems.

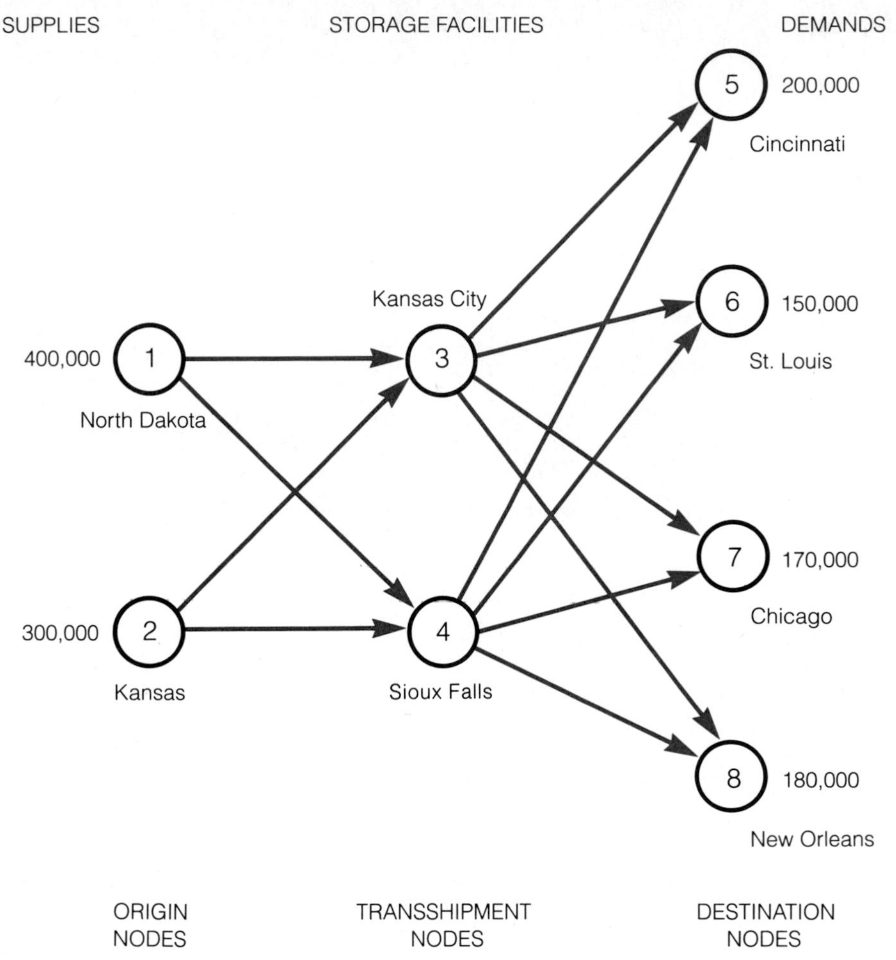

Figure 5-3
Node-arc representation of the Rice Farms transshipment problem

Table 5-29 TRANSPORTATION COSTS FOR RICE FARMS (DOLLARS PER BUSHEL)

	Transshipment Location	
Growing Location	Kansas City	Sioux Falls
North Dakota	.55	.47
Kansas	.35	.42

	Final Destination			
Transshipment	Cincinnati	St. Louis	Chicago	New Orleans
Kansas City	.60	.45	.50	.35
Sioux Falls	.55	.40	.65	.43

To help formulate Rice Farms' decision as a linear programming problem, we have numbered the nodes in Figure 5-3. With these numbers, we can define the decision variables as x_{ij}, where, for instance, x_{13} defines the amount sent from node 1 to node 3, or from North Dakota to the Kansas City storage facility. Using these decision variables, and looking at Figure 5-3, the following constraints are formulated:

1. Since Rice Farms can ship no more than 400,000 bushels from the North Dakota operation and no more than 300,000 from Kansas, we have two constraints:

$$x_{13} + x_{14} \leq 400 \qquad \text{and} \qquad x_{23} + x_{24} \leq 300$$

(For convenience, we have defined the decision variables in thousands of bushels of wheat.)

2. Assuming that no long-term storage is allowed at the transshipment facilities, everything shipped into both Kansas City and Sioux Falls must be shipped out. Therefore, for Kansas City:

$$x_{13} + x_{23} = x_{35} + x_{36} + x_{37} + x_{38}$$

which can be rewritten as:

$$x_{13} + x_{23} - x_{35} - x_{36} - x_{37} - x_{38} = 0$$

and for Sioux Falls:

$$x_{14} + x_{24} = x_{45} + x_{46} + x_{47} + x_{48}$$

rewritten as:

$$x_{14} + x_{24} - x_{45} - x_{46} - x_{47} - x_{48} = 0$$

3. To satisfy the demands at the destination nodes, we need the following set of constraints:

$$\begin{aligned} x_{35} + x_{45} &= 200 \\ x_{36} + x_{46} &= 150 \\ x_{37} + x_{47} &= 170 \\ x_{38} + x_{48} &= 180 \end{aligned}$$

The objective function is to minimize the total shipping costs along all possible routes. This becomes:

$$\begin{aligned} \text{Minimize } Z = {} & .55x_{13} + .47x_{14} + .35x_{23} + .42x_{24} + .60x_{35} + .45x_{36} + .50x_{37} \\ & + .35x_{38} + .55x_{45} + .40x_{46} + .65x_{47} + .43x_{48} \end{aligned}$$

We will use the MASTER software package to solve this problem. Figure 5-4 shows the input data necessary to run the program; the MASTER output is shown in Figure 5-5. The results are as follows:

$$\begin{array}{lll} x_{13} = 50{,}000 & x_{35} = 0 & x_{45} = 200{,}000 \\ x_{14} = 350{,}000 & x_{36} = 0 & x_{46} = 150{,}000 \\ x_{23} = 300{,}000 & x_{37} = 170{,}000 & x_{47} = 0 \\ x_{24} = 0 & x_{38} = 180{,}000 & x_{48} = 0 \end{array}$$

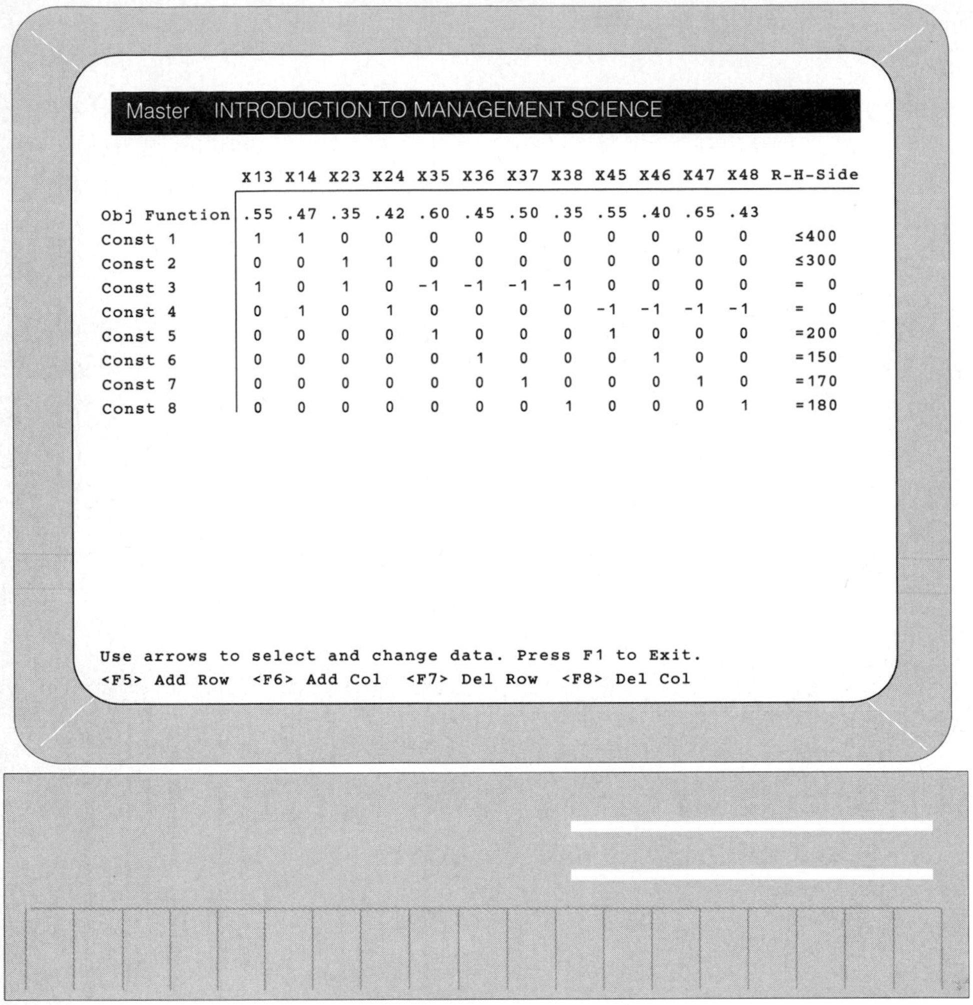

Master INTRODUCTION TO MANAGEMENT SCIENCE

	X13	X14	X23	X24	X35	X36	X37	X38	X45	X46	X47	X48	R-H-Side
Obj Function	.55	.47	.35	.42	.60	.45	.50	.35	.55	.40	.65	.43	
Const 1	1	1	0	0	0	0	0	0	0	0	0	0	≤400
Const 2	0	0	1	1	0	0	0	0	0	0	0	0	≤300
Const 3	1	0	1	0	-1	-1	-1	-1	0	0	0	0	= 0
Const 4	0	1	0	1	0	0	0	0	-1	-1	-1	-1	= 0
Const 5	0	0	0	0	1	0	0	0	1	0	0	0	=200
Const 6	0	0	0	0	0	1	0	0	0	1	0	0	=150
Const 7	0	0	0	0	0	0	1	0	0	0	1	0	=170
Const 8	0	0	0	0	0	0	0	1	0	0	0	1	=180

Use arrows to select and change data. Press F1 to Exit.
<F5> Add Row <F6> Add Col <F7> Del Row <F8> Del Col

Figure 5-4
Rice Farms problem: MASTER data entry screen

Relating these values to Figure 5-3, the optimal solution is to ship 50,000 bushels of North Dakota wheat to Kansas City and 350,000 bushels to Sioux Falls for temporary storage and cleaning. All the wheat grown in Kansas (300,000 bushels) will be shipped to the Kansas City storage facility. Then all of Chicago's and all of New Orleans' demand will be filled by shipping from Kansas City. Likewise, all of Cincinnati's and St. Louis' demand will be supplied from Sioux Falls. The total shipping cost for this transshipment problem is $615,000.

While no other shipping schedule will lead to a smaller total cost, this problem does have alternate optimal solutions. This means that other schedules will lead to the same minimum shipping cost. Depending on the solution method used, another software package might bring you to an alternate optimal solution. MASTER will warn you of alternate optimal solutions in this example when you request sensitivity analysis, but it will only print out one of the alternatives.

```
                LINEAR PROGRAMMING FORMULATION

        THE DECISION VARIABLES ARE      1   THROUGH  12
        THE SLACK VARIABLES ARE        13   THROUGH  14
        THE ARTIFICIAL VARIABLES ARE   15   THROUGH  20

                   OPTIMAL SOLUTION

  ITERATIONS =  9

  OBJECTIVE FUNCTION =        615.000


  DECISION VARIABLES:

  VARIABLE    NAME       VALUE
      1        X13        50.000
      2        X14       350.000
      3        X23       300.000
      7        X37       170.000
      8        X38       180.000
      9        X45       200.000
     10        X46       150.000


  SLACK OR SURPLUS VARIABLES:

  VARIABLE    NAME                VALUE
     13      SLACK                0.000


  DUAL RESULTS

  VARIABLE    NAME                VALUE
              X13                 0.000
              X14                 0.000
              X23                 0.000
              X24                 0.150
              X35                 0.130
              X36                 0.130
              X37                 0.000
              X38                 0.000
              X45                 0.000
              X46                 0.000
              X47                 0.070
              X48                 0.000
```

Figure 5-5
Rice Farms problem: MASTER output (figure continued on next page)

```
CONSTRAINT  1    0.000
CONSTRAINT  2    0.200
CONSTRAINT  3   -0.550
CONSTRAINT  4   -0.470
CONSTRAINT  5   -1.020
CONSTRAINT  6   -0.870
CONSTRAINT  7   -1.050
CONSTRAINT  8   -0.900
```

Figure 5-5 Continued

The advantage of solving the transshipment problem as a linear programming problem is that the formulation is very flexible. For instance, if Rice Farms could allow up to 100,000 bushels to be stored for long term in Kansas City, the appropriate constraint would become:

$$x_{13} + x_{23} - x_{35} - x_{36} - x_{37} - x_{38} \leq 100$$

If the delivery contract for Chicago was to deliver at least 150,000 bushels but no more than 200,000 bushels, the appropriate constraints would be:

$$x_{37} + x_{47} \geq 150$$
$$x_{37} + x_{47} \leq 200$$

Thus, the exact situation is modeled by incorporating the appropriate constraints into the linear programming formulation.

5-5 REHWALD & ASSOCIATES: AN ASSIGNMENT PROBLEM

Red Rehwald left the Environmental Protection Agency three years ago to start his own consulting firm, advising companies and government agencies on hazardous waste problems. During the past three years, Rehwald & Associates has grown steadily and now occupies two floors of a downtown Washington, D.C., office complex. Red has successfully recruited employees from both government agencies and private companies. He has also hired several recent graduates from some of the top universities in the country.

Red has formed teams of employees that are sent on temporary assignment to his clients' waste sites. Red's teams identify a strategy for dealing with whatever hazardous waste problem is found and they prepare a report recommending a course of action. Another department within the company will handle project management functions if the client requests assistance. Because of the makeup of the teams, some are better at handling certain types of problems than are others. This means that for some problems, certain teams will be able to complete the analysis and report faster than other teams.

Rehwald & Associates has five consulting contracts for the coming quarter. Red and his senior associates have formed five teams, which are named after the senior team member. Each contract is identified by its accounting code number. The problem is to determine how to assign the teams to the contracts.

The contracts were established on a fixed-fee basis, so the company's revenue is the same regardless of how long it takes a team to complete the work. Therefore, Red wants to assign the teams in such a way that the total time required to complete the contracts is minimized. Table 5-30 shows the completion estimates for each consulting contract by each project team.

THE LINEAR PROGRAMMING FORMULATION

An **assignment problem** involves allocating resources to meet demands. It can be represented as a linear programming problem similar to the transportation and transshipment problems presented earlier in this chapter. Assuming that Red wants to minimize the time his teams spend on the five contracts, the objective function, in general form, is:

$$\text{Minimize} \quad Z = \Sigma\, c_{ij}x_{ij}$$

where: c_{ij} = cost of assigning team i to project j
$x_{ij} = 0$ if team i is not assigned to project j
$x_{ij} = 1$ if team i is assigned to project j

The terms i and j represent the row and column number of each element in the matrix of Table 5-30.

The constraints imposed on the solution are:

$$\Sigma\, x_{ij} \leq 1 \text{ for all teams}$$

and

$$\Sigma\, x_{ij} = 1 \text{ for all contracts}$$

The first constraint ensures that all teams are assigned at most one contract. The second constraint assures all contracts are assigned to a team.

Because of how the decision variables have been defined, this formulation is a special type of linear programming called *zero-one linear programming*. Chapter 6 has a section describing zero-one linear programming and the solution procedure more fully.

While Red's assignment problem can be formulated and solved as a zero-one linear programming problem, many assignment situations involve larger numbers of rows and columns than our example. These larger problems make the linear programming formulation more complex. To overcome this problem, a special method for solving assignment problems exists.

Table 5-30 REHWALD & ASSOCIATES' COMPLETION-TIME ESTIMATES (IN WEEKS)

	Contract				
Team	1244	1379	1514	2021	1890
Elrod	15	11	17	13	16
Reed	20	23	10	16	19
Rice	23	15	18	21	24
Ferry	19	17	18	15	14
Snyder	19	21	11	17	20

THE HUNGARIAN SOLUTION METHOD

The solution procedure discussed in this section is a matrix reduction technique that was developed by D. Konig, a Hungarian mathematician, and has thus become known as the **Hungarian method.** The procedure begins with an assignment matrix like the one shown in Table 5-30.

The matrix reduction procedure is a four-step process:

Step 1 Reduce the initial matrix by subtracting the smallest value in each row from every value in that row.

Doing this for our example problem gives the following result:

	Contract				
Team	1244	1379	1514	2021	1890
Elrod	4	0	6	2	5
Reed	10	13	0	6	9
Rice	8	0	3	6	9
Ferry	5	3	4	1	0
Snyder	8	10	0	6	9

Step 1 converts the absolute times to relative times, based on how much larger they are than the smallest value in each row. *If this new matrix contains a zero in each row and column, the optimal solution will have been reached.* That would be to assign each team to the contract designated by the zero in the team row. Remember that each team must be assigned to one contract, and this would assign the fastest team to each task.

However, as you can see, step 1 does not give an optimal solution for this problem since columns 1 and 4 do not contain a zero. We proceed now to step 2.

Step 2 Further reduce the matrix by subtracting the smallest value in each column from all values in that column.

Doing this for our problem yields the following matrix:

	Contract				
Team	1244	1379	1514	2021	1890
Elrod	0	0	6	1	5
Reed	6	13	0	5	9
Rice	4	0	3	5	9
Ferry	1	3	4	0	0
Snyder	4	10	0	5	9

This reduced matrix has more zeros, one in every row and column, than the preceding one. We could assign teams to contracts based on a zero in the intersecting cell in the following manner: Elrod to 1244, Reed to 1514, Rice to 1379. Now we have two teams remaining, Ferry and Snyder, and two contracts, 2021 and 1890. However, the row for Ferry has a 0 for both contracts 2021 and 1890, implying that it would be preferable to have Ferry do both contracts. But this is not feasible. Also, the 0 in the Snyder row is for a contract already assigned to Reed. Thus, we are not yet at an optimal solution.

Table 5-31 REHWALD & ASSOCIATES EXAMPLE: RESULTS OF STEP 3 OF THE HUNGARIAN METHOD

	Contract				
Team	1244	1379	1514	2021	1890
Elrod	0	0	6	1	5
Reed	6	13	0	5	9
Rice	4	0	3	5	9
Ferry	1	3	4	0	0
Snyder	4	10	0	5	9

We need a procedure to determine if we can make an optimal assignment from a reduced matrix containing multiple zeros.

Step 3 At any point after performing steps 1 and 2, find the minimum number of lines needed to cover all the zeros in the matrix. If the minimum number of lines is equal to the number of rows (or columns) in the matrix, an optimal assignment can be made. If the minimum number of lines is less than the number of rows, continue to step 4.

Table 5-31 shows that all zeros can be covered in four lines. Since four lines are less than the five rows, we must continue.

Step 4 Working with the lined matrix in Table 5-31, locate the smallest unlined cell and subtract this value from all unlined cells in the matrix. Add this value to the cell at the intersection of any two lines. Return to step 3.

In the reduced matrix in Table 5-31, we see that 4 is the smallest value in an unlined cell. Subtracting this value from all unlined cells and adding 4 to the intersection of all lines, we find the following matrix.

	Contract				
Team	1244	1379	1514	2021	1890
Elrod	0	4	10	1	5
Reed	2	13	0	1	5
Rice	0	0	3	1	5
Ferry	1	7	8	0	0
Snyder	0	10	0	1	5

As shown in Table 5-32, the minimum number of lines required to cover the zeros is four. Since this is still less than the five rows, we must repeat step 4 by subtracting the

Table 5-32 REHWALD & ASSOCIATES EXAMPLE: STEP 3 REPEATED

	Contract				
Team	1244	1379	1514	2021	1890
Elrod	0	4	10	1	5
Reed	2	13	0	1	5
Rice	0	0	3	1	5
Ferry	1	7	8	0	0
Snyder	0	10	0	1	5

smallest unlined cell value from all unlined cell values in the matrix. Further, we add this value to all values at an intersection of two lines.

The smallest unlined value in Table 5-32 is 1. When we subtract 1 from all unlined cells and add it to the intersection of the four lines, we get the following reduced matrix:

	Contract				
Team	1244	1379	1514	2021	1890
Elrod	0	4	10	0	4
Reed	2	13	0	0	4
Rice	0	0	3	0	4
Ferry	2	8	9	0	0
Snyder	0	10	0	0	4

Now, as shown in Table 5-33, the minimum number of lines needed to cover all the zeros is five. Thus we have reached the optimal solution, since the number of lines is equal to the number of rows. The [0] values in Table 5-34 indicate the optimal assignments. The assignments shown in Table 5-34 and the estimated completion times from Table 5-30 are as follows:

	Assignment	
Team	Contract	Time
Elrod	1244	15 weeks
Reed	1514	10 weeks
Rice	1379	15 weeks
Ferry	1890	14 weeks
Snyder	2021	17 weeks
		71 weeks

Thus, the total time needed by all teams to complete all contracts is 71 weeks. No other assignments will result in lower total time.

Table 5-33 REHWALD & ASSOCIATES EXAMPLE: STEP 3 REPEATED—FINAL SOLUTION REACHED

	Contract				
Team	1244	1379	1514	2021	1890
Elrod	0	4	10	0	4
Reed	2	13	0	0	4
Rice	0	0	3	0	4
Ferry	2	8	9	0	0
Snyder	0	10	0	0	4

Table 5-34 REHWALD & ASSOCIATES EXAMPLE: ASSIGNMENT MATRIX FOR THE FINAL SOLUTION

	Contract				
Team	1244	1379	1514	2021	1890
Elrod	[0]	4	10	0	4
Reed	2	13	[0]	0	4
Rice	0	[0]	3	0	4
Ferry	2	8	9	0	[0]
Snyder	0	10	0	[0]	4

Problems Finding the Minimum Number of Lines

In some cases, covering the zeros with the fewest possible lines is more difficult than it sounds. An approach which works quite well is to start by selecting any row or column which has a single zero. If the single zero is found in a row, draw a line through the column with the zero in it. If the single zero is in a column, then draw a line through the row. Continue this process until all the zeros are covered.

If for some reason you reach what you think is the optimal solution but cannot determine a unique zero [0] assignment, then you have actually used more than the minimum number of lines to cover the zeros. When this happens, just return to the previous step and make sure the zeros are covered with the minimum number of lines.

Extending the Assignment Problem

The Rehwald & Associates example involved a **balanced assignment problem**, in which the number of contracts was equal to the number of teams. The problem was a time minimization problem, since any team could have been assigned to any of the contracts. Sometimes these conditions will not be met, but assignments still need to be made. Fortunately, the Hungarian solution method can still be used if the appropriate modifications are made in the formulation.

Number of Teams Not Equal to Number of Contracts Continuing the Rehwald & Associate example, suppose that the client with contract number 1890 notifies Rehwald that the project must be postponed for a year. This leaves Rehwald & Associates with five teams and only four contracts. Table 5-35 shows the estimated time for the four contracts, by team.

The matrix reduction solution procedure requires the number of rows in the matrix to be equal to the number of columns, but at this point we have more rows than

Table 5-35 REHWALD & ASSOCIATES EXAMPLE: COMPLETION-TIME ESTIMATES WITH ONLY FOUR CONTRACTS

	Contract			
Team	1244	1379	1514	2021
Elrod	15	11	17	13
Reed	20	23	10	16
Rice	23	15	18	21
Ferry	19	17	18	15
Snyder	19	21	11	17

Table 5-36 REHWALD & ASSOCIATES EXAMPLE: COMPLETION-TIME ESTIMATES WITH A DUMMY CONTRACT

	Contract				
Team	1244	1379	1514	2021	Dummy
Elrod	15	11	17	13	0
Reed	20	23	10	16	0
Rice	23	15	18	21	0
Ferry	19	17	18	15	0
Snyder	19	21	11	17	0

columns. To get around this problem, we assign a dummy column (dummy contract), as shown in Table 5-36.

The matrix reduction solution procedure can now be used as before. You are encouraged to work through this example to see that the following assignments are optimal:

Elrod team	To contract 1379
Reed team	To contract 1514
Ferry team	To contract 2021
Snyder team	To contract 1244
Rice team	To dummy contract

This set of assignments will have a total completion time of 55 weeks. The Rice team, which is assigned to the dummy, will be free to take on another contract.

In cases where there are fewer rows than columns, a dummy row is created and the solution procedure continues in the usual way.

Unacceptable Assignments In some situations not all teams, or sources, will be available for all assignments, or demands. For instance, suppose that due to prior involvements, Mike Reed of the Reed team has a conflict of interest and cannot work on contract 1514, to which his team was initially assigned (see Table 5-34).

To deal with this added constraint, we return to the original five-team, five-contract matrix. Table 5-37 shows that we have assigned a large completion time, M, to the appropriate cell. Such a large time will eliminate this cell from the possible set of solutions, since we are looking for a minimum total time. The value for M is set so large that it can never be the minimum row or column value.

Table 5-37 COMPLETION-TIME ESTIMATES INCORPORATING REED'S REQUEST

	Contract				
Team	1244	1379	1514	2021	1890
Elrod	15	11	17	13	16
Reed	20	23	M	16	19
Rice	23	15	18	21	24
Ferry	19	17	18	15	14
Snyder	19	21	11	17	20

Table 5-38 SPORTSCHANNEL REVENUE PROJECTIONS ($000,000s)

	Time Slot			
Game	1:30 P.M.	4:00 P.M.	7:00 P.M.	9:30 P.M.
Team 1 vs. 8	5	3	6	4
Team 2 vs. 7	7.5	9	3.5	5.5
Team 3 vs. 6	7	6	6.5	5
Team 4 vs. 5	7	8	4.5	6

Maximization Problems While the Hungarian solution procedure works for minimization problems like that facing Red Rehwald, some modifications are needed if the problem has a maximization objective. For instance, SportsChannel, a national cable television network, has received the rights to televise four games of a regional college basketball tournament. Since the teams come from different parts of the country, the size of the viewing audience for any game will depend on when the game is scheduled —and advertising revenue depends on audience size.

The tournament seeding committee has already determined the teams to be matched in each game. But the tournament directors are willing to let SportsChannel select which of the games should be played in each of the four time slots. The company's advertising department has made the estimates of advertising revenues for all combinations of games and time slots, shown in Table 5-38.

The Hungarian solution method is unique to minimization problems and so cannot directly be used on this problem, since the television executives are interested in maximizing revenues. However, we can convert this to a minimization problem if the objective is reformulated to be one of minimizing opportunity loss.

To explain opportunity loss, consider the 7:00 P.M. time slot. The maximum revenue of $650,000 will occur if the game involves the third-seeded and sixth-seeded teams. However, for a game featuring the fourth- and fifth-seeded teams, the revenue would be only $450,000. The difference of $200,000 is the **opportunity-loss value** (the projected revenue that will be lost if the channel does not have the opportunity to televise the top game). The revenue table (Table 5-38) can be converted to an opportunity-loss table by subtracting each value in a column from the maximum value in that column. The opportunity-loss representation of the problem facing SportsChannel is shown in Table 5-39.

The Hungarian method can now be used to find the assignment of games to time slots that will minimize the opportunity losses. Again, we encourage you to work

Table 5-39 SPORTSCHANNEL OPPORTUNITY-LOSS TABLE ($000,000s)

	Time Slot			
Game	1:30 P.M.	4:00 P.M.	7:00 P.M.	9:30 P.M.
Team 1 vs. 8	2.5	6	.5	2
Team 2 vs. 7	0	0	3	.5
Team 3 vs. 6	.5	3	0	1
Team 4 vs. 5	.5	1	2	0

through this problem using the Hungarian solution procedure. When you do, you should find the following solution:

Game	Time Slot
Team 1 vs. 8	7:00 P.M.
Team 2 vs. 7	4:00 P.M.
Team 3 vs. 6	1:30 P.M.
Team 4 vs. 5	9:30 P.M.

To find the revenue associated with this assignment, we will have to return to the original matrix. This value is \$2,800,000. By looking at the original revenue matrix in Table 5-38, you will see that not all time slots have the game which will generate the maximum revenue during that time. However, this occurs to allow a game with a higher relative revenue, or lower opportunity loss, to be played during that time. No other assignment of games to time periods will result in a larger revenue to Sports-Channel.

Unacceptable assignments are handled in maximization problems by putting a large cost, or $-M$, in the appropriate cell in the original assignment matrix. When subtractions are performed to convert to an opportunity-loss table, this becomes a positive M and prevents that cell from ever being a part of the solution.

Unbalanced systems for maximization are dealt with in the same manner as those for minimization problems. The needed dummy row or column is added to the matrix and the problem is then solved.

5-6 COMPUTER APPLICATIONS

The solution procedures introduced in this chapter for solving transportation and assignment problems can be performed manually. However, even though they represent an improvement over the simplex procedure in terms of complexity, the manual computations themselves can become complex. As with many of the other management science techniques introduced in this text, computer software exists for helping decision makers solve transportation, transshipment, and assignment problems. The MASTER software package which accompanies this text has those capabilities.

In addition to the linear programming module, which we have already demonstrated in this chapter, the MASTER software package contains special solution modules for transportation and assignment models. The purpose of this section is to work through examples with MASTER, showing the required input and the resulting output.

A TRANSPORTATION PROBLEM

The Norco Cookie Company has manufacturing plants at 6 locations and distribution warehouses at 5 locations, in the United States and Canada. Table 5-40 shows the transportation cost per case of cookies between each manufacturing plant and warehouse. Table 5-40 also shows the capacity (in cases) for each plant and the demand (in cases) for each warehouse. For instance, the cost per case for transporting cookies between plant 1 and warehouse 1 is \$.50. Plant 1 has a daily capacity of 10,000 cases and warehouse 1 has a daily demand for 6000 cases.

The MASTER software package has a special module for solving transportation problems. The data entry requirements are straightforward, as shown in Figure 5-6. As you can see, this figure contains the same data as the transportation matrix in Table 5-40. The user is asked to indicate whether the problem is a minimization or maximization problem. In the Norco example, we want to minimize transportation costs.

Table 5-40 NORCO COOKIE CO. TRANSPORTATION COSTS (DOLLARS PER CASE)

Plant	Warehouse 1	2	3	4	5	Capacity (cases)
1	.50	.30	.60	.40	.60	10,000
2	.70	.20	.40	.30	.50	3,000
3	.30	.40	.70	.20	.50	3,000
4	.70	.40	.40	.30	.60	7,000
5	.50	.20	.70	.40	.50	2,000
6	.60	.20	.70	.50	.10	2,000
Demand (cases)	6000	5000	4000	7000	5000	

```
Master   INTRODUCTION TO MANAGEMENT SCIENCE

         Destin   W1    W2    W3    W4    W5
Source           6000  5000  4000  7000  5000
P1       10000    .50   .30   .60   .40   .60
P2        3000    .70   .20   .40   .30   .50
P3        3000    .30   .40   .70   .20   .50
P4        7000    .70   .40   .40   .30   .60
P5        2000    .50   .20   .70   .40   .50
P6        2000    .60   .20   .70   .50   .10

Use arrows to select and change data. Press <F1> to Exit.
<F5> Add Row  <F6> Add Col  <F7> Del Row <F8> Del Col
```

Figure 5-6
Norco Cookie Co. transportation problem: MASTER data entry screen

```
     Transportation Modeling


   COST MINIMIZATION

OPTIMAL SOLUTION

          W1       W2       W3       W4       W5
P1      6000.    3000.       0.    1000.       0.
P2         0.    2000.       0.       0.    1000.
P3         0.       0.       0.    3000.       0.
P4         0.       0.    4000.    3000.       0.
P5         0.       0.       0.       0.    2000.
P6         0.       0.       0.       0.    2000.

   OBJECTIVE FUNCTION = 9500.
```

Figure 5-7
Norco Cookie Co. transportation problem: MASTER output

The MASTER results are shown in Figure 5-7. This solution represents the shipping schedule which will minimize total costs at $9500. To achieve this minimum cost, Norco will adopt the following shipping schedule:

From	To	Quantity (cases)
Plant 1	Warehouse 1	6000
Plant 1	Warehouse 2	3000
Plant 1	Warehouse 4	1000
Plant 2	Warehouse 2	2000
Plant 2	Warehouse 5	1000
Plant 3	Warehouse 4	3000
Plant 4	Warehouse 3	4000
Plant 4	Warehouse 4	3000
Plant 5	Warehouse 5	2000
Plant 6	Warehouse 5	2000

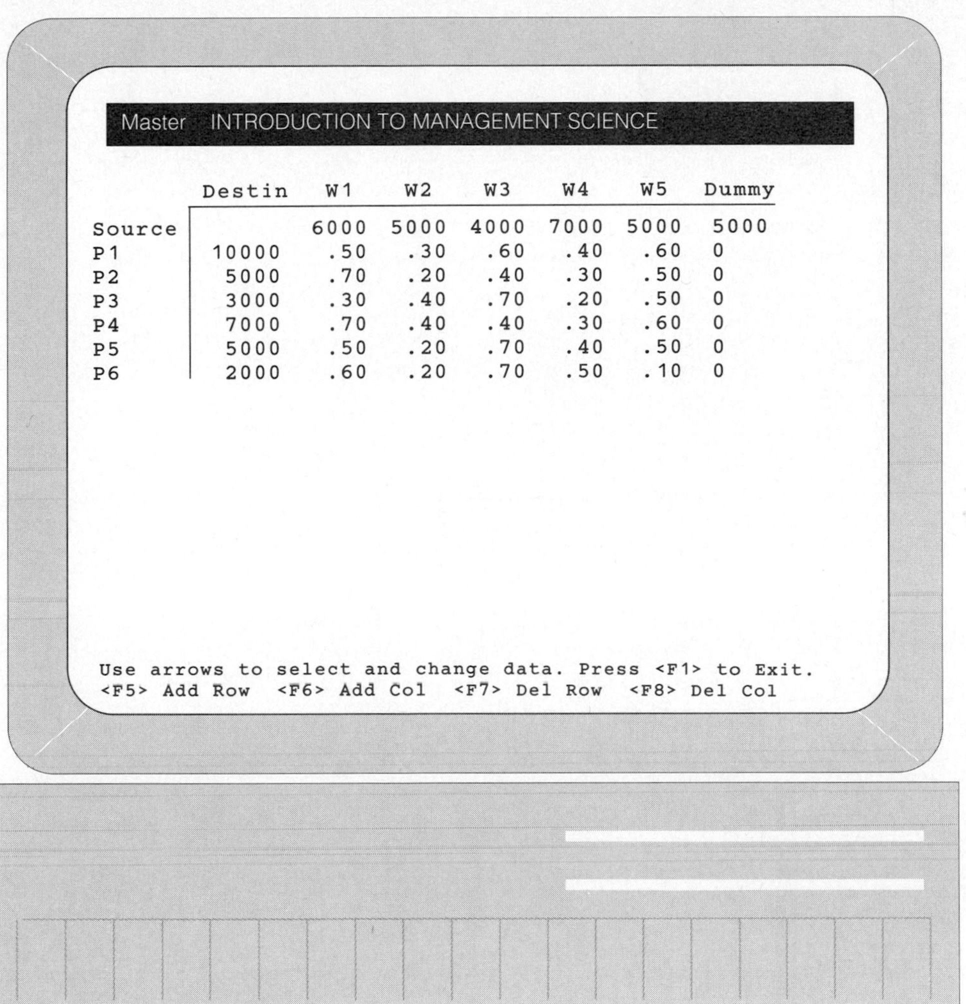

Master INTRODUCTION TO MANAGEMENT SCIENCE

	Destin	W1	W2	W3	W4	W5	Dummy
Source		6000	5000	4000	7000	5000	5000
P1	10000	.50	.30	.60	.40	.60	0
P2	5000	.70	.20	.40	.30	.50	0
P3	3000	.30	.40	.70	.20	.50	0
P4	7000	.70	.40	.40	.30	.60	0
P5	5000	.50	.20	.70	.40	.50	0
P6	2000	.60	.20	.70	.50	.10	0

Use arrows to select and change data. Press <F1> to Exit.
<F5> Add Row <F6> Add Col <F7> Del Row <F8> Del Col

Figure 5-8
Modified Norco Cookie Co. problem: MASTER data entry screen

In this example, the demand exactly equaled the capacity of the manufacturing plants. We showed earlier in this chapter that when supply and demand are not equal, we must establish either a dummy supply or a dummy demand. The same process is used by the MASTER software.

For example, suppose the capacity of plant 2 was 5000 cases rather than 3000 cases and that the capacity of plant 5 was 5000 cases rather than 2000. Assuming the warehouse demands stayed the same, the transportation problem would be out of balance by 5000 cases. To deal with this problem, we add a dummy warehouse with a demand of 5000 units. Since no cookies will actually be shipped to the dummy warehouse, the costs are set to zero between each plant and the dummy warehouse. Figure 5-8 shows the input data for the MASTER software.

Figure 5-9 shows the MASTER results. If you compare this result with that shown in Figure 5-7, you will see that the shipping schedule has changed dramatically. Most important is the fact that 5000 cases from plant 1 are scheduled to go to the dummy

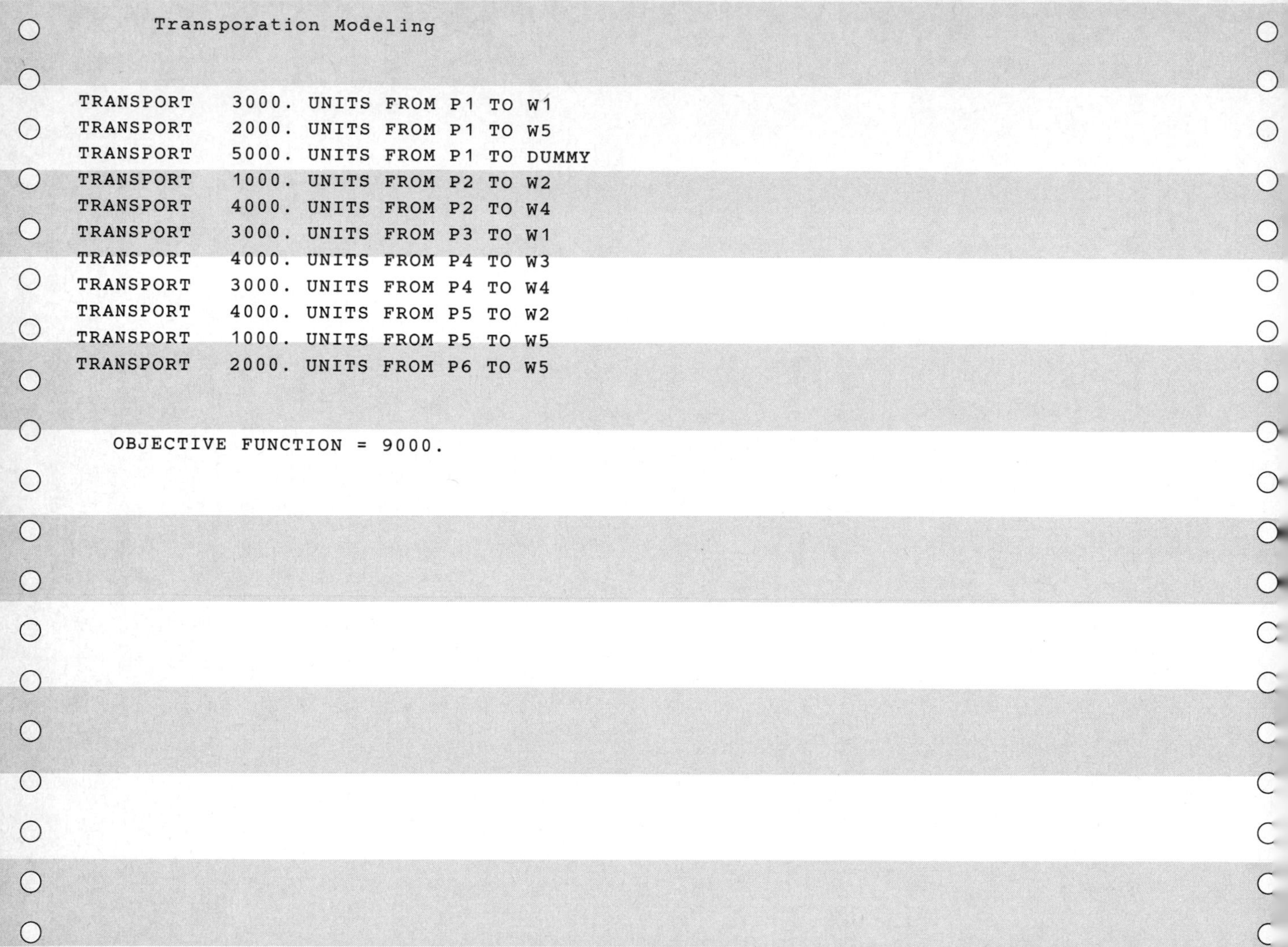

```
      Transporation Modeling

TRANSPORT    3000. UNITS FROM P1 TO W1
TRANSPORT    2000. UNITS FROM P1 TO W5
TRANSPORT    5000. UNITS FROM P1 TO DUMMY
TRANSPORT    1000. UNITS FROM P2 TO W2
TRANSPORT    4000. UNITS FROM P2 TO W4
TRANSPORT    3000. UNITS FROM P3 TO W1
TRANSPORT    4000. UNITS FROM P4 TO W3
TRANSPORT    3000. UNITS FROM P4 TO W4
TRANSPORT    4000. UNITS FROM P5 TO W2
TRANSPORT    1000. UNITS FROM P5 TO W5
TRANSPORT    2000. UNITS FROM P6 TO W5

   OBJECTIVE FUNCTION = 9000.
```

Figure 5-9

Modified Norco Cookie Co. problem: MASTER output

warehouse. This means that plant 1 will actually curtail production by 5000 units. Take note of the other changes as well. This schedule results in an overall cost of \$9000.

AN ASSIGNMENT PROBLEM

We showed earlier in this chapter that assignment problems can be solved using linear programming or by the Hungarian solution procedure. The disadvantage of using linear programming is that for large problems the formulation is fairly complex. The Hungarian solution procedure eliminates the need to formulate a linear programming problem, but the steps in reaching the solution manually can be quite cumbersome in larger problems.

To deal with these issues in solving assignment problems, many management science software packages now include assignment modules. The MASTER assignment model can be demonstrated with the following example.

The Big School Athletic Conference has 10 schools which compete in varsity football at the NCAA Division 1 level. The referees assigned to the games work as a team and will work together throughout the season. Rodney Merkle is a staff member

Table 5-41 TRAVEL COSTS FOR FOOTBALL REFEREE TEAMS

	Game Location				
Team	WAU	UC	USA	BSU	UD
1	$1400	$1760	$2120	$1500	$1900
2	$1350	$2000	$1700	$2300	$2000
3	$2700	$1900	$2200	$1800	$1600
4	$3000	$2100	$2600	$1900	$2400
5	$1700	$2000	$1800	$2350	$1950

in the Big School Conference commissioner's office, and among his other duties he is charged with scheduling game officials. Suppose he is in the process of scheduling the games for the second Saturday in October. All 10 teams are scheduled to play conference games that day, so 5 games need referees. When the 10 teams are playing within the conference like this, the league policy is to assign the 5 highest-rated officiating teams.

Rodney's problem is to determine which team to assign to which game. How the referees are assigned wouldn't matter if Rodney didn't have to consider travel costs, which are paid by the conference. The commissioner wants to assign officials in such a way that total travel costs for all officials are minimized. Since each game needs a team of officials, and since each team of officials needs a game to referee, Rodney has a classic assignment problem.

Although the referees work together as a team, they do not, as a rule, live in the same city. Instead, they tend to be scattered around the conference region. Consequently, earlier in the year Rodney developed a round-trip cost list which shows the combined travel costs for members of each officiating team for games played at each of the 10 universities. Table 5-41 shows the travel costs for the 5 top referee teams going to the schools where the 5 conference games will be played.

In order to solve this problem with the MASTER software, the user selects the Assignment Modeling option and enters the cost data from Table 5-41, as shown in Figure 5-10. The results, shown in Figure 5-11, indicate the following referee schedule:

Referee Team	School	Travel Cost
1	BSU	$1500
2	WAU	$1350
3	UD	$1600
4	UC	$2100
5	USA	$1800
		$8350

This assignment plan will cost the conference $8350. No other assignment plan will yield a lower total travel cost.

As this example and the others in this section show, computer software takes the computational burden off the user when solving transportation and assignment problems. This frees the decision maker to think more about the application and the solution and worry less about the steps required to reach the optimal solution. If you have access to either MASTER or other management science software, we encourage you to use it as you work the problems at the end of the chapter.

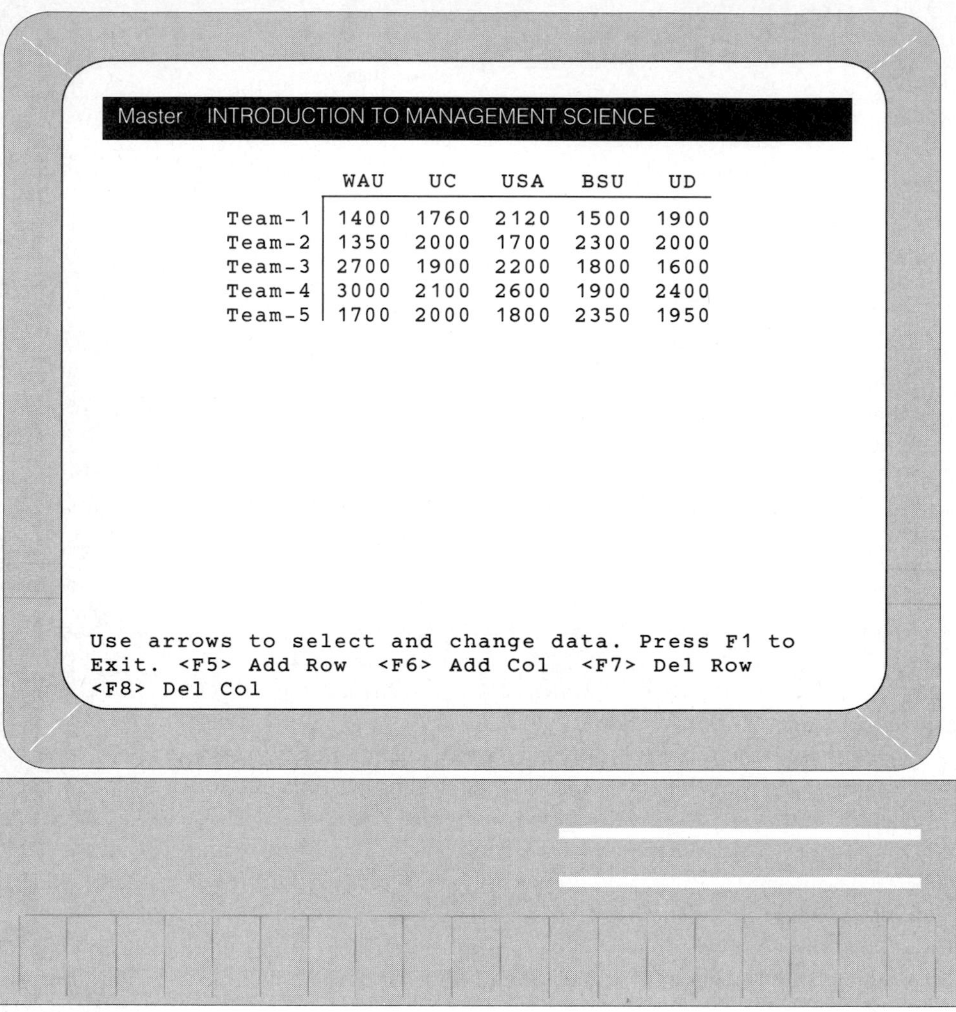

Figure 5-10
Referee assignment problem: MASTER data entry screen

5-7 SUMMARY AND CONCLUSIONS

This chapter has introduced important management science techniques for solving transportation, transshipment, and assignment problems. Transportation problems typically involve a set of two or more sources with defined capacities and a set of two or more destinations with defined demands. The cost (or some surrogate of cost) of moving items between each source and each destination is known. In many cases, the objective is to determine the shipping schedule that will minimize total costs. Transshipment problems are a variation of transportation problems. In a transshipment problem, there are source nodes and destination nodes just as in a transportation problem. However, there are also interim storage facilities which receive items from the original sources. As with transportation problems, most applications have minimization of shipping costs or shipping time as an objective.

```
         Assignment Modeling

      COST MINIMIZATION

      OPTIMAL SOLUTION

              WAU   UC   USA   BSU   UD
   Team-1     0.    0.    0.    1.    0.
   Team-2     1.    0.    0.    0.    0.
   Team-3     0.    0.    0.    0.    1.
   Team-4     0.    1.    0.    0.    0.
   Team-5     0.    0.    1.    0.    0.

      OBJECTIVE FUNCTION = 8350.
```

Figure 5-11
Referee assignment problem: MASTER output

Assignment problems are slightly different in concept from transportation or transshipment problems. In a typical assignment problem, the objective is to assign employees to tasks such that each employee is performing a single task and no task has more than one employee assigned. The objective might be to make the assignments so that the total work time is minimized.

Situations that can be described by one of these models are widely found in organizations in both the public and private sectors. Because these problems are so widespread, the solution procedures considered in this chapter are among the most useful that this text covers.

Transportation, transshipment, and assignment problems can be formulated and solved using a linear programming model. This chapter has shown examples using linear programming for each type of problem. However, in most practical applications the linear programming representations become quite large and complex. To overcome this problem, special solution procedures have been developed for all three types of problems.

This chapter has introduced the stepping-stone method for solving transportation problems and the Hungarian method for solving assignment problems. These solution procedures are mathematical algorithms which provide the optimal solution without requiring the decision maker to formulate a complex linear programming problem. Many management science software packages contain programs which use these procedures to solve transportation and assignment problems. We have demonstrated the use of MASTER, the software that accompanies this text. To use this software, the user merely inputs the transportation or assignment matrix and MASTER computes the optimal solution.

A number of the important terms introduced in this chapter are summarized in the Chapter Glossary.

Solved Problems

PROBLEM 1 Quick Freeze Corp. produces small refrigerators at three plants in the United States: Athens, Georgia; Waco, Texas; and Superior, Wisconsin. Quick Freeze has a contract with Champion Manufacturing to supply refrigerators for the travel trailers and mobile homes that Champion makes. In addition, Champion has recently become a supplier to contractors building small efficiency apartments. Champion Manufacturing has production facilities and distribution centers in New York, St. Louis, Denver, and Reno.

Plans call for Quick Freeze to supply the following number (in thousands) of refrigerators next year to the specified locations.

New York	50
St. Louis	70
Denver	60
Reno	80

The production capacities (in thousands) at Quick Freeze's three plants are as follows:

Athens	100
Waco	100
Superior	150

Because of varying production and transportation costs, the profit that Quick Freeze earns on each lot of 1000 units depends on where it was produced and which destination it was shipped to. The following table gives the accounting department's estimates of the profit per unit (shipments are made in lots of 1000 units). Because of a dispute between unions representing workers at the Quick Freeze plant in Athens and Champion's Denver plant, refrigerators cannot be shipped from Athens to Denver.

PROFIT PER UNIT ($)

	Shipped To			
Shipped From	New York	St. Louis	Denver	Reno
Athens	7	11	NA	13
Waco	20	17	12	10
Superior	8	18	13	16

Given profit maximization as the objective, how many refrigerators should be produced at each plant and where should they be shipped? What profit is associated with your recommendation?

Solution

This problem can be formulated as a transportation problem and solved using a maximization criterion. The appropriate transportation matrix is shown in Table 5-42. Notice that the infeasible route between Athens and Reno is assigned a large negative profit. Notice also that the production capacity is greater than the demand, creating an unbalanced situation. We can deal with this by adding a dummy demand column to the matrix, as shown in Table 5-43.

To solve this problem manually, we must first make an initial assignment. Using the maximum profit criterion, we first assign 50 to the Waco–New York cell, then 70 to the Superior–St. Louis cell, and 80 to Superior–Reno. This assignment fulfills the demand and exhausts the capacity at the same time, requiring that a 0 be placed somewhere in a row or column. We arbitrarily selected the Superior–Dummy route for the 0, and added 50 to the Waco–Denver cell. Finally, the Dummy demand will receive 90 from Athens, and 10 will temporarily be assigned to the unacceptable route of Athens–Denver. The initial shipping schedule is shown in Table 5-44.

Table 5-42 QUICK FREEZE PROBLEM: TRANSPORTATION MATRIX (THOUSANDS OF REFRIGERATORS)

	Champion Location				
Plant	New York	St. Louis	Denver	Reno	**Capacity**
Athens	7	11	$-M$	13	100
Waco	20	17	12	10	100
Superior	8	18	13	16	150
Demands	50	70	60	80	

Table 5-43 QUICK FREEZE TRANSPORTATION PROBLEM WITH DUMMY DEMAND (THOUSANDS OF REFRIGERATORS)

	Champion Location					
Plant	New York	St. Louis	Denver	Reno	Dummy	**Capacity**
Athens	7	11	$-M$	13	0	100
Waco	20	17	12	10	0	100
Superior	8	18	13	16	0	150
Demands	50	70	60	80	90	

Table 5-44 QUICK FREEZE PROBLEM: INITIAL ALLOCATION (THOUSANDS OF REFRIGERATORS)

	Champion Location					
Plant	New York	St. Louis	Denver	Reno	Dummy	**Capacity**
Athens	7	11	$-M$	13	0	
			10		90	100
Waco	20	17	12	10	0	
	50		50			100
Superior	8	18	13	16	0	
		70		80	0	150
Demands	50	70	60	80	90	

This problem can also be solved using a transportation software package, such as the transportation option of MASTER. (Note: If you use MASTER, you will have to substitute a large cost, say -1000, for the $-M$ in the table. You will also need to establish a dummy destination, as was done in Table 5-43.) The optimal shipping schedule should be:

Athens–Reno	10,000
Waco–New York	50,000
Waco–St. Louis	50,000
Superior–St. Louis	20,000
Superior–Denver	60,000
Superior–Reno	70,000

The Athens plant will be running at 90,000 below capacity. Quick Freeze should realize a total profit of $4,240,000 next year from its relationship with Champion Manufacturing. You are encouraged to verify this solution both manually and with a computer software package.

PROBLEM 2 International Paper has three pulp mills capable of producing the high-fiber-content paper demanded by custom publishing houses. The mills are in Minnesota, Newfoundland (Canada), and Alabama. Since the mills must be run continuously and the publishing houses have an intermittent demand for paper, International ships paper made at the three mills to distribution centers in Chicago and New York. The paper is then processed and shipped to four current customers in Boston, Cincinnati, Pittsburgh, and Albany, New York.

The weekly high-fiber capacity (in rolls of paper) at each of the mills is:

Minnesota	140
Newfoundland	200
Alabama	170

A contract with the shipping company that serves the distribution centers specifies shipping at least 200 rolls each week to each center. However, the capacity at the distribution centers limits the total rolls handled each week to a maximum of 300. Neither transshipment facility can be used to store paper. The projected weekly demand (in rolls of paper) from each of the publishing houses is:

Boston	100
Cincinnati	120
Pittsburgh	80
Albany	160

The per roll transportation costs for all routes are:

From	To	Cost
Minnesota	New York	$18
	Chicago	$14
Newfoundland	New York	$13
	Chicago	$15
Alabama	New York	$14.50
	Chicago	$13.50
New York	Boston	$11
	Cincinnati	$14
	Pittsburgh	$13.50
	Albany	$10.50

From	To	Cost
Chicago	Boston	\$15.50
	Cincinnati	\$11.50
	Pittsburgh	\$12.50
	Albany	\$14.50

Allan Wertz, the production scheduler, notes that the plants will not be able to run at full capacity because capacity exceeds projected demand. Since the production costs at the three mills are the same, the decision about which plant(s) should be cut back will be made on the basis of shipping costs. Allan needs help in determining what the operating output of each plant should be and what shipping schedule should be used.

Solution

The situation facing Allan can be formulated as a transshipment problem, as represented in Figure 5-12. To help formulate the decision as a linear programming problem, we have numbered the nodes in Figure 5-12. Using these numbers, we can define the decision variables as x_{ij}, where x_{14}

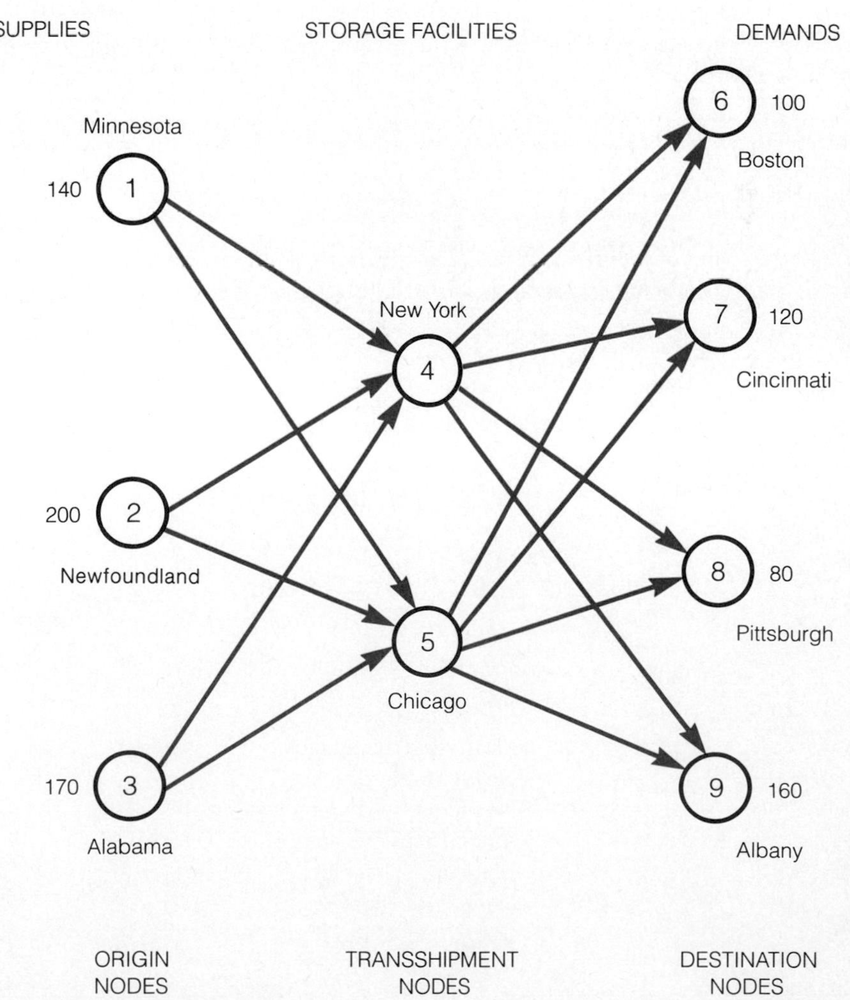

Figure 5-12
Node-arc representation of the International Paper problem

defines the amount sent from the Minnesota mill to the New York distribution center. Using these decision variables, and looking at Figure 5-12, we can develop the following constraints:

a. Since International Paper can ship no more than 140 rolls per week from the Minnesota mill, no more than 200 from the Newfoundland mill, and no more than 170 from the Alabama mill, we have the following three constraints:

$$x_{14} + x_{15} \leq 140$$
$$x_{24} + x_{25} \leq 200$$
$$x_{34} + x_{35} \leq 170$$

b. Since the two distribution centers should handle from 200 to 300 rolls per week, we have the following four constraints:

$$x_{14} + x_{24} + x_{34} \geq 200$$
$$x_{14} + x_{24} + x_{34} \leq 300$$
$$x_{15} + x_{25} + x_{35} \geq 200$$
$$x_{15} + x_{25} + x_{35} \leq 300$$

c. If International Paper allows no long-term storage at the transshipment facilities, everything shipped into both New York and Chicago must be shipped out. Therefore:

$$x_{14} + x_{24} + x_{34} = x_{46} + x_{47} + x_{48} + x_{49}$$

or $x_{14} + x_{24} + x_{34} - x_{46} - x_{47} - x_{48} - x_{49} = 0$

and $x_{15} + x_{25} + x_{35} = x_{56} + x_{57} + x_{58} + x_{59}$

or $x_{15} + x_{25} + x_{35} - x_{56} - x_{57} - x_{58} - x_{59} = 0$

d. To satisfy the demands at the destination nodes, we need the following set of constraints:

$$x_{46} + x_{56} = 100$$
$$x_{47} + x_{57} = 120$$
$$x_{48} + x_{58} = 80$$
$$x_{49} + x_{59} = 160$$

The objective function is to minimize the total shipping costs along all possible routes. This becomes:

$$\text{Minimize } Z = 18x_{14} + 14x_{15} + 13x_{24} + 15x_{25} + 14.5x_{34} + 13.5x_{35} + 11x_{46} + 14x_{47} + 13.5x_{48} + 10.5x_{49} + 15.5x_{56} + 11.5x_{57} + 12.5x_{58} + 14.5x_{59}$$

Using the linear programming option of MASTER to solve this problem, we find:

$x_{14} = 0$	Minnesota–New York
$x_{15} = 90$	Minnesota–Chicago
$x_{24} = 200$	Newfoundland–New York
$x_{25} = 0$	Newfoundland–Chicago
$x_{34} = 60$	Alabama–New York
$x_{35} = 110$	Alabama–Chicago
$x_{46} = 100$	New York–Boston
$x_{47} = 0$	New York–Cincinnati
$x_{48} = 0$	New York–Pittsburgh

$x_{49} = 160$ New York–Albany
$x_{56} = 0$ Chicago–Boston
$x_{57} = 120$ Chicago–Cincinnati
$x_{58} = 80$ Chicago–Pittsburgh
$x_{59} = 0$ Chicago–Alabama

We see that the Minnesota mill does not operate at full capacity, since it ships only 90 rolls per week. The total shipping cost for the entire system is $11,375. No other shipping schedule will have a lower cost.

General Questions and Assignments

1. Discuss in your own terms the steps involved in employing the northwest corner solution procedure to a transportation problem.
2. Discuss the differences between the type of problems that can be solved with a transportation model and those that can be solved with a transshipment model.
3. Discuss in your own terms what the stepping-stone solution method is for the transportation model.
4. In solving a transportation model, what steps must be taken if the total supply is greater than the total demand? Explain with an example of your own.
5. Define the Hungarian method for solving assignment problems. Be sure to discuss what to do when there are unacceptable assignments in the model.
6. Contact a company in your area which you think would have a need to apply either the transportation model or the transshipment model. Find out to what extent the business uses these techniques. If the techniques are not used, find out what alternative method is used to determine shipping routes and so on.
7. Locate two or more articles in the library which discuss transportation, transshipment, or assignment models. Write a paper summarizing the articles. Be sure to comment on the degree of success attained by the use of these techniques.

Exercises and Application Problems

1. Hot Air Corp. produces propane heaters at three plants in the United States: Superior, Wisconsin; Bangor, Maine; and Grand Junction, Colorado. Hot Air has distribution centers in New York, Kansas City, Dallas, and Reno. The following table gives the shipping costs from all plants to all distribution centers.

	New York	Kansas City	Dallas	Reno
Superior	13	12	15	10
Bangor	17	15	11	13
Grand Junction	12	13	14	16

Each plant can produce 2000 heaters per week. New York requires 1600 per week; Kansas City, 1200; Dallas, 1800; and Reno, 1400. The present shipping schedule is shown below:

From	To	Units Shipped
Superior	New York	1600
	Kansas City	400
Bangor	Kansas City	800
	Dallas	1200
Grand Junction	Dallas	600
	Reno	1400

a. What is the weekly cost of this distribution schedule? Is this the lowest-cost schedule possible?
b. If your answer to **a** is no, what shipping schedule would you suggest? How much would your schedule save the company?
c. Formulate and solve this problem using a linear programming model. Is your optimal solution the same one you found in part **b**?

2. Use the minimum-cost allocation method to find the initial starting solution to the distribution system given in problem 1. Is this the optimal distribution allocation?
3. Quick Freeze Corp. produces small refrigerators at three plants: Athens, Georgia; Waco, Texas; and Superior, Wisconsin. Quick Freeze has distribution centers in New York, St. Louis, Denver, and Reno. The profit the company realizes from each plant depends on the contract price at each distribution center, manufacturing costs at each plant, and shipping costs from each plant to each distribution center. The following table shows the accounting department's best estimate of these profits per refrigerator shipped.

	New York	St. Louis	Denver	Reno
Athens	11	14	15	13
Waco	18	17	14	17
Superior	15	16	12	14

Each plant can produce 1000 refrigerators per week. New York requires 800 per week; St. Louis, 600; Denver, 900; and Reno, 700. The present shipping schedule is shown below:

From	To	Units
Athens	New York	800
	St. Louis	200
Waco	St. Louis	400
	Denver	600
Superior	Denver	300
	Reno	700

a. What is the weekly profit associated with this distribution schedule? Is this the maximum profit possible?
b. If your answer to **a** is no, what shipping schedule would you suggest? How much would your schedule earn the company?
c. Formulate and solve this problem using a linear programming model. Is your optimal solution the same one you found in part **b**?

4. QTex produces and markets quality control software packages that are adaptable by most service and manufacturing companies in the country. The disks and instruction manuals are produced at three plants: Dothan, Alabama; Midland, Texas; and Arco, Idaho. QTex has distribution centers in Albany, New York; St. Paul, Minnesota; Denver, and Reno. The following table gives the shipping costs from all plants to all distribution centers.

	Albany	St. Paul	Denver	Reno
Dothan	1.20	1.55	1.40	1.30
Midland	1.45	1.65	1.10	1.35
Arco	1.70	1.35	1.05	1.45

Each plant can produce 3000 manuals and sets of disks per week. Albany requires 2000 per week; St. Paul, 1500; Denver, 2400; and Reno, 3100.

a. What shipping schedule would you suggest?
b. What is the cost of this shipping schedule?
c. Are there alternative shipping schedules which would have the same cost? How do you know?

5. Consider the situation of QTex, in problem 4. Use the minimum-cost method to determine the initial allocation. What is the cost of this solution to the transportation problem? Is this the optimal solution? If not, how many steps of the stepping-stone method will be needed to get to the optimal solution?

6. Consider the minimum-cost transportation problem shown below:

	d1	d2	d3	d4	
s_1	10	8	7	9	1500
s_2	8	12	11	10	1100
s_3	10	7	9	11	1700
	1400	800	1200	900	

a. Use the northwest corner rule to find the initial starting solution.
b. Use the minimum-cost method to find the initial starting solution.
c. What is the minimum-cost allocation to this problem?

7. Consider the maximum-profit transportation problem shown below:

	d1	d2	d3	d4	d5	
s_1	7	8	8	5	9	2100
s_2	10	9	11	8	7	1700
s_3	6	5	7	5	4	1300
s_4	9	12	10	9	8	1500
	1200	1000	1400	1600	1600	

a. Use the northwest corner rule to find the initial starting solution.
b. Use the maximum-profit method to find the initial starting solution. (This is an obvious extension of the minimum-cost method, but is used for maximization problems.)
c. What is the maximum-profit allocation to this problem?

8. Consider the situation of the Hot Air Corp., from problem 1. The Reno distributor has just called to increase her order to 2800. The company cannot meet this demand and will have to reallocate the

shipping schedule. What should the new shipping schedule be if the minimum-cost criterion continues to be the most important?

9. Once again, consider the Hot Air Corp. situation from problem 1. The Bangor plant has just been hit with a major equipment failure and output has dropped to 1200 per week. The company cannot meet the demands of all its distributors. What should the new shipping schedule be if the minimum-cost criterion continues to be the most important?
10. Return to the situation of the Quick Freeze Corp., from problem 3. The Denver distributor has just filed for bankruptcy and the court-appointed receiver has decreased the weekly order to 500. What should the new production and shipping schedule be to continue to maximize profits?
11. Once again, consider the Quick Freeze Corp. from problem 3. The Waco plant was damaged by a hurricane and has reduced weekly production to 400 refrigerators for an indefinite period. What should the new production and shipping schedule be if the maximum-profit criterion continues to be the most important?
12. Trouble continues to plague Quick Freeze (see problem 3). The Denver distributor is no longer in receivership (problem 10) and the Waco plant has recovered from the hurricane (problem 11). However, deteriorating bridges along the truck routes from Waco to New York make this transportation route impossible. How does this affect the optimal shipping schedule and the profits associated with this schedule?
13. Consider the cost-minimization transshipment problem shown in Figure 5-13.

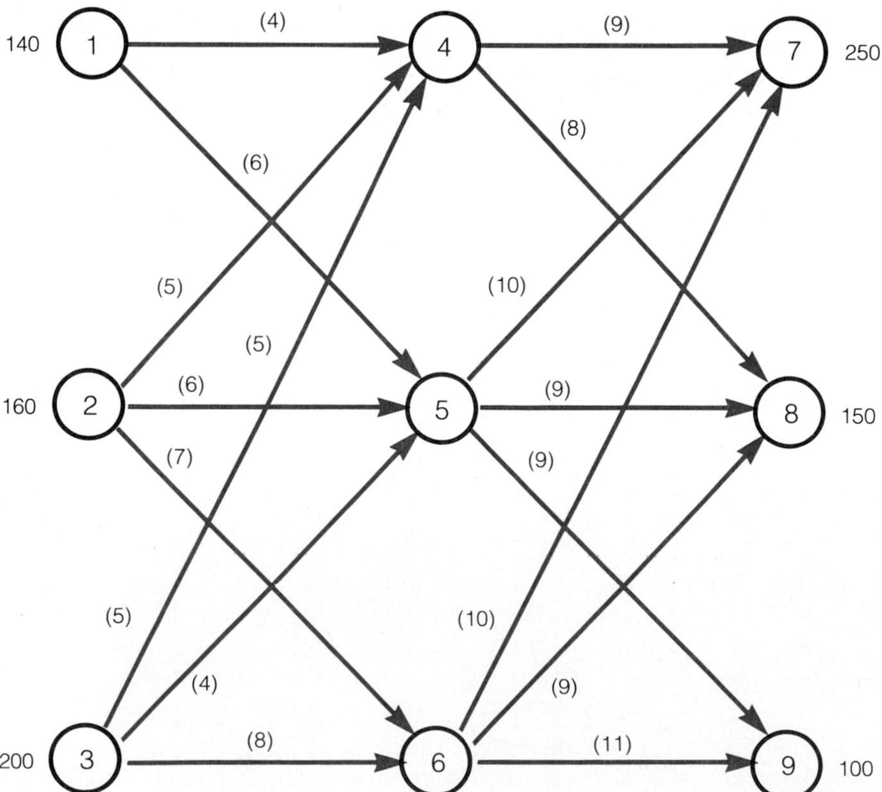

Figure 5-13
Transshipment problem: minimize costs

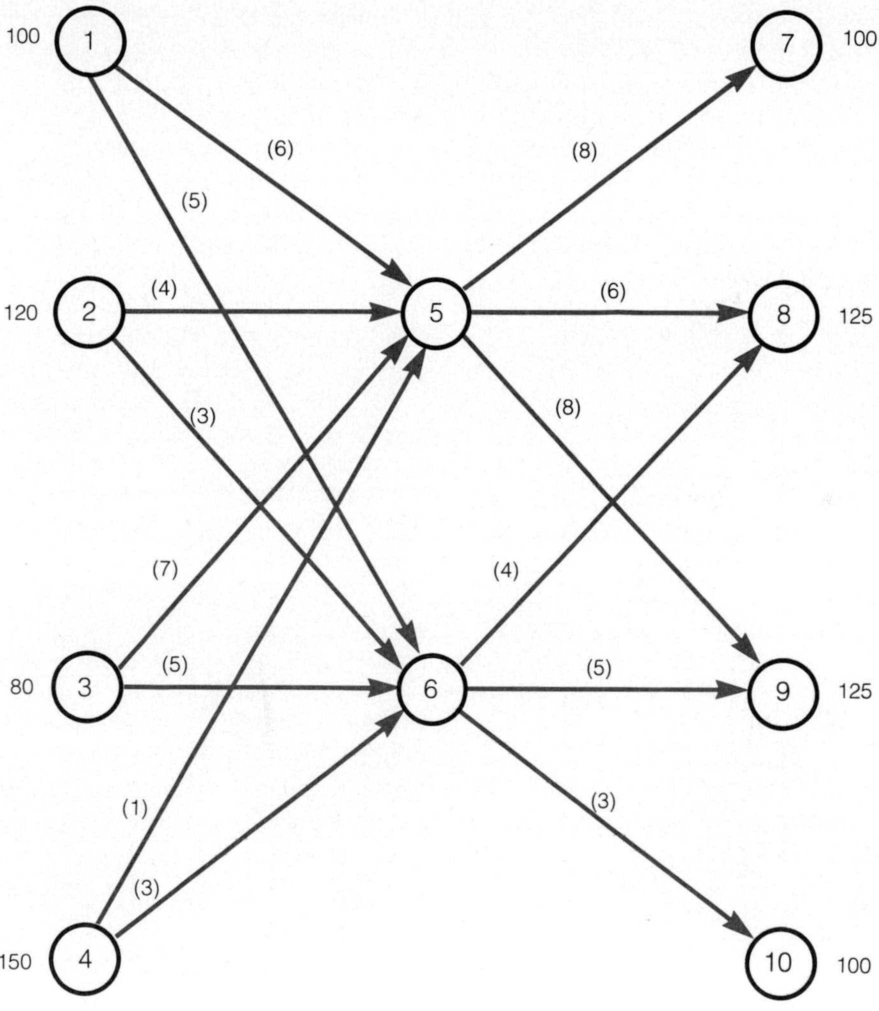

Figure 5-14
Transshipment problem: maximize profits

a. Formulate this as a linear programming problem.
b. What is the optimal shipping schedule for this problem?
c. Does this problem have any equivalent solutions?

14. Consider the profit-maximization transshipment problem shown in Figure 5-14.
a. Formulate this as a linear programming problem.
b. What is the optimal shipping schedule for this problem?
c. Does this problem have any equivalent solutions?

15. The MK Railcar Company structurally rebuilds boxcars at plants in Nevada and Texas. While these two repair facilities also have the capability to paint the cars, the painting is generally done at facilities in Boulder, Colorado, or Jacksonville, Florida. After the painting is done, any boxcar can be sent to any customer. MK presently has 75 cars available in Nevada and 90 available in Texas. A

customer in Boston wants 50, a customer in Chicago wants 80, and a customer in Fresno wants 35. The cost matrix in Table 5-45 shows unit transportation costs for all possible shipping combinations. Consider the cost of painting to be the same, no matter where it is done.

a. Draw the correct node-arc model of this situation.

b. What is the minimum-cost schedule to get cars to the three customers?

16. Because of flooding on the Mississippi River, the trains have to detour around some typically used routes, adding to the cost for MK Railcar Company (see problem 15). The new cost matrix is estimated to be as shown in Table 5-46. How will this change affect the total cost of shipping to the three customers?

17. The United Relief Fund has successfully completed a food drive to help disaster victims in the Ukraine, Chad, and El Salvador. Large stocks of food are presently located in New York, Dallas, and San Francisco. The Relief Fund maintains warehouses in London and Miami and typically routes all supplies through these two locations. In this case, however, the stocks are so large that the Fund is considering direct shipment, if this is the most cost-effective manner to distribute the food. The estimated per ton shipping costs are shown in Table 5-47.

At present, 200 tons of food are in New York, 330 tons are in Dallas, and 290 tons are in San Francisco. The plan is to divide the food equally among the three disaster areas.

a. Draw the correct node-arc model of this situation.

b. What is the minimum-cost schedule to ship the relief supplies to the three areas?

18. Midwest Airlines, a regional commuter airline, tries to station pilots in cities they are most likely to be flying from. It presently has five pilots stationed in Eau Claire, Wisconsin. At the beginning of each month, the pilots are allowed to indicate their preferences for the five routes that originate in Eau Claire. Their rankings are shown in Table 5-48. If 1 indicates a pilot's first choice and 5 the last choice, what overall route scheme will result in the highest overall rankings?

19. Wilcox and Adams is a consulting firm that assigns quality-audit teams to U.S. Navy construction projects. The purpose of these audits is to ensure that contractors follow accepted navy practices

Table 5-45 MATRIX FOR MK RAILCAR COMPANY PROBLEM

	Nevada	Texas	Boulder	Jacksonville	Boston	Chicago	Fresno
Nevada	0	100	80	150	160	130	30
Texas	90	0	70	70	190	140	90
Boulder	100	80	0	120	100	40	80
Jacksonville	140	70	130	0	60	100	200
Boston	150	180	90	80	0	60	210
Chicago	140	130	50	100	90	0	110
Fresno	40	80	70	180	200	140	0

Table 5-46 REVISED COST MATRIX

	Nevada	Texas	Boulder	Jacksonville	Boston	Chicago	Fresno
Nevada	0	100	80	190	190	180	30
Texas	90	0	70	110	200	160	90
Boulder	100	80	0	150	130	60	80
Jacksonville	200	120	170	0	60	100	250
Boston	170	210	120	80	0	60	250
Chicago	180	150	70	100	90	0	160
Fresno	40	80	70	240	270	180	0

Table 5-47 EXERCISE AND APPLICATION PROBLEMS SHIPPING COSTS (DOLLARS PER TON)

From	Destination	
	London	Miami
New York	10	8
Dallas	15	7
San Francisco	20	10

From	Destination		
	Ukraine	Chad	El Salvador
New York	25	30	18
Dallas	35	45	17
San Francisco	40	50	14

From	Destination		
	Ukraine	Chad	El Salvador
London	15	15	28
Miami	25	35	11

Table 5-48 PILOTS' RANKING OF ROUTES FROM EAU CLAIRE

Pilot	Route				
	Rockport	Madison	Milwaukee	Duluth	Des Moines
Adams	1	5	3	4	2
Garcia	1	4	3	5	2
Walker	1	4	5	3	2
Dorsett	1	5	4	3	2
Jackson	2	3	5	4	1

throughout the construction cycle. Because each team is made up of engineers with different construction specialties, the teams will spend a different amount of time on different projects. Since the audits are done on a fixed-price basis, a team spending less time on a project will mean higher profits for Wilcox and Adams. Each team is sent into the field once a week. The best estimate of how long each of the six teams will spend on the six audits scheduled for next week is shown in Table 5-49. Which teams should be sent to which projects, to minimize the overall time in the field?

20. Because of a conflict of interest, audit team E in problem 19 cannot be sent to either job 3 or job 4.
   a. Show how you would change Table 5-49 to reflect this development.
   b. What will the new maximum-profit assignment be?

21. Ted Chang of Chang's Auto Repair is considering the assignment of mechanics for tomorrow's scheduled repairs. The five jobs scheduled, and the suggested charge for each according to the standard repair manual, are shown in Table 5-50. Ted has estimated how long each of these jobs will take for each of the five mechanics on duty tomorrow. These time estimates are shown in Table 5-51.

Table 5-49 ESTIMATED TIME REQUIRED FOR AUDITS (DAYS)

	Audit					
Team	A	B	C	D	E	F
1	8	7	9	12	10	15
2	6	9	8	14	14	16
3	9	10	11	15	12	14
4	8	9	9	11	13	17
5	7	8	7	10	11	13
6	9	8	8	13	14	18

Table 5-50 REPAIR SCHEDULE

Job	Suggested Charge
A. Install new steering rack	$400
B. Install new clutch	$440
C. Rebuild an automatic transmission	$450
D. Rebuild gear box	$480
E. Replace front suspension	$440

Table 5-51 ESTIMATED MECHANICS' TIME REQUIRED FOR SCHEDULED JOBS (HOUR)

	Job				
Mechanic	A	B	C	D	E
Williams	14	16	19	17	18
Eberhart	16	15	18	17	20
Nichols	13	16	15	15	16
Sanchez	14	14	15	16	15
Earl	14	17	14	14	17

If the cost for a mechanic's time is $20 per hour, and if Ted wants to maximize total profits on these five jobs, which mechanics should work on which repair jobs?

22. Mechanic Ned Earl has just reported from the emergency medical clinic, having been treated for a partially dislocated shoulder. While this injury will not prevent him from working on any of the jobs, it would increase his estimated time on the steering rack job by 3 hours and the time on the clutch rebuild by 4 hours.
    a. Show how you would change Table 5-51 to reflect this development.
    b. What will the new maximum-profit assignment be?

Chapter Glossary

Assignment problem A problem that involves the assignment of *n* resources to *m*, where *n* must equal *m* demands on a 1-to-1 basis. Can be formulated as a linear programming problem or as a special case of a transportation problem.

Balanced assignment problem An assignment problem in which the number of individual resources equals the number of demands. When using the assignment tableaus, the number of rows equals the number of columns.

Balanced transportation problem A transportation problem where the total supply available equals the total amount demanded.

Dummy demand A demand column added to a transportation or assignment tableau to make the total demand equal the total supply. In a transportation problem, one dummy demand is added; its value is determined by the amount by which the available supply exceeds the total demand. In an assignment problem, one demand column is added for each unit difference between supply and demand.

Dummy supply A supply row added to a transportation or assignment tableau to make the total demand equal the total supply. In a transportation problem, one dummy supply is added; its value is determined by the amount by which the total demand exceeds the available supply. In an assignment problem, one supply row is added for each unit difference between supply and demand.

Hungarian method A special procedure used to solve assignment problems.

Minimum-cost method A procedure used to find a starting solution for a transportation problem, based on minimum values in the cost matrix.

Modified distribution (MODI) solution procedure An algorithm for determining the per unit improvement associated with shipping one unit over an unused route in a transportation problem.

Network A graphical technique where nodes (circles) are connected by arcs (lines); it is used to represent transportation, transshipment, and assignment problems.

Opportunity loss value The value found by subtracting the largest value in each column of an assignment problem from every other value in that column; it is used to solve maximization problems using the Hungarian method.

Stepping-stone method A solution procedure for solving transportation problems in which improved solutions are found by adding one unused route and subtracting one presently used route until the optimal schedule is found.

Transportation problem A special type of linear programming problem involving the distribution of goods or services from a set of sources to a set of demands. It can be solved as either a maximization or minimization problem.

Transshipment problem An extension of transportation problems, where goods or services are allowed to pass through intermediate points while going from original sources to final destinations.

Chapter References

BOOKS

Charnes, A., and W. W. Cooper. *Management Models and Industrial Applications of Linear Programming.* New York: Wiley, 1961.

Dantzig, G. B. *Linear Programming and Extensions.* Princeton, N.J.: Princeton, 1963.

Driebeek, Normal J. *Applied Linear Programming.* Reading, Mass.: Addison-Wesley, 1969.

Hillier, F., and G. J. Lieberman. *Introduction to Operations Research.* 4th ed. Oakland, Calif.: Holden-Day, 1986.

Loomba, N. P., and E. Turban. *Applied Programming for Management.* New York: Holt, 1974.

Wagner, H. *Principles of Operations Research with Applications to Managerial Decisions.* Englewood Cliffs, N.J.: Prentice-Hall, 1975.

Mini Case

CASE 5A

CENTRAL CITY WATER CORPORATION PART 1*

The Central City Water Corporation was franchised in 1963 to provide water for Central City and the surrounding area. The region it supplies is quite arid, and the company's own wells are insufficient to meet the needs of its customers. Thus, the company purchases water from outside the region. There are four sources of supply which can provide water for Central City's supply system. Manisento Water District, Willshire Water Company, Charmon Water and Utility, and Brenner Water. Central has five customer categories in its service region: Central City, Milltown, Flagerville, Jonestown, and Gooding.

Water from any outside supplier can be used to meet the needs of any customer. In fact, this flexibility in meeting customer needs has been a source of pride for the company for many years. However, because of the geographic locations, the cost of supplying water to each customer from each source is not the same.

In fact, these costs had Jim Kelly, the company's distribution manager, worried. In the past, the company had no real plan for allocating water supplies to customers and Jim was certain that too much was being spent to get the job done. During the past week, Jim had assigned Charlene Platt from his department the task of collecting information about water transport costs and about customer demand. At their meeting this morning, Charlene presented him with the information shown in Table 5C-1. These data indicate the costs per acre-foot of delivering water from each possible source to each possible customer. Also shown are the supply levels from each source and the projected demand amounts by each major customer.

In reviewing these data, Jim recalled the company policy which stated that the first priority was to meet the water demands of its customers. A quick check of the supply and demand totals showed Jim that, based upon Charlene's projections, the company should have more water available than demanded. At least this made Jim feel a little more at ease.

Jim had hoped the solution about how much water to ship from each supplier to each customer would be obvious from the data. But looking at the figures, Jim couldn't see the solution. He knew there had to be a way to find the least-cost water delivery

Table 5C-1 COSTS OF PROVIDING WATER FROM OUTSIDE SOURCES (DOLLARS PER ACRE-FOOT)

Water Source	Customer					Supply (ac-ft)
	Central	Milltown	Flagerville	Jonestown	Gooding	
Manisento	15	13	22	16	19	300
Willshire	30	20	14	18	24	600
Charmon	10	18	16	10	18	100
Brenner	26	14	18	22	27	600
Central	4	14	8	12	9	1100
Demand (ac-ft)	1000	300	400	700	100	

* The concept for this mini case was contributed by Professor Charles Lienert of Metropolitan State College.

schedule, short of trying all possible delivery plans—which, he thought, "would take forever!"

When Jim discussed this with Charlene, she indicated that there was a way to get the information he wanted by using a management science technique she had learned about in college. She asked for a day or two to come up with the results.

CASE 5B

CENTRAL CITY WATER CORPORATION PART 2

Jim Kelly, distribution manager for the Central City Water Corporation, examined the delivery plan that Charlene Platt had handed him two days after she had agreed to try to figure out a way to minimize delivery costs. Jim was excited about the results, but at the same time he was a little apprehensive. He didn't like to base decisions on something he didn't understand. He indicated to Charlene that he appreciated her work but that he wanted to look over the results and discuss them with her later.

Just after lunch, Jim met with Charlene to go over her report. Admitting that he still didn't understand how she had arrived at the delivery plan, Jim asked her to write a clear explanation of the method she had used to solve the minimum-cost delivery problem. Once he had that, he figured that he would have more confidence in the solution. Also, he requested that she reevaluate the plan assuming two separate possible scenarios: (1) the Brenner supply would not be available (which Jim felt was a distinct possibility because of low snowfall in its drainage area this past winter), and (2) the demand by each customer would be 20% higher than expected.

Charlene said that she thought she could have this work done in a couple of days. She indicated that she would base her work on the original data she had collected earlier (see Case 5A).

CASE 5C

IDAHO POTATO SUPPLIERS

Idaho Potato Suppliers (IPS) processes and distributes frozen potato products to restaurants and grocery stores in Seattle, Portland, Reno, Salt Lake City, and Rock Springs. IPS transports its products to customers via refrigerated trucks sent directly from IPS factories in Boise or Pocatello, or from warehouses in Spokane, Twin Falls, and Caldwell. (The map in Figure 5C-1 shows the market region.) Regardless of how delivery is made, all distribution costs are incurred by IPS.

Figure 5C-1
Idaho potato suppliers' market region

At a recent meeting, upper management expressed concern over rising transportation costs. As the meeting progressed, Robert Slone, the traffic manager, indicated that he had never performed a formal analysis of the company's distribution plans but had always assigned shipments to customers according to "whatever it takes to get the job done." Larry Craig, the marketing manager, questioned whether there was a better way to plan for supplying customers. As a result, the management group requested that Robert and his staff undertake a study to determine an optimal shipping policy.

Robert was upset by the request. He was especially troubled by the fact that upper management did not understand that some customers preferred to receive deliveries from certain factories or warehouses. In particular, Portland and Salt Lake City customers preferred to receive deliveries from the Boise factory and the Twin Falls warehouse, respectively. He reluctantly headed back to his office, knowing that he had to come up with a workable plan.

Robert decided that his best plan of attack was to develop a model which could be solved for the minimum-cost distribution pattern. This solution could then be investigated to determine whether customers preferences could be met without incurring additional costs. Toward this end, he asked colleague Cindy Gilbert to collect infor-

Table 5C-2 SHIPPING DATA FOR IDAHO POTATO SUPPLIERS

Factory Capacity (tons per week)		Warehouse Throughput (tons per week)	
Boise	120,000	Caldwell	30,000
Pocatello	87,500	Twin Falls	50,000
		Spokane	80,000

Customer Requirements (tons per week)		Customers' Preferred Supply Points
Seattle	65,000	None
Portland	50,000	Boise factory
Reno	28,750	None
Salt Lake City	47,500	Twin Falls warehouse
Rock Springs	15,000	None

Table 5C-3 TRANSPORTATION COSTS (DOLLARS PER TON SHIPPED)

	Supply Points				
	Factories		Warehouses		
Destination	Boise	Pocatello	Caldwell	Twin Falls	Spokane
Warehouses					
Caldwell	.3	*	—	—	—
Twin Falls	.7	.4	—	—	—
Spokane	1.25	*	—	—	—
Customers					
Seattle	*	*	*	*	.8
Portland	1.75	*	1.45	*	1.6
Salt Lake City	*	1.2	*	.90	*
Reno	*	*	1.80	2.25	*
Rock Springs	*	1.05	*	*	*

* Unusable route.

mation concerning weekly factory processing capacities (in tons of potatoes), distribution costs, the amounts (tons of potatoes) which can be shipped through the warehouses weekly, and each customer's weekly requirements (in tons of potatoes).

Three days later Cindy presented Robert with the data shown in Tables 5C-2 and 5C-3. As Robert examined these data, he realized that he was going to need some help in figuring out the shipping plan if he was going to be able to present it to management at next week's meeting.

Chapter 6

INTRODUCTION TO GOAL PROGRAMMING AND INTEGER PROGRAMMING

Chapter Outline

Chapter 6

Why You Need to Know

In this chapter we will discuss two extensions of linear programming that can be used in decision-making situations where a model would be useful but conventional linear programming would be inappropriate: *goal programming* and *integer programming*. These two techniques have many applications in actual decision-making situations and demonstrate typical efforts used to extend the application area of linear programming.

A linear programming model depends on an organization being able to express its goals in a decision-making situation as a single objective function. While this is acceptable for some applications, in many instances the decision situation involves multiple objectives. Goal programming is a management science technique that allows an organization to consider multiple objectives and still use the linear programming optimization technique to aid the decision-making process. With goal programming, decision makers can prioritize their goals or objectives and set target values for each objective. It is used in such situations as financial portfolio planning, marketing mix strategy, and production scheduling.

While goal programming is a useful tool when a decision maker is faced with multiple objectives, there are other situations when the assumptions of linear programming prove to be too restrictive. For instance, the divisibility assumption requires that decision variables be allowed to take on fractional values. In previous chapters, the examples and problems dealt with applications where divisibility is reasonable or where the optimal solution was assumed not to be seriously affected by rounding the solution to integer values. However, in many situations the divisibility assumption is not appropriate and rounding a linear programming solution to integer values might significantly alter the solution. In such cases, we could use integer programming, a method that uses linear programming techniques but restricts some (or all) decision variables to integer values.

Goal programming and integer programming are important extensions of linear programming, and you need to have a good understanding of when and how to apply them in decision-making situations.

Chapter Objectives

After studying the material in this chapter, you should be able to:

1. Identify situations in which goal programming is the appropriate decision-making aid.
2. Formulate goal programming problems and generally understand how the simplex method is used to solve linear programming problems with multiple objectives.
3. Discuss how the special linear programming problems of unbounded solutions, infeasible solutions, and multiple optimal solutions apply to a goal programming model.
4. Identify situations in which integer programming is the appropriate decision-making tool.
5. Solve small integer programming problems using the branch-and-bound technique.
6. Formulate problems that can be analyzed using the zero-one solution process.

6-1 A BRIEF HISTORY OF GOAL PROGRAMMING AND INTEGER PROGRAMMING

When we introduced linear programming earlier in the text, we discussed the assumptions that must be met before it can be used:

1. Divisibility of the decision variables
2. A single linear objective function and linear constraints
3. All values in the model known with certainty

To some extent, these assumptions are violated in many real-world applications. Not all decision variables can be linear, and the decision environment is rarely a certain place.

Soon after the simplex solution procedure was developed and the application of linear programming models began, decision makers started looking for ways to relax the restrictions. Early users soon determined that a major strength of the model was its adaptability to problems for which the original assumptions were not satisfied. Research led to a variety of modifications to the basic model which made it suitable for applications that violated one or more of the three basic assumptions.

George Dantzig, D. R. Fulkerson, and S. M. Johnson were the first to successfully consider situations in which the divisibility assumption was violated. In 1954 they developed an optimal schedule for a traveling salesman to visit Washington, D.C., and the capitals of the 48 continental states. The foundation for a rigorous theory of integer programming was set two years later by R. Gomory.

The problems associated with multiple goals first showed up as infeasible solutions to normal linear programming problems. (Recall that an infeasible solution can be caused by incompatible constraints.) A. Charnes and W. W. Cooper did the original work leading to the incorporation of multiple goals in a linear programming problem. Their initial work in this area was published in 1961. They considered situations in which multiple objectives were needed but each objective was still represented as a linear relationship among the set of decision variables. Others, including Sang Lee, added to the development of integer programming and its applications.

6-2 GOAL PROGRAMMING

Management writers such as Peter Drucker and, more recently, Tom Peters have stressed that to survive, all organizations must be innovative and continually changing. One of the few certainties any organization has is that the set of goods and services it is currently producing and selling is in the process of becoming obsolete. For some organizations, the obsolescence process can take a long time. For others, such as those in the high-tech electronics industry, the process may take only a few years.

Wagner Electronics is a company in the highly competitive commercial electronics industry. Milt Wagner, son of the founder of the company, recognizes that to survive, the company must not only continually improve its present product line but must also regularly introduce new products. Milt realizes that new products, and product improvements, are a direct result of research and development (R&D) efforts. From his experience, Milt estimates that a typical product improvement takes 2 worker-months of R&D time and a typical new-product development takes 8 worker-months. These are averages, since some projects require longer or shorter periods for R&D.

Wagner Electronics has budgeted a total of 1200 worker-months of R&D time in the next year. Also, for the next year, top management at Wagner Electronics has set a goal of making 250 product improvements and introducing 100 new products.

If we assign a profit level (c_1) to product improvements and a profit level (c_2) to each new product, we could formulate a linear programming problem as follows:

$$\text{Maximize} \quad Z = c_1x_1 + c_2x_2$$

Subject to:

$$\begin{aligned} x_1 \qquad &\geq 250 \quad \text{(product improvements)} \\ x_2 &\geq 100 \quad \text{(new products)} \\ 2x_1 + 8x_2 &\leq 1200 \quad \text{(R\&D time)} \end{aligned}$$

where:

x_1 = number of product improvements

x_2 = number of new products

If we attempted to solve this linear programming problem, we would see that there is no feasible solution, since the R&D time is not sufficient to meet both the new product and the product improvement constraints. This is the type of situation that led to the development of **goal programming**, an extension of the traditional linear programming technique that allows a decision maker to consider multiple objectives in the decision process.

In goal programming, the new product and product improvement constraints are treated as objectives or goals rather than constraints. (For this technique, a **goal** is defined as a numerical value representing the desired level of a specific organizational objective.) Both goals cannot be achieved, given the available R&D time ($2 \times 250 + 8 \times 100 = 1300$). If Wagner Electronics decides to concentrate on product improvements, it will not be able to introduce all 100 new products. Of course, the opposite is also true; if 100 new products are introduced, not all 250 product improvements can be made. Since both goals cannot be met simultaneously, we must allow *deviations* from the goals. These deviations are critical in the goal programming process.

FORMULATING THE GOAL PROGRAMMING MODEL

Many of the steps in formulating a goal programming model are the same as those for linear programming, but there are some important differences. The steps in the procedure are given below.

Step 1 *Establish numerical goals or objectives.*
For Wagner Electronics, the goals are:

1. Make 250 product improvements.
2. Introduce 100 new products.

Step 2 *Establish priorities for the goals.*
The priorities might be established on the basis of quantitative measures such as profit levels, or they might be based on qualitative measures and be subjectively assessed. For this example, we initially assume the goals have equal priority.

Step 3 *Identify the decision variables in the problem.*
For Wagner Electronics, the decision variables are:

x_1 = number of product improvements

x_2 = number of new products

Step 4 *Write each goal as a constraint, recognizing that deviations from the goals must be allowed.*
This is the most complicated step. Consider the first goal in this example. If it could be satisfied, it would be written as:

$$x_1 = 250$$

However, as previously indicated, since we may not be able to meet this goal, deviations must be allowed. In the general case, we must allow for deviations both above and below the stated goal. Therefore we define the deviations as:

d_1^+ = amount above the value stated for goal 1

d_1^- = amount below the value stated for goal 1

Taking into account the potential for deviations, the first goal will be stated as the following constraint:

$$x_1 = 250 + d_1^+ - d_1^-$$

which can be rewritten as:

$$x_1 - d_1^+ + d_1^- = 250$$

We define the allowable deviations from goal 2 as:

d_2^+ = amount above the value stated for goal 2

d_2^- = amount below the value stated for goal 2

The second goal is then stated as the following constraint:

$$x_2 = 100 + d_2^+ - d_2^-$$

which can be rewritten as:

$$x_2 - d_2^+ + d_2^- = 100$$

Note that we have introduced four new variables to the problem, two for each goal. These variables are called *deviation variables.*

Finally, the total R&D time constraint can be handled in the conventional manner:

$$2x_1 + 8x_2 \leq 1200$$

Step 5 *Formulate the objective function.*
This step requires some explanation. The four deviation variables (d_1^+, d_1^-, d_2^+, and d_2^-) from step 4 allow for deviations from the goals set for the company. What Milt Wagner really wants is to have 250 product improvements and 100 new products, which could be done if all four deviations were zero. In most goal programming applications, only rarely will all goals be exactly satisfied. In this example, the major concern is with falling short of meeting the goal for either new products or product improvements. Milt Wagner is probably not concerned about exceeding these goals. We will make this assumption.

Therefore, in the Wagner Electronics example, we want the negative deviations to be as small as possible and we don't care about the positive deviations. Thus, the objective function can be stated as follows:

$$\text{Minimize} \quad 0x_1 + 0x_2 + 0d_1^+ + d_1^- + 0d_2^+ + d_2^- \tag{6-1}$$

The 0 coefficients on d_1^+ and d_2^+ indicate that no penalty is assigned for exceeding either goal. The deviation variables, d_1^- and d_2^-, have coefficients of 1, indicating the two goals share equal priority. The coefficients on the two decision variables, x_1 and x_2, are zero, indicating that the values for these variables have no impact on the value of the objective function because we want them to be as large as possible.

Step 6 *Formulate as a linear programming problem and solve.*
We can go directly to a linear programming solution here, since the two goals have equal priorities. The linear programming formulation is:

$$\text{Minimize} \quad Z = 0x_1 + 0x_2 + 0d_1^+ + d_1^- + 0d_2^+ + d_2^-$$

Subject to:

$$\begin{aligned} x_1 \quad - d_1^+ + d_1^- \quad\quad\quad &= 250 \\ x_2 \quad\quad\quad - d_2^+ + d_2^- &= 100 \\ 2x_1 + 8x_2 \quad\quad\quad\quad &\le 1200 \end{aligned}$$

Solving this problem using the simplex method, we find:

$$x_1 = 250 \qquad d_1^+ = 0 \qquad d_2^+ = 0$$
$$x_2 = 87.5 \qquad d_1^- = 0 \qquad d_2^- = 12.5$$

This solution indicates that the goal of 250 product improvements has been satisfied. However, the introduction of 87.5 new products will be 12.5 short of the 100-unit goal. Now we have a potential integer problem. Obviously, 87.5 new products are not possible, and planning for 87 or 88 might not be acceptable. However, Milt is actually allocating time spent by the R&D department rather than product improvements or introductions. The goal programming solution actually tells him to plan 500 worker-months (2×250) for product improvement projects and 700 worker-months (8×87.5) for new products. This solution minimizes the deviations from the stated goals.

Goal programming problems in which the goals have equal priorities can be solved directly with linear programming if the objective function is restated to minimize deviations from the goal targets.

6-3 GOAL PROGRAMMING WITH PRIORITIES

In the previous example we assumed that the product improvement and new product introduction goals had equal priority. In many situations, managers may have multiple goals but often the goals are not of equal priority. Depending on sales last year, competitors' actions, and input from the sales force, Milt Wagner may well decide that introducing new products is more important this year than modifying present ones.

Two main approaches exist for solving goal programming models with priorities. The first requires that numerical priority weights are used as the coefficients in the objective function for each deviation variable. These values—$P_1, P_2, \ldots, P_k$—are established so that $P_1 > P_2 > P_3 > \ldots P_k$. Each deviation variable, with its respective weight, is then treated like the x_1 and x_2 decision variables and the simplex method is employed in the usual manner. In practice, establishing meaningful values for the priorities becomes difficult, especially as the number of goals increases. The advantage of this method is that when numerical weights can be established, the simplex method can be used directly to solve the goal programming problem. We will demonstrate this with an example in a later section of this chapter.

A second approach for solving a goal programming problem does not require that numerical values be assigned to $P_1, P_2, \ldots, P_k$. Rather, the decision maker is only required to be able to rank the goals such that P_1 is substantially higher than P_2 and so forth. Then a modified simplex approach is used. In this goal programming priority system, first-priority goals (P_1) will be completely satisfied before second-priority goals (P_2) are considered. Likewise, second-priority goals are completely satisfied before third-priority goals (P_3) are addressed. Furthermore, no higher-priority goal will be sacrificed in order to achieve some lower-priority goal.

SOLVING A GOAL PROGRAMMING MODEL WITH PRIORITIZED GOALS

Let us start by considering a prioritized example where numerical weights cannot be assigned. Suppose Milt has determined that the goal of introducing new products is more important than the goal of improving existing products. Let P_1 represent the first priority and P_2 represent the second priority. These become the coefficients on the deviation variables d_2^- and d_1^-, respectively. The priority goal programming model becomes:

$$\text{Minimize} \quad Z = 0x_1 + 0x_2 + 0d_1^+ + P_2 d_1^- + 0d_2^+ + P_1 d_2^-$$

Subject to:

$$\begin{aligned} x_1 \quad - d_1^+ + d_1^- \qquad\qquad &= 250 \\ x_2 \qquad\quad - d_2^+ + d_2^- &= 100 \\ 2x_1 + 8x_2 \qquad\qquad\qquad &\leq 1200 \end{aligned}$$

The method used to solve a goal programming problem with priorities involves a modification to the simplex tableau. Table 6-1 shows the initial tableau for Milt Wagner's priority problem. This tableau requires some explanation. In goal programming, each goal has a separate Z_j and $c_j - Z_j$ row. Since in this example we have two goals, we have two Z_j and $c_j - Z_j$ rows. Also, because we are not substituting one goal for another goal, terms containing the P_2 deviation variable are not shown in the Z_j and $c_j - Z_j$ rows for the P_1 deviation variable, and vice versa.

Another difference in how we formulate the simplex tableau relates to how the Z_j values are determined. For example, consider the column headed x_1. For the P_1 priority, the value Z_1 is found by:

$$Z_1 = \sum_{i=1}^{r} c_i a_{i1} \tag{6-2}$$

where:

c_i = objective-function coefficient for the ith basic variable

a_{i1} = tableau value in the ith row, column 1

r = number of variables in basis

Table 6-1 WAGNER ELECTRONICS: INITIAL TABLEAU FOR PRIORITY MODEL

		x_1	x_2	d_1^+	d_1^-	d_2^+	d_2^-	s_1	
Basis	c_j	0	0	0	P_2	0	P_1	0	b_i
d_1^-	P_2	1	0	−1	1	0	0	0	250
d_2^-	P_1	0	1	0	0	−1	1	0	100
s_1	0	2	8	0	0	0	0	1	1200
P_1	Z_j	0	1	0	0	−1	1	0	100
	$c_j - Z_j$	0	−1	0	0	1	0	0	
P_2	Z_j	1	0	−1	1	0	0	0	250
	$c_j - Z_j$	−1	0	1	0	0	0	0	

For example, using equation 6-2 and referring to Table 6-1, we would normally find Z_1 for priority P_2 as follows:

$$Z_1 = (P_2)(1) + (P_1)(0) + (0)(2)$$
$$Z_1 = P_2$$

Remember, we are not attempting to assign a numerical value to the priorities, P_1 and P_2. Therefore we can simply change Z_1 from P_2 to 1 to indicate that priority 2 is associated with variable x_1. Likewise, the value Z_2 for priority 1 is set to 1 to indicate that priority 1 is associated with variable x_2. This is shown in Table 6-1.

Once we have correctly formulated the goal programming model and constructed the modified simplex tableau, we solve the problem by applying the simplex procedure, sequentially, first to the Z_j and $c_j - Z_j$ rows corresponding to the P_1 priority. When we have completely finished with the P_1 priority, we then consider the Z_j and $c_j - Z_j$ rows for the P_2 priority. Because this is a minimization problem, we will check for negative values of $c_j - Z_j$. The variable with the most-negative $c_j - Z_j$ value will be the entering variable. Thus, for P_1 the entering variable will be x_2. The departing variable becomes d_2^-, since it has the smallest b_i/a_{ij} value, as shown in Table 6-2.

Table 6-2 WAGNER ELECTRONICS: ENTERING AND DEPARTING VARIABLES

		x_1	x_2	d_1^+	d_1^-	d_2^+	d_2^-	s_1		
Basis	c_j	0	0	0	P_2	0	P_1	0	b_i	b_i/a_{ij}
d_1^-	P_2	1	0	−1	1	0	0	0	250	n/a
d_2^-	P_1	0	1	0	0	−1	1	0	100	100*
s_1	0	2	8	0	0	0	0	1	1200	150
P_1	Z_j	0	1	0	0	−1	1	0		
	$c_j - Z_j$	0	−1	0	0	1	0	0		
P_2	Z_j	1	0	−1	1	0	0	0		
	$c_j - Z_j$	−1	0	1	0	0	0	0		
			↑ Entering variable							

* Departing variable

The simplex procedure is continued, using the P_1 priority, until all $c_j - Z_j$ values for P_1 are either zero or positive. Then we switch to the $c_j - Z_j$ row for the P_2 priority. Table 6-3 shows the simplex steps and the final simplex tableau for this goal program-

Table 6-3 WAGNER ELECTRONICS: TABLEAUS FOR P_2 PRIORITY MODEL

a.

		x_1	x_2	d_1^+	d_1^-	d_2^+	d_2^-	s_1	
		0	0	0	P_2	0	P_1	0	b_i
d_1^-	P_2	1	0	−1	1	0	0	0	250
x_2	0	0	1	0	0	−1	1	0	100
s_1	0	2	0	0	0	0	0	1	400
P_1	Z_j	0	0	0	0	−1	1	0	100
	$c_j - Z_j$	0	0	0	0	1	0	0	
P_2	Z_j	1	0	−1	1	0	0	0	250
	$c_j - Z_j$	−1	0	1	0	0	0	0	

b.

		x_1	x_2	d_1^+	d_1^-	d_2^+	d_2^-	s_1		
		0	0	0	P_2	0	P_1	0	b_i	b_i/a_{ij}
d_1^-	P_2	1	0	−1	1	0	0	0	250	250
x_2	0	0	1	0	0	−1	1	0	100	N/A
s_1	0	2	0	0	0	8	−8	1	400	200
P_1	Z_j	0	0	0	0	0	0	0	0	
	$c_j - Z_j$	0	0	0	0	0	1	0		
P_2	Z_j	1	0	−1	1	0	0	0	250	
	$c_j - Z_j$	−1	0	1	0	0	0	0		
		↑ Entering Variable								

c. **Final Tableau**

		x_1	x_2	d_1^+	d_1^-	d_2^+	d_2^-	s_1	
		0	0	0	P_2	0	P_1	0	b_i
d_1^-	P_2	0	0	−1	1	−4	4	−½	50
x_2	0	0	1	0	0	−1	1	0	100
x_1	0	1	0	0	0	4	−4	½	200
P_1	Z_j	0	0	0	0	0	0	0	0
	$c_j - Z_j$	0	0	0	0	0	1	0	
P_2	Z_j	0	0	−1	1	−4	4	−½	50
	$c_j - Z_j$	0	0	1	0	4	−4	½	

ming problem. In part (b) of Table 6-3, the entering variable will be x_1 and s_1 will be the departing variable.

The simplex procedure is continued, using the P_2 priority, until all $c_j - Z_j$ values for P_2 are either zero or positive. The one exception to this rule is when the remaining negative $c_j - Z_j$ is associated with a previous priority. For instance, in the final tableau shown in Table 6-3, the $c_j - Z_j$ for d_2^-, which is associated with P_1, is -4. Normally we would say that this variable should be brought back into basis. However, we do not wish to disturb any higher priority than the one we are working on currently. Thus, instead of entering d_2^-, we conclude that we have finished. In larger problems with more priority goals, we keep working our way down through the goals in priority order, and once a goal is satisfied, we do not reconsider it in a later step.

Table 6-3 shows the final tableau and the solution point. The values are:

$$x_1 = 200$$
$$x_2 = 100$$
$$d_1^- = 50$$

We have completely satisfied the goal of introducing 100 new products but have fallen 50 short of satisfying the goal of improving 250 products. But this solution minimizes the deviations from the original goals. Recall that this goal programming method works by first satisfying the priority 1 goal and then attempting to satisfy the priority 2 goal.

By employing the priorities specified by Milt Wagner, the decision is to allocate less R&D time ($200 \times 2 = 400$, versus 500, worker-months) toward product improvements than the previous solution, in which he chose to give equal weight to the priorities. However, more R&D time ($100 \times 8 = 800$, versus 700, worker-months) is allocated toward new product development.

6-4 ADDITIONAL GOAL PROGRAMMING EXAMPLES

Matt and Justin Pate recently took early retirement from their jobs in manufacturing companies to start their own small business. The Pate brothers are experienced woodworkers and started their business by doing part-time cabinet work for friends who were remodeling their homes. After successfully doing individual remodeling jobs for more than a year, they have received a contract to supply cabinets for an apartment complex. The contract calls for building cabinets for 120 kitchens. All 120 must be completed in the next two months, or 40 regular-time working days. Matt and Justin estimate that they can produce three sets of cabinets every 2 days (16 working hours) on the primary line of their newly completed production plant. They have a second assembly line which they can staff with two part-time workers, but the part-time staff can produce only one set of cabinets each day (8 working hours). While both the brothers and the part-time employees can work overtime, Matt and Justin would rather pay their part-time help for overtime than work overtime themselves. Specifically, they want to limit their own overtime to a total of 2 days during the construction period. In addition, they want to make sure that the part-time help is busy for all 40 regular days, plus any overtime that is needed.

To apply goal programming in an effort to assist Justin and Matt with their production resource allocation decision, we can apply the six steps identified in the previous section:

Step 1 *Establish numerical goals.*
For Justin and Matt, the goals are:

1. Make 120 cabinets.
2. Keep the part-time workers busy all 40 days.
3. Limit their own overtime to 2 days.

Step 2 *Establish priorities for the goals.*
For this example, let's assume the following priorities:

P_1 = make 120 cabinets

P_2 = keep part-time workers busy

P_3 = limit overtime for Matt and Justin to 2 days

Step 3 *Identify the decision variables in the problem.*
For Matt and Justin, the decision variables are:

x_1 = combined number of days Matt and Justin work

x_2 = number of days part-timers work

Step 4 *Write each goal as a constraint, recognizing that deviations from the goals must be allowed.*
We can define the deviations as:

d_1^+ = amount above the value stated for goal 1

d_1^- = amount below the value stated for goal 1

Allowing for deviations, the first goal for this problem is written as the following constraint:

$$3/2x_1 + x_2 = 120 + d_1^+ - d_1^-$$

which can be rewritten as:

$$3/2x_1 + x_2 - d_1^+ + d_1^- = 120$$

We define the allowable deviations from goal 2 as:

d_2^+ = amount above the value stated for goal 2

d_2^- = amount below the value stated for goal 2

The second goal can be written as the following constraint:

$$x_2 = 40 + d_2^+ - d_2^-$$

which can be rewritten as:

$$x_2 - d_2^+ + d_2^- = 40$$

Finally, we define the allowable deviations from goal 3 as:

d_3^+ = amount above the value stated for goal 3

d_3^- = amount below the value stated for goal 3

The third goal can be written as the following constraint:

$$x_1 = 42 + d_3^+ - d_3^-$$

which can be rewritten as:

$$x_1 - d_3^+ + d_3^- = 42$$

Note that in this example we have introduced six deviation variables to the problem, two for each goal.

A final set of constraints involves the total production time available for the next two months for each class of worker. These are referred to as *system constraints.* Suppose this limit is 60 working days, including 40 regular-time days and 20 overtime days. The final constraints become:

$$x_1 \leq 60$$
$$x_2 \leq 60$$

Step 5 *Formulate the objective function.*
As in the Wagner Electronics example, the objective here is to minimize the sum of the appropriate deviations. The objective function will include all the deviation variables. However, we do not care how many days the part-time workers work overtime. Thus, we assign a 0 coefficient to the d_2^+ deviation variable. The objective function is:

$$\text{Minimize} \quad P_1 d_1^+ + P_1 d_1^- + P_2 0 d_2^+ + P_2 d_2^- + P_3 d_3^+ + P_3 d_3^-$$

Step 6 *Formulate as a linear programming problem and solve.*

$$\text{Minimize} \quad Z = 0x_1 + 0x_2 + P_1 d_1^+ + P_1 d_1^- + P_2 0 d_2^+ + P_2 d_2^- + P_3 d_3^+ + P_3 d_3^-$$

Subject to:

$$\begin{aligned}
3/2x_1 + x_2 - d_1^+ + d_1^- \qquad\qquad\qquad\qquad &= 120 \\
x_2 \qquad - d_2^+ + d_2^- \qquad\qquad &= 40 \\
x_1 \qquad\qquad\qquad - d_3^+ + d_3^- &= 42 \\
x_1 \qquad\qquad\qquad\qquad\qquad &\leq 60 \\
x_2 \qquad\qquad\qquad\qquad\qquad &\leq 60
\end{aligned}$$

Table 6-4 shows the initial simplex tableau for this problem. Note that the table contains separate Z_j and $c_j - Z_j$ rows for each priority level: P_1, P_2, and P_3. We begin by examining the $c_j - Z_j$ row for the P_1 priority to determine the entering variable. The

Table 6-4 PATE BROTHERS: MODIFIED SIMPLEX INITIAL TABLEAU

		x_1	x_2	d_1^+	d_1^-	d_2^+	d_2^-	d_3^+	d_3^-	s_1	s_2	
Basis	c_j	0	0	P_1	P_1	0	P_2	P_3	P_3	0	0	b_i
d_1^-	P_1	3/2	1	−1	1	0	0	0	0	0	0	120
d_2^-	P_2	0	1	0	0	−1	1	0	0	0	0	40
d_3^-	P_3	1	0	0	0	0	0	−1	1	0	0	42
s_1	0	1	0	0	0	0	0	0	0	1	0	60
s_2	0	0	1	0	0	0	0	0	0	0	1	60
P_1	Z_j	3/2	1	−1	1	0	0	0	0	0	0	
	$c_j - Z_j$	−3/2	−1	2	0	0	0	0	0	0	0	
P_2	Z_j	0	1	0	0	−1	1	0	0	0	0	
	$c_j - Z_j$	0	−1	0	0	1	0	0	0	0	0	
P_3	Z_j	1	0	0	0	0	0	−1	1	0	0	
	$c_j - Z_j$	−1	0	0	0	0	0	2	0	0	0	

Table 6-5 PATE BROTHERS: INTERMEDIATE TABLEAUS

a. Second tableau

		x_1	x_2	d_1^+	d_1^-	d_2^+	d_2^-	d_3^+	d_3^-	s_1	s_2	
Basis	c_j	0	0	P_1	P_1	0	P_2	P_3	P_3	0	0	b_i
d_1^-	P_1	0	1	−1	1	0	0	3/2	−3/2	0	0	57
d_2^-	P_2	0	1	0	0	−1	1	0	0	0	0	40
x_1	0	1	0	0	0	0	0	−1	1	0	0	42
s_1	0	0	0	0	0	0	0	1	−1	1	0	18
s_2	0	0	1	0	0	0	0	0	0	0	1	60
P_1	Z_j	0	1	−1	1	0	0	3/2	−3/2	0	0	57
	$c_j - Z_j$	0	−1	2	0	0	0	−3/2	3/2	0	0	
P_2	Z_j	0	1	0	0	−1	1	0	0	0	0	40
	$c_j - Z_j$	0	−1	0	0	1	0	0	0	0	0	
P_3	Z_j	0	0	0	0	0	0	0	0	0	0	0
	$c_j - Z_j$	0	0	0	0	0	0	1	1	0	0	

b. Third tableau

		x_1	x_2	d_1^+	d_1^-	d_2^+	d_2^-	d_3^+	d_3^-	s_1	s_2	
Basis	c_j	0	0	P_1	P_1	0	P_2	P_3	P_3	0	0	b_i
d_1^-	P_1	0	1	−1	1	0	0	0	0	−3/2	0	30
d_2^-	P_2	0	1	0	0	−1	1	0	0	0	0	40
x_1	0	1	0	0	0	0	0	0	0	1	0	60
d_3^+	P_3	0	0	0	0	0	0	1	−1	1	0	18
s_2	0	0	1	0	0	0	0	0	0	0	1	60
P_1	Z_j	0	1	−1	1	0	0	0	0	−3/2	0	30
	$c_j - Z_j$	0	−1	2	0	0	0	0	0	3/2	0	
P_2	Z_j	0	1	0	0	−1	1	0	0	0	0	40
	$c_j - Z_j$	0	−1	0	0	1	0	0	0	0	0	
P_3	Z_j	0	0	0	0	0	0	1	−1	1	0	18
	$c_j - Z_j$	0	0	0	0	0	0	0	2	−1	0	

c. Fourth tableau

		x_1	x_2	d_1^+	d_1^-	d_2^+	d_2^-	d_3^+	d_3^-	s_1	s_2	
Basis	c_j	0	0	P_1	P_1	0	P_2	P_3	P_3	0	0	b_i
x_2	0	0	1	−1	1	0	0	0	0	−3/2	0	30
d_2^-	P_2	0	0	1	−1	−1	1	0	0	3/2	0	10
x_1	0	1	0	0	0	0	0	0	0	1	0	60
d_3^+	P_3	0	0	0	0	0	0	1	−1	1	0	18
s_2	0	0	0	1	−1	0	0	0	0	3/2	1	30
P_1	Z_j	0	0	0	0	0	0	0	0	0	0	0
	$c_j - Z_j$	0	0	1	1	0	0	0	0	0	0	
P_2	Z_j	0	0	1	−1	−1	1	0	0	3/2	0	10
	$c_j - Z_j$	0	0	−1	1	1	0	0	0	−3/2	0	
P_3	Z_j	0	0	0	0	0	0	1	−1	1	0	18
	$c_j - Z_j$	0	0	0	0	0	0	0	2	−1	0	

Table 6-5 PATE BROTHERS: INTERMEDIATE TABLEAUS *(Continued)*

d. Fifth tableau

		x_1	x_2	d_1^+	d_1^-	d_2^+	d_2^-	d_3^+	d_3^-	s_1	s_2	
Basis	c_j	0	0	P_1	P_1	0	P_2	P_3	P_3	0	0	b_i
x_2	0	0	1	0	0	−1	1	0	0	0	0	40
s_1	0	0	0	2/3	−2/3	−2/3	2/3	0	0	1	0	20/3
x_1	0	−1	0	−2/3	2/3	2/3	−2/3	0	0	0	0	160/3
d_3^+	P_3	0	0	−2/3	2/3	2/3	−2/3	1	−1	0	0	34/3
s_2	0	0	0	0	0	1	−1	0	0	0	1	20
P_1	Z_j	0	0	0	0	0	0	0	0	0	0	0
	$c_j - Z_j$	0	0	1	1	0	0	0	0	0	0	
P_2	Z_j	0	0	0	0	0	0	0	0	0	0	0
	$c_j - Z_j$	0	0	0	0	0	1	0	0	0	0	
P_3	Z_j	0	0	−2/3	2/3	2/3	2/3	1	−1	0	0	
	$c_j - Z_j$	0	0	2/3	−2/3	−2/3	2/3	0	2	0	0	34/3

entering variable will be the one with the most-negative $c_j - Z_j$ value, in this case x_1. The simplex process is continued until all three priority levels have been evaluated in order and there are no further negative values in any $c_j - Z_j$ row. Table 6-5 shows the intermediate tableaus for solving the goal programming model. We encourage you to trace through these tableaus to make sure you understand the process of moving from one goal to the next in priority order. Table 6-6 shows the final tableau for the Pate brothers example.

We see that the final solution is:

$$x_1 = 42$$
$$x_2 = 57$$
$$d_2^+ = 17$$
$$s_1 = 18$$
$$s_2 = 3$$

Table 6-6 PATE BROTHERS: FINAL TABLEAU

		x_1	x_2	d_1^+	d_1^-	d_2^+	d_2^-	d_3^+	d_3^-	s_1	s_2	
Basis	c_j	0	0	P_1	P_1	0	P_2	P_3	P_3	0	0	RHS
x_2	0	0	1	−1	1	0	0	3/2	−3/2	0	0	57
s_1	0	0	0	0	0	0	0	1	−1	1	0	18
x_1	0	1	0	0	0	0	0	−1	1	0	0	42
d_2^+	0	0	0	−1	1	1	−1	3/2	−3/2	0	0	17
s_2	0	0	0	1	−1	0	0	−3/2	3/2	0	1	3
P_1	Z_j	0	0	0	0	0	0	0	0	0	0	0
	$c_j - Z_j$	0	0	1	1	0	0	0	0	0	0	
P_2	Z_j	0	0	0	0	0	0	0	0	0	0	0
	$c_j - Z_j$	0	0	0	0	0	1	0	0	0	0	
P_3	Z_j	0	0	0	0	0	0	0	0	0	0	0
	$c_j - Z_j$	0	0	0	0	0	0	1	1	0	0	

Thus, Matt and Justin will work 40 regular days plus 2 overtime days, for a total of 42 days. The part-time employees will work a total of 57 days. The term $d_2^+ = 17$ indicates that the solution had a positive deviation of 17 days beyond the goal of 40 days for the part-time employees. Recall that no penalty was assigned to overtime for the part-time employees. The slack variables indicate that Matt and Justin could potentially work 18 more days and that the part-time workers had 3 more days before reaching the limit of 60 days.

We can examine this solution to determine how well the three goals were satisfied. The first-priority goal was to complete the 120 cabinets. Matt and Justin would produce $3/2(42) = 63$ cabinets and the part-time employees would make $1(57) = 57$ cabinets, for a total of 120. Thus, this goal is satisfied.

The second priority was to make sure the part-time employees worked at least 40 days. The solution shows that they should work 57 days. The final goal called for Matt and Justin to work a maximum of 2 overtime days. The final solution calls for them to work 40 regular-time days and 2 overtime days. Thus, all three goals have been satisfied.

GOAL PROGRAMMING WITH WEIGHTED PRIORITIES: A COMPUTER APPLICATION

The previous two examples illustrated how goal programming problems are formulated and solved using the modified simplex method. In each example, the goals were priortized by rank-ordering. No attempt was made to provide a numerical measure of the relative importance of each goal. However, as we indicated earlier, sometimes numerical weightings can be assigned to the goals. The example presented in this section shows how to formulate a goal programming problem with weighted goals and how MASTER can be used to solve this type of problem.

D. B. Silvestri and Associates manage investment portfolios. A client has approached the company with the following request:

1. Earn at least \$40,000.
2. At least half the investment must be in corporate bonds.
3. Invest no more than \$400,000.
4. No more than \$100,000 should be in common stocks.

The first goal is determined to be 3 times as important as the third goal. The third goal is 5 times as important as either goal 2 or goal 4. The following weightings can be assigned to the four goals:

Goal 1 weight = 15

Goal 2 weight = 1

Goal 3 weight = 5

Goal 4 weight = 1

Suppose that D. B. Silvestri has three alternative investment options: bonds (B), stocks (S), and real estate (R). Bonds are available in multiples of \$5000 and will earn 8.5%. Stocks average \$40 per share and can be expected to return 13.5%; shares are usually purchased in lots of 100. Real estate partnerships, which exist in \$60,000 units, will return 10%.

This situation can be formulated as a goal programming problem. First we state the goals:

Goal 1: Return must be at least \$40,000.

$$(\$5000)(.085)B + (\$40)(100)(.135)S + (\$60{,}000)(.10)R \geq \$40{,}000$$

Goal 2: Half of all dollars invested must be in bonds.

$$\$5000B - \$4000S - \$60{,}000R \geq \$0$$

Goal 3: Invest no more than $400,000 altogether.

$$\$5000B + \$4000S + \$60{,}000R \leq \$400{,}000$$

Goal 4: Invest no more than $100,000 in common stocks.

$$\$4000S \leq \$100{,}000$$

Since not all goals may be satisfied simultaneously, goal programming allows for deviations. For each goal, we must establish two deviation variables, as follows:

$$\begin{aligned}
&(1) \quad \$425B + \$540S + \$6000R - d_1^+ + d_1^- = \$40{,}000 \\
&(2) \quad \$5000B - \$4000S - \$60{,}000R - d_2^+ + d_2^- = \$0 \\
&(3) \quad \$5000B + \$4000S + \$60{,}000R - d_3^+ + d_3^- = \$400{,}000 \\
&(4) \quad \$4000S - d_4^+ + d_4^- = \$100{,}000
\end{aligned}$$

The unweighted objective would be to minimize the sum of the deviations:

$$\text{Minimize} \quad Z = 0B + 0S + 0R + 0d_1^+ + d_1^- + 0d_2^+ + d_2^- + d_3^+ + 0d_3^- + d_4^+ + 0d_4^-$$

Since the investor is not bothered by a return of more than $40,000, the deviation variable d_1^+ has a coefficient of zero. Likewise, there is no penalty for holding more than half of the investment in bonds, so d_2^+ has a coefficient of zero, and so forth.

Recall that the four goals were not equally important and that numerical weights were assigned. We incorporate the priority weights into the objective function as follows:

$$\begin{aligned}
\text{Minimize} \quad Z = {} & 0B + 0S + 0R + (15)0d_1^+ + (15)d_1^- + 0d_2^+ + d_2^- + (5)d_3^+ \\
& + (5)0d_3^- + d_4^+ + 0d_4^-
\end{aligned}$$

This goal programming problem can now be solved using the simplex method. Linear programming software such as MASTER can be used directly to determine the solution. For instance, if MASTER is used, the problem is formulated as follows:

$$\begin{aligned}
\text{Minimize} \quad Z = {} & 0B + 0S + 0R + (15)0d_1^+ + (15)d_1^- + 0d_2^+ + d_2^- + (5)d_3^+ \\
& + (5)0d_3^- + d_4^+ + 0d_4^-
\end{aligned}$$

Subject to:

$$\begin{aligned}
\$425B + \$540S + \$6000R - d_1^+ + d_1^- &= \$40{,}000 \\
\$5000B - \$4000S - \$60{,}000R - d_2^+ + d_2^- &= \$0 \\
\$5000B + \$4000S + \$60{,}000R - d_3^+ + d_3^- &= \$400{,}000 \\
0B + \$4000S + 0R - d_4^+ + d_4^- &= \$100{,}000
\end{aligned}$$

Figure 6-1 shows the output from MASTER. The objective-function value is seen to be zero. This means that the optimal solution satisfied all four goals. There were no undesirable deviations from the objectives. The optimal solution is:

$$B = 40 \qquad S = 25 \qquad R = 1.667 \qquad d_1^+ = 500.002$$

The portfolio should contain 40 bonds, each with a face value of $5000; 25 blocks of 100 shares of common stock; and 1.667 shares in the limited-partnership real estate investment. The value $d_1^+ = 500.002$ means the goal of earning a $40,000 return will be exceeded by $500.002 under this investment plan. You should verify that all four goals have been satisfied by this optimal solution.

```
                  LINEAR PROGRAMMING FORMULATION

OBJECTIVE FUNCTION:
  MINIMIZE Z =
       0.00  B +      0.00  S  +     0.00  R  +    0.00  d1+ +    15.00  d1- +
 0.00  d2+ +     1.00  d2- +      5.00  d3+  +    0.00  d3- +     1.00  d4+ +
0.00 d4-

SUBJECT TO:
    425.00B +    540.00S + 6000.00R +    -1.00d1+ +    1.00d1- +     0.00d2+ +     0.
0.00d2- +      0.00d3+ +     0.00d3- +     0.00d4+ +    0.00d4-     =  40000.00
   5000.00B + -4000.00S + -60000.00R +     0.00d1+ +    0.00d1- +    -1.00d2+ +
1.00d2- +      0.00d3+ +     0.00d3- +     0.00d4+ +    0.00d4-     =      0.00
   5000.00B +  4000.00S +60000.00R +      0.00d1+ +    0.00d1- +    0.00d2+ +     0.
0.00d2- +    - 1.00d3+ +     1.00d3- +     0.00d4+ +     0.00d4-    = 400000.00
      0.00B +  4000.00S +     0.00R +     0.00d1+ +     0.00d1- +    0.00d2+ +     0.
0.00d2- +      0.00d3+ +     0.00d3- +    -1.00d4+ +     1.00d4-    =100000.00


              THE DECISION VARIABLES ARE 1 THROUGH 11
              THE ARTIFICIAL VARIABLES ARE 12 THROUGH 15


         OPTIMAL SOLUTION


ITERATIONS =    4


OBJECTIVE FUNCTION =            0.000


DECISION VARIABLES:

VARIABLE    NAME     VALUE

   1         B       40.000
   2         S       25.000
   3         R        1.667
   4         d1+    500.002

SLACK OR SURPLUS VARIABLES:

VARIABLE    NAME              VALUE
```

Figure 6-1

D. B. Silvestri goal programming problem: MASTER output (figure continued on next page)

```
DUAL RESULTS

VARIABLE    NAME                        VALUE
            B                           0.000
            S                           0.000
            R                           0.000
            d1+                         0.000
            d1-                        15.000
            d2+                         0.000
            d2-                         1.000
            d3+                         5.000
            d3-                         0.000
            d4+                         1.000
            d4-                         0.000
            CONSTRAINT   1              0.000
            CONSTRAINT   2              0.000
            CONSTRAINT   3              0.000
            CONSTRAINT   4              0.000


   OBJECTIVE FUNCTION SENSITIVITY ANALYSIS

                                        LOWER       CURRENT      UPPER
VARIABLE   NAME      STATUS             BOUND       VALUE        BOUND

    1       B            BASIC          0.000        0.000         0.000
    2       S            BASIC      -4000.000        0.000         0.000
    3       R            BASIC          0.000        0.000         0.000
    4       d1+          BASIC        -15.000        0.000         0.000
    5       d1-      NON-BASIC          0.000       15.000      INFINITY

**************************
**  CHECK FOR MULTIPLE  **
**  OPTIMAL SOLUTIONS   **
**************************

    6       d2+      NON-BASIC        -15.000        0.000         0.000
    7       d2-      NON-BASIC          0.000        1.000      INFINITY
    8       d3+      NON-BASIC          0.000        5.000      INFINITY

**************************
**  CHECK FOR MULTIPLE  **
**  OPTIMAL SOLUTIONS   **
**************************

    9       d3-      NON-BASIC        -15.000        0.000         0.000
   10       d4+      NON-BASIC          0.000        1.000      INFINITY

**************************
**  CHECK FOR MULTIPLE  **
**  OPTIMAL SOLUTIONS   **
**************************
```

Figure 6-1

(Figure continued on next page)

11	d4-	NON-BASIC	-15.000	0.000	0.000

SENSITIVITY ANALYSIS FOR RIGHT-HAND-SIDE VALUES

VARIABLE	ORIGINAL CONSTRAINT	LOWER BOUND	CURRENT VALUE	UPPER BOUND
12	1	-INFINITY	40000.000	40500.000
13	2	-400000.000	0.000	66666.800
14	3	394594.600	400000.000	INFINITY
15	4	85714.250	100000.000	200000.000

Figure 6-1 Continued

The D. B. Silvestri Example, Modified

Suppose the investor in the previous example called to change one of her goals. Specifically, she now wants the investment portfolio to achieve a return of $70,000 instead of $40,000. All other goals remain the same, as do their priority weights. Figure 6-2 shows the MASTER software output for this modified example.

The objective-function value shown in Figure 6-2 is 442,500, which, because it is not equal to zero, indicates that one or more of the four goals was not satisfied. The number represents the sum of the weighted deviations from the targets. Looking at the optimal solution, we see the following results:

$$B = 40.0 \qquad S = 25.0 \qquad R = 1.667 \qquad d_1^- = 29{,}500$$

The solution for the three decision variables remains the same as in the previous example: purchase 40 bonds at $5000 each, buy 25 blocks of 100 shares of common stocks, and purchase 1.667 units of the real-estate limited partnership. However, since $d_1^- = 29{,}500$, the solution informs us that this portfolio will fall $29,500 short of reaching the $70,000 objective for return.

Note that even though the goal of a $70,000 return had the highest priority weight, it was not satisfied by the optimal solution. Even though the weighting process allows for interaction and trade-offs between goals, it also allows the possibility of a higher-priority goal not being achieved. When this occurs, we need to reexamine the weights used. Sensitivity analysis can help evaluate the weights we have selected. For example, in the output section showing sensitivity analysis for the objective-function coefficients, the weight on deviation variable d_1^- would have to increase from its present value of 15 to above 28.571 before the values of the decision variables would change. This does not mean that if the priority weight on the profit goal increased to 29, this goal will be completely satisfied. However, as the weight increases above 28.571, the deviation from the target of $70,000 will be reduced.

Let's increase the priority weight on d_1^- to 120 and see what impact this has on the goal programming results. Figure 6-3 shows the output from MASTER. The following results occur:

$$B = 63.636 \qquad S = 79.545 \qquad d_3^+ = 236{,}363.6 \qquad d_4^+ = 218{,}181.8$$

This means that we would purchase 63.636 bonds at $5000 each and 79.545 blocks of

```
                    LINEAR PROGRAMMING FORMULATION

OBJECTIVE FUNCTION:
  MINIMIZE Z =
       0.00  B +      0.00  S  +     0.00  R    +   0.00  d1+ +     15.00  d1- +
 0.00  d2+ +      1.00  d2- +      5.00  d3+    +   0.00  d3- +     1.00  d4+ +
0.00 d4-

SUBJECT TO:
    425.00B +  540.00S + 6000.00R +    -1.00d1+ +      1.00d1-+    0.00d2+ +     0.
00d2- +    0.00d3+ +    0.00d3- +    0.00d4+ +    0.00d4-   =  70000.00
   5000.00B  -4000.00S   -60000.00R +    0.00d1+ +    0.00d1- +    -1.00d2+ +
1.00d2- +    0.00d3+ +    0.00d3- +    0.00d4+ +     0.00d4-    =      0.00
   5000.00B + 4000.00S +60000.00R +    0.00d1+ +     0.00d1- +     0.00d2+ +     0.
00d2- +   -1.00d3+ +    1.00d3- +    0.00d4+ +    0.00d4-    = 400000.00
      0.00B + 4000.00S +    0.00R +    0.00d1+ +     0.00d1- +     0.00d2+ +     0.
00d2- +    0.00d3+ +    0.00d3- +   -1.00d4+ +    1.00d4-    = 100000.00


                 THE DECISION VARIABLES ARE     1 THROUGH 11
                 THE ARTIFICIAL VARIABLES ARE 12 THROUGH 15


            OPTIMAL SOLUTION


ITERATIONS =    4


OBJECTIVE FUNCTION =      442500.000


DECISION VARIABLES:

VARIABLE   NAME    VALUE

    1        B        40.000
    2        S        25.000
    3        R         1.667
    5        d1-   29500.000


SLACK OR SURPLUS VARIABLES:

VARIABLE   NAME             VALUE
```

Figure 6-2
D. B. Silvestri goal programming problem: MASTER output for revised goal (figure continued on next page)

DUAL RESULTS

VARIABLE NAME		VALUE
B		0.000
S		0.000
R		0.000
d1+		15.000
d1-		0.000
d2+		0.113
d2-		0.887
d3+		3.613
d3-		1.388
d4+		0.475
d4-		0.525
CONSTRAINT	1	-15.000
CONSTRAINT	2	-0.113
CONSTRAINT	3	1.388
CONSTRAINT	4	0.525

OBJECTIVE-FUNCTION SENSITIVITY ANALYSIS

VARIABLE	NAME	STATUS	LOWER BOUND	CURRENT VALUE	UPPER BOUND
1	B	BASIC	-1125.001	0.000	8875.000
2	S	BASIC	-1900.000	0.000	2100.001
3	R	BASIC	-31500.010	0.000	13500.010
4	d1+	NON-BASIC	-15.000	0.000	INFINITY
5	d1-	BASIC	0.000	15.000	28.571
6	d2+	NON-BASIC	-0.113	0.000	INFINITY
7	d2-	NON-BASIC	0.113	1.000	INFINITY
8	d3+	NON-BASIC	1.388	5.000	INFINITY
9	d3-	NON-BASIC	-1.388	0.000	INFINITY
10	d4+	NON-BASIC	0.525	1.000	INFINITY
11	d4-	NON-BASIC	-0.525	0.000	INFINITY

SENSITIVITY ANALYSIS FOR RIGHT-HAND-SIDE VALUES

VARIABLE	ORIGINAL CONSTRAINT	LOWER BOUND	CURRENT VALUE	UPPER BOUND
12	1	40500.000	70000.000	INFINITY
13	2	-400000.000	0.000	200000.000
14	3	200000.000	400000.000	718918.900
15	4	-0.008	100000.000	200000.000

Figure 6-2 Continued

```
                LINEAR PROGRAMMING FORMULATION

OBJECTIVE FUNCTION:
  MINIMIZE Z =
       0.00   B +      0.00   S   +      0.00   R   +    0.00   d1+ +   120.00   d1- +
 0.00   d2+ +      1.00   d2- +      5.00   d3+   +    0.00   d3- +     1.00   d4+ +
0.00 d4- = Z

SUBJECT TO:
    425.00B +  540.00S + 6000.00R +    -1.00d1+ +     1.00d1- +    0.00d2+ +    0.
0.00d2- +    0.00d3+ +    0.00d3- +    0.00d4+ +    0.00d4- =  70000.00
   5000.00B  -4000.00S   -60000.00R +    0.00d1+ +    0.00d1+ +    -1.00d2+ +
1.00d2- +    0.00d3+ +    0.00d3- +    0.00d4+ +    0.00d4-   =        0.00
   5000.00B + 4000.00S +60000.00R +    0.00d1+ +    0.00d1- +    0.00d2+ +    0.
0.00d2- +   -1.00d3+ +    1.00d3- +    0.00d4+ +    0.00d4- = 400000.00
      0.00B + 4000.00S +    0.00R +    0.00d1+ +    0.00d1- +    0.00d2+ +    0.
0.00d2- +    0.00d3+ +    0.00d3- +   -1.00d4+ +    1.00d4- = 100000.00


              THE DECISION VARIABLES ARE    1 THROUGH 11
              THE ARTIFICIAL VARIABLES ARE 12 THROUGH 15


         OPTIMAL SOLUTION


ITERATIONS =   6


OBJECTIVE FUNCTION =    1400000.000


DECISION VARIABLES:

VARIABLE   NAME   VALUE

   1      B             63.636
   2      S             79.545
   8      d3+       236363.600
   9      d4+       218181.800


SLACK OR SURPLUS VARIABLES:

VARIABLE   NAME            VALUE
```

Figure 6-3
D. B. Silvestri problem: MASTER output for revised priority weights (figure continued on next page)

DUAL RESULTS

VARIABLE	NAME	VALUE
	B	0.000
	S	0.000
	R	45000.030
	d1+	50.000
	d1-	70.000
	d2+	0.750
	d2-	0.250
	d3+	0.000
	d3-	5.000
	d4+	0.000
	d4-	1.000
	CONSTRAINT 1	-50.000
	CONSTRAINT 2	-0.750
	CONSTRAINT 3	5.000
	CONSTRAINT 4	1.000

OBJECTIVE-FUNCTION SENSITIVITY ANALYSIS

VARIABLE	NAME	STATUS	LOWER BOUND	CURRENT VALUE	UPPER BOUND
1	B	BASIC	-6111.116	0.000	2037.032
2	S	BASIC	-2588.230	0.000	3567.570
3	R	NON-BASIC	-45000.030	0.000	INFINITY
4	d1+	NON-BASIC	-50.000	0.000	INFINITY
5	d1-	NON-BASIC	50.000	120.000	INFINITY
6	d2+	NON-BASIC	-0.750	0.000	INFINITY
7	d2-	NON-BASIC	0.750	1.000	INFINITY
8	d3+	BASIC	2.643	5.000	6.100
9	d3-	NON-BASIC	-5.000	0.000	INFINITY
10	d4+	BASIC	0.353	1.000	1.892
11	d4-	NON-BASIC	-1.000	0.000	INFINITY

SENSITIVITY ANALYSIS FOR RIGHT-HAND-SIDE VALUES

VARIABLE	ORIGINAL CONSTRAINT	LOWER BOUND	CURRENT VALUE	UPPER BOUND
12	1	44000.010	70000.000	INFINITY
13	2	-518518.500	0.000	564705.900
14	3	-INFINITY	400000.000	636363.600
15	4	-INFINITY	100000.000	318181.800

Figure 6-3 Continued

100 common-stock shares each. This solution shows that we will achieve the \$70,000 profit goal, since d_1^+ is no longer in the basic feasible solution. However, now two lower-priority goals will not be met, and the investor will be forced to spend \$236,363.60 more than the allotted total of \$400,000 ($d_3^+ = 236{,}363.6$) and \$218,181.80 more than the \$100,000 ($d_4^+ = 218{,}181.8$) that was supposed to be spent on common stocks.

FINAL COMMENTS ON GOAL PROGRAMMING

The previous sections have introduced the basics of goal programming. As you now know, goal programming is merely an extension of linear programming, and the solution procedure commonly uses a modified simplex approach. At this introductory level, we believe that you should be able to recognize when a situation can be modeled using goal programming. You should be able to set up a goal programming problem by identifying the goals and by developing the appropriate constraints and objective function. We are not as concerned that you be able to manually solve a goal programming problem using the modified simplex procedure. Certainly by now you are capable of working through a small problem like the examples in this chapter. However, for large problems, the manual approach is not practical.

Ideally, goal programming is performed on a computer. We have demonstrated how the MASTER software package can be used to solve a goal programming problem. However, MASTER assumes that you can assign numerical priority weightings to the goals. In those cases where the goals are simply ranked, MASTER cannot be used. Very few inexpensive software packages do this type of goal programming. Sang Lee has developed a mainframe program called GPGO, and there is a personal computer package called *Micro Manager;* but in general, software for these problems is not readily available.

6-5 INTEGER PROGRAMMING

The assumption of divisibility is one of the most restrictive for the simplex algorithm. Up to this point we have not worried too much about divisibility. Divisibility is the requirement that the variables in the basis in the final solution can take on noninteger values. However, there are many situations where the final solution must contain decision variables with only integer values. Among these are certain product mix applications where the decision variables are the number of units of each product to be produced or shipped. Fractional units of a product may not be possible to produce or ship.

One approach to dealing with a noninteger linear programming solution to problems calling for integer solutions is to round the final answer to integer values. This may be acceptable, providing the optimum levels for these decision variables are very large, in which case the rounding may not seriously alter the solution. For example, the decision to produce 30,211 sheets of plywood when the linear programming solution called for 30,211.33 sheets will probably be acceptable.

However, in other applications where the decision variables have small optimal values, rounding might have adverse affects on the solution. For instance, suppose a linear programming model is used by the Morrison-Knudsen Railroad Division to help determine its product mix. If a linear programming solution calling for production of 2.42 engines and 18.35 cars is rounded to 2 engines and 18 freight cars, the value of the objective function may differ substantially from the actual optimal solution. Thus, rounding a linear programming solution to integer values may not be appropriate in certain situations.

THE BRANCH-AND-BOUND SOLUTION PROCEDURE

A linear programming problem in which all decision variables are constrained to integer values is termed an **integer programming problem**.

Several techniques exist to ensure that the outcome of a linear programming problem is restricted to integer values. In this text we present one such method, called the **branch-and-bound technique** for integer programming, introduced by A. H. Land and A. G. Doig in 1960. This solution procedure, in which only a limited number of possible solutions are examined, is illustrated in the following example.

G. W. Land Development has purchased an option to build a resort on Gull Lake in northern Michigan. Molly Coil, the managing partner, has decided to finance the development of this property by establishing a limited real estate trust. She has successfully raised \$10 million to use for both property acquisition and construction.

The resort will have a central clubhouse with spa, costing \$1.2 million, and a combination of single-family vacation homes and condominium units. Because of city planning and zoning requirements, the single-family homes will be built in groups of 6. The cost is \$1,100,000 per group. The condominium units must be completed in groups of 10 units, costing \$1,900,000 per group. Preliminary marketing research indicates that G. W. Land Development will be able to sell a maximum of 5 blocks of single-family housing units. The research indicates that more than 100 condominium groups could be sold. Company officials take this to mean that no practical marketing limitations exist for the condominium groups.

An environmental impact study has identified a potentially serious surface-water drainage problem. To meet present surface-water pollution restrictions, the development is limited to adding a maximum of 110 cubic feet of water per second (cfs) to the county's storm drain system. Each group of single-family housing units will add 20 cfs of water at peak conditions, and each group of condominium units will add 14 cfs. Annualized positive cash flow will be \$120,000 per year for each single-family housing group and \$90,000 for each condominium group.

The question facing G. W. Land Development is how many groups of single-family houses and condominiums can be built to maximize annual cash flows for the company, subject to the various constraints. If the city planning and zoning rules didn't require that entire groups of single-family houses and condominium units be completed, a linear programming model could be used to determine how many groups (or fractions of groups) of each type of housing should be built. If we didn't have the integer requirement, we could let:

X = number of single-family groups to build

Y = number of blocks of condominium units to build

The objective function for this problem is:

$$\text{Maximize} \quad Z = 120{,}000X + 90{,}000Y$$

Subject to:

$$\begin{aligned} \$1{,}100{,}000X + \$1{,}900{,}000Y &\le \$8{,}800{,}000 && \text{(available capital)} \\ X \qquad\qquad\qquad &\le 5 && \text{(housing-market restrictions)} \\ 20X + 14Y &\le 110 && \text{(surface-runoff limit)} \end{aligned}$$

But if we include the requirement for an integer solution, we add the constraint:

X and $Y \geq 0$ and integer

Since this problem has two decision variables, we can represent it graphically, as shown in Figure 6-4. The three constraints restrict the solution space to form the feasible region in the usual manner. The integer requirement further limits the potential solutions to the dots shown in Figure 6-4. Each dot in figure 6-4 represents a unique feasible solution.

In a simple problem like this one, we might evaluate the objective function at every integer solution point within the feasible region. For instance, at $X = 1$, $Y = 3$, we get $Z = 390{,}000$. At $X = 3$, $Y = 3$, we get $Z = 630{,}000$, and so forth. By inspection, the optimal integer solution is $X = 4$, $Y = 2$, giving an objective-function value of $Z = 660{,}000$.

The objective is to develop a procedure to find the optimal integer solution point within the feasible region without having to inspect all possible integer solution points. A tempting procedure is to solve it as a regular linear programming problem, ignoring the integer constraints (referred to as the *relaxed model*), and if necessary round down to the nearest integer values. Unfortunately, the rounded solution may or may not be the optimal integer solution.

The optimal corner-point solution (without the integer restriction) is $X = 3.796$, $Y = 2.434$, with $Z = 674{,}600$. If we were to round this solution down to $X = 3$ and $Y = 2$, the objective-function value would be $Z = 540{,}000$. This is substantially less than the best integer solution found by inspection, which was $Z = 660{,}000$. The

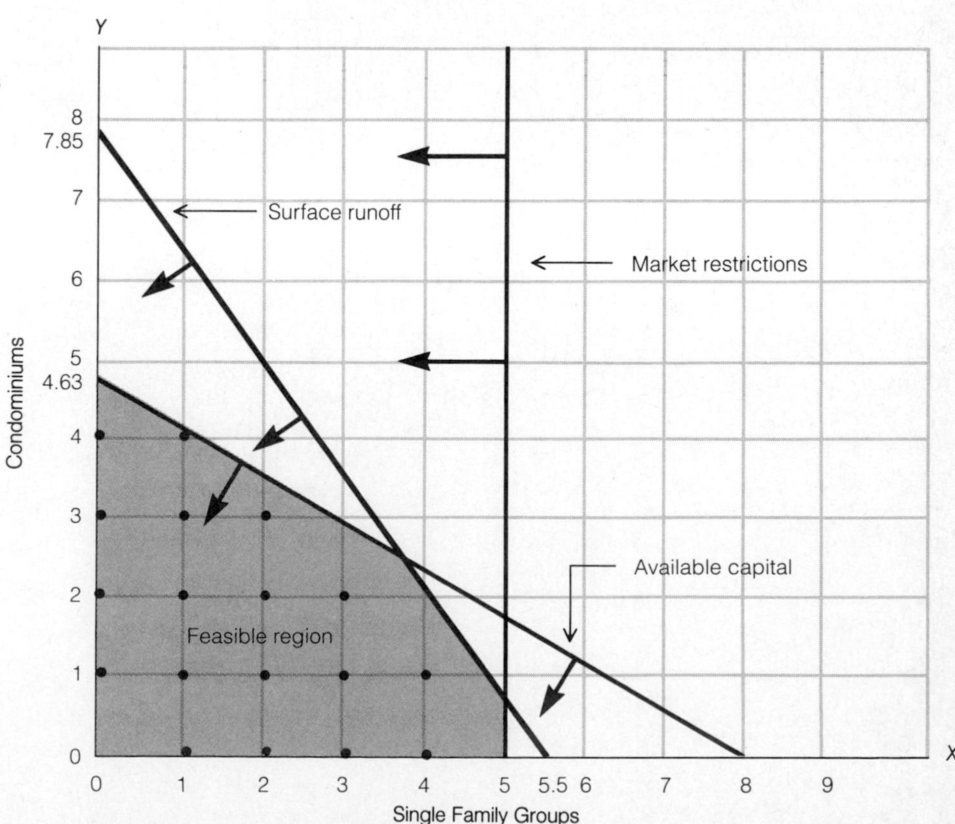

Figure 6-4
G. W. Land Development problem: possible solution points

difference between the rounded solution and the optimal integer solution is illustrated in Figure 6-5.

For small problems involving only two decision variables, we can enumerate each feasible integer solution and determine which solution optimizes the objective function. But for larger problems, we need a computational technique which will provide the optimal integer solution directly. One such procedure is the branch-and-bound technique.

Solving the Integer Problem

The branch-and-bound procedure begins with a solution space that includes all possible solutions, both integer and noninteger, and reduces the possible solution set by a series of formal steps to finally arrive at the optimal integer solution point. We will demonstrate the procedure using the G. W. Land Development example.

Step 1 *Solve the relaxed model.*
The first step is to solve the relaxed model, which is the linear programming model without the integer constraints:

$$\text{Maximize} \quad Z = 120{,}000X + 90{,}000Y$$

Figure 6-5
G. W. Land Development problem: graphical solution

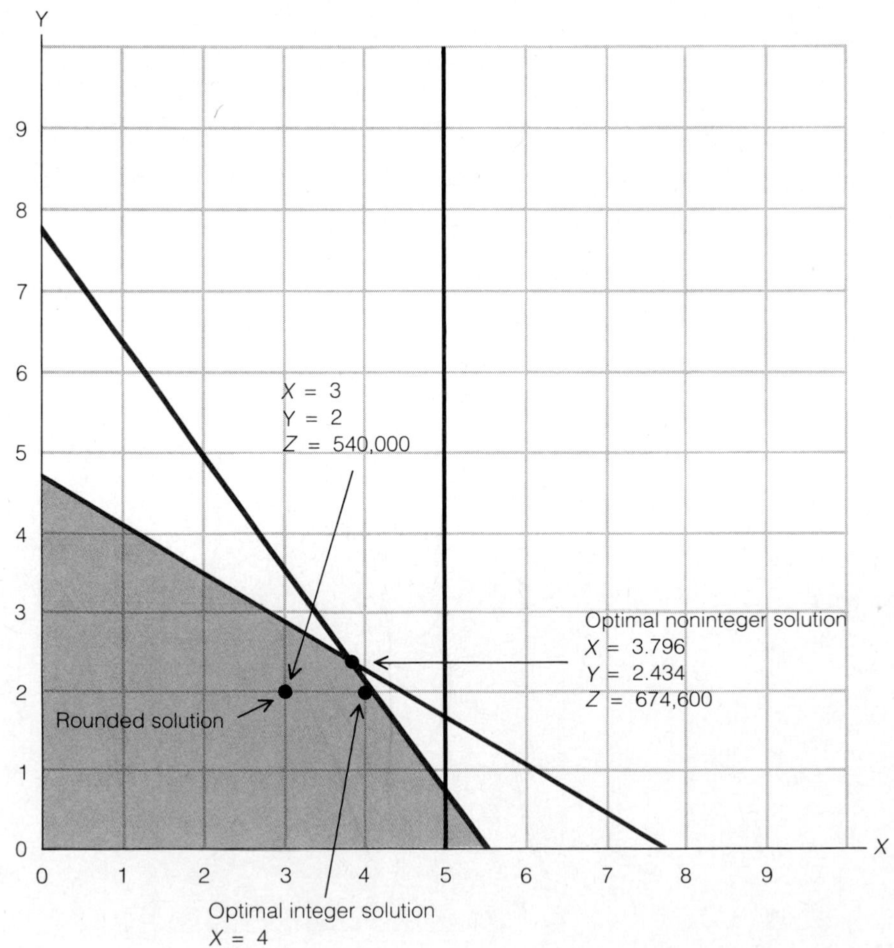

Subject to:

$$\begin{aligned} \$1{,}100{,}000X + \$1{,}900{,}000Y &\le \$8{,}800{,}000 \quad \text{(available capital)} \\ X \phantom{+ \$1{,}900{,}000Y} &\le 5 \quad \text{(housing-market restrictions)} \\ 20X + 14Y &\le 110 \quad \text{(surface-runoff limit)} \end{aligned}$$

The solution to this problem, as shown in Figure 6-5, is:

$X = 3.796$

$Y = 2.434$

$Z = 674{,}600$

The value of the objective function for the relaxed model is the upper bound of the integer programming problem. No other solution to the problem will have an objective-function value larger than this.

Step 2 *Determine the lower bound to the problem.*
While the upper bound to the problem is determined by the solution to the relaxed problem, the lower bound is found by rounding down the relaxed solution to the next lower integer values. Doing this, we get:

$X = 3$

$Y = 2$

$Z = 540{,}000$

We will not need to check any possible solution points that give us solutions with an objective-function value less than 540,000. Later, we will see how this lower bound is increased.

Step 3 *Branch on the initial solution.*
Since the relaxed model did not lead to an integer solution, we will eliminate a segment of the solution space. We will pick the solution variable with the decimal value closest to .5. This will become the branch variable. In this case, we will branch on Y, since $Y = 2.434$ has the decimal portion closest to .5. Because Y must be an integer and cannot have values between 2 and 3, we will eliminate these values by splitting the original problem into two problems. The first problem is determined by adding the constraint $Y \le 2$ to the original problem, and the second problem is determined by adding the constraint $Y \ge 3$ to the original problem. These two constraints slice the area between $Y = 2$ and $Y = 3$ out of the original solution space, as shown in Figure 6-6. We now solve these two models separately.

Model 1

$$\text{Maximize} \quad Z = 120{,}000X + 90{,}000Y$$

Subject to:

$$\begin{aligned} \$1{,}100{,}000X + \$1{,}900{,}000Y &\le \$8{,}800{,}000 \quad \text{(available capital)} \\ X \phantom{+ \$1{,}900{,}000Y} &\le 5 \quad \text{(housing-market restrictions)} \\ 20X + 14Y &\le 110 \quad \text{(surface-runoff limit)} \\ Y &\le 2 \quad \text{(added constraint)} \end{aligned}$$

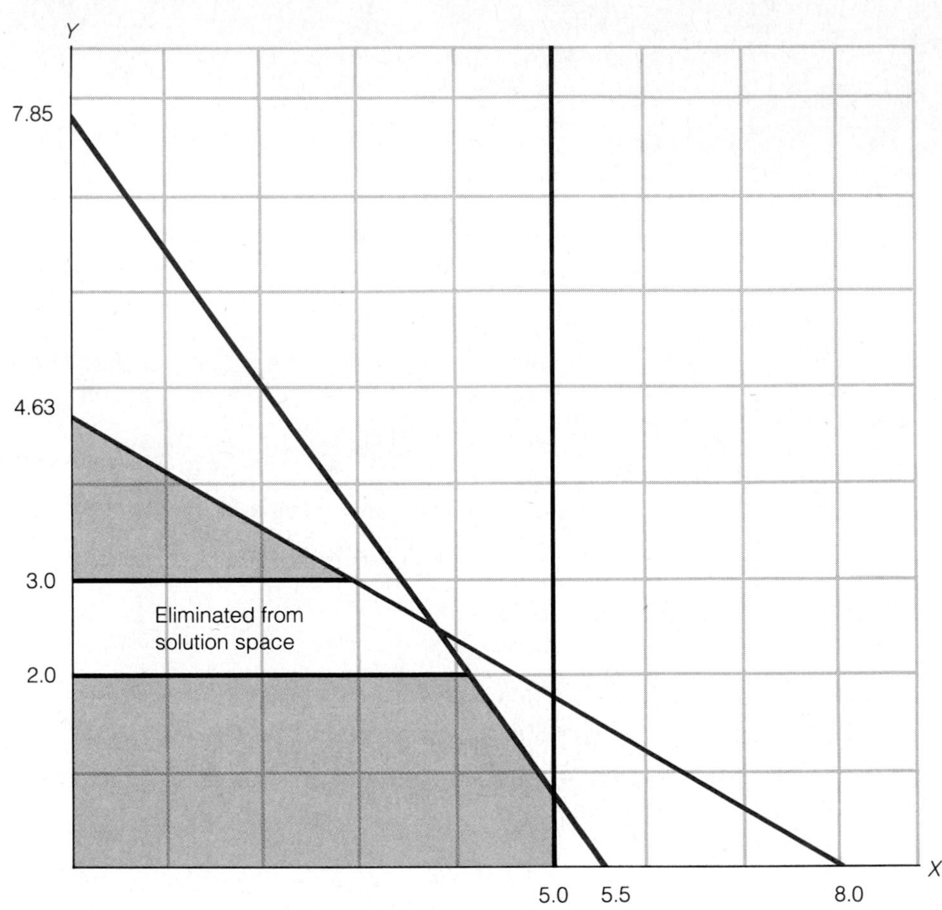

Figure 6-6
G. W. Land Development problem: reduction in solution space

This problem has the solution:

$X = 4.1$

$Y = 2$

$Z = \$672,000$

Model 2

$$\text{Maximize} \quad Z = 120{,}000X + 90{,}000Y$$

Subject to:

$\$1{,}100{,}000X + \$1{,}900{,}000Y \leq \$8{,}800{,}000$	(available capital)
$X \leq 5$	(housing-market restrictions)
$20X + 14Y \leq 110$	(surface-runoff limit)
$Y \geq 3$	(added constraint)

This problem has the solution:

$X = 2.818$

$Y = 3$

$Z = \$608,180$

This branching process is shown in Figure 6-7. Notice that by slicing out some of the solution space we have caused the solutions to the two models to have integer values for the Y variable.

Step 4 *Compare the solutions with the lower bound, and if necessary, branch again. Repeat as often as necessary.*

If we still have a noninteger solution (or a partial-integer solution) with an objective-function value greater than the lower bound, we will branch again. Since both solution values found in step 3 are larger than the lower bound, we will branch again. Given the choice, we branch on the solution point with the highest objective-function value. The model yielding the highest objective-function value has:

$$X = 4.1$$
$$Y = 2.0$$
$$Z = 672{,}000$$

Therefore, we will continue from the $Y \le 2$ branch and form two new problems, one with an $X \le 4$ constraint and the other with an $X \ge 5$ constraint. This will further restrict the solution space, as shown in Figure 6-8. This step adds the following two models:

Model 1

$$\text{Maximize} \quad Z = 120{,}000X + 90{,}000Y$$

Subject to:

$\$1{,}100{,}000X + \$1{,}900{,}000Y \le$	$\$8{,}800{,}000$	(available capital)
$X \le$	5	(housing-market restrictions)
$20X + 14Y \le$	110	(surface-runoff limit)
$Y \le$	2	(previously added constraint)
$X \le$	4	(added constraint)

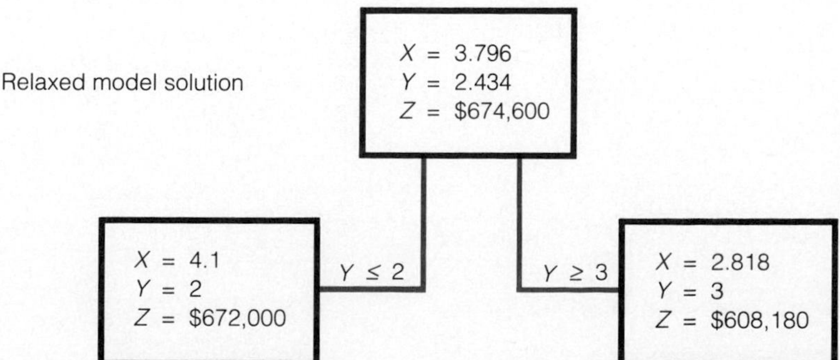

Figure 6-7
G. W. Land Development problem after initial branching

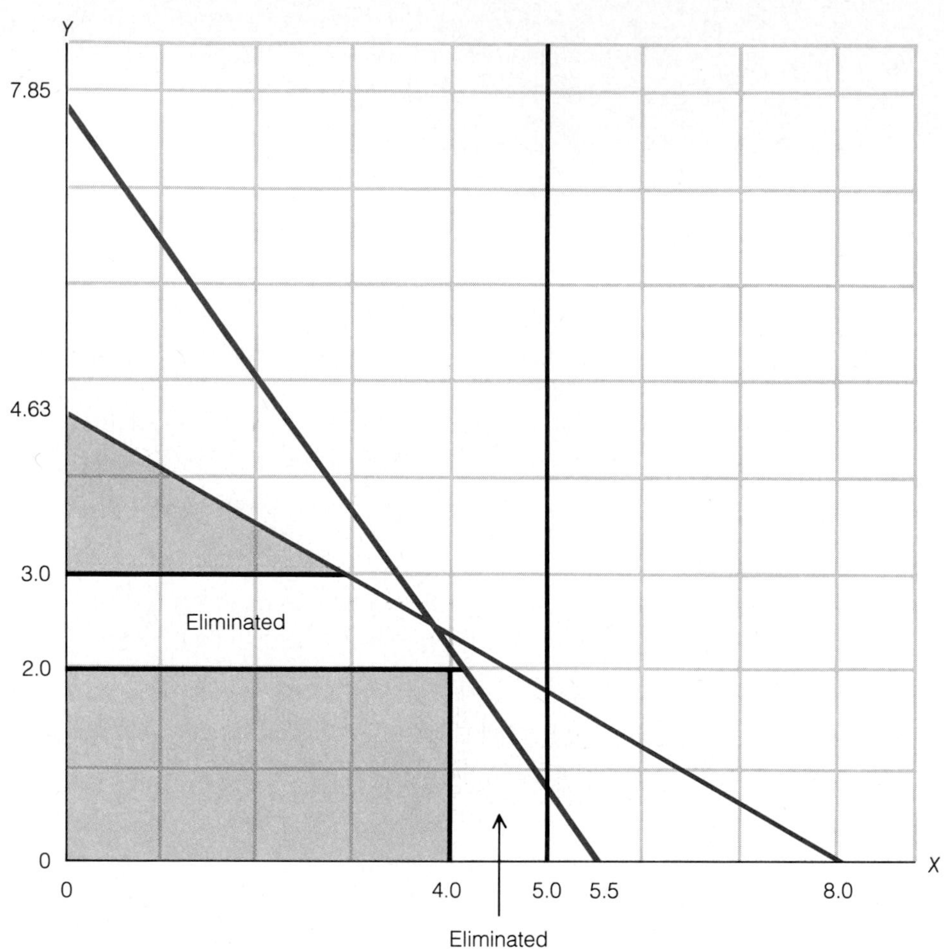

Figure 6-8
G. W. Land Development problem with further reduction in solution space

Note: Segment of line above $X = 5$ is still in solution space.

Model 2

$$\text{Maximize} \quad Z = 120{,}000X + 90{,}000Y$$

Subject to:

$\$1{,}100{,}000X + \$1{,}900{,}000Y \leq \$8{,}800{,}000$	(available capital)
$X \leq 5$	(housing-market restrictions)
$20X + 14Y \leq 110$	(surface-runoff limit)
$Y \leq 2$	(previously added constraint)
$X \geq 5$	(added constraint)

The solution to model 1 is:

$X = 4$

$Y = 2$

$Z = \$660{,}000$

The solution to model 2 is:

$X = 5$

$Y = .714$

$Z = \$664{,}290$

Notice that model 1 now provides an all-integer solution. At this point there is no assurance that this is the optimal integer solution, but it has a larger objective function than the 540,000 value found in step 2. At the very least, we have a new lower bound. Also, since the integer solution has an objective-function value greater than the objective function for the $Y \geq 3$ branch (608,180) shown in Figure 6-7, we don't have to consider that branch any further.

The results of the branching to this point are shown in Figure 6-9. Since the objective function on the $X \geq 5$ branch (664,290) is greater than the objective function on the $X \leq 4$ branch (660,000), we must further limit the solution space by branching again, as shown in Figure 6-10.

> **This is the key to branch-and-bound:** *As long as we have a noninteger solution with an objective-function value greater than the lower bound formed by the best integer solution, we will continue to branch. When all the noninteger branches have an objective-function value less than the best integer solution, the optimal integer solution is identified.*

We now have two new linear programming problems, one with the additional constraint $Y \leq 0$ and the other with the additional constraint $Y \geq 1$.

Model 1

Maximize $Z = 120{,}000X + 90{,}000Y$

Subject to:

$$\begin{array}{rcrl} \$1{,}100{,}000X + \$1{,}900{,}000Y & \leq & \$8{,}800{,}000 & \text{(available capital)} \\ X & \leq & 5 & \text{(housing-market restrictions)} \\ 20X + 14Y & \leq & 110 & \text{(surface-runoff limit)} \\ Y & \leq & 2 & \text{(previously added constraint)} \\ X & \geq & 5 & \text{(previously added constraint)} \\ Y & \leq & 0 & \text{(added constraint)} \end{array}$$

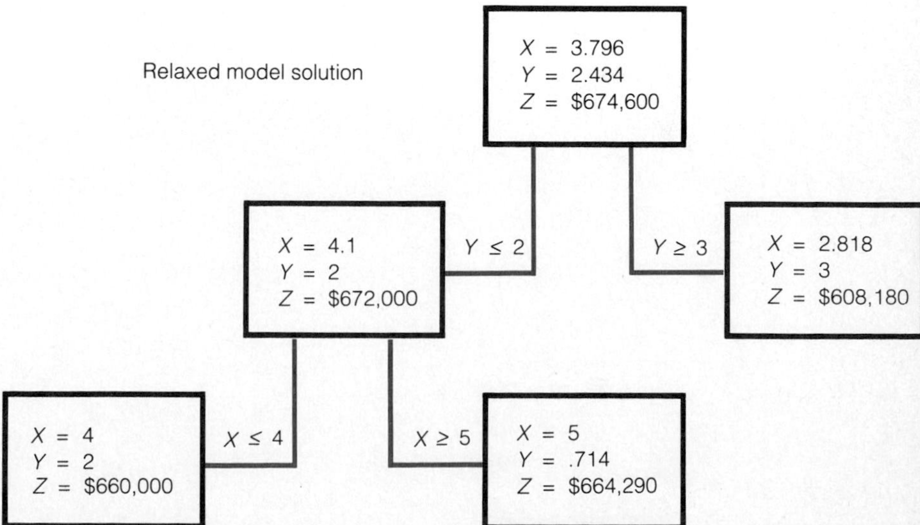

Figure 6-9
G. W. Land Development problem after second branching

Figure 6-10
G. W. Land Development problem with reduction in solution space after second branching

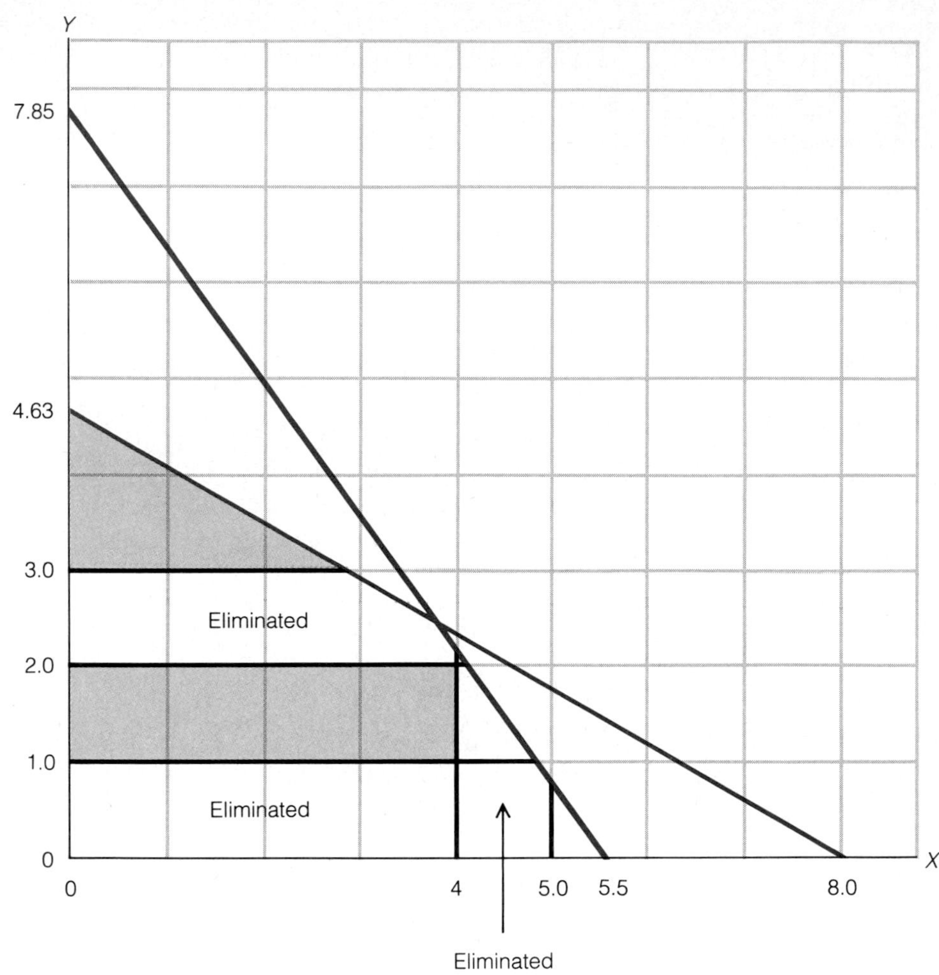

Model 2

$$\text{Maximize} \quad Z = 120{,}000X + 90{,}000Y$$

Subject to:

$\$1{,}100{,}000X + \$1{,}900{,}000Y \leq$	$\$8{,}800{,}000$	(available capital)
$X \leq$	5	(housing-market restrictions)
$20X + 14Y \leq$	110	(surface-runoff limit)
$Y \leq$	2	(previously added constraint)
$X \geq$	5	(previously added constraint)
$Y \geq$	1	(added constraint)

The solution to model 1 is:

$X = 5$
$Y = 0$
$Z = 600{,}000$

There is no feasible solution to model 2.

The final branch is shown in Figure 6-11. Notice that we have traced all branches until they have an objective-function value less than the lower bound or have an unfeasible solution. Thus, the optimal integer solution is:

$$X = 4$$
$$Y = 2$$
$$Z = 660{,}000$$

Observe that this is the same solution point as that found graphically in Figure 6-5. The G. W. Land Development Company should plan to build 4 units of single-family housing and 2 blocks of condominiums to maximize annual cash flows subject to the various constraints, including an integer solution.

While tedious, the branch-and-bound technique is straightforward and is the procedure used in virtually all linear programming software that has an integer programming option.

6-6 A MIXED-INTEGER PROGRAMMING MODEL

Just as there are examples where all the decision variables are limited to integer values, so are there many situations where some decision variables are limited to integer values while others may take on fractional parts. An application involving this mixture

Figure 6-11
G. W. Land Development problem after final branching

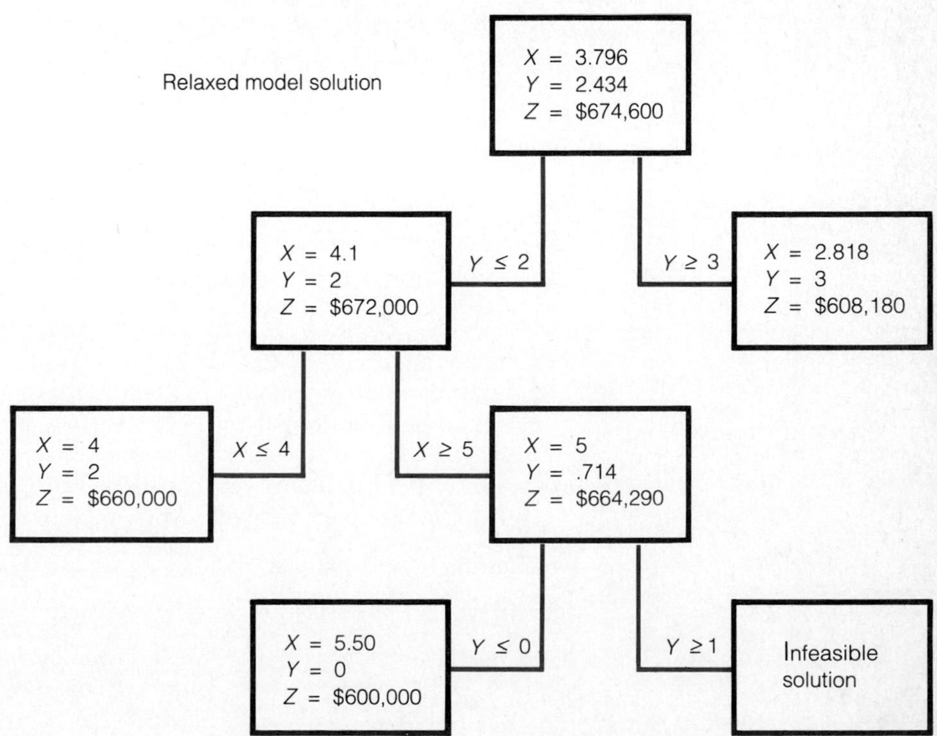

is termed a **mixed-integer programming problem**. The following example demonstrates how a mixed-integer solution model is developed.

THE DELRAY CONSULTANTS EXAMPLE

Delray Consultants is a computer consulting firm owned by Steve Delmonico and Ray Hastings. Both engineers had been employed by a large computer manufacturer but grew tired of working for someone else and decided to start their own company. Both have excellent reputations in the hardware design field and so have had no trouble finding work for their firm in the two years they have been in operation. Ray and Steve are able to act as lead engineers on consulting projects, as are two other members of their firm. In addition, Delray employs 9.5 (one engineer goes to graduate school and only works half time) other engineers and 15 electronics technicians.

Delray works on projects which can be classified into one of three categories: major design projects, trouble-shooting projects, and hourly contract work. Major design projects typically require one lead engineer, three other engineers, and four technicians. Trouble-shooting projects require one lead engineer, two other engineers, and two technicians. Hourly contract work utilizes one engineer and one technician.

Major contracts run on a yearly basis and net the company $100,000 each after costs. Steve and Ray's policy is to have at least two major contracts in place each year to give stability to the company's cash flow. Trouble-shooting contracts are generally signed on a quarterly basis and net the company $60,000 each. Hourly contract work earns $50 per hour (assume a 40-hour week and 13-week quarter).

Delray's research lab has limited space. A major project will take up 2400 square feet, and a trouble-shooting job requires 1500 square feet. A total of 7000 square feet of research space is available. Hourly contract work is carried out primarily on the client's site, but some tasks are done at Delray, requiring 500 square feet of research space.

Steve and Ray want to plan their contract placements for the next year. They also need to know whether their work force is correctly structured for their planned contract load.

This situation can be represented as a linear programming problem by following our usual procedure. First, we *define the decision variables*. Let:

x_1 = number of major projects

x_2 = number of trouble-shooting projects

x_3 = number of hours of contract work

Notice that both x_1 and x_2 must be limited to integer values but x_3 does not have an integer limitation.

Next, we *formulate the objective function*. Here we must be careful to convert all profit values to comparable time periods. That is, we cannot have yearly profits, quarterly profits, and hourly values in the same objective function. The choice of time period is up to the decision maker. For the purposes of this example, we will use quarterly values. The objective function becomes:

$$\text{Maximize} \quad Z = \$25{,}000x_1 + 60{,}000x_2 + 26{,}000x_3$$

Then, we *develop the constraints*. The constraints for this problem are:

$$\begin{aligned} x_1 \qquad\qquad &\geq 2 \quad \text{(stability requirement)} \\ x_1 + \quad x_2 \qquad &\leq 4 \quad \text{(total limit on lead engineers)} \end{aligned}$$

$$\begin{aligned} 3x_1 + \quad 2x_2 + \quad x_3 &\leq \quad 9.5 && \text{(total other engineers)} \\ 4x_1 + \quad 2x_2 + \quad x_3 &\leq \quad 15 && \text{(technicians available)} \\ 2400x_1 + 1500x_2 + 500x_3 &\leq 7000 && \text{(space available)} \end{aligned}$$

Since we have integer requirements on two of the three decision variables, we have a mixed-integer programming problem. Mixed-integer problems are solved using the branch-and-bound technique in the same manner as for the example in the previous section, except we do not have to branch on the x_3 variable since it does not have the integer constraint.

Following the procedure outlined in the previous section, we first formulate and solve the relaxed model:

Maximize $Z = \$25{,}000x_1 + 60{,}000x_2 + 26{,}000x_3$

Subject to:

$$\begin{aligned} x_1 \qquad\qquad\qquad &\geq \quad 2 && \text{(stability requirement)} \\ x_1 + \quad x_2 \qquad\quad &\leq \quad 4 && \text{(total limit on lead engineers)} \\ 3x_1 + \quad 2x_2 + \quad x_3 &\leq \quad 9.5 && \text{(total other engineers)} \\ 4x_1 + \quad 2x_2 + \quad x_3 &\leq \quad 15 && \text{(technicians available)} \\ 2400x_1 + 1500x_2 + 500x_3 &\leq 7000 && \text{(space available)} \end{aligned}$$

The relaxed model has this solution:

$x_1 = 2$

$x_2 = .9$

$x_3 = 1.7$

$Z = 148{,}200$

Notice that we have an integer value for the x_1 variable (major contracts) but not for the x_2 decision variable (trouble-shooting contracts) or the x_3 decision variable (hours of contract work). The hourly-work variable is not required to be an integer, but it does require some interpretation. Remember that we converted everything to a quarterly basis with 13 forty-hour weeks in each quarter. Therefore, $x_3 = 1.7$ really means 884 ($1.7 \times 13 \times 40$) hours of contract work.

Since we need x_2 to have an integer value, we branch on $x_2 = .9$ by forming two new linear programming models, one with the constraint $x_2 \leq 0$ and the other with the constraint $x_2 \geq 1$. This branching is shown in Figure 6-12. Since both models provide integer solutions for x_1 and x_2, we can do no further branching. The optimal mixed-integer solution has been reached after only one branch:

$x_1 = 2$

$x_2 = 1$

$x_3 = 1.4$

$Z = 146{,}400$

This means that the company should seek 2 major contracts, 1 trouble-shooting contract, and 1.4 hourly contracts (actually, $1.4 \times 13 \times 40 = 728$ hours of hourly contract work). Under this plan, Delray's quarterly profit would be \$146,400 and all

Figure 6-12
Branching for the Delray Consultants problem

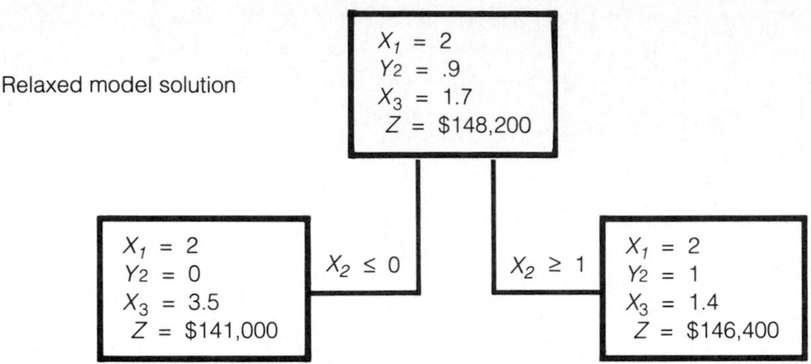

constraints would be satisfied, including the integer requirements on variables x_1 and x_2.

Steve Delmonico and Ray Hastings of Delray wanted to employ linear programming not only to determine what their optimal work mix should be during the coming quarter but also to evaluate whether their current staffing is appropriate given the desired work mix. At the optimal point, Delray has one too many lead engineers, 3.6 extra technicians and .1 extra other engineer. If the company plans to operate at this level for an extended period, the owners might consider cutting back 1 lead engineer and 3 technicians.

However, to expand beyond this optimal operating level, more space will be needed. For instance, the present research capacity of 7000 square feet is a limiting factor. They might want to rent additional space or add on to the existing research facility.

This example has demonstrated mixed-integer linear programming, which is merely an extension of integer programming. The branch-and-bound technique presented in this chapter is used to solve both integer and mixed-integer problems. The problems and cases at the end of the chapter provide additional mixed-integer applications for you to consider.

6-7 ZERO-ONE INTEGER PROGRAMMING

In many decision-making situations a manager must select one of two possible courses of action. A company president might be faced with the decision of whether to build a new plant or not. A marketing executive might need to decide whether to introduce a new product or not. The board of directors of one company may be deciding whether to attempt a takeover of a rival company. All of these decisions are of the yes-no variety.

Since yes-no decisions are some of the most common facing managers, they need models which can be used to help with these decisions. One such model is zero-one integer programming. **Zero-one integer programming** is an extension of integer linear programming where one or more of the decision variables are limited to the values zero or one. The problem is structured such that these variables are 1 if the decision is yes and 0 if the decision is no. This type of variable is called a **binary variable.** The following example is presented to introduce the zero-one integer programming technique.

THE DILBUS ASSOCIATES EXAMPLE

Barbara Shimano is the recently hired director of International Marketing for Dilbus Associates. Dilbus has seen rapid growth in the North American market for its primary family of products, software packages that improve the operation of IBM mainframe computers and compatibles. The board of directors decided to expand into the Pacific Rim and hired Barbara because of her extensive international marketing experience.

The board of directors has identified South Korea, Taiwan, Singapore, and Thailand as potential areas for expansion. Barbara has been given an overall expansion budget of $20 million and is expected to have the new system in place within the next 5 years. From an initial survey of real estate and support costs, Barbara has estimated the costs for expanding into each of the countries in the next 5 years. These costs are shown in Table 6-7. For instance, if expansion into South Korea occurs in year 1, the cost will be $6.7 million, while in year 4 the cost would be $7.0 million.

During a lengthy meeting with the long-range planning committee of the board of directors, Barbara is given the following guidelines:

1. If Dilbus is to expand into either South Korea or Taiwan, it must do so in the next 3 years, before protectionist restrictions are legislated by their governments.
2. For travel and logistical reasons, Singapore and Thailand should be treated as a pair. If Dilbus expands into one country, it will also expand into the other.
3. The board is firm that the $20 million expansion budget cannot be exceeded.

Since Barbara must make a yes-no decision on expanding into each country each year, her decision problem can be treated as a zero-one integer programming problem. The formulation of this zero-one integer programming problem can be done by following the same series of steps as for all linear programming problems.

First, we define the decision variables. The problem formulation will require 20 decision variables, each having a value of 0 or 1 and each representing the decision of whether to expand into a specific country in a specific year. We establish the following notation:

$x_{ij} = 1$ if we are to expand into country i in year j

$x_{ij} = 0$ if we are not to expand into country i in year j

$i = 1$ to 4 countries

$j = 1$ to 5 years

Then we make the following assignments:

Country 1 = South Korea

Country 2 = Taiwan

Country 3 = Singapore

Country 4 = Thailand

Table 6-7 DILBUS EXAMPLE: EXPANSION COSTS (IN MILLIONS OF DOLLARS)

	Year				
Country	1	2	3	4	5
South Korea	6.7	6.3	7.5	7.0	8.0
Taiwan	8.1	8.4	8.8	8.9	9.4
Singapore	9.1	9.7	10.0	10.8	10.2
Thailand	4.5	4.8	5.2	5.0	5.0

Thus, $x_{11} = 1$ means that we will expand into South Korea in year 1.

Next, we formulate the objective function. If the company wishes to expand into as many countries as possible, within its constraints, the objective function becomes:

$$\text{Maximize} \quad Z = x_{11} + x_{12} + x_{13} + x_{14} + x_{15} + x_{21} + x_{22} + x_{23} + x_{24} + x_{25} + x_{31} + x_{32} + x_{33} + x_{34} + x_{35} + x_{41} + x_{42} + x_{43} + x_{44} + x_{45}$$

Then, we develop the constraints. There are four different sets of constraints to consider:

1. The company can expand into a country only one time. The constraints for this condition are:

$$x_{11} + x_{12} + x_{13} + x_{14} + x_{15} \leq 1$$
$$x_{21} + x_{22} + x_{23} + x_{24} + x_{25} \leq 1$$
$$x_{31} + x_{32} + x_{33} + x_{34} + x_{35} \leq 1$$
$$x_{41} + x_{42} + x_{43} + x_{44} + x_{45} \leq 1$$

2. The total expansion budget is limited to \$20 million. This condition is handled by the following constraints:

$$6.7x_{11} + 6.3x_{12} + 7.5x_{13} + 7.0x_{14} + 8.0x_{15} + 8.1x_{21} + 8.4x_{22} + 8.8x_{23} + 8.9x_{24} + 9.4x_{25} + 9.1x_{31} + 9.7x_{32} + 10.0x_{33} + 10.8x_{34} + 10.2x_{35} + 4.5x_{41} + 4.8x_{42} + 5.2x_{43} + 5.0x_{44} + 5.0x_{45} \leq 20$$

3. Expansion into South Korea and Taiwan cannot take place after year 3. We develop the following constraints to handle this condition:

$$x_{14} = 0$$
$$x_{15} = 0$$
$$x_{24} = 0$$
$$x_{25} = 0$$

4. Expansion into Singapore and Thailand must be considered as a unit. The constraints necessary to deal with this issue are:

$$x_{31} = x_{41} \quad \text{or} \quad x_{31} - x_{41} = 0$$
$$x_{32} = x_{42} \quad \text{or} \quad x_{32} - x_{42} = 0$$
$$x_{33} = x_{43} \quad \text{or} \quad x_{33} - x_{43} = 0$$
$$x_{34} = x_{44} \quad \text{or} \quad x_{34} - x_{44} = 0$$
$$x_{35} = x_{45} \quad \text{or} \quad x_{35} - x_{45} = 0$$

Now we solve the linear programming problem. The technique for solving this problem is essentially the same as that for integer programming, except that the decision variables are restricted to 0 or 1 values. You might also recognize this problem as being a special type of assignment problem, like those in Chapter 5. While the current version of MASTER does not contain a zero-one integer programming option, a special-purpose computer program such as LINDO could be used to arrive at the optimal decision, which is:

$x_{12} = 1$ (South Korea in year 2)

$x_{31} = 1$ (Singapore in year 1)

$x_{41} = 1$ (Thailand in year 1)

The total cost of the expansion project will be $19.9 million. (Note that the optimal solution does not call for expansion into Taiwan.) This solution maximizes the number of expansions which the company can make within the budget and subject to the other constraints.

6-8 SUMMARY AND CONCLUSIONS

Decision makers often face situations that cannot be represented by a traditional linear programming model. Most often this is a result of the decision problem having conditions which violate one of the basic assumptions of the linear programming model. One of the strengths of linear programming has been its adaptability to a wider range of applications than originally considered when the technique was developed. In this chapter, we have examined two important extensions of the traditional linear programming model.

First, we considered the case where a decision involved more than one objective function. The basic linear programming model allows for only one objective function, which is either maximized or minimized. To deal with decision problems requiring multiple objective functions, a goal programming model is required. We showed how to formulate a goal programming model and illustrated how the simplex solution method is modified to solve goal programming problems.

Second, we considered situations in which the divisibility assumption of linear programming was not appropriate. Some decision problems require that one or more decision variables be restricted to integer values. The normal linear programming model allows the decision variables to take on any value, integer or noninteger. This need for a model to handle integer-only solutions has led to the development of integer and zero-one programming models. This chapter has shown examples of both integer and zero-one integer programming formulations and solutions.

The revised models presented in this chapter are extensions of the basic linear programming simplex solution procedure. Other extensions exist, such as chance-constrained linear programming, which allows for uncertainty to be incorporated into the linear programming model. Because linear programming has been such a widely used management science tool, and because of its many successful extensions, continuing research will certainly produce even more extensions to help in the decision-making process.

Solved Problem

PROBLEM The Echo Electronics Company is in the process of determining which suppliers will be given contracts to supply Echo with four different components. Four suppliers have submitted bids on the components. The following table shows the bid prices per unit for each component. (Note: A blank indicates that a supplier did not bid on a component.)

	Supplier				
Component Part	1	2	3	4	Demand (units)
1	\$20	\$23	—	\$25	10,000
2	—	\$75	\$70	\$77	25,000
3	\$25	\$23	\$28	—	5,000
4	\$35	—	—	\$37	15,000

Echo Electronics does not require sole-sourcing for its components. This means that more than one supplier can be the source of any particular component. This works out well, since some suppliers have limitations on their abilities to meet the demand for certain parts. Specifically:

Supplier 1 is limited to a maximum of 15,000 units of part 4.

Supplier 2 is limited to a maximum of 2500 units of part 1.

Supplier 4 is limited to a maximum of 12,000 units of part 2.

Supplier 4 is limited to a maximum of 3500 units of part 4.

Additionally, in a letter submitted with its bid, supplier 4 indicated that it would have to have at least \$460,000 worth of business from Echo or the bid would be withdrawn. Also, Echo does not require that contracts go strictly to the lowest bidders.

In determining how to award the contracts, Echo has established four goals. In order of priority, they are:

1. Total purchases must not exceed \$3,000,000.
2. Try to make sure that supplier 4 gets enough business so that its bid is not withdrawn. (This means that Echo Electronics wants to minimize the deviation between what would be awarded and \$460,000.)
3. Limit total contracts with any supplier to \$980,000.
4. Because of a long-standing relationship with supplier 1, keep its total contract amount to at least \$900,000.

The problem facing Echo Electronics is to determine how many units of each component part to award to each supplier in such a way as to minimize the deviations from Echo's goals.

Formulate the problem facing Echo Electronics. (Do not solve.)

Solution

We recognize this as an optimization problem with multiple goals, so the appropriate management science technique is goal programming. Our procedure will be to establish the decision variables, the deviation variables, the goal constraints, the system constraints, and the objective function.

a. Decision variables

The units of each component part assigned to each supplier constitute the decision variables. We will express these as follows:

x_{11} = units of component 1 supplied by supplier 1
x_{12} = units of component 1 supplied by supplier 2

.
.
.

x_{44} = units of component 4 supplied by supplier 4

b. Deviation variables

The deviation variables represent the amount by which a goal is exceeded or not met. In this problem we have four distinct goals to consider. Often this means two deviation variables per goal, but that is not true in this case, as we will show.

Goal 1 refers to the fact that Echo wants total component purchases not to exceed $3,000,000. Thus, two deviation variables can be defined:

d_1^+ = amount total order exceeds $3,000,000
d_1^- = amount total order is less than $3,000,000

The goal 1 constraint is written as follows:

$$20x_{11} + 23x_{12} + 0x_{13} + 25x_{14} + 0x_{21} + 75x_{22} + 70x_{23} + 77x_{24} + 25x_{31} + 23x_{32} + 28x_{33} + 0x_{34} + 35x_{41} + 0x_{42} + 0x_{43} + 37x_{44} + d_1^- - d_1^+ = 3{,}000{,}000$$

Goal 2 deals with Echo's desire to make sure that supplier 4 gets at least $460,000 worth of business so it doesn't drop out of the bid process. Thus, two further deviation variables are required:

d_2^+ = the amount over $460,000 for supplier 4
d_2^- = the amount under $460,000 for supplier 4

The goal 2 constraint is:

$$0x_{11} + 0x_{12} + 0x_{13} + 25x_{14} + 0x_{21} + 0x_{22} + 0x_{23} + 77x_{24} + 0x_{31} + 0x_{32} + 0x_{33} + 0x_{34} + 0x_{41} + 0x_{42} + 0x_{43} + 37x_{44} + d_2^- - d_2^+ = 460{,}000$$

Goal 3 indicates that the total business with individual suppliers should be limited to $980,000. This goal actually translates into four subgoals, one for each supplier. Thus, we will need two deviation variables for each of the subgoals. For instance, for supplier 1 we get:

d_3^+ = amount of business over $980,000
d_3^- = amount of business under $980,000

The goal 3 constraints are:

Supplier 1: $$20x_{11} + 0x_{12} + 0x_{13} + 0x_{14} + 0x_{21} + 0x_{22} + 0x_{23} + 0x_{24} + 25x_{31} + 0x_{32} + 0x_{33} + 0x_{34} + 35x_{41} + 0x_{42} + 0x_{43} + 0x_{44} + d_3^- - d_3^+ = 980{,}000$$

Supplier 2: $$0x_{11} + 23x_{12} + 0x_{13} + 0x_{14} + 0x_{21} + 75x_{22} + 0x_{23} + 0x_{24} + 0x_{31} + 23x_{32} + 0x_{33} + 0x_{34} + 0x_{41} + 0x_{42} + 0x_{43} + 0x_{44} + d_4^- - d_4^+ = 980{,}000$$

Supplier 3: $$0x_{11} + 0x_{12} + 0x_{13} + 0x_{14} + 0x_{21} + 0x_{22} + 70x_{23} + 0x_{24} + 0x_{31} + 0x_{32} + 28x_{33} + 0x_{34} + 0x_{41} + 0x_{42} + 0x_{43} + 0x_{44} + d_5^- - d_5^+ = 980{,}000$$

Supplier 4: $$0x_{11} + 0x_{12} + 0x_{13} + 25x_{14} + 0x_{21} + 0x_{22} + 0x_{23} + 77x_{24} + 0x_{31} + 0x_{32} + 0x_{33} + 0x_{34} + 0x_{41} + 0x_{42} + 0x_{43} + 37x_{44} + d_6^- - d_6^+ = 980{,}000$$

Goal 4 says that Echo wishes to do at least $900,000 of business with supplier 1. Thus, we establish two more deviation variables:

d_7^+ = amount exceeding $900,000 with supplier 1
d_7^- = amount under $900,000 with supplier 1

The goal 4 constraint is:

$$20x_{11} + 0x_{12} + 0x_{13} + 0x_{14} + 0x_{21} + 0x_{22} + 0x_{23} + 0x_{24} + 25x_{31} + 0x_{32} + 0x_{33} + 0x_{34} + 35x_{41} + 0x_{42} + 0x_{43} + 0x_{44} + d_7^- - d_7^+ = 900{,}000$$

In addition to the goal constraints, some system constraints must also be included in the model. These have to do with the supplier's capacity constraints and Echo's demand requirements, which were discussed in the statement of the problem. For example, supplier 1 can provide a maximum of 15,000 units of component part 4. This and the other system constraints are as follows:

Capacity constraints:

$$0x_{11} + 0x_{12} + 0x_{13} + 0x_{14} + 0x_{21} + 0x_{22} + 0x_{23} + 0x_{24} + 0x_{31} + 0x_{32} + 0x_{33} + 0x_{34} + x_{41} + 0x_{42} + 0x_{43} + 0x_{44} \leq 15{,}000$$

$$0x_{11} + x_{12} + 0x_{13} + 0x_{14} + 0x_{21} + 0x_{22} + 0x_{23} + 0x_{24} + 0x_{31} + 0x_{32} + 0x_{33} + 0x_{34} + 0x_{41} + 0x_{42} + 0x_{43} + 0x_{44} \leq 2500$$

$$0x_{11} + 0x_{12} + 0x_{13} + 0x_{14} + 0x_{21} + 0x_{22} + 0x_{23} + x_{24} + 0x_{31} + 0x_{32} + 0x_{33} + 0x_{34} + 0x_{41} + 0x_{42} + 0x_{43} + 0x_{44} \leq 12{,}000$$

$$0x_{11} + 0x_{12} + 0x_{13} + 0x_{14} + 0x_{21} + 0x_{22} + 0x_{23} + 0x_{24} + 0x_{31} + 0x_{32} + 0x_{33} + 0x_{34} + 0x_{41} + 0x_{42} + 0x_{43} + x_{44} \leq 3500$$

Demand constraints:

$$x_{11} + x_{12} + 0x_{13} + x_{14} + 0x_{21} + 0x_{22} + 0x_{23} + 0x_{24} + 0x_{31} + 0x_{32} + 0x_{33} + 0x_{34} + 0x_{41} + 0x_{42} + 0x_{43} + 0x_{44} = 10{,}000$$

$$0x_{11} + 0x_{12} + 0x_{13} + 0x_{14} + 0x_{21} + x_{22} + x_{23} + x_{24} + 0x_{31} + 0x_{32} + 0x_{33} + 0x_{34} + 0x_{41} + 0x_{42} + 0x_{43} + 0x_{44} = 25{,}000$$

$$0x_{11} + 0x_{12} + 0x_{13} + 0x_{14} + 0x_{21} + 0x_{22} + 0x_{23} + 0x_{24} + x_{31} + x_{32} + x_{33} + 0x_{34} + 0x_{41} + 0x_{42} + 0x_{43} + 0x_{44} = 5000$$

$$0x_{11} + 0x_{12} + 0x_{13} + 0x_{14} + 0x_{21} + 0x_{22} + 0x_{23} + 0x_{24} + 0x_{31} + 0x_{32} + 0x_{33} + 0x_{34} + x_{41} + 0x_{42} + 0x_{43} + x_{44} = 15{,}000$$

c. *Objective function*

Now that the system constraints and the deviation constraints have been defined, we can set up the objective function. Keep in mind that since this is a goal programming model, we seek to minimize any adverse deviations from the target values for the goals. Since the goals have different priorities, we indicate this using P_1, P_2, P_3, and P_4, respectively, for the four goals. The objective function is:

$$\text{Minimize} \quad Z = P_1 d_1^+ + P_2 d_2^- + P_3(d_3^+ + d_4^+ + d_5^+ + d_6^+) + P_4 d_7^-$$

As you can see, not all deviation variables are represented in the objective function. The omitted deviation variables would have zero coefficients. For example, with respect to goal 1, Echo managers do not care if the total expenditures for components is less than \$3,000,000, so the deviation variable, d_1^- would have a zero coefficient in the objective function. Also, goal 3 involved four subgoals, so the P_3 priority designation applies to all four deviation-plus variables (d^+) for that goal.

The instructions for this problem did not ask for a solution. If one were required, we could manually work through the modified simplex procedure discussed in this chapter or use a goal programming computer software package.

General Questions and Assignments

1. Discuss in your own terms the difference between linear programming models and goal programming models. Create an example to show the difference between goal programming and linear programming.
2. Write a short report describing the logic behind the modified simplex method for solving goal programming problems.
3. Goal programming models have decision variables and deviation variables. Discuss these by using an example of your own creation. Also indicate why the goal programming objective involves minimization of the deviation variables.
4. Referring to the discussions in this and previous chapters, list the assumptions of linear programming. In more detail than the others, discuss the divisibility assumption and indicate, through one or more of your own examples, when this assumption might not be appropriate.
5. Respond to the comment that an integer solution for one or more of the decision variables in a linear-programming problem can be achieved by rounding up or down to the nearest integer values(s). (Assume that the problem requires an integer solution.) Discuss.
6. Suppose you have a linear programming minimization problem with two decision variables and three greater-than-or-equal-to ($\geq$) constraints. Further, suppose the decision variables are required to be integer values in the final solution. Discuss the potential problems if the decision variables are determined by rounding down to the nearest integer value from the optimal linear programming results.

Exercises and Application Problems

1. The Lunch Bucket provides drive-through bag lunch service just outside the industrial park area of Bangor, Maine. All the lunches are premade and contain the same kind of fruit, juice, chips, and cookies. The only difference is the sandwich. Each day two different sandwiches are featured. They are handed out on different sides of the Lunch Bucket, as indicated by flashing signs. All the lunches cost $3.00 each. The whole operation is done so rapidly that getting a lunch takes about the same time as driving through a toll booth. Tomorrow, the bag lunches will have either a Hero or a Philly sandwich. The forecast is for 200 Hero lunches and 250 Philly lunches. Each Hero lunch requires 3 minutes to make, and each Philly lunch requires 2 minutes. Two people have been hired to come in at night and work 8 hours preparing lunches. They will be paid for 8 hours no matter how many lunches are required. If 8 hours is not enough time to produce the required number of lunches, the workers will work overtime. If too many lunches are produced and not sold, the extras are given free to local charities.

   If too few lunches are produced, customers will be turned away; profits will be lost; and customers will be disappointed. The owners of the Lunch Bucket are interested in formulating their situation as a goal programming problem which seeks to minimize overtime, lost sales, and worker idle time. Assume that all three goals have equal priority. Formulate only; do not solve.
2. Global Travel serves customers in the greater New Orleans area. The president of Global Travel establishes monthly performance objectives for the sales staff. In general, these objectives fall into two categories: providing service to business customers and providing service to vacationers. The president feels that by serving both types of customers the company will be better able to ride out downturns in economic activity. For the coming month, the following objectives have been set:
   a. Provide service to 500 business customers.
   b. Provide service to 300 vacationers.

On average, serving a business customer requires 2 hours to make all required reservations and deliver tickets (Global Travel requires each agent to personally deliver tickets to all business customers). Making all the necessary reservations for a vacationing customer requires 1.5 hours (these tickets are not personally delivered). The company will have 1200 hours of customer service time available next month. Formulate this situation as a goal programming problem.

3. Referring to problem 2, suppose that serving business customers is considered a higher priority than serving vacationers. Solve the goal programming problem for Global Travel using the modified simplex approach.
4. Dynamic Storage manufactures two different personal computer data-storage units: a 40-megabyte hard drive (which uses magnetic media) and a 40-megabyte hard card (which uses integrated circuits). The last two steps in manufacturing each product are an environmental test and a functional test. The environmental test takes 3 hours for the hard drive and 2 hours for the hard card. The functional test requires 1 hour for each device. Dynamic Storage has 90 hours per day available on its environmental test units and 60 hours per day available on its functional test units. Each hard drive yields $80 operational profit (sales price − operational costs) for the company, and each hard card makes $100.
   a. Formulate and solve this as a linear programming problem in which the objective is to maximize profits.
   b. Dynamic Storage was recently taken private through a leveraged buyout and has high debt levels. The corporate treasurer believes the company must make $4000 operational profit on these two products each day to comfortably service this debt. Formulate this new situation as a goal programming problem.
   c. Discuss the differences between the models developed in parts **a** and **b**.
5. Problem 4 considered Dynamic Storage, which manufactures a 40-megabyte hard drive and a 40-megabyte hard card. Total output is limited by the last two steps in the manufacturing process. The corporate treasurer believes the company must make $4000 operational profit on these two products each day to comfortably service this debt.

   The sales manager estimates the company will have to produce at least 20 of each product per day to remain a viable market entity. Formulate this new requirement in the goal programming problem and solve. Assume that all goals have equal priority. Use MASTER or some other software package with a linear programming module.
6. Deep Woods Products make solid oak computer desks. The Deep Woods manufacturing plant has two separate production lines. One line is operated continually and is staffed with experienced workers. The second line is activated only when demand is high. It is staffed by less-experienced, but equally paid, workers temporarily transferred from other parts of the company. The line with experienced workers can produce 5 desks per hour; the less-experienced line can produce 3 desks per hour. The operational costs for each line are the same, and each will have 40 hours of production time available next week. The production manager has formulated the following goals for next week:
   a. Produce 350 desks.
   b. Limit overtime on the experienced line to 10 hours.
   c. Make sure each line works 40 hours.

   Formulate as a goal programming model. Do not solve.
7. Referring to problem 6, suppose the highest-priority goal is the goal to produce 350 desks, followed by the limit on overtime, and finally the 40-hour goal for each line. Based on the formulation done for problem 6, solve this goal programming problem using the modified simplex approach.
8. Referring to problems 6 and 7, suppose the Deep Woods manager has elected to establish numerical weightings on the three goals as follows:

Weight	Goal
50	Produce 350 desks.
10	Limit overtime on the experienced line to 10 hours.
5	Make sure each line works 40 hours.

Using these weightings, develop a linear programming formulation to solve the goal programming problem. Use MASTER or another linear programming software package. Write a short report which discusses the solution. How many desks will be produced on each line? Be sure to discuss the degree to which each of the goals has been satisfied.

9. Refer to problems 6, 7, and 8. Assume the manager thinks the goal involving limits on overtime for the experienced line and the requirement that each line work 40 hours per week are equally important—but producing 350 desks per week is twice as important as either of them. Reformulate and solve the problem as a goal programming problem with numerical priorities. Solve using the linear programming module of MASTER or some other software package.

10. The law firm of Trendwater and Cleary is involved in an extensive product liability case. The first brief in the case is due in five working days. The rough draft of the brief is 1000 pages long and must be reworked before being presented to the court. After a team of lawyers goes over the document for legal content, it will be edited for grammar, spelling, and so on. Trendwater and Cleary employ a manuscript editing firm for this type of work. The firm can spare four manuscript editors for the next week. They charge on a per page basis, with the charge being different for each of the four editors, depending on their experience. In addition, each of the four editors is able to proof legal documents at different speeds and with different error rates. The editors also have varying amounts of time available. The four editors, their speed, error rate, available time, and charge per page are shown in the following table.

Editor	Charge per Page ($)	Speed (pages per hour)	Errors per Page	Hours Available
Min Yee	3.50	6.4	.015	50
Christy Beach	2.40	5.2	.018	40
Bill Verdon	3.75	7.5	.008	50
Luisa Huerta	3.90	8.8	.012	35

Tidewater and Cleary would like to spend no more than $3000 for editing the brief and would like to ensure that it contains no more than 12 grammatical errors. They would like to make sure that all 1000 pages are completed within the week. Assume the highest priority goal is completing the 1000 pages followed by having no more than 12 errors and limiting the costs to $3000 in that order. Formulate as a goal programming problem. Show the first tableau of the modified simplex solution procedure.

Weight	Goal
20	Finish all 1000 pages.
5	Have no more than 12 total errors.
1	Limit cost to $3000.

Using this information, formulate this goal programming problem assuming that the objective is to minimize the weighted deviations from the targets. Solve using MASTER or some other software package. Fully discuss the results, including how many pages to assign to each editor and how well the company was able to meet its objectives.

Problems 12–19 are provided to give you the opportunity to manually solve some integer programming problems that have already been formulated. The purpose is to help you better understand the solution techniques presented in this chapter.

12. Solve the following integer programming problem:

Maximize $Z = 6x_1 + 4x_2$

Subject to:

$$
\begin{aligned}
12x_1 + 8x_2 &\leq 40 \\
3x_1 + 6x_2 &\leq 20 \\
x_1, x_2 &\geq 0 \text{ and integers}
\end{aligned}
$$

13. Solve the following integer programming problem:

Maximize $Z = 3x_1 + 15x_2$

Subject to:

$$
\begin{aligned}
10x_1 + 2x_2 &\leq 75 \\
6x_1 + 7x_2 &\leq 60 \\
x_1, x_2 &\geq 0 \text{ and integers}
\end{aligned}
$$

14. Solve the following integer programming problem:

Maximize $Z = 2x_1 + 4x_2 + 6x_3$

Subject to:

$$
\begin{aligned}
5x_1 + 6x_2 + 7x_3 &\leq 90 \\
3x_1 + 4x_2 + 5x_3 &\leq 80 \\
x_1, x_2, x_3 &\geq 0 \text{ and integers}
\end{aligned}
$$

15. Solve the following integer programming problem:

Maximize $Z = 10x_1 + 8x_2 + 6x_3$

Subject to:

$$
\begin{aligned}
4x_1 + 4x_2 + 2x_3 &\leq 27 \\
3x_1 + 4x_2 + 5x_3 &\leq 22 \\
x_1, x_2, x_3 &\geq 0 \text{ and integers}
\end{aligned}
$$

16. Solve the following mixed-integer programming problem:

Maximize $Z = 3x_1 + 4x_2$

Subject to:

$$
\begin{aligned}
5x_1 + 2x_2 &\leq 15 \\
2x_1 + 4x_2 &\leq 9 \\
x_1, x_2 &\geq 0 \quad \text{and} \quad x_2 \text{ an integer}
\end{aligned}
$$

17. Solve the following mixed-integer programming problem:

Maximize $Z = 7.5x_1 + 5x_2$

Subject to:

$$12x_1 + 20x_2 \leq 180$$
$$25x_1 + 14x_2 \leq 200$$
$$x_1, x_2 \geq 0 \quad \text{and} \quad x_1 \text{ an integer}$$

18. Solve the following mixed-integer programming problem:

$$\text{Maximize} \quad Z = 5x_1 + 4x_2 + 3x_3$$

Subject to:

$$15x_1 + 12x_2 + 10x_3 \leq 250$$
$$3x_1 + 5x_2 + 6x_3 \leq 90$$
$$x_1, x_2, x_3 \geq 0 \quad \text{and} \quad x_2, x_3 \text{ integers}$$

19. Solve the following mixed-integer programming problem:

$$\text{Maximize} \quad Z = 7x_1 + 2x_2 + 3x_3$$

Subject to:

$$2x_1 + 2x_2 + 1x_3 \leq 18$$
$$5x_1 + 4x_2 + 4x_3 \leq 28$$
$$x_1, x_2, x_3 \geq 0 \quad \text{and} \quad x_1, x_2 \text{ integers}$$

20. The North Dakota Fish and Game Department is considering undertaking five new fish and wildlife projects in the next four years. The projects involve developing wetland areas on land where the department already holds options. Each project could be completed within one year, but the cost depends on when the project is started. The project costs vary, as estimated in the following table:

	Year			
Project	1991	1992	1993	1994
1	$500,000	$650,000	$ 600,000	$ 700,000
2	750,000	700,000	800,000	780,000
3	800,000	710,000	680,000	900,000
4	900,000	950,000	1,100,000	1,300,000
5	850,000	750,000	810,000	880,000

The department is constrained by the legislature in the following fashion:

a. Projects 2 and 3 must be started and finished by 1993 or not done at all.

b. Total expenses cannot exceed $2,500,000.

c. Projects 3 and 4 will be done on the same piece of land and so must be done at the same time.

Formulate as a zero-one programming problem but do not solve. Discuss why this is a zero-one linear programming problem.

21. The Help Hotline operates a telephone service for distraught people in the Tampa Bay area. The staff includes both full-time staff and volunteer members. Management is presently working on staffing schedules for Friday and Saturday, the busiest days of the week. The schedule must account for both work cycles and breaks. The number of people needed on the hotline during each hour of the 5:00

P.M. to 5:00 A.M. shift is shown below:

Hour	Number Needed
5:00–6:00 P.M.	10
6:00–7:00 P.M.	12
7:00–8:00 P.M.	12
8:00–9:00 P.M.	14
9:00–10:00 P.M.	16
10:00–11:00 P.M.	18
11:00 P.M.–midnight	18
12:00–1:00 A.M.	16
1:00–2:00 A.M.	16
2:00–3:00 A.M.	12
3:00–4:00 A.M.	10
4:00–5:00 A.M.	8

Each person starts with a 4-hour shift on the phone, followed by a 1-hour break, then another 4-hour shift. Due to the stress of the operation, no one works more than 8 hours on any Friday or Saturday. Each full-time worker is paid $10 per hour. To qualify for liability insurance, Help Hotline pays each volunteer $2 per hour. The organization has 8 full-time employees; state regulations require at least 3 of them to be on duty at any one time. Formulate an integer programming model for staffing the 12-hour block (5:00 P.M. to 5:00 A.M.) with the required number of people at the minimum cost. Do not solve.

22. The printed-circuit fabrication line at Maynard Manufacturing typically makes four types of circuit boards during each 8-hour shift. Components are put on the boards by a computerized insertion robot, which must be reprogrammed and loaded with different components each time the line shifts to a different board. The amount of time (in minutes) needed to change from the type of board the robot is presently working onto a new board is as follows, for all four boards:

	Present Board			
New Board	1011	1214	1004	1618
1011	—	20	30	25
1214	22	—	25	20
1004	18	15	—	16
1618	15	12	17	—

Formulate and solve an integer programming model for determining the optimal sequence of boards to minimize the total setup time each day.

23. The Peavy Corporation puts on quality-control seminars throughout the United States and Canada. Currently, six organizations are interested in having Peavy do a seminar within the next month. The following table shows the cost of putting on the seminar at each site, along with the expected revenue. The table also shows the number of seminar presenters that will be required at each location.

Location	Cost	Revenue	Presenters
1	$ 5,000	$15,000	4
2	11,000	24,000	7
3	9,000	14,000	4
4	7,000	13,000	2
5	13,000	22,000	11
6	17,000	21,000	5

Peavy wishes to maximize its revenues, but because of cash flow problems must limit its costs to $60,000 for the month. In addition, the maximum number of presenters the company can engage during the month is 22. Formulate and solve the appropriate model which could be used to help the Peavy Company determine which seminars to offer.

Chapter Glossary

Binary variable A decision variable whose value is restricted to 0 or 1.

Branch-and-bound technique A solution procedure for integer programming problems in which only a limited number of the possible solutions are examined.

Goal A numerical value representing the desired level of a specific organizational objective.

Goal programming An extension of the traditional linear programming technique which allows a decision maker to consider multiple objectives in the decision process.

Integer programming problem A linear programming problem in which all decision variables are constrained to integer values.

Mixed-integer programming problem A linear programming problem in which some, but not all, of the decision variables are constrained to integer values.

Zero-one integer programming problem A linear programming problem in which the decision variables represent yes-no situations and may assume values of 0 or 1.

Chapter References

BOOKS

Bradley, S. P., A. C. Hux, and T. L. Magnanti. *Applied Mathematical Programming.* Reading, Mass.: Addison-Wesley, 1977.

Garfinkle, R. S., and G. L. Nemhauser. *Integer Programming.* New York: Wiley, 1972.

Hillier, F., and G. J. Lieberman. *Introduction to Operations Research,* 4th ed. Oakland, Calif.: Holden-Day, 1986.

Lee, Sang. *Goal Programming for Decision Analysis.* Pennsauken, N.J.: Auerbach, 1972.

Wanger, H. M. *Principles of Operations Research,* 2d ed. Englewood Cliffs, N.J.: Prentice-Hall, 1975.

ARTICLES

Colling, R. W., S. I. Gass, and E. E. Rosendahl. "The ASCAR Model for Evaluating Manpower Policy." *Interfaces,* June 1983.

Crowder, H., E. L. Johnson, and M. Padberg. "Solving Large-Scale Zero-One Linear Programming Problems." *Operations Research,* September–October 1983.

Goeffrion, A. M. "A Guided Tour of Recent Practical Advances in Integer Linear Programming." *Omega,* April 1976.

Goeffrion, A. M., and P. E. Marsten. "Integer Programming Algorithms: A Framework and State-of-the-Art Survey." *Management Science,* March 1972.

Lee, Sang M., and M. J. Schniederjans. "Multicriteria Assignment Problems: A Goal Programming Approach." *Interfaces,* August 1983.

Mini Cases

CASE 6A
BIERWAG AND ASSOCIATES

Allen Bierwag founded Bierwag and Associates in late 1984, when he left General Motors Corporation. After a slow start, the company, which makes air shock units for passenger cars, has developed a solid working relationship with GM and is now one of its key suppliers of original-equipment shock absorbers. As with most other U.S. companies, the late 1980s brought a real focus on Bierwag's productivity and quality. To improve productivity, Allen has turned more and more to automation. This has meant that large capital expenditures have been required. However, like other relatively new firms, Bierwag and Associates is not in the position of being able to take on every capital expenditure that is deemed important.

Currently, Allen and his senior managers have defined four projects which have passed all their internal tests of worthiness. Table 6C-1 presents data showing the capital requirements for each of the projects over the next 6 quarters. In addition, the table shows the projected capital available during each quarter, along with the net present value of the return expected for each project.

The question facing the company is which of the four projects to commit to now. Although Allen would like to get a firm answer as to which of the projects he should go with, for now he would like you to formulate a model which could be used later to arrive at the answer.

CASE 6B
SCHWANKE PAPER PRODUCTS, INC.

As usual, William Schwanke III was hurrying to make his airline connection. This time the trip had him hitting seven cities in nine days. The schedule was hectic, and the pace that he had been operating under the past several weeks was beginning to take its toll. He actually found himself looking forward to the plane ride, since it would provide the chance to sit back and reflect on the many things that were happening.

William Schwanke III is the third-generation president of Schwanke Paper Products, Inc., located near Portland, Maine. His grandfather founded the company in the early 1900s, and his father assumed control in 1954. When his father retired in 1986, William took over. Although the company had been doing well financially prior to 1986, since William took over, business has boomed. This is partly due to William's aggressive expansion of the company's production facilities. In fact, the first stop on his current schedule takes him to a facility near Grants Pass, Oregon, where a new paper plant is within 6 months of completion. The plane ride will give William some time to sort out several issues that he wants to bring up with Evelyn Cloud, who will be general manager of the new plant. An important issue is staffing the plant when it opens.

Table 6C-1 CAPITAL REQUIRED FOR PROPOSED NEW PROJECTS ($000,000)

Proposed Project	Quarter						Net Present Value
	1	2	3	4	5	6	
1	3.5	0	0	0	0	0	270,000
2	0	7	2	3	0	0	400,000
3	1.2	3	2.5	2	2	1	400,000
4	6	2	0	0	2	1	500,000
Available capital	7	8	4	3	6	3	

Plans call for 250 production-line workers and 100 professional (engineer, manager, quality control) positions. Recruiting costs typically run about $1500 for each line worker and $4000 for each professional position. Because of promises made to the state government to gain favorable tax rates on the company's real estate, Schwanke Paper is expected to hire at least 70% of the line workers and 30% of the professional staff from within Oregon.

William jotted down several specific goals that he would propose to Evelyn with respect to the upcoming staffing at the plant:

1. Hire 250 line workers and 100 professional staff if possible. If these levels cannot be reached, get as close to them as possible.
2. Keep recruiting expenses below $800,000 if possible. If not, keep the amount over $800,000 to a minimum.
3. Try to meet the Oregon vs. non-Oregon ratios for both types of workers. If that can't be done, at least minimize the amount by which they underachieve the goal.

As William and Evelyn discussed the staffing issue on their trip between Medford and Grants Pass, Evelyn convinced William that some other issues needed to be included in the staffing plan. Specifically, she told him that prescreening work done so far indicated that hiring experienced employees from Oregon would be difficult and that training would be required. Because this would cost a substantial amount, hiring Oregon line workers would be 25% more costly than hiring experienced out-of-state employees. Also, Oregon-based professional people would be 40% more expensive. This was not the sort of thing that William wanted to hear after a long plane ride. Upon reflection, he decided that recruiting costs, while still targeted for $800,000, must not exceed $1.3 million. He also said the most important goal was to hire the necessary number of people. William figured that this goal was twice as important as that of meeting the Oregon quotas and 10 times as important as meeting the $800,000 goal.

As William and Evelyn continued to discuss the staffing issue, they began to see that some planning was needed to determine how many of each type of worker to recruit and from where. As they headed to dinner, William authorized Evelyn to get some help with this planning process.

Chapter 7

FORECASTING TECHNIQUES

Chapter Outline

Why You Need to Know

No organization, large or small, can function effectively without a forecast for the goods or services it provides. A retail clothing store must forecast the demand for shirts in various sizes. The concessionaire at Dodger Stadium in Los Angeles must forecast each game's attendance to determine how many soft drinks and hot dogs to have on hand. Your state's elected officials must forecast tax revenue in order to establish a budget each year. These are only a few of the instances in which forecasting is required. For many organizations, the success of the forecasting effort will play a major role in determining the general success of the organization.

One forecast we can make with great confidence is that when you graduate and join an organization in the public or private sector, you will be asked to prepare forecasts. You won't have access to a crystal ball on which to rely for an accurate prediction of the future. Fortunately, if you have learned the material presented in this chapter, you will have a basic understanding of forecasting and of how and when to apply various forecasting techniques. We urge you to focus on the material in this chapter and take with you the tools which will give you a competitive advantage over those who are not familiar with forecasting techniques.

Chapter Objectives

This chapter introduces some of the most frequently used forecasting models, focusing on where the models are applied and the conditions under which each is appropriate.

The specific objectives of this chapter are:

1. To introduce the basic steps in developing and implementing forecasting models.
2. To discuss the concept of time-series data and the components present in a time series.
3. To introduce the following smoothing-based forecasting models: moving average, weighted moving average, single and double exponential smoothing.
4. To introduce trend-based forecasting models, including: linear trend, nonlinear trend, seasonally adjusted trend.
5. To introduce regression-based forecasting models, including: indicator-variable models, autoregressive models, mixed models.
6. To discuss the role of qualitative forecasting techniques.

7-1 HISTORICAL OVERVIEW

The fact that individuals and organizations can make better decisions if they have good forecasts of future conditions should be obvious. In practical applications, hardly anything is more important to most organizations, including national governments, than a forecast of future economic conditions. The President of the United States has a special team of experts, called the Council of Economic Advisors, whose task is to provide and interpret economic forecasts. At the government level, forecasts are used to set taxes, and establish monetary and fiscal policies. At the organizational level, forecasts are used to make decisions on hiring, research and development, and expansion.

The need for good forecasts has been known for thousands of years. The forecast that Joseph made for the pharaoh for seven good years followed by seven bad may still be better known than any current example. Joseph's forecast was extremely accurate, and he was well rewarded. While Joseph may have had special insight into what was going to happen, over the years since then, forecasters have relied primarily on intuition, or a special feel for how conditions were going to change. Only since the 1930s has any sort of organized forecasting methodology based on quantitative techniques been developed. The field of macroeconomics is, to a large extent, an effort to explain the causes of events in the national economy and to use these explanations to predict future consequences of current actions.

The earliest efforts at forecasting generally focused on identifying causes, or groups of causes, for the general ups and downs that occur in the national economy. These efforts were largely intuitive and relied on a minimum amount of actual data, perhaps because little data were available. One of the earliest methods of forecasting was developed by Warren Persons who, early in this century, described a method of defining predictable ups and downs in national economic data. About the same time, the National Bureau of Economic research developed an alternative means for analyzing economic data.

While Person's model has been the most widely used, both it and the Bureau's model were based on relatively scarce empirical data. The stock market crash in 1929 and the severe depression that followed through the 1930s were unexpected in both severity and timing. Economists recognized the need for more sophisticated data-gathering and statistical forecasting techniques in order to better forecast these types of major changes in the economy. The purposes of the data-gathering activity during this period were to be able to understand why economic conditions were so bad and to be able to arrive at some measurement that would indicate when conditions would improve.

While government agencies and private organizations alike took up the task of data gathering in earnest, the level of analysis was limited. A number of statistical forecasting techniques were proposed between 1930 and 1960, but their general application was limited due to the computational burden imposed by the techniques when large data sets were used. However, the introduction of computers in the late 1950s opened up entirely new possibilities for forecasters. The computing capability of large computer systems meant that sophisticated analysis of large data sets could be performed. Since that time, organizations such as Data Resources Inc., Wharton Econometrics, and Chase Econometrics have been formed to provide economic forecasts for government and private clients. These companies have constructed very large mathematical models of the economy (called econometric models) that are used both to explain present movements in the economy and to predict future movements.

While large econometric models are used by organizations to predict major events in the national economy or in specific industrial sectors, they are generally too complex (and too costly to develop) to be useful for the inventory manager of a manufacturing plant trying to predict the demand next quarter for the items in the company's inventory. The problem of developing short-term forecasting models, requiring less data than the large models, was addressed by a group of people (Holt, Brown, Winters, and others) starting in the late 1950s. A broad category of forecasting techniques known as smoothing models emerged, and they are still among the most frequently used methods for making short-term forecasts.

The efforts to improve existing forecasting techniques and to develop new methods is ongoing. The references listed at the end of this chapter provide a number of alternative sources for expanding upon the historical perspective and the current status of the art of forecasting. The remaining sections of this chapter introduce you to some fundamental concepts associated with time-series analysis and forecasting.

7-2 INTRODUCTION TO FORECASTING

If you discuss forecasting with decision makers, they will often confuse forecasting and planning. **Planning** is the process of determining how to deal with the future. On the other hand, **forecasting** is the process of predicting what the future will be like. Forecasts are used as inputs for the planning process.

Experts agree that good planning is essential for an organization to be effective. Since forecasts are an important part of the planning process, decision makers need to be familiar with forecasting methods. In this section, we introduce some important terminology pertaining to forecasting and provide a basis for your study of the remaining sections in this chapter. There are two broad categories of forecasting techniques: qualitative and quantitative.

Qualitative forecasting techniques are based upon expert opinion and judgment. Section 7-7 introduces some of the more commonly used qualitative forecasting techniques. **Quantitative forecasting** techniques are based on statistical methods for analyzing historical data. Sections 7-4 through 7-6 introduce a number of frequently used quantitative forecasting approaches.

In general, quantitative forecasting techniques are used when: (1) historical data relating to the variable to be forecast exist, (2) the historical data can be quantified, and (3) one can assume that the historical pattern will continue into the future. If these conditions do not exist, qualitative forecasting techniques may be employed.

Decision makers who are actively involved in forecasting frequently say that it is both an art and a science. As in other areas of management science, the forecaster is engaged in the process of modeling a real-world system. Determining the appropriate forecasting model is a challenging task, but it can be made manageable by employing a model-building process consisting of the following three steps: (1) model specification, (2) model fitting, and (3) model diagnosis.

Model specification, or model identification, is the process of selecting the forecasting technique to be used in a particular application. As we will point out in later sections, guidelines exist for determining which techniques may be more appropriate than others in certain situations. However, you may have to specify (and try) several model forms for a given application before settling on one that is acceptable.

Model fitting is the process of determining how well a specified model fits past data. The idea is that if the future tends to look like the past, a model must adequately fit the past data to have a reasonable chance of forecasting the future. The forecaster will spend much time adjusting the model specification and estimating its parameters to reach an acceptable fit of the past data.

Model diagnosis is the process of analyzing the quality of the model employed. You will determine how well the model fits the past data, how well it performs in mock forecasting trials, and how well the model's assumptions appear to be satisfied. If the model is unacceptable in any of these areas, you will be forced to revert to the model specification step and begin again.

An important consideration when you are developing a forecasting model is to use the simplest available model which will meet your forecasting needs. The objective of forecasting is to provide good forecasts. You do not need to feel that a sophisticated approach is better if a simpler one will provide acceptable forecasts.

As in football, where some players specialize in defense and others in offense, forecasting techniques have been developed for special situations, generally dependent on the forecasting horizon. The **forecasting horizon** is the number of periods in the future covered by the forecast. This is also referred to as forecast lead time. For the purpose of categorizing forecasting techniques, the horizon or lead time is typically divided into four categories:

1. **Immediate term**—less than one month
2. **Short term**—one to three months
3. **Medium term**—three months to two years
4. **Long term**—two years or more

As we introduce various forecasting techniques, we will indicate the forecasting horizon(s) for which each is best suited.

In addition to determining the desired forecasting horizon, the forecaster must determine the forecasting period. The **forecasting period** is the unit of time for which forecasts are made. For instance, the forecasting period might be a day, a week, a month, a quarter, or year. Thus, the forecasting horizon consists of one or more forecasting periods. If quantitative forecasting techniques are to be employed, historical quantitative data must be available for a similar period. For instance, if we want weekly forecasts, weekly historical data must be available.

The frequency with which new forecasts are prepared is called the **forecasting interval.** The forecasting interval is generally the same length as the forecast period. That is, if the forecast period is one week, then we will provide a new forecast each week.

The concepts presented in this section are fundamental to forecasting. We will be introducing other important ideas in subsequent sections. In the following section, we discuss some issues related to time-series data and the components of a times series. Then, in section 7-4, we will begin our introduction to quantitative forecasting techniques.

7-3 COMPONENTS OF A TIME SERIES

Before we move on to a discussion of quantitative forecasting models, we have to lay some important groundwork. Most quantitative forecasting models have one factor in common: they use past measurements of the variable of interest to generate a forecast of the future. Past data, measured over time, are called **time-series data**.

The decision maker who plans to develop a quantitative forecasting model must analyze the relevant time-series data. Consider the case of an electronics manufacturing company which has been making videocassette recorders for the past 4 years. The company's forecast for next year should consider the pattern of sales over the prior 4 years. Relevant information would be whether sales have tended to increase or decrease and whether there have been particular times during a year when sales are typically higher than at other times. The forecasters could determine this information by performing a time-series analysis of the historical sales.

Table 7-1 presents the time-series data for the firm's VCR sales for the 4-year period. While these data can be analyzed in table form, to better observe the data's behavior a **time-series plot**—a two-dimensional representation of the time series—can be developed, as shown in Figure 7-1. By graphing the data, much can be observed about the firm's sales over the past 4 years. In fact, the time-series plot is an important tool in identifying the time-series components.

All time-series data have at least one of the following components:

1. Trend
2. Seasonality
3. Cyclical pattern
4. Random fluctuation

TREND COMPONENT

A **trend** is the long-term increase or decrease in a variable being measured over time. Figure 7-1 shows that the company's VCR sales exhibited an upward trend over the 4-year period. In other situations, the time series may exhibit a downward trend. For

Table 7-1 TIME-SERIES DATA FOR VCR SALES (THOUSANDS OF UNITS)

	Annual Sales			
Month	Year 1	Year 2	Year 3	Year 4
January	170	390	500	750
February	200	350	470	700
March	190	300	510	680
April	220	320	480	710
May	180	310	530	710
June	230	350	500	660
July	220	380	540	630
August	260	420	580	670
September	300	460	630	700
October	330	500	690	720
November	370	540	770	850
December	390	560	760	880

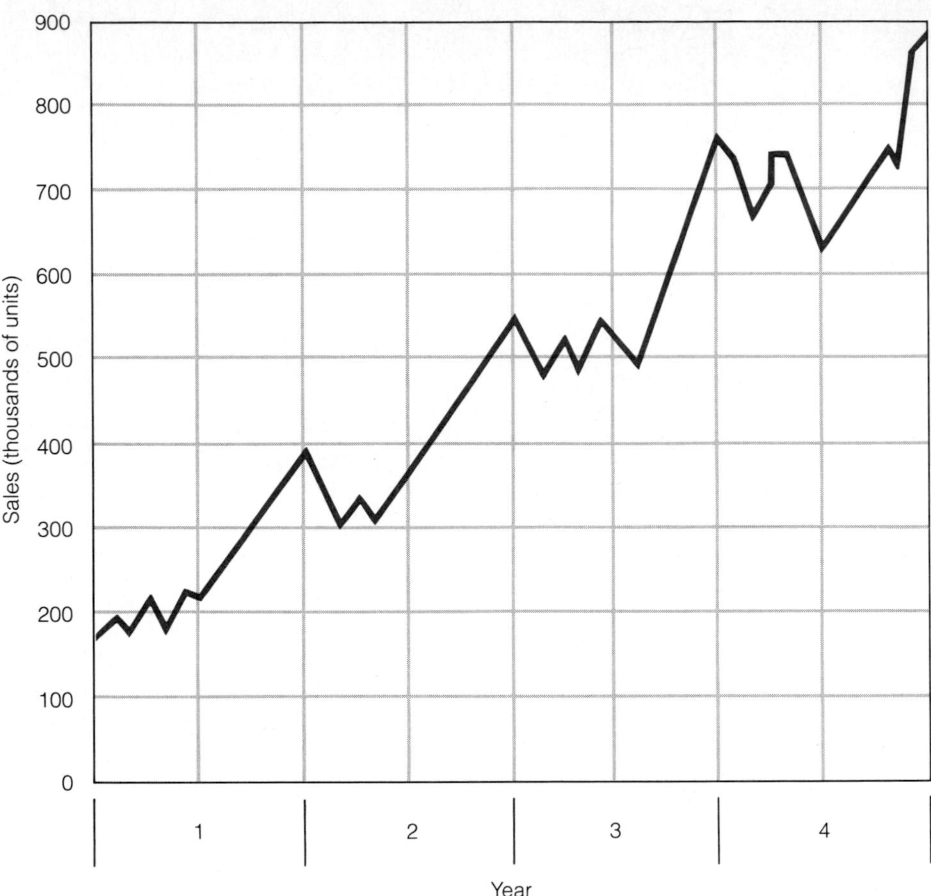

Figure 7-1
Time-series plot with upward trend: VCR sales

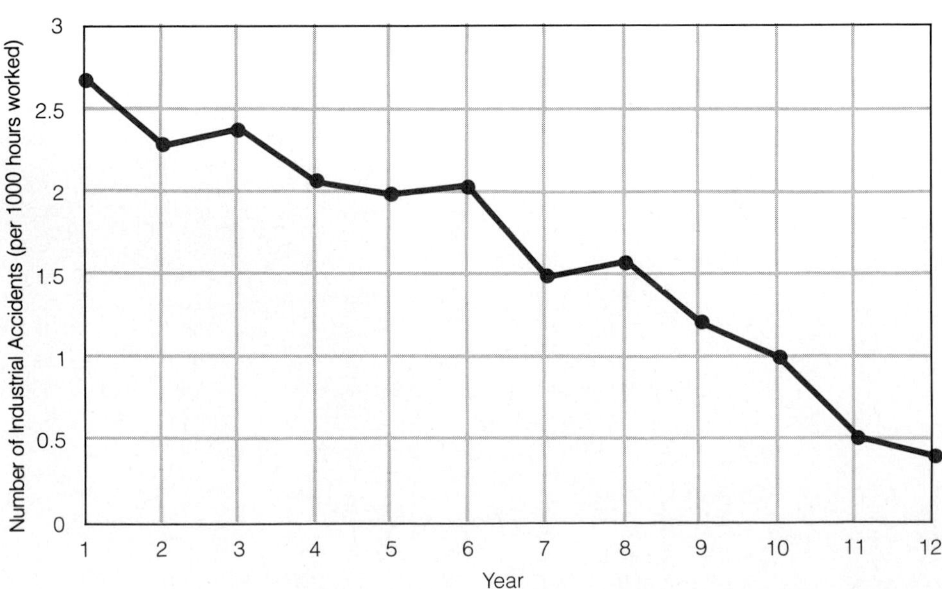

Figure 7-2
Time-series plot with downward trend

instance, Figure 7-2 shows the annual industrial accident rates at a lumber mill over the past 12 years. The managers might point to the decreasing trend in accidents as the result of improved safety practices by the company.

Trends can be classified as linear or nonlinear. A **linear trend** is a long-term increase or decrease in a time series in which the rate of change is relatively constant. In a **nonlinear trend**, the rate of change is not constant. Figure 7-3 shows examples of both classes of trends. In Figure 7-3*a*, the sales data exhibit a positive linear trend, since sales have tended to increase at a fairly constant rate. The sales data in Figure 7-3*b* show a nonlinear trend. Although sales have tended to increase over time, the rate of increase has diminished in recent periods. Figures 7-3*c* and 7-3*d* show further examples of the types of trends which a decision maker might observe.

SEASONAL COMPONENT

The **seasonal component** represents those changes, of predictable magnitude, that occur at the same time every year in the time series. For instance, in analyzing historical sales data for a retail toy store, we would see that sales increase in the fall

Figure 7-3
Linear and nonlinear trend patterns

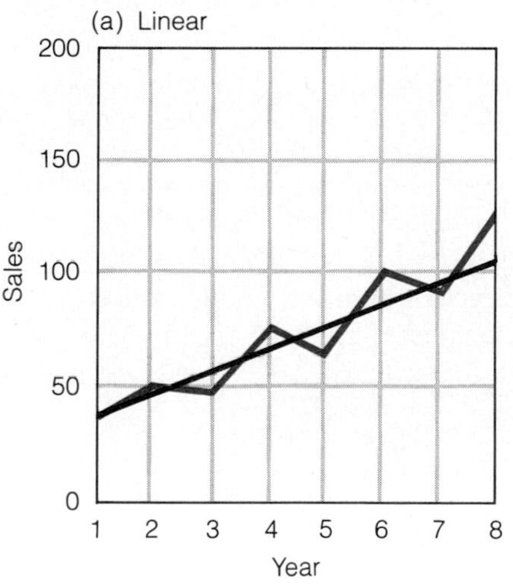

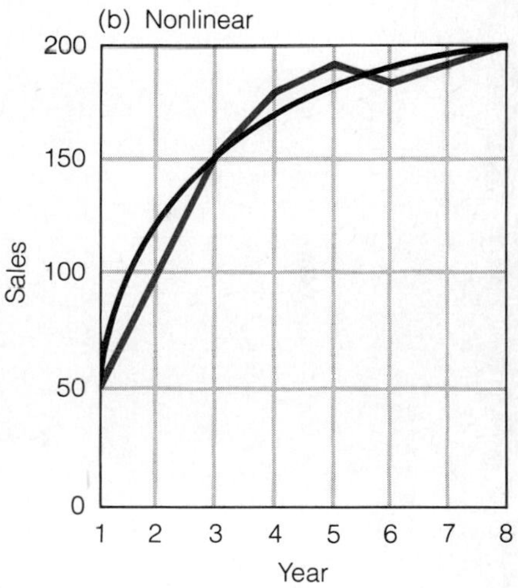

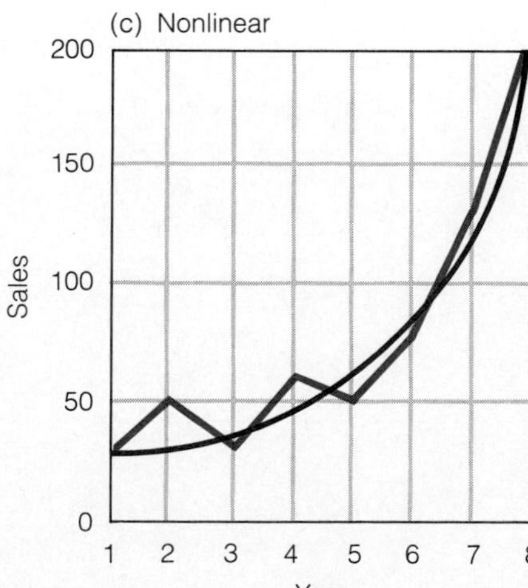

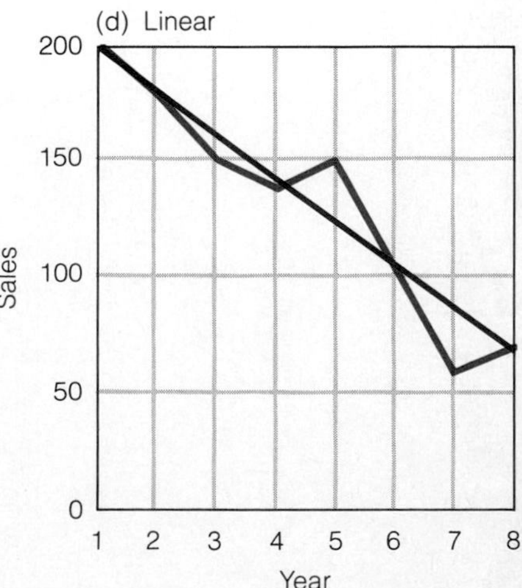

months leading into Christmas and then substantially decrease from January through March. Toy sales, then, exhibit a definite seasonal component. Automobile gasoline sales show a seasonal increase during the summer months and a decrease during the cold winter months.

In order to view seasonality in a time series, the data must be measured quarterly, monthly, weekly, or daily. Annual data will not show seasonal patterns of highs and lows. Figure 7-4 shows a plot of quarterly data for new housing starts in a county in Nebraska. As you can see, consistently higher-than-normal numbers of new homes were started in the third quarter, with lower-than-normal starts in the first quarter. The seasonality might be explained by weather factors. Figure 7-4 also presents a good example of a time series which has both a seasonal component and a trend component. While quarter 3 tends to have higher-than-normal housing starts each year, sales in the third quarter have also risen steadily over the 3 years. This increasing trend holds for the other quarters as well.

Seasonality can be observed in time-series data measured over time periods shorter than a year. For example, the number of checks processed daily by a bank may show predictable highs and lows at certain times during the month. The pattern of customers arriving at the bank during any hour may be "seasonal" within a day, with more customers arriving near opening time, around the lunch hour, and near closing time.

CYCLICAL COMPONENT

If we observe time-series data over a long enough period, we may see sustained periods of high values followed by periods of low values. The patterns of highs and lows which do not recur at fixed, predictable intervals or have fixed, predictable magnitudes over time identify the **cyclical component.** For instance, national economic measures such as the unemployment rate, gross national product, stock market indexes, and personal saving rates tend to cycle. The cycles vary in length and magnitude. That is, some cyclical time series may have longer runs of high and low values than others. Also,

Figure 7-4
Seasonality in a time series

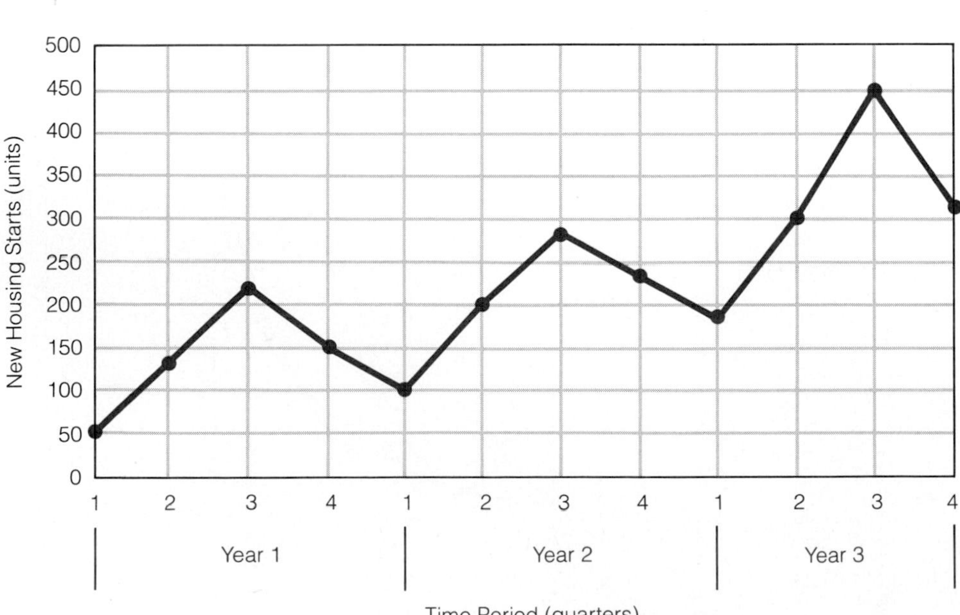

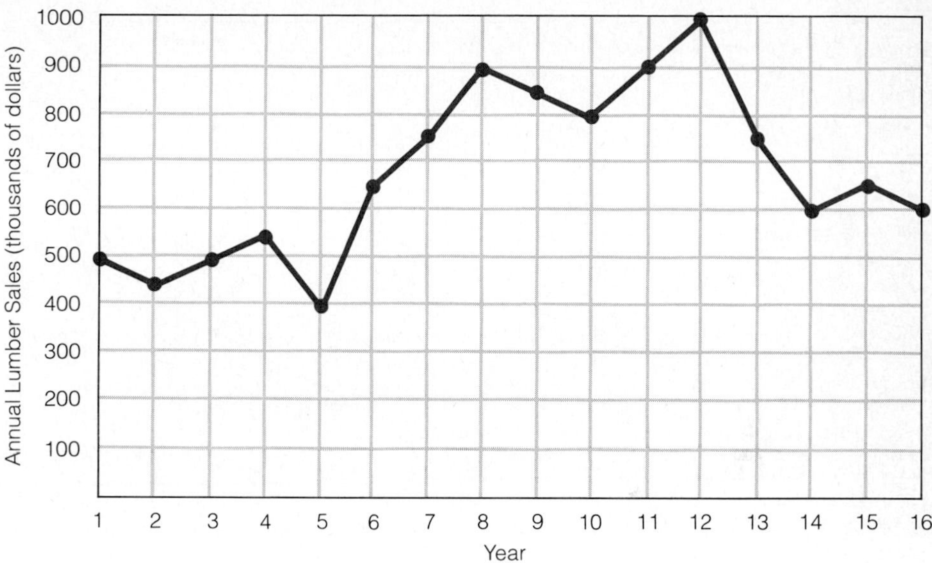

Figure 7-5
Cyclical pattern in a time series

some time series may exhibit deeper troughs and higher crests than others. Figure 7-5 shows sales data from a regional lumber company in which a cyclical pattern is present.

Companies that forecast sales for individual products often must deal with a product life cycle. That is, demand growth for a product follows an S-shaped curve, with slow growth in the early stages, followed by a period of rapid growth, and then eventual leveling off. Most products maintain the level stage for some period of time before beginning the declining stage. Figure 7-6 illustrates a typical product life-cycle curve. Most businesses are primarily concerned about how long the growth stage will last and when the declining stage will start.

RANDOM COMPONENT

While not all time series possess a trend, seasonal, or cyclical component, most will have the random component. The **random component** is the unpredictable fluctuations in a time series that cannot be attributed to a trend, seasonal, or cyclical compo-

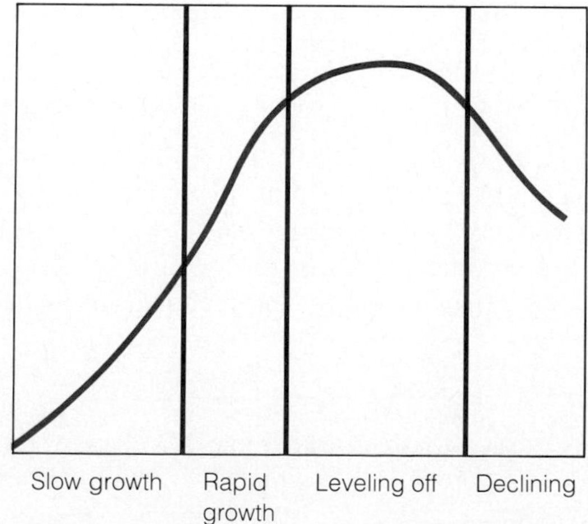

Figure 7-6
Typical product life-cycle curve

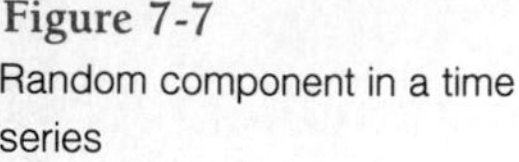

Figure 7-7
Random component in a time series

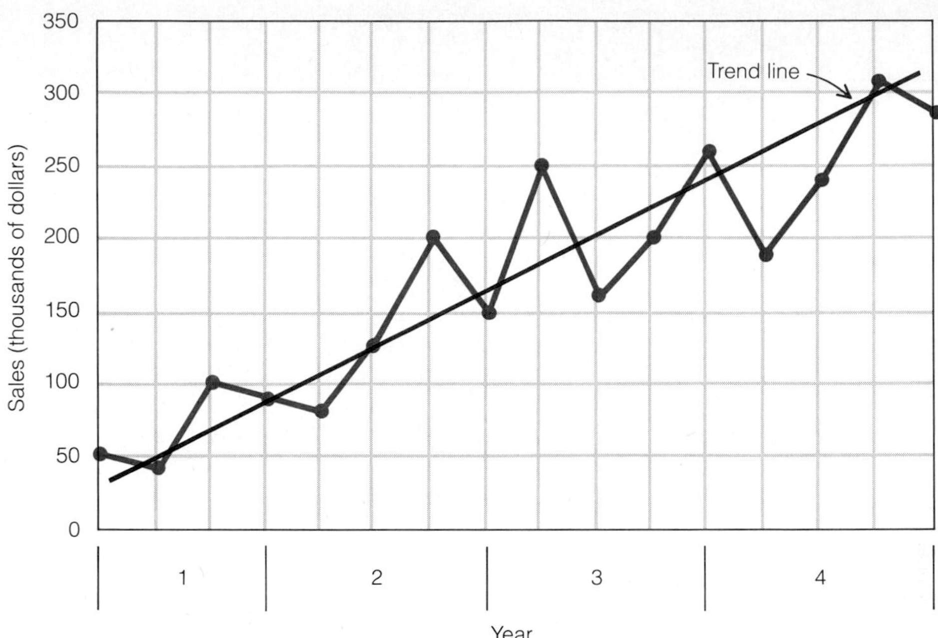

nent. It is often referred to as "noise" in the data. A time series with no pattern at all is completely random and contains only noise.

Figure 7-7 shows a time-series plot for an office furniture company's total sales. Note that there is an upward trend (represented by the trend line) in sales for the periods observed, but there are also fluctuations around the trend which are not seasonal or cyclical. These fluctuations represent the random component in the time series.

In the following sections of this chapter, you will see how various forecasting techniques deal with the time-series components. An important first step in forecasting is to identify which components are present in the time series to be analyzed. As we have shown, constructing a time-series plot is a good first step in this process.

7-4 TREND-BASED FORECASTING TECHNIQUES

As we discussed in section 7-3, some time series exhibit an increasing or decreasing trend. Further, the trend may be linear or nonlinear. A plot of the data will usually be very helpful in identifying which, if any, of these trends exist.

In this section, we introduce trend-based forecasting techniques. As the name implies, these techniques are used to identify the presence of a trend and to model that trend. Once the trend model has been defined, it is used to provide forecasts for future time periods.

LINEAR TREND FORECASTING

Figure 7-8 shows the plot for sales of ice cream produced by the Taft Ice Cream Company over a 10-year period. Table 7-2 displays the same sales data. The time-series plot in Figure 7-8 shows that sales have formed an increasing trend in the 10-year period.

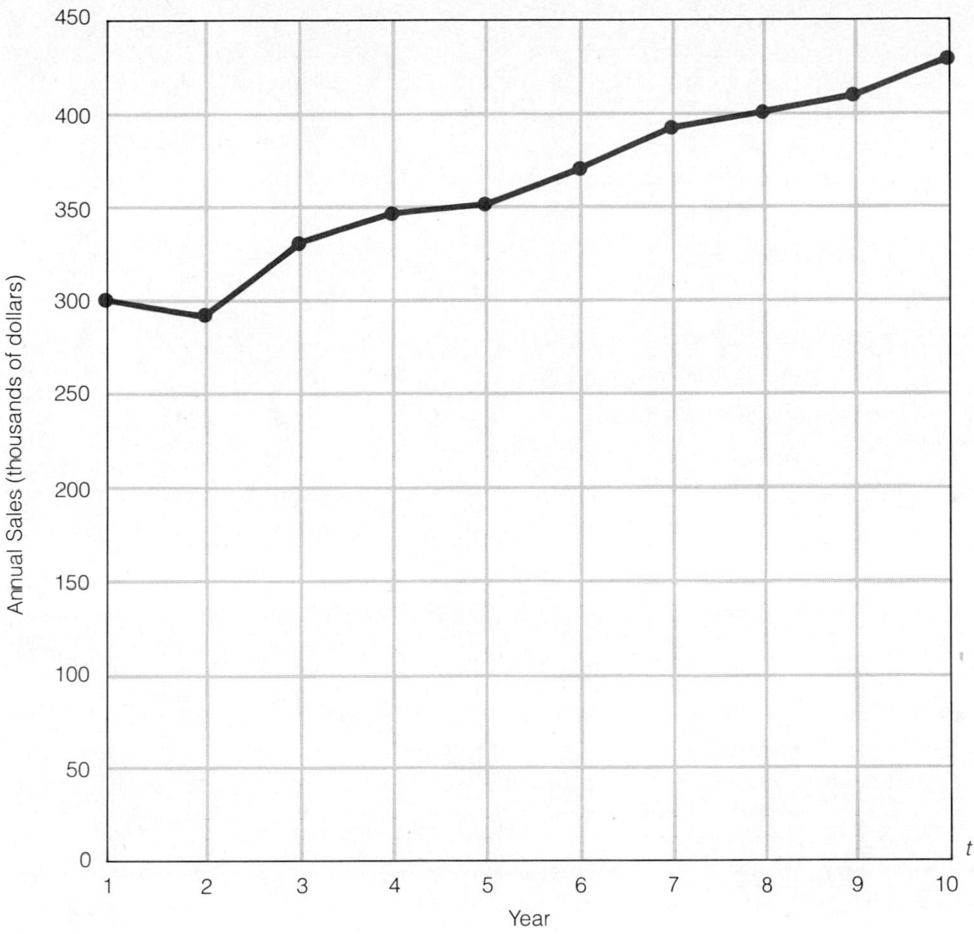

Figure 7-8
Taft Ice Cream Co. example: increasing sales trend

Executives at the Taft Ice Cream Company are considering expanding their ice cream maufacturing facilities and want to get a forecast of future sales. Recall from our earlier discussions that the forecasting process has three steps: (1) model specification, (2) model fitting, and (3) model diagnosis.

Model specification consists of identifying the appropriate forecasting technique for a given application. In the case of the Taft Ice Cream Company, we propose a linear trend (straight line) model.

In the model-fitting step, the specified model is actually fit to the historical data. Since we have specified a linear trend model, the process of fitting can be accomplished by either "eyeballing" the trend line through the data or by a statistical technique known as least-squares regression analysis.

To use the eyeballing method, the manager places a straight line through the data to "fit" the data. This method has great appeal, since it requires no formal training and can be done very quickly. However, fitting the line to the historical data is judgmental. Figure 7-9 shows two of the possible trend lines which might be placed though the Taft Ice Cream sales data by different decision makers. As you might expect, forecasts would differ depending on which trend line is selected.

Table 7-2 TAFT ICE CREAM: SALES DATA (THOUSANDS OF DOLLARS)

Year	Sales	Year	Sales
1	300	6	370
2	295	7	390
3	330	8	400
4	345	9	410
5	350	10	430

While eyeballing is a "quick-and-dirty" method for modeling the trend, a method using least-squares regression is generally preferred because it eliminates any bias which might be introduced by the forecaster. **Least-squares regression** is the process of fitting a line to a set of data to minimize the sum of the squared errors around the line.

When the model specification calls for a linear trend model, a trend line can be described as a function of time, using:

$$F_t = b_0 + b_1 t \tag{7-1}$$

where:

F_t = value of the trend at time t

b_0 = Y intercept of the trend line

b_1 = slope of the trend line

t = time

We let the first period in the time series be $t = 1$, the second period be $t = 2$, and so forth.

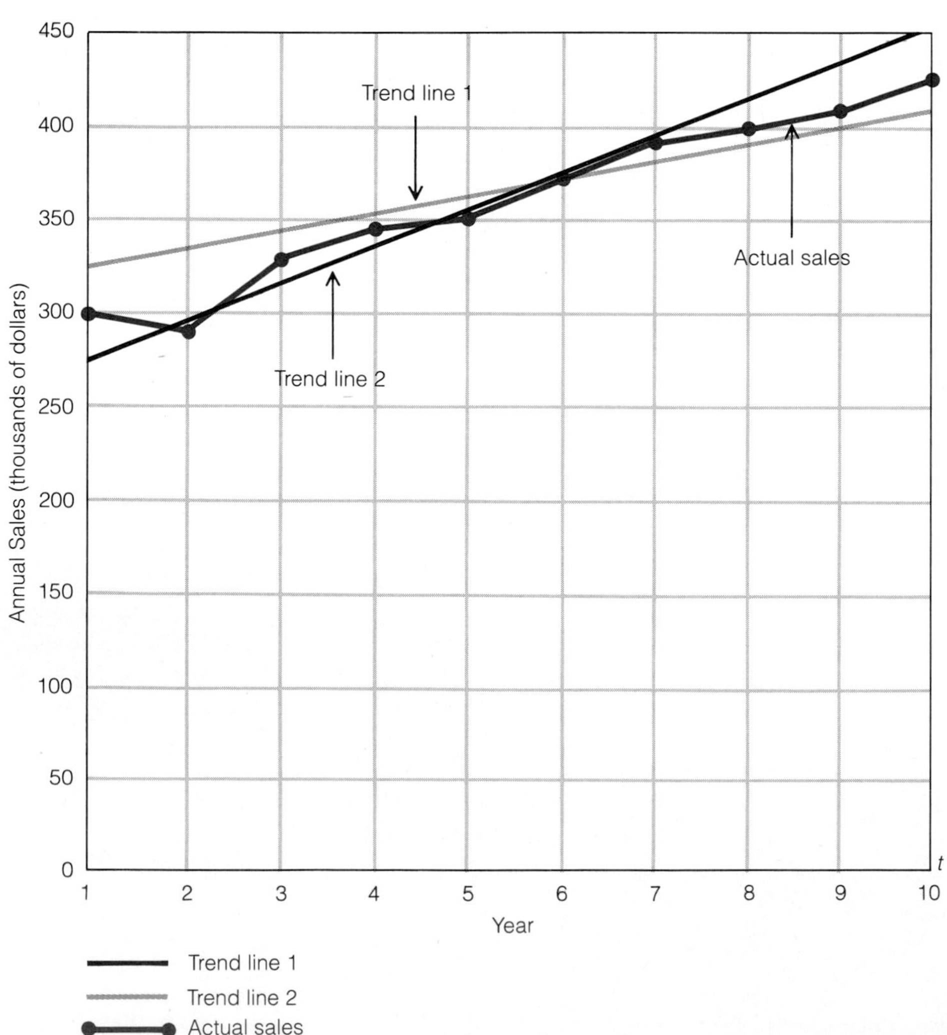

Figure 7-9
Taft Ice Cream: trend lines set by "eyeballing"

Equation 7-1 is the equation for a straight line. In Figure 7-9, each trend line could be defined by determining the appropriate intercept, b_0, and slope, b_1. When least-squares regression is used, these values are called regression coefficients and are determined so the trend line best fits the historical data. "Best fit" typically means that the sum of the squared distances between the data points, Y_t, and the trend line, F_t, is minimized. The distance between the actual value (Y_t) and the forecast value (F_t) is called the forecast **error** or **residual**. Thus, the trend line which best fits the data is the one which minimizes:

$$\Sigma(\text{error})^2$$

or:

$$\Sigma(Y_t - F_t)^2 \tag{7-2}$$

where:

Y_t = actual value of the time series at time t

F_t = trend (or forecast value) at time t

The term *least squares* refers to minimizing the quantity expressed in equation 7-2, frequently referred to as the **sum of squared errors**—the sum of the squared differences between actual and predicted values. The regression coefficients, b_0 and b_1, that will minimize the sum of squared errors are computed using

$$b_1 = \frac{\Sigma tY_t - (\Sigma t \Sigma Y_t)/n}{\Sigma t^2 - (\Sigma t)^2/n} \tag{7-3}$$

$$b_0 = \bar{Y} - b_1\bar{t} \tag{7-4}$$

where:

n = number of periods in the time series

$\bar{Y}$ = average value of the time series

$= \Sigma Y_t/n$

$\bar{t}$ = average value of t

$= \Sigma t/n$

Now let's consider the time-series data for the Taft Ice Cream Company from Table 7-2. The least-squares equation for the trend line is determined as follows:

Year t	Sales Y_t	tY_t	t^2
1	300	300	1
2	295	590	4
3	330	990	9
4	345	1,380	16
5	350	1,750	25
6	370	2,220	36
7	390	2,730	49
8	400	3,200	64
9	410	3,690	81
10	430	4,300	100
$\Sigma = 55$	$\Sigma = 3{,}620$	$\Sigma = 21{,}150$	$\Sigma = 385$

Then:

$$\bar{t} = 55/10 = 5.5$$

$$\bar{Y} = 3620/10 = 362.0$$

$$b_1 = \frac{21150 - [(55)(3620)]/10}{385 - (55)^2/10}$$

$$= 15.03$$

$$b_0 = 362.0 - 15.03(5.5)$$

$$= 279.335$$

The least-squares trend line for the Taft Ice Cream Company is:

$$F_t = 279.335 + 15.03t$$

Figure 7-10 shows this trend line plotted against the actual sales data.

Note that the above computations were performed manually. However, in most instances forecasters use statistical software to perform such computations. Solving forecasting problems using the software package MASTER, which accompanies this text, is described in section 7-8.

Comparing the Trend Line with Past Data

The slope of the trend line indicates that Taft Ice Cream Company has experienced an average increase in sales of 15.03 thousand (15,030) dollars per year over the 10-year period. The linear trend model's predicted sales value for periods $t = 1$ through $t = 10$ can be found by substituting for t in the forecast equation:

$$F_t = 279.335 + 15.03t$$

For example, for $t = 1$, we get:

$$F_1 = 279.335 + 15.03(1)$$

$$= 294.365 \text{ (or 294,365 dollars)}$$

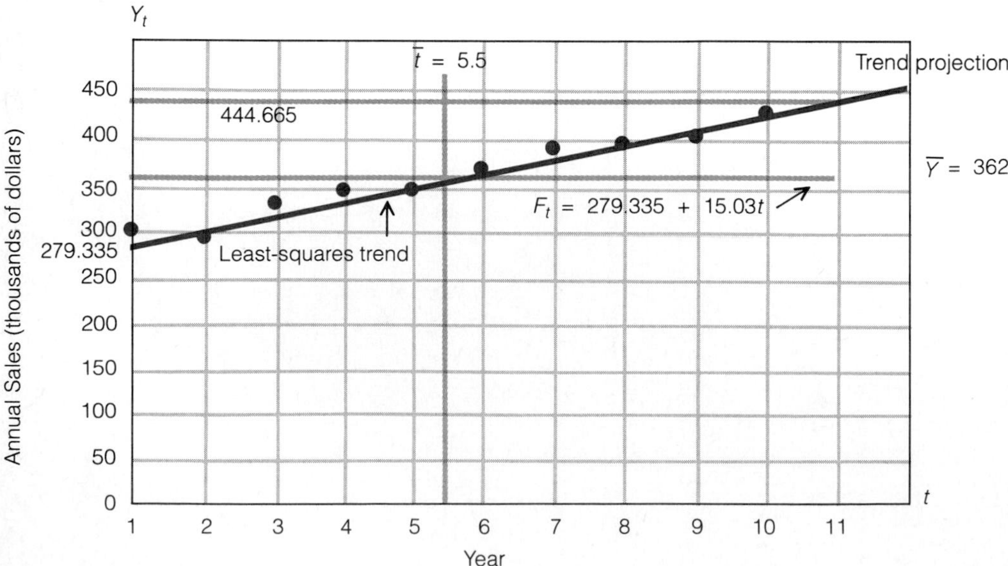

Figure 7-10
Taft Ice Cream: least-squares trend line

Table 7-3 TAFT ICE CREAM: FORECASTS AND RESIDUALS

Year t	Actual Sales Y_t	Forecast Sales F_t	Residual $(Y_t - F_t)$
1	300	294.365	5.635
2	295	309.395	−14.395
3	330	324.425	5.575
4	345	339.455	5.545
5	350	354.485	−4.485
6	370	369.515	0.485
7	390	384.545	5.455
8	400	399.575	0.425
9	410	414.605	−4.605
10	430	429.635	0.365
		Total	0.000

Note that the actual sales figures Y_1 for period 1 was 300 (or 300,000 dollars). The difference between the actual sales in time t and the forecast values found with the trend model is called the forecast error or residual. Table 7-3 shows the forecasts for periods 1–10 and the residuals.

Finding the residuals by comparing the trend-line values with actual past data is an important part of the model diagnosis step. The residuals measure how closely the model fits the actual data at each point. A perfect fit would lead to residuals of 0 each time. We would like to see small residuals and an overall good fit. In addition, the residuals should exhibit no systematic patterns. Two commonly used measures of fit are available: (1) **mean squared residual or mean squared error** (MSE), and (2) **mean absolute deviation** (MAD), which is the average of the absolute differences between the actual time-series value and the forecast value. Equations for determining MSE and MAD are given below:

$$\text{MSE} = \Sigma(Y_t - F_t)^2/n \tag{7-5}$$

$$\text{MAD} = \Sigma|Y_t - F_t|/n \tag{7-6}$$

where:

Y_t = actual value at time t

F_t = predicted value at time t

n = number of time periods

Table 7-4 shows the MSE and MAD calculations for the Taft Ice Cream example. These measures are particularly helpful when comparing two or more forecasting techniques. We can compute the MSE and/or the MAD for each forecasting technique. *The forecasting technique which gives the smallest MSE and/or MAD is generally considered to provide the best fit.*

True forecasts

While a decision maker is interested in how well a forecasting technique can fit the historical data, the real test comes with how well it forecasts future values. In the Taft example, we had 10 years of historical data. If we wish to forecast ice cream sales for

Table 7-4 TAFT ICE CREAM: MSE AND MAD COMPUTATIONS

Year t	Residual $(Y_t - F_t)$	Squared Residual $(Y_t - F_t)^2$	Absolute Residual $\lvert Y_t - F_t \rvert$
1	5.635	31.7532	5.635
2	−14.395	207.2160	14.395
3	5.575	31.0806	5.575
4	5.545	30.7470	5.545
5	−4.485	20.1152	4.485
6	0.485	0.2352	0.485
7	5.455	29.7570	5.455
8	0.425	0.1806	0.425
9	−4.605	21.2060	4.605
10	0.365	0.1332	0.365
Total	0.000	372.4240	46.970

MSE = 372.424/10 = 37.2424

MAD = 46.970/10 = 4.697

year 11 using the linear trend model, we substitute $t = 11$ into the forecast equation, as follows:

$$F_{11} = 279.335 + 15.03(11) = 444.665$$

This method of forecasting is called *trend projection*. Figure 7-10 shows how the forecast is determined graphically.

To determine how well our trend model actually forecasts, we would have to wait until the actual sales amount for period 11 is known.

Split Samples

As we just indicated, a model's true forecasting ability is determined by how well it forecasts future values, not how well it fits historical values. However, having to wait until after the forecast period to know how effective the forecast was doesn't help assess a model's effectiveness ahead of time. This problem can be partially overcome by using split samples.

Using **split samples** involves dividing the time series into two groups. We put the first (n_1) periods of historical data in the first group. These n_1 periods will be used to develop the forecasting model. The second group contains the remaining (n_2) periods of historical data, which will be used to test the model's forecasting ability. These data are called the holdout data. Usually, between 3 and 5 periods are held out, depending on the total number of periods in the time series.

In the Taft Ice Cream example, we have only 10 years of historical data, so we will hold out the last 3 periods and use the first 7 periods to develop the linear trend model. The computations are performed as before, using equations 7-3 and 7-4. Note that since we are using a different data set to develop the linear equation, we get a slightly different trend line than when all 10 periods were used. Table 7-5 shows the calculations. The trend line is:

$$F_t = 277.16 + 15.71(t)$$

This model is now used to provide forecasts for periods 8–10 by using trend projection. These forecasts are:

Year t	Actual Y_t	Forecast F_t	Residual $(Y_t - F_t)$
8	400	402.86	−2.86
9	410	418.57	−8.57
10	430	434.29	−4.29

Then we can compute the MSE and the MAD values for periods 8–10:

$$\text{MSE} = [(-2.86)^2 + (-8.57)^2 + (-4.29)^2]/3 = 33.34$$

and:

$$\text{MAD} = (|-2.86| + |-8.57| + |-4.29|)/3 = 5.24$$

These values could be compared with those produced using other forecasting techniques or evaluated against the forecaster's own standards. Other factors should also be considered. For instance, in this case, all three forecast values were higher than actual sales figures. This may imply that the linear trend model isn't the best model to use. Forecasting models which tend to overforecast or underforecast are said to contain **bias.** The quantitative measure of bias is:

$$\text{Bias} = \Sigma(Y_t - F_t)/n \tag{7-7}$$

or:

$$\text{Bias} = \Sigma(\text{error})/n$$

Table 7-5 TAFT ICE CREAM: LINEAR TREND MODEL WITH SPLIT SAMPLES

	Year t	Sales Y_t	tY_t	t^2
	1	300	300	1
	2	295	590	4
	3	330	990	9
	4	345	1380	16
	5	350	1750	25
	6	370	2220	36
	7	390	2730	49
Total	28	2380	9960	140

$$b_1 = \frac{\Sigma tY_t - (\Sigma t \Sigma Y_t)/n}{\Sigma t^2 - (\Sigma t)^2/n} \tag{7-3}$$

$$= \frac{9960 - (28)(2380)/7}{140 - (28)^2/7}$$

$$= 15.71$$

$$b_0 = \bar{Y} - b_1\bar{t} \tag{7-4}$$

$$= 340 - 15.71(4)$$

$$= 277.16$$

Bias can be either positive or negative. A positive value indicates a tendency to underforecast. A negative value indicates a tendency to overforecast. The bias in the forecasts for periods 8–10 in our example is:

$$\text{Bias} = (-2.86 + -8.57 + -4.29)/3 = -5.24$$

This means that, on average, the model overforecast sales for the 3 periods by 5.24.

Suppose, in the judgment of the decision maker, the linear trend model has done an acceptable job in forecasting periods 8–10. Then all available data (periods 1–10) would be used to develop a linear trend model, and trend projection would be used to forecast for future time periods by substituting appropriate values for t into the trend model:

$$F_t = 279.335 + 15.03t$$

However, if the linear model is judged to be unacceptable, the forecaster will need to try a different technique.

NONLINEAR TREND FORECASTING

As we indicated earlier, you may encounter a time series which exhibits a nonlinear trend. Figure 7-3 showed examples of nonlinear trends. When the historical data show a nonlinear trend, you should consider using a nonlinear trend forecasting model. A common method for dealing with nonlinear trends is to use an extension of the linear trend method. This extension calls for making a data transformation before applying the least-squares regression analysis.

Consider the situation of Harrison Equipment Company, which leases large construction equipment to contractors in the Southwest. The lease arrangements call for Harrison to perform all repairs and maintenance on leased equipment. Table 7-6 shows the repair costs for a crawler tractor on lease to a contractor in Phoenix, for the past 20 quarters. The data are also plotted in Figure 7-11.

Harrison Equipment would naturally be interested in forecasting future repair costs for the crawler tractor. The plot indicates a sharp upward trend. Recall that the first step in forecasting is model specification. Assume the forecaster starts by specifying a linear trend model. In the model fitting step we would use the least-squares equations, 7-3 and 7-4, and the time-series data in Table 7-6 to obtain the following

Table 7-6 HARRISON EQUIPMENT: EQUIPMENT REPAIR DATA

Year	Quarter	t	Repair Costs Y_t	Year	Quarter	t	Repair Costs Y_t
1	Fall	1	$1,459	4	Fall	13	$ 5,820
	Winter	2	1,620		Winter	14	5,809
	Spring	3	1,783		Spring	15	6,622
	Summer	4	1,794		Summer	16	8,092
2	Fall	5	2,191	5	Fall	17	9,426
	Winter	6	2,423		Winter	18	10,554
	Spring	7	2,677		Spring	19	10,998
	Summer	8	2,815		Summer	20	11,433
3	Fall	9	3,093				
	Winter	10	3,190				
	Spring	11	4,550				
	Summer	12	5,166				

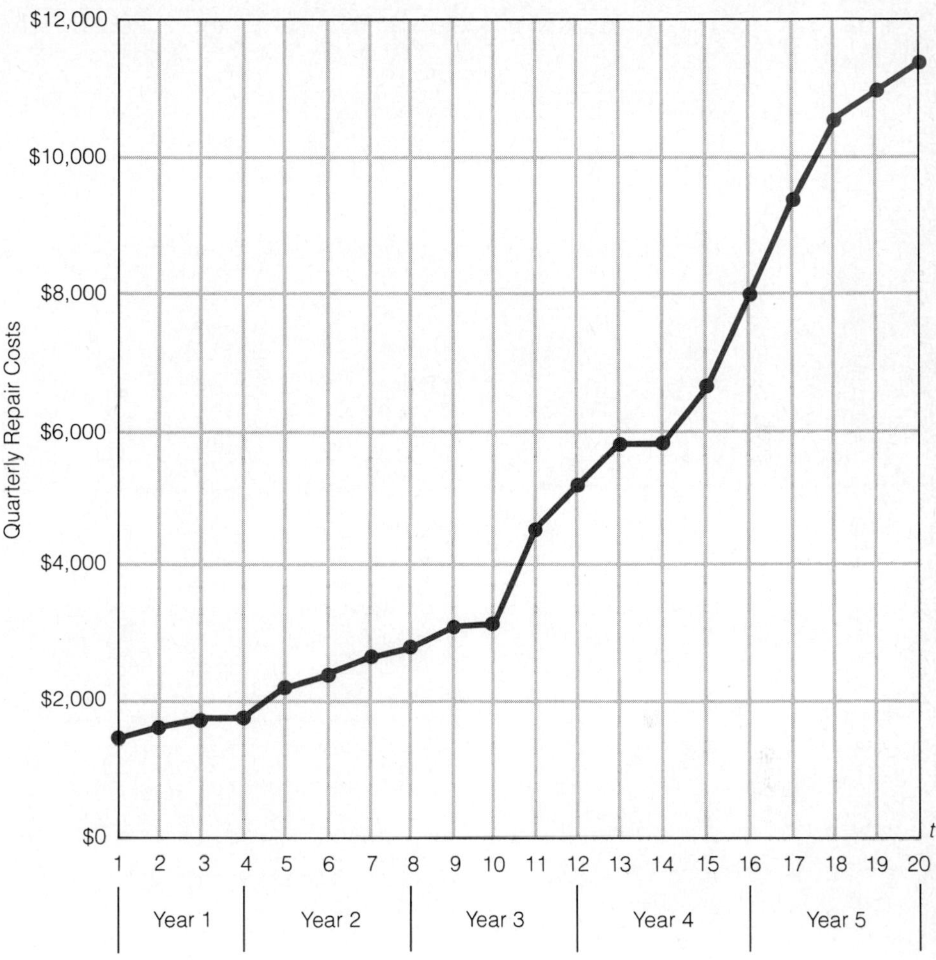

Figure 7-11
Harrison Equipment: actual repair costs (by quarter)

linear forecasting model:

$$F_t = -663.274 + 546.574(t)$$

The linear model's fit is illustrated in Table 7-7, which shows the predicted values and residuals for the 20 quarters of historical data. The MAD value is also shown. Figure 7-12 shows a plot of the trend line compared with the actual data. A close inspection of the data in Table 7-7 and the graph in Figure 7-12 indicates that the linear trend model may not be best for this case. Specifying a nonlinear trend may provide a better fit for these data.

To account for the growth trend shown in Figure 7-12, which starts out very slowly and then builds rapidly, the forecaster might consider transforming the time variable by squaring t. This transformation is suggested because the growth in costs appears to be almost exponential. Other nonlinear trends may require different types of transformations, such as taking a square root or natural log. Each situation must be analyzed separately. (See the text by Neter and Wasserman, listed in the Chapter References section, for further discussion of transformations.)

Once we have transformed the time variable by squaring each t value, we can estimate the least-squares regression trend line using equations 7-3 and 7-4 (or by

Table 7-7 HARRISON EQUIPMENT: TABLE OF RESIDUALS—LINEAR TREND

t	Y_t	F_t	$(Y_t - F_t)$		$\|Y_t - F_t\|$
1	1,459	−116.7	1575.70		1575.70
2	1,620	429.87	1190.13		1,190.13
3	1,783	976.45	806.55		806.55
4	1,794	1,523.02	270.98		270.98
5	2,191	2,069.59	121.41		121.41
6	2,423	2,616.17	−193.17		193.17
7	2,677	3,162.74	−485.74		485.74
8	2,815	3,709.32	−894.32		894.32
9	3,093	4,255.89	−1162.89		1,162.89
10	3,190	4,802.46	−1612.46		1,612.46
11	4,550	5,349.04	−799.04		799.04
12	5,166	5,895.61	−729.61		729.61
13	5,820	6,442.18	−622.18		622.18
14	5,809	6,988.76	−1179.76		1179.76
15	6,622	7,535.33	−913.33		913.33
16	8,092	8,081.91	10.09		10.09
17	9,426	8,628.48	797.52		797.52
18	10,554	9,175.05	1378.95		1,378.95
19	10,998	9,721.63	1276.37		1,276.37
20	11,433	10,268.20	1164.80		1,164.80
				Total	17,185.00

MAD = 17,185/20 = 859.25

using a computer software package like MASTER). We get the following equation:

$$F_t = 1302.3 + 26.296(t^2)$$

Table 7-8 shows the forecast values and residuals for periods 1 – 20. Figure 7-13 shows a plot of the trend line against the actual cost data. Note that the transformation of the t values provides a nonlinear trend line through the data. The model's fit is improved, as evidenced by a reduction in the MAD from \$859.25 (for the linear model) to \$288.31. Note also that the decision maker might consider trying other transformations in an attempt to achieve an even better fit to the data.

Forecasts for periods 21 and 22, using this latest model, are obtained using the trend projection method:

For $t = 21$:

$$F_{21} = 1302.3 + 26.296(21^2) = 12{,}898.84$$

For $t = 22$:

$$F_{22} = 1302.3 + 26.296(22^2) = 14{,}029.56$$

Using transformations often provides a very effective way of improving the fit of a time series. However, a forecaster should be careful not to get caught up in an exercise of "curve-fitting." One suggestion is that only explainable terms be used for transformations—terms that can be justified. For instance, in our example, we might well expect repair costs to increase at a faster rate as a tractor gets older and begins wearing out. Thus, the square transformation seems to make sense. However, a trans-

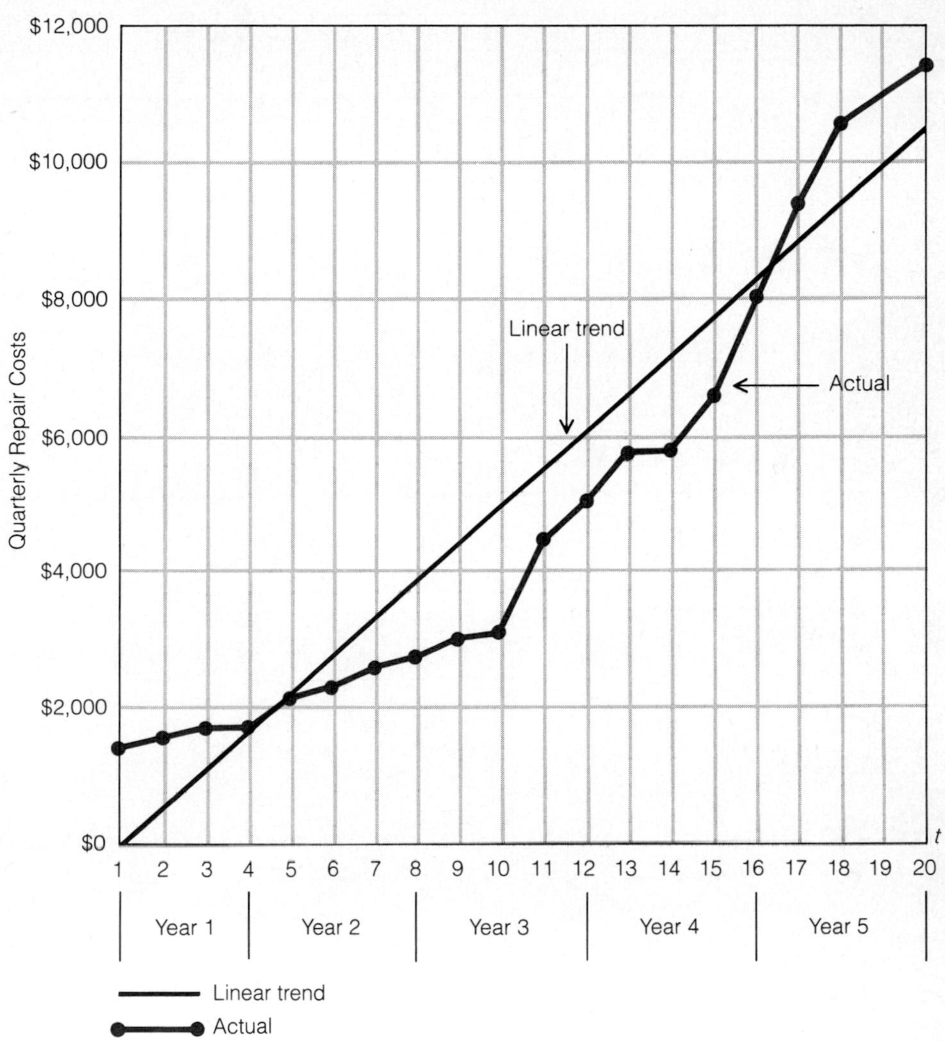

Figure 7-12
Harrison Equipment: linear trend vs. actual data

formation like sin t/cos t would be more difficult to justify, even if it did provide a better fit to the time series.

A word of caution: The trend projection method relies on the future behaving in a manner similar to the past. In the previous example, if equipment repair costs continue to follow the pattern displayed over the past 20 quarters, these forecasts may prove acceptable. However, if the future pattern changes, there is no reason to believe these forecasts will be close to actual costs.

ADJUSTING TREND FORECASTS FOR SEASONALITY

Earlier, we discussed seasonality in a time series. The seasonal component represents those changes in the time series that occur at the same time every year. Most businesses associated with the tourist industry are aware that their sales are seasonal. For example, in Fun Valley, Idaho, business peaks at two times during the year: winter for skiing and summer for golf and tennis. These peaks can be identified in a time series if the sales data are measured on at least a quarterly basis. Consider the Big Mountain Resort at Fun Valley. Table 7-9 shows total sales in each quarter for the past 4 years. The data are displayed in Figure 7-14.

Table 7-8 HARRISON EQUIPMENT: TABLE OF RESIDUALS—NONLINEAR TREND

t	Y_t	F_t	$(Y_t - F_t)$	$\|Y_t - F_t\|$	t	Y_t	F_t	$(Y_t - F_t)$	$\|Y_t - F_t\|$
1	1,459	1,328.57	130.43	130.43	11	4,550	4,484.09	65.91	65.91
2	1,620	1,407.46	212.54	212.54	12	5,166	5,088.90	77.10	77.10
3	1,783	1,538.94	244.06	244.06	13	5,820	5,746.30	73.70	73.70
4	1,794	1,723.01	70.99	70.99	14	5,809	6,456.26	−647.29	647.29
5	2,191	1,959.68	231.32	231.32	15	6,622	7,218.87	−596.87	596.87
6	2,423	2,248.93	174.07	174.07	16	8,092	8,034.05	57.95	57.95
7	2,677	2,590.78	86.22	86.22	17	9,426	8,901.82	524.18	524.18
8	2,815	2,985.22	−170.22	170.22	18	10,554	9,822.18	731.82	731.82
9	3,093	3,432.25	−339.25	339.25	19	10,998	10,795.13	202.87	202.87
10	3,190	3,931.87	−741.87	741.87	20	11,433	11,820.67	−387.67	387.67
								Total	5766.33

MAD = 5766.33/20 = 288.31

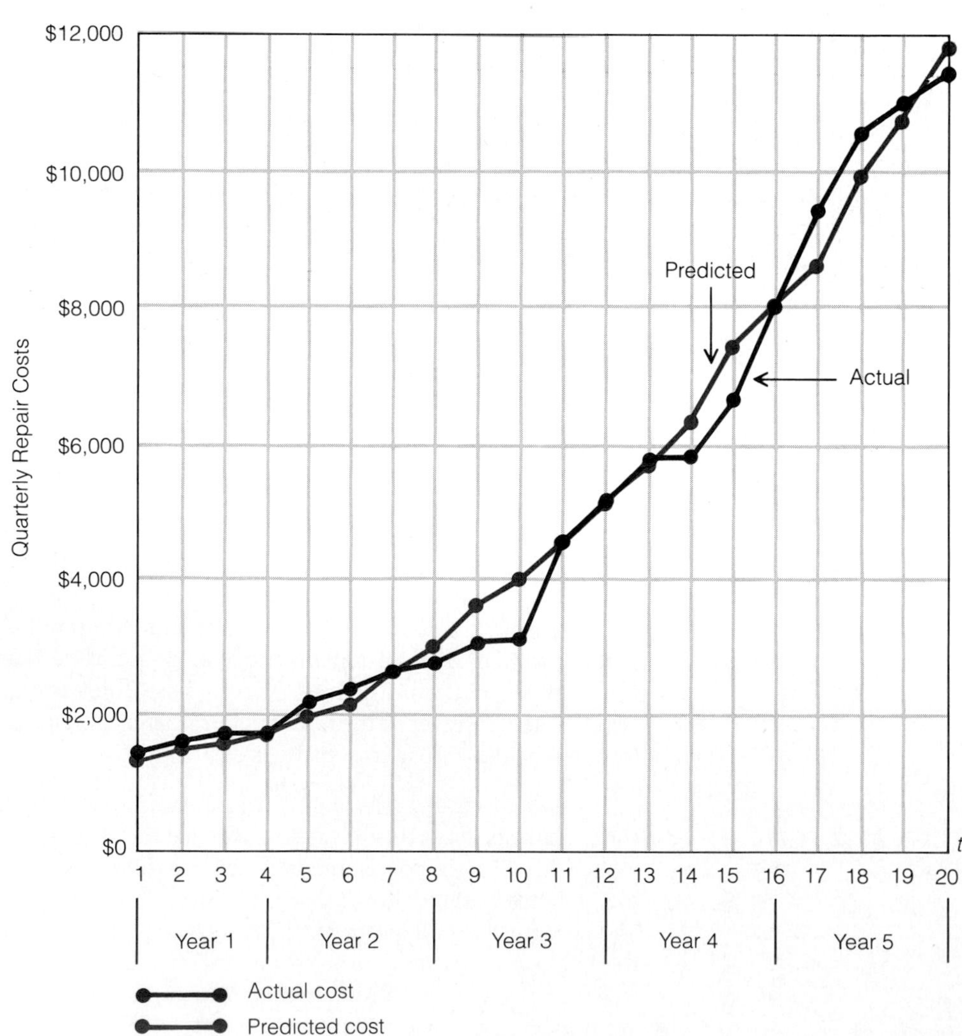

Figure 7-13
Harrison Equipment: nonlinear trend vs. actual data

Table 7-9 BIG MOUNTAIN RESORT: QUARTERLY SALES DATA

Year	Quarter	*t*	Sales ($000)	Year	Quarter	*t*	Sales ($000)
1	Winter	1	205	3	Winter	9	272
	Spring	2	96		Spring	10	110
	Summer	3	194		Summer	11	255
	Fall	4	102		Fall	12	114
2	Winter	5	230	4	Winter	13	296
	Spring	6	105		Spring	14	130
	Summer	7	245		Summer	15	270
	Fall	8	120		Fall	16	140

The time-series plot clearly shows the summer and winter quarters are the busy times. There has also been an increasing linear trend in sales over the 4 years.

Big Mountain Resort wants to forecast sales for each quarter of the coming year, and hopes to use a linear trend model. When the historical data reflect both a trend and seasonality, the trend-based forecasting model needs to be adjusted to incorporate the seasonality. This can be done by computing seasonal indexes.

A **seasonal index** is a number which quantifies the effect of seasonality for a given time period. For instance, when we have quarterly data, we can develop four seasonal indexes — one each for winter, spring, summer, and fall. A seasonal index below 1.00 indicates the quarter has values which are typically below the normal values for the year. On the other hand, an index greater than 1.00 indicates the quarter's values are higher than normal.

Computing Seasonal Indexes

The procedure for computing the seasonal indexes introduced here is the **ratio to moving-average** method. This method assumes the actual time-series data can be

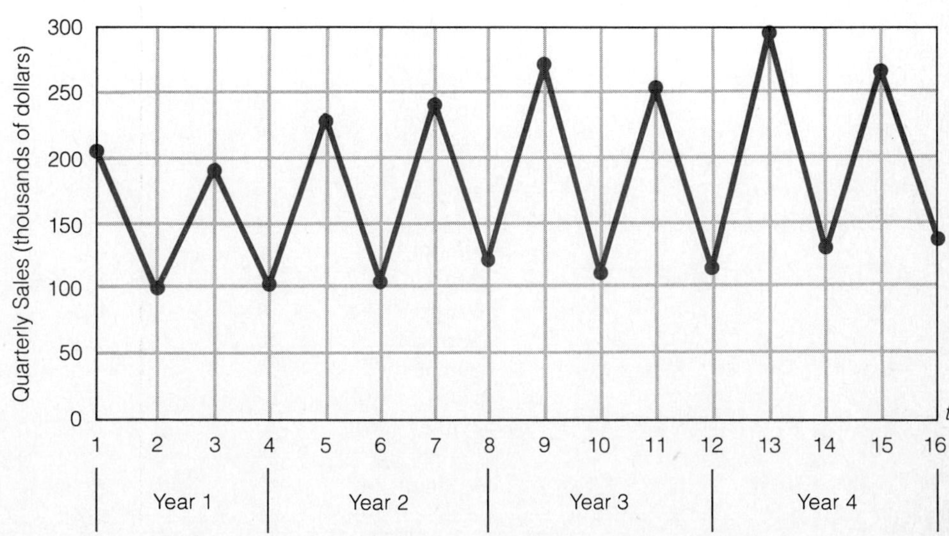

Figure 7-14
Big Mountain Resort: time-series plot for sales

represented as a product of the four time-series components and becomes the following *multiplicative model:*

$$Y_t = T_t \times S_t \times C_t \times I_t \tag{7-8}$$

where:

Y_t = value of the time series at time t

T_t = trend value at time t

S_t = seasonal value at time t

C_t = cyclical value at time t

I_t = irregular or random value at time t

The ratio to moving-average method begins by removing the seasonal and irregular components, S_t and I_t, from the data, leaving the combined trend and cyclical components, T_t and C_t. This is done by first computing successive four-period moving averages for the time series. A **moving average** is the average of n consecutive values of a time series. Using the Big Mountain sales data in Table 7-9, we find that the first moving average is:

$$(205 + 96 + 194 + 102)/4 = 149.25$$

The second moving average is found by dropping the value from period 1 and adding the value from period 5:

$$(96 + 194 + 102 + 230)/4 = 155.50$$

Table 7-10 shows the moving averages for the Big Mountain sales data. We selected a four-period moving average because we have quarterly data; with monthly data, a 12-period moving average would have been used. The moving averages in Table 7-10 are placed between quarters to properly reflect which data points are used in their computation.

Table 7-10 BIG MOUNTAIN RESORT: MOVING AVERAGES

Year	Quarter	t	Sales ($000)	Four-Period Moving Average
1	Winter	1	205	
	Spring	2	96	
				149.25
	Summer	3	194	
				155.50
	Fall	4	102	
				157.75
2	Winter	5	230	
				170.50
	Spring	6	105	
				175.00
	Summer	7	245	
				185.50
	Fall	8	120	
				186.75
3	Winter	9	272	
				189.25
	Spring	10	110	
				187.75
	Summer	11	255	
				193.75
	Fall	12	114	
				198.75
4	Winter	13	296	
				202.50
	Spring	14	130	
				209.00
	Summer	15	270	
	Fall	16	140	

Table 7-11 BIG MOUNTAIN RESORT: CENTERED MOVING AVERAGES

Year	Quarter	t	Sales ($000)	Four-Period Moving Average	Centered Moving Average
1	Winter	1	205		
	Spring	2	96		
				149.25	
	Summer	3	194		152.375
				155.50	
	Fall	4	102		156.625
				157.75	
2	Winter	5	230		164.125
				170.50	
	Spring	6	105		172.750
				175.00	
	Summer	7	245		180.250
				185.50	
	Fall	8	120		186.125
				186.75	
3	Winter	9	272		188.000
				189.25	
	Spring	10	110		188.500
				187.75	
	Summer	11	255		190.750
				193.75	
	Fall	12	114		196.250
				198.75	
4	Winter	13	296		200.625
				202.50	
	Spring	14	130		205.750
				209.00	
	Summer	15	270		
	Fall	16	140		

The next step in this procedure is to compute the *centered moving averages* by averaging each successive pair of moving averages. Table 7-11 shows these centered moving averages, which now are aligned with specific quarters. These values estimate the $T_t \times C_t$ part of the multiplicative model.

The next step is to estimate the $S_t \times I_t$ value. This is done by dividing the actual sales value for each quarter by the corresponding centered moving average. In notation form, this is:

$$S_t \times I_t = Y_t/(T_t \times C_t) \tag{7-9}$$

This value is called the *ratio to moving average*. Table 7-12 shows these values for the Big Mountain data.

The final step in determining the seasonal indexes is to average the ratios given by equation 7-9 for each of the four quarters. This is done as follows:

Year	Winter	Spring	Summer	Fall
1	—	—	1.273	.651
2	1.401	.608	1.359	.645
3	1.447	.584	1.337	.581
4	1.475	.632	—	—
Total	4.323	1.823	3.967	1.877
Average	1.441	.608	1.323	.626

Thus, the seasonal index for the winter quarter is 1.441. This indicates that winter-quarter sales for Big Mountain are 44.1 percent above normal for the year. Also, sales in the spring quarter are only 60.8% of normal for the year.

Table 7-12 BIG MOUNTAIN RESORT: RATIO TO MOVING AVERAGES

Year	Quarter	t	Sales ($000)	Centered Moving Average	Ratio to Moving Average
1	Winter	1	205	—	—
	Spring	2	96	—	—
	Summer	3	194	152.375	1.273
	Fall	4	102	156.625	0.651
2	Winter	5	230	164.125	1.401
	Spring	6	105	172.750	0.608
	Summer	7	245	180.250	1.359
	Fall	8	120	186.125	0.645
3	Winter	9	272	188.000	1.447
	Spring	10	110	188.500	0.584
	Summer	11	255	190.750	1.337
	Fall	12	114	196.250	0.581
4	Winter	13	296	200.625	1.475
	Spring	14	130	205.750	0.632
	Summer	15	270	—	—
	Fall	16	140	—	—

Deseasonalizing

A strong seasonal component may partially mask a trend in the time-series data. Consequently, to identify the trend you must first remove the effect of the seasonal component. This is called **deseasonalizing** the time series.

Again, assume the multiplicative model of equation 7-8 is appropriate:

$$Y_t = T_t \times S_t \times C_t \times I_t$$

Deseasonalizing is accomplished by dividing Y_t by the appropriate seasonal index, S_t:

$$T_t \times C_t \times I_t = Y_t/S_t \tag{7-10}$$

For time period 1, which is the winter quarter, the seasonal index is 1.441. The deseasonalized value for Y_1 is:

$$205/1.441 = 142.26$$

Table 7-13 presents the deseasonalized values for the Big Mountain sales data. The graph of these deseasonalized sales data, in Figure 7-15, indicates a gentle upward trend.

Once the data have been deseasonalized, the next step is to determine the trend. As in previous examples, we use the least-squares regression method and the deseasonalized data to compute the linear trend equation:

$$F_t = b_0 + b_1(t)$$

Equations 7-3 and 7-4 provide the values for b_1 and b_0. The resulting trend-line equation is:

$$F_t = 142.028 + 4.683(t)$$

Table 7-13 BIG MOUNTAIN SALES DATA: DESEASONALIZED TIME SERIES

Year	Quarter	t	Y_t	Y_t/S_t
1	Winter	1	205	142.26
	Spring	2	96	157.89
	Summer	3	194	146.64
	Fall	4	102	162.94
2	Winter	5	230	159.61
	Spring	6	105	172.70
	Summer	7	245	185.19
	Fall	8	120	191.69
3	Winter	9	272	188.76
	Spring	10	110	180.92
	Summer	11	255	192.74
	Fall	12	114	182.11
4	Winter	13	296	205.41
	Spring	14	130	213.82
	Summer	15	270	204.08
	Fall	16	140	223.64

We can use this trend line and the trend-projection method to forecast period $t = 17$:

$$F_{17} = 142.028 + 4.683(17) = 221.64$$

This is a **seasonally unadjusted forecast**, because the time-series data used in developing the trend line were deseasonalized. Now we need to adjust the forecast for period 17 to reflect the quarterly fluctuations. We do this by multiplying the unadjusted forecast values by the appropriate seasonal index. In this case, period 17 corresponds to the winter quarter, so the adjusted forecast is:

$$F_{17} = (221.64)(1.441) = 319.61$$

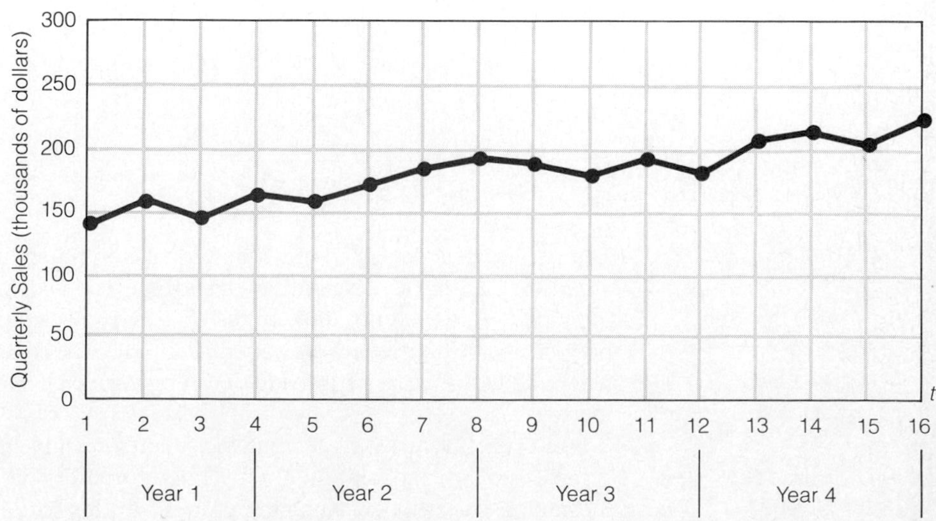

Figure 7-15
Deseasonalized sales data: Big Mountain Resort

The seasonally adjusted forecasts for each quarter in year 5 are:

Quarter (year 5)	t	Unadjusted Forecast	Index	Adjusted Forecast
Winter	17	221.64	1.441	319.61
Spring	18	226.44	.608	137.62
Summer	19	231.13	1.323	305.82
Fall	20	235.82	.626	147.54

Review of the Seasonal Adjustment Process

We can summarize the steps for performing a seasonal adjustment to a trend-based forecast as follows:

Step 1 Compute an n-period moving average where n is the number of periods in a year or season.

Step 2 Compute the centered moving averages.

Step 3 Isolate the seasonal component by computing the ratio to moving average values.

Step 4 Compute the seasonal indexes by averaging the ratio to moving averages for comparable periods.

Step 5 Deseasonalize the time series by dividing the actual data by the appropriate seasonal index.

Step 6 Use least-squares regression to develop the trend line using the deseasonalized data.

Step 7 Develop the unadjusted forecasts using trend projection.

Step 8 Seasonally adjust the forecasts by multiplying the unadjusted forecasts by the appropriate seasonal index.

You should use the seasonally adjusted trend model when the time series exhibits both a trend and seasonality. This process allows for a better identification of the trend and produces forecasts which are more sensitive to seasonality in the data.

7-5 FORECASTING USING SMOOTHING METHODS

The previous section on trend-based forecasting models applies to situations where the historical time series exhibits a trend. The least-squares approach offers a method for modeling the trend, and, by using trend projection, a forecast for future time periods can be developed. However, when the time series does not exhibit a trend, or when the least-squares approach does not work well, we need a different forecasting method.

A class of forecasting techniques called *smoothing models* is widely used in these situations. These models attempt to "smooth out" the random or irregular component in the time series by an averaging process. In this section we discuss four smoothing

Table 7-14 FIRST FIDELITY BANK: NEW ACCOUNTS DATA

Month t	New Accounts Y_t	Month t	New Accounts Y_t
1	40	7	40
2	30	8	35
3	45	9	45
4	50	10	50
5	60	11	40
6	40	12	50

techniques: moving average, weighted moving average, single exponential smoothing, and double exponential smoothing. The last of these, double exponential smoothing, offers a modification to specifically deal with trends.

MOVING-AVERAGE TECHNIQUE

We introduced the moving average in the discussion of how to seasonally adjust the trend-based forecasting model. However, the moving-average method is introduced as a stand-alone forecasting method in this section.

Consider this example involving the First Fidelity Bank. Bank managers are interested in forecasting the number of new accounts the bank will obtain next month. Table 7-14 presents historical data for the past 12 months. Figure 7-16 shows a graph of the time series. No apparent trend or seasonal components are present in these data.

A moving-average forecast model is developed by computing an n-period moving average as follows:

$$\text{Moving average} = (Y_1 + Y_2 + Y_3 + \ . \ . \ . \ Y_n)/n \tag{7-11}$$

For instance, in the First Fidelity Bank example, the first four-period moving average is found by averaging the values of Y_1 through Y_4:

$$\text{Moving average} = (40 + 30 + 45 + 50)/4 = 41.25$$

Figure 7-16
First Fidelity Bank: historical data on new accounts

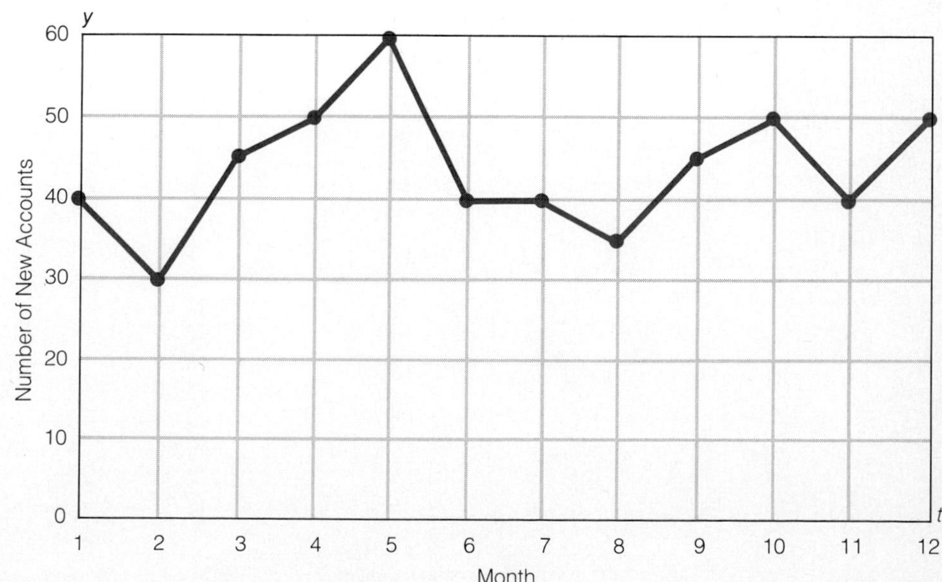

This becomes the forecast for period 5. The next moving average is determined by dropping Y_1 and picking up Y_5:

$$\text{Moving average} = (30 + 45 + 50 + 60)/4 = 46.25$$

Thus, the forecast for period 6 is 46.25 new accounts. Table 7-15 shows the four-period moving averages through period 12. Note that the forecast for period 13 is the average of the last four data values in the time series:

$$F_{13} = (45 + 50 + 40 + 50)/4 = 46.25$$

Using a four-period moving-average model, the bank managers forecast approximately 46 new accounts for next month.

The moving-average forecasting technique is an elementary smoothing method. Figure 7-17 shows a plot of the actual new accounts versus the forecast values. The forecasts follow a much smoother pattern than the original data.

The basic question when using a moving-average model is how many periods to include in the calculations. We used four periods in the First Fidelity Bank example. However, the forecast for period 13 will depend on how many periods are included. A five-period moving-average model will give a different forecast for period 13:

$$F_{13} = (35 + 45 + 50 + 40 + 50)/5 = 44$$

This forecast, produced from the average of the last five periods in the time series, is lower than the forecast from a four-period moving average.

To determine the "best" number of periods to include in a moving-average model, try various values and pick the one which gives the smallest MAD (or MSE). Keep in mind that more smoothing in the time series will occur as the number of periods in the moving average increases.

WEIGHTED MOVING AVERAGE

The **weighted moving average** is a variation of the moving-average approach. While the moving-average model assigns equal weights to each time-series value, the

Table 7-15 FIRST FIDELITY BANK: FOUR-PERIOD MOVING AVERAGE

Month t	New Accounts Y_t	Forecast F_t	Absolute Forecast Error $\lvert Y_t - F_t \rvert$
1	40	—	—
2	30	—	—
3	45	—	—
4	50	—	—
5	60	41.25	18.75
6	40	46.25	6.25
7	40	48.75	8.75
8	35	47.50	12.50
9	45	43.75	1.25
10	50	40.00	10.00
11	40	42.50	2.50
12	50	42.50	7.50
		Total	67.50

MAD = 67.50/8 = 8.4375

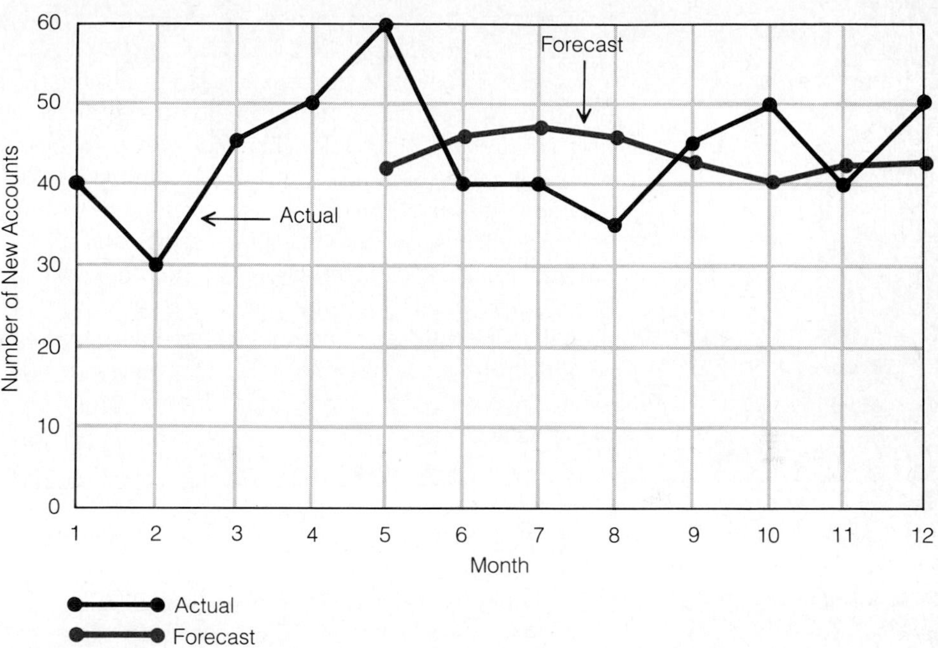

Figure 7-17
First Fidelity Bank: actual vs. forecast new accounts—four-period moving average

weighted moving-average method assigns different weights to each value. This might be practical if the decision maker believes the more current values are more important in determining the forecast.

Consider again the First Fidelity Bank example. Suppose that in a four-period moving-average model, the managers believe the most recent value should be considered 4 times as important as the oldest value. Further, the next most recent value should be considered 3 times as important as the oldest, with the third most recent value weighted twice the oldest value. Then, in obtaining the forecast for period 13, the weighted average for periods 9 through 12 is:

$$F_{13} = (\tfrac{1}{10})45 + (\tfrac{2}{10})50 + (\tfrac{3}{10})40 + (\tfrac{4}{10})50 = 46.50$$

Note that the sum of the weights must be 1.0. Note also that this model is simply an extension of the four-period moving-average model, where the weights are actually 1/4 for each value.

EXPONENTIAL SMOOTHING

The trend-based forecasting methods discussed in Section 7-4 are used in many forecasting applications. As we showed, the least-squares trend line is computed using all available historical data. Each observation is given equal input in establishing the trend line, thus allowing the trend line to reflect the past data. If the future pattern looks like the past, the forecast should be reasonably acceptable.

However, in most situations involving time-series data, the more recent the observation, the more indicative it is of possible future values. For example, this month's sales are probably a better indicator of next month's sales than would be sales from 20 months ago. However, the regression analysis approach to trend-based forecasting does not take this fact into account. The data from 20 periods ago will be given the same weight as data from this period in developing a forecasting model. This equal valuation can be a drawback to the trend-based forecasting approach. The weighted moving-average method is one means of overcoming this problem. Exponential smoothing is another.

With **exponential smoothing**, current observations are weighted more heavily than older observations in determining the forecast. Thus, if in recent periods the time-series values are much higher (or lower) than those in earlier periods, the forecast will tend to reflect this difference. The extent to which the forecast reflects the current data depends on the weights assigned by the decision maker.

We will introduce two classes of exponential smoothing models: single exponential smoothing and double exponential smoothing. Double smoothing is used when the time series exhibits a linear trend; single smoothing is used when no linear trend is present in the time series. Both single and double exponential smoothing are appropriate for short-term forecasting of one or two periods into the future and for time series which are not seasonal. Exponential smoothing models are generally considered to be the most frequently used quantitative forecasting models.

Single Exponential Smoothing

Exponential smoothing gets its name from the manner in which the influence of past data is reduced. The weight assigned to the most recent observation in an exponential smoothing model is called the **smoothing constant**, or **alpha** (α). Older data are assigned lower weights. The equation which describes this decline is:

$$\text{Weight}_t = \alpha * (1 - \alpha)^t \tag{7-12}$$

where:

t = data age

α = alpha (smoothing constant)

$0.0 < \alpha < 1.0$

In the example represented in Figure 7-18, a smoothing constant of $\alpha = .20$ is used. The weight assigned to the data for the most recent time period (age = 0) is:

$$\text{Weight}_0 = .20 * (1 - .20)^0 = .20$$

The weight assigned to data 1 period old is:

$$\text{Weight}_1 = .20 * (1 - .20)^1 = .16$$

Data 8 periods old have a weight of:

$$\text{Weight}_8 = .20 * (1 - .20)^8 = .0335$$

Figure 7-18 shows graphically that weights assigned to past observations decline in an exponential manner.

Just as their names imply, single exponential smoothing uses one smoothing constant and double smoothing uses two constants.

The equation for single exponential smoothing is:

$$F_{t+1} = F_t + \alpha\,(Y_t - F_t)$$

or:

$$F_{t+1} = \alpha\, Y_t + (1 - \alpha)F_t \tag{7-13}$$

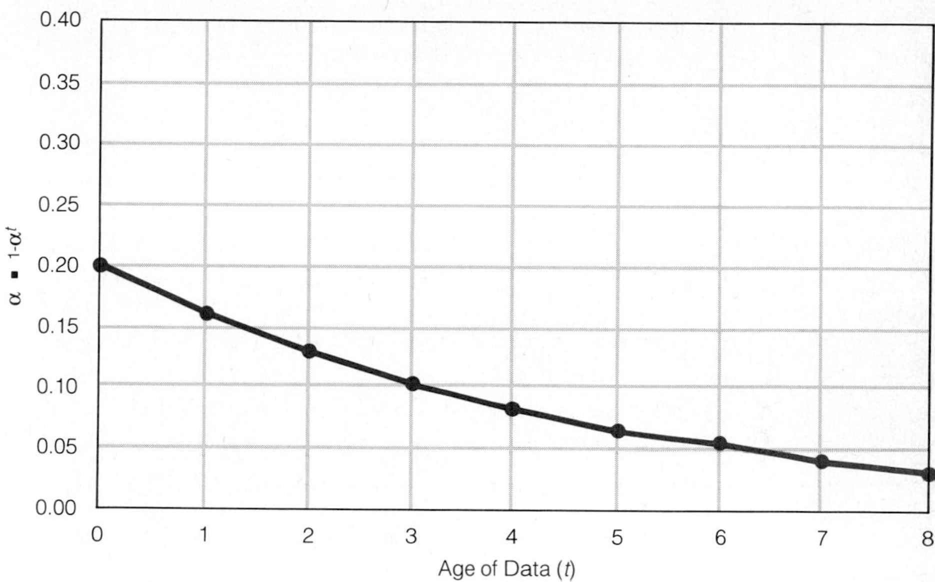

Figure 7-18 Weighting of past observations — exponential smoothing ($\alpha = .20$)

where:

F_{t+1} = forecast value for period $t + 1$

Y_t = actual value for period t

F_t = forecast value for period t

α = alpha (smoothing constant $0 \leq \alpha \leq 1$)

The logic of the exponential smoothing model is that the forecast made for the next period will equal the forecast made for this period, plus or minus some adjustment factor. The adjustment factor is determined by how far this period's forecast was from the actual value $(Y_t - F_t)$, times the smoothing value, α. The idea is that if we forecast low we will adjust next period's forecast up, but not by the entire amount of the error.

To demonstrate how the single exponential smoothing model is used, consider the 10 weekly sales figures for printed circuits at the Humboldt Electronics company in Northern California. These data are shown in Table 7-16 and are graphed in Figure 7-19. Suppose the current time period is the end of week 10 and we wish to forecast sales for week 11 using a single exponential smoothing model.

We start by selecting a value for α, the smoothing constant, between 0 and 1. The closer α is to 0, the less influence the current observations have in determining the forecast. Small α values will result in greater smoothing of the time series. Likewise, when α is near 1, the current observations have greater impact in determining the forecast and less smoothing will occur. There is no firm rule for selecting the value for the smoothing constant. However, in general, if the time series is quite stable, a small α should be used to lessen the impact of random or irregular fluctuations. Because the time series shown in Figure 7-19 appears to be relatively stable, we will use $\alpha = .20$ in this example.

The forecast value for period $t = 11$ is found using equation 7-13 as follows:

$$F_{11} = .20\, Y_{10} + (1 - .20)F_{10}$$

This demonstrates that the forecast for period 11 is a weighted average of the actual

Table 7-16 HUMBOLDT ELECTRONICS: PRINTED-CIRCUIT SALES DATA (THOUSANDS OF UNITS)

Week t	Sales Y_t	Week t	Sales Y_t
1	400	6	440
2	430	7	470
3	420	8	430
4	440	9	440
5	460	10	420

sales in period 10 and the forecast for period 10. The forecast for period 10 is determined by:

$$F_{10} = .20\ Y_9 + (1 - .20)F_9$$

Again, this forecast is a weighted average of the actual sales in period 9 and the forecast sales for period 9. We would continue in this manner until we get:

$$F_2 = .20\ Y_1 + (1 - .20)F_1$$

This requires a forecast for period 1. Since we have no sales data prior to week 1 from which to develop a forecast, a rule often used is to assume that $F_1 = Y_1$. This assumption is used to set the starting value for F. Because setting the starting value is somewhat arbitrary, you should obtain as much historical data as possible to "warm" the model and dampen out the effect of the starting value. In our example, we have 10 periods of data to warm the model before the forecast for period 11 is made. Note that when using an exponential smoothing model, the effect of the initial forecast is reduced by $(1 - \alpha)$ in the forecast for period 2, then reduced again for period 3, and so on. After sufficient periods, any error due to the initial forecast will be very small.

Before we would actually use the exponential smoothing forecast for decision-making purposes, we would want to determine how successfully the model fits the historical data. Unlike the trend-based forecast, which uses least-squares regression,

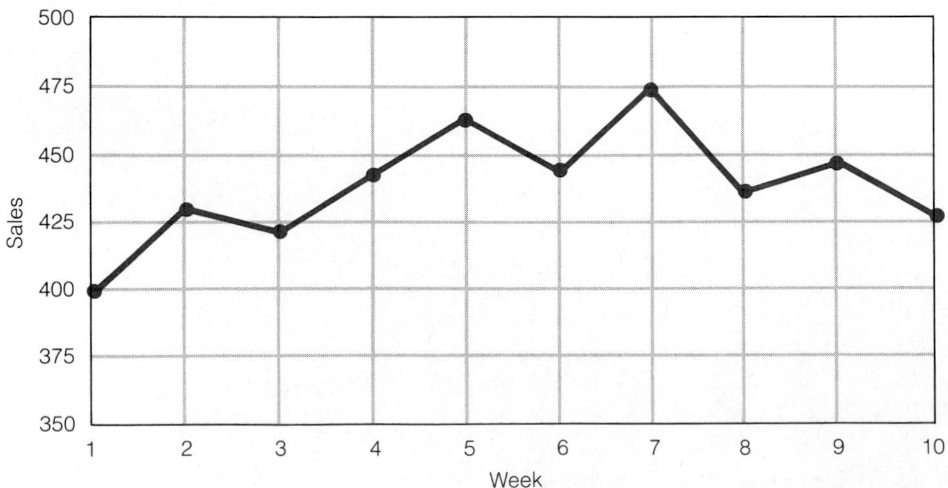

Figure 7-19 Humboldt Electronics: printed-circuit sales data

Table 7-17 HUMBOLDT ELECTRONICS: SINGLE EXPONENTIAL SMOOTHING, $\alpha = .20$

Week t	Sales Y_t	Forecast for Next Period F_{t+1}	Forecast for This Period F_t
1	400	400	400
2	430	406	400
3	420	408.8	406
4	440	415.04	408.8
5	460	424.03	415.04
6	440	427.23	424.03
7	470	435.78	427.23
8	430	434.62	435.78
9	440	435.70	434.62
10	420	432.56	435.70

there is no need to use split samples to test the forecasting ability of an exponential smoothing model, since the forecasts are "actual forecasts." The forecast for a given period is made before considering the actual value for that period.

Table 7-17 shows the results of using the single exponential smoothing equation for weeks 1 through 10. The column headed F_{t+1} represents the forecast made during period t for the next period, $t + 1$. Therefore, the last figure in that column, 432.56, is the forecast for week 11. The column headed F_t contains the actual forecasts for periods 2 through 10. These two columns sometimes cause unnecessary confusion. For example, the 406 in week 2 of the F_{t+1} column is the forecast made in week 2 (t) for week 3 ($t + 1$). It thus becomes the forecast value for week 3 in the F_t column.

Table 7-18 shows the MAD computation for the forecast model with $\alpha = .20$. Note that since you assume the forecast in time period 1 equals the actual sales in time period 1, when calculating the MAD the sum of the errors is divided by $n - 1$ rather than n. Figure 7-20 shows the plot of the forecast values and the actual values. This plot shows the smoothing that has occurred.

Table 7-18 HUMBOLDT ELECTRONICS: MAD COMPUTATION FOR SINGLE EXPONENTIAL SMOOTHING, $\alpha = .20$

Week t	Sales Y_t	Forecast F_t	Absolute Forecast Error $\lvert Y_t - F_t \rvert$
1	400	400	—
2	430	400	30
3	420	406	14
4	440	408.8	31.2
5	460	415.04	44.96
6	440	424.03	15.97
7	470	427.23	42.77
8	430	435.78	5.78
9	440	434.62	5.38
10	420	435.70	15.70
		Total =	205.76

MAD = 205.76/9 = 22.86

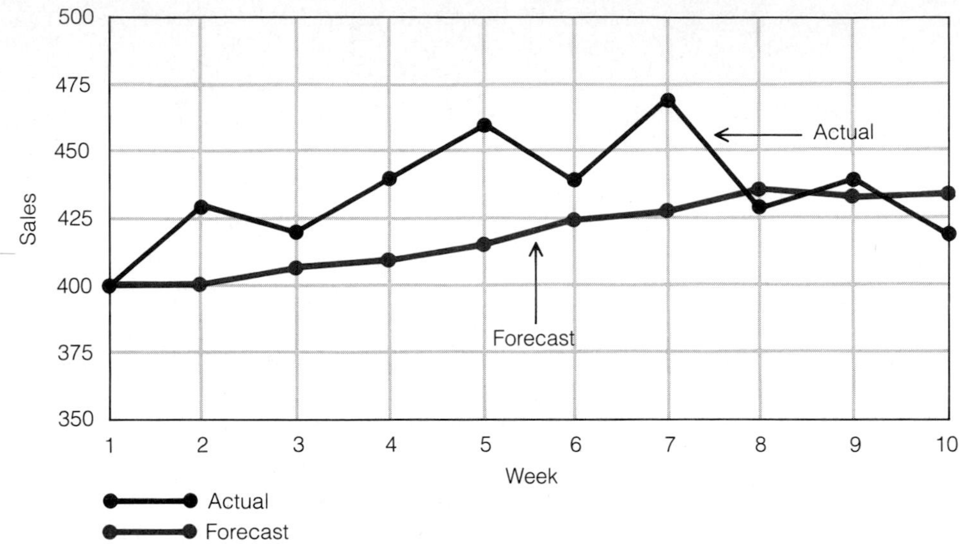

Figure 7-20
Humboldt Electronics example: actual vs. forecast sales—single exponential smoothing

Our next step would be to try a different α and repeat the process. Table 7-19 shows the results of using single exponential smoothing with $\alpha = .40$. Note that the MAD has been reduced from 22.86 to 19.51 by changing the α from .20 to .40. The forecast for period 11 using this latest model is:

$$F_{11} = .40(420) + (1 - .40)441.80 = 433.08$$

This is slightly higher than the forecast produced by the exponential smoothing model with $\alpha = .20$.

The exponential model is easy to update when new data become available. For instance, assume that sales for week 11 actually totaled 440 units. The forecast for week 12, using the model with $\alpha = .40$, is:

$$F_{12} = .40(440) + (1 - .40)433.08 = 435.85$$

Table 7-19 HUMBOLDT ELECTRONICS: MAD COMPUTATION FOR SINGLE EXPONENTIAL SMOOTHING, $\alpha = .40$

Week t	Sales Y_t	Forecast F_t	Absolute Forecast Error $\lvert Y_t - F_t \rvert$
1	400	400	—
2	430	400	30.00
3	420	412	8.00
4	440	415.2	24.80
5	460	425.12	34.88
6	440	439.07	0.93
7	470	439.44	30.56
8	430	451.67	21.67
9	440	443.00	3.00
10	420	441.80	21.80
		Total =	175.64

MAD = 175.64/9 = 19.51

As you can see, we do not need to go back and recompute the entire model, as would have been necessary with a trend-based regression model.

Double Exponential Smoothing

When the time series has an increasing linear trend, forecasts developed using a single exponential smoothing model will tend to be lower than the actual values. When the trend is decreasing, the forecasts will tend to exceed the actual values. In either of these two cases, the model exhibits bias. A double exponential smoothing model will reduce this problem because it can incorporate the trend component. The double exponential smoothing model is often referred to as *exponential smoothing with trend.*

In double smoothing, a second smoothing constant, **beta** (β) is included to account for the trend. Three equations are needed to provide the forecasts:

$$C_t = \alpha Y_t + (1 - \alpha)(C_{t-1} + T_{t-1}) \tag{7-14}$$

$$T_t = \beta(C_t - C_{t-1}) + (1 - \beta)T_{t-1} \tag{7-15}$$

$$F_{t+1} = C_t + T_t \tag{7-16}$$

where:

Y_t = actual value in time t

α = constant-process smoothing constant

β = trend-smoothing constant

C_t = smoothed constant-process value for period t

T_t = smoothed trend value for period t

F_{t+1} = forecast value for period $t + 1$

t = current time period

Equation 7-14 is used to smooth the time-series data. Equation 7-15 is used to smooth the trend, and Equation 7-16 combines the two smoothed values to form the forecast for period $t + 1$.

The Billingsley Insurance Company has maintained data on the number of automobile claims filed at its Denver office over the past 12 months. These data are listed in Table 7-20 and are graphed in Figure 7-21. The claims manager wants to forecast claims for month 13. The time series contains a strong upward trend, so a double exponential smoothing model might be selected.

As was the case with single smoothing, we must select starting values, now for C_t

Table 7-20 BILLINGSLEY INSURANCE: CLAIMS DATA

Month t	Claims Y_t	Month t	Claims Y_t
1	38	7	64
2	44	8	70
3	40	9	75
4	48	10	70
5	55	11	78
6	68	12	82

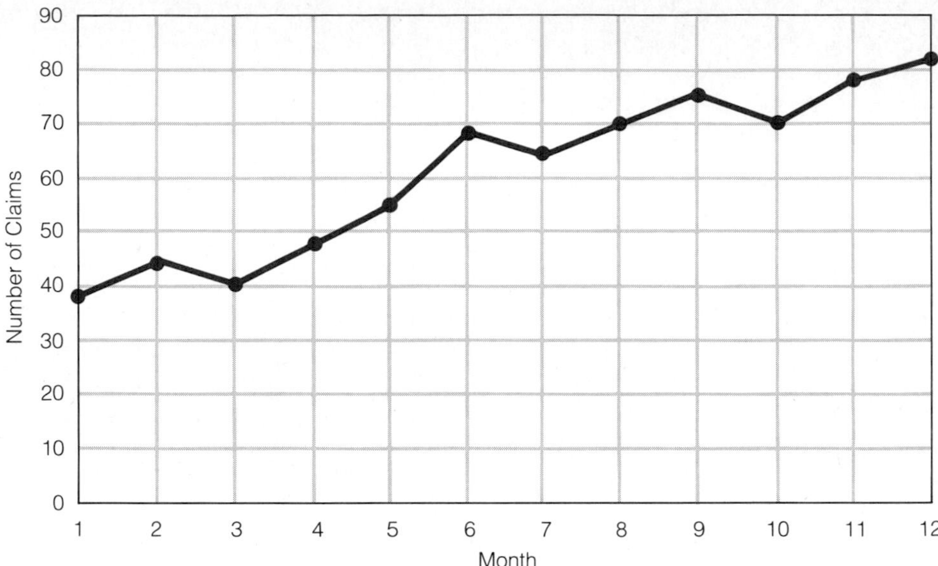

Figure 7-21
Billingsley Insurance: claims data

and T_t and also for the smoothing constants α and β. With respect to C_t and T_t, the initial values for period $t = 2$ are determined as follows:

$$C_2 = Y_1 = 38$$

and:

$$T_2 = Y_2 - Y_1 = 44 - 38 = 6$$

Keep in mind that these are arbitrary starting values and, as with single exponential smoothing, their effect will be dampened out as we proceed through the sample data to the current period.

The forecast for period 3 made at the end of period 2 is:

$$F_3 = 38 + 6 = 44$$

Table 7-21 BILLINGSLEY INSURANCE: DOUBLE EXPONENTIAL SMOOTHING, $\alpha = .20$, $\beta = .30$

t	Y_t	C_t	T_t	F_t	$\lvert Y_t - F_t \rvert$
1	38	—	—	—	—
2	44	38.00	6.00	38.00	6.00
3	40	43.20	5.76	44.00	4.00
4	48	48.768	5.7024	48.96	0.96
5	55	54.57632	5.734175	54.4704	0.5296
6	68	61.8484	6.195547	60.3105	7.6895
7	64	67.23516	5.952912	68.04395	4.04395
8	70	72.55046	5.761628	73.18808	3.18808
9	75	77.64968	5.562904	78.31209	3.31209
10	70	80.57006	4.770149	83.21258	13.21258
11	78	83.87217	4.329736	85.34021	7.34021
12	82	86.96152	3.957622	88.20191	6.20191
					Total = 56.47792

MAD = 56.47792/11 = 5.1344

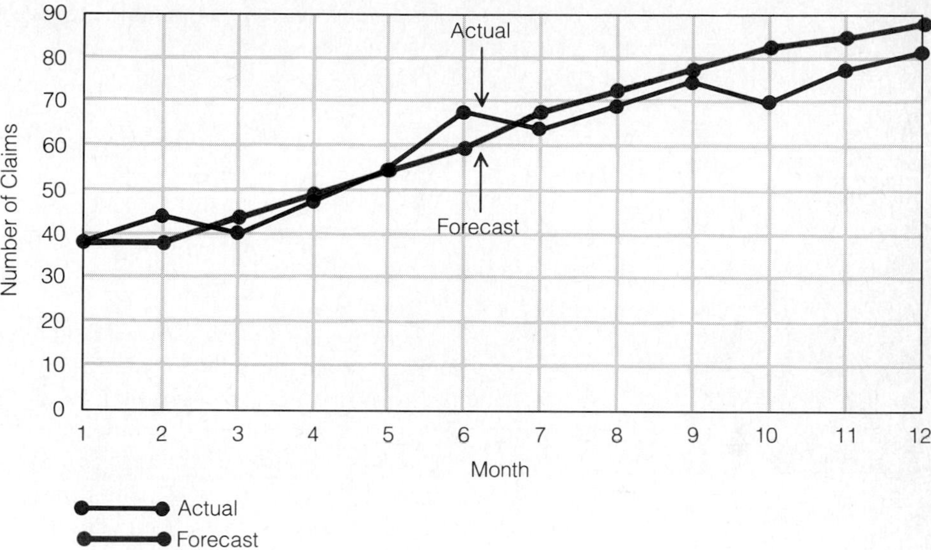

Figure 7-22
Billingsley Insurance: actual vs. forecast claims—double exponential smoothing ($\alpha = .20$ and $\beta = .30$)

The choice of smoothing constant values (α and β) depends on the same issues as those discussed earlier for single smoothing. That is, use larger smoothing constants when less smoothing is desired and values closer to 0.0 when more smoothing is desired. The larger the value, the more impact that current data will have on the forecast. Suppose we use $\alpha = .20$ and $\beta = .30$ in this example.

At the close of period 3, in which actual claims were 40, the smoothing equations are updated as follows:

$$C_3 = .20(40) + (1 - .20)(38 + 6) = 43.2$$

$$T_3 = .30(43.2 - 38) + (1 - .30)(6) = 5.76$$

Next, the forecast for period 4 is:

$$F_4 = 43.2 + 5.76 = 48.96$$

We then repeat the process through period 12 to find the forecast for period 13. Table 7-21 shows the results of the computations and the MAD value. Figure 7-22 shows the actual time series and forecasts. The forecast for period 13 is:

$$F_{13} = C_{12} + T_{12} = 90.91914$$

Thus, based on this double exponential smoothing model, the number of claims for period 13 may be forecast to be about 91. But before settling on this forecast, we would try different smoothing constants to determine whether a smaller MAD can be found.

7-6 REGRESSION-BASED FORECASTING MODELS

Section 7-4 introduced trend-based forecasting, where least-squares regression was used to determine the trend. The trend-based forecasting models used two variables: a dependent variable, Y_t, and an independent variable, time (t). Regression analysis determined that the trend line which best fit the time-series data can be defined by an equation of this form:

$$F_t = b_0 + b_1(t) \tag{7-17}$$

Forecasts were made by substituting the appropriate value for time into the trend equation.

While this use of regression analysis is common, regression analysis has a much broader application in forecasting. We will consider two additional regression models commonly used by forecasters: regression models with explanatory variables and autoregressive models.

EXPLANATORY VARIABLES

Consider the following example involving the E. J. Williams Pipe and Tool Company. The production manager needs to forecast monthly sales for a product that is made at the Dayton, Ohio, plant. The manager has monthly sales data for this product for the past 12 months. He also has monthly data available on product advertising expenditures. These data are shown in Table 7-22. Notice that the product's sales, Y_t, vary from month to month. Some people in the company think the variation in advertising spending might be partially responsible for the variation in sales. Thus, in this example, advertising is considered an explanatory variable.

A regression-based forecasting model could be developed in the following form:

$$F_t = b_0 + b_1 (X_{1t}) \tag{7-18}$$

where:

F_t = forecast value of sales in time t
b_0 = regression intercept
b_1 = regression slope
X_{1t} = value of advertising at time t

As was the case with the regression trend models, we can use the least-squares equations to determine the "best" values for b_0 and b_1:

$$b_1 = \frac{\Sigma X_{1t}Y_t - (\Sigma X_{1t}\Sigma Y_t)/n}{\Sigma(X_{1t})^2 - (\Sigma X_{1t})^2/n} \tag{7-19}$$

$$b_0 = \overline{Y} - b_1\overline{X}_1 \tag{7-20}$$

where:

$\overline{Y}$ = average value of the time series = $\Sigma Y_t/n$
$\overline{X}_1$ = average value of variable X_1 in the time series = $\Sigma X_{1t}/n$

Table 7-22 E. J. WILLIAMS PIPE AND TOOL SALES DATA

Month t	Sales (units) Y_t	Advertising ($000) X_1	Month t	Sales (units) Y_t	Advertising ($000) X_1	Month t	Sales (units) Y_t	Advertising ($000) X_1
1	100	10	5	200	20	9	250	24
2	250	23	6	240	25	10	180	22
3	150	16	7	180	20	11	220	20
4	120	15	8	300	26	12	230	25

Table 7-23 E. J. WILLIAMS PIPE AND TOOL COMPANY: MAD CALCULATION

Month t	Sales (units) Y_t	Advertising ($000) X_t	Forecast F_t	Absolute Forecast Error $\lvert Y_t - F_t \rvert$
1	100	10	83.38603	16.61397
2	250	23	229.82872	20.17128
3	150	16	150.97496	.97496
4	120	15	139.71026	19.71026
5	200	20	196.03436	3.96564
6	240	25	252.35835	12.35835
7	180	20	196.03426	16.03426
8	300	26	263.62320	36.37680
9	250	24	241.09353	8.90647
10	180	22	218.56389	38.56389
11	220	20	196.03425	23.96575
12	230	25	252.35835	22.35835
				Total = 219.99998

MAD = 219.99998/12 = 18.333

After performing the calculations required in equations 7-19 and 7-20, we find the following regression model:

$$F_t = -29.26219 + 11.2648(X_{1t})$$

Since this is the least-squares regression model, the sum of squared errors has been minimized. Table 7-23 shows the MAD calculation for the comparison between output from the explanatory-variable regression model and historical data.

To use the model to forecast sales for period 13, the production manager would need to determine the level of product advertising planned for month 13. Suppose the company plans to spend $24,000 ($X_{1,13} = 24$) for advertising. Then the sales forecast for period 13 is:

$$F_{13} = -29.26219 + 11.2648(24) = 241.09$$

Thus, the manager might plan on selling about 241 units of the product in month 13.

Multiple Regression Models

Realistically, in forecasting applications like the E. J. Williams example, there may be several potential explanatory variables which could be included in the model. A regression model with more than one independent (explanatory) variable is called a **multiple regression model.** The forecast equation would take this form:

$$F_t = b_0 + b_1X_{1t} + b_2X_{2t} + \cdots b_kX_{kt} \tag{7-21}$$

where:

F_t = forecast value for period t

b_0 = regression intercept

b_i = ith regression coefficient

X_{it} = value of ith explanatory variable measured at time t

The model described in equation 7-21 shows the X_i variables all measured at time t, corresponding to when the dependent variable is measured. Thus, to forecast for time $t + 1$, we would need to know values for each variable at time $t + 1$. This would be possible when the explanatory variable can be controlled, as was the case with the E. J. Williams advertising budget. However, when an explanatory variable cannot be controlled and its value is not known in advance, we must lag the data to have a useful forecasting equation. For instance, we might have a model which looks like:

$$F_t = b_0 + b_1X_{1t} + b_2X_{2t-1}$$

In this case, variable X_2 is measured one period before both the dependent variable and X_1. Variable X_2 is considered an **indicator variable**, an independent variable measured in time t which is used in forecasting the dependent variable at time $t + n$. The success of an explanatory regression model will depend largely on the availability of leading indicator variables which are closely related to the time series.

The multiple regression coefficients in equation 7-13 are determined such that the sum of squared errors is minimized. The computations are almost always performed using statistical software, such as the MASTER software package.

AUTOREGRESSIVE FORECASTING MODELS

Another type of regression-based forecasting approach uses as indicator variables the lagged values of the dependent variable. For instance, we might formulate a model such as:

$$F_t = b_0 + b_1Y_{t-1} + b_2Y_{t-2} \tag{7-22}$$

where:

F_t = forecast value in time t

Y_{t-1} = value of the time series at time $t - 1$

Y_{t-2} = value of the time series at time $t - 2$

Equation 7-22 represents a case in which the two most recent time periods are used as independent variables. The success of an autoregressive model depends on how closely past data are related to current data.

OTHER REGRESSION-BASED MODELS

Most other regression-based forecasting models are variations of the models discussed in this chapter. For instance, the trend projection models which use time as the independent variable can be extended to a multiple regression model of the following form:

$$F_t = b_0 + b_1t + b_2t^2 + b_3t^3 \tag{7-23}$$

where:

F_t = forecast value of the time series at time t

t = value of time at time t

t^2 = time squared

t^3 = time cubed

This format would be appropriate for a time series that exhibits particular nonlinear movements. However, one must be careful not to embark on a "curve-fitting" exercise and forget that the objective is to develop a model which will forecast effectively.

The distinguishing feature of each regression-based model is the form of the independent variable(s); that is, we get a mixed regression model when the independent variables are mixed, and so on. For instance, we might determine the following:

$$F_t = b_0 + b_1 Y_{t-1} + b_2 t^2 + b_3 X_{1t-1}$$

In this instance, the model combines autoregression, trend projection, and explanatory regression.

The art of forecasting is to determine the most appropriate form for the forecasting model. Guard against the tendency to use the same model format in all applications. What worked well in one situation may not be appropriate in others.

Remember, too, that when you develop a forecasting model, you are developing a simulation model of the system being studied—but the model is not expected to be a perfect simulator. In each situation, you will have to determine where to draw the line between the desire for a model which represents reality and what is practical to achieve.

STATISTICAL CONSIDERATIONS

The intent of this section on regression-based forecasting was to provide an overview of a very useful management science tool. There are a number of important statistical issues to consider when employing regression analysis on time-series data, but they are beyond the scope of this text. They are, however, typically included in courses focusing on business statistics and business forecasting. The Chapter References section includes some sources for additional information on this topic.

7-7 QUALITATIVE FORECASTING TECHNIQUES

In the previous sections we showed that to use quantitative forecasting techniques one must have historical data in the correct form and must assume that the conditions which gave rise to these historical data will continue over the forecasting period. While numerous situations occur where these assumptions are realistic, in other cases sufficient data may not be available, or the decision maker may be unwilling to assume that future conditions will remain unchanged. The larger the forecast time horizon, the greater the likelihood there will be unanticipated changes in the underlying patterns and relationships. The following story illustrates this point.

Abel Walker was born in Kansas in the early 1800s and was reasonably happy growing up there, but he yearned to "go west." Abel had never talked to anyone who had made the trip, so he knew nothing about what to expect when one day he gave up his job at the general store and began his journey. Since he knew nothing about what lay ahead, Abel decided to walk backward. He reasoned that by studying the country he had just passed through, he would have a good idea about what he might encounter as he traveled west! This plan worked very well as Abel crossed the Great Plains. For days upon days he encountered the same type of terrain. Then something happened. Each time Abel took a step backward, it took him higher than the previous step. At first he couldn't figure out what was happening, because he had never experienced anything like the Rocky Mountains before. Finally, after enough steps up the mountain, he began to realize that this was the way it would be for the rest of the way. So for the longest time Abel continued climbing. Then, all of a sudden, his next step was not up, but down! He was totally unprepared for this, since he knew nothing about mountain peaks. After picking himself up and continuing downhill, he finally realized that the road west might have other ups and downs and that his experience would better prepare him for what might be ahead.

This analogy might seem a bit far-fetched, but it actually closely parallels situations facing business decision makers. For instance, in the late 1960s and early 1970s, the U.S. automobile industry was flying high. Sales were expanding and the threat of foreign competition was not worth considering. When the auto company forecasters looked at their past sales data, they saw the trend was climbing steadily. However, in 1973, something happened that affected the auto industry with as much impact as hitting the peak of the Rockies affected Abel. It was in 1973 that OPEC shut off oil shipments to the United States, drastically disrupting U.S. oil supplies. This resulted in gasoline shortages and dramatic increases in gasoline prices.

American car owners suddenly quit buying Detroit's "gas guzzlers" and turned toward more economical foreign cars, such as the highly acclaimed Honda Accord from Japan. U.S. auto-makers' sales fell sharply. The industry had not forecast such an event because the historical data contained nothing like the oil embargo. In this case, looking backward did not prepare the decision makers for what was to come. Thus, forecasts based strictly on historical patterns are fine as long as the future looks like the past; but when the relationships change, time-series–based statistical forecasting tools may not be sufficient. Instead, one or more of the many qualitative forecasting techniques might prove useful.

While quantitative forecasting techniques are characterized by the use of data, qualitative techniques are characterized by the use of expert opinion. There are some well-established qualitative forecasting techniques that have been used successfully in many diverse situations. In this section, we introduce two of the most commonly used methods: the Delphi method and scenario projection. While these are often employed as stand-alone forecasting techniques, they are also routinely used in conjunction with quantitative techniques. Expert opinion is used to modify forecasts obtained from the quantitative models.

THE DELPHI METHOD

Decision makers who employ the **Delphi method** attempt to arrive at a consensus forecast from a group of experts through a systematic procedure involving a series of questionnaires. The experts are purposely kept separated throughout the process. This reduces the potential problems associated with interpersonal exchanges in which dominant personalities might sway the opinion of others. While the precise steps in implementing the Delphi method depend on the situation, the following example demonstrates the general procedure.

Identify the Issue

The first step in this process is to identify the issue. Then a study coordinator is appointed. For example, Artistic Concerns, a Dallas company, is considering building a manufacturing facility to construct the steel-framed modular homes which the company has recently patented. Management is interested in forecasting the total industry demand for this new product over the next 10 years.

Survey the Experts

In the next step, a group of experts with potential insight in this area are hired to complete an initial questionnaire relating to the building industry and the prospects for the new product. Suppose three experts make up the panel. Their responses to two key questions are as follows:

1. What will be the total number of new housing starts over the next 10 years?

Expert A	Expert B	Expert C
1,500,000	2,500,000	4,500,000

2. What number of new housing starts will be built with the steel-frame modular construction over the next 10 years?

Expert A	Expert B	Expert C
150,000	40,000	500,000

Review and Revise the Responses

Next, the panel of experts would be shown these responses without knowing which forecasts were associated with which individual. They would be given the opportunity to adjust their own responses if they wished. Suppose the revised responses were:

Question 1

Expert A	Expert B	Expert C
2,000,000	2,700,000	3,200,000

Question 2

Expert A	Expert B	Expert C
200,000	150,000	300,000

Repeat the Process until a Consensus Is Reached

These revised results would be shared with the panel, along with responses to any other questions on the questionnaire, and the revision process would be repeated. Management would continue the process until either the experts reach a consensus or cease to revise their forecasts. You should note that the objective is not to arrive at a single forecast value but to achieve a reasonably narrow spread among the experts.

The Delphi method has some drawbacks, many of which are common to all judgmental forecasts. The most common complaint is the difficulty of evaluating the actual expertise of the "experts." The process may also be sensitive to the questionnaire. However, perhaps because of its structured nature, it is the most widely used qualitative forecasting technique.

SCENARIO PROJECTION

This technique is much less structured than the Delphi method. **Scenario projection** uses a set of well-defined, self-contained assumptions to develop a plausible statement of what the future is likely to be if these assumptions hold. In an actual application, many sets of assumptions would be formulated and a corresponding number of future scenarios would be determined. The decision maker would have to choose which set of assumptions is most likely and then determine whether the related scenario is realistic.

Recall our previous discussion about what happened to the U.S. auto companies in 1973. It is a safe bet that they now have oil- and gasoline-shortage scenarios built into their forecasting methods.

7-8 COMPUTER APPLICATIONS

The statistical forecasting techniques presented in this chapter are among many such techniques available to decision makers. Each of these techniques can be done manually with the aid of a calculator. In order for you to better understand the basis for each forecasting procedure, we have used examples throughout the chapter which illustrate the steps for developing the forecast models manually.

However, as is the case for most management science tools, a computer is generally used in model development. A wide range of computer software is available, and each package has its own specific advantages. The MASTER software contains programs for applying all the statistical forecasting procedures discussed in this text. In this section, we explain how MASTER is used and show the type of output you can

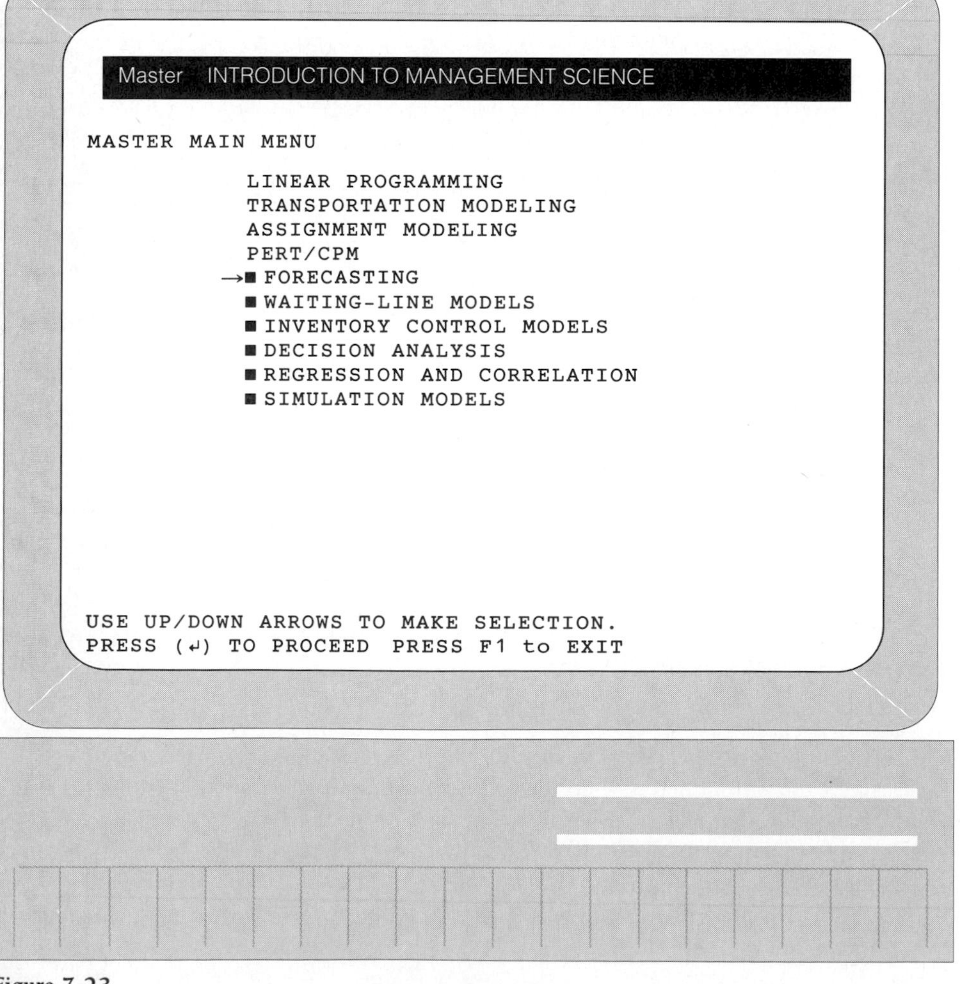

Figure 7-23
Taft Ice Cream example: MASTER main menu

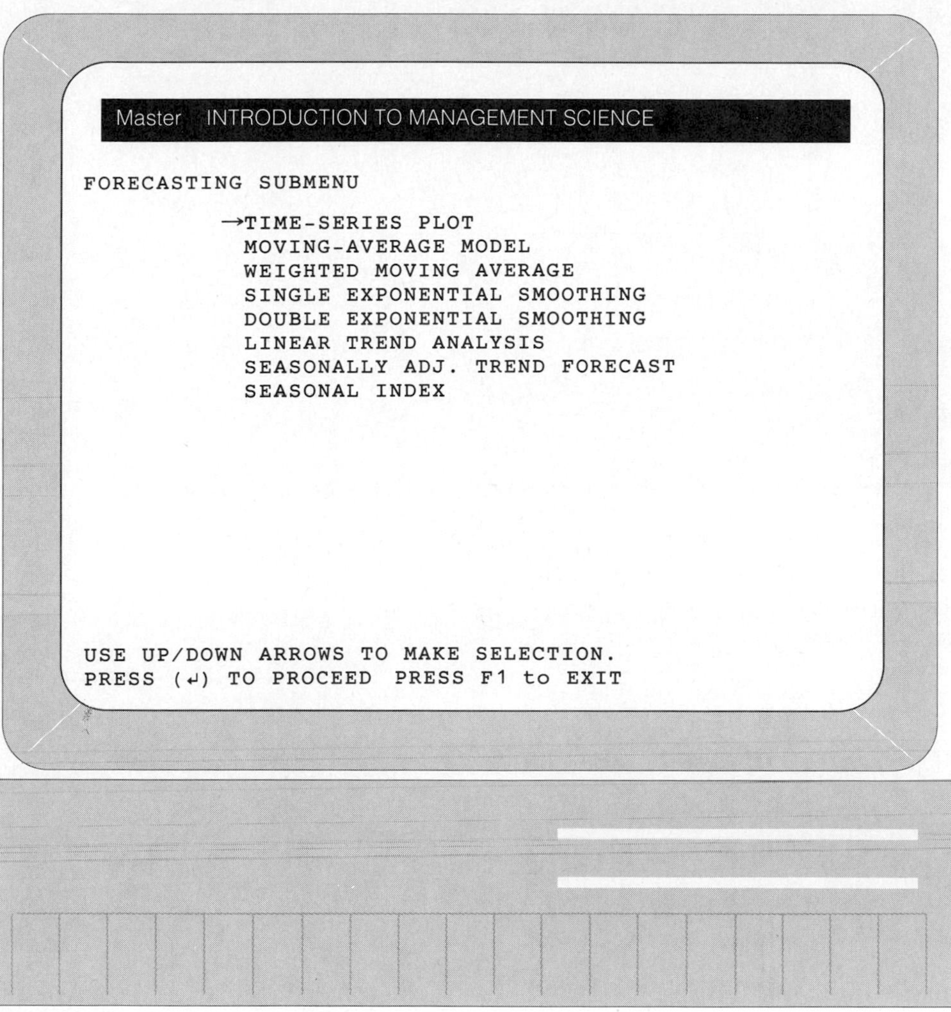

Figure 7-24
Taft Ice Cream example: MASTER forecasting submenu

expect from this or similar forecasting software. Some of the examples were presented earlier in the chapter, and you might want to compare the computer output with the manual results. Occasionally, there will be small rounding differences.

TAFT ICE CREAM COMPANY EXAMPLE

Recall the Taft Ice Cream Company example presented in Section 7-4. Sales data for 10 years are available (see Table 7-2.) The company wants to develop a forecast for year 11 based on these historical data.

To use MASTER, first select the Forecasting option on the main menu, as shown in Figure 7-23. This brings up the Forecasting submenu, shown in Figure 7-24. The plan is to first plot the data (select Time-Series Plot); and if the plot reflects a linear relationship, the linear trend option will be taken.

Figure 7-25 shows the data input screen for the example. The resulting time-series plot, shown in Figure 7-26, clearly indicates a linear pattern over the 10 years.

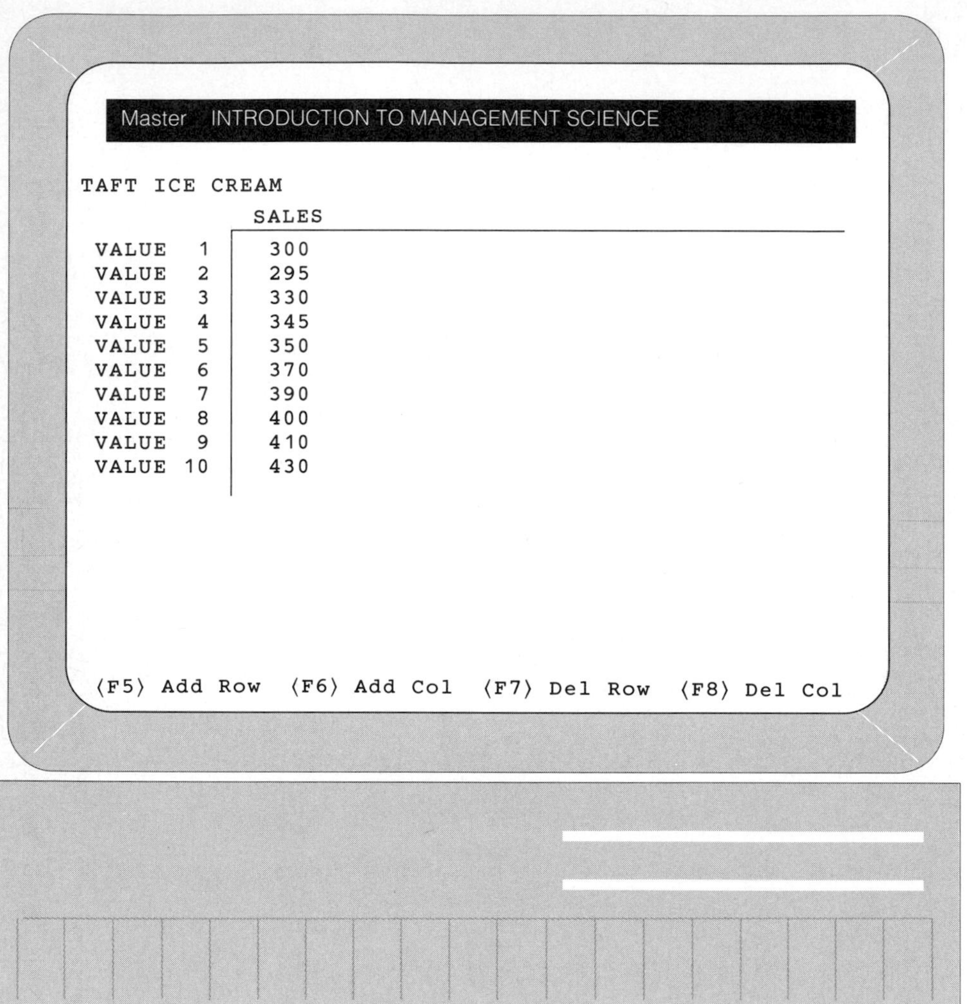

Figure 7-25
Taft Ice Cream example: MASTER scatter-plot data input screen

Given this, the next step is to access the Linear Trend Analysis program (see Figure 7-24 for submenu screen). The resulting output is shown in Figure 7-27. First, the linear trend regression equation is shown. To forecast future time periods, substitute integer values for t of 11 or higher into the trend equation.

Figure 7-27 also shows several summary statistics associated with the trend model. The R-square value of 98.0409 indicates that the linear trend line fits the time-series data very well, explaining 98.04% of the variation in the data. The standard error of the estimate (6.823) is a measure of the average deviation of sales data around the trend. Both the high R-square and the relatively low standard error imply that the linear model provides a good fit to the data. (We suggest you refer to a statistics text for a further discussion of these two terms.)

The MAD and MSE values are also output, as shown in Figure 7-27. If other forecasting models were applied to the Taft Ice Cream data, the MAD and MSE values

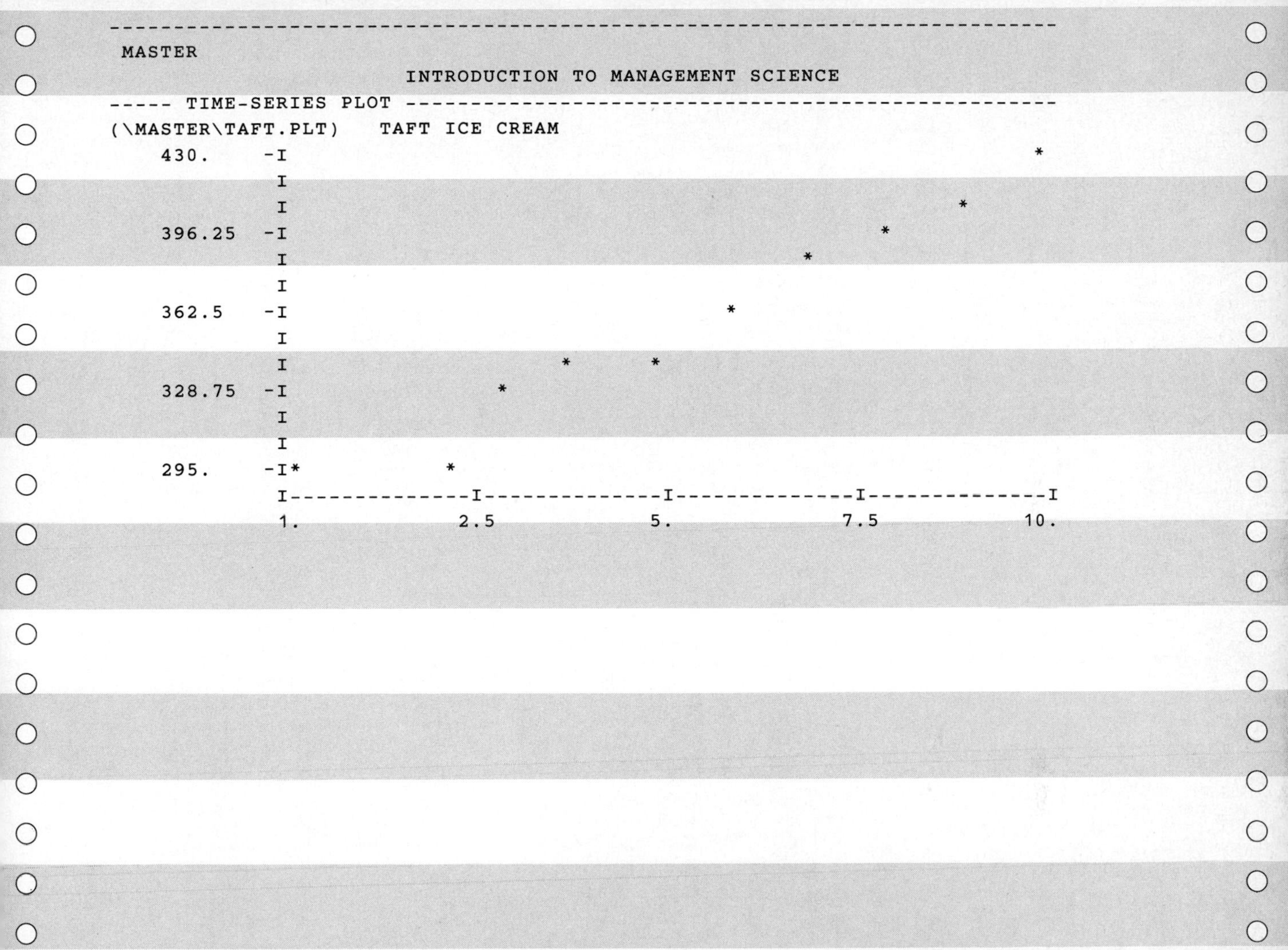

Figure 7-26
Taft Ice Cream Co. example: MASTER scatter-plot output

could be compared with those in Figure 7-27. However, the relatively small MAD of 4.697 is a further indication of the good fit established by the linear-trend model.

At the bottom of the printout in Figure 7-27, the forecast for period 11 is shown to be 444.6666. As we have indicated in other sections of this chapter, the fact that this model fits the time-series data very well does not guarantee that the forecast will be accurate. If the future looks like the past, then we might expect this linear-trend forecast to be reasonably accurate for the Taft Ice Cream Company.

HUMBOLDT ELECTRONICS EXAMPLE

In section 7-5, we introduced an example involving the Humboldt Electronics Company (see Table 7-16). In that example, the company was interested in forecasting weekly sales using exponential smoothing. Figure 7-28 shows the MASTER Forecast-

```
-------------------------------------------------------------------------
 MASTER
                      INTRODUCTION TO MANAGEMENT SCIENCE
----- LINEAR TREND ANALYSIS ----------------------------------------------
(\MASTER\TAFT.TRD)   TAFT ICE CREAM
LINEAR TREND EQUATION
      F(t)  =  279.3333  +   15.0303(t)
                      SUMMARY STATISTICS
      R-SQUARE =  98.0409     STANDARD ERROR ESTIMATE =  6.822976
                  DURBIN-WATSON STATISTIC = 2.753074
                  MAD =  4.696973
                  MSE = 37.2424
                        COEFFICIENT          ST.DEV              T-RATIO
            CONSTANT      279.3333
            TIME          15.0303            .7511849            20.00879
  TIME=t       ACTUAL VALUES   FORECASTS   RESIDUALS
    1               300         294.3636     5.636383
    2               295         309.3939   -14.39392
    3               330         324.4242     5.575775
    4               345         339.4545     5.545471
    5               350         354.4848    -4.484833
    6               370         369.5151      .4848633
    7               390         384.5454     5.454559
    8               400         399.5757      .4242554
    9               410         414.606     -4.606018
    10              430         429.6364      .3636475

    11       FORECAST =         444.6666
```

Figure 7-27
Taft Ice Cream example: MASTER linear trend output

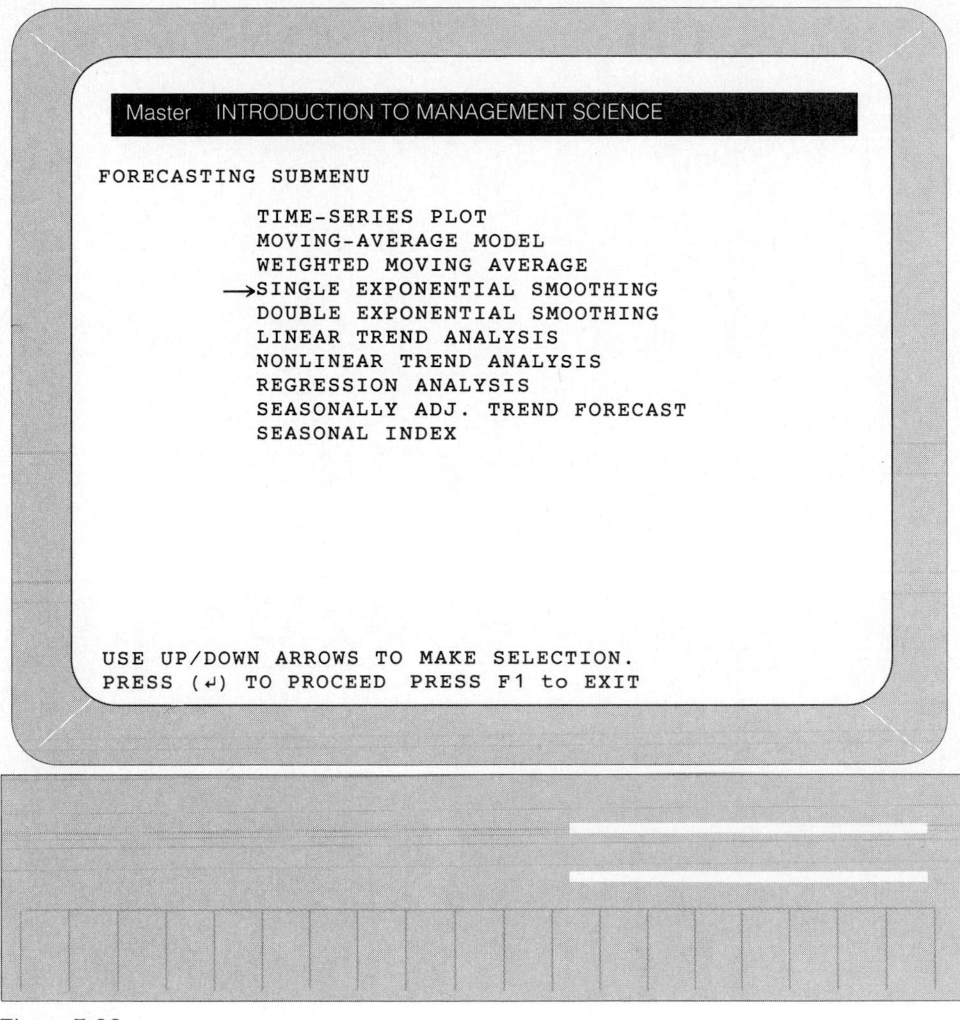

Figure 7-28
Humboldt Electronics example: MASTER forecasting submenu

ing submenu with the Single Exponential Smoothing option selected. The data entry screen is shown in Figure 7-29. Selecting the smoothing constant $\alpha = .20$ produces the output shown in Figure 7-30. The forecast for week 11 is 432.55.

This program also provides the option for smoothing-constant optimization. Near the bottom of the output in Figure 7-30, you will see that the lower limit for alpha = .1, the upper limit = .5, and the increment for analysis = .05. These values are specified interactively by the user. The program investigates values of alpha in increments of .05 from .1 to .50. The MAD and MSE for each alpha level is shown, along with the forecasts for week 11. In this case, both the MAD and the MSE decline steadily as the alpha level is increased. Thus, we need to investigate higher alpha levels to determine the optimal smoothing constant to use for these data. Note how the forecast for period 11 is affected by the choice of the smoothing constant.

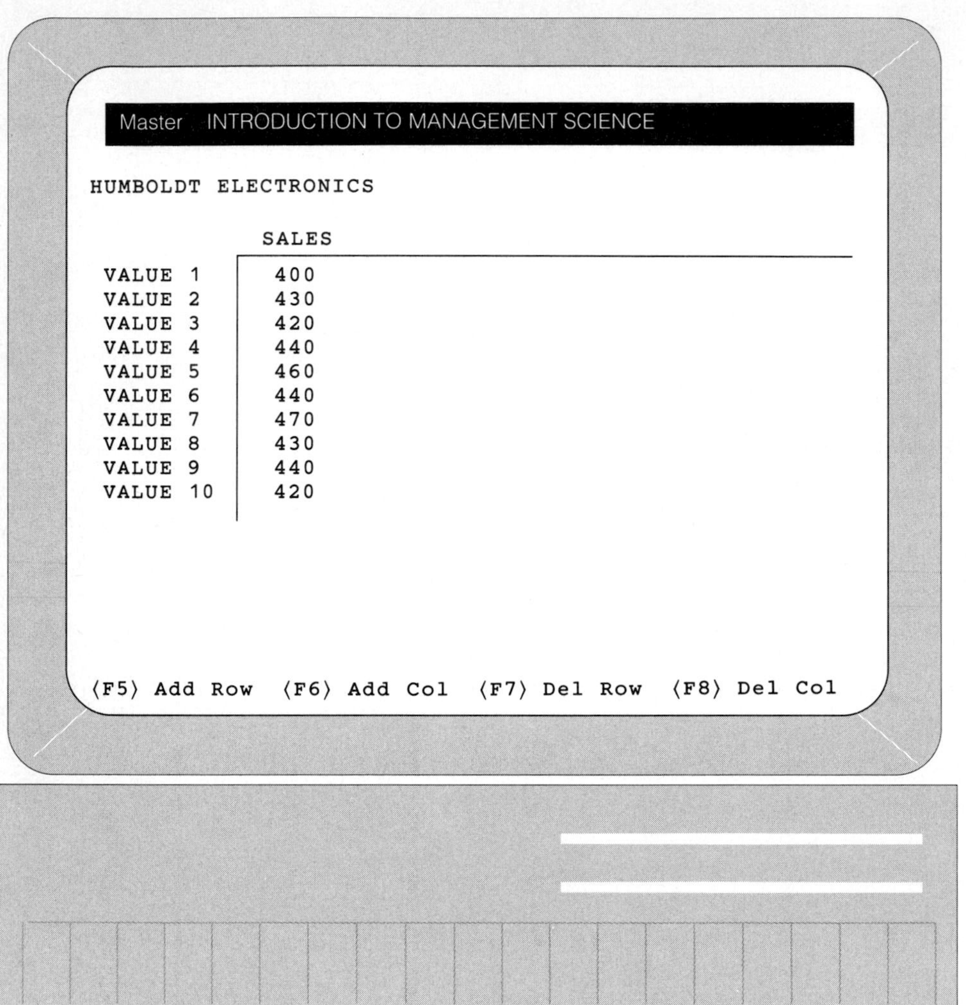

Figure 7-29
Humboldt Electronics example: MASTER data entry screen for single exponential smoothing

MASTER Summary

The examples presented in this section illustrate what can be accomplished with the MASTER software. This software will allow you to deal with any of the techniques that are presented in this text. If you take a course devoted specifically to forecasting, you will no doubt be exposed to software that offers more sophisticated techniques, in addition to those presented here. However, as is the case with all management science topics, the advantages of using a computer are to permit fast, accurate computations and to make possible more analyses in a given situation. We suggest that after you fully understand the various forecasting techniques presented in this chapter, you use a computer to work the problems at the end of the chapter. This will allow you to focus on an analysis of the results without getting bogged down in the computations.

```
-----------------------------------------------------------------------
 MASTER
                       INTRODUCTION TO MANAGEMENT SCIENCE
----- SINGLE EXPONENTIAL SMOOTHING ------------------------------------
(\MASTER\HUMBOLT.SM1)    HUMBOLDT ELECTRONICS
                    SINGLE EXPONENTIAL SMOOTHING
                            ALPHA =    .2


     PERIOD      OBSERVED VALUE        FORECAST             ERROR
        1          400.
        2          430.                  400.                30.
        3          420.                  406.                14.
        4          440.                  408.8               31.19
        5          460.                  415.04              44.95
        6          440.                  424.03              15.96
        7          470.                  427.22              42.77
        8          430.                  435.78              -5.78
        9          440.                  434.62               5.37
       10          420.                  435.69             -15.69

       11          FORECAST =        432.55
                     MEAN ABSOLUTE DEVIATION ( MAD ) =          22.86
                          MEAN SQUARED ERROR ( MSE ) =         720.47
LOWER LIMIT FOR ALPHA =        .1
UPPER LIMIT FOR ALPHA =        .5
INCREMENT FOR ANALYSIS =       .05
               SMOOTHING CONSTANT ANALYSIS
         ALPHA             MAD            MSE             PERIOD   11 FORECAST
          .1              27.21        1014.85                  423.67
          .15             24.21         836.02                  429.37
          .2              22.86         720.47                  432.55
          .25             21.72         642.86                  434.02
          .3              20.82         588.61                  434.34
          .35             20.20         549.38                  433.93
          .4              19.51         520.42                  433.07
          .45             19.21         499.07                  431.97
          .50             19.06         483.76                  430.76
```

Figure 7-30
Humboldt Electronics example: MASTER output for single exponential smoothing

7-9 SUMMARY AND CONCLUSIONS

In this chapter we have introduced the basics of forecasting. While we have included a variety of forecasting techniques, both qualitative and quantitative, our discussion is not complete. An entire semester or more could be devoted to the subject and still not do it justice. Our objective has been to provide insight into some of the more frequently used techniques and to acquaint you with some terminology of forecasting and time-series analysis.

We discussed the components of a time series and how to identify each. We also introduced a number of quantitative forecasting techniques, including:

1. Trend projection (linear and nonlinear)
2. Seasonally adjusted trend projection
3. Moving average
4. Single exponential smoothing
5. Double exponential smoothing
6. Explanatory regression models
7. Autoregressive regression models
8. Mixed autoregression models

You should also know that the success of any quantitative forecasting model is determined by two factors:

1. How well the model fits the historical time series
2. How closely the future time series resembles the past

Ultimately, the best forecasting method is the one which provides the best forecasts.

We have observed that when a short-term forecast is needed on a fairly regular basis, heavy reliance is placed on quantitative techniques. For example, a company which is determining how many units of material to purchase for the fabrication plant on a weekly basis will tend to use a quantitative model, such as exponential smoothing, and may have the forecasting process tied in with the inventory system. A periodic review will be conducted to determine whether the model is performing satisfactorily.

When the planning horizon is longer, we have observed that decision makers tend to incorporate some qualitative judgment along with the quantitative models. For instance, in the annual budgeting process, you are likely to see a manager obtain a sales forecast with a quantitative technique, such as a regression-based model, and then adjust this forecast according to the judgment of his or her managers. When long-term forecasts of 5 or more years are involved, the tendency has been to place greater reliance on qualitative methods and less reliance on quantitative models.

Finally, regardless of the length of the planning horizon, our experience is that decision makers generally combine forecasting methods to arrive at a final forecast. This involves using some form of quantitative forecasting to arrive at a base forecast, which is then adjusted through a qualitative process. This practice is consistent with the premise we reiterate throughout this text: Management science models should be used to provide information for the decision process, but the decisions are made by people.

Solved Problems

PROBLEM 1 The annual sales for Safeway, the grocery retailing giant, for a 12-year period are shown below. (Sales are in billions [10^9] of dollars.)

Year	Sales
1974	8.185
1975	9.717
1976	10.443
1977	11.249
1978	12.551
1979	13.718
1980	15.103
1981	16.580
1982	17.663
1983	18.585
1984	19.642
1985	19.651

a. Fit a least-squares regression line to the sales data, using time as the independent variable.
b. Discuss whether the linear regression line seems to be a good model to use on this data.
c. Use the regression line developed in part **a** to forecast sales for the next 2 years. How would you feel about using this as a forecasting model?

Solutions a. Using equations 7-3 and 7-4 to determine the slope and intercept of the regression line, we find:

$$b_1 = \frac{\Sigma tY_t - (\Sigma t \Sigma Y_t)/n}{\Sigma t^2 - (\Sigma t)^2/n}$$

$$= \frac{1283.059 - (173.087)(78)/12}{650 - (6084)/12}$$

$$= 158.994/143$$

$$= 1.111$$

$$b_0 = \Sigma Y_t/n - b_1 \Sigma t/n$$

$$= 173.087/12 - (1.111)(78)/12$$

$$= 7.20$$

b. We can best answer this question by comparing the values predicted by the regression line with the actual observed values.

Year	Actual	Predicted
1974	8.185	8.311
1975	9.717	9.422
1976	10.443	10.533
1977	11.249	11.644
1978	12.551	12.755
1979	13.718	13.866

Year	Actual	Predicted
1980	15.103	14.977
1981	16.580	16.088
1982	17.663	17.199
1983	18.585	18.320
1984	19.642	19.431
1985	19.651	20.542

By comparing the actual sales values with the predicted values, we see that the model does quite a good job of tracking the actual sales. Some concern may be caused by the fact that the increase in sales between 1984 and 1985 is very small. Since we know that some firms experience a leveling off in sales, we might well question whether the predicted $1.111 billion increase per year would continue in the future.

c. Assuming the model will work for the next 2 years, we would predict sales to be:

$$\text{Sales (1986)} = 7.20 + 1.111(13) = 21.643 \text{ billion}$$
$$\text{Sales (1987)} = 7.20 + 1.111(14) = 22.754 \text{ billion}$$

This forecast would be subject to the concern expressed in part **b**.

PROBLEM 2 DataKey makes keyboards and sells them to computer manufacturers. Below are the company's quarterly sales figures for the past 2 years and the current quarter, in thousands of units. DataKey has decided to try exponential smoothing as a forecasting technique.

Year	Quarter	Sales
1	1	14.7
	2	17.3
	3	15.5
	4	15.5
2	1	21.2
	2	27.1
	3	25.9
	4	23.0
3	1	33.1

a. Use a single smoothing model with $\alpha = .2$ to prepare a forecast for the next quarter. Assume your forecast for the first period is correct.
b. Use a double smoothing model with a trend-smoothing constant (β) of .3 and a process-smoothing constant (α) of .2 to prepare a forecast for the next period, quarter 10.
c. If you were to recommend one of the two models, which would you choose? Why?

Solutions a. The forecast for the next quarter is found by using equation 7-8 and determining the values in the following table.

Period t	Demand Y_t	Forecast for This Period F_t	Forecast for Next Period F_{t+1}
Year 1	14.7	14.7	14.7
	17.3	14.7	15.22
	15.5	15.22	15.28*
	15.5	15.28	15.32
Year 2	21.2	15.32	16.50
	27.1	16.50	18.62
	25.9	18.62	20.07
	23.0	20.07	20.66
Year 3	33.1	20.66	23.15

* Values from this point are rounded to the nearest .01.

b. Using equations 7-14, 7-15, and 7-16, with $\alpha = .2$ and $\beta = .3$, we find the following table of values:

t	Y_t	C_t	T_t	F_t
1	14.7	—	—	—
2	17.3	14.7	2.6	—
3	15.5	16.94	2.49*	17.3
4	15.5	18.64	2.25	19.43
5	21.2	20.95	2.27	20.9
6	27.1	24.00	2.50	23.24
7	25.9	26.38	2.46	26.51
8	23.0	27.67	2.11	28.86
9	33.1	30.44	2.31	29.81
10	—	—	—	32.78

* Values from this point are rounded to the nearest .01.

c. When comparing the results of the two smoothing models, we see that the single smoothing model lags the increasing sales. The double smoothing model does a much better job of following the sales figures. This should not surprise you, since the double smoothing model is designed to be used in situations where a trend exists.

General Questions and Assignments

1. There are two main categories of forecasting techniques. Name them and briefly describe each.
2. There are three main steps in developing a forecasting model. Name the three steps and describe each one.
3. Assume your school's athletic department is in the process of developing a budget for next year and wants to forecast ticket sales for the football season. For this budget process, what is the forecast horizon?
4. What are the four categories of forecast lead times? Describe each one and give examples for which lead time would be appropriate.
5. If a company is interested in building a new manufacturing facility, its product-demand forecast model would need to cover a long lead time. Discuss why.
6. Define the term *forecast period*.

7. Discuss the difference between a *forecast period* and a *forecasting interval*.
8. Identify three businesses in your community which might be expected to have sales that exhibit a seasonal component. Discuss.
9. If enrollments at a particular university have steadily declined over the past 10 years, which time-series component would be illustrated if enrollments were graphed for this period of time? Discuss.
10. The Willow Manufacturing Company has been in operation for 20 years. Records of annual sales have been maintained for this time period. If we graphed the data, is it likely that the data would contain a seasonal component? Discuss.
11. Discuss the difference between a *cyclical component* and a *seasonal component*.
12. Which component is more predictable, seasonal or cyclical? Discuss and illustrate with examples.
13. Is it possible for a time series to have both a trend and a seasonal pattern? Discuss. If yes, provide an example which illustrates such a time series.
14. Go to the library and find data showing the state's population for the past 20 years. Plot these data and indicate which of the time-series components are present.
15. Contact the university registrar's office for enrollment data by quarter (or semester), including summer term, for the past 6 years. Graph the data and indicate which of the time-series components are present.

Exercises and Application Problems

1. The Chesterfield Company in Omaha, Nebraska, manufactures airplane parts. Sales data for the past 22 years are as follows:

Year	Sales	Year	Sales
1	$ 133,000	12	$1,335,000
2	128,000	13	1,567,000
3	202,000	14	1,234,000
4	278,000	15	1,897,000
5	388,000	16	2,300,000
6	376,000	17	2,124,000
7	504,000	18	2,579,000
8	613,000	19	3,200,000
9	745,000	20	3,106,000
10	975,000	21	3,678,000
11	1,233,900	22	3,789,000

Graph these data and indicate whether they appear to have a linear trend. What is the sales average for the past 22 years?

2. Referring to the sales data for the Chesterfield Company in problem 1, develop a simple linear regression model with time as the independent variable. Plot the trend line against the actual data. Discuss any relationships you see between the plotted trend line and the actual data.
3. Referring to problems 1 and 2, would an exponential trend describe the sales pattern for the Chesterfield Company better than a linear trend? Develop a least-squares regression model using the square of time as the independent variable. Plot this regression line against the original data.

   Would you conclude that the exponential trend is more representative of the sales data than the linear trend? Discuss. Compare the MAD and MSE values for the two models. Also compute bias for each and discuss.

4. Sunrise Sports has experienced rapidly expanding retail sales. Its sales levels (in millions of dollars) for the past 12 years are:

Year	Sales	Year	Sales
1	1.9	7	8.6
2	3.1	8	9.3
3	2.8	9	11.0
4	4.5	10	13.9
5	5.7	11	16.6
6	5.8	12	19.4

Plot this time series on ordinary graph paper and describe the trend in the data.

5. Construct a least-squares regression line to fit the data in problem 4. How does this line explain the variation in past sales data? Comment on any patterns you see in the relationship between the actual sales values and the values predicted by the regression analysis.

6. The following are birthrates (per 1000) in the United States between 1930 and 1976. Develop a time-series plot of the data.

Year	Birthrate	Year	Birthrate	Year	Birthrate	Year	Birthrate
1930	21.3	1942	22.2	1954	25.2	1966	18.5
1931	20.2	1943	22.7	1955	24.9	1967	17.9
1932	19.5	1944	21.3	1956	25.1	1968	17.6
1933	18.4	1945	20.4	1957	25.2	1969	17.9
1934	19.0	1946	24.1	1958	24.5	1970	18.2
1935	18.7	1947	26.5	1959	24.3	1971	17.2
1936	18.4	1948	24.8	1960	23.8	1972	15.6
1937	18.7	1949	24.5	1961	23.5	1973	14.9
1938	19.2	1950	23.9	1962	22.6	1974	14.9
1939	18.8	1951	24.8	1963	21.9	1975	14.7
1940	19.4	1952	25.0	1964	21.2	1976	14.7
1941	20.3	1953	24.9	1965	19.6		

7. Referring to the birthrate data in problem 6, develop a linear-trend regression model and plot the trend line against the actual data. Comment on the degree to which the trend line fits the observed data.

8. Tran's Furniture Store has maintained monthly sales records for the past 48 months, with the following results:

Month	Sales	Month	Sales	Month	Sales	Month	Sales
1 (Jan.)	$23,500	13 (Jan.)	$23,500	25 (Jan.)	$31,000	37 (Jan.)	$32,400
2	21,700	14	23,400	26	30,400	38	35,600
3	18,750	15	21,400	27	29,800	39	31,200
4	22,000	16	24,200	28	32,500	40	34,600
5	23,000	17	26,900	29	34,500	41	36,800
6	26,200	18	29,700	30	33,800	42	35,700
7	27,300	19	31,100	31	34,200	43	37,500
8	29,300	20	32,400	32	36,700	44	40,000
9	31,200	21	34,500	33	39,700	45	43,200
10	34,200	22	35,700	34	42,400	46	46,700
11	39,500	23	42,000	35	43,600	47	50,100
12	43,400	24	42,600	36	47,400	48	52,100

Using the multiplicative model (equation 7-8), estimate the $T \times C$ portion by computing a 12-month moving average and then the centered 12-month moving average.

9. Referring to problem 8, estimate the $S \times I$ portion of the multiplicative model by finding the ratio to moving averages for the time-series data. Determine whether these ratio to moving averages are stable from year to year.
10. Referring to problems 8 and 9, extract the irregular component by taking the normalized average of the ratio to moving averages. Make a table that shows the normalized seasonal indexes. Interpret what the index for January means relative to the index for July.
11. Based on your work in problems 8–10, determine a seasonally adjusted linear-trend forecasting model. Compare this model with an unadjusted linear trend model. Use both models to forecast Tran's sales for period 49.
12. Using the models developed in problem 11, which has the lower MAD and lower MSE?
13. Lobo Theater Company operates a chain of movie theaters in the Midwest. The company recently purchased a theater in Rapid City, South Dakota. The new manager obtained ticket-sales records for the previous 36 months. She hoped to analyze these data and use them in her planning for the next 12 months. The data are as follows:

Month	Tickets Sold	Month	Tickets Sold	Month	Tickets Sold	Month	Tickets Sold
1 (Jan.)	1580	10	980	19	1580	28	1750
2	1608	11	1260	20	1680	29	1690
3	1370	12	1680	21	1560	30	1730
4	1260	13 (Jan.)	1630	22	1520	31	1690
5	1125	14	1700	23	1670	32	1780
6	1306	15	1610	24	1920	33	1670
7	1240	16	1590	25 (Jan.)	1960	34	1560
8	1340	17	1498	26	1880	35	1760
9	1090	18	1540	27	1820	36	2040

Plot these data as a time series. In a short report, describe what ticket sales have been like for this theater in the past 3 years.

14. Referring to problem 13, develop seasonal indexes for ticket sales at the Rapid City theater, based on the 36 months of data.
15. Referring to problems 13 and 14, develop two linear-trend forecasting models—one seasonally unadjusted and the other seasonally adjusted. Analyze each model and indicate which one you think is more accurate.
16. Referring to problem 15, use the seasonally adjusted linear-trend forecasting model to compute a forecast for month 37.
17. Ellial's Quality Discount Store has applied for a line of credit with the First National Bank. The line of credit is to be used primarily for financing inventory purchases. As part of the financial application, Ellial's has been asked to provide monthly inventory levels for the past 5 years. These levels (in millions of dollars) are shown at the top of page 393.
    a. Determine the seasonal index number for each month, using the ratio to moving-average method.
    b. Is there enough consistency between years to make you comfortable using seasonal index numbers?
    c. Ellial's will finance 90% of its monthly inventory through bank borrowing. The company has been able to get money at the prime rate plus 2%. However, the interest must be paid monthly,

Month	Year 1	2	3	4	5
January	5.2	4.7	6.6	7.1	7.0
February	3.3	2.9	4.0	4.0	6.2
March	2.8	3.0	3.6	2.6	4.3
April	5.3	6.3	7.2	8.0	9.5
May	9.4	10.0	11.4	7.8	12.5
June	2.6	4.3	4.0	5.4	6.4
July	6.2	7.7	8.0	9.3	8.6
August	7.2	7.5	6.8	8.2	8.4
September	6.8	5.8	6.8	7.9	6.9
October	9.7	9.6	8.9	9.3	9.8
November	13.6	13.9	14.2	16.1	16.5
December	11.8	11.9	12.7	13.8	14.6

and the value of the loan can change monthly. Estimate the value of interest payments for the next year. Use a seasonally adjusted linear-trend forecasting model.

18. Chen Computers has been operating for 24 months and has maintained monthly sales records for the entire period. The sales data are as follows:

Month	Sales	Month	Sales	Month	Sales	Month	Sales
1	$145,000	7	$126,000	13	$234,000	19	$167,000
2	95,000	8	178,000	14	176,000	20	145,000
3	135,000	9	130,000	15	78,000	21	189,000
4	206,000	10	190,000	16	150,000	22	80,000
5	176,000	11	98,000	17	180,000	23	140,000
6	90,000	12	135,000	18	89,000	24	178,000

Using a single exponential smoothing model with a smoothing constant equal to 0.10, develop a model for forecasting ahead 1 period. Evaluate the model by computing the MAD and MSE values. Discuss.

19. Referring to the data in problem 18, use single exponential smoothing to develop a forecasting model with a smoothing constant of 0.50. Compute the MAD and MSE for this model, and compare them with the MAD and MSE values computed in problem 18.

20. If you have access to exponential smoothing software (such as MASTER), determine the smoothing constant which minimizes the MSE and MAD from problem 19.

21. What factors should be considered when choosing a smoothing constant for an exponential smoothing model? Discuss.

22. Refer to problem 17, involving Ellial's Department Store. Construct a single exponential smoothing model using a smoothing constant of .20. Forecast sales for month 61. Compare this forecast with the forecast you determined using the linear-trend model in problem 17.

23. Refer to problems 17 and 22. Develop a double exponential smoothing model using $\alpha = .20$ and $\beta = .20$. Compare the single and double exponential smoothing models in terms of MSE and MAD. Also compare the forecasts for month 61 from the two smoothing models.

24. Using the Chen Computer data in problem 18, construct a four-period moving-average model. Compare the results of this model with those found in problems 18 and 19.

25. Refer to problems 18 and 24. Develop a double exponential smoothing model using $\alpha = .15$ and $\beta = .25$. Compare this model with the single exponential smoothing model in terms of MSE and MAD values.

26. Assuming you have the appropriate software, determine the optimal α and β smoothing constants for modeling the Chen Computer sales data presented in problem 18.
27. Refer to the Sunrise Sports data in problem 4. Construct a 3-year moving-average model and forecast the sales for year 13.
28. Using the Sunrise Sports data from problem 4 and $\alpha = .3$, formulate a forecast for year 13 sales based on a single exponential smoothing model.
29. Use the Sunrise Sports data from problem 4 and a double exponential smoothing model with a trend-smoothing constant of .2 and a constant-smoothing constant of .25 to forecast sales for year 13.
30. Compare the Sunrise Sports forecasts produced using the models from problems 5, 27, 28, and 29. If you were the manager of Sunrise Sports, which model would you choose? Why?
31. In the past 10 years, a medium-size Midwestern city issued the following numbers of building permits for single-family dwellings.

Year	Permits	Year	Permits
1	1500	6	1350
2	1470	7	1180
3	2100	8	1550
4	2380	9	2000
5	2050	10	2040

Construct single exponential smoothing models for the data, using α values of .2, .5, and .8. The city council needs a permit forecast for next year (year 11). Which of the three forecasting models would you recommend? Why? Indicate the year 11 forecast you would give the city council.
32. Referring to problem 31, construct double exponential smoothing models using the α values given in problem 31 and corresponding β values of .2, .4, and .6, respectively. Describe each model and indicate which one you would prefer to use to forecast building permits for year 11.
33. Consider your solutions for problems 31 and 32. If you had to forecast building permits for year 11, would you use a single or double smoothing model? Discuss.
34. You have been hired by the vice-president of your university to develop a forecasting model for admissions for the fall term. The vice-president wants a regression-based model with explanatory variables. Provide a list of potential explanatory variables and show the form of the regression model. Indicate the expected sign for each regression coefficient.
35. Referring to problem 34, collect data for the variables you have proposed, going back at least 10 years. (Note: A rule of thumb is that you need at least 4 times the number of observations as you have independent variables in the model.) Develop a regression model and provide a forecast 1 year ahead. (A computer and statistical software will be required to do this problem.)
36. Referring to the data for the Chesterfield Company in problem 1, develop a time-series regression forecasting model using time as the independent variable. Hold out 2 years of data and test the forecasting ability of the model against these two known data points.
37. Referring to problem 1, indicate what potential independent variables might be considered in forecasting sales for the Chesterfield Company. Also indicate where data for these variables might be found.
38. Discuss in your own terms what a leading-indicator variable is and provide an example of a leading indicator.
39. You have been assigned to the staff of the legislative budget office. Your task will be to help develop a forecasting model for annual state tax revenue. Develop a list of potential indicator variables that you might use in such a model.
40. Discuss the differences and similarities between judgmental and statistical forecasting methods. Discuss some advantages and disadvantages of judgmental forecasting.

41. This problem must be done with a group. After forming a group of five or six, select one person to act as the forecast coordinator. The task is to use the Delphi method to forecast the skills you will need in order to be employable in the business workplace 25 years from now.
42. This problem is designed for a group. After selecting a forecast coordinator, use the Delphi method to prepare a forecast of significant changes in the market for products of a locally important industry (e.g., steel, electronics, agriculture, oil, etc.).
43. Make three 20-year scenario projections for the steel industry in the United States. Prepare these scenarios for "best case," "worst case," and "most likely case" situations. For each of the three scenarios, discuss the kinds of companies you see as failing, surviving, and prospering.
44. Repeat problem 43 for the U.S. computer industry.

Chapter Equations

Linear Trend Projection

$$F_t = b_0 + b_1 t \qquad (7\text{-}1)$$

where:

F_t = value of the trend at time t

b_0 = Y intercept of the trend line

b_1 = slope of the trend line

t = time

Sum of Squared Errors

$$\Sigma(Y_t - F_t)^2 \qquad (7\text{-}2)$$

where:

Y_t = actual value of the time series at time t

F_t = trend (or forecast value) at time t

Least-Squares Regression Coefficients:

$$b_1 = \frac{\Sigma t Y_t - (\Sigma t \, \Sigma Y_t)/n}{\Sigma t^2 - (\Sigma t)^2/n} \qquad (7\text{-}3)$$

$$b_0 = \bar{Y} - b_1 \bar{t} \qquad (7\text{-}4)$$

where:

n = number of periods in the time series

$\bar{Y}$ = average value of the time series
$= \Sigma Y_t / n$

$\bar{t}$ = average value of t
$= \Sigma t / n$

Mean Square Error:

$$\text{MSE} = \Sigma(Y_t - F_t)^2/n \quad (7\text{-}5)$$

where:

Y_t = actual value at time t

F_t = predicted value at time t

n = number of time periods

Mean Absolute Deviation:

$$\text{MAD} = \Sigma|Y_t - F_t|/n \quad (7\text{-}6)$$

where:

Y_t = actual value at time t

F_t = predicted value at time t

n = number of time periods

Bias:

$$\text{Bias} = \Sigma(Y_t - F_t)/n \quad (7\text{-}7)$$

or:

$$\text{Bias} = \Sigma(\text{error})/n$$

Multiplicative Model:

$$Y_t = T_t \times S_t \times C_t \times I_t \quad (7\text{-}8)$$

where:

Y_t = value of the time series at time t

T_t = trend value at time t

S_t = seasonal value at time t

C_t = cyclical value at time t

I_t = irregular or random value at time t

Ratio to Moving Average:

$$S_t \times I_t = Y_t/(T_t \times C_t) \quad (7\text{-}9)$$

Deseasonalizing:

$$T_t \times C_t \times I_t = Y_t/S_t \quad (7\text{-}10)$$

Moving Average:

$$\text{Moving average} = (Y_1 + Y_2 + Y_3 + \cdots Y_n)/n \quad (7\text{-}11)$$

Exponential Smoothing Decay:

$$\text{Weight}_t = \alpha * (1 - \alpha)^t \qquad (7\text{-}12)$$

where:

t = data age

α = alpha (smoothing constant) $0.0 < \alpha < 1.0$

Single Exponential Smoothing:

$$F_{t+1} = \alpha Y_t + (1 - \alpha)F_t \qquad (7\text{-}13)$$

or

$$F_{t+1} = F_t + \alpha (Y_t - F_t)$$

where:

F_{t+1} = forecast value for period $t + 1$

Y_t = actual value for period t

F_t = forecast value for period t

α = alpha (smoothing constant), $0 \leq \alpha \leq 1$

Double Exponential Smoothing:

$$C_t = \alpha Y_t + (1 - \alpha)(C_{t-1} + T_{t-1}) \qquad (7\text{-}14)$$

$$T_t = \beta(C_t - C_{t-1}) + (1 - \beta)T_{t-1} \qquad (7\text{-}15)$$

$$F_{t+1} = C_t + T_t \qquad (7\text{-}16)$$

where:

Y_t = actual value in time t

α = constant-process smoothing constant

β = trend-smoothing constant

C_t = smoothed constant-process value for period t

T_t = smoothed trend value for period t

F_{t+1} = forecast value for period $t + 1$

t = current time period

Linear Trend Model:

$$F_t = b_0 + b_1(t) \qquad (7\text{-}17)$$

Simple Linear Regression Model:

$$F_t = b_0 + b_1(X_{1t}) \qquad (7\text{-}18)$$

where:

F_t = forecast value for period t

b_0 = regression intercept

b_1 = regression slope

X_{1t} = value of explanatory variable measured at time t

Least-Squares Coefficients:

$$b_1 = \frac{\Sigma X_{1t}Y_t - (\Sigma X_{1t}\Sigma Y_t)/n}{\Sigma (X_{1t})^2 - (\Sigma X_{1t})^2/n} \qquad (7\text{-}19)$$

$$b_0 = \overline{Y} - b_1\overline{X}_1 \qquad (7\text{-}20)$$

where:

$\overline{Y}$ = average value of the time series
$= \Sigma Y_t/n$

$\overline{X}_1$ = average value of variable X_1 in the time series
$= \Sigma X_{1t}/n$

Multiple Regression Model:

$$F_t = b_0 + b_1X_{1t} + b_2X_{2t} + \cdots b_kX_{kt} \qquad (7\text{-}21)$$

where:

F_t = forecast value for period t

b_0 = regression intercept

b_i = ith regression coefficient

X_{it} = value of ith explanatory variable measured at time t

Autoregressive Forecasting Model:

$$F_t = b_0 + b_1Y_{t-1} + b_2Y_{t-2} \qquad (7\text{-}22)$$

where:

F_t = forecast value in time t

Y_{t-1} = value of the time series at time $t - 1$

Y_{t-2} = value of the time series at time $t - 2$

Trend Projection Model:

$$F_t = b_0 + b_1t + b_2t^2 + b_3t^3 \qquad (7\text{-}23)$$

where:

F_t = forecast value of the time series at time t

t = value of time at time t

t^2 = time squared

t^3 = time cubed

Chapter Glossary

Alpha(α) The smoothing constant used in exponential smoothing to indicate the relative weight placed on the most recent observations versus the historical observations.

Beta(β) The second smoothing constant used in double exponential smoothing. It is used to weight the trend component of the model.

Bias The propensity of a forecasting model to over- or underforecast the actual value of the time series.

Cyclical component Patterns of time-series observations that are above or below the long-term trend. The frequency and magnitude of the pattern are not generally predictable.

Delphi method A qualitative forecasting technique that relies on a group of experts using a series of questionnaires to obtain a consensus about an uncertain future.

Deseasonalizing The process of removing the seasonal component from a time series.

Double exponential smoothing An exponential smoothing forecasting model which incorporates a second smoothing statistic to account for the trend in the time series.

Exponential smoothing A forecasting technique which weights the current data more heavily than the past data. The weights placed on the older observations decrease exponentially over time.

Forecast error The difference between the actual value of a time series and the forecast value; also referred to as the *residual.*

Forecasting The process of predicting what the future will be like.

Forecasting horizon The number of periods in the future covered by the forecast; sometimes referred to as the *forecast lead time.*

Forecasting interval The frequency with which new forecasts are prepared.

Forecasting period The unit of time for which forecasts are made. The period may be a day, week, month, quarter, or year.

Immediate-term horizon As defined in this text, less than one month into the future.

Indicator variable An independent variable in a regression model measured in time t which is used in forecasting the dependent variable at time $t + n$.

Least-squares regression The procedure of fitting a line to a set of data to minimize the sum of the squared errors around the line.

Linear trend A long-term increase or decrease in a time series in which the rate of change is relatively constant.

Long-term horizon As defined in this text, two years or more into the future.

Mean absolute deviation (MAD) The average of the absolute differences between the actual time-series values and the forecast values.

Mean squared error (MSE) The average of the squared differences between actual and predicted values.

Medium-term horizon As defined in this text, three months to two years into the future.

Model diagnosis The process of analyzing the quality of a model.

Model fitting The process of determining how well a specified model fits past data.

Model specification The process of selecting the forecasting technique to be used in a particular application.

Moving average The average of n consecutive values of a time series.

Multiple regression models A regression model having more than one independent (explanatory) variable.

Nonlinear trend An increase or decrease in a time series where the rate of change is not constant.

Planning The process of determining how to deal with the future.

Qualitative forecasting Forecasting techniques which are based on expert opinion and judgment.

Quantitative forecasting Forecasting techniques which are based on statistical methods for analyzing time-series data.

Random component Changes in the time-series data that are unpredictable and cannot be associated with the trend or with seasonal, or cyclical components.

Ratio to moving average The actual value of the time series divided by the centered moving average; a step in the process of constructing seasonal indexes.

Residual The difference between the actual value of the time series and the forecast value; also called the *forecast error.*

Scenario projection A qualitative forecasting technique using a self-contained set of assumptions to develop plausible descriptions of the future.

Seasonal component Those changes, of predictable magnitude, that occur at the same time every year in time-series data.

Seasonal index A number used to quantify the effect of seasonality in time-series data. Indexes exceeding 1.0 imply that the period has values higher than normal; values less than 1.0 imply that values for the period are typically lower than normal.

Seasonally unadjusted forecast A forecast made for seasonal data which does not include an adjustment for the seasonal component in the time series.

Short-term horizon As defined in this text, one to three months into the future.

Smoothing constant The value (also called *alpha*) which determines the weight placed on the most current observation in an exponential smoothing model.

Split samples The process of dividing time-series data into two groups, one used to construct the model and the second used to test the ability of the model to forecast.

Sum of squared errors The sum of the squared differences (errors) between actual and predicted values. In least-squares regression, this quantity is minimized when the model is fitted.

Time-series data Data measured over time. In most applications the period between measurements is uniform.

Time-series plot A two-dimensional plot of the time series. The vertical axis measures the variable of interest and the horizontal axis corresponds to the time periods. The points on the graph are frequently connected by straight line segments.

Trend component The long-term increase or decrease in time-series data.

Weighted moving average A moving average with weights assigned to the time-series values.

Chapter References

BOOKS

Bowerman, Bruce L., and Richard T. O'Connell. *Time Series Forecasting,* 2d ed. Boston: Duxbury, 1987.

Cryer, Johnathan D. *Time Series Analysis.* Boston: Duxbury, 1986.

Makridakis, Spyros, and Steven C. Wheelwright. *Forecasting: Methods and Applications.* New York: Wiley, 1978.

Montgomery, D. C., and L. A. Johnson. *Forecasting and Time Series Analysis.* New York: McGraw-Hill, 1976.

Neter, John, and William Wasserman. *Applied Linear Statistical Models.* Homewood, Ill.: Irwin, 1974.

ARTICLES

Armstrong, J. Scott. "Forecasting by Extrapolation: Conclusions from 25 Years of Research." *Interfaces,* Vol. 14, No. 6, 1984.

——— "The Ombudsman: Research on Forecasting—A Quarter-Century Review, 1960–1984." *Interfaces,* Vol. 16, No. 1, 1986.

Brandon, Charles, R. Fritz, and J. Xander. "Econometric Forecasts: Evaluation and Revision." *Applied Economics,* Vol. 15, No. 2, 1983.

Juster, F. T. "An Evaluation of the Recent Record in Short-term Forecasting." *Business Economics,* Vol. 7, No. 3, 1972.

McLaughlin, Robert L. "Forecasting Models: Sophisticated or Naive?" *Journal of Forecasting,* Vol. 2, No. 3, 1983.

Mini Cases

CASE 7A

THE ST. LOUIS COMPANIES

An irritated Roger Hatton finds himself sitting in the St. Louis airport after hearing that his flight to Chicago has been delayed—and, if the storm in Chicago continues, possibly cancelled. Since he must get to Chicago if at all possible, Roger is stuck at the airport. Then he decides he might as well try to get some work done, so he opens his lap-top computer and calls up the CLAIMNUM file.

Roger was recently assigned as an analyst in the worker compensation section of the St. Louis Companies, one of the biggest issuers of worker compensation insurance in the country. Until this year, the revenues and claim costs for all parts of the company were grouped together to determine any yearly profit or loss. Therefore, no one really knew if an individual department was profitable or not. Now, however, the new president is looking at each part of the company as a profit center. The clear implication is that money-losing departments may not have a future unless they can develop a clear plan to become profitable.

When Roger asked the accounting department for a listing, by client, of all policy payments and claims filed and paid, he was told that the information is available but he may have to wait 2 or 3 months to get it. He was able to determine, however, that the department has been keeping track of the clients who file frequent (at least one a month) claims and the total number of firms that purchase worker compensation insurance. Using the data from this report, Roger divides the number of clients filing frequent claims by the corresponding number of clients. These ratios, kept in the CLAIMNUM file in his computer, are as follows:

Year	Ratio (%)	Year	Ratio (%)
1	3.8	12	6.1
2	3.6	13	7.8
3	3.5	14	7.1
4	4.9	15	7.6
5	5.9	16	9.7
6	5.6	17	9.6
7	4.9	18	7.5
8	5.6	19	7.9
9	8.5	20	8.3
10	7.7	21	8.4
11	7.1		

Staring at these figures, Roger feels there should be some way to use them to project what the next several years may hold if the company doesn't change its underwriting policies.

CASE 7B

WAGNER MACHINE WORKS

Mary Lindsey has recently agreed to leave her upper-level management job at a major paper manufacturing firm and return to her hometown to take over the family machine products business. The U.S. machine products industry had a strong position of world dominance until recently, when it was devastated by foreign competition, particularly from Germany and Japan. Among the many problems facing the American industry is that it is made up of many small firms—which must compete with foreign industrial giants.

Wagner Machine Works, the company Mary is taking over, is one of the few survivors in its part of the state. But it, too, faces increasing competitive pressure. Mary's father let the business slide as he approached retirement, and Mary sees the need for an immediate modernization of their plant. She has arranged for a loan from the local bank, but now must forecast sales for the next 3 years to ensure the company has enough cash flow to repay the debt. Surprisingly, Mary finds that her father has no forecasting system in place, and she cannot afford the time, or money, to install a system like that used at her previous company.

Wagner Machine Works' quarterly sales (in millions of dollars) for the past 15 years are as follows:

	Quarter			
Year	1	2	3	4
1976	10,490	11,130	10,005	11,058
1977	11,424	12,550	10,900	12,335
1978	12,835	13,100	11,660	13,767
1979	13,877	14,100	12,780	14,738
1980	14,798	15,210	13,785	16,218
1981	16,720	17,167	14,785	17,725
1982	18,348	18,951	16,554	19,889
1983	20,317	21,395	19,445	22,816
1984	23,335	24,179	22,548	25,029
1985	25,729	27,778	23,391	27,360
1986	28,886	30,125	26,049	30,300
1987	30,212	33,702	27,907	31,096
1988	31,715	35,720	28,554	34,326
1989	35,533	39,447	30,046	37,587
1990	39,093	44,650	32,035	40,877

While looking at these data, Mary wonders whether they can be used to forecast sales for the next 3 years. She wonders how much, if any, confidence she can have in a forecast made with these data. And she also wonders if the recent increase in sales is due to growing business or just to inflationary price increases.

CASE 7C
FORECASTING AT ORE-IDA

While all organizations must forecast as they plan for future operations, in many cases goal setting and forecasting are intertwined, especially when forecasting for such factors as sales and market share. If a firm is considering a goal of increasing sales 10 percent next year, the sales forecast provides an indication of how realistic the goal is. However, one should be careful not to mistakenly consider the goal to be the forecast. At Ore-Ida, management and the forecasting staff work together to tie forecasting into the planning process.

While Ore-Ida has long had periodic planning sessions to make projections of future sales, through the 1970s these forecasts were primarily judgmental. They were typically based on sales levels for the preceding few years and incorporated a desired sales increase. In the late 1970s, management decided to develop a statistical forecasting model and hired a consultant from Data Resources Inc. (DRI) for that purpose.

The DRI consultant attempted to assess the problem. Then, daily throughout the course of the project, he gathered data and secluded himself with a computer overnight as he worked on constructing a forecasting model. At a meeting the next morning, the consultant would present his model to the Ore-Ida managers. Invariably, they would suggest changes in the format of the model—and the process would be repeated. But these efforts never produced a model that was successfully implemented, partly because of the reluctance of the Ore-Ida managers to use an unfamiliar tool that they didn't feel comfortable with.

In 1982, Don Holley, an expert in econometric forecasting, was hired to develop an in-house sales and market-share forecasting model for the frozen potato products sold by Ore-Ida. He developed a regression-based econometric forecasting model composed of three regression equations.

The first equation is used to forecast the total demand for frozen potato products. Since inflation has been a factor in forecasting since the late 1960s, all inputs are in real, inflation-adjusted terms. While the exact details of the model are confidential, the general format is:

$$Y = b_0 + b_1X_1 + b_2X_2 + b_3X_3 + b_4X_4 \tag{1}$$

where:

Y = total industry demand for frozen potatoes

X_1 = average price for frozen potato products, in real terms

X_2 = U.S. real disposable income

X_3 = price of fresh potatoes, in real terms

X_4 = Ore-Ida advertising, gross rating points

The second equation attempts to project Ore-Ida's share of the total market for frozen potato products:

$$Y = b_0 + b_1X_1 + b_2X_2 + b_3X_3 + b_4X_4 \tag{2}$$

where:

Y = Ore-Ida market share of frozen potato products

X_1 = Ore-Ida price, in real terms

X_2 = average price for all other producers, in real terms

X_3 = real disposable income

X_4 = real consumer credit

Y, X_1, X_2, X_3, X_4 all measured in time t

The third equation is for forecasting the price of fresh potatoes. The simplest of the three equations, it has the following form:

$$Y = b_0 + b_1X_1 \tag{3}$$

where:

Y = price of fresh potatoes in time t

X_1 = size of the period t fresh potato crop

The models are based on historical data beginning in 1971 and are the result of extended efforts to determine a viable forecasting system for the company's frozen potatoes. Each of the three regression equations fits the historical data well, with a coefficient of determination (R^2) in the neighborhood of .95.

In each regression equation, the dependent and independent variables are measured in the same time frame. This presents Ore-Ida with a problem in implementing the equations for forecasting, since, to forecast 1990 sales, it is necessary to know values for the independent variables for 1990. Because all of these are not available when they are needed, Ore-Ida must rely on forecasts for some of the independent variables. For instance, Wharton Econometrics, a consulting firm associated with the Wharton school at the University of Pennsylvania, provides forecasts for disposable personal income, consumer credit, and the GNP deflator. Ore-Ida also uses a consulting firm and an in-house forecasting group to project the fall potato crop. In addition, the gross rating points can be projected by the Ora-Ida marketing department, based on planned advertising and promotional efforts.

The fact that the independent variables used in providing the forecast are not known with certainty and must be forecast means that the forecasts are subject to greater potential error than indicated by the regression results. Because of this, the company managers are careful to view the regression-based forecasts as only one input into the final sales forecast.

The main purpose of the work performed by Don Holley is to help follow the progress of the company throughout the year. He continually updates the forecasts as new data become available. The various product managers compare their sales against the forecasts provided by the models month by month. The marketing department also uses the forecasting model as a planning tool by substituting different projected gross rating points and then observing the impact on demand forecasts. In addition, the model is used to help establish a guideline for the corporate sales goals. The sales level determined by Don Holley's model is used as a baseline level when management sets the sales goals for the planning period.

ASSIGNMENTS

1. Contact at least one company in your area to discuss the forecasting techniques used by its managers. Write a paper which describes the company, its products, and its forecasting methods.
2. Select an industry, such as the frozen-foods industry, for which to prepare an annual sales forecast. Collect historical data on annual sales and develop a model for forecasting annual sales for the industry. Write a paper describing your efforts and the results of your work. Be sure to discuss the various forecasting techniques you considered.

Chapter 8

INTRODUCTION TO INVENTORY CONTROL MODELS

Chapter Outline

Chapter 8

Why You Need to Know

Inventories are the parts, materials, or finished goods which a business keeps on hand, waiting to be used or sold. As a consumer of finished goods, you have already had considerable experience with inventories. At the grocery store, the shelves are stacked with food and other goods of all kinds and there is even more food in the stockroom at the back of the store. A department store's clothing section has many racks of dresses, shirts, and pants; and its shoe section has numerous boxes of shoes. An automobile dealership has several new cars in the showroom and more out on the sales lot. Your local fast-food restaurant has a supply of hamburger patties, buns, and french fries. From a consumer's standpoint, an inventory of finished goods means the items you want to buy are available when you want to buy them. This is also true for a company that manufactures personal computers. The production department is actually a consumer of parts and materials, which may be purchased from an outside supplier or fabricated by another department within the company. The production department wants the parts and materials to be available when they are needed so the production process can flow smoothly. From the consumer's viewpoint, a large inventory means that more finished goods (or parts and materials) will be on hand to meet immediate needs.

However, when you graduate and go to work for an organization, you will see the inventory picture from a different angle. You will see that carrying inventory costs money, and for some organizations it is a major expense of doing business. A typical automobile dealership might have 200–300 new cars on the sales lot at any time and have another 200 used cars which were taken as trade-ins. If the average dealer cost of a new car is $12,000, then 300 new cars would represent $3.6 million in inventory. The used-car inventory might be worth $600,000, for a total of $4.2 million in vehicle inventory. And most dealerships have a service department, which must carry a wide inventory of new parts worth, say, $400,000 to $1.0 million. Thus, the dealership might, at any given time, have as much as $5 million tied up in inventory. Money committed to inventory cannot be used for other purposes. Even if the only alternative were to invest the $5 million at 10% interest, the annual cost of carrying the inventory, due to lost investment income, might reach $500,000.

There are other costs associated with carrying inventory. For instance, storing 300 new and 200 used vehicles may require several acres of expensive real estate. Added to the real estate investment is the cost of insurance, inventory taxes, and other miscellaneous costs. Thus, a dealership incurs a large annual inventory cost so consumers can have a choice of vehicles.

Clearly, the decision of how many items to maintain in inventory involves a trade-off between always having items available for the consumer and reducing inventory costs. In this chapter, we will introduce several inventory control models which decision makers use to deal with this trade-off issue. Since inventory represents a major cost to many organizations, a good understanding of these models and the issues related to inventory management may be of great value to you in the future.

Chapter Objectives

This chapter introduces the basic concepts of inventory management and discusses the various costs associated with inventory. The trade-off between carrying too much inventory and not carrying enough is highlighted.

Specifically, the objectives of this chapter are to:

1. Define the important concepts associated with inventory management.
2. Discuss the difference between deterministic and probabilistic inventory models.

3. Introduce the basic economic order quantity (EOQ) model and show how it is applied.
4. Expand on the basic EOQ model to take into consideration business situations where planned inventory shortages are allowed.
5. Expand on the EOQ model to consider situations where quantity discounts are available.
6. Introduce the economic production lot size model and show how it is applied.

8-1 HISTORICAL PERSPECTIVE

People and organizations have experienced inventory problems throughout the ages, but not until the twentieth century had anyone attempted an analytical study of such problems. Two factors stimulated these efforts: (1) the growth of large, diverse manufacturing industries, which developed so many problems in purchasing, scheduling, storage, and production that the industry's ability to operate profitably was adversely affected; and (2) the development of industrial engineering, which stressed the scientific analysis of manufacturing operations.

The early efforts in inventory-control theory focused on constructing a mathematical equation to represent important factors in an organization's inventory situation. If a mathematical representation was possible, then the same tools being used in physics and engineering could be used to analyze possible courses of action for business. Using this approach, Ford Harris of Westinghouse developed the first inventory model in 1915. The application of scientific tools to inventory management spread rapidly; and by the 1920s, the models discussed in this chapter were being developed.

Because the early inventory control models assumed that all factors needed in the decision process were known, they are often called *deterministic models*. In reality, most inventory control problems have a large degree of uncertainty; but efforts to consider it a factor did not begin until after World War II. A discussion of some of the *probabilistic models* developed during this period is included in Chapter 9 of this text.

Since the 1960s, manufacturing techniques have undergone significant changes. In particular, some recent techniques such as Flexible Manufacturing Systems (FMS), Computer-Aided Manufacturing (CAM), Computer-Integrated Manufacturing (CIM), and Just-In-Time (JIT) manufacturing have so changed the industry that tools which worked well in the world of the 1920s and 1930s, and even the 1950s and 1960s, no longer apply. Chapter 9 also discusses some of these changes and the newest developments in inventory control theory.

8-2 THE MANAGEMENT OF INVENTORY

A specialty store at a local shopping mall sells expensive, high-quality luggage. It has a very wide selection, with literally hundreds of styles of suitcases, attaché cases, and garment bags — and not just one item of each style. There is little doubt that if someone were looking for a special type of luggage, this store would be the place to go. But we can't help wondering how much money is invested in its inventory. For this little store, a large share of its expense of doing business is obviously the large inventory it carries.

Inventory is the collection of parts, materials, work in process, and finished goods which are waiting to be used or sold. In fact, this definition can be expanded to include other factors used by an organization, such as cash and employees. Thus, broadly defined, inventory is *any* asset held by an organization. For many companies, like the luggage specialty shop, inventory is a major expense of doing business. A key to the success of any company, then, may be how well it manages its inventory.

Let's now consider the example of MacMillin Computer Stores, Inc., which operates in the Southwest. The company supplies 75 retail stores from its warehouse and headquarters in Scottsdale, Arizona. Each store sells personal computers as well as related hardware and software, but carries only a small inventory of products. Most of the company's inventory is held in the Scottsdale warehouse. On average, the warehouse has 500 computers in stock, with an average cost to MacMillin of $1000 per unit. Thus, the total cost of PC inventory at any time is approximately $500,000.

The person who manages the PC inventory has the responsibility to ship computers to the retail stores when they are needed and to order new ones from the manufacturer.

TWO TYPES OF INVENTORY MODELS

The manager in charge of an inventory continually faces two decisions:

1. *How many* or how much must be ordered to replenish inventory?
2. *When* should an order be placed?

To be useful, an inventory model must help the manager answer these questions.

Inventory models can be divided into two main categories: deterministic and probabilistic. **Deterministic models** are based on the assumption that all required information is known with certainty. For instance, one vital piece of information common to all inventory models is the demand rate, the number of units demanded during a specified time period. In Chapter 7, you learned about a number of demand forecasting techniques. The company might well use one or more of these techniques to arrive at its anticipated demand rate. In a deterministic inventory model, the forecast demand rate is assumed to be the actual demand that will occur during the period.

Probabilistic models assume that one or more items of information are not known with certainty but instead are described by a probability distribution. For instance, in a probabilistic inventory model, a point estimate for the demand rate might be forecast using the techniques introduced in Chapter 7. The model might then consider demand to be normally distributed around the point estimate; thus, the actual demand during the period is probabilistic.

This chapter focuses on several classical deterministic inventory models, and Chapter 9 discusses probabilistic models.

8-3 THE ELEMENTARY ECONOMIC ORDER QUANTITY (EOQ) MODEL

Inventory models can be further divided, according to their application, into two groups: (1) purchasing models and (2) production models. A *purchasing model* is one in which the inventory item is purchased from a supplier outside the company or from another department within the company. MacMillin Computer Stores, for instance, would use a purchasing model in making inventory decisions because the company purchases its merchandise from outside manufacturers. The purchasing model would help MacMillin's manager determine *how many* units to order and *when* to place the order.

A *production model* is one in which the inventory item is produced internally, not ordered from an outside supplier. For instance, the PC manufacturer that sells to MacMillin Computer Stores would use a production model, since it must make new PCs to replace the ones ordered by its customers. The production model would help the managers determine *how many* units to make in a production run and *when* to begin producing them.

Within a company, the same inventory item can be managed using both a purchasing model and a production model. Consider a company like Hewlett-Packard, which makes a broad line of computer products. Suppose a department within the printer division assembles the paper-feed unit for the popular HP laser printer, but the tray component is made by another department. The assembly department would use a purchasing model to manage its tray inventory, and the department which actually makes the trays would use a production model. We will begin our model development with purchasing models and then consider a production model.

INVENTORY COSTS

Recall that the two main questions an inventory manager must answer are: (1) How much to order? and (2) When should the order be placed? The early efforts to answer these questions attempted to identify, and then minimize, the costs associated with having inventory.

MacMillin Computer Stores has about \$500,000 worth of PCs in inventory at any one time. On its balance sheet, this inventory shows up as a current asset. A typical company may have inventories which represent 20 – 40% of total assets. However, you should remember that inventory represents idle resources and that most companies strive to keep their inventories as low as possible to free capital for other productive uses.

In measuring the success of a company's inventory management, the common criterion is cost. Most companies seek an inventory policy which minimizes the total inventory cost. The classical inventory models discussed in this chapter consider four cost components as defining total inventory costs. Figure 8-1 shows these four costs.

The first component is *purchase cost* or *production cost*. In some cases the unit cost is the same for any number of items purchased. In other instances, there may be a

Figure 8-1
Inventory cost components

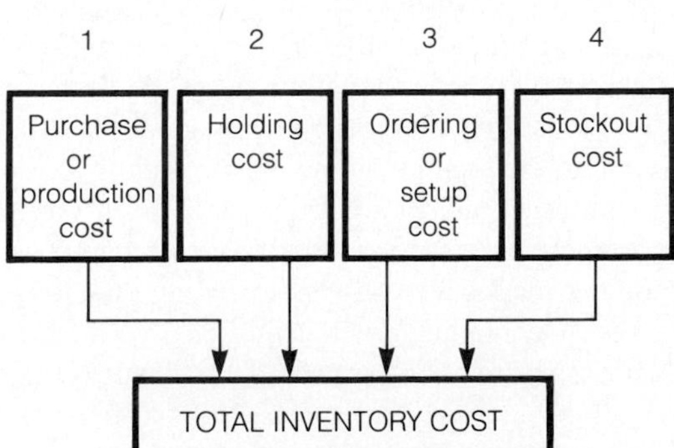

quantity discount, which is a reduction in unit cost provided to encourage larger orders. For instance, MacMillin Computer Stores pays $800 per unit for a 256K, dual-drive PC regardless of the quantity ordered. Computers with a 20-MB hard disk and 640K of RAM cost $1300, regardless of the quantity purchased. Thus, for PCs, the company does not get a quantity discount; but for other products, such as printer ribbons, MacMillin does get a reduction in the unit price as its order size increases. Likewise, in manufacturing, the unit production cost may be reduced for large runs due to efficiencies gained from running the line for a longer period of time.

The second cost component contributing to the total inventory cost is *holding cost,* or *carrying cost.* **Holding cost**, the cost associated with holding one item in inventory for a specified period, includes both opportunity costs and out-of-pocket costs. It is a function of the cost of the inventory and the length of time the inventory is on hand. Any fixed organizational costs, which are incurred regardless of the inventory size, are not included as part of the holding costs.

Consider the PC inventory carried by MacMillin Computer Stores. Suppose that on average the purchase cost of the inventory is approximately $500,000. This means that the company has $500,000 tied up in inventory which could be used for other purposes. The amount a company expects to earn on its assets is referred to as its *cost of capital.* Each company's cost of capital differs, but if MacMillin's is 12%, then on an annual basis the opportunity cost for holding this PC inventory is $\$500,000 \times .12 = \$60,000$. This is termed an *opportunity cost* because the $500,000 could have been used to generate $60,000 of income. However, if MacMillin had borrowed the $500,000 at 12% interest, the $60,000 would represent an *out-of-pocket cost.*

Other components of the holding cost include costs associated with insurance, storage space, product spoilage or deterioration, taxes, product obsolescence, and handling. Annually, total holding costs can easily amount to 25–35% of purchase costs. Holding costs are often represented as a percentage of the unit cost.

The third cost component is *ordering* or *setup* cost. This is the cost of placing an order to replenish inventory, if a purchasing model is used, or the cost of setting up the plant to produce the needed item if a production model is used. The order (or setup) cost is usually not dependent on the number of items ordered. But such components as the clerical costs of preparing, processing, and expediting an order are included in the order cost. Fixed shipping costs are also often considered a part of the ordering cost, as are personnel costs for unloading the order when it is received. In a production setting, setup costs consist of retooling and otherwise setting up machinery for the new production run. Some clerical and administrative costs associated with the setup should also be included. When increased scrap is generated at the startup of a production run, these costs are added to the other setup costs.

The final component is **stockout cost**, which is the cost associated with running out of inventory. In some situations a stockout means that a sale is lost and the customer will go somewhere else. For instance, if MacMillin Computer Stores has a stockout of PCs, a customer may well go to another vendor and MacMillin will have lost the profit from that sale. In addition, MacMillin may also lose goodwill, which will affect future sales. Assigning a dollar cost to a factor as intangible as lost goodwill is difficult, and the managers responsible should take great care not to neglect or undervalue this cost. In a production environment, a stockout may mean idle resources and lost production output. The associated costs can be significant.

In some cases, when a stockout occurs the customer may not be lost if the item can be *backordered.* Some goodwill may still be lost in this process, and there may be increased direct costs associated with processing and expediting the backorder. In this chapter, we will discuss both types of models—ones that do and ones that do not allow for backordering.

ASSUMPTIONS OF THE EOQ MODEL

We will begin our examination of classical inventory control models by addressing the question of how much to order. The introductory model used for answering this question is the elementary EOQ model, which is based on the following assumptions:

1. *Demand is known with certainty and is constant during the inventory period.* This means that the total number of units demanded during the inventory period is known and that the demand each day (or week or month) is the same. For instance, if annual demand is known to be 1200 units, demand each month will be 100 units.
2. *All items ordered are received at one time.* For example, if 200 units are ordered, the entire shipment of 200 will arrive on a particular day.
3. *Lead times are known with certainty.* This means that the time between placing an order and receiving it is a known amount.
4. *All costs are known with certainty.* This means the various inventory-related costs can be accurately determined.
5. *No stockouts are allowed.* The elementary EOQ model assumes that all demand will be filled from inventory and that no backordering will take place.
6. *No quantity discounts are given.* The per unit cost is the same regardless of the quantity ordered. Because of this assumption, the purchase cost need not be considered when using the basic EOQ model.
7. *Constant ordering and setup costs are known with certainty.* This means the order cost or setup cost is a fixed value, regardless of the number ordered, and the cost is known.

The elementary EOQ model is the most restrictive of the classical inventory models in terms of assumptions. The other models introduced in this chapter are variations of this basic model.

DEVELOPING AN EOQ MODEL

To illustrate the development of an EOQ model, we will focus on a pizza business owned by two brothers in Fargo, North Dakota. David and Robert Chessman started their business 5 years ago. Like other pizza makers, they sell pizzas with a variety of toppings; however, a common ingredient for all their pizzas is cheese purchased from the Midland Creamery in Minneapolis. Since it is essential for all the pizzas, cheese is one item that David and Robert never want to run out of.

In developing an ordering policy for cheese, the brothers identified the following:

1. Cheese cost per pound = $1.20
2. Holding-cost factor = 25%
3. Ordering cost = $50.00

The cost of $1.20 per pound is a price the Chessman brothers and Midland agreed to earlier and will be good for the next year. The holding-cost factor of 25% takes into account the opportunity cost of having resources invested in inventory which could be earning interest. It also includes the cost of some spoilage that occurs when the cheese is stored in Fargo. The brothers believe the 25% figure accurately represents their holding costs. This means, for example, that if their average annual cheese inventory value is $100, the holding cost would be $25. The $50 ordering cost includes all administrative and labor costs necessary to place an order, to make sure the order arrives, and to actually receive the order.

The final factor which will influence the ordering policy for cheese is the demand rate. Table 8-1 shows cheese use for the past 15 weeks. Because of the minimal variation in weekly demand for cheese, assuming a constant demand rate is acceptable. Both brothers agree that during the next year no growth in business is expected and that weekly cheese use will be 1600 pounds. Annual demand will total 83,200 pounds (52 weeks × 1600 pounds = 83,200 pounds) of cheese. Based on a 365-day operating year, the daily cheese demand will be just under 228 pounds.

One method to determine how many pounds of cheese to order was advanced by David when he suggested they place an order every fourth day in a quantity just large enough to last 4 days. Since they use 228 pounds every day, under this plan the order quantity, Q, would be $4 \times 228 = 912$ pounds. He argued that this plan would keep both inventory and holding costs low.

Figure 8-2 illustrates how the cheese inventory would look for the 4-day plan. When a shipment is received, 912 pounds marks the maximum inventory level. Then demand begins at a constant rate of 228 pounds per day, causing the inventory to be depleted (as shown in Figure 8-2), until the end of day 4, when the supply is exhausted and the minimum inventory level is reached. However, the next order will arrive exactly as the last of the current cheese supply is used, again boosting the cheese inventory to its maximum level of 912 pounds. The inventory depletion process is then repeated.

Figure 8-2 also shows the average inventory is $Q/2$: that is, the average inventory is equal to one-half the quantity ordered. This makes sense, since the maximum inventory level is Q, the minimum inventory level is 0, and inventory declines at a constant rate over time. Thus, on average, using this ordering plan, the Chessman Brothers Pizza Company would have 456 pounds of cheese on hand. To figure the holding cost, we establish the following notation:

H = annual holding cost for one unit

C = unit cost = \$1.20

I = inventory holding-cost factor, in decimal form = .25

Table 8-1 CHESSMAN BROTHERS PIZZA: CHEESE DEMAND (BASED ON AMOUNT USED IN A 15-WEEK PERIOD)

Week	Cheese Used (pounds)	Week	Cheese Used (pounds)
1	1,560	9	1,590
2	1,623	10	1,600
3	1,580	11	1,605
4	1,578	12	1,585
5	1,610	13	1,590
6	1,615	14	1,600
7	1,590	15	1,605
8	1,605		
			Total = 23,936
			Average = 1,595.7

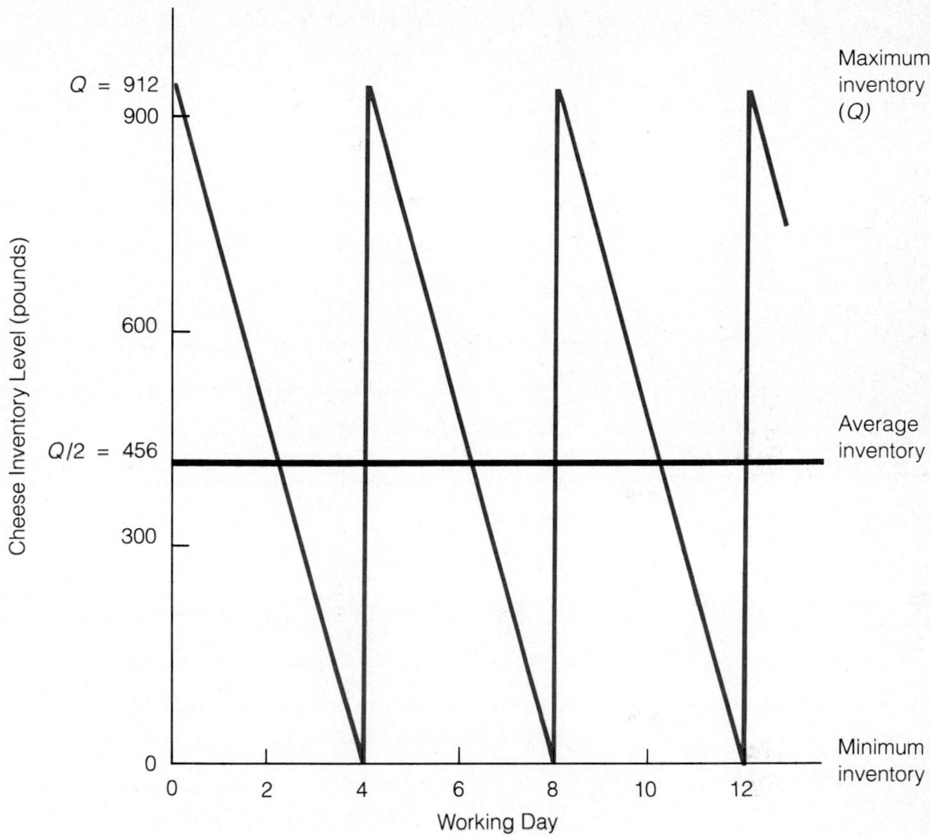

Figure 8-2
Chessman Brothers Pizza: David's inventory proposal

The cost of storing 1 pound of cheese for 1 year is:

$$\begin{aligned} H &= IC \\ &= (.25)(\$1.20) \\ &= \$.30 \end{aligned} \tag{8-1}$$

Then if, on average, the company has 456 pounds of cheese in inventory, the annual holding cost is found by multiplying the holding cost per pound, \$.30, times the average inventory level, 456 pounds:

$$\text{Annual inventory holding cost} = (\$.30)(456) = \$136.80$$

In notation form, the annual inventory holding cost is given by equation 8-2, as follows:

$$\text{Annual inventory holding cost} = (Q/2)IC \tag{8-2}$$

where:

Q = order quantity
I = inventory holding-cost factor, in decimal form
C = unit cost

In some applications, the unit holding cost, H, may be given. An alternative equation for annual inventory holding cost is:

$$\text{Annual inventory holding cost} = (Q/2)\ H \tag{8-2a}$$

where:

Q = order quantity

H = inventory holding cost per unit

Under David's proposed plan, the annual holding cost for the cheese inventory is only \$136.80. But Robert noted that this plan would require frequent orders each year. If annual demand, D, is 83,200 pounds (1600 pounds per week × 52 weeks), and if the quantity to be ordered is 912 pounds, then the number of orders made during the year is:

$$\text{Number of orders} = D/Q \tag{8-3}$$

where:

D = annual demand

Q = order quantity

Thus, Chessman Brothers Pizza will have to order:

$$83{,}200/912 = 91.2 \text{ times during the year}$$

The cost of each order, C_o, is \$50, making the annual ordering cost \$4560 (91.2 orders × \$50 per order). Equation 8-4 shows the equation for the annual ordering cost:

$$\text{Annual ordering cost} = (D/Q)\ C_o \tag{8-4}$$

where:

D = annual demand

Q = order quantity

C_o = cost to place one order

Since the brothers will not allow their cheese inventory to run out, there will be no stockout costs. Also, the purchase portion of total inventory cost will be a constant (83,200 × \$1.20 = \$99,840) and is therefore not considered in analyzing how many units to order each time an order is placed during the year. The total annual inventory cost, TC, is reduced to two components, holding cost and ordering cost, as follows:

$$TC = (Q/2)\ IC + (D/Q)\ C_o \tag{8-5}$$

For this example, the total annual inventory cost is:

$$\begin{aligned} TC &= (912/2)(\$.30) + (83{,}200/912)(\$50) \\ &= \$136.80 + \$4560 = \$4696.80 \end{aligned}$$

As the total cost value shows, while David's plan of ordering 912 pounds every 4 days does an excellent job of keeping the holding costs low, the plan would result in a large ordering cost due to the large number of orders (91.22) during the year. Is there a better ordering plan, one which will result in a lower total inventory cost? One approach to find a better value would be to try different order quantities to see whether an improvement in total cost can be achieved.

Table 8-2 CHESSMAN BROTHERS PIZZA: INVENTORY COSTS FOR VARIOUS ORDER QUANTITIES

Order Quantity (pounds)	Holding Cost ($)	Ordering Cost ($)	Total Cost ($)
912	136.80	4560.00	4696.80
1,000	150.00	4160.00	4310.00
2,000	300.00	2,080.00	2380.00
4,000	600.00	1040.00	1640.00
6,000	900.00	693.33	1593.33
8,000	1200.00	520.00	1720.00
10,000	1500.00	416.00	1916.00

Table 8-2 shows the results of several different trials where the total annual inventory costs were arrived at using equations 8-2 through 8-5. For instance, if $Q = 4000$, we get:

$$\begin{aligned}\text{Holding cost} &= (Q/2)IC \\ &= (4000/2)(.25)(\$1.20) = \$600 \\ \text{Ordering cost} &= (D/Q)C_o \\ &= (83{,}200/4000)(\$50) = \$1040 \\ \text{Total cost} &= \$600 + \$1040 = \$1640\end{aligned}$$

Table 8-2 shows that as order quantity is increased from 912 pounds, the holding cost increases but at a slower rate than the ordering cost decreases. This initially results in a lower total cost. However, for an order quantity between 6000 and 8000 pounds, total cost increases again; and it continues up as Q is increased further.

Figure 8-3, a graph of the cost curves based on the data in Table 8-2, illustrates several important concepts. First, the graph of holding costs is a linear function over

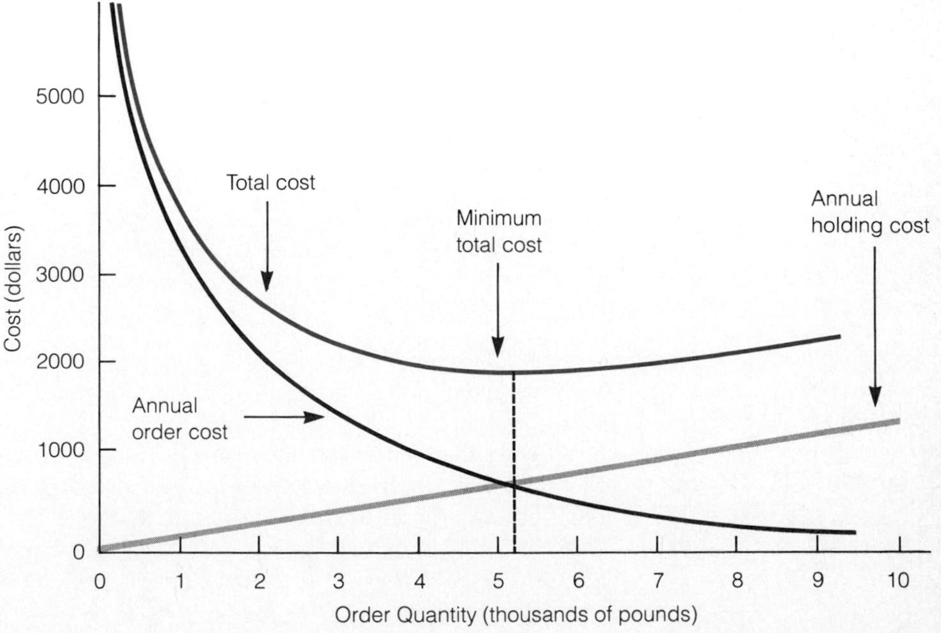

Figure 8-3
Inventory cost curves

the range of order quantities. As order quantity increases, the annual holding costs increase linearly. Second, the graph of annual ordering costs is a decreasing curve which, if we look at larger and larger order quantities, would gradually approach zero as a lifetime supply of cheese is ordered. Finally, the minimum total cost apparently occurs at the quantity where the annual holding-cost curve intersects the annual ordering-cost curve. From our graph (which is only approximate), the order quantity which minimizes total inventory cost is about 5200 pounds.

For an order quantity of 5200 pounds, we get a total cost of $1580, as follows, using equation 8-5:

$$\begin{aligned} TC &= (Q/2)IC + (D/Q)C_o \\ &= (5200/2)(\$.30) + (83{,}200/5200)(\$50) \\ &= \$780 + \$800 = \$1580 \end{aligned}$$

To test this value to see if it is the minimum-cost order quantity, we can try order quantities on either side of 5200 until we are eventually satisfied that we have reached the actual minimum cost.

This trial-and-error method for arriving at the order quantity which will minimize total annual inventory costs is adequate, but it could be very time-consuming. Keep in mind that our objective is to locate the order quantity in Figure 8-3 which corresponds to the minimum point on the total cost curve. Management scientists determined that through the application of differential calculus, an equation for the optimal economic order quantity (EOQ) can be determined which will give the value, Q^*, that minimizes the total annual inventory cost. (The Technical Appendix at the end of this chapter outlines the steps in deriving the EOQ formula shown in equation 8-6.) The EOQ formula is:

$$Q^* = \sqrt{\frac{2DC_o}{IC}} \tag{8-6}$$

Using equation 8-6 for the Chessman Brothers Pizza Company example, we get:

$$Q^* = \sqrt{2(83{,}200)(50)/.30} = 5266.25$$

Thus, the optimal order quantity is 5266.25 pounds of cheese.
The holding cost is:

$$(5266.25/2)(\$.30) = \$789.94$$

and the ordering cost is:

$$(83{,}200/5266.25)(\$50.00) = \$789.94$$

for a total annual inventory cost of:

$$\$789.94 + \$789.94 = \$1579.88$$

For Chessman Brothers Pizza, no other order quantity will result in a lower total annual inventory cost.

Recall that our graph in Figure 8-3 showed that the minimum total annual inventory cost occurred where the annual holding cost curve intersects the annual ordering cost curve. For the Chessman example, we see that annual holding cost ($789.94) equals annual ordering cost ($789.94) when Q^* is used as the order quantity. This will always be true for the elementary EOQ model.

From a practical standpoint, an order quantity of 5266.25 pounds is a bit precise. An advantage of this EOQ model is that the order quantity can be rounded to a more convenient value without leading to large changes in total cost. For instance, if the order quantity is 5000 pounds:

$$\begin{aligned}\text{Total cost} &= (5000/2)(\$.30) + (83{,}200/5000)(\$50)\\ &= \$750 + \$832 = \$1582\end{aligned}$$

If 6000 pounds of cheese is ordered:

$$\begin{aligned}\text{Total cost} &= (6000/2)(\$.30) + (83{,}200/6000)(\$50)\\ &= \$900 + \$693.33 = \$1593.33\end{aligned}$$

Determining When to Order

When a purchasing model is used, an important factor is **lead time**, the time between placing an order and receiving the shipment. Like demand, lead time can be either deterministic (known with certainty) or probabilistic (uncertain). For instance, if the Chessman Brothers know they can receive a shipment of cheese within 4 days of an order, they would assume that lead time is 4 days. However, if the lead time varies between 2 and 6 days, they might define a probability distribution, such as the normal distribution, to describe the lead time for cheese deliveries.

The Chessman brothers' records show that, almost without fail, cheese arrives 4 days from the day the order was placed, and they feel very comfortable with specifying a 4-day lead time. Therefore, lead time is known with certainty.

The EOQ formula developed earlier indicates they should order 5266.25 pounds of cheese, which can be rounded to 5270 pounds. The next important step is determining the **reorder point,** the inventory level at which a new order is placed. The current inventory level is the number of items actually on hand *plus* any items that are on order but have not been received.

The elementary EOQ model assumes there will be no stockouts and that lead time is known. This matches the Chessman Brothers case, since they must have cheese available to meet every pizza order and they know that the lead time for receiving a cheese order is 4 days. Recall that daily cheese demand is assumed to be a constant 228 pounds. Thus, an order must be placed when the inventory level equals a 4-day supply, or 912 ($228 \times 4 = 912$) pounds. Equation 8-7 shows how the reorder point is calculated:

$$ROP = dL \tag{8-7}$$

where:

ROP = reorder point
d = demand per day
L = lead time, in days

For the Chessman Brothers example, the order point is:

$$ROP = (228)(4) = 912 \text{ pounds}$$

When the inventory level drops to 912 pounds, an order will be placed for 5270 pounds. (In the EOQ model, the order point is equal to the demand during lead time.)

The number of orders placed annually will be:

$$N = D/Q^* \qquad (8\text{-}8)$$
$$= 83{,}200/5270 = 15.79 \text{ orders}$$

where:

N = annual orders
D = annual demand
Q^* = economic order quantity

The time between orders is called the **cycle time**. It is calculated using equation 8-9:

$$T = \frac{WQ^*}{D} \qquad (8\text{-}9)$$

where:

T = cycle time, in days
W = number of working days per year
Q^* = economic order quantity
D = annual demand

Since the Chessman Brothers Pizza Company operates 365 days a year, the time between orders—the cycle time—is:

$$T = \frac{(365)(5270)}{83{,}200} = 23.12 \text{ days}$$

Therefore, about every 23 days the company will place an order.

Figure 8-4 shows inventory levels over time for the Chessman Brothers Pizza Company.

A Second Example

The elementary EOQ model is applicable in any situation where the assumptions are satisfied. Let's review those assumptions:

1. Demand is known with certainty and is constant during the inventory period.
2. All items ordered are received at one time.
3. Lead time is known with certainty.
4. All costs are known with certainty.
5. No stockouts are allowed.
6. No quantity discounts are available.
7. Constant order cost is known with certainty.

These assumptions, though quite restrictive, are reasonable for some business situations.

Consider an example involving the Fairfax Manufacturing Company of Portland, Maine. The Fairfax Company makes cable TV control boxes for cable companies throughout the country. It purchases all the components from outside suppliers and assembles the control boxes at its plant in Maine. It has contracts for the next 5 years

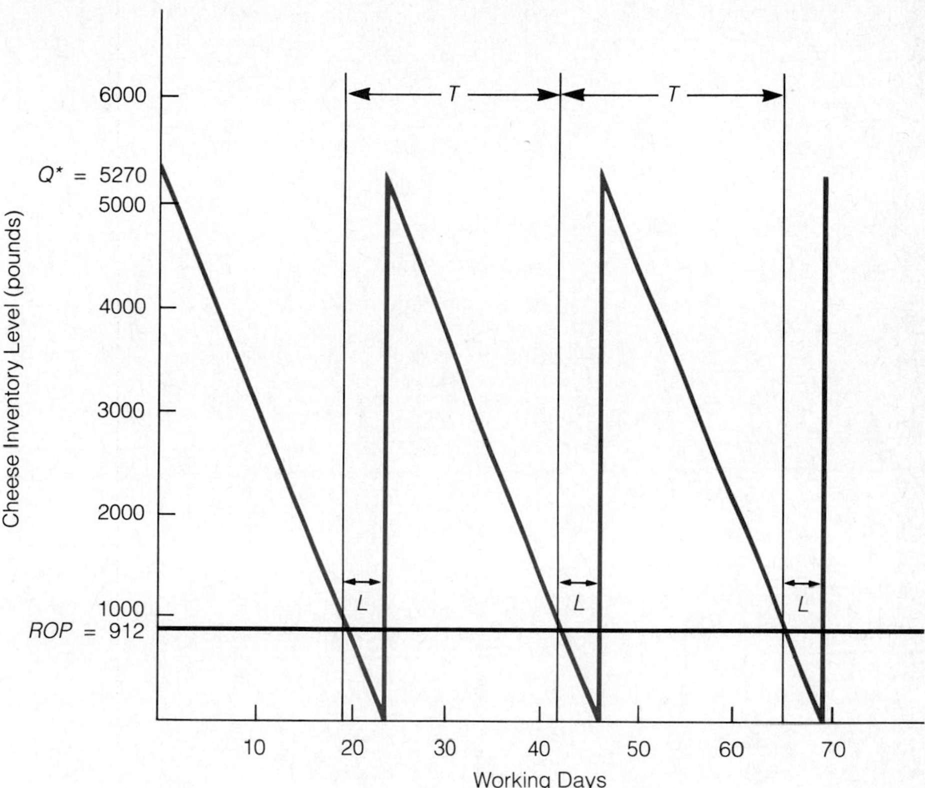

Figure 8-4
Chessman Brothers Pizza problem: cheese inventory

which require producing 300,000 control boxes per year. Each control box requires two tuners, which makes the tuner demand 600,000 per year.

Fairfax operates its plant 250 days per year, using a level production plan which calls for assembling 1200 control boxes per day—this means a constant demand for 2400 tuners per day. Each tuner costs the company $14, and no quantity discounts are available. Management figures the inventory holding-cost factor at 20%, including opportunity costs and out-of-pocket costs. The cost of placing an order is assumed to be $100, regardless of the order size. Finally, the time between placing an order and receipt of the shipment (lead time) has always been a very constant 20 days. The company's production schedule does not allow for downtime, so no stockouts are allowed.

The inventory situation facing Fairfax Manufacturing fits the assumptions of the elementary EOQ model. Once again, we need to answer the two familiar questions:

1. How many tuners should be ordered each time an order is placed?
2. When should an order be placed?

To begin, we identify the following factors:

D = annual demand = 600,000
C_o = order cost = \$100
I = holding-cost factor, in decimal form = .20
C = cost of each tuner = \$14
L = lead time = 20 days
W = working days per year = 250
d = daily demand for tuners = 2400

Equation 8-6 is used to determine the EOQ for the Fairfax Company, as follows:

$$Q^* = \sqrt{\frac{2DC_o}{IC}}$$
$$= \sqrt{\frac{(2)(600{,}000)(\$100)}{(.20)(\$14)}} = 6546.54$$

Based on the assumptions of the EOQ model, the optimal order size is 6546.54 tuners. This order size will minimize the total inventory cost. For the sake of a more practical order size, we will round it to 6550 tuners. The various inventory costs are:

$$\text{Holding cost} = (Q/2)IC$$
$$= (6550/2)(.20)(\$14) = \$9170$$
$$\text{Ordering cost} = (D/Q)C_o$$
$$= (600{,}000/6550)(\$100) = \$9160.30$$
$$\text{Total cost} = \$9170 + \$9160.30 = \$18{,}330.30$$

You might recall that when the total annual cost is minimized, the holding cost and ordering cost will be equal, since the total-cost curve will be minimized at the point where ordering cost and holding cost intersect (see Figure 8-3). The difference between the two costs in our example exists because we used $Q = 6550$ rather than $Q^* = 6546.54$ tuners. However, this rounding to make the order size more practical has not changed the total cost, as you will see if you find the cost associated with $Q^* = 6546.54$.

The question of when to place an order requires us to determine the reorder point. We use equation 8-7, as follows:

$$ROP = dL$$
$$= (2400)(20) = 48{,}000$$

When the tuner inventory drops to 48,000 units, an order should be placed for 6550 tuners.

The cycle time is the time between placing one order and the next. We find the cycle time using equation 8-9, as follows:

$$T = \frac{WQ^*}{D}$$
$$= \frac{(250)(6550)}{600{,}000} = 2.73 \text{ days}$$

An order will be placed every 2.73 working days on average, and each order will be received 20 days later.

This problem gives a rather strange relationship between the reorder point (48,000), order quantity (6550), and average inventory (6550/2 = 3275). Remember, in determining the reorder point, inventory level is defined as the total units on hand plus any on order. The fact that the order point of 48,000 units is higher than the order quantity means the Fairfax Company must begin ordering tuners 20 days ahead of the scheduled production start. During this period the company might place orders for 6550 on day −20, −18, −15, −12, −10, and so on, until total orders equal 20 days' production (2400 × 20 = 48,000 units). This will make 6550 tuners available on day 1, with new orders arriving every few working days.

As we indicated earlier, the elementary EOQ model is the most restrictive in terms of the required assumptions. It is a deterministic model, and it does not allow for backorders or quantity discounts. It also requires that each order be received in full. In the following sections, we will introduce inventory models that, while still deterministic, allow for quantity discounts, planned stockouts, and gradual receipt of inventory.

8-4 EOQ WITH PLANNED BACKORDERING

When an item is demanded but is not available for sale or use, an inventory shortage (called a stockout) exists. As a consumer, you have probably experienced stockouts, such as when you wanted to purchase an item only to be informed that the last one was sold yesterday—but that the item was *backordered*. In some situations, running out of inventory is very undesirable, especially when there is no way to substitute another item for the one demanded. When a customer can simply turn to another vendor for a substitute product, a stockout means a company has not only lost the profit from this sale, but quite possibly has lost future profits due to the loss of goodwill.

However, there are other situations where an organization might actually want to plan for stockouts. This occurs most frequently when the per item cost is extremely high and the customer or user is willing to wait for a backorder to arrive. For example, an automobile dealer carries a number of new cars in inventory but cannot possibly have a car of every color, style, and model available. If a customer wants a car which is not in inventory, it can be backordered from the manufacturer or another dealer. Providing the waiting time is not too long, most customers will wait for the car to arrive.

In this section, we extend the elementary EOQ model to allow for planned backordering. We retain the assumptions of constant demand rate, full receipt of an order at one time, known lead time, and constant and known order cost. However, the requirement that no stockouts occur will be eliminated.

DEVELOPMENT OF THE MODEL

The Big-B Tire Company, owned by Brian Bijan, is a full-service tire store in Kansas City, Missouri. It sells a wide range of tires for passenger cars and trucks. The inventory policy for most tires handled by Big-B requires that no stockouts occur, since Brian wants to have tires available when the customer wants them. This is certainly true for the four models of steel-belted radials for passenger cars and the three models of town-and-country pickup tires. However, Big-B also carries several models of specialty tires not handled by any other dealer in the city. One of these is the XR-7009, a tire used on some types of motorhomes. Because this tire is so expensive ($900 each), and because there is no other dealer for the tire in the Kansas City area, Brian has decided to allow stockouts for it. He plans on carrying some XR-7009s in inventory to meet part of the demand, and will satisfy the remaining demand through backordering.

Once Brian has decided to allow stockouts, the same two questions apply as when backordering is not allowed:

1. How many tires should be ordered each time an order is placed?
2. When should an order be placed?

To effectively answer these questions, we need an inventory model which will allow for stockouts. The stockout model we develop in this section is an extension of the basic EOQ model; it has the following assumptions:

1. Demand is known with certainty and is a constant rate during the inventory period.
2. All items ordered are received at one time.
3. Lead time is known with certainty.
4. All costs are known with certainty.
5. No quantity discounts are available.

Figure 8-5 illustrates inventory levels when planned backordering is allowed. During part of the inventory cycle, demand is satisfied from inventory. However, once the inventory is depleted, the remaining demand is assigned to the backorder. The following notation is used to describe the backorder model. The amounts shown are for the XR-9007 tire.

D = annual demand = 1000

C_o = order cost = \$100

I = holding-cost factor, in decimal form = .20

C = cost of each tire = \$900

L = lead time = 5 days

W = working days per year = 365

d = tires demanded per day = 2.74 (1000/365)

B = backordering penalty cost factor, in decimal form = .30

Q^* = optimal order quantity

S = maximum amount on backorder when an order is just received

Using this notation, and by looking at Figure 8-5, we can establish the following additional factor:

$M = Q - S$ = maximum number of units available for sale (and therefore being held) just after an order is received

When backorders are allowed, we have four components in the inventory total-cost function:

Total cost = holding cost + ordering cost + backorder cost + purchase cost (8-10)

Consider each cost component individually:

Holding cost = average inventory × carrying cost

In Figure 8-5 we see that inventory is held only during t_1 and that during t_2 there is

Figure 8-5
Big-B Tire problem: inventory system with backordering

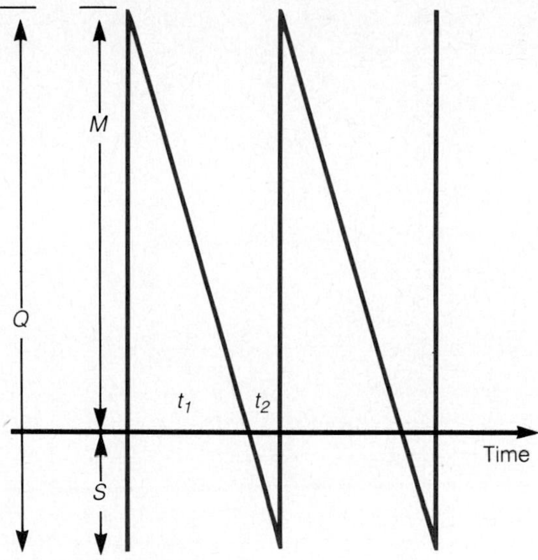

Q = order quantity
M = units to inventory
S = units on backorder
t_1 = time while filling demand from inventory
t_2 = time during backorder

no inventory. Therefore:

$$\text{Average inventory} = \frac{[(M/2)t_1 + 0t_2]}{(t_1 + t_2)}$$

but, given a daily demand of d:

$$t_1 = M/d \qquad \text{and} \qquad t_2 = S/d$$

Since $Q = M + S$, then:

$$(M + S)/d = Q/d \qquad \text{and} \qquad t_1 + t_2 = Q/d$$

Substituting for t_1 and t_2, and letting $M = Q - S$:

$$\text{Average inventory} = (Q - S)^2/2Q$$

and:

$$\text{Holding cost} = \frac{(Q - S)^2 CI}{2Q} \tag{8-11}$$

Using equation 8-4, we can determine the ordering cost by multiplying the number of orders placed per year times the cost of placing one order.

$$\text{Ordering cost} = (D/Q)C_o$$

Next we find the backorder cost, as follows:

$$\text{Backorder cost} = \text{average backorder} \times \text{backorder penalty}$$

Again, in Figure 8-5, we see we have backorders only during t_2 and that during t_1 we have no backorders. Therefore:

$$\text{Average backorders} = [0t_1 + (S/2)t_2]/(t_1 + t_2)$$

As before, $t_1 = M/d$, $t_2 = S/d$, and $t_1 + t_2 = Q/d$. We can substitute for t_1 and t_2 as follows:

$$\text{Average backorders} = S^2/2Q$$

Then we get:

$$\text{Backorder cost} = \frac{S^2BC}{2Q} \tag{8-12}$$

Finally, the purchase cost is equal to the unit cost times the number demanded:

$$\text{Purchase cost} = CD \tag{8-13}$$

Our objective in employing an inventory model is to establish the ordering policy which will minimize total inventory costs. As in the basic EOQ model, we need to determine the optimal order quantity, Q^*, which will result in the minimum overall total cost. However, in addition to determining Q^*, we must also determine S^*, the optimal maximum stockout level when an order is just received. Thus, Q^* and S^* combine to provide the information necessary for Brian to minimize his total inventory costs for the XR-7009 motorhome tire.

As was true for the basic EOQ model, differential calculus is required to determine the values of Q^* and S^* which minimize total cost. This results in equations 8-14 and 8-15:

$$Q^* = \sqrt{\frac{2C_oD}{CI} \times \frac{CI + BC}{BC}} \tag{8-14}$$

$$S^* = Q^* \sqrt{\frac{CI}{CI + BC}} \tag{8-15}$$

We can apply equations 8-14 and 8-15 to the Big-B Tire example to determine the inventory policy which will minimize Brian's total cost for the XR-7009 tire:

$$Q^* = \sqrt{\frac{2\,(100)(1000)}{(900)(.20)} \times \frac{(900)(.20) + (.30)(900)}{(.30)(900)}}$$
$$= 43.03$$

The optimal order quantity is 43.03 tires, which we could round to 43 tires. Next, we determine S^* as follows:

$$S^* = 43.03 \sqrt{\frac{(900)(.20)}{(900)(.20) + (.30)(900)}} = 17.21$$

The maximum stockout level just before an order is received is 17.21 tires, which could be rounded to 17.

We can also then solve for M^*, the optimal maximum inventory level when an order is just received:

$$M^* = Q^* - S^* = 43.03 - 17.21 = 25.82$$

Thus, at the moment an order is received, after deducting for filling the backorders for 17.21 tires, there will be 25.82 tires in inventory.

Figure 8-6 illustrates the inventory levels for Big-B, using the rounded values for Q^* and S^*. Several measures of interest are shown in Figure 8-6. First, the inventory cycle is 15.7 days. During a cycle, 9.49 days is spent filling demand from inventory and backordering will occur for 6.21 days. The maximum inventory level will be 25.82 (rounded to 26) tires.

The reorder point is determined by first finding the number of units demanded during lead time. Next, subtract the maximum number of units on backorder (17.21 tires) from the demand during lead time to get the reorder point. If this results in a negative number, the order is placed during the backorder period. If the result is positive, the order is placed before the inventory is depleted. Finally, if the result is zero, the order is placed when the inventory reaches zero.

In notation form, the reorder point is:

$$ROP = dL - S \tag{8-16}$$

where:

ROP = order point
d = daily demand rate
L = lead time, in days
S = maximum number on backorder

For the Big-B Tire Company, the daily demand is $d = 1000/365 = 2.74$. Then the reorder point is:

$$ROP = (2.74)(5) - 17.21 = -3.51 \text{ tires}$$

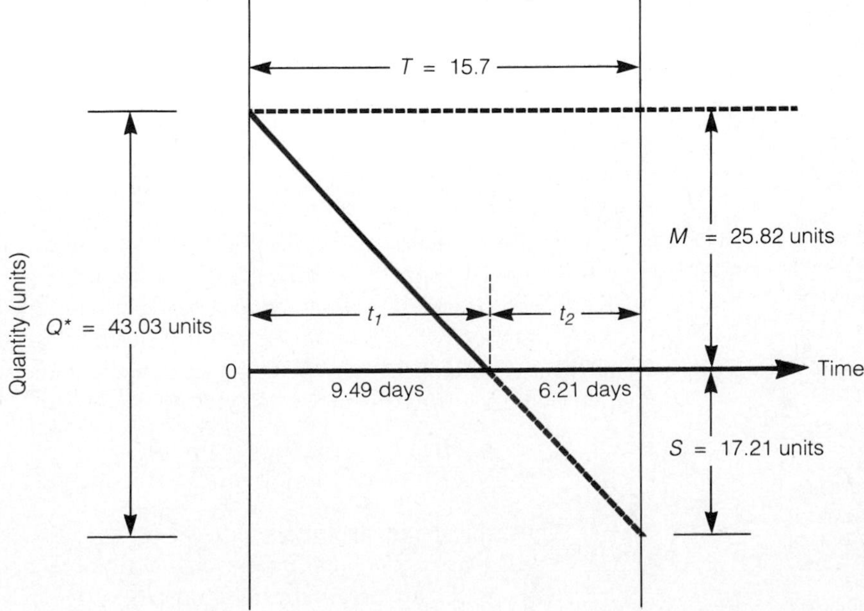

Figure 8-6
Big-B Tire problem: inventory model with planned backordering

Thus, the optimal reorder point is the point at which the inventory *shortage* reaches 3.51 (rounded to 4) tires. Note, a longer lead time would result in an earlier order. For instance, if $L = 10$ days, the reorder point is:

$$ROP = (2.74)(10) - 17.21 = 10.19$$

In this case, the company would place an order when the inventory level reached 10.19 (rounded to 10) tires.

Our purpose in using an inventory model is to determine the optimal number of units to order and when to place the order. The answers $Q^* = 43.03$ and $ROP = -3.51$ were developed with the objective of minimizing total inventory costs for the XR-7009 tire.

Using the calculated values for Q^* and S^*, we can determine the minimum total inventory cost (ignoring purchase cost) for Big-B. The holding cost is determined using equation 8-11, as follows:

$$\text{Annual holding cost} = \frac{M^2CI}{2Q} = \frac{(25.82^2)(900)(.20)}{2(43.03)} = \$1394.39$$

The ordering cost is determined using equation 8-4, as follows:

$$\text{Annual ordering cost} = (D/Q)C_o = (1000/43.03)(100) = \$2323.96$$

Finally, the backorder cost is determined using equation 8-12, as follows:

$$\text{Annual backorder cost} = \frac{S^2BC}{2Q} = \frac{(17.21)^2(.30)(900)}{2(43.03)} = \$929.23$$

Thus, the total cost (excluding purchase cost) is:

$$TC = \$1394.39 + \$2323.96 + \$929.23 = \$4647.58$$

RELATIONSHIP TO EOQ WITHOUT BACKORDERS

The cost just determined reflects the policy of allowing backorders but assumes a stockout penalty of 30% of the value of the average units on backorder. Suppose Brian Bijan was considering whether to actually adopt the backordering policy for the XR-7009 tire or whether to make sure that no shortages occur. Under the no-shortage alternative, the elementary EOQ model is in effect and we would use equation 8-6 to determine the order quantity, as follows:

$$Q^* = \sqrt{\frac{2DC_o}{CI}} = \sqrt{\frac{2(1000)(100)}{(900)(.20)}} = 33.33$$

Thus, the order quantity is reduced from 43.03 under the backorder policy to 33.33 under basic EOQ. But Brian would certainly wonder which order policy is the least expensive. To determine total costs for the EOQ without stockout, we use equation 8-5:

$$
\begin{aligned}
TC &= (Q/2)IC + (D/Q)C_o \\
&= (33.33/2)(.20)(900) + (1000/33.33)(100) \\
&= \$2999.70 + \$3000.30 = \$6000
\end{aligned}
$$

Under the no-stockout assumptions of elementary EOQ, the total inventory cost would be \$6000. This is \$1352.42 more than the total cost when backordering is allowed. Allowing backordering for the XR-7009 tire results in a savings of more than 22% in total inventory costs for this one product.

In the Big-B example, the backordering model gives a lower total cost than if no backordering is allowed. This result is not unique. In fact, backordering always gives at least as low a total cost as the elementary EOQ. The reason is that with backordering, inventory holding costs and order costs can be reduced by more than enough to offset the penalty for backordering. When the backordering penalty gets too high, the optimal backorder amount is driven to zero and we are back to the elementary EOQ result. In general, as long as backorder costs are some finite amount, allowing for backorders is cost-effective.

8-5 EOQ WITH PRICE DISCOUNTS FOR QUANTITY PURCHASES

The inventory models introduced so far have assumed the price per unit was the same regardless of the quantity ordered. Because of this assumption, we ignored the purchase cost component in the total cost equation in determining the optimal order quantity. However, quantity discounts are often given to encourage customers to purchase larger numbers of items in an order.

The number of different discount levels will vary depending on the situation. For instance, if a vendor charges \$300 per unit for a self-propelled lawn mower in orders of 10 or fewer but grants a \$30 discount for orders above 10 units, there is one discount level. However, suppose the vendor has a discount policy as follows:

Quantity	Unit Price
Under 10	\$300
11–25	\$270
Over 25	\$250

Then there are two discount levels.

At first glance you might think the buyer would automatically want to purchase enough to take full advantage of the biggest discount. But remember that large order sizes mean that average inventory will be increased, leading to increased holding costs. Thus, when faced with a quantity discount situation, we must determine the order size which minimizes total cost, which now includes the purchase price.

QUANTITY DISCOUNTS

Suppose we consider an example involving the Sheriton Appliance Company, which owns dealerships in 5 midwestern states. All buying is done through the corporate headquarters in Chicago, where the central warehouse is located. One appliance the company sells is a Space Saver microwave oven. The vendor has offered the following quantity discounts:

Purchase Quantity	Discount	Unit Price ($)
Under 50	0	$270.00
50–200	5%	$256.50
Over 200	10%	$243.00

The Sheriton managers want no possibility of a stockout and are willing to make the following assumptions:

1. Demand is known with certainty and is a constant rate during the inventory period.
2. All items ordered are received at one time.
3. Lead time is known with certainty.
4. All costs are known with certainty.
5. No stockouts are allowed.

These assumptions are the same as those for the elementary EOQ model introduced earlier, except we are now allowing quantity discounts. The following information is available for the Sheriton Appliance Company:

D = annual demand = 3000
C_o = ordering cost = $200
I = holding-cost factor, in decimal form = .24
C = cost of each oven = $270.00, $256.50, or $243.00, depending on order size
L = lead time = 10 days
W = workdays per year = 365
d = ovens demanded per day = 8.2

Step 1

First compute Q^* for each possible price level using the EOQ equation:

$$Q^* \sqrt{\frac{2DC_o}{CI}}$$

For the regular, no-discount price of $270.00, we get:

$$Q_1^* = \sqrt{\frac{2(3000)(200)}{(270.00)(.24)}} = 136.08$$

For the first-level discount price of $256.50, we get:

$$Q_2^* = \sqrt{\frac{2(3000)(200)}{(256.50)(.24)}} = 139.6$$

Finally, for the second-level price of $243.00, we get:

$$Q_3^* = \sqrt{\frac{2(3000)(200)}{(243.00)(.24)}} = 143.44$$

Now we check these order quantities to determine if they are feasible, given the vendor's pricing structure. That is, we determine whether the optimal order quantity falls within the quantity range for the price used in computing Q^*. For Q_1^*, which was computed assuming the regular, no-discount price of $270.00, the value 136.08 exceeds the limit of 49 ovens and is actually sufficient to obtain the 5% discount.

The value $Q_2^* = 139.6$ ovens, computed using the 5% discount price of \$256.50, is feasible because it falls within the 50–200 range specified for this discount level. Finally, the $Q_3^* = 143.44$ is not feasible, since it falls below the 201 lower limit required for the 10% discount. This means that even though we would like to order 143.44 ovens each time we place an order at a price of \$243.00, we can't do so because the vendor won't give us the 10% discount on such a small order.

Step 2

If any Q^* value is not feasible because it is smaller than the lower limit required to obtain the price discount, increase the order quantity until it is just large enough to get the desired discount. In this example, Q_3^* was 143.44 for the 10% discount when the required order was a minimum of 201 ovens. Thus, we change Q_3^* from 143.44 to 201.

However, since Q_1^* was actually higher than was necessary to get the price assumed (\$270.00), this Q^* can be ignored, since it cannot be the optimal order quantity.

Step 3

The final step in determining the optimal order quantity is to compute the total inventory cost for each of the Q^* values still being considered. In our example, we need only consider $Q_2^* = 139.6$ and $Q_3^* = 201$. Recall that the total inventory cost for the elementary basic EOQ model is the sum of holding costs + ordering costs + purchase costs. We must consider purchase costs now, since the quantity discount results in different purchase costs depending on what price is assumed.

The equation for total cost is:

$$TC = (Q/2)CI + (D/Q)C_o + DC \tag{8-17}$$

Then, for $Q = Q_2^* = 139.6$, we get:

$$\begin{aligned} TC &= (139.6/2)(256.50)(.24) + (3000/139.6)(200) + (3000)(256.50) \\ &= \$4296.89 + \$4297.99 + \$769{,}500.00 = \$778{,}094.88 \end{aligned}$$

And for $Q = Q_3^* = 201$, we get:

$$\begin{aligned} TC &= (201/2)(243.00)(.24) + (3000/201)(200) + (3000)(243.00) \\ &= \$5861.16 + \$2985.07 + \$729{,}000 = \$737{,}846.23 \end{aligned}$$

Table 8-3 summarizes the results of this quantity discount analysis. Considering total inventory cost, the best decision for the Sheriton Appliance Company is to order 201 ovens each time an order is placed. While this increases holding cost, the reduction in total purchase cost for the year reduces the total inventory cost.

Table 8-3 SHERITON APPLIANCE: QUANTITY DISCOUNT RESULTS

Discount Level	Unit Price (\$)	Order Quantity	Holding Cost (\$)	Ordering Cost (\$)	Purchase Cost (\$)	Total Cost (\$)
0	270	*	N/A	N/A	N/A	N/A
1	256.50	139.6	4296.89	4297.99	769,500	778,094.88
2	243.00	201.0	5861.16	2985.07	729,000	737,846.23

* The order quantity at this price level is not considered, since it cannot be the economic order quantity.

This approach to dealing with quantity discounts can be used with any inventory model. Some problems at the end of this chapter combine quantity discounts with backordering models.

8-6 ECONOMIC PRODUCTION LOT SIZE MODEL

When a company orders parts, materials, or finished goods from a vendor, the assumption that the entire order will arrive at one time is reasonable. This assumption is part of all EOQ models considered to this point. But when you think about it, in most instances the parts, materials, and finished goods were produced one at a time and the supplier accumulated the units before shipping the order to the buyer. Thus, the inventory models which are appropriate for the buyer are not necessarily appropriate for the manufacturer. This is especially true in manufacturing situations where one or more of the component parts for a finished product are manufactured internally. In such cases, the managers need an *economic production lot size model* which allows for gradual inventory buildup.

Consider an example involving Western Trailer which manufactures both camping trailers and horse trailers. A typical camping trailer requires about 1000 component parts. Western Trailer buys some of these parts from outside vendors and manufactures others internally. One part made by Western Trailer is the hitch unit used to attach the trailer to the pulling vehicle. Hitches are made in the fabrication shop, which also make other component parts. A *batch processing system* is used for producing the hitches. This means that when the shop is set up to produce hitches, a certain quantity —called a lot (or batch)—is produced before the system is reset to produce some other component.

The fabrication shop can produce trailer hitches faster than they are needed for the finished trailers. Since the production rate, P, exceeds the demand, D, while hitches are being made, some will be used to meet the current demand and the rest will go into inventory to be used later, when the shop is making some other part. Figure 8-7 illustrates an inventory system with gradual inventory buildup.

DEVELOPING THE MODEL

As with the other inventory models introduced in this chapter, the objective of the economic production lot size model is to answer two questions:

1. How many units should be produced each time a production run is started?
2. When should the production run be started?

We wish to answer these questions so that total inventory costs are minimized. The economic production lot size model is an extension of the elementary EOQ model and requires the following assumptions:

1. Demand is known with certainty and is constant during the inventory period.
2. Lead (setup) time is known with certainty.
3. All costs are known with certainty.
4. No stockouts are allowed.
5. No quantity discounts are considered.
6. Production rate exceeds the demand rate.
7. Production occurs at a constant rate during the production period.

Figure 8-7
Gradual inventory buildup (Q = economic production lot size)

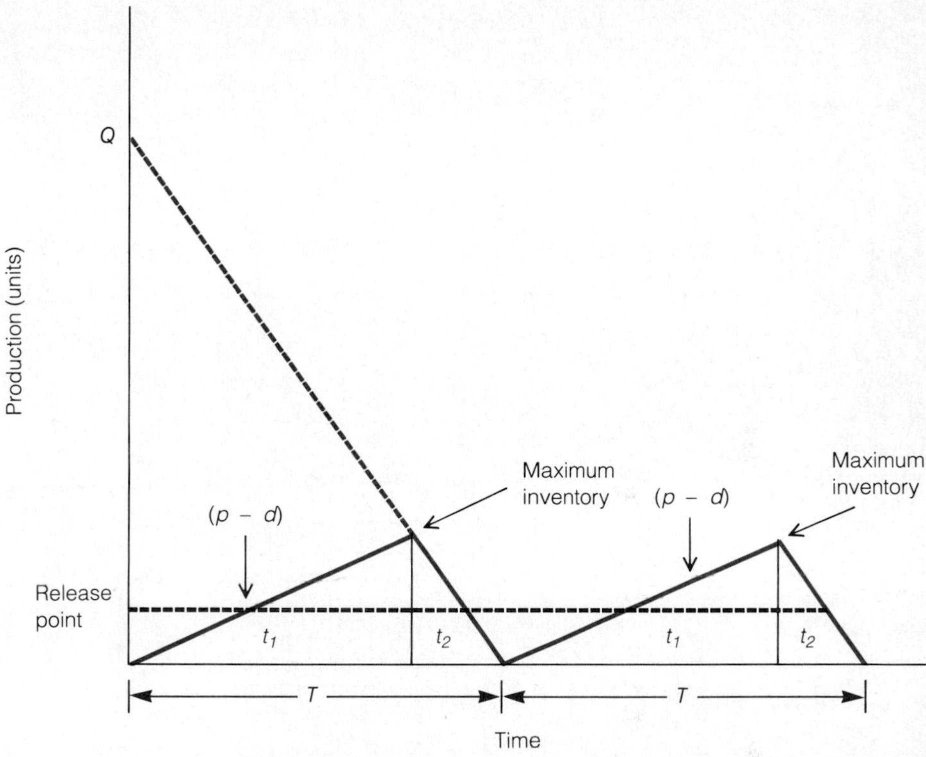

The total inventory cost (excluding production costs) is:

$$TC = \text{inventory holding cost} + \text{production setup cost} \tag{8-18}$$

The model for determining economic production lot size uses the following notation:

P = annual production rate
D = annual demand rate
p = daily production rate
d = daily demand rate
C = per unit production cost
L = lead time (time required for setup)
Q = lot or batch size
C_s = setup cost to begin producing a lot
I = inventory holding-cost factor, in decimal form
r = release point (setup point)
t_1 = time during production when inventory is being accumulated
t_2 = time when production is idle and inventory is being depleted

INVENTORY HOLDING COSTS

To determine inventory holding costs, we multiply the average number of units carried in inventory by the per unit cost of carrying the inventory. From Figure 8-7 we see that the maximum inventory level is not Q, since inventory is gradually built up. Also from Figure 8-7, we see that inventory is built up at the rate of $p - d$ for the production time t_1. Therefore:

$$\text{Maximum inventory} = (p - d)t_1$$
$$\text{Average inventory} = (p - d)t_1/2$$

Unfortunately, this average-inventory equation does not contain the optimal lot size, Q, but if we realize that Western Trailer produces hitches at the rate of p per day for t_1 days, then:

$$Q = pt_1 \qquad \text{or} \qquad t_1 = Q/p$$

So:

$$\text{Average inventory} = (p - d)Q/2p$$

$$\text{Holding cost} = \frac{(p - d)QCI}{2p} \tag{8-19}$$

Equation 8-19 can also be written as:

$$\text{Holding cost} = \frac{(P - D)QCI}{2P} \tag{8-19a}$$

This is because $P = p \times$ working days per year, and $D = d \times$ working days per year. We changed equation 8-19 to 8-19*a* by multiplying the numerator and denominator by a constant.

SETUP COST

The setup cost is analogous to the ordering cost in the elementary EOQ model. Each time the fabrication shop has to be set up to produce a certain component, such as trailer hitches, a cost is incurred for adjusting machines, rearranging the shop, and so on. The notation for setup cost is C_s. To determine total setup cost, we first determine the number of setups, as shown in equation 8-20:

$$N = D/Q \tag{8-20}$$

The annual setup cost is:

$$\text{Annual setup cost} = (D/Q)C_s \tag{8-21}$$

Thus, the total inventory cost is:

$$TC = (P - D)QCI/2P + (D/Q)C_s \tag{8-22}$$

Once again, differential calculus can be used to find the economic production lot size, Q^*, which is:

$$Q^* = \sqrt{\frac{2PDC_s}{(P - D)CI}} \tag{8-23}$$

Equation 8-23 gives a production quantity, Q^*, which will minimize the total inventory cost. Equation 8-23 can also be rewritten as:

$$Q^* = \sqrt{\frac{2DC_s}{IC} \times \frac{P}{P - D}} \tag{8-23a}$$

Note that in equation 8-23*a* the first term is the elementary EOQ and the second term is always more than 1. Thus, the economic production quantity (EPQ) always exceeds the basic economic order quantity (EOQ), since the average inventory levels are lower for given values of Q. Also, as P approaches D, the economic production quantity approaches infinity.

Western Trailer, Inc.

Recall that Western Trailer, Inc., makes camping trailers and horse trailers. It also manufactures some of its own component parts, such as trailer hitches. The plant manager believes that the factors in the production of the hitches adequately match the assumptions of the economic production lot size model. She would like to use the model to determine how many hitches to produce during each production run and when to begin each run during the year. The plant operates 250 days a year. The manager has the following information for the hitches:

P = annual production rate = 4000 per year

D = annual demand rate = 3000 per year

C = per unit production cost = \$250

L = lead time (setup time) = 3 days

C_s = setup cost to begin producing a lot = \$500

I = inventory holding-cost factor, in decimal form = .25

We can use equation 8-23 to determine the economic production lot size as follows:

$$Q^* = \sqrt{\frac{2PDC_s}{(P-D)CI}}$$

$$= \sqrt{\frac{2(4000)(3000)(500)}{(4000-3000)(250)(.25)}} = 438.18$$

Thus, using the assumptions of the economic production lot size model, Western Trailer should produce hitches in lots of about 438 units.

Now that we know how many hitches to produce, we need to determine when production should start. If the demand rate is 3000 per year, 3000 ÷ 250 = 12 hitches are used each day. The setup point is then determined by multiplying lead time, 3 days, times the daily demand rate, 12. The setup point is thus determined to be 36. Figure 8-8 is a graphical representation of the inventory levels for Western Trailer. The company should begin setup (which takes a lead time of 3 days) when the trailer-hitch inventory reaches 36 units. We can also see in Figure 8-8 that during the production stage, which lasts 40 days, inventory will build to a maximum of 110 hitches.

The total cost of this plan (ignoring production costs) is:

$$TC = \frac{(P-D)QCI}{2P} + \frac{D}{Q}C_s$$

$$TC = \frac{(4000-3000)(438.18)(250)(.25)}{(2)(4000)} + \left(\frac{3000}{438.18}\right)(500)$$

$$= \$3423.28 + \$3423.25 = \$6846.53$$

As in the elementary EOQ model, the minimum total inventory cost occurs at the point where annual holding cost equals annual setup cost.

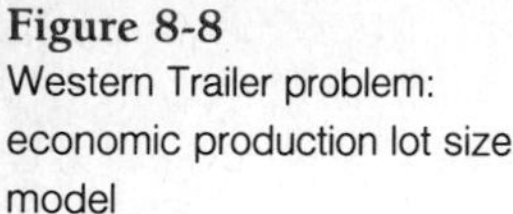

Figure 8-8
Western Trailer problem: economic production lot size model

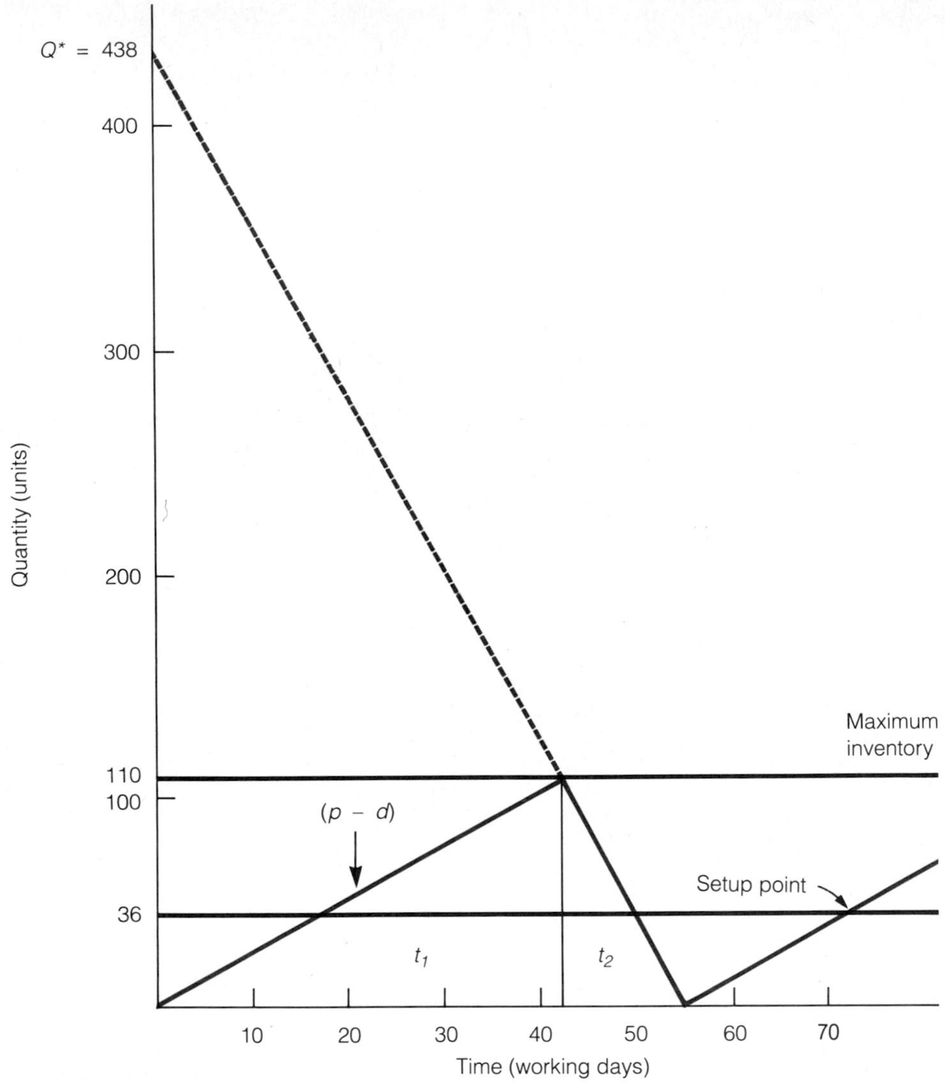

Maximum inventory = $(Q/P)(P - D)$ = (438.17/4000)(1000) = 109.54 units
Setup point = $(D/250)L$ = (3000/250)(3) = 36 units
t_1 = production run
t_2 = drawdown inventory

8-7 COMPUTER APPLICATIONS

The inventory models introduced in this chapter do not require large amounts of mathematical computation, since the equations for the optimal order quantity and production quantity are quite straightforward. However, a number of computer software packages, including MASTER, have programs for these and other inventory models.

The purpose of this section is to demonstrate several computer-assisted inventory

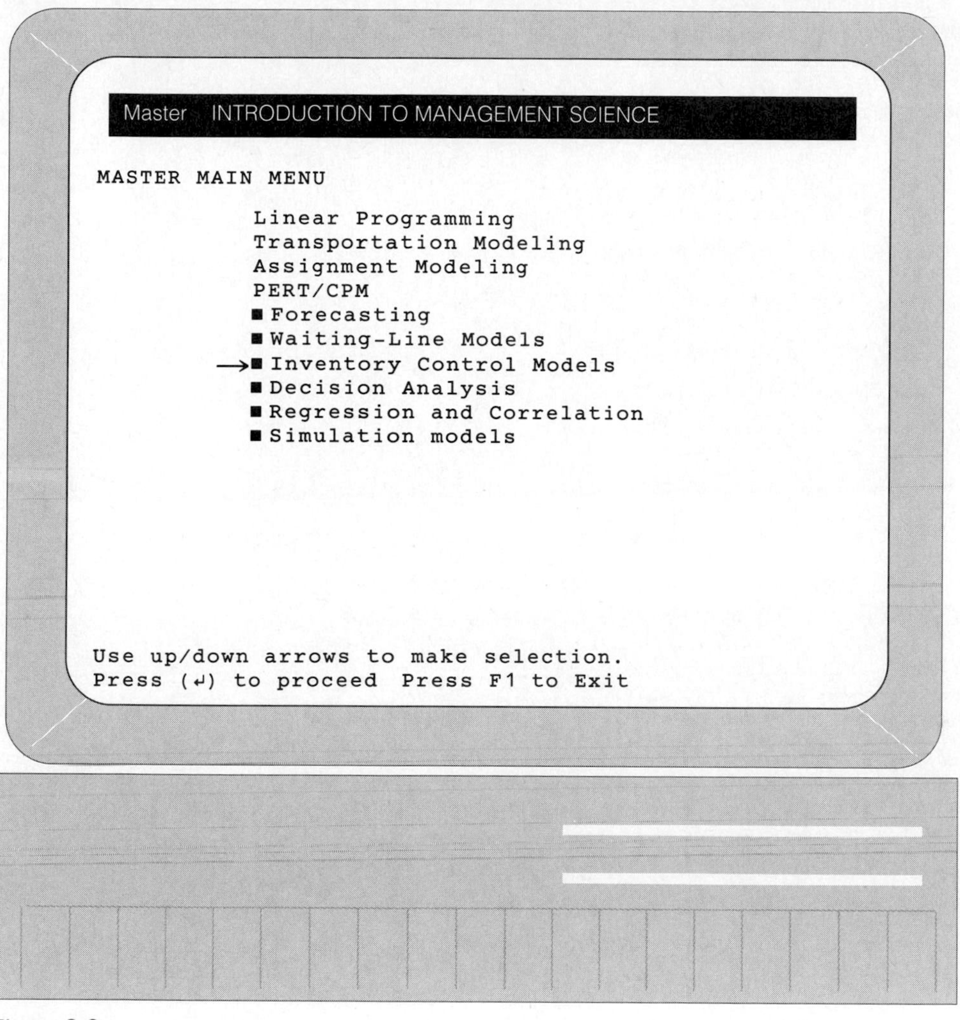

Figure 8-9
Main menu for MASTER software

model applications with the MASTER software. If you use different software, you will notice differences in the output, but generally the MASTER output in our examples is similar to that given by most other software packages. The advantage of using a computer to solve inventory model problems is that it allows you to quickly respond to What if? questions about inputs to the model. The examples that follow demonstrate this advantage.

THE ELEMENTARY EOQ MODEL

Figure 8-9 shows the main menu for the MASTER software. Selecting the Inventory Control Model option then gives us the Inventory Control Submenu shown in Figure 8-10. We will select the EOQ Model With Order Point option and use it to help Chessman Brothers Pizza Company (see section 8-3) determine how many pounds of cheese to order and when to place the order.

```
Master  INTRODUCTION TO MANAGEMENT SCIENCE

INVENTORY CONTROL SUBMENU

          →EOQ Model
           EOQ Model with Order Point
           Production Lot Size Model
           EOQ Model with Backordering
           EOQ with Quantity Discount

Use up/down arrows to make selection.
Press (↵) To Proceed  Press F1 to Exit
```

Figure 8-10
MASTER inventory model submenu

For this problem, the following inputs are used by the MASTER software:

Demand = 83,200 pounds per year

Cost = \$1.20 per pound

Order cost = \$50

Holding-cost factor = .25

Lead time = 4 days

Figure 8-11 shows the resulting MASTER output. We see that ordering 5266.24 pounds of cheese when the inventory reaches 911.78 pounds will minimize total inventory costs at \$1579.87. (*Note*: slight rounding errors may occur.)

Now, suppose an alternative cheese supplier will sell the same quality cheese for \$1.10 per pound but lead time is extended to 8 days. We can use the MASTER software, and these data modifications, to determine whether this supplier should be used. Figure 8-12 shows the output for the new situation. We see that the lower cheese

```
DAYS PER YEAR =  365
 THIS INVENTORY MODEL ASSUMES CONSTANT DEMAND AND CONSTANT LEAD TIME

        THE VALUES FOR THIS MODEL ARE:

                 DEMAND PER YEAR =  83200

                 ORDERING COST PER ORDER =     50.

                 HOLDING COST PER UNIT =       .3

               ECONOMIC ORDER QUANTITY =  5266.24

               TOTAL INVENTORY COST:
                   ORDERING COST =          789.93
                   HOLDING COST =           789.93
                                           -------
                   TOTAL COST =            1579.87

               ORDER POINT   =     911.78

               DAYS BETWEEN ORDERS   =  23.10
```

Figure 8-11
Chessman Brothers Pizza problem: original data (MASTER output)

price caused increases in the economic order quantity (5500.41 pounds) and the order point (1823.56 pounds) but lowered the total inventory cost to $1512.61. It is this capability to examine the implications of changing conditions that makes computer modeling such a valuable tool for inventory management.

EOQ WITH QUANTITY DISCOUNTS

In this chapter we have introduced a number of variations on the basic EOQ model, including an inventory model that allows for quantity discounts. To use MASTER for this analysis, go to the Inventory Control Submenu and select the option for "EOQ With Quantity Discount" (Figure 8-10).

To demonstrate, we will revisit Sheriton Appliance Company. Sheriton's supplier of Space Saver microwave ovens has recently offered the following price structure:

Purchase Quantity	Unit Price
Under 50	$270.00
51–200	256.50
Over 200	243.00

```
DAYS PER YEAR =  365
 THIS INVENTORY MODEL ASSUMES CONSTANT DEMAND AND CONSTANT LEAD TIME

        THE VALUES FOR THIS MODEL ARE:

                 DEMAND PER YEAR =  83200

                 ORDERING COST PER ORDER =      50.

                 HOLDING COST PER UNIT =        .27

               ECONOMIC ORDER QUANTITY =  5500.41

               TOTAL INVENTORY COST:
                   ORDERING COST =           756.30
                   HOLDING COST =            756.30
                                            -------
                   TOTAL COST =             1512.61

               ORDER POINT  =    1823.56

               DAYS BETWEEN ORDERS  =  24.13
```

Figure 8-12
Chessman Brothers Pizza problem: new-supplier data (MASTER output)

Other factors are:

Demand = 3000 ovens per year

Inventory holding-cost factor = .24

Ordering cost = $200

Figure 8-13 shows the MASTER output for these conditions. As you can see, the lowest cost results if Sheriton buys in quantities of 201, to take advantage of the largest price break. (This is the same answer we determined earlier by working the problem manually.)

Now, suppose that this supplier has also recently announced a price change, increasing the base price to $300 per unit. The following quantity discounts will be offered after the first of the year:

QUANTITY DISCOUNT MODEL-ASSUMES CONSTANT DEMAND

DISCOUNT LEVEL	UNIT COST	ORDER QUANTITY	HOLDING COST	ORDERING COST	PURCHASE COST	TOTAL COST
1	270.	*	*	*	*	*
2	256.5	139.6	4296.89	4297.99	769500.	778094.88
3	243.	201.	5861.16	2985.07	729000.	737846.23

Figure 8-13
Sheriton Appliance problem: original microwave-oven data (MASTER output)

Purchase Quantity	Unit Price or % Discount
Under 20	\$300
21–50	2%
51–100	5%
101–400	8%
Over 400	10%

The Sheriton managers are interested in determining how the new pricing structure would alter their ordering policy, assuming nothing else has changed. Using MASTER, we get the output shown in Figure 8-14. We see that the minimum-cost option requires ordering in quantities of 401.

QUANTITY DISCOUNT MODEL-ASSUMES CONSTANT DEMAND

DISCOUNT LEVEL	UNIT COST	ORDER QUANTITY	HOLDING COST	ORDERING COST	PURCHASE COST	TOTAL COST
1	300.	*	*	*	*	*
2	294.	*	*	*	*	*
3	285.	*	*	*	*	*
4	276.	134.59	4457.80	4457.80	828000.	836915.6
5	270.	401.	12992.4	1496.25	810000.	824488.6

Figure 8-14
Sheriton Appliance problem: new price structure (MASTER output)

In these two examples, the purchase cost has dominated, making large orders attractive. However, consider another example involving the Sheriton Appliance Company; this time the product is the hand-held Kwik Kleen vacuum. The pricing structure for this vacuum cleaner is:

Purchase Quantity	Unit Price or % Discount
Under 20	$30.00
21–50	2%
51–100	5%
101–400	8%
Over 400	10%

The demand for this product is set at 500 per year, with an ordering cost of $200 per order and an inventory holding-cost factor of .24. MASTER provides the information shown in Figure 8-15. From this, we see that the most economical ordering policy

QUANTITY DISCOUNT MODEL-ASSUMES CONSTANT DEMAND

DISCOUNT LEVEL	UNIT COST	ORDER QUANTITY	HOLDING COST	ORDERING COST	PURCHASE COST	TOTAL COST
1	30.	*	*	*	*	*
2	29.4	*	*	*	*	*
3	28.5	*	*	*	*	*
4	27.6	173.76	575.49	575.49	13800.	14951.
5	27.	401.	1299.24	249.37	13500.	15048.62

Figure 8-15
Sheriton Appliance problem: Kwik Kleen Vacuum data (MASTER output)

is to order in lots of 173.76 (rounded to 174), for a total cost of $14,951. (This order quantity is based on taking advantage of the 8% discount.)

The MASTER software also has other inventory control models (see Figure 8-10), which are typically available in most inventory software. For all applications, the principal advantage of computer software is that you can use it to analyze a wide range of options by simply changing the values for one or more input variables.

8-8 SUMMARY AND CONCLUSIONS

Virtually all businesses must manage their inventories. They must strike a balance between carrying too much inventory and not having enough to meet demand. This chapter has introduced the basics of inventory management.

Two questions must continually be answered when managing inventories:

1. What quantity should be ordered when an order is placed?
2. At what level of inventory should the order be placed?

The answers to these questions depend on the unique situations facing each business. However, as this chapter has shown, management science tools can be used to help answer these questions.

In this chapter we dealt with deterministic models, which assume that all the inputs, such as demand rate and costs, are known with certainty. We introduced four deterministic inventory models. The first, the economic order quantity (EOQ) model, requires a set of fairly restrictive assumptions. The other three models—EOQ with planned backordering, EOQ with quantity discounts, and the economic production lot size model—are all variations of the elementary EOQ model. In each case, the inventory model seeks to establish the order quantity and order point which will minimize total inventory costs. The choice of which model to use depends on the situation facing the decision maker and which assumptions are reasonable to make.

If a decision maker can apply one of the inventory models appropriately, the result will be an optimal inventory plan to minimize total inventory costs. However, even in those cases where the required assumptions are not perfectly satisfied, the models are often useful to provide general inventory guidelines.

As we indicated, the models discussed in this chapter are deterministic models which assume that all inputs are known with certainty. In most actual business situations, however, factors such as demand rate and lead time are uncertain. When uncertainty exists, inventory models which incorporate probability are needed. Chapter 9 introduces several probabilistic inventory models which can be applied in situations involving uncertainty.

Selected Chapter Equations

Elementary Economic Order Quantity (EOQ)

$$\text{Total cost} = (Q/2)IC + (D/Q)C_o \tag{8-5}$$

$$\text{EOQ (or } Q^*) = \sqrt{\frac{2DC_o}{IC}} \tag{8-6}$$

$$\text{Reorder point} = dL \tag{8-7}$$

where:

Q = order quantity
I = inventory holding-cost factor, in decimal form
C = unit cost
D = annual demand
C_o = ordering cost
d = daily demand rate
L = lead time, in days

EOQ with Backordering

$$\text{Total cost} = \frac{(Q-S)^2CI}{2Q} + (D/Q)C_o + \frac{S^2BC}{2Q} \qquad (8\text{-}11, 8\text{-}4, 8\text{-}12)$$

$$Q^* = \sqrt{\frac{2C_oD}{CI} \times \frac{CI+BC}{BC}} \qquad (8\text{-}14)$$

$$S^* = Q^* \sqrt{\frac{CI}{CI+BC}} \qquad (8\text{-}15)$$

$$\text{Reorder point} = dL - S \qquad (8\text{-}16)$$

where:

C = unit cost
I = inventory holding-cost factor, in decimal form
Q = order quantity
D = annual demand
C_o = ordering cost
S = maximum amount on backorder when an order is just received
Q^* = optimal order quantity
B = backordering penalty cost factor, in decimal form
S^* = optimal maximum stockout level when an order has just been received
d = daily demand rate
L = lead time

Economic Production Lot Run Size (Q^*)

$$\text{Total inventory cost} = \frac{(P-D)QCI}{2P} + \frac{D}{Q}C_s \qquad (8\text{-}22)$$

$$Q^* = \sqrt{\frac{2PDC_s}{(P-D)CI}} \qquad (8\text{-}23)$$

or:

$$Q^* = \sqrt{\frac{2DC_s}{IC}} \times \frac{P}{P-D} \qquad (8\text{-}23a)$$

where:

P = production rate
D = demand rate
Q = lot or batch size
C = per unit production cost
I = inventory holding-cost factor, in decimal form
C_s = setup cost to begin producing a lot

Solved Problems

PROBLEM 1 QuantPro has recently developed a thriving business in supplying add-on security protection for company computer systems. While it originally dealt exclusively with the Defense Department, QuantPro has recently found a large market in financial institutions. One method it employs is replacement of the common cables, used to connect computers to each other or to printers, with shielded cable. QuantPro purchases shielded cable from Extended Systems for \$1.50 a foot and has been buying 2000 feet at a time (based on an EOQ calculation). But yearly demand has now increased to 25,000 feet of cable, and the production schedule is constant during the year. The order cost remains at \$80 and the holding cost is estimated at \$.20 per foot per year.

a. Given the recent change in demand, what is the present optimal order quantity?
b. Assuming the previous order quantity was based on an EOQ calculation, what was the old demand level?
c. Extended Systems has recently started offering price discounts for large purchases. The present discount schedule offers 3% off purchases of at least 10,000 feet and 5% off purchases of at least 20,000 feet. Are these discounts large enough to cause QuantPro to change its order amount?

Solutions a. Since production is constant and all costs are known, this problem satisfies the assumption of the elementary EOQ model. Therefore:

$$Q^* = \sqrt{\frac{2DC_o}{IC}}$$

$$= \sqrt{\frac{(2)(25{,}000)(80)}{.20}} = 4472.14$$

b. Since the only change has been in the demand, we can again use the elementary EOQ model but solve for the previous demand by using the former 2000-foot order quantity.

$$2000 = \sqrt{\frac{2DC_o}{IC}}$$

$$2000 = \sqrt{\frac{2D80}{.20}}$$

$$\frac{(.2)(2000^2)}{(2)(80)} = D$$

$$5000 = D$$

c. Since taking either discount will increase holding costs, the question is whether the price savings are great enough to offset this increase. Determining the total costs for the EOQ point and the two discount levels, we find:

Unit Cost (\$)	Order Quantity (feet)	Holding Cost (\$)	Ordering Cost (\$)	Purchase Cost (\$)	Total Cost (\$)
1.50	4,472.14	447.21	447.21	37,500	38,394.42
1.46	10,000	970	200	36,375	37,547
1.43	20,000	1900	100	35,625	37,625

We see the total cost is minimized for an order of 10,000 feet.

PROBLEM 2 Marta Reynoso is a production scheduler for Esson Products. She is presently scheduling production for the PR-27 photo control unit. Everyone at the most recent scheduling meeting agreed on the following demand and production costs:

Demand for year = 15,000

Unit production cost = $55

Production setup costs = $150

Production rate per year = 60,000

Cost of holding a unit in inventory for 1 year = $20

The plant manager has told Marta that she is limited to scheduling production runs once a month, once a quarter, or once every 6 months.

a. Given these three scheduling choices, which is the best option?
b. How much would the company save if this restriction were not in place?

Solutions a. To determine the low-cost schedule, Marta needs to determine the cost of the three alternatives. Since production costs will be constant at 15,000 × $55 = $825,000 no matter what the run size is, this term can be ignored in the following calculations.

1. Monthly Production:

Run size = Q = 15,000/12 = 1250

Average inventory = $(p - d)Q/2p$

where:

$p = 60{,}000/365 = 164.38$

$d = 15{,}000/365 = 41.10$

Then:

$$\text{Average inventory} = \frac{(164.28 - 41.10)(1250)}{2(164.28)}$$
$$= 469.02$$

Holding cost = (average inventory)(unit holding cost)
= (469.02)($20) = $9380.40

Number of production runs = 12

Setup cost = (number of runs)(cost of 1 setup)
= (12)($150) = $1800

Total cost = holding cost + setup cost
= $9380.40 + $1800 = $11,180.40

2. Quarterly Production:

Run size = Q = 15,000/4 = 3750

$$\text{Average inventory} = \frac{(164.28 - 41.10)(3750)}{2(164.28)}$$
$$= 1405.91$$

Holding cost = (average inventory)(unit holding cost)
= (1405.91)($20) = $28,118.20

Number of production runs = 4

$$\text{Setup cost} = (\text{number of runs})(\text{cost of 1 setup}) = (4)(\$150) = \$600$$

$$\text{Total cost} = \text{holding cost} + \text{setup cost} = \$28{,}118.20 + \$600 = \$28{,}718.20$$

3. Semiannual Production:

$$\text{Run size} = Q = 15{,}000/2 = 7500$$

$$\text{Average inventory} = \frac{(164.28 - 41.10)(7500)}{2(164.28)} = 2811.82$$

$$\text{Holding cost} = (\text{average inventory})(\text{unit holding cost}) = (2811.82)(\$20) = \$56{,}236.40$$

$$\text{Number of production runs} = 2$$

$$\text{Setup cost} = (\text{number of runs})(\text{cost of 1 setup}) = (2)(\$150) = \$300$$

$$\text{Total cost} = \text{holding cost} + \text{setup cost} = \$56{,}236.40 + \$300 = \$56{,}536.40$$

Obviously, Marta should schedule monthly production runs.

b. To determine the optimal production run size, Marta should use the following formula:

$$Q^* = \sqrt{\frac{2DS}{IC} \times \frac{P}{P - D}}$$

Substituting the appropriate values:

$$Q^* = \sqrt{\frac{(2)(15{,}000)(150)}{20} \times \frac{60{,}000}{60{,}000 - 15{,}000}} = 547.72$$

The total cost for runs of this size is:

$$\text{Average inventory} = \frac{(p - d)Q}{2p}$$

where:

$$p = 60{,}000/365 = 164.38$$

$$d = 15{,}000/365 = 41.10$$

Then:

$$\text{Average inventory} = \frac{(164.28 - 41.10)(547.72)}{2(164.28)} = 205.35$$

$$\text{Holding cost} = (\text{average inventory})(\text{unit holding cost}) = (205.35)(\$20) = \$4107$$

$$\text{Number of production runs} = D/Q = 15{,}000/547.72 = 27.39$$

$$\text{Setup cost} = (\text{number of runs})(\text{cost of 1 setup}) = (27.39)(\$150) = \$4108 \text{ (rounded)}$$

$$\text{Total cost} = \text{holding cost} + \text{setup cost} = \$4107 + \$4108 = \$8215$$

The total saving if Marta can schedule the optimal run size versus the monthly alternative is: $11,180.40 − $8215 = $2965.40.

General Questions and Assignments

1. Discuss in your own terms why the total inventory cost is minimized at the point where the ordering cost equals the holding cost for the basic EOQ situation.
2. Suppose you are analyzing two inventory situations, one in which backordering is not allowed and the other in which backordering is allowed. Which situation would have lower total inventory costs? Discuss why this is the case. Under what conditions would the costs be the same?
3. Suppose a company is considering manufacturing a component part that it has been buying from an outside supplier. This part is used at the rate of 50,000 per year. The production manager figures that for at least the first year the annual production rate for the component will be 40,000. The manager would like to apply the economic production lot size model to this situation to determine how many to produce per run. What advice would you give? Discuss.
4. Discuss in your own terms how the EOQ model works when quantity discounts are applied.
5. For the basic EOQ model, why do we not consider the purchase cost in determining the economic order quantity which minimizes total inventory cost?
6. Locate at least three articles which discuss the application of inventory models. Write a paper describing the situation in which each model is used. What assumptions were made? Are these realistic assumptions? What were the benefits from employing these inventory models?
7. Visit a local business and discuss its inventory management practices. What type of inventory planning does the company use? Does it use EOQ? How are reorder points established? Write a short paper summarizing your findings.

Exercises and Application Problems

1. Folsom Chain Saw uses blades purchased from Intercity Fabrication. Folsom expects to produce 36,000 chain saws this year, with a steady flow through the production line. Intercity Fabrication charges $20.50 for each blade. If Folsom's annual holding costs are 25% of unit costs and placing each order costs $55:
   a. How many blades should be ordered each time an order is placed?
   b. What will the average inventory be per month?
   c. How many orders will be placed per year?
2. Wilson Electronics has just received its first distribution contract for a new digital-tape music system. For the 2 years of the contract, each unit will cost Wilson $900. The company projects a demand of 400 units per month. With a holding-cost factor of 2% per month and an order cost of $100:
   a. How many units should be ordered each time an order is placed?
   b. What will be the average inventory per year?
   c. How many orders will be placed per year?
   d. What will be the total cost of your recommended ordering policy?
3. Bayside Savings and Loan estimates it will use 3000 boxes of forms for recording account transactions in the coming year. Each box costs $150, and ordering and receiving costs total $60. The purchasing department has long used the policy of ordering 500 boxes each time an order is placed. If the cost of holding inventory is considered to be 30% per year, do you agree with this policy? If you recommend a different policy, how much will your policy save per year?

4. Hill Road Lumber estimates it will sell 3000 sheets of 3/4-inch red oak plywood this year. Each sheet costs $25.00. The lumberyard manager has been determining order sizes based on an estimated ordering cost of $40 and a holding-cost factor of 1.8% per month. The accounting department has just revised these costs to $55 per order and a holding cost of 2.2% per month.
   a. What was the optimal order quantity before the costs were revised?
   b. Determine the effect of changing the order cost and holding cost separately.
   c. Determine the effect of changing both the order cost and holding cost. Discuss the differences between the answers here and in part **b**.
5. Hollister Construction estimates it will use 50 carbon-tipped power-saw blades each month on construction projects it has projected over the next 2 years. Each blade costs $60, and order costs are estimated to be $75 per order. Hollister uses a cutoff rate of return of 30% per year on any expenditure.
   a. How many blades should be ordered each time an order is placed?
   b. What will be the average inventory per year?
   c. How many orders will be placed per year?
   d. What will be the total cost of your recommended ordering policy?
6. Merrill Manufacturing uses a special computer chip in its top-of-the-line iron to automatically sense when the iron is too hot for the fabric it is being used on and to automatically shut off the iron if it sits idle for 15 minutes. The chip costs $12.50. Merrill executives estimate the demand for the iron will be 12,000 per month for the next year. The chip is supplied by a company in Singapore, and ordering costs are $100 per order. Holding costs are estimated to be 28% of unit cost per year.
   a. How many chips should be ordered each time an order is placed?
   b. How many orders will be placed per year?
   c. What will be total cost per year of this ordering policy?
7. Roper Shoe Store is trying to determine the ordering policy for its most popular type of running shoe. The shoe costs Roper $40, and Roper plans to sell 1200 this year. Roper has a policy of offering a $5 rebate coupon when the shoe a customer wants is not in stock. Charles Roper estimates the cost of holding a pair of shoes is 30% of the shoe's cost and the cost of placing an order is $60.
   a. What is the optimal order size for this running shoe?
   b. What is the optimal backorder quantity?
   c. What is the total cost of this ordering policy with backorders allowed?
   d. Compare the cost of an ordering policy that allows backorders with the cost if no backorders are allowed.
8. Blacker Automotive Parts purchases electronic fuel pumps to use when replacing mechanical fuel pumps. The projected demand for the electronic pumps is 2000 per month. Each pump costs $60, holding costs are estimated to be 32% of unit cost, and placing an order costs $75.
   a. What is the optimal order quantity for this fuel pump?
   b. What is the cost of this policy?

   Blacker is deciding whether to allow backorders, at a cost estimated to be $10 per backorder.
   c. What is the optimal order quantity if backorders are allowed?
   d. Compare the cost of the policy without backorders to the cost with backorders.
9. Consider the Blacker Automotive Parts example in problem 8. In developing the policy for allowing backorders, the company is considering ordering when the backorders reach 20. Compare this policy with that developed in parts **c** and **d** of problem 8.
10. Wagner Western Wear features handmade cowboy boots costing $200. The company estimates that placing an order costs $55 and the cost of holding a pair of boots in inventory for a year costs $60. In the past, 50 pairs of boots were sold each week. Formerly, no stockouts were allowed, but now the purchasing manager has estimated the unit cost of a stockout at $10 and is considering two backorder policies. The first would allow any backorder policy that will lead to a minimum total inventory cost. The second would set the backorder level at half the weekly sales total.

a. Determine the cost of the inventory policy which allows no stockouts.
b. Compare the costs of the two backorder policies being considered.

11. Flagstaff Products offers the following discount schedule for its 4′ × 8′ sheets of quality plywood:

Order Quantity	Unit Cost
9 sheets or less	$18.00
10–50 sheets	$17.50
More than 50 sheets	$17.25

Home Sweet Home Company orders plywood from Flagstaff Products. Home Sweet Home has an ordering cost of $35, a carrying cost of 20%, and an annual demand of 100 sheets. What do you recommend as an ordering policy for Home Sweet Home? What is the total cost of this policy?

12. A small manufacturing plant currently uses about 3500 pounds of a chemical solvent each year. Currently, the firm purchases 300 pounds per order and pays $3 per pound. The supplier has just announced a 10% discount on orders of 1000 pounds or more and a 20% discount on orders of 2500 pounds or more. The firm has determined that each order will cost $80 to place and that holding the solvent in stock for one year costs 25% of the purchase price.
a. Is the current order policy, assuming no quantity discount applies, correct?
b. Would you suggest that the firm take one of the quantity discounts?
c. What is the total cost of your suggested order policy?

13. Huckabee Products uses 75,000 gallons of an iodized zinc primer for parts the company manufactures. The primer costs $17 per gallon, and Huckabee orders in lots of 10,000 gallons. The manufacturer of the primer has just offered a 10% discount for orders of more than 20,000 gallons and an additional 5% for orders above 50,000 gallons. If the cost of placing and receiving an order is $150 and the cost of holding a gallon in stock is $5 per year:
a. Is the current ordering policy, assuming no quantity discount applies, correct?
b. Would you suggest that Huckabee take one of the quantity discounts?
c. How many orders will be placed using your policy compared with the number using the present ordering policy?
d. How much will your ordering policy save the company each year?

14. Empire Trophy makes a variety of trophies and plaques for award ceremonies. A particularly popular model of trophy uses a standard base, upon which is mounted a figure of a baseball player, a basketball player, or other athlete. Its best estimates are that Empire Trophy will need 5000 bases in the coming year. Each base is made of walnut and costs $7.00. The distributor of bases will sell them for $6.00 if Empire buys more than 2000 at a time and for $5.50 if all 5000 are purchased at once. The cost of holding a base in inventory for a month is $.15, and each order costs $60. What ordering policy do you recommend? Justify your recommendation.

15. Wilshire Designs makes display cabinets used in shopping malls and grocery "superstores" in California and Arizona. While the display cabinets come in different sizes, they all have fronts made of ½″ scratch-proof plexiglass. This plexiglass comes in 8′ × 10′ sheets, each of which costs $120. Wilshire estimates the demand for the cabinets will be enough to justify purchasing 1000 sheets of plexiglass each month for the next year. Each order costs $110 to place, and the cost of holding a sheet of plexiglass in inventory is 2% of the unit cost each month. The plexiglass is purchased from a vendor who offers a 4% discount on orders of 3000 or more and an 8% discount on orders of 8000 or more.
a. What is the total cost of the optimal ordering policy, assuming no discount is given?
b. What is the total cost of inventory, assuming (1) the 3000-unit discount is taken and (2) the 8000-unit discount is taken?
c. What is your ordering recommendation?

16. You are the purchasing agent responsible for buying an expensive ($100 each) custom-made

integrated-circuit chip. Because of the chip's relatively high rate of obsolescence, your company figures yearly holding costs to be 40% of unit cost. Your department has just completed a study that estimates the cost of placing an order to be $60. The marketing department has just done a study of the demand for products that use this special chip which indicates the present estimated demand is 1000 per month.

a. You have been ordering these chips in lots of 200. Is this the best policy? What is the total cost of this policy? If you decide to change your policy, what would your new lot size be? Would there be a significant cost saving?

b. The sales representative for the vendor of the special chip has recently made an offer to reduce the unit cost by 5% if you order in lots of 500 and to reduce the cost by a total of 8% if you order in lots of 2500. Should you take either of these discounts?

17. Heath Electronics has just contracted with Sun Fish Finders to assemble 1000 units per month. The contract is renewable yearly. Since Heath has just expanded its Glenns Ferry plant, and now has the capability of assembling 4000 Fish Finders per month, it will need to use the production line for other items as well. Ted Heath is currently determining the production policy for the next year. Sun pays Heath $200 for every completed unit. Ted estimates that holding a Fish Finder in stock for a year costs $70 and changing the assembly line to produce another product costs $400.

a. What size production run would you suggest?

b. How many production runs should Heath Electronics make per year?

18. C. Y. Chang Electronics Assembly has a 3-year contract with Ion Microsystems to assemble 2000 circuit boards per month. Because its assembly line can produce 6000 of the boards per month, Chang uses it for other products besides the Ion boards. The production manager is determining the production policy for next year. She has determined that the completed boards are worth $150 each and that it costs $50 to hold a completed board in stock for a year. Changing the assembly line from one type of board to another costs about $120, due to downtime.

a. What size production run would you suggest?

b. How many production runs should be made per year?

19. Clifford Automatic Tool Works makes mounting brackets for jet engines in military fighter planes. The mounting brackets require an extensive reset and calibration of the milling machine. This reset requires 3 hours of an electronics technician's time and 4 hours of a mechanical technician's time. The electronics technician's time is billed at $40 per hour, and the mechanical technician's time is billed at $35 per hour. For a new contract with General Dynamics, an average of 400 mounting brackets, each worth $2500, will be required each month. Since the milling machine is capable of producing 2200 mounting brackets each month, it is used for several different contracts. Clifford has determined the cost of holding a completed bracket for one month to be 2.5% of the unit cost.

a. How many brackets should be made in each production run?

b. What will be the maximum bracket inventory? What will be the average bracket inventory?

c. What is the total holding and setup cost of this policy?

20. Pine Grove Press produces advertising brochures for the tourist industry in several southern states. A group in Florida recently ordered an expensive multicolor brochure. The estimated demand for the brochure is 150,000 this year. The offset press used to produce these brochures can print 1,000,000 per year. The material for each brochure costs Pine Grove Press $1.20, and printing costs are $1.70 per unit. Extensive setup is required when running this brochure, at an estimated cost of $450. Pine Grove Press estimates the cost of holding a unit in inventory to be 30% of production cost.

a. How many brochures should be printed in each production run?

b. What will be the maximum inventory? What will be the average inventory?

c. What is the total holding and setup cost of this policy?

21. Custom Car Products produces simulated-sheepskin seatcovers for sale primarily in discount stores. The seatcovers come in two basic styles, one for high-back seats and one for low-back seats. Both are produced on a machine which has the capacity of producing 400,000 high-back covers and 450,000

low-back covers each year. The projected demand for high-back covers this year is 3000 sets (2 seat covers per set) per month. Each high-back seat cover costs $30 to produce, and Custom Car estimates the unit carrying cost at $8 per year. Changing from one style to another costs $500. The present policy is to produce 10,000 of each type of cover and then switch.

a. Do you agree with the present policy?

b. If you have an alternative recommendation, compare the cost of producing high-back seat covers using your alternative with the cost of the present policy.

Chapter Glossary

Cycle time The period of time between placing one inventory order and the next.

Deterministic model An inventory model for which demand and all costs are known with certainty.

Economic order quantity (EOQ) The order quantity which minimizes total inventory cost.

Holding cost The cost associated with holding one item in inventory for a specified period of time.

Lead time The time between placing an inventory order and receiving the shipment.

Ordering cost The cost of placing one order.

Purchase cost The cost of the number of items ordered; the unit cost times the quantity ordered.

Quantity discount A reduction in unit cost provided to encourage larger order sizes.

Reorder point The inventory level at which an order is placed.

Stockout costs The cost associated with running out of inventory.

Chapter References

BOOKS

Arrow, K. J., S. Karlin, and H. Scarf. *Studies in the Mathematical Theory of Inventory and Production*. Stanford, Calif.: Stanford, 1958.

Hillier, F. S., and G. J. Lieberman. *Introduction to Operations Research,* 4th ed. Oakland, Calif.: Holden-Day, 1986.

Markland, R. E., and J. S. Sweigart. *Quantitative Methods: Applications to Managerial Decision Making*. New York: Wiley, 1987.

Silver, E. A., and R. Peterson. *Decision Systems for Inventory Management and Production Planning,* 2d ed. New York: Wiley, 1985.

Vollmann, T. E., W. L. Berry, and D. C. Whybark. *Manufacturing Planning and Control Systems,* 2d ed. Homewood, Ill.: Irwin, 1988.

ARTICLES

Austin, L. M. "Project EOQ: A Success Story in Implementing Academic Research." *Interfaces,* Vol. 7 (August), 1977.

Flowers, A. D., and J. B. O'Neill. "Application of Classical Inventory Analysis to a Spare Parts Inventory." *Interfaces,* Vol. 8 (February), 1978.

Liberatore, M. J. "EOQ under Stochastic Lead Time." *Operations Research,* Vol. 27 (March), 1979.

Muhlemann, A. P., and A. G. Lockett. "Use of Formal Inventory Control Models: A Preliminary Survey." *Omega,* Vol. 6, No. 3, 1978.

Nast, Donald A., and Stephen E. Bechtold. "The EOQ Revisited." *Decision Sciences,* Vol. 9, No. 4, 1979.

Pinney, W. E. "Correcting a Misconception about EOQ." *Decision Sciences,* Vol. 8, No. 4, 1978.

Rabak, I. W., and A. I. Schiff. "Inventory Models and Management Objectives." *Sloan Management Review,* Vol. 19, 1978.

Rothman, M. B. "Expanding the Concept of Inventory Management." *Stores,* Vol. 61 (June), 1979.

Wagner, H. M. "The Design of Production and Inventory Control Systems for Multifacility and Multiwarehouse Companies." *Operations Research,* Vol. 22, No. 3, 1974.

Woolsey, G. "Fifth Column: The Warehouse Model That Couldn't Be and the Inventory That Couldn't Be Zero." *Interfaces,* Vol. 7 (May), 1977.

Woolsey, G. "Walking through Warehouses, Toolcribs, and Shops—or, Profits through Peripatetics." *Interfaces,* Vol. 8 (February), 1978.

Mini Cases

CASE 8A
CENTRAL MANUFACTURING

Tom Barnes had never been more angry in his life! He had just been taken to task at the monthly plant scheduling meeting. Tom had been plant foreman for 15 years, and before that he had been a shift supervisor. He strongly believed he knew more about the assembly operation than anyone else in the plant—including Mary Lin, a recently hired college graduate who had never worked on an assembly line in her life.

When Tom became foreman, the assembly process was in chaos. Production runs were scheduled according to who could yell the loudest or who had the most irritated customer—with switching partway through a run being a common practice.

Central Manufacturing primarily makes machine replacement parts, for which the yearly demand is constant. Tom's scheduling procedure has always been to look at the projected demand for each product and then schedule quarterly runs for large-volume items and semiannual production runs for lower-volume items.

In the meeting just completed, Mary Lin had taken two high-volume items and two low-volume items and presented figures which "showed" significant savings could be made by using a better scheduling procedure. Now back in his office, Tom reviewed the main table from Mary's presentation:

Item	Yearly Demand	Production Cost	Present Cost	Optimal Cost
4321	25,000	$42.00	$35,250	$10,500
588B	35,000	$68.00	$75,000	$17,000
20-7	6,000	$84.00	$40,500	$10,500
5505	4,500	$17.00	$ 6,650	$ 3,900

Tom could not disagree with Mary's yearly production capacity or setup cost figures, since she had gotten them from him earlier in the month:

	4321	588B	20-7	5505
Capacity	100,000	120,000	60,000	45,000
Setup	$200	$240	$350	$320

In addition, the finance people seemed satisfied with Mary's use of a 35% rate as the cost of holding an item in inventory.

In developing his strategy, Tom decided to first verify Mary's cost figures and claim of overall savings. Also, he felt strongly that his scheduling procedures led to economies of scale that saved between 5% and 10% on production costs—savings that he knew were not taken into consideration in Mary's calculations.

CASE 8B
CLEAR LAKE COMPUTERS

Clear Lake Computers was started by Jim and Al Worthington in the early 1980s, just in time to take advantage of the explosive growth in personal computer purchases. They presently have five stores in central Oklahoma. The company was very profitable when the demand for personal computers was growing. But in the past few years, times have been hard as demand has leveled off and an increasing number of customers have started to buy from mail-order houses. Fortunately, Jim and Al predicted this trend and switched their emphasis to business hardware/software applications. The brothers believed that service was particularly important to business and so concentrated on always having high-demand items in stock.

Unfortunately, the business market has become so diverse that the Worthingtons are having a hard time keeping an adequate number of items in inventory. Because their bank has just refused to increase the line of credit they use to finance inventory, they can either cut back on the number of systems offered or cut back on the amount of inventory carried—and risk not being able to satisfy potential demand. The brothers don't like either alternative, but they also require their inventory investment to meet the same 30% return on investment criterion as the other uses of their capital.

Al suggests considering the possibility of reducing their average inventory of the new Compaq business computer. The new computer is designed to compete directly with middle-scale workstations, will retail for $9000, and will cost Clear Lake $6000. Al and Jim predict the demand for this system will average 20 per week for all stores and that the demand should be relatively constant for the next 2 years. If they reduce the average level of inventory, Al and Jim realize there will be times when customers will have to wait to have an order filled. Their best guess is that they will lose 1 out of 10 customers because of the wait.

Compaq will fill orders 10 working days after they are placed but ordering too often will rapidly increase operating costs because each order costs $1.00 to place. Jim and Al are considering a policy that will require no customer to wait more than 5 days to receive a backordered item, but they wonder just how much they will actually save.

Technical Appendix

DERIVATION OF THE BASIC EOQ FORMULA

We begin with the equation to find total cost, equation 8-5:

$$TC = (Q/2)IC + (D/Q)C_o \qquad (8\text{-}5)$$
$$= \tfrac{1}{2}Q(IC) + (D/Q)C_o$$

Through differential calculus, we can find the value of Q which minimizes TC. We begin by taking the first derivative of the total-cost equation with respect to Q:

$$\frac{dTC}{dQ} = \tfrac{1}{2}IC - (D/Q^2)C_o$$

We next set this first derivative to zero and solve for Q^*, as follows:

$$\frac{dTC}{dQ} = \tfrac{1}{2}IC - (D/Q^2)C_o = 0$$
$$\tfrac{1}{2}IC = (D/Q^2)C_o$$
$$\tfrac{1}{2}IC(Q^2) = (D)C_o$$
$$IC(Q^2) = (2D)C_o$$
$$Q^2 = \frac{(2D)C_o}{IC}$$

Then:

$$Q^* = \sqrt{\frac{(2D)\,C_o}{IC}} \qquad (8\text{-}6)$$

To check whether Q^* is a minimum, we determine whether the second derivative is positive when D, C_o, and Q are all positive. The second derivative is:

$$\frac{d^2TC}{dQ^2} = \frac{2D(C_o)}{Q^3}$$

Since this equation will be positive when D, C_o, and Q are greater than zero, we know that equation 8-6 minimizes total inventory cost.

Chapter 9

PROBABILISTIC INVENTORY MODELS AND OTHER INVENTORY TECHNIQUES

Chapter Outline

Chapter 9

Why You Need to Know

You learned in Chapter 8 that decisions involving inventory are very important to most businesses. In a competitive environment, poor inventory management can mean the end of a business. If a company carries too much inventory, the carrying costs can eat away the profit margin. On the other hand, too little inventory may result in frequent stockouts, resulting in lost profits and poor customer relations.

For all the products a company uses—whether they are finished goods, component parts, or raw materials—management must establish an effective inventory policy. To this end, two questions must continually be answered. (1) How many units of each product should be ordered? (2) When should an order be placed? In Chapter 8, you learned about four inventory control models which could be used to answer these questions. Those four models are termed **deterministic inventory models** because they assume that certainty exists for such factors as demand rate, costs, and lead time.

However, as we have often said in this text, many business situations involve uncertainty. If the demand rate or any costs are not known with certainty, or if the lead time is uncertain, deterministic models cannot be used to minimize inventory costs. Instead, management science tools which allow uncertainty in the decision process are needed. In this chapter, we introduce inventory control techniques which take into account *probabilistic* demand and lead times.

In the past 20 years, two additional techniques have been developed to answer the inventory control questions (How many do we order? and When do we order them?) These two techniques, material requirements planning (MRP) and just-in-time (JIT) manufacturing, have in some cases made alternative inventory control procedures obsolete. This chapter presents an introductory discussion of these two procedures.

Chapter Objectives

This chapter extends the discussion of inventory control models that began in Chapter 8. The primary objective of this chapter is to show how uncertainty can be incorporated into the inventory decision process through probabilistic inventory control models. The specific objectives of the chapter are to:

1. Present and discuss situations for which deterministic inventory models are not appropriate and probabilistic models should be used instead.
2. Introduce a probabilistic economic order quantity (EOQ) model for cases when demand during lead time is normally distributed.
3. Introduce a probabilistic EOQ model for single-period inventory decisions.
4. Illustrate how material requirements planning (MRP) is used as a tool for managing inventories.
5. Discuss the probable impact of just-in-time (JIT) manufacturing procedures on the use of traditional inventory control tools.

9-1 THE NEED FOR PROBABILISTIC EOQ MODELS

The elementary economic order quantity (EOQ) model introduced in Chapter 8 (section 8-3) carried with it several assumptions. Among these is that the demand rate is known with certainty. If forecast demand for next year is 3000 units, then it is assumed that demand will be exactly 3000 units. Further, the EOQ models assume this demand would be evenly spread throughout the year. If a business is open 250 days a year, the daily demand is assumed to be $3000 \div 250 = 12$ per day. These assumptions yield a graphical display of inventory levels like that shown in Figure 9-1.

While some inventory situations reasonably satisfy the assumptions of the elementary EOQ model, in many other cases the certainty assumptions are not appropriate. For instance, unit costs might change during the year because of changes in raw material costs, wage rates, energy prices, foreign competition, or a whole host of factors. Lead times may not be constant due to transportation problems, temporary shortages of materials, power outages, weather problems, and other factors.

In situations where there is significant uncertainty in such factors as demand and lead time, we need techniques which will allow us to represent the effect of uncertainty. Since uncertainty is incorporated in decision-making models by using probability distributions, the inventory techniques we introduce in this chapter are referred to as **probabilistic inventory models.**

Incorporating probability into inventory control models inreases their complexity to such an extent that a full treatment is beyond the scope of this text. In fact, in many cases where both demand and lead times are uncertain, we turn to techniques such as dynamic programming (Chapter 17), decision analysis (Chapters 13–15), and especially computer simulation (Chapter 16) to aid in analyzing the inventory situation.

In this chapter, we will look at two classes of problems for which probabilistic models can be developed: single-period problems with uncertain demand and multiperiod problems with uncertain demand during lead time.

Figure 9-1
Deterministic assumptions in basic EOQ

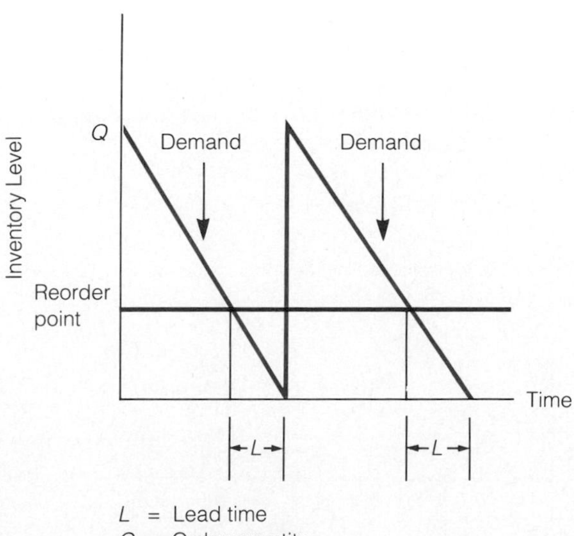

9-2 PROBABILISTIC EOQ MODEL: DEMAND DURING LEAD TIME NORMALLY DISTRIBUTED

Lead time is the time between placing and receiving an order. Deterministic inventory models assume that both the lead time and the demand during lead time are known with certainty. In the elementary EOQ model introduced in Chapter 8, the reorder point is determined assuming the order arrives just as the last item is taken from inventory. The order point was determined by finding the demand during lead time. If lead time was given in days, the demand during lead time would be found by multiplying the lead time by the daily demand.

If demand for the item under study is uncertain, then we do not know for sure how many will be demanded each day. If the length of the lead time is uncertain, then we do not know for sure the time between when an order is placed and when it arrives. The combined effect of an uncertain demand rate and an uncertain lead time is uncertainty in the *lead-time demand.* That is, we do not know for sure what the total requirements for an item will be between the time we place an order and the time the order arrives. If the lead-time demand exceeds our supply, we will be out of stock before the next order arrives. On the other hand, if the lead-time demand is less than our supply, we will have inventory remaining when the order arrives. Figure 9-2 illustrates both situations. In Figure 9-2*a*, where lead-time demand exceeds the amount on hand when the order is placed (reorder point), lost sales will result in lost profits and possibly lost goodwill. In Figure 9-2*b*, demand during lead time is less than the amount on hand when the order was placed, so excess inventory exists, resulting in inventory carrying costs that are higher than planned.

Figure 9-2
Uncertain demand during lead time

(a) Demand exceeds supply.

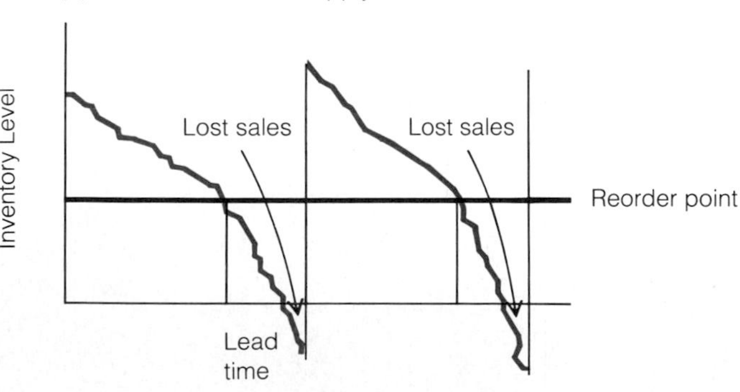

(b) Demand is less than supply.

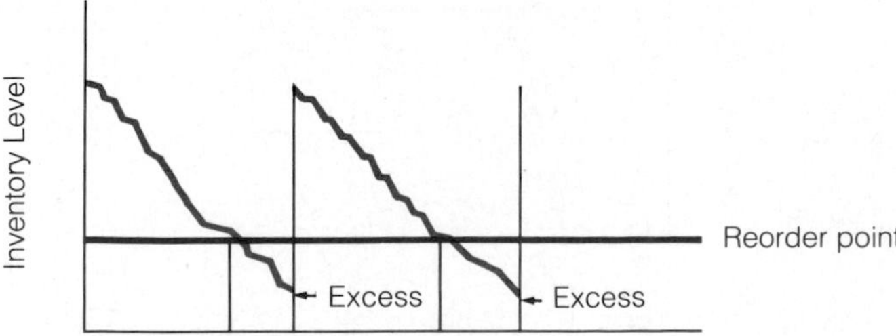

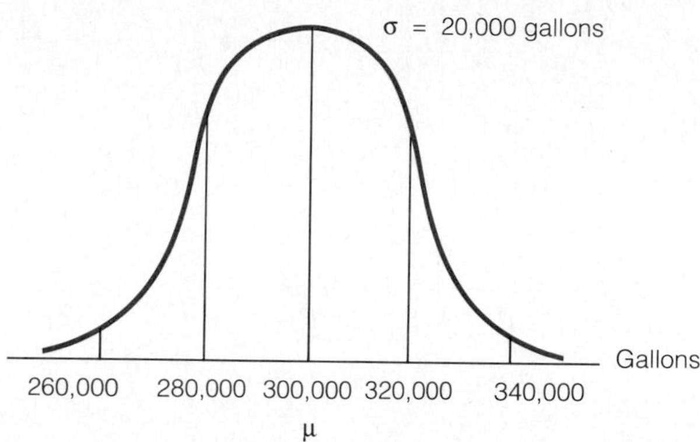

Figure 9-3
Distribution of annual demand for unleaded gasoline

Consider an example involving Gary Goldberg's service station. The annual demand for unleaded gasoline at Gary's station is uncertain, but historical records show the mean yearly demand is 300,000 gallons, with a standard deviation of 20,000 gallons. Further, the distribution of annual demand around the mean is approximately normal. Figure 9-3 illustrates this demand distribution. Each order for unleaded gasoline costs Gary $200 in paperwork and related activities. The cost factor Gary uses to determine his inventory carrying cost is .20, and his per gallon cost for unleaded gasoline is $.90.

The issues facing Gary are:

1. How many gallons of unleaded gasoline should be ordered each time an order is placed?
2. At what level of inventory should the order be placed?

DEVELOPING THE MODEL

An appropriate inventory model can provide the best answers to the above questions. The assumptions on which the present model will be based are:

1. The entire order arrives at one time.
2. The lead time is known with certainty.
3. The costs (purchase, ordering, and holding) are known with certainty.
4. No backordering is allowed.
5. No quantity discounts exist.

If you compare this list of assumptions with those for the elementary EOQ model in Chapter 8, you will see the only difference is that the assumption of certain demand is missing. In this case, the demand during lead time is uncertain but is assumed to be a random variable which follows a normal probability distribution. Recall that a **normal probability distribution** is a continuous probability distribution which is symmetrical and bell-shaped; its shape is defined by the mean and standard deviation.

Our first step is to answer the question about how much unleaded gasoline to order when an order is placed. Since Gary doesn't know what his annual demand will be, he also doesn't know what his optimal order quantity is. If we are unsure exactly what the annual demand for unleaded gasoline will be, we estimate demand using the mean, or expected value, of the distribution. The expected demand is used to approximate the order quantity using the elementary EOQ model, as follows:

$$Q^* = \sqrt{\frac{2E[D]C_o}{IC}} \tag{9-1}$$

where:

$E[D]$ = mean of the annual demand distribution
C_o = cost of placing an order
I = carrying-cost factor, in decimal form
C = purchase cost per unit

Then, substituting the values for this example, we get:

$$Q^* = \sqrt{\frac{(2)(300{,}000)(200)}{(.20)(.90)}}$$
$$= 25{,}819.89 \text{ gallons}$$

Based on the expected annual demand of 300,000 gallons, the optimal order quantity is 25,820 gallons. Using this value, Gary will place about $(D/Q) = (300{,}000 \div 25{,}820) = 11.6$ orders each year.

If demand is actually 340,000 gallons, the correct order quantity would be 27,487 gallons. If demand is 260,000 gallons, the correct order quantity would be 24,037 gallons. Therefore, the EOQ of 25,820 is a pretty good estimate, even if actual demand is 2 standard deviations higher or lower than the mean. This is true because the EOQ model is not affected by minor errors in cost and demand estimates.

Next, Gary must determine when to place an order. Assume that lead time is known to be 10 working days. The mean daily demand is: $300{,}000 \div 365 = 821.9$ gallons. For a 10-day period, the mean demand is $10 \times 821.9 = 8219$ gallons. If the annual demand was certain to be 300,000 gallons and was a constant amount each day, the demand during lead time would be 8219 gallons and the appropriate order point would be 8219 gallons. However, as shown in Figure 9-3, annual demand is not certain. The uncertainty is described by a normal probability distribution with a mean, μ, $=300{,}000$ gallons and a standard deviation, σ, $=20{,}000$ gallons. The demand during the 10-day lead time is then also described by a normal distribution with mean $= (300{,}000 \div 365)10 = 8219$ gallons (see Figure 9-4). If we assume that daily demand for gasoline is independent, we find the 10-day standard deviation as follows:

Figure 9-4
Gasoline demand during lead time

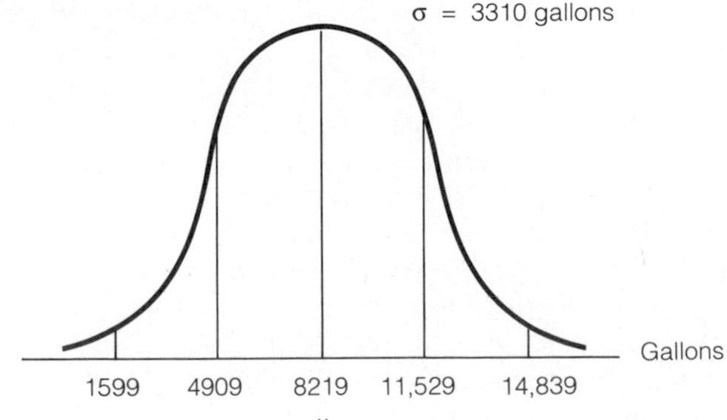

Step 1 Convert the annual standard deviation for demand to the variance by squaring the standard deviation:

$$\text{Variance} = 20{,}000^2 = 400{,}000{,}000$$

Step 2 Divide the variance by the number of operating days in the year to get the daily variance:

$$\text{Daily variance} = 400{,}000{,}000/365 = 1{,}095{,}890.4$$

Step 3 Multiply the daily variance by the number of days during lead time:

$$\text{Lead-time variance: } (1{,}095{,}890.4)(10) = 10{,}958{,}904$$

Step 4 Take the square root of the lead-time variance to get the lead-time standard deviation:

$$\text{Lead-time standard deviation} = \sqrt{10{,}958{,}904} = 3310 \text{ gallons}$$

Since demand during lead time is assumed to follow a normal distribution, if we set the reorder point at 8219 gallons, then 50% of the time demand will exceed this level and a stockout will occur. Likewise, 50% of the time demand will be less than 8219 gallons and excess inventory will accumulate. If the reorder point is raised to a level higher than 8219 gallons, the chance of stocking out is reduced but the chance of having excess inventory is increased. Likewise, if the reorder point is dropped below 8219 gallons, the chance of stocking out is increased.

In determining the order point for a probabilistic demand, decision makers must trade the cost of having too much inventory on hand against the cost of stocking out while waiting for an order. Since the cost of stocking out is often difficult to determine, decision makers may establish an order point based on a desired service level instead of incorporating the stockout costs directly into the analysis. One type of **service level** is determined by the percentage of time the manager is willing to run out of stock while waiting for a shipment to arrive. For instance, if Gary specifies a 90% service level, he is implicitly stating that he wishes to have gasoline available for customers during 9 out of 10 lead-time periods, on average. This is the same as saying he is willing to run out of unleaded gasoline while waiting for 1 out of 10 orders.

Once the service level has been specified, a reorder point can be determined such that the chance of demand during lead time being less than or equal to the reorder point is equal to the service level. Figure 9-5 illustrates this graphically.

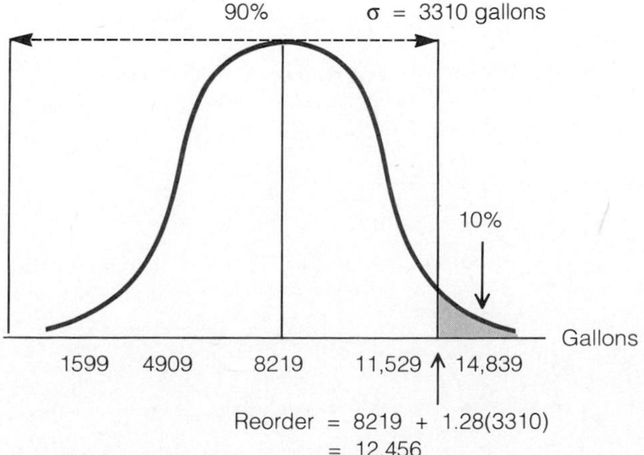

Figure 9-5
Calculating the gasoline reorder point for Gary's Station

When the demand during lead time follows a normal distribution, the reorder point is found using equation 9-2, as follows:

$$\text{Reorder point} = \text{average demand during lead time} + Z(\text{demand standard deviation during lead time}) \qquad (9\text{-}2)$$

where:

Z = a value from the standard normal distribution table (Appendix B) which corresponds to an area = (1 − service level)

For a service level of 90%, the Z value from the table is 1.28. Thus, the reorder point is:

$$8219 + 1.28(3310) = 12{,}456 \text{ gallons (rounded)}$$

When the inventory of unleaded gasoline reaches 12,456 gallons, Gary should place an order for $Q = 25{,}820$ gallons.

Note that the mean demand during lead time is 8219 gallons and the reorder point is 12,456 gallons. The difference between the reorder point and the expected demand is called **safety stock**. In this case, specifying a 90% service level, Gary's station will carry 12,456 − 8219 = 4237 gallons of unleaded gasoline as safety stock. The purpose of safety stock is to meet above-average demand during lead time. Under this plan, Gary's station should have enough gasoline available so it will run out while waiting for orders only 10% of the time. Note that the safety stock is the *average* amount of inventory that will still be on hand when an order is received. The result of carrying safety stock is that average inventory levels are increased, and so is the cost of carrying inventory.

Total Inventory Costs

Safety stock is necessary because of uncertainty associated with demand. The cost associated with this uncertainty is reflected in the added cost of holding safety stock in inventory. In essence, carrying safety stock is like buying insurance; we are willing to increase our holding cost to ensure against a stockout. Therefore, the cost of safety stock must be included when determining total inventory cost:

$$\text{Total inventory cost} = \text{normal carrying cost} + \text{ordering cost} + \text{safety-stock carrying cost}$$

In notation form, total annual inventory cost is:

$$TC = (Q/2)IC + (D/Q)C_o + (SS)IC \qquad (9\text{-}3)$$

where:

Q = order quantity
I = carrying-cost factor
C = purchase cost
D = mean annual demand
C_o = order cost
SS = safety stock

For Gary's station, we get:

$$\begin{aligned} TC &= (25{,}820/2)(.20)(.90) + (300{,}000/25{,}820)(200) + (4237)(.20)(.90) \\ &= \$2323.80 + \$2323.78 + \$762.66 \\ &= \$5410.24 \end{aligned}$$

The total inventory cost for unleaded gasoline is $5410.24. Of this total, $762.66 is for the safety stock carried to ensure against uncertain demand during lead time.

Changing Service Levels

We mentioned earlier that a cost which is not directly considered in the just-completed total cost calculations is the cost of lost sales, or stockout costs. Gary planned his reorder point based on a service level of 90%. This means he was willing to accept as much as 10% lost sales due to a shortage of inventory during lead time. Quantifying the cost associated with a lost sale is often difficult. However, when the relative cost of lost sales is high compared to the cost of carrying inventory, a high service level is appropriate.

Suppose that Gary would like to increase his service level to 98% from the present target of 90%. To achieve this higher service level, a higher safety stock will be required. The new reorder point is determined as follows:

$$\text{Reorder point} = 8219 + 2.06(3310) = 15{,}038 \text{ gallons (rounded)}$$

For a 98% service level, the Z value from the standard normal distribution table is approximately 2.06, so the reorder point is 2.06 standard deviations above the mean. The safety stock is 15,038 − 8219 = 6819 gallons. The total cost associated with this inventory plan is:

$$\begin{aligned} TC &= (25{,}820/2)(.20)(.90) + (300{,}000/25{,}820)(200) + (6819)(.20)(.90) \\ &= \$2323.80 + \$2323.78 + \$1227.42 = \$5875 \end{aligned}$$

This new cost represents an increase of $464.76 above the plan with a 90% service level. Gary must determine whether the increase in service level warrants the higher cost of carrying more safety stock.

9-3 PROBABILISTIC EOQ: SINGLE-PERIOD INVENTORY MODEL

The ordering examples presented so far in this chapter and in Chapter 8 have all involved situations where the inventory system consisted of a number of identical ordering cycles. Many businesses fit this mold. A shoe store can order shoes for its inventory many times during the year and carry inventory from one order period to the next. A manufacturer of farm implements can order component parts several times during the year and carry inventory from order period to order period. A retail bookstore can place an order for a particular book at various intervals throughout the year when inventory reaches the order point. All these examples, and those discussed in previous sections, represent *multiperiod* situations.

However, in other situations the type of business activity dictates that a single order be placed at the beginning of the inventory period. Then, at the end of the period, the inventory has either been depleted or a surplus of unsold or unused items will exist.

If unsold or unused items remain, they may or may not have a **salvage value**. This type of situation is referred to as a **single-period** inventory system.

Examples of single-period systems involve businesses which make and/or market perishable products, or are involved in seasonal business where styles change from period to period. Many food products hawked by concessionaires at college and professional football games can be managed by a single-period inventory model. Hot dogs prepared prior to a game cannot be saved for use during the next game. Most stores which sell clothes use a single-period inventory system. For example, a department store will generally place one order for winter coats of a certain style. If the inventory is exhausted, customers simply have to go to another store. If the entire stock of coats is not sold, the extras are put on sale in the "bargain basement" or disposed of in some other way. We see, then, that the elements of a single-period inventory situations are:

1. There is a finite time horizon after which the value of the item is significantly reduced.
2. There is no opportunity to reorder during the period.

NORMALLY DISTRIBUTED DEMAND

In a single-period inventory system, the question of when to place the order is generally not an issue, since lead time is often determined by manufacturers. For instance, orders for ski clothing are often made at trade shows which occur about 6 months before orders are delivered. However, the question of how much to order is still very important. If demand during the period is known with certainty, the decision of how much to order is easy—just order the quantity which will be demanded. When the demand is not known with certainty, determining the order quantity is a little more complex. The following example illustrates how order quantity is determined when the demand can be described by a normal distribution.

Goerring Publishing Company

Goerring Publishing Company, located in central Indiana, produces brochures, paperback books, and other printed items. Suppose the company has entered into a new venture in which it will publish and market the programs for Indiana University's basketball games. The multicolor programs are quite elaborate. They include photos of the Indiana team and each opponent's team, as well as paid advertising. After covering the fixed costs of typesetting, all the proceeds from advertising go directly to the university; but Goerring Publishing Company gets to keep the profits from program sales.

The first home game of the season pits Indiana University against Marquette University. The game is sold out, with nearly 16,000 people attending. However, no one knows how many programs will be sold. From past records and interviews with a number of people in the athletic department, Goerring managers believe demand is best described by a normal probability distribution with a mean = 4500 and a standard deviation = 50 programs. Figure 9–6 illustrates the demand distribution.

The programs will be sold for $3.00 each. The printing costs amount to $2.00 per copy, and unsold copies have no salvage value.

The question facing the managers at Goerring Publishing is how many programs to print. If they don't print enough programs, they forego profit; if they print too many, they incur unnecessary production costs. You should recognize these as the same trade-offs that decision makers face in multiperiod inventory systems when they

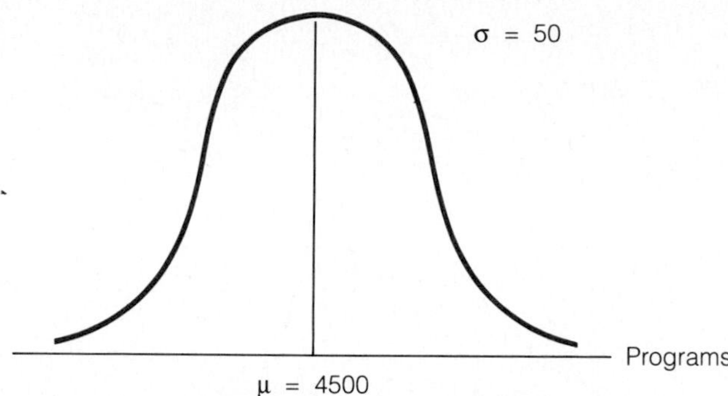

Figure 9-6
Goerring Publishing Co.: demand distribution for game programs

decide on order quantity. The method for determining the optimal order quantity for a single-period inventory system is referred to as **incremental analysis.** This technique examines the relationship between the cost of understocking (U) one additional unit and the cost of overstocking (O) one additional unit.

For Goerring Publishing Company, the cost of understocking is the lost profit associated with losing a sale because of not having a program available:

$$U = \text{price} - \text{printing cost} = \$3.00 - \$2.00 = \$1.00$$

Since the game programs have no salvage value, the cost of overstocking is:

$$O = \text{printing cost} = \$2.00$$

In employing incremental analysis, we try to balance the expected cost associated with stocking an additional unit against the expected cost of not stocking an additional unit. For instance, if we are currently planning to stock 4500 programs, what is the cost (loss) associated with stocking 4501 units versus leaving the level at 4500 units? At either stocking level, the occurrence of a loss depends on whether the demand is 4500 units or less or is more than 4500 units.

If demand is 4500 or less and we decide to stock 4501 units, we have overstocked and the incremental cost is $O = \$2.00$. On the other hand, if demand exceeds 4500 and we decide to stock only 4500 units, we have understocked and the incremental cost is $U = \$1.00$. Figure 9–7 shows that if the demand is normally distributed with a mean = 4500 units and a standard deviation = 50 units, the probability of demand $\leq$ 4500 is .50 and the probability of demand > 4500 is .50. The expected cost (loss) for each stocking level is computed as follows:

$$EL(Q = 4501) = (O)P(\text{demand} \leq 4500) = \$2.00(.50) = \$1.00$$
$$EL(Q = 4500) = (U)P(\text{demand} > 4500) = \$1.00(.50) = \$.50$$

Considering these expected-loss calculations, if we were faced with the choice of stocking 4500 or 4501 units, we would select 4500 because the expected cost (loss) is \$.50 versus \$1.00. The next step would be to examine the costs associated with stocking 4499 units versus 4500. Figure 9-8 shows the calculations for the probabilities associated with demands of 4499 or less and of more than 4499. The expected costs of these two levels are computed as follows:

$$EL(Q = 4500) = (O)P(\text{demand} \leq 4499) = \$2.00(.492) = \$.984$$
$$EL(Q = 4499) = (U)P(\text{demand} > 4499) = \$1.00(.508) = \$.508$$

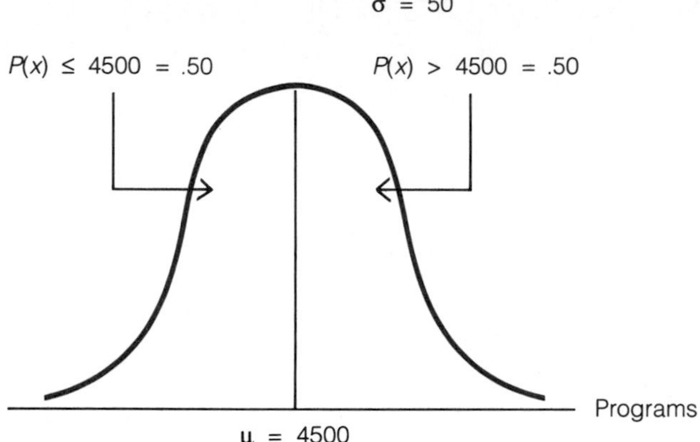

Figure 9-7
Goerring Publishing Co.: probability of demand ≤ 4500

To find: $P(x) \leq 4500$,
use standard normal distribution:

$$Z = \frac{x - \mu}{\sigma} = \frac{4500 - 4500}{50} = 0$$

From the standard normal table, $Z = 0$ is associated with probability = 0.0.
Then $P(x) \leq 4500 = .50 - 0.0 = .50$.

Thus, if we were faced with the choice of stocking 4500 versus 4499 programs, based on lower expected loss, we would select 4499 programs. We could continue checking the stocking levels of 4498, 4497, 4496, and so on until we hit an order quantity, Q, for which the incremental cost of decreasing the stocking level equals the

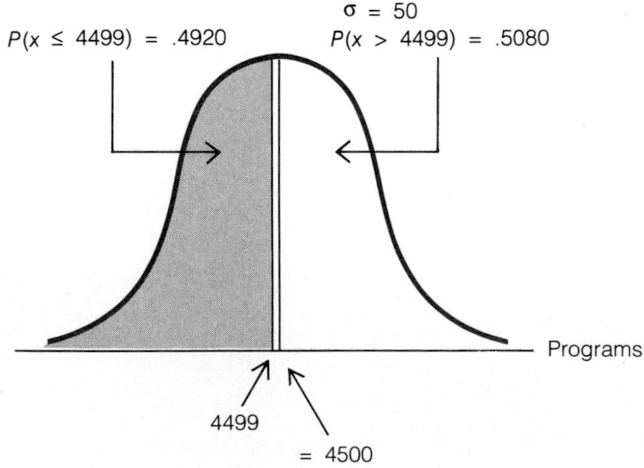

Figure 9-8
Goerring Publishing Co. problem: probability of demand ≤ 4499

Use standard normal distribution:

$$Z = \frac{x - \mu}{\sigma} = \frac{4499 - 4500}{50} = \frac{-1}{50}$$

$$Z = -.02$$

Probability from Standard Normal table for $Z = -.02$ is .0080.
Thus, $P(x \leq 4499) = .5000 - .0080 = .4920$.
Also $P(x > 4499) = 1.0 - .4920 = .5080$.

cost of staying at a level one unit higher. Through this process, we would be searching for the value Q^* where the expected loss of understocking is equal to the expected cost of overstocking an additional unit. However, this would be a complicated and extensive procedure and we would like a means for calculating Q^* which does not require the step-by-step process. We can do this by formalizing our definitions of overstocking and understocking costs. First is the expected cost of understocking an additional unit:

$$EL(Q^*) = (U)P(\text{demand} > Q^*) \tag{9-4}$$

Then the expected cost of overstocking:

$$EL(Q^* + 1) = (O)P(\text{demand} \leq Q^*) \tag{9-5}$$

Since we are dealing with probabilities, we know that:

$$P(\text{demand} > Q^*) + P(\text{demand} \leq Q^*) = 1.0 \tag{9-6}$$

or:

$$P(\text{demand} > Q^*) = 1.0 - P(\text{demand} \leq Q^*) \tag{9-7}$$

We then use equation 9-7 to rewrite equation 9-4 as:

$$EL(Q^*) = (U)[1.0 - P(\text{demand} \leq Q^*)] \tag{9-8}$$

Finally, we set the expected cost of stocking an additional unit equal to the expected cost of not stocking an additional unit, or set equation 9-5 equal to equation 9-8.

$$(O)P(\text{demand} \leq Q^*) = (U)[1.0 - P(\text{demand} \leq Q^*)] \tag{9-9}$$

Next, we solve for $P(\text{demand} \leq Q^*)$:

$$P(\text{demand} \leq Q^*) = \frac{U}{U + O} \tag{9-10}$$

Equation 9-10 can be used to determine the optimal order quantity for any single-period inventory system, regardless of the demand distribution. For the Goerring Publishing example, we get:

$$P(\text{demand} \leq Q^*) = \frac{1.00}{1.00 + 2.00}$$
$$= 1/3 = .33$$

Therefore, the optimal order quantity, Q^*, should be set such that the probability of demand being less than or equal to Q^* is .33. Figure 9-9 shows the computations necessary to find Q^*. Based on the cost figures supplied by Goerring's managers, the optimal number of programs to print is 4478. At this point, the expected loss of adding an additional program to the stock is equal to the expected cost of not adding the additional program.

Goerring Executives Reevaluate the Costs

Suppose that before printing begins, the marketing manager discovers an outlet for unused programs. She has discovered a memorabilia shop in Los Angeles which will pay $.30 each for the unsold programs. Since the number of programs to be printed for the game can be changed, the Goerring managers would like to reevaluate the order quantity.

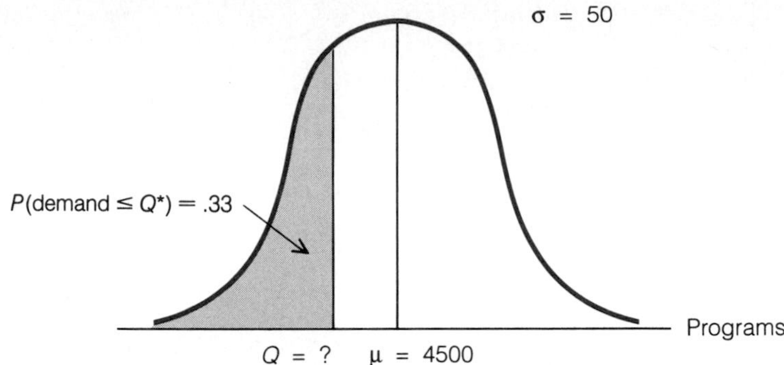

Figure 9-9
Goerring Publishing Co.: Solving for Q^*

The Z value from the standard normal table for an area = .5 − .33 = .17 is −.44.

Then:

$$Z = \frac{x - \mu}{\sigma} = \frac{Q^* - \mu}{\sigma}$$

$$-.44 = \frac{Q^* - 4500}{50}$$

$$Q^* = 4500 - .44(50) \qquad Q^* = 4478 \text{ programs}$$

Intuitively, we would think that the salvage value would increase the order size, since it reduces the cost of overstocking. To see how much effect this change has on the order size, we again use equation 9-10:

$$P(\text{demand} \le Q^*) = \frac{U}{U + O}$$

where

$$U = \text{price} - \text{printing cost} = \$3.00 - \$2.00 = \$1.00$$
$$O = \text{printing cost} - \text{salvage value} = \$2.00 - \$.30 = \$1.70$$

Now: $$P(\text{demand} \le Q^*) = \frac{\$1.00}{\$1.00 + \$1.70} = .3703$$

Figure 9-10 shows the calculations for Q^*. The new solution is to stock 4483.5 programs (rounded up to 4484). This represents an increase over the previous solution, as we suspected.

OTHER PROBABILITY DISTRIBUTIONS

In the previous example, the demand was assumed to be normally distributed. There are many instances where the normal distribution might be the appropriate distribution to use in evaluating the optimal order quantity in a single-period model. However, the methodology presented in this section is applicable when demand is represented by other probability distributions.

Figure 9-10
Goerring Publishing Co.: Solving for Q^*

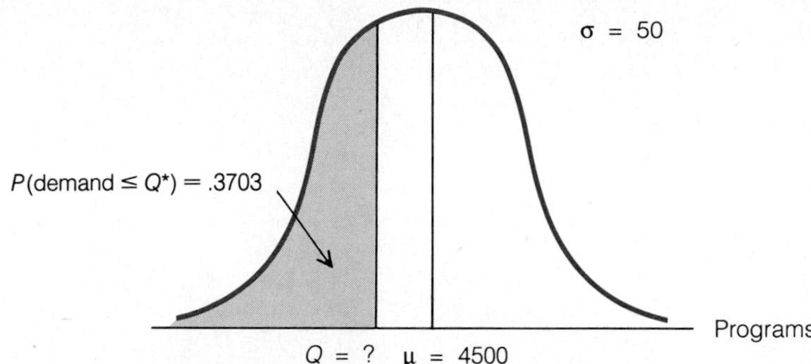

The Z value from the standard normal distribution table for an area $= .5 - .3703 = .1297$ is approximately $-.33$.

Then:

$$Z = \frac{X - \mu}{\sigma} = \frac{Q^* - \mu}{\sigma}$$

$$-.33 = \frac{Q^* - 4500}{50}$$

$$Q^* = 4500 - .33(50) \quad Q^* = 4483.5 \text{ or } 4484 \text{ programs}$$

An Example Using Poisson Distribution

Consider the following example involving Yardley Hotels, Inc., of Houston, Texas. In four weeks, the hotel will host the annual conference for the National Cattlemen's Association. Among the many amenities the hotel offers its guests is limousine service to restaurants and entertainment spots in Houston. The hotel contracts with local companies to provide the limousine service. If the hotel contracts for the service before the convention, the price is $2000 per vehicle; after the convention starts, the price is $2500 per vehicle. As a matter of policy, the hotel attempts to determine the optimal number of limousines to order before the convention to take advantage of the lower rate. However, if additional limousines are needed, they will be hired at the $2500 rate.

The hotel's convention manager recognizes that the demand for limousines is not known with certainty. However, past experience shows the demand distribution can be reasonably represented by the Poisson probability distribution. The Poisson distribution is a discrete probability distribution which requires knowing only the mean (expected value), of the distribution. From experience, the hotel's convention manager has determined that the expected number of limousines needed is 6. The Poisson distribution table in Appendix C can be used to determine the probability of 0, 1, 2, 3, . . . limousines being demanded during the convention. Table 9-1 shows these probabilities.

The issue facing the convention manager is how many limousines to order before the Cattlemen's Convention. This amount can be determined by the single-period inventory model. We know the following:

O = cost of overstocking = $2000
U = cost of understocking = $500

Table 9-1 POISSON DISTRIBUTION FOR LIMOUSINE DEMAND

Demand D	Probability* $P(D)$	Cumulative Probability	Demand D	Probability* $P(D)$	Cumulative Probability
0	.0025	.0025	9	.0688	.9161
1	.0149	.0174	10	.0413	.9574
2	.0446	.0620	11	.0225	.9799
3	.0892	.1512	12	.0113	.9912
4	.1339	.2851	13	.0052	.9964
5	.1606	.4457	14	.0022	.9986
6	.1606	.6063	15	.0009	.9995
7	.1377	.7440	16	.0003	.9998
8	.1033	.8473	17	.0001	.9999†

* To find the probabilities in the Poisson table in Appendix C, go to the column for $\lambda t = 6.00$.
† Difference from 1.0 due to the small probability for demand exceeding 17.

You might wonder why the cost of understocking is $500 when the price of a limousine hired during the convention is $2500. The $500 is the opportunity cost for not having ordered it earlier ($2500 − $2000 = $500).

Now, we can apply equation 9-10:

$$P(\text{demand} \leq Q^*) = U/(U + O)$$
$$= \$500/(\$500 + \$2000) = .20$$

The optimal order quantity, Q^*, is found by going to Table 9-1 and moving down the cumulative probability column until we hit the first value greater than .20. This is .2851, which is the probability of 4 or fewer limousines being demanded. To get Q^*, we go back one place, to 3, which is the highest demand level with a probability $\leq .20$. Thus, considering the relative costs of understocking versus overstocking, the convention manager should contract for 3 limousines.

9-4 PROBLEMS WITH TRADITIONAL EOQ-BASED INVENTORY CONTROL MODELS

The previous sections introduced several techniques for dealing with inventory decisions when the certainty assumptions associated with the traditional EOQ inventory models do not apply. Even with these probabilistic techniques taken into consideration, decision makers face still other problems in managing inventory with traditional inventory models.

Let's begin our discussion with a review of the simple EOQ model which is the basis of traditional inventory control theory considered up to this point:

$$Q^* = \sqrt{\frac{2DC_o}{IC}}$$

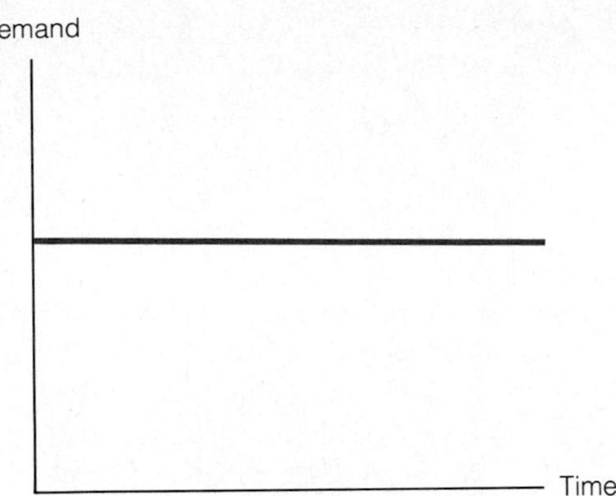

Figure 9-11
Demand in the traditional EOQ model

where:

D = demand

C_o = cost of placing one order

I = inventory carrying-cost factor, in decimal form

C = unit purchase cost

This EOQ model is deterministic; that is, it assumes all values are known with certainty. Experience indicates the two critical components in the equation are the demand, D, and the cost of holding a unit, IC (or H, in some applications). Let's take a closer look at each item and speculate on what will happen if the assumptions are violated.

The traditional EOQ model assumes that demand is constant and known with certainty, as shown in Figure 9-11. While demand rarely follows the pattern shown in this figure, for those items where demand is at least quasi-continuous, as seen in Figure 9-12, we showed earlier that expected demand, $E[D]$, can be used in the EOQ formula as a good approximation. However, in many cases, demand is neither known nor continuous over time. One situation where demand is typically not known with certainty or continuous is the batch-processing operations in production environments.

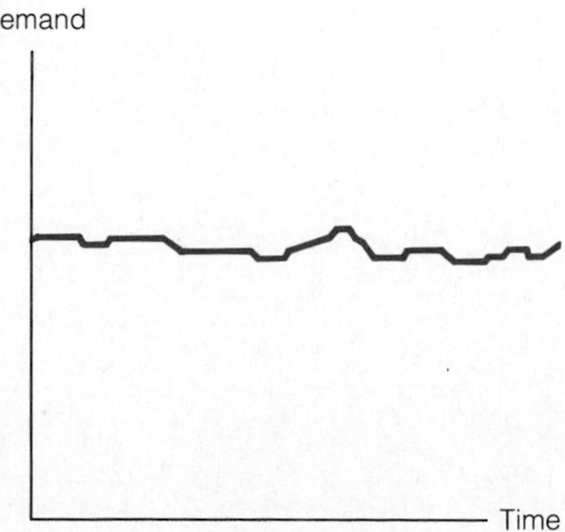

Figure 9-12
Quasi-continuous demand

BATCH-PROCESSING OPERATIONS

For some organizations, demand for a product is sufficiently large to justify one or more production lines which are fully dedicated to producing a specific product. For instance, the computer chip line at Appleton Technology is totally dedicated to producing its 640K chip. In this case, demand actually exceeds capacity. Although some industries do have dedicated assembly lines, it is more common for demand to be less than production capacity, so that a single assembly line may be used to produce a variety of items during the year.

In fact, the economic run size model developed in Chapter 8 assumed that production capacity exceeded demand. Applying this model leads to products being produced in batches; that is, a production run would last for a certain period of time, building up an inventory of finished goods, which would then be drawn down at a uniform rate. The inventory level for this situation is shown in Figure 9-13.

While batch production is common, there is often an inventory problem with the parts and materials needed to make the end item. If we purchase those parts and materials from an outside supplier, and use an EOQ model to determine the optimal order quantity, the model assumes that demand for the parts and materials is continuous at a constant rate throughout the year—when in fact the demand is discontinuous, like that shown in Figure 9-14. This assumption can produce poor results, as the following example illustrates.

McSweeney Manufacturing

McSweeney Manufacturing makes small wood-and-metal tables which most buyers use as television stands. The tables are sold through major retailers like K-Mart and Shopko. The stand is made entirely from parts supplied by outside manufacturers. Demand forecasts for next year indicate a need to manufacture 48,000 stands. This number is well below the company's production capacity. If the batches were produced continuously throughout the year, the monthly output would be 4000 units.

Figure 9-13
Inventory levels for batch production

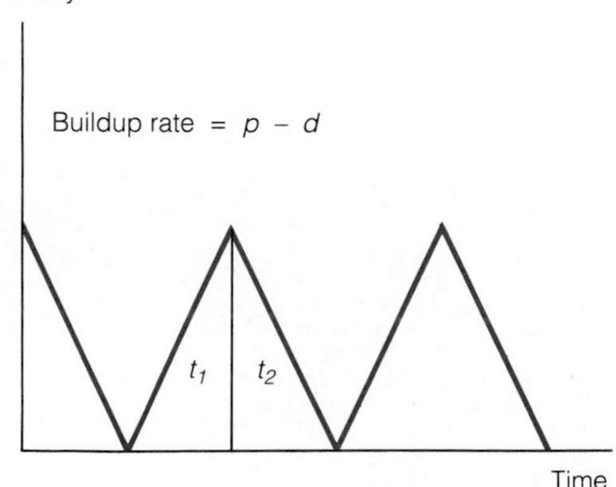

t_1 = time item is produced
t_2 = time item supplied from inventory
p = daily production rate
d = daily demand rate

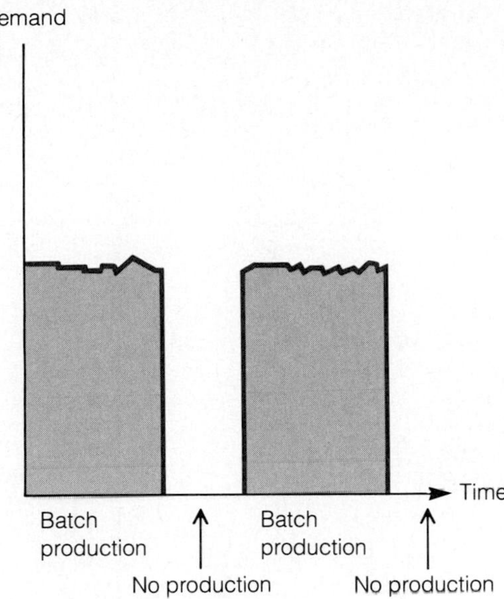

Figure 9-14
Discontinuous demand

However, this would represent a substantial underutilization of the production facilities. Instead, the following batch-processing schedule has been established:

20,000 in March
15,000 in July
13,000 in November

One part used in making the table is a Formica inlay that is part of the top. Let's consider only what will happen to this material from an inventory standpoint if it is ordered using the traditional EOQ model. Demand is 48,000 and ordering costs are \$30. The purchase price is \$4 per unit, with one unit needed for each table, and the inventory holding-cost factor is .25, making a \$1 yearly holding cost. Lead time is 6 days. Using the EOQ formula to find order quantity:

$$Q^* = \sqrt{(2)(48{,}000)(30)/1} = 1697$$

This order quantity assumes that we are using 4000 tops each month.

The ordering point is found by multiplying daily demand times lead time. In this case, daily demand is $48{,}000 \div 365 = 131.5$. Since lead time is 6 days, the ordering point is $131.5 \times 6 = 789$ units.

Figure 9-15 shows what will happen during March when this EOQ-derived order quantity is used in this batch production application. First, assume that we will enter the year with 1000 units in inventory from last year's production. These units will be held in inventory until March, when we start producing at the rate of 20,000 tables for the month. Theoretically, no orders would be placed until March production begins and inventory drops to the order point of 789 units.

If we assume that the plant is operational 31 days during March, the daily production level is $20{,}000 \div 31 = 645.16$. This means that 645 units of Formica material are needed every day. Thus, sometime on March 1, the order point will be hit

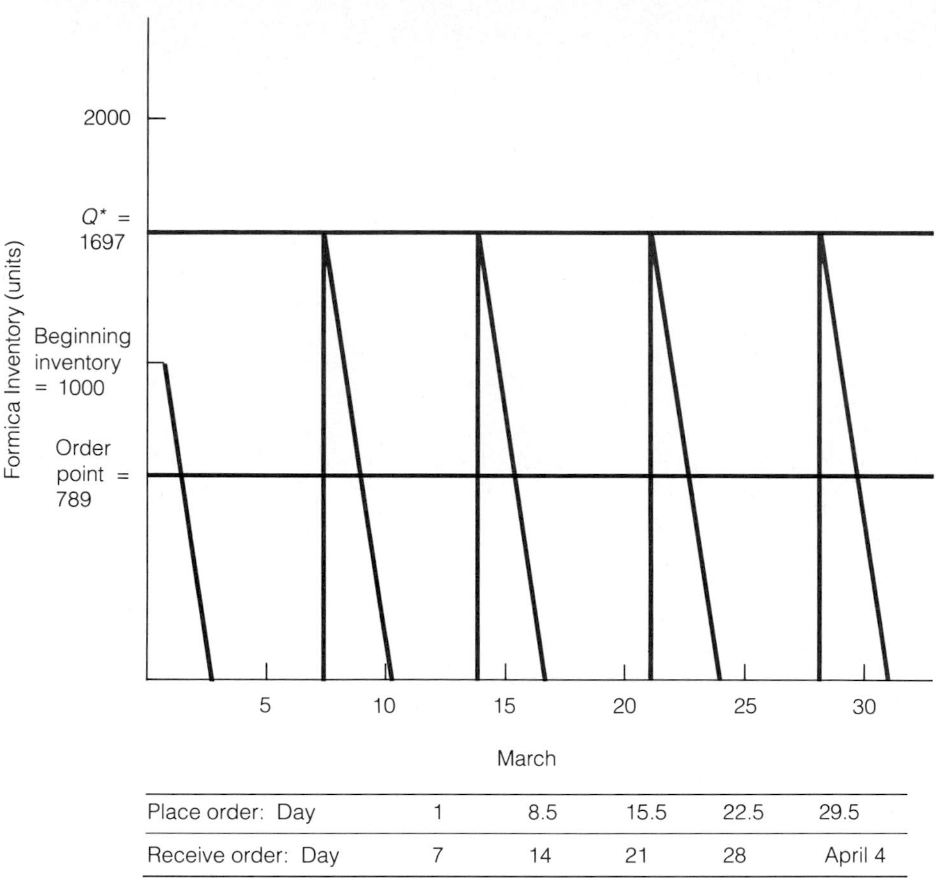

Place order: Day	1	8.5	15.5	22.5	29.5
Receive order: Day	7	14	21	28	April 4

Figure 9-15
McSweeney Manufacturing: March inventory conditions

and an order will be placed. Sometime on March 2, the plant will be forced to halt production because there is no Formica available; the order won't arrive until March 7. When this order arrives, it will be for 1697 units, enough for less than 3 days' production. The result is that the plant will be closed again. Without a change in inventory policy, this cycle of alternating production and idle time will continue throughout the month and far fewer than the planned 20,000 tables will be produced.

The traditional procedure to combat stockouts has been to increase the safety stock. If McSweeney persisted with the EOQ order point and order quantity, the required safety stock of Formica going into March would be more than 13,000 [1000 + (645/day × 19 down days) = 13,255] units. Even this would leave the company with almost no inventory at the month's end. McSweeney purchasing agents would immediately begin ordering Formica to build up a safety stock for July so production stoppages wouldn't occur then. The process would be repeated during August through October to be ready for November's production.

As you can see, *one of the consequences of using EOQ models for batch production is to either carry excess inventory in the form of safety stock or incur excessive stockout costs.*

A second major problem that occurs when applying EOQ models to a batch-processing operation involves the EOQ formula itself. To make one television stand, McSweeney needs six different items, in varying quantities:

1 Formica inlay	1 shelf
2 side assemblies	8 flat-head screws
2 top rails	8 wood screws

To use the EOQ formula, we need demands, order costs and holding costs. For this single product we will have three demand levels: 48,000; 96,000; or 384,000, depending on which item we are considering. Ordering costs will remain about the same for each of the six items, but inventory holding costs will differ since each has a different unit cost. Therefore, for the same product, we will make six different EOQ calculations and arrive at six different order quantities. For instance, if:

I = holding-cost factor = .25
C = unit cost of wood screws = \$.02

then:

$$Q^* = \sqrt{\frac{(2)(384{,}000)(30)}{(.25)(.02)}} = 67{,}882$$

And if:

I = holding-cost factor = .25
C = unit cost of flat-head screws = \$.05

then:

$$Q^* = \sqrt{\frac{(2)(384{,}000)(30)}{(.25)(.05)}} = 42{,}933$$

Therefore, by making an EOQ calculation for each item, we wind up with different order quantities, even for items used at the same rate. This leads to mismatched inventories, where we can be completely out of one item and have lots of everything else.

The problems of excessive carrying costs, excessive stockout costs, and mismatched inventories occur as a result of applying traditional EOQ inventory models to batch-processing situations. In these instances, alternative methods of inventory management are required. In order to determine what type of alternative approach is required, we must be able to categorize the demand for an item as either *dependent* or *independent.*

INDEPENDENT AND DEPENDENT DEMAND ITEMS

In the 1950s, the just-emerging computer revolution allowed organizations to greatly increase the scope and accuracy of their record-keeping systems. In an effort to improve their inventory systems, organizations started preparing forecasts for every item in inventory, using one or more of the forecasting tools introduced in Chapter 7. The forecast for demand would then be substituted into the EOQ model to determine the order quantity for the next period. In the case of McSweeney Manufacturing, an individual forecast would be made for the finished table (called an *end item*) and for each *component* part of the table. An important concept of inventory control theory is that end-item demand may differ from the demand for components.

For McSweeney, the demand for the table is different from the demand for its parts. Because the demand for completed tables is determined by purchasing agents from outside companies, and is therefore outside McSweeney's control, it is termed an **independent demand**. McSweeney's managers should spend ample time trying to forecast demand for their table; but once they have done so, they don't need to spend any time forecasting the demand for the component parts of the table. Once they decide to manufacture 48,000 tables next year, they know exactly how many of each component they will need:

48,000 Formica inlays	48,000 shelves
96,000 side assemblies	384,000 flat-head screws
96,000 top rails	384,000 wood screws

Because the demand for these component parts depends on the demand for the table, it is termed a **dependent demand**.

Further, once McSweeney Manufacturing decides to produce 20,000 tables in March, the demand for each component for March is known and does not need to be forecast. Just as important, once we know we need 20,000 Formica inlays in March, we also know we need no Formica in January, February, or April. (Although Formica may be needed for other products that the company makes during these months, we are not considering that possibility in the current example.) The same is true for all other table components: none have to be in stock during the nonproduction months. Thus, once the independent demand is forecast, the need for the dependent-demand items is established.

In the next section, we introduce a relatively new inventory management tool which utilizes the concepts of independent and dependent demand to help solve the problems associated with applying traditional EOQ models to batch production. It is called material requirements planning, or MRP.

9-5 MATERIAL REQUIREMENTS PLANNING

Certainly the problems associated with using traditional inventory control models in situations where they do not apply have occurred for many years. However, the problems were not effectively addressed until the beginning of the 1960s. The primary work in developing what is now referred to as material requirements planning, or MRP, belongs to three men: Joe Orlicky, Ollie Wight, and George Plossl.

After they began to preach MRP as a new method of answering the two inventory control questions, Orlicky, Wight, and Plossl found an ally in the American Production and Inventory Control Society (APICS), which in the 1970s launched what has been referred to as an MRP crusade. The "crusade" was very successful, and recent surveys of manufacturing and distribution organizations have consistently found that more than 75% of American firms in these categories use some sort of MRP system.

Material requirements planning is a system used to determine how many inventory items to order (or make) and when to order (make) them. MRP's prime purpose, however, is to ensure that we have enough inventory when we need it (no stockouts) and no inventory when we don't need it (no excess carrying costs). The parts of the MRP system are described in the following subsections.

MASTER SCHEDULE

The first step in developing an MRP system is to separate all inventory items into independent or dependent demand categories. As we mentioned earlier, independent demand items are those whose demand is determined outside the organization. Most often, independent demand items are those that the organization supplies to another organization. For McSweeney Manufacturing, the table is an *independent demand item,* since this is the product it sells. Using the specific terminology of MRP, an independent demand item is often called an *end item.* In a working MRP system, each distinct end item must be identifiable. For instance, if McSweeney Manufacturing makes two tables, one with an oak finish and one with a walnut finish, it has two separate end items.

Once an organization has identified its independent demand items, a master schedule is prepared for each item. A **master schedule** is a period-by-period production schedule prepared for each independent demand item based upon firm orders, demand forecasts, and plant capacity. If McSweeney manufactures 20 different items, it will have 20 different master schedules.

In MRP terminology, the time periods for which the master schedule is prepared are called **time buckets.** A master schedule may have daily, weekly, monthly, or quarterly time buckets. In fact, in a typical application the master schedule will be prepared for 18 months and have different buckets depending on the period the schedule covers. For example, an 18-month schedule might have weekly buckets for the first 3 months, then monthly buckets for the next 6 months, and quarterly buckets for the last three quarters (9 months).

The master schedule is a statement of how many of each of its end items the organization is planning to produce (or sell). It is made up of a combination of *firm orders* and *forecast orders.* For instance, McSweeney's decision to make 48,000 television tables may be based on firm orders for 30,000 tables—20,000 deliverable in April and 10,000 deliverable in August—and an additional forecast demand of 18,000. This two-component input into the master schedule is shown in Figure 9-16.

An organization would use all the forecasting tools it has available to help with the master schedule. This would include any statistical tools the organization has available and the judgment of the sales force and all managers. However, for each independent demand item, there will be one person, called the master scheduler, primarily responsible for preparing its production plan.

Part of a master schedule prepared for an under-cabinet spice rack, also manufactured by McSweeney, is shown in Figure 9-17. Notice that weekly time buckets are used so that the demand for the spice rack is forecast weekly.

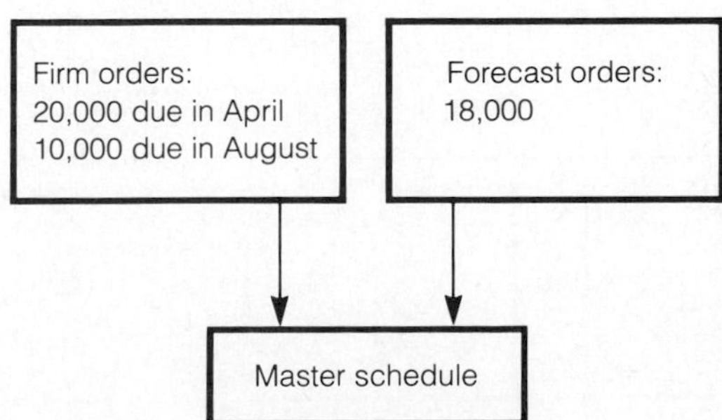

Figure 9-16
Demand sources to the Master schedule: McSweeney example

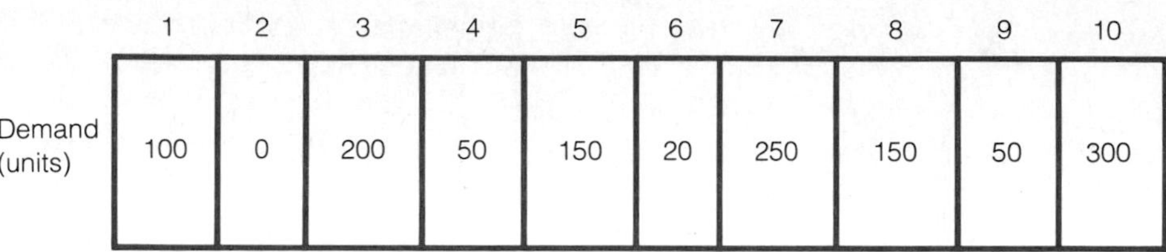

	1	2	3	4	5	6	7	8	9	10
Demand (units)	100	0	200	50	150	20	250	150	50	300

Figure 9-17
Master schedule—weekly time buckets: McSweeney example

BILL OF MATERIALS

The second necessary component for an MRP system is a bill of materials. A **bill of materials** is a structured parts and materials list; it contains a listing of all the parts and materials necessary to complete an end item and shows the order in which the parts are needed. The bill of materials is different from a parts list. Ollie Wight would make an intuitive analogy by asking someone to open a cookbook. First you see a list of all the ingredients needed for the recipe: *2 cups flour, 2 eggs, 1 cup milk,* . . . . This is the parts list. Next you see the recipe itself: *Put 2 cups flour into a bowl. Add 2 eggs and 1 cup milk.* . . . This is the bill of materials.

The bill of materials not only indicates what parts are needed to complete each end item, it also lets the decision maker know how many of each and in what order they are needed. In addition, the bill of materials indicates the timing in which the parts are needed. This information can often be combined with a product structure tree to indicate not only what parts are needed to complete the end item but also the sequence and quantity in which they are needed.

Figure 9-18 shows the product structure tree for the table produced by McSweeney Manufacturing. Notice that each part is given a unique identifier code, such as 16XY-1 for the base and 423W for the wood screws. The needed quantities of each component are also listed; for example, 2 top rails per base and 1 Formica inlay

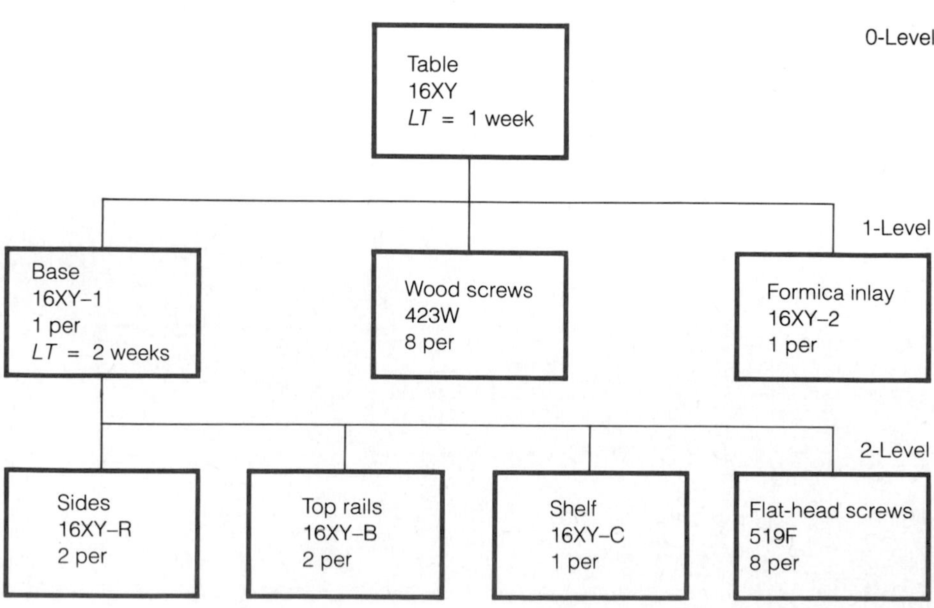

Figure 9-18
Product structure tree for McSweeney's table

per stand. Finally, for the parts assembled by McSweeney, assembly times are given on the structure tree as lead times (*LT*).

Designations of levels are indicated along the right-hand side of Figure 9-18. By definition, the end item in an MRP system is a 0- Level item. Each immediate subcomponent of a 0-Level item is a 1-Level item, and so on.

INVENTORY RECORDS

Remember, the purpose of any inventory control system is to identify how many of an item are needed and when they should be ordered or produced. The master schedule identifies the end items that are needed and when they are required. The bill of materials identifies what components are needed to produce the quantities stated in the master schedule. Next we look at the inventory records to determine what we have.

To operate effectively, an MRP system requires accurate inventory records. Ollie Wight stated that a company's inventory records must be at least 97% accurate for the system to operate correctly. This does *not* mean that the typical record can have a 3% error, but that at least 97% of all inventory records must be exactly correct. This accuracy requirement is a major stumbling block in implementing an MRP system, since many firms have thousands of items in inventory. Traditionally, many companies have had a difficult time matching *recorded inventory* with *actual inventory*.

Not only does a company have to keep track of what is physically on hand at each moment, it also must know what is presently on order and when each order is expected to arrive. Finally, the inventory records system must show what the lead time is for each item ordered from suppliers or manufactured internally.

The inventory-record information for the 16XY table is shown in Table 9-2.

ACTION REPORT

The MRP system is a procedure to take end-item requirements from the master schedule, component requirements from the bill of materials, and component availability from inventory records to generate an ordering and production schedule.

The output of the MRP system is an **action report** (also called an *MRP explosion*) which indicates an ordering schedule for the purchasing department and a production schedule for the production department. The flow of information in the MRP system is shown in Figure 9-19.

In practice, for companies that have hundreds or thousands of end items, component parts, and materials, the MRP system requires extensive computer capability to operate. However, the logic of its operation is simple, as you can see from the following discussion and the action report shown in Table 9-3.

(*Text continues on page 483.*)

Table 9-2 INVENTORY RECORDS FOR MCSWEENEY'S TABLE

Part Number	Description	On Hand	On Order	Due In	Lead Time	Lot Size
16XY	Table	1000	—	—	1 week	Lot-for-lot
16XY-1	Base	2000	—	—	2 weeks	Lot-for-lot
423W	Wood screws	20,000	—	—	1 week	100,000
16XY-2	Formica inlay	1500	—	—	2 weeks	5000
16XY-A	Sides	3000	—	—	2 weeks	4000
16XY-B	Top rails	4500	—	—	1 week	6000
16XY-C	Shelf	2000	—	—	3 weeks	5000
519F	Flat-head screws	15,000	—	—	1 week	150,000

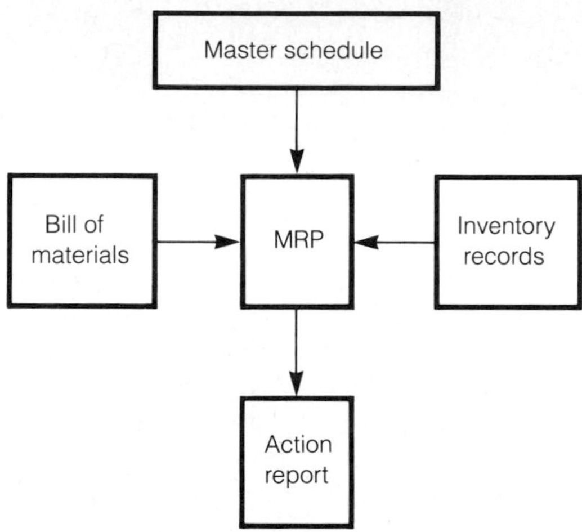

Figure 9-19
MRP system flow

Table 9-3 MCSWEENEY MANUFACTURING: MRP ACTION REPORT FOR PART 16XY, THE END ITEM

a. Table

Part 16XY
Level 0

	Period								
	Now	1	2	3	4	5	6	7	8
Gross Requirements					4000			3000	3000
Scheduled Receipts									
Projected on Hand	1000	1000	1000	1000	1000	0	0	0	0
Net Requirements					3000			3000	3000
Planned Order Receipts					3000			3000	3000
Planned Order Releases				3000			3000	3000	

b. Base

Part 16XY-1
Level 1

	Period								
	Now	1	2	3	4	5	6	7	8
Gross Requirements				3000			3000	3000	
Scheduled Receipts									
Projected on Hand	2000	2000	2000	2000	0	0	0	0	0
Net Requirements				1000			3000	3000	
Planned Order Receipts				1000			3000	3000	
Planned Order Releases		1000			3000	3000			

Table 9-3 continued

c. Wood screws

Part 432W
Level 1

	Period								
	Now	1	2	3	4	5	6	7	8
Gross Requirements				24,000			24,000	24,000	
Scheduled Receipts									
Projected on Hand	20,000	20,000	20,000	20,000	96,000	96,000	72,000	48,000	48,000
Net Requirements				4,000			0	0	
Planned Order Receipts				100,000					
Planned Order Releases			100,000						

d. Formica inlay

Part 16XY-2
Level 1

	Period								
	Now	1	2	3	4	5	6	7	8
Gross Requirements				3000			3000	3000	
Scheduled Receipts									
Projected on Hand	1500	1500	1500	1500	3500	3500	3500	500	2500
Net Requirements				1500				2500	
Planned Order Receipts				5000				5000	
Planned Order Releases		5000				5000			

e. Sides

Part 16XY-A
Level 2

	Period								
	Now	1	2	3	4	5	6	7	8
Gross Requirements		2000			6000	6000			
Scheduled Receipts									
Projected on Hand	3000	3000	1000	1000	1000	3000	1000		
Net Requirements					5000	3000			
Planned Order Receipts					8000	4000			
Planned Order Releases			8000	4000					

Table 9-3 continued

f. Top rails

Part 16XY-B
Level 2

	Period								
	Now	1	2	3	4	5	6	7	8
Gross Requirements		2000			6000	6000			
Scheduled Receipts									
Projected on Hand	4500	4500	2500	2500	2500	2500	2500	2500	2500
Net Requirements					3500	3500			
Planned Order Receipts					6000	6000			
Planned Order Releases				6000	6000				

g. Shelf

Part 16XY-C
Level 2

	Period								
	Now	1	2	3	4	5	6	7	8
Gross Requirements		1000			3000	3000			
Scheduled Receipts									
Projected on Hand	2000	2000	1000	1000	1000	3000	0	0	0
Net Requirements					2000				
Planned Order Receipts					5000				
Planned Order Releases		5000							

h. Flat-head screws

Part 519F
Level 2

	Period								
	Now	1	2	3	4	5	6	7	8
Gross Requirements		8,000			24,000	24,000			
Scheduled Receipts									
Projected on Hand	15,000	15,000	7,000	7,000	7,000	133,000	109,000	109,000	109,000
Net Requirements					17,000				
Planned Order Receipts					150,000				
Planned Order Releases				150,000					

McSweeney Manufacturing has just received an order for 10,000 tables from a major customer. The first 4000 tables are to be shipped in 4 weeks (week 4 time period). The remaining 6000 tables are to be shipped in batches of 3000 in weeks 7 and 8. These requirements are added to the master schedule in the "Gross Requirements" row for the table, part 16XY. If McSweeney currently has 10,000 tables in stock, it will be able to fill the entire order without producing any additional tables. If it has fewer than 10,000 in stock, some production will be required.

Therefore, the first step in answering the two central inventory questions is to compare the gross requirements with the quantity on hand. This value is found in the "Projected on Hand" row for part 16XY in the "Now" column. This shows a beginning inventory on hand of 1000 end items. Next, we complete the row for the number projected on hand for weeks 1–8. Since we currently have 1000 tables in stock, and have no projected demand for tables in week 1, the number projected to be on hand for week 1 will be 1000. This will also be the case for weeks 2 and 3. In week 4, we have 1000 projected on hand and a demand for 4000, which gives a net requirement of 3000 in week 4. Earlier, Table 9-2 showed that the TV table has a 1-week lead time. Therefore, to meet the net requirement for 3000 tables in week 4, McSweeney should plan on starting to produce 3000 tables in week 3. This is shown as a planned order release of 3000 in week 3.

The goal of an MRP system is to produce items on a lot-for-lot basis. *Lot for lot* means that McSweeney will produce exactly the quantity of tables needed rather than a quantity determined by an EOQ model. However, MRP will work with EOQ lot sizes or any other established order quantities. Table 9-2 shows that the table itself and the base unit are produced lot for lot and the other parts are produced or acquired in various economic lot sizes.

Assuming lot-for-lot production for the end-item table, the inventory projected on hand will drop to zero in week 4. (Note that even under a lot-for-lot production system, an inventory—such as the 1000 beginning units—can build up if actual demand differs from projected demand.) The inventory projected on hand will stay at zero until week 7 when 3000 tables will be needed. This demand will generate a net requirement in week 7, which means we have a planned order release in week 6. And because of the projected requirement for 3000 tables in week 8, a planned order release is scheduled for week 7.

The "Planned Order Receipt" row in the action report indicates how many units will be ready and in which week they can be shipped. As you can see in part **a** of Table 9-3, a receipt of 3000 units is planned for week 4 which, when combined with the 1000 units on hand, will meet the gross requirements for 4000 units in week 4. Likewise, planned order receipts are scheduled for weeks 7 and 8 to meet the gross requirements in those weeks.

We have now determined an order schedule for the tables. And when McSweeney Manufacturing decides to schedule production of 3000 tables starting in week 3, someone will have to make sure the needed parts are ready for production to begin in week 3. From the product structure tree (Figure 9-18), we can see the quantity of each component part that is needed for a complete table. Thus, to make 3000 end-item tables, McSweeney will need 3000 Formica inlay tops, 3000 bases, and 24,000 wood screws.

Once we have determined the planned order releases for the end items (independent demand items), we use these data to determine the projected gross requirements for the 1-Level items (dependent demand items). No forecasting system is needed for the 1-Level items, since their demand is entirely determined by the planned order releases for the 0-Level parent item.

The action report for the three 1-Level items is also shown in Table 9-3, parts *b–d*. In each case the on-hand quantity is found from the inventory records (Table 9-2), as are any scheduled receipts of parts. For instance, consider part 16XY-1, the table base. Beginning on-hand inventory is 2000 units. Since the action report shows a planned order release for the end item of 3000 units in week 3, there must be a planned order release for 1000 16XY-1 parts in week 1 (Table 9-2 shows a 2-week lead time for this part), so that when combined with the on-hand inventory of 2000 bases, the 3000 units will be available to meet end-item production. This will use up the on-hand inventory. Another planned order release for the 16XY-1 (base) of 3000 units must be made in week 4 so that these parts are available to begin production of 3000 end-item tables in week 6. Finally, another order release will be planned for part 16XY-1 for week 5 to meet the requirements in week 7. You should trace through Table 9-3, parts *c* and *d*, to make sure you understand the development of the MRP action report.

As you might have guessed, the planned order releases for the 1-Level items are used as the demand for the 2-Level items. The action report for the four 2-Level items are shown in parts *e–h* of Table 9-3. Notice that for several of the parts, the planned order release quantity is determined by the lot size. Therefore, even though only 17,000 flat-head screws are needed in week 4, we would order 150,000. This will leave an inventory to be carried forward to subsequent weeks. In addition, sometimes we may need to order multiples of the lot-size quantity. For instance, 8000 sides are ordered in week 2 even though the economic lot size is 4000 sides. This is because 5000 sides will be needed in week 4.

Again, we urge you to work through the entire action report shown in Table 9-3. Although real MRP applications in business would not be done by hand, you will gain valuable insight into the usefulness of MRP by working through small examples by hand. (When you take a production management course, you will get additional exposure to the implementation of MRP.)

A Demonstration of the Value of an MRP System

We indicated earlier that since the MRP "revolution" of the 1970s, a very high percentage of companies in the United States and elsewhere are now employing some form of materials requirements planning. There are numerous examples of successes (and some failures too) associated with MRP. We will discuss one example that demonstrates the value an MRP system can provide a company.

In the 1970s, a major defense contractor manufactured a jet fighter under contract to the U.S. Air Force. In turn, the U.S. government sold a number of these jets to a military ally abroad. One day, during a training mission, a pilot misjudged his landing approach and crashed into a row of parked jets on the edge of the runway. Although several planes were damaged beyond repair, two suffered only wing damage. The ally's air force contacted the manufacturer and requested that the company immediately supply two replacement wing units for the damaged planes. As you might guess, this is not a part the company stocks in its regular inventory.

The company was faced with several questions: (1) What would be the impact on the currently scheduled production activities if this order was inserted into the master production schedule? (2) How much lead time would be required to make the wings? (3) If the company decided to go ahead with the wing production, how much should it charge? At the time, the company had a large-scale MRP system on a computer. Information to answer these questions was obtained by altering the master schedule to include the demand for the two wings. A 24-hour computer run exploded the MRP system to produce action reports similar to those shown in Table 9-3, but much more extensive. From these action reports, the company was able to assess the impact on its operations if the wings were made and delivered when demanded. The project manager indicated that without the MRP system, there would have been no way of assessing this impact and easily arriving at a decision about the request. By the way, the company did supply the wings — but at a much higher price than that allocated to the original plane.

9-6 JUST-IN-TIME INVENTORY MANAGEMENT

One of the more substantial movements in industry in recent years has been toward a just-in-time (JIT) inventory and manufacturing philosophy. The JIT approach to manufacturing was first developed by the Japanese (largely by the Toyota Motor Company) in the mid 1970s, but it has been widely adopted throughout the United States and the rest of the world. While it is much more than an inventory control technique, and is not really what we might traditionally classify as a management science tool, JIT, like MRP in the previous section, is introduced to give you some exposure to alternative inventory control approaches that go beyond the more traditional deterministic and probabilistic EOQ-type models. You will get a much more in-depth exposure to JIT when you take a course in production and operations management.

UNDERLYING CONCEPTS

JIT gets its name from the practice of having parts and materials arrive just when they are needed — not sooner and not later. In a pure JIT operation, parts and materials are delivered to the plant just as they are needed and are delivered to workstations just as they are needed there. In some applications, parts and materials are delivered two or more times a day. In addition, no item is produced until a demand for it actually exists.

The movement toward JIT manufacturing has been founded on two complementary ideas. The first is that customers are not well served by high inventory levels. The second is that an organization should never be satisfied with simply improving the status quo; it should always be ready to make changes. Traditional inventory theory, when applied to finished goods, minimizes total inventory costs, with stockout costs being one component. The idea is that not everything can, or should, be in stock at all times and an organization has to try to determine the cost of *not* supplying a customer, and then factor this cost into the production-run decision. The JIT philosophy is that customer satisfaction is the first priority and should drive inventory efforts, not be factored in as an operational cost. At the same time, JIT companies recognize that customers cannot be satisfied by having unacceptably high levels of finished goods in inventory, since holding inventory costs money (and holding a lot of inventory costs a lot of money).

The alternative to achieving customer satisfaction by holding inventory is to alter the production process so that smaller run sizes are possible. This is accomplished, in the context of the traditional model, by reducing setup costs. Therefore, customer demand is satisfied from the production line and not from the finished-goods inventory.

Reducing the run size will automatically lead to smaller buffer stocks—and therefore to smaller amounts of work in process (WIP)—and will allow customer demand to be satisfied with lower levels of finished goods. Therefore, JIT will not only achieve the objective of customer satisfaction, it will lead to lower costs. By reducing WIP inventories and safety stock, other underlying production problems and inefficiencies are exposed and can be corrected.

In the context of the traditional cost model, the JIT process attacks parts and raw materials inventory by reducing the cost of placing and receiving an order. This can be done by having electronic ordering systems, consolidating shipments to reduce transportation costs, and having shipments delivered directly to the assembly line to reduce warehousing costs.

RESULTS OF CHANGING TO JIT TECHNIQUES

The positive aspects of JIT have been well documented. They include:

Reduced inventory levels
Improved quality levels
Reduced factory space requirements
Improved customer satisfaction
Improved profitability

The purpose of this list is not to advertise the benefits of JIT but to let you see that companies have substantial incentives to change manufacturing techniques. To the extent that companies change to JIT manufacturing, traditional inventory control models will become less and less applicable as computational tools. In its purest form, JIT will answer our two inventory control questions in the following manner:

1. How much do we order? *One unit at a time.*
2. When do we order? *When we need one unit.*

We should note that JIT does not work well in situations with long lead times and high setup costs. In the United States, for example, often the parts and materials suppliers are located thousands of miles from the manufacturer and/or the manufacturing plant is old and hard to change over from producing one product to producing another. This is contrasted with some Japanese situations, where suppliers (which might even be partially owned by the manufacturer) are located across the road, and the manufacturing plant can changed over from one product to another in a few hours or less.

But U.S. manufacturers are taking steps to change by modernizing their plants, including the development of *computer-automated manufacturing* systems, and by requiring vendors to be physically located close by. While MRP was the battle cry of the 1970s, JIT was the battle cry of the 1980s and will likely be an important component of production through the 1990s as well.

9-7 SUMMARY AND CONCLUSIONS

Managing inventory is an important function for most organizations. In Chapter 8 we explored several models which could be effectively used to answer two very important inventory questions: How much do we order and When do we order it? The models presented in Chapter 8 were deterministic, since they assumed that factors such as demand, lead time, and costs were known with certainty. Under the deterministic assumption, the models could provide order points and order quantities that minimized total inventory costs.

In Chapter 9, we have extended our discussion of inventory models to include situations where uncertainty exists. A model was presented for dealing with a multiperiod inventory system where demand during lead time is uncertain. We also investigated an approach for dealing with single-period inventory systems called incremental analysis. This approach allows us to determine the optimal order quantity when demand is probabilistic.

This chapter has also discussed material requirements planning (MRP), one of the more recent inventory control tools. It answers the same two questions, stated above, that all inventory models must answer. MRP has proven to be a most useful tool for ensuring that parts and materials are available when needed without the buildup of excessive safety stocks.

We have also briefly discussed the just-in-time (JIT) inventory and manufacturing philosophy. In a JIT environment, no part or material is delivered before it is needed. Under JIT, the desired lot size is reduced to one unit. There is currently a major move toward JIT inventory and production management in the United States and abroad. For organizations which can effectively implement JIT, the use and importance of more traditional inventory control techniques, such as EOQ models, will be reduced or eliminated.

However, regardless of the inventory management technique an organization uses, the basic issues of balance between excessive and insufficient inventory must be addressed. As a decision maker, you must be able to answer the two familiar questions of how many and when to order. The techniques discussed in Chapters 8 and 9 will help you answer these questions. Still, you will always have to analyze each situation and determine the appropriate technique to use in finding answers to the basic inventory questions. Regardless of the inventory management method you choose, the important thing to understand is that the goal is to have the product or component available when it is needed and to keep the overall cost of inventory as small as possible.

Chapter Equations

Basic EOQ (uncertain demand)

$$Q^* = \sqrt{\frac{2E[D]C_o}{IC}} \tag{9-1}$$

where:

Q^* = optimal order quantity

$E[D]$ = mean or expected value of annual demand distribution

C_o = ordering cost

I = carrying-cost factor, in decimal form

C = unit cost

Reorder Point (probabilistic model)

$$ROP = \text{average demand during lead time} + Z \text{ (standard deviation of demand during lead time)} \quad (9\text{-}2)$$

where:

Z = a value from the standard normal distribution table (Appendix B) which corresponds to an area equal to (1-service level)

Total Inventory Cost

$$TC = (Q/2)\ IC + (D/Q)C_o + (SS)IC \quad (9\text{-}3)$$

where:

Q = order quantity

SS = safety stock

Expected Cost of Understocking

$$EL(Q^*) = (U)P(\text{demand} > Q^*) \quad (9\text{-}4)$$

$$EL(Q^*) = (U)[1.0 - P(\text{demand} \leq Q^*)] \quad (9\text{-}8)$$

Expected Cost of Overstocking

$$EL(Q^* + 1) = (O)P(\text{demand} \leq Q^*) \quad (9\text{-}5)$$

$$(O)P(\text{demand} \leq Q^*) = (U)[1.0 - P(\text{demand} \leq Q^*)] \quad (9\text{-}9)$$

Sum of Demand Probabilities

$$P(\text{demand} > Q^*) + P(\text{demand} \leq Q^*) = 1.0 \quad (9\text{-}6)$$

$$P(\text{demand} > Q^*) = 1.0 - P(\text{demand} \leq Q^*) \quad (9\text{-}7)$$

Probability of Demand ≤ Q*

$$P(\text{demand} \leq Q^*) = \frac{U}{(U + O)} \quad (9\text{-}10)$$

Solved Problems

PROBLEM 1 Peggy Raimey is filling out her application to make a float trip down the Middle Fork of the Salmon River. The Forest Service has recently started limiting the number of trips allowed through the wilderness area. A graduate student at the University of Alaska, Peggy wants to supplement her income by acting as an outfitter for a 10-day trip this summer. She can apply for up to 40 slots in her application; unfortunately, she must pay the $200 fee for each slot at the time of application. Peggy believes she will make a profit of $150 for each person she can take on the float trip.

a. Assume that the number of customers favorably responding to Peggy's advertising can be described by a uniform distribution between 15 and 30. If Peggy will lose the fee for any unused slots, how many people should she plan to take on the trip?

b. How would your answer change if the number of favorable responses could be described by a Poisson distribution with a mean of 20?
c. How would your answers to **a** and **b** change if Peggy could sell any unused slots for \$100?

Solutions

a. Since this is a single-period order problem, we will use equation 9-10 to determine the optimal order quantity:

$$P(\text{demand} \leq Q^*) = U/(U + O)$$

For this problem, the cost of overstocking is the \$200 spent for the application and the cost of understocking is the \$150 lost profit. Putting these values in the equation, we find:

$$P(\text{demand} \leq Q^*) = 150/(150 + 200) = .429$$

To determine the order quantity corresponding to this probability, we can use the uniform distribution shown in Figure 9-20. Since the area under the distribution must equal 1, the order quantity will be the value Q^* such that the area to the left is .429. Since the distribution starts at 15 and ends at 30, we will first find the value X, which indicates how far into the distribution the optimal order quantity goes.

$$.429 = X/(30 - 15)$$
$$.429(15) = X$$
$$6.435 = X$$

Now, since the distribution starts at 15, the optimal order quantity is:

$$Q^* = 15 + 6.435 = 21.435$$

b. This is still a single-period order problem, with

$$P(\text{demand} \leq Q^*) = 150/(150 + 200) = .429$$

The order quantity can now be determined by using the Poisson distribution table in Appendix C. To use this table, we go to the column for $\lambda t = 20$ and add up the probabilities, starting with $P(0)$, until we get:

$$P(18 \text{ or less}) = .3814 \qquad \text{and} \qquad P(19 \text{ or less}) = .4702$$

Peggy would have to choose between the two values, perhaps rounding to the nearest value.

c. If Peggy could sell any unused slots, she would reduce the cost of overstocking. This should

Figure 9-20
Uniform demand distribution

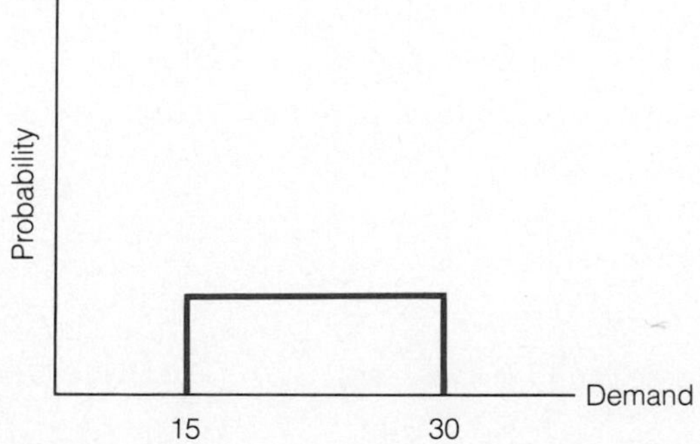

increase the number she will order, but we can determine by how much by recalculating:

$$P(\text{demand} \leq Q^*) = 150/(150 + 100) = .6$$

Using the uniform distribution, we find:

$$.6 = X/(30 - 15)$$
$$.6(15) = X$$
$$9 = X$$

Since the distribution starts at 15, the optimal order quantity is:

$$Q^* = 15 + 9 = 24$$

Using the Poisson distribution, we would continue adding until finding:

$$P(20 \text{ or less}) = .559 \qquad \text{and} \qquad P(21 \text{ or less}) = .6436$$

PROBLEM 2

Jerry Welsh is the purchasing agent responsible for the 5¼″ and 3½″ high-density disk drives used in PCComp personal computers. PCComp is a company that assembles computers from a stock of parts in response to telephone orders. Using EOQ models, Jerry has determined the correct number of 5¼″ drives to order is 1200 and the correct number of 3½″ drives is 1400. The average weekly demand for both drives is 250, based on a 5-day workweek.

Because both drives are purchased from a company in Taiwan, the shipping time is somewhat uncertain. Based on past records, the shipping time for 5¼″ drives averages 3 weeks, with a standard deviation of 1.2 weeks, and the shipping time for 3½″ drives averages 2.4 weeks, with a standard deviation of .8 week. Because speedy shipments are an advertising issue for PCComp, company policy specifies that production will be affected by stockouts for only 1 in 20 shipments.

a. Determine the appropriate order point for both disk drives.
b. How much safety stock should be held for both disk drives?

Solutions

a. Assuming a normal distribution, the appropriate order point is found using equation 9-2:

Reorder point = average demand during lead time + Z (demand standard deviation during lead time)

For the 5¼″ drive:

Average lead time = 3 weeks
Weekly demand = 250
Demand standard deviation during lead time = (1.2)(250) = 300
A service level of 19 in 20 (95%) leads to $Z = 1.645$.

Reorder point = (3)(250) + (1.645)(300) = 1243.4

For the 3½″ drive:

Average lead time = 2.4 weeks
Weekly demand = 250
Demand standard deviation during lead time = (.8)(250) = 200

Reorder point = (2.4)(250) + (1.645)(200) = 925

b. The safety-stock level is determined by how much the reorder point exceeds the average use during lead time.

For 5¼″ drives: safety stock = 1243.4 − 750 = 493.4

For 3½″ drives: safety stock = 925 − 600 = 325

General Questions and Assignments

1. Discuss the difference between *single-period* and *multiperiod* inventory control models. Develop an example of your own for each type of model.
2. Discuss what *safety stock* is and indicate the conditions under which a company might want to consider carrying safety stock.
3. Discuss the concept of *incremental analysis* as it relates to single-period inventory analysis. Clearly explain the terms *cost of understocking* and *cost of overstocking*.
4. Describe in your own words that *MRP* is and how it works. Locate at least two articles that discuss the application of *MRP* and write a short paper summarizing the articles.
5. What is the difference between *MRP* and *JIT*? What, if anything, do these two techniques have in common? Discuss.
6. Visit a company in your area to interview a manager who is responsible for managing inventory. Does this firm use *probabilistic models*? If not, how does management take into account the uncertainties associated with demand and lead time? If probabilistic inventory models are used, describe their applications.
7. Contact a company in your area that has had experience with MRP. Write a short paper outlining this company's experience. Trace the history of implementation, and indicate the problems that were encountered in getting the MRP operational.
8. Contact at least one company in your area that has had experience with JIT. Write a short paper discussing the company's experience. Supplement the paper with a review of at least three articles on JIT applications. Try to find applications in the same industry as the company you selected for your interview.

Exercises and Application Problems

1. Gotelli Distributors imports barrels of olive oil from Italy. In recent years the demand for this oil has been approximately constant during the year, averaging 5200 barrels. Each barrel costs $45, and the yearly holding cost is figured to be 33% of the purchase price. Placing an order costs $200.
   a. What is the optimal number of barrels of olive oil to order at one time?
   b. The time between placing an order and receiving the oil from Italy averages 3 weeks. What is the level of inventory when an order should be placed?
   c. If the lead time is not constant but is normally distributed with a standard deviation of 1 week, what should the order point be if the company wants to limit to 2% the chance of running out of oil while waiting for a shipment?
   d. What is the extra carrying cost associated with the safety stock found in part **c**?
2. Sakai Software is the largest retail outlet for the popular EasyWord desktop-publishing package. Each copy costs Sakai Software $250, with a cost of $100 each time an order is placed. Because of possible obsolescence due to new issues, a yearly carrying cost of 40% of the purchase price is estimated. Based on past records, estimated sales are 250 copies per week.

a. With only the given information, how many copies of the software package should be ordered in each order?
b. Because of the great demand for this package, the time between placing an order and receiving the software averages 4 weeks. At what level of inventory should an order should be placed?
c. If the demand per week is not constant but is normally distributed with a standard deviation of 50 per week, what should the order point be if Sakai Software wants to limit to 5% the chance of running out of copies of EasyWord while waiting for a shipment? Assume the lead time is constant at 4 weeks.
d. What is the extra carrying cost associated with the safety stock found in part **c**.

3. Suarez Souvenirs buys turquoise pendants from Black Hills Gold Company. The demand for pendants is constant through the year, averaging 150 per month. Each pendant costs $20, Suarez estimates the cost of holding one pendant in inventory for one year to be $6. If each order from Black Hills Gold costs $60, and the time between placing an order and receiving the pendants is ¾ month:
a. What is the optimal number of pendants to order?
b. At what level of inventory should an order be placed?
c. If the demand per month is not constant but is normally distributed with a mean of 150 and a standard deviation of 25, and if Suarez is willing to run out of inventory while waiting for a shipment only 1 in 10 times at what point should an order be placed?
d. What is the yearly cost associated with the order points found in parts **b** and **c**?

4. Hendrickson Appliance Supply stocks replacement compressor units for home freezers. In the past, the demand for these compressors has been fairly constant, averaging 600 per year. The compressors cost $130 each; the time between ordering and delivery arrives is 2 weeks. If the cost to place an order is $90, and the cost to hold a compressor in inventory for one year is $36:
a. How many compressors should be ordered each time an order is placed?
b. Hendrickson is installing a computerized ordering system that will continually monitor inventory and will automatically place an order at a preset level. What should this preset level be?
c. If the time required to receive an order averages 2 weeks, but is normally distributed with a variance of .5 week^2, how much will it cost Hendrickson Appliance to ensure the probability of running out of stock while waiting for a shipment of compressors is limited to 8%?

5. Sweet Slumber Waterbeds has just started marketing a revolutionary new mattress filled with a patented product called Textill 2. Textill 2 expands to fill the mattress bladder when it is filled with water and virtually eliminates the wave motion normally associated with a waterbed. A mattress containing Textill 2 costs $180. The price has not limited demand, which continues to be constant at 120 per week. Sweet Slumber's corporate accounting department has just finished a study which found the cost of placing an order for the waterbed mattresses is $75 and the cost of holding one unit in inventory averages 2% per month. The mattress manufacturer previously had a uniform 2-week delivery time. But now the demand for Textill 2 is so high that orders may take from 2 to 6 weeks to fill, with any time between those two values being equally probable. Sweet Slumber Waterbeds is willing to risk turning away a customer while waiting for a shipment only 2% of the time. How much has the uncertainty associated with receiving shipments added to the inventory cost of Sweet Slumber Waterbeds?

6. The time has come for the local auto dealer to place its last order for current-year sport coupes. The sales manager thinks the dealership is equally likely to sell any number between 20 and 40 before the end of the model year. The cost of the cars averages $15,000, and the dealership makes an average of 6% on each car sold. Any cars not sold to the public at the end of the year will be sold to a fleet buyer at 10% below cost. How many cars should be ordered?

7. Back Mountain Touring is trying to determine how many mountain racing bikes to order for delivery next spring. The bikes are custom-made in northern Italy, cost $600 each, and must be ordered one year before delivery. Back Mountain has a standard markup of 100% and holds no in-store sales. Any outdated merchandise is sold to a jobber at 25% below cost. The owner of Back Mountain Touring has no idea how many bikes the shop could sell, but believes that any number between 15 and 35 is equally likely. How many bikes should be ordered?
8. Sofa City Discount Furniture has been contacted about purchasing between 1 and 200 Super-Comfort Loungers from a national chain that is going out of business. The loungers can be purchased for $175 each and will be sold for $300. After 6 months any unsold loungers will be donated to a local veterans' retirement home, providing a tax deduction of 25% of the value of the loungers. The manager of the Sofa City store is not sure how many loungers will be sold in the 6-month period and so has generated the following probability distribution for projected sales:

Sales (units)	Probability
10 to 49	.3
50 to 74	.4
75 to 90	.2
91 to 100	.1

How many loungers should Sofa City order?
9. Consider the situation of Sofa City Discount Furniture, from problem 8. Upon further reflection, the store manager estimates the probable sales values will be normally distributed with a mean of 80 and a standard deviation of 20. All other values remain the same. Will the recommended order quantity be changed? If so, to what value?
10. Cosworth Milling has been offered a "special" price on bearings for its automated milling machine. The bearings usually cost $2500 a set, but Cosworth can purchase them now for $1900. Bearings periodically wear out and have to be replaced. Cosworth estimates it will use the present milling machine for 2 more years, and estimates the number of bearings required during this time will be described by a Poisson distribution with a mean of 40. Any bearings not used during the 2-year period can probably be sold, but at a 50% discount from the purchase price. How many sets of bearings should be ordered? (Hint: You may want to consult a statistics book about the normal approximation to the Poisson distribution.)
11. The local chapter of the Business Students Service Club is considering making spiced caramel apples to sell at the upcoming campus fair. The cost of making the spiced caramel apples is $.30 each, and they will be sold for $.75 each. Any unsold apples will be donated to the children's ward of the local hospital. The students estimate the following probability distribution for sales:

Apples Sold	Probability
50–100	.2
101–140	.3
141–180	.3
181–220	.1
221–260	.1

How many spiced caramel apples should be made?
12. You are the plant manager for a company that assembles industrial and sports-related machinery. You have just received an order for 40 softball pitching machines to be delivered 8 weeks from now. Information on the pitching machine is as follows:

Item	Lead Time (weeks)	Units On Hand	Subcomponent	Quantity Required per Unit
Pitching machine	2	5	A	2
	—	—	B	1
	—	—	C	3
A	3	8	E	3
	—	—	D	1
B	1	10	D	2
	—	—	F	3
C	1	50	E	2
	—	—	D	2
D	1	20	—	—
E	2	30	—	—
F	2	20	—	—

a. Develop a product structure tree for this item.
b. For all the items in this product, answer these questions: (1) How many do we order (or make)? and (2) When do we order (or start making) them?

13. Caligari Cabinets must deliver 100 units of the 10-S model 7 weeks from now. Each 10-S unit requires 1 unit of T-27 and 1.5 units of 26-V. Each unit of T-27 requires 2 units of 10X, 2 units of Y-19, and 1 unit of Z-27. Finally, each unit of 26-V requires 2 units of 10X and 3 units of Z-27. All these items are manufactured within the company. It takes 3 weeks to make a 10-S, 1 week to make a T-27, 2 weeks to make a 10X, 3 weeks to make a Y-19, 2 weeks to make a 26-V, and 1 week to make a Z-27.
a. Create a product structure tree and a gross material requirements plan for the end item. Identify all levels, parents, and components.
b. Construct a net material requirements plan from the product structure and the following on-hand inventory.

Item	On-Hand Inventory
10-S	40
26-V	30
T-27	15
10X	50
Y-19	20
Z-27	35

14. A company that makes self-propelled trenchers, sold primarily to automatic sprinkler system contractors and equipment rental firms, has just received an order for 150 trenchers to be delivered in week 9 to Gray Rentals in Orlando, Florida. The following listing indicates the availability of parts for the trenchers, as well as assembly sequence and times.

Part	Parent	Lead Time	Units On Hand
Trencher	—	2	30
Motor unit	Trencher	1	50
Drive unit	Trencher	2	60
Engine	Motor unit	3	45
Cover	Motor unit	2	25
Platform	Motor unit	2	30
Transmission	Drive unit	1	10
Chain auger	Transmission	2	30
Starter	Engine	3	20
Wheel units (4)	Platform	2	100
Steering	Platform	1	75

a. Construct a product structure tree and a gross material requirements plan for all inventory items. Identify all levels, parents, and components.

b. Construct a net material requirements plan from the product structure tree and the resulting on-hand inventory.

15. Refer to the softball pitching machine order of problem 12. Production has progressed normally for the first 2 weeks, but then the customer calls with an order change. Instead of receiving 40 machines in week 8, the customer would like to have 30 shipped in the original week 6 and an additional 30 shipped in the original week 9. Can you respond to this request without having to modify any of your lead times? What will the new material requirements plan look like?

16. Refer to the trencher manufacturer in problem 14. A quality control inspector has just found some faulty drive units in storage. Instead of the 60 units that inventory records show, a 100% inspection reveals only 25 good units. What changes will this cause in the material requirements plan you developed for problem 14?

Chapter Glossary

Bill of materials A list of all component parts needed to construct an end item and the order in which they are needed.

Dependent demand Demand for components used in fabrication of other items sold to customers outside the organization.

Deterministic inventory models Inventory models which assume demand rate, costs, and lead time are known with certainty.

End item An item whose demand is independent; it is usually made up of one or more component parts or materials.

Incremental analysis A probabilistic inventory technique which examines the relationship between the cost of understocking (*U*) one additional unit and the cost of overstocking (*O*) one additional unit.

Independent demand Demand determined outside the control of the organization; often, demand for end items.

Just-in-time (JIT) An inventory procedure in which material is supplied only when demanded, in exactly the quantity needed, and exactly when demanded.

Lead time The time between placing and receiving an order.

Master schedule A period-by-period schedule of demand prepared for each independent demand item, based on firm orders, demand forecasts, and plant capacity. It is a schedule showing how many of each end item are to be produced and when they are to be produced.

Material requirements planning (MRP) A system used to indicate how many inventory items to order (make) and when to order (make) them.

MRP action report *(or MRP explosion)* This report indicates an order schedule for the purchasing department and a production schedule for the production department.

Multiperiod systems Inventory models developed for situations where multiple orders can be placed and received during the year or season.

Normal probability distribution A well-defined continuous distribution which is symmetrical and is fully defined by knowing the mean and standard deviation.

Probabilistic inventory models Inventory models in which demand, lead time, or costs are not known with certainty.

Safety stock The difference between the reorder point and the expected demand. Safety stock is carried to meet higher than expected demand during lead time.

Salvage value Value of an item which is left over at the end of the inventory planning period.

Service level An indication of how often a decision maker is willing to run out of inventory while waiting for an order to arrive.

Single-period systems Models developed for situations where demand is uncertain and only one inventory order can be placed.

Time buckets The periods of time used on a master production schedule, usually weeks, months, or quarters.

Chapter References

ARTICLES

Bubnham, John M. "Some Conclusions about JIT Maufacturing." *Production and Inventory Management Journal,* Third Quarter, 1987.

Donovan, R. M., and S. King. "Are You Ready for MRP?" *Management Review,* Vol. 66 (October), 1977.

Hahn, C. K., P. A. Pinto, and D. J. Bragg. "Just-in-Time Production and Purchasing." *Journal of Purchasing and Materials Management,* Fall 1983.

Liberatore, M. J. "EOQ under Stochastic Lead Time." *Operations Research,* Vol. 27 (March), 1979.

Nakane, Jinichero, and Robert W. Hall. "Management Specs for Stockless Production." *Harvard Business Review,* May–June 1983.

Nast, Donald A., and Stephen E. Bechtold. "The EOQ Revisited." *Decison Sciences,* Vol. 9, No. 4, 1979.

Pinney, W. E. "Correcting a Misconception about EOQ." *Decision Sciences,* Vol. 8, No. 4, 1978.

Woolsey, G. "Fifth Column: The Warehouse Model That Couldn't Be and the Inventory That Couldn't Be Zero." *Interfaces,* Vol. 7 (May), 1977.

Zimmerman, S. M., and D. Glover. "Combining EOQ and MRP to Optimize Savings." *Journal of Purchasing and Materials Management,* Vol. 13, 1977.

BOOKS

Hillier, F. S., and G. J. Lieberman. *Introduction to Operations Research,* 4th ed. Oakland, Calif.: Holden-Day, 1986.

Markland, R. E., and J. S. Sweigart. *Quantitative Methods: Applications to Managerial Decision Making.* New York: Wiley, 1987.

Orlicky, Joseph. *Material Requirements Planning.* New York: McGraw-Hill, 1975.

Schonberger, Richard J. *Japanese Manufacturing Techniques.* New York: Free Press, 1982.

Vollmann, T. E., W. L. Berry, and D. C. Whybark. *Manufacturing Planning and Control Systems,* 2d ed. Homewood, Ill.: Irwin, 1988.

Wight, Oliver W. *MRP II: Unlocking America's Productivity Potential.* Boston: CBI Publishing, 1981.

Mini Cases

CASE 9A
MOUNTAIN SPORTING GOODS

Tom Tvedt, owner and manager of Mountain Sporting Goods, faces his typical end-of-June inventory dilemma. During the previous year, business at Mountain Sporting Goods had been brisk for all kinds of Nordic ski equipment. Since most ski equipment is manufactured overseas, orders must normally be placed in July for October delivery. Occasionally, additional inventory can be ordered during the season, but Tom tries to avoid doing so because he has to buy from a wholesaler at premium prices.

The inventory debacle 2 years ago still haunts Tom. Anticipating a good ski season, he ordered aggressively in July. Unfortunately, the snow came late that year and Christmas sales were slow. While Tom was still pondering what to do with all his inventory, two competitors started their spring sales several weeks early. By the time Mountain Sporting Goods had a spring sale, the market had become saturated. In the tiny resort town where Mountan Sporting Goods operates, you can't even give away ski equipment between late March and early November. Tom ended up carrying the excess inventory all summer and then dumping it in November at a ski swap in a large city several hundred miles away.

Now Tom is trying to decide how many skis to order. Each pair costs $100 and sells for $140. Although Tom could sell any unsold skis to a discounter, the price may be only $60, $70, or $80. In trying to forecast demand, Tom is considering three alternatives:

1. Since demand depends on an uncertain snow season, any number of skis between 100 and 250 are equally likely to be sold.
2. Assume that values at each end of the possible range are unlikely to be sold, and describe the possible sales values by a normal distribution centered at the middle of the possible sales values.
3. Base this year's sales forecast on the actual weekly sales values from last year: 5, 10, 10, 40, 60, 60, 40, 20, 20, 15, 10, 10.

CASE 9B
MOUNTAIN SPORTING GOODS Part II

Tom Tvedt has taken your advice on the number of skis to order for this winter season. However, the long-range forecast issued by the National Weather Service in September is not encouraging. Apparently the recently discovered warm spot in the Pacific Ocean, which normally stays off the coast of South America, seems to be moving north. If the warming continues, the winter storms will be pushed farther north, into Canada, and Tom's resort town will be in for a very lean year. The last time this happened, the demand for skis dropped by 40%.

Tom's major ski supplier, who has also read the weather forecast, has just called and offered a 20% price discount, but only if Tom does not reduce his order. The last time a similar weather pattern occurred, the storms hit to the east and Tom's area had little snow—and the prices that discounters offered for skis held firm. Tom wonders whether this new information should cause him to change the number ordered.

Chapter 10

PERT/CPM: AN INTRODUCTION TO PROJECT MANAGEMENT TOOLS

Chapter Outline

Why You Need to Know

Many decisions that managers make are done routinely. For instance, a production manager must determine the production schedule for each week and also regularly make decisions about ordering parts and materials. A financial investment manager must routinely evaluate the company's pension-fund investment mix, and a product distribution manager must regularly rethink shipping plans.

Decision makers who utilize management science techniques such as linear programming, forecasting, and inventory models to provide input for routine decisions usually do not consider developing a new model each time. Instead, they may update an existing model by modifying one or more of the inputs. The real modeling process occurs when the management science model is first considered in the decision process. After that, each time it is used to help make a routine decision, care must be taken to be sure that the model is still valid for the new situation.

However, not all business decisions can be categorized as routine, such as the decision to expand a manufacturing facility or to relocate a distribution center. If a management science model is used in making a one-time decision, the resulting model may be applicable only for generating input for that one decision. For instance, a large-scale linear programming model may be developed to provide input for a decision regarding which of the firm's production facilities to close. Once this decision is made, the model might have no further application.

The class of decision situations which are considered nonroutine are called projects. For some organizations, like engineering and construction companies, projects are a standard part of business. But for others, whose normal business activity is somewhat routine, a project such as expanding the plant or undertaking a major research and development effort is decidedly out of the ordinary. In either case, a large project with many activities presents decision makers with a variety of problems in planning, scheduling, and controlling.

If you are involved in managing a project from beginning to end, you undoubtedly will need a framework for planning, scheduling, and controlling the activities that must be completed. Two management science tools have been expressly developed to assist in project management: the *program evaluation and review technique (PERT)* and the *critical path method (CPM).* These tools are extremely useful and have been widely employed. Throughout your professional career, you will likely encounter many instances in which PERT/CPM will be needed in managing a project. This chapter introduces the two techniques and shows how they are used. The examples and problems in the chapter provide a wide array of situations for which PERT/CPM can be effectively employed.

Chapter Objectives

After studying the material in this chapter, you should be able to:

1. Develop the PERT/CPM network necessary to represent a unique project.
2. Formulate both single-point completion-time estimates and three-point completion-time estimates.
3. Analyze a PERT/CPM network to estimate a project's completion time.
4. Develop the appropriate tools to use PERT/CPM for both planning and control.
5. Determine the necessary relationships between activity completion times and costs, and be able to determine the least-expensive alternatives for reducing overall project completion time.

10-1 A BRIEF HISTORY OF PERT/CPM

To a large extent, PERT and CPM are quite similar, using the same methods and arriving at the same basic results. While differences do exist, they have tended to narrow over the years; therefore, in this chapter, we will concentrate on their similarities. However, the two techniques have totally different beginnings, with PERT's origin being the more colorful.

PERT is unique as a management science tool in that it was specifically developed in response to what some people saw as a national crisis. For hundreds of years the United States had been isolated from events in Europe and Asia by the Atlantic and Pacific oceans. In fact, early leaders specifically warned the nation against entering into "foreign entanglements." Although the United States occasionally became involved in events abroad, it was always able to withdraw to its own peaceful shores, protected by two vast oceans. Because of this geographic isolation, the United States, a major participant in both world wars, was spared any damage to its mainland soil.

After World War II, tension developed between the United States and the Soviet Union when it became clear that the Soviets did not intend to give up control over the Eastern European lands they had liberated from the Nazis. The hostility between the world's two superpowers—which came to be known as the cold war—took a serious turn when the Soviet Union tested its first atomic bomb in 1949. Until that time, the United States had been the only nation with "The Bomb."

Uneasiness in the United States grew as the cold war escalated in the 1950s. Still, the United States took some comfort from the knowledge that the Soviets (or even their Chinese allies) would have to fly great distances to reach the United States with an atomic bomb. But this sense of security, of being protected by two oceans, was shattered in 1957 when the Soviets launched Sputnik, the world's first artificial satellite, into orbit around the earth. The implication was obvious: If Soviet rockets could put a satellite into space, they could put a bomb or nuclear warhead anywhere in the United States!

Today, decades later, the impact on the American people at that time may be hard to comprehend, but this single event caused widespread concern—and even panic in some areas. One beneficial side effect was the increased emphasis on science and technology in schools throughout the Western world. And the budding American space program suddenly blossomed overnight—but so did the nuclear arms race.

The United States immediately rushed to develop two advanced weapon systems that would be able to survive an enemy attack: the Polaris submarine-launched nuclear missiles and the ground-based Minuteman missiles. The U.S. Navy's Office of Special Projects soon realized that its planning and control tools were not adequate for developing the Polaris project, which had hundreds of activities occurring simultaneously in hundreds of different locations, with many activities at or beyond the state of the art in technology. To add to the confusion, many activities were dependent on each other, and the Navy was under severe time pressure to bring the systems on line quickly.

The Office of Special Projects joined with the management consulting firm of Booz, Allen and Hamilton, to develop a new tool for planning and control. The result of these efforts became known as **PERT**, for **program evaluation and review technique**. PERT was credited, at least in part, with getting the Polaris system operational in record time.

The **critical path method (CPM)** was developed about the same time from efforts begun by the E. I. DuPont de Nemours Company. DuPont was interested in using computers to improve the scheduling and monitoring of its engineering projects. In 1957, a group of people from DuPont and Remington-Rand (maker of UNIVAC computers) ran a pilot program for what later became known as CPM. While developed independently by different organizations, PERT and CPM are very similar in method and purpose. In time, they came to be considered as one, now commonly referred to as PERT/CPM.

Whether PERT was instrumental in aiding the defense of the United States in the late 1950s is open to question, but what is not open to question is that PERT/CPM is now one of the most widely used managerial decision-making aids. It has proven to be so successful in helping managers ensure that projects are done on time that many government agencies require contractors to include a PERT/CPM diagram as part of any bids they submit. Numerous companies use PERT/CPM as a tool for planning and controlling projects in construction, product development, marketing, sales, and finance, to name but a few.

10-2 AN INTRODUCTION TO PERT/CPM

Shirley and Leo Knowlton have just received a permit from the U.S. Forest Service to install a dock and canoe rental hut at the campground they manage on Red Fish Lake. They have been trying to get this permit for the past 5 years. Unfortunately, the timing is not too good, since it is already late in May. Shirley and Leo believe that unless they can finish the dock, construct the rental hut, and purchase the canoes before the Fourth of July holiday they might as well postpone the project until next year. If they can complete the project in time for the holiday, they definitely want to go ahead this year. But they have never built this kind of facility before and don't know how long it will take.

Since Shirley and Leo are facing a project they have never attempted before, and since time is a consideration, they may find PERT/CPM to be a valuable decision-making aid. It will allow them to divide the overall project into a series of smaller activities which, when taken together, will lead to completion of the major project.

The first step in using PERT/CPM is to identify each specific task, or **activity**, necessary to complete the project. These activities should initially be determined without regard to the sequence in which they need to be done. Then, after the activities are identified, the sequence in which they should be performed must be determined. This is done by deciding which activities must be completed before a follow-on activity can be started and then specifying which activity or activities immediately precede another activity.

The tasks of identifying the activities and determining their sequence is very important and care should be taken to be sure they are done correctly. The results of Leo and Shirley's deliberations about activities are shown in Table 10-1. The first two columns in the table give a brief description and the unique identifier code for each activity. The third column shows the immediate predecessors, if any, of each activity.

The key to organizing activities when a short completion time is important is to perform as many activities as possible simultaneously. For example, since Leo and

Table 10-1 ACTIVITIES NECESSARY TO COMPLETE CANOE RENTAL FACILITY

Activity	Description	Immediate Predecessor
A	Prepare dock site	—
B	Prepare hut site	—
C	Install dock pilings	*A*
D	Foundation for hut	*B*
E	Build dock	*C*
F	Frame hut	*D*
G	Power to hut	*D*
H	Side the hut	*F*
I	Roof the hut	*F*
J	Order canoes	—
K	Paint hut	*H*
L	Assemble canoes	*J*
M	Finish landscaping	*L, I, K, E, G*
N	Open for business	*M*

Shirley can prepare the dock site, prepare the hut site, and order the canoes at the same time, they should do so. None of these activities have any **predecessors**—activities which must be completed before another activity can begin—and so can be started immediately.

CONSTRUCTING THE PERT/CPM NETWORK

Once the activities and their *immediate predecessors* are identified, the next step is to construct the PERT/CPM network. The network for Leo and Shirley's project is shown in Figure 10-1. The activities in the project are represented by the **branches** (lines), or arcs, in the network. The **nodes** represent the start and end of the activities. Note that the sequential arrangement identified in Table 10-1 is maintained in the network. As you can see in Figure 10-1, three activities—*A, B,* and *J*—begin at node 1, indicating that all three can be worked on simultaneously. Node 2 represents the end of activity *J*, ordering the canoes, and the start of activity *L*, assembling the canoes. Thus, regardless of how the rest of the project is progressing, once the canoes arrive, Leo and Shirley are free to assemble them.

Node 6 represents the finish of activity *D*, building the hut foundation, and the start for activities *F* and *G*, which can be performed simultaneously. In fact, activity *G*, installing power to the hut, can be done at any time while activity *F, H, I,* or *K* is being completed. However, all four of these activities plus activity *G* must be completed before activity *M* can be started. This is shown by node 9, which is the end point for activities *E, G, K, I,* and *L*, and the start for activity *M*.

While the PERT/CPM network may seem almost self-explanatory, we must be careful to follow certain rules:

1. Each activity must be represented by its own branch on the chart. An **event** is the start or end of an activity and is identified as a node in the network. Typically, activities are identified by letters and nodes are identified by numbers. The **path** is a sequence of activities leading from the beginning node to the final node.
2. The direction of time flow is indicated by arrows. An activity line meeting an event

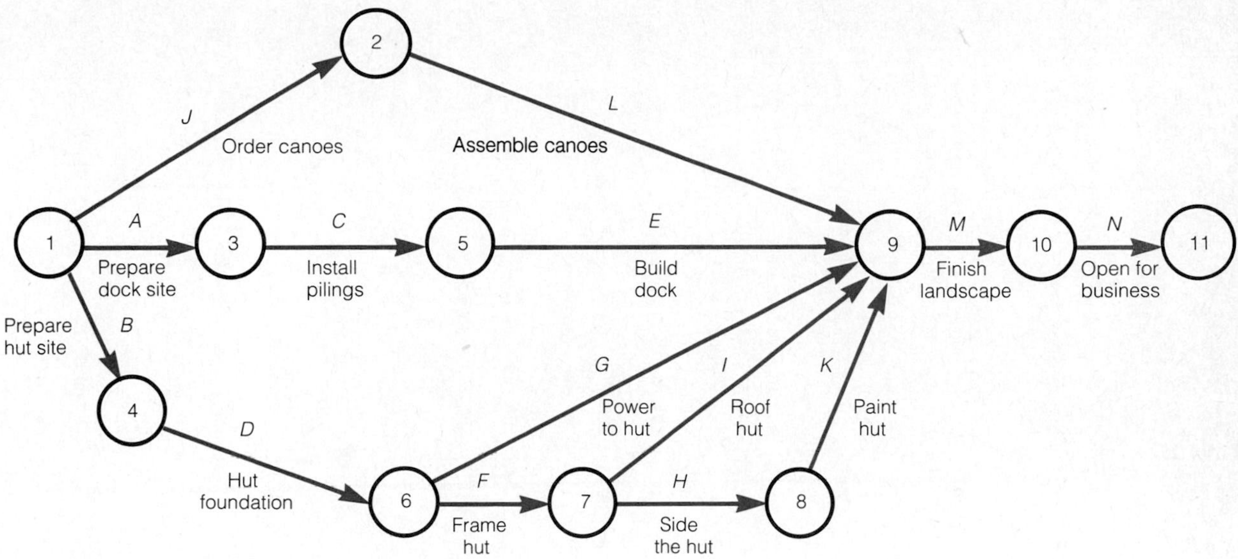

Figure 10-1
Network diagram for canoe rental project

node indicates activity completion. The length of an activity branch is not representative of the time the activity will take.

3. The relationship between activities is determined by the sequence of the branches.
4. If several activities terminate at one node, no activities starting at that node may begin until all entering activities are completed.
5. For analysis reasons, no two activities are allowed to both start and end at the same nodes. If the project network would seem to require this, a **dummy activity** must be inserted. A dummy activity has no time; it merely preserves the proper sequencing in the network diagram.

The concept of dummy activities is sometimes difficult to grasp. The following example should help. Suppose we have a project with the following activities:

Activity	Immediate Predecessor
A	—
B	*A*
C	*A*
D	*B*, *C*
E	*B*, *C*
F	*D*
G	*E*, *F*

Figure 10-2(a) appears to be the correct way to diagram this project. But as you can see, activities *B* and *C* both begin at node 2 and finish at node 3. This is not allowed in PERT/CPM networks. Figure 10-2(b) shows the proper way to diagram the project, using a dummy activity between nodes 3 and 4. This dummy activity preserves the proper sequence, showing that activities *D* and *E* can't begin until both *B* and *C* are completed. (Other examples in this chapter will also illustrate the use of dummy activities.)

(a) Two activities start and end at the same nodes.

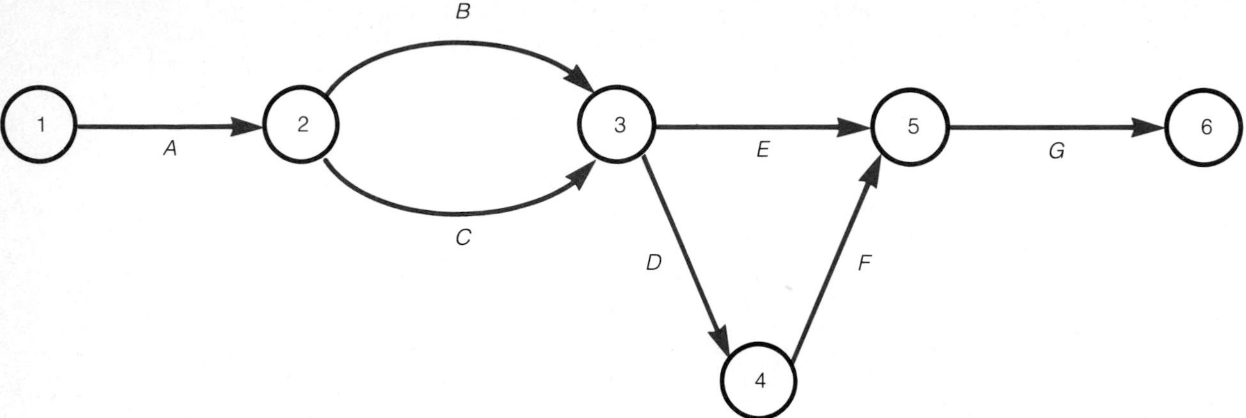

(b) Dummy activity is inserted to preserve.

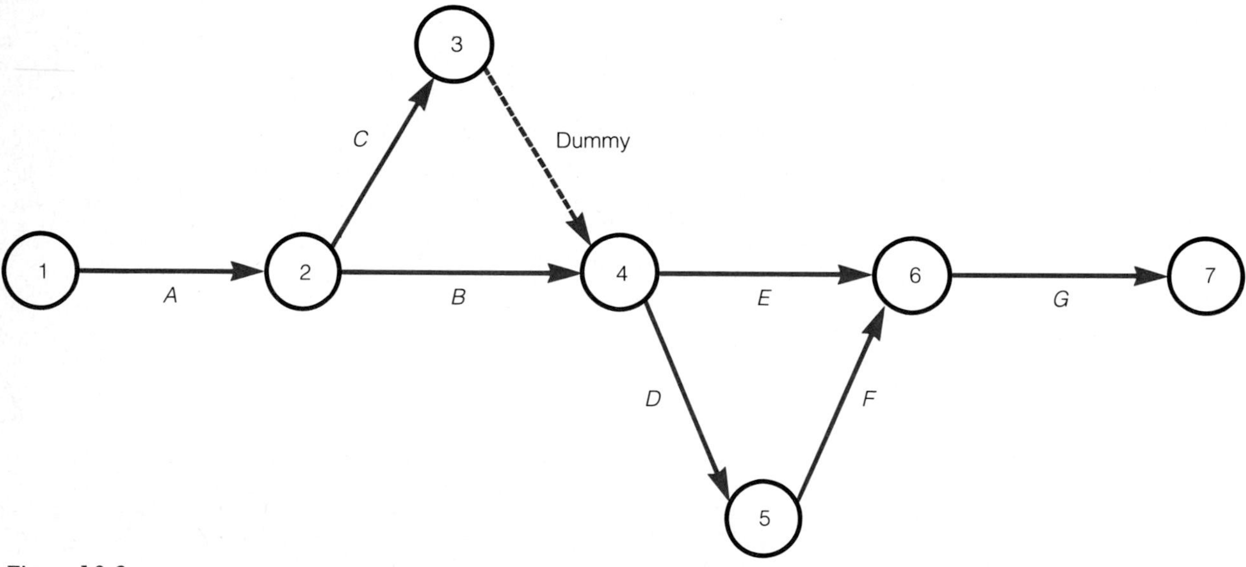

Figure 10-2
Network examples

DETERMINING ACTIVITY COMPLETION TIMES

Since Shirley and Leo are interested in knowing whether they can complete their project before the Fourth of July, their next step is to determine how long each required activity will take. The method of making these estimates is sometimes used to distinguish between PERT and CPM. CPM was originally developed to analyze engineering and construction projects which, although each overall project was unique, required activities that had been performed before and had known completion times. Therefore, in CPM, the activities were given single-point completion-time estimates. For instance, Leo and Shirley might estimate that roofing the hut will take 3 days.

PERT, on the other hand, was developed to analyze situations where, for the most part, there existed little or no historical data on which to base a single-point estimate. In the Polaris project, for example, many of the activities were being done for the very

Table 10-2 ACTIVITIES WITH SINGLE-POINT COMPLETION-TIME ESTIMATES (IN DAYS)

Activity	Description	Immediate Predecessor	Completion Time
A	Prepare dock site	—	3
B	Prepare hut site	—	4
C	Install dock pilings	*A*	6
D	Foundation for hut	*B*	3
E	Build dock	*C*	4
F	Frame hut	*D*	3
G	Power to hut	*D*	2
H	Side the hut	*F*	2
I	Roof the hut	*F*	3
J	Order canoes	—	2
K	Paint hut	*H*	4
L	Assemble canoes	*J*	10
M	Finish landscaping	*L, I, K, E, G*	4
N	Open for business	*M*	2
			52

first time. Therefore, with PERT, the activity completion times were estimated using a three-point method. These points are:

1. **Optimistic time estimate**: the completion time expected if everything involved in the activity went exactly as planned.
2. **Pessimistic time estimate**: the completion time expected if everything possible went wrong. This estimate often includes the time needed to completely start over if the planned approach fails to work.
3. **Most likely time estimate**: Based on the two values given in the optimistic and pessimistic estimates, this is the completion time expected if only the normal number of problems are encountered.

In practice, whether to use single-point completion-time estimates or three-point estimates depends on the degree of uncertainty associated with each activity. If the project is made up of activities that are commonly performed, a set of single-point estimates is generally used. However, if many or all of the activities have not been performed before, chances are the three-point system will be more effective. The conditions in a given situation will dictate whether a single-point or three-point time estimate should be used.

Since Leo and Shirley's project is made up of a set of commonly performed activities, we will use single-point estimates to analyze their problem. The single-point time estimates for each activity are given in Table 10-2.

10-3 ANALYZING A PERT/CPM NETWORK WITH SINGLE-POINT TIME ESTIMATES

The PERT/CPM technique provides the answers to three project management questions:

1. When will the project be completed?

2. Which activities are most critical to completing the project on time and when do they need to be started?
3. How much flexibility do we have in those activities that are not critical to completing the project on time?

DETERMINING THE EXPECTED COMPLETION TIME

Once the completion-time estimates for each activity have been made, we are ready to determine how long the entire project will take. From Table 10-2, we see that the total estimated activity time is 52 days; but since some of the required activities can be performed simultaneously, the calendar time from start to finish should actually be less than 52 days.

To determine the expected completion time, we must identify the critical path through the network. A **path** is the sequence of activities leading from the start of the project to the end. By reviewing Figure 10-1, we see that the network for this example has five different paths:

1: $J \rightarrow L \rightarrow M \rightarrow N$

2: $A \rightarrow C \rightarrow E \rightarrow M \rightarrow N$

3: $B \rightarrow D \rightarrow F \rightarrow I \rightarrow M \rightarrow N$

4: $B \rightarrow D \rightarrow F \rightarrow H \rightarrow K \rightarrow M \rightarrow N$

5: $B \rightarrow D \rightarrow G \rightarrow M \rightarrow N$

Not all of these paths have the same total completion time. If this network were a road map and we simply wanted to get from node 1 to node 11, we would look for the shortest path. But, this is not the case; instead, Leo and Shirley must complete all activities before the project is considered complete. And certain activities cannot be started until other activities are completed. Thus, in a project network, the **critical path** is the path with the greatest total time, since the project cannot be completed until all the activities on that path have been completed. The term *critical path* is assigned to the longest path because any delay in an activity along this path will cause a delay in completing the project. Thus, an activity on the critical path is called a **critical activity**.

For a small project like Leo and Shirley's, the critical path can be determined by listing all the paths and adding the activity times for each path. (The path with the longest total time is the critical path.) For this example, we get:

Path	Activity Times
1: $J \rightarrow L \rightarrow M \rightarrow N$	$2 + 10 + 4 + 2 = 18$ days
2: $A \rightarrow C \rightarrow E \rightarrow M \rightarrow N$	$3 + 6 + 4 + 4 + 2 = 19$ days
3: $B \rightarrow D \rightarrow F \rightarrow I \rightarrow M \rightarrow N$	$4 + 3 + 3 + 3 + 4 + 2 = 19$ days
4: $B \rightarrow D \rightarrow F \rightarrow H \rightarrow K \rightarrow M \rightarrow N$	$4 + 3 + 3 + 2 + 4 + 4 + 2 = 22$ days
5: $B \rightarrow D \rightarrow G \rightarrow M \rightarrow N$	$4 + 3 + 2 + 4 + 2 = 15$ days

Path 4 is the critical path because completion of all the listed activities, in order, will require a *minimum* of 22 days. This is the longest path through the network. If any one of the activities on the critical path takes longer than its estimated time, the overall project will take longer than 22 days to complete. (The 22-day completion time assumes that as soon as one activity on the critical path is completed, the next activity will be started.)

As this example shows, the critical path for small projects can be determined by listing the paths and adding the activity completion times. However, the applications you will encounter in business situations may have hundreds or even thousands of activities, forming far too many paths to reasonably list. The developers of PERT/CPM recognized this problem and established a methodology for determining the critical path that doesn't require listing all the paths.

This procedure, the **forward pass**, involves starting at the beginning node and working toward the final node, finding the earliest start and earliest finish times for each activity in the network. The following paragraphs describe how it works.

First, assume the project starts at time 0. Think of this as the end of day 0 just prior to the start of day 1. Assign an **earliest start time** of 0 to all activities beginning at node 1.

Next, for each activity beginning at node 1, determine the corresponding **earliest finish time.** For instance, in the dock building example, the earliest finish time for activity *A* (prepare the dock site) is day 3, because we start activity *A* at day 0 and activity *A* takes 3 days to complete. Thus, activity *A* will be required all of day 1, all of day 2, and all of day 3, finishing at the end of day 3. Likewise, the earliest finish time for activity *B* is day 4 and the earliest finish time for activity *J* is day 2.

When drawing a project network, we will use specific notation to indicate the earliest start (ES) time, the earliest finish (EF) time, and the activity times. For instance, the three activities—*A*, *B*, and *J*—which leave the starting node are shown as follows:

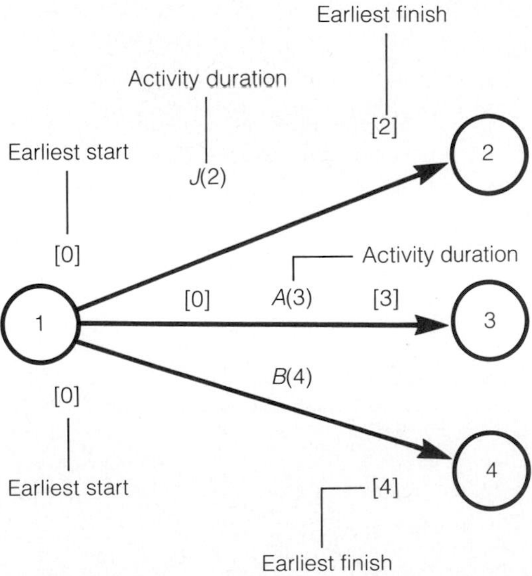

The ES times for each activity are shown within brackets near the start node for the activity. For example, [0] above node 1 indicates the earliest start for activity *J* is day 0. In this case, the earliest start for activities *A* and *B* is also day 0, as shown by [0] on the activity lines for *A* and *B*. Likewise, the EF times are shown in brackets where the arrow meets the finish node for the activity. For example, activity *J* is seen to have an EF time of day 2, as shown by [2] near node 2. Likewise, activity *A* has an EF time of day 3, indicated by the notation [3] near node 3.

The estimated times for all activities are also shown with special notation. For example, the fact that activity *J* is estimated to take 2 days is shown on the activity arrow by the notation *J*(2). Activity *A*, which will take 3 days, is shown as *A*(3) on the activity arrow. We will use this notation to work our way from the beginning node to the ending node of the network.

As we move through the network, the earliest finish for each activity is used to determine the earliest start for the succeeding activity; the only complication occurs at nodes where several activities meet. In that case, the ES time coming out of a node is determined by the greatest EF time going into the node. Refer to Figure 10-3, which shows the completed network for the canoe rental example. Node 9 is the finishing node for five different activities: *L*, *E*, *I*, *K*, and *G*. It is also the starting node for activity *M*, since activity *M* can't start until all five of these predecessor activities are completed. According to Figure 10-3, these activities have the following EF times:

Activity *L*	Day 12
Activity *E*	Day 13
Activity *I*	Day 13
Activity *K*	Day 16
Activity *G*	Day 9

This means that the ES time for activity *M* is day 16 (actually the end of day 16), since day 16 is the largest of the EF times for activities leading into node 9. Activity *M* could be finished at the end of day 20 (activity *M* requires 4 days); and activity *N*, the final activity, has an earliest start of day 20 and an earliest finish 2 days later, at the end of day 22.

Thus the question of when the project will be completed is answered in a PERT/CPM network by moving from the starting node to the ending node using the earliest start–earliest finish logic. The completion time is 22 days, as shown in Figure 10-3.

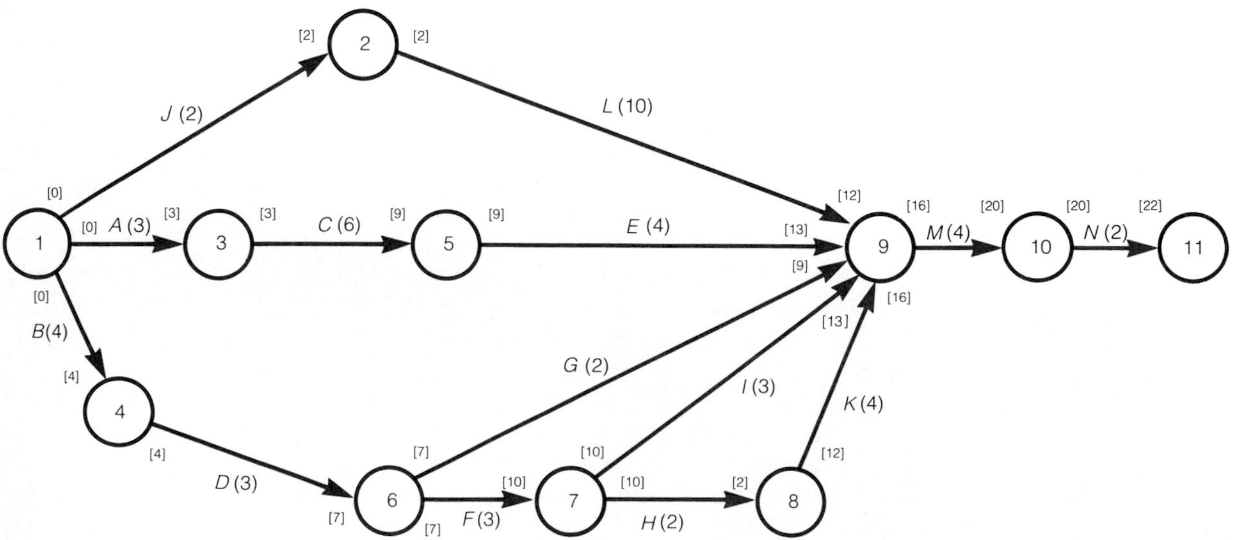

Numbers in brackets are the earliest start and finish times (in days) for each activity.

Figure 10-3

Using forward pass to determine completion time for canoe rental project

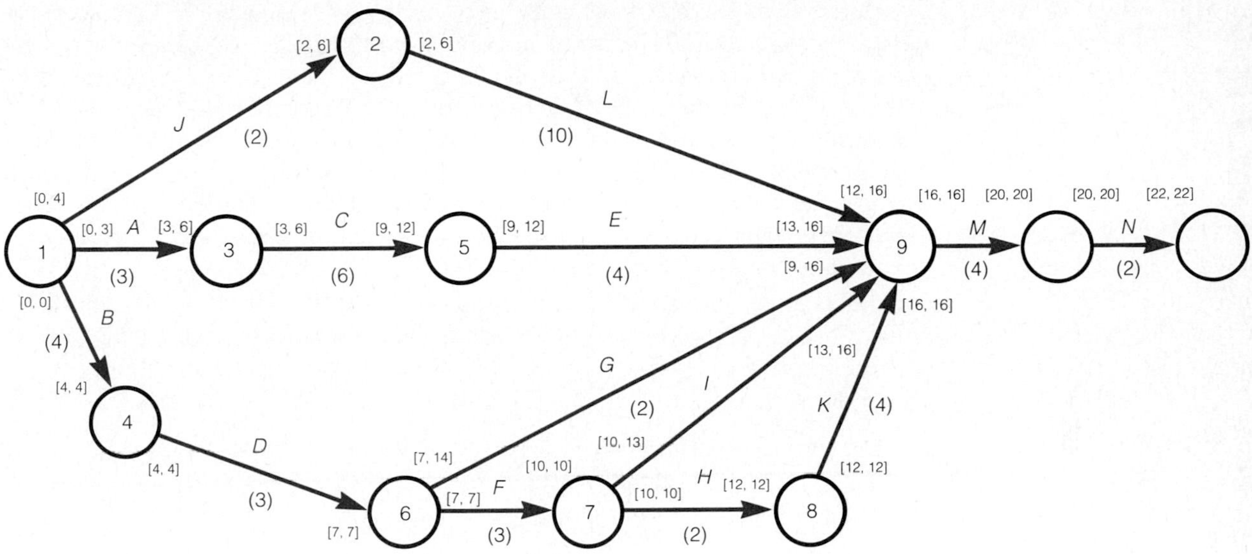

Figure 10-4
Using backward pass to determine completion time for canoe rental project

The PERT/CPM network also allows us to determine which activities are critical to completing the project on time and how much flexibility we have in activities that are not critical. These two issues are addressed with a methodology similar to that used to determine the early project completion time, except in the **backward pass** we start at the final node and move back to the starting node. Refer to Figure 10-4 as we proceed through the following discussion.

Assume we want to complete the project at day 22. To do this, the latest we can start activity *N* is day 20, because *N* has an estimated completion time of 2 days. This is called the **latest start time.** In Figure 10-4, the latest start (LS) times are placed inside the brackets, following the ES times. Thus, for activity *N*, coming out of node 10, we show [20, 20]. The second 20 indicates the latest start.

Working backward along the path, we see that if the latest start for activity *N* is day 20, then the **latest finish time** for activity *M* must be day 20. The latest finish (LF) time for activity *M* is shown as the second 20 in the brackets near the point where the activity *M* arrow enters node 10. Further, since activity *M* is estimated to take 4 days, the latest we can start activity *M* is day 16. This is noted where the activity *M* arrow leaves node 9 as [16, 16]. (The second number inside the brackets on the PERT/CPM network always represents the *latest* start or *latest* finish time.)

For activities *M* and *N*, the latest and earliest start times are the same. However, this isn't the case for all activities in the network. For example, if the latest we can start activity *M* is day 16, the latest we can finish any activity entering node 9 is day 16. However, activity *L* could be finished as early as day 12. On the network, this is noted as [12, 16] where the activity *L* arrow enters node 9. This implies an earliest finish of day 12 and a latest finish of day 16. Also, activity G could be completed as early as day 9, according to the EF times shown on the network in Figure 10-4. That is, the notation [9, 16] where activity *G* enters node 9 indicates an earliest finish of day 9 and a latest finish of day 16.

Activities which have the same ES and LS times (or the same EF and LF times) are termed *critical activities*. The critical activities form a path through the network called the *critical path*. In some applications, there may be more than one critical path. However, all activities on the critical path(s) are critical activities. For a small network like the one for this canoe rental project, we could determine critical activities and the critical path(s) by inspecting the network. However, for larger networks with many activities, it is more convenient to develop a table, like the one shown in Table 10-3. Most computer software packages (including MASTER) that do PERT/CPM analysis will produce a similar table.

Table 10-3 summarizes the earliest and latest start and finish times for the canoe rental project. Activities for which the earliest and latest times are equal are identified as the critical activities. From Table 10-3, we see that the following activities are critical:

B Prepare hut site
D Foundation for hut
F Frame hut
H Side the hut
K Paint hut
M Finish landscaping
N Open for business

Recall that earlier, when we listed all the paths in the network, the longest path (in number of days) had the same sequence of activities as the above list. If the project is to be completed in the scheduled 22 days, the critical activities must be monitored carefully to be sure they are started and finished on time.

Activities with different EF and LF (or ES and LS) times have possible slack, or float, time available and are not on the critical path. **Float** is the length of time an

Table 10-3 ACTIVITY TIMETABLE FOR CANOE RENTAL PROJECT

Activity	Earliest Start (day)	Latest Start (day)	Earliest Finish (day)	Latest Finish (day)	Critical Activity?	Float (days)
A	0	3	3	6	No	3
B	0	0	4	4	Yes	0
C	3	6	9	12	No	3
D	4	4	7	7	Yes	0
E	9	12	13	16	No	3
F	7	7	10	10	Yes	0
G	7	14	9	16	No	7
H	10	10	12	12	Yes	0
I	10	13	13	16	No	3
J	0	4	2	6	No	4
K	12	12	16	16	Yes	0
L	2	6	12	16	No	4
M	16	16	20	20	Yes	0
N	20	20	22	22	Yes	0

activity can be delayed without affecting the project completion time. It is computed as follows:

$$\text{Float} = LS - ES \tag{10-1}$$

$$\text{Float} = LF - EF \tag{10-2}$$

where:

ES = earliest start time for an activity

LS = latest start time for an activity

EF = earliest finish time for an activity

LF = latest finish time for an activity

For instance, in Table 10-3, we see that activity A (prepare dock site) has a float of 3 days. Figure 10-4 shows [0, 3] where the activity A arrow comes out of node 1. This means the earliest start is day 0 and the latest start is day 3. Using equation 10-1, we get:

$$\text{Float} = 3 - 0 = 3 \text{ days}$$

Float (or slack) for an activity provides flexibility. In this case, Leo and Shirley could wait 1, 2, or even 3 days after the start of the project to begin preparing the dock site without affecting the 22-day overall completion time. Or, if they start on day 0, they could take their time completing activity A (estimated to take 3 days) and stretch it to as much as 6 days. The only constraint on activity A is that it must be completed by the late finish time of day 6.

Table 10-3 shows the float time for all activities not on the critical path. From a project manager's perspective, float time is nice to have. However, if the float time is used up, that activity, and possibly others, become critical. So if Leo and Shirley delay starting activity A for 3 full days, activity A will become critical, since the earliest finish will then equal the latest finish. Also, this change now has a domino effect on the other activities on the path between activity A and the final node. For instance, now the earliest start for activity C will be day 6 instead of day 3. This matches the latest start for activity C, so C would also become a critical activity. Likewise, the earliest start for activity E would become day 12, matching its latest start, and it, too, would become a critical activity. Of course M and N already are critical, so they wouldn't be affected further. By using the entire float time for activity A, a second critical path is formed to join the original critical path. All activities on both paths would then have zero float time.

This example demonstrates the power of PERT/CPM as a scheduling tool. First, by using PERT/CPM you are required to define the activities and to consider their sequence. That in itself is an important step in managing a project. But PERT/CPM will also indicate what the best possible finish date for the project will be and will identify which activities are critical and which have flexibility. For a large project with many hundreds of activities, this information is extremely useful.

STEPS NEEDED TO PERFORM PERT/CPM ANALYSIS

The procedure we followed in the previous example can be outlined in a series of steps that will be followed for any PERT/CPM analysis:

1. Determine the activities needed to complete the project.

2. Determine the sequential relationship of these activities. (Remember, try to establish as many simultaneous activities as possible.)
3. Estimate the completion time for each activity.
4. Draw the PERT/CPM network, showing the relationship of activities as determined in step 2.
5. Starting with the beginning node of the network, use the earliest start–earliest finish relationships to determine the project completion time.
6. Moving to the end node of the network, use the latest start–latest finish relationships to determine the activities on the critical path and the float for activities not on the critical path.
7. Use the earliest start–earliest finish relationships found in step 5 and the latest start–latest finish relationships found in step 6 to develop an activity timetable for the project.

10-4 NETWORK ANALYSIS WITH UNCERTAIN COMPLETION TIMES

Howard Computer Specialties (HCS), founded 4 years ago, develops special-purpose software packages for professional organizations. Fred Howard started the company after spending 15 years doing applications programming for IBM. HCS has done well in the Memphis area, supplying and modifying programs for doctors and dentists, but Fred is presently negotiating for a project he thinks has the potential of leading to a market niche on the national level.

Fred has agreed in principle to develop a software package for the law firm of Liggett, Liggett & Trambull (LL&T). The package will be much more extensive than any HCS has attempted to this point. It will keep track of the time of all 85 lawyers working for the firm and assign billable hours to client accounts. It will also handle all the tax accounting and client billing, and will allocate profits among the firm's partners. Fred has agreed to meet with Laura Liggett in a week to discuss the project further. At this meeting, Fred would like to have a final proposal in hand and be able to sign a contract.

He realizes that a critical issue for both HCS and LL&T is how long the software package will take to develop. Obviously, quoting a short development time will increase his chances of landing the contract. However, promising an early completion time and then failing to deliver will not only lead to bad publicity for his firm but may even result in a lawsuit. The initial question Fred needs to answer is, How long will this project take? We will use PERT/CPM project analysis techniques to help Fred with this question; but, since HCS has never worked on a project like this before, the single-point completion-time estimates used in the canoe rental example will not be adequate. We will, however, be following the seven-step procedure outlined in the previous section.

The first step in planning for this software development is to list the activities needed to complete the project. In an initial meeting with his systems analysts, Fred determined the following activities:

A Review client's present computer use

B Determine computer competency of users

C Determine necessary elements of software package

D Design initial program
E Develop prototype of program
F Determine type of documentation needed
G Review prototype with users
H Determine structure of needed data files
I Program final package
J Develop training manuals
K Hold training sessions
L Implement program as dual system
M Modify and debug programs
N Finalize user manuals

Step 2 of the seven-step PERT/CPM procedure outlined in the previous section is to determine the order in which these activities can be completed. Since a short completion time is critical for winning the contract, Fred will want to work on as many activities as possible at the same time. The list of activities and their relationships is shown in Table 10-4.

Once the activities and their relationships have been identified, step 3 is to determine the estimated completion time for each activity. While HCS has worked on many software projects in the past, Fred has never worked with a law firm before and therefore is uncertain about the completion times. Uncertainty is generally incorporated in management science models by a probability distribution representing the value being considered.

To develop a probability distribution for the HCS project, we make a three-point estimate of completion times instead of the single-point estimate used in the canoe rental example in section 10-3. This means making an optimistic, pessimistic, and most likely time estimate for each activity. The spread between the optimistic and pessimistic estimates indicates the relative degree of uncertainty in completion times.

Table 10-4 ACTIVITIES FOR SOFTWARE DEVELOPMENT

Activity	Description	Immediate Predecessor(s)
A	Review client's present computer use	—
B	Determine computer competency of users	—
C	Determine elements needed in software package	*A*
D	Design initial program	*C, B*
E	Develop prototype of program	*D*
F	Determine type of documentation needed	*D*
G	Review prototype with users	*E*
H	Determine structure of needed data files	*A*
I	Program final package	*G, F*
J	Develop training manuals	*F, G*
K	Hold training sessions	*J*
L	Implement program as dual system	*I, K*
M	Modify and debug programs	*L*
N	Finalize user manuals	*L*

If there is no uncertainty about the completion time of some activity, all three-point estimates will be the same. Fred and the HCS systems analysts have determined the three-point completion-time estimates for each activity. These are shown in Table 10-5.

The developers of PERT determined that uncertainty in these three-point estimates can best be represented by a **beta (β) probability distribution.** Several potential β distributions are shown in Figure 10-5, with the optimistic, a; pessimistic, b; and most likely, ml, points shown on each. Note that the distributions may be skewed in either direction or they may be symmetrical. In addition, as the completion times become more certain, the distributions become narrower.

To work with the β completion-time distributions, we convert the uncertainty into a measure of **expected activity time,** t_e, and variance of completion time, σ^2. These two values are found using equations 10-3 and 10-4.

$$t_e = (a + 4ml + b)/6 \tag{10-3}$$

$$\sigma^2 = [(b - a)/6]^2 \tag{10-4}$$

where:

t_e = expected activity time

σ^2 = activity-time variance

a = optimistic completion time

ml = most likely completion time

b = pessimistic completion time

The expected completion times and variances for each activity, as identified by Fred and his analysts, are shown in Table 10-6.

Table 10-5 THREE-POINT COMPLETION-TIME ESTIMATES FOR SOFTWARE DEVELOPMENT (IN WEEKS)

Activity	Optimistic Estimate	Most Likely Estimate	Pessimistic Estimate
A	1	1	2
B	2	3	4
C	2	4	6
D	1	2	4
E	3	5	6
F	2	3	4
G	1	1	2
H	3	4	5
I	6	8	10
J	4	4	4
K	2	3	6
L	4	4	8
M	2	4	−6
N	1	1	2

Figure 10-5
Sample beta distributions

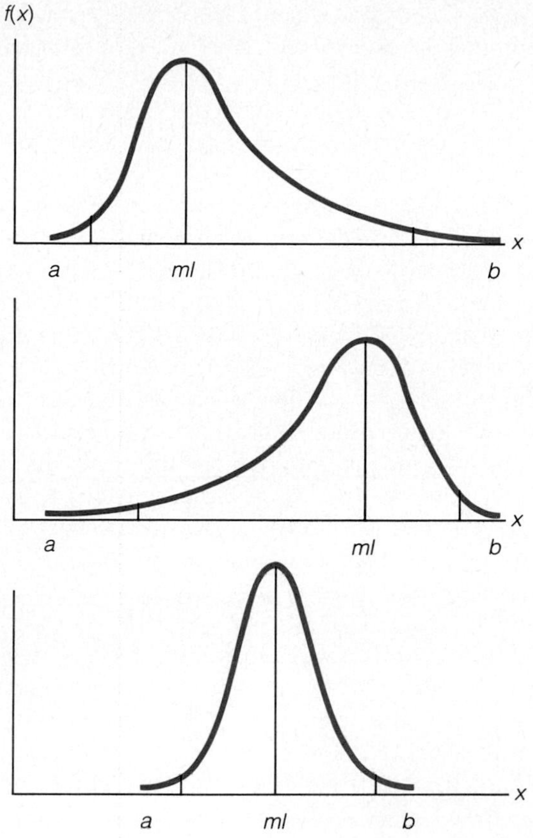

Table 10-6 EXPECTED COMPLETION TIMES AND VARIANCES FOR SOFTWARE DEVELOPMENT (IN WEEKS)

Activity	Expected Completion Time	Variance
A	$1\frac{1}{6}$	$\frac{1}{36}$
B	3	$\frac{1}{9}$
C	4	$\frac{4}{9}$
D	$2\frac{1}{6}$	$\frac{1}{4}$
E	$4\frac{5}{6}$	$\frac{1}{4}$
F	3	$\frac{1}{9}$
G	$1\frac{1}{6}$	$\frac{1}{36}$
H	4	$\frac{1}{9}$
I	8	$\frac{4}{9}$
J	4	0
K	$3\frac{1}{3}$	$\frac{4}{9}$
L	$4\frac{2}{3}$	$\frac{4}{9}$
M	4	$\frac{4}{9}$
N	$1\frac{1}{6}$	$\frac{1}{36}$

DETERMINING THE PROJECT COMPLETION TIME

Once the expected completion times have been determined, the PERT network is analyzed using the earliest start, latest start–earliest finish, latest finish (ES, LS–EF, LF) methodology developed in section 10-3. The PERT/CPM process now uses the expected activity times, t_e, instead of a point estimate. Figure 10-6 shows the PERT network with the project completion time determined. We see that the expected project completion time is 30 weeks.

The ES, LS–EF, LF listing is shown in Table 10-7. Just as in the canoe rental example in section 10-3, the critical activities are those which have ES = LS and EF = LF, and zero float time. From Figure 10-6 and Table 10-7, we see that the critical activities for HCS are *A*, *C*, *D*, *E*, *G*, *I*, *L*, and *M*. These activities must be started and completed on time if the project is to be finished in 30 weeks.

The other activities have float time, which means that the project manager will have some flexibility in deciding when they are to be started and finished. For example, activity *H* (determining data-file structure) has 16⅙ weeks of float. Since the HCS systems analysts and programmers operate on a 6-day workweek, this means that the float time is 16 weeks and 1 day. This activity can be started as early as 1 week and 1 day ($ES = 1\frac{1}{6}$ weeks) from day 0 or as late as week 17, day 2 ($LS = 17\frac{1}{3}$). Other activities with float do not have quite that much flexibility. For instance, activities *J* and *K* have only ⅔ week (4 days) float time each.

DEALING WITH VARIABILITY IN THE EXPECTED COMPLETION TIME

Fred Howard found the overall project completion time by adding the expected completion times for all the activities on the critical path. As such, this value is the average completion time expected if the software development project were worked many times. But HCS has only one chance at the LL&T project. For any single try, the completion time will be either less than, or more than, the expected value. Unfortunately, Fred will not be able to say, "We expect to be done in 30 weeks but will actually

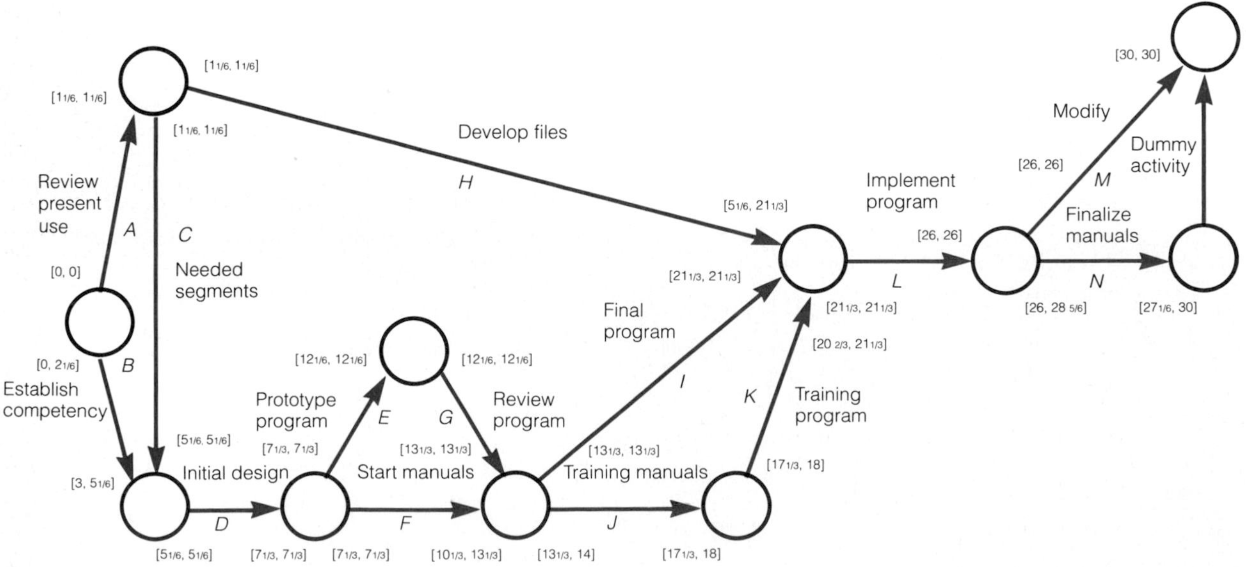

Figure 10-6
PERT network for software development project

Table 10-7 ACTIVITY COMPLETION TIME FOR SOFTWARE DEVELOPMENT (IN WEEKS)

Activity	Earliest Start	Latest Start	Earliest Finish	Latest Finish	Critical Activity?	Float
A	0	0	1⅙	1⅙	Yes	0
B	0	2⅙	3	5⅙	No	2⅙
C	1⅙	1⅙	5⅙	5⅙	Yes	0
D	5⅙	5⅙	7⅓	7⅓	Yes	0
E	7⅓	7⅓	12⅙	12⅙	Yes	0
F	7⅓	10⅓	10⅓	13⅓	No	3
G	12⅙	12⅙	13⅓	13⅓	Yes	0
H	1⅙	17⅓	5⅙	21⅓	No	16⅙
I	13⅓	13⅓	21⅓	21⅓	Yes	0
J	13⅓	14	17⅓	18	No	⅔
K	17⅓	18	20⅔	21⅓	No	⅔
L	21⅓	21⅓	26	26	Yes	0
M	26	26	30	30	Yes	0
N	26	28⅚	27⅙	30	No	2⅚

be done either sooner or later than that.'' He needs some way to include a measure of uncertainty in his completion-time estimate.

Variation in the overall project completion time is dealt with the same way variation in individual activity completion times is handled, by determining a variance. Variation in completion times along the critical path is most important. Any delay of an activity along the critical path will ensure a delay in the project completion time, unless it is offset by time saved in some other activity on the critical path. However, delay in an activity not on the critical path, if long enough, will also cause a delay in overall completion time. We will limit our discussion to the impact of variation along the critical path.

From Table 10-7 we see the critical path through the HCS network is determined by activities *A*, *C*, *D*, *E*, *G*, *I*, *L*, and *M*. The expected completion time for the overall project was found by adding the expected completion times for all the activities along the critical path. If we can assume the completion times of the activities along the critical path are *independent*, meaning that one activity taking more than the expected time to complete does not affect the probability of another activity taking more than the expected time to complete, then the variance of the overall completion time is found by adding the variances of all the activities along the critical path. This is shown in equation 10-5:

$$\sigma_c^2 = \Sigma \sigma_i^2 \tag{10-5}$$

where:

σ_c^2 = variance of critical path time

σ_i^2 = variance of *i*th activity on the critical path

Adding the variances of each critical path activity as shown in equation 10-5 gives us the overall variance shown below:

$$\begin{aligned}\sigma_c^2 &= 1/36 + 4/9 + 1/4 + 1/4 + 1/36 + 4/9 + 4/9 + 4/9 \\ &= 2\tfrac{1}{3}\end{aligned}$$

Since the standard deviation (σ) of the completion time is the square root of the variance, this value is:

$$\sigma = \sqrt{2\tfrac{1}{3}} = 1.53$$

Using this standard deviation, we can determine the probabilities of specific project completion times. These probability computations are based on the normal distribution. (Statistical theory shows the distribution formed from independent samples of a sequence of activities will approximate a normal distribution.) The resulting project completion-time distribution will be normal with a mean (μ) of 30 weeks and a standard deviation (σ) of 1.53 weeks. This distribution is shown in Figure 10-7.

In making his time estimate for the total project, Fred might like to establish a completion time large enough so that the chance the project would exceed that time is 5%. To establish this time, we begin with the following formula:

$$Z = \frac{(x - \mu)}{\sigma} \qquad (10\text{-}6)$$

where: Z = number of standard deviations x is from μ

You should recall from your statistics courses that equation 10-6 is the formula for converting to the standard normal distribution.

Now, if the completion times are normally distributed with $\mu = 30$ weeks and $\sigma = 1.53$, Figure 10-8 illustrates how a time estimate for the total project completion of 32.52 weeks is computed. Based on all the individual activity time estimates, there is a 5% chance that the project will exceed 32.52 weeks. Fred might round this up to 33 weeks and use this time estimate in his project bid. This would be a conservative estimate, which would protect HCS from understating the actual project time; but such an estimate might also hurt the company's chances of getting the contract. A lower time estimate might improve this chance but would increase the likelihood of a time overrun.

Fred Howard could perform similar calculations to determine the completion estimate that will be exceeded 10%, or even 20%, of the time. Since Fred must quote a single completion date to the law firm, he will have to trade off the fact that a shorter estimate will increase his chance of winning the contract but will also increase the probability of not completing the project on time.

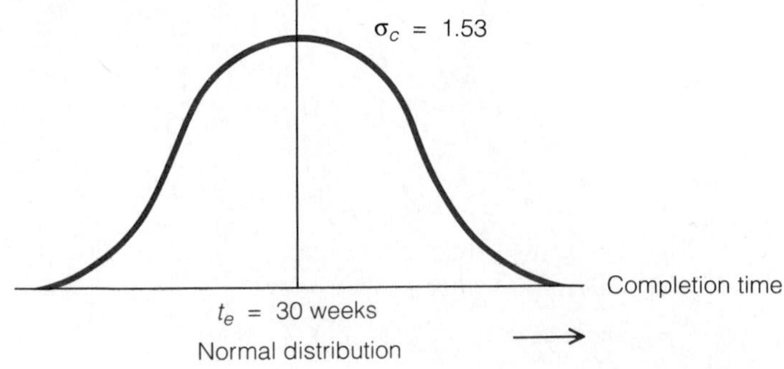

Figure 10-7
Normal distribution of completion time for software development project

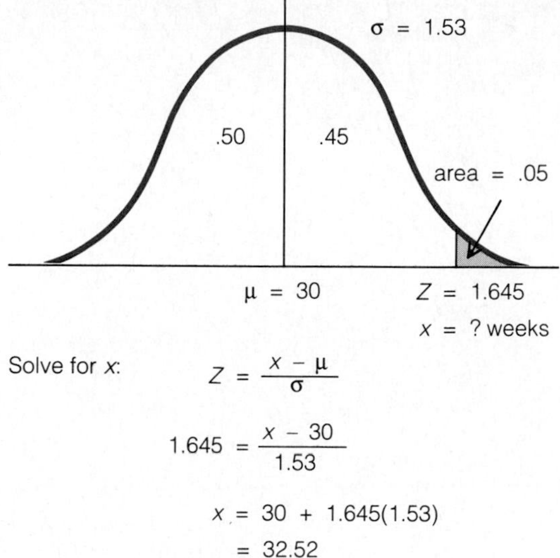

Figure 10-8
Determining completion date that will be exceeded 5% of the time

Note: $Z = 1.645$ comes from the standard normal distribution and corresponds to an area of .45 between μ and x.

10-5 USING PERT/CPM FOR PROJECT CONTROL

PERT/CPM is most often identified as a planning tool. Unfortunately, we are aware of many projects which, even though planned using PERT/CPM, did not go as scheduled —to the total surprise of the organization. However, if PERT/CPM is employed correctly, it can be just as useful for controlling a project as it is in planning the project.

To use PERT/CPM for project control, you only need to construct the ES, LS–EF, LF table (like Table 10-7), and add two new columns: Actual Start and Actual Finish. A well-respected manager we know involves his project team members in developing the PERT/CPM network and assigns a third column to the project control table: Person Responsible. If these people are included in generating the PERT/CPM network and making the completion-time estimates, they will assume a degree of ownership of the project. Then, if all the team members have a copy of the project completion table, everyone knows when every part of the project is to be completed. Table 10-8 shows a project control table for the HCS example in section 10-4.

Managers using a control table like the one shown in Table 10-8 have found they don't really have to be as personally involved in monitoring activities as they might otherwise be if no control table is used. People listed in the Person Responsible column report start and finish times and also identify any completion problems early enough for the project manager to make changes or commit needed resources to an activity that is taking longer than expected.

Peter Johnson, former president of the TRUS JOIST Corporation (now called T. J. International) and also former head of the Bonneville Power Administration, is an ardent fan of PERT/CPM. He related an interesting incident involving PERT/CPM. While he was at TRUS JOIST, an international wood products company, one division

Table 10-8 PROJECT CONTROL TABLE FOR SOFTWARE DEVELOPMENT

Activity	Earliest Start (week)	Latest Start (week)	Actual Start (week)	Earliest Finish (week)	Latest Finish (week)	Actual Finish (week)	Person Responsible
A	0	0	—	1⅙	1⅙	—	Gallup
B	0	2⅙	—	3	5⅙	—	Napier
C	1⅙	1⅙	—	5⅙	5⅙	—	Minch
D	5⅙	5⅙	—	7⅓	7⅓	—	Minch
E	7⅓	7⅓	—	12⅙	12⅙	—	Gallup
F	7⅓	10⅓	—	10⅓	13⅓	—	Napier
G	12⅙	12⅙	—	13⅓	13⅓	—	Gallup
H	1⅙	17⅓	—	5⅙	21⅓	—	Warberg
I	13⅓	13⅓	—	21⅓	21⅓	—	Gallup
J	13⅓	14	—	17⅓	18	—	Minch
K	17⅓	18	—	20⅔	21⅓	—	Minch
L	21⅓	21⅓	—	26	26	—	Howard
M	26	26	—	30	30	—	Gallup
N	26	28⅚	—	27⅙	30	—	Minch

was planning the startup for making a new product. The many activities involved in converting the production line had been organized in a PERT/CPM network and the project's critical path was identified. Within a two-day period, two project team members came to Johnson individually. One requested that, because of a heavy work load in his regular duties, he be removed from the responsibility for a critical activity. He felt the pressure would be too great and he might hold up the project completion time.

The second team member had been assigned responsibility for one critical activity and several others that were not on the critical path. She asked for a reassignment to be in charge of at least one more of the critical activities. She explained to Johnson that by working on the critical activities, she would be in a position of significant importance to the project and that her performance would be observed more closely by upper management. By succeeding in completing her assigned activities on time, she would enhance her own status and improve her chances for future promotion. Peter Johnson granted her request. While being in charge of a critical activity means that you are on the spot to perform, it also means that more eyes will be watching your efforts and your success will be noticed.

10-6 REDUCING THE PROJECT COMPLETION TIME BY CRASHING THE NETWORK

Earlier in the chapter we identified three questions that will be asked for every new project:

1. When will the project be done?
2. Which activities making up the project are most important for completing it on time and when do they need to be started?

Table 10-9 CHOOSING A NEW TRAINING METHOD

Activity	Description	Completion Time (weeks)	Immediate Predecessor
A	Develop method A	12	—
B	Develop method B	18	—
C	Test method A	20	*A*
D	Test method B	18	*B*
E	Compare methods	4	*C, D*
F	Choose and implement	8	*E*

3. How much flexibility do we have in activities that do not immediately affect the project completion time?

These three questions all deal with completion times. To this list we now need to add a fourth question, one that will also be asked for almost every project an organization undertakes:

4. How much will it cost to complete the project earlier?

There is almost always a trade-off between time and cost. In general, decreasing the completion time of an activity means adding cost, mainly as a result of working overtime, hiring additional people, adding equipment, and so on. A project manager must decide whether the reduced time for any project is worth the cost of adding resources. In a PERT/CPM application, the process of reducing the project completion time is called **crashing the network.** The issue facing the project manager in a project crash mode is to ensure the greatest reduction in completion time for the minimum additional cost.

To demonstrate the issues involved in reducing a project's completion time, consider a simple project to decide on a new company training plan, described in Table 10-9. The company is interested in whether it should organize its training efforts around a formal classroom setting (method A) or an on-the-job training effort (method B). The network formed by the six activities associated with this decision is shown in Figure 10-9.

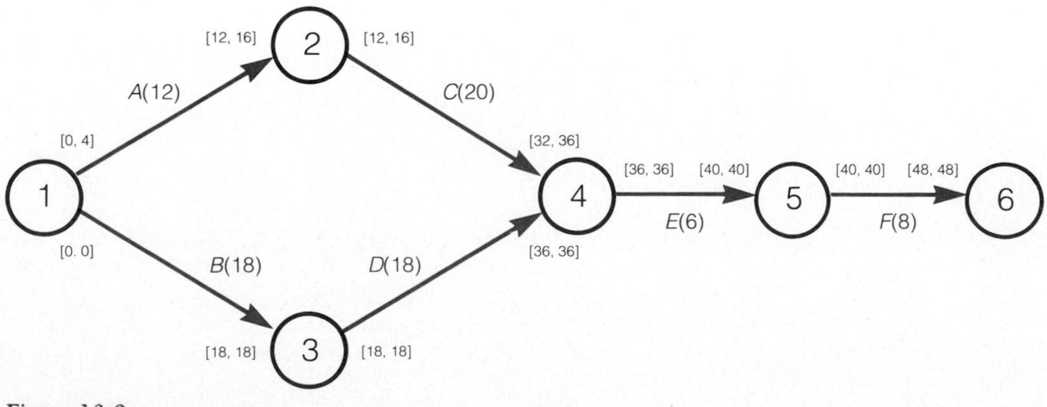

Figure 10-9
PERT/CPM network for training-method project

Table 10-10 SCHEDULE FOR TRAINING-METHOD PROJECT

Activity	Earliest Start (week)	Latest Start (week)	Earliest Finish (week)	Latest Finish (week)	Critical Activity?	Float (weeks)
A	0	4	12	16	No	4
B	0	0	18	18	Yes	0
C	12	16	32	36	No	4
D	18	18	36	36	Yes	0
E	36	36	40	40	Yes	0
F	40	40	48	48	Yes	0

Our next step after developing the network diagram is to determine the critical path. The critical activities, as identified in the schedule shown in Table 10-10, are *B*, *D*, *E*, and *F*. These activities form the longest path through the network and define an early project finish of week 48. If the project completion time is to be shorter than 48 weeks, the time of one or more critical activities must be crashed. In terms of reducing the project length, nothing is gained by crashing a noncritical activity. If a noncritical activity is crashed, the only thing accomplished is adding float to that activity.

CRASHING WITH CONSTANT COSTS

Since reducing the time to complete the project will increase the total project cost, decision makers will want to get the desired reduction for the minimum increase in cost. To determine this minimum value, we start by determining two time estimates and two cost estimates for each activity. The first estimates are the normal completion time and activity cost. The second estimates involve the minimum time necessary to complete each activity and the reduction cost per time period. For the six-activity training project, these times and costs are shown in Table 10-11. The reduction costs are weekly costs and are reported in thousands of dollars. For example, activity *A* has a normal completion-time estimate of 12 weeks. Up to 4 weeks of this time could be reduced, but at a *constant cost* of $2500 per week. If the full 4-week reduction is taken, the added cost will be $10,000.

The first step in crashing a PERT/CPM network is to identify the activities on the critical path and then determine the critical activity with the lowest per week reduction

Table 10-11 NORMAL AND CRASH DATA FOR TRAINING-METHOD PROJECT

Activity	Normal Time (weeks)	Normal Cost ($)	Crash Time (weeks)	Crash Cost ($)	Possible Reduction (weeks)	Cost per Week ($)
A	12	20,000	8	30,000	4	2500
*B**	18	30,000	15	40,000	3	3333
C	20	40,000	16	45,000	4	1250
*D**	18	50,000	16	60,000	2	5000
*E**	4	15,000	4	15,000	0	—
*F**	8	20,000	4	44,000	4	6000
		175,000				

* Critical activity.

Note: Possible reduction = normal time − crash time
Cost per week = (crash cost − normal cost)/possible reduction

Table 10-12 SCHEDULE FOR TRAINING-METHOD PROJECT AFTER STEP 1

Activity	Earliest Start (week)	Latest Start (week)	Earliest Finish (week)	Latest Finish (week)	Critical Activity?	Float (weeks)
A	0	1	12	13	No	1
B	0	0	15	15	Yes	0
C	12	13	32	33	No	1
D	15	15	33	33	Yes	0
E	33	33	37	37	Yes	0
F	37	37	45	45	Yes	0

Note: This table reflects a 3-week crash in activity *B*. No additional activities have become critical, but float times for activities *A* and *C* have been reduced.

cost. Table 10-11 shows that activity *B*, at $3333 per week, has the lowest per week reduction cost of the four critical activities. Therefore, this activity should be the first to be reduced.

Step 1 Reduce activity *B* by 3 weeks; cost = $10,000.

Next we revise the ES, EF and the LS, LF times for the network to determine if by making this reduction, any previously noncritical activities are now critical. Table 10-12 shows the revised values, with the project completion time now at 45 weeks. We see there are no new critical activities; however, the float time for activities *A* and *C* was reduced from 4 weeks to 1 week.

Step 2 Continue crashing critical activities by looking at the activity with the next lowest cost.

This is activity *D*, at a cost of $5000 per week. Table 10-11 shows that we can potentially crash this activity by 2 weeks. However, a 1-week reduction in activity *D* will reduce the completion time of path *B–D* to 32 weeks, the same as the earliest completion time of path *A – C* (see Table 10-13). After a 1-week reduction in activity *D*, we have two critical paths through the network. Crashing the PERT/CPM network often results in multiple critical paths. At this point, crashing activity *D* by more than 1 week would not reduce the completion time of the project below 44 weeks.

Thus, at step 2 we have reduced activity *D* by 1 week at a cost of $5000. Our total

Table 10-13 SCHEDULE FOR TRAINING-METHOD PROJECT AFTER STEP 2

Activity	Earliest Start (week)	Latest Start (week)	Earliest Finish (week)	Latest Finish (week)	Critical Activity?	Float (weeks)
A	0	0	12	12	Yes	0
B	0	0	15	15	Yes	0
C	12	12	32	32	Yes	0
D	15	15	32	32	Yes	0
E	32	32	36	36	Yes	0
F	36	36	44	44	Yes	0

Note: This table reflects a 1-week crash in activity *D* and follows the previous crash of activity *B* by 3 weeks. Activities *A* and *C* have become critical.

crash cost so far is $10,000 + $5000 = $15,000, and 4 weeks have been cut from the project time.

Step 3 Look for further potential crashing opportunities.

Now, however, since we have two critical paths, we must make sure that our crashing affects both paths equally. Let's take stock of where we are with respect to our potential for crashing each activity:

Activity	Crash Potential	Cost per Week
A	4 weeks	$2500
B	0	—
C	4 weeks	$1250
D	1 week	$5000
E	0	—
F	4 weeks	$6000

We see that activity *C* is the least expensive, by itself, at $1250 per week. It appears that we can shave 4 weeks off the project time for $5000 (4 × $1250 = $5000). However, keep in mind that we have two critical paths: *A, C, E, F*; and *B, D, E, F*. If activity *C* is crashed, we must make a corresponding crash in either activity *B* or *D*. But we see that no further crashing is possible for *B* and only 1 week is left for *D* (we used 1 of the 2 potential weeks in step 2). We could reduce the project by 1 more week by crashing *C* for 1 week at $1250 and *D* for one week at $5000. The total crash cost for an additional week would be $6250.

However, we see that activity *F* can be crashed for a total of 4 weeks at $6000 per week. Since activity *F* is on both paths, the project time can be reduced by crashing only activity *F*. Thus, we should choose to crash activity *F* for 4 weeks at $6000 per week, reducing the project time to 40 weeks. The total crash cost to this point is $10,000 + $5000 + $24,000 = $39,000 (see Table 10-14).

Step 4 We continue to look for further crashing possibilities.

Table 10-14 SCHEDULE FOR TRAINING-METHOD PROJECT AFTER STEP 3

Activity	Earliest Start (week)	Latest Start (week)	Earliest Finish (week)	Latest Finish (week)	Critical Activity?	Float (weeks)
A	0	0	12	12	Yes	0
B	0	0	15	15	Yes	0
C	12	12	32	32	Yes	0
D	15	15	32	32	Yes	0
E	32	32	36	36	Yes	0
F	36	36	40	40	Yes	0

Note: This table reflects a 4-week crash in activity *F*. It follows the previous crashes of activity *B* by 3 weeks and activity *D* by 1 week.

Table 10-15 CRASH PLANNING FOR TRAINING-METHODS PROJECT

Step	Crashed Activity	Weeks Crashed	Project Time (weeks)	Crash Cost per Week ($)	Total Crash Cost ($)
0	—	—	48	—	0
1	*B*	3	45	3333	10,000
2	*D*	1	44	5000	15,000
3	*F*	4	40	6000	39,000
4	*C, D*	1	39	6250	45,250

The remaining crash potential is:

Activity	Crash Potential	Cost per Week
A	4 weeks	$2500
B	0	—
C	4 weeks	$1250
D	1 week	$5000
E	0	—
F	0	—

The total project time can be reduced by 1 more week if we crash activity *C* for 1 week and activity *D* for 1 week, at a total cost of $6250. We have to crash both activities because there are two critical paths through the network. The project will not be shortened unless all critical paths are shortened.

After activities *C* and *D* are crashed for 1 week, we would be left with:

Activity	Crash Potential	Cost per Week
A	4 weeks	$2500
B	0	—
C	3 weeks	$1250
D	0	—
E	0	—
F	0	—

The only activities with further crash potential are *A* and *C*. However, both are on the same critical path. No further crashing is possible because all critical paths must be crashed by the same amount.

The steps we have gone through in this example are the same as you would use for any PERT/CPM application. At the conclusion of these steps, a crash planning table, like the one shown in Table 10-15, is usually developed. This table shows the crash sequences and costs. In this case, if full crashing is employed, the project can be shortened from 48 weeks to 39 weeks for an additional cost of $45,250.

You should be aware that the crashing order listed in Table 10-15 is for planning purposes. Never forget that once an activity has been completed, it cannot be crashed. You must decide whether to spend the money to crash an activity prior to completing the activity. Actually, in many instances, the crash decision has to be made well ahead of starting the activity. Also, in actual practice, a manager will often decide to crash fewer weeks from the project than the maximum possible because of high crashing costs. For instance, in the training-method example, suppose the project manager decides that she will spend no more than $5000 per week to reduce the project time. This means that steps 1 and 2 (see Table 10-15) will be implemented but not steps 3 and 4. Activity *B* will be crashed for 3 weeks and activity *D* for 1 week.

Now, suppose that activities *A*, *B*, *C*, and *D* are completed and it is the end of week 32. The manager can still change her mind and crash activity *F* for 4 weeks, but she has no chance of implementing the final step because activities *C* and *D* are completed. The shortest possible time for the project is now 40 weeks.

Here we should make one further point. Sometimes in actual real-world situations, activities don't get finished on time! Can you believe that? When an activity takes longer than planned, the project can be delayed. There are two situations when a project planner needs to be concerned. First, when a noncritical activity is delayed to the point that the float is exhausted. Second, when a critical activity is delayed at all. In both situations, the PERT/CPM analysis should be redone. Any activities that have already been completed should be eliminated from the network before the PERT/CPM analysis is reworked. The reason is that new critical paths through the network may be found, and certainly the ES, LS and EF, LF times will be affected for the remaining activities. In actual practice, the PERT/CPM analysis may be redone several times during the project. But experience has shown that through the careful planning and control that come from using PERT/CPM, the delays will be minimized.

USING LINEAR PROGRAMMING FOR CRASH PLANNING

The process outlined above will yield the most cost-effective means of reducing the project time. However, for large-scale PERT/CPM networks, the effort involved in completing the crash planning can be quite extensive. Certainly a computer routine for performing crashing would ease the computational burden. Some commercial PERT/CPM software packages contain these features, and linear programming offers still another approach.

For purposes of illustration, we will return to the training-method example. Refer to the network in Figure 10-9 and the crash cost data in Table 10-11. We begin by noting that the network has six event nodes. A *decision variable* is needed for each event node to indicate the occurrence time for that node. We label these decision variables as:

$x_i =$ occurrence time for event $i \qquad i = 1, 2, 3, 4, 5, 6$

Next, we need decision variables which will correspond to the number of units of crash time associated with each activity. Since we have six activities, we need six more decision variables, which we label as:

$y_i =$ crash time for activity $i \qquad i = A, B, C, D, E, F$

Without crashing, the total project cost is $175,000, as shown in Table 10-11. With crashing, the project completion time will be shortened but the total cost will be increased. The objective is to minimize total project costs (normal cost + crash cost). Since normal costs are fixed, the objective can be reduced to one of minimizing the crash costs. In linear programming notation, the objective function is:

$$\text{Minimize} \quad Z = \Sigma c_i x_i + \Sigma c_j y_j$$

where:

$c_i =$ cost associated with variable x_i

$c_j =$ cost associated with variable y_j

The x_i variables represent occurrence times for the events and do not result in any costs. Thus all c_i are zero in the objective function. The y_j variables represent the crash times and do result in costs, as shown in Table 10-11. Thus, the linear programming objective function is:

$$\text{Minimize} \quad Z = 0x_1 + 0x_2 + 0x_3 + 0x_4 + 0x_5 + 0x_6 + 2.5y_A + 3.33y_B + 1.25y_C + 5y_D + 0y_E + 6y_F$$

This objective function must be minimized subject to certain constraints, which must describe the network, limit the amount of crash time per activity, and ensure that the solution meets the project completion time. (*Note:* Values are in thousands.)

Network Description Constraints

A set of constraints must be established which describe the network. These constraints are based on the following requirements:

1. The value of x_i (the time of occurrence of event i) must be greater than or equal to the activity completion time for all preceding activities.
2. An activity start time is equal to x_i, the occurrence time of the activity's starting-event node.
3. Each activity's time is equal to its normal time less the time it is crashed, y_i.

Event Node 1: We begin by determining that $x_1 = 0$, which means that the start time from event node 1 is zero. Thus, the first constraint is:

$$x_1 = 0 \quad \text{(constraint 1)}$$

Event Node 2: For event node 2, we get:

$$x_2 \geq (n_A - y_A) + 0$$

where:

$$n_A = \text{normal project time for activity } A$$
$$(n_A - y_A) = \text{net completion time for activity } A \text{ after crashing}$$

We can rewrite this into constraint form as:

$$x_2 + y_A \geq 12 \quad \text{(constraint 2)}$$

Event Node 3: For event node 3, we get:

$$x_3 \geq (n_B - y_B) + 0$$

which we rewrite as:

$$x_3 + y_B \geq 18 \quad \text{(constraint 3)}$$

Event Node 4: For event node 4, we get:

$$x_4 \geq (n_C - y_C) + x_2 \qquad \text{and} \qquad x_4 \geq (n_D - y_D) + x_3$$

In this case, we need two constraints because there are two activities (C and D) leading into event node 4. The above inequalities are rewritten as:

$$-x_2 + x_4 + y_C \geq 20 \quad \text{(constraint 4)}$$

and:

$$-x_3 + x_4 + y_D \geq 18 \quad \text{(constraint 5)}$$

Event Node 5: For event node 5, we get:

$$x_5 \geq (n_E - y_E) + x_4$$

which we rewrite as:

$$-x_4 + x_5 + y_E \geq 4 \quad \text{(constraint 6)}$$

Event Node 6: For this final event node, we get:

$$x_6 \geq (n_F - y_F) + x_5$$

which can be converted to:

$$-x_5 + x_6 + y_F \geq 8 \quad \text{(constraint 7)}$$

Crash-Time Constraints

The previous seven constraints are used to describe the network. Because the various activities have limitations on how far they can be crashed, we must define constraints on crash time. From Table 10-11, we get the following:

$$y_A \leq 4 \quad \text{(constraint 8)}$$
$$y_B \leq 3 \quad \text{(constraint 9)}$$
$$y_C \leq 4 \quad \text{(constraint 10)}$$
$$y_D \leq 2 \quad \text{(constraint 11)}$$
$$y_E \leq 0 \quad \text{(constraint 12)}$$
$$y_F \leq 4 \quad \text{(constraint 13)}$$

Project Completion-Time Constraint

From our work earlier in this section, we know that without crashing, the project will require 48 weeks. If the manager in charge wants to complete the project in 39 weeks, one final constraint is needed:

$$x_6 \leq 39 \quad \text{(constraint 14)}$$

Table 10-16 shows the linear programming formulation with 12 variables and 14 constraints. When this linear programming model is run, we get the following solution:

$$x_1 = 0 \qquad y_A = 0$$
$$x_2 = 12 \qquad y_B = 3$$
$$x_3 = 15 \qquad y_C = 1$$
$$x_4 = 31 \qquad y_D = 2$$
$$x_5 = 35 \qquad y_E = 0$$
$$x_6 = 39 \qquad y_F = 4$$

Objective function value = 45.24 (in \$000)

Table 10-16 LINEAR PROGRAMMING FORMULATION FOR CRASHING TRAINING-METHOD PROJECT

Objective function:

$$\text{Minimize } Z = 0x_1 + 0x_2 + 0x_3 + 0x_4 + 0x_5 + 0x_6 + 2.5y_A + 3.33y_B + 1.25y_C + 5y_D + 0y_E + 6y_F$$

Subject to the following constraints:

(1) $x_1 = 0$
(2) $x_2 + y_A \geq 12$
(3) $x_3 + y_B \geq 18$
(4) $-x_2 + x_4 + y_C \geq 20$
(5) $-x_3 + x_4 + y_D \geq 18$
(6) $-x_4 + x_5 + y_E \geq 4$
(7) $-x_5 + x_6 + y_F \geq 8$
(8) $y_A \leq 4$
(9) $y_B \leq 3$
(10) $y_C \leq 4$
(11) $y_D \leq 2$
(12) $y_E \leq 0$
(13) $y_F \leq 4$
(14) $x_6 \leq 39$

and all x_i and $y_j \geq 0$ (nonnegativity constraints)

Since the y_j values represent the number of weeks each activity must be crashed to reach the 39-week project time, we see that activity B will be crashed for 3 weeks, activity C will be crashed for 1 week, and so forth. These are the same results we observed when the crash plan was developed without using linear programming (see Table 10-14).

The x_i values also provide latest and earliest start (or latest and earliest finish) times for the event nodes: $x_1 = 0$ indicates that the earliest and latest start time for event node 1 is week 0; $x_2 = 12$ indicates that, under the crash plan, the earliest start coming out of event node 2 is week 12. The earliest start out of event node 3 is week 15, as indicated by $x_3 = 15$. The value $x_4 = 31$ indicates the earliest start for the activity coming out of event node 4 is week 31. Likewise, the value $x_5 = 35$ means that the earliest start from event node 5 is week 35. Finally, $x_6 = 39$ means the earliest finish leading into event node 6 is week 39, as required in constraint 14.

This example shows how linear programming can be used to develop a crash plan. In order to use the linear programming formulation we have discussed, you must specify a desired project completion time. In our formulation, we set this at 39 weeks. We knew the project could be crashed that far because we had previously developed the crash plan. In most applications you would not know the crash limit ahead of time. Instead, as the project manager, you would usually have an objective of reducing the project time to a certain length of time. In using the linear programming approach, you start with that limit as the project-completion constraint. If that minimum time is possible, the linear program will provide the crash plan. On the other hand, if the desired project time is not possible, the linear programming formulation will be infeasible and the project completion constraint will have to be changed and the program rerun.

CRASHING WITH NONCONSTANT COSTS

While you will face decision situations where activity reduction costs are constant, in many other cases the costs of reduction will not be constant. For instance, scheduling overtime hours during the week may cost time-and-a-half, but on weekends it may cost double time. Therefore, a crash plan which calls for both weekday and weekend overtime will have nonuniform crash costs.

In other cases, reducing an activity time by 1 day (or 1 week) may be relatively inexpensive. However, each additional week may become more and more expensive because the measures needed to reduce the time require more skilled personnel or more sophisticated equipment. This, again, represents an example of nonconstant crash costs.

The methodology for project crashing is the same with nonconstant costs as with constant reduction costs; you start with the least-cost reduction on the critical path and move to the activity that is next in line from a crash-cost standpoint. The only problem is you have more costs to consider. Assume the actual weekly reduction costs of the training evaluation project are not constant but instead are as shown in Table 10-17.

To achieve a 5-week completion-time reduction, you check the per week reduction costs for the activities (*B*, *D*, *E*, and *F*) on the critical path. Of these activities, activity *B* has the lowest first-week reduction cost, at $2000, as seen in Table 10-17.

Table 10-17 NONCONSTANT REDUCTION COSTS FOR TRAINING-METHODS PROJECT

Activity	Period of Reduction	Crash Cost ($)
A	First week	1000
	Second week	2000
	Third week	3000
	Fourth week	4000
B	First week	2000
	Second week	3000
	Third week	5000
C	First week	1000
	Second week	1000
	Third week	2000
	Fourth week	2000
D	First week	2500
	Second week	2500
E	n/a	
F	First week	4000
	Second week	6000
	Third week	6000
	Fourth week	8000

Step 1: Reduce activity B by 1 week; cost = $2000.

After reducing activity *B* by 1 week, we need to find an additional 4-week reduction in the network. Looking at the per week reduction costs for the critical-path activities in Table 10-17, we see the following reductions should be made:

Step 2: Reduce activity *D* by 2 weeks; cost = $5000.

Step 3: Reduce activity B by 1 more week; cost = $3000.

At this point, we have a project completion time of 44 weeks and we have two critical paths: *A, C, E, F*; and *B, D, E, F*. Either activity *A* or *C* can be reduced by 1 week for $1000, but this would have to be accompanied by an additional 1-week reduction in activity *B*, at a third-week cost of $5000. This would make the net 1-week reduction cost $6000. An alternative is to reduce activity *F* by 1 week, costing $4000. The correct decision is:

Step 4: Reduce activity *F* by 1 week; cost = $4000.

The cost of a 5-week reduction in project completion time would be:

Cost = $5000 (2 weeks for activity *B*) + $5000 (2 weeks for activity *D*)
+ $4000 (1 week for activity *F*)
= $14,000

10-7 USING PERT/CPM IN PROJECT COST PLANNING

As we discussed at the beginning of the chapter, both PERT and CPM were developed with managing project-completion time as the driving factor. Thus, all the questions PERT and CPM were designed to answer involved time. However, project managers soon became aware that cost is also an important factor in project management. Projects that are designed to be completed within a specific time period are also usually given a budget value they are not to exceed. In addition, these budgets involve a cash-flow projection that indicates when during the project different amounts of money are needed. In many cases, money management becomes as important to project completion as effective time management.

Fortunately, the PERT/CPM scheduling techniques can be expanded to include planning and controlling cash flows as well as time considerations. The following example shows how this is done.

The president of Naylor Micron Machinery has assigned Denese Caldwell to develop a prototype flexible manufacturing workstation. The workstation will be used as part of an effort to obtain a U.S. Department of Commerce grant to allow Naylor Micron to open plants in economically depressed inner-city areas. Denese is expected to tell the president when the prototype will be ready to demonstrate; she is also expected to determine how much it will cost and when the costs will be incurred during the course of the project. The cash-flow plan is necessary, since the company will be securing a line of credit to finance the project.

The first step in associating cash with a PERT/CPM project is to determine the activities needed to complete the project. These activities are listed in Table 10-18.

Table 10-18 ACTIVITIES AND COSTS FOR PROTOTYPE WORKSTATION

Activity	Description	Immediate Predecessors	Completion Time (months)	Cost ($)
A	Design workstation	—	2.5	300,000
B	Order equipment	*A*	4	600,000
C	Install equipment	*B*	1.5	150,000
D	Arrange for facility	*A*	1.5	120,000
E	Design products	*A*	3	200,000
F	Test system	*C, D, E*	1.5	100,000
G	Demonstrate	*F*	0.5	50,000

Since cost is being considered, some effort should be taken to make sure the activity-cost relationships are realistic. In the simple examples in this chapter, this association will not become a problem. However, in realistic situations, the activity breakdown required to adequately control the timing of activities for a project may be too detailed for cost control. If this is the case, several naturally related activities can be grouped into one cost component, or **work package.**

Many projects planned and controlled by PERT/CPM will have groups of activities, or work packages, which will be subcontracted to other companies. In this case the subcontracted segments may be shown as one branch on the main contractor's PERT/CPM chart but become part of a more detailed network on the subcontractor's chart. In the example presented here, we do not have to worry about grouping activities.

The first step in solving the PERT/CPM cost problem is to determine the timing of each activity in the project and the critical path through the network. The appropriate network is shown in Figure 10-10. Table 10-19 shows the activity schedule with ES, LS and EF, LF times for the completed time analysis.

We see from Table 10-19 that the project is expected to be completed in 10 months. The next step is to determine when during this 10-month period the costs are going to occur. If we assume costs are going to occur at a constant rate during the

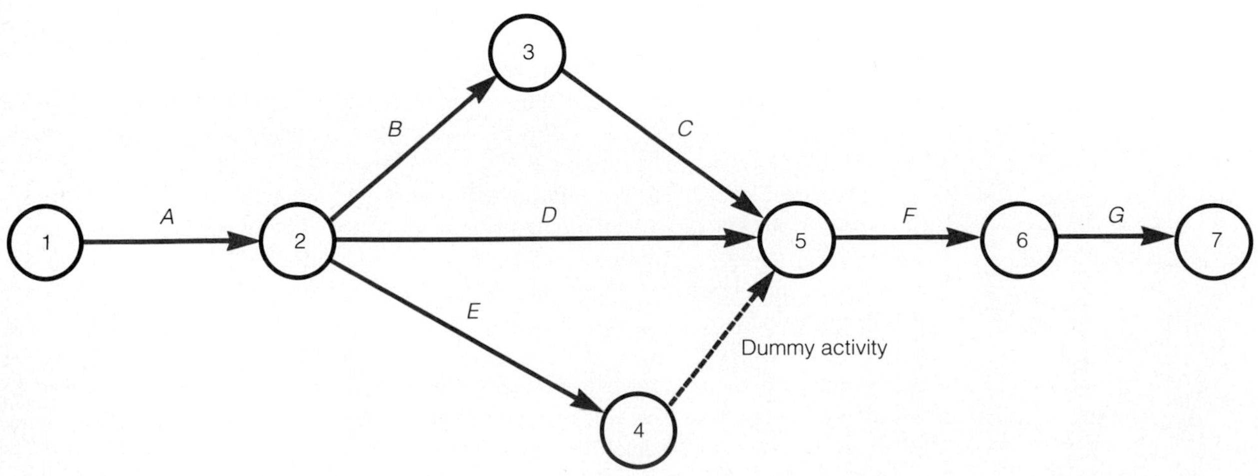

Figure 10-10
PERT/CPM network for prototype project

course of any activity, we can construct Table 10-20 which shows the monthly costs for each activity. For example, we expect activity *A* (design workstation) to take 2.5 months and cost $300,000. We will assume this means the costs will be $120,000 per month.

If Denese holds to the schedule for the project, she can assume these activity costs begin incurring sometime between the earliest and latest start times for each activity. For instance, she would expect to start spending $80,000 per month for activity *D* (arrange for facility) at the earliest in month 2.5 and at the latest in month 6.5. Using the earliest and latest start times, we can determine the range of expenditures each month, as shown in Tables 10-21 and 10-22. Denese Caldwell can use the values from

Table 10-19 COMPLETION TIMES FOR PROTOTYPE PROJECT

Activity	Earliest Start (week)	Latest Start (week)	Earliest Finish (week)	Latest Finish (week)	Critical Activity?	Float (weeks)
A	0	0	2.5	2.5	Yes	0
B	2.5	2.5	6.5	6.5	Yes	0
C	6.5	6.5	8	8	Yes	0
D	2.5	6.5	4	8	No	4
E	2.5	5	5.5	8	No	2.5
F	8	8	9.5	9.5	Yes	0
G	9.5	9.5	10	10	Yes	0

Table 10-20 COSTS FOR PROTOTYPE PROJECT

Activity	Completion Time (months)	Total Cost ($)	Monthly Cost ($)
A	2.5	300,000	120,000
B	4	600,000	150,000
C	1.5	150,000	100,000
D	1.5	120,000	80,000
E	3	200,000	66,667
F	1.5	100,000	66,667
G	0.5	50,000	100,000

Table 10-21 POTENTIAL EXPENDITURES, GIVEN EARLIEST START TIMES ($000,000)

	Month									
Activity	1	2	3	4	5	6	7	8	9	10
A	120	120	60	—	—	—	—	—	—	—
B	—	—	75	150	150	150	75	—	—	—
C	—	—	—	—	—	—	50	100	—	—
D	—	—	40	80	—	—	—	—	—	—
E	—	—	33.33	66.67	66.67	33.33	—	—	—	—
F	—	—	—	—	—	—	—	66.67	33.33	—
G	—	—	—	—	—	—	—	—	—	50
Total monthly cost	120	120	208.33	296.67	216.67	183.33	125	166.67	33.33	50
Total project cost	120	240	448.33	745	961.67	1145	1270	1436.67	1470	1520

Table 10-22 POTENTIAL EXPENDITURES FOR PROTOTYPE PROJECT GIVEN LATEST START TIMES ($000,000)

	Month									
Activity	1	2	3	4	5	6	7	8	9	10
A	120	120	60	—	—	—	—	—	—	—
B	—	—	75	150	150	150	75	—	—	—
C	—	—	—	—	—	—	50	100	—	—
D	—	—	—	—	—	—	40	80	—	—
E	—	—	—	—	66.67	66.67	66.67	—	—	—
F	—	—	—	—	—	—	—	66.67	33.33	—
G	—	—	—	—	—	—	—	—	—	50
Total monthly cost	120	120	135	150	216.67	216.67	231.67	246.67	33.33	50
Total project cost	120	240	375	525	741.67	958.34	1190	1436.67	1470	1520

these two tables to determine the required credit line on a monthly basis. For instance, the needed expenditures through month 4 of the project will be between $525,000 and $745,000.

CONTROLLING PROJECT COSTS

So far we have seen that PERT/CPM is effective not only for scheduling activity times but also for controlling projects. In a like manner, **PERT/Cost**—an extension of PERT/CPM—can be used for planning, scheduling, and controlling project costs. By using the control option of PERT/Cost, a project manager can compare cost expenditures at particular times during the project with the projected expenditures at that point, and can then determine if there is a cost overrun (actual cost above planned) or cost underrun (actual cost below planned). By identifying the activities causing the under- or overruns, the project manager can make needed adjustments.

When using PERT/CPM to monitor times, we compared actual completion times with projected completion times. We use the same procedures for controlling project costs. However, first we need a method to determine projected activity costs. In the simplest case, we can assume costs are accrued at a constant rate during the lifetime of an activity. Therefore, if the activity is 25% complete on a time basis, we expect it to be 25% complete on a cost basis. Continuing to use the activity cost figures for the prototype workstation for Naylor Micron, we will get the activity cost data shown in Table 10-23.

Table 10-23 COSTS FOR PROTOTYPE PROJECT

Activity	Projected Cost ($)
A	300,000
B	600,000
C	150,000
D	120,000
E	200,000
F	100,000
G	50,000

Now, to use PERT/Cost at any point during the project, the manager will compare actual expenditures with the projected cost based on the percent of each activity that is complete. As an example, assume Denese is 3 months into the prototype project, with the percent complete and actual cost values shown in Table 10-24. To determine the projected costs of each activity, we multiply the total cost for the activity by the percent complete, as shown in Table 10-25. By comparing the projected cost with the actual cost to date, Denese can determine which activities are costing less than expected and which are incurring cost overruns. In looking at the values in Table 10-25, we see that activities *B*, *D*, and *E* show a cost overrun and activity *A* is below the expected cost.

Table 10-24 ACTUAL COSTS AFTER THREE MONTHS

Activity	Percent Complete	Actual Cost ($)
A	90	260,000
B	10	70,000
C	0	0
D	40	60,000
E	30	70,000
F	0	0
G	0	0

Table 10-25 COST COMPARISON BASED ON CONSTANT RATE

Activity	Percent Complete	Projected Cost ($)	Actual Cost ($)	Amount Over or Under Projection ($)
A	90	270,000	260,000	10,000 under
B	10	60,000	70,000	10,000 over
C	0	0	0	0
D	40	48,000	60,000	12,000 over
E	30	60,000	70,000	10,000 over
F	0	0	0	0
G	0	0	0	0

PERT/CPM COST ANALYSIS WITH FIXED COSTS

Obviously, not all activities in a project have costs which can be realistically allocated on a percent completion basis. Frequently, activity costs involve both fixed and variable costs. Assuming variable costs can be allocated on a percent completion basis, fixed costs can be readily factored into the PERT/CPM cost-comparison system. Assume the activity costs for the flexible manufacturing prototype system are determined as shown in Table 10-26.

As soon as an activity begins, the setup cost is incurred. If the remaining project cost can be allocated on a percent completion basis, we could make a new cost/completion comparison, as shown in Table 10-27.

To determine the projected cost of each activity, multiply the total cost minus the setup cost by the percent complete and add to this value the setup cost. The results are shown in Table 10-28.

Again, by comparing the projected cost with the actual cost to date, Denese can determine which activities are progressing better than expected and which are having cost overruns. In looking at the values in Table 10-28, we see that activities *A*, *B*, and *D* show cost overruns and activity *E* has a cost underrun.

While PERT/CPM cost analysis has been shown to be an effective mechanism for cost control, it is not without problems. First, to be useful, the actual costs must be updated frequently or the cost comparisons will be meaningless. This means the technique is used primarily by organizations large enough to be able to afford this update, and on projects large enough to make this continual comparison useful. Second, while most organizations run several accounting systems, depending on who the figures are being generated for, few companies have a system like that needed to compare actual activity costs with those projected under any version of the PERT/CPM

Table 10-26 COMPARISON OF FIXED AND TOTAL COSTS

Activity	Setup ($)	Total Cost ($)
A	100,000	300,000
B	150,000	600,000
C	20,000	150,000
D	30,000	120,000
E	50,000	200,000
F	10,000	100,000
G	0	50,000

Table 10-27 REALLOCATION OF REMAINING PROJECT COSTS

Activity	Actual Cost ($)	Percent Complete
A	290,000	90
B	200,000	10
C	0	0
D	110,000	40
E	90,000	30
F	0	0
G	0	0

Table 10-28 REVISED COST PROJECTIONS

Activity	Percent Complete	Projected Cost ($)	Actual Cost ($)	Amount Over or Under Projection ($)
A	90	280,000	290,000	10,000 over
B	10	195,000	200,000	5,000 over
C	0	0	0	0
D	40	66,000	110,000	44,000 over
E	30	95,000	90,000	5,000 under
F	0	0	0	0
G	0	0	0	0

cost system we are talking about here. Therefore, the company will have to develop and maintain an additional accounting system. Finally, major differences can occur, depending on how a company allocates overhead, research and development, marketing, and other costs. Depending on the cost allocation technique, the same project can be made to show substantial overruns or underruns.

In practice, the difficulties associated with PERT/CPM cost analysis have led to its being used mainly for major projects with a substantial need for effective cost control.

10-8 COMPUTER APPLICATIONS

For reasonably small projects, like the examples described in this chapter, PERT/CPM can be performed manually. However, for more realistic projects which may have hundreds or even thousands of activities, a manual solution is not feasible. As with the other management science techniques introduced in this text, PERT/CPM computations can be handled by special computer software programs. In some instances, companies have developed their own custom PERT/CPM programs. For example, Morrison-Knudsen, a worldwide contractor and builder of hydropower dams and other large-scale projects, has its own PERT/CPM program. This program not only determines the critical path and prints out tables showing node event times and activity float, it also instructs the company's plotter to draw a picture of the project network.

Commercial PERT/CPM software packages capable of handling large-scale problems on a PC are becoming less expensive, even with increasing sophistication. The MASTER software package that accompanies this text has a PERT/CPM program for doing small-scale problems with 50 or fewer activities. In this section, we demonstrate how MASTER is used to do a PERT/CPM analysis.

Consider the situation of the accounting firm of Hindricks and Williston in Trenton, New Jersey. The firm was recently awarded a contract to perform a financial audit for a medium-size hospital in the area. Even though Hindricks and Williston have a great deal of audit experience, their practice is to establish a PERT/CPM project network and use PERT/CPM to help manage the audit to completion. Table 10-29 shows the eight major activities required for the audit and the predecessor activities. Figure 10-11 shows the network diagram.

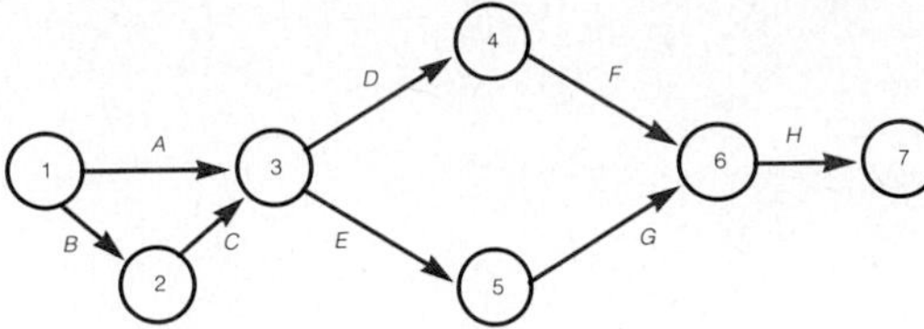

Figure 10-11
PERT/CPM network for hospital audit

Table 10-29 ACTIVITIES FOR HOSPITAL AUDIT PROJECT

Activity	Time (days)	Description	Immediate Predecessors
A	2	Set up site office at the hospital	—
B	1	Obtain copies of general ledger and other financial statements	—
C	3	Perform cash audit	*B*
D	4	Select sample of inventory records	*A*, *C*
E	6	Select samples of accounts receivable, accounts payable, and payroll transactions	*A*, *C*
F	6	Audit inventory balances	*D*
G	12	Audit receivables, payables, and payroll	*E*
H	7	Prepare audit report	*F*, *G*

```
Master   INTRODUCTION TO MANAGEMENT SCIENCE

Master Main Menu

        Linear Programming
        Transportation Modeling
        Assignment Modeling
     -->PERT/CPM
        ■ Forecasting
        ■ Waiting-Line Models
        ■ Inventory Control Models
        ■ Decision Analysis
        ■ Regression and Correlation
        ■ Simulation models

Use up/down arrows to make selection.
Press (↵) To Proceed    Press F1 to Exit
```

Figure 10-12
MASTER main menu

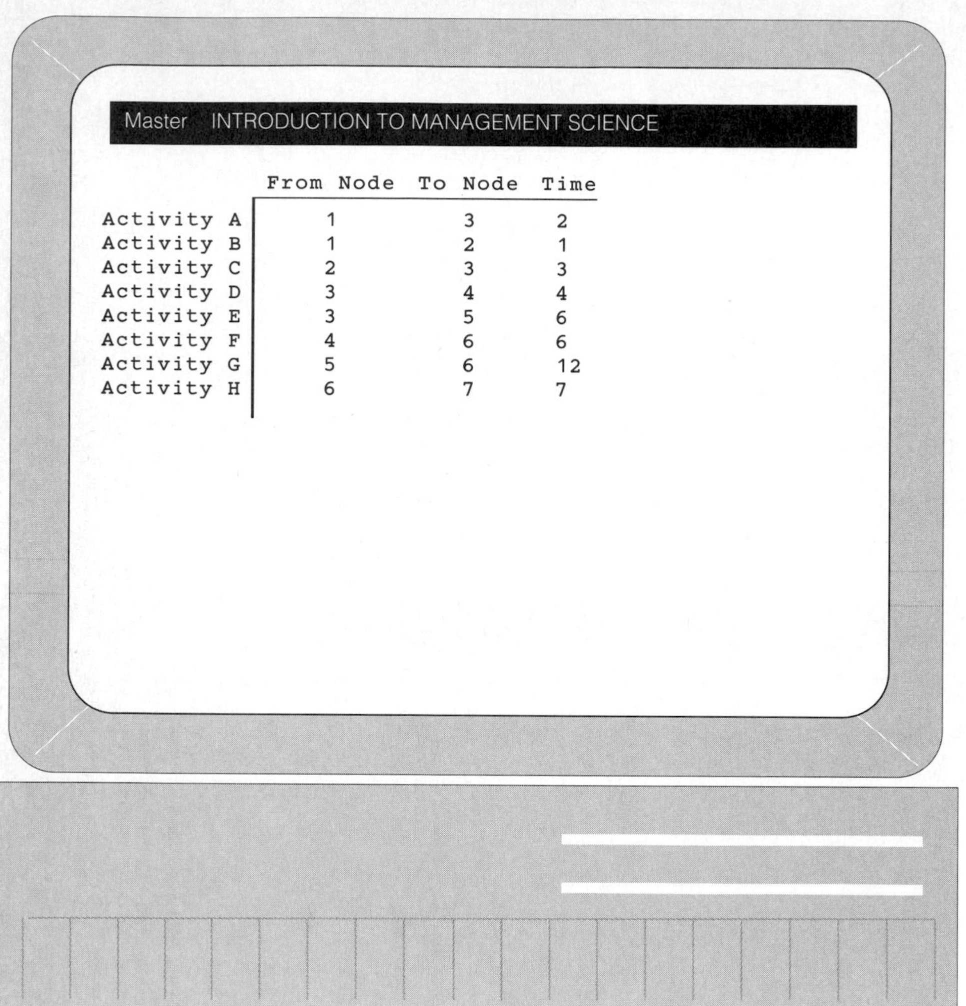

	From Node	To Node	Time
Activity A	1	3	2
Activity B	1	2	1
Activity C	2	3	3
Activity D	3	4	4
Activity E	3	5	6
Activity F	4	6	6
Activity G	5	6	12
Activity H	6	7	7

Figure 10-13
PERT/CPM data-entry screen

To use the MASTER software, select the PERT/CPM option in the main menu, as shown in Figure 10-12. The data requirements for using PERT/CPM in MASTER are to supply the starting and ending event nodes for each activity and the activity times. The data-entry screen is shown in Figure 10-13.

The output from the MASTER software (Figure 10-14) shows the earliest and latest start times (ES, LS), the earliest and latest finish times (EF, LF), and the activities on the critical path (CP). According to this PERT/CPM analysis, the audit will require a minimum of 29 days. The critical activities, as indicated by * in the output are *B*, *C*, *E*, *G*, and *H*. Activities *A*, *D*, and *F* have float times ranging from 2 to 8 days.

The PERT/CPM software in MASTER does not perform crashing directly; nor does it allow for probabilistic times. However, crashing can be performed two ways. First, you can reduce the time for an activity and quickly rerun the PERT/CPM. You can repeat this process until no further crashing is possible. Second, you can formulate the

PERT/CPM NETWORK ANALYSIS

ACTIVITY	NAME	EVENT FROM	EVENT TO	TIME
1	Activity A	1	3	2
2	Activity B	1	2	1
3	Activity C	2	3	3
4	Activity D	3	4	4
5	Activity E	3	5	6
6	Activity F	4	6	6
7	Activity G	5	6	12
8	Activity H	6	7	7

ACTIVITY		FROM	TO	TIME	ES	LS	EF	LF	FLOAT	CP
1	Activity A	1	3	2	0	2	2	4	2	
2	Activity B	1	2	1	0	0	1	1	0	*
3	Activity C	2	3	3	1	1	4	4	0	*
4	Activity D	3	4	4	4	12	8	16	8	
5	Activity E	3	5	6	4	4	10	10	0	*
6	Activity F	4	6	6	8	16	14	22	8	
7	Activity G	5	6	12	10	10	22	22	0	*
8	Activity H	6	7	7	22	22	29	29	0	*

Figure 10-14
PERT/CPM output for hospital audit

crashing problem as a linear programming problem, as shown in section 10-5, and run it using MASTER'S Linear Programming option.

The output provided by MASTER is typical of what you will see if you run any PC software package for PERT/CPM. The exact format of the output may vary slightly among programs, and some more expensive programs will offer graphical output and other project control reports. We suggest that you work a few problems in this chapter manually and then use MASTER or another PERT/CPM software package to do the others. By using a computer, you can focus more on establishing the network and interpreting the results than on performing the calculations required to determine the critical path.

10-9 SUMMARY AND CONCLUSIONS

In this chapter we have considered one of the most widely used managerial decision-making tools, PERT/CPM. Although originally developed as separate tools, over the years PERT and CPM have merged so that now they are generally treated as one technique. Developed in the late 1950s, these tools are extensively used in a wide variety of organizations to plan unique or first-time projects. PERT/CPM is specifically designed to answer the four managerial questions asked for any nonrepetitive project:

1. When will the project be completed?
2. Which activities are most important for completing the project on time and when do they need to be started?
3. How much flexibility do we have in those activities that are not critical to completing the project on time?
4. How much will it cost to complete the project earlier?

Experience has shown that organizations which use PERT/CPM are much more successful at completing projects on time and at accurately projecting costs than firms that don't use PERT/CPM. In fact, some organizations routinely require a PERT/CPM network as part of any contract bid (i.e., not including a network means the bid will be automatically rejected).

The continuing success of this technique is also partly due to its use as a control mechanism as well as a planning technique. While originally designed for situations where completion time is the most critical issue, PERT/CPM has been expanded to include cost planning and cost monitoring.

Like the other management science tools discussed in this text, PERT/CPM is a tool for *modeling* decision situations. The network represents a model of the way in which the project will be carried out. As with all models, there are trade-offs between how closely the model fits reality and its complexity. When using PERT/CPM, the decision maker must strike a balance between having the network become too large (by including every possible activity, no matter how small) and having the network become too general (by grouping too many activities together as one activity). The decision maker should focus on developing a PERT/CPM model which will best enable him or her to effectively manage a project. This requires experience that comes only from hands-on use of this very useful management science tool.

Solved Problems

PROBLEM 1 The Eastern Division of Waremart Groceries is considering opening a new "superstore" in McLean, Virginia. However, to receive funding from HJR, the holding company which owns Waremart Groceries, the plan must be approved and construction ready to start within the next 6 months. A complicating factor is that the McLean Planning and Zoning Commission must see an initial design of the store before it will approve the building permit, since the store must conform to specified architectural patterns.

The architectural planning section of Waremart's Eastern Division has determined the following list of activities necessary to receive approval from the holding company. Included are the predecessor relationships and completion-time estimates.

Activity	Description	Immediate Predecessor	Time (weeks)
A	Survey building site	—	3
B	Prepare initial design	—	8
C	Receive zoning approval	*A, B*	2
D	Select design/engineering firm	*C*	6
E	Determine needed cash flow	*C*	4
F	Review final design	*D*	3
G	Obtain corporate financing	*E, F*	3
H	Receive contractor bids	*D*	7
I	Select contractor	*H, G*	3

a. Develop the appropriate PERT/CPM network for this project.
b. Identify the critical path through the network.
c. Develop an activity schedule for this project.
d. Would you predict that the project will be ready to start within the required time constraint?

Solutions

a. The activity-predecessor relationships from the table are described by the network shown in Figure 10-15.

b. To identify the critical path through the network, we must use the earliest start–latest start relationships found by making a forward pass and then a backward pass through the network. These values are shown in Figure 10-16. The critical path is determined by activities *B, C, D, H,* and *I*. The time along the critical path is 26 weeks.

c. To develop the schedule, use Figure 10-16 to identify the earliest start, latest start, earliest finish,

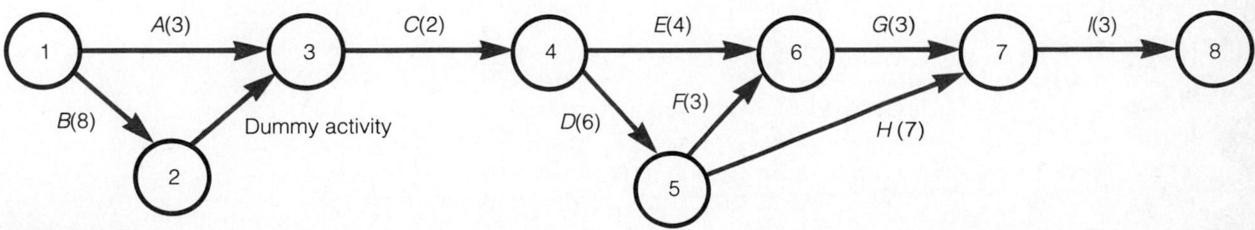

Figure 10-15
Network for Waremart problem

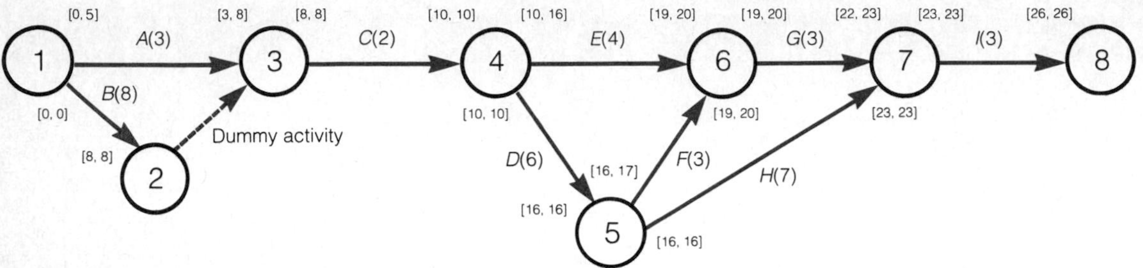

Figure 10-16
Determining the critical path

and latest finish times from Figure 10-16, as follows:

Activity	Earliest Start (week)	Latest Start (week)	Earliest Finish (week)	Latest Finish (week)	Critical Activity?	Float (weeks)
A	0	5	3	8	No	5
B	0	0	8	8	Yes	0
C	8	8	10	10	Yes	0
D	10	10	16	16	Yes	0
E	10	16	14	20	No	6
F	16	17	19	20	No	1
G	19	20	22	23	No	1
H	16	16	23	23	Yes	0
I	23	23	26	26	Yes	0

d. The time along the critical path is 26 weeks, or exactly 6 months. Assuming the completion-time estimates are correct, the project should meet the holding company's requirement.

PROBLEM 2 The Food Division vice-president at HJR (see problem 1) has been reviewing the PERT/CPM network used to show that the McLean store project will meet the timing requirements. He has expressed concern about the single-point estimates used to arrive at the project completion time, since he has been involved in numerous projects where the time estimates were not met. He asks Waremart's planning director to determine three-point estimates for each activity and then determine the probability that the 6-month requirement will be met. The planning director and her staff have arrived at the following estimates for the activity completion times.

Activity	Optimistic (months)	Most Likely (months)	Pessimistic (months)
A	2	3	5
B	6	9	10
C	2	2	4
D	5	6	7
E	3	4	6
F	2	3	4
G	2	4	5
H	6	7	10
I	2	3	3

a. Determine the new completion-time estimates for each activity and the variance of each estimate.
b. Determine the expected project completion time using these three-point estimates.
c. What is the probability that the project will be completed within the required 6-month time frame?

Solutions a. The expected time and variance for each activity can be found using equations 10-3 and 10-4. These values are:

Activity	Expected Completion Time (weeks)	Variance (weeks)
A	3.17	.25
B	8.67	.44
C	2.33	.11
D	6.0	.11
E	4.17	.25
F	3.00	.11
G	3.83	.25
H	7.33	.44
I	2.83	.03

b. While changing from single-point to three-point estimates will not change the PERT/CPM network, it will change the earliest start and finish times, and potentially the critical path. However, in this case the critical path stays the same, with the critical activities being *B, C, D, H,* and *I*. The expected completion time for the project is found by summing the expected completion times for activities on the critical path:

$$8.67 + 2.33 + 6.00 + 7.33 + 2.83 = 27.16 \text{ weeks}$$

c. The expected project completion time has increased from 26 weeks to 27.16 weeks when three-point estimates are used. However, to determine the probability the project will meet the 26-week (6-month) requirement, we must find the standard deviation of the expected completion time. To do this, we first add the variances of activities along the critical path:

$$\sigma^2 = .44 + .11 + .11 + .44 + .03 = 1.13 \text{ weeks}$$

The standard deviation of the completion time is $\sigma = 1.06$ weeks.

To determine the probability of the project being completed in 26 weeks, we use the normal distribution shown in Figure 10-17.

The probability that the project will be completed within 26 weeks is represented by the area to the left of 26 on the normal distribution. This area is found by referring to the standard normal table (Appendix B). The table shows that the probability of finding an observation between $Z = 0$ and

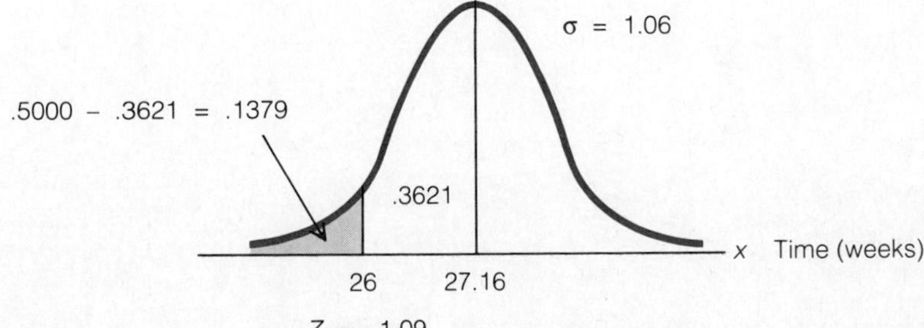

Figure 10-17
Normal distribution for Waremart problem

$Z = -1.09$ is .3621. Subtracting this probability from .50 to get the probability of finding a value less than 1.09 standard deviations below the mean, we get .1379. Thus, there is a 13.79% chance that the project will be completed in 26 weeks or less.

General Questions and Assignments

1. Discuss in your own terms the difference between an *event* and an *activity* as they relate to PERT/CPM.
2. Explain why, in a PERT/CPM analysis, if the objective is to complete a project as quickly as possible, the critical path is the network path which requires the longest time rather than the shortest.
3. Why do activities on the critical path have no float time? Also explain how activities that were once not on the critical path can come to be included on the critical path.
4. Identify a project that you are familiar with and formulate the project activities into a PERT/CPM framework. If you have actual data on activity completion times, use these to determine the project completion time and the critical-path activities.
5. Locate a business in your area which uses PERT/CPM and write a paper describing the company's use and success with PERT/CPM. Be sure to inquire about any specific problems the company might have had with this management science tool. What software is used for doing PERT/CPM? Are single- or three-point time estimates used?
6. Explain what a *dummy activity* is in a PERT/CPM analysis and discuss why dummy activities are sometimes needed. Show, through an application of your own, how a dummy activity is used. What impact do dummy activities have on total project completion times?
7. Can a dummy activity be on the critical path? Discuss why or why not. Use an example to prove your point.
8. Read at least three articles describing applications of PERT/CPM. Write a paper in which you describe these applications and summarize the advantages and/or problems the organizations encountered in using PERT/CPM.

Exercises and Application Problems

1. Gail Stratton is considering applying to the National Forest Service for a permit to build a new ski resort on federally controlled land east of Salt Lake City. Many activities must be performed before construction could start. Some potential activities are: assessing the present road system, determining the project's impact on the area's wildlife, determining the impact on established water rights, and assessing the availability of financing. The required activities have been identified as follows:

Activity	**Immediate Predecessor**
A	—
B	—
C	*A, B*
D	*A, B*
E	*B*
F	*C*
G	*D*
H	*D, F*
I	*E, G, H*

Construct the PERT/CPM network for this project.

2. Construct the appropriate PERT/CPM network for the following set of activities:

Activity	Immediate Predecessor	Activity	Immediate Predecessor
A	—	G	D
B	—	H	B
C	A	I	H
D	A	J	H
E	B	K	G, F
F	C, E	L	I

3. Construct the PERT/CPM network for the activities (listed below.) (You will have to add dummy activities to this network.)

Activity	Immediate Predecessor
A	—
B	A
C	A, B
D	A
E	C
F	C
G	D
H	F, G
I	H
J	E

4. Construct the activity–immediate predecessor list that will generate the PERT/CPM network shown in Figure 10-18.

5. The director of corporate training for Westland Manufacturing is about to begin a new training program for first-line supervisors. After identifying the activities that must be completed before the first class starts, the director found the immediate predecessors and completion times listed below. Which activities should the training director be concerned with to ensure timely project completion?

Activity	Immediate Predecessor	Completion Time (days)
A	—	15
B	A	12
C	B	6
D	B	5
E	C	3
F	—	8
G	F	8
H	F	9
I	G	7
J	G	14
K	J	6
L	H, K	4

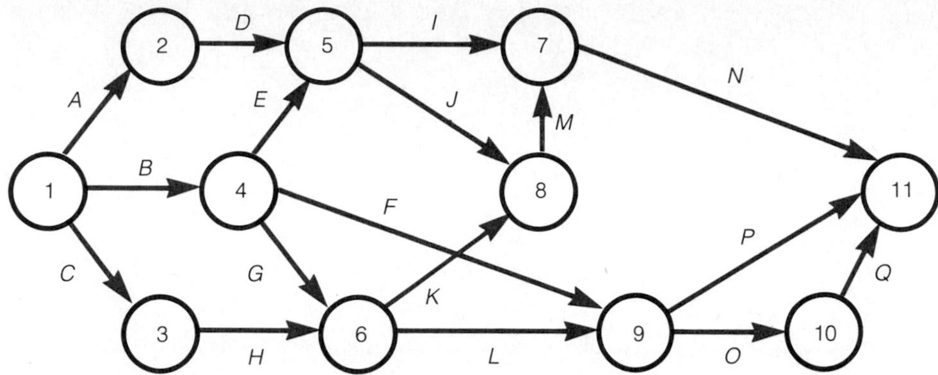

Figure 10-18
PERT/CPM network for problem 4

6. In developing an opening advertising campaign for a new liquid laundry detergent, you have identified the activities that must be completed before the product reaches the market. You have also identified the following information for the activities:

Activity	Immediate Predecessor	Completion Time (weeks)
A	—	5
B	—	3
C	A	4
D	A	7
E	D	2
F	B	10
G	B	5
H	C	4
I	C	2
J	E, F, I	4
K	G	6
L	J	3
M	H, L	10
N	J	6
O	J	4
P	K, O	9
Q	K	3
R	Q	11
S	M	7

a. Draw the appropriate PERT/CPM network for this project.
b. When will the project be complete?
c. Identify the activities on the critical path.
d. Determine the slack for all activities not on the critical path.

7. As a government auditor, you have identified the following project-activity information in conjunction with the audit you are doing on a defense contractor.

Activity	Immediate Predecessor	Completion Time (months)
A	—	2
B	—	3
C	*A*	4
D	*B*	2
E	*B*	3
F	*E*	4
G	*E*	6
H	*E*	4
I	*D, F*	3
J	*C*	4
K	*C*	6
L	*H*	2
M	*G, I, J*	1

a. Draw the appropriate PERT/CPM network for this project.
b. Your supervisor is anxious to be able to tell the overseeing Senate committee when the audit will be complete. When will this be?
c. Identify the activities on the critical path.
d. Determine the slack for all activities not on the critical path.

8. The fleet manager of Dothan Enterprises is analyzing alternatives for its automobile purchases for the next 5 years. Factors to be considered include purchase price, maintenance contracts, potential resale prices, gasoline mileage, and so on. After associating identifiers with these activities, you have determined the following immediate predecessors and completion times:

Activity	Immediate Predecessor	Completion Time (weeks)
A	—	2
B	—	1
C	*A*	3
D	*A*	2
E	*B*	4
F	*C*	3
G	*D*	5
H	*E*	3
I	*E*	2
J	*I*	3
K	*F, G*	5

a. Draw the appropriate PERT/CPM network for this project.
b. When will the fleet rental decision be made?
c. Identify the activities on the critical path.
d. Determine the slack for all activities not on the critical path.

9. The university's athletic director is attempting to organize an eight-team soccer tournament. She has determined that the following activities must be completed and has estimated the possible completion times for each activity.

	Activity	Predecessor	Estimated Completion Time (days)		
			Optimistic	Most Likely	Pessimistic
A	Select teams	—	2	3	5
B	Determine site	*A*	3	5	8
C	Make invitations	B	10	13	20
D	Arrange housing	C	5	8	11
E	Print programs and tickets	B	4	7	8
F	Sell programs and tickets	E	17	20	21
G	Complete planning	C	5	7	12
H	Schedule practices, games, fields	D	2	3	5
I	Schedule practice sessions	*G, H*	1	2	3
J	Conduct tournament	*F, I*	1	1	1

a. Draw a PERT diagram for these activities.
b. What is the critical path and the expected time to complete all the activities on this path?
c. What is the probability of organizing and completing the tournament within 30 days?
d. When should the first activity be started if the athletic director wants to have only a 2% chance of *not* having everything done when needed?

10. In problem 5, the director of corporate training for Westland Manufacturing was about to begin a new training program for first-line supervisors. In discussing the PERT/CPM network for the program, several colleagues expressed concern about meeting the original single-point time estimates. To address these concerns, the director and his staff determined the following three-point completion-time estimates:

Activity	Estimated Completion Time (days)		
	Optimistic	Most Likely	Pessimistic
A	12	15	20
B	10	12	13
C	5	6	7
D	4	6	9
E	3	3	3
F	7	8	10
G	4	8	14
H	8	9	10
I	6	7	9
J	12	16	22
K	5	6	7
L	4	4	4

a. What is the expected completion time for this project with these completion times?
b. If the training director needs to project a completion date that would have only a 5% chance of *not* being met, what time would he give?

11. Jet Stream Instruments has received exciting news from its product design group about a new "heads-up" display technique for commercial airliners. Previously, this technique, which displays instrument readings on the cockpit windshield as the pilot looks ahead, had been used only in military airplanes. The design group has identified a series of activities that must be completed before the product can be marketed. Since this is a totally new product for the company, no one can give firm estimates for the time needed to complete any of the activities. The activity identifiers and completion-time estimates are given below:

Activity	Immediate Predecessor	Estimated Completion Time (months)		
		Optimistic	Most Likely	Pessimistic
A	—	5	6	8
B	*A*	3	4	5
C	*A*	2	5	6
D	*C*	4	5	8
E	*B*	6	6	6
F	*D*	1	1	3
G	*D*	5	7	8
H	*E, F*	1	1	1
I	*E, F*	3	4	7
J	*E, F*	8	9	10
K	*G, I*	4	5	5
L	*H*	6	8	9

a. Construct the appropriate PERT/CPM network for this project.
b. Determine the expected completion time for the project.
c. Getting this product to the market before any competitors do is critical for its profitability. In particular, the executive committee estimates the system must be in production within 25 months. What is the probability that this deadline will be met?

12. Mary Mellon, personnel director for Crenshaw Enterprises, has been asked to plan the first annual work improvement conference for the company. She has determined the following list of activities:

Activity	Identifier
Identify location for conference	*A*
Plan topics for workshop session	*B*
Arrange for keynote speakers	*C*
Arrange for session moderators	*D*
Plan sequence of conference sessions	*E*
Identify specific attendees	*F*
Identify initial materials	*G*
Write and print initial materials	*H*

Mary has also determined the following sequence of activities and completion-time estimates.

Activity	Immediate Predecessor	Estimated Completion Time (days)		
		Optimistic	Most Likely	Pessimistic
A	—	5	10	15
B	—	3	5	5
C	A	10	15	20
D	A	5	5	5
E	D	3	4	5
F	B, C	10	10	15
G	E	2	3	4
H	F, G	6	8	10

a. Construct the appropriate PERT/CPM network for this project.
b. Determine the expected completion time for this project.
c. Mary is trying to set a time for the conference to start. How many workdays from now should she plan on starting if she wants to limit the probability of having to work overtime to finish the necessary activities to 5%?

13. Problem 6 discussed a potential advertising campaign. Assume the campaign has been approved and determine the PERT/CPM control chart for this project.
14. Problem 7 considered a government employee's audit of a defense contractor. Determine the control chart for this project.
15. Problem 9 considered the planning of a soccer tournament. Determine the control chart that will allow the athletic director to determine whether the project is progressing on schedule.
16. Problem 11 considered the development of a new product by Jet Stream Instruments. Determine the control chart that can be used to monitor whether this project is progressing as planned.
17. At a trade show in France, the president of Green Petrochemicals heard that its German competitor is developing a new biodegradable plastic to be used in disposable diapers. Given the recent focus on landfill problems, this development could have a great impact on Green Petrochemicals' sales. The company is now developing a project to counter this competition and has made an initial estimate of the major activities in the project, their relationships, completion-time estimates, and possible costs. All times are in months and costs are in millions of dollars.

Activity	Predecessor	Completion Time		Estimated Cost	
		Regular	Crash	Regular	Crash
A	—	6	4	40	50
B	—	7	5	65	85
C	A	5	3	60	90
D	A	9	6	90	120
E	B	7	4	45	80
F	B	9	6	70	100
G	C	8	6	20	30
H	D, E	12	10	100	140
I	F	12	8	40	70

a. What is the critical path of this project?
b. What are the regular completion time and cost of the original project?
c. If the project manager wants to reduce the completion time to 22 months, which reduction schedule would you recommend and what would be the associated costs?

18. In considering a product development project, you have determined the following set of activities, estimated completion times, and cost estimates. All times are in weeks and costs are in thousands of dollars.

Activity	Immediate Predecessor	Completion Time		Estimated Cost	
		Regular	Crash	Regular	Crash
A	—	5	3	45	50
B	A	4	2	8	10
C	A	6	4	9	12
D	A	10	7	15	20
E	B	8	5	30	40
F	C	7	5	14	18
G	C	6	6	28	28
H	D	5	4	5	8
I	E, F	8	7	14	18
J	E, F	6	3	25	35
K	H	4	3	12	15
L	G, J, K	11	9	22	28
M	H	8	5	14	28
N	I	7	6	21	26

a. Construct a PERT/CPM network representing this project.
b. What is the critical path of this network?
c. What is the projected regular completion cost of this project?
d. How much would it cost to reduce the completion time by 4 weeks? By 6 weeks?

19. The following set of activities, completion times, and costs have been identified as necessary before an emergency relief effort to a drought-stricken region in Africa can be undertaken. Times are in days and costs are in thousands of dollars.

Activity	Immediate Predecessor	Completion Time		Estimated Cost	
		Regular	Crash	Regular	Crash
A	—	4	2	5	8
B	—	5	4	10	12
C	A	6	4	9	12
D	A	8	6	12	18
E	B, C	12	9	25	35
F	B, C	10	8	16	20
G	E	6	4	12	16
H	F	4	4	8	8
I	D	6	4	12	16
J	D	8	6	24	32
K	H	4	2	8	16
L	H	15	12	30	40
M	G, J, K	5	4	22	28
N	L, M	12	9	24	34

a. Construct a PERT/CPM network representing this project.
b. What is the critical path of the network?

c. What is the projected regular completion cost of this project?
d. How much would it cost to reduce the completion time by 5 days? By 10 days?

20. The following set of activities, estimated completion times, and cost estimates have been identified by the administrator for a local children's hospital as being necessary to start the annual fund-raising drive. All times are in days and costs are in hundreds of dollars.

Activity	Immediate Predecessor	Completion Time		Estimated Cost	
		Regular	Crash	Regular	Crash
A	—	8	6	12	16
B	—	4	3	8	12
C	A	7	5	3	5
D	A	10	8	14	20
E	A	8	6	8	12
F	B	6	6	3	3
G	C	6	4	5	4
H	D	7	4	8	6
I	E, F	8	5	7	6
J	G, H	9	6	4	3
K	I	6	4	2	1

a. Draw a PERT/CPM network representing this project.
b. What is the critical path of the network?
c. What is the projected regular completion cost of this project?
d. How much would it cost to reduce the completion time by 3 days? By 5 days?
e. What is the shortest possible time in which the project can be completed?

21. Find the daily cost projections associated with the regular completion times for the activities in problem 17, for both the earliest and latest start times. Assume the costs are uniformly distributed over time.

22. Find the weekly cost projections associated with the regular completion times for the activities in problem 18, for both the earliest and latest start times. Assume the costs are uniformly distributed over time.

23. Find the daily cost projections associated with the regular completion times for the activities in problem 19, for both the earliest and latest start times. Assume that all activities have a 25% fixed cost component and after that the costs are uniformly distributed over time.

24. Find the daily cost projections associated with the regular completion times for the activities in problem 20, for both the earliest and latest start times. The fixed costs for the activities are listed below. Assume that, after the fixed costs are incurred, all additional costs are a linear function of completion time.

Activity	Fixed Cost	Activity	Fixed Cost
A	$800	G	$200
B	$300	H	$300
C	$100	I	$300
D	$400	J	$200
E	$200	K	$50
F	$100		

Chapter Glossary

Activity An individual task, or component, of an overall project. In a PERT/CPM network, an activity is represented by a branch (line) or an arc.

Backward pass A calculation procedure, beginning at the final node and moving to the starting node of a PERT/CPM network, used to determine the latest finish and latest start times for each activity.

Beta probability distribution A continuous probability distribution formed by the optimistic, pessimistic, and most likely estimates of activity completion time.

Branch A line used to represent an activity in a PERT/CPM network.

Crashing the network The process of reducing project completion time by reducing the completion time of selected activities. Usually, crashing involves increasing the overall project cost.

Critical activity An activity on the critical path.

Critical path The sequence of activities through a PERT/CPM network which takes the longest to complete.

Critical path method (CPM) A network procedure originally used to plan and control engineering and construction projects for which single-point completion-time estimates could be made.

Dummy activity An imaginary activity with no cost or completion time, used to preserve the proper sequencing in a PERT/CPM network.

Earliest finish (start) time The earliest time at which an activity may be completed (started).

Event In a PERT/CPM network, the beginning or ending of an activity.

Expected completion time In PERT/CPM, the mean of the beta distribution described by the optimistic, pessimistic, and most likely estimates of completion time.

Float The difference between an activity's earliest start and latest start times. It indicates how long an activity can be delayed before affecting overall project completion time. Also called *slack*.

Forward pass A calculation procedure, starting at the beginning node and moving to the final node of a PERT/CPM network, used to determine the earliest start and earliest finish times for each activity.

Latest finish (start) time The time by which an activity must be completed (started) so as not to delay the overall project completion time.

Most likely time estimate An activity completion-time estimate, indicating the most probable time.

Node In a PERT/CPM network, the point where an activity line begins or ends, representing an event.

Optimistic time estimate An activity completion-time estimate made by assuming all steps needed to complete the activity will proceed as planned.

Path In a PERT/CPM network, any sequence of activities leading from the beginning node to the ending node.

PERT/Cost An extension of PERT/CPM used in planning, scheduling, and controlling project costs.

Pessimistic time estimate In PERT/CPM, a completion-time estimate indicating the maximum amount of time needed to complete an activity.

Predecessor An activity which must be completed before another activity can start.

Program evaluation and review technique (PERT) A network procedure originally used to plan and control research-related projects where probabilistic completion-time estimates were required.

Work package A unit of cost control in a PERT/Cost system. A natural grouping of interrelated activities when considered on a cost basis.

Chapter References

BOOKS

Anderson, D. R., D. J. Sweeney, and T. A. Williams. *An Introduction to Management Science,* 5th ed. St. Paul, Minn.: West, 1988.

Levin, R. I., D. S. Rubin, J. P. Stinson, and E. S. Gardner, Jr. *Quantitative Approaches to Management,* 7th ed. New York: McGraw-Hill, 1989.

Shogun, Andrew W. *Management Science.* Englewood Cliffs, N.J.: Prentice-Hall, 1988.

Stevenson, William J. *Introduction to Management Science.* Homewood, Ill.: Irwin, 1989.

Weist, J., and F. Levy. *Management Guide to PERT-CPM,* 2d ed. Englewood Cliffs, N.J.: Prentice-Hall, 1977.

ARTICLES

Kaimann, R. A., and F. R. Probst. "PERT—Review Possibilities." *Journal of Systems Management,* Vol. 23 (June), 1972.

Koehler, A. B., and R. H. MacClure. "The Use of Arcs and Nodes for the Determination of Critical Paths in PERT/CPM Networks." *Decision Sciences,* Vol. 10, 1979.

Mini Case

CASE 1

MEETING PLANNERS, INC.

In May 1987, Nancy Ferguson and Mary Heaton left their jobs with a major auto parts manufacturer to start their own business, called Meeting Planners, Inc. The idea for forming their company came about somewhat by accident. For several years before her departure from the parts company, Nancy had been in charge of planning two or three major sales meetings each year. The company's entire marketing and sales staff—more than 200 people—would travel to some desirable destination for the meetings, which generally lasted two to five days each. Nancy took care of almost all the details for the meetings, such as arranging for airline flights, selecting the hotel, planning meal functions, arranging for speakers, and setting up recreational activities. She enjoyed the work a great deal and was very good at it.

But, in late 1986, the vice-president of operations made two decisions which changed things for Nancy. First, recognizing Nancy's talent for organizing and planning, he promoted her to a new position as director of corporate communications. Second, he decided that the work that Nancy had been doing would be contracted out to a professional meeting planner. At first Nancy was excited about the promotion and the new position. But after a few months, it became apparent the change had been a mistake. The focus of her work became writing and editing operations and procedures manuals for various divisions in the company. Although she was effective at this type of work, the new position wasn't what she had expected. Besides, she found that she missed the interaction with people and the challenge of meeting deadlines, which she had enjoyed so much in her old job as meeting planner.

At about this same time, Mary Heaton, from the marketing department, asked Nancy to help her plan a large meeting in another state. Nancy was happy to offer her assistance. Because the outside contractor had a schedule conflict and couldn't handle the planning for Mary's meeting, the two future partners made all the arrangements themselves. Nancy even took some time off from her regular job to attend the meeting and help Mary with last-minute details. The women worked very well together, and they were pleased to see that everything went as planned. Everyone agreed that the meeting was a big success.

During the course of this collaboration, Nancy and Mary discussed their feelings of frustration over being stuck in regular jobs they disliked. The dissatisfaction, coupled with a flood of compliments on their planning and organizational skills, both during and after the meeting, led them to explore the possibility of starting their own business. And, as the saying goes, the rest is history.

When they started Meeting Planners, Inc., in May 1987, Mary and Nancy were the only employees; now there are five full-time employees and two part-time assistants. With a lot of hard work and a bit of luck, the partners have created a successful business and enjoy the challenge of finding new clients. So far, they have planned meetings for medical associations, national accounting firms, and a variety of companies in the auto industry—even their former employer.

Last March, Meeting Planners was approached by representatives of a large professional association for help in planning a conference to be held in 2 years. The association, made up of college professors who teach quantitative business courses, wants to have its biennial national meeting somewhere in Hawaii. The association expects that more than 2000 people would attend the conference. Although the association had previously planned all its own conferences, the meetings have grown so large that the board of directors elected to contract for the services of a professional meeting planner. The association wants the planner to take care of everything: selecting the conference site, negotiating with the hotel for meeting space and hotel rooms, arranging mealtime functions, planning recreational outings and other activities, and publishing a proceedings that includes all the papers presented at the conference.

Both Nancy and Mary realized that if they took this job and successfully managed the Hawaii conference, they could probably count on more business from the association. In addition, a success would give them entree into the "big meeting" market (where the "big bucks" are). However, they knew that before committing to such a large meeting they would need to think the project through and develop a formal planning model. They decided to use PERT/CPM to help them assess the project timing. They thought that, if it accomplished nothing else, just listing the required activities and organizing them in the proper sequence would be beneficial in preparing a bid on the project.

ASSIGNMENT

Put yourself in Nancy and Mary's place. Make a list of the major required activities for the academic association's meeting. Determine which activities are predecessors and which are successors. Provide single-point time estimates (use days as the unit of measure) and develop a PERT/CPM chart which shows the critical activities and how much slack the noncritical activities have. Estimate the costs for each activity and determine what the total project will cost Meeting Planners, Inc.

Chapter 11

SPECIALIZED NETWORK MODELS

Chapter Outline

Chapter 11

Why You Need to Know

The PERT/CPM models discussed in Chapter 10 are extensively used for managing medium to large projects. However, the application of network models is not limited to project planning and control. Many organizations, particularly those which must determine the best way to handle the distribution of materials, information, people, or capacity, use one of a number of specially formulated network models.

These organizations have found that their costs or revenues may involve factors that can be represented by the node-and-arc configuration introduced in Chapter 10. For instance, a parts supply company with dispatch service will be interested in scheduling delivery calls on a route that will minimize the time needed to get from the point of dispatch to the service locations. A wholesale distribution company will be interested in how much additional capacity exists in its distribution network when considering taking on a new line of merchandise. When planning a city bus system, the decision makers will be interested in connecting all possible bus stops within a network that has minimum total travel distance.

A number of network models have been devised for situations like those just mentioned. These models, which are extensions of the PERT/CPM logic, generally seek to minimize the cost of providing a service.

Many network problems were originally formulated as linear programming problems. But because the linear programming formulations were often large and complex, specialized network models were developed to simplify the solution process. This chapter discusses three of the most widely used specialized network solution techniques. The chances are very good that when you are working in business, you will encounter situations where one or more of these techniques can be applied.

Chapter Objectives

The objective of this chapter is to introduce three widely used special-purpose network-based algorithms. In particular, we will discuss (a) the *shortest-route algorithm,* used in determining the minimum travel time or travel distance between a dispatch point and a destination; (b) the *maximum-flow algorithm,* used in determining the total flow capacity in a distribution network; and (c) the *minimum-spanning-tree algorithm,* used in determining the selection of arcs that will connect all nodes in a network according to some minimum distance, time, or cost criterion.

After studying the material in this chapter, you should be able to:

1. Identify a situation that can be represented as a shortest-route problem.
2. Formulate and solve the shortest-route algorithms for selected problems.
3. Identify a situation that can be represented as a minimum-spanning-tree problem.
4. Formulate and solve the minimum-spanning-tree algorithms for selected problems.
5. Identify a situation that can be represented as a maximum-flow problem.
6. Formulate and solve the maximum-flow algorithms for selected problems.

11-1 A BRIEF HISTORY OF SPECIALIZED NETWORK MODELS

In many ways the history of network models parallels the history of linear programming, discussed in Chapter 2. Many of the same people pioneered development in both areas, and in fact, network models can be solved as linear programming problems.

In 1947, T. C. Koopmans first associated properties of optimal and nonoptimal solutions with network models. In the following few years, Koopmans, George Dantzig, and others were busy formulating linear programming solutions to network models and generally developing the theory behind network solution procedures. By the mid-1950s, the three types of network models discussed in this chapter—shortest route, minimum spanning tree, and maximum flow—had been formulated and solved using linear programming. However, the linear programming solution to a network model is generally complex and difficult to formulate; thus, the next effort was to develop more efficient solution procedures. The three procedures discussed in this chapter resulted from that effort and were in use by the mid-1960s.

11-2 A SHORTEST-ROUTE PROBLEM

This year has been hectic for Shirley McLaughlin, director of customer service for Optic Machine Tools of Santa Ana, California. Optic Machine introduced a new visual sensing and controlling device that is compatible with most computer-controlled manufacturing machines. The demand for the device was instantaneous; and total sales and profits for Optic Machine have skyrocketed. While the sudden surge in profitability has been great for the company, it has also attracted the attention of larger companies, as well as a few well-known "takeover artists." At present, all the stock in Optic Machine is held by a small group of original investors and employees, who have not been interested in buyout overtures through the years. However, some shareholders were recently impressed after listening to representatives of a larger manufacturing company who claim they have the expertise to better manage Optic Machine's new products.

Because of the takeover pressure, Optic Machine's present management group is anxious to prove they have the experience, knowledge, and product awareness to effectively handle the surge in demand. Consequently, all levels of the organization have felt the pressure to increase productivity and "work smarter, not harder."

Customer service, Shirley McLaughlin's department, has become an increasingly important part of Optic Machine's competitive strategy. The new scanning/control unit, which is affected by wear in the machines it controls, has an internal diagnostic component that indicates when adjustment is needed, but it cannot self-adjust. A limited number of calibrations are included in the purchase price. When a unit needs recalibration, the customer calls Optic Machine's customer service department, which then schedules a call by one of the company's field representatives. Once the guaranteed number of free calibrations have been done, customers are billed for additional service calls.

The calibration procedure is a standard operation that is easily performed, but it is often quite time-consuming. Prompt customer service is an important marketing tool for Optic Machine, but now Shirley's department is feeling the same productivity challenges as the rest of the company. Currently, field representatives working out of regional service offices are randomly scheduled. Depending on the complexity of the adjustment process, a representative may be able to make only one call a day— although obviously it would be preferable to make more. Until now, each representative has simply been assigned to a service call by the dispatcher in the regional office. When the call was finished, the representative would phone the dispatcher and, if time allowed, would be given another call.

While the time spent traveling to a service call is an underlying cost, before now it had not been a scheduling consideration. Although Shirley has long felt the department could schedule its service calls more efficiently, she had not taken any steps to reduce travel costs. Now she has decided to devise a service plan which will allow the field representatives to make more calls in the same number of working days, thereby increasing productivity and reducing travel costs.

THE SERVICE NETWORK

Shirley McLaughlin has decided to try out the new scheduling procedure in the southern Indiana regional office in Bloomington. Typically, each service technician is dispatched in one direction from the office (i.e., east, south, etc.). After completing the first call, the technician phones the office and, if there is time, is given another service call in the same general area.

A limited set of possible service calls, and routings, from the Bloomington office

Figure 11-1
Service area for Bloomington regional office, Optic Machine Tools

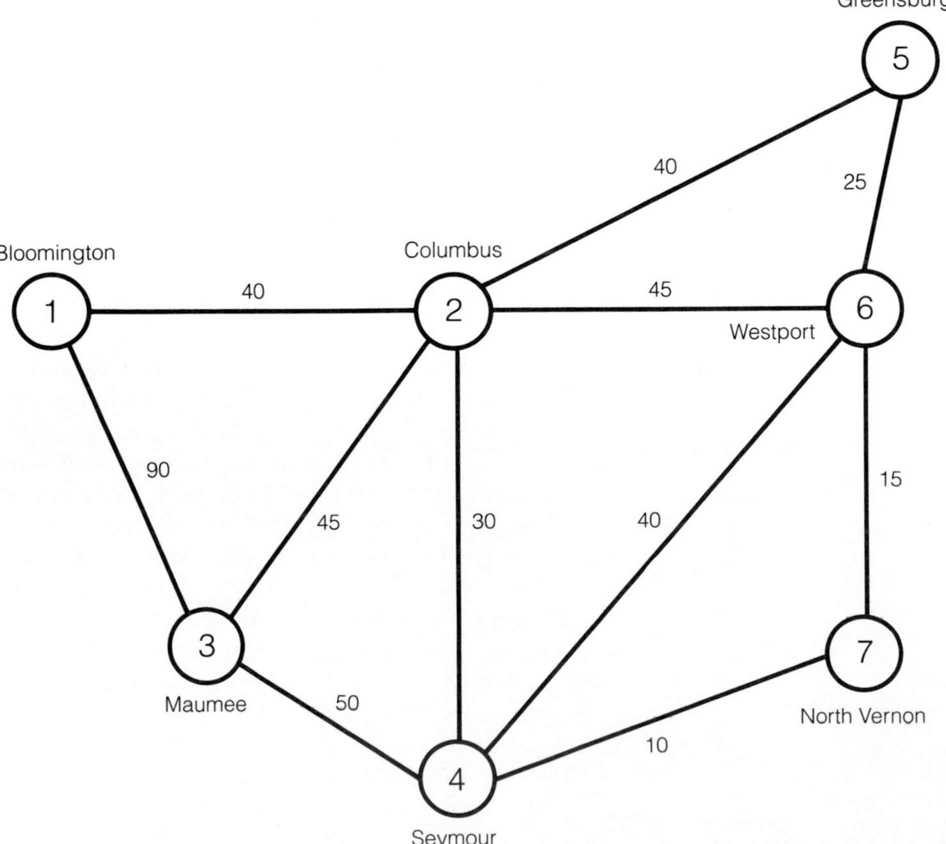

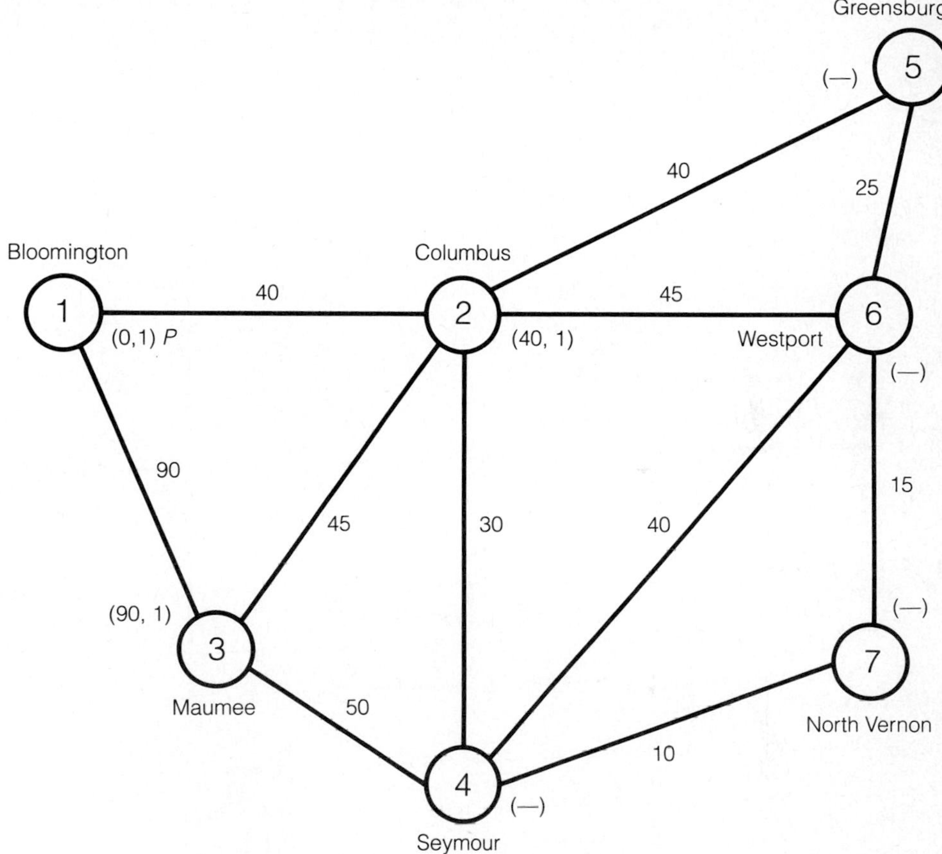

Figure 11-2
Source node and first permanent node

would involve the following cities: Columbus, Maumee, Seymour, Westport, North Vernon, and Greensburg. These locations and the driving times between them are represented by the network diagram in Figure 11-1. Recall that a **network** is a set of points, or nodes, that are connected by branches along which some item may **flow**. In this case, the network represents the flow of service calls. The **nodes**, the starting or ending points for one or more branches in the network, are numbered 1–7 and represent the cities. The **branches**, also called arcs or activities, represent the travel routes between the cities. The numbers on the arcs represent the travel times (in minutes) between cities, but arc length is *not* proportional to travel time.

THE SHORTEST-ROUTE ALGORITHM

The **shortest-route algorithm** is a model for finding the shortest path from any **source node**, or starting point, to any set of destination nodes. Recall that a **path** is a sequential series of branches providing a route between two specified nodes in a network.

The solution method we will introduce here was developed in 1959. (The Dijkstra article listed in Chapter References provides background information.) This method involves assigning each node a label, either permanent or temporary, which represents the driving time from the source node to any specified node. This label becomes permanent when we are sure the assigned time is actually the minimum from all possible routes. The solution procedure is described in the following paragraphs.

The first step is to assign a permanent label to the source node (Bloomington) and temporary labels to all other nodes that can be reached directly from Bloomington. The labels designate the travel time directly from the source node. Figure 11-2 shows

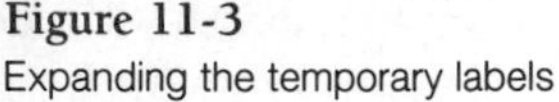

Figure 11-3
Expanding the temporary labels

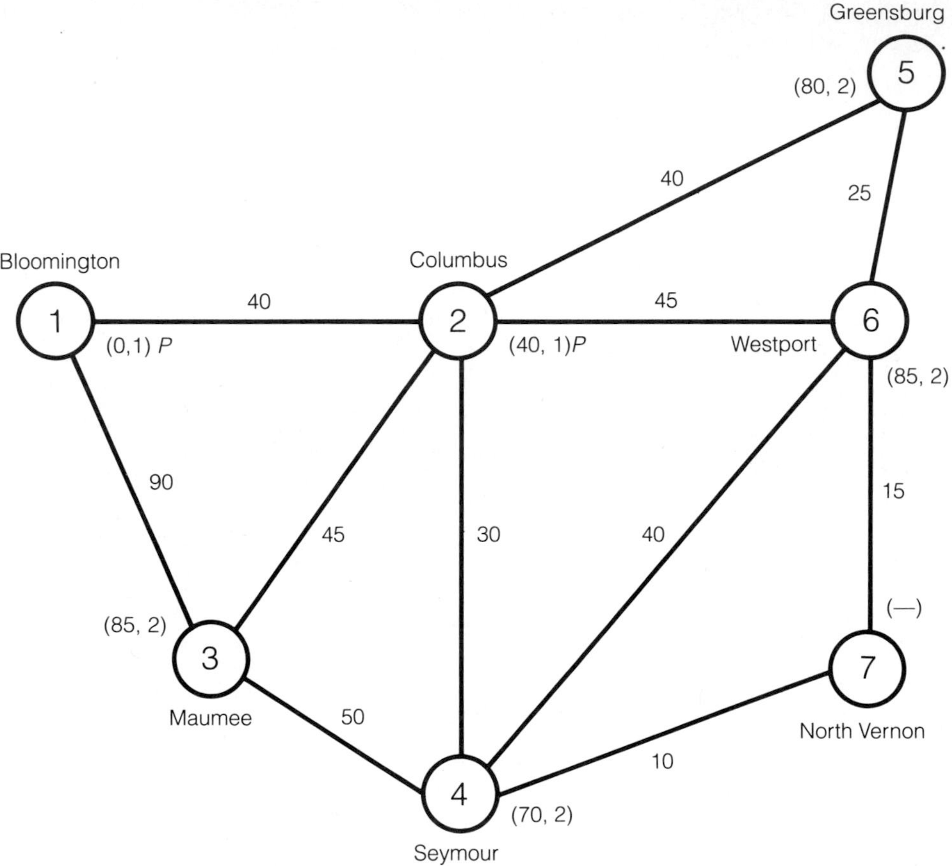

the results of this step. We have assigned the label (0, 1) to node 1, Bloomington, which indicates that Bloomington can be reached in zero driving time from Bloomington. The notation (0, 1)*P* indicates the node is permanent. Columbus (node 2) and Maumee (node 3) are given temporary labels, (40, 1) and (90, 1), indicating that we can reach Columbus in 40 minutes by driving directly from Bloomington and can reach Maumee in 90 minutes directly from Bloomington. All other locations are initially given "blank" labels, (—), indicating they cannot be reached directly from Bloomington.

In the second step, we examine the nodes that can be reached directly from the source node. Here, these are nodes 2 (Columbus) and 3 (Maumee), which have the temporary labels (40, 1) and (90, 1). We pick the temporary label with the shortest driving time and change it to a permanent label. By doing this, we reason that if we ever have to drive from Bloomington to Columbus we will go directly, since there is no faster route. The permanent designation for this label is seen in Figure 11-3.

At step 3, we consider all the nodes that can be reached from either the source node (1) or the permanent node found in step 2 (Columbus). This will only be node 3, Maumee. We can either drive directly from Bloomington in 90 minutes or first drive to Columbus in 40 minutes and then to Maumee in an additional 45 minutes (see Figure 11-1). Given the choice, we will drive to Maumee by first going to Columbus, since this will take only 85 minutes. We change the temporary label for Maumee to (85, 2), indicating we will reach node 3 through node 2 rather than directly from 1. We expand the temporary labeling of all nodes that can be reached from Columbus (node 2), as shown in Figure 11-3. The (70, 2) temporary label for node 4, for instance, indicates we can reach Seymour in 70 minutes by going through Columbus (i.e., 40 minutes from Bloomington to Columbus plus 30 minutes from Columbus to Seymour). The (80, 2) temporary label for node 5, Greensburg, indicates that getting to Greensburg through Columbus will take 80 minutes total travel time. Westport, node 6, has a temporary label of (85, 2). And, North Vernon, node 7, still has the label (—) because it can't be reached directly from Columbus.

The temporary label with the shortest driving time through Columbus (node 2) is Seymour; so we assign it a *P* (permanent), as shown in Figure 11-4. If the service schedule ever calls for a trip from Bloomington to Seymour, the shortest route is through Columbus.

In the fourth step, we continue to look at the remaining nonpermanent nodes and assign temporary labels based on the shortest driving times from the nodes with permanent designations. Looking at Figure 11-4, we see the following labels: at node 3, (85, 2); node 5, (80, 2); node 6, (85, 2); and node 7, (80, 4). Two nodes, 5 and 7, tie for the shortest driving time at 80 minutes; therefore, we change both node 5 (Greensburg) and node 7 (North Vernon) from temporary to permanent, as shown in Figure 11-4. Now only nodes 3 and 6 are temporary.

Figure 11-4
Picking the next permanent node

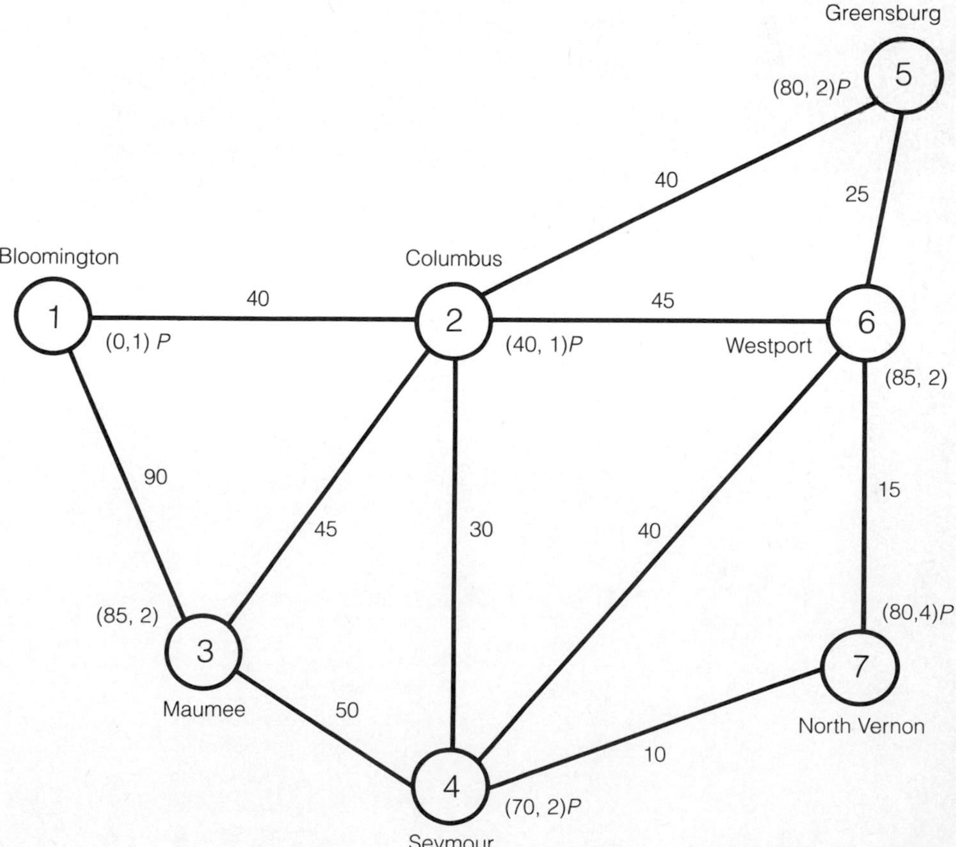

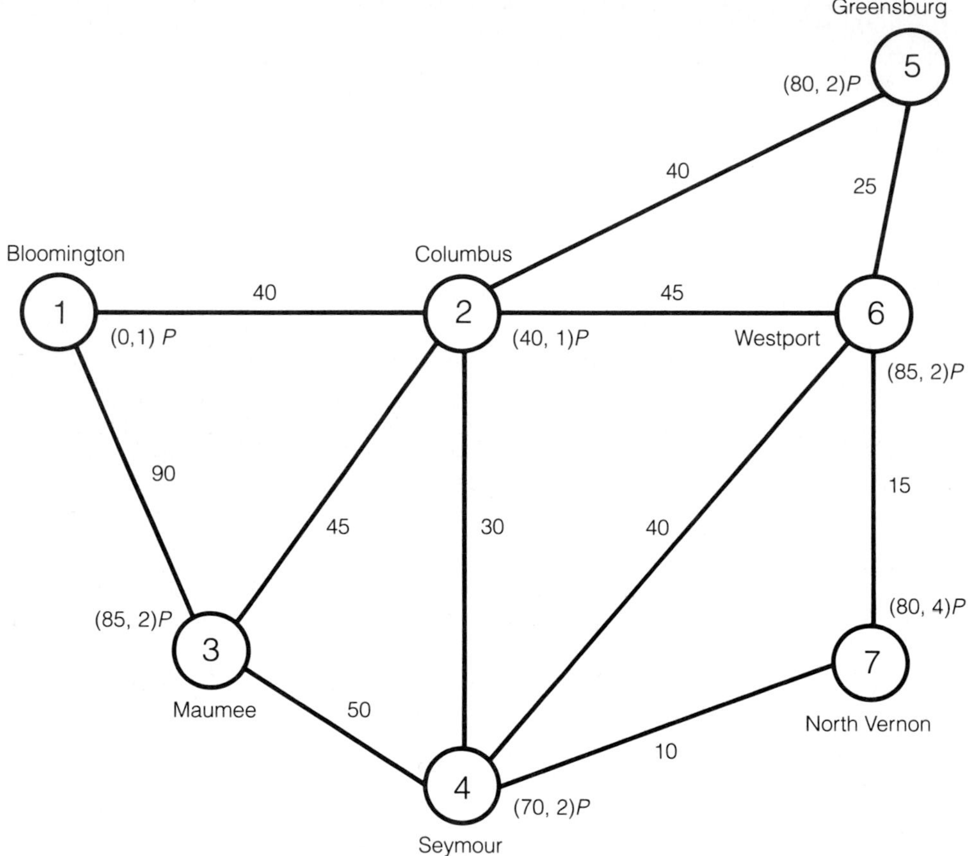

Figure 11-5
Final network for Optic Machine Tools problem

In the final step, we change the two remaining temporary nodes to permanent assignments. Since both nodes 3 (Maumee) and 6 (Westport) have a minimum travel time of 85 minutes, we change both to permanent, as shown in Figure 11-5. As there are no other nodes, the labeling process is complete.

Shirley is now able to construct a routing schedule indicating the fastest routes from Bloomington to the six potential service locations. This routing, based upon the network in Figure 11-5, is given in Table 11-1. She could develop routing lists like this using all potential service locations as source locations and would be able to specify all minimum-driving-time routes.

This example has shown how the shortest-route model can be used to find the

Table 11-1 FASTEST ROUTES FROM BLOOMINGTON TO SERVICE LOCATIONS

Destination	Fastest Route	Driving Time (minutes)
Columbus	Direct	40
Maumee	Through Columbus	85
Seymour	Through Columbus	70
Greensburg	Through Columbus	80
Westport	Through Columbus	85
North Vernon	Columbus, Seymour	80

minimum traveling time between any source and destination. An easy extension of the model would be to consider travel distance instead of time. Another alternative would be to incorporate travel costs and determine the minimum-cost travel route between any two points. Depending on the variable we are trying to minimize, we could get totally different routings. However, regardless of the unit of measure, the shortest-route model is solved in the same manner.

11-3 A MINIMUM-SPANNING-TREE PROBLEM

Carl Santos, operations director of the Key Bank of Missouri, has finally completed a series of emergency meetings. Key Bank recently installed a computer communications system linking its major information processing centers throughout Missouri. The system allows all processing centers to communicate with all other centers and greatly increases the speed of processing transactions. The system also limits the ability of someone to withdraw more than the daily limit from the automatic teller machines scattered across the state. Since the network Key Bank is using is linked to several other networks in the United States, the emergency meetings were called to consider how to deal with the possibility of a computer "virus" disrupting the system.

The risk of having the bank's records modified or destroyed by a virus is totally unacceptable to the top management committee of Key Bank, and the chairman wondered why someone had not foreseen this possibility. However, the advantages of a computer network are so great, the top management committee was unwilling to revert back to the old communications method. The agreed-on solution to the potential virus problem was to develop a dedicated network for the bank's computers.

A consultant has just made a presentation on the types of dedicated networks and

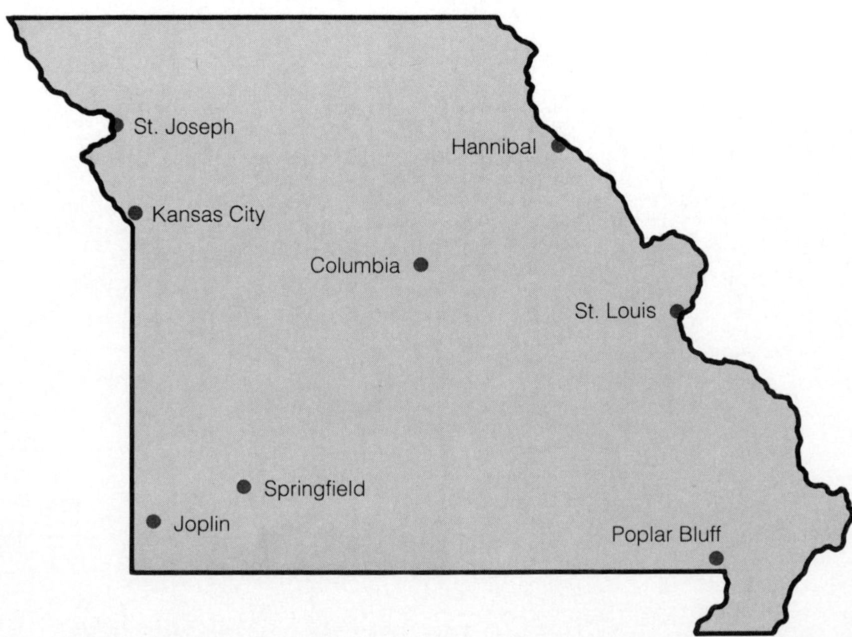

Figure 11-6
Key Bank computer centers

the costs of installing them. To a large extent, the cost of installing the network is dependent on the total distance between computers in the system. Therefore, the shortest network will generally also be the least expensive to set up.

The computer centers in the Key Bank network are shown in Figure 11-6. In the current network system, all centers are able to communicate directly with all other centers; but with only small modifications, Carl can make individual centers act as *transmission nodes* or *relay nodes*. For example, the Columbia center could communicate directly with the St. Louis center; or, if necessary, Columbia could relay information between St. Louis and Kansas City. At issue is how to connect the processing centers so that the total network cost is minimized. To do this, Carl will have to decide which centers should be transmission centers and which other centers these transmission centers should connect to.

THE MINIMUM-SPANNING-TREE ALGORITHM

To address the bank's problem, Carl can use a management science model called the **minimum-spanning-tree algorithm.** This model determines the set of branches, or arcs, in a network that provides the minimum path between all the nodes in the network. By modifying Figure 11-6 to include potential links and installation costs, as shown in Figure 11-7, we see the arrangement of nodes and arcs that has characterized our discussion of all networks to this point. The nodes represent the communication centers, and the arcs indicate the cost of installing the network between the centers.

The minimum-spanning-tree algorithm differs from most other management science tools because it is one in which making a series of "locally optimal" decisions

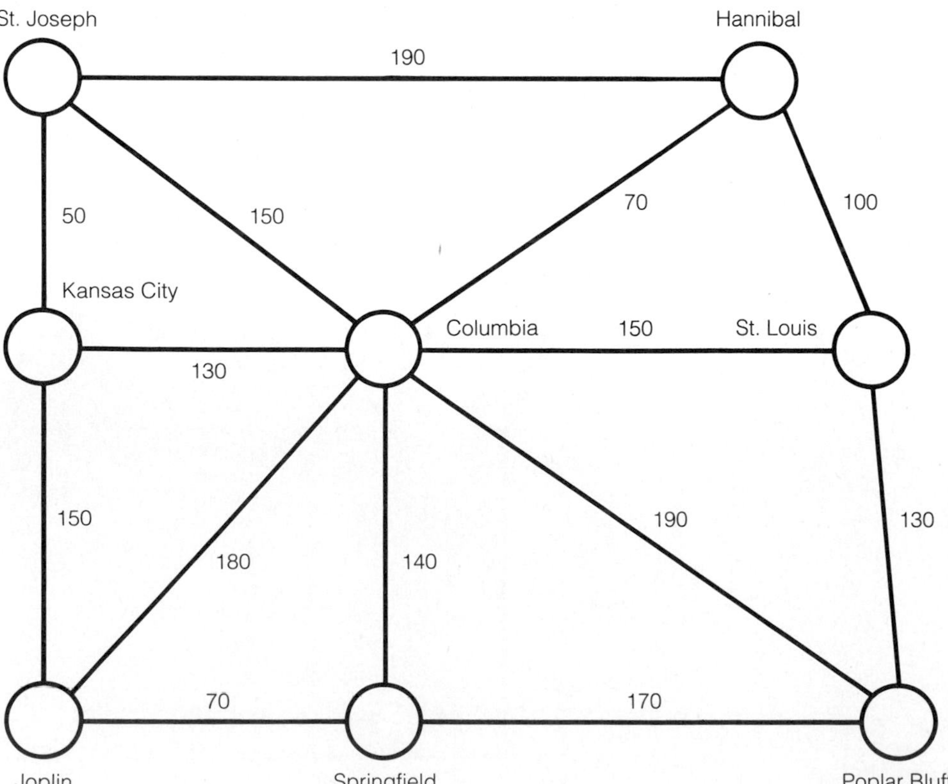

Note: Numbers on arcs represent installation costs in thousands of dollars.

Figure 11-7
Node-arc network of Key Bank computer centers

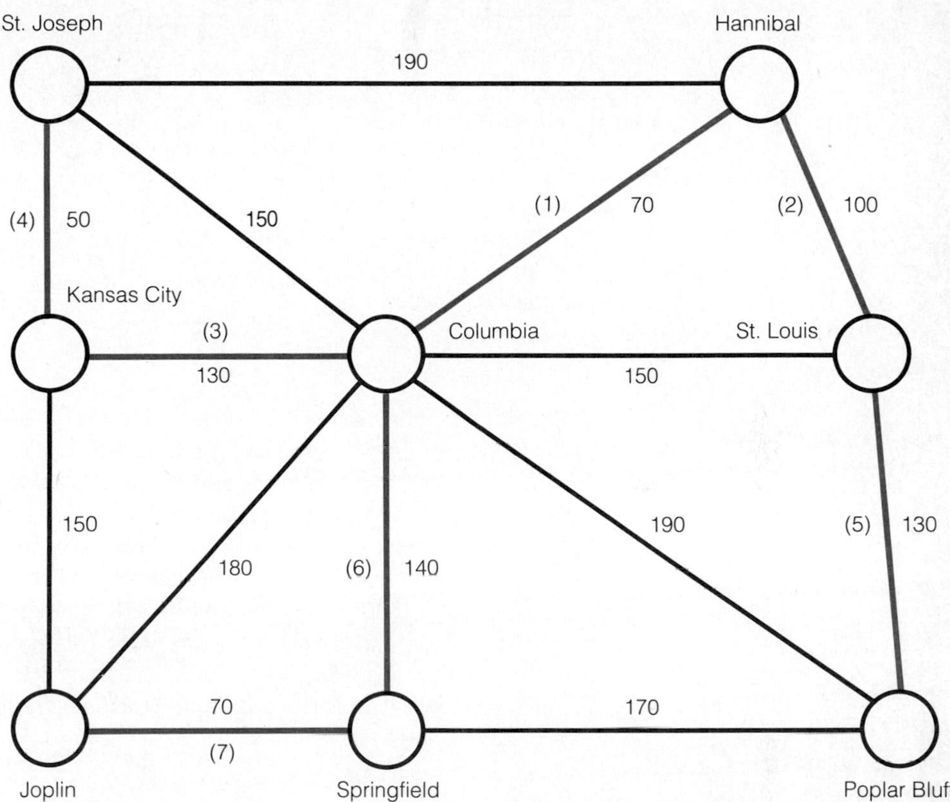

Figure 11-8
Minimum spanning tree for Key Bank network

will lead to the best overall decision. The solution procedure is as follows:

Step 1 Arbitrarily pick any node in the network and connect it to the node closest to it (i.e., the least-cost node).

Step 2 Find the unconnected node that is closest (lowest in cost) to one of the connected nodes. Connect these two nodes. Repeat this step until all the nodes are connected.

The only complicated part of the algorithm is what to do when ties occur, either in step 1 or in step 2. Although ties may be broken arbitrarily and the optimal solution will still be found; ties indicate that multiple optimal solutions may exist.

To demonstrate the solution procedure, let's return to Figure 11-7 and arbitrarily pick Columbia as the initial node. The lowest-cost node from Columbia is Hannibal. The numeral 70 indicates that a link between these two centers has a cost of $70,000. (All costs in Figures 11-7 through 11-10 are given in similar short form.) This link is shown as the color line labeled (1) in the network of Figure 11-8.

Next we consider the linking costs from both Columbia and Hannibal. After Hannibal, the least-cost link from Columbia is to Kansas City, with a cost of $130,000. The least-cost link from Hannibal is to St. Louis, at $100,000. Thus, we select the Hannibal to St. Louis arc and label it line (2), as shown in Figure 11-8.

For link (3) we have a tie, since both St. Louis to Poplar Bluff and Columbia to Kansas City have the same installation cost, $130,000. We can select either path. Suppose we arbitrarily pick Columbia to Kansas City and label it line (3) in Figure 11-8. Then the next selection will be from Kansas City to St. Joseph, at a cost of

Table 11-2 KEY BANK'S SPANNING-TREE COSTS

Arc	Cost
(1) Columbia to Hannibal	\$70,000
(2) Hannibal to St. Louis	\$100,000
(3) Columbia to Kansas City	\$130,000
(4) Kansas City to St. Joseph	\$50,000
(5) St. Louis to Poplar Bluff	\$130,000
(6) Columbia to Springfield	\$140,000
(7) Springfield to Joplin	\$70,000
	\$690,000

\$50,000. This is labeled line (4) in Figure 11-8. The St. Louis to Poplar Bluff line, at \$130,000, is next and is labeled line (5). Line (6) is the Columbia to Springfield line, at a cost of \$140,000; and line (7) is Springfield to Joplin, at \$70,000.

We have reached the final solution when all nodes in the network are connected. We see now in Figure 11-8 that all eight centers are connected with the seven lines. The total installation cost is \$690,000, the sum of the seven individual installation costs (Table 11-2). This is the minimum-cost network which will connect these eight centers. Note that several centers serve as relays for other centers. In this case, we can see that Columbia is a relay between Kansas City, Hannibal, and Springfield; and Hannibal is a relay between Columbia and St. Louis. This means that a transaction sent

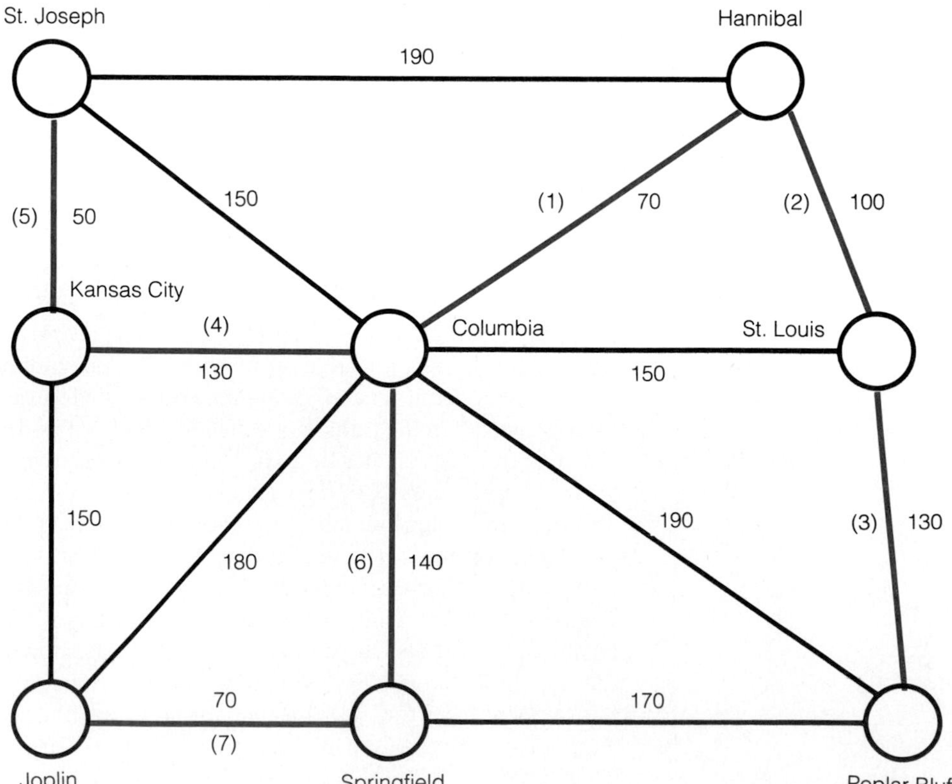

Figure 11-9
Key Bank alternate network for minimum-spanning-tree model

from Poplar Bluff to Springfield will go through St. Louis, Hannibal, and Columbia before reaching Springfield.

We mentioned earlier that when we encountered ties when solving the spanning-tree model, we have a choice as to which to select. This means there may be alternate optimal solutions. In our example, we faced a tie when forming line (3). Suppose that instead of choosing the Columbia–Kansas City link as line (3), we select St. Louis–Poplar Bluff, at the same cost, \$130,000 (see Figure 11–9). Continuing from this point, line (4) is formed between Columbia and Kansas City at a cost of \$130,000. Line (5) goes between Kansas City and St. Joseph, at a cost of \$50,000; and line (6) goes between Columbia and Springfield, at a cost of \$140,000. Finally, line (7) connects Springfield and Joplin at a cost of \$70,000. When we compare Figures 11-8 and 11-9, we see that the solutions are the same. In other examples, you may encounter multiple optimal solutions.

If you are skeptical about the ability of the spanning-tree algorithm to achieve the optimal solution regardless of the starting point, consider this additional example for the Key Bank problem. This time, suppose we start at Joplin. Figure 11-10 shows the resulting network. Line (1) will be formed between Joplin and Springfield at a cost of \$70,000; line (2), Springfield–Columbia, \$140,000; line (3), Columbia–Hannibal, \$70,000; line (4), Hannibal–St. Louis, \$100,000.

For line (5), we have a choice — Columbia–Kansas City and St. Louis–Poplar Bluff, both at \$130,000. We know that we can select either route, so we choose Columbia–Kansas City as line (5). Then, line (6) goes from Kansas City to St. Joseph, for \$50,000; and, finally, line (7), St. Louis–Poplar Bluff, \$130,000. As Figure 11-10

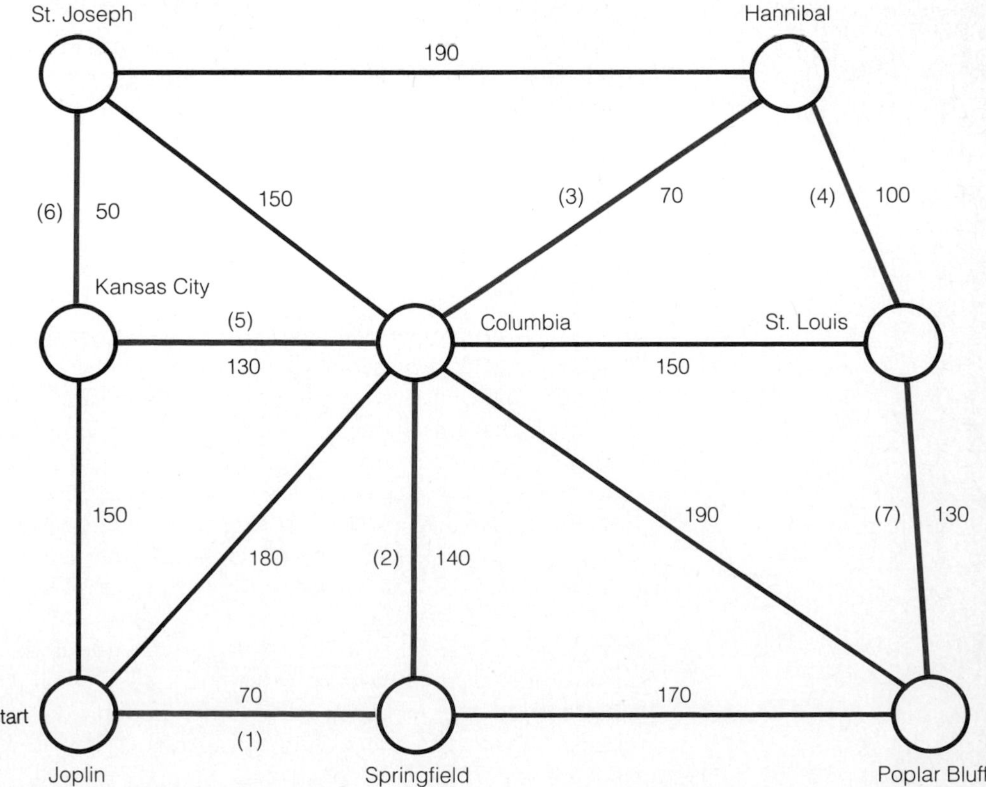

Figure 11-10
Alternate starting condition for Key Bank example

shows, the network is exactly the same as when we selected Columbia for the starting location.

The minimum-spanning-tree model is useful whenever a set of locations have to be linked and a cost is associated with each link. Key Bank's computer-linking problem is but one of a variety of situations for which this model can be used. For instance, it could be used in designing the water and sewer systems for a new subdivision. Also, companies may use the spanning-tree model to assess alternate material distribution routes, either within a large plant or between several separate locations.

Perhaps the most widespread application of the spanning-tree model is the planning of public transportation networks, where the nodes are the bus stops or train stations and the branches are the distances between the stops. A transportation planner would be interested in determining the routes that will connect all the stops in the minimum total travel distance. The model can also be expanded to include minimization of total linking time or cost, as discussed in section 11-2. The problems at the end of the chapter provide additional examples of how the minimum-spanning-tree model is used.

11-4 A MAXIMUM-FLOW PROBLEM

Midwest Natural Gas Company has just discovered a large natural gas field near Cheyenne, Wyoming. The discovery is a major event for the company, since its recoverable reserves had been declining for the past several years. Unfortunately, because the largest unfilled demand in its system is in the Chicago area, the company will have to transport the gas hundreds of miles to reach its consumers.

Robert Grisham, the gas company's operations manager, knows the company will have to construct a new gas line from the field to Cheyenne, but he hopes that sufficient capacity presently exists to transport the required gas levels from Cheyenne to Chicago. The company already has a gas line between Cheyenne and Des Moines, Iowa, which can handle some, but not all, of the new flow. Robert believes he can lease additional pipeline capacity from other carriers to cover both routes: Cheyenne – Des Moines and Des Moines – Chicago.

After considerable searching and a great many phone calls, he was able to find the leasable capacity represented by the network in Figure 11-11. Now Robert must determine the total system pipeline capacity between Cheyenne and Chicago and decide whether it is enough to transport the needed amount of gas. In addition, no matter whether the total system capacity is sufficient or not, he must determine how much of the available capacity to lease on each segment of the network. He may want to try using a management science network model called the **maximum-flow algorithm**, which can determine the maximum flow that can either enter a starting point or exit the ending point in a network for a given period of time.

THE MAXIMUM-FLOW ALGORITHM

In looking at Figure 11-11, we once again see the node and arc arrangement that characterizes all the networks we have discussed so far. In this network, the nodes represent the ends of segments of a pipeline and the arcs indicate the segments' leasable capacity. In general terms, **capacity** is defined as the amount of any item

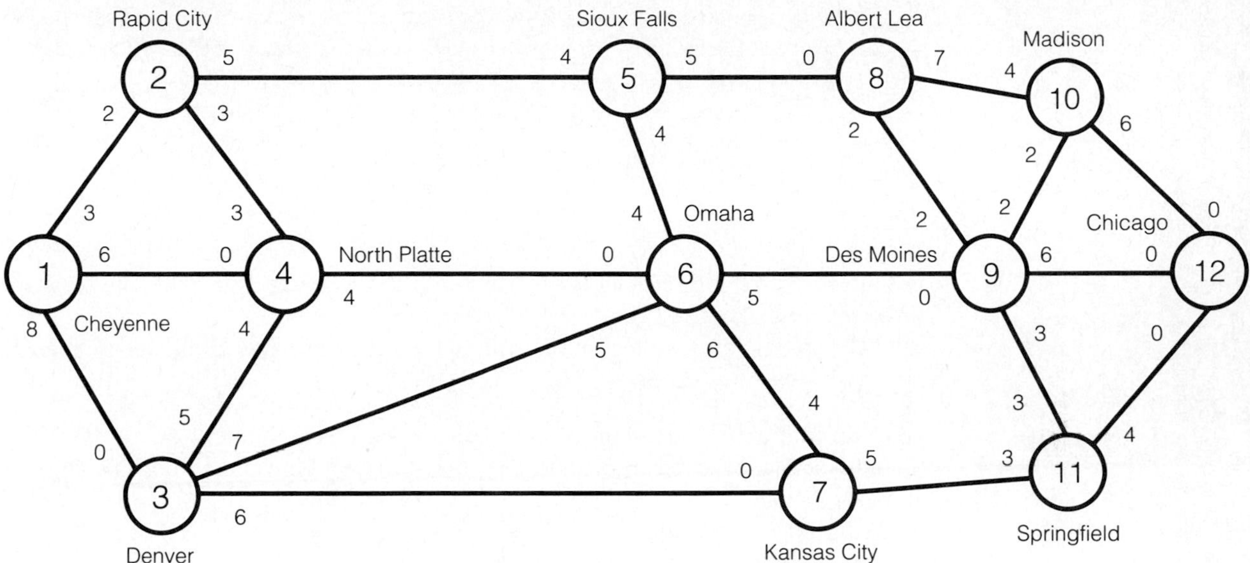

Note: Numerals on arcs represent pipeline capacity in thousands of cubic feet per minute.

Figure 11-11
Potential pipeline capacity for Midwest Natural Gas

that can move along the branch of a network; here it refers to the flow of natural gas. The starting node, Cheyenne, is called the **source**; and the ending node, Chicago, is the **sink**. Whatever flows through any network (natural gas, in this case) flows out of the source and into the sink. Because no storage is allowed at the nodes, the total amount that flows into a node must also flow *out* of the node.

In using the maximum-flow algorithm, we must recognize that some arcs of the network may allow flow in only one direction. For instance, the Omaha–Kansas City pipeline may have directional valves that allow flow only from Omaha to Kansas City but not in the reverse direction. Or the pipeline may have bidirectional valves, allowing flow in either direction. To represent this directional flow, we will use a standard notation.

Between any two nodes in the network, labeled 1 and 2 for this example, a flow of 2000 cubic feet per minute (cfm) in the direction 1 → 2, with no flow allowed in the opposite direction, 2 → 1, would be represented as follows:

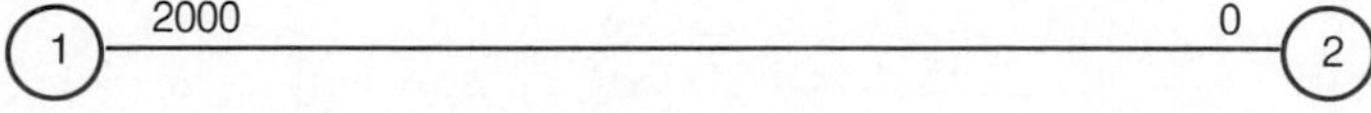

Alternatively, flows of 2000 cfm in the direction 1 → 2 and 1000 cfm in the direction 2 → 1 would be represented as:

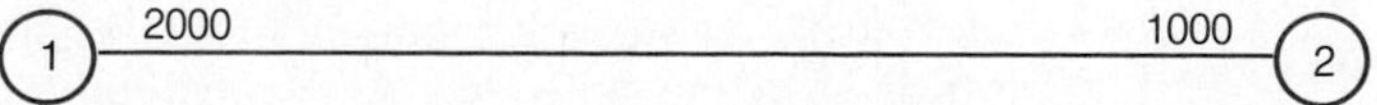

The total capacity of the line between nodes 1 and 2 is 3000 cfm, the sum of the capacities for both directions. The value that appears immediately adjacent to the node on any arc indicates the maximum amount that can flow into the line from that node.

This notation is used to represent flow capacities in the Midwest Natural Gas network (Figure 11-11). For instance, let's look at the arc between Cheyenne (node 1) and North Platte (node 4):

We see that from node 1 to node 4, there is a capacity of 6000 cfm and that no flow is permitted from node 4 to node 1. Therefore, the total capacity of the line between these two nodes is 6000 cfm.

The maximum-flow algorithm is based on the following intuitive-assignment approach:

1. Locate any path between the source node and the sink node which has positive flow (flow in the direction from source to sink) capacity between all nodes along the path.
2. Determine the minimum flow on the path selected in step 1 and let it be amount A_f. Now assume that the minimum flow amount, A_f, will pass through the entire network.
3. Decrease the flow capacity on all branches of the path identified in step 1 by the amount A_f.
4. Increase the *reverse* flow capacity of all branches identified in step 1 by the amount A_f.
5. Return to step 1 and continue as long as the total flow through the network can be increased.

Steps 1, 2, and 3 are fairly intuitive. Step 4 is the one that causes problems, since it implies either we can have flow through a network in a direction that is not physically possible or we have a total reverse flow that is greater than the capacity of the branch.

Perhaps the reasoning behind step 4 can be better understood by looking again at a branch of the network in Figure 11-11. The present capacity between Cheyenne and North Platte is 6000 cfm, and no reverse flow is allowed. If we allocate 4000 cfm to this branch, the notation becomes:

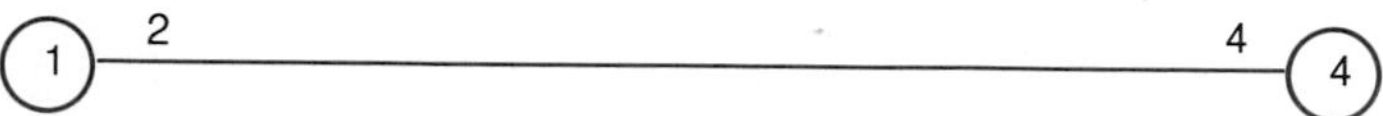

The change on the Cheyenne end of the branch should be obvious; since we have reduced the available flow out of this node from 6000 to 2000. But the change at the North Platte end (node 4) needs some explanation.

The 4000-cfm flow out of the North Platte node is termed *fictitious flow;* it indicates reduction in the original flow from Cheyenne. Fictitious flow is necessary for the maximum-flow algorithm, since it provides a mechanism for an initial assignment to be revised. For instance, we may initially make the 4000-cfm assignment on the branch from Cheyenne to North Platte but later want to reallocate some of this flow to the Cheyenne–Denver branch. Having the fictitious flow will allow us to modify the initial 4000-cfm assignment as part of the solution algorithm. If we did not have the fictitious flow, once an assignment was made it could not be reversed.

SOLVING A MAXIMUM-FLOW PROBLEM

Let's see how the solution procedure works for the Midwest Natural Gas problem.

Iteration 1

Using the previously defined five-step procedure, we will first pick a path with positive flow. Let's choose this route: Cheyenne–North Platte–Omaha–Des Moines—Chicago. The arc with the minimum capacity on this route is between North Platte and Omaha, with a value of 4 (representing 4000 cfm). We decrease the flow capacities of all routes on this path by 4 and increase the reverse flow capacities of these routes by the same amount. The results are shown in Figure 11-12.

Iteration 2

Now we choose a second path: Cheyenne–Denver–Kansas City–Springfield–Chicago. We see that the flow on this path is limited by the capacity of 4 on the Springfield–Chicago branch. Decreasing the flow capacities of all routes on this path by 4 and increasing the reverse flow capacities of these routes by the same amount gives us the results shown in Figure 11-13.

Iteration 3

Choosing the Cheyenne–Rapid City–Sioux Falls–Albert Lea–Madison–Chicago branch, we see the flow is limited by the capacity of 3 between Cheyenne and Rapid City. Performing the standard set of capacity changes gives us the results shown in Figure 11-14.

Figure 11-12
Midwest Natural Gas flow problem: iteration 1

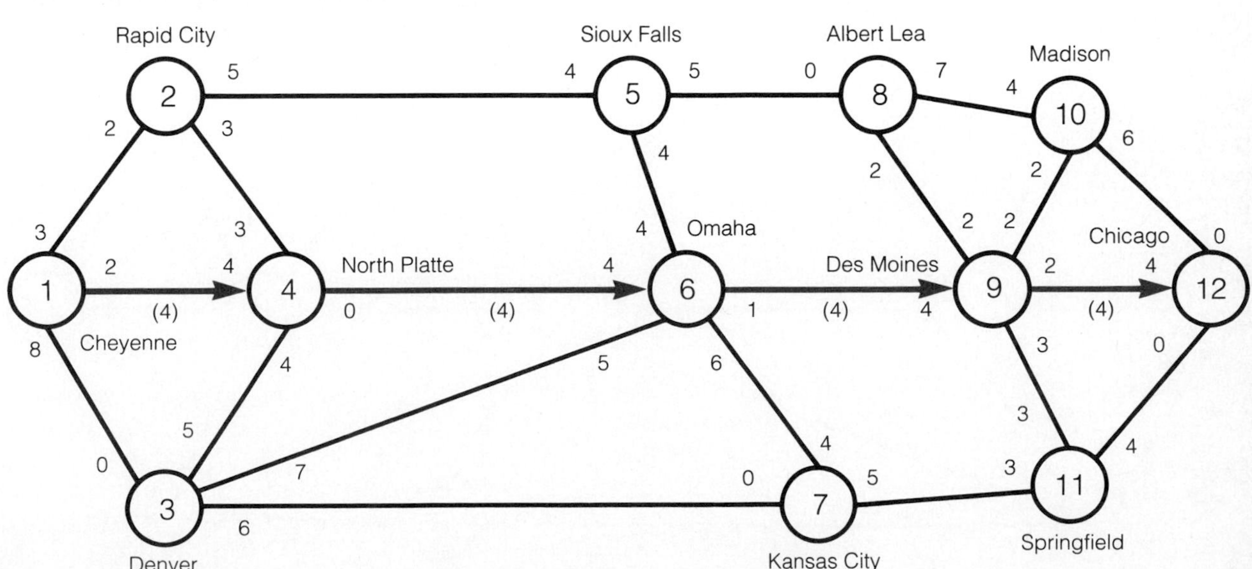

Note: Numerals in parentheses represent flow. The other numerals on the arcs represent pipeline capacity between nodes (all are in 000 cfm).

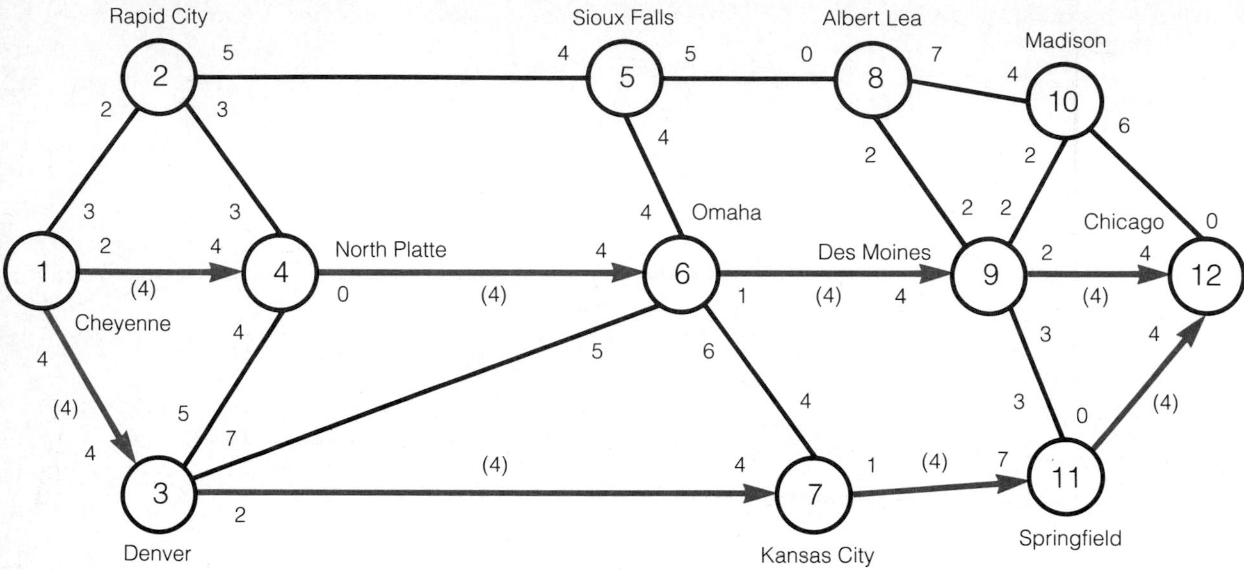

Figure 11-13
Midwest Natural Gas flow problem: iteration 2

Iteration 4

We have now picked the three obvious paths from Cheyenne; and in the case of the Cheyenne–Rapid City link, we have exhausted the pipeline capacity out of Cheyenne. However, we still have unused capacity on both the Cheyenne–North Platte link and the Cheyenne–Denver link. Let's start with the Cheyenne–North Platte route. Our problem here is that the capacity between North Platte and Omaha is exhausted; however, we can ship gas out of North Platte to Rapid City. The path analyzed on this iteration will be Cheyenne–North Platte–Rapid City–Sioux Falls–Albert Lea–

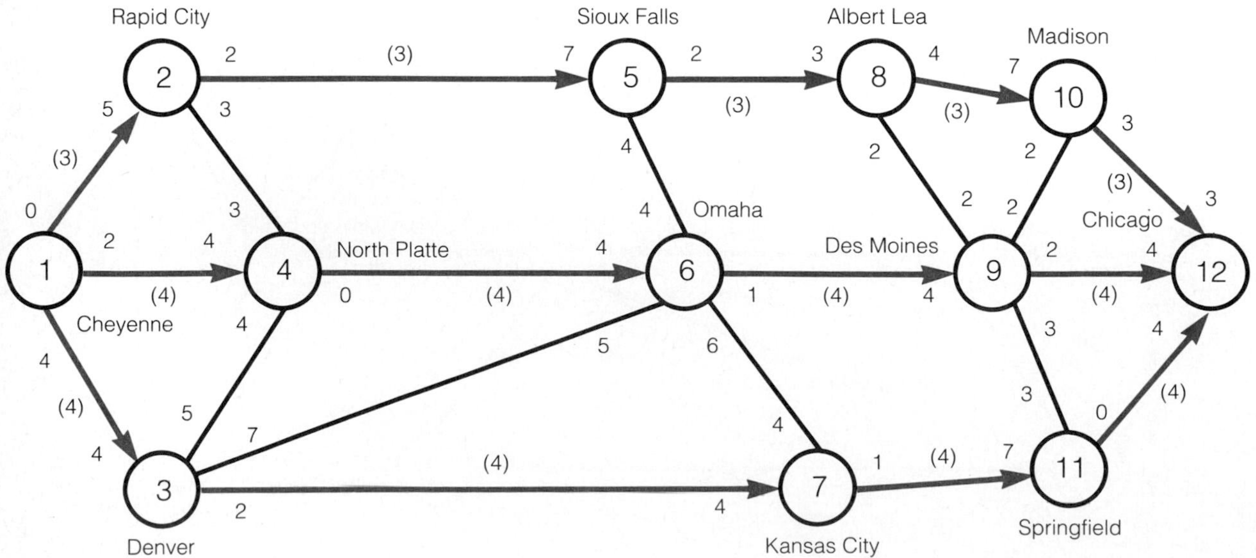

Figure 11-14
Midwest Natural Gas flow problem: iteration 3

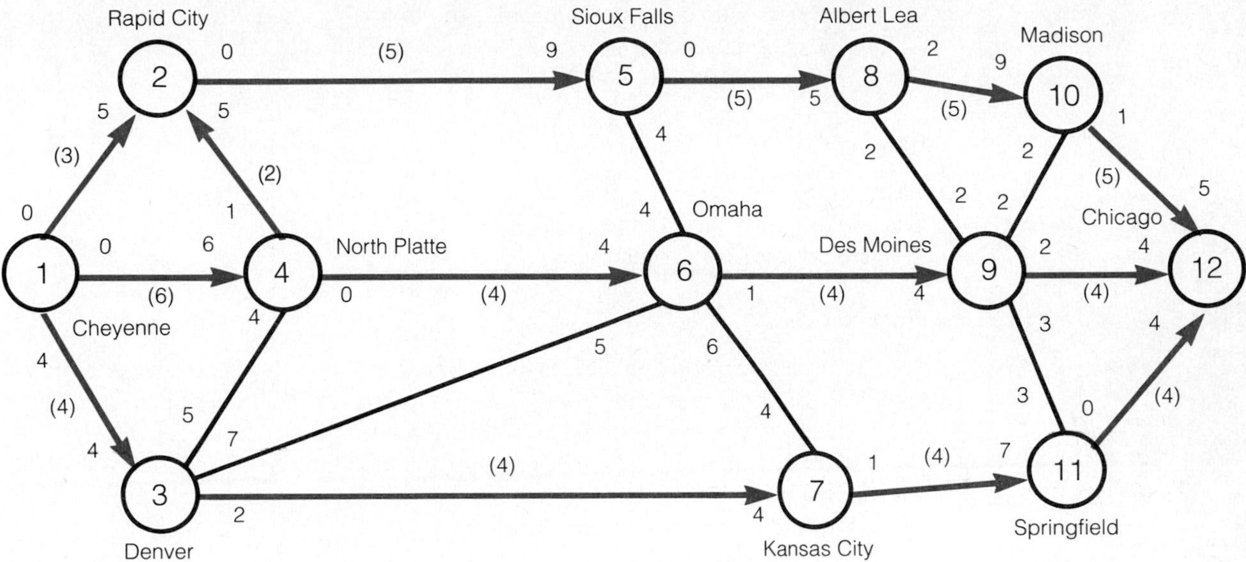

Figure 11-15
Midwest Natural Gas flow problem: iteration 4

Madison–Chicago. Looking at Figure 11-14, we see the limiting factor is 2, found on three links: Cheyenne–North Platte, Rapid City–Sioux Falls, and Sioux Falls–Albert Lea. Performing the standard capacity changes gives us the values seen in Figure 11-15.

Iteration 5

We have now exhausted the pipeline capacity out of Cheyenne to both Rapid City and North Platte, but there is still extra capacity to Denver. Looking at routes out of Denver,

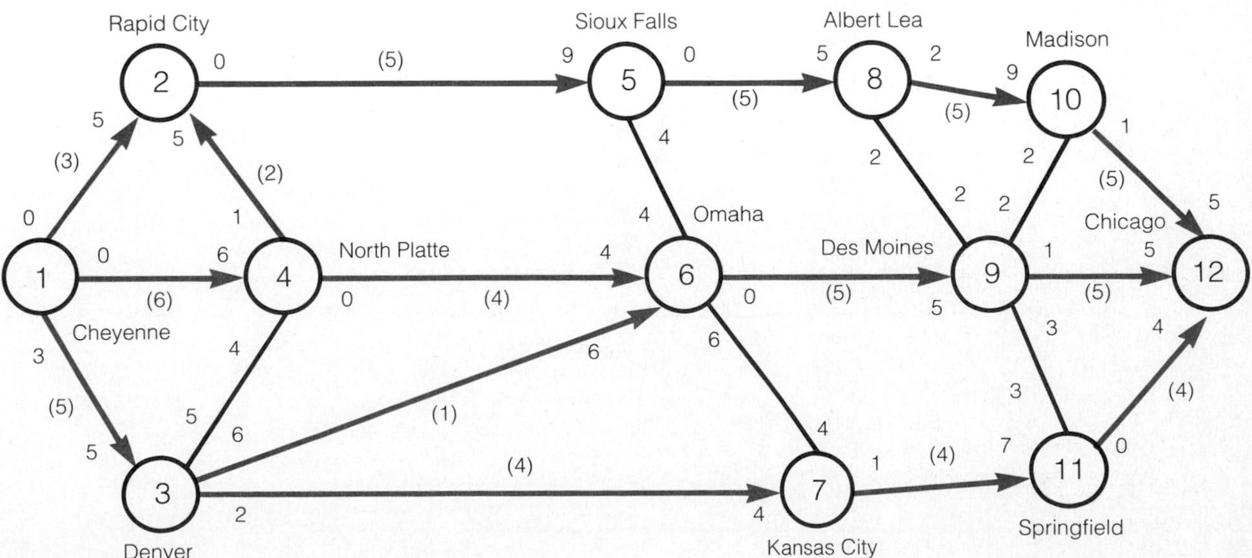

Figure 11-16
Midwest Natural Gas flow problem: iteration 5

we see some possibilities. Let's consider the following route: Cheyenne–Denver–Omaha–Des Moines–Chicago. As we can see in Figure 11-16, we can ship 1 unit (1000 cfm) on this route.

Iteration 6

Still working with the routes out of Denver, let's consider Cheyenne–Denver–Kansas City–Springfield–Des Moines–Chicago, with a limitation of 1. The results of this iteration are shown in Figure 11-17.

Final Network

Now we must stop. Although there is still extra capacity on some routes, we can find no path between the source and sink that has not reached its maximum flow on at least one of its links. The results of our process are summarized in Table 11-3.

Robert can use Table 11-3 to determine the total flow out of the source and into the sink. He can also use this information to determine how much lease capacity will be needed on each link of the network.

If the total flow possible through the network provides more gas than is needed in Chicago, selective cuts can be made in the contracted capacity. Given the routing network we have identified, 15,000 cfm is the maximum amount that can be shipped between Cheyenne and Chicago.

Some of the problems at the end of the chapter will give you additional opportunities to test your understanding of the maximum-flow algorithm.

MORE USES OF THE MAXIMUM-FLOW MODEL

The maximum-flow model can be used for situations other than the obvious ones, such as natural gas, oil, and water pipelines. It can also be used for electric power transmission and distribution networks; for transportation planning, such as regulating the flow of commuter traffic and freight deliveries; and for computer linkages and telecommunication networks. Problems at the end of the chapter will introduce some of these applications.

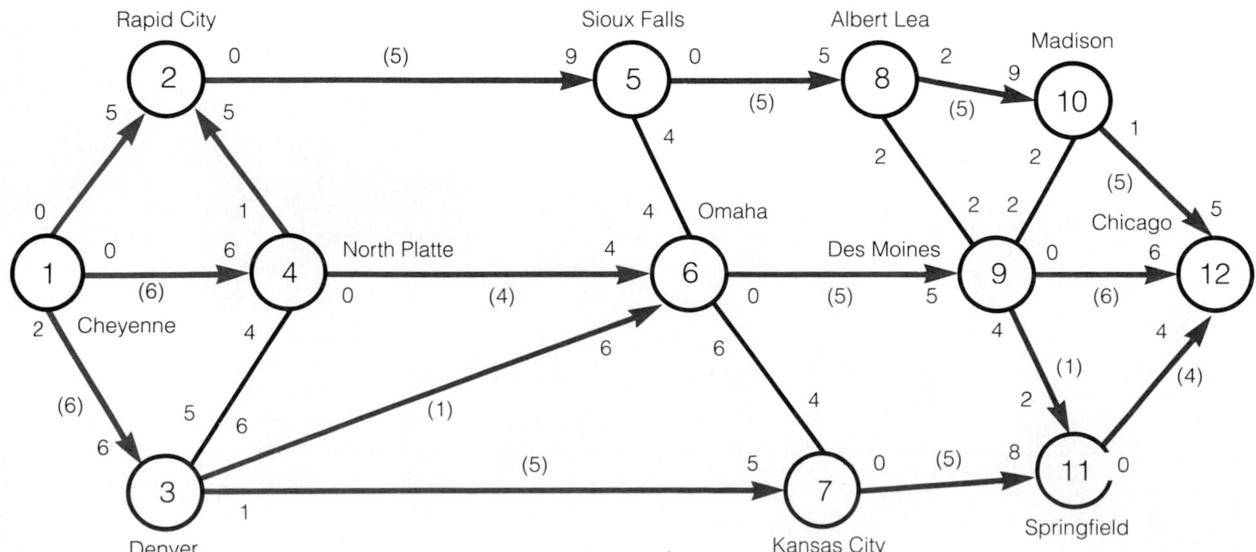

Figure 11-17
Midwest Natural Gas flow problem: iteration 6

Table 11-3 FLOW SUMMARY FOR MIDWEST NATURAL GAS PROBLEM

Pipeline Link		Iteration						
From	To	1	2	3	4	5	6	Total Flow
Cheyenne	Rapid City	—	—	3	—	—	—	3
	North Platte	4	—	—	2	—	—	6
	Denver	—	4	—	—	1	1	6
North Platte	Omaha	4	—	—	—	—	—	4
	Rapid City	—	—	—	2	—	—	2
Denver	North Platte	—	—	—	—	—	—	—
	Omaha	—	—	—	—	1	—	1
	Kansas City	—	4	—	—	—	1	5
Rapid City	Sioux Falls	—	—	3	2	—	—	5
Omaha	Sioux Falls	—	—	—	—	—	—	—
	Des Moines	4	—	—	—	1	—	5
	Kansas City	—	—	—	—	—	—	—
Sioux Falls	Albert Lea	—	—	3	2	—	—	5
Kansas City	Springfield	—	4	—	—	—	1	5
Des Moines	Albert Lea	—	—	—	—	—	—	—
	Madison	—	—	—	—	—	—	—
	Chicago	4	—	—	—	1	1	6
Albert Lea	Madison	—	—	3	2	—	—	5
Madison	Chicago	—	—	3	2	—	—	5
Springfield	Chicago	—	4	—	—	—	—	4
	Des Moines	—	—	—	—	—	1	1
Maximum total flow in network*		4	8	11	13	14	15	

Note: Flow values are in thousands of cubic feet per minute.

* These values represent the cumulative flow at the end of each iteration (e.g., iteration 2 adds a flow of 4 to the 4 from iteration 1, for a total of 8; iteration 3 adds 3 more, for a total of 11, and so on).

11-5 SUMMARY AND CONCLUSIONS

Network-based models are among the most widely used management science tools. Their appeal comes from both the wide variety of decision-making situations they can address and their ability to graphically represent a problem. This latter characteristic generally makes network models more understandable than the algebraic representations of, say, linear programming models.

In this chapter we have examined three of the most commonly used network models: the shortest-route algorithm, the minimum-spanning-tree algorithm, and the maximum-flow algorithm. Although these models are not as widely used as the PERT/

CPM techniques discussed in chapter 10, they are nonetheless very important for specific applications, particularly those involving transportation or distribution.

The Chapter Glossary lists the important terms introduced here. The problems and cases that follow this section present a variety of decision-making situations that can be addressed using the network models introduced in the chapter.

Solved Problems

PROBLEM 1 Cascade Lumber has just received permission to log seven plots of timber in the Bitterroot National Forest in Montana. To remove logs from these plots, Cascade will have to construct logging roads connecting the seven plots and an established access point. When they are no longer needed, the logging roads will be eliminated and their sites returned to their previous condition, insofar as practical. Logging in national forests has recently come under attack as being uneconomical and environmentally unsound—destroying forest habitat and big-game feeding grounds, and polluting pristine native fisheries. To mitigate damage to the environment, the lumber company is required to use the "best available technology" to prevent water pollution and other problems that might result from road construction and site restoration.

Cascade Lumber is obviously interested in building a network of roads that will allow the loggers to get their cut timber to the access point at a minimum cost. D. F. Engineering, headquartered in Ketchum, Idaho, has prepared the following cost estimates for connecting the seven plots and the access point. In some places, the terrain makes a connecting road impossible or distance makes a direct road impractical; these situations are denoted by a "blank" (—) in the cost table, below. Also in this table, the letter *A* indicates the access point and costs are given in millions of dollars.

	Plot							
Plot	A	1	2	3	4	5	6	7
A	0	1.6	—	1.1	—	—	—	—
1		0	0.9	—	2.4	—	—	—
2			0	1.7	1.7	2.7	4.7	—
3				0	—	—	—	—
4					0	1.5	—	—
5						0	1.6	2.3
6							0	2.0
7								0

a. Discuss the type of network model that can be used to solve this problem.
b. Determine how much Cascade Lumber should budget for road construction.

Solutions

a. Since Cascade Lumber is interested in constructing a minimum-cost road network, this can be treated as a minimum-spanning-tree problem where we are interested in minimizing spanning costs, not distances.

b. The seven plots of timber and the access point (*A*) are represented by the network Figure 11-18. (There is no need for actual correlation between this network and the geographic location of the plots on a map.)

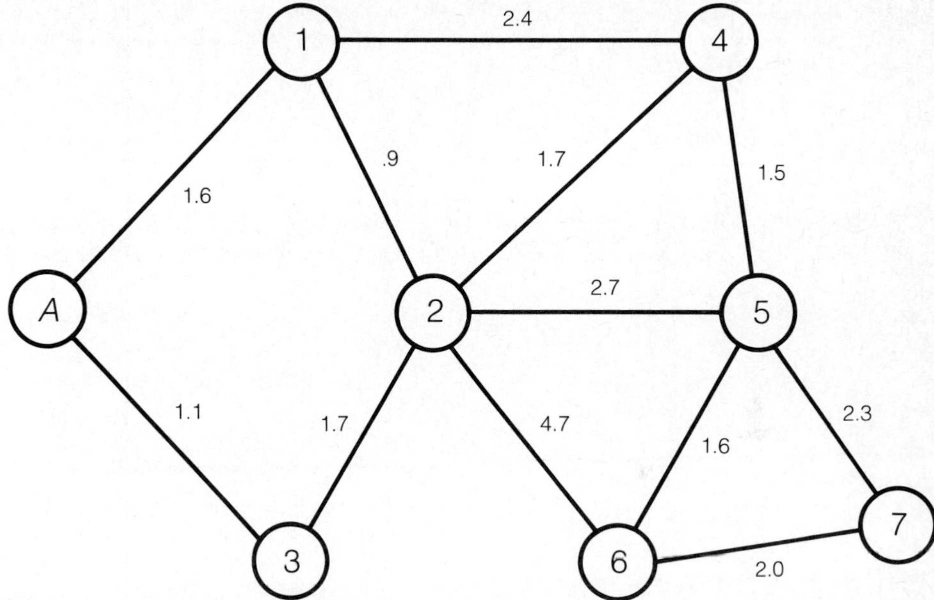

Figure 11-18
Network for Cascade Lumber problem

Note: Numbers on branches represent costs in millions of dollars.

The minimum-spanning-tree procedure is as follows:

Step 1 Arbitrarily pick any node in the network and connect it to the closest node.

Step 2 Determine which unconnected node is closest to one of the connected nodes. Then connect these two nodes. Repeat this step until all the nodes are connected.

If we arbitrarily start with plot 4, the steps in determining the minimum spanning tree are shown below.

Step	Connect Plots	Cost
1	4 and 5	1.5
2	5 and 6	1.6
3	4 and 2	1.7
4	2 and 1	0.9
5	1 and *A*	1.6
6	*A* and 3	1.1
7	6 and 7	2.0
		10.4

These steps are shown graphically in Figure 11-19. The total cost of road construction and removal will be $10.4 million.

PROBLEM 2 Gilbert Automated Accounting contracts to perform billing services for medical and dental groups. The company does all its billing with a recently purchased minicomputer and several workstations. Given the rapid pace of changes in technology, Gilbert's managers know the company can keep its present equipment a maximum of 5 years. However, they may want to replace the equipment sooner—or even several times within that period. They want to make this decision based on minimum costs.

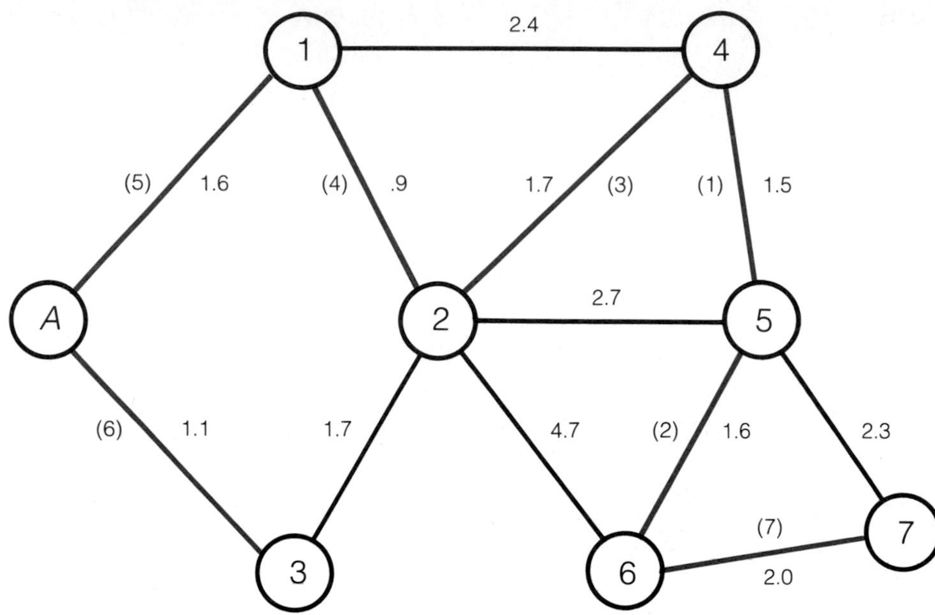

Figure 11-19
Minimum spanning tree for Cascade Lumber problem

Gilbert's upper management has made a series of cost estimates for replacing its equipment now and in each of the following four years. In all cases, the cost estimates involve the following factors:

PVP = present value of purchasing in year *i*, where *i* ranges from 0 (now) to 4 (year 5)

PVM = present value of maintenance costs for the period the equipment is used

PVS = present value of salvage cost of equipment when sold

Each cost factor is then given as $PVP + PVM - PVS$.

Although these estimates are admittedly hard to make, since they depend on predicting when new computer equipment is likely to be introduced, Gilbert's managers do have to plan for the future. The following table presents the discounted estimated costs of purchasing new equipment and selling their old equipment for each of the 5 years. All costs are in thousands of dollars.

	Year of Sale				
Year of Purchase	1	2	3	4	5
0	20	28	36	56	75
1	—	18	31	44	53
2	—	—	22	34	40
3	—	—	—	20	46
4	—	—	—	—	25

a. Determine the network model that can be used to solve this problem.
b. Recommend the equipment replacement schedule that Gilbert should follow.

Solutions

a. Gilbert's objective is to get from the present point, year 0, to the end point, year 5, at the minimum possible cost. If we substitute cost for distance or time, we see this can be considered a shortest-route

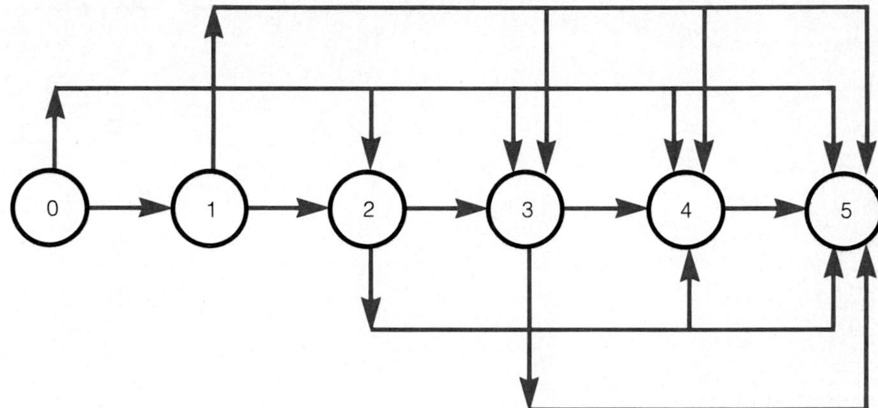

Figure 11-20
Gilbert's replacement decision represented as a shortest-route problem

problem. The replacement decision can be represented in network form, as shown in Figure 11-20. The costs provided in the table will become the values connecting the nodes.

b. Solve this problem using the shortest-route algorithm, as follows:

Step 1 Assign a permanent label to the source node, year 0, and temporary labels to the other nodes, years 1 through 5. Year 0 will be labeled (0, 0). The values in the cost table will be used to provide the temporary labels. Year 1 will be labeled (20, 0), indicating we can buy in year 0 and sell in year 1 for $20,000. Buying in year 0 and selling in year 3, represented by the arc from node 0 to node 3, will have the temporary label (36, 0). The first set of temporary labels is shown in Figure 11-21.

Step 2 Look at each node that can be reached directly from the source node, which includes all the nodes for years 1 through 5. We then pick the temporary label with the lowest cost and change it to a permanent label. This minimum-cost temporary label is the one associated with node 1. Our reasoning is that if we are to replace the computer equipment in year 1, we will be replacing equipment bought in year 0. We therefore change this temporary designation to a permanent value (*P*), as seen in Figure 11-21.

Step 3 Consider all nodes that can be reached either from the source node (0) or the permanent node found in step 2 (year 1). The reasoning for node 2 is as follows: We can buy in year 0 and replace in year 2 for a cost of $28,000, or we can replace after both year 1 and year 2 for

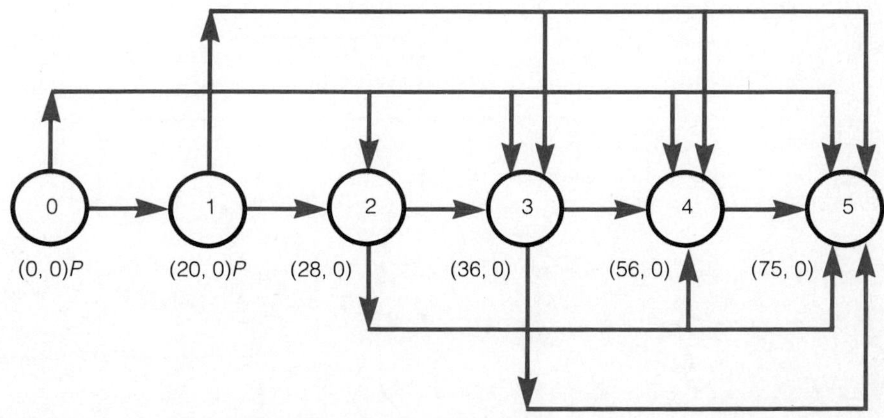

Figure 11-21
Gilbert's shortest-route problem: steps 1 and 2

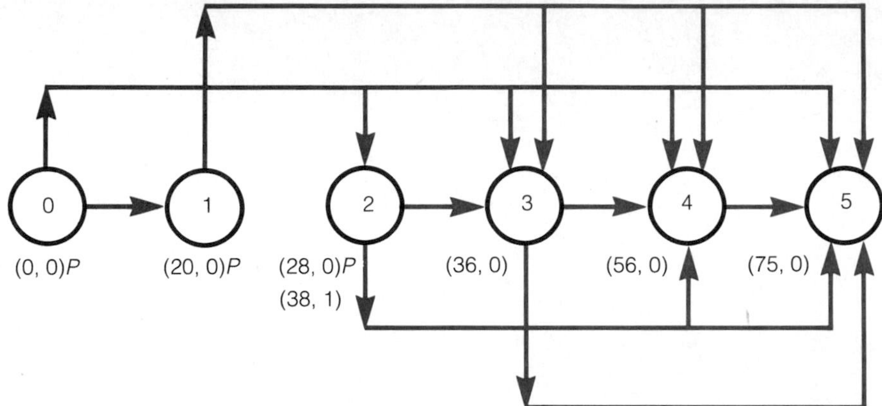

Figure 11-22
Gilbert's shortest-route problem: step 3

a cost of \$20,000 + \$18,000. Similar reasoning leads to the alternative temporary labels shown in Figure 11-22. Picking the smallest temporary label and changing it to a permanent value, we would choose the (28, 0) associated with year 2.

Step 4 We continue to look at the remaining nodes and assign temporary labels based on costs from the three permanent nodes. These are seen in Figure 11-23 for the next iteration. Once again we pick the temporary node with the smallest cost and change it to a permanent node. In this case it is the (36, 0) associated with node 3. An interesting point to note about this step is that the minimum-cost route to node 5 is now through node 2, not node 0.

Step 5 Continuing to work through the problem, we arrive at the network seen in Figure 11-24. Here we see the minimum-cost path from node 0 to node 5 is through node 2; therefore, the optimal decision is to replace the equipment after 2 and 5 years.

The sequence of temporary labels generated for this problem is summarized in the following table. The chosen permanent values are designated by an * (these are the values labeled with *P* in the network figures).

Node 0	Node 1	Node 2	Node 3	Node 4	Node 5
(0, 0)*	(20, 0)*	(28, 0)*	(36, 0)*	(56, 0)*	(75, 0)
		(38, 1)	(51, 1)	(64, 1)	(73, 1)
			(50, 2)	(62, 2)	(68, 2)*
				(56, 3)*	(82, 3)
					(81, 4)

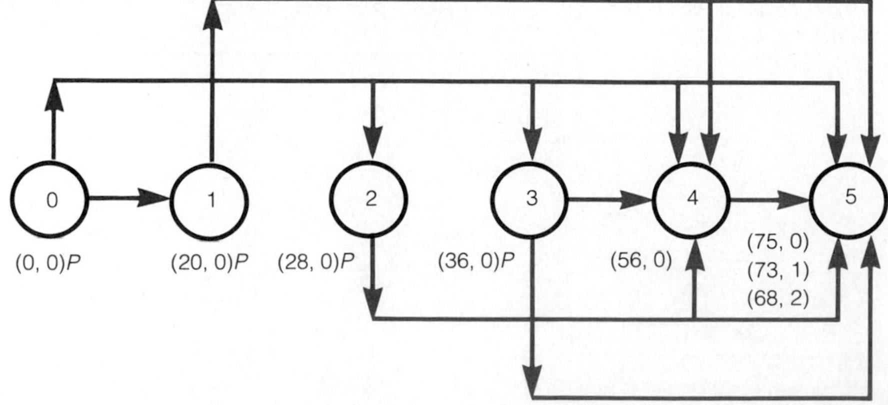

Figure 11-23
Gilbert's shortest-route problem: step 4

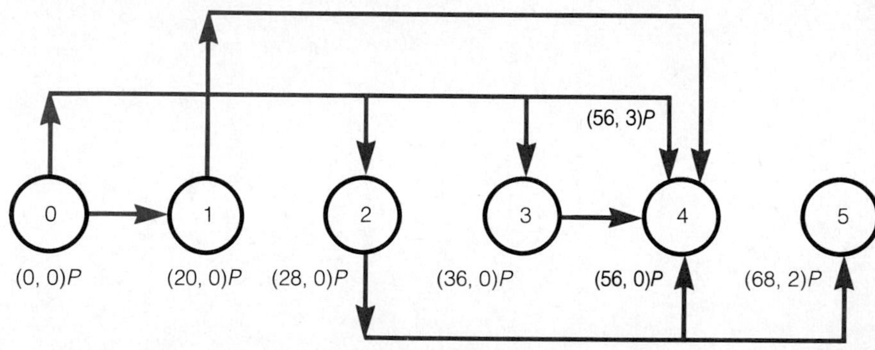

Figure 11-24
Gilbert's shortest-route problem: step 5

General Questions and Assignments

1. Explain why the shortest-route network model will yield the minimum distance, cost, or other value, starting from any location and proceeding to any other location.
2. In the shortest-route model, nodes are labeled as temporary or permanent. Explain what this means and tell how a node goes from being temporary to permanent.
3. Find one or more articles in the library which describe the use of the shortest-route model. Write a short report describing the situation in the article. Specifically, discuss what, if any, cost savings resulted from using this model.
4. The minimum-spanning-tree model works by making a series of "locally optimal" decisions which end up providing the best overall decision for the situation being modeled. In your own terms, explain how this works.
5. Develop an example of your own which shows that the minimum-spanning-tree model will always lead to the optimal result regardless of the starting point selected.
6. Explain what should be done in applying the minimum-spanning-tree model if two or more arcs have the same values. Under what conditions might this lead to multiple optimal solutions?
7. After reading the material on network models in this chapter, contact a business in your area which would be likely to use one or more of the models. If the business does use a network model, describe the application(s). If not, discuss what alternative methods are used for planning and decision making.

Exercises and Application Problems

1. Excelsior Service operates a central parts warehouse for auto dealers in the Dallas–Fort Worth area. The distances from the central warehouse to the dealerships, in driving time, are shown in Figure 11-25. Assuming this network also shows all the possible routings for Excelsior's drivers, determine the shortest route from the warehouse to each of the dealerships.
2. Billings Outfitters maintains a series of camps along established trails in the Frank Church Wilderness Area. The outfitters will pack campers and fishing parties into the wilderness area and, for groups staying a week or more, will return every two days with food and supplies. The camping areas are arranged as shown in Figure 11-26. The distances between camps are given in hours on horseback. Determine the shortest distance from Billings' two base camps to each camp area.
3. Find the shortest route between the following pairs of routes in Figure 11-27: 1–7, 1–10, 3–10, 2–9.

Figure 11-25
Auto parts delivery network

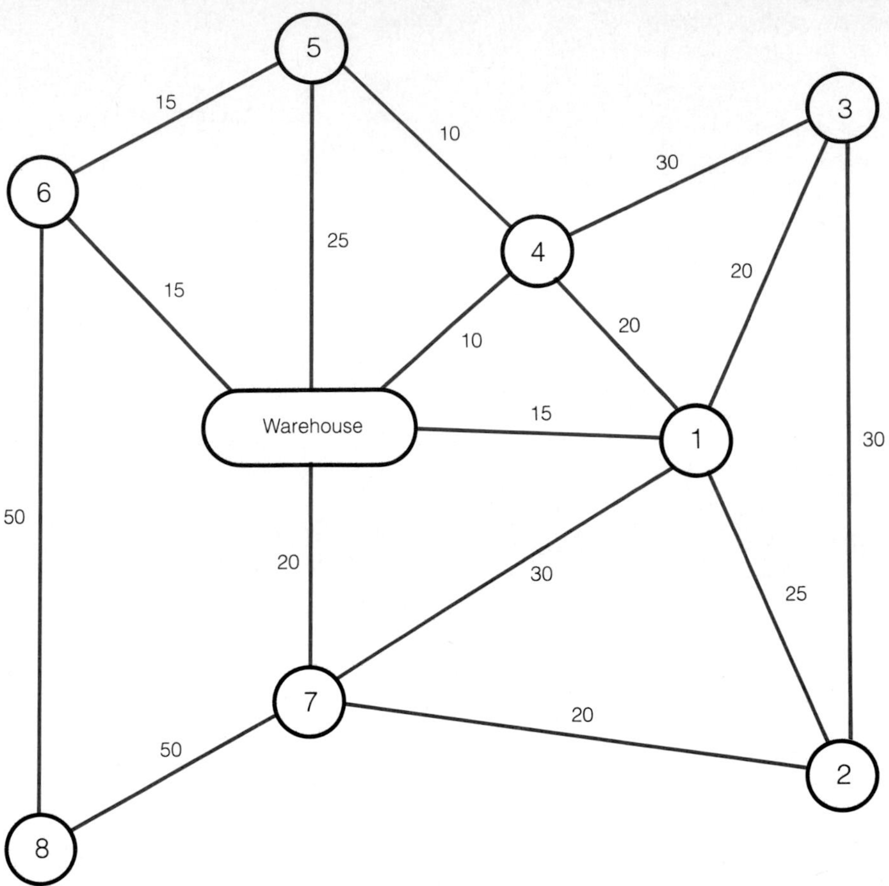

Note: Distances are driving times in minutes.

Figure 11-26
Billings Outfitters' camp network

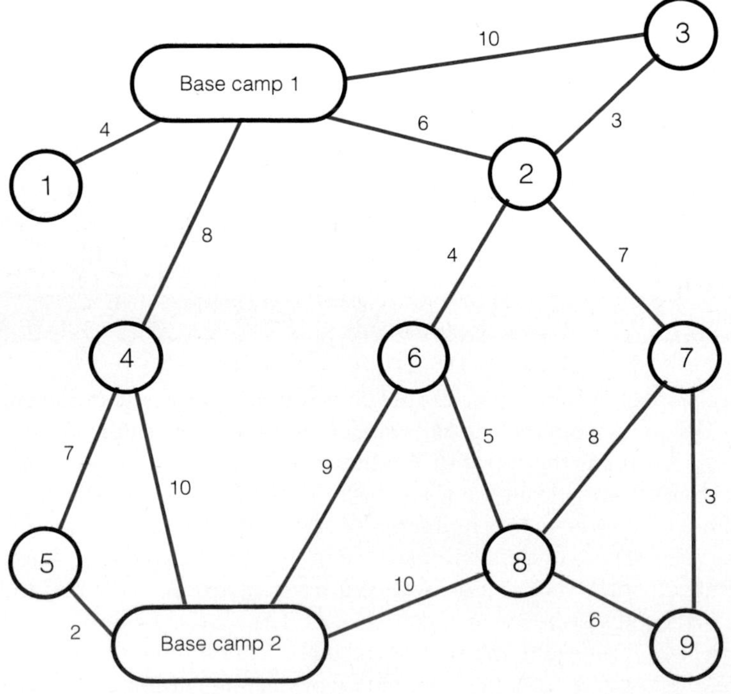

Note: All distances are in hours on horseback.

Figure 11-27
Network for problem 3

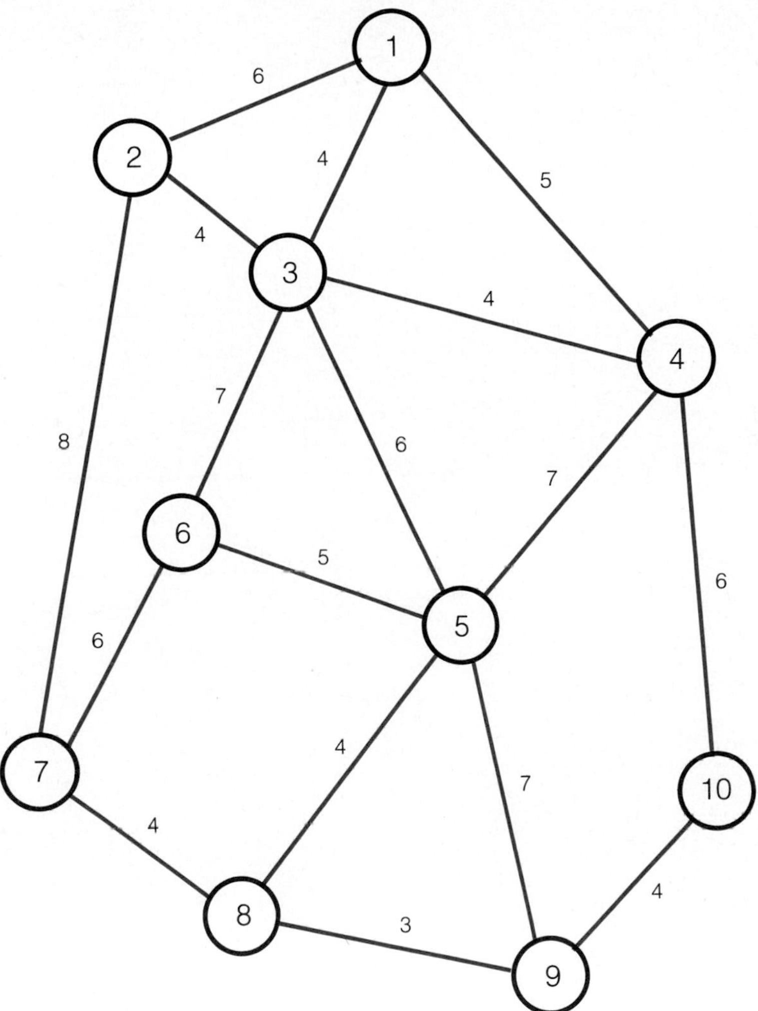

4. Maize Milling has established a thriving business with its new portable milling machine. Now, Maize employees can take the machine to local ranches and farms to mill corn and grain for animal feed. Previously, the ranchers and farmers had to drive to Maize's central mill for this service. Figure 11-28 shows the road network and all of Maize's customers located west of town. Find the shortest route between Maize's mill and each of its customers.
5. For Figure 11-29, find the shortest route between the following pairs of routes: 1–9, 2–10, 3–8, 2–9.
6. River City recently hired Ned Fiero as its new fire chief. One of the first things Ned noticed was that the fire department does not have planned routes from the fire station to possible fire locations. If a fire truck takes the wrong way to a fire, the delay could be very costly. Ned wants to determine the shortest routes between the station and various parts of the city. To begin, he has diagramed the city as a 12-square grid (Figure 11-30) and estimated the travel times between the squares, or nodes. On Figure 11-30, arrows indicate possible travel directions; if there is no arrow between two nodes, the route cannot be traveled by fire truck. Now Ned needs some help in determining the best route to take to the center of each grid square in the city so that travel time is minimized.

Figure 11-28
Maize Milling customer network

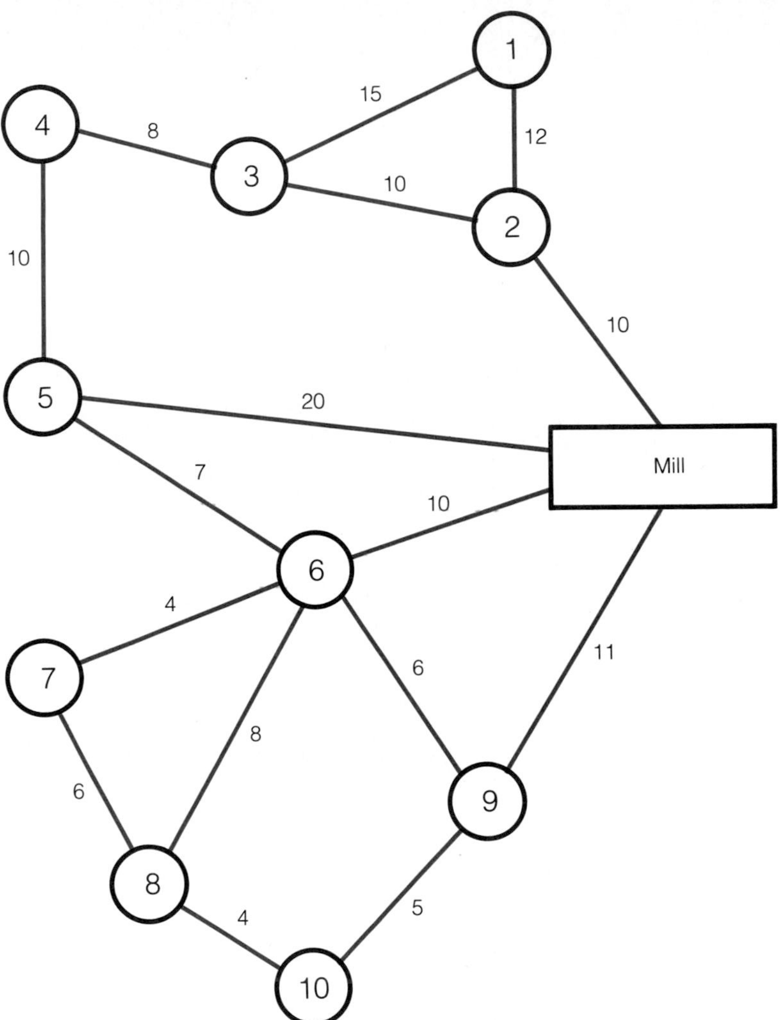

Note: All distances are driving times in minutes.

7. Elsworth Manufacturing is installing a robotized package-delivery system in its central headquarters. The robot will follow a predetermined route marked by electronic sensors in the floor of the building. Because the sensor system is so expensive, the company wants to limit the extent of the system while still making sure that it covers all the offices. Figure 11-31 shows the distances between departments (nodes), in hundreds of feet. Determine the route for the robot which will connect all the offices with the minimum number of sensors.
8. Mi Casita is a small company that makes a variety of Mexican-style food products. The company has gained market share over its bigger competitors by providing more frequent (daily, for its largest customers) deliveries from its plant. Figure 11-32 shows the locations of its largest retail distributors and the possible routes between them. If all the distributors are to be visited daily, what route will connect all the delivery stops with the minimum total distance?
9. Outdoor Adventures provides guides for fly-fishing trips in the mountains. The guides are available at an hourly rate for short trips or daily for longer excursions. Sofia Medina is a popular guide who mainly is assigned to daily guide trips—but she also plans trip routes for other guides. She knows

Figure 11-29
Network for problem 5

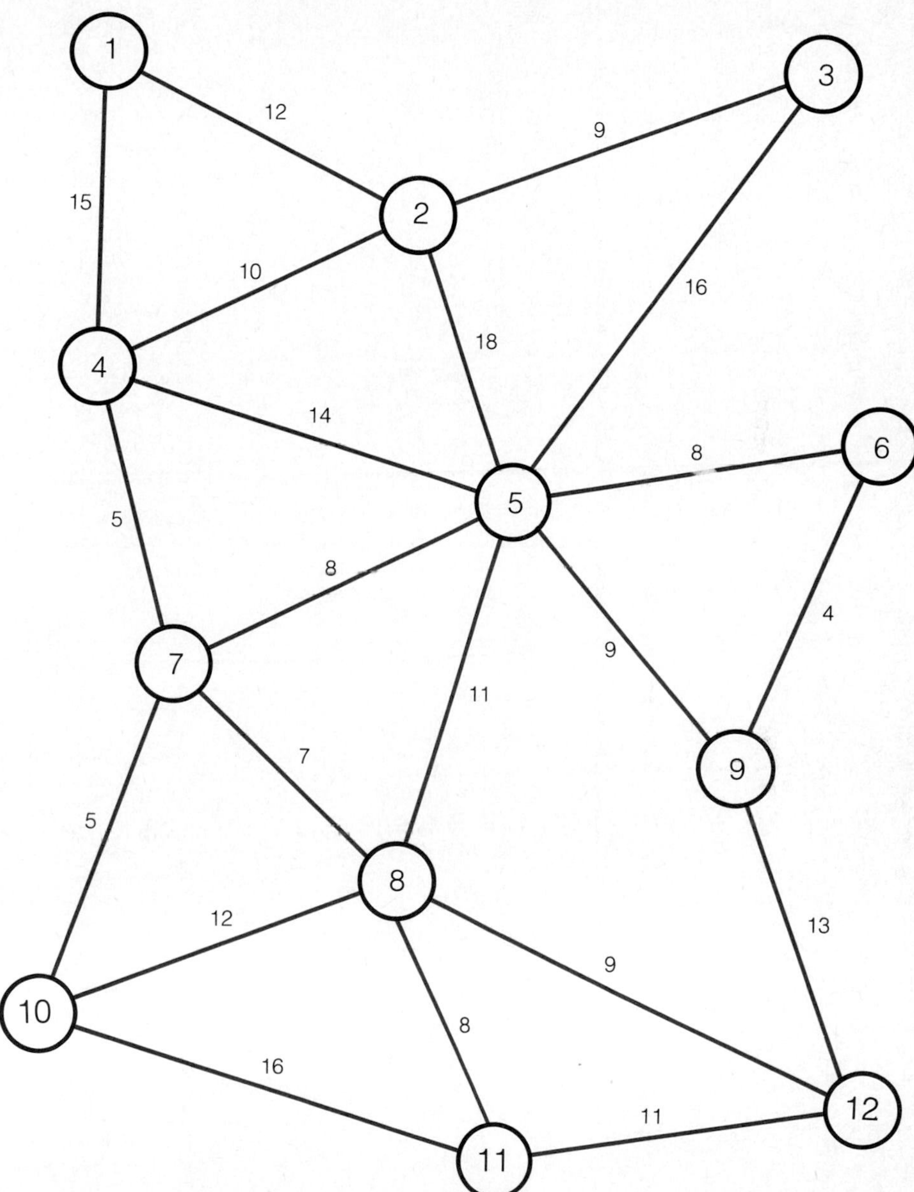

Note: Distances are travel times in hours.

Figure 11-30
Routes for fire trucks

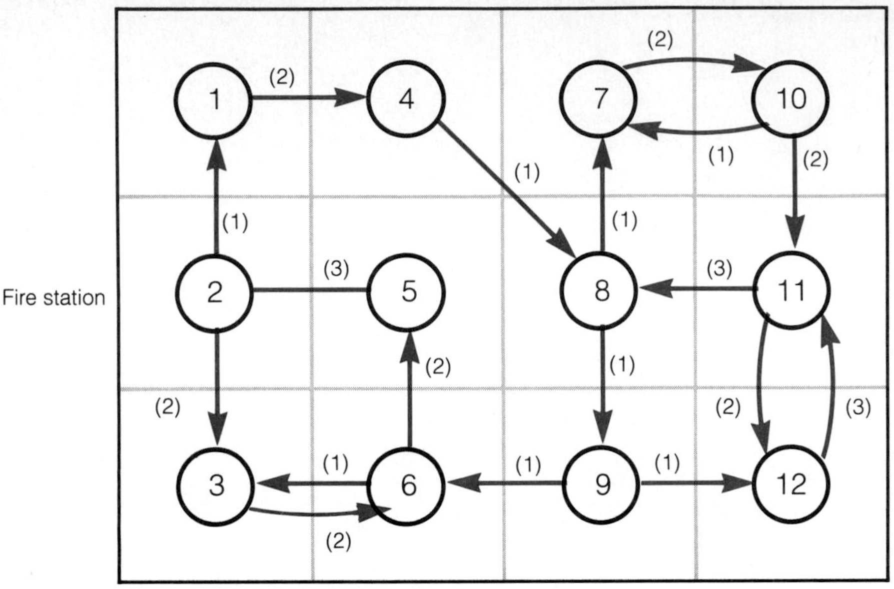

Note: Distances are travel times in minutes.

Figure 11-31
Robot delivery system

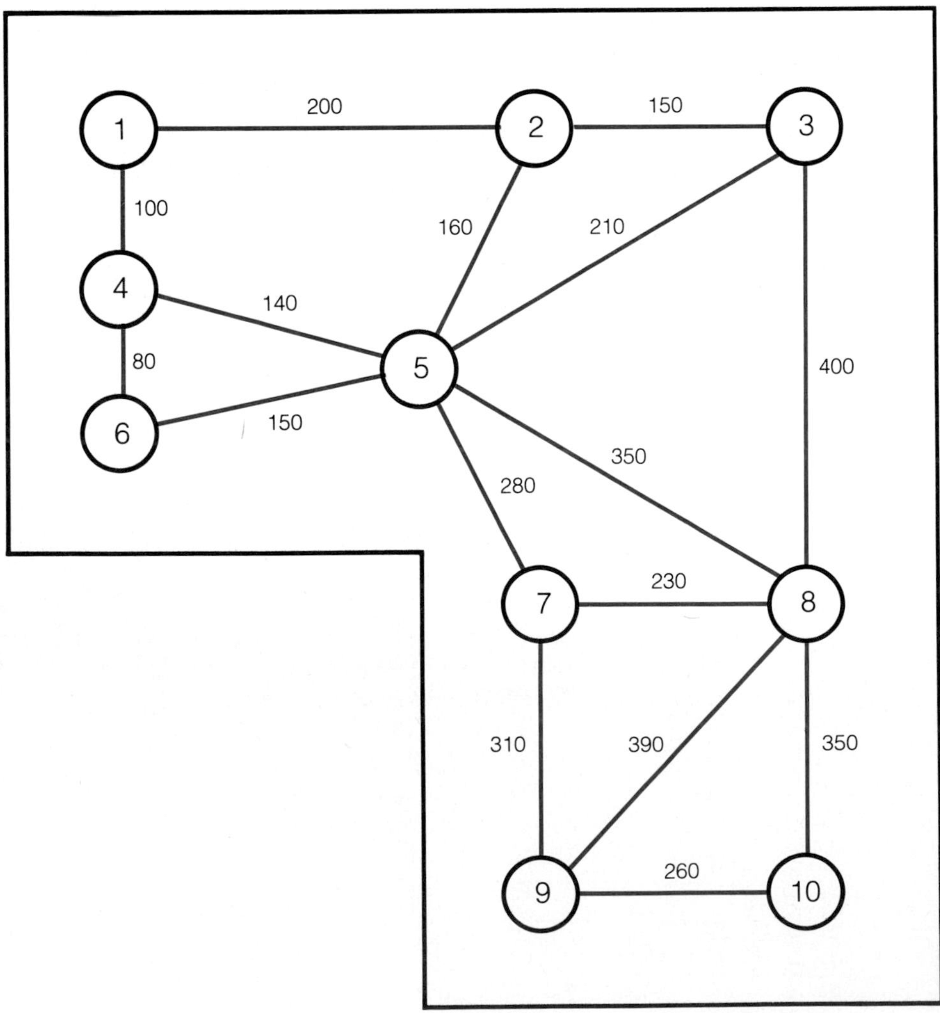

Note: Distances are in feet.

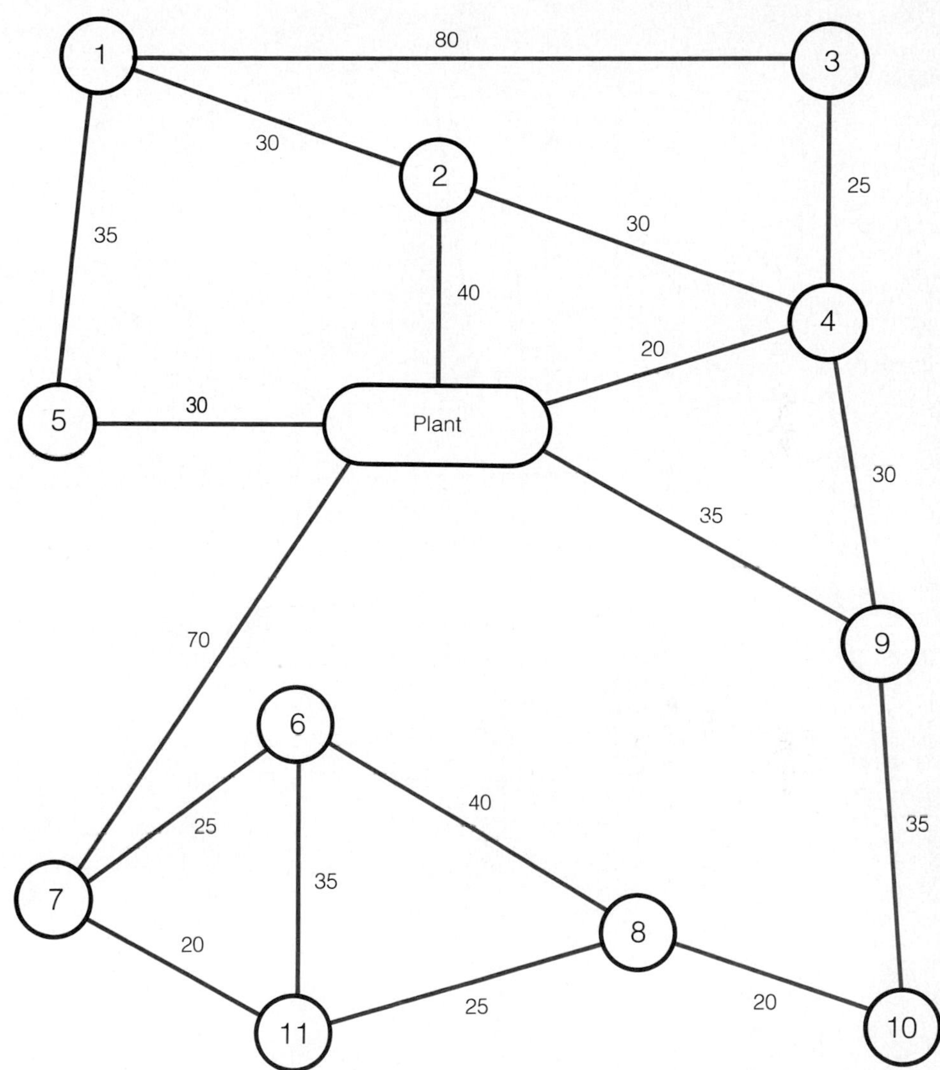

Figure 11-32
Mi Casita Foods' delivery route

that a successful trip involves not only covering the traditionally good fishing spots but also not spending excess time driving from one place to another. Figure 11-33 shows Sofia's favorite spots and the driving time between them. Assuming that she and one other guide will be making trips, in what order should Sofia visit these spots in order to minimize total driving time?

10. Mountain West Telephone has long taken pride in its reputation for providing exceptionally good customer service. Recently, however, the company's service has been criticized by several state regulatory agencies. In the past, Mountain West had always provided same-day service, with service calls being routed on a first-come, first-served basis. To experiment with a new routing policy, the service manager recorded the locations of the first 9 calls received on Monday and plotted them on a map of the town. The driving distances between these service calls are shown in Figure 11-34. First, determine the total driving distance if the service calls are made on a first-come, first-served basis. Then determine the total driving distance if the calls are covered using a minimum-spanning-tree criterion.

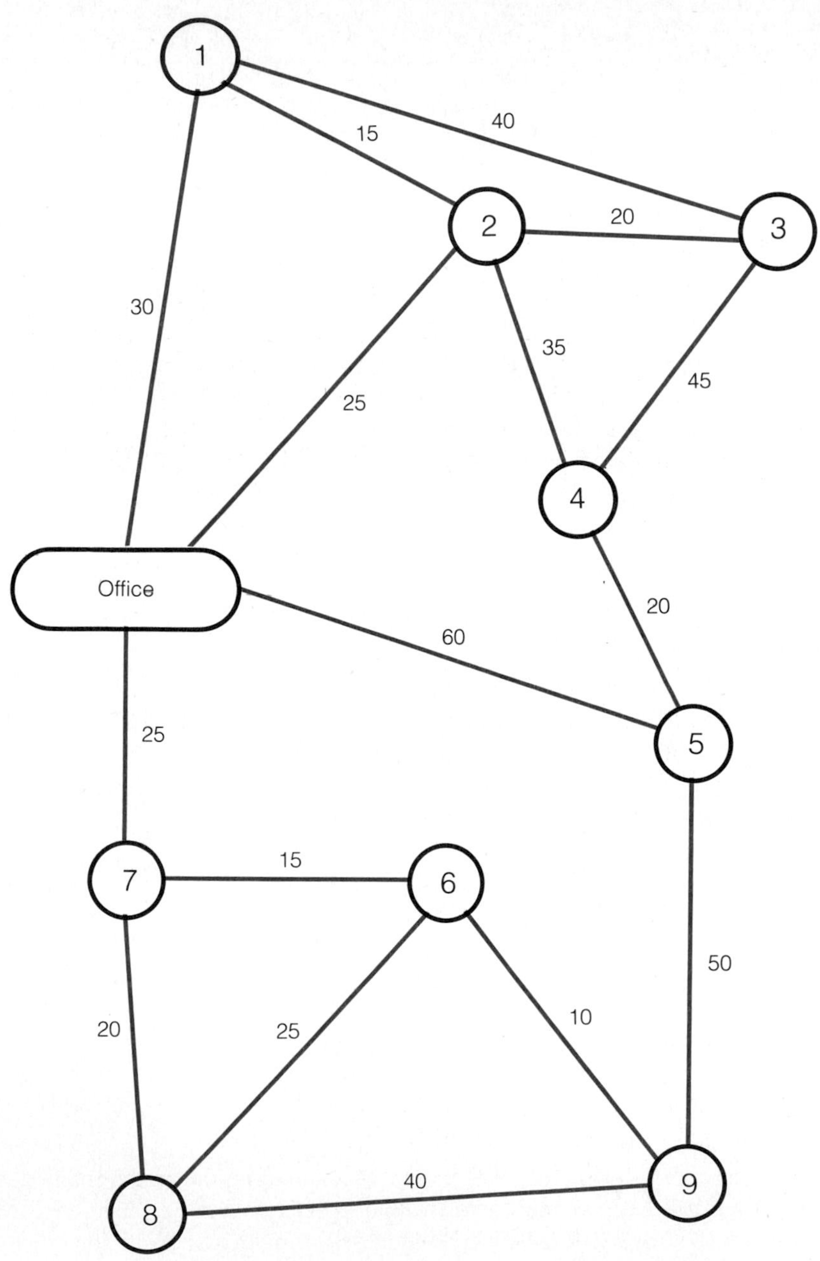

Figure 11-33
Outdoor Adventures' guided fishing trips

Note: Distances are in minutes.

Figure 11-34
Telephone service calls

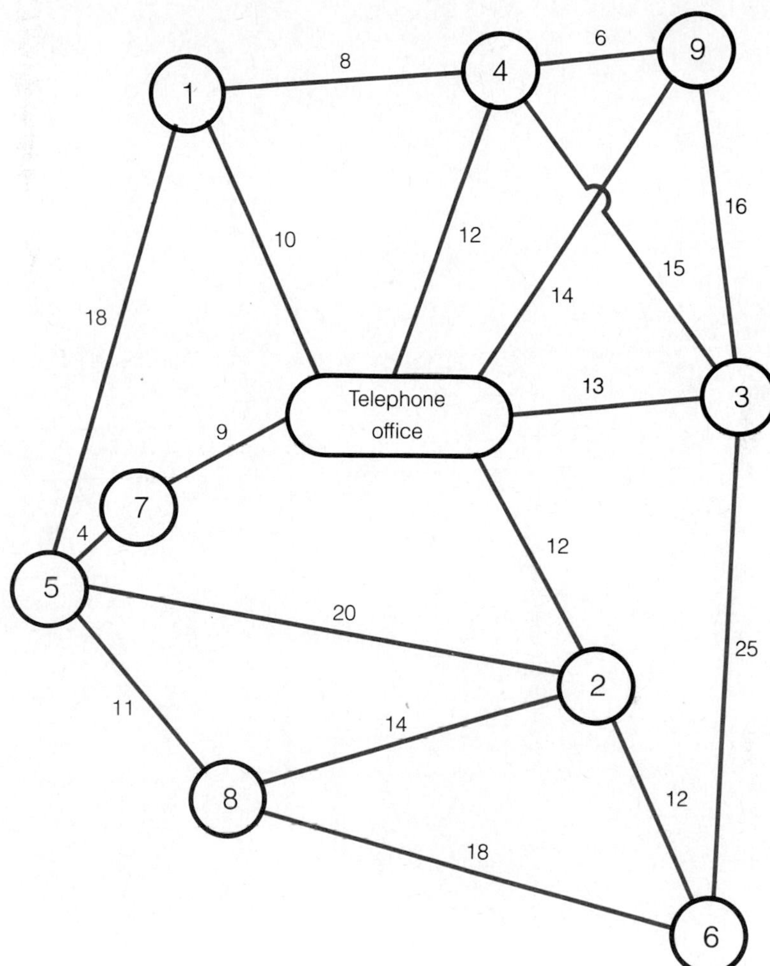

Note: Distances are in miles.

11. The Worldwide Peregrine Falcon Society is attempting to reintroduce the bird in parts of the West where it is no longer found in nature. Ten nesting boxes have been placed in the Four Corners area of Utah. Each nesting box has three peregrine falcons that were hatched in captivity. To accurately assess the progress of these birds, biologists will monitor the boxes through a closed-circuit television system, with a camera at each nesting site. The system is linked by line-of-sight microwave transmitters that can relay signals between the individual monitors and the central monitoring station. The distances between the 10 nesting boxes (and cameras) are shown in Figure 11-35. How should the microwave network be set up to minimize the total transmission distance? (Because of the mountainous terrain, actual ground distances are often greater than the straight-line distances shown on the network diagram.)
12. Eastern States Medical Center conducts research on a variety of communicable diseases. A promising form of research involves screening diseased cells with an electron microscope. The microscope is located on the third floor of the main building, and research labs are scattered throughout the 20-acre complex. A key to effective use of the microscope is the speed with which cells to be

Figure 11-35
Falcon observation network

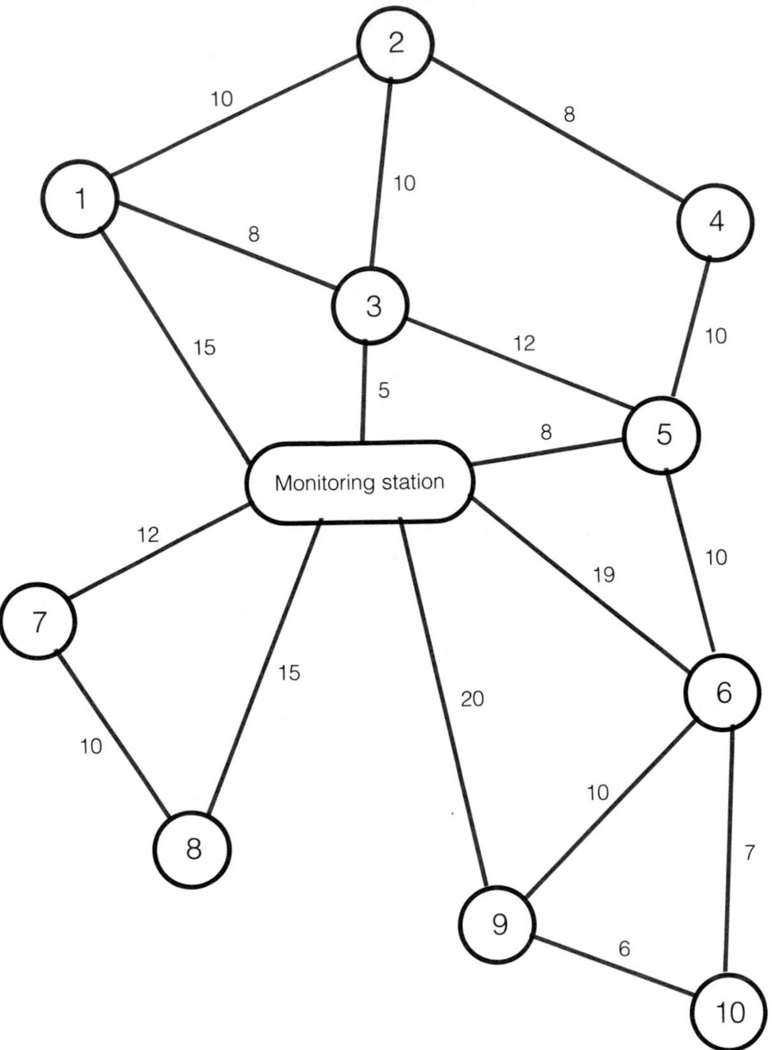

Note: Distances are in miles.

screened are transported. In fact, several promising developments have been delayed in recent months because of transportation problems. The research center has just received a grant to install a pneumatic-tube delivery system, (similar to those used by drive-in banks to carry money and other items between cars and the bank) which will allow biopsied cells to be frozen in liquid nitrogen and quickly sent to the microscope location. Since the delivery system will be so expensive, limiting its extent will be important. Figure 11-36 shows the relative locations of the microscope and various research labs. Because of the structure of the main building, not all labs can be directly connected with the microscope location or with each other. If the tube system costs $1000 per foot, what is the minimum-cost system which will connect the microscope site with all the research labs?

13. The International Famine Relief Fund has a stockpile of food products at its warehouse in Philadelphia. Fund directors have just received news of a food crisis in central Africa and want to move 100,000 tons of food within the next month. They can use cargo aircraft and merchant ships to transport the food. The possible routes, with cargo capacities given in tons per month, are shown in Figure 11-37.

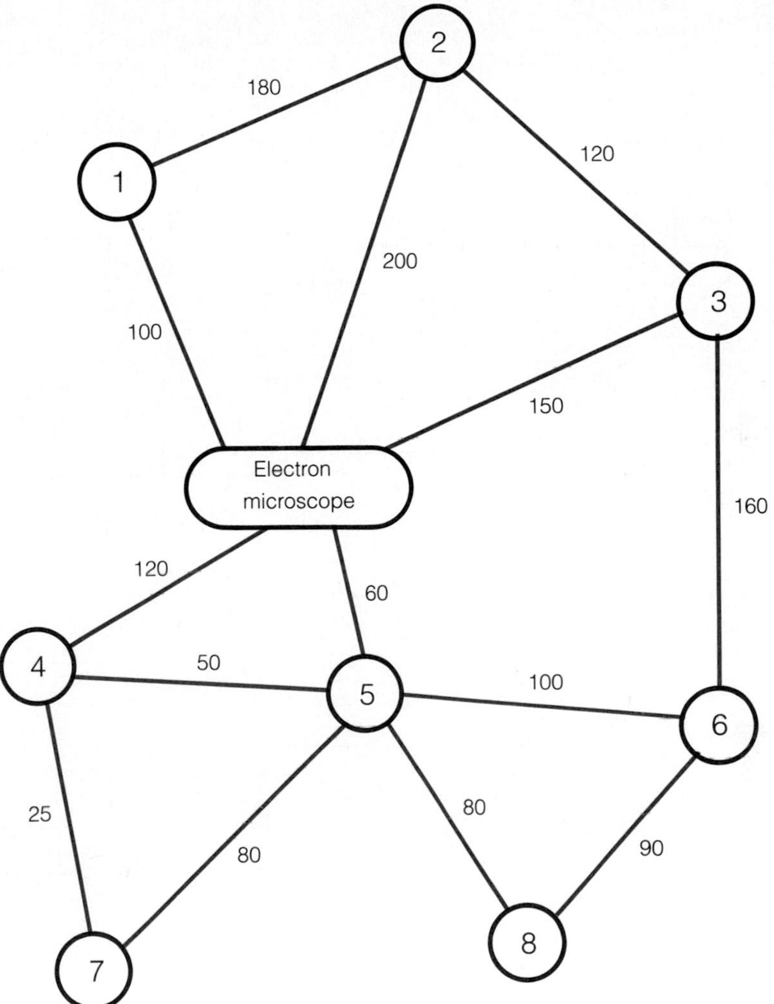

Figure 11-36
Pneumatic-tube delivery system to electron microscope

a. Considering the capacities shown in this figure, can the required amount of food be moved within a month?

b. How will overall system capacity be affected if the ship contracted for the Miami–Luanda arc is unable to sail?

14. Figure 11-38 shows the flow patterns through a petrochemical plant in Louisiana. Find the maximum flow from the plant's entry point to the exit point.

15. Referring to problem 14, suppose the flow capacity leaving node 2 was increased by 20%. What, if any, effect would this have on the maximum-flow solution you found in problem 14?

16. Figure 11-39 shows the national long-distance telephone capacities between the Washington, D.C. and Los Angeles calling areas. On Mother's Day, when long-distance calls reach a peak each year, how many calls per hour will this network be able to handle?

17. For the electric power transmission network shown in Figure 11-40, find the maximum amount of energy that can be transmitted from the power plant to the indicated destination.

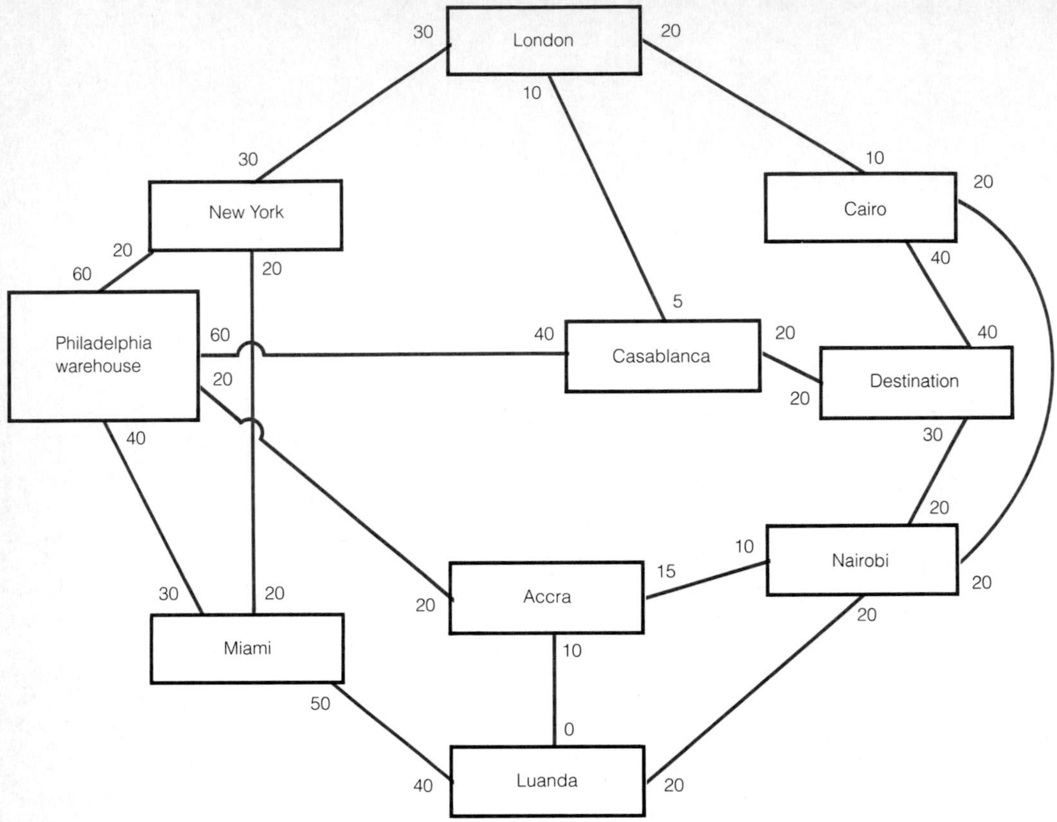

Note: Shipment capacities are in tons per month.

Figure 11-37
Food shipments

Figure 11-38
Flow pattern for Petrochemical Plant

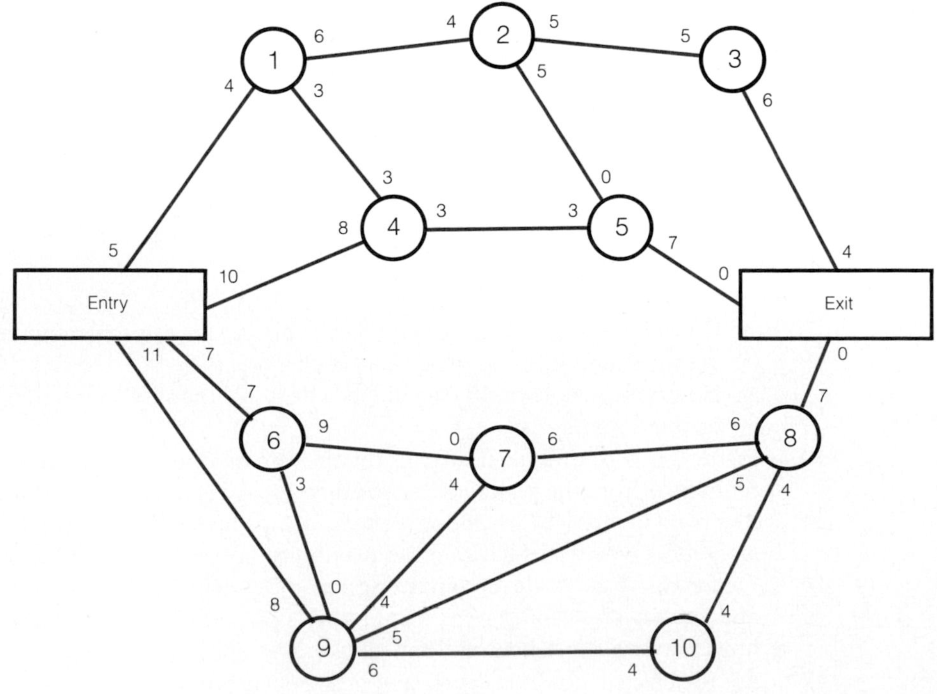

Note: Capacities are in thousands of barrels per day.

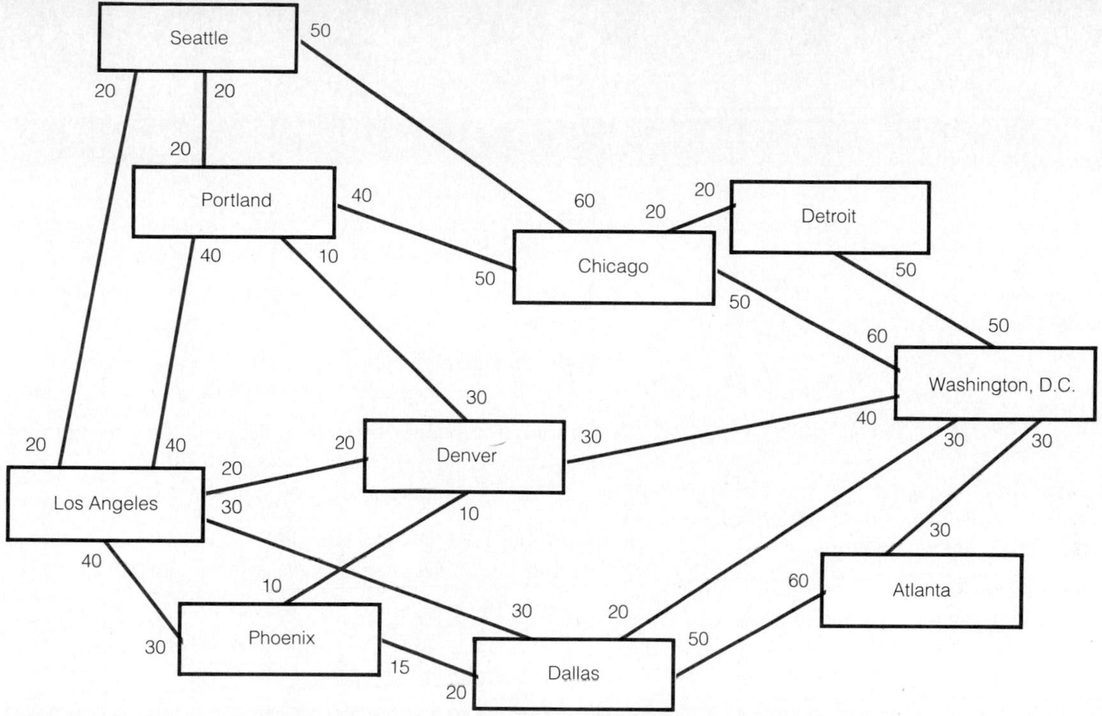

Note: Capacities are in 10,000 calls per hour.

Figure 11-39
Long-distance capacity

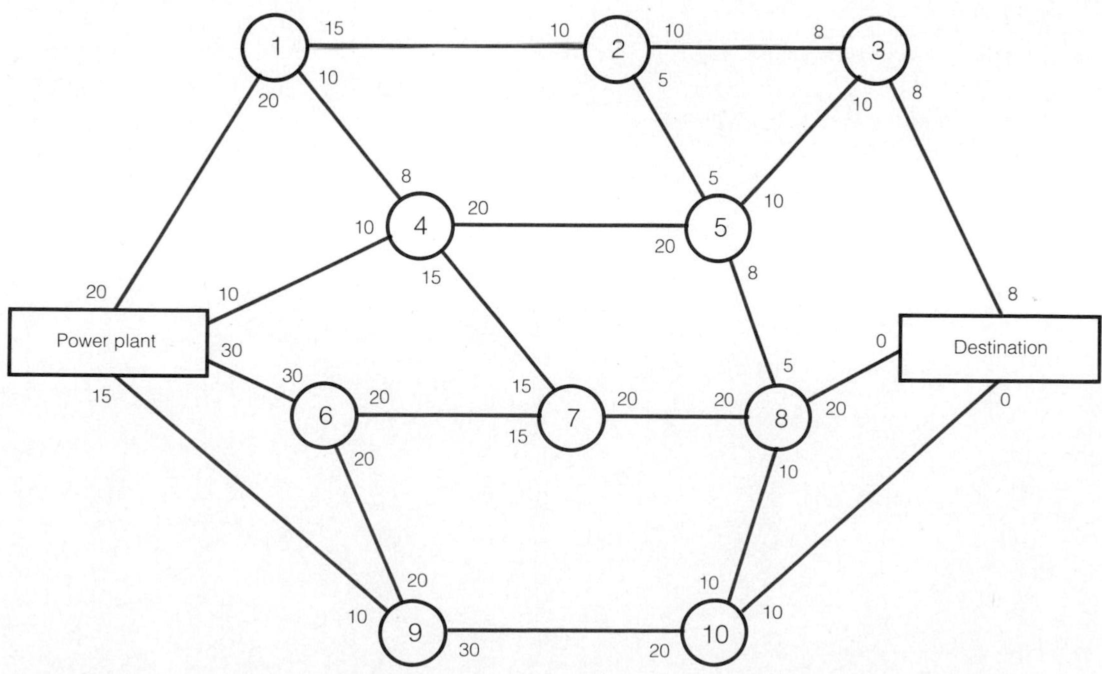

Note: Capacities are in gigawatts (100,000 kilowatts).

Figure 11-40
Electric power transmission network

Chapter Glossary

Branch The part of a network that connects two nodes; also termed *activity* or *arc*.

Capacity The amount of an item (e.g., information, materials, people, automobiles, etc.) that can move, or flow, along a branch of a network.

Flow The movement of an item (e.g., information, materials, people, automobiles, etc.) along the branch of a network.

Maximum-flow algorithm A model for determining the maximum flow that can either enter the source or exit the sink of a network during a given period of time.

Minimum-spanning-tree algorithm A model for identifying the set of branches, or arcs, in a network that provides the minimum path between all nodes in the network.

Network A set of points, or nodes, that are connected by branches along which some item may flow.

Node The starting or ending point for one or more branches in a network; also called *event*.

Path A sequential series of branches providing a route between two specified nodes in a network.

Shortest-route algorithm A model for finding the shortest path between two specified nodes of a network.

Sink The ending node in a network.

Spanning Tree A set of branches, or arcs, in a network that provide a path between all nodes in the network.

Source The starting node in a network.

Chapter References

BOOKS

Battersby, Albert. *Network Analysis for Planning and Scheduling*. New York: Wiley, 1970.

Bazarra, M. S., and J. J. Jarvis. *Linear Programming and Network Flows*. New York: Wiley, 1977.

Elmaghraby, Salah E. *Some Network Models in Management Science*. New York: Springer-Verlag, 1970.

ARTICLES

Bell, W. L., et al. "Improving the Distribution of Industrial Gases with an On-Line Computerized Routing and Scheduling Optimizer." *Interfaces*, Vol. 13 (December), 1983.

Dijkstra, E. W. "A Note on Two Problems in Connection with Graphs." *Numerische Mathematik*, Vol. 1, 1959.

Glover, F., R. Glover, J. Lorenzo, and C. McMillan. "The Passenger-Mix Problem in the Scheduled Airlines." *Interfaces*, Vol. 12 (June), 1982.

Mini Cases

CASE 11A

THE RIVERA SPRINKLER COMPANY

Like many other small business owners, Sara Rivera never envisioned owning her own company. In fact, her path after leaving high school gave no indication that owning a sprinkler installation business would be in her future. After high school, Sara attended a state university in the Southeast and earned a degree in business administration. Her specialty was finance, and after graduation she went to work as a loan officer for the state's largest bank. Six years and several transfers later, Sara realized that she needed an MBA if she planned on moving into higher management in the bank. She applied to numerous MBA programs throughout the country which she knew to have name recognition in the bank. Finally, she decided to attend a Big Ten university because it offered the largest support package. The bank gave her a leave of absence to pursue the MBA degree.

Two years later, MBA in hand, Sara did something that she hadn't planned on when she enrolled in the university—she resigned from the bank and took a position in the internal audit department of a large corporation. The main attractions were the opportunity for travel and the reasonably high starting salary. In addition, as she mulled over the offer and compared it with going back to the bank, she realized that the opportunities with her former employer would be somewhat limited over the next 10 to 15 years.

How, then, did Sara wind up as the owner of a sprinkler company? Two years after joining the large corporation, she found herself in a sticky situation during an audit of the company's executive pay plan. She uncovered what she thought were some irregularities in the way the compensation committee had assigned stock bonuses to certain key executives. Even though Sara had good evidence that these possibly illegal moves had occurred, it became clear that she would have no future with the company if she revealed what she knew. About this same time, she inherited nearly $250,000 from her late grandparents' estate.

Disillusioned with corporate life, Sara began looking for a small business that she could get into with the $250,000 and still have enough capital to operate until the company started growing. She finally settled on a sprinkler installation business in northern California. Summertime work with her father, a landscaping contractor, had given her valuable experience with sprinkler systems, which she could now use in her new venture.

From the start, Sara had two important assets that a lot of people who try their hand at small business don't have: (1) a substantial amount of capital to work with and (2) a good understanding of business concepts. Now, however, although she has been turning a pretty nice profit for the past few years, Sara thinks that she could do better in a number of areas, such as sprinkler design. Although she has always been able to design systems that worked, and her customers have always expressed satisfaction, she believes that there must be a way of determining an optimal layout which will minimize the amount of pipe required for a proper sprinkler installation.

Consider this job that Sara is working on now. Figure 11-41 shows the layout of the client's yard. The circles indicate where the sprinkler heads must be located, and the distances between sprinkler heads are shown on the lines joining the circles. If two sprinklers on the diagram have no line connecting them, it is because a structure or other impediment is between them.

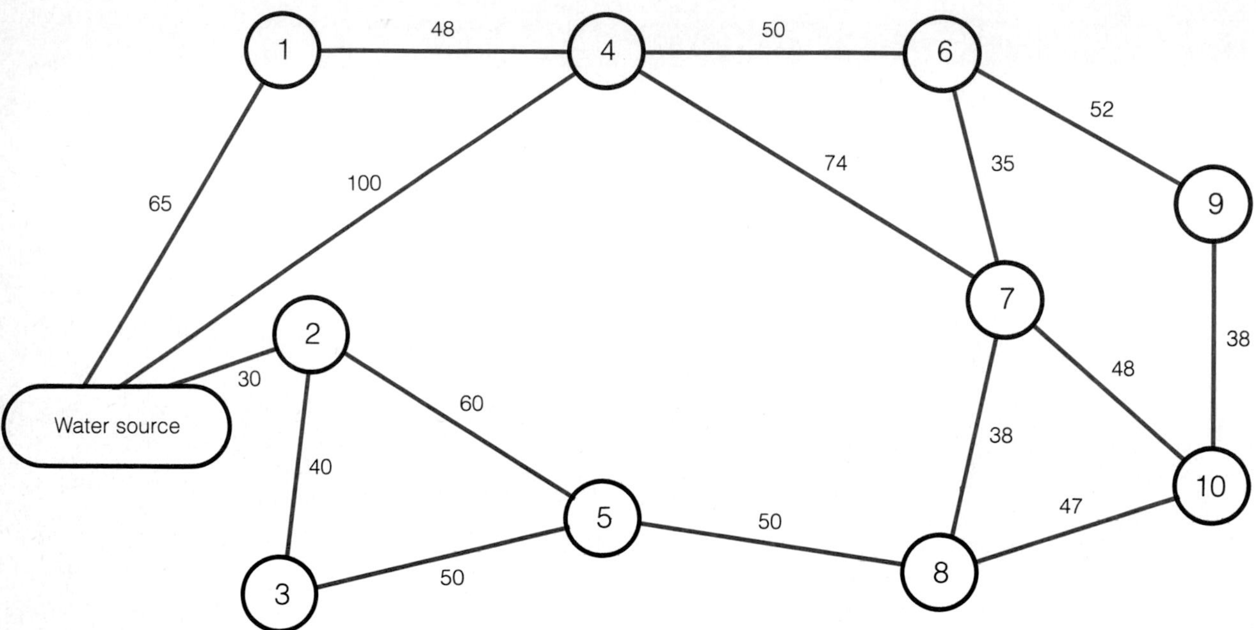

Note: Distances are in feet.
Figure 11-41
Sprinkler installation network

CASE 11B
REMINGTON BUILDERS, INC.

Phillip Remington's father founded Remington Builders in 1944, and the company went public in 1962. When his father retired in 1977, Phillip stepped in as chief executive officer and has been running the company ever since. Remington started out doing business with the automotive industry, but in the late 1960s switched its focus to aerospace and has continued doing contract work for the major aerospace companies since that time.

The company has always been very profitable, even in times when the U.S. economy was not doing particularly well. Part of the reason for this success has been Phillip's insistence on making a careful analysis of any big decisions. This emphasis on analysis has spread throughout the company. The department that Jan Aldin's manages, which makes radio controls used in military aircraft, is no exception.

Yesterday, Jan's department was awarded a 5-year contract to supply an electronic control unit that will be partially assembled by a special robot. Jan expects that each year a new model of the robot will be available. When the contract ends in 5 years, the robot will no longer be needed by Jan's department. Each new model of the robot will be only slightly different from the previous model, but a new robot will be somewhat more efficient and have lower operating costs. As the robot gets older, operating costs will increase as a result of more downtime and increased preventive maintenance requirements. The information on page 599 is available on the special robot's operating costs, trade-in value, salvage value, and purchase price for each of the next 5 years.

Jan realizes that a robot has to be available in each of the next 5 years, but she wonders what the best replacement plan would be to minimize the total costs during the contract period. Some time ago, Jan attended a seminar where she learned how to

Year	Operating Cost ($)	Trade-in Value ($)	Salvage Value ($)	Purchase Price ($)
0	20,000	—	—	100,000
1	25,000	90,000	85,000	100,000
2	30,000	80,000	75,000	100,000
3	37,000	75,000	70,000	100,000
4	44,000	70,000	65,000	100,000
5	53,000	65,000	60,000	100,000

use a shortest-route network model to deal with this type of decision, but now she has forgotten how to set up the problem and solve it.

Chapter 12

QUEUING THEORY: THE STUDY OF WAITING-LINE MODELS

Chapter Outline

Chapter 12

Why You Need to Know

Rarely does a day go by that you do not wait in some sort of line. When driving, you wait in line for traffic lights to turn green. At school, you wait in line at the cafeteria or at the book store. Lines commonly form in supermarkets, banks, and the post office; as well as at movies, concerts, and sports events. At big football games, lines form at the gate as people enter the stadium; more lines form at the concession stands; and very long lines seem to form outside the restrooms. Without thinking about it a great deal, you are a regular participant in waiting-line systems.

A waiting-line system consists of *inputs* (e.g., customers) who wait in a line to be served at a service center (e.g., a checkout stand). Certainly, as a consumer, you have been on the input side of a waiting-line system. But if you have ever worked at a fast-food store, movie theater, gasoline station, or in virtually any other organization, you have also participated as a server in a waiting-line system.

Because waiting-line systems are an integral part of business, decision makers need to understand how waiting lines function and how service centers and waiting lines interact. The formal term for the study of waiting lines is *queuing theory;* the waiting line itself is referred to as the *queue.* By applying queuing theory, businesses are able to make informed decisions about such things as how many bank teller windows to build when the bank is constructed, how many pumps to have at a gasoline station, how many ticket windows to have at a baseball stadium, how many customs inspection stations to have open at a border crossing, and so forth.

A safe bet is that no matter what type of organization you go to work for following graduation, you will be dealing with decisions that involve a waiting-line system. The material presented in this chapter provides an introduction to queuing theory as it relates to several of the most frequently encountered waiting-line systems.

Chapter Objectives

The objectives for this chapter are to introduce you to the basic concepts of waiting-line models and to help you become familiar with the types of situations for which such models can be used to aid in the decision-making process.

Specifically, after studying the material in this chapter, you should be able to:

1. Identify situations where a single-channel waiting-line model applies.
2. Compute various statistics associated with a single-channel waiting-line system.
3. Identify situations where a multiple-channel waiting-line model applies.
4. Compute various statistics associated with a multiple-channel waiting-line system.
5. Analyze the basic economic trade-offs associated with waiting-line systems.

12-1 A BRIEF HISTORY OF QUEUING THEORY

Queuing, or waiting-line, theory, exists in its present form because a Danish mathematician, A. K. Erlang, an employee of the Danish Telephone Company, wanted to determine the number of lines needed to handle various frequencies of calls. In addressing this problem, Erlang had to attach meaning to arrivals, servers, waiting-line systems, and most of the other factors presently involved in queuing theory. The publication of Erlang's pioneering work *The Theory of Probabilities and Telephone Conversation* in 1909 marks the beginning of this new field of study.

Queuing theory remained associated primarily with the telephone industry through the early 1950s, when it was expanded into other areas where waiting lines were of concern. One of the earliest applications of waiting-line theory outside the telephone industry was to aircraft landings. A few of the other areas where waiting-line theory has been applied are scheduling clinic patients, predicting arrivals at toll booths, computer networking, and loading and unloading ships.

Queuing models deal with some of the most obvious and practical problems facing businesses. Unfortunately, because the models are dependent on probability theory, they can easily become so abstract that their use by actual decision makers is limited. A recent development that may give hope to practical decision makers is the application of simulation models to waiting-line decision situations. Chapter 16 takes a look at simulation of a waiting-line system.

12-2 TYPES OF WAITING-LINE SYSTEMS

Service organizations like banks and gasoline stations are typically designed so that total service capacity exceeds total demand. However, even with excess total service capacity, a waiting line, or a **queue**, will develop at certain times. Lines will occur in a system if the demand for service is not equally spaced over time. Although most of the time the demand for service is less than the service capacity, sometimes the demand exceeds the capacity. For instance, even though the total highway capacity in a city is able to handle the total daily demand, lines occur during rush-hour traffic. Lines will also occur if the service time in the system varies. One person spending a half-hour at a bank teller's station can cause long lines in the lobby. Thus, even though on average the capacity may exceed demand, at those times when demand does exceed capacity, a waiting line will form.

If a system's service capacity is less than demand, a waiting line will quickly develop and, in theory, grow infinitely long. The line would be called an *infinite queue*. Such a situation is intolerable, and a change to increase service capacity or reduce demand is needed.

You might encounter a wide variety of waiting-line systems in decision-making situations, but all have two basic characteristics: They all have an arrival (demand) subsystem and a server (supply) subsystem. Figure 12-1 shows examples of three basic waiting-line systems. Since the arrival and service subsystems vary from situation to situation, a different waiting-line model is needed to describe each combination.

Figure 12-1
Examples of waiting-line systems

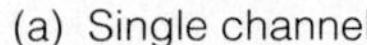

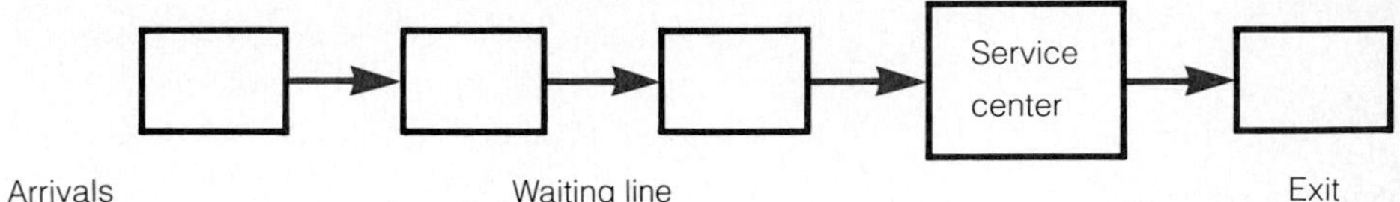

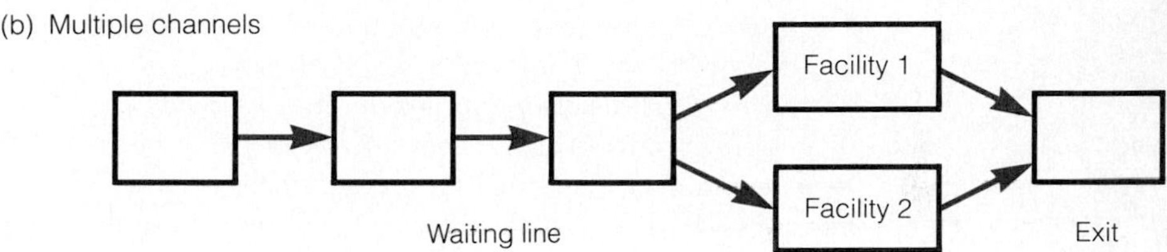

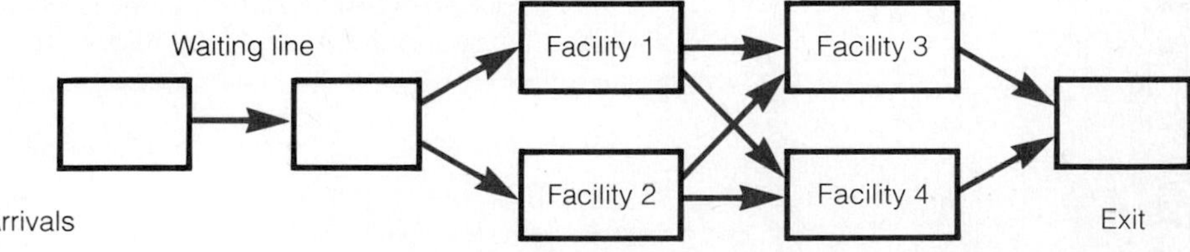

ARRIVAL CHARACTERISTICS

The factors which differentiate arrival (demand) subsystems generally pertain to the way customers arrive at the service facility. (Note that we refer to the demand entities as "customers." The "customer" may actually be a person (a customer in the usual sense), a phone call to a 911 emergency number, or a product in an assembly line.) Some of these distinguishing factors are described in the following paragraphs.

The customer population can be *finite* or *infinite*. In most business situations, the population is finite. For instance, the number of potential patients arriving at an emergency room for treatment is finite, since the number of people in the emergency-room service area is limited. However, when the potential customer base is large, the assumption of an infinite population is often acceptable—it also simplifies modeling.

The customer source can be either a *single population* or *multiple populations*. Consider again the example of patients arriving at a hospital emergency room. If we don't distinguish between the type of treatment required, for modeling purposes the customers come from a single population. But if we distinguish between trauma patients, psychiatric patients, and all others, there are multiple populations.

The waiting-line system can exert *total control, partial control,* or *no control* over the arrival of customers. For example, the arrival of automobiles at the painting station on an assembly line is totally controlled by the production staff. The arrival of logging trucks at a lumber mill can be partially controlled by scheduling their departure from the forest, but some lack of control enters the process when the trucks leave the forest and start traveling the highway system on their way to the mill. Finally, a bank has no control over the arrival of customers at its teller windows.

Customers may arrive in *groups* or as *individuals*. Bookstore customers typically arrive as individuals, but restaurant customers tend to arrive in groups of two or more.

Arrivals can be either *independent* or *dependent*. For instance, on a soft-drink production line, the bottles are filled automatically, capped, and then scanned to detect any foreign substances. If the scanner detects something, a gate opens and the bottle is sent down an alternate conveyor belt to be manually inspected. When the filling process is operating normally, the chance of one bottle having a foreign substance is independent of whether the previous bottle was contaminated and bottles would arrive for manual inspection independently. However, when the filling machine malfunctions and a series of bottles are affected, then bottle arrivals for inspection are dependent.

Arrivals are either *deterministic* or *probabilistic*. In a deterministic system, both the number of arrivals per time period and the time between arrivals are known with certainty. This situation occurs when arrivals are totally controlled, as in an auto assembly line. Arrivals are probabilistic if both the number of arrivals per time period and the time between arrivals are random. Most waiting-line applications have probabilistic arrivals.

If arrivals are probabilistic, the distribution which describes customer arrivals can be either *empirical* or *theoretical*. Suppose data on the number of vehicles arriving at a highway toll booth between 8:00 and 11:00 A.M. were collected for 80 days and used to generate the following frequency distribution:

Vehicles Arriving	Frequency Observed	Fraction
Under 100	5 days	.0625
100–200	40 days	.5000
201–400	8 days	.1000
Over 400	27 days	.3375
Total	80 days	

This empirical probability distribution might be used to represent the arrival pattern for vehicles at the toll booth.

When no data are available to build an empirical distribution, a theoretical distribution must be assumed. The *Poisson distribution*, which we will discuss later, is the theoretical distribution most often used to describe customer arrivals.

SERVICE CHARACTERISTICS

Service subsystems also differ according to how service occurs and how the waiting customers are handled. Some of the main service characteristics of a waiting-line system are described in the paragraphs below.

Service may be performed on a *first-come, first-served* basis. Many waiting-line systems have this service pattern. For instance, cars arriving at a "quick lube" business for an oil change and lube job are served in the order they arrive. This rule is sometimes called the "fairness" rule.

Service may also be performed in a *last-come, first-served* order. For instance, firewood is used in reverse order of how it was stacked. This service rule is much less common than the first-come, first-served rule.

Random-order service rules are occasionally used when there is no clear indication of the order of arrivals or when the service capacity is limited and not everyone will be served. For example, if customers can enter a clothing store by any of several different doors, clerks may wait on whichever customer they happen to notice first. Random-order service might also occur when a store has only a limited supply of a particular item, numerous customers want to purchase the item, and there is no clear way of determining which customer should have preference. For example, a few years ago, Cabbage Patch Kids were in great demand at Christmastime. A local department store, which had completely sold out of the dolls, suddenly received a shipment of five at 11:00 A.M. The store manager had no way of determining which five customers should have the chance to buy the dolls, so he set up a random lottery for all customers who were in the store at 11:00 A.M. and who wanted to buy a Cabbage Patch Kid.

The service rule can be based on a *priority scheme,* which means that the customers with the highest priority will be served first. One place where priority service rules are commonly used is the hospital emergency room. Many people go to the emergency room for treatment of nonemergency problems such as flu and colds; they are served as long as no true emergencies exist. The emergency room is also a good example of *preemptive* service, which means that a customer presently being served (or next in line) is bumped back to waiting status by a customer with a higher priority. For instance, a person being treated for a sore throat will be returned to the waiting room when paramedics bring in a heart attack victim for treatment. (Most of us would accept being preempted under such circumstances, but imaging being bumped from your table in a restaurant by a "more important" customer!)

While preemptive service rules in hospital emergency rooms are fairly standard, hospital operating rooms generally function under a *nonpreemptive* service rule. That is, once an operation begins it is generally not interrupted, even by patients with higher priorities.

Service systems can have *single* or *multiple channels.* A single-channel system is characterized by having only one server, as in the case of a local movie house that has just one ticket seller even though the building contains four small theaters. Likewise, a multiple-channel service subsystem has two or more servers, like the multiple tellers in a bank. In self-serve situations, the customer actually becomes his or her own server.

In a multiple-channel system, the servers can be arranged in *parallel* or in *series* or in a combination of both. For example, many fast-food restaurants use the **multiple-server system**, in which identical servers are arranged in parallel. This system produces multiple lines, since several cash registers are placed along the counter and customers can line up to order at any one of them. On the other hand, a production situation may have the servers arranged in series. For instance, if a part must be drilled, then sanded, and then painted, three service stations would be arranged so that the products move from one server to the next, in order. A production facility could have several assembly lines, each performing these three operations.

The time it takes to service a customer can be *deterministic* or *probabilistic.* If the time is deterministic, we know exactly how long it takes to serve each customer and therefore how many customers can be served in a given time period. If the service times are probabilistic, then they will be described by an *empirical* distribution or a *theoretical* distribution. Empirical distributions are based on observed data, and theoretical distributions are based on what should, in theory, occur. The most commonly used theoretical distribution for describing service times is the *exponential distribution.*

WAITING-LINE BEHAVIOR

Waiting-line systems are characterized by their arrival and service subsystems, but another important factor is the behavior of "customers" in the line. The following paragraphs introduce some of the most common types of waiting-line behavior, which you will no doubt recognize from your own personal experience.

For instance, if a line is too long, some customers arriving for service will refuse to enter the system. This practice is called **balking.** Recently a family-oriented seafood restaurant opened in our town. On our first visit we were greeted by a line out the front door and an expected wait of 50–75 minutes before we could be seated. We balked and drove down the street to another restaurant—which had no waiting line.

When a customer joins a line and then, after waiting for a period of time, leaves the line, the customer has "truncated the queue." This practice of leaving a line before being served is also called **reneging.** Truncating, or reneging, often occurs when the line is long and/or the waiting time is long. For example, customers who call computer software service hotlines (usually toll calls) often are put in a queue and told their call will be answered by the next available service representative. After waiting for a while, some callers hang up without receiving the answers to their questions. They have truncated the queue.

If the waiting-line system has a maximum queue length and it is filled to capacity, a customer will be *rejected.* A gasoline station has limited space for cars to wait in line; after that point, customers may be forced to wait illegally in the street. When a parking lot fills up, new arrivals may form informal queues as customers drive around looking for vacant stalls or come back later to obtain the desired service.

Customers may *jockey* between waiting lines in an attempt to reduce their waiting time. For instance, in the fast-food example presented earlier, with multiple lines to parallel servers, customers will jump from line to line if they think one line is moving faster than another.

So far we have discussed a number of arrival and service characteristics, as well as several alternative waiting-line behaviors. A variety of waiting-line systems can be formed by different combinations of arrival, service, and queue behavior. For instance, we could have a system with constant arrivals, constant service rates, multiple-channel parallel servers, and queue jockeying allowed. We could change it slightly by assuming Poisson-distributed arrivals and leaving the other factors the same. There are many possible waiting-line systems, and some are extremely complicated to analyze. In fact, the mathematics underlying some waiting-line systems is so complex that the only reasonable means for analysis is simulation (see Chapter 16).

In this chapter, we will examine three fundamental waiting-line systems:

1. Single channel with constant arrivals, constant service times, and first-come, first-served service.
2. Single channel with Poisson-distributed arrivals, exponential service, and first-come, first-served service.
3. Multiple parallel channels with Poisson-distributed arrivals, exponential service, and first-come, first-served service.

12-3 SINGLE-CHANNEL WAITING-LINE MODELS

DETERMINISTIC ARRIVAL AND SERVICE RATES

The Dart Assembly Company makes carburetors for major U.S. car manufacturers at a fully automated plant outside Detroit. Near the end of the assembly process, lacquer is sprayed on the carburetors by an automatic spray gun. The production manager has complete control over the carburetors' **arrival rate,** defined as the number of units arriving for service per unit of time, and over how long lacquering each carburetor will take. Since the manager controls the **service time**—the time a unit spends being

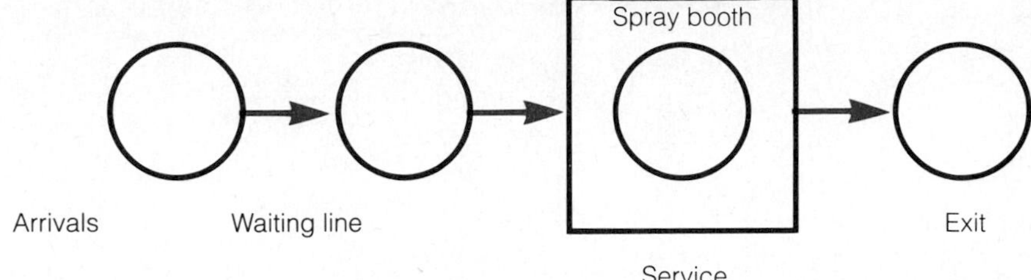

Figure 12-2
Dart Assembly waiting-line system: (single-channel system with deterministic arrivals and service rates)

served (lacquered, in this case), he therefore controls the **service rate**, defined as the number of units served per unit of time.

Figure 12-2 shows the Dart system, which has one waiting line and one server. This type of system is referred to as a *single-channel system.* Since the arrival rate and service rate are both totally controllable, they are deterministic.

Situation 1: No Queue, No Idle Time

Suppose the production manager sets the carburetor arrival rate at 20 per hour. This means that carburetors will arrive at the spray station with an **interarrival** time, or time between units arriving for service, of 3 minutes. Further suppose that the spray process, or service time, is set to take exactly 3 minutes. In this situation, no waiting line will form because a carburetor will arrive at just the moment the spraying is completed for the previous carburetor. Further, no idle time will occur in the spray station because as soon as one carburetor is finished, another will be moved into the spray booth. **Idle time** is the time a service facility is sitting empty waiting to provide service.

Table 12-1 shows how the system would operate during the first 30 minutes. Note that the queue length and idle time are always zero. This will be the case as long as the arrival rate and the service rate are equal and constant.

Table 12-1 DART ASSEMBLY SITUATION 1: NO QUEUE, NO IDLE TIME

Arrival rate: 1 each 3 minutes (20 per hour)
Service rate: 3 minutes each (20 per hour)
Assumptions: Constant arrivals, constant service
Starting conditions: Unit 1 starting service
All times are in minutes.

Elapsed Time	Unit	Time in Service	Time out of Service	Idle Time	Queue Length
0	1	0	3	0	0
3	2	3	6	0	0
6	3	6	9	0	0
9	4	9	12	0	0
12	5	12	15	0	0
15	6	15	18	0	0
18	7	18	21	0	0
21	8	21	24	0	0
24	9	24	27	0	0
27	10	27	30	0	0
30	11	30	33	0	0

Situation 2: No Queue, Positive Idle Time

In situation 1, the arrival rate matched the service rate. Suppose the production manager adjusts the spray rate so that 30 carburetors per hour could be sprayed, or 1 carburetor every 2 minutes. The carburetor arrival rate is left at a constant of 20 per hour (1 every 3 minutes). We have changed the system so that hourly service capacity exceeds hourly demand. This means a waiting line will not form but there will be idle time in the system. When both arrival rate and service time are constant, we can compute the fraction of the time the service facilities will be idle as follows:

$$\text{Idle-time fraction} = 1 - A/S \tag{12-1}$$

where:

A = arrival rate per time period

S = service capacity per time period

In this example, we have:

$A = 20$ per hour and $S = 30$ per hour

Then, using equation 12-1, the idle-time fraction is:

$$1 - A/S = 1 - 20/30 = 10/30 = 1/3$$

Thus, with these production control settings, the spray booth will sit idle for one-third of each hour. Table 12-2 shows how the waiting-line system will function for the first 11 arrivals. Notice that the system is idle 1 out of every 3 minutes and that the queue length is always zero.

Table 12-2 DART ASSEMBLY SITUATION 2: NO QUEUE, POSITIVE IDLE TIME

Arrival rate: 1 each 3 minutes (20 per hour)
Service rate: 2 minutes each (30 per hour)
Assumptions: Constant arrivals, constant service
Starting conditions: Unit 1 starting service
All times are in minutes.

Elapsed Time	Unit	Time in Service	Time out of Service	Idle Time	Queue Length
0	1	0	2	0	0
3	2	3	5	1	0
6	3	6	8	1	0
9	4	9	11	1	0
12	5	12	14	1	0
15	6	15	17	1	0
18	7	18	20	1	0
21	8	21	23	1	0
24	9	24	26	1	0
27	10	27	29	1	0
30	11	30	32	1	0
				10	

Situation 3: Queue Buildup, No Idle Time

Suppose the Dart production manager finds that with the spray booth set at 30 per hour, the quality of work deteriorates. To overcome this problem, he sets the spray rate back to 20 per hour (1 every 3 minutes). However, suppose the carburetor arrival rate is increased to 30 per hour (1 every 2 minutes). Both the arrival and service rates are constant.

Now the carburetors are arriving faster than the spray booth can accommodate and a waiting line will develop. The *queue buildup* is the rate at which the waiting line grows. When the arrival and service rates are constant, the queue buildup is computed as follows:

$$\text{Queue buildup} = A - S \tag{12-2}$$

where:

A = arrival rate per time period

S = service capacity per time period

For this example, the waiting line will grow at the rate of 10 per hour, as calculated using equation 12-2:

$$A - S = 30 - 20 = 10$$

In a 30-minute period, the waiting line would grow by 5 units, as shown in Table 12-3. Take a close look at Table 12-3 to see how the queue lengths were determined. Also

Table 12-3 DART ASSEMBLY SITUATION 3: QUEUE BUILDUP, NO IDLE TIME

Arrival rate: 1 each 2 minutes (30 per hour)
Service rate: 3 minutes each (20 per hour)
Assumptions: Constant arrivals, constant service
Starting conditions: Unit 1 starting service
All times are in minutes.

Elapsed Time	Unit	Time Arrived	Time in Service	Time out of Service	Idle Time	Queue Length
0	1	0	0	3	0	0
2	2	2	3	6	0	1
4	3	4	6	9	0	1
6	4	6	9	12	0	1
8	5	8	12	15	0	2
10	6	10	15	18	0	2
12	7	12	18	21	0	2
14	8	14	21	24	0	3
16	9	16	24	27	0	3
18	10	18	27	30	0	3
20	11	20	30	33	0	4
22	12	22	33	36	0	4
24	13	24	36	39	0	4
26	14	26	39	42	0	5
28	15	28	42	45	0	5
30	16	30	45	48	0	5

note the **waiting time**, the length of time some of the units will have to wait for service. For instance, unit 16 will arrive at time 30 but won't enter the paint booth until time 45; this is a 15-minute wait.

If the production system operated at these rates for 2 hours, the waiting line would reach 20 units; in 3 hours, the line would reach 30, and so on. In fact, the waiting line will grow indefinitely when the arrival rate exceeds the service rate. The production manager will have to slow down arrivals, figure out some way to get acceptable-quality spraying at a rate of 30 per hour or higher, or perhaps work overtime.

These examples for the Dart Assembly Company assume constant arrival and service rates. Although such cases do exist, more frequently you will encounter probabilistic arrival and/or service rates. These situations present a slightly more complicated waiting-line system, as you will see in the next example.

PROBABILISTIC ARRIVAL AND SERVICE RATES

Consider a second waiting-line example, involving the Clean Look Car Wash Company, founded by Everett Wilson in 1986 in Fresno, California. Everett had owned and operated several car wash businesses in and around Fresno for 14 years. During that time, he had intermittently worked on designing an improved automatic car-washing system. In the summer of 1985, he installed his prototype Turbo-Washer in Fresno. Using the summer to make minor technical adjustments, he applied for a patent in late 1985. The patent was granted in June 1986 and Everett formed the Clean Look Car Wash Company in July.

The feature which made the Turbo-Washer patentable was its computer sensing device, which determines the shape of a vehicle and automatically selects the appropriate spray pattern and brush units. The sensor can, for instance, distinguish between a sedan and a pickup truck. An even more sophisticated feature is the sensor's ability to assess how dirty a vehicle is and adjust the spray strength and soap content to maximize cleaning capability at a minimum cost.

The Clean Look Car Wash Company, under Everett Wilson's management, has sold more than 200 Turbo-Washer franchises throughout California and other western states. However, before Everett will sell a franchise, he works with the buyer to determine what size Turbo-Washer to install and what configuration the location should have to accommodate customers. For this purpose, his analysis includes a waiting-line model.

A Single-Channel System

Let's look at an example of how Everett uses the single-channel waiting-line model. Recently, Everett negotiated a deal with Donald Mitchell, who owns a lot at the corner of 18th and Grant in Eugene, Oregon. Figure 12-3 shows the general lot location and the proposed layout for the Clean Look Car Wash. Eighteenth is one of Eugene's busiest streets, and both Don and Everett agreed the entrance should be from 18th to attract the most business. Because of the lot's size and the buyer's financial position, a single-stall Turbo-Washer is being considered. Figure 12-4 shows the waiting-line system which will develop at the car wash. Vehicles will arrive and enter the Turbo-Washer one at a time, on a first-come, first-served basis. When the wash is complete, the vehicles will exit the system. A single line will form to enter the Turbo-Washer, since there is only one Turbo-Washer stall for all arriving vehicles, thus constituting a single-channel system.

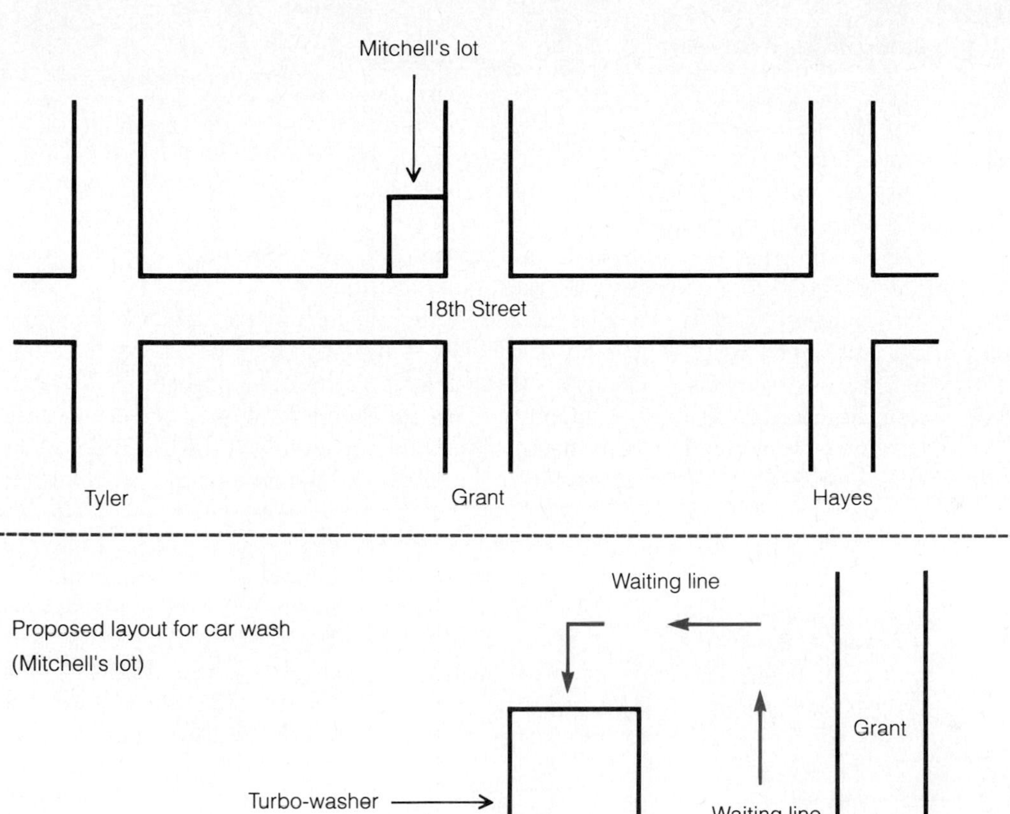

Figure 12-3
Clean Look Car Wash waiting-line analysis

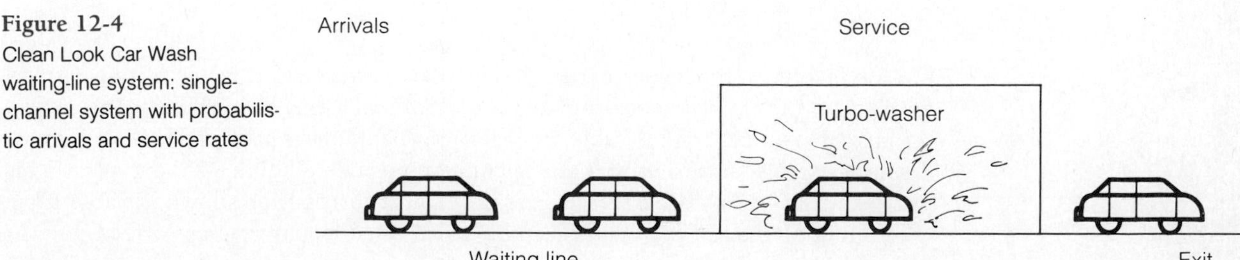

Figure 12-4
Clean Look Car Wash waiting-line system: single-channel system with probabilistic arrivals and service rates

Probabilistic Arrivals

In the Dart Assembly Company example, carburetors arrive at the paint booth at a constant rate determined by the speed of the assembly line. However, in most customer service situations, like this car wash example, arrivals cannot be controlled, since obviously there is no way to control the number of people who choose to drive east on 18th or to control when a car will turn into the Clean Look Car Wash lot. The arrivals are therefore probabilistic, and the number of customers arriving in a given time period can be described by a probability distribution.

Numerous empirical studies have supported the idea that for many waiting-line situations, the Poisson probability distribution is appropriate for describing the number of arrivals at a service facility in a given period. The **Poisson probability distribution** assumes arrivals occur randomly and are independent of one another. Because customers would tend to arrive randomly and independently at the Clean Look Car Wash in Eugene, we will assume the number of arrivals per time period has a Poisson distribution.

The Poisson distribution is described by a single parameter, λ (lambda), which is the mean number of arrivals in the designated time period. Thus, if the mean number of customers arriving at the car wash per hour is 10, then we set $\lambda = 10$; if the mean is 8, then $\lambda = 8$.

Even though customers may arrive at an average rate of 8 per hour, in some hours arrivals may total 6, 7, 8, 9, or some other number. We can find the probability of any reasonable arrival rate occurring by using the Poisson probability distribution formula:

$$P(x) = \frac{\lambda^x e^{-\lambda}}{x!} \tag{12-3}$$

where:

$x =$ number of arrivals per time period

$e = 2.71828$

Using this formula, we get:

$$P(5) = \frac{8^5 e^{-8}}{5!} = .0916$$

$$P(6) = \frac{8^6 e^{-8}}{6!} = .1221$$

$$P(7) = \frac{8^7 e^{-8}}{7!} = .1396$$

$$P(9) = \frac{8^9 e^{-8}}{9!} = .1241$$

In fact, even though we expect 8 customers to arrive each hour, there is a small probability (.0003) that no customers will arrive and a small probability (.0001) that 21 customers may arrive. A table of Poisson probabilities is provided in Appendix C. Using this table or performing the calculations using equation 12-3 for all arrivals between 0 and 21 will give the discrete probability distribution shown in Table 12-4.

Similar Poisson probabilities can be determined for any average arrival rate. As part of Everett's buyer assistance program, he helps Don estimate lambda (the mean

Table 12-4 POISSON PROBABILITY DISTRIBUTION FOR $\lambda = 8$

Arrivals per Hour	Probability
0	.0003
1	.0027
2	.0107
3	.0286
4	.0573
5	.0916
6	.1221
7	.1396
8	.1396
9	.1241
10	.0993
11	.0722
12	.0481
13	.0296
14	.0169
15	.0090
16	.0045
17	.0021
18	.0009
19	.0004
20	.0002
21	.0001

number of arrivals per time period) for the proposed car wash. After conducting a traffic study and performing a market analysis, they arrived at a "best estimate" of $\lambda = 7$, indicating that an average of 7 vehicles will arrive per hour, and the actual number of arrivals will follow a Poisson probability distribution.

Probabilistic Service Rates

In the Dart Assembly example, the painting time was strictly controlled and was constant. However, in many service situations, service time cannot be maintained at a constant level. Such is the case with the Turbo-Washer at a Clean Look Car Wash. The time needed to wash a vehicle depends on both the vehicle type and how dirty it is. Everett sells three models of the Turbo-Washer, which differ in price based upon washing speed. (The faster the wash, the higher the price.) However, the average wash time will depend on the types of vehicles being washed and how dirty they are.

If the service rate is not constant, it is probabilistic and should be described by a probability distribution. If service times are assumed to be independent (that is, the time required to wash one vehicle does not influence the time needed to wash any other vehicle), the times can be described by an **exponential probability distribution.**

The exponential probability distribution can be used to find the probability that a customer can be served within some time, t, using the following formula:

$$P(\text{service time} \leq t) = 1 - e^{-\mu t} \qquad (12\text{-}4)$$

where: μ = average number of customers the facility can serve in a unit of time

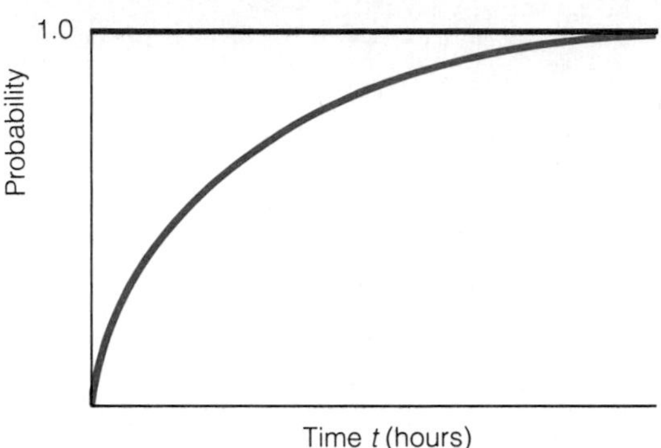

Figure 12-5
Probability a vehicle will be washed within time t

Thus if, on average, a vehicle can be washed in 10 minutes (1/6 hour), then $\mu = 6$ units per hour. (We convert 10 minutes to a fraction of an hour because μ is given in units per hour.) Since not every car will take 10 minutes to wash, we can use equation 12-4 to find the probability that a car will be done in a specified period of time. For instance, to find the probability that a car can be washed within 5 minutes:

$$P(\text{service time} \leq 5/60 \text{ hour}) = 1 - e^{-6(5/60)} = 1 - e^{-.5} = 1 - .6065 = .2935$$

(Again, we have converted minutes into a fraction of an hour.) We could perform similar calculations to find the probability that a car will be washed within 12 minutes.

$$P(\text{service time} \leq 12/60 \text{ hour}) = 1 - e^{-6(12/60)} = 1 - e^{-1.2} = 1 - .3012 = .6988$$

We could, in fact, use this distribution to find the probability that a vehicle will be washed in any specified period of time. The probability of service-time distribution represented by these calculations is shown in Figure 12-5.

Everett also helps his customers estimate mean washing rates by analyzing the distribution of vehicle types and dirt characteristics in the market area. For instance, agricultural areas have more pickups with "tougher" dirt than metropolitan areas do. Both factors increase the average wash time. For the Eugene area, Everett's analysis yields the following mean hourly service rates for the three levels of Turbo-Washers:

Level 1	Level 2	Level 3
$\mu = 6$	$\mu = 8$	$\mu = 10$

Waiting-Line Characteristics

When the arrivals are assumed to be Poisson-distributed and the service times are assumed to follow an exponential distribution, the single-channel waiting-line system is well defined. That is, the system's behavior is well understood and can be predicted. While the mathematical development is beyond the scope of this text, a number of its waiting-line operating characteristics can be computed to help decision makers understand their waiting-line system. These characteristics relate to the waiting line and to the service facility itself.

The waiting-line characteristics assume that $\mu > \lambda$. If the service rate does not exceed the arrival rate, the system will develop an infinite queue. *Waiting-line formulas cannot be used if* $\mu \leq \lambda$. This means that (for the purposes of our waiting-line analysis) Don Mitchell cannot consider the Level 1 Turbo-Washer since it can wash only 6 vehicles per hour on average ($\mu = 6$) and the average arrival rate for his proposed car wash is estimated to be 7 per hour.

Probability of the Server Being Idle

As mentioned earlier, when a service facility is not being used, it is idle. Unless some other productive use can be found (such as routine maintenance), this idle time is an opportunity cost to the owner. Therefore, decision makers need to know the percentage of time the facility will be idle.

The equation for determining the probability of an idle service facility is:

$$P_0 = 1 - \lambda/\mu \qquad (12\text{-}5)$$

Thus, if Donald Mitchell purchases the Level 2 Turbo-Washer, with $\mu = 8$ and the average number of customer arrivals per hour (λ) is 7, the probability the facility will be idle is:

$$P_0 = 1 - 7/8 = .125$$

Therefore, Don can expect .125 of each hour to be idle time with the Level 2 Turbo-Washer, which might be an acceptably low amount of idle time. However, other waiting-line characteristics will also influence his decision about which machine to buy.

Average Waiting Time

When a customer arrives for service but the service facility is busy, the customer must wait. The length of the wait will vary, depending on how many customers are already in line. The expected, or average, waiting time for a customer is found by equation 12-6:

$$W_q = \frac{\lambda/\mu}{\mu - \lambda} \qquad (12\text{-}6)$$

For the Level 2 Turbo-Washer, the expected waiting time is:

$$W_q = \frac{7/8}{8 - 7} = .875 \text{ hour}$$

This means that, on average, a customer will wait .875 hour ($.875 \times 60 = 52.5$ minutes) just to get into the Turbo-Washer. This long average waiting time occurs because the arrival rate and the service rate for the Level 2 machine are so close.

Average Time in the System

Equation 12-6 provides the average time an arrival will wait for service, but a customer is actually in the system for a longer period than that, on average. Equation 12-7 shows the equation for computing average total time in the system:

$$W_s = \frac{1}{\mu - \lambda} \qquad (12\text{-}7)$$

In this case, the average, or expected, time in the system (waiting and being served) is:

$$W_s = \frac{1}{8 - 7} = 1 \text{ hour}$$

Equations 12-6 and 12-7 address the issue of average waiting time and average time in the system. These values are important to a decision maker, since costs are associated with making customers wait; these costs are generally opportunity costs and lost goodwill. In situations like the Clean Look Car Wash, a long average wait on the first trip will discourage customers from returning to the business. An average wait of 52.5 minutes may be excruciating, and an average of 60 minutes waiting and service time is probably excessive.

For most people, the aggravation associated with being in a waiting-line system arises from waiting for service. Amazingly, our attitudes seem to change as soon as service begins. Thus, if the average time spent in the system is to be long, most of that time should be spent being served rather than waiting for service. Unfortunately, in this example, 52.5 minutes is the average time waiting for service and only 7.5 minutes on average will be spent in the Turbo-Washer.

Average Number Waiting for Service

While the average waiting time and average time in the system are important values to know, so is the average length of the waiting line. Equation 12-8 will determine the average number of customers waiting for service in this system:

$$L_q = \frac{\lambda^2/\mu}{\mu - \lambda} \tag{12-8}$$

For this example, we get:

$$L_q = \frac{7^2/8}{8-7} = 6.125$$

Average Number in the System

Equation 12-8 provides the average number of customers waiting for service. We can also determine the average number of customers in the system (both waiting and being served), as follows:

$$L_s = \frac{\lambda}{\mu - \lambda} \tag{12-9}$$

For our example, we get:

$$L_s = \frac{7}{8-7} = 7$$

Thus, on average, 7 units will be in the system at any one time.

The queue-length statistics are important to a decision maker in facility planning, since obviously space must be provided to accommodate those waiting. But if we expect an average of 7 vehicles in the system, does this mean that we should have room for 6 vehicles in line for the Turbo-Washer? Not necessarily. Although 7 is the average, sometimes more than 7 vehicles will be in the system, sometimes less. To more fully analyze the waiting area requirements, you will need to determine the probability distribution for the number of customers waiting for service.

Probability of Having *n* Units in the Waiting Line

Using Equation 12-8, we found the average line length to be 6.125 units. But we know that sometimes the line would be shorter than 6.125 units and sometimes it would be longer. In planning the number of waiting spaces, we can compute the probability distribution for the number waiting for service. Equation 12-10 is used for this purpose:

$$P_n = (1 - \lambda/\mu)(\lambda/\mu)^n \tag{12-10}$$

For our example, we can determine the probability of having any number waiting in line. For instance, the probability of exactly 10 units waiting is:

$$P_{10} = (1 - 7/8)(7/8)^{10} = .0329$$

Equation 12-10 can be used to determine the values in Table 12-5, which shows the probability distribution of various waiting-line lengths.

This probability distribution can be very useful to a decision maker in evaluating the waiting-line system. Suppose the car-wash parking lot has room for a maximum of 10 vehicles. We can find the probability that a customer would not have room to wait by summing the probabilities of 11 or more, in Table 12-5. We see the chance is slightly more than 23% that more customers could be waiting than there is room for. Since the available spaces are taken, the extra customers will *balk the queue* or be forced to park illegally in the street. From a decision-making standpoint, Don must decide whether he can accept a 23% chance of this happening.

Table 12-5 PROBABILITY DISTRIBUTION FOR QUEUE LENGTH

Units Waiting (n)	Probability P_n
0	.1250
1	.1094
2	.0957
3	.0837
4	.0733
5	.0641
6	.0561
7	.0491
8	.0430
9	.0376
10	.0329
11	.0288
12	.0252
13	.0220
14	.0193
15	.0169
More than 15	.1179
	1.0000

Decision Based on Waiting-Line Analysis

The waiting-line characteristics computed above were based on a Poisson arrival distribution with $\lambda = 7$ customers per hour and installing the Level 2 Turbo-Washer, which has an exponential service rate of $\mu = 8$ units per hour. While the probability of facility idle time was fairly small, the expected waiting time (52.5 minutes) and the expected time in the system (60 minutes) are probably excessive. Likewise, the 23% chance of a waiting line exceeding the 10-vehicle limit is quite high. (The purpose of analyzing waiting-line models is to discover these problems before the facility is actually constructed.)

The Level 3 Turbo-Washer sells for more money but is faster than the Level 2 unit. The service rate for the Level 3 machine is also exponential, with $\mu = 10$ units per hour compared with $\mu = 8$ for the Level 2 machine. Equations 12-5 through 12-10 can be used to compute new waiting-line characteristics based on the faster service rate. Table 12-6 shows these values for both the Level 2 and Level 3 Turbo-Washers. As you can see, the faster Turbo-Washer results in much lower average waiting times and queue lengths. The average waiting time would decrease from .875 hour (52.5 minutes) to .233 hour (13.98 minutes). The average number of customers waiting would decrease from 6.125 to 1.633.

Table 12-7 shows the probability distribution for the number waiting if the Level 3 Turbo-Washer is used. Now, the probability of the waiting line exceeding the 10-vehicle space limit is only .0198, which is substantially lower than the 23% probability for the Level 2 Turbo-Washer.

The improvements in waiting-line characteristics resulting from installing a Level 3 machine instead of a Level 2 machine are striking. However, the faster Level 3 car wash also means more idle time. As shown in Table 12-6, the chance of the facility being idle is increased from .125 to .300, which means that the more expensive car-washing unit will sit idle 30% of the time.

The increase in idle time points out the paradox of waiting-line analysis. That is, decreases in most waiting line characteristics are countered by increases in facility idle time. Likewise, steps which cut back facility idle time will increase average waiting times and lengths of waiting lines. As a decision maker, you will be faced with analyzing these trade-offs in light of the social and economic costs associated with customers waiting versus facility idle time. Section 12-5 introduces the techniques of performing economic analysis on waiting line systems.

Table 12-6 COMPARISON OF WAITING-LINE STATISTICS FOR TWO TURBO-WASHERS

	Level 2	Level 3
Probability of facility idle time (P_0)	.125	.300
Average number of units waiting (L_q)	6.125	1.633
Average number of units in system (L_s)	7.000	2.333
Average waiting time (W_q)	.875	.233
Average time in the system (W_s)	1.00	.333
Probability of a unit waiting ($1 - P_0$)	.875	.700

Table 12-7 PROBABILITY DISTRIBUTION FOR QUEUE LENGTH WITH LEVEL 3 TURBO-WASHER ($\mu = 10$)

Units Waiting (n)	Probability $P(n)$
0	.3000
1	.2100
2	.1470
3	.1029
4	.0720
5	.0504
6	.0353
7	.0247
8	.0173
9	.0121
10	.0085
11 or more	.0198
	1.0000

12-4 MULTIPLE-CHANNEL WAITING-LINE MODELS

Many service situations can be described as multiple-channel systems. *A multiple-channel system is characterized by two or more service facilities operating in parallel.* Examples of multiple-channel systems abound. Banks have multiple tellers, fast-food stores have several cash registers for multiple lines, racetracks have numerous betting windows, gasoline stations often have several bays of pumps, a post office has several clerks, and so on.

While all multiple-channel systems have two or more parallel service facilities, a system can have different numbers of queues. Figure 12-6 shows two alternatives: (a) multiple service facilities with a single queue and (b) multiple service facilities with multiple queues. As we can see in part (a) of Figure 12.6, when any one of the service facilities is free, the customer at the front of the line goes to that service facility. Service is performed on a first-come first-served basis in this system. This is a familiar type of waiting-line system. Banks often put up ropes in the lobby to guide customers into a single line. Customers move through the line, often in a zigzag pattern, until it is their turn to be served by a teller. This setup is also used at ticketing areas in many large airports. The prime advantage of this single-queue, multiple-channel system is that it ensures a first-come, first-served operation.

Part (b) of Figure 12-6 diagrams a *multiple-queue, multiple-channel* system, which has a separate waiting line for each service facility. You are probably familiar with this system too, as it is commonly used by fast-food stores such as Burger King and McDonald's. With this setup, customers arrive and are allowed to choose which line they want to join. If the service times are not constant for all customers, the lines will not move at the same speed. Thus, you may join a line, begin waiting, and see someone in another line who arrived after you did get served first. On the other hand, if you happen to pick the "fast" line, you will get in and out faster than someone who got

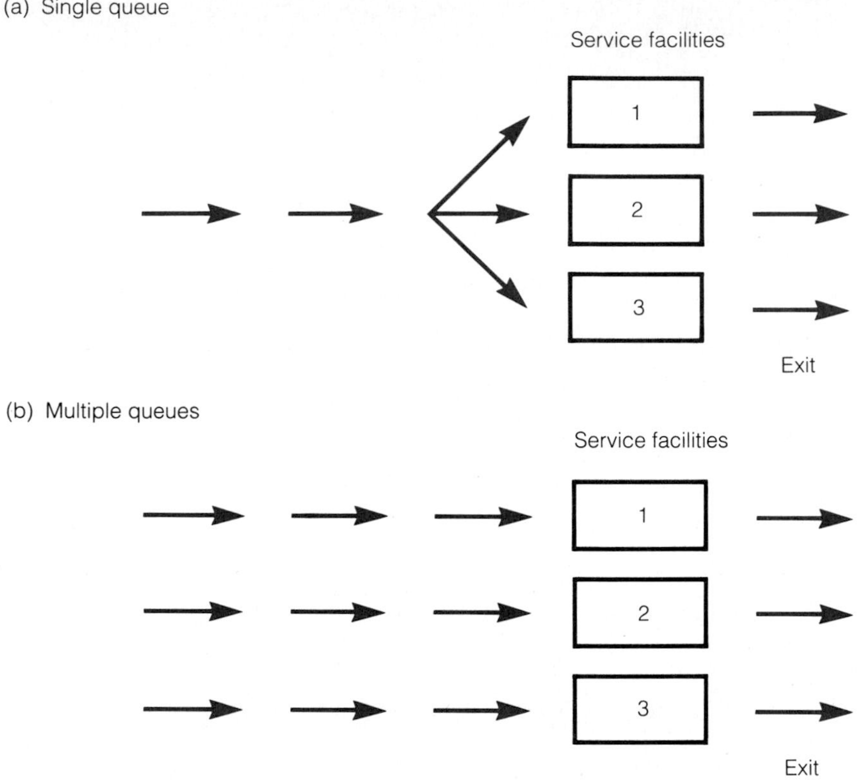

Figure 12-6
Queue types in multiple-channel waiting-line systems

there before you. In this system, you will observe line-jockeying behavior as customers seek to minimize their personal waiting time by finding the fastest line.

In section 12-5, we will discuss the economics of waiting lines and will address the factors associated with designing a waiting-line system.

A SINGLE-QUEUE SYSTEM

Many people visit a state unemployment office for a variety of services when they are out of work. They must first go to the office to establish their eligibility for unemployment benefits and then return each week to show they are still unemployed and looking for work.

The building where the local unemployment office has been located for the past 14 years is too small for current needs. Over the years, the number of people served has increased substantially as a result of growth in the area population. To meet the increasing demand, the office has been remodeled numerous times and service facilities added. (A *service facility* consists of a small area large enough to hold a desk, file cabinet, and two chairs.) No further expansion is possible at the existing facility, and on any given day the waiting times are excessively long—occasionally, some clients have to wait outside.

These conditions led the state legislature to authorize a move to a new facility. Before the move is made, a careful study of facility needs is required. Waiting-line analysis is a major part of this study.

The option under consideration is for a single waiting line leading to multiple parallel servers. Part (a) of Figure 12-6 diagrams this type of system. The key questions to be answered are, How many service facilities are needed? and How much space should be available for the waiting line?

Studies done at the current location indicate that clients arrive randomly and independently, according to a Poisson probability distribution, at a rate of $\lambda = 30$ per hour. Further, the service rate at each service desk is probabilistic; from the studies performed, it can be described by an exponential distribution with $\mu = 5$ per hour. (Keep in mind that $\mu = 5$ per hour applies to each service facility.) In order to analyze the system using waiting-line statistics, *the combined service rate must exceed the arrival rate.* Equation 12-11 specifies this important consideration.

$$\text{System service rate} = k\mu \qquad \text{when } k\mu > \lambda \tag{12-11}$$

where:

k = number of servers

μ = service rate for each server

λ = arrival rate

Based on an arrival rate of $\lambda = 30$ per hour and a single service rate of $\mu = 5$ per hour, a minimum number of 7 servers is needed to make sure the waiting line doesn't grow without bound.

Just as with the single-server system discussed in the previous section, a multiple-channel waiting-line analysis requires that we determine values for the facility idle time and other waiting-line characteristics. The equations presented in the following discussion assume a single waiting line leading to 2 or more parallel servers. These equations also assume that $k\mu > \lambda$, the arrivals are Poisson-distributed, and service rates are exponentially distributed.

The equations in this section are slightly more complex than those for the single-channel system. If you take additional course work in queuing theory, you will find that as complexities are added to the waiting-line system, the equations for computing the characteristics become increasingly complicated. In fact, for some systems, the only practical form of analysis is through simulation.

Probability of All Servers Being Idle

If no customers are being served, the system is idle. Since all the employees are on salary, when the staff is idle, they are being paid for unproductive time. Equation 12-12 is used to calculate the probability of all servers in the system being idle:

$$P_0 = \frac{1}{\sum_{n=1}^{k-1} \frac{(\lambda/\mu)^n}{n!} + \frac{(\lambda/\mu)^k}{(k-1)!} \cdot \frac{\mu}{k\mu - \lambda}} \tag{12-12}$$

Therefore, if clients arrive at $\lambda = 30$ per hour on average and each staff member can serve at an average rate of $\mu = 5$ per hour, with 7 servers the probability of all servers being idle is:

$$P_0 = \frac{1}{\frac{(30/5)^0}{0!} + \frac{(30/5)^1}{1!} + \frac{(30/5)^2}{2!} + \frac{(30/5)^3}{3!} + \frac{(30/5)^4}{4!} + \frac{(30/5)^5}{5!} + \frac{(30/5)^6}{6!} + \left[\frac{(30/5)^7}{7!} \cdot \frac{5}{(35-30)}\right]}$$

$$P_0 = .0016$$

Thus, the chance of having a time when all 7 staff members are idle is very small. This means that almost always at least 1 staff member will be busy. However, what is the probability that 6 of the 7 servers will be idle? Or what about the probability that 5 of the 7 servers will be idle? Another way of asking these questions is: What is the probability 1 customer will be in the system? What is the probability 2 customers will be in the system? and What is the probability n customers will be in the system?

Probability of *n* Units Being in the System

Equations 12-13 and 12-14 are used to determine the probability of n items being in the system.

$$P_n = \frac{(\lambda/\mu)^n}{k!k^{n-k}} P_0 \qquad (n > k) \tag{12-13}$$

$$P_n = \frac{(\lambda/\mu)^n}{n!} P_0 \qquad (0 \leq n \leq k) \tag{12-14}$$

where:

$n =$ number of arrivals in the system

$k =$ number of servers

If we are concerned with the chances of 6 idle servers in our example, which is the same as having only 1 person in the system, we would determine P_1 using equation 12-14: (Note: $P_0 = .0016$ from equation 12-12.)

$$P_1 = \frac{(30/5)^1}{1!} P_0 = .0096$$

The chance of having exactly 5 servers idle is found by again using equation 12-14 to get the probability of 2 people in the system:

$$P_2 = \frac{(30/5)^2}{2!} P_0 = .0288$$

We can also compute the probability of only 1 server of the 7 being idle by using equation 12-14. (Note that we are actually determining the probability of 6 customers in the system.)

$$P_6 = \frac{(30/5)^6}{6!} P_0 = .1037$$

The decision maker in charge of planning the new office must consider facility idle time when determining how many service facilities to design for the building. But as we observed in the Clean Look Car Wash example, an inverse relationship exists between facility idle time and customer waiting time; thus, both factors must be considered.

Average Number of Units Waiting for Service

In designing the facility, the waiting area must be planned so it is large enough to handle clients waiting for service. A factor that is useful in determining the space required for a waiting room is the average (or expected) number of units in the queue waiting for service. Equation 12-15 is used to compute this value:

$$L_q = \frac{(\lambda/\mu)^k (\lambda)(\mu)}{(k-1)!(k\mu - \lambda)^2} P_0 \qquad (12\text{-}15)$$

where:

k = number of servers

If we continue to consider a facility with 7 staff members (servers), the average number of people waiting for service (customers) is:

$$L_q = \frac{(30/5)^7(30)(5)}{(7-1)![7(5)-30]^2}(.0016) = 3.683$$

Of course, this is an average, and if the building is designed to accommodate 7 servers with a waiting area for 4 people, it would be the right size on average, but sometimes it would be too small. Suppose the waiting area is designed large enough to handle 10 people. We can use equation 12-13 to determine the chances that there will be 17 people (10 waiting and 7 being served) in the system as follows:

$$P_{17} = \frac{(30/5)^{17}}{7!7^{17-7}}(.0016) = .019$$

Since the chance that as many as 10 people will be waiting at any one time is very small, designing a waiting room with space for 10 people should be more than sufficient.

Average Number of Units in the System

While the waiting-room space required for the facility with 7 servers could be established as discussed above, we still have not fully examined the waiting-line issues. For instance, we might be interested in the average number of customers in the system at any given time. This will include those being served plus those waiting for service. Equation 12-16 shows that the average number of units in the system is the sum of the average number waiting plus the average number being served.

$$L = L_q + \lambda/\mu \qquad (12\text{-}16)$$

where:

L_q = average number waiting

λ/μ = average number of units in service

For our example, we already know the average number waiting will be 3.683 and on average $\lambda/\mu = 30/5 = 6$ people will be meeting with a staff member, giving this total in the system:

$$L = 3.683 + (30/5) = 9.683$$

Average Time a Unit Spends Waiting for Service

An important consideration in analyzing any waiting-line system is the time the arriving units spend waiting for service. In this unemployment office example, the arriving units are people needing assistance with their unemployment benefits. We can determine the average time an arrival spends waiting to see a staff member by using equation 12-17:

$$W_q = L_q/\lambda \tag{12-17}$$

where:

L_q = average number of units waiting for service

With an office having 7 staff members and a Poisson arrival rate of $\lambda = 30$ per hour, the average time spent in the line waiting for service will be:

$$W_q = 3.683/30 = .123 \text{ hour}$$

Average Time a Unit Spends in the System

The average time it takes clients from the time they enter the office until they receive the service they came for can be determined using equation 12-18:

$$W = W_q + 1/\mu \tag{12-18}$$

where:

W_q = average time a unit spends waiting for service

Not surprisingly, the average total time in the system is the sum of the average waiting time and the average service time. In this case, the average time a customer will spend in the system is:

$$\begin{aligned} W &= .123 \text{ hour} + 1/5 \text{ hour} = .323 \text{ hour} \\ &= .323 \times 60 = 19.38 \text{ minutes} \end{aligned}$$

Of the average amount of time (just under 20 minutes) a customer will spend in the office, 7.38 minutes will be spent waiting and 12 minutes will be spent being served.

Probability of an Arriving Unit Waiting for Service

We used equation 12-18 to determine the average time a customer will spend in the system. It combined the average waiting time with the average service time. While all customers who arrive will be served, not all customers will have to wait for service. Anytime a customer arrives and one or more servers is free, there will be no waiting. Equation 12-19 shows how the probability of a unit waiting for service is calculated:

$$P_w = \frac{1}{k!}\left(\frac{\lambda}{\mu}\right)^k \left(\frac{k\mu}{k\mu - \lambda}\right) P_0 \tag{12-19}$$

where:

k = number of servers

P_0 = probability of all servers being idle

With $k = 7$ servers, the chance of a customer having to wait is:

$$P_w = \frac{1}{7!}\left(\frac{30}{5}\right)^7 \frac{7(5)}{7(5) - 30}(0.0016) = .6138$$

Since just over 61% of all arrivals will have to wait for service, about 39% of all arrivals will be served without waiting.

Table 12-8 WAITING-LINE VALUES FOR UNEMPLOYMENT OFFICE EXAMPLE

Arrival rate: $\lambda = 30$/hour
Service rate: $\mu = 5$/hour
Number of servers: 7

Probability of all servers being idle	.0016
Average number of units waiting	3.683
Average number of units in the system	9.683
Average waiting time for service (hour)	.123
Average time in the system (hour)	.323
Probability of a unit waiting	.6138

DECISION BASED ON WAITING-LINE MODEL

The current unemployment office is not large enough to effectively handle the volume of people arriving for service. The organization has been authorized to move to a new facility. A waiting-line model is used to provide input into the planning process. The system studied is a *single-queue multiple-channel system*. In this system, two or more servers operate in parallel, with a single line feeding the servers (see Figure 12-6). Based on the assumption of Poisson arrivals and exponential service rates, a number of waiting-line characteristics can be computed by using equations 12-12 through 12-19. Assuming an average arrival rate of $\lambda = 30$ per hour, 7 servers in the system, and an average service rate of $\mu = 5$ per hour, the values shown in Table 12-8 were computed. As a decision maker, you would examine these values to determine whether the idle-time probabilities and waiting-time values are acceptable.

A natural question to ask is, What would happen if the number of servers is increased from 7 to 8? or even 9? Table 12-9 shows a comparison of facilities with 7, 8, 9, and 10 servers. As the number of service facilities increases, the probability of the system being idle increases (but still remains quite low) and the waiting-line characteristics improve. For instance, with 10 servers, the probability of a customer having to wait is reduced to .1013, and the average waiting time drops to .005 hour ($.005 \times 60 = .30$ minute), and the average number of customers waiting at any one time is only .152. To gain these improvements, the office must increase funding for staff from 7 to 10 and must also increase the service facility space. This added space could possibly be offset by a smaller waiting area, since fewer customers will have to wait.

Of course, as we have seen before, these improvements in customer waiting times are countered by more idle time for the servers. For instance, if we look at the

Table 12-9 COMPARATIVE WAITING-LINE VALUES WHEN $\lambda = 30$/hr and $\mu = 5$/hr

	Number of Servers			
	7	8	9	10
Probability of an idle system	.0016	.0021	.0024	.0024
Average number of units waiting	3.683	1.071	.392	.152
Average units in the system	9.683	7.071	6.392	6.152
Average waiting time (hours)	.123	.036	.013	.005
Average time in the system (hours)	.323	.236	.213	.205
Probability of waiting	.6138	.3570	.1960	.1013

probability of one or more servers being idle at any given time, we get:

$$P(\text{1 or more idle servers}) = 1 - P_w \quad (12\text{-}20)$$

where:

P_w = probability of a unit waiting for service

With 7 servers, we get: P(1 or more idle servers) = 1 − .6138 = .3862.

With 10 staff members, we get: P(1 or more idle servers) = 1 − .1013 = .8987.

Thus, if we increase the staffing from 7 to 10, we increase the probability of 1 or more staff member being idle from about 39% to nearly 90%.

As a decision maker, you must weigh the benefits of having your customer waiting times be short on average against the cost of adding service facilities and the increased chance of having idle servers. In many cases, the analysis comes down to a cost-benefit trade-off. In section 12-5, we will look at the issue of economic analyses of waiting lines.

As one additional consideration, suppose several of the people responsible for making this new facility decision are concerned about future demand increases. The question that has been raised is how the system will behave if the arrival rate increases to 40 or 50 or even 60 per hour in the future. Table 12-10 shows the waiting-line values for 13, 14, and 15 servers when $\lambda = 60$ customers per hour. Recall that equations 12-12 through 12-19 require $k\mu > \lambda$. This means that the minimum number of servers which can be considered with this waiting-line model is 13. We see, in Table 12-10, there is essentially no chance (zero to 4 decimal places) that the system will be completely idle with from 13 to 15 servers. However, with 13 servers, the number of people waiting for service, on average, is 8.453; the average waiting time is .141 hour, or almost 8.5 minutes; and the probability of someone having to wait is over 70%. The waiting statistics improve considerably with 14, and especially with 15, servers. With 15 servers, the probability of waiting drops to just under 32% and the average waiting time drops to .021 hour (.021 × 60 = 1.26 minutes).

If the decision makers are concerned with the potential to handle heavier workloads, they will need to plan ahead and make space available for more staff. Ultimately, the decision on exactly how many servers to plan for depends on the trade-offs between the cost of providing servers and the costs of having the customers wait for service.

Before proceeding, recall that equations 12-12 through 12-19 can be applied to

Table 12-10 COMPARATIVE WAITING-LINE VALUES WHEN $\lambda = 60$/hr and $\mu = 5$/hr

	Number of Servers		
	13	14	15
Probability of an idle system	.0000	.0000	.0000
Average number of units waiting	8.453	2.890	1.277
Average units in the system	20.453	14.890	13.277
Average waiting time (hour)	.141	.048	.021
Average time in the system (hour)	.341	.248	.221
Probability of waiting	.7044	.4817	.3192

model a waiting-line system which satisfies the following conditions:

1. Poisson-distributed arrivals
2. Exponentially distributed service times
3. Two or more servers operating in parallel
4. Average service times the same for each server
5. Single queue; arriving units served on first-come, first-served basis
6. Combined service rate, $k\mu$, exceeds arrival rate, λ (or, $k\mu > \lambda$)

12-5 ECONOMIC CONSIDERATIONS IN WAITING-LINE ANALYSIS

You should have noted a common characteristic in applying the waiting-line models introduced thus far. From a customer's perspective, improved service results from decreases in both the average number waiting and the average time spent waiting. But these improvements are not achieved without a cost. First, increasing the service rate usually requires additional resources; and second, when the service rate is increased, facility idle time will increase. And idle facilities incur an opportunity cost.

The underlying question then becomes, What is the optimal service level when both cost of waiting and costs associated with faster service and additional idle time are considered? Figure 12-7 is a graphical representation of the economic trade-offs associated with increasing the service rate. You can see that service cost and the cost of waiting move in opposite directions. As the service rate increases, idle-time costs and service costs increase but waiting time and its cost decrease. Decision makers should try to operate at the minimum cost point on the total cost curve, as shown in Figure 12-7.

SERVICE COST

The service cost is generally fairly easy to determine. Suppose we have a single-channel system, as in the Clean Look Car Wash example. To increase the service rate (i.e.,

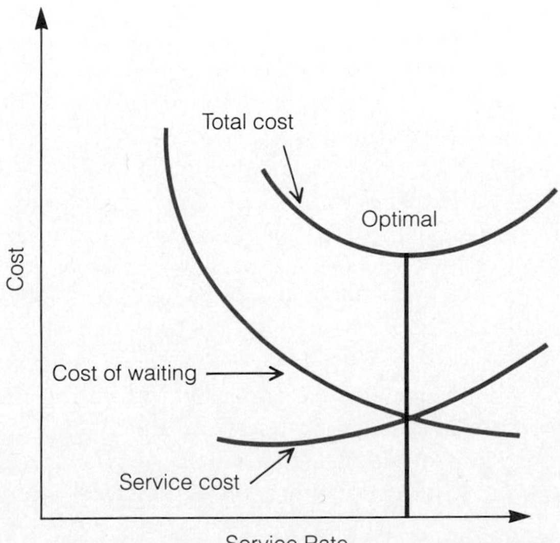

Figure 12-7
Economic trade-offs for increasing service rate

reduce the per unit service time), a faster Turbo-Washer could be purchased for a known price. In another example, if increasing the service rate means hiring better-trained workers, the costs associated with better workers are generally available. If we are dealing with a multiple-channel system, the cost of adding each extra server is usually known.

WAITING COST

While the process of determining the service cost is generally straightforward, determining waiting costs is often more difficult. If the waiting units are products or people internal to your organization, you probably can adequately assess a waiting cost. For instance, if the waiting-line system is for access to the company's copying machines, the hourly cost of clerical help can be determined and the per hour or per minute cost of waiting could be estimated.

But in situations where the arriving units come from outside the organization, such as customers arriving for service at a bank, assessing the cost of waiting is more difficult. First, the longer a customer has to wait, the more agitated he or she becomes. This creates ill will and may adversely affect future business. Second, if a customer arrives for service and discovers a long line, he or she may balk. By refusing to join the service line, the customer may take his or her business elsewhere. Third, if the wait is too long, not only does ill will become a factor, some customers will truncate or renege the queue and take their business elsewhere. In some cases the cost of waiting can be extreme, as in the case of injured persons waiting for treatment at a hospital emergency room or waiting for a paramedic unit to arrive at the scene of an accident.

Regardless of the situation, waiting costs are difficult to assess accurately. Consequently, most waiting-line studies which seek to define the optimal service level from an economic viewpoint use a technique called *marginal analysis,* which requires only that the relationship between waiting costs and service costs be estimated.

MARGINAL ANALYSIS

Marginal analysis seeks to determine the service level that minimizes the total service plus waiting costs. It works by setting the service rate at an arbitrary level and determining total queuing costs (waiting costs plus service costs). Then the service rate is changed (increased or decreased) by a small amount and the total queuing cost is recalculated. If this cost is less than the previously detemined cost, the service rate is changed again in the same direction and the queuing cost determined. The service rate keeps changing for as long as a reduction in total cost occurs. The marginal analysis ends when no further improvement can be achieved by changing the service rate.

In actual practice, this stepwise approach to marginal analysis is not efficient. Instead, differential calculus can be used to derive an equation which gives the optimal service rate directly. A different equation will be found for each waiting-line system being analyzed.

In this section, we will introduce the marginal-analysis model for a single-channel system which assumes no cost associated with customers who balk or renege the line. The analysis also assumes that service- and waiting-cost functions are linear, that arrivals are Poisson-distributed, and that service times are exponential. The total queuing cost of such a system can be represented by equation 12-21:

$$T_c = (C_s)(\mu) + (C_w)(L_s) \tag{12-21}$$

where:

T_c = total queuing cost
C_s = marginal cost of service
μ = average customers served per time period
C_w = cost of a customer waiting per unit of time
L_s = average number of units in the system

By substituting equation 12-9 for L_s in equation 12-21, we get:

$$T_c = (C_s)(\mu) + (C_w)[\lambda/(\mu - \lambda)] \tag{12-22}$$

Using calculus, we take the first derivative of T_c with respect to μ, set it equal to zero, and solve for μ. This gives:

$$\mu^* = \lambda + [(C_w/C_s)(\lambda)]^{1/2} \tag{12-23}$$

where:

μ^* = optimal service rate to minimize total queuing costs

To demonstrate the marginal-analysis approach to service-rate optimization, consider this example involving a lumber mill in Wisconsin. Loaded logging trucks arrive at the mill at the rate of 6 per hour, but they can't be unloaded until the logs have been scaled. Scaling is a process for calculating the number of usable board feet in a log by measuring its length and diameter and rating it for knots and uniformity. Although the mill has only one scaling station, more than one scaler can be assigned to work a load of logs. Figure 12-8 illustrates the single-channel system at the scaling station.

The lumbermill manager wants to determine the optimal number of trucks to be scaled per hour to minimize waiting plus service costs. To use equations 12-22 and 12-23 to find the optimal scaling rate and total cost, the manager must first determine the service and waiting costs. However, using equation 12-23 to determine the optimal service rate does not require knowing the actual service and waiting costs, since the equation uses only the ratio C_w/C_s. Thus, the manager need only assess the relative relationship between the two cost factors.

Suppose the mill manager is struggling with a proper assessment of waiting costs and has concluded, after careful study, that the waiting cost per hour for a truck is about half the cost of scaling an additional truck. Therefore, 1/2 can be used for C_w/C_s in equation 12-23, as follows:

$$\mu^* = 6 + [(1/2)(6)]^{1/2} = 7.73$$

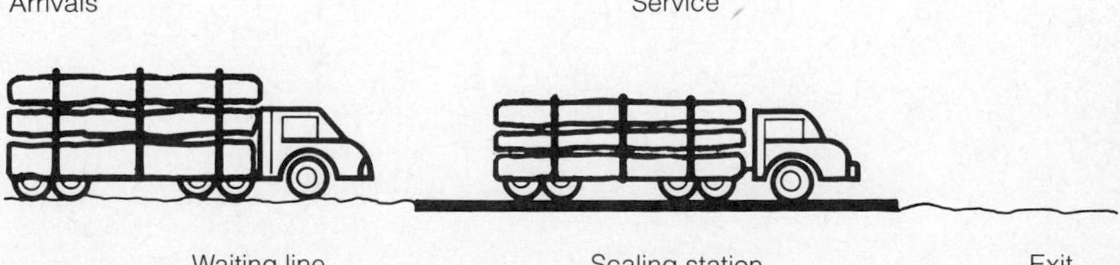

Figure 12-8
Single-channel system for log scaling

Thus, the optimal service rate would be to have enough scalers at the station to scale an average of 7.73 trucks per hour.

The minimum total queuing cost can't be determined (equation 12-22) without knowing the service and waiting costs. If the mill manager knows that scaling an additional truck per hour will require \$40 in scaler wages, then, assuming that waiting cost per hour is half the service cost, the manager assigns a cost of \$20 per hour to each waiting truck.

Given these costs, the minimum total queuing cost, based on an average service level of 7.73 trucks per hour, is:

$$T_c = (\$40)(7.73) + (\$20)\ [6/(7.73 - 6)] = \$309.20 + 69.36 = \$378.56$$

In summary, determining the optimal service rate for any waiting-line system requires analyzing the trade-offs between the cost of waiting and the cost of serving. The example in this section applies to a single-channel waiting-line model with certain specified conditions. However, regardless of the system being considered, the concept of marginal economic trade-offs still applies.

12-6 OTHER WAITING-LINE MODELS

As a decision maker, you will probably encounter many situations where waiting-line analysis will be useful. However, as we have stressed many times in this text, the technique should always fit the application. Thus, you must first define the system to be studied and then attempt to model that system by applying the appropriate technique.

The models introduced in this chapter can be applied only in specific types of situations. For instance, the single-channel model discussed in the car wash example assumes that arriving units are served on a first-come, first-served basis. If an actual situation being studied permits priority service, the characteristics computed using the same model as the car wash problem would not apply.

Likewise, if the single-queue multiple-channel model introduced in section 12-4 were applied in a situation with multiple queues, the conclusions reached from the waiting-line calculations might be misleading. The point to remember here is that you will encounter many situations in the real world that do not correspond to the specific waiting-line models discussed in this chapter. Here are some common variations on the models introduced in this chapter:

1. Arrivals following other than a constant or Poisson distribution
2. Service rates following other than an exponential or constant distribution
3. Units arriving for service in groups rather than singly
4. Multiple-channel models with different channels having different service rates
5. Systems in which the service rate depends on the number waiting for service
6. Service systems where an item passes through a sequence of servers

The models we have introduced are the most elementary waiting-line models. As the assumptions and conditions vary, the complexity of the models increases; and in fact, the complexity can increase to the point that a mathematical representation of the queuing system is not feasible at all. In those cases, decision makers often turn to computer simulation as a tool for analyzing the waiting-line system. Chapter 16 will introduce computer simulation and illustrate several waiting-line applications.

12-7 COMPUTER APPLICATIONS

Unlike management science techniques such as linear programming, waiting-line analysis does not require extensive computations. Each model has a series of equations which provide the required waiting-line characteristics, and in most cases these equations can be solved using only a calculator. Even so, many computer software packages have queuing analysis capability. These packages have two advantages. First, if the proper inputs are provided, the resulting calculations will be accurate. Second, as a decision maker, you will probably want to perform sensitivity analysis as you study the waiting-line system. The computer software allows you to run numerous What if? analyses in a short amount of time.

The MASTER software package which accompanies this text has several waiting-line programs.

MASTER WAITING-LINE OPTIONS

MASTER has four waiting-line models:

1. Single-channel model
2. Sensitivity analysis, single-channel model
3. Economic analysis, single-channel model
4. Single-queue multiple-channel model

All the models assume arrivals are Poisson-distributed and service times are exponential.

Single-Channel Model

Consider the following single-channel waiting-line situation. The Select-a-Seat Company provides computerized ticket sales for college and professional sports, concerts, and theater productions in a West Coast city. All Select-a-Seat locations are connected to a central computer, which can serve all locations simultaneously.

Each Select-a-Seat location has its own microcomputer, which is connected to the central computer, and its own ticket printer. When a customer arrives to buy a ticket, the clerk determines the event and ticket price range the customer wishes and then accesses the central computer to determine seat availability. The clerk then gives the customer several seating options and, once a selection is made, enters the request. Then the tickets are paid for and printed. The time to complete this process varies. Studies have shown that the service time is exponential, with an average of 5 minutes per customer, so the service rate is 12 per hour.

At one location, studies have shown the customer arrival rate is 6 per hour and the arrivals can be described by a Poisson distribution. The Select-a-Seat manager wants to know the waiting-line characteristics for this location. We can use the Single Channel Model option of MASTER to describe this system. The program requires just two inputs: the average number arriving per time period, λ; and the average number served per time period, μ; it also requires $\mu > \lambda$. Using $\lambda = 6$ and $\mu = 12$, MASTER produces the output shown in Figure 12-9. As you can see, MASTER provides the waiting-line characteristics and also the probability of having a different number of units in the system.

From the MASTER output (Figure 12-9), the manager sees that, on average, a customer must wait .08 hour ($.08 \times 60 = 4.8$ minutes) for service and the chance of any customer waiting is .50.

```
        SINGLE CHANNEL WAITING LINE MODEL

                POISSON ARRIVALS
            EXPONENTIAL SERVICE TIMES

             MEAN ARRIVAL RATE =   6.00
             MEAN SERVICE RATE =  12.00

PROBABILITY THAT THE SERVICE FACILITY IS IDLE = 0.5000
THE AVERAGE NUMBER OF UNITS WAITING FOR SERVICE =     0.50
THE AVERAGE NUMBER OF UNITS IN THE SYSTEM =     1.00
THE AVERAGE TIME A UNIT SPENDS WAITING FOR SERVICE =     0.08
THE AVERAGE TIME A UNIT SPENDS IN THE SYSTEM =     0.17
THE PROBABILITY THAT A UNIT HAS TO WAIT FOR SERVICE = 0.5000

          PROBABILITY OF X UNITS BEING IN THE SYSTEM

               UNITS                PROBABILITY
                 X                     P(X)
       ---------------------------------------

                 0                    0.5000
                 1                    0.2500
                 2                    0.1250
                 3                    0.0625
                 4                    0.0313
                 5                    0.0516
```

Figure 12-9
MASTER output for single-channel waiting-line model

Sensitivity Analysis Option

In most decision-making situations, a manager would be interested in performing a sensitivity analysis on one or more of the input values. If the Select-a-Seat manager wanted to determine the change in waiting-line characteristics for diferent arrival rates, she could simply rerun the single-channel model using the new λ values.

If the manager wants to observe the change in the waiting-line characteristics for various service rates, she can select the sensitivity analysis option, which allows the user to specify a λ value and up to 5 different service rates. For instance, suppose the Select-a-Seat manager wants to know the waiting-line characteristics for service rates of 11, 12, 13, 14, and 15 customers per hour when the arrivals average 6 per hour. Figure 12-10 shows the output generated by MASTER. You can see that as the service rate is increased, facility idle time increases but is offset by decreases in the average number waiting, the average waiting time, and the probability of waiting.

```
                   SINGLE CHANNEL WAITING LINE MODEL
                          POISSON ARRIVALS
                       EXPONENTIAL SERVICE TIMES

ARRIVAL RATE = 6.00
                                               MEAN SERVICE RATE
                                     11.00  12.00  13.00  14.00  15.00

----------------------------------------------------------------------
-
PROBABILITY OF IDLE FACILITY         0.4545 0.5000 0.5385 0.5714 0.6000

AVERAGE NUMBER OF UNITS WAITING         0.7    0.5    0.4    0.3    0.3

AVERAGE UNITS IN THE SYSTEM             1.2    1.0    0.9    0.8    0.7

AVERAGE TIME WAITING FOR SERVICE      0.109  0.083  0.066  0.054  0.044

AVERAGE TIME IN THE SYSTEM            0.200  0.167  0.143  0.125  0.111

PROBABILITY OF WAITING               0.5455 0.5000 0.4615 0.4286 0.4000
```

Figure 12-10
MASTER output for sensitivity analysis in waiting-line model

Economic Analysis

MASTER also contains a module for determining the optimal service rate for a single-channel model when the costs of waiting and service are considered. This model determines the service level which will minimize total queuing cost.

Suppose the Select-a-Seat Manager estimates customer waiting costs to be 8 times the per customer service cost. Since data show that the total cost of serving a customer is \$1.00, the manager is considering the waiting cost to be \$8.00 per hour. To use the MASTER software to perform economic optimization, the manager must input λ, the customer arrival rate; μ, the current service rate; and the costs of waiting and service. Figure 12-11 shows the MASTER output for these inputs: $\lambda = 6$, $\mu = 12$, waiting cost = \$8.00 and unit service cost = \$1.00. (MASTER assumes linear waiting and service costs.)

As you can see in Figure 12-11, the service level which minimizes total hourly queuing cost is 12.93 customers per hour. This is quite close to the current service level

```
                    SINGLE CHANNEL SYSTEM

ASSUMES:
    POISSON INTER-ARRIVAL TIMES
    EXPONENTIAL SERVICE TIMES

INPUTS
      MEAN ARRIVAL RATE =  6.00
      MEAN SERVICE RATE = 12.00
              SYSTEM COSTS :
                  WAITING COST =      8.00
                  SERVICE COST =     12.00
                    TOTAL COST =     20.00

       TO MINIMIZE TOTAL COST:
            OPTIMAL SERVICE RATE =      12.93

       COSTS ASSUMING OPTIMAL SERVICE RATE:
               WAITING COST =     6.93
               SERVICE COST =    12.93
                 TOTAL COST =    19.86
                                   COST SAVINGS = 0.14
```

Figure 12-11
MASTER output for economic optimization analysis of waiting-line model

of 12 per hour. The cost savings from increasing the service level to 12.93 per hour is only $.14 per hour. This comes from a $1.07 decrease in waiting costs (due to shortened waiting times) being offset by a $.93 increase in service costs.

Other software packages may feature different types of waiting-line models and may present the output in a different format. In any case, the advantages of all computer software programs used for waiting-line analysis are primarily speed and accuracy.

```
SYSTEM STATISTICS:
                                          SERVICE RATE
                                  ORIGINAL              OPTIMUM
                                    12.00                 12.93

CHANCE OF SYSTEM BEING IDLE =       0.500                 0.536
AVERAGE UNITS WAITING =              1.00                  0.87
AVERAGE WAITING TIME =               0.17                  0.14
AVERAGE TIME IN SYSTEM               0.25                  0.22
CHANCE OF UNIT WAITING =            0.500                 0.464
```

Figure 12-11 Continued

12-8 SUMMARY AND CONCLUSIONS

Waiting lines occur in one form or another in virtually every phase of every business. This chapter has introduced the basic concepts associated with analyzing various types of waiting lines. A number of new terms have also been introduced and are summarized in the Chapter Glossary.

Since there are many different types of waiting-line systems, a wide variety of models have been developed to analyze them. Some, such as the models in this chapter, are relatively simple; others are very complicated. The choice of which waiting-line model to use obviously depends on the individual situation. The waiting-line models introduced in this chapter use a series of equations to find the various waiting-line characteristics. These equations are summarized in the Chapter Equations section.

Waiting-line models can be categorized as being either deterministic or probabilistic and can represent a single- or multiple-channel system. We saw how the behavior of arrivals influences the choice of models. Do customers balk or truncate the queue? In a single-channel system, is customer service on a first-come, first-served basis or is a priority scheme involved? All of these factors and more must be considered in determining which queuing model best represents any situation being analyzed.

Regardless of which model is used, a basic trade-off exists between facility idle time and customer waiting time. As the service rate improves, facility idle time will increase and customer waiting time will decrease. In addition to the time factors, this chapter addressed the economic trade-offs between waiting costs and service costs, an issue which will become very real to you as a decision maker. It is very likely that you will apply waiting-line analysis in your future professional activities. The material in this chapter should provide a solid foundation for doing so.

Solved Problems

PROBLEM 1 United Service is a new regional commuter airline based in Tennessee. The airline has limited funds and is interested in strictly controlling expenses, but it also recognizes the importance of customer service. One important part of customer service is being able to talk to a reservation agent on the phone and not be put on hold. However, idle reservation agents add a fixed cost to the airline's operation.

The management of United Service has hired a limited number of full-time reservation agents and supplements them with part-time help brought in for 2-hour blocks. The reservation manager is presently analyzing the 2:00–4:00 P.M. time slot, a period when calls arrive at the rate of 80 per hour. While service times vary, on the average each agent can handle 12 calls per hour. The airline has a policy that the average time customers should have to wait for service should be no more than 1/2 minute. Assuming that arrivals can be described by a Poisson distribution and service times by an exponential distribution,

a. How many reservation agents should be on duty from 2:00 to 4:00 P.M.?

b. What are the waiting-line characteristics for the system with the number of agents determined for part **a**?

Solutions **a.** This is a single-line multiple-channel problem. The criterion for this part of the problem is that average waiting time be no more than 1/2 minute, which (to have consistent units) we convert to a fraction of an hour: 1/120 = .0083 hour. The number of reservation agents that will satisfy this criterion can be found as follows, starting with equation 12-17.

Average time waiting for service: $W_q = L_q/\lambda$

where: $$L_q = \frac{(\lambda/\mu)^k(\lambda)(\mu)}{(k-1)!(k\mu-\lambda)^2} P_0$$

Since the mean service rate per server times the number of servers must be greater than the average arrival rate, we know we need at least 7 reservation agents. Starting with 7 agents and working up, we find the following average waiting times:

Number of Agents	Average Waiting Time (hours)
7	.215
8	.033
9	.011
10	.004
11	.002

The first number of agents with an average waiting time less than 1/2 minute is 10.

b. The waiting-line system characteristics for this single-line 10-agent system can be found using equation 12-11 through 12-17. (These values can also be found with MASTER.)

System service rate: $k\mu = 120$

Probability of all servers being idle: $P_0 = \dfrac{1}{\sum_{n=1}^{k-1} \dfrac{(\lambda/\mu)^n}{n!} + \dfrac{(\lambda/\mu)^k}{(k-1)!} \cdot \dfrac{\mu}{k\mu - \lambda}} = .0012$

Average number waiting: $L_q = \dfrac{(\lambda/\mu)^k(\lambda)(\mu)}{(k-1)!(k\mu - \lambda)^2} P_0 = .349$

Average number in the system: $L = L_q + \lambda/\mu = 7.016$

Average time waiting for service: $W_q = L_q/\lambda = .004$

Average time in the system: $W = W_q + 1/\mu = .088$

Probability of waiting: $P_w = \dfrac{1}{k!}\left(\dfrac{\lambda}{\mu}\right)^k \left(\dfrac{k\mu}{k\mu - \lambda}\right) P_0 = .1746$

PROBLEM 2 BusinessServ Computer Systems has recently opened a new sales center in Jacksonville, Florida. Management has observed that most computer stores feature sales staff who are primarily interested in making a sale and are therefore not willing to spend much time actually helping customers. To solve this problem, BusinessServ hires highly qualified software and hardware specialists and pays them at an hourly rate instead of on commission. At the Jacksonville location, an average of 2 customers seeking information arrive each hour and a service representative will spend an average of 1 hour with each customer. If the service representatives are paid $25 per hour, and if corporate guidelines indicate that customer waiting time is 3 times as expensive as a service representative's time, then:

a. How many service representatives should be at the Jacksonville location?

b. What are the waiting-line characteristics of the system?

Solutions a. To answer this question we will perform a marginal analysis comparing the cost of waiting with the cost of service. Remember, we are interested in a service system that will minimize the total cost (service plus waiting). Here we once again have a single-line multiple-channel model and so will have to use equations 12-11 through 12-17.

We will first find the average time spent waiting for service for different numbers of service representatives:

Average time waiting for service: $W_q = L_q/\lambda$

where:

$$L_q = \frac{(\lambda/\mu)^k(\lambda)(\mu)}{(k-1)!(k\mu - \lambda)^2} P_0$$

Service Representatives	Time Spent Waiting (hours)
3	.444
4	.087
5	.020

We can now determine a total hourly cost for both service representatives' time and customer waiting time, using:

Total cost per hour = \$25 (number of servers) + (2 arrivals) (\$75) (average wait)

Number of Servers	Total Cost
3	\$141.60
4	\$113.05
5	\$128.00

Therefore, the minimum-cost point is to have 4 service representatives in the Jacksonville store.

b. The characteristics of this single-channel multiple-server system are:

System service rate: $k\mu = 4$

Probability of all servers being idle: $P_0 = \dfrac{1}{\sum_{n=1}^{k-1} \dfrac{(\lambda/\mu)^n}{n!} + \dfrac{(\lambda/\mu)^k}{(k-1)!} \cdot \dfrac{\mu}{k\mu - \lambda}} = .1304$

Average number waiting: $L_q = \dfrac{(\lambda/\mu)^k(\lambda)(\mu)}{(k-1)!(k\mu - \lambda)^2} P_0 = .174$

Average number in the system: $L = L_q + \lambda/\mu = 2.174$

Average time waiting for service: $W_q = L_q/\lambda = .087$

Average time in the system: $W = W_q + 1/\mu = 1.087$

Probability of waiting: $P_w = \dfrac{1}{k!}\left(\dfrac{\lambda}{\mu}\right)^k \left(\dfrac{k\mu}{k\mu - \lambda}\right) P_0 = .1739$

General Questions and Assignments

1. Identify a decision-making situation (other than those discussed in this chapter) in which a single-channel waiting-line model would be appropriate. Fully describe the situation. Use any means at your disposal to determine the average arrival rate and the average service time for this system.
2. Discuss why a waiting-line system will generate infinite line lengths if the average arrival rate exceeds the average service rate.
3. After reading the material in this chapter, discuss—using examples based on personal experience—the different types of waiting-line behaviors.
4. Identify a situation other than those discussed in this chapter in which a multiple-channel waiting-line model would be appropriate. Fully describe the situation. Use any means at your disposal to determine the average arrival rate and the average service time for this system.
5. Library assignment: Locate three or more articles which describe decision-making applications of queuing theory. Write a paper describing these situations and discuss the results that were achieved using queuing theory.
6. Locate a business in your area which has waiting-line problems. Visit with the managers and

employees who work with the waiting line to assess what they have done to minimize total waiting-line costs. If waiting costs are considered most important, discuss why the company has taken that position. If idle-time costs are considered most critical, discuss why the company has taken that view.

Exercises and Application Problems

1. A bank proof operator receives checks on a conveyor belt at a constant rate of 35 per minute and enters the amounts in the proofing machine. After several years at this job, the operator is able to enter the amounts from 40 checks every minute. How many minutes will this proof operator be idle every hour?
2. The arrival of customers wanting to pay their bills at the local gas company follows a Poisson distribution and averages 10 customers per hour.
   a. What is the probability that 8 customers will arrive in an hour?
   b. What is the probability that between 4 and 9 customers will arrive in an hour?
   c. What is the probability that more than 7 customers will arrive in an hour? Assume an 8-hour day.
3. Suppose the gas company discussed in problem 2 has only one clerk to receive the customers and process their payments. From historical data, we know that this clerk is capable of handling 15 customers per hour on average. Suppose the service time distribution follows an exponential distribution with a mean of 15. Further suppose the customers form a single line and are served on a first-come, first-served basis.
   a. Discuss why this system fits the single-channel waiting-line model described in this chapter.
   b. What is the probability the clerk will be idle during the entire first hour the office is open?
   c. What will be the average waiting time for customers in this system?
   d. On average, how much time (waiting time and service time) will a customer spend in the system?
   e. If the waiting room will hold 3 people, what is the probability that a customer will arrive to find the waiting room full?
   f. Using the queuing statistics for this system, write a short report assuming you are the manager of the gas company. In the report, assess the overall acceptability of the system as it now stands and make recommendations for how the system could be improved.
4. Customers arriving at the LightenUp Exercise Club arrive according to a Poisson distribution with a mean rate of 20 per hour. The club has only one clerk at the check-in desk. This clerk has to sign in the customers, record their weight and blood pressure, and assign them lockers. This service requires an average of 1.5 minutes per customer.
   a. Assume that the arrival and service rates are constant. Create a table which shows the queues, waiting times, and idle times for 1/2 hour at the club. What is the maximum queue length that develops in this time? What is the average waiting time for customers who have to wait? How much waiting time occurs during this 1/2-hour period.
   b. After completing part **a**, assume arrivals are Poisson-distributed, with the stated average arrival rate, and that service times are exponentially distributed with the stated service rate. What is the probability that the waiting line will exceed 3 people? What is the expected number of people in the queue at any one time? What proportion of the clerk's time will be spent assisting customers?
5. The LightenUp Exercise Club (see problem 4) has decided to run a special program to generate more business. If this program works as expected, the number of people who arrive per hour at the club will increase by 50%. If this happens and the club does not add any help at the check-in counter to speed up service, what will be the expected waiting time for someone to get checked in? What will be the average number of people in the system at any one time? Write a short report to management using these and any other queuing statistics to discuss how effective the check-in system will be if the new plan is implemented and arrivals increase by 50%.

6. Refer to problems 4 and 5 for the LightenUp Exercise Club. Suppose the managers have decided to go ahead with the promotion and increase the number of arrivals per hour to 30. In addition, they have decided to hire a second person to work the check-in counter. This person will take blood pressures and weights but will not do any of the other check-in tasks. The managers feel this will reduce the average check-in time to 1.0 minute. Using appropriate queuing statistics, write a report which discusses the advisability of this move and what the possible consequences might be.
7. At the Star Gasoline Station, the time required to fill a car's tank averages 5 minutes and can be described by an exponential distribution.
   a. What is the probability that if you pull into the gas station your car will be filled in less than 3 minutes?
   b. What is the mean service rate, in cars per hour?
   c. What percentage of cars entering the service station will need more than 5 minutes to fill their tanks?
8. The number of students arriving at the statistics lab the night before a big exam averages 5 every hour. There is only one instructor there and the average time to assist each student is 7.5 minutes.
   a. What is the probability that the instructor will *not* be answering a student's question when another student enters the room?
   b. What will be the average waiting time for students needing assistance?
   c. What is the average time students will be in the lab if they leave once their questions are answered?
   d. What will be the average number of students waiting for assistance?
   e. Assuming students leave when their questions are answered, what will be the average number of students in the lab?
9. Holubar Outdoors is a mail-order business specializing in outdoor clothing. New orders, which are processed by a single clerk, have a mean arrival rate of 15 per half-hour. The clerk is able to process 40 per hour. Assume an 8-hour day, that arrivals are Poisson-distributed, and that service times are exponentially distributed.
   a. What is the average time, in hours, that an order spends waiting to begin processing?
   b. What is the average number of orders waiting to be processed or being processed?
   c. What is the probability that 2 or more orders are waiting to be processed?
   d. Use any appropriate queuing statistics to analyze the present system for processing orders. In your written analysis, comment on the strengths and weaknesses of the system. Do you think the cost of waiting should be considered more important than the cost of idle time? Discuss.
10. Phil's Tire Center is a one-person service business that advertises speedy installation of snow tires. His slogan is "On your way in 30 minutes or less." During December, business gets hectic when people want to get snow tires put on before they go skiing. During that month, cars arrive at the rate of 16 per day (assume an 8-hour day) and the average installation time is 25 minutes. Determine if Phil is able to meet his advertisement. Assume arrivals are Poisson-distributed and service times are exponentially distributed.
11. A local grocery store manager has decided to provide a check-cashing service. She would like to have only one clerk handling this service. She expects that customers will arrive at a rate of 35 per hour and that service time will average 1.5 minutes per customer.
   a. Determine what percentage of time the clerk will be cashing checks.
   b. On average, how many customers will be waiting in line to have checks cashed?
   c. How long can a customer expect to be in the store if the only thing he is doing is having his check cashed?
   d. What is the probability that 2 or fewer customers will be waiting in line?
12. Engineers at a computer chip manufacturing company are designing a special machine for the second stage of a coating operation. The silicon disks arrive at this stage at an average of one every 10 minutes. If the disks are kept waiting for more than 3 minutes, the first-stage coating is destroyed

and the disk is unusable. The machine prototype which the engineers have developed for the second stage can coat a disk every 5 minutes. If you assume the arrivals follow a Poisson distribution and the service times follow an exponential distribution, what percentage of silicon disks will be damaged before they enter the second stage? Suppose the engineers could improve the machine design so that the coating time could be reduced to 3 minutes per disk. Comment on what effect this would have on the percentage of damaged disks.

13. The accounting firm of Goldman and Silverton has only two CPAs on staff, H. P. Goldman and Larry Silverton. Because of the amount of work processed, the office has two personal computers and two clerks for data entry. When either Goldman or Silverton has work that needs to be entered on the computer, he gives it to the office supervisor, who then assigns it (in order received) to the first available data-entry clerk. A study has shown that during tax season (January 1 to April 15) the accountants generate work at an average rate of 10 jobs per day. These jobs are not all the same and take varying amounts of time to enter on the computer. On average, each data-entry clerk can process 6 jobs per day.
   a. What type of waiting-line system is described by this situation?
   b. If the jobs arrive according to a Poisson distribution, and if the service times follow an exponential distribution, answer the following questions:

      What percentage of the time will both data-entry clerks be available with no work?

      What is the probability that, at some time during a day, 6 jobs will be in the system either waiting or being keyed?

      What is the average number of jobs in the queue waiting to be entered?

      What is the average waiting time for jobs that are submitted for data entry?

      What percentage of jobs will arrive and have to wait for some amount of time before being entered?

14. Referring to problem 13, suppose Goldman and Silverton hire a new CPA and the workload increases such that, on average, the number of jobs submitted for data entry increases to 15 per day. Also suppose there is no increase in the number of data-entry clerks or computers. Now assume the number of jobs submitted is constant at 15 per day and that each data-entry clerk can finish exactly 6 jobs per day. Write a short report describing the behavior of the system. Comment on what is likely to happen over the tax season.

15. Referring to problem 14, suppose that Goldman and Silverton decided on two courses of action. First, they bought new software that is supposed to decrease the data-entry time for a typical job. Second, they purchased a new personal computer to have available if needed, with the office supervisor using that machine. This means that each machine (and data entry clerk) can process 8 jobs per day on average.
   a. Draw a diagram which depicts the waiting-line system for the Goldman and Silverton firm.
   b. Suppose that, after several days of having the new computer, the office supervisor tells the two partners that she is spending so much time on data entry she can't get any of her regular work done. If you were asked to analyze the situation, given the job arrival rate and the service rate, what percentage of time should the office supervisor be expected to be doing data entry?

16. A family practice dental office currently has two dentists. Patients see whichever dentist is available first after they arrive. On Saturdays, the dentists perform examinations only, without appointments, and patients arrive at an average of 6 per hour. Each dentist averages 4 exams every hour.
   a. What is the probability that a patient entering the office will have to wait?
   b. What is the probability that 5 or fewer patients will be in the office at any one time?
   c. What is the average number of patients sitting in the waiting room?
   d. What is the average time a patient will spend in the office, from arrival to departure?

17. Referring to problem 16, suppose the dentists are considering adding another dentist to their staff

who can perform examinations at the same rate as the first two. Looking at this proposal from both the patients' standpoint and the dentists', use any appropriate queuing statistics in a short report discussing the merits of adding a third dentist.

18. The Hair Affair has three stylists working at any one time. No appointments are taken, so customers walk in and are served by the next available stylist. Customers arrive on the average of 10 every hour. Each stylist averages 15 minutes per customer.
    a. What is the probability that when a customer enters the hair salon a stylist will be free?
    b. What is the probability that 6 or more customers will be in the salon at the same time?
    c. What is the average time a customer will spend waiting to see a stylist?
    d. What is the average number of customers in the salon at any one time?

19. Recall from problem 10 that Phil advertised he could have customers in and out of his tire service center in 30 minutes or less. Suppose that Phil wanted to offer a $10 refund to anyone waiting more than 30 minutes. The market research Phil conducted relative to this idea indicated that business would increase to 40 arrivals per day on the average (5 per hour). Service was still expected to average 25 minutes per customer. Phil recognized that he couldn't keep up with this demand and that he would have to add more service bays and hire more people. His initial idea was to add 2 tire changers and 2 service areas. Phil has asked you to prepare a complete report outlining the feasibility of his plan. Base your report on all pertinent queuing data.

20. Referring to problem 8, concerning the statistics lab, suppose the university figured the waiting cost per hour for a student is about a third the cost of providing service to each additional student. From these cost estimates, determine the optimal service rate to minimize the total cost. Suppose the cost of assisting students was $10 per hour. What would be the total cost at the optimal service rate?

21. The Hamburger Hut has one drive-through window. A worker has been hired to handle only this window. Customers arrive at a rate of 20 per hour and the mean service time is 2 minutes per customer. The Hamburger Hut has determined that the waiting cost per hour for a customer is about 70% of the cost of serving each additional customer. Determine the optimal service rate to minimize waiting plus service costs.

22. Refer to problem 11, concerning the grocery store manager who has decided to add a check-cashing service. Recall that the store has estimated arrivals to average 35 per hour with service time averaging 1.5 minutes per customer. If the cost to serve customers is estimated to be $15 per hour and the cost of having a customer wait is $40 per hour, what is the total system cost as the situation currently stands? What would the service rate have to be to minimize the total system cost?

23. The Bijou Cinema Complex has six movie theaters. Currently, customers can purchase tickets at only one window. People have been complaining lately about having to wait in line too long to purchase a ticket. After surveying customers waiting in line, the manager has determined the time people must stand in line should be less than 2 minutes. If, in the future, customers are expected to arrive at an average rate of 300 per hour and the average service time is 30 seconds, how many ticket windows must be open to keep the average time waiting in line below 2 minutes? Assume the cost of keeping windows open is such that the manager wants to be as close to 2 minutes as possible without going over.

24. Assume that the theater manager in problem 23 decides the total time of being in line and purchasing a ticket should be less than 2 minutes. Does this change the number of windows that must be open?

Chapter Equations

Constant arrival, constant service rate

Idle-time fraction $= 1 - A/S$ (12-1)

Queue buildup $= A - S$ (12-2)

where:

$A =$ arrival rate per time period

$S =$ service capacity per time period

Poisson probability function

$P(x) = \lambda^x e^{-\lambda}/x!$ (12-3)

Probabilistic service rate

$P(\text{service time} \leq t) = 1 - e^{-\mu t}$ (12-4)

Single line, single server

Probability of server being idle $P_0 = 1 - \lambda/\mu$ (12-5)

Average waiting time $W_q = \dfrac{\lambda/\mu}{\mu - \lambda}$ (12-6)

Average time in the system $W_s = \dfrac{1}{\mu - \lambda}$ (12-7)

Average number waiting for service $L_q = \dfrac{\lambda^2/\mu}{\mu -}$ (12-8)

Average number in the system $L_s = \dfrac{\lambda}{\mu - \lambda}$ (12-9)

Probability of n units in line $P_n = (1 - \lambda/\mu)(\lambda/\mu)^n$ (12-10)

Single line, multiple servers

System service rate $= k\mu$ (12-11)

Probability of all servers being idle

$$P_0 = \frac{1}{\sum_{n=1}^{k-1} \frac{(\lambda/\mu)^n}{n!} + \frac{(\lambda/\mu)^k}{(k-1)!} \times \frac{\mu}{k\mu - \lambda}} \qquad (12\text{-}12)$$

Probability of n units in the system

$$P_n = \frac{(\lambda/\mu)^n}{k!k^{n-k}} P_0 \qquad (n > k) \qquad (12\text{-}13)$$

$$P_n = \frac{(\lambda/\mu)^n}{n!} P_0 \qquad (0 \leq n \leq k) \qquad (12\text{-}14)$$

Average number waiting for service

$$L_q = \frac{(\lambda/\mu)^k(\lambda)(\mu)}{(k-1)!(k\mu - \lambda)^2} P_0 \qquad (12\text{-}15)$$

Average number in the system $L = L_q + \lambda/\mu$ (12-16)

Average time waiting for service $W_q = L_q/\lambda$ (12-17)

Average time in the system $W = W_q + 1/\mu$ (12-18)

Probability of waiting for service $P_w = \frac{1}{k!}\left(\frac{\lambda}{\mu}\right)^k \left(\frac{k\mu}{k\mu - \lambda}\right) P_0$ (12-19)

Probability of servers being idle

$P(1 \text{ or more idle servers}) = 1 - P_w$ (12-20)

Total queuing cost $T_c = (C_s)(\mu) + (C_w)(L_s)$ (12-21)

$T_c = (C_s)(\mu) + (C_w)[\lambda/(\mu - \lambda)]$ (12-22)

Optimal service rate to minimize total queuing costs $\mu^* = \lambda + [(C_w/C_s)\lambda]^{1/2}$ (12-23)

Chapter Glossary

Arrival rate The average number of units arriving for service in a waiting-line system per unit of time.

Balking Customers arriving for service but refusing to join the waiting line because of its length.

Exponential probability distribution A probability distribution often used to describe the service times in a waiting-line system.

Idle The situation when no customers are in the system.

Interarrival time The time between two units arriving for service.

Multiple-server systems A queuing system in which identical servers are arranged in parallel.

Poisson probability distribution A probability distribution often used in waiting-line models to describe the random arrival of customers at a service facility.

Queue (waiting line) One or more units waiting for service.

Reneging Customers leaving a waiting line before reaching the service facility.

Service rate The average number of units served in a waiting-line system per unit of time.

Service time In a waiting-line system, the time a customer spends being served.

Waiting time The time a customer spends in line waiting for service to start.

Chapter References

BOOKS

Beckman, P. *Introduction to Elementary Queueing Theory and Telephone Traffic.* Boulder, Colo.: Golem, 1968.

Cooper, R. B. *Introduction to Queuing Theory.* New York: Macmillan, 1972.

Gross, D., and C. M. Harris. *Fundamentals of Queuing Theory.* New York: Interscience-Wiley, 1971.

Panico, Joseph A. *Queuing Theory: A Study of Waiting Lines for Business and Economics.* Englewood Cliffs, N.J.: Prentice-Hall, 1969.

ARTICLES

Cosmetatos, G. P. "Value of Queuing Theory—A Case Study." *Interfaces,* Vol. 9 (May), 1979.

Green, L., and P. Kolesar. "Testing the Validity of a Queuing Model of Police Patrol." *Management Science,* Vol. 35 (February), 1989.

Jordan, S. "Analysis and Approximation of a JIT Production Line." *Decision Sciences,* Vol. 19, 1988.

Kaimann A., and R. J. Asebrook. "Waiting Line Theory: Useful Auditing Tool." *Internal Auditor,* Vol. 35 (February), 1978.

McKeown, P. G. "Application of Queuing Analysis to the New York State Child Abuse and Maltreatment Register Telephone Reporting System." *Interfaces,* Vol. 9 (May), 1979.

———. "Modeling the Queue." *Datamation,* Vol. 25 (June), 1979.

Skiena, S. S. "A Fairer Scoring System for Jai-Alai." *Interfaces,* Vol. 18 (November–December), 1988.

Mini Case

CASE 12A

QUAL-TECH MANUFACTURING

Qual-Tech Manufacturing, located in Santa Ana, California, is one of hundreds of firms that supply component parts to the high-tech industries in Silicon Valley. The company opened in the early 1980s, when a trio of Hewlett-Packard engineers decided they could do a better job of supplying component parts for HP's minicomputer division than HP was getting from its current suppliers. Jerry Brown, Clint Bixby, and Harold Eck pooled their life savings and obtained additional capital from a Houston-based investor to open a manufacturing facility in a small warehouse near their current location.

Because of their connections at HP, they were able to get a small contract to supply casing units for a disk drive in the HP product line. Qual-Tech's commitment to the highest possible quality levels paid off when the casing units exceeded HP's expectations and led to larger contracts for this part. Soon, contracts were coming in for related components, first from HP and then from other companies in the area. Although sales increased rapidly during the first few years, so did expenses and the need for capital investment. However, the partners remained committed to quality and would not skimp on anything that might affect customer relations.

While the past five years have had their ups and down, Qual-Tech has become a very profitable enterprise, with sales of $27,000,000 last year. During this period, the three partners decided to divide up their management responsibilities. Jerry Brown now heads up the marketing and sales effort, Clint Bixby focuses on purchasing and finance, and Harold Eck is in charge of production and research and development. Even though they have separate responsibilities, the three partners still communicate daily about company operations.

As Qual-Tech has grown, so has the competition. Suddenly many competitors are capable of producing high-quality components and no customers can be taken for granted. The competition from domestic and international firms requires that Qual-Tech seek the most efficient means of performing every manufacturing process.

This brings us to a meeting that Harold Eck held recently with his production supervisors on Condor line. The Condor line makes the outside housing for laser printers. These housings are made of molded plastic formed to the customer's specifications. One of the final steps in the process is to paint the housing and apply appropriate decals. The line opened a year ago with substantial excess capacity, producing strictly on an as-ordered basis, but business was such that the line could be operated continuously at about 50% of capacity.

In the past three months, Jerry Brown negotiated a deal with a U.S. computer company for a quantity of printer housings that all three partners agreed would tax the Condor line's capacity. However, Harold Eck thought that through careful scheduling, the existing line could accommodate the extra orders. For a while things went pretty smoothly, with only an occasional crisis, but recently the process flow was backing up at the paint station. The paint station consists of a computer-controlled sprayer which is programmed to spray paint on all sides of the housing unit. The units arrive at the spray station on a conveyor and are manually hung on an overhead hook, which moves the housing into the spray booth when the previous unit is finished. Because of the various models of housings, the spraying times differ. The operator enters a code into the computer to indicate the proper spraying time.

The housing units arrive at the spray booth in a random manner, depending on production schedules. The problem is that arrivals at the spray booth sometimes exceed the booth's service capacity. When that happens, unpainted housings back up. This situation is affecting production schedules and causing missed deliveries. In addition, the floor in the painting area is "a real mess," according to one supervisor.

A meeting between Eck and the line supervisors focused on what to do about the situation. The paint booth operator wrote some data on the board to help explain the problem. He said that printer housings have recently been arriving at an average rate of 40 per hour. He also noted that average painting time is 2 minutes per unit. It didn't take the group long to see why the queues were developing. The supervisor offered that the only way they had managed to this point was by running the paint booth while the rest of the line was down for routine maintenance. He was worried that this schedule was not allowing adequate preventive maintenance for the paint operation and that problems might soon occur.

The group made several suggestions. One was to slow down the production line; another was to cut the unit painting time. But both suggestions were dismissed. A slowdown in production would increase the number of missed deliveries and hurt customer relations. Reducing the spray time would adversely affect painting quality. One suggestion that created a lot of interest was made by Mike Stern, a new supervisor on the Condor line. He suggested replacing the sprayer with a new model that could cut the painting time from an average of 2 minutes per unit to about 30 seconds. But he also warned that the new model costs about three times as much as the current model. The remainder of the discussion focused on whether this was the way to go. When the meeting broke up, Harold was not convinced and thought there ought to be some way to analyze the situation without actually spending money on the machine.

CASE 12B

QUAL-TECH MANUFACTURING

Harold Eck (see case 12A) spent the evening studying the queuing statistics prepared by Henry Dutzar. Henry, a graduate of the college of business at one of the state's universities, had joined Qual-Tech in 1989 as head of the personnel department. Although once employed as a statistical analyst, Henry had always preferred working people instead of numbers and enjoyed his job at Qual-Tech. He communicated well with people at all levels of the organization, and they felt free to call on him at any time — especially when they needed assistance with modeling and other management science problems.

When Harold left his meeting with the production supervisors, now confused about whether to purchase the new model paint sprayer, he had phoned Henry and explained the situation. The report that was now occupying Harold's evening was very complete. It showed Harold what he could expect from the system if printer housings continued to arrive at the paint station at the same average rate, and if the new model sprayer could actually do the same quality paint job in one-fourth the current time. Harold was impressed, not only by the completeness of the report but also by the fact that it had taken Henry only a couple of days to generate it.

However, in the two days while Henry was preparing the queuing report, Harold and his supervisors were still thinking and discussing the problem. Earlier that morning, the swing-shift paint booth operator called Harold with an idea that he said was "probably crazy." The idea was to remodel the paint spray booth so that two additional spray units could be installed. These could be the old model spray units, which cost less than the new model. He figured the cost of buying two additional machines plus the remodeling would be about the same as buying the new style sprayer. He indicated that printer housings could be channeled into whichever spray unit became available first. The computer program that now controlled the one sprayer could be modified quite easily to handle any number of sprayers.

The more Harold thought about this latest idea, and the more he studied Henry's report, the more he realized that he needed more information before making the decision. Even though his watch showed 9:40 P.M., he reached for the phone and dialed Henry's home number. He explained the latest idea and asked Henry to prepare an analysis of the multiple-sprayer option. He asked for a report that assumed two sprayers and another one which assumed three sprayers. Finally, he asked that Henry compare the multiple-sprayer option with the previous option of buying a new-model sprayer. As he hung up, Harold made a mental note to talk to his partners about Henry Dutzar's value to the organization.

Chapter 13

INTRODUCTION TO DECISION ANALYSIS

Chapter Outline

Why You Need to Know

The management science techniques presented so far in this text were originally designed to help decision makers answer particular questions. As you have seen, these techniques have widespread applications and cover all the functional business areas. For the most part, these techniques assume the situation being modeled is stable and the appropriate physical parameters are known with certainty. For instance, in a linear programming model, the objective-function coefficients are assumed to be known, as are the constraint coefficients and the right-hand-side values. The inventory models introduced in Chapter 8 assume that such factors as demand and lead time are known with certainty, and the network models in Chapters 11 and 12 often assume that activity times and costs are known.

While certainty is often assumed in decision-making situations, more often than not the real decision environment is uncertainty. We dealt with uncertainty when we discussed how to incorporate probability distributions in inventory models and PERT/CPM networks. In our discussion of linear programming models, uncertainty was addressed through the use of sensitivity analysis. However, this was simply adding a level of complexity to a model originally developed assuming a certain environment. Many business decisions require multistage, multiperiod decision models incorporating many levels of uncertainty.

As future business leaders, you need to be prepared to make complex multiperiod decisions in situations where the assumption of certainty is not realistic. Over the past 30 years, *decision analysis* (also referred to as decision theory) has been developed to provide a framework for dealing with such situations. Since the use of decision analysis is increasing rapidly in business and government, you need to be familiar with the techniques and be able to recognize when and how to apply them.

Chapter Objectives

The objectives of this chapter are to introduce the fundamentals of decision analysis and to show, through examples, how several basic decision-analysis tools are used in the decision-making process.

Specifically, the objectives of this chapter are to:

1. Describe the two decision environments: certainty and uncertainty.
2. Show how to construct a payoff table and an opportunity-loss table.
3. Introduce and define the expected-value criterion.
4. Show how the expected-value criterion is applied in decision situations.
5. Show how to compute the value of perfect information.
6. Illustrate how to develop a decision tree and show how it can aid decision making in an uncertain environment.

13-1 A BRIEF HISTORY OF DECISION ANALYSIS

While in a way this entire book is devoted to discussing tools managers can use to help analyze decisions, the term *decision analysis* has a specialized meaning in management science. It applies to the set of tools, covered in this and the following two chapters, that have been developed to help managers analyze multistage decisions that must be made in an uncertain environment.

Putting together this set of tools has been a relatively recent development, starting in the late 1950s, initially by faculty at the Harvard Business School. The individual tools themselves are considerably older than decision analysis, however, and come from three theoretical areas of thought: (1) Bayesian statistics, (2) game theory, and (3) risk-preference analysis.

The bedrock of decision analysis was formed by the eighteenth-century work of the Reverend Thomas Bayes, one of the most enigmatic figures in scientific history. He is credited with being the first person to give a rational account of how statistical inference can be used as a process for understanding situations in the real world. But, his pioneering work was not published until after his death in 1761, and during his lifetime he was a scientific unknown. Now, however, he has become so popular that a whole group of decision analysts refer to themselves as "Bayesians."

A second contribution to modern decision analysis is the game-theory concept of John Von Neumann and Oskar Morgenstern. They demonstrated that the "correct" decision in any situation depends on the objectives of the decision maker and actions likely to be taken by competitors.

The third area is the work of such economists as Milton Friedman and L. J. Savage. They showed that a person's attitude toward risk depended on the person's circumstances; and therefore different decision makers, when facing the same decision, may make different choices because of their differing attitudes.

The academic subject area of decision analysis was formulated from these three bodies of work by such people as Robert Schlaifer, Howard Raiffa, Ralph Keeney, D. V. Lindley, Rex Brown, Andrew Kahr, Cameron Peterson, and Robert Winkler. They and others have been responsible for organizing the decision-sciences discipline and bringing it to the business community. Since its introduction in the late 1950s, decision analysis has become a common feature in MBA programs and has influenced thousands of decision makers in government and industry.

13-2 DECISION-MAKING ENVIRONMENTS

In business, you will encounter a wide variety of decision situations. The analytic methods you use to deal with each situation will depend largely on the *decision environment*. The two primary decision environments are *certainty* and *uncertainty*. In this section, we define these environments and show how they affect decision making. In the following sections, we will introduce some techniques for making decisions in an uncertain environment.

CERTAINTY

Sometimes you will encounter a decision situation where you can be certain of the outcome for each alternative. This type of decision environment, in which the results of each alternative are known before the decision is made, is termed a **certainty** environment. Consider, for example, a decision faced by the Gorden Company, which makes frozen hamburger patties for fast-food stores and grocery chains. The national sales manager has just received a message from a regional sales representative indicating that she has negotiated a deal with a new customer for 1 million patties at $.50 each. However, the customer wants the patties to be packaged in groups of 6 rather than the usual 24 per package. The sales representative points out that the company can modify its packaging equipment "quite easily" to accommodate this change. She urges a quick decision, since a delay is likely to force the customer to go elsewhere and the efforts to attract this new business will be lost.

Needing information on which to base his decision, the national sales manager contacts the industrial engineering and accounting staffs. He is told that the total production costs for the product grouped 6 to a package will be $.44 per patty.

Table 13-1 shows the projected profits and losses for the two decision alternatives—accept the offer or reject the offer. Since all costs and revenues are known for each alternative, the decision is straightforward: The $30,000 profit associated with accepting the offer exceeds the $0 profit associated with not accepting the offer; therefore, the offer should be accepted.

As this example shows, once a certainty model has been specified, the best decision is evident. By "best decision," we mean the alternative course of action, using all available information, that best satisfies the decision criterion. In the Gorden Company example, the decision criterion was highest profit. Given that the decision model displayed in Table 13-1 utilized all available information, the best decision was to accept the offer. Since this is a certainty environment, the decision will result in an outcome of $30,000 profit. Thus, in a certainty environment, the best decision will always be associated with the best outcome.

If business decisions were always made in a certainty environment, you would probably not need the academic training you are now receiving to be successful. How many of us would have chosen to reject the offer in the Gorden Company example if Table 13-1 reflected the total decision picture? In reality, the typical business decision-making environment is not one of certainty but, rather, uncertainty.

UNCERTAINTY

The certainty environment is predicated on the fact that the outcome from each alternative course of action is known. If we choose alternative A, outcome Y will occur. If alternative B is selected, outcome Z will occur. This makes choosing between the alternatives straightforward.

Table 13-1 GORDEN COMPANY: PROFITS AND LOSSES FOR TWO ALTERNATIVES

	Alternatives	
Revenues and Expenses	Accept Offer	Reject Offer
Revenues		
Sales (1 million @ $.50 each)	$500,000	0
Costs		
Production (1 million @ $.44 each)	$440,000	0
Selling (5% of sales)	$25,000	0
Overhead (1% of revenue)	$5,000	0
Profit	$30,000	0

However, in most business situations, while we may be able to specify the possible outcomes for each alternative, we will be uncertain about which outcome will occur. In an environment of **uncertainty**, the outcome which will occur from selecting an alternative course of action is not known. Consider the real estate speculator who is trying to decide whether to purchase a property with the hopes of reselling it next year at a profit. If the speculator elects not to purchase the property, the net change in his financial position will be zero. He knows this for sure. However, if he chooses to buy the property, just what will the outcome be? Will he make $10,000 or $20,000, or will he lose $5000? Identifying the possible outcomes is difficult enough, but knowing for certain what outcome definitely will occur is impossible in a competitive real estate market. Thus, the speculator must decide to buy or not buy in an environment of uncertainty.

Consider this example of the Eagle Lumber Company in Glenns Ferry, Wisconsin. About 3 weeks ago, the manager received 4000 board feet of 2″ × 6″ tongue-and-groove knotty pine, which is used primarily for floors and ceilings. The product is hard to get, since the supplier makes only a limited quantity each month. The wholesale price for the recent shipment was $360 per thousand board feet. Two days after receiving the material, a customer came in and bought the entire shipment for $450 per thousand board feet. However, the customer wanted Eagle Lumber to store the material for 8 weeks.

Three weeks later, another customer arrived and wanted to purchase as much 2″ × 6″ tongue-and-groove knotty pine as possible for immediate use. The only stock on hand at the lumber company is the 4000 board feet, which has already been sold. After seeing the paid-for knotty pine, the new customer asked whether the manager would consider selling him the 4000 board feet now and replacing the material before the previous customer returned to pick it up in about 5 weeks.

In a certain environment, the decision would be relatively easy. If the lumber could be replaced at a known price before the first customer returned, the manager could resell the material and both customers would be happy. If the lumber could not be replaced before the first customer returned, the second customer would be turned away.

Unfortunately, the decision environment facing Eagle's manager is not one of certainty. For one thing, he does not know whether he will be able to replace the stock within 5 weeks. Furthermore, if he is able to replace the material, he does not know exactly what the cost will be. Therefore, he is uncertain about what price to charge the second customer. He is also uncertain about whether the first customer will arrive early to take his material. As you can see, a seemingly simple situation is actually quite complex due to the uncertainties involved.

The decision-analysis techniques presented in this and the following two chapters do not eliminate the uncertainty associated with a decision, but they do provide a framework for dealing with the uncertainty. These techniques help you make good decisions under uncertain conditions, but good decisions don't necessarily result in good outcomes. For instance, suppose after considering all available information, the best decision is not to sell to the new customer. Then, a week later, the original customer calls to say he will be 6 weeks late picking up the material. If the manager had known this, he could have sold the materials to the new customer and received the additional profit. Thus, the best decision at the time did not result in a good outcome.

This concept of decision analysis is contrary to how many people view situations. The tendency is to look at the outcome and, if it is not good, we second-guess our decision. However, if we have properly used all available information in making the decision, it was a good decision. Decision makers must realize that in an uncertain environment, where they don't have total control over the outcomes of their decisions, bad outcomes will sometimes occur. Decision makers must also continually remind themselves there is a difference between a good *decision* and a good *outcome*.

> The goal of decision analysis is to focus on making good decisions, which in the long run should result in an increased number of good outcomes.

DECISION SITUATIONS REQUIRING DECISION ANALYSIS

Not all decisions require the use of decision analysis, particularly those which lack complexity and can be based on programmed rules. For instance, in Chapter 8, we discussed fixed-order-point inventory models, where orders are made when the inventory level reaches a specified order point. The decision to order is automatic until the rule is changed. In fact, in many companies, a computer determines when an order is needed and automatically prints out the order form. This type of repetitive decision typically does not require decision analysis.

The complexity of the decision situation usually determines the usefulness of decision analysis. The more complex the decision, the greater the potential benefit from decision analysis. Several factors affect the complexity of a decision, including the number of alternatives available to the decision maker, the number of possible outcomes associated with each alternative, and the general level of uncertainty associated with the decision. For example, marketing decisions regarding product design, product pricing, and distribution are very complex, and decision-analysis tools can be helpful to the decision maker. Of course, any decision involving product design or pricing also involves other areas in an organization, including production and finance.

Another characteristic of situations where decisions can be aided by decision analysis is that they often extend to multiple functional areas of the organization. Production decisions including process design, aggregate planning, and facilities planning all lend themselves to decision analysis because of their complexity and long-term importance to the organization. Such financial decision areas as capital budgeting, project financing, and pension investing clearly can benefit from the application of decision analysis.

The types of decisions mentioned here are only a few of those where decision analysis can be effectively applied. Throughout the remainder of this chapter and in Chapters 14 and 15 we will present further examples of areas where decision analysis can be used.

13-3 DECISION CRITERIA

Campbell Specialty Publishing has been in business for 10 years in Memphis, Tennessee. The company was started by Jan Campbell as a part-time business when she decided to stay home to care for her young children. Jan had worked for a book publisher before starting her business and saw a market for publishing company newsletters, annual reports, advertising brochures, and the like. Campbell Specialty concentrated on small businesses that could not afford to have their own in-house publishing capability or to contract a large publishing organization to do the work. The production process was labor-intensive, with manual typesetting and page makeup.

Business had been extremely good until 2 years ago, when sales fell drastically. By contacting past customers, Jan determined the drop in sales was due to the increase in relatively inexpensive computer desktop publishing capability. Small companies were now finding it economical to do their publications in-house.

This finding made Jan realize that her company must change to computerized publishing to be competitive, but she is uncertain about the extent of the investment needed. Jan feels she has three potential courses of action (alternatives):

A_1: A large investment, which would involve purchasing a minicomputer with multiple communication ports to allow direct data transfer to customer facilities, high-speed multicolor laser printers, and facsimile transmission capability. This equipment would give Jan much more capability than she now has.

A_2: A medium investment, which would enable computerizing the labor/mechanical functions. This alternative would provide most of the equipment of alternative A_1 but would omit the communication capabilities. Communicating with customers would still be done in person or by mail or telephone.

A_3: A small investment, which would involve purchasing a desktop publishing system such as the Apple Macintosh and a laser printer. This alternative effectively means that Jan would concentrate on the smaller customers who do not have their own desktop publishing capabilities.

Obviously, the alternative Jan selects should depend on the future demand for the service her company provides. She has identified three potential directions this demand can take. In decision-analysis terminology, these three demand levels are referred to as **states of nature**, or the possible outcomes in a decision situation over which the decision maker has no control. For Jan, they are:

S_1: Rapidly increasing demand due to the high-quality low-cost service that computerized publishing provides.

S_2: Demand at about the same level as now.

S_3: Decreasing demand as more businesses add their own in-house capability.

Jan would like to base her investment decision on yearly profit values, but as we can see, there are three potential profit levels, due to the three states of nature, for each alternative. The outcome associated with any combination of state of nature and alternative is called a **payoff**. Since Jan's decision involves three alternatives and three states of nature, she has nine possible payoffs to consider, as shown in the payoff table (Table 13-2).

Table 13-2 CAMPBELL SPECIALTY PUBLISHING: PAYOFF TABLE

	Demand (states of nature)		
Alternative	S_1: Increasing	S_2: Stable	S_3: Decreasing
A_1: Large investment	\$60,000	\$40,000	−\$26,000
A_2: Medium investment	\$25,000	\$50,000	−\$10,000
A_3: Small investment	\$20,000	\$15,000	\$12,000

Note: These values are Jan Campbell's estimates of the profit associated with each combination of alternative and state of nature.

In order to decide among the three alternatives, Jan must have some basis for comparing them and so must establish decision criteria. There are two main categories of decision criteria: *nonprobabilistic* and *probabilistic*. Nonprobabilistic criteria are used when either the probabilities associated with the possible payoffs are unknown or the decision maker lacks confidence and/or information with which to assess probabilities for the various payoffs.

NONPROBABILISTIC DECISION CRITERIA

Several specific decision criteria fall into the nonprobabilistic category. One of these is the **maximax criterion**, which leads us to select the alternative that carries with it the highest possible payoff. For Jan Campbell, using this criterion would mean making a major investment in computer publishing, since that is the alternative with the highest possible payoff, $60,000 per year (Table 13-2). The maximax criterion might be chosen by optimistic decision makers.

If we are not optimistic, we might select the alternative whose worst possible outcome is higher than the worst possible outcome from any other alternative. This pessimistic (or conservative) criterion is called the **maximin criterion**. For Jan, using the maximin criterion would mean selecting the small-investment alternative, since its worst outcome, $12,000, is better than any other alternative's worst outcome.

A disadvantage of the maximax and maximin criteria is they use only one value from the payoff table to make the decision. In analyzing the decision situation, Jan may be interested in determining how much damage may be caused by making the wrong choice. For instance, suppose she decides on the medium-cost alternative and later finds the market for her services has expanded greatly. Her medium-investment decision leads to a $25,000 yearly profit while, given perfect hindsight, the best decision of making a large investment would have earned $60,000. The difference between the actual payoff and the optimal payoff for a given state of nature is an *opportunity loss;* in Jan's case, it is $35,000. If she decides to use the minimax regret criterion to help her make a decision, she will need to know the value of the opportunity loss.

The **minimax regret criterion** considers the results of selecting the "wrong" alternative. The first step is to construct an opportunity-loss, or *regret,* table by finding, for each state of nature, the difference between the payoff for the best decision and the payoffs for all the other alternatives. Table 13-3 shows how this is done. The next step is to find the maximum regret for each alternative. These values are shown in Table 13-4. The minimax regret criterion now requires selecting the minimum of these maximum regret values. Using this criterion, Jan should choose the medium-investment decision, since the maximum opportunity loss of $35,000 is lower than the maximum opportunity loss for either of the other two alternatives.

Table 13-3 CAMPBELL SPECIALTY PUBLISHING: OPPORTUNITY-LOSS TABLE

	Demand (states of nature)		
Alternative	S_1: Increasing	S_2: Stable	S_3: Decreasing
A_1: Large investment	$0	$10,000	$38,000
A_2: Medium investment	$35,000	$0	$22,000
A_3: Small investment	$40,000	$35,000	$0

Note: The values in this table were found by subtracting each column value in Table 13-2 from the largest value in that column.

Table 13-4 CAMPBELL SPECIALTY PUBLISHING: MAXIMUM REGRET TABLE

Alternative	Maximum Opportunity Loss, or Regret
A_1: Large investment	\$38,000
A_2: Medium investment	\$35,000
A_3: Small investment	\$40,000

Observe that all three criteria lead to different decisions; therefore Jan should determine which criterion best describes her decision-making philosophy and use it to help her choose.

The maximax, maximin, and minimax regret decision criteria are examples of nonprobabilistic decision criteria. Nonprobabilistic criteria do not take into account the probability associated with the outcomes for each alternative; they merely focus on the dollar value of the outcomes. The criticism of nonprobabilistic decision criteria is their failure to include important information about the chances of each outcome occurring. It is often argued that if the payoff probabilities are known or can be assessed, a probabilistic decision criterion should be employed.

PROBABILISTIC DECISION CRITERIA

Some decision criteria take into account the probabilities associated with each outcome. One of these is the expected-value criterion.

Expected-Value Criterion

You have probably encountered the term *expected value* in a statistics course; it refers to the long-run average outcome for a given alternative. In order to determine an expected value, we must have probabilities for each possible outcome. The expected value is computed as follows:

$$E(x) = \Sigma x_i P(x_i) \tag{13-1}$$

where:

x_i = the ith outcome of the specified alternative measured in some units, such as dollars

$P(x_i)$ = the probability of outcome x_i occurring

and:

$$\Sigma P(x_i) = 1.0 \tag{13-2}$$

$$0.0 \leq P(x_i) \leq 1.0 \tag{13-3}$$

Equation 13-1 shows that the expected value is the sum of the weighted outcomes for a specified alternative. This means that if the alternative is repeatedly selected, over the long run the average outcome will equal $E(x)$, the expected value.

Consider the following simple decision situation that involves flipping a coin. If the head turns up, you will be paid \$10; if the tail turns up, you must pay \$5. If you choose not to play, you will neither gain nor lose anything. In this case, the no-play option has a constant \$0 payoff and the play alternative has uncertain outcomes. Let $x_1 = \$10$ (head) and $x_2 = -\$5$ (tail). Then, if you are using a fair coin, the following probability distribution exists:

x	$P(x)$
\$10	.50
−\$5	.50
	1.00

The expected value is:

$$E(x) = (\$10)(.50) + (-\$5)(.50) = \$2.50$$

This means that over the long run you would average \$2.50 per flip if you elected to play. However, on any given flip, you would either win \$10 or lose \$5. If you don't play, the expected gain is \$0, since that payoff is a constant for the don't-play alternative.

When applying the **expected-value criterion**, the best decision is to select the alternative with the highest average payoff or the lowest average loss. In the coin example, the best decision, using the expected-value criterion, is to play, since \$2.50 > \$0. The advantage of the expected-value criterion is that it takes into account the information contained in the probabilities. For instance, if the coin is unfair and the chance of a head is only .10 instead of .50, the expected value of the play option would be:

$$E(x) = (\$10)(.10) + (-\$5)(.90) = -\$3.50$$

Then, given this new information about the coin, the best decision, based on the expected-value criterion, would be the don't-play option, since \$0 > −\$3.50.

The disadvantage of the expected-value criterion is that it does not take into account the decision maker's attitude toward risk. For instance, in the first case for the coin example, the expected value was \$2.50. Clearly, on the basis of expected value we should play the game, since \$2.50 > \$0. However, if we can play only one time, we could lose \$5. Thus, depending on how averse we are to this outcome, we might decide not to play after all. Chapter 15 deals specifically with the issue of risk preferences.

Expected value is the decision criterion around which the techniques of decision analysis are built and is the one emphasized throughout this chapter and in Chapters 14 and 15.

Probability Assessment

In the coin example, we assumed that the probability of a head turning up was known and that, if the coin is fair, the chances of winning are 50-50. In fact, probabilities are known for most games of chance, and in casino games, serious players always know the probabilities of winning and losing. The assessment method used in these cases is called *classical probability assessment*. It assumes that individual outcomes are equally likely and that:

$$P(a) = \frac{\text{number of ways } a \text{ can occur}}{\text{total number of ways any outcome can occur}} \tag{13-4}$$

For instance, if a fair six-sided die is rolled, the probability that the number showing will be 3 or greater is determined by counting the number of ways a 3 or higher can occur:

$$\{3 \quad 4 \quad 5 \quad 6\} = 4 \text{ ways}$$

Then we divide this number by the total number of ways any outcome can occur, which is:

$$\{1 \quad 2 \quad 3 \quad 4 \quad 5 \quad 6\} = 6 \text{ ways}$$

Thus, $P(x \geq 3) = 4/6$.

Although classical probability assessment works well for games of chance, it is not appropriate for situations in which individual outcomes are not equally likely. For instance, suppose your university is considering whether or not to continue to keep the computer lab open on Friday evening. The administrator agrees to do so only if 12 or more people will show up to use the lab. She might begin by attempting to assess the chances that 12 or more people will show up. The classical probability assessment method will not work, since neither denominator nor numerator values, required for using equation 13-4, are known. A sample of 50 Friday evenings shows that on 20 occasions 12 or more people were in the lab. With this information, she could use the *relative frequency of occurrence method* to assess the probabilities. This method equates the probability of an outcome occurring to the ratio of the number of times the outcome has occurred in the past to the total number of observations. In this case, the probability is $P(x \geq 12) = 20/50$. In general notation, this is stated as:

$$P(x) = \frac{\text{number of times } x \text{ occurs}}{n} \tag{13-5}$$

where: n = number of observances

This method of probability assessment is often used in business. For instance, a production control manager would assess the probability of a defective part being produced on a production line by examining a sample of n parts and counting how many were defective. The ratio of the number of defectives to the sample size gives the probability assessment.

In order for the relative frequency of occurrence method to be appropriate, the sample size has to be sufficiently large and each observation must be taken under similar conditions. A construction firm estimating the chances of winning a bid on a project may have had only two equivalent experiences. But winning both previous bids should not lead the company to believe the chance of winning the new bid is 100% even though $P(\text{win}) = 2/2 = 1.0$. The sample size is just too small. However, the sample size might be increased by including all contract bids in the last 10 years. But even if n increases to 250, the situations for the past 250 contracts will not match this current contract; so a relative frequency of occurrence assessment would not be appropriate.

In many decision-making situations that require a probability assessment, neither the classical method nor the relative frequency of occurrence method is satisfactory. Instead, the decision maker will have to make a subjective probability assessment.

Subjective assessments are based upon individual experiences and available information. A *subjective probability* is a measure of a personal conviction that an outcome will occur. Therefore, a subjective probability assessment represents the decision maker's state of mind, or degree of belief, regarding the chance that the outcome will occur.

Decision makers constantly make subjective probability assessments and incorporate them into their decisions. When the tools of decision analysis are employed, these probability assessments must be quantified and expressed openly. For example, suppose a company manager has to decide which of two numerically controlled milling machines to purchase. One criterion to be used in the decision is monthly

Table 13-5 PROBABILITY DISTRIBUTION FOR MONTHLY REPAIR COSTS

Machine A		Machine B	
Repair Cost	Probability	Repair Cost	Probability
$0	.10	0	.20
$1,000	.50	$1,000	.30
$5,000	.30	$5,000	.40
$10,000	.10	$10,000	.10

expected repair costs. Table 13-5 shows the possible repair costs for each machine and the subjectively assessed probability for each level. These probabilities reflect the state of mind of the manager. If someone else were to assess the probabilities, he or she would probably arrive at different assessments based on different experiences and a different state of mind.

The expected monthly repair cost for each of the two machines is computed in Table 13-6. Since lower repair costs are preferred, the best decision using the expected-value criterion is to select machine A, since $\$3000 < \$3300$. The expected value is computed using the decision maker's subjective probabilities. In assessing these probabilities, it is important that the decision maker incorporate all available information and experience in order to accurately reflect his or her state of mind at the time the decision is being made.

13-4 COST OF UNCERTAINTY

The advantage of making decisions in a certainty environment is that the best decision always yields the best outcome. In an uncertain environment, the best decision might not result in the best outcome. Thus, there is a cost of uncertainty associated with not knowing in advance which outcome will occur. An example will show what we mean.

Dennon Concessions sells hot dogs and other items at a minor league baseball park in Ohio. The business is owned and operated by two sisters. Before each game, they must determine how many hot dogs to make. The hot dogs must be precooked, and any unsold hot dogs are donated to a local homeless shelter. Harriet, the senior partner, thinks that the minimum number of hot dogs demanded during next Saturday's game will be 700 and the maximum will be 1100. If this is true, then the actual

Table 13-6 EXPECTED-VALUE COMPUTATION FOR MONTHLY REPAIR COSTS

Machine A			Machine B		
Repair Cost x	Probability $P(x)$	$xP(x)$	Repair Cost y	Probability $P(y)$	$yP(y)$
$0	.10	$0	0	.20	$0
$1,000	.50	$500	$1,000	.30	$300
$5,000	.30	$1500	$5,000	.40	$2000
$10,000	.10	$1000	$10,000	.10	$1000
	Expected repair cost	$3000		Expected repair cost	$3300

Table 13-7 DENNON CONCESSIONS: PROBABILITY ASSESSMENT

Demand (number of hot dogs)	Probability
700	.05
800	.10
900	.20
1000	.40
1100	.25
	1.00

demand could be any number between 700 and 1100. To simplify the analysis, Table 13-7 lists only five possible demand levels, along with Harriet's subjective assessments of the probability that each of these demand levels will occur.

The fixed cost of setting up to cook the hot dogs is \$350, variable costs amount to \$.30 per hot dog, and the selling price is \$.70 each. With this information, we find the payoffs associated with different production levels by using the following equation:

$$\text{Payoff} = \$.70(s) - \$350 - \$.30(p)$$

where:

s = number of units sold

p = number of units produced

Thus, the payoff when production is 700 and demand is 700 is:

$$\text{Payoff} = \$.70(700) - \$350 - \$.30(700) = -\$70.00$$

If 800 hot dogs are cooked and 1000 are demanded, the payoff is:

$$\text{Payoff} = \$.70(800) - \$350 - \$.30(800) = -\$30.00$$

(Notice that even though demand is 1000, sales are limited to 800 because only 800 were produced. The payoffs associated with all combinations of production and demand are displayed in the *payoff table* (Table 13-8). The demand levels are labeled "states of nature," since demand is outside the control of the decision maker.

Table 13-9 shows the payoff table and the probabilities associated with each demand level. The expected values for each production alternative are shown. These are computed by summing the payoffs times the probabilities. For example, the

Table 13-8 DENNON CONCESSIONS: PAYOFF TABLE

	Demand (states of nature)				
Production	700	800	900	1000	1100
700	−\$70	−\$70	−\$70	−\$70	−\$70
800	−\$100	−\$30	−\$30	−\$30	−\$30
900	−\$130	−\$60	\$10	\$10	\$10
1000	−\$160	−\$90	−\$20	\$50	\$50
1100	−\$190	−\$120	−\$50	\$20	\$90

Table 13-9 DENNON CONCESSIONS: EXPECTED VALUES

	Demand (states of nature)					
Production	700 ($p = .05$)	800 ($p = .10$)	900 ($p = .20$)	1000 ($p = .40$)	1100 ($p = .25$)	E(payoff)
700	−\$70	−\$70	−\$70	−\$70	−\$70	−\$70.00
800	−\$100	−\$30	−\$30	−\$30	−\$30	−\$33.50
900	−\$130	−\$60	\$10	\$10	\$10	−\$4.00
1000	−\$160	−\$90	−\$20	\$50	\$50	\$11.50
1100	−\$190	−\$120	−\$50	\$20	\$90	−\$1.00

expected payoff for a production level of 900 hot dogs is:

$$\begin{aligned} E(\text{payoff}) &= -\$130(.05) + -\$60(.10) + \$10(.20) + \$10(.40) + \$10(.25) \\ &= -\$4.00 \end{aligned}$$

Therefore, in the long run, Dennon Concessions can expect to lose \$4.00 per game if they cook 900 hot dogs. The other expected values are computed in a similar manner.

From Table 13-9 we see that if the decision criterion of highest expected payoff is used, the best decision is to cook 1000 hot dogs at each game, for an expected payoff of \$11.50 per game. This production level has a higher expected payoff than any other production alternative. However, for any single game, the actual payoff from a decision to cook 1000 hot dogs could be either −\$160, −\$90, −\$20, or \$50. This means that for any single situation, the best decision might not give the best outcome. Thus, there is a cost of being uncertain about which demand level will occur.

If Harriet Dennon could obtain perfect information about the demand level, her decision environment would change to one of certainty. If she knew in advance how many hot dogs would be demanded, she could select the production level that will maximize the payoff in each case. For example, if she knew the demand was going to be 900, she would decide to cook 900 hot dogs, for a profit of \$10.00. If she knew demand would be 1100, she would decide to cook 1100 hot dogs, for a profit of \$90.00.

However, having perfect information about what is going to happen does not mean that we can control what will happen. Even though the highest profit will occur when demand is 1100 and production is also, 1100, Harriet cannot *make* the demand be 1100. The demand for hot dogs is outside her control.

If the demand level is assumed to occur according to the subjectively assessed probability distribution, the *expected value under certainty (EVUC)* can be computed. We first assume we know what the demand will be for each game. Therefore we are able to achieve the optimal decision each time. To determine our overall expected profit, we multiply the probability of each demand level times the payoff associated with the best decision *given* that demand level occurs. Therefore, if Harriet Dennon had perfect information (certainty) about what the demand was going to be for each game, her expected payoff would be computed as follows:

$$\begin{aligned} EVUC &= -\$70(.05) + -\$30(.10) + \$10(.20) + \$50(.40) + \$90(.25) \\ &= \$38.00 \end{aligned}$$

Thus, with perfect information, Dennon Concessions would make, on average, a profit of \$38.00 per game.

We determined earlier that the expected payoff under uncertainty was \$11.50. The expected cost of uncertainty is the difference between the expected payoff given perfect information and the expected payoff under uncertainty. This is:

$$\text{Expected cost of uncertainty} = \$38.00 - \$11.50 = \$26.50$$

Another term for the cost of uncertainty is the *expected value of perfect information (EVPI)*. The EVPI in this case is \$26.50, which is the most Harriet would be willing to pay for perfect information about the hot dog demand at any game. Any information that is not perfect would be worth less than \$26.50 per game. Chapter 14 discusses how to establish the value of imperfect information in the context of decision analysis.

OPPORTUNITY-COST TABLES

We can also analyze the Dennon Concessions problem using opportunity-cost tables. As we saw earlier, an *opportunity cost* (also called *opportunity loss*) is the difference between the payoff which would occur from a particular decision and the payoff which would have resulted from the optimal decision when the state of nature is known in advance. Referring to the payoff table (Table 13-8), if 700 units are demanded but 800 are produced, the payoff will be −\$100. But with this demand level, Harriet should have decided to cook 700 hot dogs, for a payoff of −\$70. The difference in payoffs [−\$70 − (−\$100) = \$30] is the opportunity cost of not having made the optimal decision.

If demand is 1000 and production is 800, the payoff will be −\$30. However, the best decision for a demand of 1000 is to produce 1000 hot dogs, for a payoff of \$50. Thus, the opportunity loss in this case is [\$50 − (−\$30) = \$80].

Table 13-10 shows the opportunity-loss table for Dennon Concessions. Note that the opportunity losses (or regret values) are all positive. Table 13-11 shows the expected opportunity losses associated with each production alternative. These expected values were computed in the same manner as the expected payoffs. For example, the expected opportunity loss for the production of 700 hot dogs is:

$$\begin{aligned} E(\text{cost}) &= \$0(.05) + \$40(.10) + \$80(.20) + \$120(.40) + \$160(.25) \\ &= \$108 \end{aligned}$$

When opportunity losses are used, the decision criterion is to select the alternative which provides the smallest expected loss. In Table 13-11, we see that the best decision is to produce 1000 hot dogs for an expected opportunity loss of \$26.50. You should note that this is the same decision (i.e., produce 1000) that was reached using the payoff-table approach.

A second item of interest is that the minimum expected opportunity loss is equal to the expected cost of uncertainty and is therefore equal to the EVPI. This is true for

Table 13-10 DENNON CONCESSIONS: OPPORTUNITY-LOSS TABLE

	Demand (states of nature)				
Production	700	800	900	1000	1100
700	\$0	\$40	\$80	\$120	\$160
800	\$30	\$0	\$40	\$80	\$120
900	\$60	\$30	\$0	\$40	\$80
1000	\$90	\$60	\$30	\$0	\$40
1100	\$120	\$90	\$60	\$30	\$0

Table 13-11 DENNON CONCESSIONS: EXPECTED OPPORTUNITY COSTS

	Demand (states of nature)					
Production	700 ($p = .05$)	800 ($p = .10$)	900 ($p = .20$)	1000 ($p = .40$)	1100 ($p = .25$)	*E*(cost)
700	$0	$40	$80	$120	$160	$108.00
800	$30	$0	$40	$80	$120	$71.50
900	$60	$30	$0	$40	$80	$42.00
1000	$90	$60	$30	$0	$40	$26.50
1100	$120	$90	$60	$30	$0	$39.00

any decision-analysis problem. Earlier we computed the cost of uncertainty to be $26.50. We see in Table 13-11 that the best decision also has an expected opportunity loss of $26.50. With perfect information, we would have $0 opportunity loss. The difference between the expected opportunity cost ($26.50) and $0 is the cost of being uncertain.

Most decision problems can be structured in terms of either payoffs or opportunity losses; it makes no difference which approach is used. The expected-value analysis will lead to the same best decision.

13-5 DECISION-TREE ANALYSIS

When decision analysis is applied to a real business problem, the process can become quite complex. The decision maker must identify the outcomes for each decision alternative, assess probabilities associated with each outcome, assign cash flows in the form of payoffs or opportunity costs, and somehow keep the sequence of decisions and outcomes in the proper order. Decision-tree analysis is very helpful in dealing with these complex decisions in an orderly manner. A *decision tree* provides a "road map" of the decision problem. In this section, we illustrate the steps involved in using decision trees to help with the decision process.

Consider the decision facing the Harris Publishing Company, which recently received a manuscript written by a former government official about the private life of a very influential member of the United States government. The author will grant Harris full rights to the book for a guaranteed up-front payment of $200,000 plus a per copy royalty if the book is published. The basic question facing Harris's management is whether or not to sign the contract with this author or risk losing the book to another publisher. Even if they sign, Harris will publish the book only if the manuscript receives a favorable review from the editorial board. But several uncertainties make this decision difficult. Laurel Anaya, executive editor and the person ultimately responsible for making the decision, has outlined the following items for consideration:

1. There is an 80% (.80) chance that the content of the book is accurate. If the content is accurate, the author will be paid $1.00 per copy for each hardcover book sold and $.40 per copy for each paperback. No royalties will be paid if the manuscript is not accurate.
2. If the content is not accurate, there is a .90 chance that a libel suit will be filed; and if so, experience indicates the publisher will settle out of court for $900,000.

3. For hardcover publication, the following demand distribution has been assessed:

Demand	Probability
100,000 copies	.40
1,000,000 copies	.60

4. The fixed production costs for the hardcover book will be $350,000 before any copies are printed; the cost of printing and binding is $8.00 each. The number of copies to be printed can match any projected demand. The wholesale selling price of the hardcover book will be $12.00.
5. For paperback publication, the following demand distribution has been assessed:

Demand	Probability
50,000 copies	.30
1,500,000 copies	.70

6. The fixed costs for paperback publication are $200,000, the printing and binding cost is $1.00 per copy, and the wholesale selling price is $4.00 each.
7. The accuracy of the book's content will be known only after the book has been published and sold.
8. Laurel Anaya has assessed the probability the manuscript will get a favorable review from the editorial board as .80.

The decision is complicated by the uncertainties involved; thus, a decision tree can be used to provide a framework for helping make the decision. A **decision tree** is a diagram of the decision alternatives and outcomes arranged in the order in which they will occur. The diagram appears like a tree lying on its side, with the alternatives and outcomes forming the branches.

GROWING THE TREE

The decision tree is developed by starting with the initial decision facing the publisher: sign the contract or don't sign the contract. Figure 13-1 shows the beginnings of the decision tree. The box represents a *decision fork,* the point where a decision must be made.

If the publisher does not sign the contract, the issue is settled. There are no further branches on that side of the tree. However, if the contract is signed, other branches are needed. Keep in mind that the decision tree is a model of the decision in which alternatives (decisions) are followed by the outcomes (events) that they influence. Usually, but not always, the ordering of alternatives and outcomes follows a chronological sequence. Thus, if the contract is signed, the next step is the review by the editorial board. The outcome of this review is considered an event and is not within control of the company, since it is determined by how well the book is written. A small circle is used to designate an event fork on the decision tree, as is shown in Figure 13-2.

If the editorial review is unfavorable, the book will not be published. If the manuscript review is favorable, the book will be published. Then the company must decide between hardcover or paperback books. This decision fork is shown in Figure 13-3.

Following the hardcover/paperback decision, the book will go on sale and the true demand will be known. (Recall it was assumed that production can be set to match demand.) The level of demand is an event and is not controlled by the company. Figure 13-4 shows the event forks and branches associated with demand.

After the book goes on sale, the company will find out whether the content is

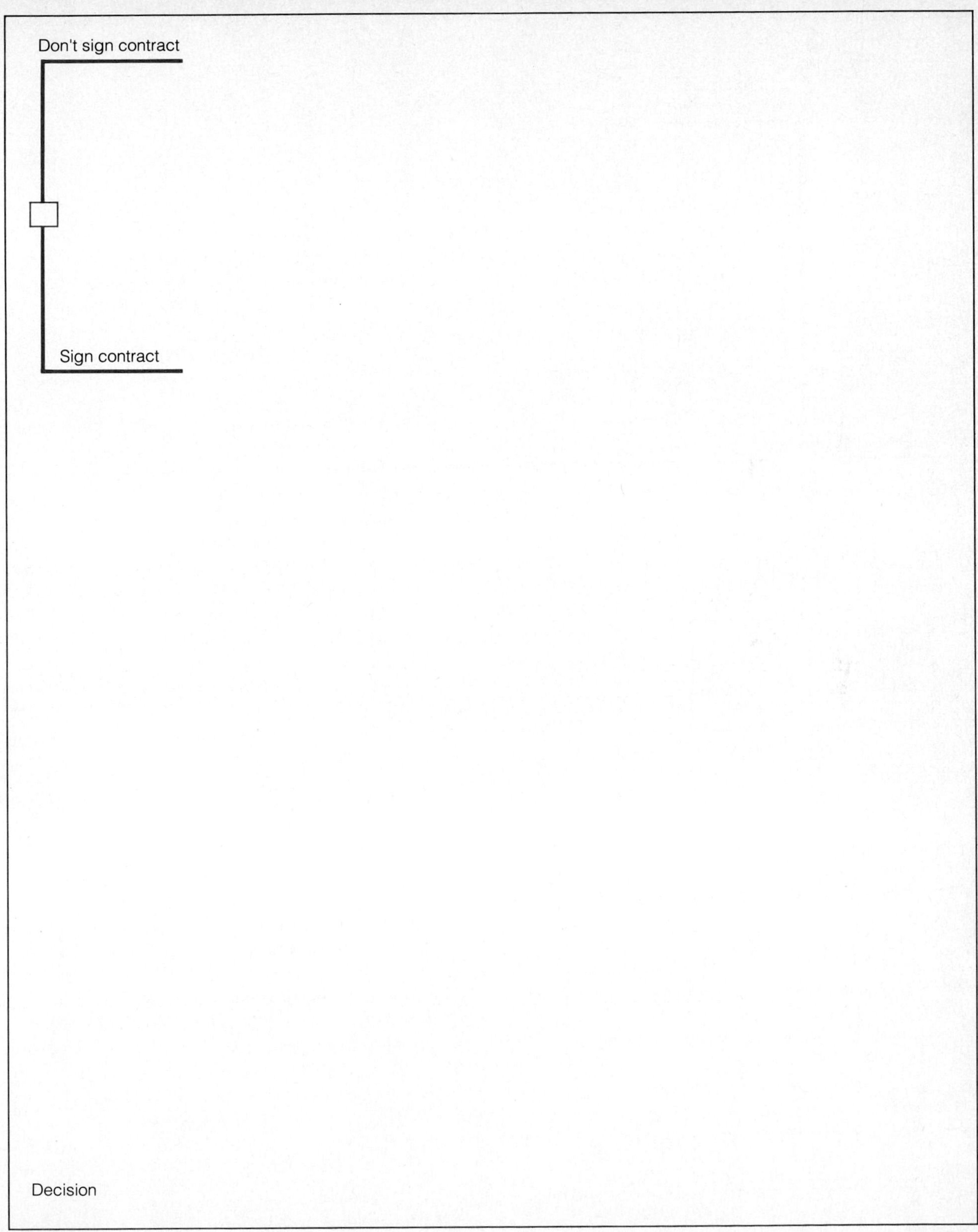

Figure 13-1
Harris Publishing Co. decision tree: step 1

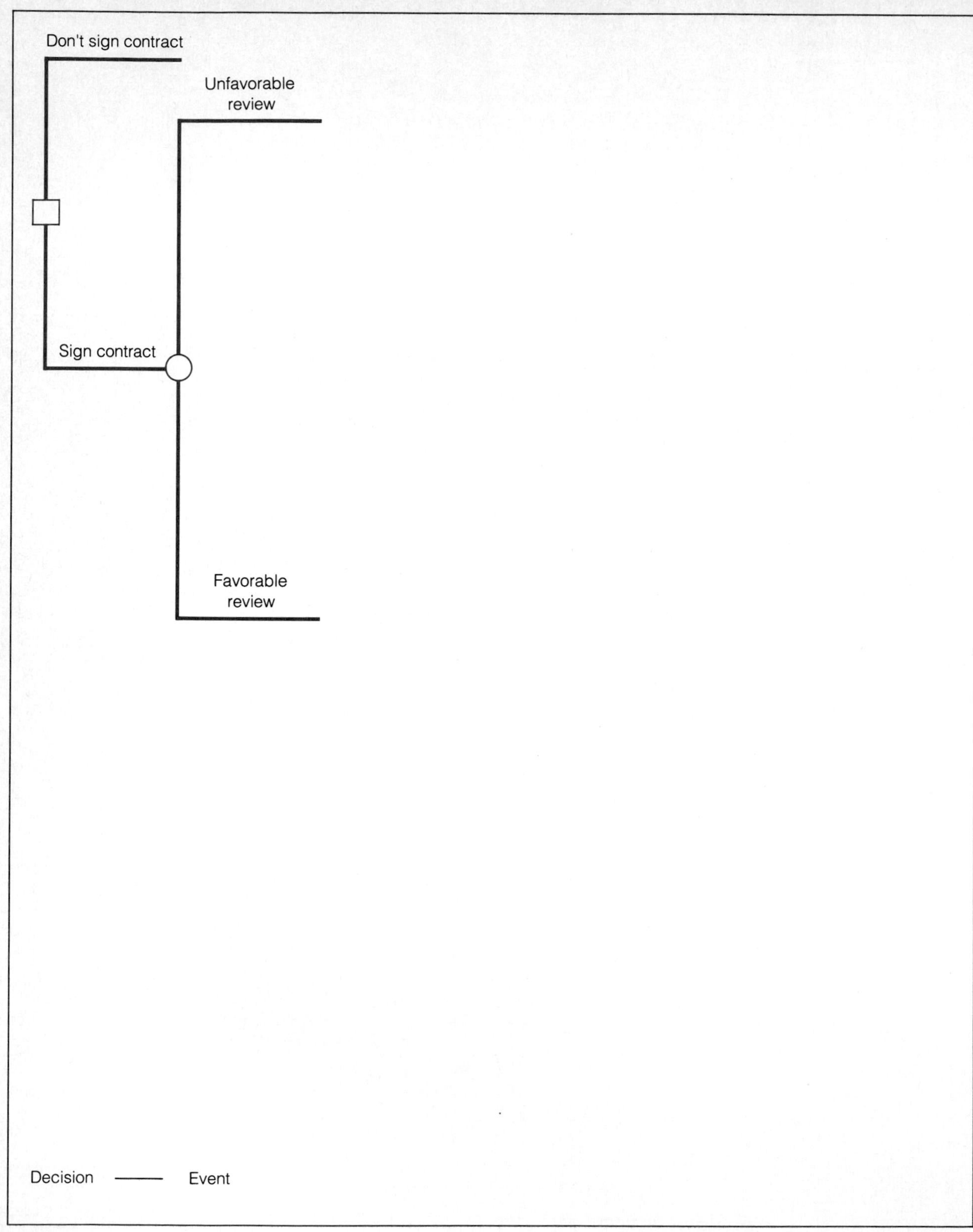

Figure 13-2
Harris Publishing Co. decision tree: step 2

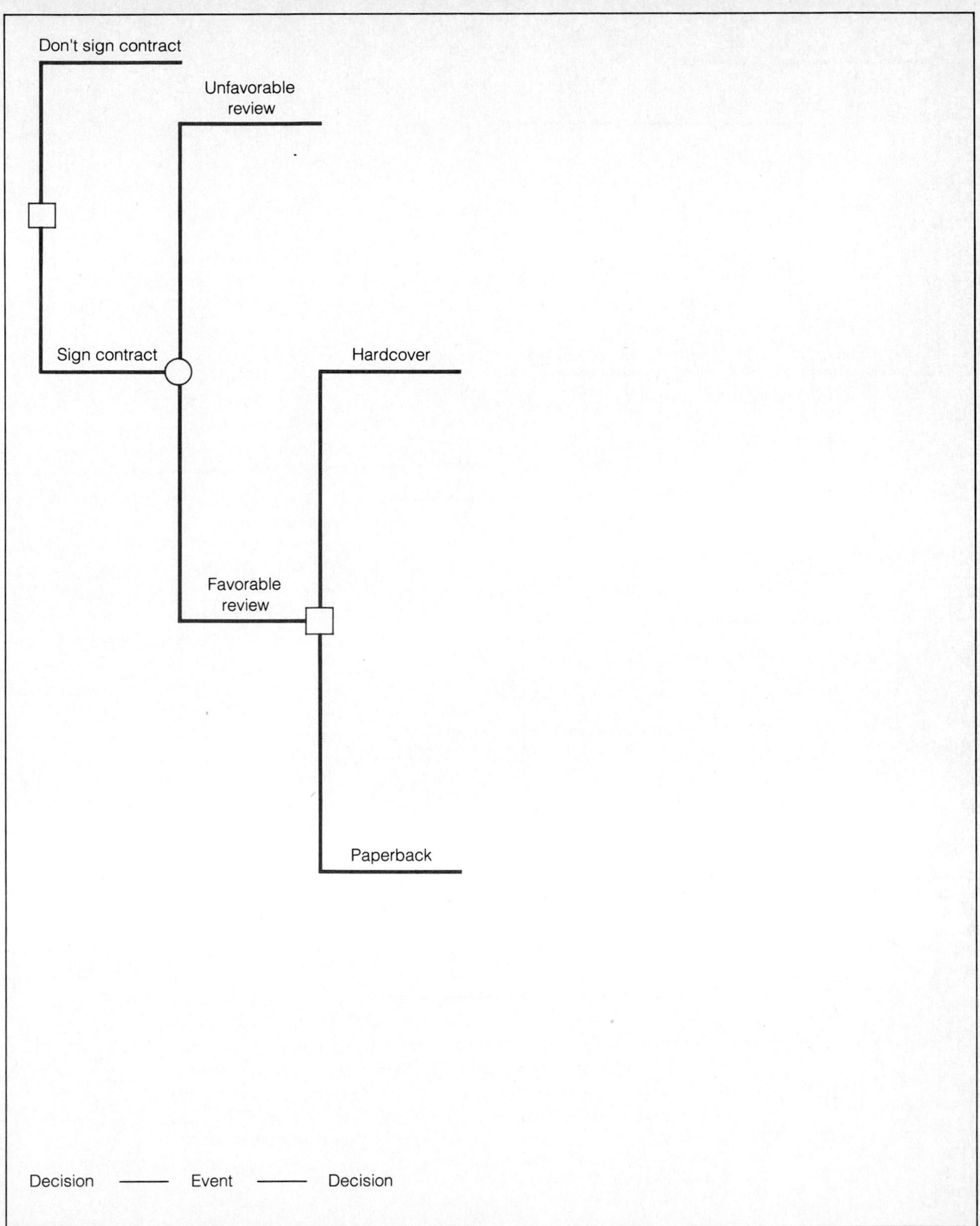

Figure 13-3
Harris Publishing Co. decision tree: step 3

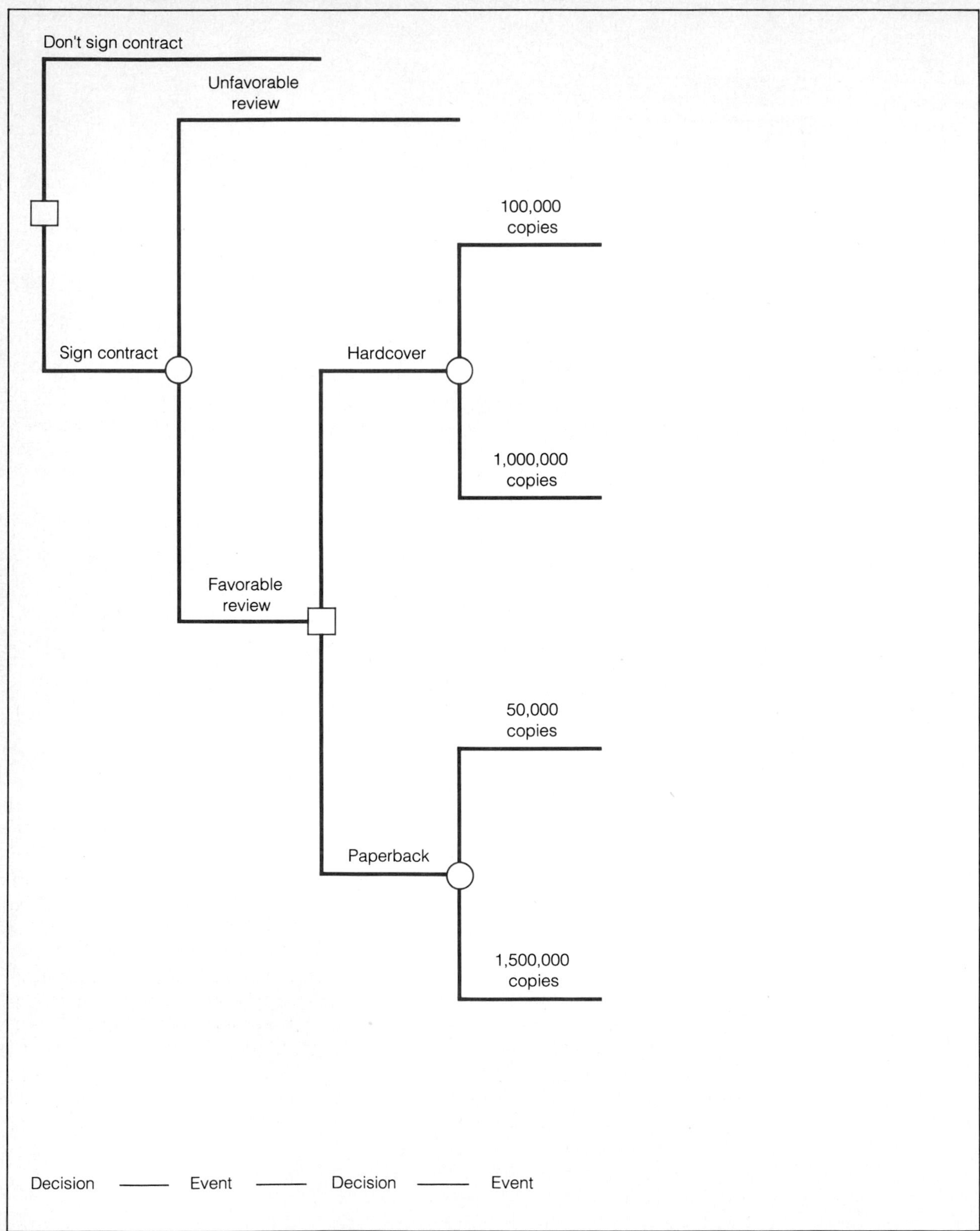

Figure 13-4
Harris Publishing Co. decision tree: step 4

accurate. This is an event beyond the decision maker's control. Figure 13-5 shows these event branches. As you can see, the tree is growing.

Figure 13-6 shows the final set of branches, which relate to the possibility of a libel suit. If we have correctly described the decision problem, this tree is a model of the decision facing the Harris Publishing Company. After reaching the point when you think the tree is complete, conferring with someone who has not been involved in developing the tree can be helpful. A fresh perspective is often useful in finding oversights and inconsistencies in a decision tree. *The decision tree should reflect the decision problem as accurately as possible before any further analysis is performed using the tree.*

ASSIGNING THE PROBABILITIES

The decision tree contains a number of *event forks,* represented by small circles. The branches leaving these event forks represent possible outcomes from an uncertain event. To make full use of decision-tree analysis, probabilities must be assigned to each of these event branches. As indicated earlier, these probabilities can come from classical assessment, relative frequency of occurrence or, most likely, subjective assessment.

In the Harris Publishing Company example, the probabilities were subjective assessments by the executive editor, Laurel Anaya, based on her experience and the available information. We can summarize these as follows:

1. The probability that a manuscript review will be favorable is .80; unfavorable, .20.
2. If a hardcover edition is printed, there is a .40 chance that demand will be 100,000 copies and a .60 chance that demand will be 1 million copies.
3. If a paperback edition is printed, there is a .30 chance that 50,000 copies will be sold and a .70 chance that 1.5 million copies will be sold.
4. There is an .80 chance that the content of the book will prove accurate.
5. There is a .90 chance the publisher will be sued for libel if the book turns out not to be accurate.

Figure 13-7 shows the decision tree with the probabilities assigned. Remember, probabilities must be assigned to every event branch. The sum of the probabilities for each event fork must be 1.

ASSIGNING THE CASH FLOWS

Once probabilities have been assigned to each event, the next step is to assign the cash flows. A *cash flow* is defined here as any dollar change in the decision maker's asset position. For instance, any income or expense which is expressed in dollar terms is considered a cash flow. (In some applications, the "cash flows" might be expressed in something other than dollars, but in this text we will limit our definition of cash flows to dollars.) The cash flows are displayed on the tree branches indicating the time at which they will occur. Unlike probabilities, which are assigned only to events, cash flows can occur for both decisions and events. For Harris Publishing Company, the first cash flow will occur when the author signs the contract. This will be an expense of $200,000. Figure 13-8 shows this as −$200,000 directly under the *Sign contract* branch. The *Don't sign contract* branch has a cash flow of $0, indicating that if this decision is made, there will be no change in the company's asset position.

The editorial review is done by salaried staff members. Thus, we can treat this cost as part of administrative overhead and not assign any cash flows to the review branches in Figure 13-8. When the decision to publish hardcover or paperback books is made, a fixed expense occurs. The expense is $350,000 for hardcover and $200,000 for

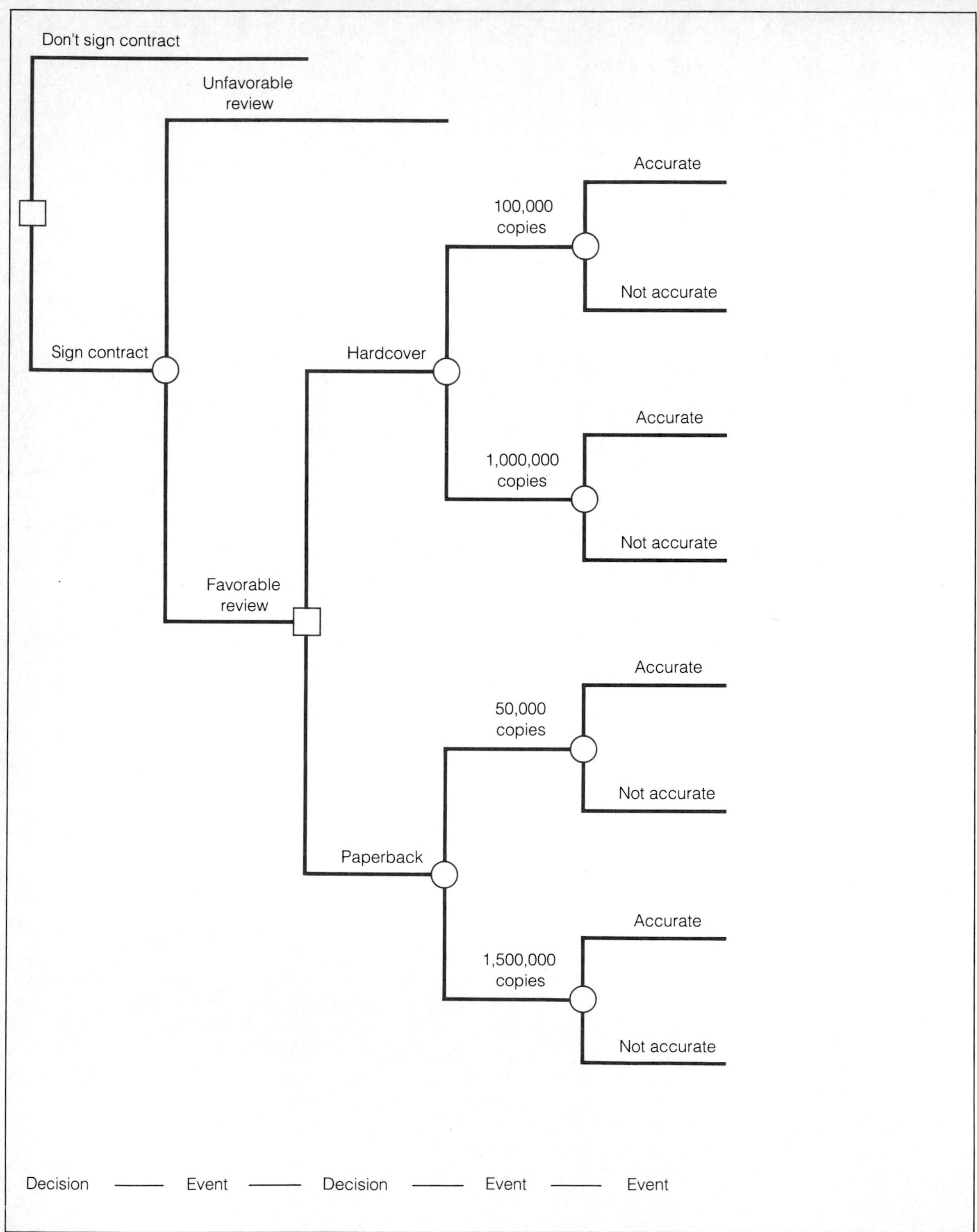

Figure 13-5
Harris Publishing Co. decision tree: step 5

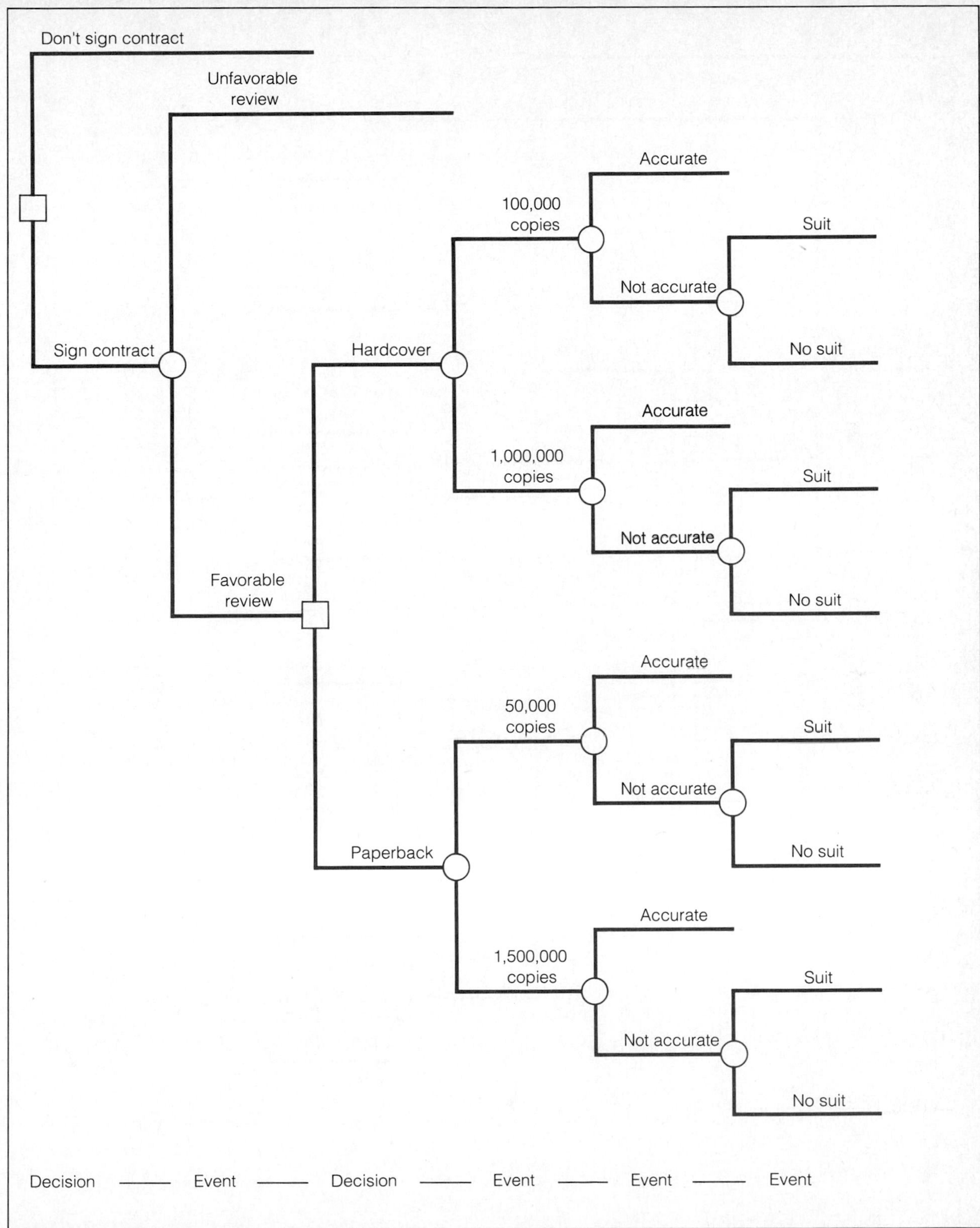

Figure 13-6
Harris Publishing Co. decision tree: step 6, final tree

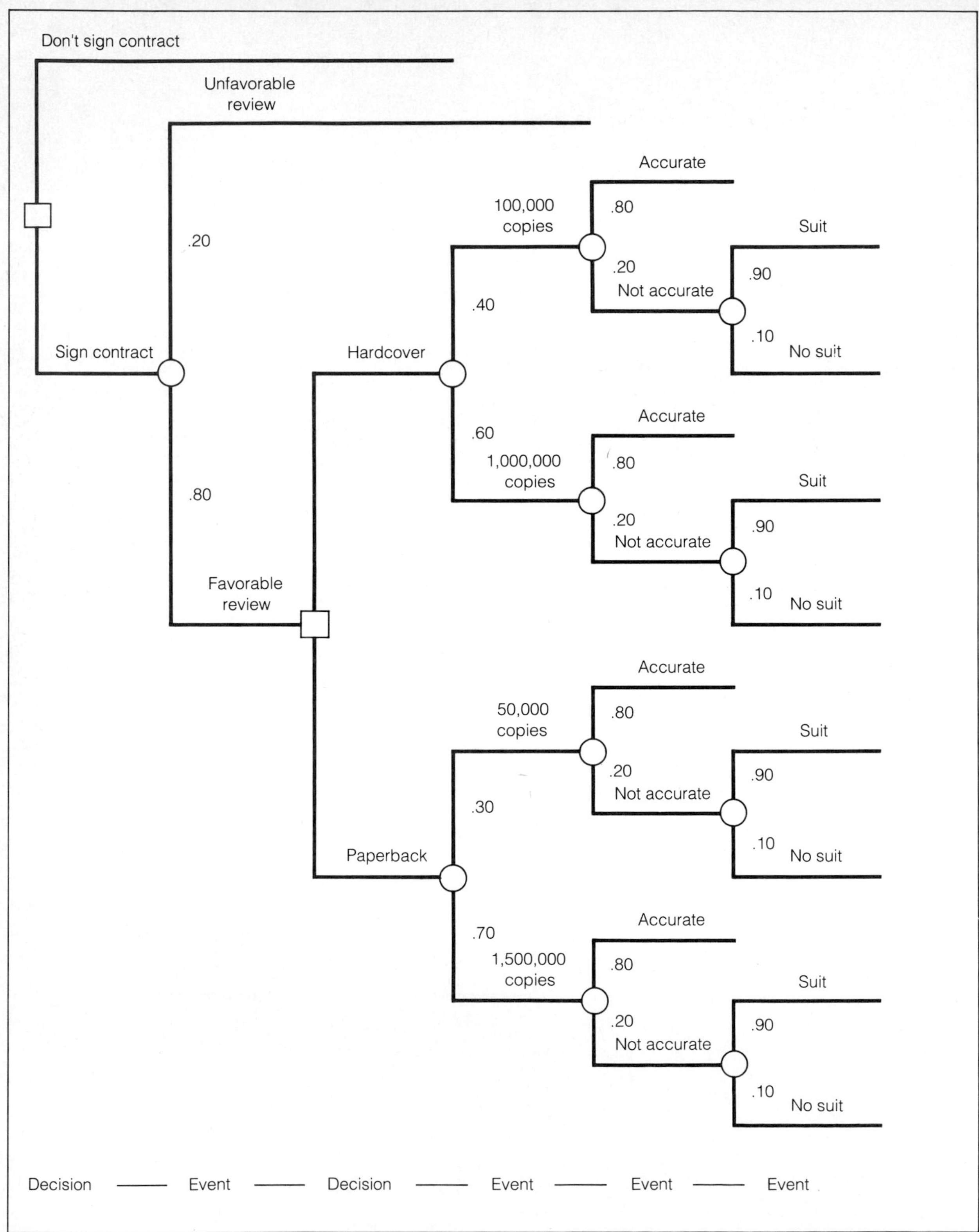

Figure 13-7
Harris Publishing Co. decision Tree: step 7, assigning probabilities

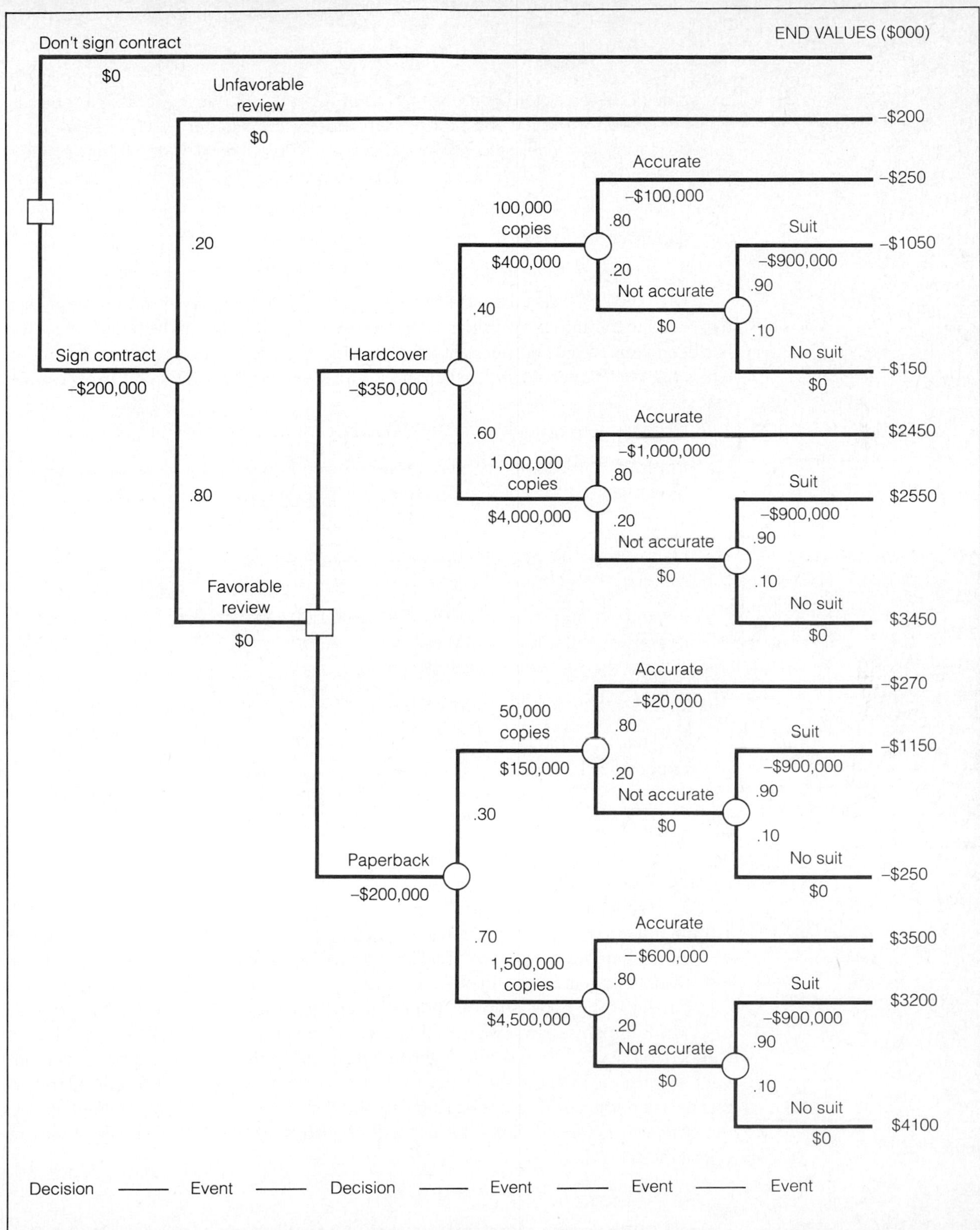

Figure 13-8
Harris Publishing Co. decision tree: assigning cash flows

paperback. These cash flows are displayed in Figure 13-8. Next, we assign the cash flows associated with the demand levels for hardcover and paperback. For example, if the hardcover decision is selected and demand is 100,000 copies, the following cash flow will occur:

Revenue	100,000 at $12.00 each =	$1,200,000
Expenses	100,000 at $8.00 each =	− 800,000
	Net cash flow =	$400,000

This $400,000 cash flow is shown in Figure 13-8. You may be wondering what happened to the author's royalties. These are to be paid only when the book's accuracy has been verified. For purposes of this decision, this is the same as paying the author when the books are sold and having him return the money if the book proves to be inaccurate.

If the hardcover book sells 1,000,000 copies, the cash flow will be:

Revenue	1,000,000 at $12.00 each =	$12,000,000
Expenses	1,000,000 at $8.00 each =	− 8,000,000
	Net cash flow =	$4,000,000

Likewise, if the paperback option is selected, the cash flow associated with 50,000 copies will be:

Revenue	50,000 at $4.00 each =	$200,000
Expenses	50,000 at $1.00 each =	− 50,000
	Net cash flow =	$150,000

The total cash flow for 1,500,000 copies will be:

Revenue	1,500,000 at $4.00 each =	$6,000,000
Expenses	1,500,000 at $1.00 each =	−1,500,000
	Net cash flow =	$4,500,000

These cash flows are shown in Figure 13-8.

Now, if the book turns out to be accurate, the publisher must pay the author royalties based on the number of books sold. For a hardcover book, the royalty rate is $1.00 per copy; for a paperback, it is $.40 per copy. For example, if the paperback sells 1.5 million copies, the author must be paid $600,000. The royalty costs are shown under the branches labeled *Accurate* in Figure 13-8. If the book proves to be inaccurate, the author gets no royalties; so $0 cash flow is shown on the *Not accurate* branch.

Finally, if the book is not accurate, the publisher might be sued for libel. In that case, the company's lawyer has told Laurel the government official who was libeled will be paid $900,000 to settle (Figure 13-8). Laurel agrees that this amount is more than adequate to stop the suit. Since there are no other cash flows to be considered in this decision, the last step is to accumulate the cash flows from left to right and put the net cash flow for each branch to the right of each branch in Figure 13-8. These are called the *end values.*

FOLDING BACK THE TREE

Figure 13-9 shows the completed decision tree for Harris Publishing Company. (We have removed the intermediate values from the branches and have expressed the end values in thousands to make the numbers easier to work with.) This sets the stage for the process of *folding back the decision tree,* a process employed whenever the decision

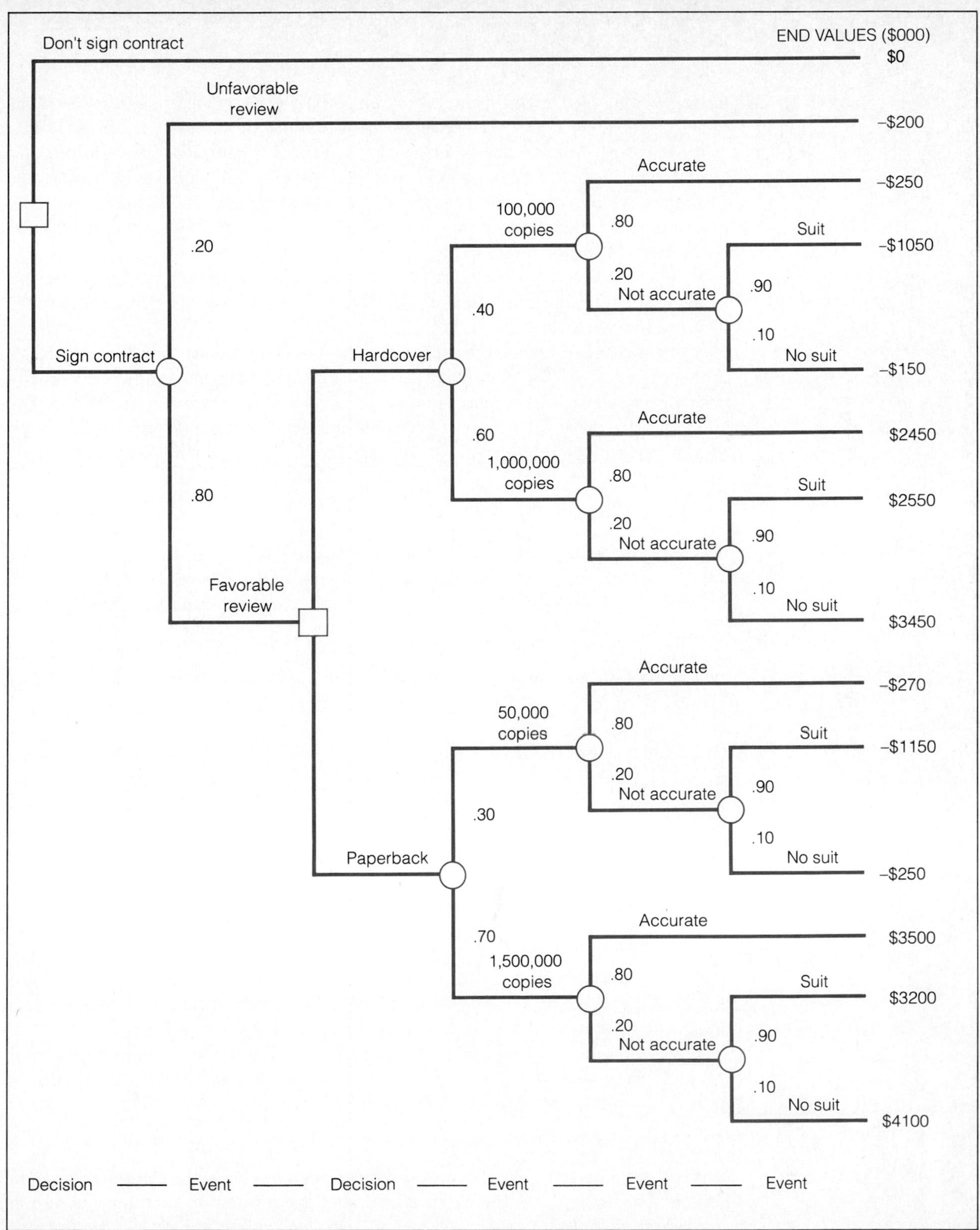

Figure 13-9
Harris Publishing Co. problem: final decision tree

criterion being used is the expected-value criterion. Recall that Harris Publishing plans to select the alternative with the highest expected payoff.

Remember that the decision tree is a diagram of the sequence of decisions and events. To fold back the decision tree, we begin with the end values at the right of the tree and work our way back to the initial decision at the far left. To do this, we must determine the expected value of each decision branch. (Please refer to Figure 13-10 as we discuss the foldback steps.)

Since the *Don't sign contract* branch has no following uncertain events, the end value of $0 is the expected value of that decision alternative. This expected value is displayed in a box near the decision fork.

The process of finding the expected value for the *Sign contract* branch requires a little more effort. To begin, we go to each event branch where *Suit* and *No suit* are the possible outcomes. We compute the expected values of these events by multiplying the end value times the probability of each outcome. For instance, for the event branch emanating from the *Hardcover, 100,000 copies, not accurate* branch, the expected value is:

$$EV = -\$1050(.90) + -\$150(.10) = -\$960$$

This expected value is displayed inside the oval between the two event branches. We use the same procedure to find expected values for all *Suit/No suit* event branches, as shown in Figure 13-10. (*Note:* All dollar amounts are in thousands.)

Next, we determine the expected value of the event *Accurate/Not accurate* in each instance in the tree where the event appears. To illustrate, we will use the event emanating from the *Hardcover; 100 copies* branch. The expected value is:

$$EV = -\$250(.80) + -\$960(.20) = -\$392$$

This value is shown in the oval between the two event branches. Note that in computing the expected value, we used $-\$960$, the expected value of the *Suit/No suit* event. This value was multiplied by the .20 probability that the content of the manuscript will not be accurate. The .80 chance that the manuscript will be accurate is multiplied by $-\$250$, since that is the expected value of the *Accurate* branch.

The expected value of the *Accurate/Not accurate* event emanating from the *Hardcover, 1,000,000 copies* branch is:

$$EV = \$2450(.80) + \$2640(.20) = \$2488$$

This value is also shown in Figure 13-10, in the oval between the two outcome branches. The same methodology is used in the lower portion of the tree. This process of moving from right to left is what we mean by "folding back the tree."

We continue by determining the expected values of the demand events. For instance, the expected value for the demand event emanating from the *Hardcover* branch is:

$$EV = -\$392(.40) + \$2488(.60) = \$1336$$

This value, shown in Figure 13-10, is also the expected value of the *Hardcover* decision branch. This means that the expected value of the hardcover alternative is $1336 (actually $1,336,000).

The expected value for the demand event emanating from the *Paperback* decision branch is:

$$EV = -\$428(.30) + \$3458(.70) = \$2292.20$$

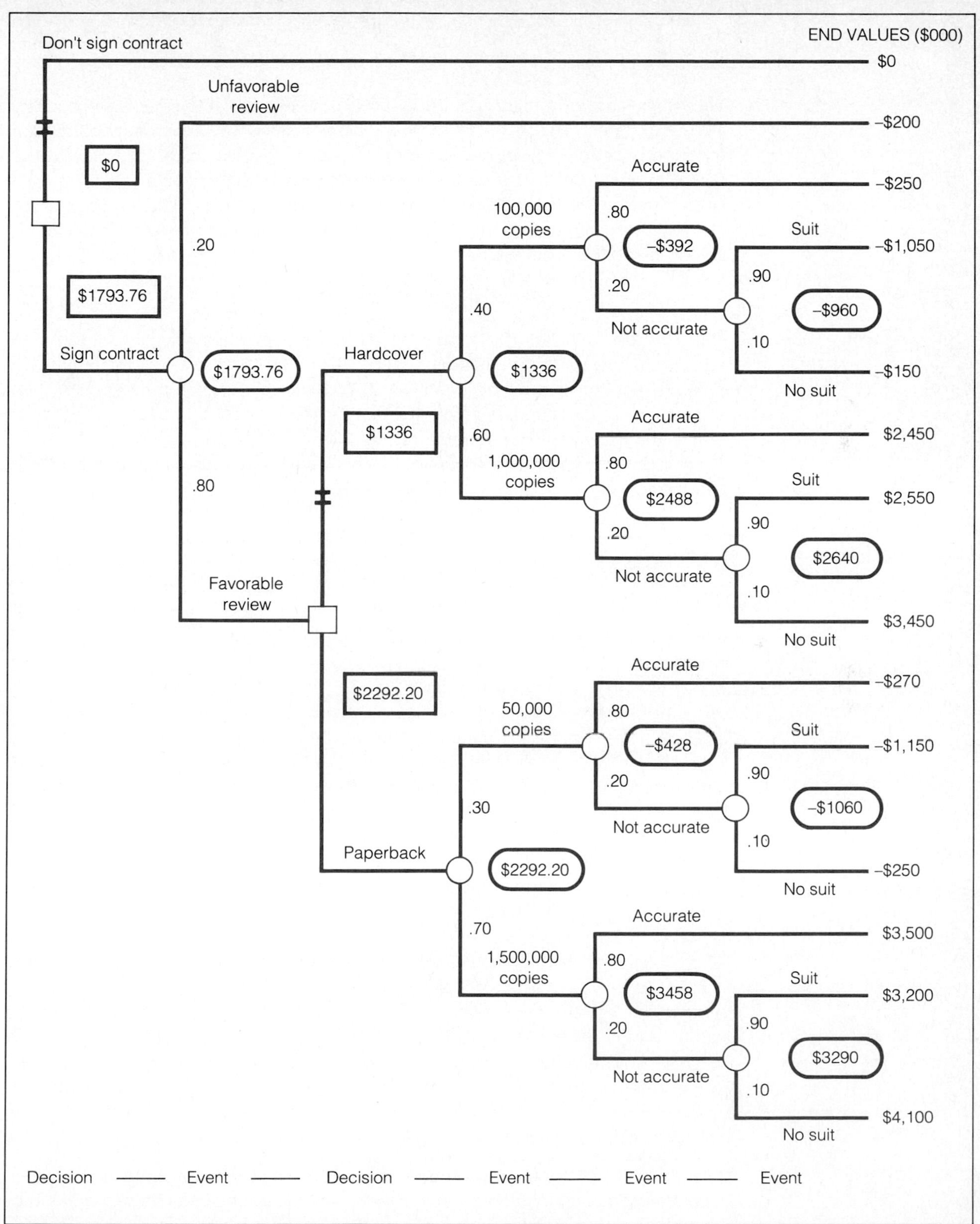

Figure 13-10
Harris Publishing Co. problem: folding back the decision tree

This value, shown in Figure 13-10, is the expected value of the *Paperback* decision alternative. Since \$2292.20 > \$1336, the best decision for Laurel Anaya is to select the paperback option if she reaches that decision point. She would expect a net payoff of \$2292.20 (actually \$2,292,200) from the paperback decision. Note that the hardcover decision branch is blocked, indicating that it is not the best decision.

The final step in the foldback process is to determine the expected value of the review event. We again multiply the appropriate cash flows by their probabilities.

$$EV = -\$200(.20) + \$2292.20(.80) = \$1793.76$$

Thus, as shown in Figure 13-10, the expected value is \$1793.76, which is the expected value of the *Sign contract* branch. This means that if the company signs the publishing contract, its expected payoff is \$1793.76 (actually \$1,793,760). Since \$1793.76 exceeds the \$0 expected payoff for the *Don't sign contract* branch, the best decision is to sign the contract. If the editorial review is favorable, then publish in paperback. (Notice that the *Don't sign* branch is blocked, indicating this alternative won't be selected.)

This example demonstrates the use of a decision tree to help in making a decision under uncertainty. The decision tree provides a framework for analyzing alternatives and dealing with uncertainties. The decision reached is the best decision given the expected value criterion. However, as we indicated earlier, the best decision does not always lead to the best outcome. For instance, if the contract is signed and the book is published in paperback, demand may be only 50,000 copies and, worse yet, the contents might not be accurate. If this chain of events occurred, Harris Publishing would lose \$1,150,000 on the deal. Thus, a "bad outcome" can occur from this one-time decision. But then again, an extremely good outcome could occur if the demand for the book is 1.5 million copies, the book proves inaccurate, and no suit is filed. The payoff under this scenario is \$4,100,000. The expected-value criterion takes into consideration all the possible payoffs and the probabilities of those payoffs occurring.

This example illustrates an important virtue of decision-tree analysis. That is, the tree allows future decisions which have an influence on the current decision to be systematically considered. Chronologically, the decision about whether to publish in hardcover or paperback comes after the initial decision of whether to sign a contract. However, the decision to sign or not is made only after the expected profits associated with publishing in hardcover and paperback are determined. In this case, Laurel Anaya decided to publish in paperback before her analysis indicated the contract should be signed. The ability to use projected future events to help make a current decision is a natural part of the foldback process.

The Solved Problem section at the end of this chapter presents another decision-tree example. Please review that problem to make sure you fully understand the process. The same steps are used whenever decision-tree analysis is applied to any decision situation. They are:

1. Arrange the decisions and events in the order in which they will occur. This is often difficult with complex decision problems, but unless the decision tree accurately represents the situation, the decision made may not be the best decision.
2. Make the necessary probability assessments and show them on the event branches. These probabilities can be determined using classical assessment, relative frequency of occurrence, or subjective techniques. (Remember, probabilities are associated with the uncertain events and not with the decision alternatives.)

3. Assign cash flows by showing costs and payoffs on the branches where they occur. Accumulate these cash flows and determine the end value for each branch of the decision tree.
4. Fold back the decision tree. At each decision fork, select the decision that maximizes expected payoff or minimizes expected cost.

SENSITIVITY ANALYSIS

In a decision problem like the one facing Harris Publishing Company, uncertainty in the events is measured by the probabilities assessed for each event outcome. The expected-value criterion utilizes these probability assessments. But a question that arises when decision analysis is applied is how *sensitive* is the decision to the probabilities being assessed. For instance, Laurel Anaya might want to know how much the probability of a favorable review would have to change to make not signing the contract the best decision.

To answer this question, refer to Figure 13-10. Instead of using .80 for the probability of a favorable review, let the probability be P. Then the probability of an unfavorable review is $1 - P$. We next solve for P such that the expected value of the *Sign contract* alternative ($2292.20) is the same as the expected value of the *Don't sign contract* alternative, which in this case is $0.

$$\begin{aligned} 0 &= 2292.20(P) + -200(1 - P) \\ 0 &= 2292.20P - 200 + 200P \\ 200 &= 2492.20P \\ 200/2492.20 &= P \\ .0803 &= P \end{aligned}$$

Thus, the probability of a favorable report would have to decrease from .80 to less than .0803 in order for the best decision to be not to sign the contract. This means the decision is quite insensitive to the probability assessed for a favorable editorial review, and there is probably no need to investigate this assessment any further.

Another question might be, How sensitive is the decision to publish softcover to the probability assessment associated with the number of hardcover books that might be sold? That is, how much higher than .60 would the probability of selling 1 million copies have to be before the best decision would be to go with the hardcover books? The approach to answering this question is essentially the same as before. We let $P =$ the probability of selling 1 million copies and $1 - P$ be the probability of selling 100,000 copies. We then solve for P such that the expected payoff for hardcover is equal to that for paperback: $2292.20 (see Figure 13-10). We solve for P as follows:

$$\begin{aligned} 2292.20 &= 2488(P) + -392(1 - P) \\ 2292.20 &= 2488P - 392 + 392P \\ 2684.20 &= 2880P \\ 2684.20/2880 &= P \\ .9320 &= P \end{aligned}$$

Thus, the probability of selling 1 million books would have to be higher than .9320 for the best decision to be to publish a hardcover book. When this is compared with the current assessment of .60, we see the decision is not very sensitive to this probability assessment. Depending on how much information and thought went into the original probability assessment, there does not appear to be a need to direct substantial resources to study the hardcover demand issue further.

Sensitivity analysis can also investigate how much a cash-flow value would have to change before the decision would change. The method for determining the sensitivity of a cash-flow item is the same as for a probability. Let the cash-flow value in question equal X and then solve for X such that the decision branches have the same expected payoff.

When sensitivity analysis indicates that the resulting decision is sensitive to a probability or cash-flow value, you will want to spend extra time studying this factor before arriving at the final decision.

RISK-PREFERENCE ANALYSIS

An inherent assumption when the expected-value criterion is applied to a decision tree with dollar payoffs or costs is that the decision maker is an "averages player." An averages player will select the alternative with the highest expected payoff, or lowest expected cost, without regard to the individual outcomes represented by the end values of the "best decision" branch. For instance, as an averages player, Laurel Anaya will elect to sign the contract with the author and, if the editorial review is favorable, the book will be published in paperback. This decision strategy has an expected value of $1,793,760. However, the actual payoff will be one of the following:

−$270,000
−$1,150,000
−$250,000
$3,500,000
$3,200,000
$4,100,000

These are the end values for the *Paperback* decision path in Figure 13-10. Three of the possible payoffs exceed $3 million. There is no question that Laurel Anaya and Harris Publishing Company would like to see one of these outcomes. However, there are also three negative payoffs, one of which is a loss of $1.15 million. Certainly these negative payoffs are not what Laurel and the company want to see. There is a *risk* involved in the decision, since the favored outcome might not occur.

The decision maker who decides to use the expected-value criterion on payoffs or costs is considered *risk-neutral*, A risk-neutral decision maker is not influenced by large positive or negative payoffs but simply relies on expected values to guide his or her decision. But most people are not risk-neutral. Instead, we tend to let the potential outcomes influence our decisions and would not strictly abide by the expected-value decision. For instance, suppose you were facing the following decision situation. A fair coin will be flipped one time. If a head turns up, you will win $10; for a tail, you will lose $5. Alternatively, you can choose not to play—for a payoff of $0.

The expected value of the play decision is:

$$E(\text{play}) = .5(\$10) + .5(-\$5) = \$2.50$$

If you are risk-neutral, you would play, since $\$2.50 > \$0$. However, some people would choose not to play even though the expected payoff of playing is higher. The reason is that they would prefer to avoid the 50% chance of losing $5 even if it means giving up the potential to gain $10. What would you do?

Suppose we change the numbers a bit. Now, instead of winning $10 for a head, suppose the payoff is $10,000; but on the other hand, you must pay $5000 if a tail turns up. The expected value of playing is $2500. Remember, the expected value is the long-run average payoff per play if the coin is flipped a very large number of times; but on one flip, you will either make $10,000 or lose $5000. If you were actually faced with the decision to play or not, we suspect that you would consider all the wonderful things you could do with the $10,000, but you would also have to consider what would happen if you had to come up with $5000 today. Now what would you do? In these instances, decision makers who would choose not to play would be exhibiting *risk-averse* behavior.

Suppose we consider another example, in which you have the option of spending a dollar for a lottery ticket. In this game, you must select six numbers between 1 and 60. If your numbers match the six numbers randomly selected by the lottery's computer, you win the grand prize. The prize starts at $2 million and goes up by $2 million each week until someone wins. The stated probability of winning on a single $1 ticket is about 1 in 13 million, or .0000000769. The chances of losing your dollar are $1 - .0000000769 = .9999999231$. If the prize is $2 million, the expected payoff is:

$$\begin{aligned} E(\text{payoff}) &= .0000000769(\$2 \text{ million}) + .9999999231(-\$1) \\ &= \$.1538 + -\$.9999999231 = -\$.8461 \end{aligned}$$

Thus, the expected payoff is approximately a $-\$.85$ per ticket. (This assumes that no one else would match your numbers and cause a split in prize money.)

However, as you know, many people buy lottery tickets even though the expected value is negative. They do so because their desire to win a large sum of money outweighs the overwhelming odds that they will lose their dollar. Decision makers who willingly make such a decision are exhibiting *risk-seeking* behavior.

Chapter 15 presents a more extensive discussion of risk-preference analysis and shows how attitudes toward risk can be incorporated into decision analysis.

13-6 COMPUTER APPLICATIONS

The MASTER computer software package that accompanies this text contains a series of decision-analysis programs. Among them is a program which creates a payoff table, and another which creates a payoff table and determines the expected payoff for each decision alternative. To demonstrate how these programs are used, let's return to the Dennon Concessions example presented in section 13-4. Recall that the question facing the company was how many hot dogs to prepare for sale at each baseball game. The demand distribution was subjectively assessed as follows:

Demand	Probability
700	.05
800	.10
900	.20
1000	.40
1100	.25
	1.00

The hot dogs sell for $.70 each, and have a per unit variable cost of $.30 and a fixed cost of $350. The task is to develop a payoff table and determine the best decision regarding the number of hot dogs to prepare, based on expected payoff.

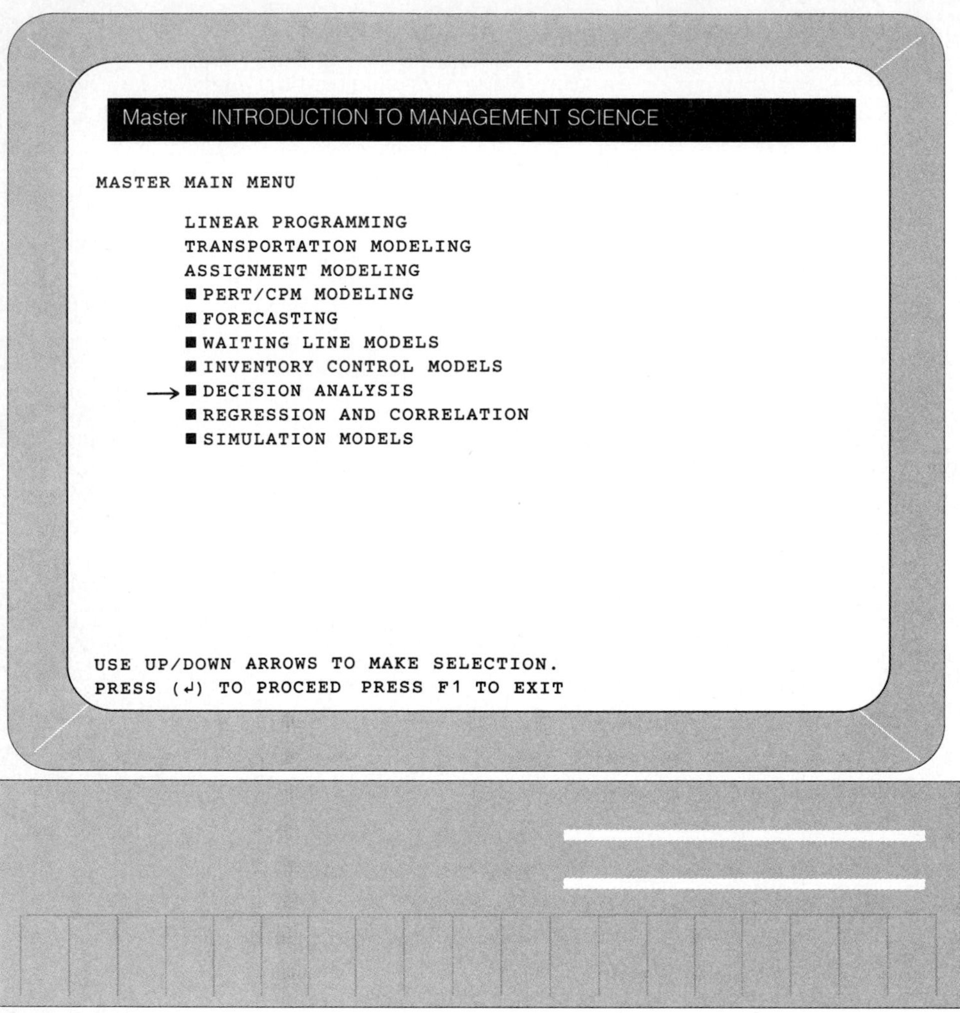

Figure 13-11
MASTER main menu

Figure 13-11 shows the MASTER main menu. To use MASTER for this problem, we select the Decision Analysis option to call up the submenu screen shown in Figure 13-12. We then select the Expected Value–Payoff Table option from the submenu. Next, we enter the states of nature (Units) and the probabilities (Priors), as shown in Figure 13-13. Figure 13-14 shows the output produced by the MASTER software. (Note: This program asks the user to interactively input the per unit revenue, \$.70; the per unit variable cost, \$.30; and the fixed cost, \$350.)

From the output in Figure 13-14, we see that the best decision, based on expected value, is to prepare 1000 hot dogs for an expected payoff of \$11.50. The cost of uncertainty is \$26.50. These are the same values we determined earlier when we solved the problem manually.

```
Master  INTRODUCTION TO MANAGEMENT SCIENCE

DECISION ANALYSIS SUB MENU

  PAYOFF TABLE
→EXPECTED VALUE-PAYOFF TABLE
  BAYESIAN POSTERIOR ANALYSIS-BINOMIAL SAMPLING
  BAYESIAN POSTERIOR ANALYSIS-SUBJECTIVE CONDITIONALS
  OPTIMAL SAMPLE SIZE ANALYSIS

USE UP/DOWN ARROWS TO MAKE SELECTION.
PRESS(↵) TO PROCEED  PRESS F1 TO EXIT
```

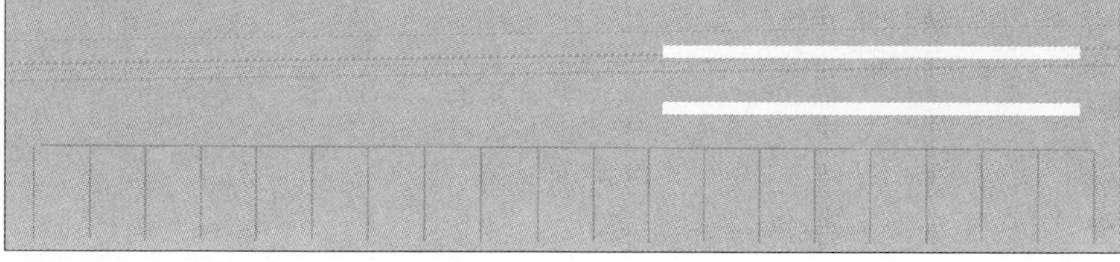

Figure 13-12
MASTER decision-analysis submenu

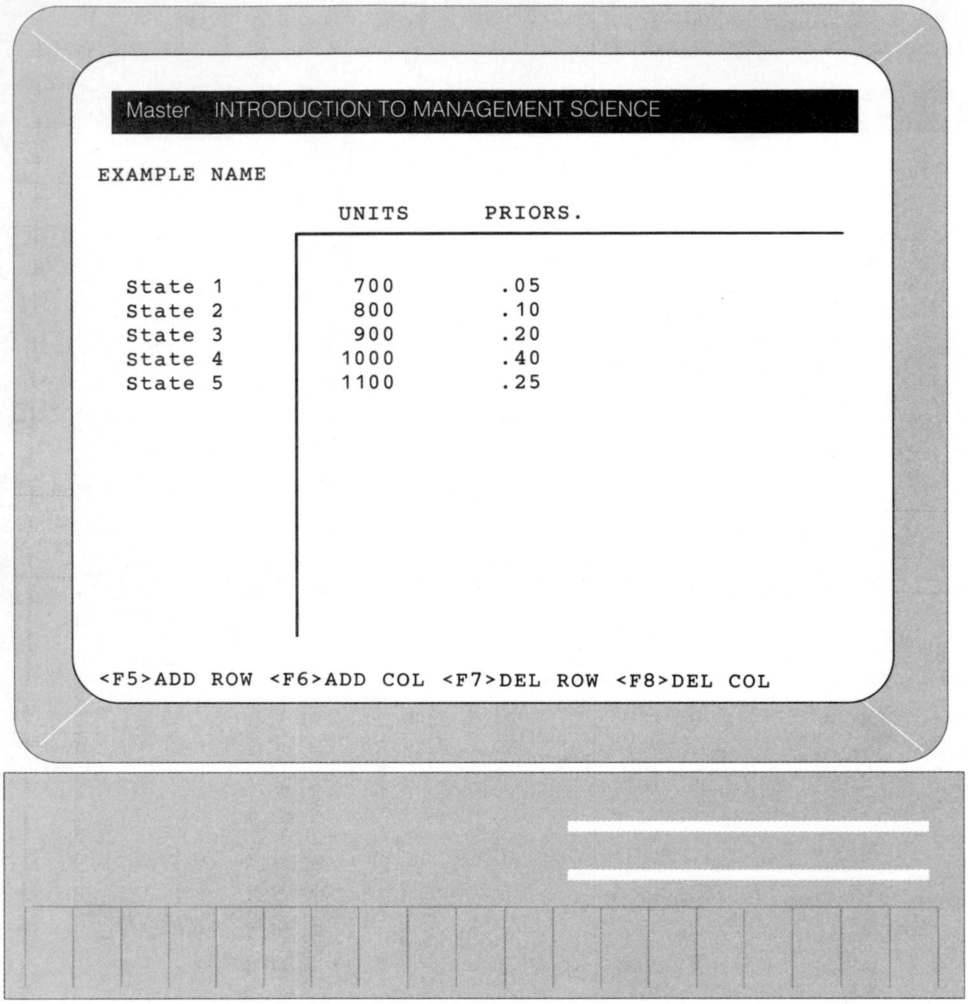

Master INTRODUCTION TO MANAGEMENT SCIENCE

EXAMPLE NAME

	UNITS	PRIORS.
State 1	700	.05
State 2	800	.10
State 3	900	.20
State 4	1000	.40
State 5	1100	.25

<F5>ADD ROW <F6>ADD COL <F7>DEL ROW <F8>DEL COL

Figure 13-13
Dennon Concessions: payoff data-entry screen

PAYOFF TABLE

ALTERNATIVES	STATES OF NATURE 700	800	900	1000	1100
700	-70.00	-70.00	-70.00	-70.00	-70.00
800	-100.00	-30.00	-30.00	-30.00	-30.00
900	-130.00	-60.00	10.00	10.00	10.00
1000	-160.00	-90.00	-20.00	50.00	50.00
1100	-190.00	-120.00	-50.00	20.00	90.00
PROBABILITIES	0.05	0.10	0.20	0.40	0.25

ALTERNATIVES	EXPECTED VALUES
700	-70.00
800	-33.50
900	-4.00
1000	11.50
1100	-1.00

ALTERNATIVE WITH HIGHEST EXPECTED PAYOFF IS: 1000
EXPECTED PAYOFF = $ 11.50
COST OF UNCERTAINTY = 26.50

Figure 13-14
Dennon Concessions: payoff table output

One of the main advantages of using a computer is that it allows a decision maker to try different scenarios. For instance, Harriet Dennon is considering packaging hot dogs in a heat-sealing wrapper, which will add $.10 to the per unit variable cost. She plans to sell the hot dog in the new wrapper for $1.00 rather than $.70. The increase in price is expected to affect the demand distribution. Based on all available information, she has assessed the following probabilities for each demand level:

Demand	Probability
700	.20
800	.30
900	.20
1000	.20
1100	.10

To enter the new data, we use the EDIT/CHANGE DATA command. Figure 13-15 shows the screen with the revised probabilities. The resulting output is shown in Figure 13-16. The results indicate that if the new wrapper is introduced, the best decision is to prepare only 900 hot dogs, for an expected payoff of $120.00. Since $120.00 > $11.50, the option of using the new wrapper and charging a higher price is preferred over the original wrapper and $.70 price.

Chapters 14 and 15 illustrate the use of the other decision-analysis options that MASTER offers (Figure 13-12). Several commercial software packages, such as Arborist and Supertree, are designed specifically for decision-tree analysis.

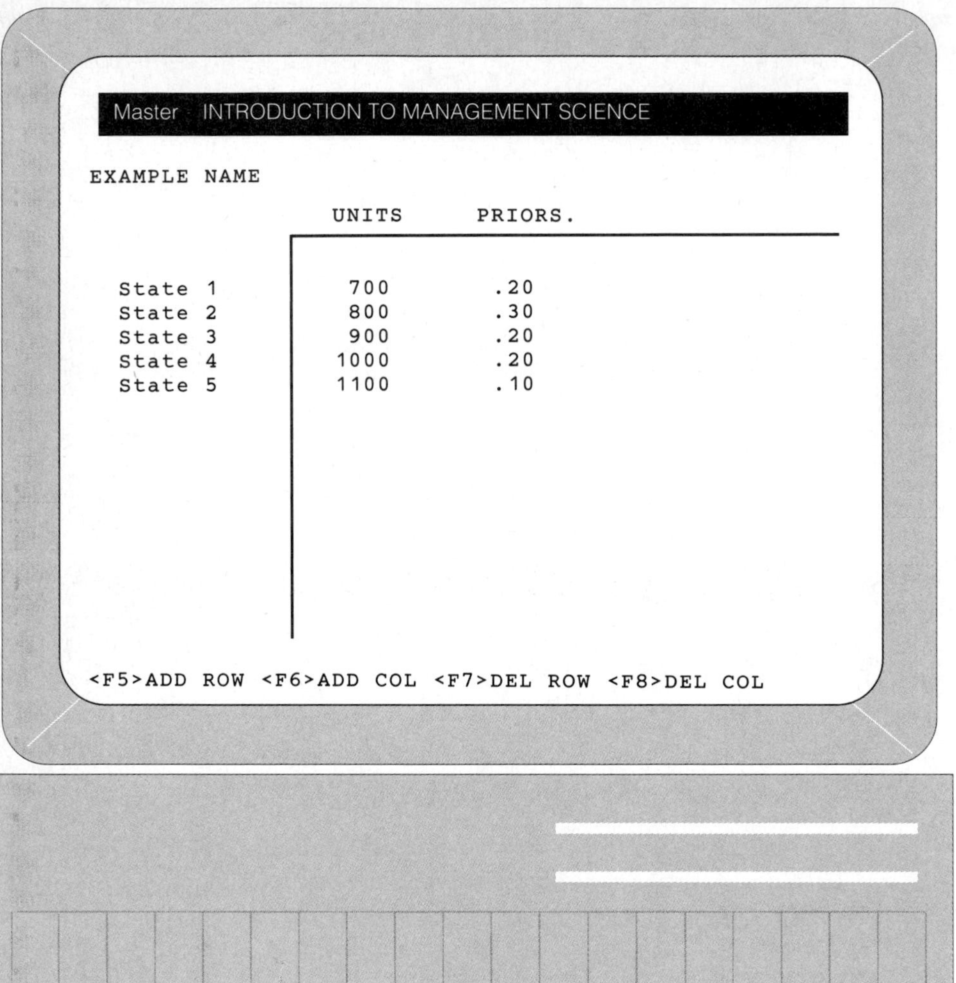

Figure 13-15
Data-entry screen for payoff table Dennon Concessions

PAYOFF TABLE

ALTERNATIVES	STATES OF NATURE				
	700	800	900	1000	1100
700	70.00	70.00	70.00	70.00	70.00
800	30.00	130.00	130.00	130.00	130.00
900	-10.00	90.00	190.00	190.00	190.00
1000	-50.00	50.00	150.00	250.00	250.00
1100	-90.00	10.00	110.00	210.00	310.00
PROBABILITIES	0.20	0.30	0.20	0.20	0.10

ALTERNATIVES	EXPECTED VALUES
700	70.00
800	110.00
900	120.00
1000	110.00
1100	80.00

ALTERNATIVE WITH HIGHEST EXPECTED PAYOFF IS: 900
EXPECTED PAYOFF = $ 120.00
COST OF UNCERTAINTY = 52.00

Figure 13-16
Dennon Concessions: payoff table output

13-7 SUMMARY AND CONCLUSIONS

Making decisions under uncertainty is a regular part of business. Although decision makers usually cannot eliminate uncertainty, they can use the tools of decision analysis to help deal with it.

In this chapter we explained the steps for constructing a payoff table and an opportunity-loss table. We also introduced nonprobabilistic decision criteria, such as minimax, maximax, and minimax regret. More importantly, we discussed the expected-value criterion, which utilizes probabilities assigned to the uncertain outcomes. We demonstrated how to determine the cost of uncertainty and to determine an upper limit on the value of new information using either a payoff or opportunity-cost approach.

One of the most important decision-analysis tools is the decision tree, which provides a chronological ordering of the decisions and events involved in making a decision. In this chapter, we illustrated how to use a decision tree in making a decision under uncertainty. In addition, we showed how decision-tree analysis, through the foldback process, takes into account future decisions which affect the current decision.

Chapter 14 extends the discussion presented in this chapter by introducing a formal process for incorporating new information into the decision process. It also shows how to determine the value of this new information. Chapter 15 continues the general topic by showing how a decision maker's attitude toward risk can be incorporated into the decision analysis.

Remember, the objective of decision analysis is to assist the decision maker in making the "best decision," defined as the one which, utilizing all available information, best satisfies the decision criterion. In an uncertain environment, however, the best decision does not always result in the best outcome. By helping the decision maker deal with uncertainty, decision analysis improves the quality of the decision.

Solved Problems

PROBLEM 1 Pacific Rim Exercise Equipment contracts with Asian manufacturers to produce a variety of products, which Pacific Rim then sells by mail order. The company's very successful marketing strategy solely relies on television advertising on cable networks and late-night programs on local stations. Pacific Rim executives have recently decided to market a new exercise machine, a cross-country-skiing simulator. They have found a manufacturer in Singapore that will sell them a minimum of 10,000 and a maximum of 50,000 of these exercisers for $50 each; unfortunately, the manufacturer will guarantee only one shipment at that price.

Pacific Rim plans to advertise the exerciser for $89.95 and is confident of making a profit, since comparable equipment is sold in sporting-goods stores for more than $200. However, since the company is still feeling the effects of negative publicity resulting from unfilled orders after a recent rowing-machine sales campaign, the executives have found an alternative supplier that will ship any quantity demanded, but for a price of $120 each. In the event Pacific Rim does not sell the ordered number of exercisers, any remainders can be sold to a European distributor for $25 each.

From past experience, Pacific Rim's marketing and distribution department predicts that one of the following demand levels will occur: 5000; 15,000; 20,000; 60,000.

a. Set up a table showing the payoffs for all combinations of demand and order quantity.
b. Use the maximax, maximin, and minimax regret criteria to arrive at the appropriate decision.
c. The following probabilities have been subjectively assessed for the previously defined demand levels.

Demand Level	Probability
5,000	.2
15,000	.4
20,000	.3
60,000	.1

Use the expected-value criterion to arrive at the best decision.

Solutions a. To set up the payoff table, we use the following formula to determine the payoff for each combination of demand and order quantity:

$$\text{Payoff} = -\text{fixed cost} - \text{variable cost} + \text{revenue} + \text{salvage} - \text{penalty}$$

where:

Fixed cost = 0
Variable cost = $50
Revenue = $89.95
Salvage = $25
Penalty = $120 − $89.95 = $30.05

The payoff table is given below.

Order quantity	Demand (states of nature)			
	5000	15,000	20,000	60,000
10,000	74,750	249,250	99,000	−1,103,000
15,000	−50,250	599,250	449,000	−753,000
20,000	−175,250	474,250	799,000	−403,000
60,000	−1,875,250	−1,225,750	−901,000	1,697,000

Note: The minimum order quantity is 10,000. All payoff values are in dollars.

b. Using the optimistic maximax criterion, we would order 60,000 exercisers and expect to make $1,697,000. Using the maximin criterion, we would order 20,000, since this quantity has the best minimum payoff of −175,250.

To use the minimax regret criterion, we must construct an opportunity-loss table, as follows:

Order quantity	Opportunity Loss (states of nature)			
	5000	15,000	20,000	60,000
10,000	0	350,000	700,000	2,800,000
15,000	125,000	0	300,000	2,450,000
20,000	250,000	125,000	0	2,100,000
60,000	1,950,000	1,825,000	1,700,000	0

Note: The minimum order quantity is 10,000. All loss values are in dollars.

Using this criterion, we would order 60,000 because this alternative has the smallest maximum opportunity loss.

c. To use the expected-value criterion, we multiply the assessed probabilities times the appropriate payoffs for each decision alternative. For instance:

$$E(\text{order } 10{,}000) = .2(\$74{,}750) + .4(\$294{,}250) + .3(\$99{,}000) + .1(-\$1{,}103{,}000)$$
$$= \$34{,}050$$

In a similar manner, we can find:

$$E(\text{order } 15{,}000) = \$289{,}050$$
$$E(\text{order } 20{,}000) = \$354{,}050$$
$$E(\text{order } 60{,}000) = -\$965{,}950$$

So, using the expected-value criterion, we would suggest ordering 20,000 exercisers because this quantity leads to the highest expected payoff.

PROBLEM 2 Bighorn Oil Company owns a parcel of land in Wyoming which may or may not contain an oil reserve. A competitor has offered to lease the land for $200,000 cash in return for the drilling rights and all rights to any oil that might be found. This offer will expire in three days. If Bighorn takes the deal, it gets a cash payment of $200,000. If it doesn't take the deal, Bighorn will be faced with the decision of whether to drill for oil on its own. Drilling costs are projected to be $400,000. There are four possible production outcomes if Bighorn decides to drill: The hole will produce (1) nothing (dry hole), (2) natural gas, (3) natural gas and some oil, or (4) only oil.

If drilling yields only a dry hole, the land will be basically worthless, since it is in the badlands of Wyoming and at present has little value beyond its potential for oil and gas development. If natural gas is discovered, Bighorn will recover the drilling costs but little more. If natural gas and some oil are found, the revenue will be double the original drilling costs. Finally, if the hole produces only oil, the payoff will be four times as great as the drilling costs.

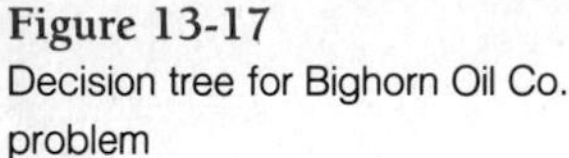

Figure 13-17
Decision tree for Bighorn Oil Co. problem

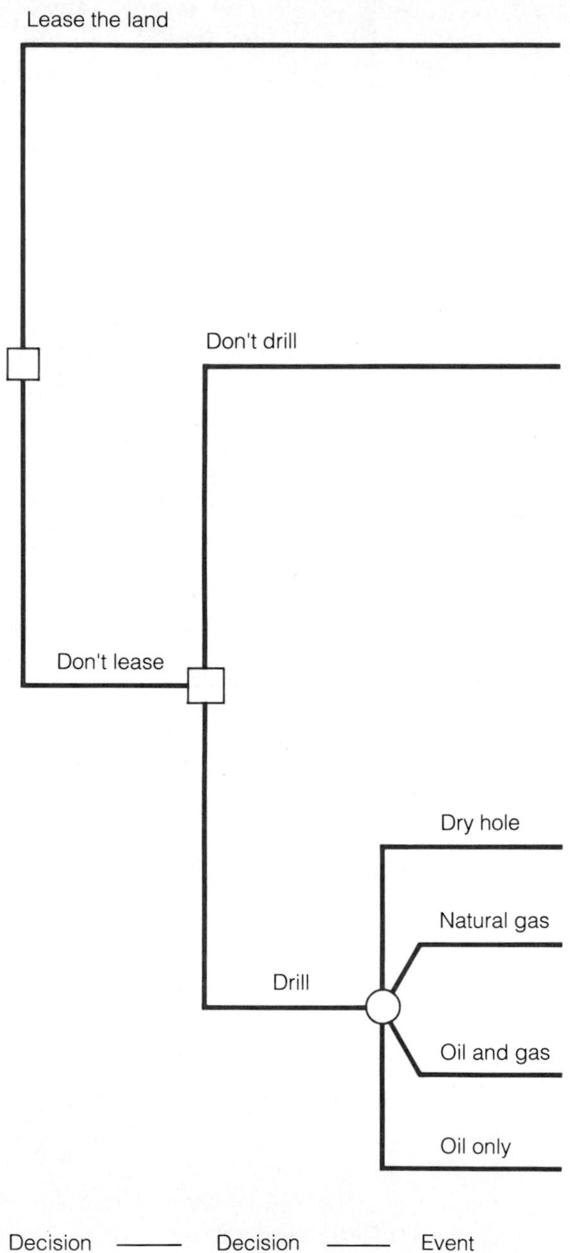

The following probabilities have been assessed by Bighorn's managers, based upon their experience with similar land:

Outcome	Probability
Dry hole	.2
Natural gas	.4
Gas and oil	.3
Oil	.1

Figure 13-18
Completed decision tree for Bighorn Oil Co. problem

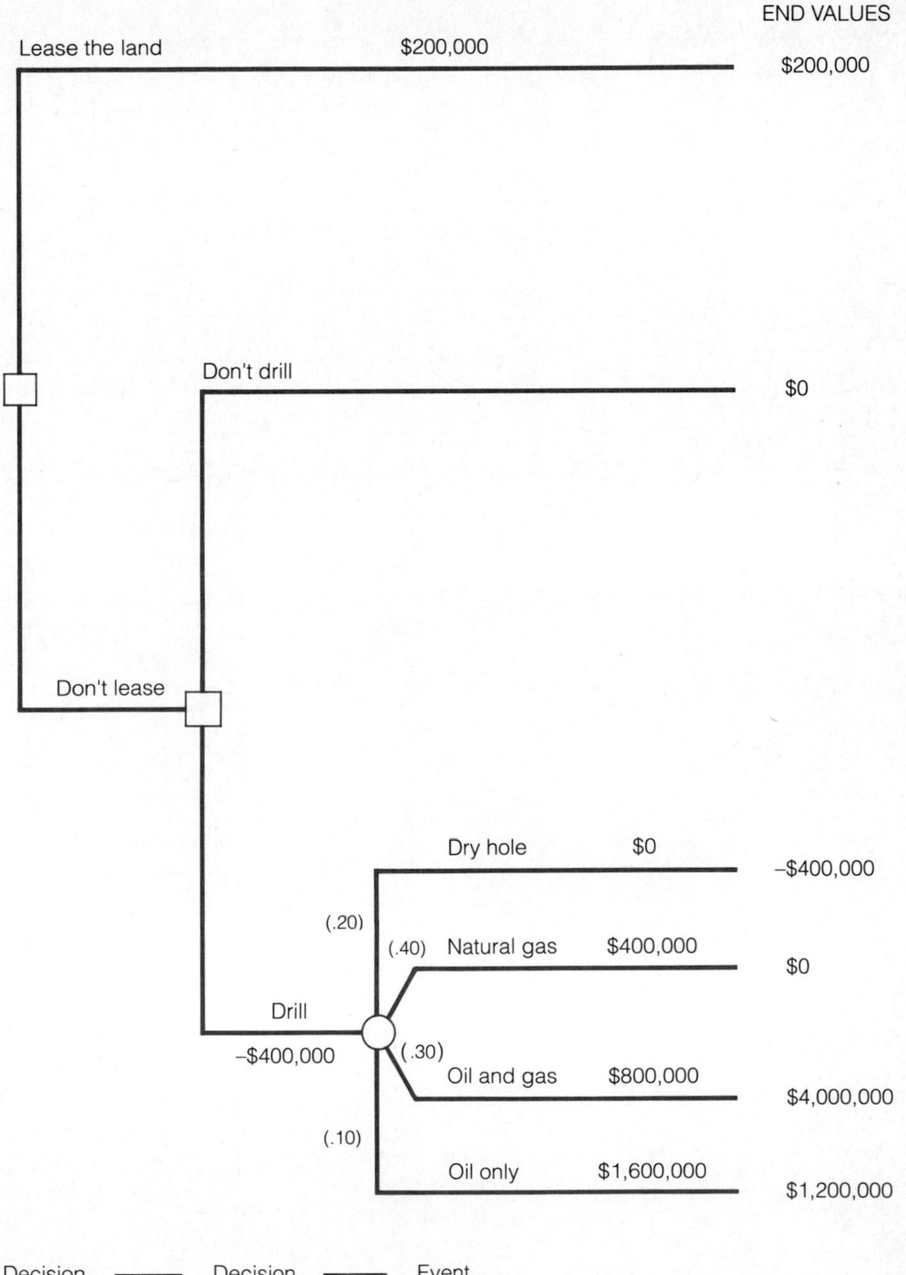

a. Develop the decision tree which models the decision facing Bighorn Oil Company.
b. Assign the probabilities and cash flows to the decision tree and compute the end values.
c. Fold back the tree and determine the decision Bighorn should make, using the criterion of maximizing expected profit.

Solutions

a. The decision tree representing Bighorn's decision situation is shown in Figure 13-17.
b. The probabilities, cash flows, and end values are shown in Figure 13-18.

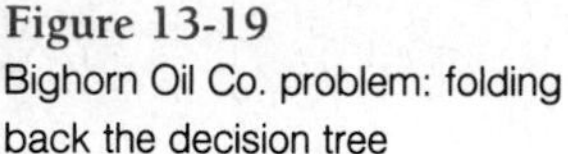

Figure 13-19
Bighorn Oil Co. problem: folding back the decision tree

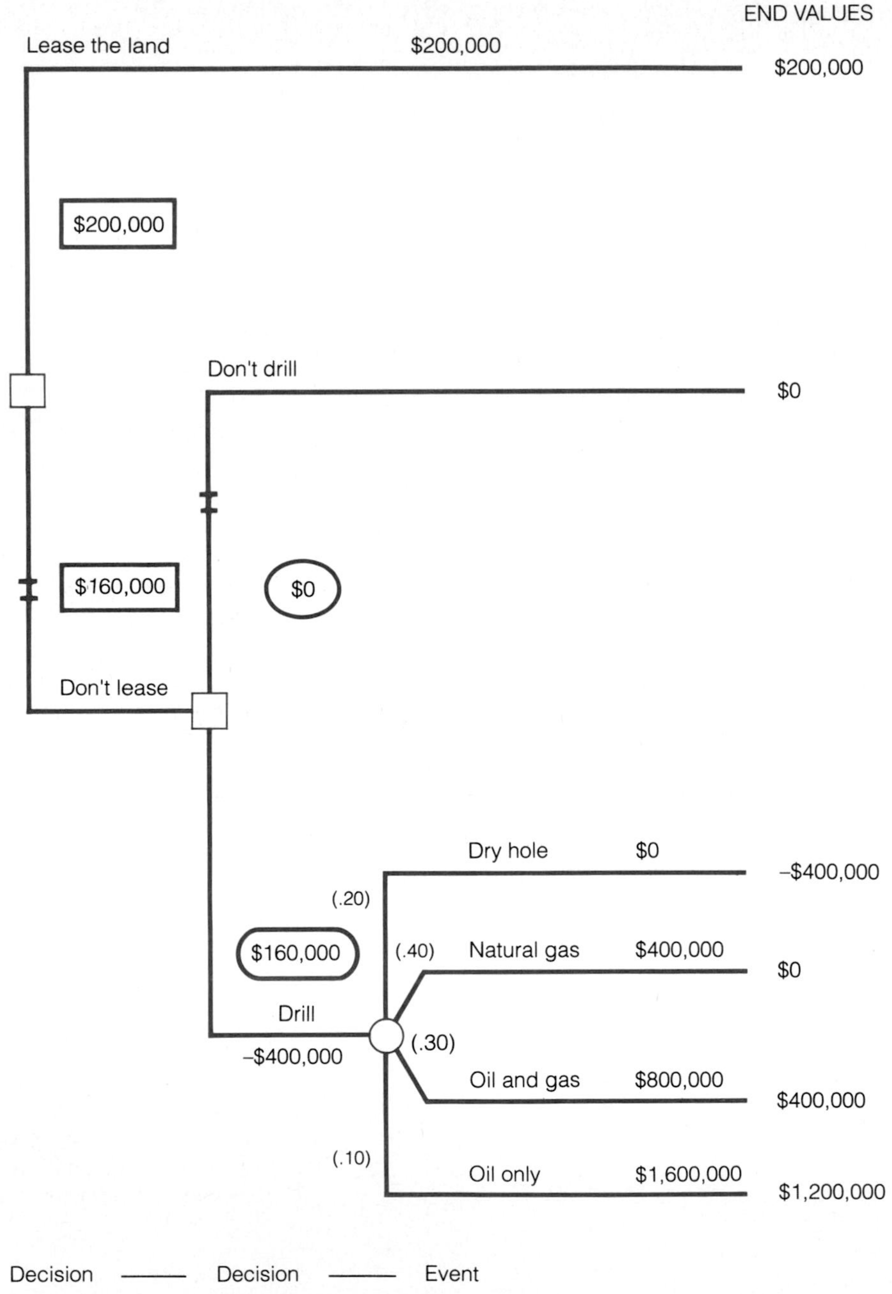

c. The decision tree is folded back as shown in Figure 13-19. The expected value of the *Drill* branch is found as follows:

$$E(\text{drill}) = .20(-\$400{,}000) + .40(\$0) + .30(\$400{,}000) + .10(\$1{,}200{,}000)$$
$$= \$160{,}000$$

If the decision is *not* to lease the land, the company may want to drill rather than not drill. However, the lease option has an expected value of $200,000, which exceeds the no-lease option of $160,000. Thus, the best decision is to lease the land.

General Questions and Assignments

1. For each of the following situations, indicate whether the decision environment is one of certainty or uncertainty and explain your reasoning:
   a. A major company is considering expansion into a new market area but is concerned about whether the economy in that market area will remain strong.
   b. A major car rental company is going to make a decision regarding which auto maker it will purchase cars from for next year. The decision will be based on unit price as quoted by the manufacturer.
   c. A company is considering changing the heating system in its plant from electric to natural gas, on the basis of monthly heating costs.
   d. A regional ski resort is considering whether to put in a new chair lift and is basing its decision on the projected number of season tickets that will be sold over the next two years.
2. Discuss the characteristics you would use to distinguish between decision making under *certainty* and under *uncertainty*.
3. How can *subjective probabilities* be a useful tool if all a decision maker must do to change an outcome is change his or her state of mind? Discuss.
4. Expected value is the basic decision criterion used in decision analysis. Explain what *expected value* means and dicuss the advantages and disadvantages of using it.
5. Think of a major decision that you have either made recently or expect to be making in the near future and create a decision tree for it. Assign probabilities to the event outcomes and "cash flows" to the appropriate branches of the tree. Fold back the tree and reach a decision based upon expected values. Write a report clearly describing your procedure and reasoning.
6. Discuss what is meant by the *expected cost of uncertainty* and explain why it is really the same as the expected value of perfect information.
7. Contact a business in your area and discuss with a manager whether or not the company uses decision trees or other decision-analysis techniques. If so, prepare a short report describing one or more of the company's applications. If the business does not use decision analysis, find out why not and explain the reasons in your report.
8. Locate two or more articles which describe actual applications of decision analysis. Write a short paper describing these applications and discuss the degree of success that resulted from using decision-analysis techniques in these situations.
9. The administrator of the Back Bay Blood Bank has estimated the odds of running short of blood this month are 5 to 3. Translate these odds into a subjective probability assessment.
10. Wilbur Marshall, a concert promoter for MegaHit Productions, was recently criticized for his poor subjective probability assessments. The criticism was based on his overly optimistic estimate of the crowd that would attend a recent rock concert in the Hill Street Coliseum. Wilbur assessed the chance that the concert crowd would exceed 12,000 to be 75%, but only 10,000 paying fans actually attended. Because MegaHit had a fixed-price contract with the featured group instead of basing the fee on ticket sales, the producers lost money on the concert. Is the criticism of Wilbur justified? Why or why not?
11. Maggie Wing, a foreign-trade analyst for the U.S. Department of Commerce, recently completed an extensive research project to determine whether agricultural exports would increase during the coming year. Feeling uncertain about her conclusions, she stated them in the form of a probability distribution, as shown below:

    $$P(\text{increase in value}) = .82$$
    $$P(\text{no increase in value}) = .24$$

    Comment on Maggie's probability assessments.

Exercises and Application Problems

1. Varsity Contracting has recently started negotiating to provide custodial service for a local manufacturer at several facilities in the area. The manufacturer has offered to contract for Varsity's services at the rate of $.10 per square foot per month. To provide nightly custodial service for the 100,000-square-foot plant, Varsity would have to hire two more workers at $8.00 per hour. The new service would require 8 hours per night, 5 nights a week. Supplies would cost $200 per week, and overhead would be charged at 20% of the labor cost.

   Given the information presented here, what decision environment exists? Why do you think so? Would you recommend that Varsity sign this contract?
2. Cooke Collectibles produces fine pocelain miniatures representing famous people and historical events. To avoid production and scheduling problems, Cooke's policy is to make all copies of a figure in one production run. In the event that the demand for any figure exceeds the number produced, the customer's money is returned along with a coupon good for $10.00 toward the purchase of another Cooke miniature. If the company makes too many figures, the extras are sold to a discounter, who agrees to hold them for 6 months, for $50 each. This price is half the variable production cost of a figure.

   Cooke Collectibles has recently agreed to pay $200,000 for the rights to produce a miniature representing a famous singer. The company plans to sell the figures for $250 each. The marketing department predicts that actual demand will equal one of these possible demand levels: 20,000; 40,000; 60,000; 80,000.
   a. Set up a table showing the payoffs for all combinations of production and demand.
   b. Use the maximin criterion to arrive at the appropriate decision. Contrast this decision with the one made using the maximax criterion instead.
3. Referring to problem 2, suppose the marketing manager at Cooke Collectibles has analyzed the possible demand levels and subjectively assessed the following probabilities for the various demand levels:

Demand Level	Probability
20,000	.10
40,000	.30
60,000	.40
80,000	.20
	1.00

   Use the expected-value criterion to arrive at the best decision for Cooke.
4. The Special Occasions Company, a nationwide distributor of flowers and greeting cards, has just contracted with Global Floral to purchase up to 500,000 dozen red and yellow roses for sale in the week before Valentine's Day. Special Occasions supplies flower shops and other retail outlets from regional distribution centers throughout the country. The problem now facing the company is how many dozen roses to buy. If the company doesn't buy enough, it loses potential business; if it buys more than are demanded, it loses the costs of purchasing and shipping these unsold roses. Any unsold roses are given to local hospitals and retirement homes or disposed of at the area landfill.

   The contract calls for a basic payment of $150,000 plus $5 for each dozen roses bought by Special Occasions. The company's accounting department has determined that the cost of shipping the roses from Global Floral's greenhouses averages $1.50 per dozen. The marketing department has estimated the demand for roses, and its probability distribution, as follows:

Demand Level	Probability
100,000	.10
150,000	.40
200,000	.20
225,000	.20
250,000	.10
	1.00

Assuming the roses sell for an average of $18 per dozen, set up the payoff table and use the expected-value criterion to find how many dozen roses should actually be purchased for the next Valentine's Day sales.

5. Baker Enterprises, a produce wholesaler that supplies fruits and vegetables to local grocery stores and restaurants, has just received notice that a frost in Florida will have a serious impact on this winter's orange harvest. If Baker's buyer waits until the time he normally buys Florida oranges, the price could be very high. Consequently, Sara Baker, the owner, has decided to enter into a contract now. The Florida supplier will guarantee any quantity of oranges this winter, but only on the following terms:

Fixed finder's fee	$10,000
Fewer than 1001 boxes	$3.00 per box
1001–5000 boxes	$2.80 per box
More than 5000 boxes	$2.50 per box

The sales manager has identified the following possible demand levels for boxes of oranges this winter: 500, 1000, 2000, 4000, 7000. The expected selling price will be $9.00 per box, and unsold boxes will be given away.

Set up a payoff table for this decision problem and use the minimax regret decision criterion to determine how many boxes of oranges Baker Enterprises should buy.

6. Referring to problem 5, suppose the managers at Baker Enterprises have discussed the situation and, on the basis of their past experience with orange sales, have assessed the following probabilities for each possible demand level:

Demand	Probability
500	.15
1000	.20
2000	.20
4000	.30
7000	.15

Incorporate these probabilities into your analysis and determine the "best decision" for Baker Enterprises, using the expected-value criterion.

7. Referring to problems 5 and 6, suppose Sara Baker has found an alternative supplier of Florida oranges. The new supplier will not charge a finder's fee but will charge $4.50 per box regardless of the quantity purchased. If Sara Baker decides to buy from the new supplier, how many boxes of oranges should she buy in order to maximize expected profit? Which supplier should she choose? Explain.

Problems 8 through 12 refer to Duckland Enterprises, which is considering bidding on one or all of the first five franchises offered by a popular Japanese fast-food operation. Each franchise requires a yearly $100,000 payment and the construction of a building at an average cost of $250,000. Duckland plans to keep the franchises for a year and, if the businesses are successful, should be able to sell them for $600,000 *each, including the buildings. If the operations are not successful, Duckland will close them down and sell the buildings for $150,000.*

8. Referring to the Duckland franchise situation described above, use the maximax decision criterion to determine how many franchises Duckland should purchase.
9. How many franchises should Duckland purchase if the maximin decision criterion is used?
10. Suppose Duckland Enterprises has three options for constructing the buildings for its franchises. One option is to construct the buildings as originally planned, at a cost of $250,000 each. A second option is to build smaller facilities in established malls, with building expenses totaling $150,000 each. If the mall operations are not successful, Duckland can recover $100,000 of the $150,000 building cost; and if they are successful, they can be sold for $500,000 each. A third option is to construct larger buildings, at a cost of $400,000 each. If successful, these operations can be sold for $1,000,000 each; and if they are not successful, the buildings can be sold for $200,000 each.

    Construct a payoff table describing these new alternatives for Duckland Enterprises.
11. Determine how many franchises Duckland should acquire under each building-cost option described in problem 10. Provide separate answers using the maximin and maximax decision criteria.
12. Referring to problem 11, suppose Duckland Enterprises assesses the following probability distributions for the number of successful franchises at each building-cost level.

$150,000		$250,000		$400,000	
Number	P(success)	Number	P(success)	Number	P(success)
0	.05	0	.06	0	.09
1	.10	1	.10	1	.15
2	.15	2	.20	2	.25
3	.25	3	.40	3	.40
4	.30	4	.12	4	.07
5	.15	5	.12	5	.04

For each building alternative, use the expected-payoff criterion to determine the optimal number of franchises to purchase. Then determine which building-cost level Duckland should use for its franchises.

Problems 13 through 16 refer to the Far Horizons Development Corporation, which is considering building a vacation condominium project on the Maine coast. The question facing the company is how many units to build.

Because of their central-utility design, the units must be built in blocks of 10. Assume that, for each block of 10, the land will cost $200,000 and construction will cost $250,000 plus an additional $70,000 for each unit. Given that the company has decided to build, the possible production levels are as follows: 10, 20, 30, 40, 50.

Each unit will be priced at $200,000 for the regular market. However, if demand does not meet supply, Far Horizons will be forced to auction the units at an average price of $75,000.

13. Referring to the Far Horizons condominium project described above, set up a payoff table assuming the following possible demand levels: 0, 10, 20, 30, 40, 50.
14. Referring to the payoff table from problem 13, what is the best decision if the maximin criterion is used? Show how you arrived at your answer.
15. What is the best decision for Far Horizons if the maximax criterion is used with the payoff table from problem 13? Show how you arrived at your answer.
16. Assume that Far Horizons has assessed the following probability distribution for condominium demand:

Demand	Probability
0	.05
10	.10
20	.25
30	.25
40	.20
50	.15
	1.00

Use the expected-value criterion to determine how many units should be built. What is the expected value of this alternative?

Problems 17 through 20 refer to the following situation. The production manager for a video-game company has been asked to help upper management decide whether or not to market a new game based on a popular cartoon character. If the new game is successful, the company will make $50 million; but if it is a failure, the company will lose an estimated $20 million in production and advertising expenses.

17. The video-game production manager in the situation described above believes that there is a 60% chance the new game will be successful. Construct the payoff table for the decision faced by the video-game company.

18. What decision should the managers of the video-game company make if they wish to maximize the expected payoff?

19. Suppose that marketing personnel have determined there are several levels of success and failure possible with the proposed video game. These possibilities (states of nature) and the assessed probabilities are as follows:

Success Level	Probability
Excellent ($70,000,000)	.30
Good ($50,000,000)	.30
Fair ($10,000,000)	.10
Poor (−$20,000,000)	.30
	1.00

Develop the payoff table that reflects these states of nature.

20. Given the payoff table you developed in problem 19, what decision should the company's managers make if they wish to maximize the expected payoff?

21. The manager of the Pink Flounder restaurant must decide how many orders of its special butter-broiled catfish to make for Thursday's lunch special. The orders must be made in advance, since the restaurant guarantees lunch-time service in less than 15 minutes and the catfish special takes 45 minutes to prepare. Each order costs $3.50 to prepare and is sold for $7.00. Any leftover orders can be used in the restaurant's fish gumbo, for a saving of $1.50. People who order catfish after it has run out are given a free catfish dinner on their next visit. Sales records from past Thursdays indicate that demand should have the following probability distribution:

Demand Level	Probability
3	.10
4	.30
5	.25
6	.20
7	.10
8	.05
9 or more	0
	1.00

Develop a payoff table for the Pink Flounder's decision problem.

22. Referring to problem 21, how many orders of catfish should be prepared on Thursday?
23. Problems 2 and 3 discussed the situation of Cooke Collectibles, which was considering making a porcelain miniature of a famous singer for sale to the public. As part of solving that problem, you constructed a payoff table. Use the values in that table to determine the expected value, given perfect information. Then determine the expected cost of uncertainty for this problem.
24. In problem 4, you considered the decision faced by the Special Occasions Company, which was determining how many dozen roses to purchase for sale in the week before Valentine's Day. As part of that problem, you constructed a payoff table. Use the values in that table to determine the expected value, given perfect information. Then determine the expected cost of uncertainty for this problem.
25. Referring to problems 4 and 24, construct an opportunity-loss table for the Special Occasions Company and determine the quantity of roses to order which will minimize the expected opportunity loss. Compare the expected opportunity loss with the expected cost of uncertainty you found in problem 24. Why are these the same?
26. In problem 12 you constructed payoff tables for the Duckland Enterprises franchise decision. Use the values in those tables to determine the expected value, given perfect information for each situation. Then determine the expected cost of uncertainty for each approach.
27. Referring to problems 12 and 26, construct opportunity-loss tables and determine the decision for each franchise approach which minimizes the expected opportunity loss. Compare these values with the costs of uncertainty that you found in problem 26. Why are they the same?
28. Referring to the situation of Baker Enterprises in problems 5 through 7, develop opportunity-loss tables for both alternatives. What is the best choice for the number of boxes of oranges to be purchased under each alternative? Base your response on the criterion of minimizing expected opportunity loss. For each alternative, find the EVPI value. Which alternative should Baker select? Discuss.
29. In problems 13–16 you constructed a payoff table and used expected values to determine the appropriate number of condominiums for Far Horizons to build in Maine. Convert this table to an opportunity-loss table. Using expected opportunity loss as the decision criterion, determine how many units should be built. In this case, what is the EVPI? Suppose someone offered to sell the company perfect information about demand for $10,000. Would the information be worth that price? Explain.
30. In problems 21 and 22 you used the expected-value criterion to determine the optimal number of catfish orders to prepare. Convert the table you used in making your decision to an opportunity-loss table. Make the appropriate decision using the opportunity-loss table. What is the EVPI? What is the expected cost of uncertainty?
31. East Coast Imports is considering two alternative advertising and marketing plans for a new line of consumer products it buys from a manufacturer in Singapore. The first plan involves contracting with a television shopping channel and is projected to have a monthly cost of $200,000. East Coast's marketing director has analyzed this alternative and, after a joint meeting with the shopping-channel's manager, believes that the following probability distribution for additional profit generated is accurate:

Increased Revenue	Probability	Increased Revenue	Probability
$120,000	.10	260,000	.20
150,000	.10	290,000	.10
200,000	.20	320,000	.10
230,000	.20		1.00

The second marketing alternative—to rely on advertising in airline magazines and newspaper inserts—is projected to have a monthly cost of $120,000. However, the marketing director thinks that this approach would not be as effective for generating added monthly revenue as the shopping-channel approach. This is reflected in the following probability distribution:

Increased Revenue	Probability
$70,000	.10
90,000	.10
110,000	.25
140,000	.25
170,000	.20
200,000	.10
	1.00

Because of the fear of "overkill," the company has decided not to try both approaches simultaneously. However, the managers did agree that if the print-advertising approach is chosen and results in $90,000 or less in added revenues, they can switch to the shopping channel for an additional cost of $20,000. They assume the probabilities would not be affected, but all profit projections will be reduced by this cost.

a. Set up the appropriate decision tree for this problem.

b. Using the criterion of maximizing the expected increase in net revenues, what marketing strategy should be chosen?

Problems 32 through 35 refer to the Major League Corporation, which makes sports-related items at a plant in South Carolina. Before the baseball season, the company was approached by representatives from the Sports Connection, a company that supplies baseball items to be sold at major league parks and at sports souvenir stores. The Sports Connection has offered to contract to buy 300,000 baseball hats for $3.00 each. The company's production capacity is 500,000 hats. The problem facing Major League is whether to accept this offer or to attempt to independently sell all its baseball hats. If the demand for hats is high, the company will be able to sell hats for much more than $3.00 each; but if demand is low, the hats will have to be sold for much less than $3.00.

At least two uncertainties exist which will affect the demand for hats. First, if the league races are tight the demand will be high; clear leaders early in the season will lead to low demand. Second, if the players strike this year, demand will be reduced. Using available information on injury levels and team strength analysis, Major League's executives estimate a 60% probability that the league races will be tight. In addition, the executives estimate the probability of a strike this year to be 30%. Assuming the two events, tight races and a player strike, are independent, the following table shows the possible selling prices for the company's hats and the associated probabilities.

	League Races	
Players' Strike	Tight	Not Tight
No	$5.00 $p = .42$	$2.50 $p = .28$
Yes	$4.00 $p = .18$	$2.00 $p = .12$

32. Assuming Major League will sell its entire output, should it accept the the Sports Connection's offer if it wishes to maximize its expected revenue?

33. Suppose Major League's executives believe the company will be able to negotiate the following deal with the Sports Connection: The contract price for hats will be reduced to \$2.70 per hat; Major League will commit to delivering 150,000 hats at this price with the option of supplying the remaining 150,000 hats at \$2.70 each after it determines whether the players will strike. This decision must be made before the status of the league races is known.

This proposal, if made, will require the services of legal counsel, with a fee estimated to be \$25,000. Determine the decision tree describing this situation.

34. Should Major League make the proposal specified in problem 33? Base your recommendation on expected values.

35. Assume you are the purchasing manager for the Sports Connection. If you receive the offer proposed in problem 33, would you recommend that it be accepted if your only other alternative is to buy 300,000 baseball hats on the open market? Assume that you have assessed the same probabilities as Major League regarding league races and player strikes. Base your conclusion on expected costs.

36. The Gregston Corporation has purchased a petroleum lease tract in the Pacific Ocean which may contain extensive oil deposits. Drilling a dry hole would be very expensive, so Gregston's managers are considering conducting a test to determine whether or not the geologic structure is favorable for the presence of oil. Unfortunately, the test is not perfect. Construct a decision-tree diagram for the problem facing Gregston's managers.

37. Referring to problem 36, suppose Gregston's managers have determined the correct structure will be found 70% of the time when the reading is positive. Recent industry evidence with the test has shown a correct structure will be found 40% of the time when the reading is negative. Further, records show that when this test was conducted in this region in the past, 40% of the time the reading was positive. However, records also show that oil is struck for only 10% of all holes drilled worldwide.

The test will cost the company \$400,000 to perform, and the cost of drilling the hole is \$2 million. If Gregston does drill and hit oil, there are three possible outcomes:

Oil Outcome	Revenue	Probability
Small find	\$2 million	.40
Medium find	\$5 million	.40
Large find	\$10 million	.20

Considering this information, what decision should Gregston make? Base your decision on expected profits.

38. In problem 37, Gregston's managers did not take into account the fact that they had already paid \$500,000 for the drilling lease. What, if any, effect does this new information have on the decision facing the company? Discuss.

39. Referring to problem 37, how sensitive is the decision to the probability assessment that the tester will give a positive reading in this region of the ocean? That is, how much would this probability have to change in order to change the decision that Gregston will make?

40. New Age Marketing is considering two alternative advertising plans for a client. The first plan uses radio and television commercials that will cost \$100,000. The account executive estimates a 40% chance that the client's revenues will increase by \$80,000, a 25% chance that revenues will increase by \$110,000, and a 35% chance that revenues will increase by \$120,000 as a result of this advertising approach.

The second plan is to use newspaper and magazine advertisements, at a cost of \$20,000. However, print media are thought to be less effective than radio and television. The account executive estimates the chances are 20% that this plan will increase revenues by \$14,000, a 50% chance that revenues will increase by \$30,000, and a 30% chance that revenues will increase by \$40,000.

If the newspaper and magazine option is chosen, New Age can later take the radio and TV option, but expected revenue will decline by $10,000 from what it would have been had that been the first choice. The account executive has indicated that it would not be feasible to try the newspaper and magazine approach after first choosing radio and TV.

Use a decision-tree approach to determine what decision(s) the New Age agency should make.

Chapter Equations

Expected value

$$E(x) = \Sigma x_i P(x_i) \quad (13\text{-}1)$$

where:

x_i = the ith outcome of the specified alternative measured in some units, such as dollars

$P(x_i)$ = the probability of outcome x_i occurring

and:

$$\Sigma P(x_i) = 1.0 \quad (13\text{-}2)$$

$$0.0 \leq P(x_i) \leq 1.0 \quad (13\text{-}3)$$

Classical probability assessment

$$P(a) = \frac{\text{number of ways } a \text{ can occur}}{\text{total number of ways any outcome can occur}} \quad (13\text{-}4)$$

Relative frequency of occurrence

$$P(x) = \frac{\text{number of times } x \text{ occurrs}}{n} \quad (13\text{-}5)$$

where: n = number of observances

Chapter Glossary

Certainty A decision environment in which the results of selecting each alternative are known before the decision is made.

Decision tree A diagram that illustrates the correct ordering of actions and events in a decision-analysis problem. Each act or event is represented by a node on the decision tree.

Expected-value criterion A decision criterion that employs probability to select the alternative that will produce the greatest average payoff or minimum average loss.

Maximax criterion An optimistic decision criterion for dealing with uncertainty without using probability. For each option, the decision maker finds the maximum possible payoff and then selects the option with the greatest maximum payoff.

Maximin criterion A pessimistic (conservative) decision criterion for dealing with uncertainty without using probability. For each option, the decision maker finds the minimum possible payoff and selects the option with the greatest minimum payoff.

Minimax regret criterion A decision criterion that considers the results of selecting the "wrong" alternative. For each state of nature, the decision maker finds the difference between the best payoff and each other alternative and uses these values to construct an opportunity-loss table. The decision maker then selects the alternative with the minimum opportunity loss (or regret).

Payoff The outcome (profit or loss) for any combination of alternative and state of nature. The outcomes of all possible combinations of alternatives and states of nature constitute a *payoff table*.

State of nature The possible outcome in a decision situation over which the decision maker has no control.

Uncertainty A decision environment in which the decision maker does not know what outcome will result when an alternative is selected.

Chapter References

BOOKS

Baird, Bruce F. *Managerial Decision Making under Uncertainty*. New York: Wiley, 1989.

Brown, R. V., A. S. Kahr, and C. Peterson. *Decision Analysis for the Manager*. New York: Holt, 1974.

Bunn, D. W. *Applied Decision Analysis*. New York: McGraw-Hill, 1984.

Felson, J. *Decision Making under Uncertainty*. New York: CBS Educational and Professional Publishing, 1979.

Gregory, G. *Decision Analysis*. New York: Plenum, 1988.

Holloway, C. *Decision Making under Uncertainty: Models and Choices*. Englewood Cliffs, N.J.: Prentice-Hall, 1979.

Keeney, R. L., and H. Raiffa. *Decisions with Multiple Objectives: Preferences and Value Trade-offs*. New York: Wiley, 1976.

Raiffa, H. *Decision Analysis*. Reading, Mass.: Addison-Wesley, 1968.

Sampson, D. *Managerial Decision Analysis*. Homewood, Ill.: Irwin, 1988.

Schlaifer, R. *Analysis of Decisions under Uncertainty*. New York: McGraw-Hill, 1969.

Winkler, R. *Introduction to Bayesian Inference and Decision*. New York: Holt, 1972.

ARTICLES

Bell, D. "Regret in Decision Making under Uncertainty." *Operations Research*, Vol. 30, 1982.

Berger, P. D., and A. Gerstenfeld. "Decision Analysis for Increased Highway Safety." *Sloan Management Review*, Spring 1971.

Brown, R. V. "Do Managers Find Decision Theory Useful?" *Harvard Business Review*, January–February 1970.

Hespos, R. F., and P. A. Strassmann. "Stochastic Decision Trees for the Analysis of Investment Decisions." *Management Science*, Vol. 11, 1965.

Howard, R. A. "An Assessment of Decision Analysis." *Operations Research*, Vol. 28, 1980.

Keeney, R. L. "Decision Analysis: An Overview." *Operations Research*, Vol. 30, 1982.

Ulvila, J. W., and R. V. Brown. "Decision Analysis Comes of Age." *Harvard Business Review*, September 1982.

Mini Case

CASE 13

ROCKSTONE INTERNATIONAL, PART 1

Rockstone International is one of the world's largest diamond brokers. The firm purchases rough stones and has them cut and polished for sale in the United States and Europe. The diamond business has been very profitable, and from all indications it will continue to be so. However, R. B. Randall, president and chief executive officer for Rockstone, has stressed the need for effective management decisions throughout the organization if the firm is to remain profitable and competitive.

Normally, R. B. does not involve herself in personnel decisions, but today's situation is not typical. Beth Harkness, Rockstone's personnel manager, is considering whether or not to hire Hans Marquis, a world-famous diamond cutter, to replace Omar Barboa, who broke both his hands in a freak skateboard accident almost a month ago. If he is hired, Hans Marquis will be paid on a commission basis at the rate of $5000 for each stone he cuts successfully. (Because of his professional pride, Hans will accept no fee if he is unsuccessful in cutting a stone.)

In the past, the decision of whether to hire Hans would have been simple. If he was available, he would be hired. However, 6 months ago, the Liechtenstein Corporation introduced the world's first diamond-cutting machine. This machine, which can be leased for $1 million per year, is guaranteed to cut stones successfully 90% of the time.

Although Hans Marquis has an excellent reputation, Rockstone International cannot be sure about his success rate because of the extreme secrecy among people in the diamond business. Hans claims that his success rate is 95%, but he has been known to exaggerate. Rockstone executives have made the following assessments, based on all the information they could obtain:

Success Rate	Probability
0.97	.10
0.95	.40
0.90	.30
0.85	.10
0.80	.10
	1.00

Rockstone purchases gemstones at a cost of $15,000 each. A successful cut yields four diamonds that can be sold at an average price of $35,000 each. Harry Winkler, sales and purchasing manager, reports that his projections for the next year indicate a need for 100 stones to be cut.

R. B. Randall knows there must be a way to decide whether to hire Hans Marquis or lease the new cutting machine.

Chapter 14

BAYESIAN REVISION ANALYSIS AND THE VALUE OF INFORMATION

Chapter Outline

Why You Need to Know

Most decisions are made in an *uncertain* environment. Chapter 13 introduced some important tools of decision analysis, including decision trees. The expected-value criterion was introduced as the primary means of comparing decision alternatives. The advantage of the expected-value criterion is that it fully utilizes the decision maker's probability assessments about the uncertain events involved in a decision.

When probability assessments are based on subjective evaluation, they represent the decision maker's opinion, or state of mind, regarding the chances that an outcome will occur. The subjective assessments are based on personal experiences and all available information up to the point at which the probabilities are assessed. However, if new information becomes available, the decision maker should use the new information to revise his or her probability assessments. For instance, a sales representative for a national sporting goods manufacturer might have assessed the chances of making a sale to a particular client to be .60, given all available information. A day before her sales call, she learns that the client has just closed one of its stores in the city for financial reasons. This new information would seem to affect the chances of making a sale. The sales representative might then revise her probability estimate downward, to .40.

Revising probability assessments is a normal part of decision making; people do it informally all the time. Think back to when you signed up for this course. You no doubt had formed some sort of expectation about the class and the instructor from comments by friends who had previously taken the class. Now think back to the first day of class. By then you probably had purchased this text, and may have browsed through it to get an idea of the topics to be covered. As you listened to the instructor go over the course outline, explain the grading requirements, and so on, your expectations about the course were changing. Each person in the class began with different expectations and then processed the new information differently; however, you all went through the same revision of your expectations. (In fact, this process has no doubt continued throughout the term.)

Because the process of using new information to revise original probability assessments is a natural part of decision making, it is an important part of decision analysis. In this chapter, we introduce the Bayesian revision analysis technique, which is a formal means by which new information about events is incorporated into the decision process and used to revise the original probability assessments about those events. Bayesian revision is a very important component of decision analysis.

New information does not often come without a cost. As a decision maker, you will need to know how to place a value on potential new information. For instance, a company needs to know how much to spend for additional market research before making a decision about introducing a new product into a specific market area. Certainly the company won't want to spend more for the information than it is worth. The steps involved in determining the value of information are also discussed in this chapter.

Chapter Objectives

This chapter introduces the Bayesian process for revising probability assessments to account for new information and discusses how to determine the value of this new information. Specifically, the objectives of this chapter are to:

1. Explain how to use the Bayesian revision process when the new information comes from a sample taken from a binomial process.
2. Show you how to apply the Bayesian revision process when the new information is qualitative.
3. Explain how to determine the value of a sample before actually selecting the sample.

14-1 INTRODUCTION TO BAYESIAN REVISION ANALYSIS

At some time, most likely in a statistics or mathematics course, you should have been introduced to the rules of probability. During that introduction, you no doubt learned about the concept of **conditional probability**—the probability that event A will occur, *given* that a second event, B, has already occurred. In simple notation form, we can state this as:

$$P(A|B) = ?$$

where the symbol | represents *given*. For instance, you might recall the familiar problem of drawing a bead from an urn, and the instructor posing a question like this one: If you have an urn with exactly 10 green beads and 10 white beads, what is the probability of getting a green bead on the second draw from the urn, *given* that the first bead drawn was also green and that it was not returned to the urn?

Using the above notation, we can restate the instructor's question as follows:

$$P(G_2|G_1) = ?$$

Since the beads are drawn without replacement, the probability of getting green on the second draw is *conditional* on the outcome of the first draw. For example, if the first draw produced a white bead, 10 of the remaining 19 beads are green and the chances of getting a green on the second draw are 10 in 19, or 10/19. However, if the first draw yielded a green bead, then 9 of the remaining 19 beads are green and the probability of getting a green on the second draw—*given* that the first bead drawn was green—is 9/19.

In statistics class, you used conditional probabilities each time you tested a hypothesis. The p-value associated with the test of a hypothesis is the conditional probability of observing the sample statistic, given that the null hypothesis is true.

Conditional probability can be used for making decisions in many types of business situations. Suppose a company has two production facilities, one in Ohio and one in Virginia. The Ohio facility makes 60% of the company's total output, and the remaining 40% is made by the Virginia plant. After extensive sampling, the quality assurance manager has determined that 5% of the items produced in Ohio and 10% of the items produced in Virginia are defective. All finished products from both facilities are sent to a central warehouse, but then are intermingled rather than being stored separately. When the company sells a defective product, it incurs not only the cost of replacing the item but also the loss of goodwill. The vice president for production would like to allocate these costs fairly between the two plants. To do so, he knows that he must first determine the probability that a defective item was produced by a particular production facility. Specifically, he needs to answer these questions:

1. What is the probability that an item was produced at the Ohio plant, given that the item is defective?
2. What is the probability that an item was produced at the Virginia plant, given that the item is defective?

In notation form, with D representing the occurrence of a defective item, what the manager wants to know is:

$$P(\text{Ohio plant}|D) = ?$$
$$P(\text{Virginia plant}|D) = ?$$

The general rule for determining conditional probability is:

$$P(A_1|B) = \frac{P(B \text{ and } A_1)}{P(B)} = \frac{P(A_1)\ P(B|A_1)}{P(B)} \tag{14-1}$$

The denominator in equation 14-1, $P(B)$, which is the probability of the event given to have occurred, is found by:

$$P(B) = \Sigma\ P(B \text{ and } A_i) = \Sigma\ P(A_i)\ P(B|A_i) \tag{14-2}$$

where A_i is a collection of mutually exclusive and collectively exhaustive events.

Another way of writing equation 14-1 is shown below:

$$P(A_1|B) = \frac{P(A_1)\ P(B|A_1)}{\Sigma\ P(A_i)\ P(B|A_i)} \tag{14-3}$$

We can use equation 14-3, known as *Bayes's rule,* for the manufacturing example. First, we are looking for:

$$P(\text{Ohio plant}|D) = \frac{P(\text{Ohio plant})\ P(D|\text{Ohio plant})}{P(D)}$$

$$P(\text{Virginia plant}|D) = \frac{P(\text{Virginia plant})\ P(D|\text{Virginia plant})}{P(D)}$$

We already know the probability that an item comes from the Ohio plant is $P(\text{Ohio plant}) = .60$. Likewise, we know the probability that an item comes from the Virginia facility is $P(\text{Virginia plant}) = .40$. We also know the chances of an item being defective, given its production facility:

$$P(D|\text{Ohio plant}) = .05 \qquad \text{and} \qquad P(D|\text{Virginia plant}) = .10$$

Thus, we can substitute into equation 14-1 as follows:

$$P(\text{Ohio plant}|D) = \frac{(.60)(.05)}{P(D)}$$

$$P(\text{Virginia plant}|D) = \frac{(.40)(.10)}{P(D)}$$

As you can see, we have values for everything but the overall probability of a defective item, $P(D)$; but we can use equation 14-2 to find it, as follows:

$$\begin{aligned} P(D &= P(\text{Ohio plant})\ P(D|\text{Ohio plant}) + P(\text{Virginia plant})\ P(D|\text{Virginia plant}) \\ &= (.60)(.05) + (.40)(.10) = .07 \end{aligned}$$

Now we can use equation 14-3, Bayes's rule, to find the conditional probabilities we originally sought:

$$P(\text{Ohio plant}|D) = \frac{(.60)(.05)}{.07} = .428$$

$$P(\text{Virginia plant}|D) = \frac{(.40)(.10)}{.07} = .572$$

Given that an item is found to be defective, there is a .428 chance that it came from the Ohio facility and a .572 chance that it came from the Virginia plant. Thus, 42.8% of the defective-item costs should be allocated to the Ohio plant and 57.2% to the plant in Virginia.

In the manufacturing example, in the absence of any additional information, we knew that the probability of an item being produced in Ohio was .60. This is called the *prior probability*. In more formal terms, **prior probability** is the probability that an event will occur (or a condition will exist), as assessed prior to the acquisition of any additional relevant information.

After learning that the item was defective, we used Bayes's rule (equation 14-3) to revise the probability downward to .428. Termed the **posterior probability**, this revised probability combines the *prior probability* and new information from the sample.

The importance of Bayes's rule to the study and application of decision analysis is that it gives decision makers a means of incorporating new information into the decision process. The *Bayesian revision analysis* procedures discussed in the remaining sections of this chapter provide a systematic method for using new information to revise prior opinions as well as a basis for determining the economic value of this new information.

14-2 USING BAYESIAN REVISION ANALYSIS

The Dexter Company supplies electrical lighting fixtures, bulbs, and replacement parts to office buildings in the Southeast. Replacement bulbs for fluorescent lights are a key product in Dexter's line, and the firm's purchasing agents are always on the lookout for manufacturers whose bulbs will help Dexter keep its costs low.

Dexter currently buys its fluorescent bulbs from a Georgia company called Compu-Lite. This supplier produces a good product and, as determined from historical records of shipments to Dexter, has the following distribution of defective lights:

Proportion Defective	Probability
.01	.50
.02	.40
.03	.10
	1.00

Because of its emphasis on quality, Dexter guarantees its products and replaces any defective fluorescent items at no cost to the customer. Dexter's cost accountants have pegged the overall cost of each defective bulb, including lost goodwill, at $5.

The marketing department anticipates that Dexter will sell 100,000 fluorescent bulbs next year. If all 100,000 bulbs are purchased from Compu-Lite, the probability distribution for the number of defective bulbs and their overall cost is:

Proportion Defective	Number Defective	Overall Cost	Probability
.01	1000	$5,000	.50
.02	2000	$10,000	.40
.03	3000	$15,000	.10
			1.00

The expected replacement cost for Dexter if all 100,000 bulbs are purchased from Compu-Lite is:

Cost x	Probability $P(x)$	$xP(x)$
\$5,000	.50	\$2500
\$10,000	.40	\$4000
\$15,000	.10	\$1500
		\$8000 = expected cost

For the year, Dexter could expect to incur an \$8000 cost for replacing defective fluorescent lights purchased from Compu-Lite.

While attending the National Lighting Dealers Convention and Trade Show in Las Vegas recently, two Dexter managers were approached by representatives of a French manufacturer. The French sales reps offered to supply all the fluorescent lights Dexter would need at a cost of \$.25 per unit less than Compu-Lite's price. This was an intriguing offer since, on 100,000 lights, an added profit of \$25,000 was theoretically possible. The only uncertainty was the quality of the French lights.

After a number of phone calls to the French company and several of its customers, Dexter representatives subjectively developed the following probability distribution for the French manufacturer's defect rate:

Proportion Defective	Subjective Probability
.01	.10
.02	.20
.03	.40
.10	.20
.15	.10
	1.00

This probability distribution reflects the collective opinion of Dexter's quality engineers and thus reflects the state of mind of the decision makers regarding the quality of the French bulbs. The probability distribution indicates a good chance (.70) that the defect rate will be 3% or less. However, the distribution also reflects Dexter's concern that the French company's products might have a defect rate of 10% or even 15%.

If the French company and Compu-Lite are the only suppliers under consideration by Dexter, which one should Dexter purchase from to minimize expected costs? To make this decision, Dexter managers must determine the expected cost of buying from the French company and compare it with the expected cost of buying from Compu-Lite.

The expected cost of replacing defective lights supplied by the French company is found as follows:

Proportion Defective	Number Defective	Cost x	Probability $P(x)$	$xP(x)$
.01	1,000	\$5,000	.10	\$500
.02	2,000	\$10,000	.20	\$2,000
.03	3,000	\$15,000	.40	\$6,000
.10	10,000	\$50,000	.20	\$10,000
.15	15,000	\$75,000	.10	\$7,500
			1.00	\$26,000

If we compare only expected replacement costs, we get:

E(Compu-Lite cost) = \$8000 and E(French company cost) = \$26,000

Since $\$8000 < \$26{,}000$, the choice based only on expected replacement costs would be to stay with Compu-Lite. This decision assumes no difference in the purchase price that Dexter pays per light. However, since the French company has quoted a price which is \$.25 per unit less than Compu-Lite's price, now Compu-Lite's price is \$.25 per unit (or \$25,000 per 100,000 lights) higher than the French price. This cost must be added to the expected cost of replacing Compu-Lite's defective bulbs, as follows:

$$E(\text{Compu-Lite cost}) = \$8000 + \$25{,}000 = \$33{,}000$$

Now, if we consider all the costs, and base our decision solely on expected costs, the French company is the better alternative, since $\$26{,}000 < \$33{,}000$. The expected savings (and therefore higher profit earned) from changing suppliers is \$7000.

However, suppose the long-term business relationship that Dexter has enjoyed with Compu-Lite has caused Dexter's managers to give some more thought to their decision. They finally decide that before the relationship is severed, they need more information about the French product. Now Dexter requests that a random sample of 50 lights from the French manufacturer be tested by an independent testing service. Dexter officials plan to use the information from the sample tested, along with their prior probability distribution, in making the final decision. The technique of incorporating sample information into the decision process is called **Bayesian revision analysis.**

CONSTRUCTING A POSTERIOR PROBABILITY TABLE

A random sample of $n = 50$ lights was selected from the French manufacturer's inventory. We will assume a *binomial distribution* represents the sampling process in which a fluorescent bulb can be judged either good or defective. The Bayesian revision analysis for Dexter's decision is described in the following paragraphs.

First, recall that the possible outcomes in terms of the proportion of defectives and the associated prior probability distribution were subjectively assessed as:

Proportion Defective	**Subjective Probability**
.01	.10
.02	.20
.03	.40
.10	.20
.15	.10
	1.00

Next, in the second step, we determine the *conditional probability* of the sample result, given that the population of lights contains a particular proportion of defectives. Suppose the sample of 50 contains $x_1 = 6$ defectives. Remember that this is just one possible sample taken from the entire population of lights in the French manufacturer's inventory. The chances of seeing this sample result depends on what fraction of the total population actually are defective.

In the first step, the probability distribution indicated that the defect rate might be .01, ... ,.15. Now, for each possible defect rate, we must determine the conditional probability of finding 6 defectives in a sample of 50 lights. We have assumed that the process can be described by a binomial distribution and that the probabilities can be determined by using the tables in Appendix A, as follows: (1) locate the binomial table for $n = 50$, (2) find the row for $x_1 = 6$, and (3) locate the p-value corresponding to a specific proportion defective. For instance, to find the probability for the first propor-

Table 14-1 CONDITIONAL PROBABILITIES FOR DEXTER EXAMPLE

Defect Rate (p)	Prior Probability	Conditional Probability
.01	.10	.0000
.02	.20	.0004
.03	.40	.0030
.10	.20	.1541
.15	.10	.1419
	1.00	

Note: Conditional probability $= P(x_1, n|p)$, where $x_1 = 6$, $n = 50$.

tion defective, .01, we locate the intersection of the column headed $P = .01$ and the row for $x_1 = 6$. We find this value is .0000, which means there is essentially no chance that there would be 6 defectives in a sample of $n = 50$, given the proportion of defectives is .01.

Table 14-1 shows the conditional probabilities for all possible defect levels in the Dexter example. (Make sure you can find these probabilities. A common mistake is to set $p =$ prior probability instead of $p =$ proportion defective. Please don't do this!)

The third step in the Bayesian posterior analysis is to compute the joint probabilities. **Joint probability** is the probability of the simultaneous occurrence of two or more events. It represents the chances of observing both the sample information and a particular state of nature. In the Dexter example, it is the probability of a specific defective rate and the conditional probability of the sample information, given the defective rate. The joint probabilities, which form the numerator in Bayes's rule (equation 14-3), are calculated by multiplying the prior probability times the conditional probability. These values for the Dexter example are shown in Table 14-2.

The denominator in Bayes's rule is the sum of the joint probabilities; in this case, it is the overall probability of getting 6 defectives in a sample of 50, given prior knowledge about the defective rate of the French products. Thus, there is a .04629 chance that we would get 6 defectives in a sample of 50 from this supplier.

Table 14-2 JOINT PROBABILITIES FOR DEXTER EXAMPLE

Defect Rate (p)	Prior Probability	Conditional Probability	Joint Probability
.01	.10	.0000	.00000
.02	.20	.0004	.00008
.03	.40	.0030	.00120
.10	.20	.1541	.03082
.15	.10	.1419	.01419
	1.00		.04629

Note:

Joint probability = prior probability × conditional probability $= P(x_1)P(x_1, n|p)$

where: $P(x_1) =$ prior probability
$P(x_1, n|p) =$ conditional probability

and $x_1 = 6$, $n = 50$

Table 14-3 POSTERIOR PROBABILITIES FOR THE DEXTER EXAMPLE

Defect Rate (p)	Prior Probability	Conditional Probability	Joint Probability	Posterior Probability
.01	.10	.0000	.00000	.00000
.02	.20	.0004	.00008	.00173
.03	.40	.0030	.00120	.02592
.10	.20	.1541	.03082	.66580
.15	.10	.1419	.01419	.30655
	1.00		.04629	1.00000

Note:

$$\text{Posterior probability} = \frac{\text{joint probability}}{\text{sum of joint probabilities}}$$

$$= \frac{P(x_1)\,P(x_1,\, n|p)}{\sum_{i=1}^{k} P(x_i)\,P(x_i,\, n|p)}$$

where: $P(x_1)$ = prior probability of state 1
$P(x_1, n|p)$ = conditional probability
k = number of possible states

and $x_1 = 6$, $n = 50$

The fourth step is to compute the *posterior probabilities* by dividing each joint probability by the sum of the joint probabilities. Table 14-3 shows the results of the completed Bayesian revision analysis.

The posterior probabilities reflect the combination of information from the prior probabilities and the sample data. Dexter now has a different view of the French company, since the posterior probabilities are quite different from the prior probabilities. Whereas before, Dexter officials thought there was a 70% chance that the defect rate would be .03 or less, the posterior probabilities indicate that the chance is actually slightly less than 3% (i.e., .00000 + .00173 + .02592 = .02765). Dexter officials now believe the French company is far more likely to supply a greater number of defective bulbs than they had estimated before the sample was tested. The fact that the sample contained 12% defectives was the key to this change in attitude. The posterior probabilities reflect Dexter officials' current state of mind about the French company's defect rate.

In the final step of the Bayesian revision analysis for the Dexter example, we use the posterior probabilities to reevaluate the decision situation. The revised cost distribution for the French supplier and the computation of expected cost of replacing defectives, are given below.

Proportion Defective	Number Defective	Cost x	Probability $P(x)$	$xP(x)$
.01	1,000	$5,000	.00000	$0
.02	2,000	$10,000	.00173	$17.30
.03	3,000	$15,000	.02592	$388.80
.10	10,000	$50,000	.66580	$33,290.00
.15	15,000	$75,000	.30655	$22,991.25
			1.00000	$56,687.35

After incorporating the sample information with the prior probability distribution, we find that expected cost of replacing defectives from the French company is $56,687.35, which now exceeds the $33,000 expected cost for Compu-Lite. Therefore, using the decision criterion of minimizing expected costs, the Dexter Company should continue to buy from Compu-Lite. The sample information caused this change from the initial decision.

SUMMARY OF THE BAYESIAN REVISION PROCESS

The Bayesian revision process applies Bayes's rule (equation 14-3) in a manner which allows new information to be included in the decision process. To review, the steps in the analysis are:

1. Develop the prior probability distribution and evaluate the decision on the basis of the prior probabilities.
2. Collect new information and compute the conditional probabilities.
3. Compute the joint probabilities as the product of the conditional probability and the prior probability. The sum of the joint probabilities reflects the overall probability of observing the new information, given the prior state of knowledge about the population of interest.
4. Compute the posterior probabilities by dividing each joint probability by the sum of the joint probabilities.
5. Reevaluate the decision by computing the expected payoff, or cost, using the newly calculated posterior probabilities.

THE DEXTER EXAMPLE CONTINUES

You no doubt learned in your statistics course that the potential for sampling error exists whenever sampling is used. Sampling error is measured by the difference between a calculated sample value and the corresponding actual population value. The French supplier's production manager believes that his company has been a victim of bad luck and severe sampling error. He feels the defect rate found in the sample of 50 is much higher than the actual defect rate in the bulbs his company produces. He is willing to pay for testing another sample of 50 lights in the hope that the new information will cause Dexter to decide to buy lights from his company. Since there is no cost to Dexter, its officials are happy to obtain more information. However, Dexter's managers inform the French production manager that they won't ignore the first sample and will use the newly formed posterior probabilities as the prior probabilities in their analysis for the second round of sampling.

What is about to take place in the Dexter example is very typical of business decision making. That is, we begin with a set of prior probabilities ("priors") which reflect our "current" state of mind. We observe information and revise our priors accordingly. The posterior probabilities become a new set of priors. We then review more information and revise the priors again. This revision process continues as long as new information is made available before the final decision must be made. Each time, *the posteriors become the priors for the next round of revisions.*

Suppose that the test of the second sample of 50 lights yielded only 1 defective bulb. Table 14-4 shows the results of the new Bayesian revision analysis, including the new posterior probabilities. (You should perform all the necessary calculations to be sure you fully understand the steps involved in computing the posterior probabilities using the new defect rate.)

Now we can compute a new expected cost, using the posterior probabilities from Table 14-4. Because the second sample of 50 had only 1 defective bulb, the probabili-

Table 14-4 POSTERIOR PROBABILITIES BASED ON NEW SAMPLE

Defect Rate (p)	Prior Probability	Conditional Probability	Joint Probability	Posterior Probability
.01	.00000	.3056	.00000	.00000
.02	.00173	.3716	.00064	.02190
.03	.02592	.3372	.00874	.29911
.10	.66580	.0286	.01904	.65161
.15	.30655	.0026	.00080	.02738
	1.00000		.02922	1.00000

Note:

$$\text{Posterior probability} = \frac{\text{joint probability}}{\text{sum of joint probabilities}}$$

$$= \frac{P(x_1)\,P(x_1,\,n|p)}{\sum_{i=1}^{k} P(x_i)\,P(x_i,\,n|p)}$$

where: $P(x_1)$ = prior probability of state 1
$P(x_1, n|p)$ = conditional probability
k = number of possible states

and $x_1 = 1$, $n = 50$

ties now shift back somewhat, lowering the expected cost from $56,687.35 to $39,339.65. However, even after the new analysis, Dexter's best decision is to continue buying from Compu-Lite, since $33,000 < $39,339.15.

Proportion Defective	Number Defective	Cost x	Probability $P(x)$	$xP(x)$
.01	1,000	$5,000	.00000	$0
.02	2,000	$10,000	.02190	$219.00
.03	3,000	$15,000	.29911	$4,486.65
.10	10,000	$50,000	.65161	$32,580.50
.15	15,000	$75,000	.02738	$2,053.50
			1.00000	$39,339.65

IS ONE BIG SAMPLE DIFFERENT FROM TWO SMALL SAMPLES?

After learning of Dexter's decision to stay with Compu-Lite, despite the favorable results of the second sample, the French company's managers lamented the fact that they had provided two samples of 50 instead of one sample of 100. Suppose that initially they had selected a random sample of 100 and found 7 defective bulbs, the same total number of defectives found in the two 50-bulb samples. Table 14-5 shows the revised probabilities based on the sample of $n = 100$ and $x_1 = 7$ defectives. With small differences for rounding, these posterior probabilities are equal to those in Table 14-4, which were computed after two successive samples of 50 each, with a total of 7 defectives.

As you can see, the conclusions reached from the two smaller samples and one larger sample are the same. The sum of the information in several small samples is exactly the same as the information in a large sample that is equal in size to the sum of the small samples. However, an argument is sometimes made for planning a series of small samples if the per unit cost of sampling cost is high, since the results of the first few small samples may be sufficient for making a decision.

Table 14-5 POSTERIOR PROBABILITIES BASED ON ONE 100-UNIT SAMPLE

Defect Rate (p)	Prior Probability	Conditional Probability	Joint Probability	Posterior Probability
.01	.10	.0001	.00001	.00037
.02	.20	.0031	.00062	.02263
.03	.40	.0206	.00824	.30073
.10	.20	.0889	.01778	.64890
.15	.10	.0075	.00075	.02737
	1.00		.02740	1.00000

Note:

$$\text{Posterior probability} = \frac{\text{joint probability}}{\text{sum of joint probabilities}}$$

$$= \frac{P(x_1)\,P(x_1,\, n|p)}{\sum_{i=1}^{k} P(x_i)\,P(x_i,\, n|p)}$$

where: $P(x_1)$ = prior probability of state 1
$P(x_1, n|p)$ = conditional probability
k = number of possible states

and $x_1 = 7$, $n = 100$

14-3 BAYESIAN REVISION USING SUBJECTIVE CONDITIONAL PROBABILITIES

In the Dexter Company example in the previous section, sample information was obtained from the French bulb manufacturer. We assumed the sample was selected with a process that had two possible outcomes on each trial and therefore could be described as a binomial process. Selecting a defective (or nondefective) bulb on each trial was assumed to be independent of what was selected on any previous trial. We used the binomial distribution table in Appendix A to find the conditional probability of the sample result, given each possible defective rate. These conditional probabilities were combined with the prior probabilities to form the posterior probabilities.

But sample information does not always come from a binomial process. In fact, new information may not even be in the form of sample data. In this section, we will show how prior probabilities can be revised when the new information is qualitative rather than quantitative, which means that we will assess *subjective conditional probabilities.*

Consider this brief example involving the Zeejax Corporation. Several managers recently considered writing a proposal to bid on the design and manufacture of a nuclear breeder reactor. The proposal, to be submitted to the Department of Energy, will be very expensive to develop. These managers are concerned that the federal government may decide to place a moratorium on building new nuclear power plants, resulting in the loss of the money spent to develop the proposal. Using all the information available as of March 1, the managers assessed the following prior probabilities:

Event	Prior Probability
Moratorium	.20
No moratorium	.80
	1.00

Because the prior probabilities are favorable for no moratorium, the managers decided to go ahead with developing the proposal. However, two weeks later, the managers learned that the Department of Energy transferred two nuclear energy experts, who formerly worked in the proposal review department, to a different department. Although this transfer could mean nothing, there is a great deal of speculation within Zeejax that the moratorium is going to be ordered.

At the weekly progress meeting, the decision to develop the proposal is reevaluated. After careful consideration, the managers agree that there is a .90 chance that the two experts were transferred because the moratorium will be imposed. In addition, there is a .40 chance that they would have been transferred anyway, even if no moratorium is planned. These are the conditional probabilities that the new information would have occurred under each possible state of nature facing the managers. Bayesian revision analysis can be used to determine the revised probabilities of a moratorium and no moratorium, as shown below.

Moratorium	Prior Probability	Conditional Probability	Joint Probability	Posterior Probability
Yes	.20	.90	.18	.36
No	.80	.40	.32	.64
	1.00		.50	1.00

Considering the new information about the employee transfers, the managers now feel that a nuclear moratorium is more likely (probability = .36) than before. This change in thinking might be sufficient to alter their decision about going ahead with the proposal.

The preceding example is a simple case illustrating how new qualitative information can be incorporated into a decision analysis through the Bayesian revision process. As more new information became available to the ZeeJax managers, it could also be used to revise the prior probabilities and could be factored into the decision process.

14-4 THE VALUE OF INFORMATION

We saw in sections 14-2 and 14-3 that Bayes's rule can be used to incorporate new information into the decision process. Presumably, the new information has a value, and in this section we will explain how to determine the value of new information.

Consider the example of Amalgamated Manufacturing, which uses numerous small, highly tempered cams in its production process. Amalgamated cannot produce this part and purchases it from an outside supplier. In the past, this supplier has always provided the component at a 2% defect rate. Amalgamated's purchasing department has located an alternative supplier which will sell the cam for $.01 less than the original supplier. Since Amalgamated will order 100,000 cams this year, it stands to save $1000 if it buys them from the new supplier. However, Amalgamated emphasizes product quality, and the purchasing department is uncertain about the defect rate of parts from the new supplier. After some investigation, the head of the purchasing department has assessed the following probability distribution for the proportion of defective cams which would be received from the new supplier:

Proportion Defective	Probability
.01	.10
.02	.20
.04	.30
.06	.40
	1.00

Even though both suppliers guarantee free replacement for defective parts, locating and replacing the defective cams costs Amalgamated \$.50 each. Thus, the yearly costs associated with a defect rate of .02 from either supplier is \$1000 (100,000 × .02 × \$.50 = \$1000).

Figure 14-1 shows the decision tree for the problem facing Amalgamated. As you can see, the expected cost for buying from the old supplier is \$2000 (\$1000 for defective parts and \$1000 due to the price differential). After folding back the decision tree, we see that the expected cost of purchasing from the new supplier is \$2050. Thus, on the basis of minimum expected costs, the best decision is to stay with the old supplier, at an expected cost of \$2000.

Suppose, however, that before actually making the decision about suppliers, Amalgamated inspects a sample of $n = 100$ cams from the new supplier and finds

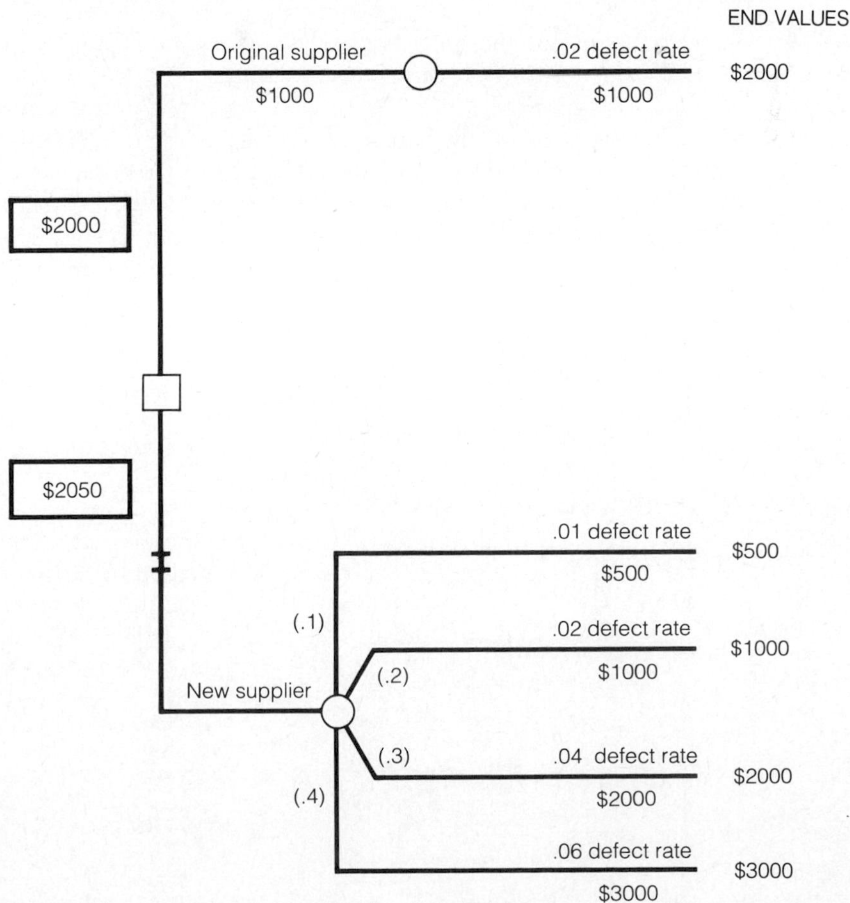

Figure 14-1
Decision tree for Amalgamated Manufacturing example

$x_1 = 5$ defectives. Bayesian revision analysis can be used to incorporate this new information into the decision in the usual manner. Table 14-6 shows the Bayesian posterior probabilities for this case, with conditional probabilities computed assuming a binomial distribution. (You should verify the probabilities in Table 14-6 to make sure you understand the revision process. Use the binomial table in Appendix A to find the conditional probabilities.)

Figure 14-2 shows the decision tree with expected costs computed using the posterior probabilities. We see that, considering the sample information, the expected cost associated with the new supplier is \$2481, versus \$2000 for the old supplier. The decision remains to stay with the old supplier.

Now the question becomes, What is the value of this sample information? From one perspective, the sample information has no value, since it did not change our decision. This conclusion comes from the following definition for the value of sample information.

> The value of a sample after its results are known is equal to the absolute difference between the expected cost (or payoff) associated with the best decision prior to receiving the information and the expected cost (or payoff) associated with the best decision after the new information has been taken into account.

For the Amalgamated Manufacturing example, the expected cost of the best decision before sampling was \$2000 and the expected cost of the best decision after sampling was also \$2000. Thus, according to this definition for the value of sample information, the sample of $n = 100$ with $x_1 = 5$ defectives had no value. Because it did not change the decision, the information had no value in terms of the decision process.

However, an alternative view of the value of sample information holds that a sample has value if it reduces the cost of uncertainty. The value in this case is psychological rather than monetary, assuming the following definition of psychological value:

> The psychological value of sample information evaluated after the sample has been observed is the difference between the expected cost of uncertainty prior to sampling and the expected cost of uncertainty after the sample information has been incorporated.

In Chapter 13, we showed that the expected cost of uncertainty is the same as the expected value of perfect information (EVPI). For the Amalgamated example

Table 14-6 AMALGAMATED EXAMPLE: POSTERIOR PROBABILITIES WHEN $n = 100$, $x_1 = 5$

Defect Rate (p)	Prior Probability	Conditional Probability	Joint Probability	Posterior Probability
.01	.10	.0029	.00029	.002
.02	.20	.0353	.00706	.059
.04	.30	.1595	.04785	.396
.06	.40	.1639	.06556	.543
	1.00		.12076	1.000

Figure 14-2
Decision tree with posterior probabilities

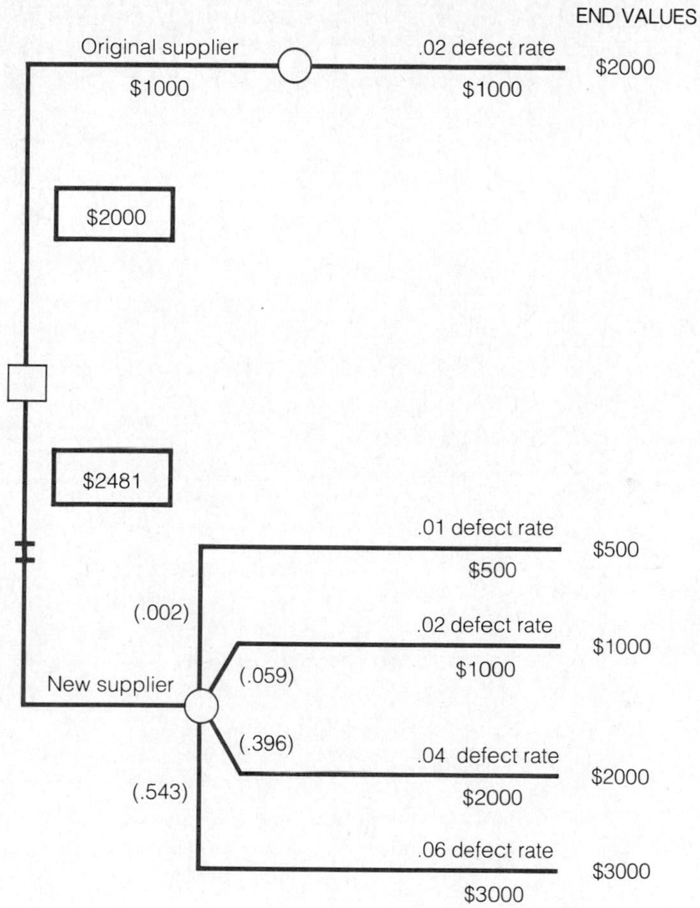

the expected value of perfect information before sampling is:

EVPI = expected cost given uncertainty
− expected cost given perfect information (14-4)

The expected cost given uncertainty is the expected cost of the best decision, or $2000. The expected cost given perfect information is determined by the sum of the costs of the optimal decision for each possible defect rate times the probability of that defect rate occurring. For example, if perfect information indicated the new supplier would have a .01 defect rate, the best decision would be to go with the new supplier, since the $500 cost associated with this defective rate is less than $2000. The probability of this cost occurring is .10, according to the prior probability distribution. We then find $500 × .10 = $50.

If we were certain the new supplier would have a defect rate of .06, the best decision would be to stay with the old supplier, since $2000 < $3000. With a .40 chance that this defect rate will occur, we find $2000 × .40 = $800, which we add to the $50 determined previously. We continue in this manner until all possible defect rates have been considered, as follows:

Expected cost given perfect information = $500(.10) + $1000(.20) +
$2000(.30) + $2000(.40)
= $1650

Thus, the expected value of perfect information is $2000 − $1650 = $350. This is also the cost of uncertainty prior to sampling.

Now, to determine the cost of uncertainty after sampling, we go through the same steps, except we use the posterior probabilities as the defect rates for the new supplier. The expected cost of the best decision under uncertainty is still $2000, even after sampling. The expected cost given perfect information is determined as follows:

$$\$500(.002) + \$1000(.059) + \$2000(.396) + \$2000(.543) = \$1938$$

The EVPI after sampling is: $2000 − $1938 = $62.

Since the EVPI is also the cost of uncertainty, after sampling the cost of uncertainty is $62. Therefore, the expected cost of uncertainty has been reduced: $350 − $62 = $288. This means that while we would have paid $350 for perfect information prior to sampling, after seeing this sample result we would now pay only $62 for perfect information. The difference of $288 is the psychological value of this sample result. The sample information has a psychological value because it helped confirm our earlier decision. We should point out, however, that under this definition of the cost of uncertainty, a sample can actually increase the cost of uncertainty and therefore have negative psychological value.

VALUE OF SAMPLE BEFORE RESULTS ARE KNOWN

Regardless of which viewpoint you subscribe to about the value of sample information, from a practical standpoint, both approaches have a problem because the valuation is done *after* the sample result is known. In most actual situations, the decision maker cannot know the sample results *before* deciding to sample. Since the decision maker is concerned with whether to invest in new information—and if so, how much to pay—he or she must determine the expected value of the sample prior to sampling.

Let's reconsider the Amalgamated Manufacturing example. This time, assume the purchasing manager is considering selecting a sample of 100 components and is concerned with the expected value of the information in a sample of 100. He wants to know the value of the sample information before actually observing the sample results.

To make this determination, we must first recognize that the possible outcomes of the sample range from 0 to 100 defectives. In the earlier example we learned that if the new supplier's 100-unit sample has 5 defective cams, the best decision is to remain with the present supplier. If the sample has more than 5 defectives, the new supplier will look even worse, and the decision will continue to remain with the original supplier. But what would the decision be if fewer than 5 defectives are found?

Let us consider what happens if we find 3 defectives in the sample of 100. Table 14-7 shows the Bayesian revision and the resulting posterior probabilities. We can

Table 14-7 POSTERIOR PROBABILITIES WHEN $n = 100$, $x_1 = 3$

Defect Rate (p)	Prior Probability	Conditional Probability	Joint Probability	Posterior Probability
.01	.10	.0610	.00610	.045
.02	.20	.1823	.03646	.267
.04	.30	.1973	.05919	.434
.06	.40	.0864	.03456	.254
	1.00		.13631	1.000

Table 14-8 POSTERIOR PROBABILITIES WHEN $n = 100$, $x_1 = 4$

Defect Rate (p)	Prior Probability	Conditional Probability	Joint Probability	Posterior Probability
.01	.10	.0149	.00149	.011
.02	.20	.0902	.01804	.136
.04	.30	.1994	.05982	.450
.06	.40	.1338	.05352	.403
	1.00		.13287	1.000

now calculate the expected cost for the new supplier:

$$E(\text{new supplier cost}) = \$500(.045) + \$1000(.267) + \$2000(.434) + \$3000(.254) = \$1919.50$$

The expected cost of staying with the original supplier is \$2000. Thus, if the sample yields 3 defectives, the new supplier would be selected, since $\$1919.50 < \$2000$. If fewer than 3 defectives were observed, the new supplier would look even better and would be the choice based upon expected cost.

Since we now know the sample has 5 or more defectives, the best decision is to remain with the present supplier; with 3 or fewer defectives, the best decision is to switch suppliers. To finalize the decision rule, we need to determine what happens when 4 defectives are found.

Table 14-8 shows the Bayesian revision and the posterior probabilities when 4 defectives are found in the sample of 100. Using these posterior probabilities, the expected cost for the new supplier is:

$$E(\text{new supplier cost}) = \$500(.011) + \$1000(.136) + \$2000(.450) + \$3000(.403) = \$2250.50$$

Since $\$2250.50 > \$2000$, the best decision—if 4 defectives are observed in the sample of 100—is not to switch suppliers.

We now have our completed decision rule: If $x_1 \leq 3$, $n = 100$, switch suppliers; if $x_1 > 3$, $n = 100$, remain with the present supplier.

Now, assuming that we use this decision rule, the next step in determining the value of sample information is to consider the sample as yielding only two possible outcomes: switch suppliers ($x_1 \leq 3$) or remain with the present supplier ($x_1 > 3$). Table 14-9 shows the Bayesian revision assuming the sample information has $x_1 \leq 3$. The conditional probabilities are *cumulative probabilities* found by adding the probabilities of 3 or fewer defectives: $P(0) + P(1) + P(2) + P(3)$. Note that the posterior

Table 14-9 POSTERIOR PROBABILITIES WHEN $n = 100$, $x_1 \leq 3$

Defect Rate (p)	Prior Probability	Conditional Probability	Joint Probability	Posterior Probability
.01	.10	.9816	.09816	.215
.02	.20	.8590	.17180	.377
.04	.30	.4295	.12885	.283
.06	.40	.1430	.05720	.125
	1.00		.45601	1.000

probabilities reflect the general information that the sample had $x_1 \leq 3$ defectives. If $x_1 \leq 3$ defectives occur, according to the decision rule the new cam supplier would be chosen. The expected cost associated with choosing the new supplier, assuming the decision rule is applied, is:

$$E(\text{new supplier cost}) = \$500(.215) + \$1000(.377) + \$2000(.283) + \$3000(.125) = \$1425.50$$

This is the *expected cost from the sampling plan* if $x_1 \leq 3$ defectives are observed.

The sum of the joint probabilities in Table 14-9 is .45601. This is the probability the sample will have $x_1 \leq 3$ defectives, given the prior state of mind about the new supplier's defect rate. Thus, there is a .45601 chance that the decision will be to switch suppliers.

If the number of defectives in the sample is greater than 3, the decision will be to stay with the present supplier, for an expected cost of $2000. The probability that this will occur is .54399 (1.0 − .45601). Thus, the expected cost given the sampling plan is:

$$E(\text{cost}|\text{sampling plan}) = \$1425.50(.45601) + \$2000(.54399) = \$1738.02$$

Therefore, before the results of the sample are known, Amalgamated can expect costs of $1738.02 if the sampling plan is used. We can compare this with the expected cost of $2000 with no sampling (see the earlier analysis, prior to sampling). Thus, the expected value of the sampling information (EVSI) from a sample of $n = 100$ is:

$$EVSI = \$2000 - \$1738.02 = \$261.98$$

The Amalgamated Manufacturing Company would be willing to pay as much as $261.98 for a sample of 100 components, given the prior state of knowledge about the prospective new supplier's defective rate, and would pay this price before knowing the sample results.

COMPUTING EXPECTED NET GAIN FROM SAMPLING

In the Amalgamated example we have so far not mentioned the cost of sampling; our computations have centered strictly on the value of the sample. However, in most cases, sampling does not come without a price. Quite often some fixed sampling costs occur regardless of the number of units sampled; in addition, generally a variable sampling cost occurs that depends on the number of units sampled. We can compute the total sampling cost (*TSC*) as follows:

$$TSC = \text{fixed cost} + \text{variable cost} \tag{14-5}$$

where variable cost is the cost per unit times the number of units.

Then, the **expected net gain from sampling** (ENGS) is the average net benefit from the information associated with a sample of a given size when the costs of sampling are considered. It is computed by finding the difference between the expected value of the sample and the total sampling cost:

$$ENGS = EVSI - TSC \tag{14-6}$$

Suppose the fixed cost of sampling in the Amalgamated example is $100.00 and the variable cost per unit is $.10. Then the total sampling cost is:

$$TSC = \$100.00 + (\$.10)(100) = \$110.00$$

The net gain from sampling is:

$$ENGS = \$261.98 - \$110.00 = \$151.98$$

Thus, in determining a sample size, we would be willing to increase the size as long as the net gain from sampling remains positive. In the next section, we will show how you can use the MASTER computer software to determine the net gain from sampling and determine the optimal sample size.

14-5 COMPUTER APPLICATIONS

The decision-analysis techniques introduced in this chapter can be performed manually if you have the patience to work through the computations. However, like most of the other management science techniques introduced in this text, decision analysis is easier with the aid of a computer. The MASTER software which accompanies this text contains several decision-analysis programs, including programs to perform Bayesian revision analysis and to determine the net gain from sampling when the sampling distribution is binomial. By continuing the Amalgamated Manufacturing example, we will demonstrate the use of MASTER to deal with the net gain from sampling and to determine the optimal sample size.

Figure 14-3 shows the MASTER main menu. We select the Decision Analysis option to call up the Decision Analysis Submenu (Figure 14-4), and then select Optimal Sample Size Analysis. The data-entry screen for this program (Figure 14-5) shows that we are using the same data we used in section 14-4. (Since this example is based on selecting the alternative with the minimum expected cost and all values are costs, the values entered are in the form of negative payoffs.) MASTER determines the net gain from sampling for a range of user-specified sample sizes. In this example, we have specified sample sizes of 100 to 120.

The resulting output is shown in Figure 14-6. First, we are given information based only on priors. As we found when we worked the problem manually, the best decision is to go with the original supplier (alternative 2), since the expected value of $-\$2000 > -\$2050$ for alternative 1. The expected value given perfect information is $-\$1650$ which means that the cost of uncertainty is \$350. Next, Figure 14-6 shows the optimal decision rule for each of the sample sizes investigated. We see that for this range of sample sizes (100–120), the decision rule is always the same: if the number of defectives (x_1) is greater than (GT) 3, take alternative 2; otherwise, take alternative 1.

The final output shown in Figure 14-6 is the net gain from sampling for each sample size. Note that the net gain for a sample of 100 is \$151.83, which is the same

Figure 14-3
MASTER main menu

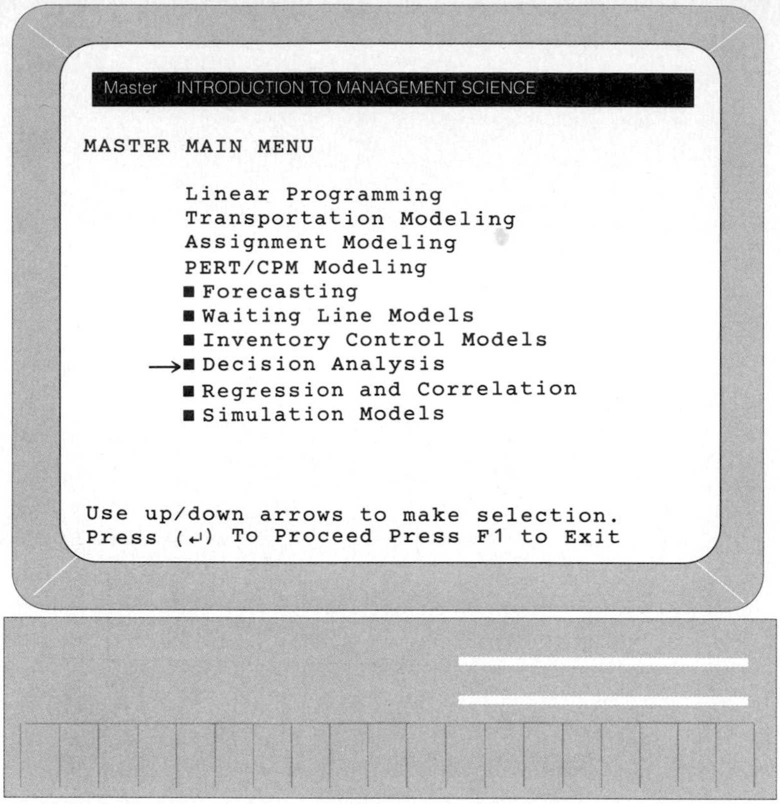

```
Master   INTRODUCTION TO MANAGEMENT SCIENCE

MASTER MAIN MENU

         Linear Programming
         Transportation Modeling
         Assignment Modeling
         PERT/CPM Modeling
         ■ Forecasting
         ■ Waiting Line Models
         ■ Inventory Control Models
      →  ■ Decision Analysis
         ■ Regression and Correlation
         ■ Simulation Models

Use up/down arrows to make selection.
Press (↵) To Proceed Press F1 to Exit
```

Figure 14-4
MASTER submenu for decision analysis

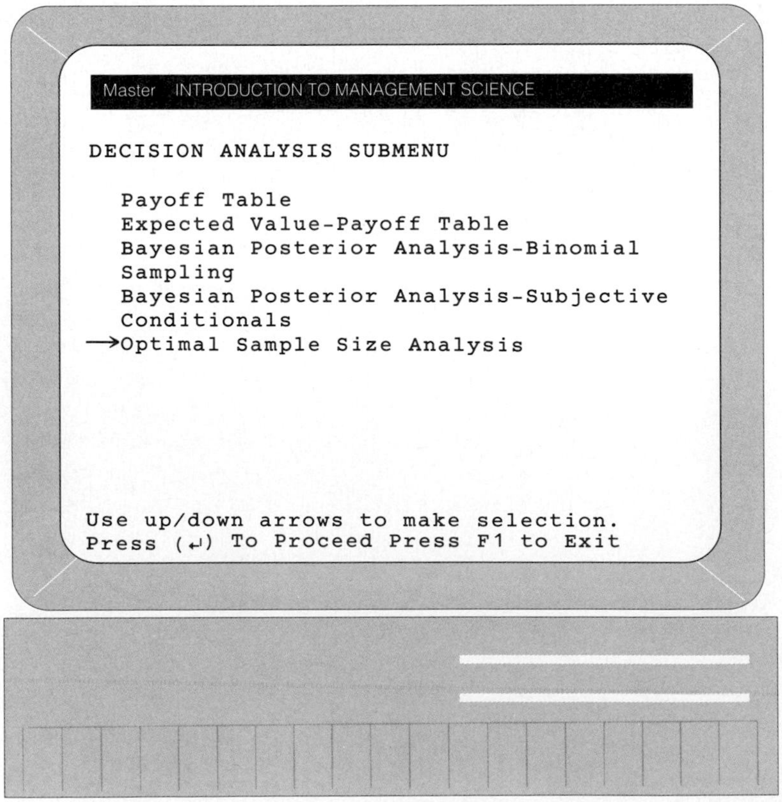

```
Master   INTRODUCTION TO MANAGEMENT SCIENCE

DECISION ANALYSIS SUBMENU

   Payoff Table
   Expected Value-Payoff Table
   Bayesian Posterior Analysis-Binomial
   Sampling
   Bayesian Posterior Analysis-Subjective
   Conditionals
 →Optimal Sample Size Analysis

Use up/down arrows to make selection.
Press (↵) To Proceed Press F1 to Exit
```

Master INTRODUCTION TO MANAGEMENT SCIENCE

EXAMPLE NAME

	Values	State	Priors	$ Payoff
# States	4	.01	.10	-500
Altern $	-2000	.02	.20	-1000
Fixed Cost	100	.04	.30	-2000
Var Cost	.10	.06	.40	-3000
n-Low	100			
n-High	120			

<F5> Add Row <F6> Add Col <F7> Del Row <F8> Del Col

Figure 14-5

Data-entry screen for optimal sample size analysis

```
                 ALTERNATIVE 1 STATES OF NATURE

FRACTION      PRIORS       PAYOFF

 0.0100       0.1000       -500.00
 0.0200       0.2000      -1000.00
 0.0400       0.3000      -2000.00
 0.0600       0.4000      -3000.00

                 ALTERNATIVE   2   PAYOFF = $       -2000.00

            INFORMATION BASED ONLY ON PRIORS

       BEST DECISION IS TO SELECT ALTERNATIVE 2

            EXPECTED VALUE FOR ALT. 1 = $       -2050.00

            VALUE OF ALTERNATIVE 2 = $       -2000.00

       EXPECTED VALUE GIVEN PERFECT INFORMATION =       -1650.00

       COST OF UNCERTAINTY GIVEN BEST DECISION =       350.00

       OPTIMAL DECISION RULE FOR GIVEN SAMPLE SIZE

SAMPLE SIZE =  100      IF X1 GT   3 TAKE ALTERNATIVE  2
                        IF X1 LE    3 TAKE ALTERNATIVE  1
SAMPLE SIZE =  101      IF X1 GT   3 TAKE ALTERNATIVE  2
                        IF X1 LE    3 TAKE ALTERNATIVE  1
SAMPLE SIZE =  102      IF X1 GT   3 TAKE ALTERNATIVE  2
                        IF X1 LE    3 TAKE ALTERNATIVE  1
SAMPLE SIZE =  103      IF X1 GT   3 TAKE ALTERNATIVE  2
                        IF X1 LE    3 TAKE ALTERNATIVE  1
SAMPLE SIZE =  104      IF X1 GT   3 TAKE ALTERNATIVE  2
                        IF X1 LE    3 TAKE ALTERNATIVE  1
SAMPLE SIZE =  105      IF X1 GT   3 TAKE ALTERNATIVE  2
                        IF X1 LE    3 TAKE ALTERNATIVE  1
SAMPLE SIZE =  106      IF X1 GT   3 TAKE ALTERNATIVE  2
                        IF X1 LE    3 TAKE ALTERNATIVE  1
SAMPLE SIZE =  107      IF X1 GT   3 TAKE ALTERNATIVE  2
                        IF X1 LE    3 TAKE ALTERNATIVE  1
SAMPLE SIZE =  108      IF X1 GT   3 TAKE ALTERNATIVE  2
                        IF X1 LE    3 TAKE ALTERNATIVE  1
SAMPLE SIZE =  109      IF X1 GT   3 TAKE ALTERNATIVE  2
                        IF X1 LE    3 TAKE ALTERNATIVE  1
SAMPLE SIZE =  110      IF X1 GT   3 TAKE ALTERNATIVE  2
                        IF X1 LE    3 TAKE ALTERNATIVE  1
```

Figure 14-6

MASTER output for optimal sample size analysis (figure continued on next page)

```
SAMPLE SIZE =  111       IF X1 GT   3 TAKE ALTERNATIVE  2
                         IF X1 LE    3 TAKE ALTERNATIVE  1
SAMPLE SIZE =  112       IF X1 GT   3 TAKE ALTERNATIVE  2
                         IF X1 LE    3 TAKE ALTERNATIVE  1
SAMPLE SIZE =  113       IF X1 GT   3 TAKE ALTERNATIVE  2
                         IF X1 LE    3 TAKE ALTERNATIVE  1
SAMPLE SIZE =  114       IF X1 GT   3 TAKE ALTERNATIVE  2
                         IF X1 LE    3 TAKE ALTERNATIVE  1
SAMPLE SIZE =  115       IF X1 GT   3 TAKE ALTERNATIVE  2
                         IF X1 LE    3 TAKE ALTERNATIVE  1
SAMPLE SIZE =  116       IF X1 GT   3 TAKE ALTERNATIVE  2
                         IF X1 LE    3 TAKE ALTERNATIVE  1
SAMPLE SIZE =  117       IF X1 GT   3 TAKE ALTERNATIVE  2
                         IF X1 LE    3 TAKE ALTERNATIVE  1
SAMPLE SIZE =  118       IF X1 GT   3 TAKE ALTERNATIVE  2
                         IF X1 LE    3 TAKE ALTERNATIVE  1
SAMPLE SIZE =  119       IF X1 GT   3 TAKE ALTERNATIVE  2
                         IF X1 LE    3 TAKE ALTERNATIVE  1
SAMPLE SIZE =  120       IF X1 GT   3 TAKE ALTERNATIVE  2
                         IF X1 LE    3 TAKE ALTERNATIVE  1

     NET GAIN FROM SAMPLING

             SAMPLES OF 100 TO 120

          FIXED COST OF SAMPLING = $      100.00

          VARIABLE COST OF SAMPLING = $      0.10
SAMPLE SIZE =  100     NET GAIN =         151.83
SAMPLE SIZE =  101     NET GAIN =         152.98
SAMPLE SIZE =  102     NET GAIN =         154.06
SAMPLE SIZE =  103     NET GAIN =         155.07
SAMPLE SIZE =  104     NET GAIN =         156.00
SAMPLE SIZE =  105     NET GAIN =         156.87
SAMPLE SIZE =  106     NET GAIN =         157.67
SAMPLE SIZE =  107     NET GAIN =         158.40
SAMPLE SIZE =  108     NET GAIN =         159.07
SAMPLE SIZE =  109     NET GAIN =         159.68
SAMPLE SIZE =  110     NET GAIN =         160.22
SAMPLE SIZE =  111     NET GAIN =         160.71
SAMPLE SIZE =  112     NET GAIN =         161.14
SAMPLE SIZE =  113     NET GAIN =         161.51
SAMPLE SIZE =  114     NET GAIN =         161.82
SAMPLE SIZE =  115     NET GAIN =         162.08
SAMPLE SIZE =  116     NET GAIN =         162.30
SAMPLE SIZE =  117     NET GAIN =         162.45
SAMPLE SIZE =  118     NET GAIN =         162.56
SAMPLE SIZE =  119     NET GAIN =         162.62
SAMPLE SIZE =  120     NET GAIN =         162.64
```

Figure 14-6 Continued

(except for rounding differences) as we manually computed earlier. This takes into account the $100 fixed cost of sampling and the $.10 per unit sampling cost. We see that as the sample size is increased to 120, the net gain also increases, indicating that the information value of each additional unit sampled is greater than the $.10 marginal cost of sampling the unit.

This program takes several minutes to run because of all the computations required to determine the optimal decision rule and the net gain from sampling. However, it is certainly far faster than trying to do the work manually. The computer enables the decision maker to explore a wider range of issues than could be explored otherwise. For instance, if you are using MASTER, we suggest that you modify the sampling-cost figures by making the fixed cost lower and the per unit cost higher, and observe the impact on the net gains for various sample sizes. You should find that as the incremental sampling cost increases, a point will be reached where additional sampling is not justified.

14-6 SUMMARY AND CONCLUSIONS

The idea of incorporating sample information into a decision-analysis problem has great intuitive appeal, since new information affects the decision maker's state of mind about the likelihood of uncertain outcomes. This chapter has presented a formal means for introducing new information into the decision process through the use of Bayes's rule. We showed how to merge the information in the prior probability distribution with the information in the sample to arrive at a posterior probability distribution. The Bayesian revision process is a central part of decision analysis and is a significant step toward making it more accessible to decision makers.

This chapter has demonstrated the use of Bayes's rule for situations when the sampling distribution is binomial. We have also demonstrated the Bayesian revision process when the sample information, like the priors, is subjective. Mini Case 14H, at the end of this chapter, illustrates a situation in which the Poisson distribution is used in the Bayesian revision process.

While incorporating new information into the decision analysis is desirable, the value of the new information must exceed its cost. In this chapter, we introduced two approaches for determining the value of sample information after the information has been observed. One approach is based upon the increase that occurs in the expected payoff for the best decision after the sample information is known. Under this approach, if the sample information does not lead us to change our decision, the sample information has no value. From a psychological viewpoint, we define the value of the sample information as the diference between the cost of uncertainty before the sample and the cost of uncertainty after the sample. However, under this approach, the sample information can actually increase the cost of uncertainty and therefore have negative value. Both approaches have their limitations.

However, while the two approaches to valuing information after the information is known have shortcomings, in most instances the real problem facing the decision maker is how much the sample information will be worth before the results of the sample are known. This chapter has shown how to evaluate a sample of a given size before selecting the sample.

Chapter Equations

Rules for determining conditional probability

$$P(A_1|B) = \frac{P(B \text{ and } A_1)}{P(B)} = \frac{P(A_1)\ P(B|A_1)}{P(B)} \quad (14\text{-}1)$$

$$P(B) = \Sigma\ P(B \text{ and } A_i) = \Sigma\ P(A_i)\ P(B|A_i) \quad (14\text{-}2)$$

$$P(A_1|B) = \frac{P(A_1)\ P(B|A_1)}{\Sigma\ P(A_i)\ P(B|A_i)} \quad (14\text{-}3)$$

Expected value of perfect information

$$EVPI = \text{expected cost given uncertainty} - \text{expected cost given perfect information} \quad (14\text{-}4)$$

Total sampling cost

$$TSC = \text{fixed cost} + \text{variable cost} \quad (14\text{-}5)$$

where: variable cost = unit cost × number of units

Expected net gain from sampling

$$ENGS = EVSI - TSC \quad (14\text{-}6)$$

Solved Problem

PROBLEM The American Press Corporation is considering setting up a division to publish a weekly newsmagazine. Upper management estimates that the weekly fixed cost of establishing the division will be \$300,000 and that the variable cost per magazine printed will be \$.50. The magazine will sell for \$1.50 per copy. The marketing department estimates that of the company's current 1 million subscribers, the following possibilities exist with respect to the percentage who will buy this new magazine:

Proportion Buying	Prior Probability
.20	.10
.30	.30
.40	.40
.50	.20
	1.00

a. Considering only the prior information, should the company go ahead with the magazine idea? Base your decision on expected profits.

b. Suppose a random sample of 20 newspaper subscribers are selected and 5 say they will buy the magazine. Assuming that the binomial distribution applies, determine the posterior probability distribution for the proportion of customers who will buy the new magazine.

c. Given the sample information and the posterior probabilities found in part **b**, what decision should the company now make?

Solution a. The first step is to determine the profit for each possible level of demand, as follows:

Proportion Buying	Profit	Prior Probability
.20	−$100,000	.10
.30	$ 0	.30
.40	$100,000	.40
.50	$200,000	.20

The expected profit associated with publishing the magazine is:

$$E(\text{profit}) = -\$100{,}000(.10) + \$0(.30) + \$100{,}000(.40) + \$200{,}000(.20) = \$70{,}000$$

Since $70,000 is greater than $0 (which would be the "profit" if the magazine is not published), the best decision is to publish the magazine, for an expected profit of $70,000.

b. The posterior probabilities are found by constructing a Bayesian revision table, using $n = 20$ and $x_1 = 5$.

Proportion Buying	Prior Probability	Conditional Probability	Joint Probability	Posterior Probability
.20	.10	.1746	.01746	.1680
.30	.30	.1789	.05367	.5164
.40	.40	.0746	.02984	.2871
.50	.20	.0148	.00296	.0285
	1.00		.10393	1.0000

c. To determine the best decision after observing the sample information, we find the expected profit using the posterior probabilities, as follows:

$$\begin{aligned} E(\text{profit}) &= -\$100{,}000(.1680) + \$0(.5164) + \$100{,}000(.2871) + \$200{,}000(.0285) \\ &= \$17{,}610 \end{aligned}$$

Although the expected profit is smaller than before the sample information was known, $17,610 is still greater than $0 so the decision would not change. (Note that we could argue that the information in this sample had no value since it did not change the decision.)

General Questions and Assignments

1. Discuss the difference between a *prior* probability distribution and a *posterior* probability distribution.
2. Suppose you were faced with selecting between two competing brands of diskettes for a corporate purchase of 200,000 diskettes. The two competitors charge the same price. One competitor is known to provide 98% defect-free diskettes. Less is known about the other competitor. You have decided to sample from the second competitor's inventory. Discuss whether there is an advantage in taking several small samples totaling 100 diskettes or just sampling the full 100 at one time.
3. Discuss in your own terms the steps in the *Bayesian revision process*.
4. The chapter discussed two approaches for determining the value of sample information after the information is known. Discuss these two approaches and their differences.
5. Discuss why determining the value of a sample prior to sampling is more practical than waiting until after the sample information has been observed.
6. Describe in your own words the process for determining the value of sample information prior to taking the sample.

7. Locate several articles in the library which deal with the value of sample information. Write a report discussing these articles. As part of your discussion, comment on how useful you think these articles would be to a manager.

Exercises and Application Problems

1. Sylvia Taylor Manufacturing produces PC keyboards at three plants in the Baltimore area. Plant 1 makes 50% of the keyboards, of which 5% contain some defect. Plant 2 accounts for 30% of the keyboards and has a 7% defect rate. Finally, plant 3 makes 20% of the keyboards, of which only 3% are defective. After production, the keyboards are packed in identical boxes and sent to a centralized warehouse, where they are shelved in such a random manner that there is no way to determine their origin.

   Sylvia Taylor Manufacturing offers a 1-year replacement warranty on defective parts, and last year the company incurred a warranty cost of $900,000. The corporate accountants want to divide this cost among the three plants according to the rate of defective keyboards produced by each plant. Calculate this cost breakdown for the accountants.
2. The Crown Sealant Company has three plants where it mixes silicon-based sealing materials used extensively in new home construction. Forty percent of all the material is mixed at plant A, 50% at plant B, and 10% at plant C. Although Crown would like to believe it has a good quality control system at each plant, sometimes bad batches do get through. For instance, in the past, 10% of the batches produced by plant A have been bad, as have 8% from plant B and 12% from plant C.

   Suppose a bad batch has just been discovered at a construction site. Which plant most likely provided the bad material?
3. The New York Tax Commission has randomly selected a taxpayer for a basic audit. Past records indicate that in the area from which this taxpayer filed, 20% of the returns have some sort of error. In a basic audit, the entire return is examined. But basic audits are not perfect; sometimes they indicate a problem when no problem exists and at other times indicate no problem when, in fact, a problem does exist. The chance that a basic audit will indicate no problem when there is a problem is 20%. The probability that the basic audit will indicate a problem when, in fact, no problem exists is 5%. Suppose the basic audit of this taxpayer indicates a problem. What is the probability that there really is a problem with the tax return?
4. A manufacturer of hard disk drives for personal computers has two suppliers of the magnetic media used in the drives. Vendor 1 supplies 40% of the magnetic media and vendor 2 supplies 60%. Tests have shown that 15% of vendor 1's magnetic media have defective spots which result in bad sectors on the disks. Conversely, 5% of vendor 2's media result in bad sectors. The disk manufacturer has just found some bad magnetic media in its inventory. Which vendor most likely supplied these materials?
5. As part of a VCR manufacturer's quality control procedures, an inspector judgmentally selects 15% of all the VCRs produced and gives them a thorough inspection. Experience has shown that 15% of all the VCRs made at this plant have problems with magnetic-sensing head alignment. Past records show that of those VCRs selected for inspection, 30% were actually good. This means that the inspector does provide some value in the selection process, since proportionally fewer good VCRs (30%) than the population as whole (85%) actually get inspected needlessly. Suppose that a recently purchased VCR proves to be good. What is the probability it was completely inspected?

Problems 6 through 8 refer to the following situation.

When the Oliviera Milling and Frame Company has correctly set up its manufacturing process, only 5% of the products off the line are defective. But when the process is set up incorrectly, 20% of the products are defective. Past experience indicates a 90% chance that the process will be set up properly.

6. Suppose a sample of 10 items has been randomly selected and 3 have been found defective. Use this sample information to revise the probability that the process is set up correctly.
7. After the initial sample of 10 taken in problem 6, a second sample of 15 yielded 4 defective products. Combine this new sample information with the revised probabilities found in problem 6 to arrive at new posterior probabilities.
8. How would the posterior probabilities calculated in problem 7 differ from the posterior probabilities that would be determined if one sample of 25 was selected and 7 defectives observed? Show the calculations to support your answer.
9. Executives of a cable TV network are considering forming an affiliated cable service to offer exclusive sporting events. They estimate the monthly fixed cost of the affiliate will be $5,000,000 and the monthly variable cost per subscriber will be $2.50. The network will charge each subscriber $4.50 per month for the service. The marketing department estimates that of the network's present 10 million customers, the following possibilities exist with respect to the percentage who will subscribe to the new channel:

Proportion Subscribing	Prior Probability
.10	.10
.20	.30
.30	.40
.40	.20
	1.00

   a. Considering only this prior information, should the network go ahead with the new service if its goal is to maximize expected profits?
   b. Suppose a random sample of 20 present subscribers is selected and 7 indicate they will select the new service if it is offered. Assuming the binomial distribution applies, determine the revised or posterior probability for each possible proportion of customers who will subscribe to the service.
   c. Given the sample information in part **b**, what should the network do?
10. Western Bell is considering installing a new message recording system in its service area. The equipment necessary for the system can be leased for $6 million per year, and the annual incremental cost per user is estimated at $60. Western Bell will charge each customer served $10 per month, or $120 per year.

    There are currently 4 million telephone customers in Western Bell's area. The company's marketing department has assessed the following probability distribution for the proportion who will subscribe to the new service:

Proportion Subscribing	Probability
.02	.20
.04	.30
.06	.40
.08	.10
	1.00

   a. Determine the payoffs for each possible proportion.
   b. Analyze the problem facing Western Bell using only prior information. Determine the best decision using the expected-value criterion.

Problems 11 through 13 refer to the following situation.

Green Mountain Corporation has just developed a drug which may be effective in treating arthritis in hunting dogs. Because of the wide variety of genetic patterns in hunting dogs, the company realizes that no drug will be effective in all cases. However, if the drug is a "good" product, improvement will be shown by 80% of the dogs that are treated. If the drug is a "fair" product, 60% of the dogs will show improvement, and if it is a "poor" product, 30% will show improvement. On the basis of their laboratory studies, Green Mountain executives believe the following probabilities apply:

Effectiveness Level	Probability
Good	.30
Fair	.30
Poor	.40
	1.00

11. Suppose a random sample of 25 hunting dogs take the drug and 14 show improvement. Determine the posterior probability for each effectiveness level.
12. Referring to problem 11, two more samples of 25 dogs were given the drug, resulting in improvement for 12 dogs in one sample and 15 dogs in the other. Determine the posterior probability for each effectiveness level.
13. Green Mountan has a policy of not marketing a drug unless the chance that its effectiveness will be at least "fair" exceeds 90%. Using the posterior probabilities determined in problem 12, should the drug be marketed?

Problems 14 through 17 refer to the following situation.

Greg Wojtkowski, operations manager of a company which makes remote-controlled model cars, has to decide whether to lease a new assembly robot or have the current assembly line repaired at a cost of $30,000. Leasing the robot will cost $120,000, but it will decrease the assembly cost of each model car to $10 per unit. The current assembly line, after repair, will assemble the cars sat a cost of $15 each. The finished model cars sell for $20 each. Because consumer buying habits are unpredictable, the demand for the cars is not known with certainty but is expected to occur according to the following probability distribution:

Demand Level	Probability
10,000	.05
15,000	.15
20,000	.20
30,000	.40
50,000	.20
	1.00

14. Construct a payoff table listing the decision alternatives and the payoff associated with each alternative for Greg's decision.
15. What decision should Greg make if his objective is to maximize the expected payoff? Provide a practical justification for your answer.
16. Suppose an independent market research firm has been hired by the model-car manufacturer. The market research report is based in part on sample information gathered by the firm and in part on the researchers' "expert analysis." The results of the marketing study are examined by Greg Wojtkowsi. The report is basically optimistic, but Greg doesn't want to ignore the prior assessments, and in fact wants to include both the prior assessments and the market survey information in the decision. Greg assesses the conditional probability of observing the results of the market survey,

given each possible demand level. These conditional probabilities are:

Demand Level	Conditional Probability P(optimistic survey|demand)
10,000	.05
15,000	.10
20,000	.30
30,000	.50
50,000	.80

Use this information to determine the revised or posterior probability associated with each demand level.

17. Considering the posterior probabilities calculated in problem 16, should Greg fix the current assembly line or lease the robot?

Problems 18 through 20 are related to problem 9, which discussed the television network that was considering developing a new cable sports service. The marketing department determined the following distribution for the percentage of present subscribers who would sign up for the new service.

Proportion Subscribing	Prior Probability
.10	.10
.20	.30
.30	.40
.40	.20
	1.00

18. Network executives have contracted with Fredricka Goldman, a media consultant, to analyze the new service. Goldman has reported the following distribution, indicating her assessment of the number of customers who would subscribe to the new service.

Proportion Subscribing	Probability
.10	.30
.20	.30
.30	.20
.40	.20
	1.00

What decision do you recommend to the network executives, using only Goldman's probability distribution and the expected-value criterion?

19. Upon further reflection, the executives decide they would like to use both the initial assessment from the marketing department and Goldman's assessment in making their decision. Perform the necessary calculations to combine the two distributions and indicate the correct decision.
20. Now combine the probability assessments from both the marketing department and Goldman with the sample information to determine the recommended decision for the network. Does this decision depend on whether Goldman's distribution is considered before or after the sample information is gathered?
21. The Civic Opera Company is considering whether to have a party for the 4000 people whose donations allow them to be termed "friends of the opera." Assume the following distribution represents those who would attend the party:

Proportion Attending	Probability
.20	.30
.25	.40
.30	.20
.35	.10
	1.00

Cost estimates indicate a fixed setup and advertising cost of $30,000 plus a variable cost of $20 per person attending. Tickets will be sold for $40. Considering only this information, should the party be held? Also determine the expected value of perfect information.

Problems 22 through 24 refer to the following situation.

The Minch Artificial Intelligence Group has the opportunity to participate in a medical research project at Georgetown Medical Center. If the project is successful, the Minch Group will net $7.5 million. If the project is a failure, the group will lose $4.5 million. The executive committee has worked out the following probability assessments for the three possible outcomes:

State of Nature	Prior Probability
Successful ($7,500,000)	.30
Marginally successful ($1,250,000)	.30
Failure (−$4,500,000)	.40
	1.00

If the Minch Group does not participate in this project, it will accept an Internal Revenue Service contract with a sure profit of $400,000.

22. Considering only the prior probabilities, what decision should the Minch Group make if it wishes to maximize expected profit?
23. Suppose the Minch Group could obtain perfect information about the medical research project. What would its value be to the group? What is the cost of being uncertain?
24. If the Minch Group could hire consultants to provide some information about the outcomes of the proposed project, what is the absolute maximum the group should be willing to pay for this information? Under what conditions would it pay this much?

Problems 25 through 29 are based on the following situation.

A major automobile manufacturer currently buys the sound systems for its cars from Everson Electronics, but it is considering changing to Krado Audio Systems. Everson's charge of $201 for each sound system includes a 5-year warranty. Over the past few years, 5% of Everson's systems have required replacement under the warranty. However, the auto maker ultimately covers the warranty costs because the system price is set to reflect the possibility of repair.

Krado, which proposes to charge $200 for each sound system, claims its product is more reliable than Everson's. After initial testing, the auto maker has assessed the following probability distribution for the proportion of Krado systems requiring warranty work.

Proportion Requiring Work	Prior Probability
.03	.20
.04	.30
.05	.20
.06	.20
.07	.10
	1.00

25. If the auto maker wants to buy 100,000 sound systems, which supplier should it buy them from, using only prior information as a basis for the decision?
26. Suppose the auto maker can obtain perfect information about the proportion of Krado's systems which will require replacement. What would be the value of this perfect information?
27. Suppose Krado has offered a free sample of 100 sound systems to the auto maker for testing. Test results indicate that 6 sound systems will require warranty work. Given this sample information, what is the best decision for the auto maker?
28. Considering the information in problem 27, what is the value of this sample information after the sample has been selected?
29. Suppose the cost of sampling is broken into two parts, a fixed cost of $500 and a variable cost of $10 per unit sampled. What is the ENGS for a sample size of 100?

Chapter Glossary

Bayesian revision analysis The technique of incorporating sample information into the decision process.

Conditional probability The probability that event *A* will occur, given that a second event, *B*, has already occurred.

Expected net gain from sampling (ENGS) The average net benefit from the information associated with a sample of a given size when the costs of sampling are considered.

Joint probability The probability of the simultaneous occurrence of two or more events; it represents the chances of observing both the sample information and a particular state of nature.

Posterior probability The revised probability which combines the prior probability and new information from the sample.

Prior probability Probability that an event will occur, as assessed prior to the acquisition of any additional relevant information.

Chapter References

BOOKS

Baird, Bruce F. *Managerial Decision Making under Uncertainty.* New York: Wiley, 1989.

Brown, R. V., A. S. Kahr, and C. Peterson. *Decision Analysis for the Manager.* New York: Holt, 1974.

Bunn, D. W. *Applied Decision Analysis.* New York: McGraw-Hill, 1984.

Felson, J. *Decision Making under Uncertainty.* New York: CBS Business and Professional Publishing, 1979.

Gregory, G. *Decision Analysis.* New York: Plenum, 1988.

Holloway, C. *Decision Making under Uncertainty: Models and Choices.* Englewood Cliffs, N.J.: Prentice-Hall, 1979.

Keeney, R. L., and H. Raiffa. *Decisions with Multiple Objectives: Preferences and Value Trade-offs.* New York: Wiley, 1976.

Raiffa, H. *Decision Analysis.* Reading, Mass.: Addison-Wesley, 1968.

Sampson, D. *Managerial Decision Analysis.* Homewood, Ill.: Irwin, 1988.

Schlaifer, R. *Analysis of Decisions under Uncertainty.* New York: McGraw-Hill, 1969.

Winkler, R. *Introduction to Bayesian Inference and Decision.* New York: Holt, 1972.

ARTICLES

Bell, D. "Regret in Decision Making under Uncertainty." *Operations Research,* Vol. 30, 1982.

Berger, P. D., and A. Gerstenfeld. "Decision Analysis for Increased Highway Safety." *Sloan Management Review,* Spring 1971.

Brown, R. V. "Do Managers Find Decision Theory Useful?" *Harvard Business Review,* January–February 1970.

Hespos, R. F., and P. A. Strassmann. "Stochastic Decision Trees for the Analysis of Investment Decisions." *Management Science,* Vol. 11, 1965.

Howard, R. A. "An Assessment of Decision Analysis." *Operations Research,* Vol. 28, 1980.

Keeney, R. L. "Decision Analysis: An Overview." *Operations Research,* Vol. 30, 1982.

Ulvila, J. W., and R. V. Brown. "Decision Analysis Comes of Age." *Harvard Business Review,* September 1982.

Mini Cases

CASE 14A
THE NFL DRAFT

Each spring, the entire National Football League (NFL) conducts a draft of available players. The draft has 26 rounds; if a team has not traded its draft picks to another team, it will have one pick in each round. The order of picks in each round depends on how the team finished in its league the year before. The teams pick in inverse order, with the last-place team having first pick in each round. The object of the draft is for a team to select players who can help them win in the future.

Suppose our team has the sixth pick in each round this year. Typically, the most promising prospects are selected in the first three rounds, so a team's first selections are very important. The teams keep their draft choices a closely guarded secret. Since several teams often want to draft the same player, by the time a team gets a turn to pick, its choice for that round may have already been selected. Each team plans a draft strategy to try to ensure that it gets the players it wants.

Our team is very interested in two top players, a quarterback and a defensive lineman, and would like to draft both. However, there are some uncertainties involved. While we feel certain that both players will be available on our first pick, we are unsure whether the player not drafted first will still be available for our second pick. On the morning of the draft, considering all available information, we subjectively assess the following probability distributions for each player being available on the second round:

Quarterback		**Defensive Lineman**	
Availability	Probability	Availability	Probability
Yes	.40	Yes	.70
No	.60	No	.30

Since both players are considered equally desirable choices by our team's general manager, we decide to make our first pick the player with the least chance of being available in the second round. Considering current information, we think there is only a .40 chance that the quarterback will be available, compared with a .70 chance for the lineman. The decision is to draft the quarterback and hope to get the lineman in round 2.

However, 4 hours prior to draft time, a trade is announced between two other teams. Team A has traded away two backup defensive linemen and a wide receiver for the number 14 selection in the first round. Team A now has two selections in the draft ahead of our round 2 slot. The wheels start turning in our team's temporary draft headquarters. Does the trade mean team A will now be more interested in our lineman choice? Will team A draft him before we get a chance in round 2? How does this affect the chances that the quarterback would be taken before our pick in round 2? After considering this issue carefully, the general manager thinks there is a .2 chance that team A would have made this trade given it was not planning to pick our lineman. He also assesses a .6 chance that team A would have made this trade given it was planning to take our lineman. The general manager believes that team A's trade has no particular bearing on the quarterback's status.

Clearly this trade information ought to affect our assessment of the defensive lineman's availability for our second round pick. However, the general manager is unclear about how to use this information and is not sure what to do in round 1 of the draft.

CASE 14B

QUALITY BAKERY

Quality Bakery, managed by R. D. Poteet, makes specialty breads for distribution through retail outlets in several western states. Poteet recently read an article in a trade magazine describing a sequential quality control sampling system. The sequential sampling system involves a process whereby a specified number of loaves are tested and the numbers of good and defective loaves are recorded. After looking at the results of this sample, the bakery can decide to either test more loaves in the same batch or stop sampling and make an accept/reject decision regarding the batch. Depending on the cost of sampling and the time available, the sequential sampling can have any number of stages, with any number of loaves tested at each stage until the sample information indicates that a final decision should be made.

Poteet has been somewhat concerned lately that his bakery's quality control is slipping. A suggestion in the journal article was to introduce the system by sampling one loaf and, if necessary, one more. Thus, initially the sampling would be limited to two stages with a total of two loaves tested.

At Quality Bakery, a batch contains 400 loaves. Cost accountants have determined that each loaf costs Quality \$.10 to make, including labor and raw materials. Packaging and shipping account for an additional \$.01 per loaf. (If a batch is rejected, the loaves are not packaged or shipped.) The selling price of the loaves is \$.25 each.

If a defective loaf is sold, the cost to Quality in lost goodwill is estimated to be \$1 per loaf. From past experience, Poteet knows the following proportions of defective loaves are possible and should occur with a frequency represented by the associated probabilities:

Proportion Defective	Prior Probability
.00	.40
.01	.30
.02	.20
1.00	.10
	1.00

This probability distribution indicates that a batch will be either good, fairly good, or completely defective, depending on the mixing process. A totally bad batch will occur if an ingredient is left out or if bad yeast is used in the mixing process.

R. D. Poteet is attempting to establish the decision rules under the two-stage sampling plan with a sample size of one loaf at each stage. He has decided to ignore sampling costs.

CASE 14C

ARTISTIC AMERICANS, INC.

Artistic Americans, Inc., a company that produces television specials, has just been approached with a new idea for a holiday special. The cost of producing this special is estimated at \$825,000. To finance this type of program, Artistic must secure television advertising contracts to underwrite part or all of the cost. Advertisers have established the following financing policy based on ratings:

Show Rating	Percent Financing
A	100
B	80
C	40
D	0

If the show is given an A rating by Troody and Good's Rating Service, Artistic will be able to contract with the advertisers for the full $825,000. (Note that the advertisers pay for the right to advertise and receive no other money if the show is a success.) If the rating is B or C, Artistic will be forced to finance the remaining part of the production cost. Unfortunately, the rating cannot be determined until after the show has been taped.

The televison networks will accept the show for a one-time presentation if it receives an A, B, or C rating from Troody and Good's, with the following payment schedule:

Show Rating	Payment
A	$500,000
B	$400,000
C	$150,000

Thus, if the special receives an A rating, it will be 100% financed by the advertisers and the network will pay Artistic $500,000 for rights to a one-time showing.

Suppose Artistic's management has assessed the following probabilities with respect to the potential ratings for the latest proposed special:

Show Rating	Prior Probability
A	.20
B	.30
C	.40
D	.10
	1.00

Carmen Zamora is responsible for making a decision for Artistic and wishes to present the analysis in a logical way to the other members of the management team.

CASE 14D

AMERICAN NATIONAL PART 1

American National provides consumer credit to people all over the world through its own credit card, which it offers eligible persons for a small annual fee.

Each month American National encloses a "special purchase" offer in its cardholder statement. Currently, American National is considering offering its customers the opportunity to purchase a set of fancy carving knives at a "reduced" price of $15. (Customers can have the amount added to their next statement.)

American National must pay $200,000 for the right to sell the knives plus $10 per set sold. At present, American National has 100,000 customers. The marketing department has assessed the following probabilities for potential demand:

Proportion Buying	Probability
.10	.10
.15	.30
.20	.30
.25	.20
.30	.10
	1.00

Fred Turner, American National's executive vice-president, is currently trying to determine whether to offer the knives and also the absolute maximum he would be willing to pay for a market research study.

CASE 14E
AMERICAN NATIONAL PART 2

American National's marketing department has stated that the total cost of sampling its customers to estimate the proportion who will buy the carving knives (see case 14D) consists of a \$3000 fixed cost, plus \$25 per person sampled if the work is done by American National employees.

Turner wants his eventual decision to be based on as much information as possible. He has asked his executive assistant to determine whether a sample of $n = 50$ would produce information worth its cost.

CASE 14F
AMERICAN NATIONAL PART 3

Shortly after hearing his executive assistant's report (see case 14E), Fred Turner received a phone call from an old Army pal, Barry Britten, who is now a market researcher with a consulting firm in Dallas. During their conversation, Fred mentioned his decison about the knife sales campaign (cases 14D and 14E). Barry offered to randomly sample 20 of American National's customers and report back with the percentage who will buy.

Fred has agreed to call Barry later in the day with a price he is willing to pay for the information that could be obtained from the sample of 20 customers.

CASE 14G
ROCKSTONE INTERNATIONAL PART 2

Charley Diamante, Rockstone's corporate controller, happened to walk into the conference room just as R. B. Randall announced her decision on hiring Hans Marquis (see the Mini Case in Chapter 13 for background information). R. B. explained the analysis used in arriving at the decision.

Although Charley was impressed by their methods, he offered the following suggestion. "Why not hire Marquis on a temporary basis and have him cut five stones? Then, after seeing these results, you could make the final decision." He added, "It seems to me that this approach would reduce our cost of uncertainty."

R. B. liked the idea but wondered how this could be done. She also wondered whether the value of the information would be worth the added cost.

CASE 14H
THE HAMILTON COMPANY

The Hamilton Company sells tax-sheltered annuities (TSAs). With a TSA, an employee is allowed to allocate part of his or her monthly paycheck directly to a designated company. These deposits are not subject to federal or state income tax until they are withdrawn after the person reaches age 59½.

Sheryl Peterson, marketing manager for Hamilton, is concerned each time she hires a new salesperson, since she would like to hire only successful salespeople. From past experience, Sheryl believes that TSA salespeople can be divided into four categories: excellent, good, fair, and poor. By her definition, an excellent salesperson will sell an average of 1 TSA per day; a good salesperson will average .5; a fair salesperson will average .20; and a poor salesperson will average .10. Sheryl feels comfortable assuming the number of sales per day for any category salesperson is Poisson-distributed.

Yesterday Sheryl hired a young man to be a sales representative for the Hamilton Company. After a complete review of his credentials and a lengthy personal interview, she feels there is a 20% chance that he will be an excellent salesperson, a 40% chance that he will be good, a 30% chance that he will be fair, and a 10% chance that he will be poor.

The company policy has always been to hire new salespeople for a 10-day trial period. After the 10-day trial, the employee will either be given a permanent position or be released. The purpose of the 10-day trial is to collect data about the employee's performance in sales.

Hamilton pays its sales representatives a fixed rate of $120 per day, regardless of the number of TSAs sold. The company nets $300 for each TSA sold.

Henry Wrentz, Hamilton's vice president, questioned Sheryl's judgment in hiring the young man. She replied that her assessment of his sales potential indicated he would be an asset to the company. Nonetheless, Henry asked Sheryl to present quantifiable data to support her contention.

Sheryl decided to wait until after the 10-day trial period to submit her report. Then she would submit two reports: one based on her prior judgment and a second incorporating both her prior judgment and the actual sales data from the trial period. The young man sold 7 TSAs in the 10 days.

Chapter 15

INTRODUCTION TO RISK-PREFERENCE ANALYSIS

Chapter Outline

Chapter 15

Why You Need to Know

Why do some people travel to Nevada or Atlantic City to gamble when they know that the odds are not in their favor? Why do some people pay $10 a day for damage insurance when they rent a car and others choose not to? Why do some people buy lottery tickets? In most cases, the answers to all these questions relate to the individuals' preference for risk.

People who purchase collision insurance on their automobiles are indicating their preference for paying an annual premium to protect them against having to pay for repairs in the unlikely event the vehicle is damaged in an accident. By paying the insurance premium, the individual is trading a relatively small insurance payment for the potentially large (but unlikely) cost of an accident. In most cases, the expected cost of the premiums is greater than the expected cost of not buying the insurance.

Individuals who go against the expected value in making a decision in order to guard against extreme "bad" outcomes are *risk avoiders.* On the other hand, people who buy lottery tickets or gamble in casinos are *risk seekers.* They choose to play a game which has a negative expected payoff in the hopes of winning a very large jackpot. The gambler's preference for a big payoff overshadows his or her concern with losing the cost of buying a lottery ticket or playing a casino game.

Interestingly enough, often the same person who buys collision insurance when he or she rents a car will also be willing to gamble at a slot machine. Thus, a person may exhibit different attitudes toward risk in different decision-making situations.

Because of the way individuals incorporate preferences for risk into their personal decisions, attitudes toward risk are an important part of business decision making. This chapter will show you how to formally incorporate risk preference attitudes into the decision process as an extension of the decision-analysis techniques introduced in Chapters 13 and 14. You need to know how to deal with risk preferences in order to effectively model the decision process.

Chapter Objectives

In this chapter we introduce the concepts of risk-preference analysis and show how to incorporate attitudes toward risk into the decision-making process. After reading this chapter you should be able to:

1. Identify risk-seeking or risk-avoiding behavior by examining the decision which has been made.
2. Construct an individual risk-preference function and use it in decision analysis.
3. Compute the risk premium for a risk avoider.
4. Recognize the importance of including attitudes toward risk in the decision-analysis process.

15-1 RISK-PREFERENCE ATTITUDES

Not all people select the same alternative when faced with the same decision situation. For instance, managers often disagree over which course of action should be taken by a company facing the prospect of expansion. Decision makers might reach different conclusions about whether to hire an applicant for an important position. One important reason why the choices could be different is that the decision makers have different attitudes about taking a risk. Referred to as "risk preference," the decision maker's attitude toward risk influences his or her view of the potential outcomes associated with the various alternatives. In decision analysis, the risk-preference attitudes are commonly classified as follows:

1. Risk-neutral
2. Risk-averse
3. Risk-seeking

In this section, we will discuss these three types of decision behavior and show how a decision maker's risk preference can be incorporated into the decision-analysis model.

RISK-NEUTRAL

In Chapters 13 and 14, the expected-value criterion was used as the primary means for deciding between alternatives. This meant that we always selected the alternative with the highest expected payoff or the lowest expected cost. Decision makers who strictly apply the expected-value criterion and select the highest payoff or lowest cost are considered **risk-neutral.** For example, suppose a risk-neutral decision maker is given the following options:

1. Play a game consisting of tossing a fair coin one time. If a head turns up, the player will be paid $10; if a tail turns up, the player will lose $6.
2. Don't play the game.

This decision is diagrammed as follows:

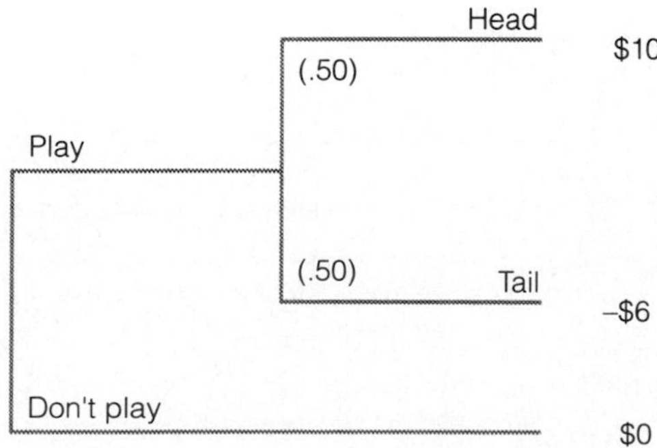

If the coin is fair, the chance of a head turning up is .5, the same as for a tail. The risk-neutral decision maker would compute the expected value of both alternatives as follows:

$$E(\text{play}) = \$10(.5) + -\$6(.5) = \$5 - \$3 = \$2$$

$$E(\text{don't play}) = \$0$$

Then, choosing strictly on the basis of expected value, the decision maker would select the *Play* alternative, since $2 > $0.

Consider a similar decision, diagrammed as follows:

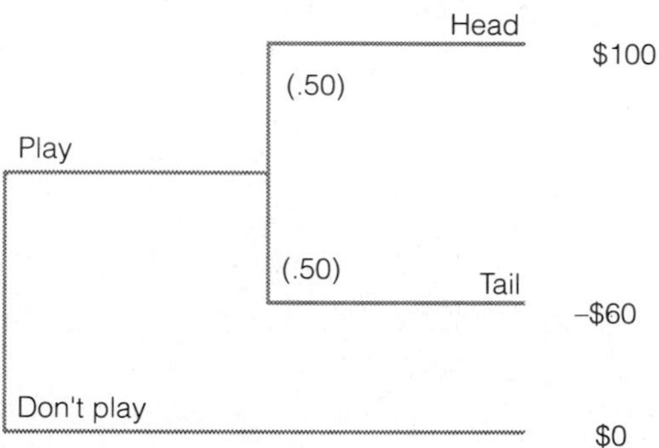

Now the expected values of the alternatives in this case are:

$$E(\text{play}) = \$100(.5) + -\$60(.5) = \$20$$
$$E(\text{don't play}) = \$0$$

Deciding strictly on the basis of expected value, the risk-neutral decision maker will choose to play, since $20 > $0.

While most of us would like to win the $10 in the first example, our day would not be totally ruined if we lost and had to pay the $6. In the second example, we would very much like the $100 payoff, but the loss of $60 would hurt a bit. The risk-neutral decision maker doesn't let such thoughts affect the decision, and would make the same choice even if the game had payoffs of $10,000 and −$6000, as follows:

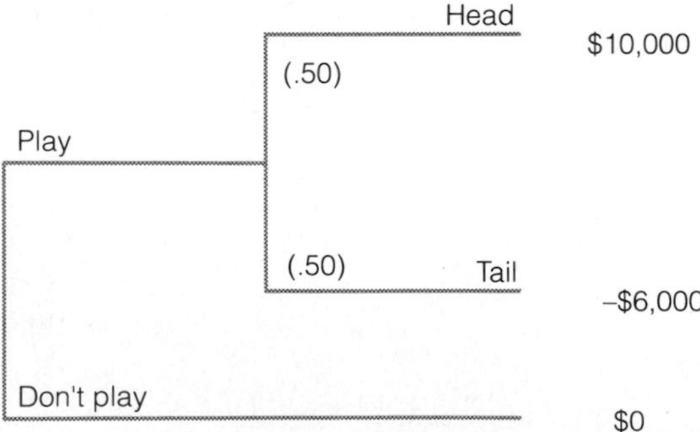

The expected value of the *Play* alternative is $2000, which clearly makes the "best decision" to play the game. Right?

If you were faced with this latest decision situation, what would you do, given your current financial status? Just think how nice it would be to add $10,000 to your bank account—if a head turns up. However, how would you feel if a tail turns up and you suddenly *owe* $6000? Most of us would tend to look at the values of the possible outcomes and balance our desire for the $10,000 gain versus our dislike for losing $6000, before actually making our decision.

Considering end values and letting our attitude toward these values influence the decision means we are not risk-neutral. Further, when considering the end values in a decision situation, rarely will someone be risk-neutral over a wide range of decision situations. If a decision maker is not risk-neutral, then he or she is said to be either a *risk avoider* or a *risk seeker*. In either instance, the expected value of a decision alternative is not the sole decision criterion.

RISK-AVERSE

Consider the following situation. An investment option exists that will require you to invest $10,000. There is a .50 chance that you will walk away with $20,000; but there is also a .50 chance that you will end up with $0. The expected value is:

$$E(\text{payoff}) = .5(\$20{,}000) + .5(\$0) = \$10{,}000$$

Thus, on average, you would break even. You would be paying $10,000 to earn back an average of $10,000. This is an *actuarially fair gamble*. Risk-neutral decision makers would be indifferent; they could take the investment option or leave it. A **risk-averse** individual would not take this investment option; in fact, a risk avoider would be willing to pay some certain amount, called a *certainty equivalent*, to get out of taking the gamble. Consider your own personal situation. If you were told that you had to ante up $10,000 for an investment option where the flip of a coin would determine whether you get either $20,000 or nothing, how would you feel? Would you be willing to pay some amount right now to get out of taking the gamble? How much would you pay? The more you would be willing to pay, the more risk-averse you are for this gamble.

Most people are risk avoiders, choosing to guard against the extreme "bad" outcome. Insurance companies rely on this fact. Consider the decision of whether to purchase health insurance for $600 per year. The policy has a $1000-deductible clause, meaning you pay the first $1000 in medical bills during each year, and it covers 90% of the costs over $1000. Figure 15-1 shows a decision tree for this situation. Three possible outcomes are possible under each alternative. These outcomes and the subjectively assessed probabilities are:

Medical Cost	Probability
$100	.90
$500	.09
$25,000	.01

The probabilities reflect the decision maker's assessment of each possible outcome. There is a high chance that the medical costs during the year will be $500 or less and only 1 chance in 100 that a major medical problem costing $25,000 will occur.

Figure 15-1 shows that the expected cost is $385 for the *No insurance* alternative and $769 for the *Buy insurance* option. On the basis of expected value, the "best decision" is not to buy insurance, since $345 < $769. However, most people will buy the insurance anyway, exhibiting a preference to avoid the risk of the potentially worst outcome.

Risk avoidance is also prevalent in business decision making. The reasons for this are at least twofold. First, since the individual is likely to be a risk avoider in many personal situations, this behavior will extend to business decisions, even though now it is the company's resources—not the decision maker's personal resources—that are at stake. Second, the reward structure in many organizations provides an incentive for people to avoid choosing alternatives with risky outcomes. While a good outcome may result in a bonus for the decision maker, often this bonus does not outweigh the possible consequences of an extremely negative outcome, such as being fired.

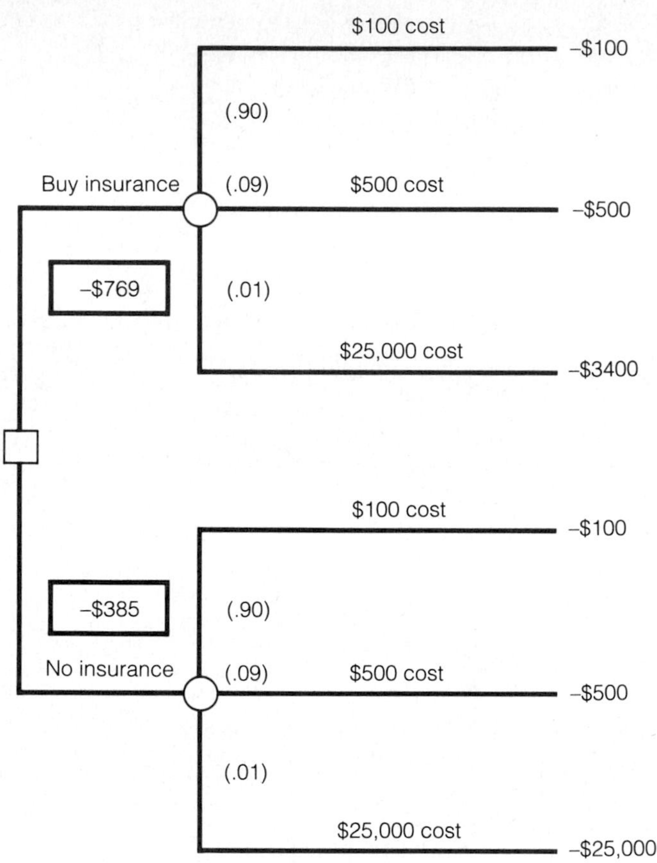

Figure 15-1
Decision tree for Health Insurance example

In practice, risk-avoiding behavior in an organization tends to be more prevalent at the lower and middle management levels. Often this runs somewhat counter to the desires of upper management which, publicly at least, talks about the need to take chances and being willing to fail.

RISK-SEEKING

Not everyone is a risk avoider. Clearly, there are many situations in which people exhibit **risk-seeking** behavior. For instance, consider another investment alternative which requires a $10,000 investment. There is a .10 chance that you would walk away with $80,000 and a .90 chance that you would lose your $10,000 and end up with $0. The expected payoff is:

$$E[\text{payoff}] = .10(\$80{,}000) + .90(\$0) = \$8000$$

Thus, on average, an investor would leave with $8000 after making a $10,000 investment, providing an expected loss of $2000. A risk-neutral decision maker would choose not to invest; so would a risk avoider. However, some people would want to invest to have the chance at $80,000. These individuals are called risk seekers. In fact, if faced with the prospect of losing out on the investment option, a risk seeker might agree to pay some additional amount just to keep the investment opportunity open.

A good example of risk-seeking behavior is what happens when someone enters a "sweepstakes" contest sponsored by a magazine publishing company. For instance, in a contest held in 1990, the person who had the winning number would receive $10 million. To be eligible to win, all a contestant had to do was mail in the entry form, which required spending $.25 for a stamp. The stated chance of winning was 1 in 100,000,000. The tree for this decision is shown in Figure 15-2. Even though the expected value was −$.15, millions of people entered this contest. They were willing to risk a $.25 stamp for the chance to make $10 million.

Risk-seeking behavior is typically associated with situations in which one possible outcome is perceived by the decision maker to have the potential to markedly change his or her life. Winning the contest and receiving $10 million is that type of outcome. States with government-run lotteries have found that they get more players if they offer a major prize of several million dollars instead of more, but smaller, prizes. People are more willing to take a risk in hopes of obtaining the big prize.

Business decision makers can also engage in risk-seeking behavior. About 5 years ago, a young accountant saw an advertisement in the Portland *Oregonian* newspaper offering for sale 5 franchises for a popular hamburger chain in the Eugene area. After reviewing the situation, assessing the possible gains and losses, and determining that the decision's expected value was negative, he invested anyway. The potentially high payoff meant more to him than a negative expected value.

The same person may be risk-averse in some situations and risk-seeking in others, depending on the range of outcomes. For example, if you were asked to spend $1 on a lottery ticket that offered a 1 in 1000 chance of winning $500, you might consider it, even though the expected value is −$.50. If you play, you are a risk seeker. On the other hand, if you were offered a chance to buy a $10,000 ticket in a lottery with a .25 chance of winning $100,000, you might refuse the offer, even though the expected value is $15,000. If you refuse, you are exhibiting risk-averse behavior. In the first case, the range of payoffs was −$1 to $500 and the worst outcome was to lose only $1. However, when the possible loss is greater, such as the −$10,000 in the second example, you might select an alternative which would protect you against this bad outcome.

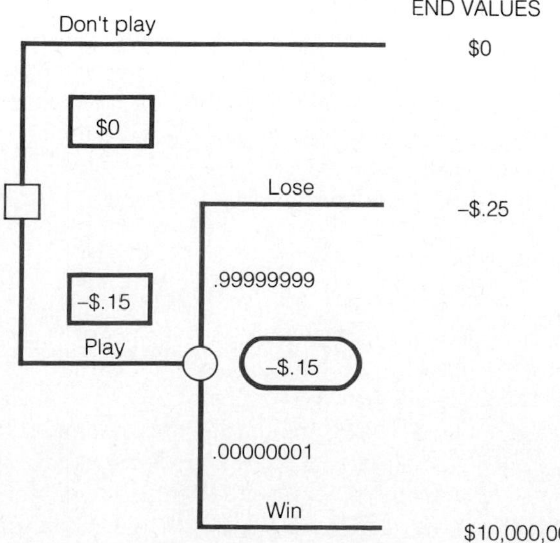

Figure 15-2
Decision tree for publisher's sweepstakes

15-2 DEVELOPING A RISK-PREFERENCE FUNCTION

The expected-value criterion suits the attitude of a risk-neutral decision maker. For this group of decision makers, the best decision is the one which maximizes the expected payoff or minimizes the expected cost. However, because not all (or even most) decision makers are risk-neutral, a method for formally incorporating risk-averse and risk-seeking attitudes into the decision process is needed.

The method used in decision analysis is to develop a **risk-preference function** that describes the decision maker's relative preferences for all outcomes within a specified range. (The preference function is commonly plotted as a line or curve on a graph.)

THE STANDARD GAMBLE APPROACH

Several methods can be used to establish a decision maker's risk-preference function. The method illustrated in this text, called the **standard gamble approach**, involves setting up a series of 50-50 gambles between two payoffs and determining the certainty equivalents. We begin by using a simple example to demonstrate how a standard gamble is used to develop risk-neutral, risk-averse, and risk-seeking preference functions. We will then follow with an example showing how preference functions are used in the decision-making process.

Risk-Neutral Preference Function

To develop a risk-preference function, we must have a range of possible outcomes measured in dollars. The outcomes typically range from the highest possible end value on a decision tree to the lowest possible end value. Suppose you are the decision maker analyzing a decision tree where the highest possible payoff is $10,000 and the lowest possible payoff is −$2000. Further assume that you are risk-neutral.

The first step in developing your risk-preference function is to assign preference quotients to the highest and lowest possible outcomes. A **preference quotient** is a measure of the relative utility for the outcomes of a decision on a scale between 1.0 and 0.0. Let q represent the preference quotient. The higher the q value, the greater the relative preference for the dollar outcome. The highest possible payoff is assigned a value of $q = 1.0$, since that value is preferred over all other payoffs. The lowest possible payoff is assigned $q = 0.0$, indicating that you would prefer any other payoff over the lowest payoff. When dealing with costs instead of payoffs, we reverse this reasoning and assign a value of 1.0 to the lowest-cost alternative and 0.0 to the highest-cost alternative. For this example, we get:

Payoff	q
$10,000	1.0
−$2,000	0.0

The next step in developing the risk-preference function is to pose a series of *standard gambles.* The first one is diagrammed in Figure 15-3. The alternatives are either to play a game with a .50 chance of winning $10,000 and a .50 chance of losing $2000 or not to play the game. The payoffs associated with the "Play" alternative are the same payoffs for which we have already assigned q values. This decision is referred to as a standard gamble because the chance of each payoff occurring is set at .50.

You must next determine what certain outcome for the *Don't play* branch would

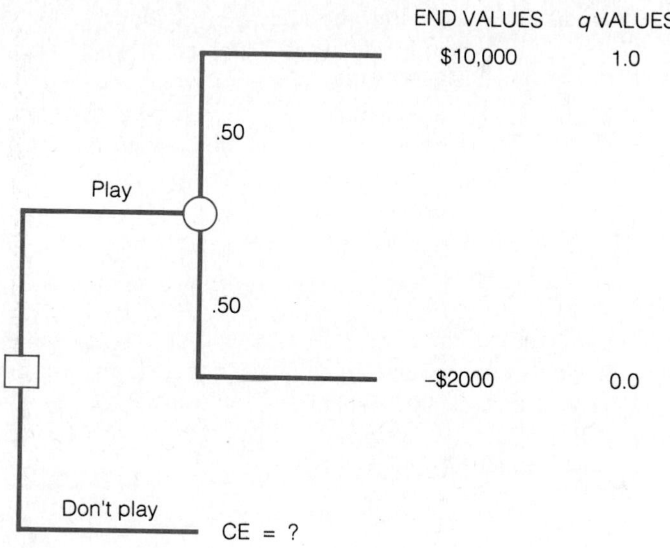

Figure 15-3
Assessing the risk-preference function: standard gamble 1

make you indifferent between playing and not playing. This value is termed the **certainty equivalent** (or *CE* value) of the gamble. You can think of it as the amount you would take to give up the opportunity to play the game.

The expected value of the *Play* branch is:

$$EV = \$10{,}000(.50) + -\$2000(.50) = \$4000$$

This means that, on average, you would make $4000 by selecting the *Play* alternative. A risk-neutral decision maker always selects the option with the highest expected payoff. If the payoff for the *Don't play* branch exceeds $4000, then the choice would be not to play. If the payoff for the *Don't play* alternative is less than $4000, then the *Play* branch would be selected. Thus, for a risk-neutral decision maker, the certainty equivalent for this standard gamble is the expected value, $4000. If the *Don't play* branch had a certain payoff of $4000, the risk-neutral decision maker would be indifferent between the two alternatives.

Since we are assuming you are risk-neutral, the next step is to determine the q value for a payoff of $4000. This is done by determining the expected q value for the *Play* branch based on the q values already assigned to the payoffs of $10,000 and −$2000:

$$E(q) = 1.0(.50) + 0.0\ (.50) = .50$$

Thus, the preference quotient, q, for a payoff of $4000 is .50. We now have the following q values:

Payoff	q
$10,000	1.0
$4,000	0.5
−$2,000	0.0

Note that the decision tree may not have an end value of $4000; but this does not present a problem, since our objective is to develop a risk-preference curve which can be used to determine the relative preference for any value between \$10,000 and −\$2000. We now have three points on this preference curve.

To determine additional points, we pose a second standard gamble, as shown in Figure 15-4. The *Play* alternative now shows a .50 chance at \$10,000 and a .50 chance at \$4000. We have previously assigned q values to each of these outcomes and must now determine the *CE* value for this gamble. Remember, *CE* will be the point of indifference between playing and not playing.

The expected value of the *Play* branch is:

$$EV = \$10{,}000(.50) + \$4000(.50) = \$7000$$

On average, the *Play* alternative will yield a \$7000 payoff. A risk-neutral decision maker would be indifferent between playing and not playing if the *Don't play* alternative had a certain outcome of \$7000. Then, for a risk-neutral decision maker, $CE = \$7000$. We determine the q value for \$7000 by finding the expected q value for this standard gamble:

$$E(q) = 1.0(.50) + .50(.50) = .75$$

The preference quotient for a payoff of \$7000 is .75. We now have four values:

Payoff	q
\$10,000	1.00
\$ 7,000	0.75
\$ 4,000	0.50
−\$2,000	0.00

We can pose still another standard gamble, as shown in Figure 15-5. The expected value of the *Play* branch is:

$$EV = \$4000(.50) + -\$2000(.50) = \$1000$$

A risk-neutral decision maker would be indifferent between the alternatives if the certain outcome of the *Play* branch was \$1000. Thus, the *CE* for this standard gamble is

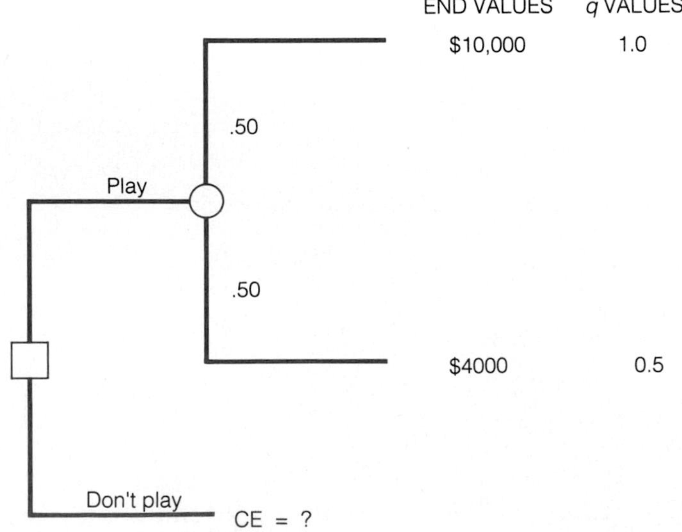

Figure 15-4
Assessing the risk-preference function: standard gamble 2

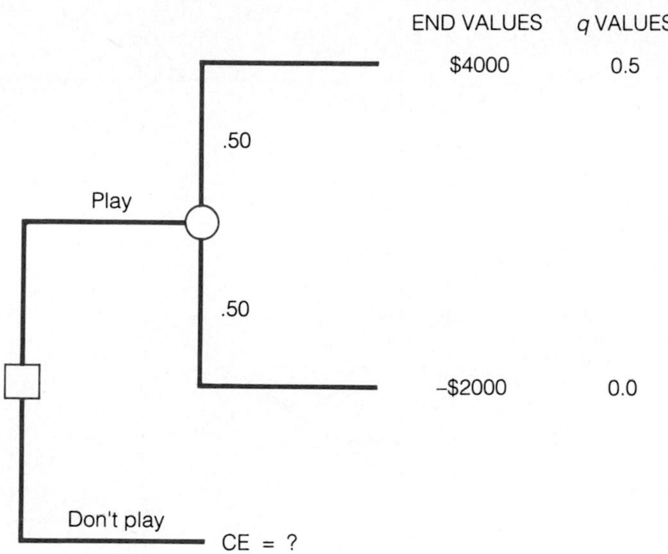

Figure 15-5
Assessing the risk-preference function: standard gamble 3

$1000. We determine the q value for a $1000 payoff as follows:

$$E(q) = .50(.50) + 0.0(.50) = .25$$

The preference quotient for a $1000 payoff is .25, giving the following results so far:

Payoff	q
$10,000	1.00
$ 7,000	0.75
$ 4,000	0.50
$ 1,000	0.25
−$2,000	0.00

This process can be repeated as often as necessary until enough q values have been determined to allow us to graph the preference function. Let's use the five points we have so far to see how things look.

Figure 15-6 is a graph of this preference function. The horizontal axis shows the payoffs, and the q values are shown on the vertical axis. As you can see, the risk-neutral preference function is linear. You can use the preference function graphed in Figure 15-6 to determine the relative preference for any payoff between $10,000 and −$2,000 by going from the payoff number on the horizontal axis up to the preference-function line and then over to the vertical axis, for the q value. Figure 15-7 shows how we found the q value of approximately .61 for a payoff of $5000. Other q values can be determined in the same way.

Risk-Averse Preference Function

The linear preference function shown in Figure 15-6 is for a risk-neutral decision maker. The preference function is linear because the *CE* values for each standard gamble were always the expected value of the *Play* alternative. However, we indicated earlier that most decision makers are not risk-neutral but instead are risk-averse or risk-seeking. Let's reconsider the same decision problem as before, with the highest

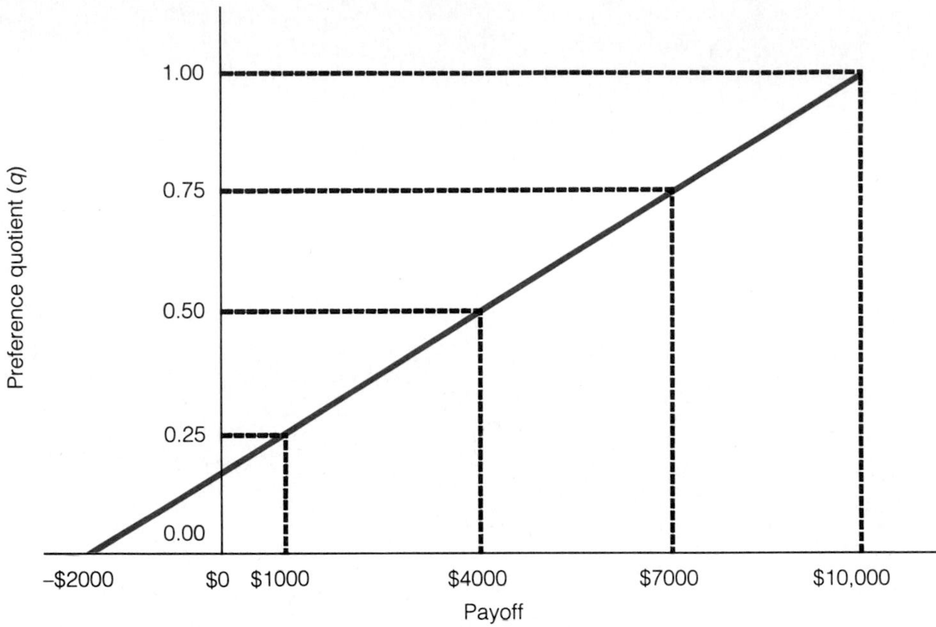

Figure 15-6
Risk-neutral preference-function example

payoff of $10,000 and lowest payoff of −$2,000, but now suppose the decision maker is *risk-averse.*

A risk-averse decision maker will pick a certainty equivalent that is less than the expected payoff for a standard gamble. However, there are different degrees of risk aversion. The extent to which a person is risk-averse will be reflected in his or her risk-preference function.

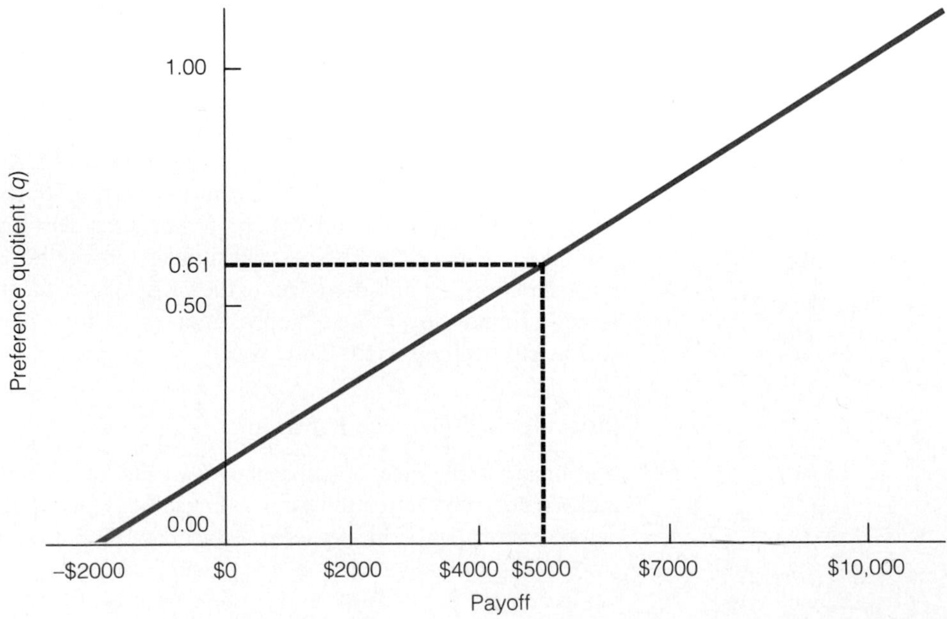

Figure 15-7
Risk-neutral preference function

The steps in assessing a risk-averse decision maker's preference function are essentially the same as for a risk-neutral or risk-seeking decision maker. We begin by assigning $q = 1.0$ to the highest possible payoff, in this case \$10,000, and assign $q = 0.0$ to the lowest possible payoff, −\$2000. This again gives:

Payoff	q
\$10,000	1.0
−\$2,000	0.0

Next, we pose the standard gamble shown earlier in Figure 15-3. Recall that the expected value for the *Play* alternative is \$4000. A risk-neutral individual would set $CE = \$4000$. But this will not be the case for a risk-averse decision maker. The *CE* (certainty equivalent) is the certain value associated with the *Don't play* branch which would make the decision maker indifferent between the two options. A risk-averse person's indifference point will be less than \$4000. How much less depends on how risk-averse he or she is.

Usually a decision maker has trouble directly assessing the *CE* for a standard gamble like the one shown in Figure 15-3. Someone helping assess the decision maker's risk-preference function might begin by asking whether he would pay \$1500 to avoid taking the play gamble. If the response is no, ask whether the decision maker would pay \$500 to get out of the gamble. As long as the decision maker prefers the gamble to the certain dollar figure, the point of indifference has not been reached.

Suppose that after several iterations the indifference point is determined to be \$0; that is, the decision maker would be indifferent between playing and not playing if the *Don't play* alternative has a certain payoff of \$0. Then the *CE* for the standard gamble posed in Figure 15-3 is \$0. We next find the q for \$0, as follows:

$$E(q) = 1.0(.50) + 0.0(.50) = .50$$

This gives us the following three values:

Payoff	q
\$10,000	1.0
\$0	0.5
−\$2,000	0.0

You should note that this decision maker was willing to accept a \$0 payoff instead of the gamble with an expected payoff of \$4000. The difference between the expected value and the *CE* is called the **risk premium.** Risk-averse decision makers have positive risk premiums. In effect, this decision maker is willing to pay a premium, in the form of a lost expected payoff, of \$4000 to avoid the possibility of losing \$2000. The risk premium is:

$$\text{Risk premium} = \$4000 - \$0 = \$4000$$

Does this seem like an excessive premium to pay? Ask yourself whether today you would risk losing \$2000 for the chance to win \$10,000 on the flip of a coin. If you would walk away from this gamble and take a \$0 payoff, you are at least as risk-averse as the decision maker in our example. If you wouldn't give up the gamble so easily, then you are less risk-averse than this decision maker.

We now have three points on the preference function but need more. Our next step is to pose still another standard gamble, like the one shown in Figure 15-8. Now

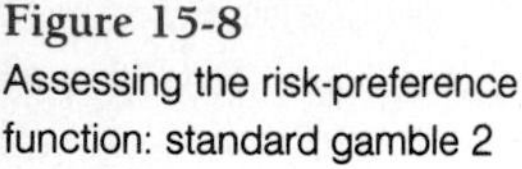

Figure 15-8
Assessing the risk-preference function: standard gamble 2

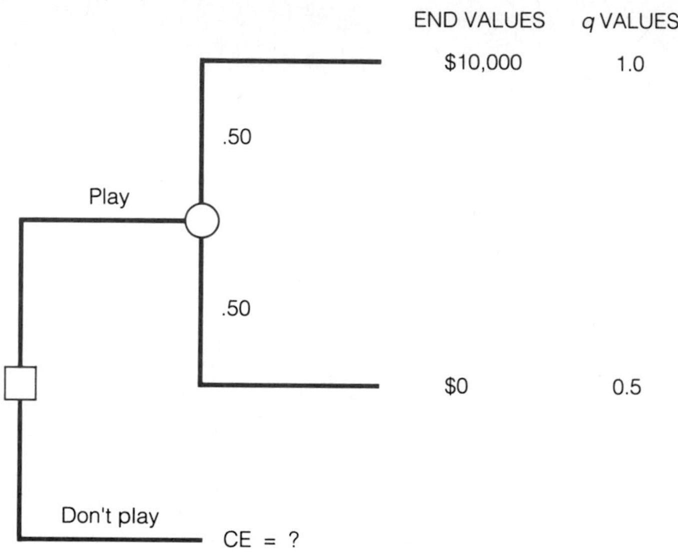

the decision maker must determine the certain payoff of not playing, which would make him or her indifferent between playing and not playing. Using the same procedure as before, we would determine the indifference point. Assume the decision maker settles on \$2750 as the *CE* for this latest standard gamble. This means that he or she would be indifferent between taking the 50-50 gamble with payoffs of \$10,000 or \$0 and the sure payoff of \$2750.

The expected payoff for the gamble is:

$$EV = \$10{,}000(.50) + \$0(.50) = \$5000$$

The difference between the expected value and the certainty equivalent is the risk premium. In this case, we get:

$$\text{Risk premium} = \$5000 - \$2750 = \$2250$$

This risk premium is less than the \$4000 risk premium associated with the earlier gamble. Therefore the decision maker is not as risk-averse over the range \$10,000 to \$0 as he or she was over the range \$10,000 to −\$2000.

The q value for the \$2750 *CE* is:

$$E(q) = 1.0(.50) + .50(.50) = .75$$

We have now determined four q values:

Payoff	q
\$10,000	1.00
\$2,750	0.75
\$0	0.50
−\$2,000	0.00

You should determine as many q values as necessary to feel comfortable about drawing the risk-preference function. Let's find one more value, using the standard gamble diagrammed in Figure 15-9. Suppose the *CE* for this gamble is determined to

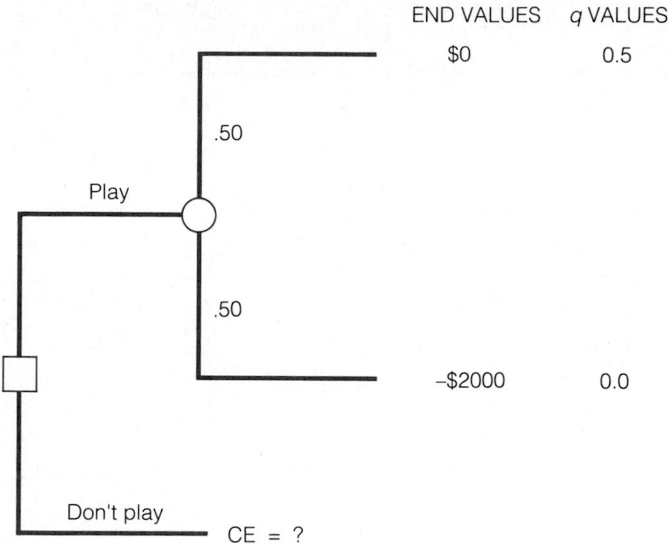

Figure 15-9
Assessing the risk-preference function: standard gamble 3

be −$1250. This decision maker would be willing to pay $1250 to avoid a 50-50 chance of losing $2000 or breaking even.

The expected value of the gamble shown in Figure 15-9 is −$1000, and the risk premium is:

$$\text{Risk premium} = -\$1000 - (-\$1250) = \$250$$

The q value for this −$1250 *CE* is:

$$E(q) = .50(.50) + 0.0(.50) = .25$$

We now have the following q values:

Payoff	q
$10,000	1.00
$2,750	0.75
$0	0.50
−$1,250	0.25
−$2,000	0.00

Figure 15-10 shows these five points connected to form the risk-preference function. Five is the minimum number of points to use for a risk-averse decision maker. We can use Figure 15-10 to determine the preference quotients for any value between $10,000 and −$2000. For instance, Figure 15-11 shows that the q value for a payoff of $5000 is approximately .91. Other q values would be determined in the same manner.

At this point, we can state three general conclusions regarding risk-preference functions. First, all risk-neutral preference functions are linear. Second, risk-averse preference functions are concave from the origin. You need only look at the general shape of the risk-preference function to determine whether the decision maker is risk-neutral or risk-averse. Third, the risk premium for a risk-averse decision maker will be positive, since the certainty equivalent will be less than the expected value of the standard gamble.

Figure 15-10
Risk-averse preference function

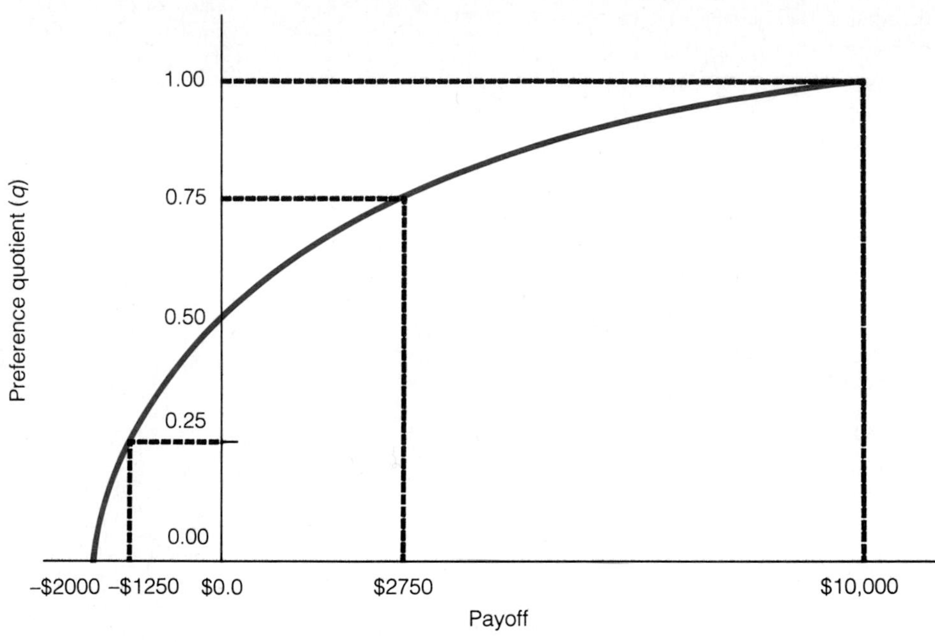

Risk-Seeking Preference Function

The steps required to assess the preference function of a risk seeker are the same as those for a risk avoider. The only difference is that a risk seeker will have a certainty equivalent which exceeds the expected value of the standard gamble. This means that the risk premium for a risk seeker is negative. An example will show what we mean.

Let us once again consider the decision with payoffs ranging from \$10,000 to −\$2000. We again set $q = 1.0$ for the \$10,000 payoff and $q = 0.0$ for the −\$2000

Figure 15-11
Risk-averse preference function

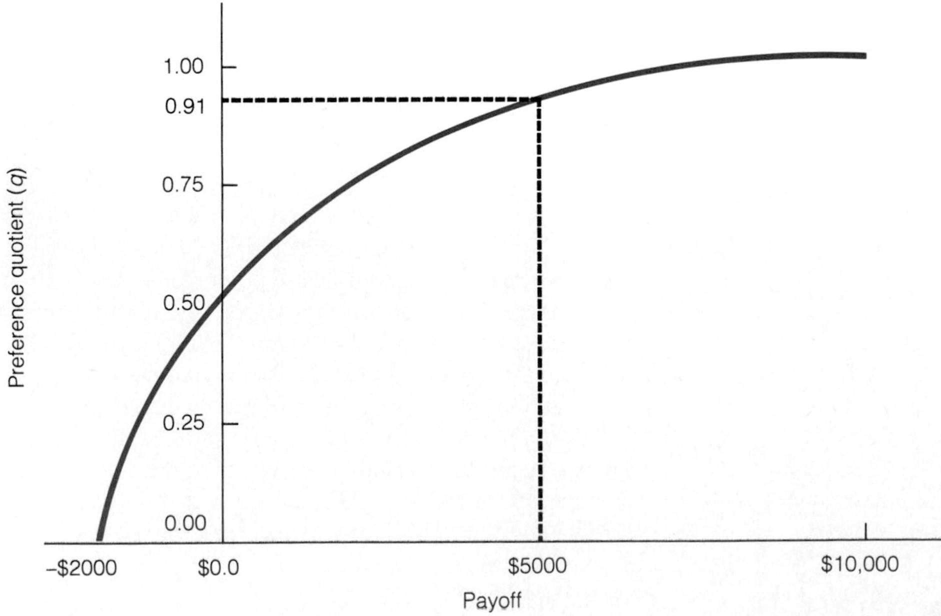

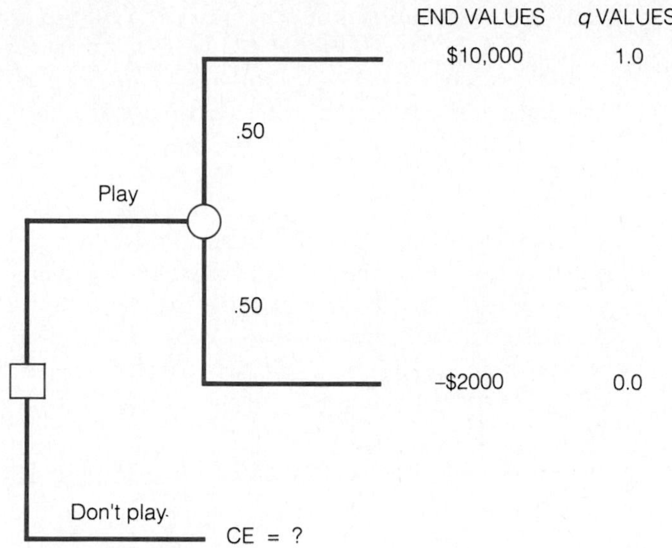

Figure 15-12
Assessing the risk-preference function: standard gamble 1

payoff. Now we propose the standard gamble shown in Figure 15-12. The gamble has an expected value of $4000. A risk-neutral decision maker would set the *CE* at $4000. We saw previously that a risk-averse decision maker would have a *CE* of less than $4000 ($0 in the earlier example).

A risk seeker will demand a certain payoff in excess of $4000 not for playing. This demand reflects his or her desire for the $10,000 payoff. The exact *CE* chosen will depend on how much of a risk taker the decision maker is. Suppose the *Don't play* branch would have to have a certain payoff of $6500 to make the decision maker indifferent between the options of playing and not playing. Recall that the expected

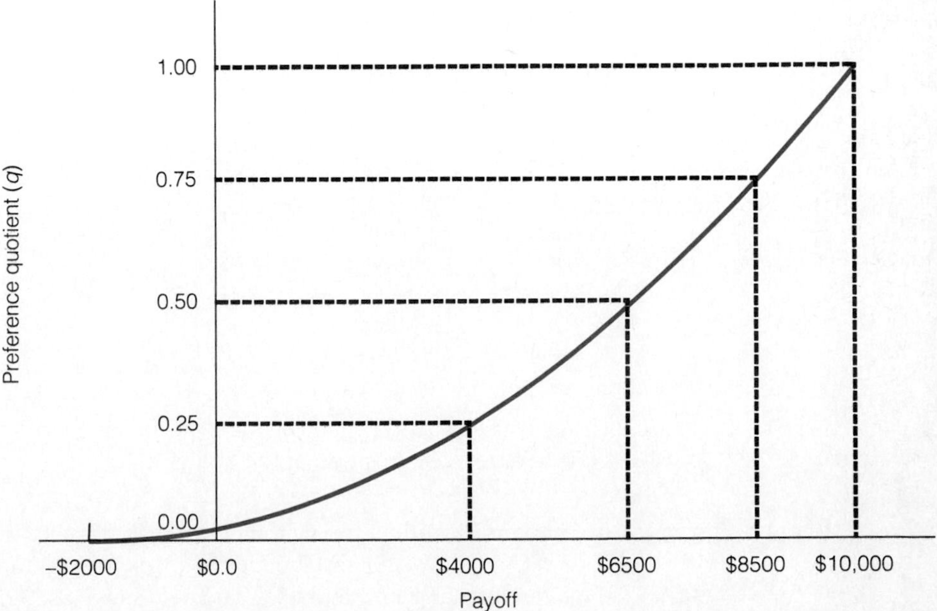

Figure 15-13
Risk-seeking preference function

value of the *Play* option is $4000; thus, $CE > EV$, indicating a negative risk premium:

$$\text{Risk premium} = \$4000 - \$6500 = -\$2500$$

The preference quotient value for the *CE* of $6500 is found as before:

$$E(q) = 1.0(.50) + 0.0(.50) = .50$$

We would continue proposing standard gambles to the risk-seeking decision maker and determine both the certainty equivalent and preference quotient for each gamble. After determining at least five preference quotients and certainty equivalents, we would be ready to determine the preference function. Figure 15-13 shows the completed risk-preference function for this risk seeker. This preference function can be used to determine q values for any payoff between $10,000 and −$2000. Figure 15-13 also shows that the risk-preference function for a risk seeker is convex from the origin.

15-3 INCORPORATING RISK PREFERENCES INTO THE DECISION ANALYSIS

The previous section explained the steps involved in developing a risk-preference function for risk-neutral, risk-averse, and risk-seeking decision makers. In this section, we show how to incorporate risk preferences into the decision analysis. As you will see, once the preference function is developed, the method is very straightforward.

Betty Feeney has just received a surprising $8000 inheritance from the estate of a relative she had not seen for 20 years. Betty has decided to invest the money for 2 years until her oldest child enters college and then use it for tuition. She must decide between two alternative investments: a mutual fund and real estate. Figure 15-14 shows her completed decision tree. At the end of 2 years, Betty estimates her shares in the mutual fund could be sold for $16,000, $11,000, or $6000, depending on how the stock market performs and how well the mutual fund is managed. The property could be sold at the end of the investment period for $18,000, $10,000, or $8000, depending on the demand for real estate in the area.

Betty has subjectively assessed the following probability distributions:

Mutual Fund			Real Estate		
Selling Price	Net Cash Position	Probability	Selling Price	Net Cash Position	Probability
$16,000	$8000	.30	$18,000	$10,000	.20
$11,000	$3000	.40	$10,000	$2,000	.40
$6,000	−$2000	.30	$8,000	$0	.40

The end values to the right of the decision tree in Figure 15-14 represent Betty's projected net cash position at the end of 2 years.

A RISK-NEUTRAL INVESTOR

In Chapters 13 and 14, you learned how to fold back a decision tree using end values. Figure 15-15 shows the result of this foldback process for Betty's decision. We see that the expected value of the mutual fund alternative is $3000, versus $2800 for the real

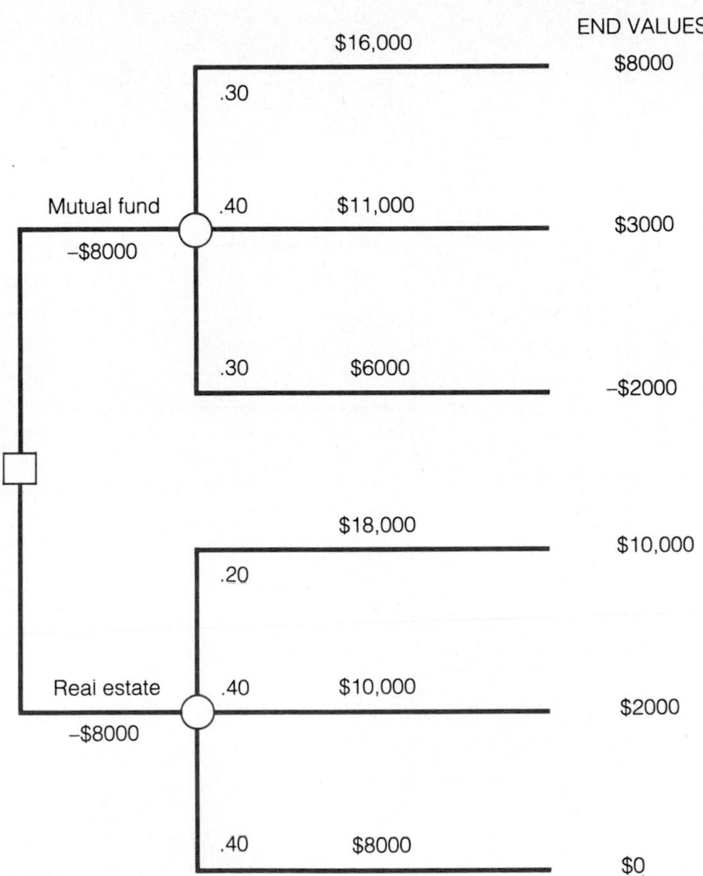

Figure 15-14
Decision tree for the investment example

estate. Thus, based upon the expected values, Betty's "best decision" is to invest in the mutual fund.

The procedure of using the end values directly in the foldback process assumes that Betty is risk-neutral. Earlier, we indicated that a risk-neutral decision maker will make a decision strictly on the basis of expected value. Thus, for a risk-neutral decision maker, we can use an alternative method of decision-tree analysis. This method utilizes the risk-preference function.

We showed earlier that the preference function for a risk-neutral person is linear. Figure 15–6 illustrates a risk-neutral preference function that can be used for this example, since the preference function includes the same highest possible payoff ($10,000) and lowest possible payoff (−$2000) as the investment decision. Incorporating the risk-preference function into the decision-tree analysis is quite easy. You begin by substituting the q value from the preference function for each end value on the decision tree. This is done by locating each end value on the horizontal axis on the preference-function graph. Then go up to the preference function and across to the vertical axis to find the preference quotient, q. Figure 15-16 shows this process for each end value on the decision tree for the investment example. For instance, the q value for a $3000 payoff is .43.

Figure 15-17 shows the decision tree with the q values to the right of the tree. The decision tree is now folded back, but we have used q values instead of dollar end values.

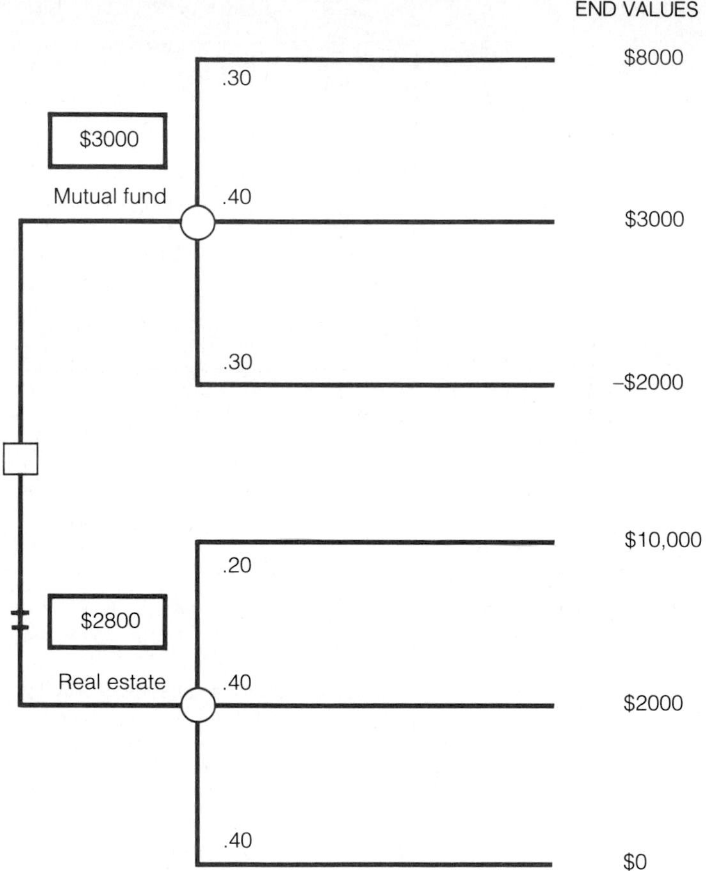

Figure 15-15
Folding back the decision tree for the investment example: Risk-neutral

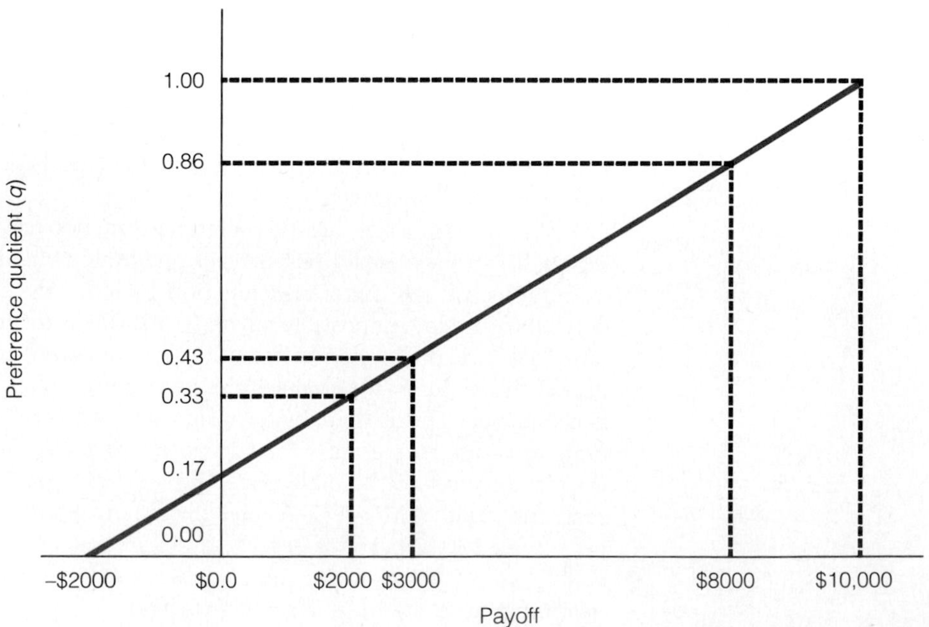

Figure 15-16
Risk-neutral preference function for the investment example

Figure 15-17
Folding back the decision tree, using q values, for the investment example: Risk-neutral

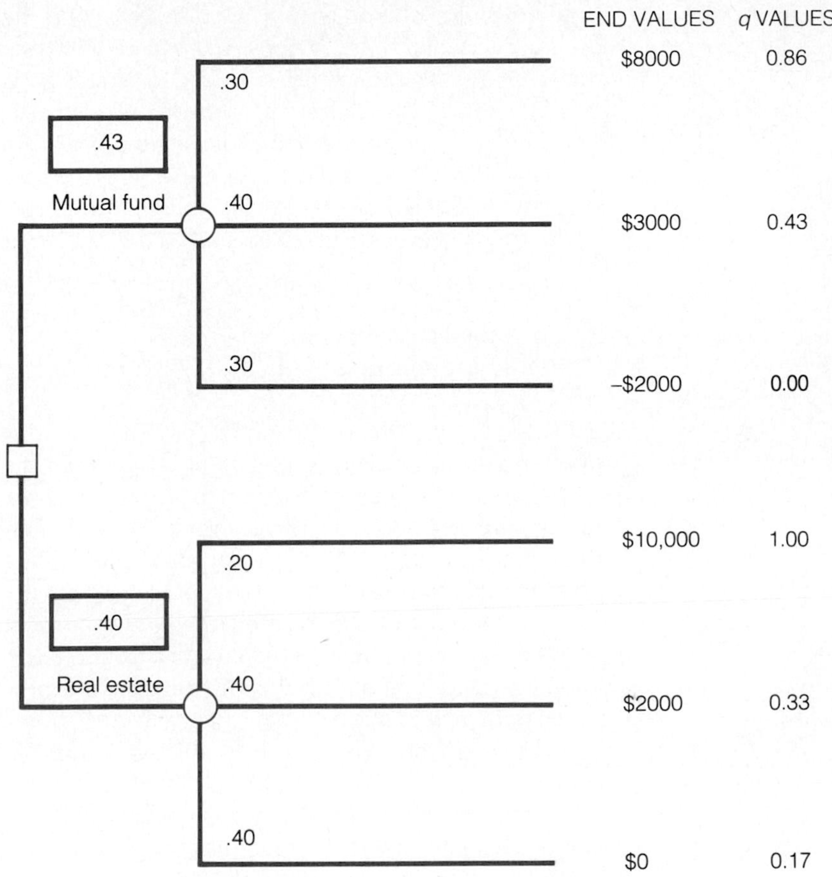

We move from right to left, computing expected q values instead of expected payoffs. The "best decision" is the one which gives the highest expected q value. For this example, the expected q value for the mutual fund alternative is:

$$E(q) = .86(.30) + .43(.40) + 0(.30) = .43$$

and for the real estate alternative, it is:

$$E(q) = 1.0(.20) + .33(.40) + .17(.40) = .40$$

Then, since $.43 > .40$, the "best decision" is to invest in the mutual fund.

Because a risk-neutral preference function is linear, a risk-neutral decision maker will make the same decision using dollar payoffs or q values. The q value for the $3000 expected value of the mutual fund alternative is .43, the same as the expected q value for this alternative in Figure 15-17. However, this equivalence holds only for risk-neutral decision makers.

A RISK-AVERSE DECISION MAKER

We just showed that for a risk-neutral person, using the actual dollar payoffs to fold back the decision tree leads to the same decision as using risk-preference quotients (q values). However, if the decision maker is not risk-neutral, a different decision can be reached.

Risk-averse decision makers are willing to pay a risk premium to avoid alternatives with undesirable outcomes. To illustrate how we incorporate risk-averse attitudes into the decision process, suppose that Figure 15-18 shows the risk-preference function for Betty's investment decision. We see that Betty is risk-averse, since the preference function is concave, curving up from the origin. Figure 15-18 shows the q values for each payoff level associated with the investment decision.

Figure 15-19 shows the decision tree with the q values on the right side; these q values are folded back instead of the dollar payoffs. The best decision at any decision fork is the one having the highest expected q value. For the mutual fund alternative:

$$E(q) = .98(.30) + .79(.40) + 0(.30) = .61$$

For the real estate alternative:

$$E(q) = 1.0(.20) + .71(.40) + .50(.40) = .684$$

Since .6834 > .61, the best decision for Betty, as a risk-averse decision maker, is to invest in real estate. This is a different choice than the risk-neutral decision maker would have made. The reason is that the decision shown in Figure 15-19 incorporates this risk-averse attitude. Being risk-averse, Betty is willing to take an alternative with a lower expected value ($2800) rather than an alternative that has a higher expected value ($3000) but also the possibility of losing $2000.

In this example, the decision changed from mutual fund to real estate when Betty's risk-averse attitude was taken into account. But decisions don't always change; in some instances, the alternative with the highest expected payoff will also be the least risky. In other cases, the decision maker's degree of risk aversion will not be sufficient to lead to a different decision. Each decision situation must be evaluated independently.

If the decision maker has a risk-seeking preference function, the process for incorporating his or her preferences into the decision analysis is the same as for a

Figure 15-18
Risk-averse preference function for the investment example

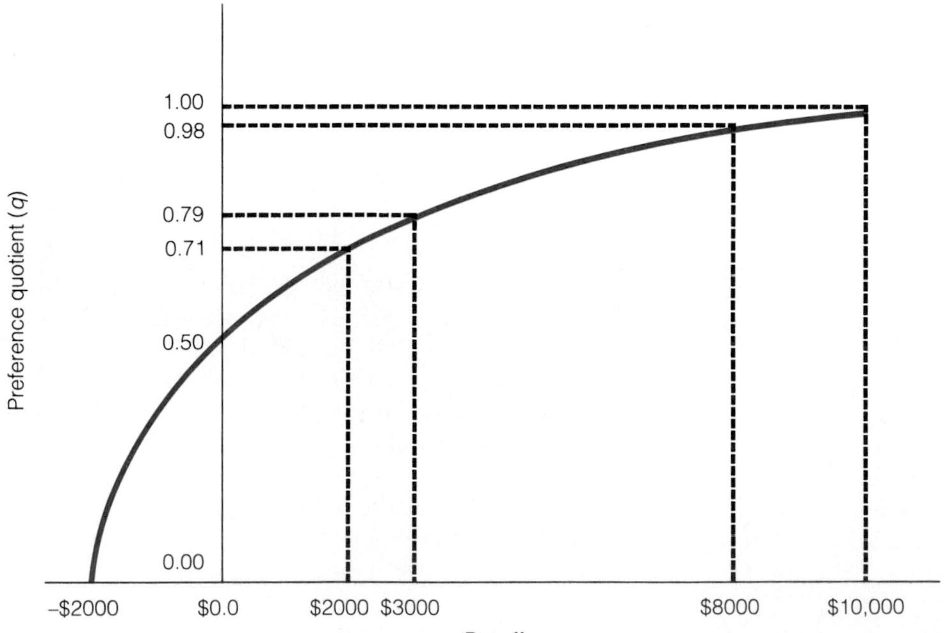

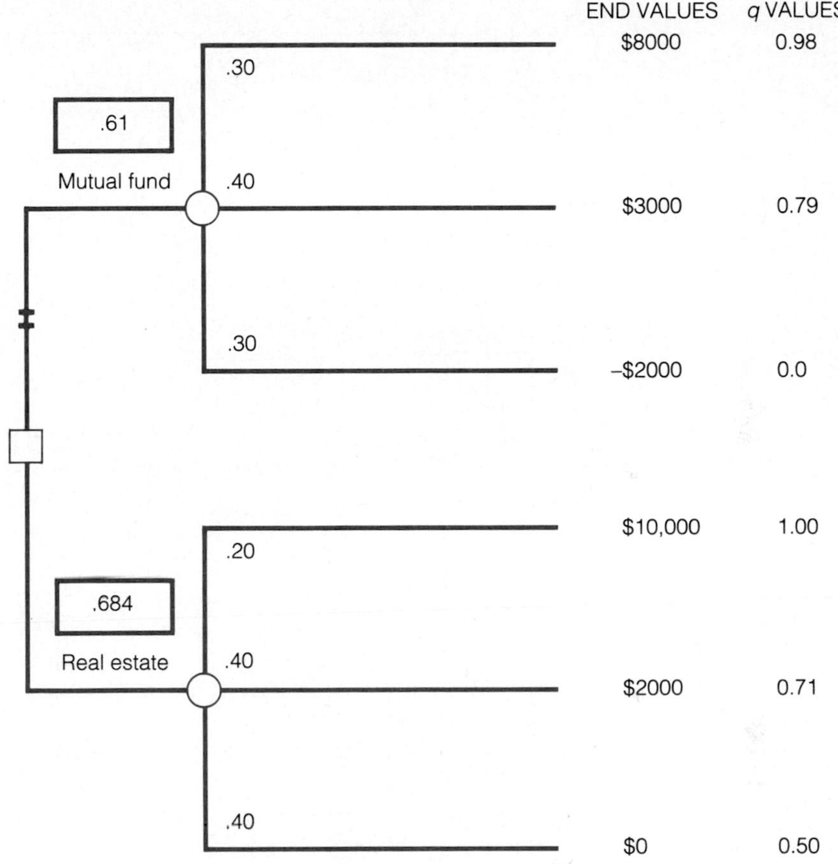

Figure 15-19
Decision tree, folding back the decision tree, using q values, for the investment example: Risk-averse

risk-averse individual. The tendency will be to select alternatives offering higher potential payoffs but with more risk of low or negative payoffs. We suggest that you use the risk-preference function in Figure 15-13 to analyze this investment decision.

15-4 USING RISK PREFERENCES: HARRIS PUBLISHING COMPANY EXAMPLE REVISITED

In Chapter 13, we used an example involving the Harris Publishing Company to introduce decision-tree analysis methodology. You might recall that Laurel Anaya was faced with deciding whether to sign a contract to publish a book about the personal life of an important former government official. Figure 15-20 shows the final results of the decision-tree analysis assuming that Laurel is risk-neutral. Under this assumption, the "best decision" is to sign the contract. If the editorial review is favorable, then publish the book in paperback.

Now suppose that Laurel is risk averse rather than risk-neutral. What effect might this have on her decision? To answer these questions, the risk-preference function must be assessed and then preference quotients used rather than dollar payoffs in folding back the decision tree. Figure 15-21 shows the risk-preference function determined using the standard gamble approach. The shape of the function clearly indicates that Laurel Anaya is risk-averse.

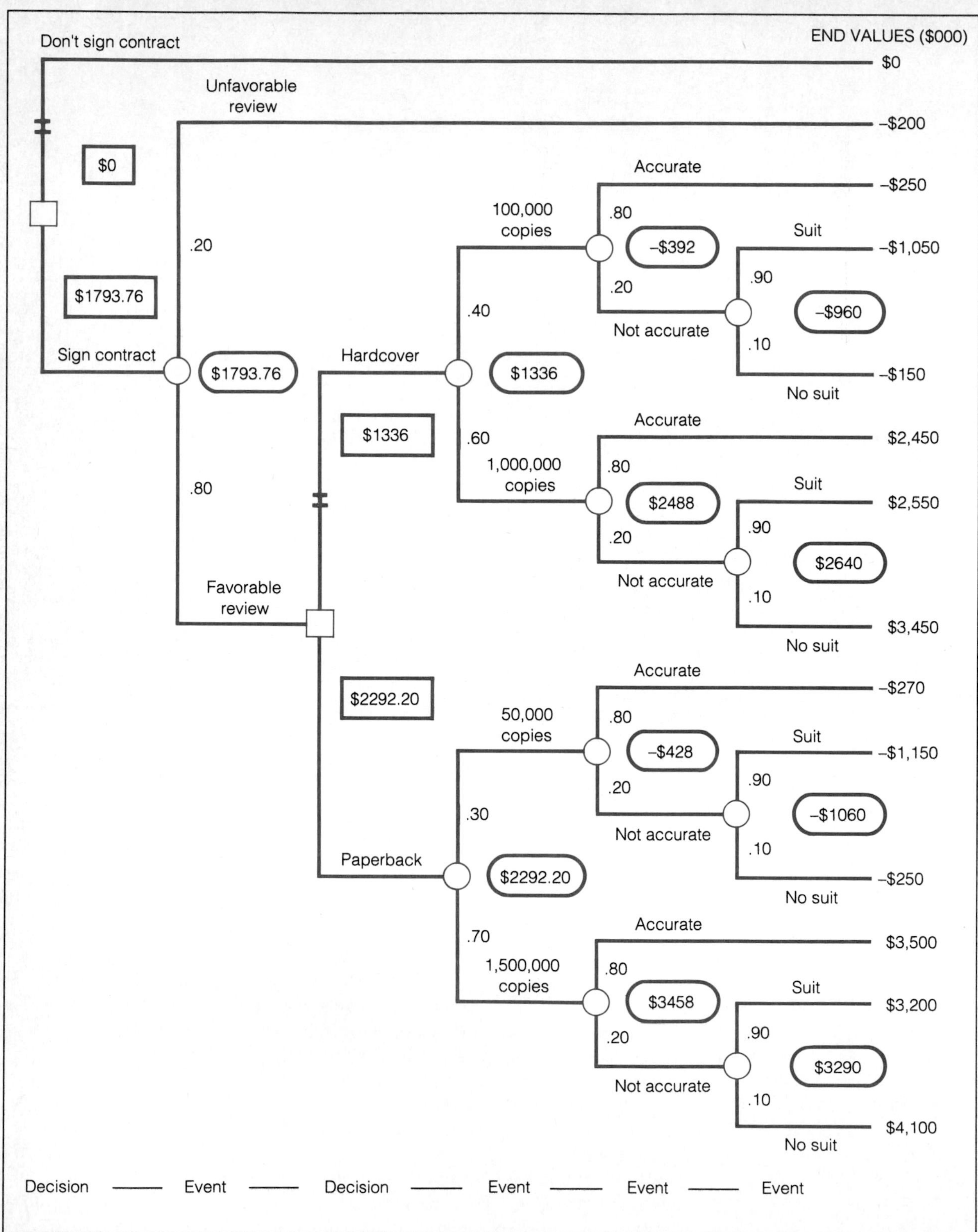

Figure 15-20
Decision tree for Harris Publishing example: Risk-neutral decision

Figure 15-21
Risk-preference function for Harris Publishing Company

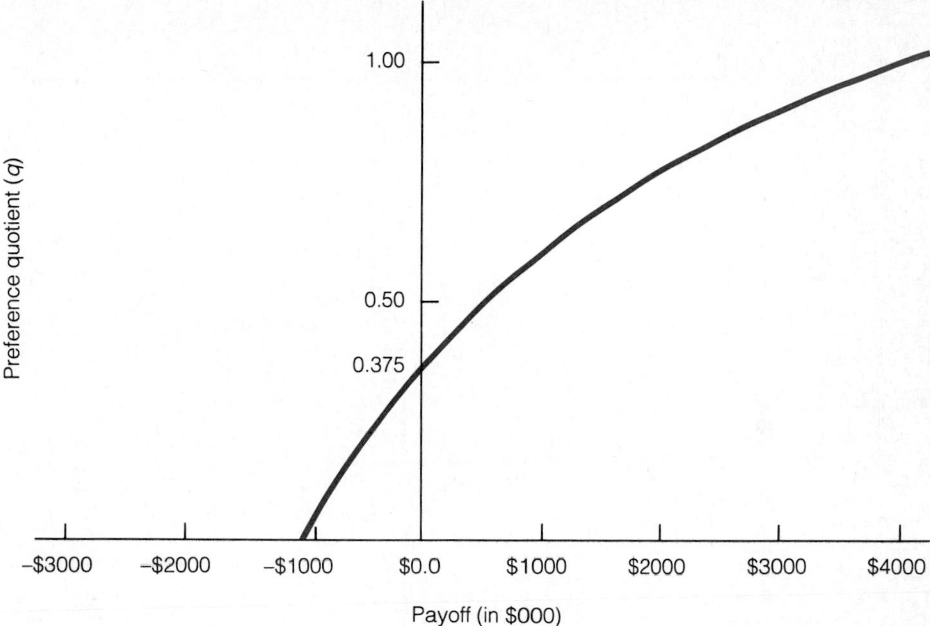

We use the risk-preference function in Figure 15-21 to obtain a preference quotient, q, for each end value on the decision tree in Figure 15-20. Figure 15-22 shows the decision tree with the q values for each end value at the far right side. Note that the payoff of $4100 ($4,100,000) has a q value of 1.0, indicating that this payoff is preferred over all others. The payoff −$1150 (−$1,150,000) has a q value of 0.0, indicating it is the least-preferred payoff.

Figure 15-22 also shows the results of folding back the decision tree using preference quotients rather than dollar values. The foldback process involves computing expected q values and, at decision points, selecting the alternative with the highest expected q value. As you can see, even though Anaya is risk-averse, the "best decision" is to sign the contract and, if the review is favorable, publish in paperback. The expected risk-preference quotient for this decision strategy is .6666, which is greater than $q = .37$ for the decision not to sign the contract. The potential payoffs are substantial enough to offset Laurel's dislike for the bad outcomes, and the decision remains the same as it was when analyzed from a risk-neutral viewpoint.

15-5 SUMMARY AND CONCLUSIONS

Not all decision makers are willing to make decisions strictly on the basis of the highest expected payoff or lowest expected cost. Many people will select an alternative which has a lower expected payoff than another alternative if doing so reduces the possibility of a bad outcome. Another decision maker will pick an alternative with a lower expected value just for the chance of a high payoff. Thus, not all decision makers are risk-neutral; in fact, most are not. The majority tend to be risk avoiders, and others are risk seekers.

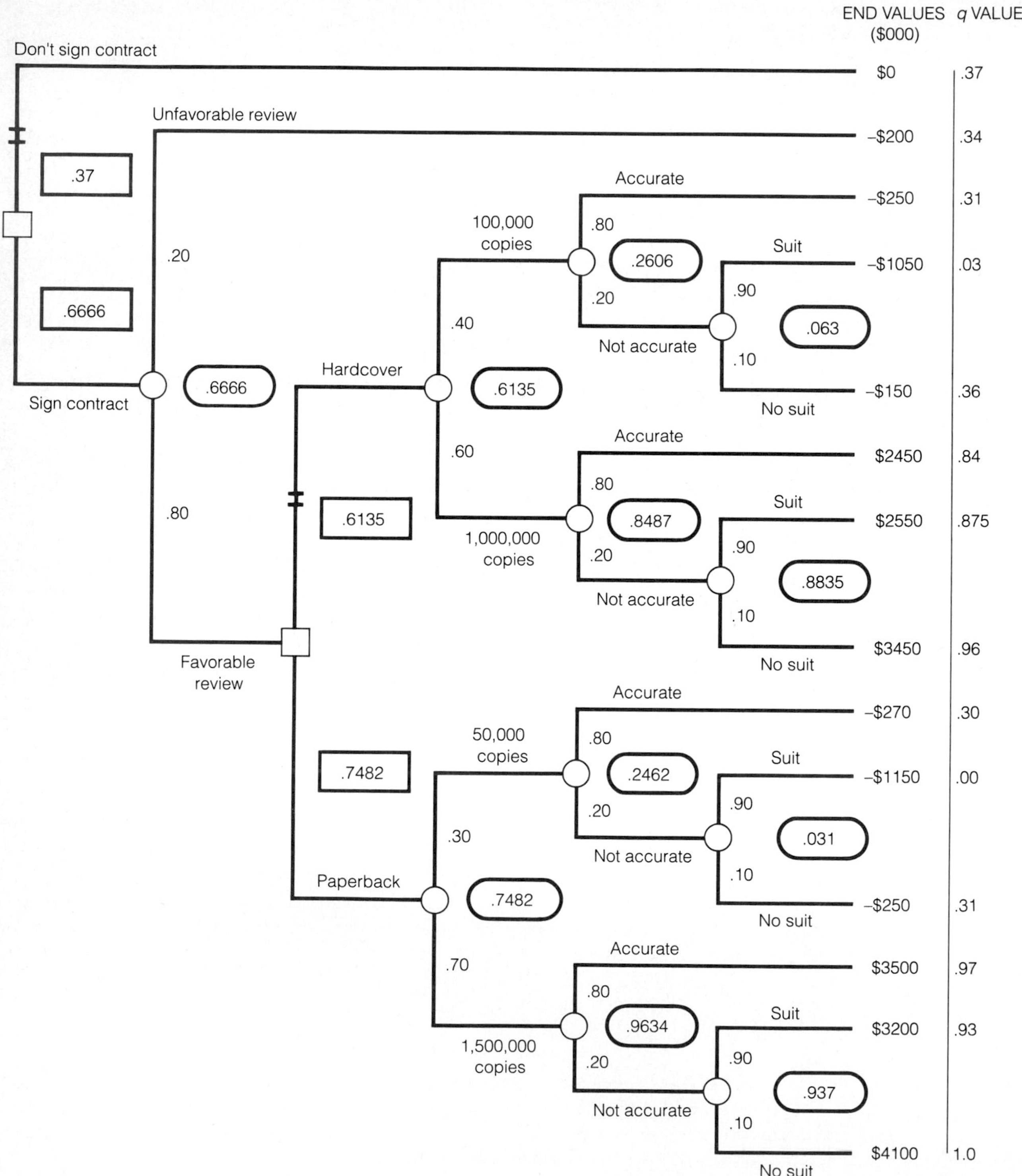

Figure 15-22
Decision tree for Harris Publishing example: Risk-averse

This chapter has introduced the concept of risk preference and showed how attitudes toward risk are incorporated into the decision process. We explained how risk-preference functions are developed using the standard gamble approach, and we discussed the concept of risk premium. We showed how to incorporate information from a risk-preference function into a decision-tree analysis; instead of folding back the dollar payoffs or costs, you fold back the q values for each payoff. Then, at each decision point, select the alternative with the highest q value.

A decision analysis is not complete, and would not accurately model the decision maker's state of mind, if it does not take into account his or her attitude toward risk. The basics introduced in this chapter will get you started in incorporating risk preferences into decision analysis. We suggest that you consult the Chapter References for sources of information on risk-preference analysis.

Solved Problem

PROBLEM Use the standard gamble approach to construct a risk-preference function for the range of payoffs between \$100,000 and −\$50,000. Assume the decision maker is risk-averse.

Solution We start by assigning preference quotients for the two extreme outcomes, as follows:

Payoff	q
\$100,000	1.0
−\$50,000	0.0

This indicates that the most preferred outcome is \$100,000 and the least preferred outcome is −\$50,000. Now we ask the decision maker what his or her certainty equivalent (*CE*) is for a 50-50 gamble at \$100,000 or −\$50,000. The expected value is:

$$E(\text{payoff}) = .50(\$100{,}000) + .50(-\$50{,}000) = \$25{,}000$$

A risk-averse decision maker will have a *CE* less than \$25,000. Suppose that after careful discussion with the decision maker, we set the *CE* at −\$3000. This means that the decision maker is indifferent between paying \$3000 and taking the 50-50 gamble.

Now we determine the risk-preference quotient for the *CE* value by finding the expected q value for the gamble:

$$E(q) = .50(1.0) + .50(0.0) = .50$$

We now have the following:

Payoff	q
\$100,000	1.00
−\$3,000	0.50
−\$50,000	0.00

We continue by establishing another standard gamble between \$100,000 and −\$3000. The expected value of a 50-50 gamble between these two values is:

$$E(\text{payoff}) = .50(\$100{,}000) + .50(-\$3000) = \$48{,}500$$

A risk-averse decision maker will have a *CE* lower than \$48,500. Suppose, after much discussion, the CE is set at \$40,000. The q value for this new CE is found by:

$$E(q) = .50(1.0) + .50(.50) = .75$$

We now have:

Payoff	q
\$100,000	1.00
\$40,000	0.75
−\$3,000	0.50
−\$50,000	0.00

We can continue by setting up a standard gamble for the payoffs −\$3000 and −\$50,000. The expected value for this gamble is:

$$E(\text{payoff}) = .50(-\$3000) + .50(-\$50{,}000) = -\$26{,}500$$

A risk-averse decision maker will have a CE less than −\$26,500. Suppose this figure is −\$40,000. The q value for this value is found by:

$$E(q) = .50(.50) + .50(0.0) = .25$$

We have now determined the following q values:

Payoff	q
\$100,000	1.00
\$40,000	0.75
−\$3,000	0.50
−\$40,000	0.25
−50,000	0.00

Although more points could be established, these five values are sufficient to develop a plot of the risk-preference function, as shown in Figure 15-23.

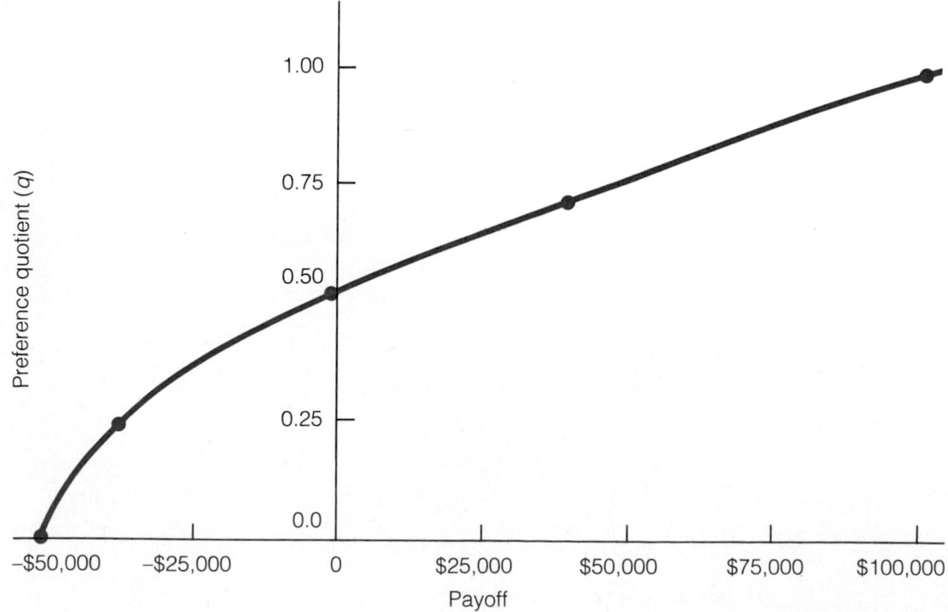

Figure 15-23
Preference-function curve

General Questions and Assignments

1. Discuss why the expected-value criterion is used in decision analysis for one-time decisions even though expected value represents the long-run average outcome.
2. The concept of *risk premium* is discussed in this chapter. Use an example of your own to illustrate what is meant by a risk premium.
3. Discuss the three types of risk-preference attitudes and present an example describing each one.
4. Could two people, one a risk avoider and the other a risk seeker, reach the same decision for a given application? Discuss. Formulate an example which supports your position.
5. Locate three or more articles which deal with using risk preferences for decision problems. Write a short paper discussing the situations described in these articles.
6. Contact a local business and meet with a lower-level manager. Construct a sample decision problem and show this manager the decision tree with the range of end values. Then use the standard gamble approach to construct his or her risk-preference function. Write a short report describing your experiences.
7. Referring to question 6, contact a higher-level manager in the same company, and go through the same process. Compare the preference functions for the two managers. Write a short report discussing the differences and/or similarities between the two.

Exercises and Application Problems

Problems 1 through 9 refer to the following situation.

Russell Smith is assessing his options as the planting season for his 1000-acre farm nears. The problem is this has so far been a bad snow year and Russell's farm is dependent on irrigation water from the Magic Valley Reservoir. If the remaining spring snowfall in the mountains that feed the reservoir is below average, his farm will run out of irrigation water in August. If the spring snowfall is average, he will have water for the entire season, but at 75% of the normal level. If the snowfall is above average, Russell will have his normal allocation of water. Russell has three options: (1) not plant at all, and collect federal idle-land payments, (2) plant oats, and (3) plant potatoes. While not planting at all will guarantee a payment, the federal money will not cover the loan payment due at the bank. However, spending the money necessary to plant either of the two crops will be lost if the spring snowfall is light. The following table lists the potential income values arising from the three possible snow levels and Russell's three planting alternatives.

		Snowfall	
Alternative	Light	Average	High
Don't plant	−$10,000	−$10,000	−$10,000
Plant oats	−$20,000	$30,000	$30,000
Plant potatoes	−$50,000	$10,000	$60,000

1. Without any information about what level of snowfall is likely, what alternative should Russell choose if he is risk-neutral and uses the *maximin* decision criterion?
2. Without any information about what level of snowfall is likely, what alternative should Russell choose if he is risk-neutral and uses the *maximax* decision criterion?
3. The long-range forecast from the National Weather Service indicates the precipitation forecast for the next three months is: *P*(light snow) = .5, *P*(average snow) = .3, *P*(heavy snow) = .2. On the

basis of this information, and using the expected-value criterion, what alternative would you recommend for Russell?

4. Before making his decision, Russell constructs a risk-preference function. The following are several points on his curve.

Outcome	Preference
−$75,000	0.00
$0	0.58
$10,000	0.62
$40,000	0.78
$100,000	1.00

Use these values to sketch the appropriate risk-preference curve for this problem and to construct a risk-preference table for the decision facing Russell.

5. Using the risk-preference table determined in problem 4 and the probability assessments in problem 3, choose the appropriate planting strategy for Russell, using the expected-risk preference criterion.
6. Russell Smith's neighbor has deep wells drilled on his farm. He is willing to sell Russell extra water, which will ensure normal water levels, if the wells do not run dry. To use this potential water, Russell will have to install a temporary pipeline costing $10,000. In addition, the extra water will cost $15,000 and will be used only if snowfall is light or average. Russell assesses the probability the wells will not run dry as 75%. Draw the appropriate decision tree including this new alternative. Assess this decision tree assuming Russell is risk-neutral.
7. Use the decision tree from problem 6 and the risk-preference curve determined in problem 4 to decide whether Russell should arrange to purchase water from his neighbor.
8. In addition to considering purchasing water from his neighbor, Russell is also considering the alternative of buying drought insurance for the first time. The cost of this insurance will be $5000 and will pay off only if no water is received, starting in August. Russell estimates the payoff will be $20,000 if he receives any insurance money. Add this new factor to the decision tree developed in problem 6. Again, assuming Russell is a risk-neutral decision maker, recommend a course of action for him.
9. Use the decision tree from problem 8 and the risk-preference curve determined in problem 4 to recommend a course of action for Russell.

Problems 10 through 15 refer to the following situation.

Hatchman Electronics makes specialized fuel injection units for automobile engines. The company is presently completing its 5-year strategic plan. A major component is this plan involves analyzing the following situation.

Hatchman presently makes an injection unit which it sells to automobile manufacturers for $200. The operating profit (revenue − direct manufacturing costs) for this unit is $90. The company estimates the probability is 80% that demand for this product will continue, at the same price, for the next 5 years. But if a competitor introduces a better unit, the selling price will be dropped to $140 to maintain the company's market share. Hatchman Electronics is considering trying to develop an improved fuel injector. Whether the product is successful or not, the development costs will be amortized by adding $20 to the cost of every injector sold for the next 5 years. If the development effort is successful, the improved unit will still be sold for $200 but direct manufacturing costs will be reduced to $70. The research and development department estimates the probability of the development effort being successful is 60%.

10. Develop a decision tree representing the Hatchman Electronics decision situation.
11. Assuming the Hatchman Electronics board of directors is willing to consider this problem from a risk-neutral perspective, should they decide to develop the new product?

12. Since the fuel injection unit is a high-volume product for Hatchman Electronics, the company may not be willing to analyze the decision from a risk-neutral perspective. Assume the preference function shown in Figure 15-24 applies to the decision. What is the best decision about producing the new product now?
13. Hatchman Electronics has the option of contracting with Stewart Consultants to analyze the feasibility of developing the new fuel injection unit. The feasibility study will cost $5 million and will be added to the production cost of each of the 1 million units the company is planning to make over the next 5 years. If the study indicates the new development is feasible, the probability of the product being successfully developed will be increased to 90%. If the study indicates the new development is not feasible, the product may still be developed but the probability of its being successful drops to 20%. Hatchman's managers don't have enough information to speculate about the probability the feasibility study will indicate a success; so they assess each outcome—success and not a success—as equally likely. Develop the decision tree for this new situation.
14. Assuming the Hatchman Electronics board of directors is still willing to consider this problem from a risk-neutral perspective, should they hire Stewart Consultants? What is the new sequence of decisions that should be taken?
15. Hatchman's president has read that companies that take no risks do not remain competitive in today's environment. Put yourself in the president's position and draw a risk seeker's preference function. Using this preference function, what is the best decision about producing the new product now?

Problems 16 through 21 refer to the following situation.

The Grimm Group presents in-house training seminars to organizations throughout the United States. The company presently presents seminars on three topics: quality control, material management, and just-in-time (JIT) manufacturing. The quality control seminar costs each participant $500, and the Grimm Group's gross margin (revenue − direct expenses) is 40% of this amount. The material management seminar costs $450 for each attendee and also has a 40% gross margin; the JIT seminar costs $600 and has a 35% gross margin. After 5 years of expansion, attendance at the seminars has declined more than 10% in

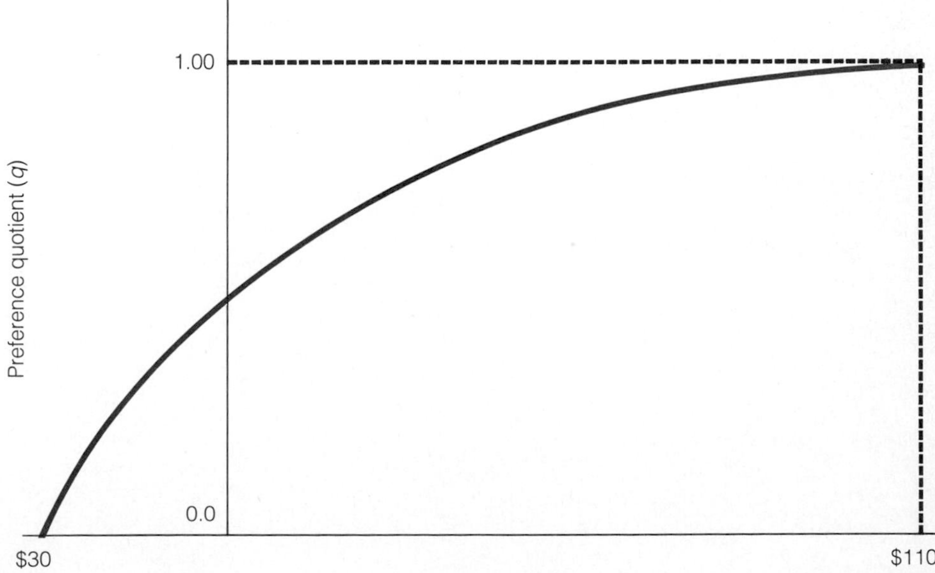

Figure 15-24
Risk-preference curve for Hatchman Electronics

the past year. The revenues from the three operations last year were: quality control, $1,200,000; material management, $900,000; JIT, $1,400,000.

At the yearly forecasting meeting, Graciela Grimm, the company's founder, projects that if no changes are made in marketing philosophy, revenues will be stagnant this year. She is, however, considering two options which should increase demand for the three seminars. The first option is to incorporate a computer simulation game as part of each seminar. Projections indicate that adding this type of game will increase the demand for the quality control seminar by 10% and the demand for the other two seminars by 15%. Adding a game will increase the cost associated with each seminar participant by $50; but, because the market is very competitive, the company will have to hold the line on the price change. The second option is to offer 3-day training seminars on the same topics but at 60% of the price of the 5-day seminars. Unfortunately, the cost of presenting the 3-day seminars will be reduced by only 20% from the cost of the original seminars. The president estimates the demand for the shorter seminars this year will generate revenues equal to 50% of the revenues realized from each 5-day seminar in the past year. Also, adding the shorter seminars will reduce the projected demand for the original seminars to 75% of last year's level.

16. Develop a decision tree describing the Grimm Group's decision situation.
17. Assuming President Grimm is risk-neutral for this decision, what alternative would you recommend?
18. Assume the president's attitude about risk can be represented by the preference curve developed for a previous project (Figure 15-25). What alternative would you recommend now?
19. An initial market survey of the acceptance of simulation games indicates they are so popular that there is a 70% chance the Grimm Group will be able to raise the price of the seminars by enough to maintain its previous margins without affecting the demand. Incorporate this new information into your previous problem analysis.
20. Assume that Graciela Grimm is risk-neutral for the decision situation as amended by problem 19. Now what alternative would you recommend?
21. Using Figure 15-25 to assess Grimm's attitude about risk, what alternative do you recommend as the decision for problem 19?

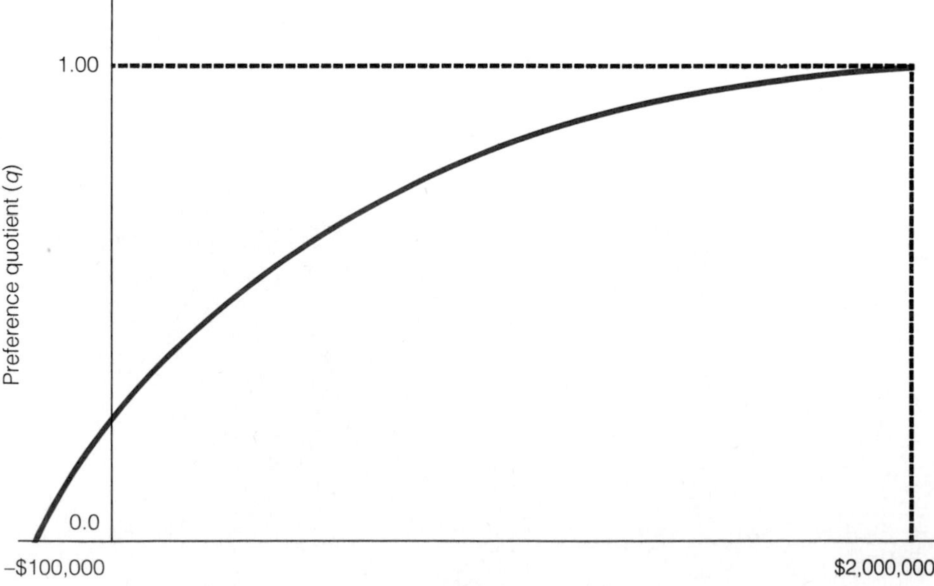

Figure 15-25
Risk-preference curve for the Grimm Group

Chapter Glossary

Certainty equivalent The value that would make a decision maker indifferent between taking an uncertain gamble versus taking that value; the amount a decision maker would pay to give up the opportunity to take the gamble.

Preference quotient A measure of the relative utility for the outcomes of a decision on a scale between 1.0 and 0.0.

Risk-averse attitude The preference for risk under which the risk premium will be positive.

Risk-neutral attitude The preference for risk under which the alternative with the highest expected payoff or lowest expected cost will be selected.

Risk-preference function A graph of the decision maker's risk-preference quotients over the range of possible payoffs.

Risk premium The difference between the expected value of an event and the certainty equivalent. The risk premium will be zero for a risk-neutral decision maker, positive for a risk-averse decision maker, and negative for a risk-seeking decision maker.

Risk-seeking attitude The preference for risk under which the risk premium will be negative.

Standard gamble approach The approach for assessing risk-preference functions which involves setting up a series of 50-50 gambles between two payoffs and determining the certainty equivalent for each gamble.

Chapter References

BOOKS

Baird, Bruce F. *Managerial Decision Making under Uncertainty*. New York: Wiley, 1989.

Brown, R. V., A. S. Kahr, and C. Peterson. *Decision Analysis for the Manager*. New York: Holt, 1974.

Bunn, D. W. *Applied Decision Analysis*. New York: McGraw-Hill, 1984.

Felson, J. *Decision Making under Uncertainty*. New York: CBS Business and Professional Publishing, 1979.

Fishburn, P. C. *Utility Theory for Decision Making*. New York: Wiley, 1970.

Gregory, G. *Decision Analysis*. New York: Plenum, 1988.

Holloway, C. *Decision Making under Uncertainty: Models and Choices*. Englewood Cliffs, N.J.: Prentice-Hall, 1979.

Keeney, R. L., and H. Raiffa. *Decisions with Multiple Objectives: Preferences and Value Trade-offs*. New York: Wiley, 1976.

Raiffa, H. *Decision Analysis*. Reading, Mass.: Addison-Wesley, 1968.

Sampson, D. *Managerial Decision Analysis*. Homewood, Ill.: Irwin, 1988.

Schlaifer, R. *Analysis of Decisions under Uncertainty*. New York: McGraw-Hill, 1969.

Winkler, R. *Introduction to Bayesian Inference and Decision*. New York: Holt, 1972.

ARTICLES

Arrow, K. J. "Utilities, Attitudes, Choices: A Review Note." *Econometrica*, Vol. 26, 1958.

Bell, D. "Regret in Decision Making under Uncertainty." *Operations Research*, Vol. 30, 1982.

Davidson, F. "Dimensions of Utility in a Regional Planning Context." *Decision Sciences*, January 1974.

Farquhar, P. "Utility Assessment Methods." *Management Science*, Vol. 30, 1984.

Friedman, M., and L. J. Savage. "The Utility Analysis of Choices Involving Risk." *Journal of Political Economy*, August 1948.

Hammond, J. S. "Better Decisions with Preference Theory." *Harvard Business Review*, Vol. 45 (November–December), 1967.

Stimson, D. H. "Utility Measurement in Public Health Decision Making." *Management Science*, Vol. 16, 1969.

Swalm, R. O. "Utility, Theory Insights into Risk Taking," *Harvard Business Review*, November–December 1966.

Mini Cases

CASE 15A
HADDEN MATERIALS AND SUPPLIES, INC. PART 1

Mark Hadden and his son, Greg, began Hadden Materials and Supplies, Inc., in the mid-1980s. Both Mark and Greg had had successful careers with major U.S. corporations, but after several years of talking about it they came to the conclusion that they wanted to work together in their own business. They also concluded that they wanted to be in manufacturing, where they could take advantage of their previous experience and business contacts.

From the beginning, Mark has run the production shop and Greg has concentrated on sales. About two years ago, they got a contract to make an electronic component for natural gas heaters. At first they made this part exclusively for one company, but about 6 months ago they started making the same component for other heater manufacturers. The component is produced in large volume and sells for $30. The variable production cost per unit is $13, making this a very profitable product for the company.

However, until recently there was no way to determine whether a component would work properly until it had actually been installed in the heater unit. Whenever the heater manufacturer found a defect, Hadden Materials and Supplies would refund the full $30 plus pay a penalty of $10. Although the company has made major improvements in its quality control program, this particular component is very difficult to build and to have work properly. As a result, the defect rate has been approximately 25%.

A week ago, the company was approached by a representative of Tech-Notics, Inc., who said her company had a device for testing components like the one Hadden makes for gas heaters. By using this tester, Hadden could determine before shipping whether the component would work or not. This was one sales call that really got Mark and Greg's attention, and the sales representative agreed to bring a unit by for a trial the next morning. Greg called their largest customer and made some arrangements to "test the tester" at the customer's plant the next afternoon.

Over the next two days, Mark, Greg, and the Tech-Notics sales representative tested 400 components. Of these, 320 tested positive, indicating that they would turn out to be good; however, of the 320 that tested positive, 72 ended up actually being defective. In addition, of the components that got a negative reading, 8 were found to be good. Although the testing device was not perfect, the Haddens were still encouraged.

The sales representative explained that her company preferred to lease the testers, with a financial arrangement that called for the lessor to pay $3 per test. (The tester had an automatic counter.) If the unit were sold outright, it would cost $6 million. Mark and Greg realized there was no way that they could afford to purchase the unit, so that option was immediately eliminated. However, they were interested in the lease plan and told the sales representative they would call her soon with their decision.

As Mark and Greg conferred over lunch, they estimated the heater component would remain in production for about 2 more years. During that time, they could expect orders for about 100,000 units. They also agreed that if they leased the tester, they would use it to test every component that they built. As Greg said, "Why should we lease it if we don't use it!" They also concluded that if an item tested negative, it would be scrapped and not shipped.

CASE 15B

HADDEN MATERIALS AND SUPPLIES PART 2

About 2 hours after Mark Hadden had phoned the Tech-Notics sales representative to tell her of his company's tentative decision, he placed a call to Diane Rogers. Diane is a former colleague of Mark's who now serves as a consultant to manufacturing companies. After Mark explained the details of the decision he and Greg had made, Diane asked whether they had considered their risk preferences in their analysis. Mark said that they thought they had, but he didn't quite know what Diane was referring to.

Before long, Mark was offering to cover the expenses if Diane and Fred, her husband, would fly out for a long weekend—and if Diane would provide some advice on this decision. They agreed to get their work out of the way Friday evening and leave the rest of the weekend for some fun and relaxation.

Friday afternoon, after making sure that Diane and Fred had arrived and were settled into their hotel, Mark arranged to drive Diane to the plant to meet with Greg. As they discussed the decision situation, Diane made some notes. She remarked that it appeared Mark and Greg had not formally considered their preferences for risk; instead, they had conducted their analysis as if they were risk-neutral. She also noted that the decision regarding the tester should be analyzed as if only one component was being built instead of 100,000.

Diane suggested that together they try to develop a risk-preference function for this deal. First, she asked the partners to determine the highest possible addition and the biggest possible reduction in the company's net cash position that might result from the decision. Greg indicated that these ranged from a high of +\$17 per unit to a low of −\$26 per unit. Then Diane posed a series of questions, beginning with this one: "Suppose you are faced with an event that will give you a 50-50 chance at making \$17 versus losing \$26. Further suppose that you will be forced to participate. Do you want to?"

Both Mark and Greg agreed that it didn't seem like a very good deal. Diane then

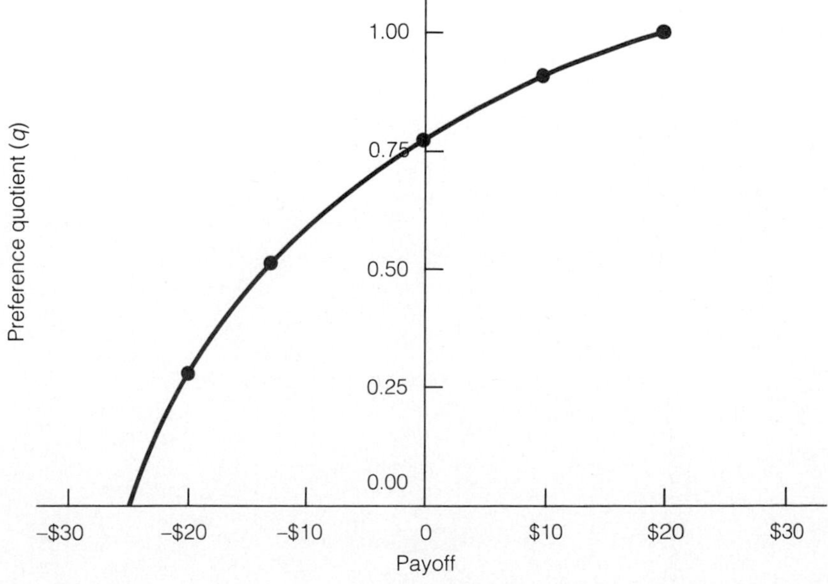

Figure 15-26
Risk-preference curve for Mini Case 15B

asked, "Suppose I will let you out of the deal for a fee. would you pay me $20 right now to get out of the deal?"

Mark and Greg conferred and decided that they would not pay $20 but they would pay $16 to get out of the deal. Diane wrote this down and continued asking similar questions until she finally announced, "Now we have enough information about your risk preferences to develop a risk-preference curve, which we can then use in your decision analysis."

The curve that Diane drew is shown in Figure 15-26. The group then set out to determine whether this finding would alter the decision Mark and Greg had made before conferring with Diane.

After making arrangements for an early tennis game Saturday morning, Mark asked Diane if she would take some time on Saturday to explain clearly what they had done this afternoon and why the results were the way they were, compared with the decision that Mark and Greg had reached earlier.

Chapter 16

INTRODUCTION TO SIMULATION MODELING

Chapter Outline

Chapter 16

Why You Need to Know

The first 15 chapters of this text have introduced a wide variety of useful and important management science techniques. We have stressed that, as a decision maker, you will be faced with situations in which applying one or more of these techniques may be helpful. We have also stressed that the choice of which technique to use must be based on the specific problem being analyzed, rather than trying to fit the problem to a certain technique.

Thus, your task will be to identify the problem that needs to be solved, or the decision to be made, and to fully understand the circumstances which surround the problem or decision. Then you can use the particular management science technique which best models the situation. For example, if the problem has characteristics which are consistent with those modeled by linear programming, you will want to develop and solve a linear programming model. If an inventory decision has the characteristics of the basic EOQ model, such as constant demand and known lead time, then the basic EOQ inventory technique could be used to model the decision situation.

However, for many business decisions, the underlying characteristics will contain features that are to some extent inconsistent with the assumptions of any specific management science model. The decision maker may decide to go ahead and apply the "most appropriate" management science technique realizing that the "optimal" output from the model may be only a reasonable solution for the true situation. This is sometimes referred to as "satisficing" as opposed to optimizing, since the decision maker is willing to settle for a satisfactory, rather than optimal, solution. Alternatively, the decision maker may feel that the situation is too much in conflict with the assumptions of an existing management science model and that the results from using any model would be misleading. In these cases, developing an appropriate unique mathematical model may be very difficult, if not impossible.

In situations for which developed management science models are judged to be inappropriate, decision makers have increasingly been using simulation models. In somewhat formal terms, **simulation** is the use of a model to represent the critical characteristics of a system and to observe the system's operation over time. By the strictest definition, much of what we have covered so far in the text can be classified as simulation, since a management science model is used to model a physical situation. In practice, however, simulation models are characterized by (1) being developed as a computer routine, (2) dealing with situations involving uncertainty by running repeated trials of the computer program, and (3) monitoring the decision situation over time.

Once a simulation model is developed, the decision maker can experiment with various aspects of the real system by observing the results from the model. For instance, a simulation model of a lumber mill could be used to test the effect of adding a second shift or to see the impact if the supply of logs is interrupted. A simulation model of a bank could be used to determine the improvement in service if additional teller windows are provided in the bank lobby.

Simulation is a very versatile and powerful tool for decision makers. With computers being so readily available, computer simulation models are heavily used in business and government. Because of its increasing use, you need to have a good understanding of the fundamentals of how simulation models are developed and employed. After studying the material in this chapter, you should have gained this understanding.

Chapter Objectives

The objectives of this chapter are to introduce the basic steps in building a simulation model and to illustrate several examples of where simulation models have been used in business decision situations. After studying the material in this chapter, you should:

1. Have a good understanding of how simulation models are used in business decision making.
2. Know the steps involved in developing a simulation model.
3. Be able to design and develop small-scale simulation models.
4. Be able to recognize situations for which simulation models are an appropriate management science technique.

16-1 A BRIEF HISTORY OF SIMULATION

Simulation, as a management science technique, has evolved from early models developed by engineers and scientists almost a century ago. In the late 1800s, engineers and scientists used **analog simulation models**—physical models representing real systems—of fluid flows to help design dams and other projects involving fluid transfers. In the early 1900's, engineers relied heavily on physical simulation models of direct current to solve electric-power-distribution problems. By the late 1920s, scientists and engineers began to develop large-scale analog simulation models. Through the 1930s, widespread use was made of mechanical methods for solving complex algebraic and differential equations. During the war years of the 1940s, physical simulation models were used to help solve military distribution problems. Automobile engineers began using wind-tunnel simulations to help design more efficient cars.

However, using simulation in business and economic analysis didn't really begin until the late 1950s, when digital computers became available. At this point the focus shifted from analog to digital simulation methods. There were virtually no articles published before 1955 about business simulation. For a variety of reasons, including programming difficulties, the slow processing speed of the computer, and limited memory capacity, the early computerized business simulation examples were quite basic. The models were of simple inventory systems, simple waiting-line systems, and small-scale economic systems.

However, as computer capabilities increased and more became known about the power of computer simulation, the applications and uses became much more sophisticated. In management science, simulation is used in Markov chain models (presented later, in Chapter 18), complex queuing models, stochastic inventory systems, and many other areas. Simulation has been heavily used in production scheduling applications to estimate such factors as resource availability, process cycle time, machine breakdowns, production volume, and facility idle times. In the 1970s, computer simulation was used to study the effects of such factors as lot-size and lead-time uncertainty on the performance of a materials requirements planning (MRP) system. And in the 1980s, simulation studies were used to examine numerous situations involving just-in-time (JIT) manufacturing.

Simulation has also had a major role in marketing. For instance, the Pillsbury Company uses a simulation model of consumer behavior to measure the effect of marketing and promotional alternatives for specific products. Anheuser-Busch and Corning Glass, among many others, use simulation models to forecast product sales.

People working in finance have developed many applications for simulation. One of the earliest uses of simulation for financial analysis was by Geoffrey Clarkson, in 1962, when he simulated the decision process used by a bank trust officer in selecting investment policies for particular accounts and in developing portfolios for the accounts. David Hertz published an article in 1964 in which he used simulation to develop the probability distribution for the present value of an investment alternative.

In 1968, the Sun Oil Company developed one of the first corporate financial models, which provided management with fast, reliable information about the financial position of the firm and allowed the managers to test "What if?" scenarios. By the way, the Sun Oil simulation model required 13 person-years to complete, and another 10 person-years were required to make the model workable. The total elapsed time for the model's development was 2.5 years. Boise Cascade, a wood products and paper company, followed with a simulation model called the Pacific Northwest Planning Model, which is used to simulate the effects that timberland purchases and capital expenditures have on profits.

By the early 1970s, most major companies were using simulation for one purpose or another. IBM, Xerox, Hewlett-Packard, and General Motors are just a few of the companies that have invested heavily in computer simulation as a tool for decision making. The trend through the 1980s was for even greater emphasis on simulation. The availability of low-cost, high-speed, personal computers has now made simulation accessible to medium and small businesses.

Throughout the 1990s, there will be increasing emphasis on the application of simulation to help decision makers deal with an even broader range of decision situations. More powerful personal computers, with capabilities previously seen only in large mainframes, make simulation analysis even more accessible to managers at all levels. And current simulation software will be enhanced to provide for the modeling of more complicated decision situations.

Simulation has not been limited to the private sector, however. Many public agencies have long used simulation as a tool for analyzing policy alternatives. For example, in 1978, voters in Idaho passed an initiative limiting property taxes to 1% of the property's actual market value. The Tax Commission sponsored a simulation model which was used to explore a wide variety of implementation strategies. The model, which shows the revenue impact on all the tax districts in Idaho, has been used extensively to help answer questions posed by legislators and other government officials regarding proposed changes in the property tax system.

16-2 STEPS IN DEVELOPING A SIMULATION MODEL

The previous chapters in this text have introduced a number of important and useful management science techniques, all of which have applications in business decision making. However, each technique is restricted by assumptions which limit its use to those cases where the assumptions apply. The most widely used models are obviously those where the actual decision-making situation corresponds most often to these assumptions. In addition, in those cases where they can be applied, techniques such as linear programming, PERT, and inventory models provide "optimal results" for the system at a particular point in time. However, this is often too restrictive for a decision maker who wishes to observe the behavior of the system over a longer period.

Simulation is a management science technique which allows the analyst to model an actual system and then use the model to observe how the system behaves over time. Being able to observe a system's behavior over time is what separates simulation from the other management science techniques. There are many situations where this is a desirable feature. In addition, simulation models are particularly useful when experimenting on an actual system will be either too expensive or time-consuming, or both. To demonstrate what we mean, consider the plan by the city of Denver to build a new airport, replacing the outmoded Stapleton. Among other factors, the designers will have to consider the appropriate number of air traffic controllers, the best number of runways, and the appropriate size of the baggage-handling facility. Of course, the new airport could be built and these factors could be determined by trial and error, but this could be very expensive if any changes were needed. A model would simulate airline arrivals and departures over time, and the designers could observe such factors as number and length of landing and takeoff delays, number of accidents or near misses, and/or baggage delivery problems as they varied the model's components.

The National Forest Service could use a simulation model of a forest to observe, over time, how different harvest strategies would impact the forest system and the availability of trees used to make paper. The decision makers might use the model to simulate such phenomena as tree growth, trees lost to disease or fire, and environmental impacts.

An oil company planning to construct a new refinery might use a simulation model to test the effects of various designs on the cost and quality of the refined oil. The model would simulate oil refining over a period of time, and the analysts would collect observations from the model.

A key advantage of simulation is that it allows decision makers to examine the effects of changes to a system without incurring the costs and time delays of actually making the physical changes. Imagine the expense of trying an airport with both four and six runways! As another example, suppose a bank is considering building a new drive-up teller facility. Among the many considerations in the design would be how many teller windows and driving lanes to add and how large a vehicle waiting area to pave. A simulation model of this system would allow the decision makers to try different numbers of teller windows and different configurations of vehicle access. The various options could be examined without the expense of actually having to build the facility.

Consider also a city faced with traffic congestion in the downtown area. The city planners and transportation specialists could develop a simulation model of the downtown traffic flow and then examine the various routing and traffic patterns by running the simulation for various time periods. The decision makers would be able to see the effects on traffic waiting, accidents, and flow without actually having to physically try the patterns with real cars on real roads.

WHEN IS SIMULATION APPROPRIATE?

As indicated in the previous examples, simulation models are used to run experiments on a real system without actually having to alter, or build, the real system. There are several disadvantages to direct experimentation on a real system which are overcome by using simulation, as discussed in the following paragraphs.

First, a company's normal day-to-day operations would almost certainly be disrupted if physical changes to the system were made to facilitate experiments. Suppose a company which makes frozen French fries wanted to experiment with its production process to see what plant settings would improve the quality of the final product. To actually perform the experiments in the plant during normal processing runs would interfere with production, reduce output, and result in french fries of varying quality.

If people are an important part of the system, they may react differently during the experiments and adversely influence the results. For instance, suppose the management of a large company wishes to perform experiments on its mailroom operations by making changes in such factors as layout and work-force size. Because people are such an important part of the mailroom system, the experimental results would be tainted if the employees work differently during the experiments.

Also, maintaining the same operating conditions for each run of a physical experiment is difficult. For instance, in the plant that makes French fries, the quality of the raw potatoes coming into the plant has a great effect on the end product. An experiment to see how different cutting techniques affect the quality of the end product will be unreliable because the quality of the incoming raw potatoes is not constant. Thus, any differences in the end product caused by the cutting techniques may be difficult to determine because of this variability in the incoming potatoes.

In most realistic situations, valid conclusions cannot be reached after only one trial; in fact, many runs of an experiment may be required to achieve statistical significance. But this may be too time-consuming and costly if physical experiments are performed. Consider a commercial lawn-fertilizing company which wishes to experiment with different application techniques. To achieve the desired level of confidence may require that each application process be tested 50 to 100 times under identical conditions. Needless to say, this would be very costly and require extensive time.

In some cases, a manager may simply not be able to explore certain alternatives on the real system. For instance, an investment manager may be interested in testing a variety of investment strategies with his clients' money. However, because of moral and legal obligations, the manager cannot actually implement the experimental strategies.

These drawbacks to physical experimentation with the real system provide the reasons for performing experiments through simulation. When one or more of the following conditions exist, simulation should be considered:

1. If developing a complete mathematical model of the system is not possible or is too difficult to complete.
2. If the mathematical models, while possible, are so complex that simulation provides a more effective means of answering questions about the system.
3. If you are interested in observing the behavior of the system over time, in addition to estimating certain values of the system.
4. If running experiments using the real system are either not possible or are too expensive.
5. If you need to compress the time required to observe the physical experiment. For instance, a corporate model may simulate the company's operations for the next 5 years under various operating scenarios. Obviously, the company could not wait 5 years to see the effect of one operating strategy, then try a second strategy and wait 5 more years, and so on. Simulation would allow the effective passage of 5 years in a few minutes of computer time.

In addition to all the reasons that simulation is an important management science tool, it has great intuitive appeal to decision makers who are not trained in management science. We think this is a prime reason to consider simulation models. In one case, a manager who could not understand a model using complex queuing formulas was able to easily follow a simulation model of the same system. Consequently, he tended to ignore the queuing-model output and give substantial weight to the simulation results.

While simulation is one of the most frequently used management science techniques, there are also times when it is not the most effective or most efficient means of providing the needed information. The following are some of the major drawbacks to simulation:

1. Developing a simulation model is usually very costly and time-consuming and requires employees (or consultants) who are very experienced in such development.
2. Simulation models may not correctly describe the real system. Thus, the results from the simulation may not accurately portray how the real system would operate under the same experimental conditions.
3. Simulation models do not provide precise answers to questions about the system. Additionally, there is no way to determine how imprecise the results of the simulation are.

These three points could be made about all the models discussed in the text. The common point is that, before employing simulation, decision makers must weigh the advantages and disadvantages of simulation against their objectives. Although it is another useful tool, it is best used by managers who remember that it is only a useful aid to decision making.

THE ROLE OF COMPUTERS IN SIMULATION

When we refer to simulation, we are really referring to *computer simulation*. Computers have allowed decision makers to develop and use simulation models for a wide range of applications. Because computer simulation models can keep track of many different system values and can quickly simulate system operations over long periods, they can be used to easily test many variations of a system.

In the early stages of computer simulation, the models were programmed in machine language or in general-purpose languages such as FORTRAN and PL/1. In fact, many models still in use were programmed in these languages. As people gained experience with simulation models, they discovered that different systems often included similar functions. For instance, in simulating both production and service situations, the computer must have assigned clocks to keep track of arrival times, service times, and so forth; in any situation involving people or products waiting for service, the model has to keep track of waiting times and the length of waiting lines.

As the use of simulation increased, special-purpose computer languages were developed to aid in constructing models for situations that had similar functions, such as GPSS (General Purpose Systems Simulator), DYNAMO (developed at the Massachusetts Institute of Technology), SIMSCRIPT (developed by RAND Corporation and General Electric), SIMPAC (from Systems Development Corporation), and GASP (developed by United States Steel, the present USX Corporation.) Each language has specific advantages, depending on the system being simulated. For example, GPSS is especially useful for modeling queuing systems because it easily keeps track of arrivals, service times, waiting times, and so forth.

Since the purpose of this chapter is to introduce the concept of simulation, we will not look at specific programming models. It is likely that the information systems or computer science department at your college or university offers a course in computer simulation; taking that course will give you some experience in actually developing simulation models.

MASTER, the microcomputer software package which accompanies this text, contains two simulation routines, one for inventory and the other for waiting-line modeling. The next two sections present examples using the MASTER simulation software.

STEPS IN CONSTRUCTING AND APPLYING A SIMULATION MODEL

Constructing and applying a computer simulation model to a decision-making situation generally involves six steps:

1. Defining the problem.
2. Analyzing and modeling the system to be simulated.
3. Formulating the computer program.
4. Validating the model.
5. Designing the simulation experiments.
6. Analyzing data from the experiments.

The amount of time and effort required for each step depends on the complexity of the system being simulated.

Defining the Problem

As is the case when using any management science tool, the first step in constructing a simulation model is to define the problem. This means explicitly stating the objectives of the simulation. You need to determine what questions are to be answered, what hypotheses are to be tested, and what effects are to be estimated with the simulation model. You must also determine the type of output required to address these issues before starting to construct the model.

Analyzing and Modeling the System

Once the problem is defined, the next step in developing a simulation model is to analyze and model the system. This means you must examine the system and determine the relationship between the exogenous (or input) variables and the endogenous (or output) variables. **Exogenous variables** are the variables determined by forces outside the system. For instance, in a simulation model of emergency-room activity at a hospital, the arrival rate of trauma patients is an exogenous variable. **Endogenous variables** are the dependent variables in the system. In the emergency-room model, the number of patients waiting for emergency service is an endogenous variable; another might be the time a patient spends in the emergency room, from time of entry until discharge. The relationship between the exogenous and endogenous variables is determined by **controllable variables**, which are those factors within the system that can be controlled. For instance, the hospital can control the number of emergency-room beds and the number of doctors and nurses on call.

The endogenous, or dependent, variables are generally identified when the simulation objectives are determined. For example, in the emergency-room simulation, the problem statement will identify whether waiting time and queue length are variables whose values we want to monitor with the model. Determining what controllable and exogenous variables to include in the model is generally more difficult. Very complex systems have many exogenous and controllable variables. If we include too few of these variables in the model, the simulation will not represent the real system. On the other hand, if we attempt to include too many, the model development may become so complex that time or cost considerations make it infeasible. In the end, developing a simulation model always involves a trade-off between attempting to accurately represent the "true system" at a high cost and extensive time versus developing a simulation model that is too simplistic and does not provide valid information about the system.

Many simulation modelers use a flowchart to help analyze the system. A **flowchart** is a diagram using geometric symbols and arrows which represents the time flow and activities of the system. The decision maker can use a flowchart to more clearly define the relationship between variables in the system. Figure 16-1 is a simplified flowchart for the emergency room at a local hospital. If you trace through this flowchart, you get a pretty good idea of how the emergency room functions. However, the chart does not include every detail about the process; some variables have been left out. For instance, variables representing nurses and doctors on duty have not been included. Likewise, the diagnosis of trauma patients is limited to two levels: serious or not serious. Also not included are variables representing the availability of equipment and supplies needed to treat the emergency-room patients. By excluding these variables, a trade-off is being made between modeling reality and what is feasible to accomplish given time and cost considerations.

Formulating the Computer Program

Once the system has been analyzed and modeled, the computer program can be written. The specific programming language to be used depends on the situation being modeled, the availability of the simulation language, and the ability and experience of the programmer. The flowchart is an important guide for the programmer, since the program must match the logical relationships between the variables and be able to generate the time flow of the simulated system. The program must also be capable of producing the desired output reports. For instance, for the emergency-room simulation example, one required report might be like that shown in Table 16-1. Note that the status of the system is displayed for every hour and the cumulative statistics are presented at the end of each hour.

Another important step in developing the computer program is preparing the program documentation. The documentation specifies what data inputs are required and their form. It also provides a listing of the program, flowcharts, sample output reports, and other information pertaining to hardware requirements and other matters. Poor or nonexistent documentation is an increasing problem in many organizations. Model designers seldom want to take the time to accurately document their programs, often feeling that other tasks are more important. Unfortunately, if such a model must be modified when its designer is not available, it is likely that no one else can understand the program and the model must be reconstructed from the beginning.

Table 16-1 REPORT FORMAT FOR EMERGENCY-ROOM SIMULATION MODEL

Hour	Arrivals	Total Arrivals	Queue Length	Maximum Queue Length	Average Wait (min.)	Facility Use %
1	8	8	3	4	9.2	77.6
2	3	11	0	5	5.0	48.9
3	—	—	—	—	—	—
—	—	—	—	—	—	—
—	—	—	—	—	—	—
—	—	—	—	—	—	—

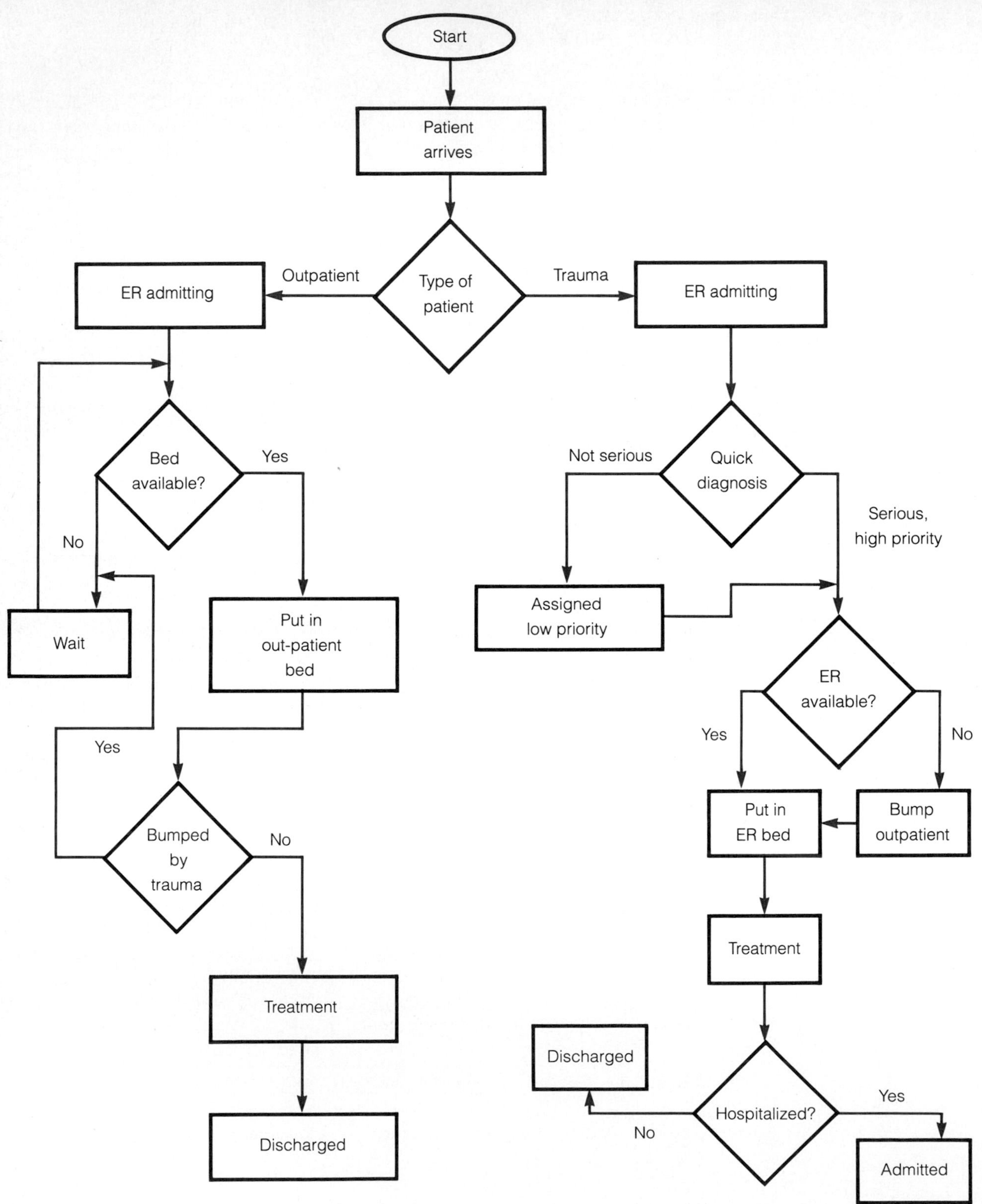

Figure 16-1
Flowchart for emergency-room simulation model

We cannot overemphasize the importance of thorough and accurate program documentation; it may well save you (or someone else) a great deal of time and effort in the future.

Validating the Model

Validation refers to determining how accurately the simulation model represents the real system. This is an important step, since our confidence in inferences we make about the system is determined by our confidence in the model. Four ways of validating a simulation model are described below.

First, we can determine how well the model duplicates the past by comparing its output with historical data. For example, in the emergency-room model, we could supply patient arrivals in the same sequence as those that actually occurred during the previous three months. Then we could compare the model's output for such endogenous variables as facility use, average queue length, and average waiting time with the actual results for those variables during the three-month period.

A second method of validation is to determine how well the model conforms to what we would expect, based on what we know about the system. For instance, in the emergency-room simulation, does the model indicate that waiting times are reduced, as we would expect, when the number of emergency beds is increased? And if so, how realistic is the reduction?

Another way is to determine to what extent the model is acceptable to other model designers. This step requires that we have the model examined by others inside and/or outside our own organization to determine its **face validity**. These "experts" will examine the model to see whether the functional relationships between variables appear to be reasonable. The experts' role should be to challenge the model by asking probing questions about the assumptions and formulation.

A fourth method of validating a simulation model is to determine whether the model is acceptable to those who are actually going to use it. That is, do the decision makers have confidence in the model and see it as a useful source of information about their system?

Although these steps are important in validating a simulation model, they do not necessarily ensure a valid model. However, by carefully applying these validation procedures and judging the model according to its defined purpose, we have the best chance of developing a useful simulation model. The true test of validation for a simulation model is to compare the model's "forecasts" with the actual future behavior of the system.

Designing the Simulation Experiments

The purpose of developing a simulation model is to be able to conduct experiments on the system without actually having to physically alter the system. Thus, a very important step in the simulation process is to design the experiments to be conducted. While a complete treatment of experimental design is beyond the scope of this text, we will discuss some important concepts to consider.

Two important terms related to experimental design are *factor* and *response,* which refer to variables in the simulation. Whether a variable is considered a factor or a response depends on the experiment being conducted. Let's consider two variables, X and Y, to explain the difference. If we want to determine how changes in variable X affect variable Y, then X is the factor and Y is the response. Thus, the **factor variable** must be an *exogenous* variable in the model. Conversely, the **response variable** in an experiment is an *endogenous* variable in the model. For example, in the emergency-room simulation model, we might be interested in assessing how an increase in the arrival rate of trauma patients affects the average outpatient waiting time. Thus, the arrival rate is the factor variable and the outpatient waiting time is the response variable.

An experiment may contain multiple factor and response variables. For instance, we might be interested in finding out how changing both trauma-patient arrival rates and the number of emergency-room beds will affect the average waiting time for all patients as well as maximum queue length in the system. In this case, the factor variables are trauma-patient arrival rate and number of emergency-room beds; the response variables are average waiting time for all patients and maximum queue length. In the experiment, we would vary the factor variables, holding all other exogenous variables constant, and observe the behavior of the response variables.

Table 16-2 is an example of the experimental design layout for the two-factor emergency-room experiment with average waiting time as the response variable. The arrival-rate factor has 6 levels, and the ER-beds factor has 4 levels. Since $6 \times 4 = 24$, we now know that 24 experiments must be conducted to complete the design. As we said earlier, to deal with the uncertainty in the model, we will need **replications** of each experiment; this means we will rerun the simulation using the same starting conditions and values for the input variables. Assuming we use 50 replications for each cell, the simulation model must be run 1200 (50×24) times to complete the design. In some cases, more than 50 runs at each level may be needed to achieve the desired precision, so the total number of runs may go beyond 1200.

As the preceding discussion demonstrates, the required number of runs of a simulation model can grow rapidly. As the number of factors and/or the number of levels per factor is increased, the size of the experiment grows quickly. Consequently, for practical reasons, the decision maker should give a great deal of thought to what factors and levels of factors to use in the experiment.

Table 16-2 EXPERIMENT DESIGN FOR EMERGENCY-ROOM EXAMPLE
(response variable: average waiting time)

Trauma-Patient Arrival Rate (arrivals/hour)	Number of Emergency-Room Beds			
	3	4	5	6
2				
3				
4				
5				
6				
7				

Analyzing Data from the Experiments

A full discussion of data analysis based upon results from simulation models is beyond the scope of this text. The techniques typically used are analysis of variance and regression analysis, which you may have learned about in a statistics course. These techniques are used to determine whether significant differences in the response variable exist for different factor levels and to determine which combination of factor levels yields the optimal value for the response variable.

Each of the six steps described above is important to the success of the simulation analysis. However, the procedure can best be understood by working through a problem. The next two sections present examples of simulation models to reinforce the importance of following these steps.

16-3 A QUEUING SIMULATION EXAMPLE

The First State Bank and Trust Company is considering building a drive-in banking facility adjacent to the bank's downtown location. The facility would be designed so that an entering driver selects a service lane, moves ahead in that lane to the service window, and, after completing the transaction, exits so that the next vehicle can move to the service window. Figure 16-2 diagrams a system with two service windows.

THE PROBLEM

The problem facing the bank's architects is to determine how many service windows to build at this location. The minimum number is one, although the lot will accommodate as many as five windows. The lot is long enough so that each service lane can hold five vehicles, four waiting plus one at the window. If all the service lanes are full, an arriving vehicle will not be able to enter the queue and will leave. Thus, too few service windows means that some customers won't be able to use the drive-in facility; also, too few service windows will result in long waiting times for those that do get into the system. Conversely, if too many service windows are built, the bank will have spent excessive money on facilities that are not efficiently used. The problem is to determine

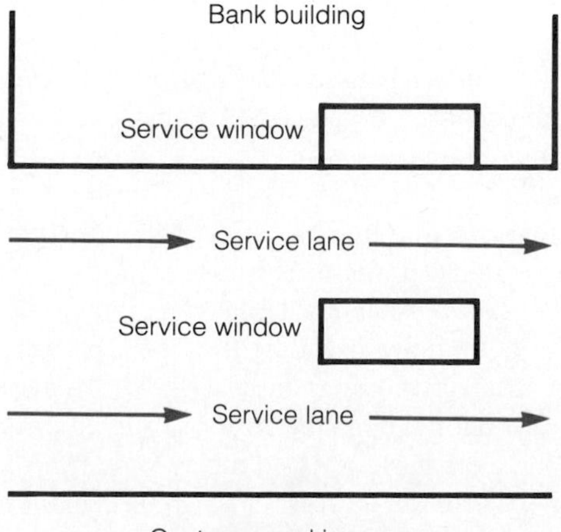

Figure 16-2
Drive-in banking system with two servers

the best number of service windows to build, considering the conflicting objectives of heavily utilizing the facilities while having short waiting times and not turning away customers.

THE MODEL

Chapter 12 introduced queuing theory, the study of waiting lines. You should recognize the bank drive-in as a queuing system. Specifically, it is a *multiple-line multiple-channel* system. As shown in Figure 16-2, when customers arrive, they select one of the service lanes and wait in line until the service facility is free.

There are two primary exogenous, or input, variables in the system: the *interarrival rate* of vehicles coming to the bank and the *service rate* for vehicles at the teller window. There is one controllable variable: the number of service windows. Among the endogenous, or output, variables are the following: number of vehicles turned away, average waiting time, facility utilization rate, average queue length, and maximum queue length.

A system can be defined as either deterministic or stochastic, depending on the relationship between the input and output variables. In a **deterministic system,** the output variables can be predicted with certainty if the values of the input variables are known. Thus, in a deterministic system, a given input always leads to the same output. For example, an accountant who develops a *pro forma* income statement is developing a deterministic simulation model; based upon given inputs for revenues and expenses, the output variable—net income—will be known. It should be apparent that the drive-in bank model cannot be deterministic, since customers arrive at different rates during the day and during the week, and these customers have a variety of banking needs, each requiring different service times.

A **stochastic system** is one in which values of the output variables cannot be predicted with certainty for a given input. In a stochastic system, the same set of inputs will lead to a range of possible outputs. In the First State Bank and Trust example, the same average arrival and service rates may lead to different output values from trial to trial. Although the average arrivals per time period may be known, the actual time between individual arrivals will vary from vehicle to vehicle. For instance, if the drive-in window stays open until 6:00 P.M., the bank may see a surge of customers just before it closes, not evenly distributed between 5:00 and 6:00 o'clock. The same is true for service rate. The actual time required to serve a customer will not be uniform and will be higher or lower than the average service rate. The actual interarrival times and service times occur according to some probability distribution.

When one or more of the input variables is described by a probability distribution, **Monte Carlo simulation** is used. Since all the simulation models discussed in the remainder of this chapter are stochastic (or probabilistic), we will use Monte Carlo simulation to solve them.

In our discussion of queuing theory (Chapter 12), we indicated that for many waiting-line situations, the number of arrivals per time period is assumed to be described by a Poisson distribution. For this distribution to apply, the interarrival times must be exponentially distributed. Likewise, many studies have shown that service times are also exponentially distributed. In the First State Bank and Trust example, we will assume the interarrival times and service times are exponentially distributed. An exponential distribution is described by only one parameter, its average. Assume that a consultant for the bank has estimated the average time between customer arrivals will be 4 minutes (240 seconds). Further, studies at similar drive-in branches show that the average service time per vehicle is 5 minutes (300 seconds).

Figure 16-3 is the simulation flowchart for the First State Bank and Trust drive-in system. Note that this is a general flowchart for the system; a more detailed flowchart would most likely be developed before the computer programming actually started.

This bank model is a next-event simulation model. In **next-event simulation**, the time clock is advanced when each event occurs (remember, keeping track of the system over time is the main characteristic of simulation models). The time advance will vary, depending on the time between events. In this example, the master clock is advanced when each arrival occurs and the departure clock is advanced when waiting and service occur.

An alternative type of model uses fixed-time simulation. With **fixed-time simulation**, the time clock is advanced in fixed units of time, during which a certain number of events may occur. For instance, if the fixed time interval is 10 minutes, the model would simulate activity during a 10-minute period. An example of a fixed-time simulation model is presented in section 16-4.

Figure 16-3 shows the general flow through the system for the bank example. First, all clocks are set to zero and the **starting conditions**, which define the status of the system at the beginning of the simulation run, are established. As you know, at the beginning of a day, the drive-in bank facility will be empty. We could choose to start the simulation in this empty state, or we could start the simulation at some nonempty level that might occur after the start of business, say, at 10:00 A.M. The issues involved in determining appropriate starting conditions are very complex and will be left for a course devoted entirely to simulation modeling. You should be aware, however, that the output seen from any simulation model can be affected by the starting conditions. In this example, we will start with an empty system. This means that all clocks are set to zero and the queues and service facilities are empty.

We must next set values for the controllable variables. In this model the only controllable variable is the number of service facilities. Remember, because of space constraints, the number of service windows must be set between one and five. For the first experiment, suppose we set the system at two windows.

Referring to Figure 16-3, once the initial conditions are set, the next step is to generate an arrival. This means we must determine an arrival time based upon the probability distribution for the specified interarrival time. With Monte Carlo simulation, the interarrival time is determined by sampling from an exponential distribution with a mean of 4 minutes.

A frequently used formula for obtaining a value from an exponential distribution is:

$$T = -(\mu) * \ln(R) \tag{16-1}$$

where:

R = uniform random number between 0 and 1

μ = mean of the exponential distribution

We first obtain a uniformly distributed random number, R, between 0 and 1, and then find the interarrival time, T, by multiplying the natural logarithm of R times the negative of the mean value of the distribution.

For modeling purposes, for R we will use a **pseudorandom number**, a computer-generated number that has the statistical properties of a true random number. Virtually all programming languages, including general-purpose languages like BASIC and

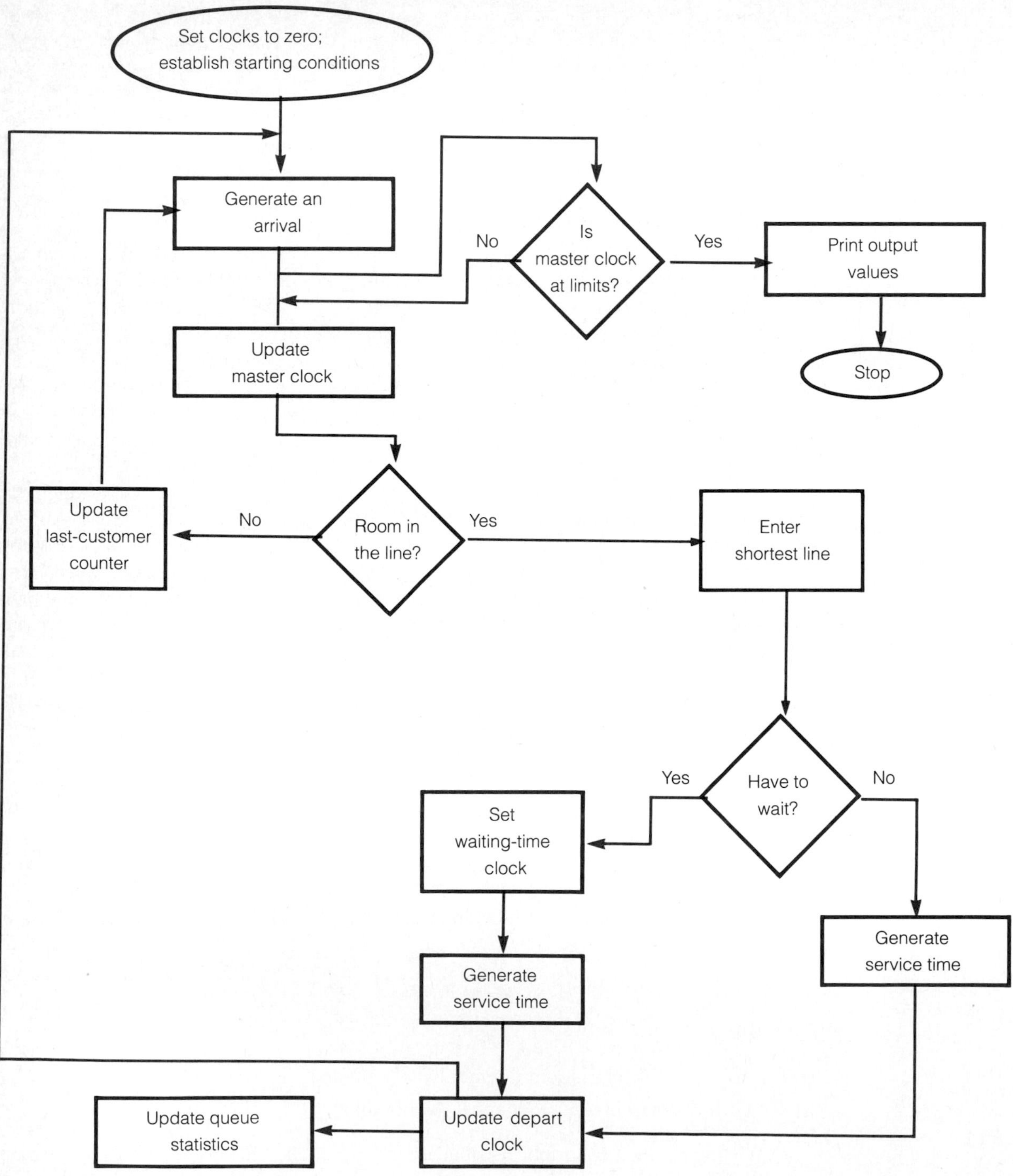

Figure 16-3
Next-event simulation flowchart for bank example

FORTRAN, contain built-in functions for generating these pseudorandom numbers which can be used to supply the R value.

Suppose the first simulated arrival occurs 5 minutes and 45 seconds (345 seconds) into the day. We will record this as $AR(1) = 345$. The master clock (MC) must be updated to indicate the passage of time. We record this as $MC = 345$. Again referring to Figure 16-3, we check the master clock to see whether the simulated day is complete (7 hours = 25,200 seconds). The first arrival occurs well short of this value, so we will continue with the simulation.

The model must next check to see if the service lines are full. (Recall that the service line can accommodate 4 vehicles plus the one being served.) Since this is the first arrival of the day, the lines are empty and the vehicle can enter line 1 and proceed directly to the service window. We will specify that a vehicle will always enter line 1 when all lines are empty; otherwise it will enter the shortest line. In general, if two or more lines are equally short, the vehicle will enter the lowest-numbered line.

When a vehicle arrives at a service window, a service time must be generated using the exponential distribution with a mean of 5 minutes. Using equation 16-1, suppose we obtain a service time (ST) for vehicle 1 at window 1 of 6 minutes and 35 seconds (395 seconds). This value is $ST(1, 1) = 395$. The exit clock for window 1 must be updated by adding 395 to the arrival time of 345, giving $EX(1, 1) = 740$, indicating that facility 1 will be open for a new vehicle at time 740 seconds. (If a vehicle has to wait in line for service, the waiting time will be added to the service time and arrival time to give the exit time. This will be demonstrated later.)

We can prepare an interim simulation report, like the one shown in Table 16-3, to help keep track of the simulation results. The first line in the report shows the status of the system for the first arriving vehicle. A new line will be generated for each subsequent vehicle.

The model would next update the interim values needed to compute the specific output variables: number of vehicles turned away, average waiting time, facility utilization rate, facility idle time, and facility utilization percentage. Table 16-4 shows the interim computations for the first vehicle. As you can see, the vehicle did not balk (leave without service) and incurred no waiting time. The queue length facing this vehicle was 0 and the service time was 395 seconds.

The model will now generate a new arrival. Suppose the interarrival time is 44 seconds. Now $AR(2) = 345 + 44 = 389$, meaning the second vehicle arrived 389 seconds after the bank opened, and the master clock is updated ($MC = 345 + 44 =$

Table 16-3 INTERIM SIMULATION REPORT FOR BANK EXAMPLE

Vehicle (i)	$AR(i)$	MC	$ST(i, 1)$	$ST(i, 2)$	$WT(i, 1)$	$WT(i, 2)$	$EX(i, 1)$	$EX(i, 2)$
1	345	345	395	—	0	—	740	—

Table 16-4 INTERIM CALCULATIONS FOR OUTPUT VARIABLES

Vehicle (i)	Balked? (yes = 1)	Waiting Time	Queue Length (1)	Queue Length (2)	Service Time (1)	Service Time (2)
1	0	0	0	0	395	0

Table 16-5 INTERIM SIMULATION REPORT—UPDATED

Vehicle (i)	AR(i)	MC	ST(i, 1)	ST(i, 2)	WT(i, 1)	WT(i, 2)	EX(i, 1)	EX(i, 2)
1	345	345	395	—	0	—	740	—
2	389	389	—	666	—	0	0	1055

Table 16-6 INTERIM CALCULATIONS FOR OUTPUT VARIABLES—UPDATED

Vehicle (i)	Balked? (yes = 1)	Waiting Time	Queue Length (1)	Queue Length (2)	Service Time (1)	Service Time (2)
1	0	0	0	0	395	0
2	0	0	0	0	0	666

389). Since 389 is well short of the 25,200 seconds per day, the model continues. The model will determine whether all service lines are full. At time 389, vehicle 1 is being served in facility 1 and no other vehicles are in the system; therefore vehicle 2 will be served immediately. The model next determines which service facility has the shorter queue. At this point, both queues are empty; but because a vehicle is being served by window 1, vehicle 2 will proceed directly to window 2.

Assume the model generates a service time of 666 seconds. Tables 16-3 and 16-4 are updated as shown in Tables 16-5 and 16-6. Table 16-5 shows that at time $MC = 389$, both servers are busy. Server 1 will be free at $EX(1, 1) = 740$ seconds; so if a vehicle arrives before 740, it will have to wait for service.

Suppose the interarrival time for vehicle 3 is 100 seconds. The master clock is set to $MC = 489$ $(389 + 100)$. The model determines that while there are no vehicles waiting for service in either line, both service windows are busy and vehicle 3 will have to wait. The model will send the vehicle into the lower-numbered line, since both lines have equally short queue lengths. (Note that the shortest queue might not always be the line with the earliest exit time—a stroke of bad luck everyone can relate to.) This seems realistic, since a driver would have no way of knowing how long the service for either vehicle will take.

The waiting time is computed by subtracting $MC = 489$ from the exit time of the vehicle being served in line 1: $EX(1, 1) = 740$, giving $W(3, 1) = 251$. The simulation model then generates a service time of 120 seconds for vehicle 3. Table 16-7 shows the results for vehicle 3, whose exit time from window 1 will be 860 seconds after the service day starts.

If both servers are busy and vehicles are in the queue, the waiting time will be the difference between the highest exit time for a window and the arrival time for the vehicle entering the line for that window. Table 16-8 shows the updated statistics after the third vehicle has arrived. The queue length for facility 1 is now 1 unit and the total waiting time for the system is 251 seconds.

The simulation will continue in this manner until the end of the day (25,200 seconds). At that point, no further arrivals will be accepted and any vehicles remaining

Table 16-7 INTERIM SIMULATION REPORT—UPDATED

Vehicle (*i*)	*AR*(*i*)	*MC*	*ST*(*i*, 1)	*ST*(*i*, 2)	*WT*(*i*, 1)	*WT*(*i*, 2)	*EX*(*i*, 1)	*EX*(*i*, 2)
1	345	345	395	—	0	—	740	—
2	389	389	—	666	—	0	0	1055
3	489	489	120	—	251	—	860	—

Table 16-8 INTERIM CALCULATIONS FOR OUTPUT VARIABLES—UPDATED

Vehicle (*i*)	Balked? (yes = 1)	Waiting Time	Queue Length (1)	Queue Length (2)	Service Time (1)	Service Time (2)
1	0	0	0	0	395	0
2	0	0	0	0	0	666
3	0	251	1	0	120	0

in the system will be served. We suggest that you manually simulate additional arrivals and track them through the system by updating Tables 16-7 and 16-8. Feel free to make up interarrival and service times or use equation 16-1 and the table of uniform random numbers in Appendix D.

THE EXPERIMENTS

As you can see, manually simulating a waiting-line system like that for the First State Bank and Trust example is a tedious process. The purpose of walking you through a few arrivals manually was to make sure you understand how the model operates. If you are to program the model (or communicate the model requirements to a programmer), you must first understand how it will work.

In an actual application, you would use a computer simulation model. Since this is not a programming class, we will not show the programming code necessary to relate the input and output variables; instead, we will demonstrate using the queuing simulation model in the MASTER software package. This program allows the user to specify from 1 to 10 servers in a queuing problem. It also allows having one waiting line for each server or a single waiting line feeding all servers (you should recognize these as single-line, multiple-channel or multiple-line, multiple-channel models from Chapter 12). The user also specifies the maximum queue length, the average interarrival time, the average service time, the simulation time per replication, and the number of replications desired.

Figure 16-4 shows the inputs for the bank example. Note that since the average service time and average interarrival time are set in seconds, the output values will also be in seconds. We are asking for one replication that is 25,200 seconds (7 hours) in duration. Figure 16-5 shows the resulting output. (The model has been programmed to generate different random-number sequences each time it is run; so a second run with the same input values would yield slightly different results.)

A total of 108 simulated customers arrived for service during the day. The two service facilities were busy 52.34% of the day. Seven customers were turned away

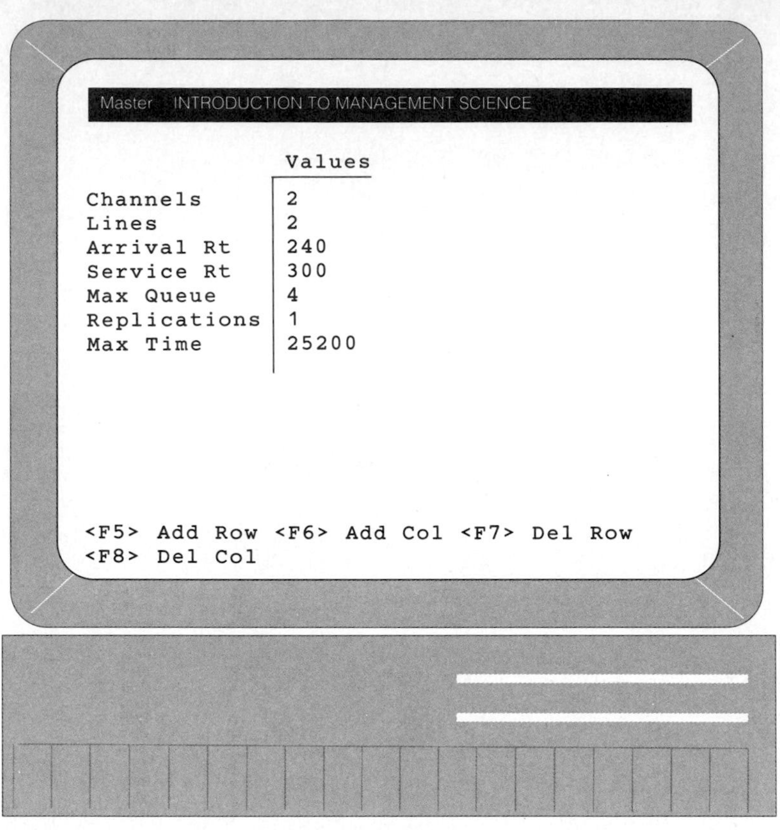

Figure 16-4
Initial input data for MASTER simulation of bank problem

```
                         QUEUING SIMULATION RESULTS
MODEL FORM:
              NUMBER OF CHANNELS = 2
              NUMBER OF LINES = 2
              AVERAGE TIME BETWEEN ARRIVALS 240.00
              AVERAGE SERVICE TIME 300.00
              MAXIMUM QUEUE LENGTH =    4
              NUMBER OF REPLICATIONS =    1
              NUMBER OF TIME UNITS PER REPLICATION =     25200

                        OUTPUT STATISTICS:

              NUMBER OF ARRIVALS =      108

              ACTUAL AVERAGE TIME BETWEEN ARRIVALS =    233.00

              ACTUAL AVERAGE SERVICE TIME       265.74

              FACILITY UTILIZATION PERCENTAGE =  52.34

              PERCENTAGE WAITING = 82.41

              AVERAGE WAITING TIME-ALL ARRIVALS =     462.24

              AVERAGE WAITING TIME-THOSE WAITING ONLY =    560.92

              AVERAGE NUMBER TURNED AWAY =       7
```

Figure 16-5
Initial MASTER simulation output for bank example with 2 servers

```
                         QUEUING SIMULATION RESULTS
MODEL FORM:
              NUMBER OF CHANNELS = 2
              NUMBER OF LINES = 2
              AVERAGE TIME BETWEEN ARRIVALS 240.00
              AVERAGE SERVICE TIME 300.00
              MAXIMUM QUEUE LENGTH =    4
              NUMBER OF REPLICATIONS =   20
              NUMBER OF TIME UNITS PER REPLICATION =     25200

                        OUTPUT STATISTICS:

              NUMBER OF ARRIVALS =     2163

              ACTUAL AVERAGE TIME BETWEEN ARRIVALS =    229.78

              ACTUAL AVERAGE SERVICE TIME =    296.71

              FACILITY UTILIZATION PERCENTAGE =  56.45

              PERCENTAGE WAITING = 80.31

              AVERAGE WAITING TIME-ALL ARRIVALS =    675.30

              AVERAGE WAITING TIME-THOSE WAITING ONLY =    840.91

              AVERAGE NUMBER TURNED AWAY =       9
```

Figure 16-6
MASTER simulation output for 20 replications, 2 servers

because the two waiting lines were full when they arrived. Of those who were not turned away, just over 82% had to wait. The average waiting time for the 101 customers who were served was 462.24 seconds (7.7 minutes). However, the average waiting time for the customers who actually had to wait was 560.92 seconds (9.3 minutes).

The output shown in Figure 16-5 represents the results of only one replication of the simulation model. As we indicated earlier, the output of a Monte Carlo simulation model is subject to variation and a second run would yield slightly different results. Consequently, before drawing inferences about the behavior of the simulated system, a decision maker should observe the results from a number of replications. The process of determining the appropriate number of replications for a model is a statistical matter beyond the scope of this text.

For demonstration purposes, suppose we run 20 replications of the MASTER software program using the same input values. Figure 16-6 shows the output values from the 20 replications. A total of 2163 customers arrived during the 20-day simu-

```
                    QUEUING SIMULATION RESULTS
MODEL FORM:
              NUMBER OF CHANNELS = 3
              NUMBER OF LINES = 3
              AVERAGE TIME BETWEEN ARRIVALS 240.00
              AVERAGE SERVICE TIME 300.00
              MAXIMUM QUEUE LENGTH =   4
              NUMBER OF REPLICATIONS =   20
              NUMBER OF TIME UNITS PER REPLICATION =     25200

                    OUTPUT STATISTICS:

              NUMBER OF ARRIVALS =     2105

              ACTUAL AVERAGE TIME BETWEEN ARRIVALS =    237.75

              ACTUAL AVERAGE SERVICE TIME =     289.39

              FACILITY UTILIZATION PERCENTAGE =  40.18

              PERCENTAGE WAITING = 17.67

              AVERAGE WAITING TIME-ALL ARRIVALS =       61.76

              AVERAGE WAITING TIME-THOSE WAITING ONLY =    349.50

              AVERAGE NUMBER TURNED AWAY =       0
```

Figure 16-7
MASTER simulation output: 3 servers

lated period. The two service facilities were used an average of 56.45% of the time. On average, 9 customers balked each day because both waiting lines were full. Of those that were served, 80.31% were forced to wait for service. Overall, the average waiting time was 675.30 seconds (11.3 minutes). For those who actually had to wait, the average waiting time was 840.91 seconds (14.01 minutes). Compare Figures 16-5 and 16-6 to see that the results from a single replication may differ substantially from the average of 20 replications.

Figure 16-6 shows the simulated output assuming that First State Bank and Trust builds 2 drive-in service windows and uses 2 waiting lines. One purpose of developing a simulation model is to observe the effects of changes to the system. For instance, Figure 16-7 shows the output for 20 replications of the model with 3 service windows and 3 waiting lines. When we compare these results with those in Figure 16-6 (2 servers, 2 lines) we observe that adding an additional window causes the facility utilization to drop from 56.45% to 40.18%. On the other hand, with 3 servers and 3

```
                    QUEUING SIMULATION RESULTS
MODEL FORM:
            NUMBER OF CHANNELS = 4
            NUMBER OF LINES = 4
            AVERAGE TIME BETWEEN ARRIVALS 240.00
            AVERAGE SERVICE TIME 300.00
            MAXIMUM QUEUE LENGTH =    4
            NUMBER OF REPLICATIONS =   20
            NUMBER OF TIME UNITS PER REPLICATION =      25200

                    OUTPUT STATISTICS:

            NUMBER OF ARRIVALS =     2101

            ACTUAL AVERAGE TIME BETWEEN ARRIVALS =    238.06

            ACTUAL AVERAGE SERVICE TIME =     288.58

            FACILITY UTILIZATION PERCENTAGE =  30.07

            PERCENTAGE WAITING =  3.81

            AVERAGE WAITING TIME-ALL ARRIVALS =      11.72

            AVERAGE WAITING TIME-THOSE WAITING ONLY =    307.67

            AVERAGE NUMBER TURNED AWAY =       0
```

Figure 16-8
MASTER simulation output: 4 servers

waiting lines, no customers would have been turned away and the percentage of all customers having to wait dropped to 17.67% from 80.31%. Additionally, adding the third server and waiting line caused the average waiting time for those actually having to wait to drop to only 349.50 seconds (5.8 minutes), from 840.91 seconds (14.01 minutes).

Since the location can accommodate as many as 5 drive-in windows, we will also run the simulation model using 4 and 5 service windows and waiting lines. Figure 16-8 shows the results when the system has 4 servers, and Figure 16-9 shows the results with 5 servers. As expected, the facility utilization percentage continues to decline as servers are added to the system. With 5 servers (Figure 16-9), the utilization rate has dropped to 24.05%. Likewise, as windows and lines are added, the waiting statistics improve; for instance, with 5 servers, only 0.45% of the customers have to wait and the average waiting time for those actually having to wait is 171.93 seconds (2.9 minutes).

```
                    QUEUING SIMULATION RESULTS
MODEL FORM:
              NUMBER OF CHANNELS = 5
              NUMBER OF LINES = 5
              AVERAGE TIME BETWEEN ARRIVALS 240.00
              AVERAGE SERVICE TIME 300.00
              MAXIMUM QUEUE LENGTH =    4
              NUMBER OF REPLICATIONS =   20
              NUMBER OF TIME UNITS PER REPLICATION =     25200

                         OUTPUT STATISTICS:

              NUMBER OF ARRIVALS =     2103

              ACTUAL AVERAGE TIME BETWEEN ARRIVALS =    237.09

              ACTUAL AVERAGE SERVICE TIME =     288.21

              FACILITY UTILIZATION PERCENTAGE =  24.05

              PERCENTAGE WAITING =  0.48

              AVERAGE WAITING TIME-ALL ARRIVALS =       0.82

              AVERAGE WAITING TIME-THOSE WAITING ONLY =    171.93

              AVERAGE NUMBER TURNED AWAY =       0
```

Figure 16-9
MASTER simulation output: 5 servers

The role of the decision maker is to review the outputs in Figures 16-6 through 16-9 and weigh the advantages, in improved customer service, of adding more servers against the disadvantage of larger construction and operating costs.

SENSITIVITY ANALYSIS

Recall that **sensitivity analysis** is the process of altering the input variables in a simulation model and observing the effects on the output variables. We can apply it to the bank example, as described below.

You should recall that both the average interarrival time and the average service time inputs to the model were based on studies done by the bank's consultants. Since these values were estimates, a conscientious decision maker would probably want to determine how sensitive the output values are to different assumptions about average interarrival times and/or average service times. For instance, we might be interested in the effect on the output values if the average interarrival rate is 150 seconds rather than 240. This would represent a much heavier demand for drive-in bank services than the

```
                         QUEUING SIMULATION RESULTS
MODEL FORM:
              NUMBER OF CHANNELS = 3
              NUMBER OF LINES = 3
              AVERAGE TIME BETWEEN ARRIVALS 150.00
              AVERAGE SERVICE TIME 300.00
              MAXIMUM QUEUE LENGTH =    4
              NUMBER OF REPLICATIONS =  20
              NUMBER OF TIME UNITS PER REPLICATION =     25200

                        OUTPUT STATISTICS:

              NUMBER OF ARRIVALS =     3438

              ACTUAL AVERAGE TIME BETWEEN ARRIVALS =    145.58

              ACTUAL AVERAGE SERVICE TIME =    297.67

              FACILITY UTILIZATION PERCENTAGE =  64.78

              PERCENTAGE WAITING = 73.71

              AVERAGE WAITING TIME-ALL ARRIVALS =     467.39

              AVERAGE WAITING TIME-THOSE WAITING ONLY =    634.13

              AVERAGE NUMBER TURNED AWAY =       3
```

Figure 16-10

MASTER simulation output: 3 servers, interarrival time = 150 seconds consultants had estimated. Figure 16-10 shows the results for 20 replications with 3 servers. Note that the average service time remains at 300 seconds (5 minutes).

To see the impact of the change in arrival rate, we need to compare the new results in Figure 16-10 with the original simulation results shown in Figure 16-7. First, note that the number of arrivals has increased from 2105 to 3438, which results in an average of 3 customers per day being turned away compared with none before. As expected, the facility utilization percentage increases (from 40.18% to 64.78%). On the other hand, the waiting statistics get worse. The percentage of served customers having to wait increases from slightly less than 18% to almost 74%. Also, the average waiting time for the served customers has increased from 349.5 seconds to 634.13 seconds.

The sensitivity analysis could be continued by testing other average interarrival times and/or other average service times. If you have access to MASTER, we encourage you to perform a variety of these sensitivity analyses.

16-4 AN INVENTORY SIMULATION EXAMPLE

Roger and Dale Erickson started their wine distribution business in 1984 and have worked hard since then to develop a profitable company with customers in 11 western states. Erickson Brothers, Inc., distributes wines produced in California, Washington, and Idaho; its customers mainly grocery stores, liquor stores, and restaurants.

THE PROBLEM

Managing inventories has long been one of the most difficult parts of the business for Roger and Dale. Their tendency has been to carry too much inventory and tie up money that could be put to more productive use. The problem is exacerbated by the fact that nothing about their business is constant. Demand fluctuates each day, and the time needed to receive shipments of wines (lead time) also varies. In the past, Roger and Dale just determined their longest lead time and highest demand and then used an EOQ model to find the order points and order quantities for each product—but that led to excessive inventories.

THE MODEL

Instead of using an EOQ model, Roger and Dale can use an inventory simulation model. The model can be programmed to simulate their inventory system with such features as stochastic demand and lead times built in. In addition, the possibility of losing backorders can be considered. Using the simulation model, Roger and Dale can explore the effects of various order points and order quantities and can observe the simulated results of operating their business without actually implementing the inventory policies and suffering the consequences of poor strategies.

Figure 16-11 shows the system flowchart for the inventory simulation model. As in the previous example, the First State Bank and Trust simulation model, we will manually go through a few steps of the simulation and then turn to a computer model available in MASTER. To illustrate the inventory simulation model for the Ericksons, let's consider one wine, the St. Chapelle Johannesburg Riesling. Since this is an inventory simulation, we will have to address the same costs we consider for all other inventory problems. As we can see in Figure 16-12, Erickson Brothers pays $20 per case for this wine, holding cost is assumed to be 15% of the purchase cost per year (or .00041 per day), the cost of placing an order is $40, and the cost of receiving an order

Figure 16-11
Flowchart for Erickson Brothers' simulation program

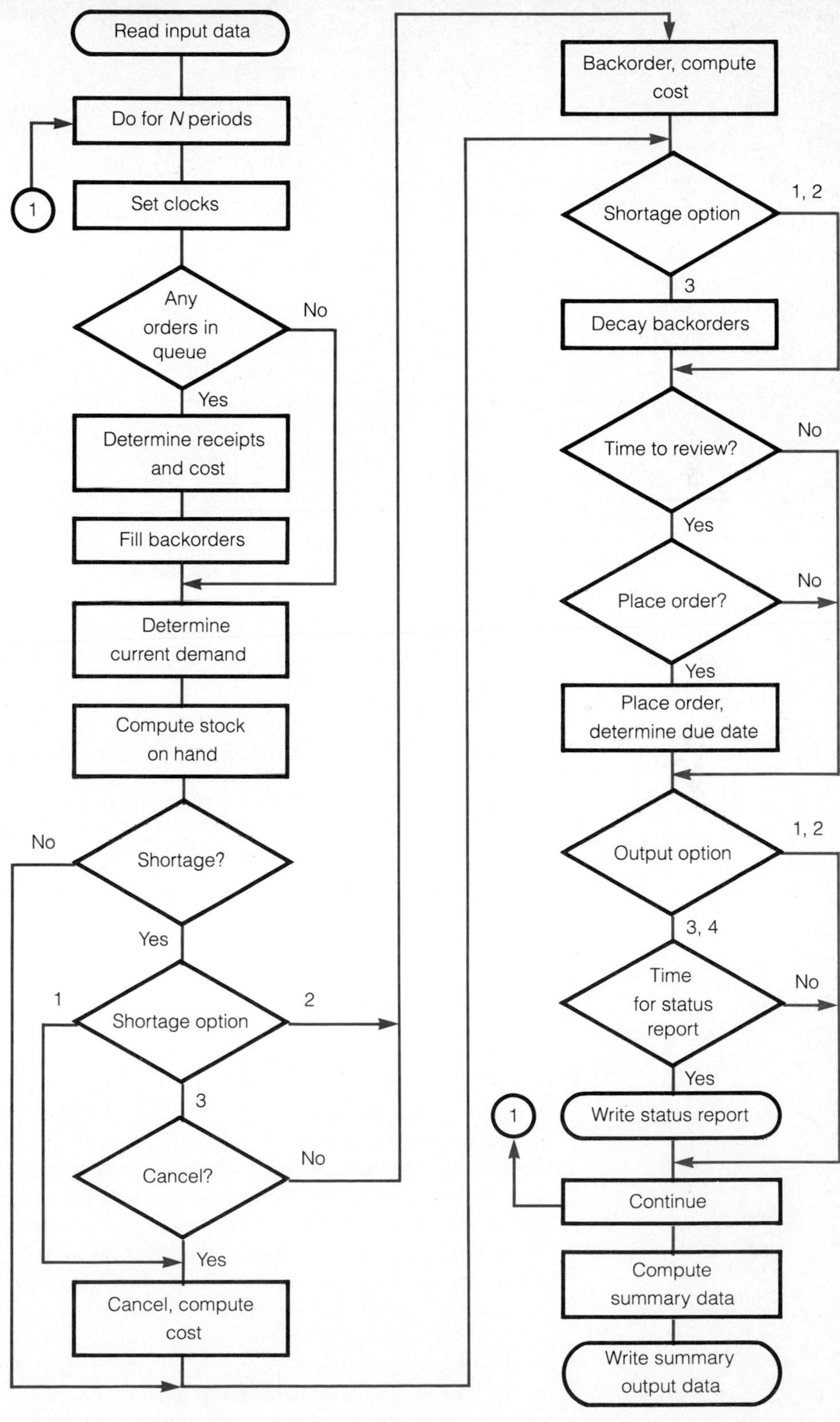

```
Master   INTRODUCTION TO MANAGEMENT SCIENCE

                Values  Period  Probability
Periods        | 50        0         .25
Price          | 20        1         .00
Beg Inv        | 4000      2         .30
Ord Point      | 3000      3         .50
Ord Qty        | 10000     4         .75
Ord Cost       | 40        5        1.00
Rec Cost       | 200
Back Cost      | 100
Lost Cost      | 60
Hold Factor    | .00041
Ave Dem        | 1000
St Dev Dem     | 200
Ave Lead       | 4
St Dev Lead    | 2

<F5> Add Row <F6> Add Col <F7> Del Row <F8> Del Col
```

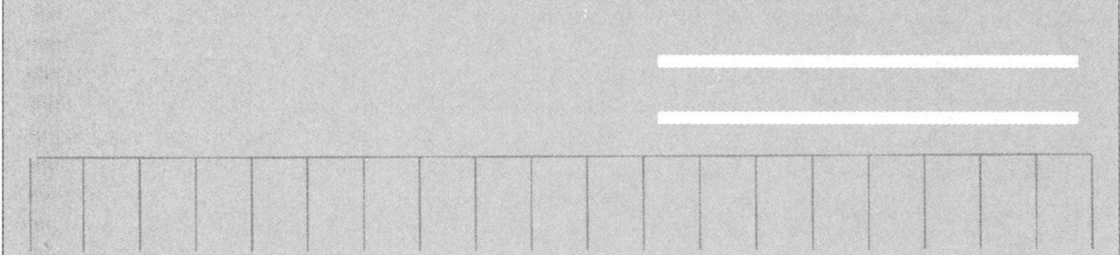

Figure 16-12
Input for MASTER inventory simulation

is \$200. Backordering is possible, but the cost is \$100 per backorder. Also, when backordering is necessary, a customer may cancel the order, and the chance of cancellation increases with the number of periods until the backorder is received. Table 16-9 shows the probability distribution for losing backorders, based on past data for this wine. There is a 25% chance that a customer will not accept any backordering. However, a customer who does accept a backorder will certainly not cancel the order within the first day, but the order will definitely be lost if the number of backorder days is 5 or more. Roger and Dale have estimated the cost of failing to have inventory to meet the demand to be \$60 per case in lost profit and goodwill.

Demand for this wine changes from day to day. However, during the planning period, the Ericksons have forecast an average daily demand of 1000 cases. Judging from their historical data, they think the actual daily demand will be normally distributed around the average of 1000 cases, with a standard deviation of 200 cases. The lead time, or time from when an order is placed until it is received, has not been constant

Table 16-9 ERICKSON BROTHERS: PROBABILITY OF LOSING BACKORDERS

Number of Periods Backordered	Probability of Loss
0	.25
1	.00
2	.30
3	.50
4	.75
5	1.00

either. Past data show that lead time has been normally distributed, with a mean of 4 days and a standard deviation of 2 days.

For this example, let's assume the beginning inventory is 4000 cases, no units are on backorder, and no orders are pending. We will start with an order point (the inventory level at which a new order is placed) of 3000 cases and an order quantity of 10,000 cases. Suppose we elect to run the model for 50 periods (i.e., 50 days of simulated business activity). The simulation model we are going to use is a fixed-time simulation model, which advances time in fixed intervals, such as hours, days, weeks and so on. (Recall that the queuing simulation model introduced in section 16-3 was a next-event simulation model.)

We begin by determining the demand for period 1, $D(1)$. We know that daily demand is normally distributed, with a mean of 1000 cases and a standard deviation of 200 cases. To select a value from a normal distribution, we use a process very similar to the one we used in section 16-3 for an exponential distribution. A common method for generating values from a normal distribution has two steps:

1. Select 12 uniformly distributed random numbers between 0 and 1, sum the 12 values, and call this value *SUM*.
2. Compute X, the normally distributed value, as follows:

$$X = SD * (SUM - 6.0) + M \qquad (16\text{-}2)$$

where:

X = normally distributed value

SD = standard deviation of the normal distribution

M = mean of the normal distribution

For this example, $SD = 200$ and $M = 1000$. Recall that most computer languages have algorithms for generating the uniform random numbers between 0 and 1. (A table of uniform random numbers is provided in Appendix D.)

Suppose, using the above procedure, we find that the simulated demand on day 1 is 1096 cases. The model then checks the stock on hand to determine if sufficient inventory exists to meet this demand. Since the inventory going into period 1 is 4000 cases, the first day's demand can be filled from existing inventory.

The model also checks the inventory for each period to determine whether an order should be placed. At the end of period 1, the inventory is reduced from 4000 units to 2904 (4000 − 1096 = 2904). Since the order point of 3000 units has been reached, an order is issued. Table 16-10 shows an interim status report for the simulation model after period 1. The first line shows the reduced inventory due to the

Table 16-10 INVENTORY STATUS REPORT AFTER PERIOD 1

Period	Number On Hand	Number On Order	Number Due In	Demand	On Backorder	Backorder	Lost Sales	Cost
1	2904	0	—	1096	0	—	—	—
1	2904	10,000	8	—	—	—	—	$40

demand in period 1. Line 2 shows that an order for 10,000 units was placed and is due to be received in period 8. Recall that lead time is assumed to be normally distributed with a mean of 4 days and a standard deviation of 2 days. The process for randomly generating lead times is the same as that for generating demands. If we let $SUM = 8.14$, we can use equation 16-2, as follows:

$$L = 2.0 * (8.14 - 6.0) + 4.0 = 4.28 + 4.0$$
$$= 8.28 \text{ (which is rounded to 8 days)}$$

The minimum lead time will be 1 day.

The second line of the status report (Table 16-10) shows the ordering cost of $40. We will use this column to track the inventory costs as they occur.

After updating the various output values generated during the simulation run, we proceed to period 2. We begin by generating the demand for period 2. Suppose this value is determined to be 972. The model would check to see whether the current inventory of 2904 cases is sufficient to meet this demand. Since 2904 is greater than 972, the demand can be met. The inventory level will be reduced by 972 cases, to 1932. Table 16-11 presents the interim status report for period 2.

Moving on to period 3 (Table 16-12), suppose we generate a demand for 1109 cases. The existing inventory of 1932 cases is sufficient to meet this demand, but the inventory is reduced to 823 cases.

For period 4 (Table 16-13), the simulated demand is 1127 cases, which exceeds the 823-case inventory by 304. The first thing we do now is reduce the inventory level to zero. Next we check to see whether the 304 units can be backordered. To do this, a random number between 0 and 1 is selected from a uniform distribution. From Table

Table 16-11 INVENTORY STATUS REPORT AFTER PERIOD 2

Period	Number On Hand	Number On Order	Number Due In	Demand	On Backorder	Backorder	Lost Sales	Cost
1	2904	0	—	1096	0	—	—	—
1	2904	10,000	8	—	—	—	—	$40
2	1932	10,000	—	972	0	—	—	—

Table 16-12 INVENTORY STATUS REPORT AFTER PERIOD 3

Period	Number On Hand	Number On Order	Number Due In	Demand	On Backorder	Backorder	Lost Sales	Cost
1	2904	0	—	1096	0	—	—	—
1	2904	10,000	8	—	—	—	—	$40
2	1932	10,000	—	972	0	—	—	—
3	823	10,000	—	1109	—	—	—	—

Table 16-13 INVENTORY STATUS REPORT AFTER PERIOD 4

Period	Number On Hand	Number On Order	Number Due In	Demand	On Backorder	Backorder	Lost Sales	Cost
1	2904	0	—	1096	0	—	—	—
1	2904	10,000	8	—	—	—	—	$40
2	1932	10,000	—	972	0	—	—	—
3	823	10,000	—	1109	—	—	—	—
4	0	10,000	—	1127	304	304	—	$100

16-9, we see that if this number is .25 or less, the demand will be immediately recorded as lost sales and no backordering will occur. If the random number is greater than .25, then a backorder will be placed. Suppose the random number is .8706. Since .8706 > .25, a backorder will be recorded, at a cost of $100. The customers will wait at least 1 day for this backorder to arrive.

We enter period 5 (Table 16-14) without any inventory on hand and the next shipment not due in until period 8. Consequently, a demand for 608 cases in period 5 cannot be filled. We again check to see whether this demand can be backordered. This time, the random number is .1392. Since .1392 ≤ .25, this demand is lost. This lost order for 608 cases, at $60 per case, means a cost of $36,480. But we can't forget the existing backorder of 304 cases placed in period 4. Since we are still out of inventory in period 5, we must determine whether to cancel the backorder or whether the customers will wait until day 6. Referring to Table 16-9, we see there is a .30 chance the order will be lost if it cannot be filled within 2 days. If we select a uniform random number between 0 and 1 that is .30 or less, the backorder requiring 2 days will be canceled and the sales will be lost. Suppose the random number selected is .0911. This means that we will now incur a cost of $18,240 (304 cases at $60 per case) for lost sales.

As you can see, Erickson Brothers will be out of inventory until period 8, when the order for 10,000 units is scheduled to arrive. During periods 6 and 7, the model must again consider backordering. Any backorders which exist when the shipment arrives in period 8 will be filled before any new demand is considered.

USING THE COMPUTER SIMULATION MODEL

The simulation would continue in the previous manner for the designated 50 periods. Rather than continuing manually, we will use the inventory simulation module in the MASTER software. Figure 16-12 shows the input data needed to run the simulation

Table 16-14 INVENTORY STATUS REPORT AFTER PERIOD 5

Period	Number On Hand	Number On Order	Number Due In	Demand	On Backorder	Backorder	Lost Sales	Cost
1	2904	0	—	1096	0	—	—	—
1	2904	10,000	8	—	—	—	—	$40
2	1932	10,000	—	972	0	—	—	—
3	823	10,000	—	1109	—	—	—	—
4	0	10,000	—	1127	304	304	—	$100
5	0	10,000	—	608	304	—	608	$36,480
5	0	10,000	—	—	—	—	304	$18,240

```
                INVENTORY SIMULATION

MODEL FORM:
                NUMBER OF TIME PERIODS:     50
                PRODUCT PRICE PER UNIT:     20
                BEGINNING INVENTORY    :    4000
                ORDER POINT            :    3000
                ORDER QUANTITY         :    10000
                COST OF PLACING ORDER  :    40
                COST TO RECEIVE ORDER  :    200
                BACKORDERING COST      :    100
                LOST SALES COST        :    60
                INTEREST RATE/PERIOD   :    .00041

DEMAND IS NORMALLY DISTRIBUTED
                AVERAGE DEMAND IS      :    1000
                DEMAND STANDARD DEV.   :    200

LEAD TIME IS NORMALLY DISTRIBUTED
                AVERAGE LEAD TIME IS   :    4
                ST. DEV. LEAD TIME IS  :    2

                SUMMARY STATISTICS

TOTAL DEMAND =    51307
AVERAGE INVENTORY =   4368.06
CARRYING COST = $     1790.90
NUMBER OF ORDERS PLACED =      5
ORDER COST = $     200.00
NUMBER OF ORDERS RECEIVED =      5
RECEIVING COST = $     1000.00
NUMBER OF SALES UNITS LOST =      2670
COST OF LOST SALES = $ 160200.00
SERVICE FACTOR =   94.80
NUMBER OF BACKORDERS =      4

TOTAL INVENTORY COST =   163590.90
```

Figure 16-13
MASTER inventory output

that we began manually. The per period holding rate (Hold Factor) of .00041 represents an annual rate of 15% divided by 365 (.15/365 = .00041). The numbers in the Probability column represent the chances of losing backorders, according to how long ago they were placed (see Table 16-9).

The MASTER inventory simulation program offers the user the option of getting detailed status reports and a summary or just the summary information. Figure 16-13 shows the summary statistics for one replication of 50 days. The total cost (excluding purchase price) for this inventory system for 50 days is $163,590.90. Of this amount, $160,200 is attributed to lost sales of 2670 cases of wine. The entry Service Factor = 94.80 indicates that 94.8% of all demand was filled.

```
                 INVENTORY SIMULATION

    MODEL FORM:
                 NUMBER OF TIME PERIODS:     365
                 PRODUCT PRICE PER UNIT:     20
                 BEGINNING INVENTORY    :    4000
                 ORDER POINT            :    3000
                 ORDER QUANTITY         :    10000
                 COST OF PLACING ORDER  :    40
                 COST TO RECEIVE ORDER  :    200
                 BACKORDERING COST      :    100
                 LOST SALES COST        :    60
                 INTEREST RATE/PERIOD   :    .00041

    DEMAND IS NORMALLY DISTRIBUTED
                 AVERAGE DEMAND IS      :    1000
                 DEMAND STANDARD DEV.   :    200

    LEAD TIME IS NORMALLY DISTRIBUTED
                 AVERAGE LEAD TIME IS   :    4
                 ST. DEV. LEAD TIME IS  :    2

                 SUMMARY STATISTICS

    TOTAL DEMAND =   368139
    AVERAGE INVENTORY =   4373.92
    CARRYING COST = $   13091.15
    NUMBER OF ORDERS PLACED =    35
    ORDER COST = $    1400.00
    NUMBER OF ORDERS RECEIVED =    34
    RECEIVING COST = $    6800.00
    NUMBER OF SALES UNITS LOST =    23069
    COST OF LOST SALES = $1384140.00
    SERVICE FACTOR =   93.73
    NUMBER OF BACKORDERS =    40

    TOTAL INVENTORY COST = 1409431.00
```

Figure 16-14
MASTER inventory simulation

Figure 16-14 shows the results for the same inventory system for one replication of 365 days. The service factor is 93.73%, and again the majority of the total inventory cost is attributed to the lost sales.

Suppose Roger and Dale want to experiment with a higher order point, 5000 cases of wine, and a higher order quantity, 20,000 cases, in an effort to lower the total inventory cost. We suspect that this would lower the lost-sales cost and increase the inventory carrying cost. Figure 16-15 shows the summary results for one replication of 365 days. For this run, the cost of lost sales is reduced from $1,384,140 to $590,160, and carrying cost increased from $13,091.15 to $33,803.59. The direction of these changes is as we predicted.

```
                INVENTORY SIMULATION

MODEL FORM:
                NUMBER OF TIME PERIODS:     365
                PRODUCT PRICE PER UNIT:     20
                BEGINNING INVENTORY    :    4000
                ORDER POINT            :    5000
                ORDER QUANTITY         :    20000
                COST OF PLACING ORDER  :    40
                COST TO RECEIVE ORDER  :    200
                BACKORDERING COST      :    100
                LOST SALES COST        :    60
                INTEREST RATE/PERIOD   :    .00041

DEMAND IS NORMALLY DISTRIBUTED
                AVERAGE DEMAND IS      :    1000
                DEMAND STANDARD DEV.   :    200

LEAD TIME IS NORMALLY DISTRIBUTED
                AVERAGE LEAD TIME IS   :    4
                ST. DEV. LEAD TIME IS  :    2

                SUMMARY STATISTICS

TOTAL DEMAND =   366944
AVERAGE INVENTORY = 11294.22
CARRYING COST = $   33803.59
NUMBER OF ORDERS PLACED =    19
ORDER COST = $     760.00
NUMBER OF ORDERS RECEIVED =    19
RECEIVING COST = $    3800.00
NUMBER OF SALES UNITS LOST =     1635
COST OF LOST SALES = $  48100.00
SERVICE FACTOR =  99.55
NUMBER OF BACKORDERS =     4

TOTAL INVENTORY COST =  136863.40
```

Figure 16-15
MASTER inventory simulation

One of the problems represented by this model is the uncertainty in demand and lead times. The demand distribution has a standard deviation of 200 cases, which is 20% of the average demand of 1000 cases per day. Suppose Roger and Dale were able to work with their sales representatives on a plan that would reduce the standard deviation in daily demand to 100 cases. More consistent demand should result in lower inventory costs for the company. Suppose, too, that they were successful in reducing the lead-time standard deviation from 2 days to 1. This improvement in lead-time consistency should also help reduce inventory costs. Figure 16-16 shows the summary results for one replication of 365 days' activity with the new standard

```
                 INVENTORY SIMULATION

MODEL FORM:
                 NUMBER OF TIME PERIODS:      365
                 PRODUCT PRICE PER UNIT:      20
                 BEGINNING INVENTORY    :     4000
                 ORDER POINT            :     5000
                 ORDER QUANTITY         :     20000
                 COST OF PLACING ORDER  :     40
                 COST TO RECEIVE ORDER  :     200
                 BACKORDERING COST      :     100
                 LOST SALES COST        :     60
                 INTEREST RATE/PERIOD   :     .00041

DEMAND IS NORMALLY DISTRIBUTED
                 AVERAGE DEMAND IS      :     1000
                 DEMAND STANDARD DEV.   :     100

LEAD TIME IS NORMALLY DISTRIBUTED
                 AVERAGE LEAD TIME IS   :     4
                 ST. DEV. LEAD TIME IS  :     1

                 SUMMARY STATISTICS

TOTAL DEMAND =   365800
AVERAGE INVENTORY = 10698.53
CARRYING COST = $   32020.71
NUMBER OF ORDERS PLACED =    19
ORDER COST = $     760.00
NUMBER OF ORDERS RECEIVED =    19
RECEIVING COST = $    3800.00
NUMBER OF SALES UNITS LOST =      1593
COST OF LOST SALES = $ 95580.00
SERVICE FACTOR =   99.56
NUMBER OF BACKORDERS =     1

TOTAL INVENTORY COST =   132260.70
```

Figure 16-16
MASTER inventory simulation

deviation. (Note that the order point is left at 5000 units and the order quantity is 20,000 units.) As you can see from the figure, the total inventory cost is reduced to $132,260.70 and the service factor is 99.56%. These values are better than any previous results.

THE NEED FOR REPLICATIONS

In section 16-3, we discussed the importance of replications in a simulation study. The output from a Monte Carlo simulation study based on only one replication is like estimating a population value based on a sample size of 1. To demonstrate, we will use the same input data used to generate the output results in Figure 16-16 and rerun the

```
                    INVENTORY SIMULATION

MODEL FORM:
                    NUMBER OF TIME PERIODS:     365
                    PRODUCT PRICE PER UNIT:     20
                    BEGINNING INVENTORY    :    4000
                    ORDER POINT            :    5000
                    ORDER QUANTITY         :    20000
                    COST OF PLACING ORDER  :    40
                    COST TO RECEIVE ORDER  :    200
                    BACKORDERING COST      :    100
                    LOST SALES COST        :    60
                    INTEREST RATE/PERIOD   :    .00041

DEMAND IS NORMALLY DISTRIBUTED
                    AVERAGE DEMAND IS      :    1000
                    DEMAND STANDARD DEV.   :    100

LEAD TIME IS NORMALLY DISTRIBUTED
                    AVERAGE LEAD TIME IS   :    4
                    ST. DEV. LEAD TIME IS  :    1

                    SUMMARY STATISTICS

TOTAL DEMAND =   364039
AVERAGE INVENTORY = 11041.19
CARRYING COST = $   33046.29
NUMBER OF ORDERS PLACED =    19
ORDER COST = $     760.00
NUMBER OF ORDERS RECEIVED =    19
RECEIVING COST = $    3800.00
NUMBER OF SALES UNITS LOST =          0
COST OF LOST SALES = $          0
SERVICE FACTOR = 100.00
NUMBER OF BACKORDERS =     0

TOTAL INVENTORY COST =    37606.29
```

Figure 16-17
MASTER inventory simulation

simulation. (Note that MASTER produces a different string of random numbers each time the simulation model is run.)

Figure 16-17 shows the results of this second replication. As you can see, it produced substantially different results from those in Figure 16-16, with no lost sales and a reduction in total inventory cost to $37,606.29. Thus, in order to more accurately evaluate the performance of a system through simulation, a decision maker will need to run a number of replications and evaluate the average values of the output variables.

16-5 SUMMARY AND CONCLUSIONS

Computer simulation is a powerful and effective management science tool. Its use by decision makers in both public and private organizations has grown steadily since the early 1950s. Simulation provides decision makers with a means for observing the effect that certain changes have on the behavior of a system without actually making the physical changes.

The steps involved in developing a simulation model are:

1. Defining the problem
2. Analyzing and modeling the system to be simulated
3. Formulating the computer program
4. Validating the model
5. Designing the simulation experiments
6. Analyzing data from the experiments

In this chapter we have introduced the basic concepts of simulation and discussed two specific simulation models. The queuing model introduced in section 16-3 illustrates how a waiting-line system can be analyzed using simulation. In section 16-4, we introduced an inventory simulation model. Both of these models are examples of *Monte Carlo simulation*. During the simulation runs, sample values are selected from predefined probability distributions. In the case of the queuing model, the interarrival times and the service times were assumed to be exponentially distributed. These times were randomly generated to simulate arrivals to the system and service of the customers. In the inventory model, the demand and lead time were normally distributed. A random selection process was used to generate demand and lead times from the specified normal distributions.

The waiting-line and inventory examples represent two distinct types of simulation models. The queuing example used a *next-event model,* a type of model in which the time increment is based on the occurrence of the next event. The randomly generated interarrival time for a customer advances the clock. The inventory model is an example of a *fixed-time simulation,* in which each cycle through the model simulates a time period of a specific length (e.g., one day or one week).

Computer simulation is often a useful alternative to other management science tools. In cases where the system being modeled is not suited to a more traditional technique, simulation can sometimes be used to help understand the system's behavior. However, unlike many other management science tools, such as linear programming, simulation does not locate the "optimal value" or "optimal solution." Instead, simulation models represent what will happen with the system if it is operated under specific conditions. The objective of a simulation model is to search for the "optimal" values for one or more decision variables through experimental runs of the model.

With simulation, as with other management science models, you will face the trade-off between being able to accurately model the system versus being able to complete the modeling project. The simulation model will be a representation of the real system, but it won't be a perfect representation. As with all models, a decision maker will have to decide on the trade-off between a more accurate model and the time and expense necessary to generate such a model. We also, once again, need to emphasize that a simulation model is only a tool to be used in the decision process.

Solved Problem

PROBLEM

The vice-president for gaming at the Players' Casino in Atlantic City is interested in simulating a betting strategy for the roulette wheel. The strategy will be:

1. Starting with a bankroll of $100, bet $5 on red.
2. If red occurs, increase the bankroll by the amount of the bet and repeat step 1.
3. If black or green occurs, decrease the bankroll by the amount of the bet and double the previous bet. Continue doubling the bet until red occurs or until the bankroll is gone.

Manually simulate this betting strategy, continuing until the bankroll is gone or until you have played 40 times, whichever comes first.

Solution

We begin by defining the roulette game. Suppose there are 52 slots on the wheel: 25 are red, 25 are black, and 2 are green. We can develop the following probability distribution:

Event (color)	Probability
Win (red)	25/52
Lose (black)	25/52
Lose (green)	2/52
	52/52 = 1.00

We combine the chances of losing on black and green to get the following probabilities:

Event	Probability
Win	25/52 = .4807
Lose	27/52 = .5193

Next we must establish a mechanism for determining whether a win or a loss occurs on each play of the roulette wheel. Monte Carlo simulation will be used to model this problem and a sample will be selected from a uniform distribution with values ranging from 0 to 1. As shown in the diagram below, if the random number is .4807 or less, the roulette spin will be a win; otherwise, it will be a loss. Through this process, in the long run, the number of wins should approach 48.07%.

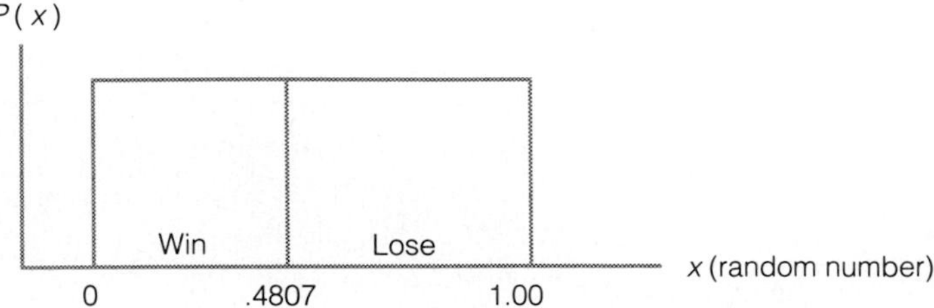

You can use the table of uniform random numbers (Appendix D) in the sampling process.

The flow diagram in Figure 16-18 represents the sequence of events for this system. We set the starting values as follows: bankroll = $100, spin = 1, and bet = $5. The table below shows the spin-by-spin results of the simulation.

Spin	Bet	Random Number	Result	Payoff	Bankroll
0	0				$100
1	$5	.1394	Win	+5	$105
2	$5	.0697	Win	+5	$110

Spin	Bet	Random Number	Result	Payoff	Bankroll
3	$5	.5474	Lose	−5	$105
4	$10	.9405	Lose	−10	$95
5	$20	.2060	Win	+20	$115
6	$5	.1319	Win	+5	$120
7	$5	.0999	Win	+5	$125
8	$5	.6484	Lose	−5	$120
9	$10	.3672	Win	+10	$130
10	$5	.9060	Lose	−5	$125
11	$10	.1272	Win	+10	$135
12	$5	.6847	Lose	−5	$130
13	$10	.5591	Lose	−10	$120
14	$20	.3320	Win	+20	$140
15	$5	.2295	Win	+5	$145
16	$5	.2160	Win	+5	$150
17	$5	.6709	Lose	−5	$145
18	$10	.4281	Win	+10	$155
19	$5	.2099	Win	+5	$160
20	$5	.7368	Lose	−5	$155
21	$10	.0449	Win	+10	$165
22	$5	.7903	Lose	−5	$160
23	$10	.5747	Lose	−10	$150
24	$20	.5700	Lose	−20	$130
25	$40	.9764	Lose	−40	$90
26	$80	.0931	Win	+80	$170
27	$5	.0335	Win	+5	$175
28	$5	.3664	Win	+5	$180
29	$5	.2140	Win	+5	$185
30	$5	.5888	Lose	−5	$180
31	$10	.9988	Lose	−10	$170
32	$20	.6050	Lose	−20	$150
33	$40	.4594	Win	+40	$190
34	$5	.6080	Lose	−5	$185
35	$10	.0864	Win	+10	$195
36	$5	.0929	Win	+5	$200
37	$5	.8674	Lose	−5	$195
38	$10	.0594	Win	+10	$205
39	$5	.6152	Lose	−5	$200
40	$10	.4654	Win	+10	$210

Note: Percent wins = 22/40 = .55; longest win streak = 4; longest loss streak = 4; lowest balance = $90; highest balance = $210; final cash balance = $210; highest bet = $80.

This simulation shows that, starting with $100, a person would have a balance of $210 at the end of 40 plays. However, you would want to replicate the procedure many more times before drawing any firm conclusions about this betting system.

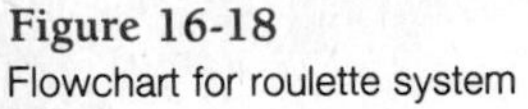

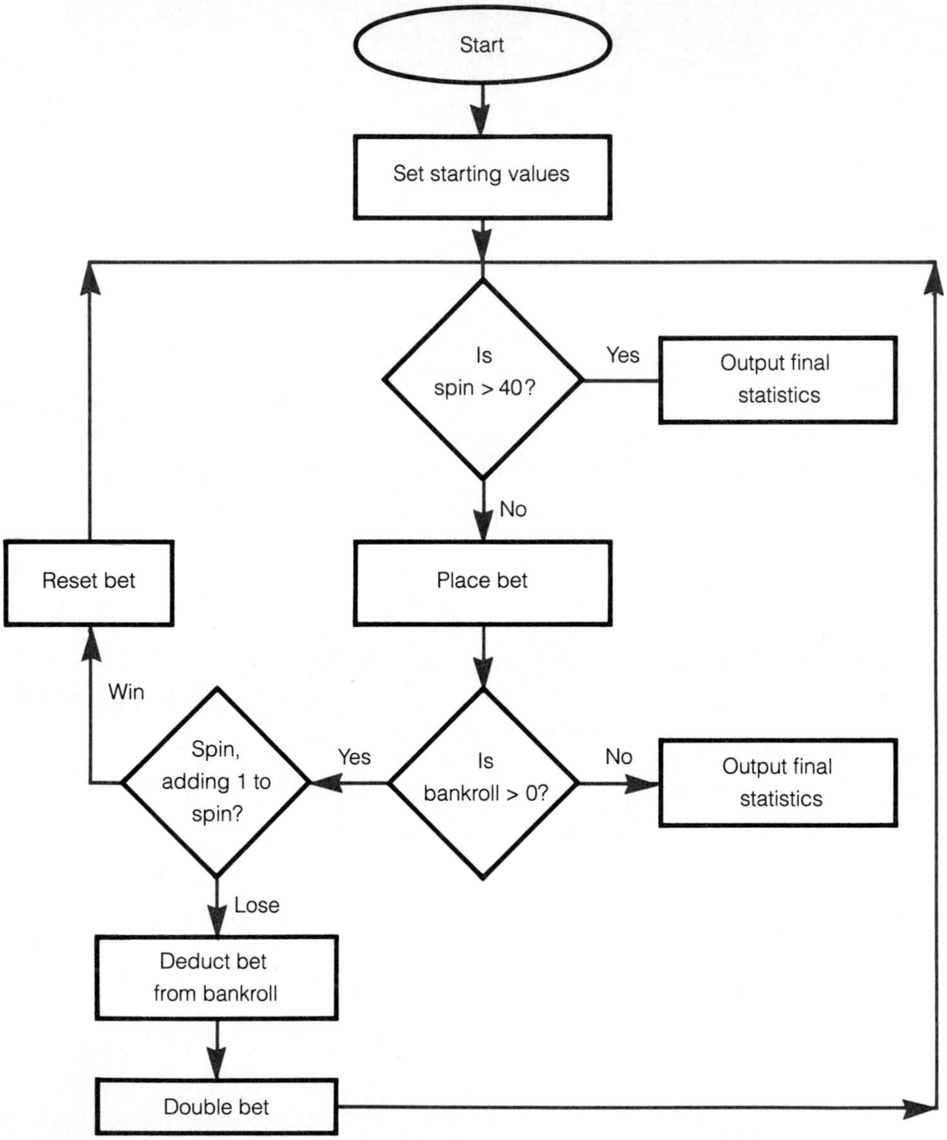

Figure 16-18
Flowchart for roulette system

General Questions and Assignments

1. What are the basic steps in developing a simulation model? Discuss each step in your own terms.
2. Discuss what is meant by *validating* the simulation model. Discuss the approaches to model validation.
3. Discuss the difference between a *deterministic* simulation model and a *stochastic* simulation model.
4. Discuss, using examples of your own, what *exogenous* and *endogenous* variables are as they relate to simulation modeling.
5. Suppose that a simulation experiment has 5 factors: the first two factors have 3 levels, factor 3 has 5

levels, and factors 4 and 5 have 4 levels. The decision maker wishes to have 40 replications of each experiment. How many runs of the model will be required?

6. What is meant by the term *Monte Carlo simulation?*
7. Drawing from the discussion in this chapter and your coursework in statistics, discuss why replications of a simulation model should be run before using the results to assist in decisions about the system being modeled.
8. Identify a waiting-line system on your campus which fits either the single-line, multiple-channel model or the multiple-line, multiple-channel model. Collect data on average time between arrivals and average service time. If you have access to MASTER, use these data and simulate the system for 40 time periods (or use a time period that makes sense for the system you have observed). Write a report describing the model output and compare the results with what you have actually observed in the system.
9. Discuss the difference between *next-event* simulation models and *fixed-time* simulation models. Use an example of your own to illustrate the differences.
10. Contact a local business or other organization that uses simulation models and determine the type(s) of model used. Write a short report describing one or more of these simulation models and the type of application for which it is used.
11. Locate at least three articles which describe applications of computer simulation. Write a paper summarizing the articles and comment on how successful these applications were for the users.

Exercises and Application Problems

1. A service technician for a major computer company is trained to service two models of the computer: BT3000 and CT4000. Approximately 70% of the technician's service calls are for the CT4000 and 30% are for the BT3000. The service time distributions for the two models are as follows:

BT3000		CT4000	
Time (minutes)	Relative Frequency	Time (minutes)	Relative Frequency
20	.40	15	.50
30	.20	25	.15
40	.30	30	.10
50	.10	40	.25

   a. Show the random-number intervals that can be used to simulate the type of machine to be serviced and the length of the service time.
   b. Simulate 25 service calls. What is the total time the technician spends on the 25 calls?

2. A restaurant is planning to offer drive-through service and needs to determine whether to install one or two windows. The following probability distributions regarding arrival intervals and service times have been developed from historical data from another restaurant in a city of similar size:

Arrival Interval (minutes)	Probability	Service Time (minutes)	Probability
1	.15	2	.30
2	.50	3	.45
3	.20	4	.20
4	.10	5	.05
5	.05		

For the two-window system, assume that a car will always join the shorter line. When the lines are the same length, there is a .50 probability the driver will enter either queue.

a. Develop a flowchart for the two-window system.
b. Develop a manual simulation experiment based on a 40-minute arrival period for both the one- and two-window systems. Compute the average queue length, waiting time, and percentage utilization of each system.
c. Which system should the restaurant install?

3. A bicycle shop carries a popular brand of bike that sells for $175. The owner wants to determine how many of these bicycles to order and when to order them. Demand is not known with certainty. The lead time is 10 days. The cost of the bikes depends on the quantity ordered. Placing an order costs $30, and a stockout is assumed to cost $40 per unit. The daily cost of carrying inventory is 1% of the selling price of the bicycle. No backordering is allowed.

Historical Frequency of Demand		**Price Schedule**	
Demand per Day	Probability	Order Quantity	Unit Price
0	.08	Under 15	$125
1	.12	15–25	$115
2	.38	Over 25	$110
3	.22		
4	.16		
5	.04		

a. Develop a flowchart for simulating the inventory policy that requires ordering 20 bikes when the total number of bikes on hand plus bikes on order reaches 15 or fewer.
b. Manually simulate this policy for a 20-day period (assume a beginning inventory of 10 bikes and no bikes on order).

4. The Come-on-In Beauty Salon currently has one stylist. Since business has been increasing, the owner is considering hiring another stylist. Customer arrivals are Poisson-distributed at a rate of 2 per hour. The time it takes to style a customer's hair is exponentially distributed, with a mean of 20 minutes. The owner has noticed that if 3 customers are waiting for service, a potential new customer will generally not stay. The cost of each service is $10, and a new stylist would cost $120 per 5-day week. Use simulation to help decide whether or not to hire the additional stylist. (If you have access to MASTER or another software package, use it for the simulation; if not, perform 10 replications manually.)

5. A door-to-door cleaning-products salesman has compiled some useful information from his historical sales records. For instance, he has learned that if he talks to a man in the household, there is a 30% chance of making a sale. But if the woman of the house answers the door, there is only a 20% chance of making a sale. The probability distributions for the number of products ordered by a man and woman are as follows:

Man's Order		**Woman's Order**	
Products	Probability	Products	Probability
2	.50	1	.45
3	.30	2	.35
4	.20	3	.15
		4	.05

The salesman has found that no one answers the door at about 35% of the houses contacted. When the door is answered, there is a 50% chance that it will be a man. The salesman's profit is $3.00 for each product sold.

a. Prepare a flowchart for a simulation of this problem, with output being the salesman's profit.
b. Manually simulate this problem and show the house-by-house results for 30 calls. What is the total profit from these 30 calls?
c. Based on your results from part **b**, how many products should the salesman expect to sell if he calls on 90 houses? What is his expected profit?

6. A retail firm has the following inventory policy:

   Order size = 6 units

   Reorder point = 2 units

   Holding costs = 20% per year

   Ordering cost = $8 per order

   Stockout cost = $20 per unit

   Unit price = $12.00

   Daily demand is thought to be normally distributed, with a mean of 8.0 and a standard deviation of 3.2. Lead time is also normally distributed, with a mean of 10 days and a standard deviation of 6 days. Customers will not backorder.

   The firm has a beginning inventory balance of 3 units. All orders are received at the beginning of the day. Develop a simulation experiment to replicate this firm's inventory policy for 100 days. Replicate the experiment 10 times using MASTER or another simulation software package. (Assume that the store is open 365 days per year.)

7. Referring to problem 6, suppose the retail store works with its vendor and is able to cut the average lead time to 5 days and reduce the standard deviation to 1.5 days. Use MASTER or another software package to simulate 100 days of inventory activity. Replicate the experiment 10 times and compare the results with those of problem 6.

8. Referring to problems 6 and 7, suppose the store is trying to determine what the appropriate order size should be. Use simulation to test several different order sizes. Simulate for 100 days and use 10 replications of each experiment. Use MASTER or another simulation software package.

9. The time between arrivals at a self-service car wash is exponentially distributed, with a mean of 3.5 minutes. The time taken to wash a car is also exponentially distributed, with a mean of 9 minutes. Assume that the car wash is a multiple-line, multiple-channel system and is open 8 hours a day. Use MASTER or another simulation model to describe the operation of the system.
   a. Simulate the system for 30 replications of an 8-hour period, assuming that there is just one car-washing bay and a maximum queue length of 4. Write a short report describing the results. Discuss what happens when the arrival rate exceeds the service rate.
   b. Simulate the system for 30 replications of 8 hours each, assuming there are two car-washing bays with a maximum queue length of 4 at each bay. How do these results compare with those for part **a**?

10. Referring to the simulation results for problem 9, how many car-washing bays would you recommend? What factors are you considering? Write a short report explaining your position.

11. Jobs arrive at the Ace Machine Shop according to a Poisson distribution at an average of 6 per hour. The shop has 3 work centers that can be used to do any of the jobs. The time required for each job at each center varies, depending upon the type of job, and is considered to be exponentially distributed with a mean of 12 minutes. Assume that jobs wait in a single line for the next available center. The shop has space for a maximum of 10 jobs to be waiting. Use MASTER or another software package to simulate the system in the machine shop for fifteen 8-hour days using a first-come, first-served rule. Write a report describing the behavior of this system.

12. Referring to problem 11, suppose that the system is changed so that jobs go into a queue behind a given work center, where each line is limited to 10 jobs. When a job arrives, it goes into the shortest

queue. Simulate this system for fifteen 8-hour days. Write a short report comparing these results with the results for problem 11.

13. Jog-Along Corp. wants to develop a policy for order quantity and reorder point to minimize the total costs associated with the company's inventory of $350 jogging machines. The historical daily demand has been normally distributed, with a mean of 2.6 and a standard deviation of 1.2.

    The lead time on past orders has also been normally distributed, with a mean of 10 days and standard deviation of 3 days. The inventory holding costs are $2 per unit per week, the ordering cost is $15 per order, the stockout cost is $30 per unit, and the beginning inventory is 5 units. If demand occurs and cannot be filled, no backordering will be done.

    The company is considering using an order quantity of 10 and a reorder point of 6. Use simulation to evaluate the operation of this inventory system. Simulate for 365 days, using MASTER or another simulation software package.

14. Referring to the Jog-Along Corp. in problem 13, suppose its managers are considering increasing the order quantity to 100 units. Simulate this system for 365 days and compare the results with those for problem 13.

15. The managers of Greene Trucking have recently studied the loading-dock area at the central warehouse facility. They have found that trucks arrive according to a Poisson distribution at the rate of 10 per hour. The loading (or unloading) time is exponentially distributed, with an average of 50 minutes. When trucks arrive, they are sent to the next available loading dock. The waiting area has room for 10 trucks at any one time. Any trucks turned away will be unloaded after hours, with overtime paid to the loading-dock crew and truck drivers. Greene Trucking currently has 6 loading docks but is considering closing down 1 or 2 of them to add more warehouse space. Simulate this system for 20 days (assume 8 hours per day), using MASTER or another software package. Write a report based on the simulation results and give your recommendation about closing the loading docks.

16. The owner of a magazine stand is trying to decide how many copies of *Business Monthly* to stock. He purchases copies for $.90 and sells them for $2.50 each. If he has old magazines at the end of the month, they can be sent back to the publisher for $.35 per magazine (assume the publisher picks up the shipping cost). The demand distribution for the magazine is given below:

Number of Magazines	Probability	Number of Magazines	Probability
40	.03	60	.33
45	.08	65	.18
50	.13	70	.02
55	.23		

    Use a manual simulation model to determine the number of magazines to be purchased for sale at the newsstand. Use purchase levels equal to possible demand levels. Simulate for 10 periods.

17. The manager of Yum-Yum Bakery would like to determine how many glazed doughnuts to produce each day to maximize profits. Production costs are $.10 per doughnut, and the selling price is $.30 each. Any doughnuts not sold by the end of the day are priced at $.05 as day-old goods. Assume the bakery has the following data covering the daily demand for last month (30 days of operation):

Daily Demand	Frequency	Daily Demand	Frequency
30	3	50	4
35	5	55	3
40	8	60	1
45	6		

    Develop a 10-day simulation for production sizes equivalent to each of the daily demands above. What appears to be the best production size?

18. Consider a medium-size community that has only one city park. City managers are currently trying to determine the best location for a second park. What would be the objective for this problem? Explain how computer simulation might be used to evaluate alternative locations.
19. A local medical group has asked you to help them determine the number of examination rooms to include in their new clinic. How could computer simulation assist in reaching a good decision? What factors would you consider in a simulation model of this problem?

Note: Problems 20–23 require the use of MASTER or another simulation software package.

20. Consider a bank with 4 tellers. Customers arrive at a rate of 60 per hour and go directly to a teller if one is idle. If all tellers are busy, the customer enters a single waiting line and then goes to the first available teller. Customers who find the waiting line to be 10 or more leave immediately. Customers who join the waiting line will stay in the system until they are served. Each teller serves at the same average rate of 4 minutes per customer. Develop a simulation model for an 8-hour day and perform 25 replications. Determine the facility utilization percentage, the average waiting time in the system, and the average number of customers turned away. Write a short report describing the system's behavior.
21. How would the results of problem 20 change if there was a separate line for each teller and everything else remained constant? Write a report showing the comparison.
22. Price Motors purchases a certain model automobile for $9000. To finance the purchase of this auto, Price must pay interest at a 15% annual rate on borrowed capital. Orders for additional cars can be placed each week, but a minimum order of 15 cars is required. Orders are received within an average of 3 weeks, with a standard deviation of 1 week. The cost of placing an order is $100. Currently, Price has 20 cars of this model in inventory. Demand is normally distributed, with an average demand of 4 cars per week and a standard deviation of 1.5 cars per week. If demand occurs and no car is available, the car may be backordered, but the cost of placing a backorder is $400. There is a 20% chance that the customer will not backorder. If backordering is acceptable to the customer, the following distribution represents the cumulative probability that the customer will cancel the backorder in a given number of weeks.

Weeks on Backorder	Probability	Weeks on Backorder	Probability
0	.20	3	.70
1	.10	4	.90
2	.30	5	1.00

If a backorder is canceled, a lost-goodwill cost of $300 per car is incurred. Simulate this system for 52 weeks and write a report discussing the results. Assume a reorder point of 10 cars and that the minimum number of cars are ordered.
23. Refering to problem 22, suppose the minimum order quantity is reduced to 10 cars. After finding the output for a simulation of 52 weeks, would you recommend that the company change its order size from 15 to 10?

Chapter Glossary

Analog simulation models A physical model used to represent a real system (e.g., a wind tunnel simulates the pressures that wind exerts on cars, aircraft, etc.).

Controllable variables Those factors within the system that can be controlled.

Deterministic system A system whose output values can be predicted with certainty if the values of the input variables are known.

Endogenous Variables The output (or dependent) variables in a simulation model.

Exogenous Variable The input (or independent) variables in a simulation model; they are determined by forces outside the system.

Face validity A judgment that the simulation model has the functional relationships between variables arranged in a reasonable manner.

Factor variable An exogenous variable in a simulation study.

Fixed-time simulation A simulation model in which the time clock is incremented in fixed units of time, during which a certain number of events may occur.

Flowchart A diagram using geometric symbols and arrows which represents the time flow and activities of the system.

Monte Carlo simulation A simulation model in which one or more of the input variables is described by a probability distribution.

Next-event simulation A simulation model in which the time clock is incremented when each event occurs.

Pseudorandom numbers A computer-generated number that has the statistical properties of a true random number.

Replications A rerun of a simulation using the same starting conditions and values for the input variables.

Response variable An endogenous variable in a simulation experiment.

Sensitivity analysis The process of altering the input variables of a simulation model and observing the effects on the output variables.

Simulation The use of a model to represent the critical characteristics of a system and to observe the system's operation over time.

Starting conditions The status of the system at the beginning of the simulation run.

Stochastic system A system in which values of the output variables cannot be predicted with certainty for a given input.

Chapter References

BOOKS

Hoover, S. V., and R. F. Perry. *Simulation: A Problem-Solving Approach.* Reading, Mass.: Addison-Wesley, 1989.

Maisel, Herbert, and Giuliano Gnugnoli. *Simulation of Discrete Stochastic Systems.* Chicago: SRA, 1972.

Meir, R. C., W. T. Newell, and H. L. Pazer. *Simulation in Business and Economics.* Englewood Cliffs, N.J.: Prentice-Hall, 1969.

Naylor, Thomas H. *Computer Simulation Experiments with Models of Economic Systems.* New York: Wiley, 1971.

Roberts, Nancy, et al. *Introduction to Computer Simulation.* Reading, Mass.: Addison-Wesley, 1983.

Shannon, R. E. *Systems Simulation: The Art and Science.* Englewood Cliffs, N.J.: Prentice-Hall, 1975.

ARTICLES

Brown, J. J., and J. J. Kelly. "Simulation of Elevator Systems for World's Tallest Buildings." *Transportation Science,* Vol. 2, 1968.

de Kluyver, C. A., and McNally, G. M. "Corporate Planning Using Simulation." *Interfaces,* Vol. 10, 1980.

Godin, V. B. "The Dollars and Sense of Simulation." *Decision Sciences,* Vol. 7, 1976.

Golovin, L. "Product Blending: A Simulation Case Study in Double Time." *Interfaces,* Vol. 9, 1979.

Grant, F. H. "Reducing Voter Waiting Time." *Interfaces,* Vol. 10, 1980.

Hertz, D. B. "Risk Analysis in Capital Budgeting." *Harvard Business Review,* January–February, 1964.

Taylor, R. J., and W. F. Evans. "Showing That the Low-Cost Route to More Data Processing Capacity Will Work." *Interfaces,* Vol. 12, 1982.

Shannon, P. W., et al. "Using Simulation in Implementing Property Tax Reform." *Simulation,* Vol. 33, 1979.

Mini Cases

CASE 16A
VARSITY TICKET SALES*

Varsity Ticket Sales was founded in 1986 to sell tickets for athletic events, plays, concerts, and other activities in the Tulsa metropolitan area. It has 15 outlets throughout the community where people can buy advance tickets to events through a computerized vending machine, which works much like a bank teller machine. Varsity also has an office at the Tulsa Events Center in downtown Tulsa where people can make purchases directly from ticket agents at walk-up windows.

When Thomas McKay took over as general manager of Varsity Ticket Sales in the spring of 1990, he began to look for opportunities to improve service to the public. One area that concerned him was the ticket operation at the Tulsa Events Center. Although he observed long waiting lines on many occasions and had to answer numerous customer complaints about excessive waiting times, he also noticed many instances when the ticket sellers were not busy.

In June, he decided to study the situation and hired a local consulting firm to prepare recommendations. The consultants started by collecting data for two types of activity: (1) sales during peak busy times, on the day of a major event, and (2) sales during slow times, when no major events were scheduled within 5 days. This information would give them a good idea of the range of activity at the ticket office. They found the following:

	Peak Time	Slow Time
Average interarrival rate	0.6 minute	8.2 minutes
Average service time	3.4 minutes	4.4 minutes

The ticket center currently has 10 ticket windows but not all are staffed all the time. In fact, even during busy times in the past, at most 5 ticket sellers were on duty because the previous manager did not want to pay for idle time. The consultants also noted that the waiting-line system was set up for first come, first served—when customers arrived, they joined a single waiting line and then were served by the first available ticket agent.

When Tom met with the consultants to review these data, he asked whether there was some way to analyze the system as it now stood. He said that he was most concerned with the behavior of the system during peak demand periods and said he was willing to increase the number of ticket agents on duty, change the way the lines operated, or whatever it would take to help the situation. He asked for a full report explaining all his options, supported by statistics.

CASE 16B
GOLDEN VALLEY CARS

Julia Bosco is negotiating to buy Golden Valley Cars from Les Chandler. Les is being forced to sell the dealership because Eastern First National, Golden Valley's bank, has refused to extend the line of credit the company needs to finance its inventory. All auto dealers have to stock an inventory of cars, which they usually finance with a continuous bank loan. Generally, bank managers like making this type of loan, as long as they feel comfortable about being able to close out the loan if necessary. But times have been hard for car dealers recently, and Golden Valley is no exception. When the bank manager observed that the inventory of cars had been steadily building because sales

* Note: MASTER or another simulation software package must be used to solve this case.

were down, he concluded that Golden Valley had been using its line of credit for normal operations, not restocking. Bank regulators, who have been under increasing pressure to ensure that loans are secured by reliable assets or operations, will be vitsiting Eastern First National within the month. Facing critical scrutiny of his bank's loans, the manager decided not to continue to finance an inventory that was not moving.

Julia will be taking over the dealership after a successful career as a sales manager in Phoenix. However, this will be the first time she has had to be responsible for the entire operation of a company: managing all the departments, including parts and service; maintaining records; controlling expenses; and determining promotion activities. All the lending agencies Julia has contacted are aware of the sluggish sales in the auto industry, and everyone wants assurances that she has an effective plan for managing the inventory.

Julia's first response to the lenders' concern about inventory was simple: "We'll just sell it!" But the lenders required a more complete response. In particular, one bank officer, Bob Vick, offered the following scenario to provide some insight into the decision-making strategy of a car dealer.

"For the sake of simplicity, assume you sell only one model car, with a unit cost of \$10,000. You have 15 cars in inventory now, but the cost of carrying the inventory, including interest charges, is 24% per year. The cost of placing an order is \$250, and the cost of receiving an order is \$500." Bob then produced the following distribution table to describe daily demand for the car:

Daily Demand	Proportion of Time
0	5%
1	5%
2	5%
3	10%
4	10%
5	20%
6	10%
7	10%
8	10%
9	10%
10	5%

Then Bob continued, "When an order is placed, the lead time is uncertain. Unfortunately, if a customer comes in to buy a car and one is not on the lot, the sale is lost—and so is the average \$300 profit. So you can see the importance of knowing as much as possible about lead time—the time between placing and receiving an order." Bob said as he handed Julia this table describing the lead-time distribution:

Number of Days	Proportion of Time
10	10%
15	40%
20	20%
25	20%
30	10%

Now Bob expects Julia to determine the order point and order quantity that will minimize the total inventory cost for the example.

Julia asks for some time to respond—and immediately calls her daughter, Jill, who is attending graduate school and majoring in computer science. Jill claims she can write a program to simulate the operation of this inventory situation if Julia can outline the important information and cost flows.

Chapter 17

DYNAMIC PROGRAMMING

Chapter Outline

Why You Need to Know

Linear programming, with all its variations, is a very powerful decision-making tool; but it is not appropriate for certain types of decision situations. For example, the manager of a shoe store must determine how many pairs of all the various styles to purchase for the year in order to maximize profit. The decision depends on a variety of constraints, such as demand, shelf space, advertising costs, and so on. If this were simply a product-mix problem, linear programming could be used to find the optimal number of each type of shoe to order for the season. However, in practice, the manager is likely to make an initial ordering decision and then revise it after seeing data on actual sales for the first week or month. Because linear programming assumes a decision situation is static and does not easily allow for changes, or *dynamic* adjustments, this decision problem would have to be reformulated after the first month to update the ordering decision. In another application, advertising executives may plan a campaign that will allow them to shift advertising among various media, depending on which one proves most effective in a particular area. Linear programming is not well equipped to deal with these types of dynamic decision processes.

Typically, many actual decision-making situations also change over time. Given today's rapidly changing world, businesses and other organizations simply cannot afford to make any long-term decisions without the option of revising their course periodically. For instance, a company may decide to stop making a product partway through the year because of skyrocketing materials costs. A company may even need to suspend operations in a foreign country because of military or political events or a natural disaster. In such cases, the decision approach must be flexible enough to adapt to unexpected change. Earlier, we said that linear programming models are inherently static, or fixed. This means that, to build a model, we gather as much information about the decision variables and constraints as possible and then assume that the optimal set of solution variables, and their values, can be determined from this information. But in the real world, a great many decision-making situations are dynamic, or changeable, and require revised decisions as conditions or information change. Managers can choose from several techniques to aid in decision making when conditions are uncertain, or likely to change. One of the best-known decision tools for this purpose is *dynamic programming.* Since it is likely that you will often face situations in which the optimal decision will depend on unforeseen outcomes, or the decision must be made in stages, you need to be aware of the characteristics and applications of dynamic programming models.

Chapter Objectives

The purpose of this chapter is to introduce dynamic programming, one of the earliest techniques for developing models that allow decision makers to account for the changeable nature of many actual decision situations. As you will see, dynamic programming shares some common characteristics with linear programming, but the two techniques also have some fundamental differences. In this chapter, we will identify these similarities and differences and will also examine the strengths and weaknesses of each.

Dynamic programming is not as structured as linear programming, a decision process that requires us to determine a set of decision variables, an objective function, and a series of constraints for every problem. In this chapter, we will use examples to illustrate the principles of dynamic programming and to explain the procedure for formulating the decision model.

After studying the material in this chapter, you should be able to:

1. Identify the characteristics of situations which can be modeled using dynamic programming.
2. Formulate dynamic programming models for a variety of situations.
3. Discuss the differences between linear programming and dynamic programming models.

17-1 A BRIEF HISTORY OF DYNAMIC PROGRAMMING

The inability of traditional linear programming models to incorporate uncertainty or to handle decisions that take place in stages was recognized soon after the simplex procedure was introduced. The initial management science effort to attack these problems focused on multistage inventory decisions involving uncertain demands. And the work of one person, Richard Bellman, led to the decision technique now known as dynamic programming. Initially referred to as "linear programming under uncertainty" or "stochastic linear programming," this technique was developed as part of the surge of management science tools introduced in the 1950s.

Dynamic programming is a general problem-solving procedure that can be applied to sequential decision situations; it allows a complex, hard-to-solve decision problem to be separated into a series of smaller, easier-to-solve problems. But it lacks the well-defined structure of tools like linear programming and therefore depends on the ability of the decision maker to correctly identify the form of the problem being considered. Certainly, the technique has not been as successful, or as widely applicable, as its proponents predicted in the 1950s and 1960s. Whether this is due to the nature of the technique itself or to a lack of skill on the part of decision makers using it is open for conjecture. Nonetheless, dynamic programming remains a powerful management science tool for helping decision makers deal with certain types of decision situations.

17-2 CHARACTERISTICS OF DYNAMIC PROGRAMMING MODELS

In formulating the linear programming models earlier in this text, we proceeded through a set of standardized steps. We identified the model's decision variables, the objective the decision maker was trying to achieve, and the set of constraints which restricted the possible values the decision variables could assume. The situations which can be represented by dynamic programming models also have a particular set of characteristics, but they are generally not as well structured as those for linear programming.

Overall, dynamic programming models are most useful in situations where a series of incremental decisions will have future effects that occur within the time horizon of the decision-making model. For instance, your graduation depends on the series of decisions you make regarding the courses to take each term. In another situation, a sales representative may be trying to decide whether to book orders this quarter, to help her make a yearly quota, or to place the orders next quarter; the decision will affect her income both this year and next. A plant manager may be deciding whether to postpone planned maintenance this year in order to produce at higher profit levels now, even though he knows this will increase maintenance time and costs next year.

Although the pattern for a dynamic programming model is not as well defined as that for linear programming, dynamic programming problems do have some specific characteristics, as discussed in the following paragraphs.

First, the problem can be divided into a series of **stages**, or interrelated subproblems (often defined by time), where decisions have to be made. Continuing with the college analogy, the stages might be semesters or quarters, since at the end of each term (stage), you are required to decide which courses to take next term. For a manufacturer, a stage may occur monthly, when a new set of production-run decisions must be made. For a television network executive, it may be a one- or two-month period after the new fall shows are introduced and decisions must be made about which programs to continue and which ones to cancel. Whatever the actual situation, all the decisions made from stage to stage in a dynamic programming problem are *interrelated.* For instance, the courses you are able to take next term are related to the courses you are taking now and to ones you completed in earlier terms.

Second, all dynamic programming models have *state variables.* **States** are the conditions a problem can assume either entering or leaving different stages, as described by the specific state variables for the system. In deciding which major to pursue in college, the state variables in your decision may include the grades you received in past courses, the subjects you found interesting, perceived future job opportunities, and the advice of friends and relatives. In a production decision, the state variables may include production capacity, stocks of raw materials, demand for products, and items in inventory. The dynamic programming procedure becomes more complex as the number of state variables increases. (Since this is an introductory treatment, we will limit our examples to ones with easily defined state variables.)

At each stage of the problem, when a decision is made, the current state variables may assume different values for the next stage. However, the decisions made at any stage are based on the values of the state variables at that time, and in dynamic programming, the decision offers the opportunity to change these values, often in a probabilistic manner. For instance, you may decide to change majors because of the grades you have received in the past and your perception of the grades you are likely to receive in future courses required to complete your current major. Because these future grades are uncertain, you are incorporating uncertainty into your decision-making process. A television network executive may decide to cancel or add programs on the basis of ratings for the present set of shows and a perception (uncertain) of the likely ratings for new programs. A plant manager may decide to postpone scheduled maintenance because of the high level of demand at present and a perception (uncertain) that demand will decrease in the future.

Third, given the situation facing the decision maker at the current stage, the optimal policy for the future is independent of how he or she arrived at the present point. What this means for decision makers using a dynamic programming model is that someone can make decisions which have poor outcomes during early decision time periods and still make good decisions, resulting in good outcomes, in future time periods. This characteristic assumes the conditions at the present point are independent of the routes the decision maker took in getting to this point. In many cases this is a realistic assumption. For instance, a production manager with a particular set of inventory values and production capacity is not interested in whether the inventory was added last month or earlier in the year. In other cases, however, this is not a realistic assumption. For example, the future career of a salesperson who has attained a certain level of sales will be affected by how prior sales were generated; that is, did his or her sales technique alienate customers or build a loyal clientele?

Fourth, and last, the decision problem is structured to establish a **recursion relationship**—a mathematical relationship linking the optimal decision for the last stage to the optimal decisions for the prior stages. This recursion relationship must be definable for the duration of the decision, but it allows us to start at the end and work back through the problem to the first stage. The dynamic programming solution procedure involves identifying the optimal decision for the last stage (n) of the problem, using the recursion relationship to determine the optimal decision at stage $n - 1$, and then $n - 2$, and so on, to the beginning of the problem. (This is the same concept used in folding back a decision tree, as discussed in Chapter 13.)

These four characteristics are admittedly vague. This vagueness is both a strength and a weakness of dynamic programming. The strength is that the method can be extended to a wide variety of decision-making situations. The weakness is that the technique relies as much on the experience of the decision maker as it does on its procedures. The best way to gain experience with dynamic programming is to see it demonstrated in a variety of decision-making situations. Therefore, we will work through several examples in the next three sections of this chapter.

17-3 THE BASICS OF DYNAMIC PROGRAMMING: A ROUTING PROBLEM

The first dynamic programming model we will consider is an updated version of the classic stagecoach problem (see Harvey Wagner's text listed in the Chapter References). Our problem involves a computer sales representative, Kathy Beach, who has to travel from her home office in Chicago to New Delhi, India, to complete a sale. Although her starting point and ending point are fixed, Kathy has a choice of many different flights, all of which are interconnected. For instance, she may start her trip by flying first to New York, Washington, D.C., or Atlanta. From any of these cities, she may then fly to London, Paris, Frankfurt, or Rome. And from any of the latter cities, she may fly to either Athens or Cairo and then to New Delhi. Her possible connections between Chicago and New Delhi are shown in Figure 17-1.

The computer company allows its sales force to make their own airline reservations. Given the recent series of plane crashes, terrorist bombings, and equipment problems on airlines, Kathy is concerned about her safety. She assumes that companies offering flight insurance are much more capable of analyzing airline safety than she is, so she decides to use their rates to determine which routes are safest. Her theory is that she should book the routes which have the lowest insurance costs, since they should be the safest. She compiled information on the cost per $500,000 of insurance for each of the possible flights, as shown in Table 17-1. The question facing Kathy is which series of flights minimizes the total insurance cost and hence should be considered the safest route.

FORMULATING THE MODEL

In the previous section, we identified several specific characteristics of dynamic programming models. To formulate the model for Kathy Beach's problem, we must first identify those characteristics in this problem.

1. Recall that the stages of a problem are the points where *decisions* are made. Notice in Figure 17-1 that each group of destinations is a point at which decisions can be made; these points correspond to the stages of the model.
2. At each stage, Kathy must decide which flight to take. Because these are the factors that will change from one stage to another, the flight choices are the *state variables.*
3. The insurance cost of flying from, say, Frankfurt to any other destination is independent of what route Kathy took to get to Frankfurt. Thus, the *independence* requirement of the modeling process is satisfied for this problem.

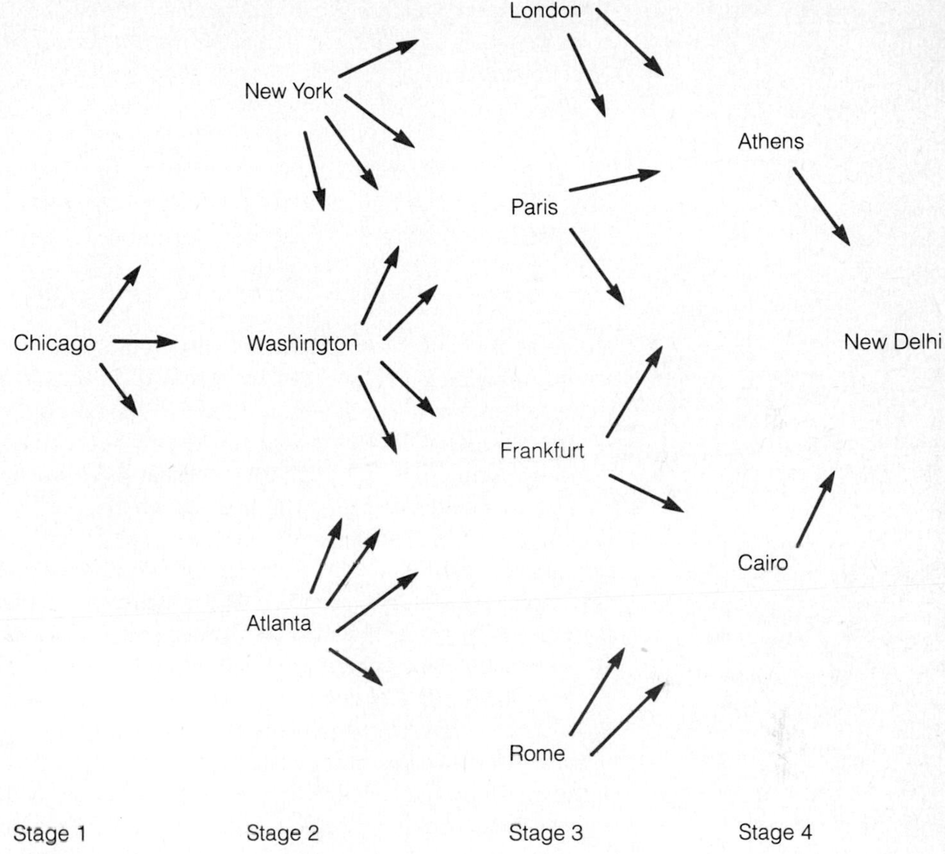

Figure 17-1
Possible routings for Kathy Beach's trip

Table 17-1 INSURANCE COSTS FOR VARIOUS ROUTES (cost per $500,000)

Stage 1	**To**		
From	New York	Washington	Atlanta
Chicago	$2	$3	$3

Stage 2	**To**			
From	London	Paris	Frankfurt	Rome
New York	$5	$6	$7	$6
Washington	$6	$6	$7	$7
Atlanta	$3	$3	$5	$2

Stage 3	**To**	
From	Athens	Cairo
London	$6	$7
Paris	$7	$7
Frankfurt	$8	$12
Rome	$7	$7

Stage 4	**To**
From	New Delhi
Athens	$6
Cairo	$4

4. The *recursion relationship* links the cost decisions made at all stages of the problem and enables us to find the sum of the insurance costs for the combinations of flights considered.

SOLUTION PROCEDURE

The first point to note about situations which can be represented by dynamic programming models is that they are often full of suboptimization opportunities. In this case, if Kathy selects each flight on the basis of insurance cost, in sequence her route would be:

$$\text{Chicago} \xrightarrow{\$2} \text{New York} \xrightarrow{\$5} \text{London} \xrightarrow{\$6} \text{Athens} \xrightarrow{\$6} \text{New Delhi}$$

The total insurance cost for these flights would be $19. As in other situations where suboptimization is an issue, sacrificing a little in one stage of the decision can lead to greater savings at future stages. In this case, the cost of flying from Chicago to London via Atlanta instead of New York would be only $6, which is less than the $7 overall cost found by taking the least expensive alternative from each city, in sequence.

Kathy could determine the least expensive (safest) route by listing all possible combinations of flights from Chicago to New Delhi. While we could present an exhaustive enumeration to illustrate this textbook problem, in real situations the number of possible solution routes through a sequential decision problem can be extensive — and you may mistakenly miss some routes. In this case you would have to list 24 possible routes between Chicago and New Delhi.

Approaching this decision situation as a dynamic programming problem will allow us to arrive at the correct routing with less effort than doing an exhaustive enumeration of all possible combinations of routes. The dynamic programming solution procedure involves dividing the large problem, which is difficult to solve, into a series of small problems, each of which is much less difficult to solve than the large one.

Since stages are the points where decisions can be made, Kathy's problem has four stages, as you can see in Figure 17-1. In the previous section we stated that dynamic programming problems are solved by starting at the end of the problem and using the recursion relationship to move to the beginning decision. So here, we start by assuming that Kathy is at the last stage (stage 4) and is in either Athens or Cairo; now she has only one possible decision: fly to New Delhi. The insurance costs for these flights are $6 (Athens) and $4 (Cairo).

Now, moving back to stage 3, assume Kathy is in London. Should she fly to Athens or to Cairo? Insurance for the flight to Athens costs only $6, compared with $7 for flying to Cairo; but flying from Cairo to New Delhi is less expensive by $2 than flying from Athens to New Delhi. Thus, the least-cost decision from London should be to fly to New Delhi via Cairo, for a total cost of $11.

Continuing at stage 3, assume Kathy is in Paris. The insurance cost of flying from Paris to Athens is $7, the same as from Paris to Cairo; but it costs $2 less to fly to New Delhi from Cairo than from Athens. Therefore, if she is in Paris, Kathy's decision should be to fly to New Delhi via Cairo for a total cost of $11.

Following the same logic, we find that the least costly choices for the remaining alternatives in stage 3 are:

Frankfurt ⟶ Athens ⟶ New Delhi $14

Rome ⟶ Cairo ⟶ New Delhi $11

These decisions, and their associated costs, are summarized in Table 17-2.

Table 17-2 LEAST EXPENSIVE ROUTES IN STAGE 3

From	Best Route	Total Insurance Cost
London	Cairo→New Delhi	$11
Paris	Cairo→New Delhi	$11
Frankfurt	Athens→New Delhi	$14
Rome	Cairo→New Delhi	$11

Moving to stage 2 of the problem, we apply the same logic, except since we have already determined the cheapest route from each city in stage 3, we can now work with the costs shown in Table 17-2. Therefore, if we assume that Kathy will fly out of New York, the trip to New Delhi via London will cost a total of $16 ($5 for New York to London plus $11 for London to New Delhi via Cairo).

We then analyze each of the other three flight options from New York in the same manner. For example, flying through Paris will cost $17 ($6 cost for New York to Paris plus $11 for Paris to New Delhi via Cairo). Likewise, the total cost from New York to New Delhi through Frankfurt is $21, and the total cost through Rome is $17. Thus, the least-cost alternative from New York is:

New York ⟶ London ⟶ Cairo ⟶ New Delhi $16

To complete stage 2, we need to perform similar calculations for departures from Washington, D.C., and Atlanta. Table 17-3 shows the least-cost routes from each of these intermediate locations. Note that two options from Washington, D.C., have the same minimum insurance cost; going through either London or Paris will cost $17.

We now move back one more stage, to stage 1, the Chicago starting location. According to Table 17-1, Kathy can fly to New York for an insurance cost of $2. Table 17-3 shows that the least-expensive route from New York will cost an additional $16, for a total of $18. If she flies from Chicago to Washington, D.C., for $3, she will continue to either London or Paris for an additional $17, making the total cost through Washington, D.C., equal to $20. Flying from Chicago to Atlanta costs $3; from Atlanta, the least-cost route to New Delhi is through Rome, for an additional $13—or a total trip cost of $16. To summarize:

Chicago ⟶ New York ⟶ London ⟶ Cairo ⟶ New Delhi $18
Chicago ⟶ Washington ⟶ London ⟶ Cairo ⟶ New Delhi $20
Chicago ⟶ Washington ⟶ Paris ⟶ Cairo ⟶ New Delhi $20
Chicago ⟶ Atlanta ⟶ Rome ⟶ Cairo ⟶ New Delhi $16

Table 17-3 LEAST EXPENSIVE ROUTES IN STAGE 2

From	Best Route	Total Insurance Cost
New York	London→Cairo→New Delhi	$16
Washington	Paris→Cairo→New Delhi	$17
	London→Cairo→New Delhi	$17
Atlanta	Rome→Cairo→New Delhi	$13

Thus, the optimal route for Kathy is to fly from Chicago to New Delhi via Atlanta, Rome, and Cairo, for an insurance cost of $16. If her assumptions about insurance rates and safety hold true, this will also be the safest route.

What we did in this example is typical of the dynamic programming approach to model building; by separating the decision into sequential stages, we were actually able to reverse the decision flow. We started at the final decision in the sequence and worked back to the beginning. This process will be an inherent part of all the models we will build in this chapter.

17-4 DYNAMIC PROGRAMMING FOR RESOURCE ALLOCATION

Industrial engineers at ElectroSignal Manufacturing have spent the past year training five special three-person quality control teams. These teams will work with employees in the company's manufacturing plants to set up effective quality control procedures. After concentrating on a specific operation in the manufacturing process for 3 months, the team should have developed the appropriate procedures and will be able to move on to the next operation. Sam Bates, the vice-president of manufacturing, must determine how to allocate these five teams for their first assignments.

Although ElectroSignal has eleven manufacturing plants, Sam has decided to start with the four plants that have the poorest quality records. Using information supplied by a consultant, Sam developed the values in Table 17-4, showing the reductions in end-item defects associated with assigning the five teams to the four target plants. (It's possible that all five teams could be assigned to the same plant.)

Sam has been pushing this approach to improve ElectroSignal's quality but has met with resistance from some other executives. Therefore, he is interested in showing the greatest possible improvement after the first set of assignments. He needs to decide how many teams to assign to each of the four target plants to maximize the total reduction in end-item defects. This decision situation can be modeled as a dynamic programming problem.

FORMULATING THE PROBLEM

Initially, we must somehow identify the parts of this decision problem that correlate to the characteristics shared by all dynamic programming models. Since this problem has no readily identified time sequence, the sequential nature of the decision is not as

Table 17-4 REDUCTION IN END-ITEM DEFECTS

Number of Teams Assigned	Plant			
	A	B	C	D
0	0	0	0	0
1	5	3	6	4
2	7.5	5	9	8
3	9	8	10	12
4	10.5	12	11	14
5	12	15	12	16

Note: The values in columns A–D represent tens of thousands of defective items per quarter.

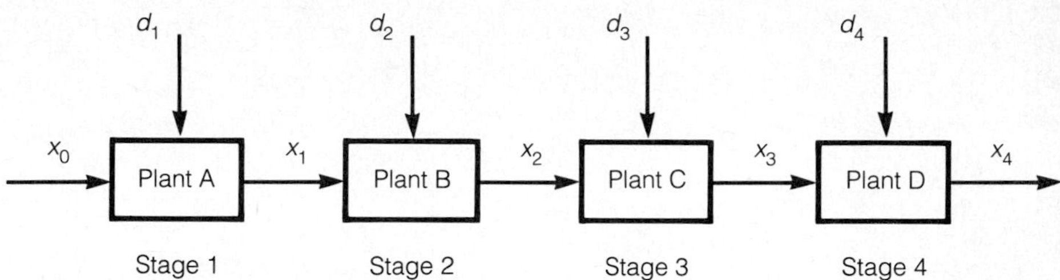

Figure 17-2
Stages in team assignment problem

obvious as that in the routing example. And as we shall see, this makes the problem harder to formulate. Also, in this example we will introduce some of the notation commonly used in dynamic programming models.

Our first step is to identify the *stages* of the problem. Even though the allocation of teams will actually occur at the same time, the decision of how many teams to send to a particular plant is related to the decision of how many teams to send to each of the other plants. Therefore, we can consider the four plants to be the stages of the problem. The fact that the stages in a dynamic programming problem need not be time-oriented greatly expands the applicability of the dynamic programming technique.

Next, we must identify the *state variables* of the problem, the factors that change as we move from one stage to the next. Determining the state variables requires careful consideration; in this problem, they are the factors that change as we move from one plant to another. Because Sam's decision is how to allocate teams to all four plants, the state variables will be the number of teams still available to be assigned at each stage. We can now diagram the problem as shown in Figure 17-2. We also introduce the following notation to be used in solving the problem:

d_i = decisions associated with stage i

x_i = state variables associated with stage i

f_i = value of the decision criteria at stage i

SOLUTION PROCEDURE

Even though this allocation problem has no real time sequence, we can still subdivide it into smaller problems by establishing an order to the plants (stages). We label the plants A, B, C, and D (Figure 17-2) and let plant A be the starting point in the defined sequence. Then, using the *recursion relationship* approach, we will begin the analysis at the end (plant D) and move back to the front (plant A).

First we assume that we are at plant D (stage 4) in the decision sequence. At this point, depending on what we will have decided to do at the other three plants, there may be any number from zero to five teams still available to be assigned. Since all available teams entering this stage *must* be assigned, Sam can use the defect-reduction values for plant D developed earlier (Table 17-4) to construct Table 17-5 for stage 4.

In Table 17-5, we are using the notation introduced above. The x_4 column represents the state variables associated with plant D. Any number of teams, from zero to five, may still be available at stage 4 of the problem. Since Sam wants to assign all teams, any team available at stage 4 will be assigned to plant D. Thus, the x_4* column shows the number of teams assigned to plant D under each possible value for x_4. The $f(x_4)$ column shows the value of the decision criterion (defect reductions) for each state variable.

Using the recursion relationship to move to plant C, we can determine the defect-reduction values shown in Table 17-6. The method used to determine the values in this

Table 17-5 ASSIGNMENT OF TEAMS AT STAGE 4

Teams Available x_4	Defect Reduction $f(x_4)$	Teams Assigned x_4^*
0	0	0
1	4	1
2	8	2
3	12	3
4	14	4
5	16	5

Table 17-6 ASSIGNMENT OF TEAMS AT STAGE 3

Teams Available	Teams Assigned to Plant C						Optimal Assignment to Plant C
x_3	0	1	2	3	4	5	x_3^*
0	0						—
1	4	(6)					1
2	8	(10)	9				1
3	12	(14)	13	10			1
4	14	(18)	17	14	11		1
5	16	20	(21)	18	15	12	2

Note: Circles indicate maximum defect reductions for all numbers of teams (0 to 5) available for assignment to plants C and D.

table requires some explanation. For example, suppose Sam enters the plant C decision point (stage 3) with two teams available for assignment. He now has these options:

1. Assign both teams to plant C, leaving none remaining to be assigned to plant D.
2. Assign one team to plant C and one to plant D.
3. Assign no teams to plant C and both to plant D.

Using the defect-reduction values for these options from Table 17-4, we can fill in the appropriate row values in Table 17-6. Again assume that two teams are available when plant C is entered. Table 17-4 indicates that if both teams are assigned to plant C, a reduction of 9 will occur. Thus, we place the value 9 in the "$x_3 = 2$" row under the "teams assigned = 2" column. However, we might assign one team to plant C and the other team to plant D, when it is reached. In that case, the one team at plant C will achieve a defect reduction of 6 (see Table 17-4) and the one team at plant D will achieve a defect reduction of 4, for a total of 10 units of defect reduction. This is shown in the "$x_3 = 2$" row and "teams assigned = 1" column of Table 17-6.

Finally, if we don't assign any teams to plant C, zero reduction will occur at that plant; but the two teams will be assigned to plant D, for a defect reduction of 8 units (see Table 17-4). This value is shown in the "$x_3 = 2$" row and "teams assigned = 0" column in Table 17-6. Thus, if two teams are available when plant C is entered, the largest defect reduction (10 units) occurs by assigning one team to plant C and then one team to plant D. Table 17-6 shows the optimal assignments in the x_3* column.

We use the same logic to consider the possibilities of having all the other numbers of teams from zero to five available to assign to plants C and D. In Table 17-6, the circled values are the maximum defect reductions for all options at this stage of the problem. Therefore, no matter how many teams are available entering this stage, Table 17-6 provides the best allocation decision for plants C and D.

We now move back to plant B and follow the same procedure as for plant C. In stage 2, the available teams can be assigned to plant B, plant C, or plant D. The number of teams to be assigned to plant B will depend on the total defect reductions possible at plants C and D, which we have just determined in Table 17-6. The results of the stage 2 analyses are shown in Table 17-7.

To see how to find the values for Table 17-7, let's assume that three teams are available at this stage. If Sam assigns all three teams to plant B, then no teams are available for either plant C or plant D and the total reduction for plants B, C, and D will be 8, as we can see from Table 17-4. The applicable values in Table 17-4 are as follows: 8 (for three teams assigned to plant B), 0 (for no teams assigned to plant C, and 0 (for no teams assigned to plant D); the sum is $8 + 0 + 0 = 8$. From Table 17-6, we see that with zero teams available at plant C, there will be no defect reduction for that plant or plant D.

If two of the three available teams are assigned to plant B, the defect reduction will be 5, as shown in Table 17-4, *plus* the optimal 6 from Table 17-6, which is the reduction that will occur when the remaining one team is assigned to plant C. This plan results in a total defect reduction of $5 + 6 = 11$ units. This value is shown in Table 17-7 in the "teams available = 3" row and "teams assigned = 2" column. By completing Table 17-7 for all possibilities of available teams and assignments to plant B, we have determined the optimal assignment policy for plant B, no matter how many teams are available entering this stage of the decision.

The final step is to move back to plant A. The number of teams assigned to plant A should depend on the relative defect reduction that can be made at this plant *and* the optimal assignment policy for the following three plants. Since this is the first plant, all five teams are available. Thus, we can construct Table 17-8 to show the total reduction in defects for each assignment strategy at plant A.

To demonstrate how the values in this table are computed, we start by assigning zero teams to plant A; this means that no reduction will occur at plant A and all five

Table 17-7 ASSIGNMENT OF TEAMS AT STAGE 2

Teams Available	Teams Assigned to Plant B						Optimal Assignment to Plant B
x_2	0	1	2	3	4	5	x_2^*
0	0						0
1	(6)	3					0
2	(10)	9	5				0
3	(14)	13	11	8			0
4	(18)	17	15	14	12		0
5	(21)	(21)	19	18	18	15	0 or 1

Table 17-8 ASSIGNMENT OF TEAMS AT STAGE 1

Teams Available	Teams Assigned to Plant A						Optimal Assignment to Plant A
x_1	0	1	2	3	4	5	x_1^*
5	21	23	21.5	19	16.5	12	1

teams will be available at plant B. Now we look at Table 17-7 to find the maximum possible defect reduction when five teams are available for assignment to plants B, C, and D. Table 17-7 shows that the optimal reduction will occur by assigning either zero or one team to plant B. The total defect reduction for that plant and all subsequent plants will be 21. This value appears in the "teams assigned = 0" column in Table 17-8.

Next, if we decide to allocate one team to plant A, the defect reduction at that plant will be 5, as shown in Table 17-4. This would leave four teams available for plants B through D. We see from Table 17-7 that the best decision when four teams are available is to assign no teams to plant B. The total defect reduction from this strategy will be 18, which is more than the reduction for any other option.

Table 17-6 shows that the optimal reduction for plant C when four teams are available is 18, which results from assigning one team to this plant. The remaining three teams will be assigned to plant D. Overall, the total defect reduction when one team is assigned to plant A is $5 + 18 = 23$ (given in Table 17-8 in the assignment = 1 column).

We repeat this process to assign the remaining two through five teams, with the results as shown in Table 17-8. Thus, the optimal assignment policy is as follows: one team to plant A, zero teams to plant B, one team to plant C, and the final three teams to plant D. Table 17-8 indicates that this assignment strategy will result in a total four-plant defect reduction of 23 (230,000) units.

The preceding example is a common type of dynamic programming problem referred to as *distribution of effort.* It is characterized by having a single resource (quality control teams) to be allocated among a number of demands (plants) in the most effective manner (here, measured by the total reduction in defective parts). When formulated as a dynamic programming problem, the individual demands always correspond to the stages of the problem. The decision required at each stage is how much of the resource to allocate to the demand at that stage, and the state variable is the amount of the resource available (initial allocation minus the amount assigned at all previous stages) at each stage of the problem.

17-5 DYNAMIC PROGRAMMING UNDER UNCERTAINTY

The previous dynamic programming examples have assumed that all factors were known with certainty. That is, once Kathy Beach decided to fly from Rome to Cairo, we assumed that she knew how much the flight insurance would cost for each leg of the trip. In that example, the certainty assumption may be fairly reasonable.

However, in the team assignment example, we assumed that the defect reduction for each combination of teams and plants was known. If Sam Bates decided to commit two quality control teams to plant C, we assumed he knew exactly how many defects would be reduced. As you might guess, this level of certainty in quality control work is not possible. There is an element of uncertainty in these defect-reduction data which should be incorporated in the decision about the team assignments. This type of uncertainty can be built into the dynamic programming model, but the formulation is somewhat complicated, as the following example will demonstrate.

The Hunter Racing Team is preparing cars for the upcoming Indianapolis 500. The Hunter team feels they have an excellent chance of winning this year's race, especially since they have developed a special modification for the standard Indy-car racing engine. Understandably, this modification is expensive and time-consuming, involving a special setup and production run in the engine shop. Setting up to produce and then test the modified engines has a fixed cost of $200,000. After the setup costs, considering the time and materials necessary, each modified engine costs $150,000, and even then the engine may not perform properly. In any given production run, any number of engines can be built.

The only way to find out how an engine will perform under racing conditions is to install it in one of the team's race cars and make a series of runs on the test track. This special modification goes beyond the current state of the art in engine technology, and test results indicate that each engine produced has only a 40% chance of operating as expected when installed in a race car. Thus, there is a 60% chance that an engine will not make the grade.

The Hunter team needs two good engines for the qualifying time trials, which start two weeks before the actual race. If the team doesn't have two good engines by that time, the decision will be not to compete and the preparation costs will be lost. The estimated cost of not racing—including lost sponsorships, prize money, and endorsements—is set at $3 million.

Between now and the time when qualifying starts, the team has time to make three engine production and test runs. Rick Hunter, the team's crew chief, is responsible for determining how many engines to build during each production run. Now he needs to establish a schedule that will minimize total expected costs.

FORMULATING THE PROBLEM

The first step is to relate the parts of this decision problem to the characteristics common to all dynamic programming models. Since this problem has a readily identified time sequence, its stages are easy to define; but it is complicated by the fact that the outcome at each stage is uncertain. That is, if Rick decides to produce three engines, then he may find that zero, one, two, or all three are good; but he won't know how many are actually acceptable until after all three are produced and tested.

The first step is to identify the stages of the problem. Because of their obvious time sequence, the three possible production runs form the three stages. The decision at each stage is how many engines to produce. (Remember, more than one engine can be made in any production run.)

Next, we establish the state variables, the factors that change as we move from one stage of the problem to the next; in this case, they are the number of good engines still needed at each stage. And the recursion relationship linking the decisions made in the problem is the cost associated with each decision.

SOLUTION PROCEDURE

As always, the solution procedure starts with the final stage of the problem and works back to the first stage. Thus, we begin by examining the options at the third production run (stage 3). If by this point two good engines have already been produced and tested, the best decision is not to produce the third engine. The cost for this stage will be zero. But this situation will exist only if the production runs in the first two stages yielded two good engines.

However, if at stage 3 only one or no good engines are available, then additional engines are needed. The decision at this stage will be how many new engines to produce. The cost of producing each possible number of engines (n_i) has the following components:

$$\text{Cost} = \text{fixed setup cost} + \text{cost of producing } n_i \text{ engines} + \text{cost of not racing}$$

Since the number of good engines in any production run is uncertain, the costs at any stage are probabilistic. To deal with this uncertainty, we will work with expected costs. If:

$$x_i = \text{value of the state variable (engines needed)}$$
$$c_i = \text{cost of a particular } x_i$$
$$P(x_i) = \text{probability that } x_i \text{ will occur}$$

Then

$$\text{Expected cost} = \Sigma P(x_i)c_i \tag{17-1}$$

Working with uncertainty, and therefore probabilities, makes the recursion relationship more complex than in the two problems we solved previously. Let's assume that Rick is at stage 3 and knows that he already has one good engine. Since he still needs one more good engine, he needs to know how many more engines to produce. If he decides to produce only one engine, the expected total cost is:

$$E(\text{total cost}) = [\$200{,}000 \text{ (setup)}] + [1 \times \$150{,}000 \text{ (production)}] + [\$3{,}000{,}000 \times P(0 \text{ good engines, given 1 produced})]$$

$$E(\text{total cost}) = \$200{,}000 + \$150{,}000 + (\$3{,}000{,}000 \times .60) = \$2{,}150{,}000$$

The $3,000,000 cost of not racing will be incurred if the team does not have two good engines by qualifying time. In this case, one engine is still needed. If only one engine is built at stage 3, there is a 60% chance that it will fail (as determined earlier). Therefore, we multiply the $3,000,000 cost times the .60 probability to get the expected cost of not racing. This expected cost is added to the fixed and variable costs of the production run to get the expected total cost for this stage.

Another option, if one engine is needed at stage 3, is to produce two engines. For that decision, the expected total cost is:

$$E(\text{total cost}) = [\$200{,}000 \text{ (setup)}] + [2 \times \$150{,}000 \text{ (production)}] + [\$3{,}000{,}000 \times P(0 \text{ good engines, given 2 are produced})]$$

We continue to assume a 60% chance that any given engine will be defective, regardless of the number produced in a single production run. So the probability of getting zero good and two defective engines if two engines are produced is:

$$P(2 \text{ defective}) = .60 \times .60 = .36$$

Thus:

$$E(\text{total cost}) = \$200{,}000 + \$300{,}000 + (\$3{,}000{,}000 \times .36) = \$1{,}580{,}000$$

Table 17-9 shows the expected total costs for zero, one, or two engines needed and production levels of zero to nine engines. The value 1.58 ($1,580,000) appears at the intersection of "engine needed = 1" row and the "number to produce = 2" column. To make sure you understand how the values in this table are determined, consider the option in which one engine is needed and the production decision is for six engines. The expected total cost from this point on is:

$$E(\text{total cost}) = [\$200{,}000 \text{ (setup)}] + [6 \times \$150{,}000 \text{ (production)}] + [\$3{,}000{,}000 \times P(0 \text{ good engines, given 6 are produced})]$$

Table 17-9 EXPECTED COSTS AT LAST PRODUCTION RUN (in $ millions)

Engines Needed	Number of Engines to Produce (n_1) 0	1	2	3	4	5	6	7	8	9
0	0									
1	3.000	2.150	1.580	1.298	1.189	1.183	1.240	1.334	1.450	1.580
2	3.000	3.000	3.020	2.594	2.226	1.961	1.800	1.726	1.719	1.769

Minimum cost per number produced:
If 0 engines needed, produce 0: expected cost = $0
If 1 engine needed, produce 5: expected cost = $1,183,000
If 2 engines needed, produce 8: expected cost = $1,719,000

The probability that all six engines will fail is:

$$P(0 \text{ good}) = .60 \times .60 \times .60 \times .60 \times .60 \times .60$$
$$= .60^6 = .046656$$

Then:

$$E(\text{total cost}) = \$200{,}000 + \$900{,}000 + (\$3{,}000{,}000 \times .046656)$$
$$= \$1{,}239{,}968$$

This figure is rounded up and corresponds to the 1.240 value at the intersection of the "engines needed = 1" row and the "number to produce = 6" column (Table 17-9).

Now let's consider one final example, in which two engines are still needed at stage 3. If the decision is to produce four engines, the expected total cost is:

$$E(\text{total cost}) = [\$200{,}000 \text{ (setup)}] + [4 \times \$150{,}000 \text{ (production)}]$$
$$+ [\$3{,}000{,}000 \times P(0 \text{ good engines, given 4 are produced})]$$
$$+ [\$3{,}000{,}000 \times P(1 \text{ good engine, given 4 are produced})]$$

Note that in this case if two engines are needed, the team can end up not racing if none of those produced at stage 3 are good *or* if only one engine in the production run is good. Thus, we need to find the probabilities for each event and multiply the sum of these probabilities by the $3,000,000 cost of not racing. A direct means for determining these probabilities is to use the binomial formula, as follows:

$$P(x) = \frac{n!}{x!(n-x)!} p^x q^{n-x} \tag{17-2}$$

where:

x = number of outcomes of interest

n = sample size

p = probability of a success

$q = 1 - p$

Therefore, if we want to know the chance of getting no good engines (four defectives) in a production run of $n = 4$, we use equation 17-2, as follows:

$$P(4) = \frac{4!}{4!\,0!}(.6^4)(.4^0)$$
$$= (1)(.6^4) = .1296$$

Next, we find the probability that three of the four engines will be defective:

$$P(3) = \frac{4!}{3!\ 1!}(.6^3)(.4^1)$$
$$= (4)\ (.6^3)\ (.4^1) = .3456$$

We computed these binomial probabilities using equation 17-2, but we could have found the same values in the binomial distribution table, Appendix A, by going to the section for $n = 4$ and finding the column headed $p = .40$. We then locate the rows for $x_1 = 0$ and $x_1 = 1$ to find the probabilities of zero good and one good engine. Then we add these probabilities: $.1296 + .3456 = .4752$.

We are now ready to finish our calculation for the expected total cost:

$$E(\text{total cost}) = \$200{,}000 + (4 \times \$150{,}000) + (\$3{,}000{,}000 \times .4752)$$
$$= \$2{,}225{,}600$$

Rounded up to $2,226,000, this corresponds to the 2.226 value where the engines needed = 2 row and the production = 4 column intersect in Table 17-9.

From Table 17-9, we can also determine the optimal production strategy for stage 3 for either zero, one, or two engines needed. If the Hunter Racing Team enters stage 3 needing no additional engines, none will be built and the cost of this decision is $0. If one additional engine is needed, the minimum-expected-cost decision is to make five engines, for $1,183,000. If two engines are still needed at stage 3, eight should be built, for a minimum expected cost of $1,719,000.

Now we are ready to step back to stage 2 and go through the same type of calculations for this stage. Depending on what happened at stage 1, the team may need zero, one, or two good engines at stage 2. Now the recursion relationship becomes more complicated. If no engines are needed, none will be built and the cost is $0. If one good engine is needed, the number to be produced will be based on minimum expected cost. As at stage 3, the cost relationship will be:

$$\text{Cost} = \text{fixed setup cost} + \text{cost of producing } n_i \text{ engines} + \text{cost of not racing}$$

Note that now the cost of not racing will not be $3,000,000, as in stage 3, but $1,183,000 (from Table 17-9), which is the expected cost of the best production decision at stage 3 if one engine is needed in the third stage. (We use the "engines needed = 1" row to get the cost of not racing because we are assuming that at stage 2 we already have one good engine. Thus, the only way that the team won't be prepared for qualifying is if no good engines are produced at stage 2 and one good engine is still needed at stage 3.) The total-cost function for stage 2 is then:

$$E(\text{total cost}) = [\$200{,}000 \text{ (setup)}] + [n_i \times \$150{,}000 \text{ (production)}]$$
$$+ [\$1{,}183{,}000 \times p(0 \text{ good engines, given } n_i \text{ produced})]$$

To see how the expected costs are determined, let's assume one good engine is needed, and Rick decides to produce four engines at stage 2. We first need to compute the probability of no good engines (or four defectives) in a production run of $n = 4$. As before, this is:

$$P(4) = .6^4 = .1296$$

Then the expected total cost is:

$$E(\text{total cost}) = \$200{,}000 + (4 \times \$150{,}000) + (\$1{,}183{,}000 \times .1296)$$
$$= \$953{,}000$$

Table 17-10 COSTS EXPECTED AT SECOND PRODUCTION RUN (in $ millions)

Engines Needed	Number of Engines to Produce (n_i) 0	1	2	3	4	5	6
0	0						
1	1.183	1.060	0.926	0.906	0.953	1.042	1.155
2	1.719	1.855	1.687	1.532	1.432	1.390	1.401

Minimum cost per number produced:
If 0 engines needed, produce 0: expected cost = $0
If 1 engine needed, produce 3: expected cost = $906,000
If 2 engines needed, produce 5: expected cost = $1,390,000

By performing similar calculations, we can find the costs in the engine needed = 1 row of Table 17-10. (Recall that if only one engine is needed at stage 2 [because one is already on hand], two engines cannot be needed at stage 3.)

The cost calculations in the engines needed = 2 row of Table 17-10 are slightly more complex than before, since now potentially one or two good engines could still be needed at stage 3. If one engine is needed at stage 3, the appropriate carry-on cost (the cost of not racing) is $1,183,000. If two engines are needed, the appropriate cost is $1,769,000. Thus the total-cost function for this row is:

$$\begin{aligned} E(\text{total cost}) = {} & [\$200{,}000 \text{ (setup)}] + [n_i \times \$150{,}000 \text{ (production)}] \\ & + [\$1{,}183{,}000 \times p(1 \text{ good engine, given } n_i \text{ produced})] \\ & + [\$1{,}719{,}000 \times p(0 \text{ good engines, given } n_i \text{ produced})] \end{aligned}$$

For example, assume Rick Hunter decides to produce four engines at stage 2 and two are still needed. Using the binomial distribution table for $n = 4$ (Appendix A), we get:

$$\begin{aligned} E(\text{total cost}) &= \$200{,}000 + (4 \times \$150{,}000) + (\$1{,}183{,}000 \times .3456) \\ &\quad + (\$1{,}719{,}000 \times .1296) \\ &= \$1{,}432{,}000 \text{ (or 1.432 in Table 17-10)} \end{aligned}$$

We use the same procedure to calculate the other production possibilities. Table 17-10 shows that if two engines are needed at stage 2, the minimum-expected-cost decision is to produce five engines (1.390 = $1,390,000). Likewise, if at stage 2 the team still needs one engine, the minimum-expected-cost decision is to produce three engines (.906 = $906,000).

We are now ready to move to stage 1. At this point we know we need two good engines. The appropriate expected-total-cost function at stage 1 is:

$$\begin{aligned} E(\text{total cost}) = {} & [\$200{,}000 \text{ (setup)}] + [n_i \times \$150{,}000 \text{ (production)}] \\ & + [\$906{,}000 \times p(1 \text{ good engine, given } n_i \text{ produced})] \\ & + [\$1{,}390{,}000 \times p(0 \text{ good engines, given } n_i \text{ produced})] \end{aligned}$$

We use this function to determine the expected costs shown in Table 17-11. We can see from the table that the best decision at stage 1 is to have a production run of four or five engines, for an expected cost of $1,293,000.

Now, through the use of this dynamic programming model, Rick Hunter can

Table 17-11 COSTS AT FIRST PRODUCTION RUN (in $ millions)

Engines Needed	Number of Engines to Produce (n_i) 0	1	2	3	4	5	6
2	1.390	1.546	1.435	1.342	1.293	1.293	1.334

Minimum cost decision: Produce 4 or 5 engines at an expected cost = $1,293,000.

establish an engine production plan that minimizes the expected total costs:

Stage 1:	Produce 4 or 5 engines	Expected cost = $1,293,000
Stage 2:	0 engines needed ⟶ produce 0	
	1 engine needed ⟶ produce 3	$906,000
	2 engines needed ⟶ produce 5	$1,390,000
Stage 3:	0 engines needed ⟶ produce 0	
	1 engine needed ⟶ produce 5	$1,183,000
	2 engines needed ⟶ produce 8	$1,719,000

Note that in stage 1 the expected cost of this decision plan is $1,293,000. However, the expected costs at subsequent stages depend on the production results from the previous stage(s). That is why if two engines are still needed at stage 3, the best decision (to produce eight more engines) has an *expected* total cost of $1,719,000. But if five engines were produced in stage 1 and five in stage 2, the *actual* cost for production prior to stage 3 would be:

$$\text{Actual cost} = (2 \times \$200{,}000) + (5 \times \$150{,}000) + (5 \times \$150{,}000)$$
$$= \$1{,}900{,}000$$

The Hunter Racing Team example illustrates that incorporating uncertainty into a dynamic programming model greatly increases the formulation and computational difficulties. However, adding the probabilistic element enhances the usefulness of this decision-making technique.

17-6 A COMPARISON OF DYNAMIC AND LINEAR PROGRAMMING

The three examples presented so far in the chapter demonstrate both the strengths and weaknesses of dynamic programming. First, the technique is specifically designed to operate as a sequential decision-making procedure, which more accurately reflects the way in which managers usually make decisions. In this respect, it has an advantage over techniques such as linear programming which require the entire situation to be specified before the model can be used and also require that the decision situation be static.

Dynamic programming allows "mistakes" to be made in the first stages of the decision process. That is, if the decision made at the first stage does not produce the desired outcome, the decision strategy at subsequent stages is flexible enough to provide an optimal solution from that point forward. For example, in the Hunter Racing Team example, regardless of what happens in the first production run, an optimal strategy for the second production run exists. This is a considerable improvement over linear programming, which would require the entire production schedule to be set at one time. Then, as new information about production success was learned, the linear programming model would have to be respecified and rerun.

While dynamic programming attempts to maximize or minimize an objective function—and in that respect it is similar to linear programming—the form of the objective function can be more flexible than with linear programming. In the Hunter example we showed how uncertainty could be included in the dynamic programming process; but an equivalent extension of linear programming would require a much more complicated procedure.

While it may not be apparent from the examples in this chapter, dynamic programming offers a substantial reduction in computational effort over exhaustive enumeration of all alternatives. For instance, a realistic problem with 10 stages, 10 states, and 10 possible decisions at each stage could require 10^{10} calculations to list all the possible alternatives! But a dynamic programming formulation would require only 10 calculations at each state for each stage, or 10^3 calculations—an amazing difference.

Although dynamic programming offers some specific advantages over linear programming, its implementation is more difficult. For instance, identifying the sequential nature of the decision-making process often depends on the intuitive insight of the decision maker and his or her experience with building dynamic programming models. Since the sequential nature of the decision-making process often does not depend on time, it may not be properly recognized by a decision maker. The widely divergent situations to which dynamic programming models can be applied means that the technique is usually learned by studying and working through examples rather than learning a structured format, as in linear programming. Also, for many people, the structured format of linear programming models is easier to apply to a variety of decision-making situations than is the changing recursion relationship of a dynamic programming model.

The economic interpretations associated with linear programming models, such as the economic values associated with shadow prices and marginal rates of substitution, do not have corollary values in dynamic programming models. Thus, one of the main strengths of linear programming is absent from dynamic programming models. Likewise, the ease with which sensitivity analysis is performed in linear programming is not duplicated in dynamic programming models.

Finally, because of the structured format, linear programming models are fairly easy to program and a wide variety of linear programming software is available at relatively low cost. For example, MASTER, the software package which accompanies this text, has a linear programming module, and other software packages contain similar programs. Also, some relatively inexpensive commercial packages are capable of solving large, complex linear programming problems very quickly. However, very little software exists for the more loosely structured dynamic programming models. And the software that does exist consists mainly of special-purpose programs and is not adaptable to a wide range of applications. This lack of computer software has greatly hindered the use of dynamic programming as a management science technique.

17-7 SUMMARY AND CONCLUSIONS

Dynamic programming is a powerful technique for making a sequence of interrelated decisions. As such, it effectively describes the process associated with many managerial decision-making situations. The procedure is forgiving in that it accepts the conditions of the current situation and allows the decision maker to determine the correct decision sequence from that point on. Changes in the problem's conditions can be incorporated easily into the procedure without adjusting all parts of the model, thus allowing a smaller computational effort than some alternative models.

Dynamic programming probably has not lived up to the potential seen for it when the technique was developed in the 1950s. Progress has been made incrementally as problems have been solved and the solution procedure reported in the literature. Also, other management science techniques have been developed to address some of the same types of time-sequenced decisions as dynamic programming. For instance, the decision-tree analysis introduced in Chapter 13 can be used in place of dynamic programming in some situations. And these other techniques are often easier to understand and use. Even so, dynamic programming is an important concept for students of decision-making models to understand, since it provides a means for correctly identifying the sequential nature of many decision situations.

Dynamic programming models can incorporate uncertainty into the decision process through the use of probability distributions. This feature allows the decision maker to establish as his or her objective the maximization (or minimization) of an expected value. Chance-constrained programming, a linear programming technique, also deals with uncertainty in decision making, but its complexity puts it beyond the scope of this text.

Solved Problem

PROBLEM

Allen and Medlin is a rapidly growing accounting firm serving primarily the California and Arizona markets. Most of its clients fall into one of four industrial categories: aerospace, medical electronics, computer hardware, and computer software. The firm has an extensive training program that familiarizes newly hired accountants with the four types of clients, using videotapes and workbooks, and then provides more specialized training through projects in the industry areas where individual accountants will work. The various training sessions, and the estimated time to complete each one, are listed in Table 17-12.

Because of the content of the training sessions, there are some restrictions on the order in which they must be completed. For instance, session A2 can be followed by B1 or B3 but not by B2 or B4. The possible relationships among the training sessions are listed in Table 17-13.

Table 17-12 TRAINING-SESSION COMPLETION TIMES (in weeks)

Aerospace		Medical Electronics		Computer Hardware		Computer Software	
Session	Weeks	Session	Weeks	Session	Weeks	Session	Weeks
A1	10	B1	9	C1	10	D1	11
A2	8	B2	5	C2	7	D2	6
A3	18	B3	6	C3	12	D3	5
—	—	B4	4	—	—	D4	14

Table 17-13 RELATIONSHIPS OF TRAINING SESSIONS

Session	Can Be Followed By:
A1	B1, B2, B3
A2	B1, B3
A3	B2, B4
B1	C1, C2
B2	C1, C2
B3	C1, C3
B4	C2, C3
C1	D2, D3
C2	D1, D4
C3	D2, D3
D1	Finish
D2	Finish
D3	Finish
D4	Finish

Traditionally, the newly hired accountants have first been distributed equally among the three initial aerospace training sessions and then randomly assigned to later sessions on the other topics. Sarah Medlin, a partner in the firm, is considering how to better schedule this training. Specifically, she needs to answer two questions:

a. What is the minimum time schedule to follow once an accountant has finished the aerospace modules?

b. How much difference does the initial session assignment make in total training time?

Solution **a.** The most important step in developing a dynamic programming model is to identify the sequential nature of the problem. This problem has some characteristics similar to those of the routing example in section 17-3 and the assignment example in section 17-4. Often, drawing a diagram is helpful, as we have done for this problem (Figure 17-3). You should recognize that this figure looks like the one for Kathy Beach's flight-routing problem (Figure 17-1). We will solve this problem in a similar manner, starting at stage 4 and moving to stage 1.

1. A trainee at stage 4 has no option but to complete either session D1, D2, D3, or D4.
2. A trainee at stage 3 should be assigned to the allowable session in stage 4 that can be completed in the shortest possible time. Therefore:

   If at C1, assign to D3 Training time: 5 weeks
   If at C2, assign to D1 Training time: 11 weeks
   If at C3, assign to D3 Training time: 5 weeks

3. Moving to stage 2, we now need to consider both stage 3 and its follow-on assignments. Therefore:

   If at B1, assign to C1 Time to finish: 15 weeks
   If at B2, assign to C1 Time to finish: 15 weeks
   If at B3, assign to C1 Time to finish: 15 weeks
   If at B4, assign to C3 Time to finish: 17 weeks

Figure 17-3
Possible sequences of training sessions

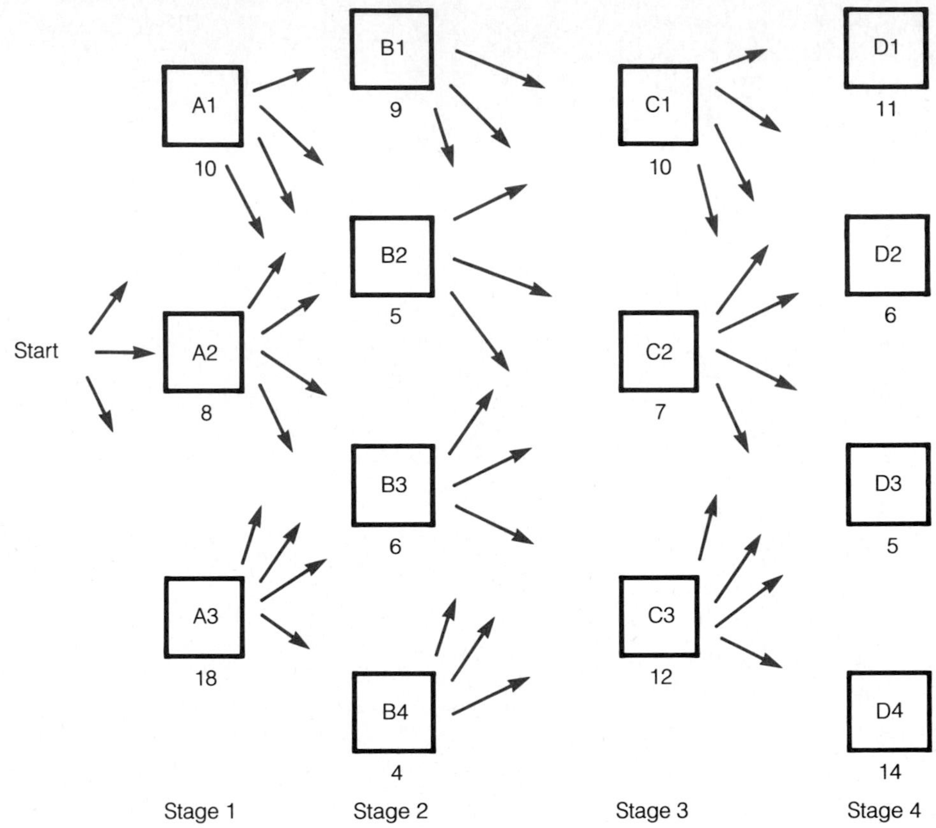

Numbers are training-session completion times, in weeks.

4. Moving to stage 1, and considering the optimal routes from stage 2, Sarah can determine the minimum-time assignment sequences. Her reasoning is that a trainee at A1 can proceed to B1, B2, or B3 and should be sent to the session that will lead to the minimum total training time. Since all three assignments will lead to a finish time of 15 weeks, the choice should be based on which one, by itself, can be completed soonest. From Table 17-12, we see that the decision should be:

   If at A1, assign to B2 Time to finish: 20 weeks
   If at A2, assign to B3 Time to finish: 21 weeks
   If at A3, assign to B2 Time to finish: 20 weeks

b. Since the trainees are randomly assigned to one of the three aerospace training sessions, we can simply add these times to the times we found in part **a**.

   If assigned to A1, total training time: $10 + 20 = 30$ weeks
   If assigned to A2, total training time: $8 + 21 = 29$ weeks
   If assigned to A3, total training time: $18 + 20 = 38$ weeks

[*Note:* The solutions to parts **a** and **b** above do not show the detailed computations. You are encouraged to work through the details yourself to be sure that you can reach the solutions given here.]

General Questions and Assignments

1. Discuss in your own terms the *stages* and *state variables* in a dynamic programming model.
2. Dynamic programming is a management science technique which addresses the concept of *suboptimization*. In your own terms, explain this concept. Use an original example.
3. Discuss in your own terms the steps in formulating and solving a dynamic programming model.
4. What are the advantages and disadvantages of dynamic programming compared with linear programming? Discuss.
5. Locate one or more articles about an application (or applications) of dynamic programming. Write a paper describing the application(s). Discuss the results and to what extent they were beneficial. Could linear programming or some other management science technique have been used instead of dynamic programming? Discuss.

Exercises and Application Problems

1. Item 2 in the application problems section at the end of Chapter 11 asked you to solve the following shortest-route problem. (See Chapter 11 for the figure referred to here.)

   Billings Outfitters maintains a series of camps along established trails in the Frank Church Wilderness Area. The outfitters will pack campers and fishing parties into the wilderness area and, for groups staying a week or more, will return every two days with food and supplies. The camping areas are arranged as shown in Figure 11-26. The distances between camps are given in hours on horseback. Determine the shortest distance from Billings' two base camps to each camp area.

   Now solve the problem using dynamic programming and prepare a summary comparing the two solution procedures. As a decision maker, would you prefer one technique over the other for (a) ease of application and (b) insight gained?
2. Item 6 in the application problems section at the end of Chapter 11 asked you to solve the following shortest-route problem. (See Chapter 11 for the figure referred to here.)

   River City recently hired Ned Fiero as its new fire chief. One of the first things Ned noticed was that the fire department does not have planned routes from the fire station to possible fire locations. If a fire truck takes the wrong way to a fire, the delay could be very costly. Ned wants to determine the shortest routes between the station and various parts of the city. To begin, he has diagramed the city as a 12-square grid (Figure 11-30) and estimated the travel times between the squares, or nodes. On Figure 11-30, arrows indicate possible travel directions; if there is no arrow between two nodes, the route cannot be traveled by fire truck. Now Ned needs some help in determining the best route to take to the center of each grid square in the city so that travel time is minimized.

   Now solve this problem using dynamic programming and prepare a summary comparing the two procedures. As a decision maker, would you prefer one technique over the other for (a) ease of application and (b) insight gained?
3. Allied Engineering has decided to hire as many as eight new engineers to handle its backlog of hazardous waste disposal projects. Most of the project contracts have a bonus clause for early completion. The estimated profits for each project associated with allocating the possible new hires to the five most pressing projects are listed below. (Profit values are times \$10,000; the additional salaries are accounted for in profits.)

Project	Number of Engineers Assigned								
	0	1	2	3	4	5	6	7	8
A	23	35	42	49	53	55	56	57	58
B	17	25	30	33	35	36	37	38	38
C	30	36	40	44	48	50	52	54	55
D	12	24	36	40	40	40	40	40	40
E	5	20	30	35	39	43	47	49	50

a. What is the optimal assignment of new engineers to the five projects if eight engineers are hired? What is the total projected increase in profits associated with the allocation?

b. What is the optimal assignment of new engineers to the five projects if only five engineers are hired? What is the total projected increase in profits associated with the allocation?

4. On a whim, Bob James submitted a sealed bid for eight four-wheel-drive pickups to be auctioned off by the U.S. Forest Service. Much to his surprise, his was the high bid and he got the trucks. He wants to keep one for himself and sell the others. He has contacted three used-car dealers and has received bids on various quantities of trucks, from one to all seven. However, all the trucks need some maintenance work, which must be done before the dealers will accept them. Bob's estimates of the total profit from selling none to all seven of the trucks are as follows:

Number Sold	Used-Car Dealer		
	A	B	C
0	0	0	0
1	200	150	180
2	280	250	260
3	350	360	300
4	400	420	320
5	420	450	330
6	430	470	330
7	430	480	330

How many trucks should Bob sell to each car dealer to maximize his expected profit?

5. Refer to problem 4. How would Bob's total profit be affected if he kept two of the seven remaining trucks?

6. A recent hurricane caused extensive damage in many parts of the Southeast. Palmetto Construction Company has offered to donate the services of five work crews to the repair efforts for one week. Five areas in the county have been severely damaged, and the work crews would be able to restore services to the residents of these areas. A county official prepared an estimate of the number (in thousands) of people in each of these five areas who can have their services restored, using varying numbers of construction crews.

Number of Crews	Area				
	A	B	C	D	E
1	20	12	5	17	15
2	32	26	9	22	27
3	38	35	13	25	35
4	40	39	15	25	42
5	40	43	16	27	45

How should the construction crews be assigned to maximize the number of people whose service will be restored?

7. DynaWeights, Inc., manufactures dynamic weighing equipment used by state highway departments to monitor the weights of heavy trucks that may be avoiding official weigh stations. The company has just received a combined order for 28 units from two neighboring states and has committed to the following delivery schedule:

Month	Number
April	4
May	8
June	6
July	10

The units sell for $175,000 each and have a direct manufacturing cost of $75,000. DynaWeights presently has no dynamic weighers on hand and has a policy of maintaining no inventory of this unit. Setting up a production run costs $50,000, and a new setup would be made each month. Because of the plant's other manufacturing requirements, no more than 12 units can be produced in any month. To minimize inventory, DynaWeights requires a 5% per month holding cost for any finished goods kept in inventory. What manufacturing schedule will meet the delivery requirements, ensure that no inventory is on hand at the end of July, and minimize costs?

8. Refer to problem 7. Suppose DynaWeights starts production in April with four units on hand and wants to end July with two units to use for demonstration at a trade show. How would these changes affect the production schedule determined in problem 7?

9. Your company has decided to follow the example of Illinois Tool and has decided to replace its large Ahmdahl computer with a set of personal computers connected through a local area network. Used mainframe computers are sold in an established market on a weekly basis. You are responsible for selling the computer. The only criteria your manager has established are that the sale must be made in the next 4 weeks and that you should receive as high a price as possible.

You have established the following prices and probabilities by finding bid-asked prices for similar computers sold over the past 2 months.

Price	Probability
$1,500,000	.3
1,750,000	.5
2,000,000	.2

You expect these prices and probabilities to apply for the next 4 weeks. Use dynamic programming to formulate the best selling strategy.

10. NASA has 20,000 pounds of payload capacity remaining on an upcoming shuttle flight. Four groups have offered to "rent" this space to support research experiments to be carried out in space. Because of NASA requirements, all the proposed projects are modular, so that an experiment can be expanded just by adding modules. The four experimental projects, the weight of a single module for each experiment, and the revenue NASA will receive is given below.

Type of Experiment	Module Weight	Revenue
Insect reproduction	1000 pounds	$300,000
Light diffusion	2000 pounds	$800,000
Plant germination	3000 pounds	$1,300,000
Crystal growth	4000 pounds	$1,700,000

Use dynamic programming to decide how many modules for each experiment should be chosen to maximize revenues to NASA.

11. The law firm of Bixby and Wong is considering expanding into three possible new market areas and has budgeted a total of $10 million for the expansion effort, which includes setting up offices and advertising their services in the new area. The firm judges the success of any proposed new office by projecting the potential annual billings for the location and comparing them with the actual annual billings generated by its most successful office, in Charleston. Therefore, an office rated at .7 would be expected to generate 70% as much business as the Charleston office. The following table presents the firm's best estimates of the amount of business that could be expected during the first year at each of the three locations (as a percentage of Charleston's billings) for each amount of money that might be spent on the expansion. The maximum investment at any one location is $5 million.

Expansion Money	Ratings of Projected First-Year Billings		
	Location 1	Location 2	Location 3
$0	0	0	0
$1,000,000	.10	.25	.40
$2,000,000	.20	.35	.40
$3,000,000	.25	.45	.50
$4,000,000	.30	.50	.55
$5,000,000	.35	.50	.60
$6,000,000	.40	.50	.60
$7,000,000	.45	.50	.60
$8,000,000	.50	.60	.60
$9,000,000	.55	.70	.60
$10,000,000	.60	.80	.60

How should the expansion money be distributed to maximize the total billing for the first year?

12. Refer to problem 11. Under what conditions (first-year billing ratings) would:
    a. Only one of the three possible locations would be used?
    b. Two of the three possible locations would be used?
    c. All three of the locations would be used?

13. The Gourmet Cheese Company makes a special cheese in limited amounts. Only one production run is made each month. The minimum amount of cheese produced is 1000 pounds, and the maximum is 10,000 pounds, in 1000-pound increments. In some months, none of this cheese is produced. The cheese is aged for a month in a warehouse that has limited, and varying, capacity. If cheese can be supplied from inventory, the production setup charge of $500 can be avoided. Because of changes in milk prices and the inventory-transfer conditions at the warehouse, both production and storage costs vary each month. Below are the projected demands and projected costs for this cheese for the next 3 months.

Month	Demand (pounds)	Costs (per 1000 pounds)		Storage Capacity (1000 pounds)
		Production	Storage	
April	8,000	$55	$25	15
May	8,000	$45	$30	18
June	9,000	$60	$40	14

Any cheese made in one month can be used to satisfy the next month's demand, with storage costs being charged starting in the month of production and thereafter at the beginning of the month. The company is starting with an inventory of 10,000 pounds and wants to have at least 8000 pounds available at the start of July. What is the minimum-cost production schedule to satisfy this demand?

14. The maintenance superintendent for the company in problem 13 wants to shut down production at the plant in June to install new temperature-control equipment.
    a. Can the total 3-month projected demand be met with the present production and storage capacity?
    b. If the answer to part **a** is no, how much capacity must be added during April and May to meet the total projected demand?
    c. If the answer to **a** is yes, how much will the shutdown add to the total cost of production and storage?

Chapter Glossary

Dynamic programming A general problem-solving procedure that can be applied to sequential decision-making situations. It allows a complex, hard-to-solve decision problem to be separated into a series of smaller, easier-to-solve problems.

Recursion relationship A mathematical relationship that links the optimal decision for the last stage of a decision problem to the optimal decisions for the prior stages.

Stages The interrelated subproblems (often based on time) into which a dynamic programming problem is divided.

States The conditions a problem can assume either entering or leaving different stages.

Chapter References

BOOKS

Bellman, R. E. *Dynamic Programming.* Princeton, N.J.: Princeton, 1957.

Bellman, R. E., and S. E. Dreyfus. *Applied Dynamic Programming.* Princeton, N.J.: Princeton, 1962.

Loomba, N. P., and E. Turban. *Applied Programming for Management.* New York: Holt, 1974.

Nemhauser, G. L. *Introduction to Dynamic Programming.* New York: Wiley, 1966.

Wagner, H. M. *Principles of Operations Research.* Englewood Cliffs, N.J.: Prentice-Hall, 1975.

ARTICLES

Elton, E. J., and M. J. Gruber. "Dynamic Programming Applications in Finance." *Journal of Finance,* May 1971.

Lembersky, M. R., and U. H. Chi. "Weyerhaeuser Decision Simulator Improves Timber Profits." *Interfaces,* January–February 1986.

Rosenblatt, M. J. "The Dynamics of Plant Layout." *Management Science,* January 1986.

Terry, L. A. et al. "Coordinating the Energy Generation of the Brazilian National Hydrothermal Electric Generating System." *Interfaces,* January–February 1986.

Waddell, Richard. "A Model for Equipment Replacement Decisions and Policies." *Interfaces,* August 1983.

Mini Cases

CASE 17A
SOLAR POWER, INC. (PART 1)

Elsa Newell, a senior design engineer for Solar Power, Inc., is part of the new design team for a radio telescope that is scheduled to be launched into earth orbit 5 years from now. She is responsible for the design and production of the three servomotors that will allow the telescope to be controlled by signals sent by the research team in Houston. Satellite design always involves trade-offs between weight and reliability considerations; but now, because of recent funding cuts, cost is also an issue. Elsa recently attended a meeting of the design team to discuss initial specifications and requirements. The servomotors will be powered by batteries to be recharged by independent banks of photoelectric cells. Since the batteries are the control-system element most likely to fail, each motor will be connected to a redundant set of two or more batteries. Elsa's initial task is to determine just how many batteries to connect to each servomotor.

The overall consideration in designing the control system is the expected 15-year life of the radio telescope. The design team would like to maximize the probability that none of the servomotors will fail, since correct operation of the telescope requires all three. Using data from past designs, Elsa has developed a table showing the probabilities of failure for each of the three motors related to the number of batteries connected to the motor.

	Probability of Failure		
Number of Batteries	Motor 1	Motor 2	Motor 3
1	.20	.15	.08
2	.14	.11	.06
3	.08	.07	.03
4	.02	.03	.01
5	.01	.01	.01

Each battery weighs 12 pounds, and the initial overall design specifications call for a maximum allowance of 125 pounds for batteries.

Elsa is to report next month on whether the overall reliability goal of 95% for this part of the system can be met while also meeting the weight specifications. If the specifications cannot be met, Elsa is to report how much additional weight will be required.

CASE 17B
SOLAR POWER, INC. (PART 2)

A group of accountants from Hugheson Aerospace, the primary contractor for the radio telescope, attended the second meeting of the design team. They are at the meeting (as accountants often are) to make sure the design team is also aware of the cost restrictions in the contract. In particular, they have developed a set of cost estimates for each component in the telescope system. Their cost estimates for the servomotor system are given below.

Number of Batteries	Estimated Cost of Servomotor System ($ millions)		
	Motor 1	Motor 2	Motor 3
1	30	38	27
2	37	42	33
3	40	44	36
4	41	45	37
5	42	46	38

Although Elsa and the other engineers object to having cost restrictions imposed on such important scientific efforts, they are mindful of congressional hearings on excessive cost overruns by aerospace contractors. For the next meeting, Elsa is asked to answer the following questions:

1. Can the system she proposed (see solution to case 17A) meet a budgeted amount of $350 million for this part of the satellite?
2. What is the minimum cost of a system that will have 95% reliability?
3. What is the reliability of the best system that can be built for the budgeted amount, not considering the weight restriction?

Chapter 18

MARKOV-PROCESS MODELS

Chapter Outline

Why You Need to Know

In the earlier chapters, we introduced complicated but well-structured management science models that generally dealt with situations in which conditions were known with certainty. For example, we assumed that we knew the objective-function coefficients and constraining values in a linear programming model, the ordering and holding costs in an inventory control model, and the activity times in a PERT model. In addition, we generally used these models for single-period decisions; and if, over time, we learned new information that would affect the decision, we would have to reformulate the entire model to change the decision.

For some subjects, such as inventory control, we eventually introduced models that added both uncertainty and multiperiod decisions; but we tried to model the entire decision situation so the best course would be decided at the beginning. Then we demonstrated how dynamic programming can be used to model more complicated situations involving a series of decisions; that is, one decision would lead to a result that would then require a further decision. The models we constructed for such problems had a finite number of decisions. In some situations, however, managers face decisions which are without a well-defined end point. Consider the following examples.

Ann Dante, brand manager for a new dental product, has worked with the company's marketing staff and an outside advertising agency to develop a campaign to introduce the product. She knows that the major competitors in this country will counter with their own advertising blitz. Then, after Ann and her staff see the competitors' response, they will most likely have to revise their initial advertising plan—which will result in a further response from the competition, and on and on.

Jim Potakar, financial officer for Hill Leasing, is considering two primary options for obtaining financing for a major equipment purchase: the long-term debt market or the equity market. Choosing equity financing now will affect the chance to obtain both equity and debt financing in the future, should the company need additional capital. In making his decision, Jim must consider the continual stream of financing that Hill Leasing will need in the future.

Nancy Merrill is considering what proportion of assembly-line equipment to replace at the three Merrill Ball Bearing plants in Georgia. Replacing equipment now means that new technology can be incorporated to update the manufacturing process. To cost-justify the new equipment, the company plans to keep it for at least 10 years. Choosing the lower-cost option of repairing rather than replacing the equipment now means that implementation of new technology will be put on hold. However, new technology will continue to be developed and the equipment can be replaced later, but replacement costs are expected to increase over time.

As you can see, many business decisions are only one part of a series of potential decisions. And in many actual situations, the outcome of a decision may not be known with certainty. If Nancy Merrill decides to repair equipment now, she may not know exactly how much future replacement equipment will cost. Jim Potakar knows that the decision to use equity financing will affect future financing options, but he can't be sure of exactly what the impact will be.

Clearly, managers need a technique for analyzing a decision, under uncertainty, which is part of a stream of future decision. One tool that can help in certain types of situations with those characteristics is the *Markov-process model*.

Chapter Objectives

The purpose of this chapter is to introduce the Markov-process model, a management science technique used to represent multiperiod decision-making situations in which the outcome of a decision may not be known with certainty. Because the development of the theory behind Markov-process models is beyond the scope of this text, we will limit our discussion to the characteristics of the Markov process and to the formulation of a few basic models.

After studying the material in this chapter, you should be able to:

1. Discuss the characteristics of decision-making situations which can be represented as Markov processes.
2. Be familiar with the terminology associated with Markov models.
3. Be able to formulate Markov models for simple multiperiod decision-making situations.

18-1 A BRIEF HISTORY OF MARKOV-PROCESS MODELS

Markov-process models are somewhat different from the models introduced earlier in this text in that they are based on a mathematical technique which was first used in physical science. Andrei Markov, a young Russian mathematician, developed the technique to describe the movement of gas molecules in a closed container. The earliest applications of this procedure, in the 1940s, were in physics, followed by applications in biology and genetics.

In the 1950s, management scientists began to recognize that the technique could be adapted to decision situations which fit the pattern Markov described—now known as a Markov chain or Markov process. The **Markov process** is defined as a stochastic process in which the transition from one state to the next is determined by a known set of probabilities that are independent of how the system arrived at its present state.

Articles on Markov processes started appearing in management science journals in the early 1960s. Since then, the procedure has been used to describe plant maintenance decisions, stock market movements, accounts-receivable projections, marketing strategies, and many other situations. However, while the procedure correctly identifies the time-phased decision process commonly found in organizations, the mathematics necessary to analyze a realistic system can become very complex. As a result, businesses have been much slower to adopt this decision-making tool than most of the techniques introduced in earlier chapters.

18-2 CHARACTERISTICS OF MARKOV-PROCESS MODELS

Situations which can be modeled using Markov procedures are in many respects similar to those which can be described by dynamic programming models, with two major differences. The first is that dynamic programming models deal with situations in which a manager is required to make a limited number of incremental decisions within a given time, or decision horizon, whereas Markov models can be used to represent the outcome of a large number of occurrences in an unlimited time frame. The second difference is that in dynamic programming, once the decision maker reaches a particular stage of the process, a known state can be selected. Markov models, on the other hand, are used to describe the outcome of a series of events that are not directly under the decision-maker's control. Characteristics of Markov-process modeling and of problems for which it can be used are discussed in the following paragraphs.

First, the problem contains a definite *time structure* within which a specific set of *outcomes* may occur. For a registrar monitoring a student's progress through college, this time structure would be quarters or semesters; since, within each term, a certain number of students graduate, change majors, elect to drop out of school, are dropped because of failing grades, and so on. For a manufacturer, the time structure may involve the weekly scheduling meeting, when the current set of orders are booked into the production schedule. For a television network, the time structure may be a week, when viewers either decide to watch the same show as last week, watch a new show, or not watch television at all.

Second, all Markov models contain *state variables*. These are the variables that describe the condition, or **state**, of the system at each trial or period of the process. For the college registrar, the state variables would include such factors as a student's class standing, major, and grade-point average. For the marketing manager in a household-products company, the state variable may indicate whether someone purchases the same laundry detergent again this week or changes brands. (Since this is an introductory treatment of Markov models, we will limit our examples to ones with easily defined state variables.)

Third, at a specific point, often the beginning or end of a time period in the process, the condition being monitored may change from one state to another. For example, someone who purchased one brand of detergent last week may switch brands this week. At the end of a semester, a student may change his major from business to art history.

Fourth, the decision maker is often uncertain about whether the state variable will change or remain the same; and this uncertainty is reflected in a set of transition probabilities. These **transition probabilities** reflect the chance that the conditions being monitored will change at specified points in the process. Assuming the system is in state i during the current trial or period of the process, the transition probability, p_{ij}, represents the chance the condition will change to state j during the next period. For instance, what is the probability someone who purchased brand X detergent last week will switch to brand Y this week? What is the probability that a junior-year finance major will switch to art history? As we shall show, these transition probabilities will be placed in a **transition matrix** to be used in the model.

Finally, at a given point in the structure of the process, the set of transition probabilities representing the uncertainty of moving to any future state depend only on the current state. The probability a shopper will switch from brand X to brand Y this week would be assumed independent of how many weeks prior to this the person bought brand X, or whether he or she has ever bought brand Y in the past. The probability a television viewer will decide to watch news on a different channel this week would be assumed independent of how many weeks in the past he or she has been watching another channel. In statistical terms, this means the conditional probability of each next state, given the value of the current state, is independent of any previous states. This is similar to the independence assumption of dynamic programming, and often it is a realistic assumption. Many marketing studies have shown that for certain types of products, consumers are not brand-loyal and will, for instance, readily buy whichever brand is currently on sale. In some cases, however, this is not a realistic assumption. A senior who expects to graduate next term is much less likely to change majors than a sophomore.

As with dynamic programming, the characteristics of a Markov process are sometimes difficult to recognize in practical applications. In the next three sections, we will present basic examples of Markov models and will more fully describe the characteristics of a Markov process.

18-3 PREDICTING MARKET SHARES AMONG COMPETING BRANDS

For the past decade or so, as health concerns have prompted people to change their eating habits, consumption of poultry in North America has been increasing. Chicken production has become big business, and some brands are distributed nationally. In recent years, the Midwest market has been dominated by two brands, Golden Pride and Home Glow; but last year, Armstrong Packing introduced a new brand, Farm's Best. After an extensive advertising campaign, Farm's Best has become a recognized presence in the market.

Armstrong Packing subscribes to CompuScan, a market research service which collects information on a carefully selected sample of families. Each family has an individual identification code, which is presented at the supermarket each time a family member makes a purchase. The product readout from the supermarket's optical scanning system at the checkout stand is transmitted directly to CompuScan's customer data base. By tracking the buying patterns of CompuScan's families, companies are able to learn much about consumer preferences and the effect of advertising campaigns on buying habits.

Armstrong Packing, the only one of the three major chicken producers to subscribe to this service, hopes the information will provide a competitive advantage. Bob Horn, a market research analyst, is reviewing a compilation of data gathered since the Farm's Best product was introduced. Since Farm's Best is a recent entry in the market, its share is still a relatively low 10%, but the company hopes to increase its share in the future.

Estimating future market share is important, since it will be used to determine production capacity, distribution networks, work-force requirements, storage capacity needed, and a host of other business variables. Bob is wondering whether he can use any of the information from CompuScan to predict how big a share of the final market Farm's Best may eventually have.

FORMULATING THE MODEL

Markov models can become complicated very rapidly, and so for this situation we still make two simplifying assumptions. The first is that customers make meat purchases once a week. The second is that customers buy one of three brands of chicken each week—Golden Pride, Home Glow, or Farm's Best. Given these assumptions, we can determine the following characteristics needed for a Markov model.

1. The *time structure* is the period of time when a set of outcomes occurs; here, the time period is a week.
2. The *state variables* specify the brand of chicken purchased each week, as follows: state 1, Golden Pride; state 2, Home Glow; state 3, Farm's Best.
3. The *transition probabilities*, as determined from CompuScan's records, are given in Table 18-1.

Table 18-1 TRANSITION PROBABILITIES FOR THREE BRANDS

Brand Purchased This Period	Brand Purchased Next Period		
	Golden Pride	Home Glow	Farm's Best
Golden Pride	.80	.05	.15
Home Glow	.10	.70	.20
Farm's Best	.10	.10	.80

The probabilities would be determined, for instance, by counting the number of customers who bought a Golden Pride chicken last week and then recording which brand they bought this week. The same counts would be made for the other two brands. Bob Horn has found records on 500 families and has determined that of those who purchased Golden Pride last week, 80% also bought Golden Pride this week, 5% changed to Home Glow, and 15% switched to Farm's Best. By determining the same probabilities for the families that bought Home Glow and Farm's Best last week, he can determine the transition probabilities needed for the model (Table 18-1).

Note that the probabilities in each row of Table 18-1 add to 1.00. This is simply an indication that a family which bought a Golden Pride chicken this week will buy one of the three possible brands next week. The fact that the probabilities in the *columns* do not add to 1 indicates the present market share of the three brands will change. The probabilities on the main diagonal of the table indicate the brand loyalty of the three brands, since they represent the probability that a family will buy the same brand from one week to the next.

Finally, to develop a Markov model of this situation, we must assume the transition probabilities will remain constant over the time period of the model and that they are the same for all families in the market area. To make the model easier to solve, we will represent the table of transition probabilities as a matrix, **P**. Where:

$$\mathbf{P} = \begin{bmatrix} p_{11} & p_{12} & p_{13} \\ p_{21} & p_{22} & p_{23} \\ p_{31} & p_{32} & p_{33} \end{bmatrix} = \begin{bmatrix} .80 & .05 & .15 \\ .10 & .70 & .20 \\ .10 & .10 & .80 \end{bmatrix}$$

Here, the probabilities, p_{ij}, are the transition probabilities of moving from state i in period n to state j in period $n + 1$.

SOLUTION PROCEDURE

A Markov model allows a decision maker to use the table of transition probabilities to move from some starting point to an end state. This ending position is often called the *steady-state condition* of the system. For this example, the steady-state condition will determine the final market shares among the three brands.

To understand the logic of solving the model, refer to Figure 18-1. We have used a decision tree to represent the possible states, and transitions, of the first three time periods in the process for a family initially buying a Golden Pride chicken. The numbers on the branches leaving the node at period 0 are the probabilities of purchasing each of the three brands in period 1 (week 1). Each of the first three branches gains three branches (leaving period 1) for the decision moving to week 2. (Obviously, constructing a tree diagram is feasible only for decisions with a few states and a limited number of time periods, but it is useful for clearly showing the logic of the process.)

The week 2 probabilities, at the right-hand side of the tree, indicate the probabilities of moving along that path. We see that the probability of purchasing a Golden Pride

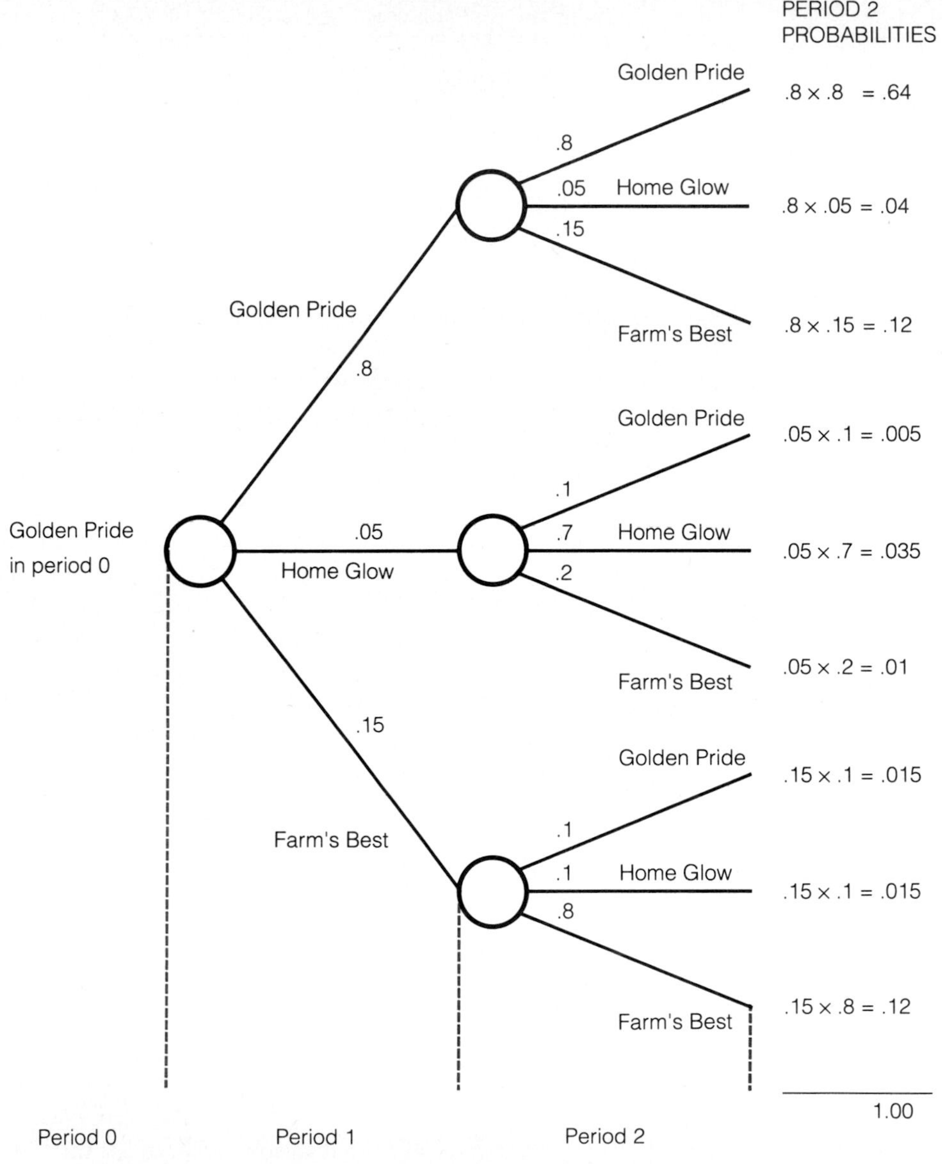

Figure 18-1
Decision tree for possible brand choices

chicken in both week 1 and week 2 is .8 × .8 = .64. The probability that a family which purchased a Golden Pride chicken in week 0 will also purchase a Golden Pride chicken in week 2, regardless of the brand purchased in week 1, can be found by adding the week 2 probabilities of all the Golden Pride branches (values for Golden Pride are always on the topmost of the three branches): .64 + .005 + .015 = .66.

The logic we are using to solve Bob Horn's problem is: (1) If we consider the three possible states in period 0—that is, a family will start by purchasing a Golden Pride, Home Glow, or Farm's Best brand chicken, and (2) if we can determine the ending probabilities *many* periods in the future (as we did for period 2 in Figure 18-1 for all three starting decisions), we can use these ending probabilities as the end market share of the three brands.

Returning to Figure 18-1, we see that if a family purchases a Golden Pride chicken in week 0, the probability that family will also purchase a Golden Pride chicken in week 2 is .66. Let's represent the probability of this outcome, *o*, as:

$$o_i(n) = \text{probability the system will be in state } i \text{ during period } n$$

Using this representation (since Golden Pride is identified as state 1), the three conditions in Figure 18-1 would be:

$$o_1(0) = 1.0$$
$$o_1(1) = .8$$
$$o_1(2) = .66$$

To make the calculations easier to follow, let's specify an *outcome vector*, **O**, which will identify the probability of a family being in one of the three possible states (buying one of the three brands) at any time period. Since Bob Horn's example has three possible states during each time period, the outcome vector will be:

$$\mathbf{O}(n) = [o_1(n) \quad o_2(n) \quad o_3(n)]$$

For a family which purchased a Golden Pride chicken during week 0, this vector would be:

$$\mathbf{O}(0) = [o_1(0) \quad o_2(0) \quad o_3(0)] = [1 \quad 0 \quad 0]$$

For a family which purchased a Home Glow chicken (state 2) during week 0, this vector would be:

$$\mathbf{O}(0) = [o_1(0) \quad o_2(0) \quad o_3(0)] = [0 \quad 1 \quad 0]$$

For a family which purchased a Farm's Best chicken (state 3) during week 0, this vector would be

$$\mathbf{O}(0) = [o_1(0) \quad o_2(0) \quad o_3(0)] = [0 \quad 0 \quad 1]$$

Suppose we know that a family bought a Golden Pride chicken at week 0. What is the probability the same family will purchase Golden Pride during week *n*? We can answer this question using the initial outcome vector and the transition probabilities in the following manner:

$$\mathbf{O}(n) = \mathbf{O}(n-1)\mathbf{P}$$

To see how this works, assume we start with a family which purchases a Golden Pride chicken in week 0. We know the initial vector is:

$$\mathbf{O}(0) = [1 \quad 0 \quad 0]$$

To determine the corresponding vector for period 1, we perform the matrix multiplication:

$$\begin{aligned}\mathbf{O}(1) &= \mathbf{O}(0)\mathbf{P} \\ &= [1 \quad 0 \quad 0]\begin{bmatrix} .8 & .05 & .15 \\ .1 & .70 & .20 \\ .1 & .10 & .80 \end{bmatrix} \\ &= [.8 \quad .05 \quad .15]\end{aligned}$$

Notice that this new vector represents the probabilities on the branches leaving the period 0 node in Figure 18-1.

In case you are rusty on matrix multiplication, we will show how the above multiplication was carried out:

Step 1 Multiply each element in the vector by each element in column 1 of the matrix and add the results. This gives the new value for the first position of the revised vector:

$$(1 \times .8) + (0 \times .1) + (0 \times .1) = .8$$

Step 2 Multiply each element in the original vector by each element in column 2 of the matrix and add the results. This gives the new value for the second position of the revised vector:

$$(1 \times .05) + (0 \times .7) + (0 \times .1) = .05$$

Step 3 Multiply each element in the original vector by each element in column 3 of the matrix and add the results. This gives the new value for the third position of the revised vector:

$$(1 \times .15) + (0 \times .2) + (0 \times .8) = .15$$

To determine the probabilities of being at each of the three states at time period 2, we continue the matrix multiplication by multiplying the revised output vector times the matrix of transition probabilities:

$$\begin{aligned} \mathbf{O}(2) &= \mathbf{O}(1)\mathbf{P} \\ &= [.8 \quad .05 \quad .15] \begin{bmatrix} .8 & .05 & .15 \\ .1 & .70 & .20 \\ .1 & .10 & .80 \end{bmatrix} \\ &= [.66 \quad .09 \quad .25] \end{aligned}$$

These are the same probabilities we get by adding the week 2 probabilities from Figure 18-1.

In a similar manner, we can determine the outcome vector for period 3:

$$\begin{aligned} \mathbf{O}(3) &= \mathbf{O}(2)\mathbf{P} \\ &= [.66 \quad .09 \quad .25] \begin{bmatrix} .8 & .05 & .15 \\ .1 & .70 & .20 \\ .1 & .10 & .80 \end{bmatrix} \\ &= [.562 \quad .121 \quad .317] \end{aligned}$$

If we continue to determine the probabilities associated with the output vectors, we will find the values shown in Table 18-2.

Note that, as the model moves from one time period to the next the probabilities change, but each change becomes smaller. If we continued for many periods, we would

Table 18-2 PROBABILITIES FOR GOLDEN PRIDE CHICKEN

	Period											
State	0	1	2	3	4	5	6	7	8	9	10	SS*
$o_1(n)$	1	.80	.66	.562	.493	.445	.412	.388	.372	.360	.352	.333
$o_2(n)$	0	.05	.09	.121	.145	.162	.175	.184	.191	.196	.200	.208
$o_3(n)$	0	.15	.25	.317	.362	.393	.413	.427	.437	.444	.448	.459

* SS = steady-state condition

Table 18-3 PROBABILITIES FOR HOME GLOW CHICKEN

	Period											
State	0	1	2	3	4	5	6	7	8	9	10	SS*
$o_1(n)$	0	.1	.170	.219	.253	.227	.294	.306	.314	.320	.324	.333
$o_2(n)$	1	.7	.515	.400	.329	.285	.257	.240	.228	.221	.217	.208
$o_3(n)$	0	.2	.315	.381	.417	.438	.449	.455	.457	.459	.459	.459

PROBABILITIES FOR FARM'S BEST CHICKEN

	Period											
State	0	1	2	3	4	5	6	7	8	9	10	SS*
$o_1(n)$	0	.1	.170	.219	.253	.277	.294	.306	.314	.320	.324	.333
$o_2(n)$	0	.1	.155	.185	.200	.207	.210	.212	.212	.211	.211	.208
$o_3(n)$	1	.8	.675	.597	.547	.516	.459	.483	.474	.469	.465	.459

* SS = steady-state condition

reach the steady-state condition, where further changes would become insignificant. To show that these final steady-state conditions are independent of the starting conditions, in Table 18-3 we show the outcome probabilities for families who bought a Home Glow or Farm's Best chicken in period 0. The **steady-state probabilities** are the probabilities of the consumer represented by the initial vector being in any of the outcome states after a large number of periods or trials of the system.

Since the steady-state probabilities indicate the chance a family will buy each of the three brands, for a large number of families, N, we can find:

Families that will buy Golden Pride = $N(.333)$

Families that will buy Home Glow = $N(.208)$

Families that will buy Farm's Pride = $N(.459)$

These probabilities indicate the market share each of the three brands will eventually have, which answers Bob Horn's initial question. Unfortunately, we had to perform a large number of matrix multiplications to arrive at these values. But there is an easier way to find the ending point, or steady-state probabilities.

DIRECTLY DETERMINING STEADY-STATE PROBABILITIES

We know that the state probability vector for any period $n + 1$ can be determined by multiplying the probability vector for period n by the transition matrix **P**. This is shown as:

$$[o_1(n+1) \quad o_2(n+1) \quad o_3(n+1)] = [o_1(n) \quad o_2(n) \quad o_3(n)] \begin{bmatrix} p_{11} & p_{12} & p_{13} \\ p_{21} & p_{22} & p_{23} \\ p_{31} & p_{32} & p_{33} \end{bmatrix}$$

But, by looking at the sequence of probabilities in Tables 18-2 and 18-3, we see that as n gets very large, the probabilities in period $n + 1$ are essentially the same as the probabilities in period n. Therefore, for large values of n, we can use:

$$[o_1(n) \quad o_2(n) \quad o_3(n)] = [o_1(n) \quad o_2(n) \quad o_3(n)] \begin{bmatrix} p_{11} & p_{12} & p_{13} \\ p_{21} & p_{22} & p_{23} \\ p_{31} & p_{32} & p_{33} \end{bmatrix}$$

Substituting the transition probabilities for the three-brand example into the matrix and performing the multiplication, we find the following three equations:

$$o_1(n) = .8\, o_1(n) + .1\, o_2(n) + .1\, o_3(n) \tag{18-1}$$
$$o_2(n) = .05\, o_1(n) + .7\, o_2(n) + .1\, o_3(n) \tag{18-2}$$
$$o_3(n) = .15\, o_1(n) + .2\, o_2(n) + .8\, o_3(n) \tag{18-3}$$

Rearranging equations 18-1 through 18-3, we get the following results:

$$.2\, o_1(n) = .1\, o_2(n) + .1\, o_3(n) \tag{18-4}$$
$$.3\, o_2(n) = .05\, o_1(n) + .1\, o_3(n) \tag{18-5}$$
$$.2\, o_3(n) = .15\, o_1(n) + .2\, o_2(n) \tag{18-6}$$

In addition, because the probabilities must sum to 1, we know:

$$o_1(n) + o_2(n) + o_3(n) = 1 \tag{18-7}$$

Picking equation 18-7 and any two from equations 18-4 through 18-6, we will have three equations and three unknowns. Solving for the steady-state probabilities, we find:

$$o_1(n) = .333$$
$$o_2(n) = .208$$
$$o_3(n) = .459$$

Note that these are the same as the steady-state probabilities in Tables 18-2 and 18-3.

Therefore, even though the Farm's Pride brand has a small share of the present market, Bob Horn knows that, if the transition probabilities remain constant, Farm's Pride will eventually become the market leader. We know, however, that once they see what is happening, the two competitors will not give up market share easily and will try strategies to change the transition probabilities. (The Solved Problem example at the end of the chapter presents a problem with changing transition probabilities.)

18-4 ESTIMATING SUCCESSFUL COMPLETION OF TRAINING

Hillview Center operates a group of residential treatment facilities for people with chemical dependencies and eating disorders in the New England area. The most effective part of the center's popular 3-month recovery program seems to be the group sessions, run by Hillview-trained counselors. These counselors are key employees in the operation, and Rachelle Polanski is in charge of hiring and training them. All candidates must have at least a master's degree and be certified counselors. The company provides an extensive training program for those who are hired. However, Rachelle has found that not every person hired has the temperament to be a treatment counselor. As they go through the training program, counselors are classified as follows:

1. Qualified counselor
2. Minimum supervision required
3. Extensive supervision required
4. Switched to other duties; training terminated

Newly hired counselors enter at level 3, because they require extensive supervision, and are evaluated weekly to determine whether a change in status is called for.

Although Rachelle has records on past counselor training, her present problem is the center's imminent need for 100 additional counselors to be hired for a new treatment facility. How many does she need to hire to be sure that 100 will successfully complete the training program?

FORMULATING THE MODEL

We can analyze Rachelle's problem as a Markov process if we identify the following states:

1. Qualified counselor
2. Switched to other duties; training terminated
3. Minimum supervision required
4. Extensive supervision required

(We reordered the states to facilitate computation, but the order does not affect the final steady-state condition.)

The time period associated with the model is one week. From records charting past counselors' movements between the states, Rachelle can construct the following transition matrix:

$$\mathbf{P} = \begin{bmatrix} 1.0 & 0.0 & 0.0 & 0.0 \\ 0.0 & 1.0 & 0.0 & 0.0 \\ 0.4 & 0.1 & 0.3 & 0.2 \\ 0.1 & 0.3 & 0.1 & 0.5 \end{bmatrix}$$

This problem is different from the previous market-share example in that two of the states are absorbing states. This means that once counselors reach state 1 (qualified) or state 2 (switched), they are effectively "trapped" at that state. More formally stated, an **absorbing state** is one for which the probability of leaving in any future period is zero.

SOLUTION PROCEDURE

Since every counselor starts in the extensive-supervision category, the starting outcome vector is:

$$\mathbf{O}(0) = [0 \quad 0 \quad 0 \quad 1]$$

The state vector showing the distribution after the first week is:

$$\mathbf{O}(1) = [0 \quad 0 \quad 0 \quad 1] \begin{bmatrix} 1.0 & 0.0 & 0.0 & 0.0 \\ 0.0 & 1.0 & 0.0 & 0.0 \\ 0.4 & 0.1 & 0.3 & 0.2 \\ 0.1 & 0.3 & 0.1 & 0.5 \end{bmatrix}$$

$$= [.1 \quad .3 \quad .1 \quad .5]$$

Thus, after one week, Rachelle can expect 10% of those in training to have reached the qualified state, 30% to have been switched to other duties, 10% to require minimum supervision, and 50% to still need extensive supervision.

After the second week, the state vector becomes:

$$\mathbf{O}(2) = [.1 \quad .3 \quad .1 \quad .5] \begin{bmatrix} 1.0 & 0.0 & 0.0 & 0.0 \\ 0.0 & 1.0 & 0.0 & 0.0 \\ 0.4 & 0.1 & 0.3 & 0.2 \\ 0.1 & 0.3 & 0.1 & 0.5 \end{bmatrix}$$

$$= [.19 \quad .46 \quad .08 \quad .27]$$

Table 18-4 PROBABILITIES FOR ENTRY-LEVEL COUNSELORS

	Period											
State	0	1	2	3	4	5	6	7	8	9	10	SS*
$o_1(n)$	0	.1	.19	.249	.285	.305	.317	.324	.328	.330	.332	.333
$o_2(n)$	0	.3	.46	.549	.599	.628	.645	.654	.659	.663	.664	.667
$o_3(n)$	0	.1	.08	.051	.030	.018	.010	.006	.003	.002	.001	.000
$o_4(n)$	1	.5	.27	.151	.086	.049	.028	.016	.009	.005	.003	.000

* SS = steady-state condition

Now, 19% will have reached the qualified state, 46% will have washed out, 8% will require only minimum supervision, and 27% will still require extensive supervision.

Table 18-4 shows the state probabilities for the first 10 weeks of counselor training and the steady-state conditions. By looking at the steady-state probabilities, we see that only a third of those who start the training make it to state 1, or become full counselors. This means that if Rachelle needs 100 counselors, the company will have to hire 300 to start the training.

18-5 FORECASTING BAD DEBTS IN ACCOUNTS RECEIVABLE

Cecil Anderson, the newly appointed controller of Risch Mail Order Sales, moved into the job when the previous controller asked to take early retirement—after he had substantially underestimated the company's tax liability. His low forecast of the tax liability resulted from a large miscalculation in the allowance for bad-debt accounts. Cecil realizes his future could be affected unless he develops a system to better forecast the amount of bad debt.

Risch Mail Order has found it must sell its merchandise on credit to be competitive. As with any credit operation, the store must be willing to take a loss on its charge accounts. The only benefit associated with these losses is that they can be written off against the company's profit and reduce the company's tax liability. However, if the company overestimates the credit losses, the budgeted tax liability will be understated; in such a case, at tax time the company will be forced to come up with a larger tax payment than expected. This can have an adverse impact on the company's cash flow, as was the case last year.

As is common in credit operations, Risch "ages" its credit accounts, classifying each account into one of four categories:

1. Accounts paid in full within the current billing cycle
2. Accounts with a balance due, payment received in the last billing cycle
3. Accounts with a balance due, no payment received in the last billing cycle
4. Bad accounts; balance due but no payment received within the last four months

Accounts in category 4 are classified as noncollectible and are sold to a collection agency for 15% of their face value; they are also written off for tax purposes.

Cecil's immediate problem is to determine how much of the current outstanding credit should be set aside as bad accounts. He has done extensive research on past accounts and has traced the monthly flow of credit dollars over time, primarily to observe the movement of credit accounts to the bad-debt category. The progression of accounts into any of the four categories can be modeled as a Markov process, as discussed below.

FORMULATING THE PROBLEM

We can formulate this problem as a Markov model if we first identify the following states:

1. Account paid in full (o_1)
2. Account classified as a bad debt (o_2)
3. Balance due, payment made in current cycle (o_3)
4. Balance due, no payment made in current cycle (o_4)

We have once again rearranged the order in which the states are listed. (The reason for this change will be explained in the next section.) The time period associated with this model is one billing cycle, or one month.

By selecting a random sample of accounts in the two balance-due categories (3 and 4), Cecil has estimated a transition-probability matrix (Table 18-5) to describe the chances of an account moving from one category to another on a monthly basis.

As Table 18-5 indicates, once an account is moved into either of the first two categories (fully paid or bad account), it will not move out of that category. Also, an account cannot be moved from category 3 (balance due, current) to category 4 (bad account) in one month.

SOLUTION PROCEDURE

Cecil's problem is to determine how much of the amount in each of the two balance-due categories, states 3 and 4, will eventually be fully paid (state 1) and how much will be written off as a bad debt (state 2). To determine this movement for state 3, we define the following initial outcome vector:

$$\mathbf{O}(0) = [0 \quad 0 \quad 1 \quad 0]$$

Multiplying this vector by the transition matrix, we find the outcomes for period 1:

$$\mathbf{O}(1) = [0 \quad 0 \quad 1 \quad 0] \begin{bmatrix} 1.0 & 0.0 & 0.0 & 0.0 \\ 0.0 & 1.0 & 0.0 & 0.0 \\ 0.5 & 0.0 & 0.4 & 0.1 \\ 0.3 & 0.1 & 0.3 & 0.3 \end{bmatrix}$$

$$= [.5 \quad 0 \quad .4 \quad .1]$$

This indicates a .5 chance that these accounts will be paid and 0 chance that they will move into the bad-debt category in period 1. There is also a .4 chance that the account

Table 18-5 TRANSITION PROBABILITIES FOR CREDIT ACCOUNTS

	This Month's Status			
			Balance Due	
Last Month's Status	Fully Paid	Bad Account	Current	Not Current
Fully paid	1.0	0.0	0.0	0.0
Bad account	0.0	1.0	0.0	0.0
Balance due, account current	0.5	0.0	0.4	0.1
Balance due, account not current	0.3	0.1	0.3	0.3

Table 18-6 PROBABILITIES FOR STATE 3 CHARGE ACCOUNTS

State	Period 0	1	2	3	4	5	6	7	8	9	10	SS
$o_1(n)$	0	0.5	.73	.846	.907	.939	.956	.965	.969	.972	.973	.975
$o_2(n)$	0	0.0	.01	.017	.021	.023	.024	.025	.025	.025	.025	.025
$o_3(n)$	1	0.4	.19	.097	.051	.027	.014	.007	.004	.002	.001	.000
$o_4(n)$	0	0.1	.07	.040	.022	.012	.006	.003	.002	.001	.001	.000

will remain in its current state and a .1 chance that the account will deteriorate to state 4 (balance due, payment not made) during this billing cycle.

If we continue to perform the matrix multiplications for subsequent periods, we will reach the steady-state probabilities shown in Table 18-6. From the steady-state column in the table, we see that for each dollar of credit presently in state 3 (balance due, payment made), 2.5 cents ($.025) will eventually move into the bad-debt category (o_2).

Continuing to category 4 (balance due, no current payment), we perform the matrix multiplication with the revised state vector:

$$\mathbf{O}(0) = [0 \quad 0 \quad 0 \quad 1]$$

$$\mathbf{O}(1) = [0 \quad 0 \quad 0 \quad 1]\begin{bmatrix} 1.0 & 0.0 & 0.0 & 0.0 \\ 0.0 & 1.0 & 0.0 & 0.0 \\ 0.5 & 0.0 & 0.4 & 0.1 \\ 0.3 & 0.1 & 0.3 & 0.3 \end{bmatrix}$$

$$= [.3 \quad .1 \quad .3 \quad .3]$$

By continuing the series of matrix multiplications, we find the state probabilities shown in Table 18-7. From the table, we see that for every dollar in category 4 (balance due, no current payment) 15.4 cents ($.154) will eventually be classified as bad debt.

With the steady-state probabilities shown in Tables 18-6 and 18-7, Cecil will be able to determine the required allowance for bad debts. If Risch Mail Order currently has $3 million in category 3 (balance due, current payment) and $5 million in category 4 (balance due, no current payment), Cecil should plan on having:

$$\$.025(3{,}000{,}000) + \$.154(5{,}000{,}000) = \$845{,}000$$

of nonpaying accounts. Since he can sell bad-debt accounts to a collection agency for 15% of their face value, the total amount of bad debt will be .85($845,000) = $718,250. We will look at a different way to analyze this problem, and to more quickly assess the impact of policies which will change the transition matrix, in the next section.

Table 18-7 PROBABILITIES FOR STATE 4 CHARGE ACCOUNTS

State	Period 0	1	2	3	4	5	6	7	8	9	SS
$o_1(n)$	0	.3	.54	.681	.758	.799	.820	.832	.838	.841	.846
$o_2(n)$	0	.1	.13	.142	.148	.151	.153	.154	.154	.154	.154
$o_3(n)$	0	.3	.21	.120	.065	.035	.009	.010	.005	.003	.000
$o_4(n)$	1	.3	.12	.057	.029	.015	.008	.004	.002	.001	.000

18-6 USING THE FUNDAMENTAL MATRIX

In the preceding section we analyzed a common application of Markov models, the accounts-receivables life cycle. That model had two end states which we classified as *absorbing states* since, once an outcome reached one of these states, no further movement was possible. We demonstrated that a model with absorbing states could be analyzed using the same matrix multiplication procedure as a problem without absorbing states. We also saw that if we cycled the model through enough time periods, only the two absorbing states would contain nonzero probabilities. However, the matrix structure of the transition probabilities allows us to determine the steady-state probabilities without cycling the model through a large number of time periods.

The Risch problem in the previous section had this transition matrix:

$$\mathbf{P} = \begin{bmatrix} 1.0 & 0.0 & 0.0 & 0.0 \\ 0.0 & 1.0 & 0.0 & 0.0 \\ 0.5 & 0.0 & 0.4 & 0.1 \\ 0.3 & 0.1 & 0.3 & 0.3 \end{bmatrix}$$

We can partition the transition matrix into four parts, as follows:

$$\mathbf{P} = \left[\begin{array}{cc|cc} 1.0 & 0.0 & 0.0 & 0.0 \\ 0.0 & 1.0 & 0.0 & 0.0 \\ \hline 0.5 & 0.0 & 0.4 & 0.1 \\ 0.3 & 0.1 & 0.3 & 0.3 \end{array}\right] = \begin{array}{c|c} \mathbf{I} & \mathbf{O} \\ \hline \mathbf{A} & \mathbf{N} \end{array}$$

The four subcomponents of the transition matrix are defined below:

$$\mathbf{I} = \begin{bmatrix} 1 & 0 \\ 0 & 1 \end{bmatrix}$$

The matrix **I** is an *identity* matrix which represents the probability of remaining in an absorbing state once such a state is reached.

$$\mathbf{O} = \begin{bmatrix} 0 & 0 \\ 0 & 0 \end{bmatrix}$$

The **O** matrix represents the probability of moving from an absorbing state to one of the nonabsorbing states.

$$\mathbf{A} = \begin{bmatrix} 0.5 & 0.0 \\ 0.3 & 0.1 \end{bmatrix}$$

The **A** matrix represents the probability of moving from one of the nonabsorbing states to an absorbing state.

$$\mathbf{N} = \begin{bmatrix} .4 & .1 \\ .3 & .3 \end{bmatrix}$$

Finally, the **N** matrix represents the probability of moving from one of the nonabsorbing states to another nonabsorbing state.

The key to directly determining the final probability that an initial state will move to one of the absorbing states is to determine the model's fundamental matrix. For a given starting state, the **fundamental matrix** determines the average number of periods a process will remain in a nonabsorbing state before finally entering an absorbing state.

The fundamental matrix, **F**, can be determined from the partitioned transition matrix as follows:

$$\mathbf{F} = (\mathbf{I} - \mathbf{N})^{-1}$$

Using the Risch transition matrix, we find:

$$(\mathbf{I} - \mathbf{N})^{-1} = \left[\begin{bmatrix} 1 & 0 \\ 0 & 1 \end{bmatrix} - \begin{bmatrix} .4 & .1 \\ .3 & .3 \end{bmatrix}\right]^{-1}$$

$$= \begin{bmatrix} .6 & -.1 \\ -.3 & .7 \end{bmatrix}^{-1}$$

The fundamental matrix, then, is:

$$\mathbf{F} = (\mathbf{I} - \mathbf{N})^{-1} = \begin{bmatrix} 1.79 & 0.26 \\ 0.77 & 1.54 \end{bmatrix}$$

Since states 3 and 4 are the two nonabsorbing states (accounts in those categories can still change status), the fundamental matrix gives the number of times an outcome in either state 3 or 4 will move, on average, before reaching an absorbing state.

Beginning State	**Number of Steps to Absorption**
S_3	$1.79 + 0.26 = 2.05$
S_4	$0.77 + 1.54 = 2.31$

The **probability of absorption** represents the probability that a system currently in a nonabsorbing state will move to an absorbing state in the next period of the system. For this problem, the absorption probabilities can be found by:

$$\text{Probability of absorption} = \mathbf{FA}$$

$$= \begin{bmatrix} 1.79 & 0.26 \\ 0.77 & 1.54 \end{bmatrix} \begin{bmatrix} 0.5 & 0.0 \\ 0.3 & 0.1 \end{bmatrix}$$

$$= \begin{bmatrix} .975 & .025 \\ .846 & .154 \end{bmatrix}$$

Putting the current and future states on the absorption-probability matrix, we see:

	Future State	
Current State	S_1	S_2
S_3	.975	.025
S_4	.846	.154

The first row of this matrix represents the probability that an outcome currently in state 3 will eventually move to either state 1 or state 2. Notice that these values, .975 and .025, are the same as the steady-state values found in Table 18-6. The second row in the matrix represents the probability that an outcome currently in state 4 will eventually move to either of the two absorbing states. As you can see, these probabilities, .846 and .154, are the same as the steady-state values found in Table 18-7.

The amount of total credit outstanding that will move to each of the two absorbing states can be determined directly from the absorption-probability matrix. If we again assume the total amount of credit in state 3 is $3,000,000 and the amount in state 4 is $5,000,000, we can represent this condition as the following vector:

$$\text{Credit} = [3{,}000{,}000 \quad 5{,}000{,}000]$$

Multiplying this vector by the absorption-probability matrix, we get:

$$[3{,}000{,}000 \quad 5{,}000{,}000] \begin{bmatrix} .975 & .025 \\ .846 & .154 \end{bmatrix}$$

$$= [7{,}155{,}000 \quad 845{,}000]$$

Therefore, of the total $8,000,000 credit currently on the books, $7,155,000 is expected to be collected by Risch and $845,000 is expected to be sold to a collection agency. These are the same values we found in section 18-5, but we did not have to cycle the model until the steady-state conditions were found.

18-7 SUMMARY AND CONCLUSIONS

In this chapter, we explained the fundamental structure of Markov models and presented examples of decision-making applications for these models. We saw that the structure of Markov models is similar to that of dynamic programming models, except movement from one state of the model to the next is determined by a distribution of transition probabilities instead of a choice made by the decision maker. We showed how these transition probabilities can be used to assess the condition of the process at any time period in the future. We also showed how, after many cycles, the system would move into a steady-state condition, and then we showed how to find the steady-state probabilities. Of special interest were systems with absorbing states: Once a process outcome moves into an absorbing state, no further movement is possible.

Because Markov models can rapidly become very complicated, our discussion in this text has been on the most elementary level possible. Our examples covered some of the applications for which Markov models are commonly used, such as marketing analysis to study brand swtiching, and financial analysis to examine the behavior of accounts receivable. In general, Markov models can also be used for many other types of decision situations that involve predicting the future behavior of a system by analyzing historical data on the system's past behavior.

Solved Problem

PROBLEM

Fred's Superfair has just expanded into a western state that has been dominated by the Jacobson and Foodtown supermarket chains. Fred's Superfair timed its entry to correspond with the establishment of a state lottery and has instituted a very effective marketing scheme. Each Fred's store electronically posts five numbers which change each hour. At checkout, customers whose receipts have three, four, or five of the posted numbers will receive a grocery credit of $10, $20, or $50.

This game has proved very popular, and Fred's executives are happy with the current market share. The company's research department has surveyed shoppers in the area to determine how

Table 18-8 TRANSITION PROBABILITIES FOR FRED'S SUPERFAIR

	Store Chosen Next Period		
Store Chosen This Period	Jacobson's	Foodtown	Fred's
Jacobson's	.85	.05	.10
Foodtown	.10	.75	.15
Fred's	.10	.10	.80

they select supermarkets. Using this sample information, they constructed the transition matrix shown in Table 18-8.

a. Fred's currently has a 5% market share in the area, Jacobson has a 50% share, and Foodtown has 45%. Use the transition matrix (Table 18-8) to predict their final market shares. (Assume weekly time periods.) How large will the market share of all three competitors be in 6 weeks?

b. After seeing the effectiveness of Fred's marketing campaign, executives at Foodtown institute a matching coupon system which affects consumers' shopping patterns. The coupon system, which began 6 weeks after Fred's campaign, seems to give the transition matrix shown in Table 18-9. How will the introduction of Foodtown's coupon system affect the final projection of Fred's market share?

Solution **a.** We are interested in both the market share after 6 weeks and the final, or steady-state, probabilities. We can find the market share after 6 weeks by performing a series of matrix multiplications. For example, if we begin by considering shoppers who start at Jacobson's, we have this initial multiplication:

$$[1 \quad 0 \quad 0]\begin{bmatrix} .85 & .05 & .10 \\ .10 & .75 & .15 \\ .10 & .10 & .80 \end{bmatrix}$$

By performing this multiplication, we get:

$$[.85 \quad .05 \quad .10]$$

This vector represents the probabilities that a Jacobson's shopper in one period will shop at each of the three supermarkets the next period. For example, if the shopper starts out as a Jacobson shopper, there is .85 chance he or she will still be a Jacobson shopper after period 1. There is a .05 chance that an original Jacobson's shopper will be a Foodtown shopper after period 1, and a .10 chance that a shopper who starts out as a Jacobson's shopper will shop at Fred's after period 1.

Table 18-9 REVISED TRANSITION PROBABILITIES FOR FRED'S

	Store Chosen Next Period		
Store Chosen This Period	Jacobson's	Foodtown	Fred's
Jacobson's	.80	.10	.1
Foodtown	.05	.85	.1
Fred's	.05	.15	.8

We continue the multiplication process for period 2, as follows:

$$[.85 \quad .05 \quad .10] \begin{bmatrix} .85 & .05 & .10 \\ .10 & .75 & .15 \\ .10 & .10 & .80 \end{bmatrix} = [.7375 \quad .0900 \quad .1725]$$

Thus, the chances of a shopper starting at Jacobson's and still being a Jacobson's shopper after two periods is .7375. A shopper who starts at Jacobson's has a .0900 chance of being a Foodtown shopper after two periods, and a shopper starting at Jacobson's has a .1725 chance of being a Fred's shopper after two periods.

We continue in this manner through period 6, with the following results:

	Probabilities for Shoppers Starting at Jacobson's		
Period	Jacobson	Foodtown	Fred's
1	.8500	.1000	.1000
2	.7375	.0900	.1725
3	.6530	.1220	.2250
4	.5900	.1460	.2640
5	.5420	.1660	.2920
6	.5070	.1810	.3130

Therefore, of the people who initially shopped at Jacobson's in week zero, 50.7% will shop there in week 6, 18.1% will shop at Foodtown, and 31.3% will shop at Fred's. Determining the same 6-week probabilities for shoppers who start at Foodtown and Fred's in week zero, we find the values shown below:

Probabilities for Shoppers Starting at Foodtown			
Period	Jacobson	Foodtown	Fred's
6	.329	.307	.364

Probabilities for Shoppers Starting at Fred's			
Period	Jacobson	Foodtown	Fred's
6	.329	.232	.439

Recall that the initial market share for Jacobson's was 50%. The market share at the end of 6 periods is calculated by determining the percentage that will stay with Jacobson's and the percentage that will switch to Jacobson's from the other two stores. This is computed as follows:

$$.50(.507) + .45(.329) + .05(.329) = .417$$

Thus, under the assumptions of this problem, Jacobson's market share will slip from 50% to 41.7% by period 6.

The process is the same for Foodtown and Fred's. For Foodtown, which started with a 45% market share, we get:

$$.50(.181) + .45(.307) + .05(.232) = .24025$$

Thus, Foodtown's market share is expected to drop from 45% to about 24%. For Fred's, we get:

$$.50(.313) + .45(.364) + .05(.439) = .343$$

As we can see, Fred's market share would improve from 5% to 34.3% by period 6.

Instead of stopping at period 6, we could continue to perform the multiplications until the steady state is reached. At that point, the market shares will be: Jacobson's, 40%; Foodtown, 22.9%; and Fred's 37.1%.

b. By introducing its coupon system, Foodtown has changed the transition matrix. Since customers have already gone through 6 weeks of shopping, we start with the shopping patterns at that point. These are the ones associated with period 6 in part **a** and are reproduced below. We find the following steady-state conditions:

Probabilities for Shoppers Starting at Jacobson's

Period	Jacobson	Foodtown	Fred's
6	.507	.181	.313

Probabilities for Shoppers Starting at Foodtown

Period	Jacobson	Foodtown	Fred's
6	.329	.307	.364

Probabilities for Shoppers Starting at Fred's

Period	Jacobson	Foodtown	Fred's
6	.329	.232	.439

We continue performing the matrix multiplications, now using the new transition matrix. For example, for the original Jacobson shopper for week 7:

$$[.507 \quad .181 \quad .313] \begin{bmatrix} .80 & .10 & .1 \\ .05 & .85 & .1 \\ .05 & .15 & .8 \end{bmatrix} = [.430 \quad .251 \quad .319]$$

Notice that Foodtown's decline has been reversed. We could perform similar calculations for the original Foodtown and Fred's shoppers, but if we move directly to the steady-state probabilities, we find the following market shares: Jacobson's, 20%; Foodtown, 40%; and Fred's, 40%.

We suspect, however, that after seeing the trend determined by Foodtown's coupon program, Jacobson's executives would implement a strategy that would again change the transition matrix.

General Questions and Assignments

1. Discuss the similarities and differences between *Markov-process models* and *dynamic programming models*.
2. Discuss in your own terms what decision situation characteristics fit the Markov-process model.

3. In a Markov model, transition probabilities are used in the analysis. Discuss what transition probabilities are. Use an original example to show how the transition probabilities would be generated.
4. Using an example from your major area of study, write a short case or problem which can be analyzed using a Markov model.
5. Explain in your own terms what is meant by the *steady state* in a Markov model.
6. Locate two or more articles describing applications of the Markov-process model. Write a paper summarizing these applications. Comment on how useful the model was in these situations.

Exercises and Application Problems

1. The registrar at State University has been asked by the executive vice-president to perform a study of student enrollment. Specifically, the vice-president wants to know what the real increase in enrollment will be at the end of four years if 200 new students are admitted each year. The school has no graduate programs; student classifications are freshman, sophomore, junior, and senior.

   After studying past records, the registrar determined the following transition matrix:

	To					
From	Quit	Freshman	Sophomore	Junior	Senior	Graduate
Quit	1.00	0.00	0.00	0.00	0.00	0.00
Freshman	0.52	0.10	0.38	0.00	0.00	0.00
Sophomore	0.24	0.00	0.08	0.68	0.00	0.00
Junior	0.18	0.00	0.00	0.10	0.72	0.00
Senior	0.00	0.00	0.00	0.00	0.13	0.87
Graduate	0.00	0.00	0.00	0.00	0.00	0.00

   Based on these data, what would the enrollment be after 4 years of admitting 200 new students each year?
2. Referring to problem 1, suppose the recruiting plan is to admit 50 new students in year 1, 100 new students in year 2, 150 students in year 3, and 200 new students in year 4. How will this admittance policy affect total enrollment over 4 years?
3. Suppose four major manufacturers of golf balls supply a given market. The following data show the sales by each company during the previous month:

Company	Sales
A	1000 dozen
B	1500 dozen
C	4000 dozen
D	500 dozen

   Golfers tend to change equipment periodically, including the brand of golf ball they use. Suppose managers for company D have been tracking this particular market and have determined the following probabilities that golfers will change brands on their next purchase:

	To			
From	A	B	C	D
A	.30	.20	.40	.10
B	.10	.40	.20	.30
C	.25	.15	.55	.05
D	.05	.10	.05	.80

a. Considering the current market shares for the four companies, what market share should company D expect in the long run? Use a Markov-process model.

b. State clearly all assumptions that must be made to apply the Markov model in part **a**.

4. Referring to problem 3, suppose company D plans to offer a discount on its golf balls. The marketing director thinks this discount will affect the brand-switching probabilities, as follows:

	To			
From	A	B	C	D
A	.30	.10	.35	.25
B	.10	.30	.15	.45
C	.20	.15	.50	.15
D	.05	.05	.05	.85

a. What effect will the cost reduction have on long-term market share?

b. Suppose that in a given month the total demand in the market area will be 10,000 dozen golf balls. What advice would you give company D if the proposed price cut was $2 per dozen?

5. Referring to problems 3 and 4, suppose company D plans to offer the discount ($2 per dozen golf balls) for only 3 months. Should the company go ahead with the plan? Assume demand is 10,000 dozen balls per month.

6. Referring to problems 3–5, suppose that company D does run the sale for 3 months and then rolls the price back to the original (prediscount) level. Further suppose the probabilities of brand switching shown in problem 4 hold during the sale but the probabilities shown in problem 3 take over again after period 3. What will be the long-term market share for each of the four companies? What assumptions must be made to analyze this problem using a Markov-process model?

7. The Guardian National Bank has three branches. Currently, 30% of its customers use branch A, 50% use branch B, and the rest use branch C. However, Guardian National has noticed that customers sometimes switch from one branch to another. Assume the following table shows the probabilities of customers switching between the branches:

	To Branch		
From Branch	A	B	C
A	.70	.20	.10
B	.25	.60	.15
C	.20	.20	.60

a. If the above probabilities remain in effect, what will be the customer distribution at the three branches after two periods?
b. Suppose the above branch-switching probabilities stay in effect indefinitely. What will be the long-term distribution of customers using the three branches?

8. Referring to problem 7, suppose the Guardian National Bank has changed its banking practices, offering attractive incentives to discourage customers from switching to another branch once they start banking at branch A. The new policy has been well received and has effectively reduced to zero the movement out of branch A. The revised branch-switching probabilities are shown below:

	To Branch		
From Branch	A	B	C
A	1.00	0.00	0.00
B	0.25	0.60	0.15
C	0.20	0.20	0.60

Using these data, and assuming that the initial distribution of use is the same as for problem 7, what will be the long-term effect of this new policy on distribution of use at the three branches?

9. A local video rental store has three outlets. Currently, customers must return a video to the same outlet it was rented from. The most recent data indicate that 30% of the rentals occurred at outlet A, 30% at outlet B, and the remainder at outlet C. However, the owner is considering a new policy that would allow customers to return a video to any of the three outlets, regardless of where it was rented, on the condition that the next video is rented at the return location. On the basis of a survey done recently, the manager has determined that the following probabilities reflect the distribution of video returns:

	Returned To		
Rented From	A	B	C
A	.80	.15	.05
B	.20	.70	.10
C	.05	.10	.85

a. If we can assume that 1400 people each rent a single video each week, what is the expected number of videos that will be returned to outlet B after 3 weeks under the new policy?
b. Suppose the manager decided to continue this policy indefinitely. What would be the expected percentage of returns to each outlet at some point in the future? Would you recommend that the manager institute this policy? What factors would have to be considered?

10. The Bronco Athletic Association (BAA), the booster group for the university's athletic department, raises money by selling memberships in the group. There are four BAA membership categories:

Colt ($30)	Stallion ($100)
Bronco ($50)	Steed ($500)

Currently, 40% of the memberships are Colts, 30% are Broncos, 20% are Stallions, and 10% are Steeds. In an effort to raise more money, the BAA is planning a new marketing program. In addition to attracting new members, they hope that they can get people to increase the level of their membership. The company that is consulting with the BAA on the marketing campaign has assessed the following transition probabilities, based on its experience in other locations:

	To Membership Category				
From	Colt	Bronco	Stallion	Steed	Quit
Colt	.60	.20	.10	.00	.10
Bronco	.30	.40	.20	.05	.05
Stallion	.10	.20	.50	.15	.05
Steed	.05	.10	.20	.60	.05

a. If the BAA goes ahead with this plan next year, what will be the net change in revenue from membership sales to existing members, assuming that total revenues this year were $500,000?
b. In the long run, what percentage of the current members will have quit the BAA?

Chapter Glossary

Absorbing state A state for which the probability of making a transition out is zero. Once an outcome reaches an absorbing state, it will remain there forever.

Fundamental matrix Determined only for processes with absorbing states, this matrix determines the average number of periods a process will remain in a nonabsorbing state before finally entering an absorbing state.

Markov process A stochastic process in which the transition from one state to the next is determined by a known set of probabilities that are independent of how the system arrived at its present state.

Probability of absorption The probability that a system currently in a nonabsorbing state will move to an absorbing state in the next trial or period of the system.

State The condition of the system at each trial or period of the process.

Steady-state probabilities The probabilities of finding the process in any of the outcome states after a large number of periods or trials of the system; once reached, further trials of the system will not change the steady-state probabilities.

Transition matrix A matrix formed of all p_{ij} transition probabilities.

Transition probabilities Assuming the system is at state i during the current trial or period of the process, the transition probability, p_{ij}, represents the probability the process will move to state j during the next period.

Chapter References

BOOKS

Freedman, D. *Markov Chains.* Orlando, Fla.: Academic, 1970.

Hillier, F., and G. J. Lieberman. *Introduction to Operations Research*, 4th ed. Oakland, Calif.: Holden-Day, 1986.

Kemeny, J. G., A. Schleifer, Jr., J. L. Snell, and G. L. Thompson. *Finite Mathematics with Business Applications.* Englewood Cliffs, N.J.: Prentice-Hall, 1972.

Martin, J. J. *Bayesian Decision Problems and Markov Chains.* New York: Wiley, 1967.

ARTICLES

Bessent, W. E., and A. M. Bessent. "Student Flow in a University Department: Results of a Markov Analysis." *Interfaces*, Vol. 10, 1980.

Brodheim, E., and G. P. Prastacos. "The Long Island Blood Distribution System as a Prototype for Regional Planning." *Interfaces*, Vol. 9, 1979.

Flamholts, E., G. Geis, and R. Perle. "A Markovian Model for the Evaluation of Human Assets Acquired by an Organizational Purchase." *Interfaces*, Vol. 14, 1984.

Kamal, G., R. B. Kulkarni, and G. B. Way. "A Statewide Pavement Management System." *Interfaces*, Vol. 12, 1982.

Liebman, L. H. "A Markov Decision Model for Selecting Optimal Credit Control Policies." *Management Science*, Vol. 18, 1972.

Meridith, J. "A Markovian Analysis of a Geriatric Ward." *Management Science*, Vol. 19, 1973.

Mini Case

CASE 18
SALISBURY PHARMACEUTICALS

Dick Salisbury has started to question the advice he has been getting about his long-distance telephone service. Several years ago, Dick both subscribed to 800 long-distance service and installed a fax machine to allow his sales staff to contact more customers and, hopefully, to reduce the sales cost-to-revenue ratio. Now Dick has begun to wonder if all customers react the same, regardless of whether service is by telephone or fax, or whether he should develop a differentiated sales strategy. As a starting point in this analysis, Dick classified customers into three categories:

A. Long-term, loyal customers who purchase substantial amounts
B. Long-term customers who purchase varying amounts
C. Recent customers who purchase varying amounts

Each category A company represents an operational profit (before sales expense) of $100,000 for Salisbury Pharmaceuticals. Each category B company nets $50,00; and each category C company, $10,000.

Dick is considering three sales strategies:

1. Quarterly personal sales calls, frequent phone calls and fax messages
2. Monthly personal sales calls, frequent phone calls and fax messages
3. Weekly personal sales calls, infrequent phone calls and fax messages

The projected yearly costs of these strategies, per customer, are: strategy 1, $10,000; strategy 2, $16,000; and strategy 3, $24,000.

Since category A companies are the most profitable for Salisbury, the company's overall goal is to have as many customers in this category as possible. Currently, 40% of all customers fall into this category and 30% are in each of the other two categories. Having taken a course in management science, Dick is familiar with transition probabilities and has constructed the following tables for the three strategies:

STRATEGY 1

Category Next Period	Category This Period A	B	C
A	.92	.05	.03
B	.04	.85	.11
C	.02	.08	.90

STRATEGY 2

Category Next Period	Category This Period A	B	C
A	.94	.04	.02
B	.08	.85	.07
C	.06	.09	.85

STRATEGY 3

Category Next Period	Category This Period A	B	C
A	.97	.02	.01
B	.12	.86	.02
C	.09	.10	.81

Dick wants to stress the sales strategy that has the best long-term impact on the profitability of the firm.

Appendixes

A Binomial Distribution

B Standard Normal Distribution

C Poisson Probability Distribution

D Uniform Random Number

APPENDIX A BINOMIAL DISTRIBUTION

$$P(x_1) = \frac{n!}{x_1!(n - x_1)!} p^{x_1}(q)^{n - x_1}$$

$n = 1$

x_1	$p = .01$	$p = .02$	$p = .03$	$p = .04$	$p = .05$	$p = .06$	$p = .07$	$p = .08$	$p = .09$	$p = .10$	$n - x_1$
0	.9900	.9800	.9700	.9600	.9500	.9400	.9300	.9200	.9100	.9000	1
1	.0100	.0200	.0300	.0400	.0500	.0600	.0700	.0800	.0900	.1000	0
	$q = .99$	$q = .98$	$q = .97$	$q = .96$	$q = .95$	$q = .94$	$q = .93$	$q = .92$	$q = .91$	$q = .90$	
x_1	$p = .11$	$p = .12$	$p = .13$	$p = .14$	$p = .15$	$p = .16$	$p = .17$	$p = .18$	$p = .19$	$p = .20$	$n - x_1$
0	.8900	.8800	.8700	.8600	.8500	.8400	.8300	.8200	.8100	.8000	1
1	.1100	.1200	.1300	.1400	.1500	.1600	.1700	.1800	.1900	.2000	0
	$q = .89$	$q = .88$	$q = .87$	$q = .86$	$q = .85$	$q = .84$	$q = .83$	$q = .82$	$q = .81$	$q = .80$	
x_1	$p = .21$	$p = .22$	$p = .23$	$p = .24$	$p = .25$	$p = .26$	$p = .27$	$p = .28$	$p = .29$	$p = .30$	$n - x_1$
0	.7900	.7800	.7700	.7600	.7500	.7400	.7300	.7200	.7100	.7000	1
1	.2100	.2200	.2300	.2400	.2500	.2600	.2700	.2800	.2900	.3000	0
	$q = .79$	$q = .78$	$q = .77$	$q = .76$	$q = .75$	$q = .74$	$q = .73$	$q = .72$	$q = .71$	$q = .70$	
x_1	$p = .31$	$p = .32$	$p = .33$	$p = .34$	$p = .35$	$p = .36$	$p = .37$	$p = .38$	$p = .39$	$p = .40$	$n - x_1$
0	.6900	.6800	.6700	.6600	.6500	.6400	.6300	.6200	.6100	.6000	1
1	.3100	.3200	.3300	.3400	.3500	.3600	.3700	.3800	.3900	.4000	0
	$q = .69$	$q = .68$	$q = .67$	$q = .66$	$q = .65$	$q = .64$	$q = .63$	$q = .62$	$q = .61$	$q = .60$	
x_1	$p = .41$	$p = .42$	$p = .43$	$p = .44$	$p = .45$	$p = .46$	$p = .47$	$p = .48$	$p = .49$	$p = .50$	$n - x_1$
0	.5900	.5800	.5700	.5600	.5500	.5400	.5300	.5200	.5100	.5000	1
1	.4100	.4200	.4300	.4400	.4500	.4600	.4700	.4800	.4900	.5000	0
	$q = .59$	$q = .58$	$q = .57$	$q = .56$	$q = .55$	$q = .54$	$q = .53$	$q = .52$	$q = .51$	$q = .50$	

$n = 2$

x_1	$p = .01$	$p = .02$	$p = .03$	$p = .04$	$p = .05$	$p = .06$	$p = .07$	$p = .08$	$p = .09$	$p = .10$	$n - x_1$
0	.9801	.9604	.9409	.9216	.9025	.8836	.8649	.8464	.8281	.8100	2
1	.0198	.0392	.0582	.0768	.0950	.1128	.1302	.1472	.1638	.1800	1
2	.0001	.0004	.0009	.0016	.0025	.0036	.0049	.0064	.0081	.0100	0
	$q = .99$	$q = .98$	$q = .97$	$q = .96$	$q = .95$	$q = .94$	$q = .93$	$q = .92$	$q = .91$	$q = .90$	

x_1	$p = .11$	$p = .12$	$p = .13$	$p = .14$	$p = .15$	$p = .16$	$p = .17$	$p = .18$	$p = .19$	$p = .20$	$n - x_1$
0	.7921	.7744	.7569	.7396	.7225	.7056	.6889	.6724	.6561	.6400	2
1	.1958	.2112	.2262	.2408	.2550	.2688	.2822	.2952	.3078	.3200	1
2	.0121	.0144	.0169	.0196	.0225	.0256	.0289	.0324	.0361	.0400	0
	$q = .89$	$q = .88$	$q = .87$	$q = .86$	$q = .85$	$q = .84$	$q = .83$	$q = .82$	$q = .81$	$q = .80$	
x_1	$p = .21$	$p = .22$	$p = .23$	$p = .24$	$p = .25$	$p = .26$	$p = .27$	$p = .28$	$p = .29$	$p = .30$	$n - x_1$
0	.6241	.6084	.5929	.5776	.5625	.5476	.5329	.5184	.5041	.4900	2
1	.3318	.3432	.3542	.3648	.3750	.3848	.3942	.4032	.4118	.4200	1
2	.0441	.0484	.0529	.0576	.0625	.0676	.0729	.0784	.0841	.0900	0
	$q = .79$	$q = .78$	$q = .77$	$q = .76$	$q = .75$	$q = .74$	$q = .73$	$q = .72$	$q = .71$	$q = .70$	
x_1	$p = .31$	$p = .32$	$p = .33$	$p = .34$	$p = .35$	$p = .36$	$p = .37$	$p = .38$	$p = .39$	$p = .40$	$n - x_1$
0	.4761	.4624	.4489	.4356	.4225	.4096	.3969	.3844	.3721	.3600	2
1	.4278	.4352	.4422	.4488	.4550	.4608	.4662	.4712	.4758	.4800	1
2	.0961	.1024	.1089	.1156	.1225	.1296	.1369	.1444	.1521	.1600	0
	$q = .69$	$q = .68$	$q = .67$	$q = .66$	$q = .65$	$q = .64$	$q = .63$	$q = .62$	$q = .61$	$q = .60$	
x_1	$p = .41$	$p = .42$	$p = .43$	$p = .44$	$p = .45$	$p = .46$	$p = .47$	$p = .48$	$p = .49$	$p = .50$	$n - x_1$
0	.3481	.3364	.3249	.3136	.3025	.2916	.2809	.2704	.2601	.2500	2
1	.4838	.4872	.4902	.4928	.4950	.4968	.4982	.4992	.4998	.5000	1
2	.1681	.1764	.1849	.1936	.2025	.2116	.2209	.2304	.2401	.2500	0
	$q = .59$	$q = .58$	$q = .57$	$q = .56$	$q = .55$	$q = .54$	$q = .53$	$q = .52$	$q = .51$	$q = .50$	

$n = 3$

x_1	$p = .01$	$p = .02$	$p = .03$	$p = .04$	$p = .05$	$p = .06$	$p = .07$	$p = .08$	$p = .09$	$p = .10$	$n - x_1$
0	.9703	.9412	.9127	.8847	.8574	.8306	.8044	.7787	.7536	.7290	3
1	.0294	.0576	.0847	.1106	.1354	.1590	.1816	.2031	.2236	.2430	2
2	.0003	.0012	.0026	.0046	.0071	.0102	.0137	.0177	.0221	.0270	1
3	.0000	.0000	.0000	.0001	.0001	.0002	.0003	.0005	.0007	.0010	0
	$q = .99$	$q = .98$	$q = .97$	$q = .96$	$q = .95$	$q = .94$	$q = .93$	$q = .92$	$q = .91$	$q = .90$	
x_1	$p = .11$	$p = .12$	$p = .13$	$p = .14$	$p = .15$	$p = .16$	$p = .17$	$p = .18$	$p = .19$	$p = .20$	$n - x_1$
0	.7050	.6815	.6585	.6361	.6141	.5927	.5718	.5514	.5314	.5120	3
1	.2614	.2788	.2952	.3106	.3251	.3387	.3513	.3631	.3740	.3840	2
2	.0323	.0380	.0441	.0506	.0574	.0645	.0720	.0797	.0877	.0960	1
3	.0013	.0017	.0022	.0027	.0034	.0041	.0049	.0058	.0069	.0080	0
	$q = .89$	$q = .88$	$q = .87$	$q = .86$	$q = .85$	$q = .84$	$q = .83$	$q = .82$	$q = .81$	$q = .80$	

x_1	$p=.21$	$p=.22$	$p=.23$	$p=.24$	$p=.25$	$p=.26$	$p=.27$	$p=.28$	$p=.29$	$p=.30$	$n-x_1$
0	.4930	.4746	.4565	.4390	.4219	.4052	.3890	.3732	.3579	.3430	3
1	.3932	.4015	.4091	.4159	.4219	.4271	.4316	.4355	.4386	.4410	2
2	.1045	.1133	.1222	.1313	.1406	.1501	.1597	.1693	.1791	.1890	1
3	.0093	.0106	.0122	.0138	.0156	.0176	.0197	.0220	.0244	.0270	0
	$q=.79$	$q=.78$	$q=.77$	$q=.76$	$q=.75$	$q=.74$	$q=.73$	$q=.72$	$q=.71$	$q=.70$	
x_1	$p=.31$	$p=.32$	$p=.33$	$p=.34$	$p=.35$	$p=.36$	$p=.37$	$p=.38$	$p=.39$	$p=.40$	$n-x_1$
0	.3285	.3144	.3008	.2875	.2746	.2621	.2500	.2383	.2270	.2160	3
1	.4428	.4439	.4444	.4443	.4436	.4424	.4406	.4382	.4354	.4320	2
2	.1989	.2089	.2189	.2289	.2389	.2488	.2587	.2686	.2783	.2880	1
3	.0298	.0328	.0359	.0393	.0429	.0467	.0507	.0549	.0593	.0640	0
	$q=.69$	$q=.68$	$q=.67$	$q=.66$	$q=.65$	$q=.64$	$q=.63$	$q=.62$	$q=.61$	$q=.60$	
x_1	$p=.41$	$p=.42$	$p=.43$	$p=.44$	$p=.45$	$p=.46$	$p=.47$	$p=.48$	$p=.49$	$p=.50$	$n-x_1$
0	.2054	.1951	.1852	.1756	.1664	.1575	.1489	.1406	.1327	.1250	3
1	.4282	.4239	.4191	.4140	.4084	.4024	.3961	.3894	.3823	.3750	2
2	.2975	.3069	.3162	.3252	.3341	.3428	.3512	.3594	.3674	.3750	1
3	.0689	.0741	.0795	.0852	.0911	.0973	.1038	.1106	.1176	.1250	0
	$q=.59$	$q=.58$	$q=.57$	$q=.56$	$q=.55$	$q=.54$	$q=.53$	$q=.52$	$q=.51$	$q=.50$	

$n = 4$

x_1	$p=.01$	$p=.02$	$p=.03$	$p=.04$	$p=.05$	$p=.06$	$p=.07$	$p=.08$	$p=.09$	$p=.10$	$n-x_1$
0	.9606	.9224	.8853	.8493	.8145	.7807	.7481	.7164	.6857	.6561	4
1	.0388	.0753	.1095	.1416	.1715	.1993	.2252	.2492	.2713	.2916	3
2	.0006	.0023	.0051	.0088	.0135	.0191	.0254	.0325	.0402	.0486	2
3	.0000	.0000	.0001	.0002	.0005	.0008	.0013	.0019	.0027	.0036	1
4	.0000	.0000	.0000	.0000	.0000	.0000	.0000	.0000	.0001	.0001	0
	$q=.99$	$q=.98$	$q=.97$	$q=.96$	$q=.95$	$q=.94$	$q=.93$	$q=.92$	$q=.91$	$q=.90$	
x_1	$p=.11$	$p=.12$	$p=.13$	$p=.14$	$p=.15$	$p=.16$	$p=.17$	$p=.18$	$p=.19$	$p=.20$	$n-x_1$
0	.6274	.5997	.5729	.5470	.5220	.4979	.4746	.4521	.4305	.4096	4
1	.3102	.3271	.3424	.3562	.3685	.3793	.3888	.3970	.4039	.4096	3
2	.0575	.0669	.0767	.0870	.0975	.1084	.1195	.1307	.1421	.1536	2
3	.0047	.0061	.0076	.0094	.0115	.0138	.0163	.0191	.0222	.0256	1
4	.0001	.0002	.0003	.0004	.0005	.0007	.0008	.0010	.0013	.0016	0
	$q=.89$	$q=.88$	$q=.87$	$q=.86$	$q=.85$	$q=.84$	$q=.83$	$q=.82$	$q=.81$	$q=.80$	
x_1	$p=.21$	$p=.22$	$p=.23$	$p=.24$	$p=.25$	$p=.26$	$p=.27$	$p=.28$	$p=.29$	$p=.30$	$n-x_1$
0	.3895	.3702	.3515	.3336	.3164	.2999	.2840	.2687	.2541	.2401	4
1	.4142	.4176	.4200	.4214	.4219	.4214	.4201	.4180	.4152	.4116	3
2	.1651	.1767	.1882	.1996	.2109	.2221	.2331	.2439	.2544	.2646	2
3	.0293	.0332	.0375	.0420	.0469	.0520	.0575	.0632	.0693	.0756	1
4	.0019	.0023	.0028	.0033	.0039	.0046	.0053	.0061	.0071	.0081	0
	$q=.79$	$q=.78$	$q=.77$	$q=.76$	$q=.75$	$q=.74$	$q=.73$	$q=.72$	$q=.71$	$q=.70$	

x_1	$p=.31$	$p=.32$	$p=.33$	$p=.34$	$p=.35$	$p=.36$	$p=.37$	$p=.38$	$p=.39$	$p=.40$	$n-x_1$
0	.2267	.2138	.2015	.1897	.1785	.1678	.1575	.1478	.1385	.1296	4
1	.4074	.4025	.3970	.3910	.3845	.3775	.3701	.3623	.3541	.3456	3
2	.2745	.2841	.2933	.3021	.3105	.3185	.3260	.3330	.3396	.3456	2
3	.0822	.0891	.0963	.1038	.1115	.1194	.1276	.1361	.1447	.1536	1
4	.0092	.0105	.0119	.0134	.0150	.0168	.0187	.0209	.0231	.0256	0
	$q=.69$	$q=.68$	$q=.67$	$q=.66$	$q=.65$	$q=.64$	$q=.63$	$q=.62$	$q=.61$	$q=.60$	

x_1	$p=.41$	$p=.42$	$p=.43$	$p=.44$	$p=.45$	$p=.46$	$p=.47$	$p=.48$	$p=.49$	$p=.50$	$n-x_1$
0	.1212	.1132	.1056	.0983	.0915	.0850	.0789	.0731	.0677	.0625	4
1	.3368	.3278	.3185	.3091	.2995	.2897	.2799	.2700	.2600	.2500	3
2	.3511	.3560	.3604	.3643	.3675	.3702	.3723	.3738	.3747	.3750	2
3	.1627	.1719	.1813	.1908	.2005	.2102	.2201	.2300	.2400	.2500	1
4	.0283	.0311	.0342	.0375	.0410	.0448	.0488	.0531	.0576	.0625	0
	$q=.59$	$q=.58$	$q=.57$	$q=.56$	$q=.55$	$q=.54$	$q=.53$	$q=.52$	$q=.51$	$q=.50$	

$n=5$

x_1	$p=.01$	$p=.02$	$p=.03$	$p=.04$	$p=.05$	$p=.06$	$p=.07$	$p=.08$	$p=.09$	$p=.10$	$n-x_1$
0	.9510	.9039	.8587	.8154	.7738	.7339	.6957	.6591	.6240	.5905	5
1	.0480	.0922	.1328	.1699	.2036	.2342	.2618	.2866	.3086	.3280	4
2	.0010	.0038	.0082	.0142	.0214	.0299	.0394	.0498	.0610	.0729	3
3	.0000	.0001	.0003	.0006	.0011	.0019	.0030	.0043	.0060	.0081	2
4	.0000	.0000	.0000	.0000	.0000	.0001	.0001	.0002	.0003	.0004	1
5	.0000	.0000	.0000	.0000	.0000	.0000	.0000	.0000	.0000	.0000	0
	$q=.99$	$q=.98$	$q=.97$	$q=.96$	$q=.95$	$q=.94$	$q=.93$	$q=.92$	$q=.91$	$q=.90$	

x_1	$p=.11$	$p=.12$	$p=.13$	$p=.14$	$p=.15$	$p=.16$	$p=.17$	$p=.18$	$p=.19$	$p=.20$	$n-x_1$
0	.5584	.5277	.4984	.4704	.4437	.4182	.3939	.3707	.3487	.3277	5
1	.3451	.3598	.3724	.3829	.3915	.3983	.4034	.4069	.4089	.4096	4
2	.0853	.0981	.1113	.1247	.1382	.1517	.1652	.1786	.1919	.2048	3
3	.0105	.0134	.0166	.0203	.0244	.0289	.0338	.0392	.0450	.0512	2
4	.0007	.0009	.0012	.0017	.0022	.0028	.0035	.0043	.0053	.0064	1
5	.0000	.0000	.0000	.0001	.0001	.0001	.0001	.0002	.0002	.0003	0
	$q=.89$	$q=.88$	$q=.87$	$q=.86$	$q=.85$	$q=.84$	$q=.83$	$q=.82$	$q=.81$	$q=.80$	

x_1	$p=.21$	$p=.22$	$p=.23$	$p=.24$	$p=.25$	$p=.26$	$p=.27$	$p=.28$	$p=.29$	$p=.30$	$n-x_1$
0	.3077	.2887	.2707	.2536	.2373	.2219	.2073	.1935	.1804	.1681	5
1	.4090	.4072	.4043	.4003	.3955	.3898	.3834	.3762	.3685	.3601	4
2	.2174	.2297	.2415	.2529	.2637	.2739	.2836	.2926	.3010	.3087	3
3	.0578	.0648	.0721	.0798	.0879	.0962	.1049	.1138	.1229	.1323	2
4	.0077	.0091	.0108	.0126	.0146	.0169	.0194	.0221	.0251	.0283	1
5	.0004	.0005	.0006	.0008	.0010	.0012	.0014	.0017	.0021	.0024	0
	$q=.79$	$q=.78$	$q=.77$	$q=.76$	$q=.75$	$q=.74$	$q=.73$	$q=.72$	$q=.71$	$q=.70$	

x_1	$p = .31$	$p = .32$	$p = .33$	$p = .34$	$p = .35$	$p = .36$	$p = .37$	$p = .38$	$p = .39$	$p = .40$	$n - x_1$
0	.1564	.1454	.1350	.1252	.1160	.1074	.0992	.0916	.0845	.0778	5
1	.3513	.3421	.3325	.3226	.3124	.3020	.2914	.2808	.2700	.2592	4
2	.3157	.3220	.3275	.3323	.3364	.3397	.3423	.3441	.3452	.3456	3
3	.1418	.1515	.1613	.1712	.1811	.1911	.2010	.2109	.2207	.2304	2
4	.0319	.0357	.0397	.0441	.0488	.0537	.0590	.0646	.0706	.0768	1
5	.0029	.0034	.0039	.0045	.0053	.0060	.0069	.0079	.0090	.0102	0
	$q = .69$	$q = .68$	$q = .67$	$q = .66$	$q = .65$	$q = .64$	$q = .63$	$q = .62$	$q = .61$	$q = .60$	

x_1	$p = .41$	$p = .42$	$p = .43$	$p = .44$	$p = .45$	$p = .46$	$p = .47$	$p = .48$	$p = .49$	$p = .50$	$n - x_1$
0	.0715	.0656	.0602	.0551	.0503	.0459	.0418	.0380	.0345	.0312	5
1	.2484	.2376	.2270	.2164	.2059	.1956	.1854	.1755	.1657	.1562	4
2	.3452	.3442	.3424	.3400	.3369	.3332	.3289	.3240	.3185	.3125	3
3	.2399	.2492	.2583	.2671	.2757	.2838	.2916	.2990	.3060	.3125	2
4	.0834	.0902	.0974	.1049	.1128	.1209	.1293	.1380	.1470	.1563	1
5	.0116	.0131	.0147	.0165	.0185	.0206	.0229	.0255	.0282	.0313	0
	$q = .59$	$q = .58$	$q = .57$	$q = .56$	$q = .55$	$q = .54$	$q = .53$	$q = .52$	$q = .51$	$q = .50$	

$n = 10$

x_1	$p = .01$	$p = .02$	$p = .03$	$p = .04$	$p = .05$	$p = .06$	$p = .07$	$p = .08$	$p = .09$	$p = .10$	$n - x_1$
0	.9044	.8171	.7374	.6648	.5987	.5386	.4840	.4344	.3894	.3487	10
1	.0914	.1667	.2281	.2770	.3151	.3438	.3643	.3777	.3851	.3874	9
2	.0042	.0153	.0317	.0519	.0746	.0988	.1234	.1478	.1714	.1937	8
3	.0001	.0008	.0026	.0058	.0105	.0168	.0248	.0343	.0452	.0574	7
4	.0000	.0000	.0001	.0004	.0010	.0019	.0033	.0052	.0078	.0112	6
5	.0000	.0000	.0000	.0000	.0001	.0001	.0003	.0005	.0009	.0015	5
6	.0000	.0000	.0000	.0000	.0000	.0000	.0000	.0000	.0001	.0001	4
7	.0000	.0000	.0000	.0000	.0000	.0000	.0000	.0000	.0000	.0000	3
8	.0000	.0000	.0000	.0000	.0000	.0000	.0000	.0000	.0000	.0000	2
9	.0000	.0000	.0000	.0000	.0000	.0000	.0000	.0000	.0000	.0000	1
10	.0000	.0000	.0000	.0000	.0000	.0000	.0000	.0000	.0000	.0000	0
	$q = .99$	$q = .98$	$q = .97$	$q = .96$	$q = .95$	$q = .94$	$q = .93$	$q = .92$	$q = .91$	$q = .90$	

x_1	$p = .11$	$p = .12$	$p = .13$	$p = .14$	$p = .15$	$p = .16$	$p = .17$	$p = .18$	$p = .19$	$p = .20$	$n - x_1$
0	.3118	.2785	.2484	.2213	.1969	.1749	.1552	.1374	.1216	.1074	10
1	.3854	.3798	.3712	.3603	.3474	.3331	.3178	.3017	.2852	.2684	9
2	.2143	.2330	.2496	.2639	.2759	.2856	.2929	.2980	.3010	.3020	8
3	.0706	.0847	.0995	.1146	.1298	.1450	.1600	.1745	.1883	.2013	7
4	.0153	.0202	.0260	.0326	.0401	.0483	.0573	.0670	.0773	.0881	6
5	.0023	.0033	.0047	.0064	.0085	.0111	.0141	.0177	.0218	.0264	5
6	.0002	.0004	.0006	.0009	.0012	.0018	.0024	.0032	.0043	.0055	4
7	.0000	.0000	.0000	.0001	.0001	.0002	.0003	.0004	.0006	.0008	3
8	.0000	.0000	.0000	.0000	.0000	.0000	.0000	.0000	.0001	.0001	2
9	.0000	.0000	.0000	.0000	.0000	.0000	.0000	.0000	.0000	.0000	1
10	.0000	.0000	.0000	.0000	.0000	.0000	.0000	.0000	.0000	.0000	0
	$q = .89$	$q = .88$	$q = .87$	$q = .86$	$q = .85$	$q = .84$	$q = .83$	$q = .82$	$q = .81$	$q = .80$	

x_1	$p = .21$	$p = .22$	$p = .23$	$p = .24$	$p = .25$	$p = .26$	$p = .27$	$p = .28$	$p = .29$	$p = .30$	$n - x_1$
0	.0947	.0834	.0733	.0643	.0563	.0492	.0430	.0374	.0326	.0282	10
1	.2517	.2351	.2188	.2030	.1877	.1730	.1590	.1456	.1330	.1211	9
2	.3011	.2984	.2942	.2885	.2816	.2735	.2646	.2548	.2444	.2335	8
3	.2134	.2244	.2343	.2429	.2503	.2563	.2609	.2642	.2662	.2668	7
4	.0993	.1108	.1225	.1343	.1460	.1576	.1689	.1798	.1903	.2001	6
5	.0317	.0375	.0439	.0509	.0584	.0664	.0750	.0839	.0933	.1029	5
6	.0070	.0088	.0109	.0134	.0162	.0195	.0231	.0272	.0317	.0368	4
7	.0011	.0014	.0019	.0024	.0031	.0039	.0049	.0060	.0074	.0090	3
8	.0001	.0002	.0002	.0003	.0004	.0005	.0007	.0009	.0011	.0014	2
9	.0000	.0000	.0000	.0000	.0000	.0000	.0001	.0001	.0001	.0001	1
10	.0000	.0000	.0000	.0000	.0000	.0000	.0000	.0000	.0000	.0000	0
	$q = .79$	$q = .78$	$q = .77$	$q = .76$	$q = .75$	$q = .74$	$q = .73$	$q = .72$	$q = .71$	$q = .70$	

x_1	$p = .31$	$p = .32$	$p = .33$	$p = .34$	$p = .35$	$p = .36$	$p = .37$	$p = .38$	$p = .39$	$p = .40$	$n - x_1$
0	.0245	.0211	.0182	.0157	.0135	.0115	.0098	.0084	.0071	.0060	10
1	.1099	.0995	.0898	.0808	.0725	.0649	.0578	.0514	.0456	.0403	9
2	.2222	.2107	.1990	.1873	.1757	.1642	.1529	.1419	.1312	.1209	8
3	.2662	.2644	.2614	.2573	.2522	.2462	.2394	.2319	.2237	.2150	7
4	.2093	.2177	.2253	.2320	.2377	.2424	.2461	.2487	.2503	.2508	6
5	.1128	.1229	.1332	.1434	.1536	.1636	.1734	.1829	.1920	.2007	5
6	.0422	.0482	.0547	.0616	.0689	.0767	.0849	.0934	.1023	.1115	4
7	.0108	.0130	.0154	.0181	.0212	.0247	.0285	.0327	.0374	.0425	3
8	.0018	.0023	.0028	.0035	.0043	.0052	.0063	.0075	.0090	.0106	2
9	.0002	.0002	.0003	.0004	.0005	.0006	.0008	.0010	.0013	.0016	1
10	.0000	.0000	.0000	.0000	.0000	.0000	.0000	.0001	.0001	.0001	0
	$q = .69$	$q = .68$	$q = .67$	$q = .66$	$q = .65$	$q = .64$	$q = .63$	$q = .62$	$q = .61$	$q = .60$	

x_1	$p = .41$	$p = .42$	$p = .43$	$p = .44$	$p = .45$	$p = .46$	$p = .47$	$p = .48$	$p = .49$	$p = .50$	$n - x_1$
0	.0051	.0043	.0036	.0030	.0025	.0021	.0017	.0014	.0012	.0010	10
1	.0355	.0312	.0273	.0238	.0207	.0180	.0155	.0133	.0114	.0098	9
2	.1111	.1017	.0927	.0843	.0763	.0688	.0619	.0554	.0494	.0439	8
3	.2058	.1963	.1865	.1765	.1665	.1564	.1464	.1364	.1267	.1172	7
4	.2503	.2488	.2462	.2427	.2384	.2331	.2271	.2204	.2130	.2051	6
5	.2087	.2162	.2229	.2289	.2340	.2383	.2417	.2441	.2456	.2461	5
6	.1209	.1304	.1401	.1499	.1596	.1692	.1786	.1878	.1966	.2051	4
7	.0480	.0540	.0604	.0673	.0746	.0824	.0905	.0991	.1080	.1172	3
8	.0125	.0147	.0171	.0198	.0229	.0263	.0301	.0343	.0389	.0439	2
9	.0019	.0024	.0029	.0035	.0042	.0050	.0059	.0070	.0083	.0098	1
10	.0001	.0002	.0002	.0003	.0003	.0004	.0005	.0006	.0008	.0010	0
	$q = .59$	$q = .58$	$q = .57$	$q = .56$	$q = .55$	$q = .54$	$q = .53$	$q = .52$	$q = .51$	$q = .50$	

$n = 20$

x_1	$p=.01$	$p=.02$	$p=.03$	$p=.04$	$p=.05$	$p=.06$	$p=.07$	$p=.08$	$p=.09$	$p=.10$	$n-x_1$
0	.8179	.6676	.5438	.4420	.3585	.2901	.2342	.1887	.1516	.1216	20
1	.1652	.2725	.3364	.3683	.3774	.3703	.3526	.3282	.3000	.2702	19
2	.0159	.0528	.0988	.1458	.1887	.2246	.2521	.2711	.2818	.2852	18
3	.0010	.0065	.0183	.0364	.0596	.0860	.1139	.1414	.1672	.1901	17
4	.0000	.0006	.0024	.0065	.0133	.0233	.0364	.0523	.0703	.0898	16
5	.0000	.0000	.0002	.0009	.0022	.0048	.0088	.0145	.0222	.0319	15
6	.0000	.0000	.0000	.0001	.0003	.0008	.0017	.0032	.0055	.0089	14
7	.0000	.0000	.0000	.0000	.0000	.0001	.0002	.0005	.0011	.0020	13
8	.0000	.0000	.0000	.0000	.0000	.0000	.0000	.0001	.0002	.0004	12
9	.0000	.0000	.0000	.0000	.0000	.0000	.0000	.0000	.0000	.0001	11
	$q=.99$	$q=.98$	$q=.97$	$q=.96$	$q=.95$	$q=.94$	$q=.93$	$q=.92$	$q=.91$	$q=.90$	

x_1	$p=.11$	$p=.12$	$p=.13$	$p=.14$	$p=.15$	$p=.16$	$p=.17$	$p=.18$	$p=.19$	$p=.20$	$n-x_1$
0	.0972	.0776	.0617	.0490	.0388	.0306	.0241	.0189	.0148	.0115	20
1	.2403	.2115	.1844	.1595	.1368	.1165	.0986	.0829	.0693	.0576	19
2	.2822	.2740	.2618	.2466	.2293	.2109	.1919	.1730	.1545	.1369	18
3	.2093	.2242	.2347	.2409	.2428	.2410	.2358	.2278	.2175	.2054	17
4	.1099	.1299	.1491	.1666	.1821	.1951	.2053	.2125	.2168	.2182	16
5	.0435	.0567	.0713	.0868	.1028	.1189	.1345	.1493	.1627	.1746	15
6	.0134	.0193	.0266	.0353	.0454	.0566	.0689	.0819	.0954	.1091	14
7	.0033	.0053	.0080	.0115	.0160	.0216	.0282	.0360	.0448	.0545	13
8	.0007	.0012	.0019	.0030	.0046	.0067	.0094	.0128	.0171	.0222	12
9	.0001	.0002	.0004	.0007	.0011	.0017	.0026	.0038	.0053	.0074	11
10	.0000	.0000	.0001	.0001	.0002	.0004	.0006	.0009	.0014	.0020	10
11	.0000	.0000	.0000	.0000	.0000	.0001	.0001	.0002	.0003	.0005	9
12	.0000	.0000	.0000	.0000	.0000	.0000	.0000	.0000	.0001	.0001	8
	$q=.89$	$q=.88$	$q=.87$	$q=.86$	$q=.85$	$q=.84$	$q=.83$	$q=.82$	$q=.81$	$q=.80$	

x_1	$p=.21$	$p=.22$	$p=.23$	$p=.24$	$p=.25$	$p=.26$	$p=.27$	$p=.28$	$p=.29$	$p=.30$	$n-x_1$
0	.0090	.0069	.0054	.0041	.0032	.0024	.0018	.0014	.0011	.0008	20
1	.0477	.0392	.0321	.0261	.0211	.0170	.0137	.0109	.0087	.0068	19
2	.1204	.1050	.0910	.0783	.0669	.0569	.0480	.0403	.0336	.0278	18
3	.1920	.1777	.1631	.1484	.1339	.1199	.1065	.0940	.0823	.0716	17
4	.2169	.2131	.2070	.1991	.1897	.1790	.1675	.1553	.1429	.1304	16
5	.1845	.1923	.1979	.2012	.2023	.2013	.1982	.1933	.1868	.1789	15
6	.1226	.1356	.1478	.1589	.1686	.1768	.1833	.1879	.1907	.1916	14
7	.0652	.0765	.0883	.1003	.1124	.1242	.1356	.1462	.1558	.1643	13
8	.0282	.0351	.0429	.0515	.0609	.0709	.0815	.0924	.1034	.1144	12
9	.0100	.0132	.0171	.0217	.0271	.0332	.0402	.0479	.0563	.0654	11
10	.0029	.0041	.0056	.0075	.0099	.0128	.0163	.0205	.0253	.0308	10
11	.0007	.0010	.0015	.0022	.0030	.0041	.0055	.0072	.0094	.0120	9
12	.0001	.0002	.0003	.0005	.0008	.0011	.0015	.0021	.0029	.0039	8
13	.0000	.0000	.0001	.0001	.0002	.0002	.0003	.0005	.0007	.0010	7
14	.0000	.0000	.0000	.0000	.0000	.0000	.0001	.0001	.0001	.0002	6
	$q=.79$	$q=.78$	$q=.77$	$q=.76$	$q=.75$	$q=.74$	$q=.73$	$q=.72$	$q=.71$	$q=.70$	

x_1	$p=.31$	$p=.32$	$p=.33$	$p=.34$	$p=.35$	$p=.36$	$p=.37$	$p=.38$	$p=.39$	$p=.40$	$n-x_1$
0	.0006	.0004	.0003	.0002	.0002	.0001	.0001	.0001	.0001	.0000	20
1	.0054	.0042	.0033	.0025	.0020	.0015	.0011	.0009	.0007	.0005	19
2	.0229	.0188	.0153	.0124	.0100	.0080	.0064	.0050	.0040	.0031	18
3	.0619	.0531	.0453	.0383	.0323	.0270	.0224	.0185	.0152	.0123	17
4	.1181	.1062	.0947	.0839	.0738	.0645	.0559	.0482	.0412	.0350	16
5	.1698	.1599	.1493	.1384	.1272	.1161	.1051	.0945	.0843	.0746	15
6	.1907	.1881	.1839	.1782	.1712	.1632	.1543	.1447	.1347	.1244	14
7	.1714	.1770	.1811	.1836	.1844	.1836	.1812	.1774	.1722	.1659	13
8	.1251	.1354	.1450	.1537	.1614	.1678	.1730	.1767	.1790	.1797	12
9	.0750	.0849	.0952	.1056	.1158	.1259	.1354	.1444	.1526	.1597	11
10	.0370	.0440	.0516	.0598	.0686	.0779	.0875	.0974	.1073	.1171	10
11	.0151	.0188	.0231	.0280	.0336	.0398	.0467	.0542	.0624	.0710	9
12	.0051	.0066	.0085	.0108	.0136	.0168	.0206	.0249	.0299	.0355	8
13	.0014	.0019	.0026	.0034	.0045	.0058	.0074	.0094	.0118	.0146	7
14	.0003	.0005	.0006	.0009	.0012	.0016	.0022	.0029	.0038	.0049	6
15	.0001	.0001	.0001	.0002	.0003	.0004	.0005	.0007	.0010	.0013	5
16	.0000	.0000	.0000	.0000	.0000	.0001	.0001	.0001	.0002	.0003	4
	$q=.69$	$q=.68$	$q=.67$	$q=.66$	$q=.65$	$q=.64$	$q=.63$	$q=.62$	$q=.61$	$q=.60$	

x_1	$p=.41$	$p=.42$	$p=.43$	$p=.44$	$p=.45$	$p=.46$	$p=.47$	$p=.48$	$p=.49$	$p=.50$	$n-x_1$
0	.0000	.0000	.0000	.0000	.0000	.0000	.0000	.0000	.0000	.0000	20
1	.0004	.0003	.0002	.0001	.0001	.0001	.0001	.0000	.0000	.0000	19
2	.0024	.0018	.0014	.0011	.0008	.0006	.0005	.0003	.0002	.0002	18
3	.0100	.0080	.0064	.0051	.0040	.0031	.0024	.0019	.0014	.0011	17
4	.0295	.0247	.0206	.0170	.0139	.0113	.0092	.0074	.0059	.0046	16
5	.0656	.0573	.0496	.0427	.0365	.0309	.0260	.0217	.0180	.0148	15
6	.1140	.1037	.0936	.0839	.0746	.0658	.0577	.0501	.0432	.0370	14
7	.1585	.1502	.1413	.1318	.1221	.1122	.1023	.0925	.0830	.0739	13
8	.1790	.1768	.1732	.1683	.1623	.1553	.1474	.1388	.1296	.1201	12
9	.1658	.1707	.1742	.1763	.1771	.1763	.1742	.1708	.1661	.1602	11
10	.1268	.1359	.1446	.1524	.1593	.1652	.1700	.1734	.1755	.1762	10
11	.0801	.0895	.0991	.1089	.1185	.1280	.1370	.1455	.1533	.1602	9
12	.0417	.0486	.0561	.0642	.0727	.0818	.0911	.1007	.1105	.1201	8
13	.0178	.0217	.0260	.0310	.0366	.0429	.0497	.0572	.0653	.0739	7
14	.0062	.0078	.0098	.0122	.0150	.0183	.0221	.0264	.0314	.0370	6
15	.0017	.0023	.0030	.0038	.0049	.0062	.0078	.0098	.0121	.0148	5
16	.0004	.0005	.0007	.0009	.0013	.0017	.0022	.0028	.0036	.0046	4
17	.0001	.0001	.0001	.0002	.0002	.0003	.0005	.0006	.0008	.0011	3
18	.0000	.0000	.0000	.0000	.0000	.0000	.0001	.0001	.0001	.0002	2
	$q=.59$	$q=.58$	$q=.57$	$q=.56$	$q=.55$	$q=.54$	$q=.53$	$q=.52$	$q=.51$	$q=.50$	

$n = 25$

x_1	$p = .01$	$p = .02$	$p = .03$	$p = .04$	$p = .05$	$p = .06$	$p = .07$	$p = .08$	$p = .09$	$p = .10$	$n - x_1$
0	.7778	.6035	.4670	.3604	.2774	.2129	.1630	.1244	.0946	.0718	25
1	.1964	.3079	.3611	.3754	.3650	.3398	.3066	.2704	.2340	.1994	24
2	.0238	.0754	.1340	.1877	.2305	.2602	.2770	.2821	.2777	.2659	23
3	.0018	.0118	.0318	.0600	.0930	.1273	.1598	.1881	.2106	.2265	22
4	.0001	.0013	.0054	.0137	.0269	.0447	.0662	.0899	.1145	.1384	21
5	.0000	.0001	.0007	.0024	.0060	.0120	.0209	.0329	.0476	.0646	20
6	.0000	.0000	.0001	.0003	.0010	.0026	.0052	.0095	.0157	.0239	19
7	.0000	.0000	.0000	.0000	.0001	.0004	.0011	.0022	.0042	.0072	18
8	.0000	.0000	.0000	.0000	.0000	.0001	.0002	.0004	.0009	.0018	17
9	.0000	.0000	.0000	.0000	.0000	.0000	.0000	.0001	.0002	.0004	16
10	.0000	.0000	.0000	.0000	.0000	.0000	.0000	.0000	.0000	.0001	15
	$q = .99$	$q = .98$	$q = .97$	$q = .96$	$q = .95$	$q = .94$	$q = .93$	$q = .92$	$q = .91$	$q = .90$	

x_1	$p = .11$	$p = .12$	$p = .13$	$p = .14$	$p = .15$	$p = .16$	$p = .17$	$p = .18$	$p = .19$	$p = .20$	$n - x_1$
0	.0543	.0409	.0308	.0230	.0172	.0128	.0095	.0070	.0052	.0038	25
1	.1678	.1395	.1149	.0938	.0759	.0609	.0486	.0384	.0302	.0236	24
2	.2488	.2283	.2060	.1832	.1607	.1392	.1193	.1012	.0851	.0708	23
3	.2358	.2387	.2360	.2286	.2174	.2033	.1874	.1704	.1530	.1358	22
4	.1603	.1790	.1940	.2047	.2110	.2130	.2111	.2057	.1974	.1867	21
5	.0832	.1025	.1217	.1399	.1564	.1704	.1816	.1897	.1945	.1960	20
6	.0343	.0466	.0606	.0759	.0920	.1082	.1240	.1388	.1520	.1633	19
7	.0115	.0173	.0246	.0336	.0441	.0559	.0689	.0827	.0968	.1108	18
8	.0032	.0053	.0083	.0123	.0175	.0240	.0318	.0408	.0511	.0623	17
9	.0007	.0014	.0023	.0038	.0058	.0086	.0123	.0169	.0226	.0294	16
10	.0001	.0003	.0006	.0010	.0016	.0026	.0040	.0059	.0085	.0118	15
11	.0000	.0001	.0001	.0002	.0004	.0007	.0011	.0018	.0027	.0040	14
12	.0000	.0000	.0000	.0000	.0001	.0002	.0003	.0005	.0007	.0012	13
13	.0000	.0000	.0000	.0000	.0000	.0000	.0001	.0001	.0002	.0003	12
14	.0000	.0000	.0000	.0000	.0000	.0000	.0000	.0000	.0000	.0001	11
	$q = .89$	$q = .88$	$q = .87$	$q = .86$	$q = .85$	$q = .84$	$q = .83$	$q = .82$	$q = .81$	$q = .80$	

x_1	$p = .21$	$p = .22$	$p = .23$	$p = .24$	$p = .25$	$p = .26$	$p = .27$	$p = .28$	$p = .29$	$p = .30$	$n - x_1$
0	.0028	.0020	.0015	.0010	.0008	.0005	.0004	.0003	.0002	.0001	25
1	.0183	.0141	.0109	.0083	.0063	.0047	.0035	.0026	.0020	.0014	24
2	.0585	.0479	.0389	.0314	.0251	.0199	.0157	.0123	.0096	.0074	23
3	.1192	.1035	.0891	.0759	.0641	.0537	.0446	.0367	.0300	.0243	22
4	.1742	.1606	.1463	.1318	.1175	.1037	.0906	.0785	.0673	.0572	21
5	.1945	.1903	.1836	.1749	.1645	.1531	.1408	.1282	.1155	.1030	20
6	.1724	.1789	.1828	.1841	.1828	.1793	.1736	.1661	.1572	.1472	19
7	.1244	.1369	.1482	.1578	.1654	.1709	.1743	.1754	.1743	.1712	18
8	.0744	.0869	.0996	.1121	.1241	.1351	.1450	.1535	.1602	.1651	17
9	.0373	.0463	.0562	.0669	.0781	.0897	.1013	.1127	.1236	.1336	16
10	.0159	.0209	.0269	.0338	.0417	.0504	.0600	.0701	.0808	.0916	15
11	.0058	.0080	.0109	.0145	.0189	.0242	.0302	.0372	.0450	.0536	14
12	.0018	.0026	.0038	.0054	.0074	.0099	.0130	.0169	.0214	.0268	13
13	.0005	.0007	.0011	.0017	.0025	.0035	.0048	.0066	.0088	.0115	12
14	.0001	.0002	.0003	.0005	.0007	.0010	.0015	.0022	.0031	.0042	11
15	.0000	.0000	.0001	.0001	.0002	.0003	.0004	.0006	.0009	.0013	10
16	.0000	.0000	.0000	.0000	.0000	.0001	.0001	.0002	.0002	.0004	9
17	.0000	.0000	.0000	.0000	.0000	.0000	.0000	.0000	.0001	.0001	8
	$q = .79$	$q = .78$	$q = .77$	$q = .76$	$q = .75$	$q = .74$	$q = .73$	$q = .72$	$q = .71$	$q = .70$	

x_1	$p = .31$	$p = .32$	$p = .33$	$p = .34$	$p = .35$	$p = .36$	$p = .37$	$p = .38$	$p = .39$	$p = .40$	$n - x_1$
0	.0001	.0001	.0000	.0000	.0000	.0000	.0000	.0000	.0000	.0000	25
1	.0011	.0008	.0006	.0004	.0003	.0002	.0001	.0001	.0001	.0000	24
2	.0057	.0043	.0033	.0025	.0018	.0014	.0010	.0007	.0005	.0004	23
3	.0195	.0156	.0123	.0097	.0076	.0058	.0045	.0034	.0026	.0019	22
4	.0482	.0403	.0334	.0274	.0224	.0181	.0145	.0115	.0091	.0071	21
5	.0910	.0797	.0691	.0594	.0506	.0427	.0357	.0297	.0244	.0199	20
6	.1363	.1250	.1134	.1020	.0908	.0801	.0700	.0606	.0520	.0442	19
7	.1662	.1596	.1516	.1426	.1327	.1222	.1115	.1008	.0902	.0800	18
8	.1680	.1690	.1681	.1652	.1607	.1547	.1474	.1390	.1298	.1200	17
9	.1426	.1502	.1563	.1608	.1635	.1644	.1635	.1609	.1567	.1511	16
10	.1025	.1131	.1232	.1325	.1409	.1479	.1536	.1578	.1603	.1612	15
11	.0628	.0726	.0828	.0931	.1034	.1135	.1230	.1319	.1398	.1465	14
12	.0329	.0399	.0476	.0560	.0650	.0745	.0843	.0943	.1043	.1140	13
13	.0148	.0188	.0234	.0288	.0350	.0419	.0495	.0578	.0667	.0760	12
14	.0057	.0076	.0099	.0127	.0161	.0202	.0249	.0304	.0365	.0434	11
15	.0019	.0026	.0036	.0048	.0064	.0083	.0107	.0136	.0171	.0212	10
16	.0005	.0008	.0011	.0015	.0021	.0029	.0039	.0052	.0068	.0088	9
17	.0001	.0002	.0003	.0004	.0006	.0009	.0012	.0017	.0023	.0031	8
18	.0000	.0000	.0001	.0001	.0001	.0002	.0003	.0005	.0007	.0009	7
19	.0000	.0000	.0000	.0000	.0000	.0000	.0001	.0001	.0002	.0002	6
	$q = .69$	$q = .68$	$q = .67$	$q = .66$	$q = .65$	$q = .64$	$q = .63$	$q = .62$	$q = .61$	$q = .60$	

x_1	$p=.41$	$p=.42$	$p=.43$	$p=.44$	$p=.45$	$p=.46$	$p=.47$	$p=.48$	$p=.49$	$p=.50$	$n-x_1$
0	.0000	.0000	.0000	.0000	.0000	.0000	.0000	.0000	.0000	.0000	25
1	.0000	.0000	.0000	.0000	.0000	.0000	.0000	.0000	.0000	.0000	24
2	.0003	.0002	.0001	.0001	.0001	.0000	.0000	.0000	.0000	.0000	23
3	.0014	.0011	.0008	.0006	.0004	.0003	.0002	.0001	.0001	.0001	22
4	.0055	.0042	.0032	.0024	.0018	.0014	.0010	.0007	.0005	.0004	21
5	.0161	.0129	.0102	.0081	.0063	.0049	.0037	.0028	.0021	.0016	20
6	.0372	.0311	.0257	.0211	.0172	.0138	.0110	.0087	.0068	.0053	19
7	.0703	.0611	.0527	.0450	.0381	.0319	.0265	.0218	.0178	.0143	18
8	.1099	.0996	.0895	.0796	.0701	.0612	.0529	.0453	.0384	.0322	17
9	.1442	.1363	.1275	.1181	.1084	.0985	.0886	.0790	.0697	.0609	16
10	.1603	.1579	.1539	.1485	.1419	.1342	.1257	.1166	.1071	.0974	15
11	.1519	.1559	.1583	.1591	.1583	.1559	.1521	.1468	.1404	.1328	14
12	.1232	.1317	.1393	.1458	.1511	.1550	.1573	.1581	.1573	.1550	13
13	.0856	.0954	.1051	.1146	.1236	.1320	.1395	.1460	.1512	.1550	12
14	.0510	.0592	.0680	.0772	.0867	.0964	.1060	.1155	.1245	.1328	11
15	.0260	.0314	.0376	.0445	.0520	.0602	.0690	.0782	.0877	.0974	10
16	.0113	.0142	.0177	.0218	.0266	.0321	.0382	.0451	.0527	.0609	9
17	.0042	.0055	.0071	.0091	.0115	.0145	.0179	.0220	.0268	.0322	8
18	.0013	.0018	.0024	.0032	.0042	.0055	.0071	.0090	.0114	.0143	7
19	.0003	.0005	.0007	.0009	.0013	.0017	.0023	.0031	.0040	.0053	6
20	.0001	.0001	.0001	.0002	.0003	.0004	.0006	.0009	.0012	.0016	5
21	.0000	.0000	.0000	.0000	.0001	.0001	.0001	.0002	.0003	.0004	4
22	.0000	.0000	.0000	.0000	.0000	.0000	.0000	.0000	.0000	.0001	3
	$q=.59$	$q=.58$	$q=.57$	$q=.56$	$q=.55$	$q=.54$	$q=.53$	$q=.52$	$q=.51$	$q=.50$	

$n = 50$

x_1	$p=.01$	$p=.02$	$p=.03$	$p=.04$	$p=.05$	$p=.06$	$p=.07$	$p=.08$	$p=.09$	$p=.10$	$n-x_1$
0	.6050	.3642	.2181	.1299	.0769	.0453	.0266	.0155	.0090	.0052	50
1	.3056	.3716	.3372	.2706	.2025	.1447	.0999	.0672	.0443	.0286	49
2	.0756	.1858	.2555	.2762	.2611	.2262	.1843	.1433	.1073	.0779	48
3	.0122	.0607	.1264	.1842	.2199	.2311	.2219	.1993	.1698	.1386	47
4	.0015	.0145	.0459	.0902	.1360	.1733	.1963	.2037	.1973	.1809	46
5	.0001	.0027	.0131	.0346	.0658	.1018	.1359	.1629	.1795	.1849	45
6	.0000	.0004	.0030	.0108	.0260	.0487	.0767	.1063	.1332	.1541	44
7	.0000	.0001	.0006	.0028	.0086	.0195	.0363	.0581	.0828	.1076	43
8	.0000	.0000	.0001	.0006	.0024	.0067	.0147	.0271	.0440	.0643	42
9	.0000	.0000	.0000	.0001	.0006	.0020	.0052	.0110	.0203	.0333	41
10	.0000	.0000	.0000	.0000	.0001	.0005	.0016	.0039	.0082	.0152	40
11	.0000	.0000	.0000	0000	.0000	.0001	.0004	.0012	.0030	.0061	39
12	.0000	.0000	.0000	.0000	.0000	.0000	.0001	.0004	.0010	.0022	38
13	.0000	.0000	.0000	.0000	.0000	.0000	.0000	.0001	.0003	.0007	37
14	.0000	.0000	.0000	.0000	.0000	.0000	.0000	.0000	.0001	.0002	36
15	.0000	.0000	.0000	.0000	.0000	.0000	.0000	.0000	.0000	.0001	35
	$q=.99$	$q=.98$	$q=.97$	$q=.96$	$q=.95$	$q=.94$	$q=.93$	$q=.92$	$q=.91$	$q=.90$	

x_1	$p = .11$	$p = .12$	$p = .13$	$p = .14$	$p = .15$	$p = .16$	$p = .17$	$p = .18$	$p = .19$	$p = .20$	$n - x_1$
0	.0029	.0017	.0009	.0005	.0003	.0002	.0001	.0000	.0000	.0000	50
1	.0182	.0114	.0071	.0043	.0026	.0016	.0009	.0005	.0003	.0002	49
2	.0552	.0382	.0259	.0172	.0113	.0073	.0046	.0029	.0018	.0011	48
3	.1091	.0833	.0619	.0449	.0319	.0222	.0151	.0102	.0067	.0044	47
4	.1584	.1334	.1086	.0858	.0661	.0496	.0364	.0262	.0185	.0128	46
5	.1801	.1674	.1493	.1286	.1072	.0869	.0687	.0530	.0400	.0295	45
6	.1670	.1712	.1674	.1570	.1419	.1242	.1055	.0872	.0703	.0554	44
7	.1297	.1467	.1572	.1606	.1575	.1487	.1358	.1203	.1037	.0870	43
8	.0862	.1075	.1262	.1406	.1493	.1523	.1495	.1420	.1307	.1169	42
9	.0497	.0684	.0880	.1068	.1230	.1353	.1429	.1454	.1431	.1364	41
10	.0252	.0383	.0539	.0713	.0890	.1057	.1200	.1309	.1376	.1398	40
11	.0113	.0190	.0293	.0422	.0571	.0732	.0894	.1045	.1174	.1271	39
12	.0045	.0084	.0142	.0223	.0328	.0453	.0595	.0745	.0895	.1033	38
13	.0016	.0034	.0062	.0106	.0169	.0252	.0356	.0478	.0613	.0755	37
14	.0005	.0012	.0025	.0046	.0079	.0127	.0193	.0277	.0380	.0499	36
15	.0002	.0004	.0009	.0018	.0033	.0058	.0095	.0146	.0214	.0299	35
16	.0000	.0001	.0003	.0006	.0013	.0024	.0042	.0070	.0110	.0164	34
17	.0000	.0000	.0001	.0002	.0005	.0009	.0017	.0031	.0052	.0082	33
18	.0000	.0000	.0000	.0001	.0001	.0003	.0007	.0012	.0022	.0037	32
19	.0000	.0000	.0000	.0000	.0000	.0001	.0002	.0005	.0009	.0016	31
20	.0000	.0000	.0000	.0000	.0000	.0000	.0001	.0002	.0003	.0006	30
21	.0000	.0000	.0000	.0000	.0000	.0000	.0000	.0000	.0001	.0002	29
22	.0000	.0000	.0000	.0000	.0000	.0000	.0000	.0000	.0000	.0001	28
	$q = .89$	$q = .88$	$q = .87$	$q = .86$	$q = .85$	$q = .84$	$q = .83$	$q = .82$	$q = .81$	$q = .80$	

x_1	$p = .21$	$p = .22$	$p = .23$	$p = .24$	$p = .25$	$p = .26$	$p = .27$	$p = .28$	$p = .29$	$p = .30$	$n - x_1$
0	.0000	.0000	.0000	.0000	.0000	.0000	.0000	.0000	.0000	.0000	50
1	.0001	.0001	.0000	.0000	.0000	.0000	.0000	.0000	.0000	.0000	49
2	.0007	.0004	.0002	.0001	.0001	.0000	.0000	.0000	.0000	.0000	48
3	.0028	.0018	.0011	.0007	.0004	.0002	.0001	.0001	.0000	.0000	47
4	.0088	.0059	.0039	.0025	.0016	.0010	.0006	.0004	.0002	.0001	46
5	.0214	.0152	.0106	.0073	.0049	.0033	.0021	.0014	.0009	.0006	45
6	.0427	.0322	.0238	.0173	.0123	.0087	.0060	.0040	.0027	.0018	44
7	.0713	.0571	.0447	.0344	.0259	.0191	.0139	.0099	.0069	.0048	43
8	.1019	.0865	.0718	.0583	.0463	.0361	.0276	.0207	.0152	.0110	42
9	.1263	.1139	.1001	.0859	.0721	.0592	.0476	.0375	.0290	.0220	41
10	.1377	.1317	.1226	.1113	.0985	.0852	.0721	.0598	.0485	.0386	40
11	.1331	.1351	.1332	.1278	.1194	.1089	.0970	.0845	.0721	.0602	39
12	.1150	.1238	.1293	.1311	.1294	.1244	.1166	.1068	.0957	.0838	38
13	.0894	.1021	.1129	.1210	.1261	.1277	.1261	.1215	.1142	.1050	37
14	.0628	.0761	.0891	.1010	.1110	.1186	.1233	.1248	.1233	.1189	36
15	.0400	.0515	.0639	.0766	.0888	.1000	.1094	.1165	.1209	.1223	35
16	.0233	.0318	.0417	.0529	.0648	.0769	.0885	.0991	.1080	.1147	34
17	.0124	.0179	.0249	.0334	.0432	.0540	.0655	.0771	.0882	.0983	33
18	.0060	.0093	.0137	.0193	.0264	.0348	.0444	.0550	.0661	.0772	32
19	.0027	.0044	.0069	.0103	.0148	.0206	.0277	.0360	.0454	.0558	31
20	.0011	.0019	.0032	.0050	.0077	.0112	.0159	.0217	.0288	.0370	30
21	.0004	.0008	.0014	.0023	.0036	.0056	.0084	.0121	.0168	.0227	29
22	.0001	.0003	.0005	.0009	.0016	.0026	.0041	.0062	.0090	.0128	28
23	.0000	.0001	.0002	.0004	.0006	.0011	.0018	.0029	.0045	.0067	27
24	.0000	.0000	.0001	.0001	.0002	.0004	.0008	.0013	.0021	.0032	26
25	.0000	.0000	.0000	.0000	.0001	.0002	.0003	.0005	.0009	.0014	25
26	.0000	.0000	.0000	.0000	.0000	.0001	.0001	.0002	.0003	.0006	24
27	.0000	.0000	.0000	.0000	.0000	.0000	.0000	.0001	.0001	.0002	23
28	.0000	.0000	.0000	.0000	.0000	.0000	.0000	.0000	.0000	.0001	22
	$q = .79$	$q = .78$	$q = .77$	$q = .76$	$q = .75$	$q = .74$	$q = .73$	$q = .72$	$q = .71$	$q = .70$	

x_1	$p = .31$	$p = .32$	$p = .33$	$p = .34$	$p = .35$	$p = .36$	$p = .37$	$p = .38$	$p = .39$	$p = .40$	$n - x_1$
4	.0001	.0000	.0000	.0000	.0000	.0000	.0000	.0000	.0000	.0000	46
5	.0003	.0002	.0001	.0001	.0000	.0000	.0000	.0000	.0000	.0000	45
6	.0011	.0007	.0005	.0003	.0002	.0001	.0001	.0000	.0000	.0000	44
7	.0032	.0022	.0014	.0009	.0006	.0004	.0002	.0001	.0001	.0000	43
8	.0078	.0055	.0037	.0025	.0017	.0011	.0007	.0004	.0003	.0002	42
9	.0164	.0120	.0086	.0061	.0042	.0029	.0019	.0013	.0008	.0005	41
10	.0301	.0231	.0174	.0128	.0093	.0066	.0046	.0032	.0022	.0014	40
11	.0493	.0395	.0311	.0240	.0182	.0136	.0099	.0071	.0050	.0035	39
12	.0719	.0604	.0498	.0402	.0319	.0248	.0189	.0142	.0105	.0076	38
13	.0944	.0831	.0717	.0606	.0502	.0408	.0325	.0255	.0195	.0147	37
14	.1121	.1034	.0933	.0825	.0714	.0607	.0505	.0412	.0330	.0260	36
15	.1209	.1168	.1103	.1020	.0923	.0819	.0712	.0606	.0507	.0415	35
16	.1188	.1202	.1189	.1149	.1088	.1008	.0914	.0813	.0709	.0606	34
17	.1068	.1132	.1171	.1184	.1171	.1133	.1074	.0997	.0906	.0808	33
18	.0880	.0976	.1057	.1118	.1156	.1169	.1156	.1120	.1062	.0987	32
19	.0666	.0774	.0877	.0970	.1048	.1107	.1144	.1156	.1144	.1109	31
20	.0463	.0564	.0670	.0775	.0875	.0965	.1041	.1098	.1134	.1146	30
21	.0297	.0379	.0471	.0570	.0673	.0776	.0874	.0962	.1035	.1091	29
22	.0176	.0235	.0306	.0387	.0478	.0575	.0676	.0777	.0873	.0959	28
23	.0096	.0135	.0183	.0243	.0313	.0394	.0484	.0580	.0679	.0778	27
24	.0049	.0071	.0102	.0141	.0190	.0249	.0319	.0400	.0489	.0584	26
25	.0023	.0035	.0052	.0075	.0106	.0146	.0195	.0255	.0325	.0405	25
26	.0010	.0016	.0025	.0037	.0055	.0079	.0110	.0150	.0200	.0259	24
27	.0004	.0007	.0011	.0017	.0026	.0039	.0058	.0082	.0113	.0154	23
28	.0001	.0003	.0004	.0007	.0012	.0018	.0028	.0041	.0060	.0084	22
29	.0000	.0001	.0002	.0003	.0005	.0008	.0012	.0019	.0029	.0043	21
30	.0000	.0000	.0001	.0001	.0002	.0003	.0005	.0008	.0013	.0020	20
31	.0000	.0000	.0000	.0000	.0001	.0001	.0002	.0003	.0005	.0009	19
32	.0000	.0000	.0000	.0000	.0000	.0000	.0001	.0001	.0002	.0003	18
33	.0000	.0000	.0000	.0000	.0000	.0000	.0000	.0000	.0001	.0001	17
	$q = .69$	$q = .68$	$q = .67$	$q = .66$	$q = .65$	$q = .64$	$q = .63$	$q = .62$	$q = .61$	$q = .60$	

x_1	$p = .41$	$p = .42$	$p = .43$	$p = .44$	$p = .45$	$p = .46$	$p = .47$	$p = .48$	$p = .49$	$p = .50$	$n - x_1$
8	.0001	.0001	.0000	.0000	.0000	.0000	.0000	.0000	.0000	.0000	42
9	.0003	.0002	.0001	.0001	.0000	.0000	.0000	.0000	.0000	.0000	41
10	.0009	.0006	.0004	.0002	.0001	.0001	.0001	.0000	.0000	.0000	40
11	.0024	.0016	.0010	.0007	.0004	.0003	.0002	.0001	.0001	.0000	39
12	.0054	.0037	.0026	.0017	.0011	.0007	.0005	.0003	.0002	.0001	38
13	.0109	.0079	.0057	.0040	.0027	.0018	.0012	.0008	.0005	.0003	37
14	.0200	.0152	.0113	.0082	.0059	.0041	.0029	.0019	.0013	.0008	36
15	.0334	.0264	.0204	.0155	.0116	.0085	.0061	.0043	.0030	.0020	35
16	.0508	.0418	.0337	.0267	.0207	.0158	.0118	.0086	.0062	.0044	34
17	.0706	.0605	.0508	.0419	.0339	.0269	.0209	.0159	.0119	.0087	33
18	.0899	.0803	.0703	.0604	.0508	.0420	.0340	.0270	.0210	.0160	32
19	.1053	.0979	.0893	.0799	.0700	.0602	.0507	.0419	.0340	.0270	31
20	.1134	.1099	.1044	.0973	.0888	.0795	.0697	.0600	.0506	.0419	30
21	.1126	.1137	.1126	.1092	.1038	.0967	.0884	.0791	.0695	.0598	29
22	.1031	.1086	.1119	.1131	.1119	.1086	.1033	.0963	.0880	.0788	28
23	.0872	.0957	.1028	.1082	.1115	.1126	.1115	.1082	.1029	.0960	27
24	.0682	.0780	.0872	.0956	.1026	.1079	.1112	.1124	.1112	.1080	26
25	.0493	.0587	.0684	.0781	.0873	.0956	.1026	.1079	.1112	.1123	25
26	.0329	.0409	.0497	.0590	.0687	.0783	.0875	.0957	.1027	.1080	24
27	.0203	.0263	.0333	.0412	.0500	.0593	.0690	.0786	.0877	.0960	23
28	.0116	.0157	.0206	.0266	.0336	.0415	.0502	.0596	.0692	.0788	22
29	.0061	.0086	.0118	.0159	.0208	.0268	.0338	.0417	.0504	.0598	21
30	.0030	.0044	.0062	.0087	.0119	.0160	.0210	.0270	.0339	.0419	20
31	.0013	.0020	.0030	.0044	.0063	.0088	.0120	.0161	.0210	.0270	19
32	.0006	.0009	.0014	.0021	.0031	.0044	.0063	.0088	.0120	.0160	18
33	.0002	.0003	.0006	.0009	.0014	.0021	.0031	.0044	.0063	.0087	17
34	.0001	.0001	.0002	.0003	.0006	.0009	.0014	.0020	.0030	.0044	16
35	.0000	.0000	.0001	.0001	.0002	.0003	.0005	.0009	.0013	.0020	15
36	.0000	.0000	.0000	.0000	.0001	.0001	.0002	.0003	.0005	.0008	14
37	.0000	.0000	.0000	.0000	.0000	.0000	.0001	.0001	.0002	.0003	13
38	.0000	.0000	.0000	.0000	.0000	.0000	.0000	.0000	.0001	.0001	12
	$q = .59$	$q = .58$	$q = .57$	$q = .56$	$q = .55$	$q = .54$	$q = .53$	$q = .52$	$q = .51$	$q = .50$	

$n = 100$

x_1	$p = .01$	$p = .02$	$p = .03$	$p = .04$	$p = .05$	$p = .06$	$p = .07$	$p = .08$	$p = .09$	$p = .10$	$n - x_1$
0	.3660	.1326	.0476	.0169	.0059	.0021	.0007	.0002	.0001	.0000	100
1	.3697	.2707	.1471	.0703	.0312	.0131	.0053	.0021	.0008	.0003	99
2	.1849	.2734	.2252	.1450	.0812	.0414	.0198	.0090	.0039	.0016	98
3	.0610	.1823	.2275	.1973	.1396	.0864	.0486	.0254	.0125	.0059	97
4	.0149	.0902	.1706	.1994	.1781	.1338	.0888	.0536	.0301	.0159	96
5	.0029	.0353	.1013	.1595	.1800	.1639	.1283	.0895	.0571	.0339	95
6	.0005	.0114	.0496	.1052	.1500	.1657	.1529	.1233	.0895	.0596	94
7	.0001	.0031	.0206	.0589	.1060	.1420	.1545	.1440	.1188	.0889	93
8	.0000	.0007	.0074	.0285	.0649	.1054	.1352	.1455	.1366	.1148	92
9	.0000	.0002	.0023	.0121	.0349	.0687	.1040	.1293	.1381	.1304	91
10	.0000	.0000	.0007	.0046	.0167	.0399	.0712	.1024	.1243	.1319	90
11	.0000	.0000	.0002	.0016	.0072	.0209	.0439	.0728	.1006	.1199	89
12	.0000	.0000	.0000	.0005	.0028	.0099	.0245	.0470	.0738	.0988	88
13	.0000	.0000	.0000	.0001	.0010	.0043	.0125	.0276	.0494	.0743	87
14	.0000	.0000	.0000	.0000	.0003	.0017	.0058	.0149	.0304	.0513	86
15	.0000	.0000	.0000	.0000	.0001	.0006	.0025	.0074	.0172	.0327	85
16	.0000	.0000	.0000	.0000	.0000	.0002	.0010	.0034	.0090	.0193	84
17	.0000	.0000	.0000	.0000	.0000	.0001	.0004	.0015	.0044	.0106	83
18	.0000	.0000	.0000	.0000	.0000	.0000	.0001	.0006	.0020	.0054	82
19	.0000	.0000	.0000	.0000	.0000	.0000	.0000	.0002	.0009	.0026	81
20	.0000	.0000	.0000	.0000	.0000	.0000	.0000	.0001	.0003	.0012	80
21	.0000	.0000	.0000	.0000	.0000	.0000	.0000	.0000	.0001	.0005	79
22	.0000	.0000	.0000	.0000	.0000	.0000	.0000	.0000	.0000	.0002	78
23	.0000	.0000	.0000	.0000	.0000	.0000	.0000	.0000	.0000	.0001	77
24	.0000	.0000	.0000	.0000	.0000	.0000	.0000	.0000	.0000	.0000	76
	$q = .99$	$q = .98$	$q = .97$	$q = .96$	$q = .95$	$q = .94$	$q = .93$	$q = .92$	$q = .91$	$q = .90$	

x_1	$p = .11$	$p = .12$	$p = .13$	$p = .14$	$p = .15$	$p = .16$	$p = .17$	$p = .18$	$p = .19$	$p = .20$	$n - x_1$
0	.0000	.0000	.0000	.0000	.0000	.0000	.0000	.0000	.0000	.0000	100
1	.0001	.0000	.0000	.0000	.0000	.0000	.0000	.0000	.0000	.0000	99
2	.0007	.0003	.0001	.0000	.0000	.0000	.0000	.0000	.0000	.0000	98
3	.0027	.0012	.0005	.0002	.0001	.0000	.0000	.0000	.0000	.0000	97
4	.0080	.0038	.0018	.0008	.0003	.0001	.0001	.0000	.0000	.0000	96
5	.0189	.0100	.0050	.0024	.0011	.0005	.0002	.0001	.0000	.0000	95
6	.0369	.0215	.0119	.0063	.0031	.0015	.0007	.0003	.0001	.0001	94
7	.0613	.0394	.0238	.0137	.0075	.0039	.0020	.0009	.0004	.0002	93
8	.0881	.0625	.0414	.0259	.0153	.0086	.0047	.0024	.0012	.0006	92
9	.1112	.0871	.0632	.0430	.0276	.0168	.0098	.0054	.0029	.0015	91
10	.1251	.1080	.0860	.0637	.0444	.0292	.0182	.0108	.0062	.0034	90
11	.1265	.1205	.1051	.0849	.0640	.0454	.0305	.0194	.0118	.0069	89
12	.1160	.1219	.1165	.1025	.0838	.0642	.0463	.0316	.0206	.0128	88
13	.0970	.1125	.1179	.1130	.1001	.0827	.0642	.0470	.0327	.0216	87
14	.0745	.0954	.1094	.1143	.1098	.0979	.0817	.0641	.0476	.0335	86
15	.0528	.0745	.0938	.1067	.1111	.1070	.0960	.0807	.0640	.0481	85
16	.0347	.0540	.0744	.0922	.1041	.1082	.1044	.0941	.0798	.0638	84
17	.0212	.0364	.0549	.0742	.0908	.1019	.1057	.1021	.0924	.0789	83
18	.0121	.0229	.0379	.0557	.0739	.0895	.0998	.1033	.1000	.0909	82
19	.0064	.0135	.0244	.0391	.0563	.0736	.0882	.0979	.1012	.0981	81
20	.0032	.0074	.0148	.0258	.0402	.0567	.0732	.0870	.0962	.0993	80
21	.0015	.0039	.0084	.0160	.0270	.0412	.0571	.0728	.0859	.0946	79
22	.0007	.0019	.0045	.0094	.0171	.0282	.0420	.0574	.0724	.0849	78
23	.0003	.0009	.0023	.0052	.0103	.0182	.0292	.0427	.0576	.0720	77
24	.0001	.0004	.0011	.0027	.0058	.0111	.0192	.0301	.0433	.0577	76
25	.0000	.0002	.0005	.0013	.0031	.0064	.0119	.0201	.0309	.0439	75
26	.0000	.0001	.0002	.0006	.0016	.0035	.0071	.0127	.0209	.0316	74
27	.0000	.0000	.0001	.0003	.0008	.0018	.0040	.0076	.0134	.0217	73
28	.0000	.0000	.0000	.0001	.0004	.0009	.0021	.0044	.0082	.0141	72
29	.0000	.0000	.0000	.0000	.0002	.0004	.0011	.0024	.0048	.0088	71
30	.0000	.0000	.0000	.0000	.0001	.0002	.0005	.0012	.0027	.0052	70
31	.0000	.0000	.0000	.0000	.0000	.0001	.0002	.0006	.0014	.0029	69
32	.0000	.0000	.0000	.0000	.0000	.0000	.0001	.0003	.0007	.0016	68
33	.0000	.0000	.0000	.0000	.0000	.0000	.0000	.0001	.0003	.0008	67
34	.0000	.0000	.0000	.0000	.0000	.0000	.0000	.0001	.0002	.0004	66
35	.0000	.0000	.0000	.0000	.0000	.0000	.0000	.0000	.0001	.0002	65
36	.0000	.0000	.0000	.0000	.0000	.0000	.0000	.0000	.0000	.0001	64
37	.0000	.0000	.0000	.0000	.0000	.0000	.0000	.0000	.0000	.0000	63
	$q = .89$	$q = .88$	$q = .87$	$q = .86$	$q = .85$	$q = .84$	$q = .83$	$q = .82$	$q = .81$	$q = .80$	

x_1	$p = .21$	$p = .22$	$p = .23$	$p = .24$	$p = .25$	$p = .26$	$p = .27$	$p = .28$	$p = .29$	$p = .30$	$n - x_1$
7	.0001	.0000	.0000	.0000	.0000	.0000	.0000	.0000	.0000	.0000	93
8	.0003	.0001	.0001	.0000	.0000	.0000	.0000	.0000	.0000	.0000	92
9	.0007	.0003	.0002	.0001	.0000	.0000	.0000	.0000	.0000	.0000	91
10	.0018	.0009	.0004	.0002	.0001	.0000	.0000	.0000	.0000	.0000	90
11	.0038	.0021	.0011	.0005	.0003	.0001	.0001	.0000	.0000	.0000	89
12	.0076	.0043	.0024	.0012	.0006	.0003	.0001	.0001	.0000	.0000	88
13	.0136	.0082	.0048	.0027	.0014	.0007	.0004	.0002	.0001	.0000	87
14	.0225	.0144	.0089	.0052	.0030	.0016	.0009	.0004	.0002	.0001	86
15	.0343	.0233	.0152	.0095	.0057	.0033	.0018	.0010	.0005	.0002	85
16	.0484	.0350	.0241	.0159	.0100	.0061	.0035	.0020	.0011	.0006	84
17	.0636	.0487	.0356	.0248	.0165	.0106	.0065	.0038	.0022	.0012	83
18	.0780	.0634	.0490	.0361	.0254	.0171	.0111	.0069	.0041	.0024	82
19	.0895	.0772	.0631	.0492	.0365	.0259	.0177	.0115	.0072	.0044	81
20	.0963	.0881	.0764	.0629	.0493	.0369	.0264	.0182	.0120	.0076	80
21	.0975	.0947	.0869	.0756	.0626	.0494	.0373	.0269	.0186	.0124	79
22	.0931	.0959	.0932	.0858	.0749	.0623	.0495	.0376	.0273	.0190	78
23	.0839	.0917	.0944	.0919	.0847	.0743	.0621	.0495	.0378	.0277	77
24	.0716	.0830	.0905	.0931	.0906	.0837	.0736	.0618	.0496	.0380	76
25	.0578	.0712	.0822	.0893	.0918	.0894	.0828	.0731	.0615	.0496	75
26	.0444	.0579	.0708	.0814	.0883	.0906	.0883	.0819	.0725	.0613	74
27	.0323	.0448	.0580	.0704	.0806	.0873	.0896	.0873	.0812	.0720	73
28	.0224	.0329	.0451	.0580	.0701	.0799	.0864	.0886	.0864	.0804	72
29	.0148	.0231	.0335	.0455	.0580	.0697	.0793	.0855	.0876	.0856	71
30	.0093	.0154	.0237	.0340	.0458	.0580	.0694	.0787	.0847	.0868	70
31	.0056	.0098	.0160	.0242	.0344	.0460	.0580	.0691	.0781	.0840	69
32	.0032	.0060	.0103	.0165	.0248	.0349	.0462	.0579	.0688	.0776	68
33	.0018	.0035	.0063	.0107	.0170	.0252	.0352	.0464	.0579	.0685	67
34	.0009	.0019	.0037	.0067	.0112	.0175	.0257	.0356	.0466	.0579	66
35	.0005	.0010	.0021	.0040	.0070	.0116	.0179	.0261	.0359	.0468	65
36	.0002	.0005	.0011	.0023	.0042	.0073	.0120	.0183	.0265	.0362	64
37	.0001	.0003	.0006	.0012	.0024	.0045	.0077	.0123	.0187	.0268	63
38	.0000	.0001	.0003	.0006	.0013	.0026	.0047	.0079	.0127	.0191	62
39	.0000	.0001	.0001	.0003	.0007	.0015	.0028	.0049	.0082	.0130	61
40	.0000	.0000	.0001	.0002	.0004	.0008	.0016	.0029	.0051	.0085	60
41	.0000	.0000	.0000	.0001	.0002	.0004	.0008	.0017	.0031	.0053	59
42	.0000	.0000	.0000	.0000	.0001	.0002	.0004	.0009	.0018	.0032	58
43	.0000	.0000	.0000	.0000	.0000	.0001	.0002	.0005	.0010	.0019	57
44	.0000	.0000	.0000	.0000	.0000	.0000	.0001	.0002	.0005	.0010	56
45	.0000	.0000	.0000	.0000	.0000	.0000	.0000	.0001	.0003	.0005	55
46	.0000	.0000	.0000	.0000	.0000	.0000	.0000	.0001	.0001	.0003	54
47	.0000	.0000	.0000	.0000	.0000	.0000	.0000	.0000	.0001	.0001	53
48	.0000	.0000	.0000	.0000	.0000	.0000	.0000	.0000	.0000	.0001	52
	$q = .79$	$q = .78$	$q = .77$	$q = .76$	$q = .75$	$q = .74$	$q = .73$	$q = .72$	$q = .71$	$q = .70$	

x_1	$p = .31$	$p = .32$	$p = .33$	$p = .34$	$p = .35$	$p = .36$	$p = .37$	$p = .38$	$p = .39$	$p = .40$	$n - x_1$
15	.0001	.0001	.0000	.0000	.0000	.0000	.0000	.0000	.0000	.0000	85
16	.0003	.0001	.0001	.0000	.0000	.0000	.0000	.0000	.0000	.0000	84
17	.0006	.0003	.0002	.0001	.0000	.0000	.0000	.0000	.0000	.0000	83
18	.0013	.0007	.0004	.0002	.0001	.0000	.0000	.0000	.0000	.0000	82
19	.0025	.0014	.0008	.0004	.0002	.0001	.0000	.0000	.0000	.0000	81
20	.0046	.0027	.0015	.0008	.0004	.0002	.0001	.0001	.0000	.0000	80
21	.0079	.0049	.0029	.0016	.0009	.0005	.0002	.0001	.0001	.0000	79
22	.0127	.0082	.0051	.0030	.0017	.0010	.0005	.0003	.0001	.0001	78
23	.0194	.0131	.0085	.0053	.0032	.0018	.0010	.0006	.0003	.0001	77
24	.0280	.0198	.0134	.0088	.0055	.0033	.0019	.0011	.0006	.0003	76
25	.0382	.0283	.0201	.0137	.0090	.0057	.0035	.0020	.0012	.0006	75
26	.0496	.0384	.0286	.0204	.0140	.0092	.0059	.0036	.0021	.0012	74
27	.0610	.0495	.0386	.0288	.0207	.0143	.0095	.0060	.0037	.0022	73
28	.0715	.0608	.0495	.0387	.0290	.0209	.0145	.0097	.0062	.0038	72
29	.0797	.0710	.0605	.0495	.0388	.0292	.0211	.0147	.0098	.0063	71
30	.0848	.0791	.0706	.0603	.0494	.0389	.0294	.0213	.0149	.0100	70
31	.0860	.0840	.0785	.0702	.0601	.0494	.0389	.0295	.0215	.0151	69
32	.0833	.0853	.0834	.0779	.0698	.0599	.0493	.0390	.0296	.0217	68
33	.0771	.0827	.0846	.0827	.0774	.0694	.0597	.0493	.0390	.0297	67
34	.0683	.0767	.0821	.0840	.0821	.0769	.0691	.0595	.0492	.0391	66
35	.0578	.0680	.0763	.0816	.0834	.0816	.0765	.0688	.0593	.0491	65
36	.0469	.0578	.0678	.0759	.0811	.0829	.0811	.0761	.0685	.0591	64
37	.0365	.0471	.0578	.0676	.0755	.0806	.0824	.0807	.0757	.0682	63
38	.0272	.0367	.0472	.0577	.0674	.0752	.0802	.0820	.0803	.0754	62
39	.0194	.0275	.0369	.0473	.0577	.0672	.0749	.0799	.0816	.0799	61
40	.0133	.0197	.0277	.0372	.0474	.0577	.0671	.0746	.0795	.0812	60
41	.0087	.0136	.0200	.0280	.0373	.0475	.0577	.0670	.0744	.0792	59
42	.0055	.0090	.0138	.0203	.0282	.0375	.0476	.0576	.0668	.0742	58
43	.0033	.0057	.0092	.0141	.0205	.0285	.0377	.0477	.0576	.0667	57
44	.0019	.0035	.0059	.0094	.0143	.0207	.0287	.0378	.0477	.0576	56
45	.0011	.0020	.0036	.0060	.0096	.0145	.0210	.0289	.0380	.0478	55
46	.0006	.0011	.0021	.0037	.0062	.0098	.0147	.0212	.0290	.0381	54
47	.0003	.0006	.0012	.0022	.0038	.0063	.0099	.0149	.0213	.0292	53
48	.0001	.0003	.0007	.0012	.0023	.0039	.0064	.0101	.0151	.0215	52
49	.0001	.0002	.0003	.0007	.0013	.0023	.0040	.0066	.0102	.0152	51
50	.0000	.0001	.0002	.0004	.0007	.0013	.0024	.0041	.0067	.0103	50
51	.0000	.0000	.0001	.0002	.0004	.0007	.0014	.0025	.0042	.0068	49
52	.0000	.0000	.0000	.0001	.0002	.0004	.0008	.0014	.0025	.0042	48
53	.0000	.0000	.0000	.0000	.0001	.0002	.0004	.0008	.0015	.0026	47
54	.0000	.0000	.0000	.0000	.0000	.0001	.0002	.0004	.0008	.0015	46
55	.0000	.0000	.0000	.0000	.0000	.0000	.0001	.0002	.0004	.0008	45
56	.0000	.0000	.0000	.0000	.0000	.0000	.0000	.0001	.0002	.0004	44
57	.0000	.0000	.0000	.0000	.0000	.0000	.0000	.0001	.0001	.0002	43
58	.0000	.0000	.0000	.0000	.0000	.0000	.0000	.0000	.0001	.0001	42
59	.0000	.0000	.0000	.0000	.0000	.0000	.0000	.0000	.0000	.0001	41
	$q = .69$	$q = .68$	$q = .67$	$q = .66$	$q = .65$	$q = .64$	$q = .63$	$q = .62$	$q = .61$	$q = .60$	

x_1	$p = .41$	$p = .42$	$p = .43$	$p = .44$	$p = .45$	$p = .46$	$p = .47$	$p = .48$	$p = .49$	$p = .50$	$n - x_1$
23	.0001	.0000	.0000	.0000	.0000	.0000	.0000	.0000	.0000	.0000	77
24	.0002	.0001	.0000	.0000	.0000	.0000	.0000	.0000	.0000	.0000	76
25	.0003	.0002	.0001	.0000	.0000	.0000	.0000	.0000	.0000	.0000	75
26	.0007	.0003	.0002	.0001	.0000	.0000	.0000	.0000	.0000	.0000	74
27	.0013	.0007	.0004	.0002	.0001	.0000	.0000	.0000	.0000	.0000	73
28	.0023	.0013	.0007	.0004	.0002	.0001	.0000	.0000	.0000	.0000	72
29	.0039	.0024	.0014	.0008	.0004	.0002	.0001	.0000	.0000	.0000	71
30	.0065	.0040	.0024	.0014	.0008	.0004	.0002	.0001	.0001	.0000	70
31	.0102	.0066	.0041	.0025	.0014	.0008	.0004	.0002	.0001	.0001	69
32	.0152	.0103	.0067	.0042	.0025	.0015	.0008	.0004	.0002	.0001	68
33	.0218	.0154	.0104	.0068	.0043	.0026	.0015	.0008	.0004	.0002	67
34	.0298	.0219	.0155	.0105	.0069	.0043	.0026	.0015	.0009	.0005	66
35	.0391	.0299	.0220	.0156	.0106	.0069	.0044	.0026	.0015	.0009	65
36	.0491	.0391	.0300	.0221	.0157	.0107	.0070	.0044	.0027	.0016	64
37	.0590	.0490	.0391	.0300	.0222	.0157	.0107	.0070	.0044	.0027	63
38	.0680	.0588	.0489	.0391	.0301	.0222	.0158	.0108	.0071	.0045	62
39	.0751	.0677	.0587	.0489	.0391	.0301	.0223	.0158	.0108	.0071	61
40	.0796	.0748	.0675	.0586	.0488	.0391	.0301	.0223	.0159	.0108	60
41	.0809	.0793	.0745	.0673	.0584	.0487	.0391	.0301	.0223	.0159	59
42	.0790	.0806	.0790	.0743	.0672	.0583	.0487	.0390	.0301	.0223	58
43	.0740	.0787	.0804	.0788	.0741	.0670	.0582	.0486	.0390	.0301	57
44	.0666	.0739	.0785	.0802	.0786	.0739	.0669	.0581	.0485	.0390	56
45	.0576	.0666	.0737	.0784	.0800	.0784	.0738	.0668	.0580	.0485	55
46	.0479	.0576	.0665	.0736	.0782	.0798	.0783	.0737	.0667	.0580	54
47	.0382	.0480	.0576	.0665	.0736	.0781	.0797	.0781	.0736	.0666	53
48	.0293	.0383	.0480	.0577	.0665	.0735	.0781	.0797	.0781	.0735	52
49	.0216	.0295	.0384	.0481	.0577	.0664	.0735	.0780	.0796	.0780	51
50	.0153	.0218	.0296	.0385	.0482	.0577	.0665	.0735	.0780	.0796	50
51	.0104	.0155	.0219	.0297	.0386	.0482	.0578	.0665	.0735	.0780	49
52	.0068	.0105	.0156	.0220	.0298	.0387	.0483	.0578	.0665	.0735	48
53	.0043	.0069	.0106	.0156	.0221	.0299	.0388	.0483	.0579	.0666	47
54	.0026	.0044	.0070	.0107	.0157	.0221	.0299	.0388	.0484	.0580	46
55	.0015	.0026	.0044	.0070	.0108	.0158	.0222	.0300	.0389	.0485	45
56	.0008	.0015	.0027	.0044	.0071	.0108	.0158	.0222	.0300	.0390	44
57	.0005	.0009	.0016	.0027	.0045	.0071	.0108	.0158	.0223	.0301	43
58	.0002	.0005	.0009	.0016	.0027	.0045	.0071	.0108	.0159	.0223	42
59	.0001	.0002	.0005	.0009	.0016	.0027	.0045	.0071	.0109	.0159	41
60	.0001	.0001	.0002	.0005	.0009	.0016	.0027	.0045	.0071	.0108	40
61	.0000	.0001	.0001	.0002	.0005	.0009	.0016	.0027	.0045	.0071	39
62	.0000	.0000	.0001	.0001	.0002	.0005	.0009	.0016	.0027	.0045	38
63	.0000	.0000	.0000	.0001	.0001	.0002	.0005	.0009	.0016	.0027	37
64	.0000	.0000	.0000	.0000	.0001	.0001	.0002	.0005	.0009	.0016	36
65	.0000	.0000	.0000	.0000	.0000	.0001	.0001	.0002	.0005	.0009	35
66	.0000	.0000	.0000	.0000	.0000	.0000	.0001	.0001	.0002	.0005	34
67	.0000	.0000	.0000	.0000	.0000	.0000	.0000	.0001	.0001	.0002	33
68	.0000	.0000	.0000	.0000	.0000	.0000	.0000	.0000	.0001	.0001	32
69	.0000	.0000	.0000	.0000	.0000	.0000	.0000	.0000	.0000	.0001	31
	$q = .59$	$q = .58$	$q = .57$	$q = .56$	$q = .55$	$q = .54$	$q = .53$	$q = .52$	$q = .51$	$q = .50$	

APPENDIX B STANDARD NORMAL DISTRIBUTION

To illustrate: 19.85% of the area under a normal curve lies between the mean, μ_x, and a point 0.52 standard deviation units away.

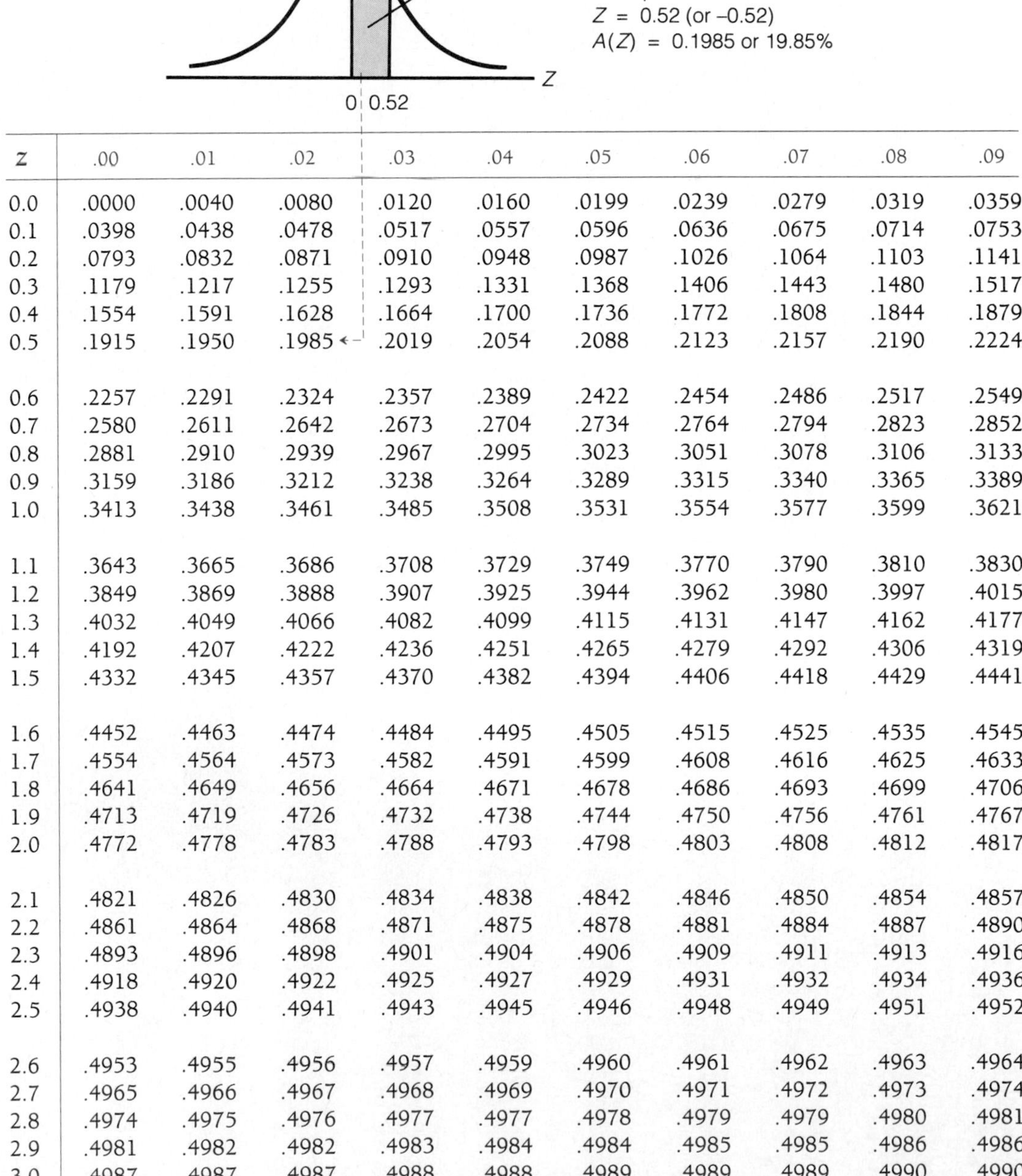

z	.00	.01	.02	.03	.04	.05	.06	.07	.08	.09
0.0	.0000	.0040	.0080	.0120	.0160	.0199	.0239	.0279	.0319	.0359
0.1	.0398	.0438	.0478	.0517	.0557	.0596	.0636	.0675	.0714	.0753
0.2	.0793	.0832	.0871	.0910	.0948	.0987	.1026	.1064	.1103	.1141
0.3	.1179	.1217	.1255	.1293	.1331	.1368	.1406	.1443	.1480	.1517
0.4	.1554	.1591	.1628	.1664	.1700	.1736	.1772	.1808	.1844	.1879
0.5	.1915	.1950	.1985 ←	.2019	.2054	.2088	.2123	.2157	.2190	.2224
0.6	.2257	.2291	.2324	.2357	.2389	.2422	.2454	.2486	.2517	.2549
0.7	.2580	.2611	.2642	.2673	.2704	.2734	.2764	.2794	.2823	.2852
0.8	.2881	.2910	.2939	.2967	.2995	.3023	.3051	.3078	.3106	.3133
0.9	.3159	.3186	.3212	.3238	.3264	.3289	.3315	.3340	.3365	.3389
1.0	.3413	.3438	.3461	.3485	.3508	.3531	.3554	.3577	.3599	.3621
1.1	.3643	.3665	.3686	.3708	.3729	.3749	.3770	.3790	.3810	.3830
1.2	.3849	.3869	.3888	.3907	.3925	.3944	.3962	.3980	.3997	.4015
1.3	.4032	.4049	.4066	.4082	.4099	.4115	.4131	.4147	.4162	.4177
1.4	.4192	.4207	.4222	.4236	.4251	.4265	.4279	.4292	.4306	.4319
1.5	.4332	.4345	.4357	.4370	.4382	.4394	.4406	.4418	.4429	.4441
1.6	.4452	.4463	.4474	.4484	.4495	.4505	.4515	.4525	.4535	.4545
1.7	.4554	.4564	.4573	.4582	.4591	.4599	.4608	.4616	.4625	.4633
1.8	.4641	.4649	.4656	.4664	.4671	.4678	.4686	.4693	.4699	.4706
1.9	.4713	.4719	.4726	.4732	.4738	.4744	.4750	.4756	.4761	.4767
2.0	.4772	.4778	.4783	.4788	.4793	.4798	.4803	.4808	.4812	.4817
2.1	.4821	.4826	.4830	.4834	.4838	.4842	.4846	.4850	.4854	.4857
2.2	.4861	.4864	.4868	.4871	.4875	.4878	.4881	.4884	.4887	.4890
2.3	.4893	.4896	.4898	.4901	.4904	.4906	.4909	.4911	.4913	.4916
2.4	.4918	.4920	.4922	.4925	.4927	.4929	.4931	.4932	.4934	.4936
2.5	.4938	.4940	.4941	.4943	.4945	.4946	.4948	.4949	.4951	.4952
2.6	.4953	.4955	.4956	.4957	.4959	.4960	.4961	.4962	.4963	.4964
2.7	.4965	.4966	.4967	.4968	.4969	.4970	.4971	.4972	.4973	.4974
2.8	.4974	.4975	.4976	.4977	.4977	.4978	.4979	.4979	.4980	.4981
2.9	.4981	.4982	.4982	.4983	.4984	.4984	.4985	.4985	.4986	.4986
3.0	.4987	.4987	.4987	.4988	.4988	.4989	.4989	.4989	.4990	.4990

APPENDIX C POISSON PROBABILITY DISTRIBUTION: VALUES OF $P(x) = (\lambda t)^x e^{-\lambda t}/x!$

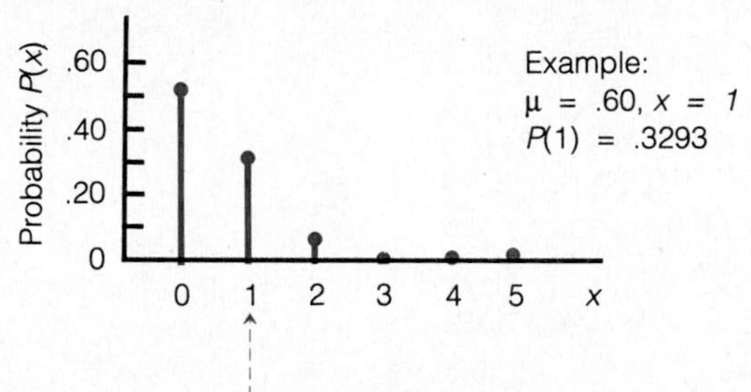

x_1	λt .005	.01	.02	.03	.04	.05	.06	.07	.08	.09
0	.9950	.9900	.9802	.9704	.9608	.9512	.9418	.9324	.9231	.9139
1	.0050	.0099	.0192	.0291	.0384	.0476	.0565	.0653	.0738	.0823
2	.0000	.0000	.0002	.0004	.0008	.0012	.0017	.0023	.0030	.0037
3	.0000	.0000	.0000	.0000	.0000	.0000	.0000	.0001	.0001	.0001

x_1	λt 0.10	0.20	0.30	0.40	0.50	0.60	0.70	0.80	0.90	1.00
0	.9048	.8187	.7408	.6703	.6065	.5488	.4966	.4493	.4066	.3679
1	.0905	.1637	.2222	.2681	.3033	.3293	.3476	.3595	.3659	.3679
2	.0045	.0164	.0333	.0536	.0758	.0988	.1217	.1438	.1647	.1839
3	.0002	.0011	.0033	.0072	.0126	.0198	.0284	.0383	.0494	.0613
4	.0000	.0001	.0002	.0007	.0016	.0030	.0050	.0077	.0111	.0153
5	.0000	.0000	.0000	.0001	.0002	.0004	.0007	.0012	.0020	.0031
6	.0000	.0000	.0000	.0000	.0000	.0000	.0001	.0002	.0003	.0005
7	.0000	.0000	.0000	.0000	.0000	.0000	.0000	.0000	.0000	.0001

x_1	λt 1.10	1.20	1.30	1.40	1.50	1.60	1.70	1.80	1.90	2.00
0	.3329	.3012	.2725	.2466	.2231	.2019	.1827	.1653	.1496	.1353
1	.3662	.3614	.3543	.3452	.3347	.3230	.3106	.2975	.2842	.2707
2	.2014	.2169	.2303	.2417	.2510	.2584	.2640	.2678	.2700	.2707
3	.0738	.0867	.0998	.1128	.1255	.1378	.1496	.1607	.1710	.1804
4	.0203	.0260	.0324	.0395	.0471	.0551	.0636	.0723	.0812	.0902
5	.0045	.0062	.0084	.0111	.0141	.0176	.0216	.0260	.0309	.0361
6	.0008	.0012	.0018	.0026	.0035	.0047	.0061	.0078	.0098	.0120
7	.0001	.0002	.0003	.0005	.0008	.0011	.0015	.0020	.0027	.0034
8	.0000	.0000	.0001	.0001	.0001	.0002	.0003	.0005	.0006	.0009
9	.0000	.0000	.0000	.0000	.0000	.0000	.0001	.0001	.0001	.0002

x_1	λt 2.10	2.20	2.30	2.40	2.50	2.60	2.70	2.80	2.90	3.00
0	.1225	.1108	.1003	.0907	.0821	.0743	.0672	.0608	.0550	.0498
1	.2572	.2438	.2306	.2177	.2052	.1931	.1815	.1703	.1596	.1494
2	.2700	.2681	.2652	.2613	.2565	.2510	.2450	.2384	.2314	.2240
3	.1890	.1966	.2033	.2090	.2138	.2176	.2205	.2225	.2237	.2240
4	.0992	.1082	.1169	.1254	.1336	.1414	.1488	.1557	.1622	.1680
5	.0417	.0476	.0538	.0602	.0668	.0735	.0804	.0872	.0940	.1008
6	.0146	.0174	.0206	.0241	.0278	.0319	.0362	.0407	.0455	.0504
7	.0044	.0055	.0068	.0083	.0099	.0118	.0139	.0163	.0188	.0216
8	.0011	.0015	.0019	.0025	.0031	.0038	.0047	.0057	.0068	.0081
9	.0003	.0004	.0005	.0007	.0009	.0011	.0014	.0018	.0022	.0027
10	.0001	.0001	.0001	.0002	.0002	.0003	.0004	.0005	.0006	.0008
11	.0000	.0000	.0000	.0000	.0000	.0001	.0001	.0001	.0002	.0002
12	.0000	.0000	.0000	.0000	.0000	.0000	.0000	.0000	.0000	.0001

x_1	λt 3.10	3.20	3.30	3.40	3.50	3.60	3.70	3.80	3.90	4.00
0	.0450	.0408	.0369	.0334	.0302	.0273	.0247	.0224	.0202	.0183
1	.1397	.1304	.1217	.1135	.1057	.0984	.0915	.0850	.0789	.0733
2	.2165	.2087	.2008	.1929	.1850	.1771	.1692	.1615	.1539	.1465
3	.2237	.2226	.2209	.2186	.2158	.2125	.2087	.2046	.2001	.1954
4	.1734	.1781	.1823	.1858	.1888	.1912	.1931	.1944	.1951	.1954
5	.1075	.1140	.1203	.1264	.1322	.1377	.1429	.1477	.1522	.1563
6	.0555	.0608	.0662	.0716	.0771	.0826	.0881	.0936	.0989	.1042
7	.0246	.0278	.0312	.0348	.0385	.0425	.0466	.0508	.0551	.0595
8	.0095	.0111	.0129	.0148	.0169	.0191	.0215	.0241	.0269	.0298
9	.0033	.0040	.0047	.0056	.0066	.0076	.0089	.0102	.0116	.0132
10	.0010	.0013	.0016	.0019	.0023	.0028	.0033	.0039	.0045	.0053
11	.0003	.0004	.0005	.0006	.0007	.0009	.0011	.0013	.0016	.0019
12	.0001	.0001	.0001	.0002	.0002	.0003	.0003	.0004	.0005	.0006
13	.0000	.0000	.0000	.0000	.0001	.0001	.0001	.0001	.0002	.0002
14	.0000	.0000	.0000	.0000	.0000	.0000	.0000	.0000	.0000	.0001

	λt									
x_1	4.10	4.20	4.30	4.40	4.50	4.60	4.70	4.80	4.90	5.00
0	.0166	.0150	.0136	.0123	.0111	.0101	.0091	.0082	.0074	.0067
1	.0679	.0630	.0583	.0540	.0500	.0462	.0427	.0395	.0365	.0337
2	.1393	.1323	.1254	.1188	.1125	.1063	.1005	.0948	.0894	.0842
3	.1904	.1852	.1798	.1743	.1687	.1631	.1574	.1517	.1460	.1404
4	.1951	.1944	.1933	.1917	.1898	.1875	.1849	.1820	.1789	.1755
5	.1600	.1633	.1662	.1687	.1708	.1725	.1738	.1747	.1753	.1755
6	.1093	.1143	.1191	.1237	.1281	.1323	.1362	.1398	.1432	.1462
7	.0640	.0686	.0732	.0778	.0824	.0869	.0914	.0959	.1002	.1044
8	.0328	.0360	.0393	.0428	.0463	.0500	.0537	.0575	.0614	.0653
9	.0150	.0168	.0188	.0209	.0232	.0255	.0280	.0307	.0334	.0363
10	.0061	.0071	.0081	.0092	.0104	.0118	.0132	.0147	.0164	.0181
11	.0023	.0027	.0032	.0037	.0043	.0049	.0056	.0064	.0073	.0082
12	.0008	.0009	.0011	.0014	.0016	.0019	.0022	.0026	.0030	.0034
13	.0002	.0003	.0004	.0005	.0006	.0007	.0008	.0009	.0011	.0013
14	.0001	.0001	.0001	.0001	.0002	.0002	.0003	.0003	.0004	.0005
15	.0000	.0000	.0000	.0000	.0001	.0001	.0001	.0001	.0001	.0002

	λt									
x_1	5.10	5.20	5.30	5.40	5.50	5.60	5.70	5.80	5.90	6.00
0	.0061	.0055	.0050	.0045	.0041	.0037	.0033	.0030	.0027	.0025
1	.0311	.0287	.0265	.0244	.0225	.0207	.0191	.0176	.0162	.0149
2	.0793	.0746	.0701	.0659	.0618	.0580	.0544	.0509	.0477	.0446
3	.1348	.1293	.1239	.1185	.1133	.1082	.1033	.0985	.0938	.0892
4	.1719	.1681	.1641	.1600	.1558	.1515	.1472	.1428	.1383	.1339
5	.1753	.1748	.1740	.1728	.1714	.1697	.1678	.1656	.1632	.1606
6	.1490	.1515	.1537	.1555	.1571	.1584	.1594	.1601	.1605	.1606
7	.1086	.1125	.1163	.1200	.1234	.1267	.1298	.1326	.1353	.1377
8	.0692	.0731	.0771	.0810	.0849	.0887	.0925	.0962	.0998	.1033
9	.0392	.0423	.0454	.0486	.0519	.0552	.0586	.0620	.0654	.0688
10	.0200	.0220	.0241	.0262	.0285	.0309	.0334	.0359	.0386	.0413
11	.0093	.0104	.0116	.0129	.0143	.0157	.0173	.0190	.0207	.0225
12	.0039	.0045	.0051	.0058	.0065	.0073	.0082	.0092	.0102	.0113
13	.0015	.0018	.0021	.0024	.0028	.0032	.0036	.0041	.0046	.0052
14	.0006	.0007	.0008	.0009	.0011	.0013	.0015	.0017	.0019	.0022
15	.0002	.0002	.0003	.0003	.0004	.0005	.0006	.0007	.0008	.0009
16	.0001	.0001	.0001	.0001	.0001	.0002	.0002	.0002	.0003	.0003
17	.0000	.0000	.0000	.0000	.0000	.0001	.0001	.0001	.0001	.0001

x_1	λt 6.10	6.20	6.30	6.40	6.50	6.60	6.70	6.80	6.90	7.00
0	.0022	.0020	.0018	.0017	.0015	.0014	.0012	.0011	.0010	.0009
1	.0137	.0126	.0116	.0106	.0098	.0090	.0082	.0076	.0070	.0064
2	.0417	.0390	.0364	.0340	.0318	.0296	.0276	.0258	.0240	.0223
3	.0848	.0806	.0765	.0726	.0688	.0652	.0617	.0584	.0552	.0521
4	.1294	.1249	.1205	.1162	.1118	.1076	.1034	.0992	.0952	.0912
5	.1579	.1549	.1519	.1487	.1454	.1420	.1385	.1349	.1314	.1277
6	.1605	.1601	.1595	.1586	.1575	.1562	.1546	.1529	.1511	.1490
7	.1399	.1418	.1435	.1450	.1462	.1472	.1480	.1486	.1489	.1490
8	.1066	.1099	.1130	.1160	.1188	.1215	.1240	.1263	.1284	.1304
9	.0723	.0757	.0791	.0825	.0858	.0891	.0923	.0954	.0985	.1014
10	.0441	.0469	.0498	.0528	.0558	.0588	.0618	.0649	.0679	.0710
11	.0245	.0265	.0285	.0307	.0330	.0353	.0377	.0401	.0426	.0452
12	.0124	.0137	.0150	.0164	.0179	.0194	.0210	.0227	.0245	.0264
13	.0058	.0065	.0073	.0081	.0089	.0098	.0108	.0119	.0130	.0142
14	.0025	.0029	.0033	.0037	.0041	.0046	.0052	.0058	.0064	.0071
15	.0010	.0012	.0014	.0016	.0018	.0020	.0023	.0026	.0029	.0033
16	.0004	.0005	.0005	.0006	.0007	.0008	.0010	.0011	.0013	.0014
17	.0001	.0002	.0002	.0002	.0003	.0003	.0004	.0004	.0005	.0006
18	.0000	.0001	.0001	.0001	.0001	.0001	.0001	.0002	.0002	.0002
19	.0000	.0000	.0000	.0000	.0000	.0000	.0000	.0001	.0001	.0001

x_1	λt 7.10	7.20	7.30	7.40	7.50	7.60	7.70	7.80	7.90	8.00
0	.0008	.0007	.0007	.0006	.0006	.0005	.0005	.0004	.0004	.0003
1	.0059	.0054	.0049	.0045	.0041	.0038	.0035	.0032	.0029	.0027
2	.0208	.0194	.0180	.0167	.0156	.0145	.0134	.0125	.0116	.0107
3	.0492	.0464	.0438	.0413	.0389	.0366	.0345	.0324	.0305	.0286
4	.0874	.0836	.0799	.0764	.0729	.0696	.0663	.0632	.0602	.0573
5	.1241	.1204	.1167	.1130	.1094	.1057	.1021	.0986	.0951	.0916
6	.1468	.1445	.1420	.1394	.1367	.1339	.1311	.1282	.1252	.1221
7	.1489	.1486	.1481	.1474	.1465	.1454	.1442	.1428	.1413	.1396
8	.1321	.1337	.1351	.1363	.1373	.1382	.1388	.1392	.1395	.1396
9	.1042	.1070	.1096	.1121	.1144	.1167	.1187	.1207	.1224	.1241
10	.0740	.0770	.0800	.0829	.0858	.0887	.0914	.0941	.0967	.0993
11	.0478	.0504	.0531	.0558	.0585	.0613	.0640	.0667	.0695	.0722
12	.0283	.0303	.0323	.0344	.0366	.0388	.0411	.0434	.0457	.0481
13	.0154	.0168	.0181	.0196	.0211	.0227	.0243	.0260	.0278	.0296
14	.0078	.0086	.0095	.0104	.0113	.0123	.0134	.0145	.0157	.0169
15	.0037	.0041	.0046	.0051	.0057	.0062	.0069	.0075	.0083	.0090
16	.0016	.0019	.0021	.0024	.0026	.0030	.0033	.0037	.0041	.0045
17	.0007	.0008	.0009	.0010	.0012	.0013	.0015	.0017	.0019	.0021
18	.0003	.0003	.0004	.0004	.0005	.0006	.0006	.0007	.0008	.0009
19	.0001	.0001	.0001	.0002	.0002	.0002	.0003	.0003	.0003	.0004
20	.0000	.0000	.0001	.0001	.0001	.0001	.0001	.0001	.0001	.0002
21	.0000	.0000	.0000	.0000	.0000	.0000	.0000	.0000	.0001	.0001

	λt									
x_1	8.10	8.20	8.30	8.40	8.50	8.60	8.70	8.80	8.90	9.00
0	.0003	.0003	.0002	.0002	.0002	.0002	.0002	.0002	.0001	.0001
1	.0025	.0023	.0021	.0019	.0017	.0016	.0014	.0013	.0012	.0011
2	.0100	.0092	.0086	.0079	.0074	.0068	.0063	.0058	.0054	.0050
3	.0269	.0252	.0237	.0222	.0208	.0195	.0183	.0171	.0160	.0150
4	.0544	.0517	.0491	.0466	.0443	.0420	.0398	.0377	.0357	.0337
5	.0882	.0849	.0816	.0784	.0752	.0722	.0692	.0663	.0635	.0607
6	.1191	.1160	.1128	.1097	.1066	.1034	.1003	.0972	.0941	.0911
7	.1378	.1358	.1338	.1317	.1294	.1271	.1247	.1222	.1197	.1171
8	.1395	.1392	.1388	.1382	.1375	.1366	.1356	.1344	.1332	.1318
9	.1256	.1269	.1280	.1290	.1299	.1306	.1311	.1315	.1317	.1318
10	.1017	.1040	.1063	.1084	.1104	.1123	.1140	.1157	.1172	.1186
11	.0749	.0776	.0802	.0828	.0853	.0878	.0902	.0925	.0948	.0970
12	.0505	.0530	.0555	.0579	.0604	.0629	.0654	.0679	.0703	.0728
13	.0315	.0334	.0354	.0374	.0395	.0416	.0438	.0459	.0481	.0504
14	.0182	.0196	.0210	.0225	.0240	.0256	.0272	.0289	.0306	.0324
15	.0098	.0107	.0116	.0126	.0136	.0147	.0158	.0169	.0182	.0194
16	.0050	.0055	.0060	.0066	.0072	.0079	.0086	.0093	.0101	.0109
17	.0024	.0026	.0029	.0033	.0036	.0040	.0044	.0048	.0053	.0058
18	.0011	.0012	.0014	.0015	.0017	.0019	.0021	.0024	.0026	.0029
19	.0005	.0005	.0006	.0007	.0008	.0009	.0010	.0011	.0012	.0014
20	.0002	.0002	.0002	.0003	.0003	.0004	.0004	.0005	.0005	.0006
21	.0001	.0001	.0001	.0001	.0001	.0002	.0002	.0002	.0002	.0003
22	.0000	.0000	.0000	.0000	.0001	.0001	.0001	.0001	.0001	.0001

x_1	λt 9.10	9.20	9.30	9.40	9.50	9.60	9.70	9.80	9.90	10.00
0	.0001	.0001	.0001	.0001	.0001	.0001	.0001	.0001	.0001	.0000
1	.0010	.0009	.0009	.0008	.0007	.0007	.0006	.0005	.0005	.0005
2	.0046	.0043	.0040	.0037	.0034	.0031	.0029	.0027	.0025	.0023
3	.0140	.0131	.0123	.0115	.0107	.0100	.0093	.0087	.0081	.0076
4	.0319	.0302	.0285	.0269	.0254	.0240	.0226	.0213	.0201	.0189
5	.0581	.0555	.0530	.0506	.0483	.0460	.0439	.0418	.0398	.0378
6	.0881	.0851	.0822	.0793	.0764	.0736	.0709	.0682	.0656	.0631
7	.1145	.1118	.1091	.1064	.1037	.1010	.0982	.0955	.0928	.0901
8	.1302	.1286	.1269	.1251	.1232	.1212	.1191	.1170	.1148	.1126
9	.1317	.1315	.1311	.1306	.1300	.1293	.1284	.1274	.1263	.1251
10	.1198	.1210	.1219	.1228	.1235	.1241	.1245	.1249	.1250	.1251
11	.0991	.1012	.1031	.1049	.1067	.1083	.1098	.1112	.1125	.1137
12	.0752	.0776	.0799	.0822	.0844	.0866	.0888	.0908	.0928	.0948
13	.0526	.0549	.0572	.0594	.0617	.0640	.0662	.0685	.0707	.0729
14	.0342	.0361	.0380	.0399	.0419	.0439	.0459	.0479	.0500	.0521
15	.0208	.0221	.0235	.0250	.0265	.0281	.0297	.0313	.0330	.0347
16	.0118	.0127	.0137	.0147	.0157	.0168	.0180	.0192	.0204	.0217
17	.0063	.0069	.0075	.0081	.0088	.0095	.0103	.0111	.0119	.0128
18	.0032	.0035	.0039	.0042	.0046	.0051	.0055	.0060	.0065	.0071
19	.0015	.0017	.0019	.0021	.0023	.0026	.0028	.0031	.0034	.0037
20	.0007	.0008	.0009	.0010	.0011	.0012	.0014	.0015	.0017	.0019
21	.0003	.0003	.0004	.0004	.0005	.0006	.0006	.0007	.0008	.0009
22	.0001	.0001	.0002	.0002	.0002	.0002	.0003	.0003	.0004	.0004
23	.0000	.0001	.0001	.0001	.0001	.0001	.0001	.0001	.0002	.0002
24	.0000	.0000	.0000	.0000	.0000	.0000	.0000	.0001	.0001	.0001

x_1	λt 11.	12.	13.	14.	15.	16.	17.	18.	19.	20.
0	.0000	.0000	.0000	.0000	.0000	.0000	.0000	.0000	.0000	.0000
1	.0002	.0001	.0000	.0000	.0000	.0000	.0000	.0000	.0000	.0000
2	.0010	.0004	.0002	.0001	.0000	.0000	.0000	.0000	.0000	.0000
3	.0037	.0018	.0008	.0004	.0002	.0001	.0000	.0000	.0000	.0000
4	.0102	.0053	.0027	.0013	.0006	.0003	.0001	.0001	.0000	.0000
5	.0224	.0127	.0070	.0037	.0019	.0010	.0005	.0002	.0001	.0001
6	.0411	.0255	.0152	.0087	.0048	.0026	.0014	.0007	.0004	.0002
7	.0646	.0437	.0281	.0174	.0104	.0060	.0034	.0019	.0010	.0005
8	.0888	.0655	.0457	.0304	.0194	.0120	.0072	.0042	.0024	.0013
9	.1085	.0874	.0661	.0473	.0324	.0213	.0135	.0083	.0050	.0029
10	.1194	.1048	.0859	.0663	.0486	.0341	.0230	.0150	.0095	.0058
11	.1194	.1144	.1015	.0844	.0663	.0496	.0355	.0245	.0164	.0106
12	.1094	.1144	.1099	.0984	.0829	.0661	.0504	.0368	.0259	.0176
13	.0926	.1056	.1099	.1060	.0956	.0814	.0658	.0509	.0378	.0271
14	.0728	.0905	.1021	.1060	.1024	.0930	.0800	.0655	.0514	.0387
15	.0534	.0724	.0885	.0989	.1024	.0992	.0906	.0786	.0650	.0516
16	.0367	.0543	.0719	.0866	.0960	.0992	.0963	.0884	.0772	.0646
17	.0237	.0383	.0550	.0713	.0847	.0934	.0963	.0936	.0863	.0760
18	.0145	.0256	.0397	.0554	.0706	.0830	.0909	.0936	.0911	.0844
19	.0084	.0161	.0272	.0409	.0557	.0699	.0814	.0887	.0911	.0888
20	.0046	.0097	.0177	.0286	.0418	.0559	.0692	.0798	.0866	.0888
21	.0024	.0055	.0109	.0191	.0299	.0426	.0560	.0684	.0783	.0846
22	.0012	.0030	.0065	.0121	.0204	.0310	.0433	.0560	.0676	.0769
23	.0006	.0016	.0037	.0074	.0133	.0216	.0320	.0438	.0559	.0669
24	.0003	.0008	.0020	.0043	.0083	.0144	.0226	.0329	.0442	.0557
25	.0001	.0004	.0010	.0024	.0050	.0092	.0154	.0237	.0336	.0446
26	.0000	.0002	.0005	.0013	.0029	.0057	.0101	.0164	.0246	.0343
27	.0000	.0001	.0002	.0007	.0016	.0034	.0063	.0109	.0173	.0254
28	.0000	.0000	.0001	.0003	.0009	.0019	.0038	.0070	.0117	.0181
29	.0000	.0000	.0001	.0002	.0004	.0011	.0023	.0044	.0077	.0125
30	.0000	.0000	.0000	.0001	.0002	.0006	.0013	.0026	.0049	.0083
31	.0000	.0000	.0000	.0000	.0001	.0003	.0007	.0015	.0030	.0054
32	.0000	.0000	.0000	.0000	.0001	.0001	.0004	.0009	.0018	.0034
33	.0000	.0000	.0000	.0000	.0000	.0001	.0002	.0005	.0010	.0020
34	.0000	.0000	.0000	.0000	.0000	.0000	.0001	.0002	.0006	.0012
35	.0000	.0000	.0000	.0000	.0000	.0000	.0000	.0001	.0003	.0007
36	.0000	.0000	.0000	.0000	.0000	.0000	.0000	.0001	.0002	.0004
37	.0000	.0000	.0000	.0000	.0000	.0000	.0000	.0000	.0001	.0002
38	.0000	.0000	.0000	.0000	.0000	.0000	.0000	.0000	.0000	.0001
39	.0000	.0000	.0000	.0000	.0000	.0000	.0000	.0000	.0000	.0001

Source: Stephen P. Shao, *Statistics for Business and Economics*. 3d ed. (Columbus, Ohio: Merrill Publishing Company, 1976), pp. 782–86. Used with permission.

APPENDIX D UNIFORM RANDOM NUMBERS

.0354	.9371	.8689	.3502	.5134	.8901
.0990	.6425	.9385	.9586	.1114	.2012
.7245	.4643	.2538	.0458	.6257	.7062
.9413	.9933	.0030	.1642	.0470	.4870
.3395	.9519	.5426	.6742	.0058	.5197
.3892	.7343	.2758	.6083	.6776	.4573
.5926	.4512	.0192	.0714	.0836	.2285
.1866	.3215	.3265	.7696	.0039	.7974
.3648	.5064	.4879	.5116	.9735	.6766
.2383	.7275	.1746	.7766	.0783	.0378
.0029	.2646	.9456	.6922	.5214	.5141
.0325	.1759	.0871	.0164	.1770	.0376
.8666	.8345	.5032	.9675	.6016	.3056
.3119	.1255	.6247	.9944	.2213	.7196
.1249	.8963	.5578	.8335	.6633	.8906
.9961	.5051	.9388	.4433	.4504	.0546
.8034	.5607	.2147	.6623	.5282	.9921
.3535	.1974	.3188	.6830	.3424	.2953
.0810	.4786	.9589	.6863	.4365	.0763
.4228	.7736	.9884	.2295	.7867	.4612
.8368	.2001	.5773	.2325	.3446	.4621
.6850	.4777	.1530	.6545	.5056	.0728
.4470	.7844	.3301	.2070	.4714	.6802
.9857	.4612	.2961	.6948	.7264	.1360
.8317	.6585	.3734	.8297	.0954	.0825
.7063	.2669	.7264	.6115	.1029	.3761
.7517	.7273	.4306	.6180	.6015	.7017
.1864	.5637	.3749	.7996	.8880	.7228
.3557	.7323	.7142	.6216	.7780	.3604
.3954	.1308	.8413	.6472	.3547	.0443
.9770	.8615	.0978	.9068	.3633	.0309
.8545	.0922	.6912	.6450	.4684	.1315
.1801	.6085	.5383	.2911	.8431	.4440
.8084	.4009	.0030	.7456	.8091	.9325
.0579	.8818	.7473	.3270	.4967	.9487
.6476	.5736	.1645	.9728	.7425	.0372
.7788	.3646	.1131	.5371	.6945	.6216
.5797	.6745	.9200	.2811	.8427	.4113
.3827	.1237	.8727	.8977	.4445	.6263
.5517	.5504	.6673	.6651	.5633	.3810
.8291	.4691	.5336	.5738	.1892	.8226
.4216	.3143	.0040	.5189	.1600	.8670
.2927	.0633	.5458	.9034	.8527	.6259
.3806	.0806	.5252	.2451	.8620	.8693
.7114	.2807	.2233	.6314	.1372	.1167
.6247	.9488	.8697	.1147	.2939	.2013
.5823	.8171	.9164	.3944	.0704	.4000
.2765	.2381	.0172	.3763	.1478	.4743

.0091	.5490	.4335	.4553	.8017	.2144
.5576	.9719	.8349	.6150	.1050	.3317
.9990	.6427	.7127	.6868	.6498	.7919
.2096	.6122	.8750	.3627	.0081	.9338
.0090	.9141	.7439	.8068	.3991	.9668
.1670	.0434	.4207	.9568	.2825	.6915
.7435	.4379	.7407	.8620	.8465	.5355
.4783	.8077	.7838	.6494	.6085	.2512
.2007	.4068	.5622	.9627	.5987	.8656
.4780	.5886	.8512	.9676	.8433	.7292
.9697	.2413	.3848	.2672	.1187	.7554
.2089	.9455	.8818	.3217	.1926	.1956
.7772	.9485	.6242	.2156	.0231	.5431
.0935	.2983	.5536	.8657	.6327	.4093
.2845	.7320	.1073	.0151	.6282	.4666
.8561	.1616	.2603	.6058	.5823	.8017
.1343	.8511	.4939	.3736	.7479	.2723
.6946	.6291	.6583	.7601	.8241	.7117
.2479	.7300	.9488	.4843	.7398	.0749
.7026	.1080	.4637	.3682	.6773	.8696
.3713	.3174	.0634	.2603	.8021	.4666
.5407	.3032	.4988	.1502	.4188	.1320
.8731	.6957	.0279	.8187	.5212	.8767
.3592	.4521	.9895	.6164	.9557	.4655
.7904	.9405	.0529	.2152	.6676	.1804
.9692	.8084	.1117	.4262	.7466	.1815
.1264	.2301	.0414	.4281	.2434	.5590
.2649	.3770	.7885	.9982	.9737	.4207
.3969	.2044	.5107	.5931	.7793	.6085
.8955	.8980	.7368	.3689	.9650	.8870
.4273	.5749	.7643	.4876	.8807	.6994
.1868	.0815	.7644	.3023	.8656	.8324
.3994	.9836	.3134	.2648	.0255	.5862
.3134	.0912	.3169	.6496	.5600	.2911
.1484	.1125	.5494	.4383	.6102	.2663
.7201	.2798	.2743	.9579	.8438	.5636
.7095	.0431	.6654	.1164	.2474	.0897
.7945	.1726	.9981	.3303	.8455	.9517
.1152	.8658	.8281	.4866	.3123	.1184
.7882	.7021	.6281	.5347	.6987	.7425
.4419	.5389	.5995	.5499	.7396	.7357
.9889	.6925	.6293	.3637	.4636	.4427
.1066	.9984	.6095	.1048	.0705	.5054
.1425	.5939	.5890	.2433	.2990	.2632
.4144	.5172	.4766	.9826	.7496	.2815
.1246	.4668	.2630	.0930	.8845	.8533
.3546	.3145	.9810	.5307	.6715	.5673
.8626	.2164	.8733	.4347	.0916	.2853
.6482	.4151	.4856	.3477	.9780	.1250
.5076	.0770	.6545	.7522	.9065	.2887
.0442	.7589	.6083	.2675	.1049	.8349
.8561	.3465	.6506	.1006	.6013	.7343
.8672	.5602	.1436	.5939	.0787	.8048

.0222	.3704	.7622	.9657	.1562	.3693
.8136	.9170	.2349	.5845	.0637	.7296
.3591	.7766	.0432	.3733	.9311	.8009
.9988	.6707	.7958	.1856	.1586	.5002
.6310	.9597	.2478	.2486	.5880	.7314
.2541	.5150	.1826	.0162	.4438	.0634
.4353	.8149	.6270	.0258	.2623	.4418
.6734	.3556	.1156	.6027	.2778	.5309
.8743	.7233	.9760	.5068	.9848	.5269
.4101	.9196	.8514	.8630	.8444	.5389
.4770	.7852	.9307	.9716	.3540	.8791
.7243	.6144	.6044	.8409	.9494	.8574
.3709	.3052	.5147	.5367	.4573	.9232
.2792	.6379	.2192	.6908	.0677	.2494
.7043	.5266	.9362	.7650	.0437	.1006
.6883	.3372	.0918	.9114	.6398	.5807
.3176	.6153	.6349	.5251	.9446	.6035
.3121	.8181	.3422	.8310	.6190	.1788
.6655	.8943	.5787	.1007	.7468	.3597

SOLUTIONS TO ODD-NUMBERED PROBLEMS

Chapter 1

9. **a.** x_1 = ⅜-in plywood; x_2 = ½-in plywood **b.** The value of z **c.** All coefficients of x_1 and x_2; \$3.40, \$5.76, 8, 5, 1.5, and 3.0 **d.** Perhaps a cost accounting study **e.** $z = \$3.40x_1 + \$5.50x_2$; value trying to optimize **f.** 30,000 and 17,500; place limits on possible values of the independent variables.

Chapter 2

1. Max $z = 30A + 11B + 15C$
Subject to
$$\begin{aligned} 2A + 2B + 2C &\le 500 \\ .8A + .4B + .3C &\le 160 \\ .1A + .16B + .18C &\le 80 \end{aligned}$$

3. Let C = artificial cream
M = milk
Min $z = .5C + .8M$
Subject to
$$\begin{aligned} 6C + 10M &\le 40 \\ C - 2M &\ge 0 \\ C/8 + M/5 &= 1 \end{aligned}$$

5. Let w = wheat
o = oats
b = barley

Min $z = .05w + .07o + .04b$
Subject to
$$\begin{aligned} 15w + 25o + 12b &\ge 150 \\ 10w + 20o + 16b &\ge 100 \end{aligned}$$

7. Let A = stock A
B = bond B
T = treasury bill

Max $z = .15A + .13B + .1T$
Subject to
$$\begin{aligned} A + B &\le 1{,}125{,}000 \\ A &\le 450{,}000 \\ A + B + T &= 1{,}500{,}000 \end{aligned}$$

9. Let x_1 = amount of Haitian in premium
x_2 = amount of Colombian in premium
x_3 = amount of Peruvian in premium
x_4 = amount of Haitian in deluxe
x_5 = amount of Colombian in deluxe
x_6 = amount of Peruvian in deluxe

Max $z = 5x_1 + 3.5x_2 + 3x_3 + 3.5x_4 + 2x_5 + 1.5x_6$
Subject to
$$\begin{aligned} x_1 + x_4 &\le 300 \\ x_2 + x_5 &\le 500 \\ x_3 + x_6 &\le 350 \\ x_1 + x_2 + x_3 &\ge 400 \\ x_4 + x_5 + x_6 &\ge 500 \\ .7x_1 - .3x_2 - .3x_3 &\le 0 \\ -.3x_1 + .7x_2 - .3x_3 &\ge 0 \\ -.5x_1 - .5x_2 + .5x_3 &\ge 0 \\ .6x_4 - .4x_5 - .4x_6 &\ge 0 \\ -.4x_4 + .6x_5 - .4x_6 &\ge 0 \\ -.2x_4 - .2x_5 + .8x_6 &\le 0 \end{aligned}$$

11. Let x_1 = Sleeper
x_2 = Spinner
Max $z = 2x_1 + 2x_2$
Subject to
$$\begin{aligned} 1x_1 + 2x_2 &\le 14{,}400 \\ 2x_1 + 8x_2 &\le 48{,}000 \end{aligned}$$

13. Max $z = 11D + 13M$
Subject to
$$\begin{aligned} 2D + 2M &\le 10{,}000 \\ 1D + 3M &\le 9{,}000 \\ 2D + 3M &\le 12{,}000 \end{aligned}$$

15. Max $z = 20R + 28.50B$
Subject to
$$\begin{aligned} 14R + 10B &\le 4000 \\ 5R + 12B &\le 4500 \\ R &\ge 50 \\ B &\ge 50 \\ 5R &\ge 1500 \\ 12B &\ge 300 \end{aligned}$$

17. Let x_1 = letter size
x_2 = legal size
Max $z = 51x_1 + 55.50x_2$
Subject to
$36x_1 + 54x_2 \leq 120{,}000$
$2x_1 + 3x_2 \leq 10{,}000$
$4x_1 + 2x_2 \leq 8{,}000$
$41x_1 + 52x_2 \leq 375{,}000$

23.

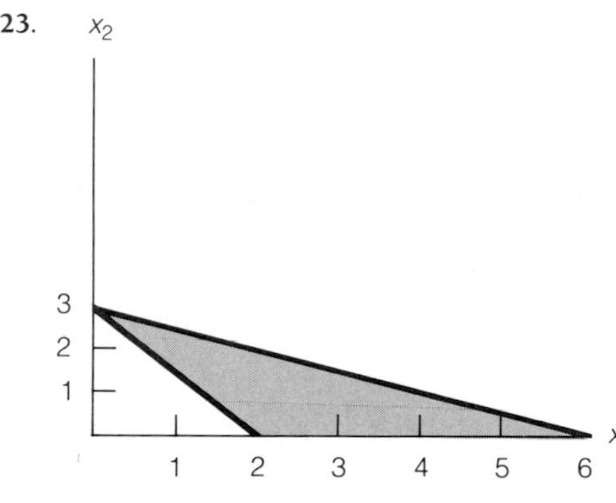

25.

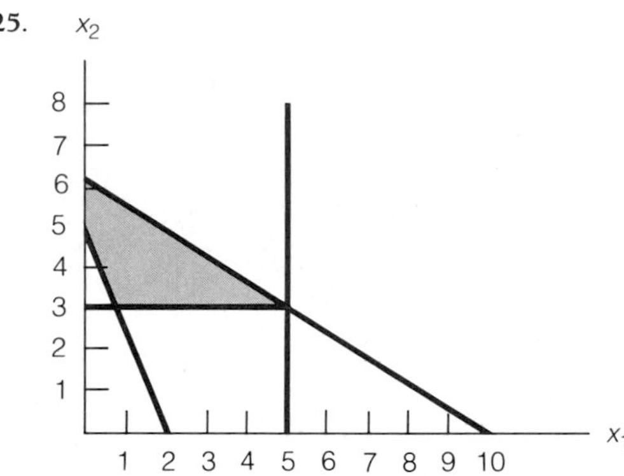

27. Optimum solution:
$z = 40.25$
$x_1 = 5.75$
$x_2 = 0$

29. Optimum solution:
$z = .176$
$x_1 = 1.875$
$x_2 = 1.50$

31. Optimum solution:
$z = 97.5$
$x_1 = 75$
$x_2 = 40$

33. **a.** Let x_1 = fence posts
x_2 = fence panels
Max $z = 1.5x_1 + 2x_2$
Subject to
$4x_1 + 12x_2 \leq 18{,}000$
$4x_1 + 10.5x_2 \leq 2{,}450$

b. $z = 918.75$
$x_1 = 612.5$
$x_2 = 0$

c. Wood constraint binding; labor time not all used.

35. Optimum solution:
Max $z = 22.5x_1 + 60x_2$
Subject to
$x_1 + x_2 \leq 300$
$3x_1 + x_2 \leq 360$
$z = 27{,}000$
Tourister = 120
Traveller = 0

37. Max $z = 20R + 28.50B$
Subject to
$14R + 10B \leq 4000$
$5R + 12B \leq 4500$
$R \geq 50$
$B \geq 50$

Optimum solution:
$z = 10{,}405$
B = 330
R = 50

39. Let t = number of telephone contacts
m = number of mail contacts
Min $z = 1.5t + 1m$
Subject to
$.5t + .35m \geq 200$
$.5t - 1.05m \geq 0$

41. Let x_1 = number from Boise to Baton Rouge
x_2 = number from Minneapolis to Baton Rouge
x_3 = number from Kansas City to Baton Rouge
x_4 = number from Boise to Fayetteville
x_5 = number from Minneapolis to Fayetteville
x_6 = number from Kansas City to Fayetteville
x_7 = number from Boise to Salinas
x_8 = number from Minneapolis to Salinas
x_9 = number from Kansas City to Salinas

Min $z = 7x_1 + 6x_2 + 2x_3 + 4x_4 + 8x_5 + 2x_6 + 1x_7 + 3x_8 + 4x_9$
Subject to
$x_1 + x_2 + x_3 = 200$
$x_4 + x_5 + x_6 = 400$
$x_7 + x_8 + x_9 = 500$
$x_1 + x_4 + x_7 \leq 300$
$x_2 + x_5 + x_8 \leq 800$
$x_3 + x_6 + x_9 \leq 600$

43. Optimum solution:
$z = 62$
$x_1 = 3$
$x_2 = 2.6$

45. Optimum solution:
$z = 466.667$
$x_1 = 0$
$x_2 = 9.333$

47. Optimum solution:
$z = 245$
$x_1 = 3$
$x_2 = 1$

49. Optimum solution:
Cost 2.133
Lamb = 37.33
Soybean = 10.67

51. Optimum solution:
Cost 6600
Liquid A = 6200
Liquid B = 400

Chapter 3

5. a. $x_1 = 0, x_2 = 0, z = 0$
$x_1 = 0, x_2 = 8, z = 48$
$x_1 = 4, x_2 = 0, z = 32$
$x_1 = 60/11, x_2 = 48/11, z = 768/11$

b. Max $z = 8x_1 + 6x_2 + 0s_1 + 0s_2 + 0s_3$
Subject to
$x_1 + x_2 + s_1 = 10$
$2x_1 + 3x_2 + s_2 = 24$
$3x_1 - x_2 + s_3 = 12$
$x_1, x_2, s_1, s_2, s_3 \geq 0$

c.

		x_1	x_2	s_1	s_2	s_3	
Basis	c_i	8	6	0	0	0	b_i
s_1	0	1	1	1	0	0	10
s_2	0	2	3	0	1	0	24
s_3	0	3	−1	0	0	1	12
z_j		0	0	0	0	0	0
$c_j - z_j$		8	6	0	0	0	

7. Iteration 0: $x_1 = 0, x_2 = 0, z = 0$
Iteration 1: $x_1 = 4, x_2 = 0, z = 32$
Iteration 2: $x_1 = 60/11, x_2 = 48/11, z = 768/11$

9. Max $z = 24x_1 + 15x_2 + 19x_3$
Subject to
$11x_1 + 9x_2 + 8x_3 \leq 600$
$8x_1 + 10x_2 + 8x_3 \leq 480$
$6x_1 + 7x_2 + 13x_3 \leq 400$

Solution: $x_1 = 48.421$
$x_2 = 0$
$x_3 = 8.421$
$z = 1322.105$

13. Max $z = 35x_1 + 30x_2 + 25x_3$
Subject to
$x_1 + x_2 + x_3 \leq 25{,}000$
$x_2 - 2x_3 \geq 0$
$x_1 \geq 6{,}000$
$x_2 \geq 4{,}500$
$x_3 \geq 2{,}600$

Solution: $x_1 = 17{,}200$
$x_2 = 5{,}200$
$x_3 = 2{,}600$
$z = 823{,}000$

15. $x_1 = 5$
$x_2 = 3\frac{1}{8}$
$z = 656\frac{1}{4}$

17. Max $z = 28.5B + 20R$
Subject to
$12B + 5R \leq 4500$
$10B + 14R \leq 4000$
$B \geq 50$
$R \geq 50$

Solution: $B = 330$
$R = 50$
$z = 10{,}405$

19. $x_1 = 1.875$
$x_2 = 1.5$
$z = .176$

23. Min $z = 10x_1 + 8.5x_2 + 5x_3$

Subject to
$$\begin{aligned} 10x_1 + 8.5x_2 + 5x_3 &\le 1500 \\ -2x_1 - 2x_2 + x_3 &\le 0 \\ x_1 + x_2 + x_3 &\ge 100 \\ x_1 &\ge 10 \end{aligned}$$

Solution: $x_1 = 10$, $x_2 = 23\frac{1}{3}$, $x_3 = 66\frac{2}{3}$, $z = 631\frac{2}{3}$

25. Min $z = 1.5T + 1M$

Subject to
$$\begin{aligned} .5T + .35M &> 200 \\ .5T - 1.05M &\ge 0 \end{aligned}$$

Solution: $T = 300$, $M = 142.857$, $z = 592.857$

27. $x_1 = 5$, $x_2 = 2$, $z = 32$

29. Min $z = 1A + 1B$

Subject to
$$\begin{aligned} .5A + .25B &\ge 3200 \\ A &\ge 550 \\ B &\ge 400 \end{aligned}$$

Solution: $A = 6200$, $B = 400$, $z = 6600$

31. Banana Computer = 6,000,000
NBM Computer Bonds = 3,600,000
Star Oil Co. Bonds = 9,600,000
Bears Dept. Store Stock = 3,600,000
Bears Dept. Store Bonds = 1,200,000
$z = 2,688,000$

33. Radio = $10\frac{2}{3}$
Flyers = 5
Direct mail = 5
$z = 346,666.7$

35. Sharon—station E
Eddie—station D
Charlene—station B
Darlene—stations A and C
Objective function = 33

37. Tulsa to Minneapolis 52
Oklahoma City to Salinas 16
Oklahoma City to Lincoln 1
Denver to Lincoln 70
Denver to Wichita 15
St. Louis to Wichita 50
Lawrence to Salinas 11
Lawrence to Kansas City 83
Omaha to Salinas 72
Objective function = 778

39. $x_1 = 136.364$, $x_3 = 36.364$, $x_4 = 45.455$, $x_5 = 81.818$, $z = 1372.727$

41. No dogs—during week = $333\frac{1}{3}$
No dogs—weekends = 666.67
1 or 2 dogs—during week = 600
More than 2—during week = 400
$z = 28,000$

43. Multiple optimum solutions

45. Unbounded solution

47. Optimum solution at the origin

49. Solution: $x_1 = 1\frac{2}{3}$, $x_2 = 0$, $x_3 = 13\frac{1}{3}$, $z = 50$
No problems

Chapter 4

1. a. Min $30y_1 + 20y_2$

Subject to
$$\begin{aligned} 3y_1 + 5y_2 &\ge 6 \\ 5y_1 + 2y_2 &\ge 3 \end{aligned}$$

b.

Primal	Dual
$x_1 = 2.105$	$y_1 = .158$
$x_2 = 4.737$	$y_2 = 1.105$
$z = 26.842$	$z = 26.842$

c.

Primal	Dual
Dual values	Dual values
Variable 1 = 0	Variable 1 = 0
Variable 2 = 0	Variable 2 = 0
Constraint 1 = .158	Constraint 1 = −2.105
Constraint 2 = 1.105	Constraint 2 = −4.77

3. a. Max $18y_1 + 40y_2 + 3.5y_3$

Subject to
$$\begin{aligned} 2y_1 + 4y_2 &\le .08 \\ 4y_1 + 10y_2 + y_3 &\le .04 \end{aligned}$$

b.

Primal	Dual
$x_1 = 0$	$y_1 = .01$
$x_2 = 4.5$	$y_2 = 0$
$z = .18$	$y_3 = 0$
	$z = .18$

c.

Primal	Dual
Dual values	Dual values
Variable 1 = .06	Variable 1 = 0
Variable 2 = 0	Variable 2 = 5
Constraint 1 = − .01	Variable 3 = 1
Constraint 2 = 0	Constraint 1 = 0
Constraint 3 = 0	Constraint 2 = 4.5

5. a. Max $.2x_1 + .15x_2 + .17x_3 + .1x_4$

Subject to
$$\begin{aligned} x_1 + x_3 &\le 5{,}000{,}000 \\ x_1 &\le 3{,}500{,}000 \\ x_2 &\le 3{,}500{,}000 \\ x_3 &\le 3{,}500{,}000 \\ x_4 &\le 3{,}500{,}000 \\ x_1 + x_2 + x_3 + x_4 &\le 10{,}000{,}000 \\ x_4 &\ge 2{,}500{,}000 \end{aligned}$$

b. Min $5{,}000{,}000y_1 + 3{,}500{,}000y_2 + 3{,}500{,}000y_3 + 3{,}500{,}000y_4 + 3{,}500{,}00y_5 + 10{,}000{,}000y_6 - 2{,}500{,}000y_7$

Subject to
$$\begin{aligned} y_1 + y_2 + y_6 &\ge .2 \\ y_3 + y_6 &\ge .15 \\ y_1 + y_4 + y_6 &\ge .17 \\ y_5 + y_6 - y_7 &\ge .1 \end{aligned}$$

c.

Primal	Dual
$x_1 = 3{,}500{,}000$	$y_1 = .02$
$x_2 = 2{,}500{,}000$	$y_2 = .03$
$x_3 = 1{,}500{,}000$	$y_3 = 0$
$x_4 = 2{,}500{,}000$	$y_4 = 0$
$z = 1{,}580{,}000$	$y_5 = 0$
	$y_6 = .15$
	$y_7 = .05$
	$z = 1{,}580{,}000$

d.

Primal		Dual	
Dual values		Dual values	
Variable 1 =	0	Variable 1 =	0
Variable 2 =	0	Variable 2 =	0
Variable 3 =	0	Variable 3 =	1,000,000
Variable 4 =	0	Variable 4 =	2,000,000
Constraint 1 =	.02	Variable 5 =	1,000,000
Constraint 2 =	.03	Variable 6 =	0
Constraint 3 =	0	Variable 7 =	0
Constraint 4 =	0	Constraint 1 =	−3,500,000
Constraint 5 =	0	Constraint 2 =	−2,500,000
Constraint 6 =	.15	Constraint 3 =	−1,500,000
Constraint 7 =	−.05	Constraint 4 =	−2,500,000

7. a. The primal will have 20 decision variables and 9 constraints.

b. The dual will have 9 decision variables and 20 constraints.

c. Solution:

Vivian	A
Vivian	D
Waylon	E
Jennifer	C
Howard	B

9. Solution: $x_1 = 6$, $x_2 = 2$, $z = 33$

Ranges $0 \le x_1 \le \infty$, $0 \le x_2 \le \infty$

11. Solution: $x_1 = 6$, $x_2 = 0$, $x_3 = 0$, $z = 3000$

Ranges $400 \le x_1 \le 533.33$, $750 \le x_2 \le 1000$, $900 \le x_3 \le \infty$

13. Solution: Sport = 1000, Career = 1000, Formal = 9666.667, Profit = 434,666.7

Ranges $-\infty \le$ Budget ≤ 26.667

$-\infty \le$ Career ≤ 31.11

$36 \le$ Insignia $\le \infty$

15. a. Purchase resource 2. b. No, have to increase above 13.125. c. Between 5.417 and ∞

17. Solution: $x_1 = 10$, $x_2 = 5$, $z = 75$

Ranges $90 \le b_1 \le \infty$, $0 \le b_2 \le 11$, $3.75 \le b_3 \le 5.625$, $110 \le b_4 \le \infty$

19. Solution: $x_1 = 6$, $x_2 = 1$, $x_3 = 0$, $z = 300$

Ranges $-\infty \le b_1 \le 31$, $-\infty \le b_2 \le 14$, $6 \le b_3 \le \infty$, $-\infty \le b_4 \le 6$, $0 \le b_5 \le 5$

21. Let x_1 = men's clothing
x_2 = women's clothing
x_3 = housewares
x_4 = auto supplies

a. Max $z = 3x_1 + 5x_2 + 2.5x_3 + 2.75x_4$

Subject to
$$\begin{aligned}
12x_1 + 15x_2 + 10x_3 + 20x_4 &\le 1{,}500{,}000\\
x_2 &\le 22{,}500\\
-.25x_1 - .25x_2 - .25x_3 + x_4 &\le 0\\
x_1 &\ge 10{,}000\\
x_2 &\ge 15{,}000\\
x_3 &\ge 8{,}000\\
x_4 &\ge 5{,}000\\
x_1 + x_2 + x_3 + x_4 &= 75{,}000
\end{aligned}$$

b. Constraint 2, 3
Constraint 4, 3

c. Ranges
$991{,}500 \le b_1 \le \infty$
$15{,}000 \le b_2 \le 52{,}000$
$-12{,}000 \le b_3 \le \infty$
$-\infty \le b_4 \le 39{,}500$
$-\infty \le b_5 \le 22{,}500$
$0 \le b_6 \le 37{,}500$
$0 \le b_7 \le 15{,}000$
$45{,}500 \le b_8 \le 117{,}375$

23. a. 5 by air freight; 490 by truck; 5 by piggyback b. Biggest restriction is shipping by piggyback.

Chapter 5

1. a. 81,600
b.

Superior—Kansas City	600
—Reno	1400
Bangor—Kansas City	200
—Dallas	1800
Grand Junction—New York	1600
—Kansas City	400

Objective function = 68,400

3. a. 40,200
b.

Athens—Denver	900
—Reno	100
Waco—New York	800
—Reno	200
Superior—St. Louis	600
—Reno	400

Objective function = 47,800

5.

Dolthan—Albany	2000
—Reno	1000
Midland—St. Paul	900
—Reno	2100
Arco—St. Paul	600
—Denver	2400

Not optimum, 1 step to optimum

7. a.
S_1—D_1 = 1200
—D_2 = 900
S_2—D_2 = 100
—D_3 = 1400
—D_4 = 200
S_3—D_4 = 1300
S_4—D_4 = 100
—D_5 = 1400

b. One way
S_1—D_1 = 700
—D_5 = 1400
S_2—D_1 = 300
—D_3 = 1400
S_3—D_1 = 200
—D_5 = 1100
S_4—D_2 = 1000
—D_4 = 500

c.
S_1—D_3 = 700
—D_5 = 1400
S_2—D_1 = 1200
—D_3 = 500
S_3—D_3 = 200
—D_4 = 1100
S_4—D_2 = 1000
—D_4 = 500

9. Add dummy source; get:
Superior—Kansas City = 600
—Reno = 1400
Bangor—Dallas = 1200
Grand Junction—Kansas City = 400
—New York = 1600

11. Add dummy source; get:
Athens—Denver = 900
—Reno = 100
Waco—New York = 400
Superior—New York = 400
—St. Louis = 600

13. a. Min $z = 4x_1 + 6x_2 + 5x_3 + 6x_4 + 7x_5 + 5x_6 + 4x_7 + 8x_8 + 9x_9 + 8x_{10} + 10x_{11} + 9x_{12} + 9x_{13} + 10x_{14} + 9x_{15} + 11x_{16}$

Subject to $x_1 + x_2 \le 140$
$x_3 + x_4 + x_5 \le 160$
$x_6 + x_7 + x_8 \le 200$
$x_1 + x_3 + x_6 = x_9 + x_{10}$
$x_2 + x_4 + x_7 = x_{11} + x_{12} + x_{13}$
$x_5 + x_8 = x_{14} + x_{15} + x_{16}$
$x_9 + x_{11} + x_{14} = 250$
$x_{10} + x_{12} + x_{15} = 150$
$x_{13} + x_{16} = 100$

b. Node 1—node 4 = 140
Node 2—node 4 = 160
Node 2—node 6 = 0
Node 3—node 4 = 100
Node 3—node 5 = 100
Node 4—node 7 = 250
Node 4—node 8 = 150
Node 5—node 10 = 100

c. yes

15. a. All nodes connected with costs as found in Table 5-45; can eliminate some routes.

b. Nevada—Boulder 40
Texas—Boulder 40
Nevada—Fresno 35
Texas—Jacksonville 50
Boulder—Chicago 80
Jacksonville—Boston 50
Objective function = 16,750

17. a.

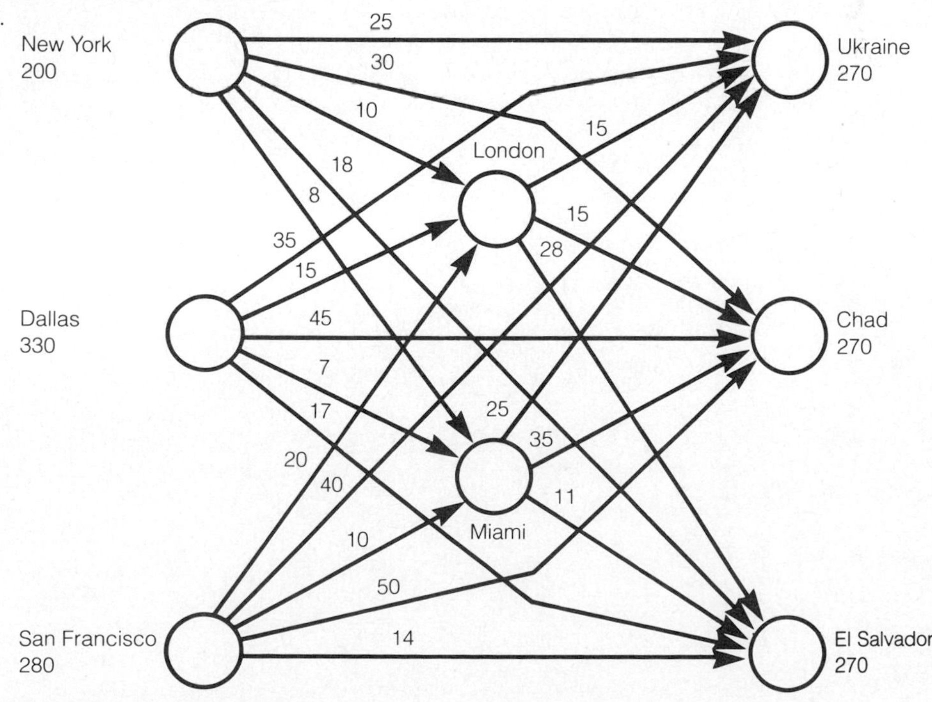

b. Ship: New York→Ukraine = 200
Dallas→London = 330
San Francisco→London = 10
San Francisco→El Salvador = 270
London→Ukraine = 70
London→Chad = 270
Objective function = 19,030

19. Team 1: Audit E
Team 2: Audit A
Team 3: Audit F
Team 4: Audit D
Team 5: Audit C
Team 6: Audit B
Objective function = 33

21. Williams: Job 1
Eberhart: Job 2
Nichols: Job 4
Sanchez: Job 5
Earl: Job 3
Objective function = 750

Chapter 6

1. x_1 = Hero
x_2 = Philly
Min $z = 0x_1 + 0x_2 + d_1^+ + d_1^- + 0d_2^+ + d_2^- + 0d_3^+ + d_3^-$
Subject to $3x_1 + 2x_2 - d_1^+ + d_1^- = 960$
$x_1 - d_2^+ + d_2^- = 200$
$x_2 - d_3^+ + d_3^- = 250$

3. x_1 = business customers served
x_2 = vacationers served
Min $z = 0x_1 + 0x_2 + 0d_1^+ + P_1d_1^- + 0d_2^+ + P_2d_2^-$
Subject to $x_1 - d_1^+ + d_1^- = 500$
$x_2 - d_2^+ + d_2^- = 300$
$2x_1 + 1.5x_2 \leq 1200$
Solution: $x_1 = 500$
$x_2 = 133\frac{1}{3}$

5. x_1 = hard drive
x_2 = hard card
Min $z = 0x_1 + 0x_2 + 0d_1^+ + d_1^- + 0d_2^+ + d_2^- + 0d_3^+ + d_3^-$
Subject to $80x_1 + 100x_2 = 4000 + d_1^+ - d_1^-$
$x_1 = 20 + d_2^+ - d_2^-$
$x_2 = 20 + d_3^+ - d_3^-$
$3x_1 + 2x_2 \leq 90$
$x_1 + x_2 \leq 60$
Solution: $x_1 = 7.143$
$x_2 = 34.286$

7. x_1 = desks by experienced line
x_2 = desks by less experienced line
Min $z = 0x_1 + 0x_2 + 0d_1^+ + P_1d_1^- + P_2d_2^+ + 0d_2^- + 0d_3^+ + P_3d_3^- + 0d_4^+ + P_30d_4^-$
Subject to $x_1 + x_2 = 350 + d_1^+ - d_1^-$
$x_1/5 = 40 + d_2^+ - d_2^-$
$x_2 \div 3 = 40 + d_3^+ - d_3^-$
$x_1 \div 5 = 50 + d_4^+ - d_4^-$
Solution: $x_1 = 230$
$x_2 = 120$

9. $x_1 = 229.988$
$x_2 = 120.012$

11. x_1 = Min Yee pages
x_2 = Christy Beach pages
x_3 = Bill Verdon pages
x_4 = Luisa Huerta pages
Min $z = 0x_1 + 0x_2 + 0x_3 + 0x_4 + d_1^+ + 1d_1^- + 5d_2^+ + 5d_2^- + 20d_3^+ + 20d_3^-$
Subject to $3.5x_1 + 2.4x_2 + 3.75x_3 + 3.9x_4 = 3000 + d_1^+ - d_1^-$
$.015x_1 + .018x_2 + .008x_3 + .012x_4 = 12 + d_2^+ - d_2^-$
$x_1 + x_2 + x_3 + x_4 = 1000 + d_3^+ - d_3$
$x_1/6.4 \leq 50$
$x_2 \div 5.2 \leq 40$
$x_3 \div 7.5 \leq 50$
$x_4 \div 8.8 \leq 35$

Solution: $x_1 = 320$
$x_2 = 208$
$x_3 = 375$
$x_4 = 97$

13. $x_1 = 0$
$x_2 = 8$
$z = 120$

15. $x_1 = 6$
$x_2 = 0$
$x_3 = 0$
$z = 60$

17. $x_1 = 5$
$x_2 = 5.357$
$z = 64.286$

19. $x_1 = 5$
$x_2 = 0$
$x_3 = .75$
$z = 37.25$

21. Let x_1 = number full time starting at 5:00 P.M.
x_2 = number full time starting at 6:00 P.M.
$\vdots$
x_{12} = number full time starting at 4:00 A.M.
x_{13} = number part time starting at 5:00 P.M.
$\vdots$
x_{24} = number part time starting at 4:00 A.M.

Min $z = 80x_1 + 80x_2 + \cdots + 80x_{12} + 16x_{13} + \cdots + 16x_{24}$

Staffing constraints:
$x_1 + x_{13} \geq 10$
$x_1 + x_2 + x_{13} + x_{14} \geq 12$
$x_1 + x_2 + x_3 + x_{13} + x_{14} + x_{15} \geq 12$
$x_1 + x_2 + x_3 + x_4 + x_{13} + x_{14} + x_{15} + x_{16} \geq 14$
$x_2 + x_3 + x_4 + x_5 + x_6 + x_{14} + x_{15} + x_{16} \geq 16$
etc.

Full-time employee constraints:
$x_1 \leq 8$
$x_1 + x_2 \leq 8$
$x_1 + x_2 + x_3 \leq 8$
etc.

State regulation constraints:
$x_1 \geq 3$
$x_1 + x_2 \geq 3$
$x_1 + x_2 + x_3 \geq 3$
etc.

23. Let x_1 = location 1
x_2 = location 2
etc.

Max $z = 15{,}000x_1 + 24{,}000x_2 + 14{,}000x_3 + 13{,}000x_4 + 22{,}000x_5 + 21{,}000x_6$

Subject to $5000x_1 + 11{,}000x_2 + 9000x_3 + 7000x_4 + 13{,}000x_5 + 17{,}000x_6 \leq 60{,}000$
$4x_1 + 7x_2 + 4x_3 + 2x_4 + 11x_5 + 5x_6 \leq 22$
All $x_i = 0$ or 1

Solution: $x_1 = 1$
$x_2 = 1$
$x_3 = 1$
$x_4 = 1$
$x_5 = 0$
$x_6 = 1$
$z = 87{,}000$

Chapter 7

1. Average sales = $1,472,000

3. Linear trend: MAD = 257.94
MSE = 94,041.61
Exponential trend: MAD = 99.49
MSE = 20,405.32
Bias = 0 for both models

5. $R^2 = .94$
Sales = $-1.40 + 1.53t$
Residuals show nonlinear pattern.

7. Birthrate = 22.53 − .07 year; $R^2 = .08$; poor model

9. Indexes (Jan.–Dec.)

1	.8488	7	.9660
1	.8627	8	1.0161
3	.7889	9	1.0754
4	.8662	10	1.1348
5	.9250	11	1.2561
6	.9329	12	1.3272

11. Unadjusted trend:
Sales = $23{,}424 + 420.89t$
$R^2 = .54$
MAD = 4409.36
Forecast = 44,048

Seasonally adjusted trend:
Sales = $(25{,}249 + 339.97t)$ monthly adjustment
MAD = 4489.49
$R^2 = .517$
Forecast = 35,570

15. Unadjusted:
Tickets = 1271.02 + 16.38t
R^2 = .49
MAD = 137.94
MSE = 30,423.62
Seasonally adjusted:
Tickets = (1224.64 + 19.05t) monthly adjustment
R^2 = .475
MAD = 140.33
MSE = 31,198.71

17. **a.** Jan.–Dec.: 78.6, 51.9, 41.37, 94.88, 127.99, 60.72, 100.82, 96.05, 87.64, 120.23, 182.50, 157.30
c. Depends on present prime rate. Use: Inventory = (6.28 + .052t) adjustment factor. To estimate inventory, multiply by .9 and monthly interest.

19. With α = .1 MAD = 36.96
MSE = 2004.86
With α = .5 MAD = 43.92
MSE = 2910.11

23. With α = .2 MAD = 2.91
MSE = 12.55
Forecast = 11.04
With α = .2
β = .2 MAD = 3.527
MSE = 19.010
Forecast = 11.677

25. With α = .1 MAD = 36.96
MSE = 2004.86
With α = .15
β = .25 MAD = 87.143
MSE = 11,319.05

27. Forecast = 16.63

29. Forecast = 18.455

31. For α = .2 MAD = 391.79
MSE = 205,148.8
α = .5 MAD = 379.75
MSE = 207,774
α = .8 MAD = 370.78
MSE = 183,994
α = .8 slightly better forecast = 2012

33. Best double smoothing model: α = .8, β = .2, MAD = 401.155, MSE = 219,197. Pick single-smoothing model.

Chapter 8

1. **a.** EOQ = 879.02
b. Average inventory = 439.51
c. 40.95

3. Present cost = $11,610
EOQ = 89.44
Cost of EOQ quantity = $4024.92
Savings = $7585.08

5. **a.** EOQ = 70.41
b. 35.355
c. 8.49
d. 1272.80

7. **a.** 201.99
b. 142.58
c. 712.91
d. Without back orders, cost = $1314.54.

9. Optimum cost = $4865.31; alternate cost, assume Q = 739.93: cost = $9319.36

11. Order 51; total cost = $1881.54

13. **a.** No, EOQ = 2121.75.
b. Yes, order 50,000.
c. 1.5 vs. 7.5
d. 110,903

15. **a.** 1,448,719.6
b. 1,424,312, 1,430,949
c. Q = 3000

17. **a.** 427.62
b. 28.06

19. **a** 20.17
b. Maximum = 16.50
Average = 8.25
c. Holding = 5156.64
Set up = 5156.64

21. Cost of present policy = $36,400; alternative, Q = 3310.88: cost = $21,746.50

Chapter 9

1. **a.** 374.26 **b.** 300 **c.** 505 **d.** 3044.25

3. **a.** 189.74
b. 112.5
c. 139.56
d. 112.5 **5.** Added cost = \$20,321.28 **7.** $Q = 31$ **9.** $Q = 78.8$ **11.** 153.33

13. **a.** Structure tree

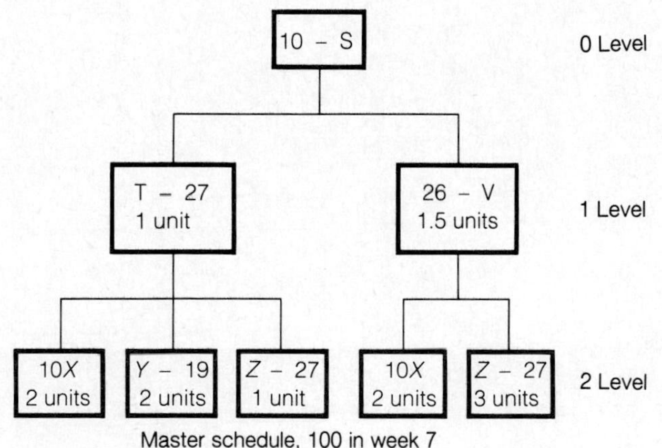

Master schedule, 100 in week 7

b. Net requirements
10-S, 60 in week 7
T-27, 45 in week 6
26-V, 60 in week 5
10X, 40 in week 4
120 in week 3
Z-27, 10 in week 5
180 in week 5
Y-19 70 in week 3

15. No, have to cut two weeks.

Chapter 10

1.

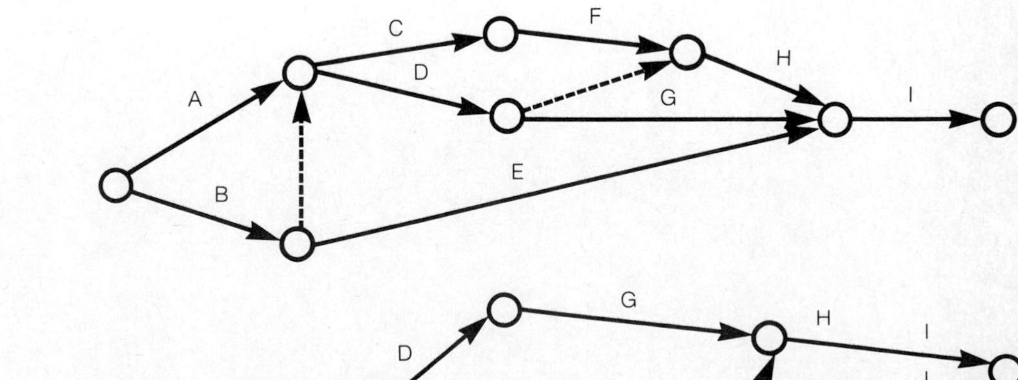

3.

5. Critical activities: F, G, J, K, L

7. a.

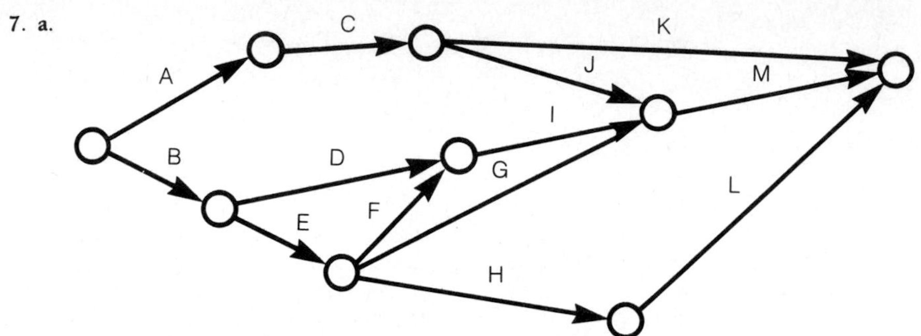

b. 14 mo c. Activities: B, E, F, I, M

d. Activity A, slack 2
Activity C, slack 2
Activity D, slack 5
Activity G, slack 1
Activity H, slack 2
Activity J, slack 3
Activity K, slack 2
Activity L, slack 2

9. a.

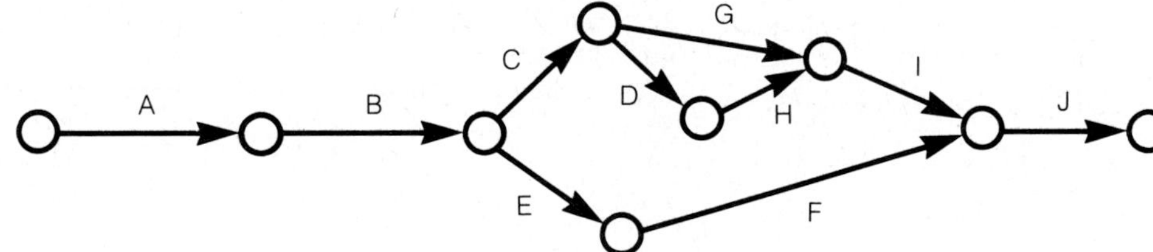

b. Critical path: A, B, C, D, H, I, J; 36.18 c. Less than 1% d. 40.8

11. a.

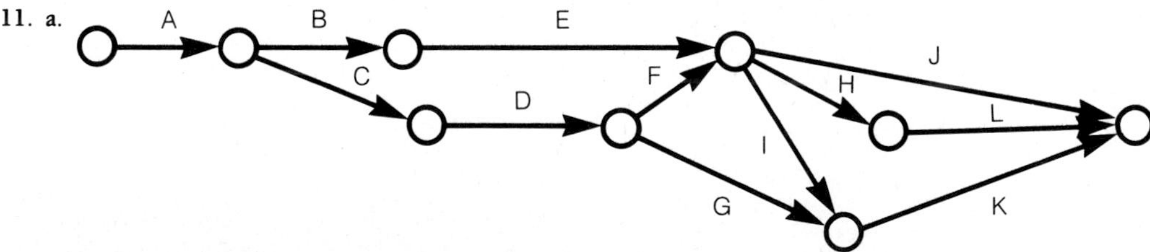

b. 27.83 c. .89%

13.

	Activity	From	To	Time	ES	LS	Actual Start	EF	LF	Actual Finish
1.	Activity 1	1.	2.	5.00	0.00	0.00		5.00	5.00	
2.	Activity 2	1.	3.	3.00	0.00	1.00		3.00	4.00	
3.	Activity 3	2.	4.	4.00	5.00	8.00		9.00	12.00	
4.	Activity 4	2.	5.	7.00	5.00	5.00		12.00	12.00	
5.	Activity 5	5.	7.	2.00	12.00	12.00		14.00	14.00	
6.	Activity 6	3.	7.	10.00	3.00	4.00		13.00	14.00	
7.	Activity 7	3.	6.	5.00	3.00	13.00		8.00	18.00	
8.	Activity 8	4.	9.	4.00	9.00	17.00		13.00	21.00	
9.	Activity 9	4.	7.	2.00	9.00	12.00		11.00	14.00	
10.	Activity 10	7.	8.	4.00	14.00	14.00		18.00	18.00	
11.	Activity 11	6.	10.	6.00	8.00	18.00		14.00	24.00	
12.	Activity 12	8.	9.	3.00	18.00	18.00		21.00	21.00	
13.	Activity 13	9.	11.	10.00	21.00	21.00		31.00	31.00	
14.	Activity 14	8.	13.	6.00	18.00	32.00		24.00	38.00	
15.	Activity 15	8.	10.	4.00	18.00	20.00		22.00	24.00	
16.	Activity 16	10.	13.	9.00	22.00	29.00		31.00	38.00	
17.	Activity 17	10.	12.	3.00	22.00	24.00		25.00	27.00	
18.	Activity 18	12.	13.	11.00	25.00	27.00		36.00	38.00	
19.	Activity 19	11.	13.	7.00	31.00	31.00		38.00	38.00	

Project completion time = 38.00

15.

Activity	Early Start	Late Start	Actual Start	Early Finish	Late Finish	Actual Finish
A	0	0		3.17	3.17	
B	3.17	3.17		8.34	8.34	
C	8.34	8.34		22.01	22.01	
D	22.01	22.01		30.01	30.01	
E	8.34	8.84		15.01	15.51	
F	15.01	15.51		34.68	35.18	
G	22.01	25.68		29.51	33.18	
H	30.01	30.01		33.18	33.18	
I	33.18	33.18		35.18	35.18	
J	35.18	35.18		36.18	36.18	

17. **a.** B, F, I **b.** 28, $530 million

c. 1. I by 1
2. A by 1, I by 1
3. A by 1, B by 1
4. B by 1, D by 1
5. H by 2, I by 2
Cost = $110 million

19. **a.**

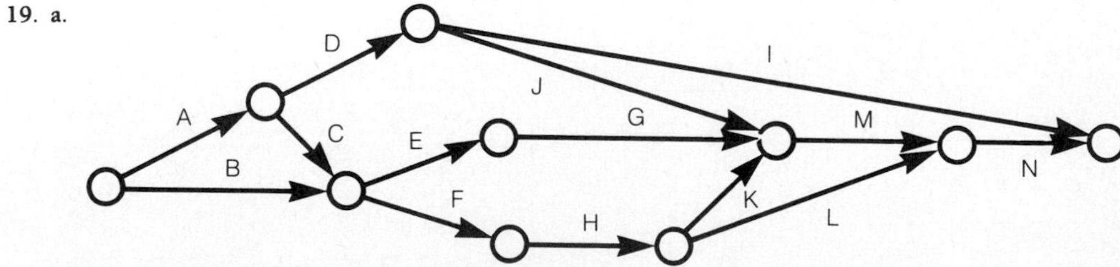

b. A, C, F, H, L, N **c.** 21,700,000 **d.** 800,000; 2,333,333

21.

Activity	Completion time (months)	Total cost (millions)	Monthly cost (millions)
A	6	40	6.667
B	7	65	9.286
C	5	60	12.000
D	9	90	10.000
E	7	45	6.429
F	9	70	7.778
G	8	20	2.500
H	12	100	8.333
I	12	40	3.333

Earliest Start Cash Flow

Activity	1	2	3	4	5	6	7
A	6.667	6.667	6.667	6.667	6.667	6.667	
B	9.286	9.286	9.286	9.286	9.286	9.286	9.286
C							12
D							10
E							
F							
G							
H							
I							
Monthly cost	15.953	15.953	15.953	15.953	15.953	15.953	31.286

Activity	8	9	10	11	12	13	14
A							
B							
C	12	12	12	12			
D	10	10	10	10	10	10	10
E	6.429	6.429	6.429	6.429	6.429	6.429	6.429
F	7.778	7.778	7.778	7.778	7.778	7.778	7.778
G					2.5	2.5	2.5
H							
I							
Monthly cost	36.207	36.207	36.207	36.207	26.707	26.707	26.707

Activity	15	16	17	18	19	20	21
A							
B							
C							
D	10						
E							
F	7.778	7.778					
G	2.5	2.5	2.5	2.5	2.5		
H		8.333	8.333	8.333	8.333	8.333	8.333
I			3.333	3.333	3.333	3.333	3.333
Monthly cost	20.278	18.611	14.166	14.166	14.166	11.666	11.666

Activity	22	23	24	25	26	27	28
A							
B							
C							
D							
E							
F							
G							
H	8.333	8.333	8.333	8.333	8.333	8.333	
I	3.333	3.333	3.333	3.333	3.333	3.333	3.333
Monthly cost	11.666	11.666	11.666	11.666	11.666	11.666	3.333

Latest start monthly cash flows:

Month 1: 9.286
Month 2–7: 15.953
Month 8–9: 17.778
Month 10–15: 24.207
Month 16: 36.207
Month 17–20: 23.666
Month 21–28: 14.166

23.

Activity	Completion time (days)	Total cost (×100,000)	Fixed cost (×100,000)	Daily cost (×100,000)
A	4	5	1.25	.938
B	5	10	2.5	1.5
C	6	9	2.25	1.125
D	8	12	3	1.125
E	12	25	6.25	1.563
F	10	16	4	1.2
G	6	12	3	1.5
H	4	8	2	1.5
I	6	12	3	1.5
J	8	24	6	2.25
K	4	8	2	1.5
L	15	30	7.5	1.5
M	5	22	5.5	3.3
N	12	24	6	1.5

Earliest start daily cash flows:

Day 1:	6.188	Day 22:	3.063
Day 2–4:	2.438	Day 23:	6
Day 5:	9	Day 24:	3
Day 6–10:	2.25	Day 25:	4
Day 11:	15.138	Day 26–28:	4.5
Day 12:	3.888	Day 29:	10.3
Day 13:	15.513	Day 30–33:	4.8
Day 14–18:	6.513	Day 34–39:	1.5
Day 19–20:	5.013	Day 40:	7.5
Day 21:	5.063	Day 41–53:	1.5

Latest start daily cash flows:

Day 1:	2.188	Day 25:	11.688
Day 2–4:	.938	Day 26:	4.188
Day 5:	3.375	Day 27:	11.313
Day 6:	5.125	Day 28:	5.313
Day 7–10:	2.625	Day 29–30:	8.25
Day 11:	6.2	Day 31–34:	8.75
Day 12–16:	1.2	Day 35:	10.3
Day 17:	9.013	Day 36–39:	3.8
Day 18:	2.763	Day 40:	7.5
Day 19:	6.888	Day 41–45:	1.5
Day 20:	5.088	Day 46:	6
Day 21:	7.188	Day 47–51:	3
Day 22–24:	4.188		

Chapter 11

1. Warehouse—node 1 = 15
   Warehouse—node 1—node 2 = 40
   Warehouse—node 1—node 3 = 35
   Warehouse—node 4 = 10
   Warehouse—node 4—node 5 = 20
   Warehouse—node 6 = 15
   Warehouse—node 7 = 20
   Warehouse—node 6—node 8 = 65

3. Node 1—2—7 = 14
   Node 1—4—10 = 11
   Node 3—4—10 = 10
   Node 2—7—8—9 = 15

5. Node 1—4—7—5—9 = 37
   Node 2—5—9 = 27
   Node 3—5—8 = 27
   Node 2—4—7—10 = 20

7. Node 1—4
4—6
4—5
5—2
2—3
5—7
7—8
7—9
9—10
Distance = 1710

9. Other guide: shop—2—4—3—2—1—shop
Sophia: shop—7—8—6—9—5—shop

11. Station—node 3 = 5
Station—node 5 = 8
Station—node 7 = 12
Node 3—node 1 = 8
Node 3—node 2 = 10
Node 2—node 4 = 8
Node 5—node 6 = 10
Node 6—node 10 = 7
Node 10—node 9 = 6
Node 7—node 8 = 10
Total distance = 84

13. **a.** No; maximal flow = 75,000 tons. **b.** Reduce flow to 60,000 tons.

15. No effect; maximal flow = 16,000.

17.

From	To	Flow
Plant	1	8
Plant	6	5
Plant	9	15
Plant	9	10
1	2	8
4	5	8
4	7	2
6	7	5
5	8	8

From	To	Flow
7	8	7
10	8	5
9	10	10
9	10	10
2	3	8
3	Destination	8
10	Destination	10
8	Destination	20

Maximal flow = 1,800,000

Chapter 12

1. 7.5 min

3. **b.** .0000 **c.** .13 hr **d.** .2 hr **e.** $P(x > 3) = .1976$

5. Waiting time = .08 hr
Average number in system = 3

7. **a.** .4512 **b.** 12/hr **c.** .3679

9. **a.** .08 hr **b.** 3 **c.** .5625

11. **a.** .875 **b.** 6.13 **c.** .2 hr **d.** .330

13. **a.** Single line, multiple server
b. p(both idle) = .0909
p(6 in system) = .0079
Average in queue = 3.788
Average time waiting = .379
p(waiting) = .7576

15. **a.**

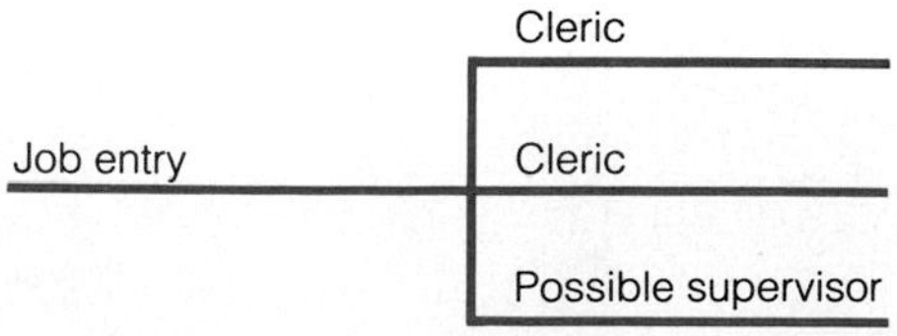

Job entry — Cleric / Cleric / Possible supervisor

b.

	2 entering	3 entering
Number waiting	13.609	.646
Time waiting	.907	.043
Time in system	1.032	.168
Probability of waiting	.9073	.3874

For 3 bays

17.

	2 dentists	3 dentists
p(no patients)	.1429	.2105
Average number waiting	1.929	.237
Average in system	3.43	1.74
Time waiting	.321	.039
Time in system	.571	.289
p(waiting)	.6429	.2368

19. p(waiting) = .485
Average waiting time = .221 hr
Average time in system = .638 hr
Most customers get rebate.

21. Optimum service rate = 23.74
Cost = $75.81

23. 2 servers: line grows infinitely long
3 servers: average waiting time = .72 min

Chapter 13

1. Certainty; sign; revenue = $10,000; cost = $3,872
3. 60,000; EV = 676,000
5. Order 7000.
7. Buy 2000; EV = 5180; new company
9. If purchase required, purchase 1. Otherwise purchase 0.

11. Original option: Maximin—select 0—value = 0
Maximax—select 5—value = 1,250,000
Second option: Maximin—select 0—value = 0
Maximax—select 5—value = 1,250,000
Third option: Maximin—select 0—value = 0
Maximax—select 5—value = 2,500,000

13.

	Demands					
Alternatives	0	10	20	30	40	50
10	−.4	.85	.85	.85	.85	.85
20	−.8	.45	1.7	1.7	1.7	1.7
30	−1.2	.05	1.3	2.55	2.55	2.55
40	−1.6	−.35	.9	2.15	3.4	3.4
50	−2.0	−.75	.5	1.75	3.0	4.25

Payoffs × 100,000

15. Build 50; payoff = 4,250,000.

17.

	Outcomes	
Alternatives	Success (.6)	Failure (.4)
Market	50,000,000	−20,000,000
Don't market	0	0

19.

	Outcomes			
Alternatives	**Excellent (.3)**	**Good (.3)**	**Fair (.1)**	**Poor (.3)**
Market	70,000,000	50,000,000	10,000,000	−20,000,000
Don't market	0	0	0	0

21.

	Demands					
Produced	3	4	5	6	7	8
3	10.50	7.00	3.50	0.00	−3.50	−7.00
4	8.50	14.00	10.50	7.00	3.50	0
5	6.50	12.00	17.50	14.00	10.50	7.00
6	4.50	10.00	15.50	21.00	17.50	14.00
7	2.50	8.00	13.50	19.00	24.50	21.00
8	.50	6.00	11.50	17.00	22.50	28.00

23. EVPI = 1,140,000; cost of uncertainty = $1,140,000

25.

	Demands				
Ordered	100,000	150,000	200,000	225,000	250,000
100,000	0	58,000	1,150,000	1,440,000	1,730,000
150,000	32,000	0	57,000	86,000	1,150,000
200,000	65,000	33,000	0	29,000	58,000
225,000	81,000	49,000	16,000	0	29,000
250,000	97,000	65,000	32,000	16,000	0

Order 200,000; expected opportunity loss = $31,300.

27. $150,000 option:

	Successes					
Franchises	0	1	2	3	4	5
0	0	250,000	500,000	750,000	1,000,000	1,250,000
1	150,000	0	250,000	500,000	750,000	1,000,000
2	300,000	150,000	0	250,000	500,000	750,000
3	450,000	300,000	150,000	0	250,000	500,000
4	600,000	450,000	300,000	150,000	0	250,000
5	750,000	600,000	450,000	300,000	150,000	0

Choose 4; opportunity loss = $195,000.

$250,000 option:

	Successes					
Franchises	0	1	2	3	4	5
0	0	250,000	500,000	750,000	1,000,000	1,250,000
1	200,000	0	250,000	500,000	750,000	1,000,000
2	400,000	200,000	0	250,000	500,000	750,000
3	600,000	400,000	200,000	0	250,00	500,000
4	800,000	600,000	400,000	200,000	0	250,000
5	10,000,000	800,000	600,000	400,000	200,000	0

Choose 4; opportunity loss = $206,000.

$400,000 option:

	Successes					
Franchises	0	1	2	3	4	5
0	0	500,000	1,000,000	1,500,000	2,000,000	2,500,000
1	300,000	0	500,000	1,000,000	1,500,000	2,000,000
2	600,000	300,000	0	500,000	1,000,000	1,500,000
3	900,000	600,000	300,000	0	500,000	1,000,000
4	1,200,000	900,000	600,000	300,000	0	500,000
5	1,500,000	1,200,000	900,000	600,000	300,000	0

Choose 4; opportunity loss = $321,000.

29.

	Demands					
Alternatives	0	10	20	30	40	50
0	0	.85	1.7	2.55	3.4	4.25
10	.4	0	.85	1.7	2.55	3.4
20	.8	.4	0	.85	1.7	2.55
30	1.2	.8	.4	0	.85	1.7
40	1.6	1.2	.8	.4	0	.85
50	2.0	1.6	1.2	.8	.4	0

Opportunity losses × 100,000

EVPI = 745,000

31. **a.**

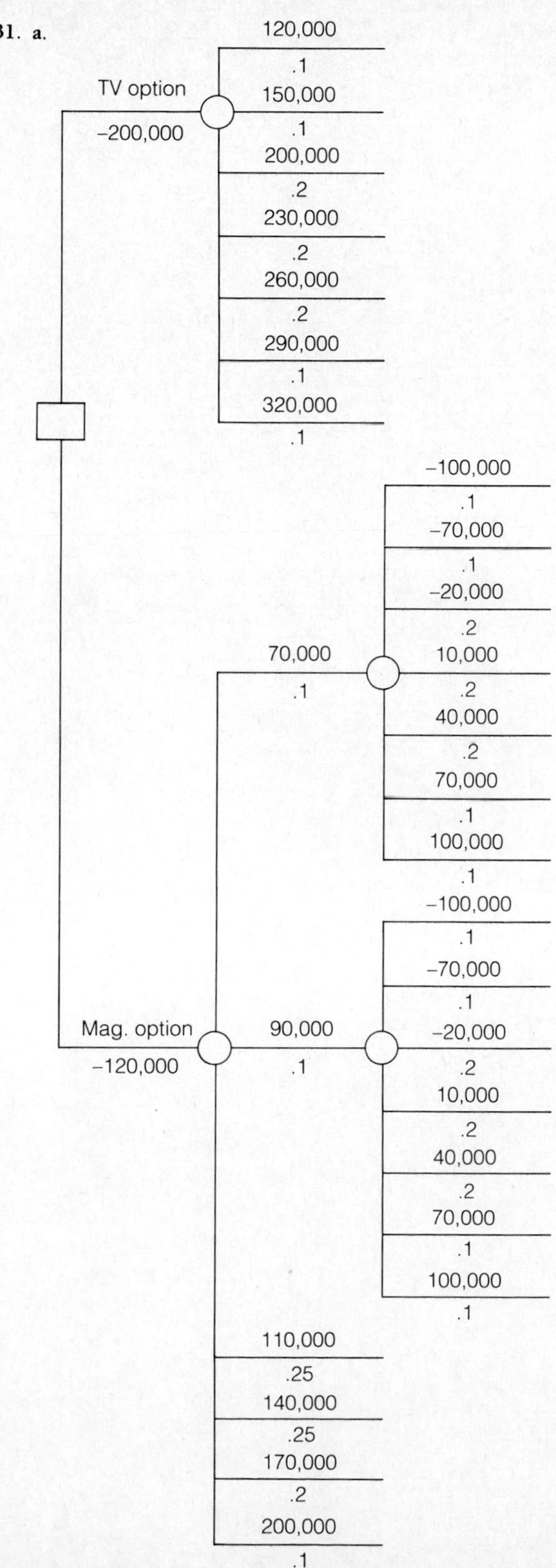

b. TV option EV = 26,000

33.

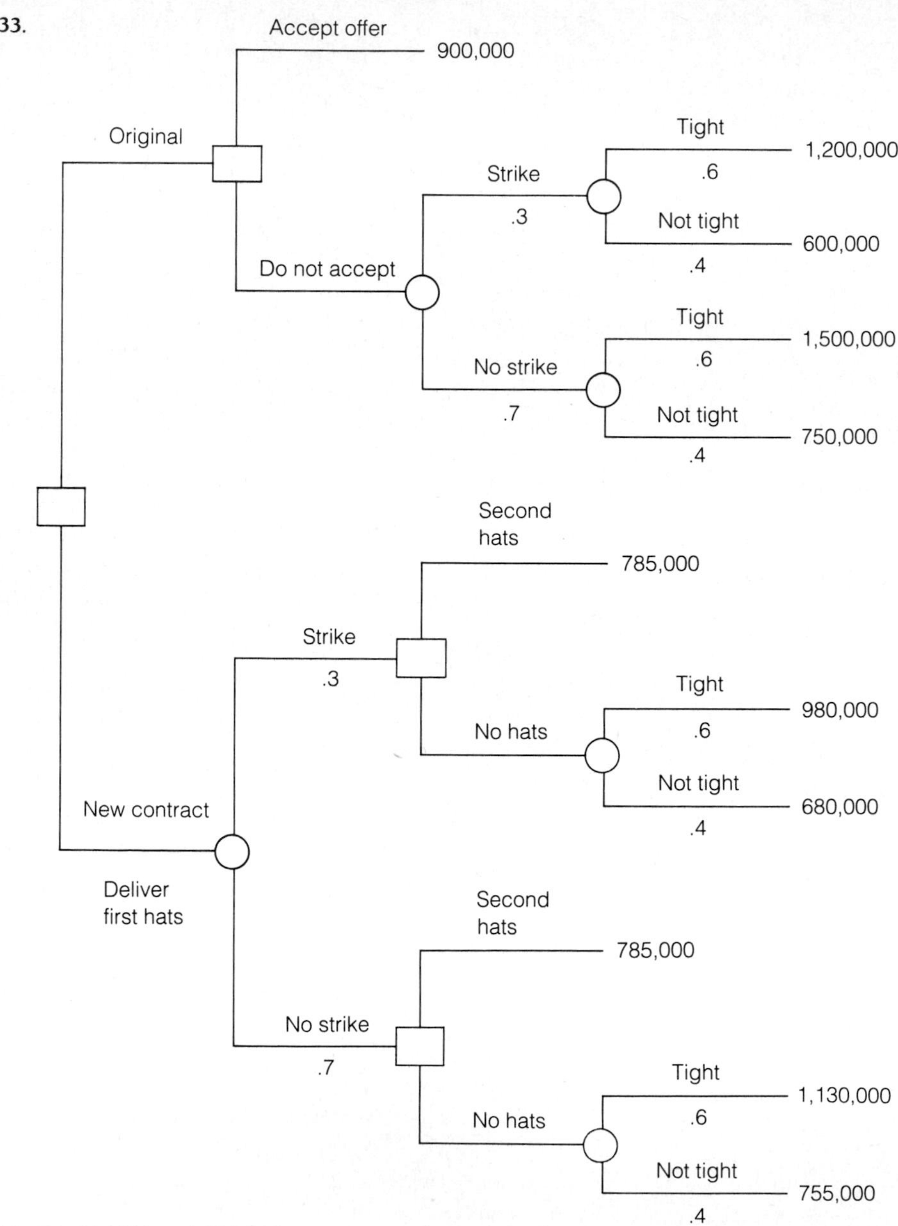

35. Yes; 944,000 vs. 1,128,000.

37.

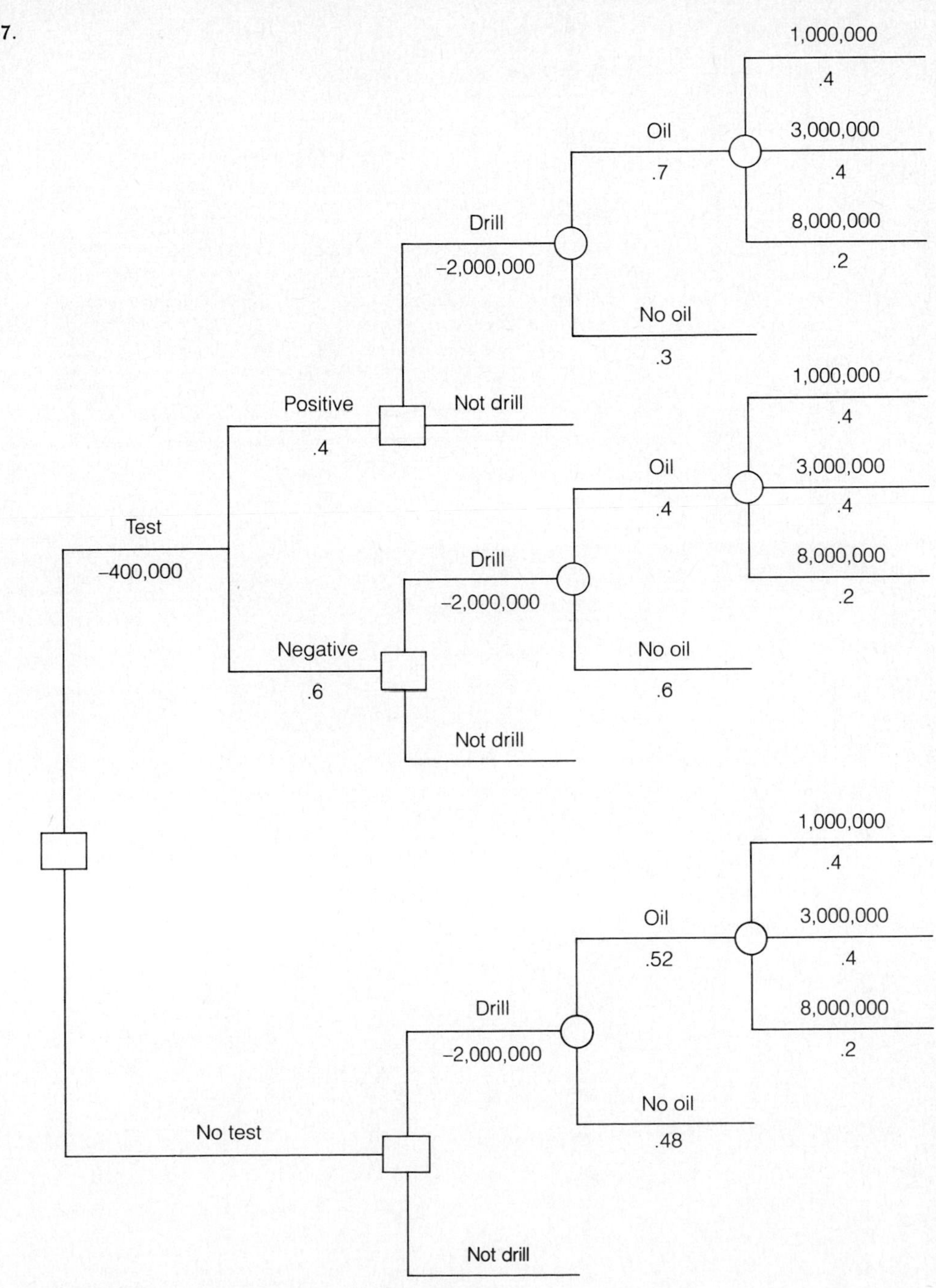

No test. Drill.
EV = 1,456,000

39. EV = 0 at $p = 1.07$, impossible.
Always drill without test.

Chapter 14

1. Plant 1 = 432,000
   Plant 2 = 360,000
   Plant 3 = 108,000

3. .8   5. .053   7. Posteriors: .012, .988

9. a. No; expected payoff = −1,250,000.
   b. Posteriors: .0017, .1418, .5692, .2874
   c. Form affiliate; expected payoff = 350,000.

11. Good—.0257
    Fair—.9383
    Poor—.0360

13. Yes; p(fair) + p(good) = .9999. 15. Lease robot; produce 30,000; payoff = 75,000. 17. Lease robot; produce 30,000; payoff = 140,000. 19. Don't form; expected payoff = 1,560,000 if do. 21. No; expected payoff = −12,400; EVPI = 2,800. 23. 1,960,000 25. Buy from Krado; save $65,000. 27. Stay with Everson, $15,000 less expensive. 29. ENGS = 53,220

Chapter 15

1. Don't plant. 3. Plant oats. 5. Plant oats. 7. Install pipe; purchase water for light or average snowfall. 9. Install pipe; purchase both water and insurance; plant potatoes. 11. Yes, work on improved model.

13.

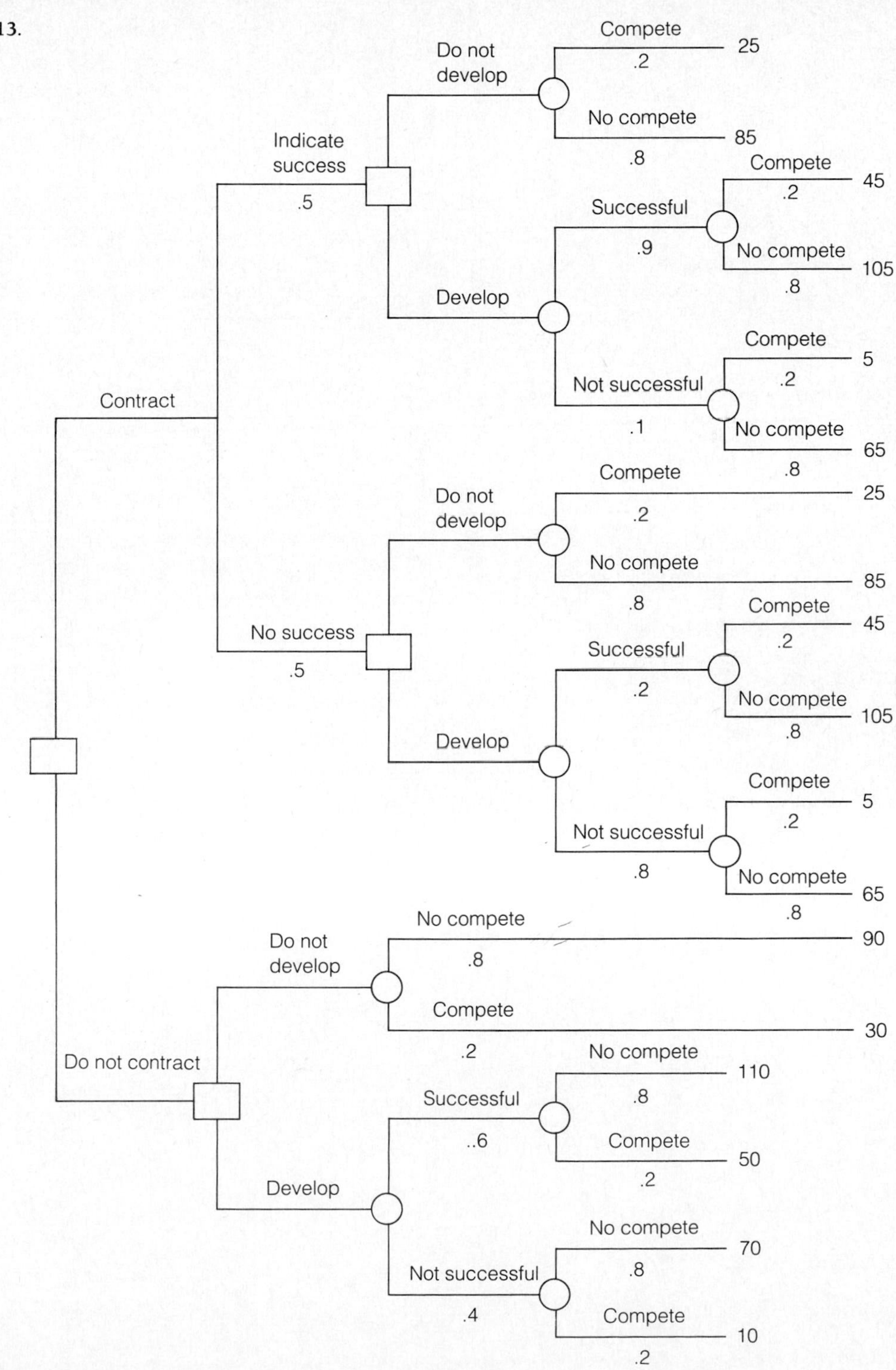

15. Depending on preference curve, don't sign contract. Develop model. 17. Do nothing.

19.

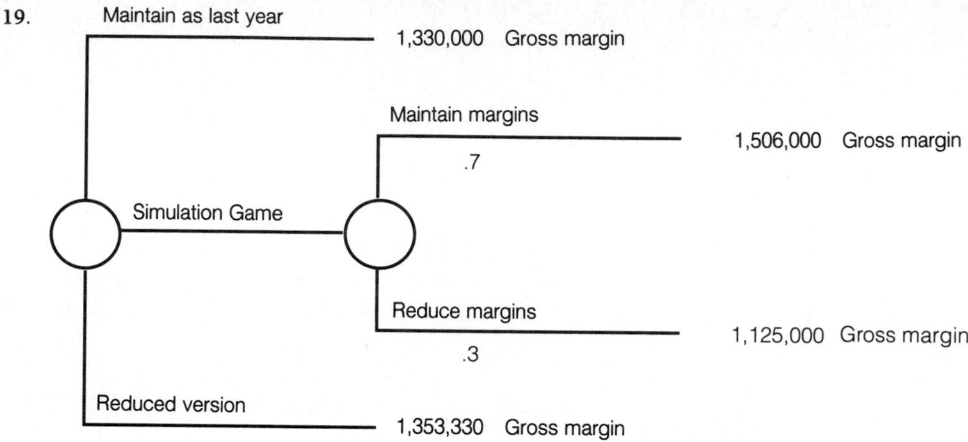

21. Add Simulation Game.

Chapter 16

1. a. Type of machine: $0 \le$ random number $< .70$, BT3000
$.70 \le$ random number < 1.00, cT4000

BT3000 service time: $0 \le$ random number $< .4$, 20 min
$.4 \le$ random number $< .6$, 30 min
$.6 \le$ random number $< .9$, 40 min
$.9 \le$ random number < 1.00, 50 min

cT 4000 service time: $0 \le$ random number $< .5$, 15 min
$.5 \le$ random number $< .65$, 25 min
$.65 \le$ random number $< .75$, 30 min
$.75 \le$ random number < 1.00, 40 min

b.

Arrival	Random number	Machine	Random number	Time
1	.34	BT	.65	40
2	.69	BT	.30	20
3	.58	BT	.16	20
4	.43	BT	.60	40
5	.57	BT	.74	40
6	.57	BT	.41	30
7	.03	BT	.15	20
8	.48	BT	.98	50
9	.28	BT	.04	20
10	.82	cT	.77	40
11	.85	cT	.66	30
12	.09	BT	.20	20
13	.20	BT	.12	20
14	.14	BT	.50	30
15	.89	cT	.94	40
16	.79	cT	.91	40
17	.14	BT	.48	30
18	.19	BT	.42	30
19	.47	BT	.62	40
20	.35	BT	.10	20
21	.69	BT	.91	50
22	.59	BT	.40	30
23	.75	cT	.59	25
24	.91	cT	.35	15
25	.44	BT	.72	40

Total time = 780 min

3. a.

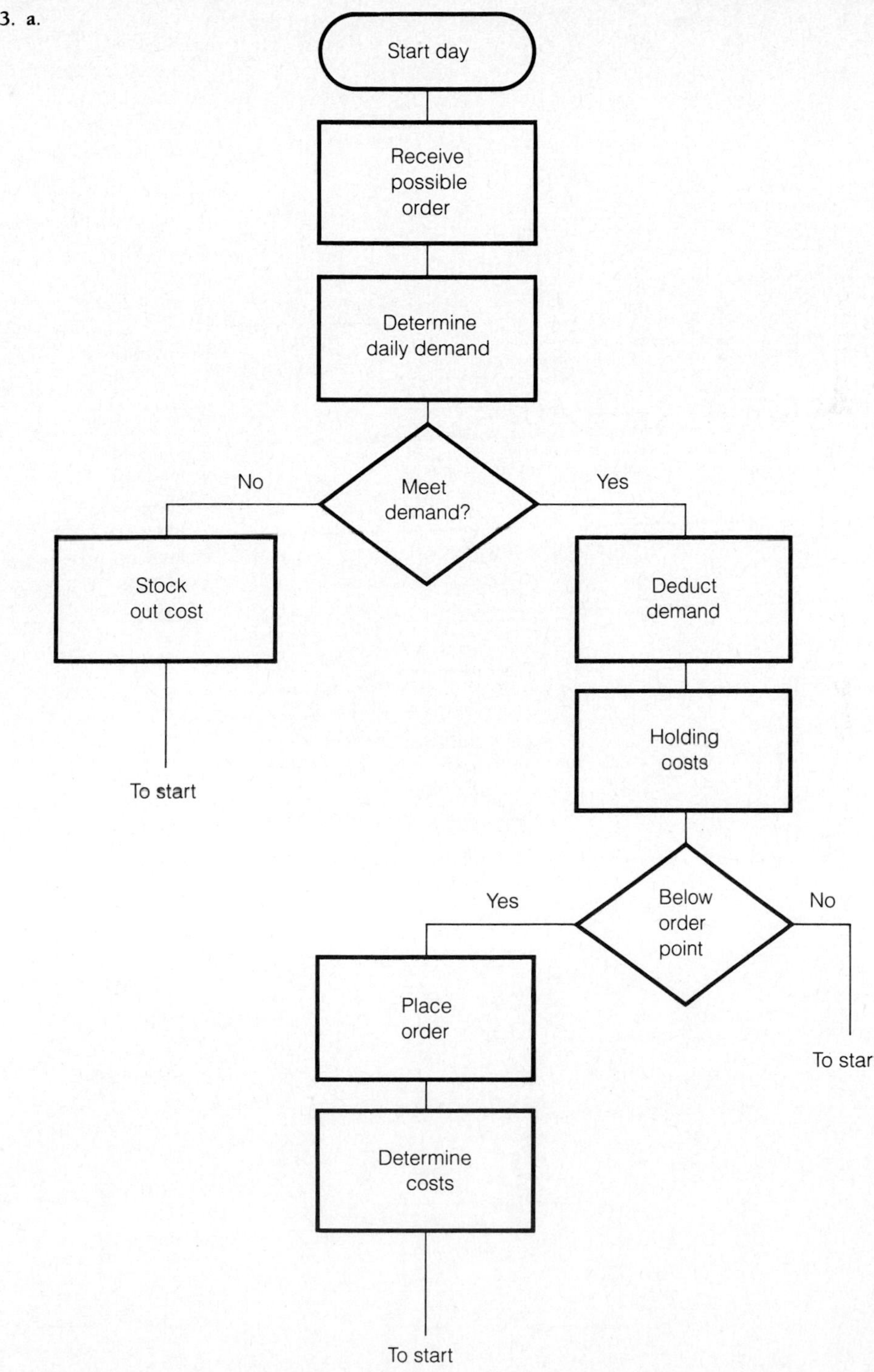
Start day
Receive possible order
Determine daily demand
Meet demand?
No
Yes
Stock out cost
To start
Deduct demand
Holding costs
Below order point
Yes
No
Place order
Determine costs
To start
To start

b.

Day	Random number	Demand	On hand	Order	Costs
1	.67	3	7	20	Order 30.00
					Cost 2300.00
					Holding 12.25
2	.16	1	6		Holding 10.50
3	.39	2	4		Holding 7.00
4	.87	4	0		
5	.12	1	0		Stockout 40.00
6	.66	3	0		Stockout 120.00
7	.73	3	0		Stockout 120.00
8	.11	1	0		Stockout 40.00
9	.56	2	0		Stockout 80.00
10	.00	0	0		
11	.67	3	17		Holding 29.70
12	.60	3	14	20	Order 30.00
					Cost 2300.00
					Holding 24.50
13	.01	0	14		Holding 24.50
14	.62	3	11		Holding 19.25
15	.87	4	7		Holding 12.25
16	.45	2	5		Holding 8.75
17	.46	2	3		Holding 5.25
18	.57	2	1		Holding 1.75
19	.43	2	0		Stockout 40.00
20	.03	0	0		

5. a.

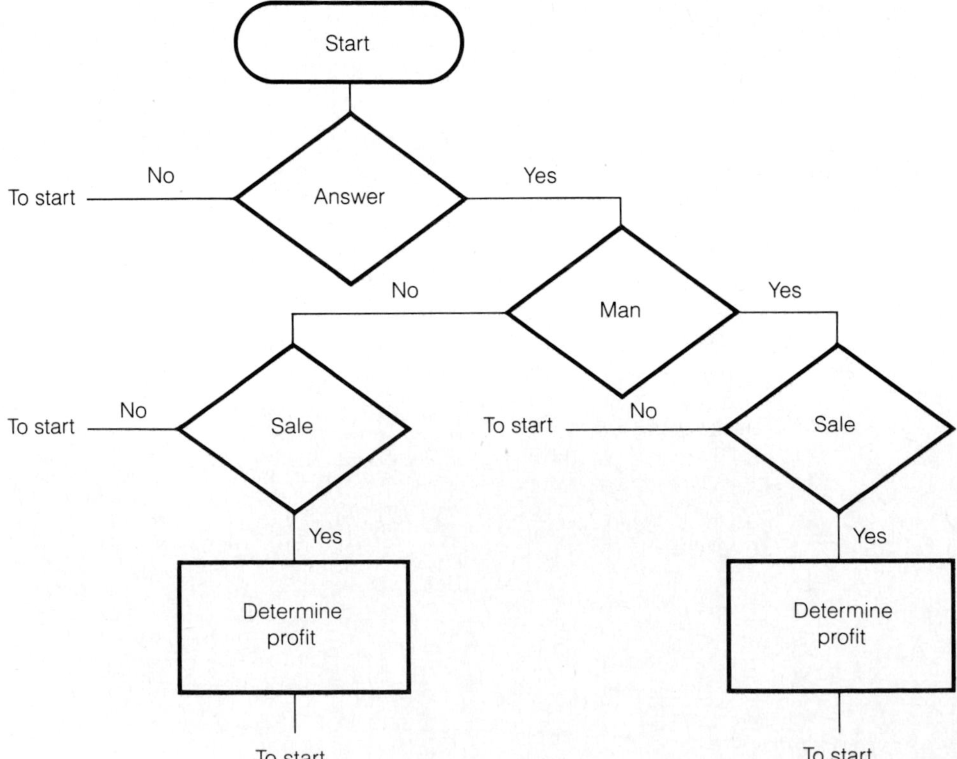

b.

Day	Random number	Answer	Random number	Man	Random number	Sale	Random number	Profit
1	.08	No						
2	.14	No						
3	.85	Yes	.84	No	.79	No		
4	.42	Yes	.42	Yes	.34	No		
5	.15	No						
6	.26	No						
7	.12	No						
8	.02	No						
9	.80	Yes	.12	Yes	.74	No		
10	.90	Yes	.96	No	.07	Yes	.88	9.00
11	.94	Yes	.81	No	.80	No		
12	.41	Yes	.73	No	.32	No		
13	.04	No						
14	.56	Yes	.34	Yes	.83	No		
15	.06	No						
16	.03	No						
17	.82	Yes	.94	No	.05	Yes	.46	6.00
18	.97	Yes	.20	Yes	.57	No		
19	.14	No						
20	.12	No						
21	.26	No						
22	.19	No						
23	.12	No						
24	.61	Yes	.23	Yes	.30	No		
25	.20	No						
26	.28	No						
27	.75	Yes	.34	Yes	.93	No		
28	.05	No						
29	.45	Yes	.08	Yes	.05	Yes	.71	9.00
30	.89	Yes	.28	Yes	.17	Yes	.68	9.00

Total profit = $33.00

c. Total products = 33
Total profit = $99.00

7. Actual differences will vary. Total cost should decrease.

9. a. Results will vary. Typical values:
   Utilization = 73%
   Average service time = 500 sec
   Average waiting time — those waiting = 1875 sec
   Average turned away = 90
   b. Actual differences vary between simulations.
   Biggest difference in number turned away.

11. Typical values in report:
   Facility utilization = 40%
   Percent waiting = 17%
   Waiting time — those waiting = 25 min
   Number turned away = 0

13. Typical values in report:
   Average inventory = 1.71
   Carrying cost = 177.78
   Number of orders = 32
   Ordering cost = 480
   Sales lost = 453
   Cost of lost sales = 13,590

15. Major factors: extra space vs. increase in overtime

17.

Demand	Frequency	Relative frequency	Cumulative
30	3	.100	.100
35	5	.167	.267
40	8	.267	.534
45	6	.200	.734
50	4	.133	.867
55	3	.100	.967
60	1	.033	1.000
	30		

Make 30:

	Random number	Demand	Revenue	Loss	Total
1	.579	45	6.00	—	6.00
2	.533	40	6.00	—	6.00
3	.033	30	6.00	—	6.00
4	.208	35	6.00	—	6.00
5	.698	45	6.00	—	6.00
6	.017	30	6.00	—	6.00
7	.363	40	6.00	—	6.00
8	.352	40	6.00	—	6.00
9	.314	40	6.00	—	6.00
10	.458	40	6.00	—	6.00
					60.00

Make 35:

	Random number	Demand	Revenue	Loss	Total
1	.005	30	6.00	.25	5.75
2	.048	30	6.00	.25	5.75
3	.415	40	7.00	—	7.00
4	.202	35	7.00	—	7.00
5	.369	40	7.00	—	7.00
6	.131	35	7.00	—	7.00
7	.967	55	7.00	—	7.00
8	.349	40	7.00	—	7.00
9	.416	40	7.00	—	7.00
10	.941	55	7.00	—	7.00
					67.50

Make 40:

	Random number	Demand	Revenue	Loss	Total
1	.838	50	8.00		8.00
2	.574	45	8.00		8.00
3	.442	35	7.00	.25	6.75
4	.895	55	8.00		8.00
5	.127	35	7.00	.25	6.75
6	.137	35	7.00	.25	6.75
7	.277	40	8.00		8.00
8	.022	30	6.00	.50	5.50
9	.292	40	8.00		8.00
10	.834	50	8.00		8.00
					73.75

Make 45:

	Random number	Demand	Revenue	Loss	Total
1	.122	35	7.00	.50	6.50
2	.482	40	8.00	.25	7.75
3	.575	45	9.00		9.00
4	.894	55	9.00		9.00
5	.730	45	9.00		9.00
6	.776	50	9.00		9.00
7	.626	45	9.00		9.00
8	.133	35	7.00	.50	6.50
9	.683	55	9.00		9.00
10	.141	35	7.00	.50	6.50
					81.25

Make 50:

	Random number	Demand	Revenue	Loss	Total
1	.602	45	9.00	.25	8.75
2	.634	45	9.00	.25	8.75
3	.288	40	8.00	.50	7.50
4	.073	30	6.00	1.00	5.00
5	.589	45	9.00	.25	8.75
6	.864	50	10.00		10.00
7	.194	35	7.00	.75	6.25
8	.643	45	9.00	.25	8.75
9	.117	35	7.00	.75	6.25
10	.243	35	7.00	.75	6.25
					76.25

Make 55:

	Random number	Demand	Revenue	Loss	Total
1	.960	55	11.00	—	11.00
2	.118	35	7.00	1.00	6.00
3	.648	45	9.00	.50	8.50
4	.581	45	9.00	.50	8.50
5	.341	40	8.00	.75	7.25
6	.073	30	6.00	1.25	4.75
7	.929	55	11.00	—	11.00
8	.928	55	11.00	—	11.00
9	.018	30	6.00	1.25	4.75
10	.914	55	11.00	—	11.00
					83.75

Make 60:

	Random number	Demand	Revenue	Loss	Total
1	.352	40	8.00	1.00	7.00
2	.349	40	8.00	1.00	7.00
3	.608	45	9.00	.75	8.25
4	.963	55	11.00	.25	10.75
5	.045	30	6.00	1.50	4.50
6	.853	50	10.00	.50	9.50
7	.291	40	8.00	1.00	7.00
8	.011	30	6.00	1.50	4.50
9	.465	40	8.00	1.00	7.00
10	.181	35	7.00	1.25	5.75
					71.25

Make 55.

21. Most values about the same; fewer customers turned away.
23. Depends on simulation; holding cost down; lost sales up.

Chapter 17

1. Shortest route:

To camp	From base camp	Time
1	1	4
2	1	6
3	1	9
4	1	8
5	2	2
6	2	9
7	1	13
8	2	10
9	1 or 2	16

3. a.

Project	Engineers assigned	Profit
A	3	$ 49
B	1	25
C	0	30
D	2	36
E	2	30
		$170

Total profit 170 × 10,000 = $1,700,000

b.

Project	Engineers assigned	Profit
A	1	$ 35
B	0	17
C	0	30
D	2	36
E	2	30
		$148

Profit = $148 × 10,000 = $1,480,000

5. Solution:

Lot	Trucks sold	Profit
A	1	$200
B	3	360
C	1	180
		$740

Profit reduced from $900 to $740

7. April: Build 4.
May: Build 8.
June: Build 6.
July: Build 10.
Carrying cost tends to outweigh set-up cost.

9. Week 1. Sell only if receive 2,000,000.
EV(week 1) = $1,859,000
Week 2. Sell only if receive 2,000,000.
EV(week 2) = $1,824,000
Week 3. Sell if receive 2,000,000 or 1,750,000.
EV(week 3) = $1,780,000
Week 4. Must sell.
EV(week 4) = $1,725,000

11. Multiple optimum solutions (two examples):
a. loc(1) = $2 million; loc(2) = $3 million; loc(3) = $5 million; total rating = 1.25.
b. loc(1) = $3 million; loc(2) = $3 million; loc(3) = $4 million; total rating = 1.25.

13. Production schedule: April—5,000 units; May—10,000 units; June—3,000 units; total cost = $2,065.

Chapter 18

1. 237 additional students; 52 additional graduates

3. a. 41.2% b. Transition probabilities remain constant and apply to all golfers.

5. Total sales, present policy = 4730 dozen.
   Total sales with discount = 7650 dozen.
   Consider cost of increased sales.

7. a. A—.375; B—.4; C—.225 b. A—43.3%; B—33.3%; C—23.3%

9. a. Total returned = 1243(rounded)
   Returned week 3 = 410 (rounded)
   b. A—37.8%; B—29.7%; C—32.4%
   Consider store size, cost, etc.

INDEX